brief contents

contents

LIFE-SPAN
DEVELOPMENT

Fourteenth Edition

JOHN W. SANTROCK
University of Texas at Dallas

Mc Graw Hill

Connect
Learn
Succeed™

The McGraw·Hill Companies

Connect
Learn
Succeed™

LIFE-SPAN DEVELOPMENT, FOURTEENTH EDITION

Published by McGraw-Hill, a business unit of The McGraw-Hill Companies, Inc., 1221 Avenue of the
Americas, New York, NY 10020. Copyright © 2013 by The McGraw-Hill Companies, Inc. All rights
reserved. Printed in the United States of America. Previous editions © 2011, 2009, and 2008. No part of
this publication may be reproduced or distributed in any form or by any means, or stored in a database or
retrieval system, without the prior written consent of The McGraw-Hill Companies, Inc., including, but not
limited to, in any network or other electronic storage or transmission, or broadcast for distance learning.

Some ancillaries, including electronic and print components, may not be available to customers outside the
United States.

This book is printed on acid-free paper.

1 2 3 4 5 6 7 8 9 0 QVR/QVR 1 0 9 8 7 6 5 4 3 2

ISBN 978-0-07-131868-6
MHID 0-07-131868-2

All credits appearing on page or at the end of the book are considered to be an extension of the copyright
page.

The Internet addresses listed in the text were accurate at the time of publication. The inclusion of a website
does not indicate an endorsement by the authors or McGraw-Hill, and McGraw-Hill does not guarantee the
accuracy of the information presented at these sites.

www.mhhe.com

With special appreciation to
my mother, Ruth Santrock, and
the memory of my father, John Santrock

about the author

John W. Santrock

John Santrock received his Ph.D. from the University of Minnesota in 1973. He taught at the University of Charleston and the University of Georgia before joining the Program in Psychology and Human Development at the University of Texas at Dallas, where he currently teaches a number of undergraduate courses and was given the University's Effective Teaching Award in 2006. In 2010, he created the UT-Dallas Santrock undergraduate scholarship, an annual award that is given to outstanding undergraduate students majoring in developmental psychology to enable them to attend research conventions.

John Santrock, teaching in his undergraduate course in life-span development.

John has been a member of the editorial boards of *Child Development* and *Developmental Psychology*. His research on father custody is widely cited and used in expert witness testimony to promote flexibility and alternative considerations in custody disputes. John also has authored these exceptional McGraw-Hill texts: *Children* (12th edition), *Adolescence* (14th edition), *A Topical Approach to Life-Span Development* (6th edition), and *Educational Psychology* (5th edition).

For many years, John was involved in tennis as a player, teaching professional, and coach of professional tennis players. At the University of Miami (Fl), the tennis team on which he played still holds the NCAA Division I record for most consecutive wins (137) in any sport. His wife, Mary Jo, has a master's degree in special education and has worked as a teacher and a Realtor. He has two daughters—Tracy, who also is a Realtor, and Jennifer, who is a medical sales specialist. He has one granddaughter, Jordan, age 21, currently an undergraduate student at Southern Methodist University, and two grandsons, Alex, age 8, and Luke, age 6. In the last two decades, John also has spent time painting expressionist art.

SECTION 3   INFANCY   106

SECTION 4 EARLY CHILDHOOD 206

SECTION 7   **EARLY ADULTHOOD   418**

SECTION 8 MIDDLE ADULTHOOD 480

expert consultants

Life-span development has become an enormous, complex field, and no single author, or even several authors, can possibly keep up with all of the rapidly changing content in the many periods and different areas of life-span development. To solve this problem, author John Santrock has sought the input of leading experts about content in a number of areas of life-span development. These experts have provided detailed evaluations and recommendations in their area(s) of expertise.

The following individuals were among those who served as expert consultants for one or more of the previous editions of this text:

Urie Bronfenbrenner	*Cornell University*	Margie Lachman	*Brandeis University*
K. Warner Schaie	*Pennsylvania State University*	James Garbarino	*Cornell University*
Paul Baltes	*Max Planck Institute, Berlin*	Elena Grigorenko	*Yale University*
Tiffany Field	*University of Miami*	William Hoyer	*Syracuse University*
James Birren	*University of Southern California*	Ross Parke	*University of California—Riverside*
Jean Berko Gleason	*Boston University*	Ross Thompson	*University of California—Davis*
Gilbert Gottlieb	*University of North Carolina*	Phyllis Moen	*University of Minnesota*
Karen Adolph	*New York University*	Ravenna Helson	*University of California—Berkeley*
Joseph Campos	*University of California—Berkeley*	Toni Antonucci	*University of Michigan*
Jean Mandler	*University of California—San Diego*	Arthur Kramer	*University of Illinois*
James Marcia	*Concordia University*	Karen Fingerman	*Purdue University*
Andrew Meltzoff	*University of Washington*	Cigdem Kagitcibasi	*Koc University*
Elizabeth Susman	*Pennsylvania State University*	Robert Kastenbaum	*Arizona State University*
John Schulenberg	*University of Michigan*		

Following are the biographies and photographs of the expert consultants for the fourteenth edition of this text, who (like the expert consultants for the previous seven editions) literally represent a Who's Who in the field of life-span development.

K. Warner Schaie K. Warner Schaie is widely recognized as one of the pioneers who created the field of life-span development and continues to be one of its leading experts. He is currently the Evan Pugh Professor Emeritus of Human Development and Psychology at Pennsylvania State University. Dr. Schaie also holds an appointment as Affiliate Professor of Psychiatry and Behavioral Sciences at the University of Washington. He received his Ph.D. in psychology from the University of Washington, an honorary Dr. Phil. from the Friedrich-Schiller University of Jena, Germany, and an honorary Sc.D. degree from West Virginia University. He received the Kleemeier Award for Distinguished Research Contributions and the Distinguished Career Contribution to Gerontology Award from the Gerontological Society of America, the MENSA lifetime career award, and the Distinguished Scientific Contributions award from the American Psychological Association. He is author or editor of 62 books, including the textbook *Adult Development and Aging* (5th edition, with S. L. Willis) and the *Handbook of the Psychology of Aging* (6th edition, with J. E. Birren). He has directed the Seattle Longitudinal Study of cognitive aging since 1956 and is the author of more than 300 journal articles and chapters on the psychology of aging. His current research interests focus on the life course of adult intelligence, its antecedents and modifiability, the impact of cognitive activity in midlife on the integrity of brain structures in old age, the early detection of risk for dementia, and methodological issues in the developmental sciences.

"I believe John Santrock has done a marvelous job of crafting a comprehensive presentation of psychological development across the life span. It is factually

and scholarly sound and discusses findings that have stood the test of time as well as integrating the most recent advances in research methods and research findings. Each of the chapters is a comprehensive presentation of a particular phase or aspect of development but is expertly linked to earlier phases to keep the reader intrigued to follow the entire story from beginning to end. I believe this text to be undoubtedly the classic presentation of the psychology of the lifespan, easiest to teach, and most accessible for the average student."*
—**K. Warner Schaie** *University of Washington*

Kirby Deater-Deckard Dr. Deater-Deckard is a leading expert on biological foundations of development, heredity-environment interaction, and parenting. He obtained his Ph.D. from the University of Virginia and currently is a professor and the director of graduate programs in psychology at Virginia Polytechnic Institute and State University. Dr. Deater-Deckard's research focuses on the development of individual differences in childhood and adolescence, with an emphasis on gene-environment processes. He has written papers and book chapters in the areas of developmental psychology and psychopathology. His current research on parenting and children's development is funded by the NICHD. Dr. Deater-Deckard has been joint editor of the *Journal of Child Psychology and Psychiatry,* and currently is on the editorial boards of *Infant and Child Development, Journal of Family Psychology,* and *Parenting: Science and Practice.*

"As with Dr. Santrock's other books, the research base for this updated edition of Life-Span Development remains very timely and focused on the

most important concepts and findings with respect to the biological beginnings of humans. The chapter provides quite comprehensive coverage of behavioral/molecular genetic and gene-environment transaction concepts and findings. . . . Dr. Santrock's books are written at just the right level for a wide variety of students. The prose is clear and concise, without sacrificing content." —**Dr. Kirby Deater-Deckard** *Virginia Tech University*

Maria Hernandez-Reif Dr. Maria Hernandez-Reif is a leading expert on prenatal development, birth, and infant perception. She currently is a professor in the Department of Human Development and Family Studies and the director of the Pediatric Development Research (PDR) laboratory at the University of Alabama. Dr. Hernandez-Reif's research expertise and interests are in infant perception and development, as well as massage therapy. She has conducted numerous research studies with Dr. Tiffany Field on the effects of massage therapy in improving various developmental outcomes for preterm and low birth weight babies. She recently established the Pediatric Development Research Laboratory at the University of Alabama. Her current research continues to focus on massage therapy and also on the role that maternal depression plays in developmental outcomes for young children.

". . . the chapters were comprehensive and read seamlessly from section to section. Moreover, the writing style is easy to follow and engages the reader. I feel that the narrative and perspective reflect the most current scholarship in the field. . . . The level of detail provided in Chapters 3 and 4 is impressive. . . . the chapters will be a great addition for students enrolled in a life-span development course." —**Maria Hernandez-Reif** *University of Alabama*

Ross Thompson Ross Thompson is one of the world's leading experts on children's socioemotional development. He currently is Professor of Psychology at the University of California–Davis, where he directs the Social and Emotional Development Lab. A developmental psychologist, Dr. Thompson studies early parent-child relationships, the development of emotion understanding and emotion regulation, early moral development, and the growth of self-understanding in young children. He also works on the applications of developmental research to public policy concerns, including school readiness and its development, early childhood investments, and early mental health. Dr. Thompson is a founding member of the National Scientific Council on the Developing Child. Dr. Thompson has twice been Associate Editor of *Child Development*. He received the Boyd McCandless Young Scientist Award for Early Distinguished Achievement from the American Psychological Association, the Scholarship in Teaching Award, and the Outstanding Research and Creative Activity Award from the University of Nebraska, where he was also a lifetime member of the Academy of Distinguished Teachers.

"The writing is clear and engaging, and students are moved in a logical and effortless manner from topic to topic. John Santrock does a remarkable job of maintaining currency with the field, such that students are given a brief but state-of-the-art introduction to each of the relevant issues for each chapter." —**Ross Thompson** *University of California–Davis*

Diane Hughes Diane Hughes is a leading expert on diversity and children's development. Following her doctoral work at the University of Michigan, she became a professor in the Department of Psychology at New York University and currently is a faculty member in the Steinhardt Department of Applied Psychology at New York University. Dr. Hughes is a community and

developmental psychologist who examines ethnicity and race as contexts for parenting and adolescent development. She seeks to discover how parents from a range of ethnic backgrounds communicate information about ethnicity and race in the course of their everyday routines and practices. Dr. Hughes and her colleagues have been awarded multi-million-dollar grants from the National Science Foundation to establish and maintain the Center for Research on Culture, Development, and Education at New York University.

"It was a pleasure reading the manuscript of the new edition of John Santrock's book, Life-Span Development. I imagine it will be very engaging and informative for students and easy to plan with and lecture from for professors. . . . thank you for the opportunity to read this." —**Diane Hughes** *New York University*

William Hoyer William Hoyer is one of the world's leading experts on cognitive aging. He currently is professor of psychology and senior scientist at the Center for Health and Behavior at Syracuse University, where he teaches courses in adult development and aging. At Syracuse, he also is an associate of the Gerontology Center, director of the Graduate Training Program in Experimental Psychology, and research professor of ophthalmology at Upstate Medical University. Dr. Hoyer obtained an undergraduate degree in psychology from Rutgers College, and his M.S. and Ph.D. in experimental psychology from West Virginia University. His research interests center on skill learning, memory, and cognitive expertise from a developmental perspective. Dr. Hoyer is currently the principal investigator on a five-year research grant titled "Aging of Cognitive Mechanisms" from the National Institute on Aging. His publications include seven books and over 100 articles in such journals as *Developmental Psychology, Psychology and Aging*, and *Journal of Gerontology: Psychological Sciences*. Dr. Hoyer is a Fellow of the American Psychological Association, the American Psychological Society, and the Gerontological Society of America. He serves or has served on a number of grant review panels and on the editorial boards for journals, including *Developmental Psychology; Journals of Gerontology: Psychological Sciences; Aging, Neuropsychology, and Cognition;* and *Psychology and Aging*.

"The distinctions that influence adoption I think have largely to do with the match to students in terms of difficulty and breadth/depth of coverage, author credibility, and currency. . . . John Santrock again is positioned to stay ahead of the curve on these critical dimensions. He somehow manages to know about the latest work in the field. . . . New materials for the fourteenth edition look great!" —**William Hoyer** *Syracuse University*

John Schulenberg Dr. John Schulenberg is a leading expert on adolescent development and emerging adulthood. He currently is a professor of psychology in the Institute of Social Research and the Center for Human Growth and Development at the University of Michigan. His research expertise focuses on developmental transitions in adolescence and emerging adulthood that involve health and well-being, substance use and abuse, and conceptualization of developmental change. Dr. Schulenberg is one of the key members of the research team that conducts the ongoing Monitoring the Future study at the Institute of Social Research. He recently became President of the Society for Research on Adolescent Development.

"Great chapter (Physical and Cognitive Development in Adolescence), covering all major topics from my perspective, with many up-to-date references. . . . From my view, this chapter (Socioemotional Development in Adolescence) read well, covers the major topics, and has up-to-date references included." —**John Schulenberg** *University of Michigan*

Phyllis Moen Dr. Moen is a leading expert on adult socioemotional development. She currently holds the McKnight Presidential Chair in Sociology at the University of Minnesota. Across a number of decades, she has been a leading researcher on career development, gender, families, and well-being. She considers herself a life course scholar, which means that she is interested in *time*. A major current research project focuses on flexible work and well-being. In her own words, she describes her research interests as follows:

> Specifically, what are the patterned ways jobs, retirement, civic engagement, families, and lives play out over the life course? And what are the impacts of these different pathways? Individuals and families make key decisions—about jobs, about retirement, about community participation, about relationships, about health practices—at all life stages. But their "choices" are shaped by the culture and structure of age, gender, organizations, communities, and social policies in which they are embedded, as well as by their previous experiences, along with any broad-scale social changes along the way. Diverse pathways over the life course, in turn, result in disparities in health, stress, and life quality in the middle and later adult years. Improving life chances and life quality of individuals and families often means changing the multilayered contexts of their lives.

Dr. Moen's books include *It's About Time: Couples and Careers* and *The Career Mystique: Cracks in the American Dream* (co-authored with Patricia Roehling).

"Chapter 13 (Physical and Cognitive Development in Early Adulthood): Good discussion of obesity . . . great discussion of Csikszentmihalyi . . . good discussion of dual-earner families . . . Chapter 16 (Socioemotional Development in Middle Adulthood): Good discussion of theories . . . Good discussion of Almeida's work . . . Good discussion of grandparent literature . . . Chapter 19 (Sociemotional Development in Late Adulthood): Good discussion of Carstensen . . . Good discussion of marriage and the family . . . Nice to end on successful aging." —**Phyllis Moen** *University of Minnesota*

David Almeida David Almeida is one of the world's leading experts on stress and coping in the field of life-span development. He obtained his Ph.D. from the University of Victoria and currently is Professor of Human Development at Pennsylvania State University. Dr. Almeida's research focuses on how daily experiences in families and other social contexts, such as work and leisure, influence health and well-being in adulthood and aging. His research has been funded by grants from the National Institute of Mental Health, the National Institute of Aging, the MacArthur Foundation, the Kellogg Foundation, and the Sloan Foundation. Dr. Almeida has published extensively in leading research journals in adult development and aging and recently contributed a chapter titled "The Speedometer of Life: Stress, Health, and Aging" to the *Handbook of the Psychology of Aging* (Almeida, Piazza, Stawski, & Kline, 2011).

"The number of new citations is wonderful. Each page I read had findings from new studies published after 2010. It really gave me the sense that I was reading the most up-to-date work in human development. The Topical Connection is not only a great learning device, it encourages developmental thinking. This will help instructors to drive home important developmental issues of looking backward and looking forward as a way of understanding individuals." —**David Almeida** *Pennsylvania State University*

Crystal Park Crystal Park is a leading expert on religious beliefs and religious coping, stress, and death and dying. She currently is Professor of Psychology at the University of Connecticut. Dr. Park has developed a comprehensive model of meaning-making coping that focuses on how people find meaning or create meaning out of negative life events. Her research has been funded by the Templeton Foundation, the Lance Armstrong Foundation, and the National Center for Complementary and Alternative Medicine. Dr. Park also is associate editor of *Psychology of Religion; Psychology and Health;* and the *International Journal of the Psychology of Religion*. She was a recipient of the Early Career Award from the Psychology of Religion division of the American Psychological Association.

"In reading through these chapters, I once again am amazed and inspired by how much solid research is accurately and succinctly being presented. These chapters cover so much material and yet are very specific and grounded in empirical literature." —**Crystal Park** *University of Connecticut*

Arthur Kramer is the Director of the Beckman Institute for Advanced Science & Technology and the Swanlund Chair and Professor of Psychology and Neuroscience at the University of Illinois. He received his Ph.D. in Cognitive/Experimental Psychology from the University of Illinois in 1984. He holds appointments in the Department of Psychology, Neuroscience program, and the Beckman Institute. Professor Kramer's research projects include topics in Cognitive Psychology, Cognitive Neuroscience, Aging, and Human Factors. A major focus of his recent research is the understanding and enhancement of cognitive and neural plasticity across the life span. He is a former Associate Editor of *Perception* and *Psychophysics* and is currently a member of six editorial boards. Professor Kramer is also a fellow of the American Psychological Association, American Psychological Society, a former member of the executive committee of the International Society of Attention and Performance, and a recent recipient of a NIH Ten Year MERIT Award. Professor Kramer's research has been featured in a long list of print, radio, and electronic media including the *New York Times, Wall Street Journal, Washington Post, Chicago Tribune, CBS Evening News, Today Show, NPR,* and *Saturday Night Live.*

". . . I very much enjoyed reading Chapters 17 (Physical Development and Aging) and 18 (Cognitive Development and Aging) of the 13th edition of Life-Span Development. The material is up-to-date and the different connections that are integrated within the chapters render the material quite accessible to today's students." —**Arthur Kramer** *University of Illinois at Urbana-Champaign*

McGraw-Hill Connect Lifespan Development

adaptive learning system

McGraw-Hill Connect® Psychology is our response to today's student. The groundbreaking adaptive learning system helps students "know what they know" while helping them learn what they don't know through engaging interactive exercises, click/drag activities, the Milestones program, and video clips. Instructors using Connect are reporting that their students' performance is improving by a letter grade or more. Through this unique tool, *Life-Span Development* gives instructors the ability to identify struggling students quickly and easily, *before* the first exam.

Connect Psychology's adaptive diagnostic tool develops an individualized learning plan for every student. Confidence levels tailor the next question to each individual, helping students to identify what they don't know. If a student is doing well, the adaptive diagnostic tool will challenge the student with more applied and conceptual questions. If the student is struggling, the system identifies problem areas and directs the student to the exact page they need to read. In doing so, it works like a GPS, helping students master key concepts efficiently and effectively.

Regardless of individual study habits, preparation, and approaches to the course, students will find that *Life-Span Development* connects with them on a personal, individual basis and provides a road map for success in the course.

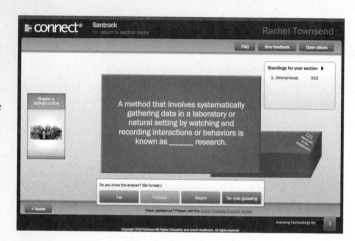

milestones

Experience life as it unfolds

- Engage with real children developing over time.
- Test your ability to apply course content to real children, adolescents, and adults.

McGraw Hill's Milestones is a powerful tool that allows students to experience life as it unfolds, from infancy to late adulthood.

Milestones consists of two essential components that work together to capture key changes throughout the lifespan—**Milestones of Child Development and Milestones: Transitions.**

In **Milestones of Child Development,** students track the early stages of physical, social, and emotional development. By watching one child over time or comparing various children, Milestones provides a unique, experiential learning environment that can only be achieved by watching real human development as it happens—all in pre-, transitional, and post-milestone segments.

In **Milestones: Transitions,** students meet a series of people—from teenagers to individuals in late adulthood—to hear individual perspectives on changes that occur throughout the the life span. Through a series of interviews, students are given the opportunity to think critically while exploring the differences in attitudes on everything from body image to changes in emotion, sexuality, cognitive processes, and death and dying.

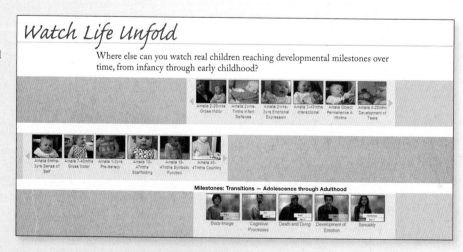

Watch Life Unfold

Where else can you watch real children reaching developmental milestones over time, from infancy through early childhood?

Milestones: Transitions — Adolescence through Adulthood

assignable and assessable activities keyed to learning objectives

Whether a class is face-to-face, hybrid, or entirely online, *Life-Span Development* provides the tools needed to reduce the amount of time and energy that instructors must expend to administer their course. At the end of each chapter, assignable and assessable activities are correlated with key topic areas.

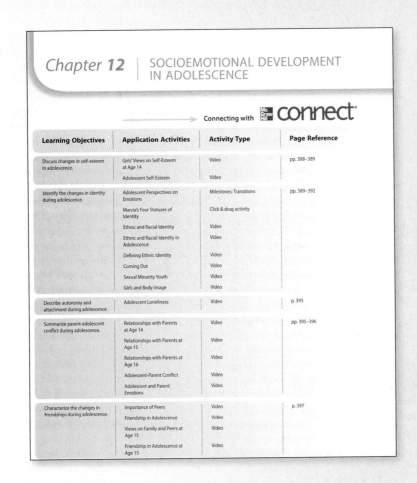

MCGRAW-HILL/BB/DO MORE

Through McGraw-Hill's partnership with Blackboard®, *Life-Span Development* offers a seamless integration of content and tools:

- Seamless gradebook between Blackboard and Connect
- Single sign-on providing seamless integration between McGraw-Hill content and Blackboard
- Simplicity in assigning and engaging your students with course materials

create

Craft your teaching resources to match the way you teach! With McGraw-Hill Create™ (www.mcgrawhillcreate.com), you can easily rearrange chapters, combine material from other content sources, and quickly upload content you have written, such as your course syllabus or teaching notes. Find the content you need in Create by searching through thousands of leading McGraw-Hill textbooks. Arrange your book to fit your teaching style. Create even allows you to personalize your book's appearance by selecting the cover and adding your name, school, and course information. Order a Create book and you'll receive a complimentary print review copy in three to five business days or a complimentary electronic review copy (eComp) via e-mail in about an hour. Go to www.mcgrawhillcreate.com today and register. Experience how McGraw-Hill Create empowers you to teach *your* students *your* way.

tegrity

McGraw-Hill Tegrity® is a service that makes class time available all the time by automatically capturing every lecture in a searchable format for students to review when they study and complete assignments. With a simple, one-click start and stop process, users capture all computer screens and corresponding audio. Students replay any part of any class with easy-to-use, browser-based viewing on a PC or Mac. Educators know that the more students can see, hear, and experience class resources, the better they learn. With Tegrity, students quickly recall key moments by using Tegrity's unique search feature. This search helps students efficiently find what they need, when they need it, across an entire semester of class recordings. Help turn all your students' study time into learning moments immediately supported by your lecture.

CourseSmart

This text is available as an eTextbook at www.CourseSmart.com. At CourseSmart your students can take advantage of significant savings off the cost of a print textbook, reduce their impact on the environment, and gain access to powerful Web tools for learning. CourseSmart eTextbooks can be viewed online or downloaded to a computer. The eTextbooks allow students to do full text searches, add highlighting and notes, and share notes with classmates. CourseSmart has the largest selection of eTextbooks available anywhere. Visit www.CourseSmart.com to learn more and to try a sample chapter.

Making Connections . . . From My Classroom to *Life-Span Development* to You

Having taught life-span development every semester for 27 years now, I'm always looking for ways to improve my course and *Life-Span Development*. Just as McGraw-Hill looks to those who teach the life-span development course for input, each year I ask the almost 200 students in my life-span development course to tell me what they like about the course and the text, and what they think could be improved. What have my students told me lately about my course and text? Students said that highlighting connections among the different aspects of life-span development would help them to better understand the concepts. As I thought about this, it became clear that a *connections* theme would provide a systematic, integrative approach to the course material. I used this theme to shape my current goals for my life-span development course, which, in turn, I've incorporated into *Life-Span Development*:

1. **Connecting with today's students** To help students learn about life-span development more effectively

2. **Connecting research to what we know about development** To provide students with the best and most recent theory and research in the world today about each of the periods of the human life span

3. **Connecting developmental processes** To guide students in making developmental connections across different points in the human life span

4. **Connecting development to the real world** To help students understand ways to apply content about the human life span to the real world and improve people's lives; and to motivate them to think deeply about their own personal journey through life and better understand who they were, are, and will be

Connecting with Today's Students

In *Life-Span Development,* I recognize that today's students are as different in some ways from the learners of the last generation as today's discipline of life-span development is different from the field 30 years ago. Students now learn in multiple modalities; rather than sitting down and reading traditional printed chapters in linear fashion from beginning to end, their work preferences tend to be more visual and more interactive, and their reading and study often occur in short bursts. For many students, a traditionally formatted printed textbook is no longer enough when they have instant, 24/7 access to news and information from around the globe. Two features that specifically support today's students are the adaptive diagnostic tool and the learning goals system.

The Learning Goals System

My students often report the life-span development course to be challenging because of the amount of material covered. To help today's students focus on the key ideas, the Learning Goals System I developed for *Life-Span Development* provides extensive learning connections throughout the chapters. The learning system connects the chapter opening outline, learning goals for the chapter, mini-chapter maps that open each main section of the chapter, *Review, Connect, and Reflect* at the end of each main section, and the chapter summary at the end of each chapter.

The learning system keeps the key ideas in front of the student from the beginning to the end of the chapter. The main headings of each chapter correspond to the learning goals, which are presented in the chapter-opening spread. Mini-chapter maps that link up with

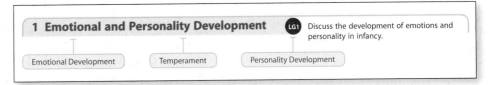

1 Emotional and Personality Development **LG1** Discuss the development of emotions and personality in infancy.

Emotional Development — Temperament — Personality Development

xxi

Prenatal Development and Birth

| 1 Prenatal Development | **LG1** Describe prenatal development. |

The Course of Prenatal Development

• Prenatal development is divided into three periods: germinal (conception until 10 to 14 days later), which ends when the zygote (a fertilized egg) attaches to the uterine wall; embryonic (two to eight weeks after conception), during which the embryo differentiates into three layers, life-support systems develop, and organ systems form (organogenesis); and fetal (from two months after conception until about nine months, or when the infant is born), a time when organ systems have matured to the point at which life can be sustained outside the womb. The growth of the brain during prenatal development is nothing short of remarkable. By the time babies are born, they have approximately 100 billion neurons, or nerve cells. Neurogenesis is the term for the formation of new neurons. The nervous system begins with the formation of a neural tube at 18 to 24 days after conception. Proliferation and migration are two processes that characterize brain development in the prenatal period. The basic architecture of the brain is formed in the first two trimesters of prenatal development.

the learning goals are presented at the beginning of each major section in the chapter.

Then, at the end of each main section of a chapter, the learning goal is repeated in *Review, Connect, and Reflect,* which prompts students to review the key topics in the section, connect to existing knowledge, and relate what they learned to their own personal journey through life. *Reach Your Learning Goals,* at the end of the chapter, guides students through the bulleted chapter review, connecting with the chapter outline/learning goals at the beginning of the chapter and the *Review, Connect, and Reflect* questions at the end of major chapter sections.

Connecting Research to What We Know about Development

Over the years, it has been important for me to include the most up-to-date research available. I continue that tradition in this fourteenth edition by looking closely at specific areas of research, involving experts in related fields, and updating research throughout. **Connecting through Research** describes a study or program to illustrate how research in life-span development is conducted and how it influences our understanding of the discipline. Topics range from *Do Children Conceived through In Vitro Fertilization Show Significant Differences in Developmental Outcomes in Adolescence?* (Chapter 2) to *How Much Does the Environment Affect Intelligence?* (Chapter 9) to *What Is the Relationship Between Fitness in Young Adults and Cardiovascular Health in Middle Age?* (Chapter 15).

The tradition of obtaining detailed, extensive input from a number of leading experts in different areas of life-span development also continues in this edition. Biographies and photographs of the leading experts in the field of life-span development appear on pages xiv to xvi, and the chapter-by-chapter highlights of new research content are listed on pages xxv to xxxix. Finally, the research discussions have been updated in every period and topic. I expended every effort to make this edition of *Life-Span Development* as contemporary and up-to-date as possible. To that end, there are more than 1,200 citations from 2011, 2012, and 2013 in the text.

connecting through research

Which Children Are Most Likely to Benefit From Early Intervention?

Fast Track is an intervention that attempts to lower the risk of juvenile delinquency and other problems (Conduct Problems Prevention Research Group, 2010, 2011; Dodge & McCourt, 2010; Jones & others, 2010; Miller & others, 2011). Schools in four areas (Durham, North Carolina; Nashville, Tennessee; Seattle, Washington; and rural central Pennsylvania) were identified as high-risk based on neighborhood crime and poverty data. Researchers screened more than 9,000 kindergarten children in the four schools and randomly assigned 891 of the highest-risk and moderate-risk children to intervention or control groups. The average age of the children when the intervention began was 6.5 years.

The 10-year intervention consisted of parent behavior management training, child social cognitive skills training, reading tutoring, home visitations, mentoring, and a revised classroom curriculum that was designed to increase socioemotional competence and decrease aggression. Outcomes were assessed in the third, sixth, and ninth grades for conduct disorder (multiple instances of behaviors such as truancy, running away, fire setting, cruelty to animals, breaking and entering, and excessive fighting across a six-month period), oppositional defiant disorder (an ongoing pattern of disobedient, hostile, and defiant behavior toward authority figures), attention deficit hyperactivity disorder (as

described in Chapter 9, being characterized by one or more of these characteristics over a period of time: inattention, hyperactivity, and impulsivity), any externalizing disorder (presence of any of the three disorders previously described), and self-reported antisocial behavior (a list of 34 behaviors, such as skipping school, stealing, and attacking someone with an intent to hurt them).

The extensive intervention was successful only for children and adolescents who were identified as having the highest risk in kindergarten, lowering their incidence of conduct disorder, attention deficit hyperactivity disorder, any externalized disorder, and antisocial behavior (Dodge & McCourt, 2010). Positive outcomes for the intervention occurred as early as the third grade and continued through the ninth grade. For example, in the ninth grade the intervention reduced the likelihood that the highest-risk kindergarten children would develop conduct disorder by 75 percent, attention deficit hyperactivity disorder by 53 percent, and any externalized disorder by 43 percent. Recently, data have been reported through age 19 (Miller & others, 2011). Findings indicate that the comprehensive Fast Track intervention was successful in reducing youth arrest rates (Conduct Problems Prevention Research Group, 2011).

Connecting Developmental Processes

Development through the life span is a long journey, and too often we forget or fail to notice the many connections from one point in development to another. I have substantially increased these connections made in the text narrative. I also created two new features to help students connect topics across the periods of development.

Developmental Connections, which appear multiple times in each chapter, points readers to where the topic is discussed in a previous or subsequent chapter. *Developmental Connections* highlight links across age periods of development *and* connections between biological, cognitive, and socioemotional processes. These key developmental processes are typically discussed in isolation from each other, and students often fail to see their connections. Included in the

developmental **connection**

Personality

Two key points in development when there is a strong push for independence are the second year of life and early adolescence. Chapter 12, p. 395

Developmental Connections is a brief description of the backward or forward connection. For example, consider the development of the brain. In recent editions, I have significantly expanded content on the changes in the brain through the life span, including new coverage of changes in the brain during prenatal development and an expanded discussion of the aging brain in older adults. The prenatal brain discussion appears in Chapter 3 and the aging brain is described in Chapter 17. An important brain topic that we discuss in Chapters 3 and 17 is neurogenesis, the production of new neurons. In this new edition, connections between these topics in Chapters 3 and 17 are highlighted through *Developmental Connections*.

Topical Connections: Looking Back and **Looking Forward** begin and conclude each chapter by placing the chapter's coverage in the larger context of development. The Looking Back section reminds the reader of what happened developmentally in previous periods of development.

Looking Forward prepares the student for what is to happen in a future period of development. Together, these new features help students construct a topical understanding of development alongside a chronological one.

Finally, a *Connect* question appears in the section self-reviews—*Review, Connect, and Reflect*—so students can practice making connections between topics. For example, in Chapter 9, students are asked to connect what they learned in Chapter 7 about the genetic links of autism to what they have just read about specific brain abnormalities associated with autism spectrum disorders.

-topical **connections** -----------

Genes form the biological basis of our development. They are passed on through mitosis, meiosis, and, ultimately, fertilization. The impact of our genes involves the genetic principles of dominate-recessive genes, sex-linked genes, genetic imprinting, and polygenically determined characteristics. Approximately 10 to 15 percent of U.S. couples have problems with fertility. Some of these problems can be solved through surgery, drugs, or in vitro fertilization. Whether a pregnancy occurs naturally or with assistance, the resulting infant's development is shaped both by his or her genes (nature) and environment (nurture).

◄--- *looking back* ---------------

-topical **connections** -----------

This chapter marks the beginning of our chronological look at the journey of life. In the next three chapters that comprise Section 3 of the book, we will follow the physical, cognitive, and socioemotional development of infants, including the theories, research, and milestones associated with the first 18 to 24 months of life. You will learn about the remarkable and complex physical development of infants' motor skills, such as learning to walk; trace the early development of infants' cognitive skills, such as the ability to form concepts; and explore infants' surprisingly sophisticated socioemotional capabilities, as reflected in the development of their motivation to share and to perceive others' actions as intentionally motivated.

looking **forward** ---►

Connecting Development to the Real World

In addition to helping students make research and developmental connections, *Life-Span Development* shows the important connections between the concepts discussed and the real world. In recent years, students in my lifespan development course have increasingly told me that they want more of this type of information. In this edition, real-life connections are explicitly made through the chapter opening vignette, *Connecting Development to Life*, the new Milestones program that helps students watch life as it unfolds, and *Connecting with Careers*.

Each chapter begins with a story designed to increase students' interest and motivation to read the chapter.

Connecting Development to Life describes the influence of development in a real-world context on topics including From Waterbirth to Music Therapy (Chapter 3), Increasing Children's Self-Esteem (Chapter 10), and Health Care Providers and Older Adults (Chapter 17).

The **Milestones** program shows students what developmental concepts look like by watching actual humans develop. Starting from infancy, students track several individuals, seeing them achieve major developmental milestones, both physically and cognitively. Clips continue through adolescence and adulthood, capturing attitudes toward issues such as family, sexuality, and death and dying.

Connecting with Careers profiles careers ranging from an educational psychologist (Chapter 1) to a toy designer (Chapter 7) to a marriage and family therapist (Chapter 8) to the director of an organization that promotes positive adolescent development (Chapter 11) to a geriatric nurse (Chapter 17), each of which requires knowledge about human development.

---

connecting development to life

Increasing Children's Self-Esteem

Ways to improve children's self-esteem include identifying the causes of low self-esteem, providing emotional support and social approval, helping children achieve, and helping children cope (Bednar, Wells, & Peterson, 1995; Harter, 2006, 2012).

• *Identify the causes of low self-esteem.* Intervention should target the causes of low self-esteem. Children have the highest self-esteem when they perform competently in domains that are important to them. Therefore, children should be encouraged to identify and value areas of competence. These areas might include academic skills, athletic skills, physical attractiveness, and social acceptance.

• *Provide emotional support and social approval.* Some children with low self-esteem come from conflicted families or conditions in which they experienced abuse or neglect—situations in which support was not available. In some cases, alternative sources of support can be arranged either informally through the encouragement of a teacher, a coach, or another significant adult, or more formally, through programs such as Big Brothers and Big Sisters.

• *Help children achieve.* Achievement also can improve children's self-esteem. For example, the straightforward teaching of real skills to children often results in increased achievement and, thus, in enhanced self-esteem. Children develop higher self-esteem because they know the important tasks that will achieve their goals, and they have performed them or similar behaviors in the past.

• *Help children cope.* Self-esteem often increases when children face a problem and try to cope with it, rather than avoid it. If coping rather than avoidance prevails, children face problems realistically, honestly, and nondefensively. This produces favorable self-evaluative thoughts, which lead to the self-generated approval that raises self-esteem.

How can parents help children develop higher self-esteem?

As discussed in the "Emotional Development" section of Chapter 8, which parenting approach might help accomplish the last goal mentioned here? How?

Darla Botkin, Marriage and Family Therapist

Darla Botkin is a marriage and family therapist who teaches, conducts research, and engages in marriage and family therapy. She is on the faculty of the University of Kentucky. Botkin obtained a bachelor's degree in elementary education with a concentration in special education and then went on to receive a master's degree in early childhood education. She spent the next six years working with children and their families in a variety of settings, including child care, elementary school, and Head Start. These experiences led Botkin to recognize the interdependence of the developmental settings that children and their parents experience (such as home, school, and work). She returned to graduate school and obtained a Ph.D. in family studies from the University of Tennessee. She then became a faculty member in the Family Studies program at the University of Kentucky. Completing further coursework and clinical training in marriage and family therapy, she became certified as a marriage and family therapist.

Botkin's current interests include working with young children in family therapy, addressing gender and ethnic issues in family therapy, and exploring the role of spirituality in family wellness.

Darla Botkin (*left*) conducting a family therapy session.

For more information about what marriage and family therapists do, see page 47 in the Careers in Life-Span Development appendix.

The careers highlighted extend from the Careers Appendix in Chapter 1 that provides a comprehensive overview of careers in life-span development to show students where knowledge of human development could lead them.

Part of applying development to the real world is understanding its impact on oneself. An important goal I have established for my life-span development course and this text is to motivate students to think deeply about their own journey of life. To further encourage students to make personal connections to content in the text, *Reflect: Your Own Personal Journey of Life* appears in the end-of-section review in each chapter. This feature involves a question that asks students to reflect on some aspect of the discussion in the section they have just read and connect it to their own life. For example, in Chapter 1, students are asked:

Do you think there is, was/will be a best age for you to be? If so, what is it? Why?

I always include this question in the first content lecture I give in life-span development and it generates thoughtful and interesting class discussion. Earlier in that section of Chapter 1 is a research discussion on whether there is a best age to be, which includes recent research on the topic and in this edition a new self-assessment that lets students evaluate their own life satisfaction. In addition, students are asked a number of personal connections questions in the photograph captions.

Content Revisions

Following are the main chapter-by-chapter changes that were made in this new edition of *Life-Span Development.*

Chapter 1: Introduction

- Extensive updating of research citations
- Update on life expectancy in the United States (U.S. Census Bureau, 2011)
- Expanded discussion of poverty and children, including updated statistics on the percentage of U.S. children under 18 years of age living in poverty (U.S. Census Bureau, 2012)
- Description of a recent study of more than 300,000 U.S. adults that revealed an increase in psychological well-being after 50 years of age (Stone & others, 2010)
- New Figure 1.9, How Satisfied Am I with My Life? that gives students an opportunity to evaluate their life satisfaction on the most widely used measure in research on life satisfaction (Diener, 2012; Diener & others, 1985)
- Revised and updated commentary about social age and its links to happiness and longevity (Carstensen & others, 2011)
- New Figure 1.18 showing neuroimages of the brains of two adolescents (one a non-drinker, the other a heavy drinker) while they are engaging in a memory task
- Inclusion of recent research and commentary on Millennials involving ethnic diversity and technology based on a recent national survey by the Pew Research Center (2010)
- New Figure 1.19 comparing various generations, their historical periods, and their characteristics

Chapter 2: Biological Beginnings

- Extensive editing and updating of chapter based on detailed reviews by leading experts Kirby Deater-Deckard and David Moore
- New discussion of the genome-wide association study that is increasingly used to identify genetic variations in individuals who have a disease compared with those who don't (National Human Genome Research Institute, 2012)
- New coverage of some diseases for which genome-wide association studies recently have been conducted: childhood obesity (Early Growth Genetics Consortium & others, 2012), Alzheimer disease (Raj & others, 2012), and cardiovascular disease (Lusis, 2012)
- Expanded and updated material on modifications in DNA expression as a result of stress, radiation, and temperature (Georgakilas, 2011)
- Description of a recent study that found exposure to radiation changes the rate of DNA synthesis (Lee & others, 2011)
- Updated and expanded coverage of gene-gene interaction to include recent studies of immune system functioning (Reijmerink & others, 2011), asthma (Su & others, 2012), cancer (Bushel & others, 2012), cardiovascular disease (Xiao & others, 2012), and arthritis (Ronninger & others, 2012)
- Updated material on noninvasive prenatal diagnosis (NIPD) (Chiu & Lo, 2012; Geaghan, 2012)
- New information about being able to determine the sex of the fetus at an earlier point in pregnancy through new noninvasive procedures (Kolialexi, 2012)
- Discussion of a recent meta-analysis indicating that a baby's sex can be determined as early as 7 weeks into pregnancy (Devaney & others, 2011)

- Coverage of recent reviews regarding child and adolescent outcomes for individuals conceived using new reproductive technologies (Golombok, 2011a, b; Golombok & Tasker, 2010)
- New material indicating that many U.S. adoptions now involve other family members (aunts/uncles/grandparents): 30 percent of U.S. adoptions are made by relatives and slightly more than 50 percent of U.S. adoptions involve the foster care system (Ledesma, 2012)
- New description of research on the age at which children are adopted and whether they engage in juvenile delinquency (Laubjerg & Petersson, 2011)
- Discussion of a recent study of improved cognitive development in children who were adopted after they had lived in foster homes and institutions (van den Dries & others, 2010)
- Addition of information about epigenetic mechanisms involving the actual molecular modification of the DNA strand as a result of environmental inputs in ways that alter gene functioning (Feil & Fraga, 2012; Meaney, 2010)
- Updated coverage of the concept of $G \times E$, which involves the interaction of a specific measured variation in the DNA sequence and a specific measured aspect of the environment (Bihagi & others, 2012; Petersen & others, 2012; Zannas & others, 2012)
- Description of recent research indicating that variations in dopamine-related genes interact with supportive or unsupportive environments to influence children's development (Bakermans-Kranenburg & van IJzendoorn, 2011)

Chapter 3: Prenatal Development and Birth

- Description of a recent study that found cigarette smoke weakened and increased oxidative stress in the fetal membranes from which the placenta develops (Menon & others, 2011)
- Inclusion of information from a recent research review indicating that high amounts of caffeine consumption by pregnant women do not increase the risk of miscarriage, congenital malformations, or growth retardation (Brent, Christian, & Diener, 2011)
- Coverage of recent research that found deficiencies in the brain pathways involved in the working memory of children with FASD (Diwadkar & others, 2012)
- Discussion of a recent meta-analysis linking maternal smoking during pregnancy to a modest increase in risk for childhood non-Hodgkin lymphoma (Antonopoulos & others, 2011)
- Information about a recent study that found environmental tobacco smoke exposure during pregnancy was linked to diminished ovarian functioning in female offspring (Kilic & others, 2012)
- Update on the most consistent negative outcomes of cocaine use during pregnancy (Gouin & others, 2011)
- Coverage of a recent research review that concluded cocaine quickly crosses the placenta to reach the fetus (De Giovanni & Marchetti, 2012)
- Description of recent research on the negative effects of cocaine exposure prenatally on children's attention and externalizing problems (Minnes & others, 2010; Richardson & others, 2011)
- New information from research on a link between prenatal cocaine exposure and elevated blood pressure at 9 years of age (Shankaran & others, 2010)

- Coverage of a recent study that found prenatal meth exposure was associated with smaller head circumference, neonatal intensive care unit (NICU) admission, and referral to child protective services (Shah & others, 2012)

- Discussion of prenatal methamphetamine exposure and decreased brain activation, especially in the frontal lobes, in 7- to 15-year-olds (Roussotte, 2011)

- Expanded description of the possible negative outcomes for the off-spring of women with syphilis (Caddy & others, 2011; Ishaque & others, 2011)

- Description of a recent large-scale study that found children whose mothers had diabetes during pregnancy had lower expressive language scores than mothers who did not have diabetes during pregnancy (Krakowiak & others, 2012)

- Update on guidelines for eating certain types of fish during pregnancy (American Pregnancy Association, 2012; Mayo Clinic, 2012)

- Description of recent research on more than 30,000 offspring regarding the time during prenatal development when maternal exposure to stress was most likely to increase the risk of preterm birth (Class & others, 2011)

- Coverage of a recent research review that linked maternal depression to preterm birth (Dunkel Schetter, 2011)

- Description of a recent study that revealed paternal smoking around the time of the child's conception was linked to an increased risk of the child developing leukemia (Milne & others, 2012)

- Coverage of a recent research review indicating an increased risk of spontaneous abortion, autism, and schizophrenic disorders in offspring for whom the father is 40 years of age and older (Reproductive Endocrinology and Infertility Committee & others, 2012)

- New discussion of how much weight gain during pregnancy is best for obese women, as well as the importance of their losing weight and increasing exercise prior to becoming pregnant (Simmons, 2011)

- New discussion of the increasing inclusion of exercise in prenatal care programs (Streuling & others, 2011)

- Coverage of a recent study indicating that the risk of exercise-related injury during pregnancy was low (Vladutiu, Evenson, & Marshall, 2010)

- Description of a recent experimental study that found a 3-month aerobic exercise program improved pregnant women's health-related quality of life (Montoya Arizabaleta & others, 2010)

- Inclusion of recent research indicating that exercise during pregnancy improved mothers' perceptions of their health (Barakat & others, 2011)

- Discussion of a recent study that revealed yoga and massage therapy sessions resulted in decreased levels of depression, anxiety, and back and leg pain (Field & others, 2012)

- Coverage of a recent research review that concluded practicing yoga during pregnancy is associated with a number of positive outcomes for mothers and a reduction in the incidence of low birth weight infants (Babbar & others, 2012)

- Description of a recent study that found group prenatal care provided a broad network of social support for pregnant women (McNeil & others, 2012)

- Coverage of a recent experimental study of the effects of a Centering-Pregnancy Plus program on high-stress pregnant women (Ickovics & others, 2011)

- Discussion of a recent research review of prenatal home visits and their link to improved prenatal care use but less evidence for their influence on newborns' birth weight (Issel & others, 2011)

- New material on the recent increase in home births to non-Latino White women (Macdorman, Declercq, & Menacker, 2011)

- Description of a recent research review that found positive outcomes for midwife-led care compared with physician-led care in low-risk women (Sutcliffe & others, 2012)

- Discussion of a recent study that found waterbirth was linked with a shorter second stage of labor (Cortes, Basra, & Kelleher, 2011)

- Updated coverage of the increased evidence that acupuncture can have positive effects on labor and delivery (Citkovitz, Schnyer, & Hoskins, 2011)

- Discussion of the results of two recent research reviews that indicated massage therapy reduces pain during labor (Jones & others, 2012; Smith & others, 2012)

- Update on the dramatic increase in cesarean deliveries in the United States (Solheim & others, 2011)

- Discussion of a recent study indicating that low Apgar scores are linked with developing ADHD in childhood (Li & others, 2011)

- Updated coverage of the percentage of infants born preterm in the United States, including the overall rate and ethnic variations in 2009 (National Center for Health Statistics, 2011)

- Description of a recent research review that concluded kangaroo care reduced the risk of mortality in low birth weight infants (Conde-Agudelo, Belizan, & Diaz-Rossello, 2011)

- Coverage of a recent study that revealed the mechanisms responsible for weight gain in massaged preterm infants (Field, Diego, & Hernandez-Reif, 2011)

- New coverage of the incidence of fathers having elevated depressive symptoms when their wives have postpartum depression (Letourneau & others, 2012; Ramchandani & others, 2011)

Chapter 4: Physical Development in Infancy

- Changes in coverage of the development of the brain based on comments from leading expert consultant Martha Ann Bell

- Addition of John Richards and his colleagues (2009, 2010; Mallin & Richards, 2012; Richards, Reynolds, & Courage, 2010) for conducting important research on the development of the brain in infancy

- Update on the role of myelination in providing energy for neurons (Fancy & others, 2012; Harris & Attwell, 2012)

- New section, The Neuroconstructivist View, that describes an increasingly popular perspective on the brain's development (Diamond, 2013; Johnson, 2012; Westerman, Thomas, & Karmiloff-Smith, 2011; Peltzer-Karpf, 2012)

- Description of a recent research review of sleep patterns in infancy (Galland & others, 2012)

- Inclusion of information about a recent study that revealed by 6 months of age, a majority of infants slept through the night, awakening their mothers only once or twice a week (Weinraub & others, 2012)

- Discussion of a recent study that revealed nighttime wakings at 12 months of age predicted a lower level of sleep efficiency at four years of age (Tikotzky & Shaashua, 2012)

- Coverage of a recent study linking maternal emotional availability to fewer infant sleep problems (Teti & others, 2010)

- Discussion of a recent study indicating that paternal involvement in infant care was related to fewer infant sleep problems (Tikotzky, Sadeh, & Glickman-Gavrieli, 2010)

- Description of recent research on early life risk factors that are linked to infant sleep duration (Nevarez & others, 2010)

- Updated information about infant-parent bed sharing and an increasing trend of recommending that this not occur until the infant is at least six months old (McIntosh, Tonkin, & Gunn, 2010)
- Discussion of a recent meta-analysis linking breastfeeding to a lower incidence of SIDS (Hauck & others, 2011)
- New material on recent research indicating that as many as 10 to 15 percent of SIDS cases are linked to heart arrhythmias, with gene mutations being involved in the arrhythmias (Brion & others, 2012; Van Norstrand & others, 2012)
- Updated data on recent increases in the percentage of infants who are overweight (Centers for Disease Control and Prevention, 2010)
- Description of a recent study that found the introduction of solid foods before 4 months of age was linked to an increased risk of obesity at 3 years of age (Huh & others, 2011)
- Description of recent research that found low maternal sensitivity when infants were 15 and 24 months of age was linked to a higher risk of obesity in adolescence (Anderson & others, 2012)
- Inclusion of the American Academy of Pediatrics Section on Breastfeeding's (2012) reconfirmation of its recommendation of exclusive breast feeding in the first six months, followed by continued breast feeding as complementary foods are introduced, and further breast feeding for one year or longer as mutually desired by the mother and infant
- Updated data on the percentage of U.S. mothers who breast feed their infants in the hospital and for the first 6 months (Centers for Disease Control and Prevention, 2011)
- Discussion of a recent study of infant feeding practices in 28 developing countries that found the practices were far from optimal (Arabi & others, 2012)
- Description of a longitudinal study that revealed malnourished Barbadian infants had persisting attentional deficits when they were 40 years old (Galler & others, 2012)
- Updated coverage of the WIC program, including recent research, in the *Connecting Development to Life* interlude (WIC New York, 2011)
- New discussion of a recent literacy intervention program with Spanish-speaking families in the Los Angeles WIC program that increased literacy resources and activities in homes, which in turn led to a higher level of school readiness in children (Whaley & others, 2011)
- A number of changes made in the material on motor development based on leading expert Karen Adolph's feedback
- Description of a recent study by Karen Adolph and her colleagues (2012) that found 12- to 19-month-olds took 2,368 steps and fell 17 times an hour during free play, suggesting the extensiveness of locomotor experience
- Inclusion of recent research indicating that training infants to use sticky mittens resulted in advances in their reaching behavior (Libertus & Needham, 2010)
- New coverage of Rachel's Keen's (2011) research indicating that tool use is an excellent context for studying problem solving in children less than 3 years old because motor behavior can indicate how the infant plans to reach a goal
- Updated discussion of the new perspective on infant reflexes arguing that reflexes are not exclusively inborn, genetic mechanisms but rather that infants can deliberately control such movements (Adolph & Berger, 2013; Adolph & Robinson, 2013)
- New coverage of recent research indicating that alternating leg movements occur during the fetal period and at birth (Adolph & Robinson, 2013)

- Revised information about the percentage of infants who do not crawl in some cultures with information that about one-fourth of infants in Jamaica don't crawl (Hopkins, 1991)
- Revised and updated information about cultural variations in promoting or restricting motor development and outcomes of these practices (Adolph, Karasik, & Tamis-LeMonda, 2010)
- A number of changes in the discussion of perceptual development based on feedback from leading experts Scott Johnson and Rachel Keen
- Much expanded and updated coverage of the dramatic increase in the use of sophisticated eye-tracking equipment in the study of infant perception (Aslin, 2012; Oakes, 2012)
- Description of a recent eye-tracking study in which 1-year-old infants were less efficient in looking at an educational video than their older counterparts (Kirkorian, Anderson, & Keen, 2012)
- Coverage of a recent fMRI study that confirmed the fetus can hear at 33 to 34 months into the prenatal period by assessing fetal brain responses to auditory stimuli (Jardri & others, 2012)
- Discussion of a recent study that found 7-month-old infants can process simultaneous pitches when they hear voices but they are more likely to encode the higher-pitched voice (Marie & Trainor, 2012)
- Updated information about learning tastes prenatally through the amniotic fluid (Mennella, 2009)
- Coverage of a recent study indicating that young infants looked longest at reddish hues and shortest at greenish hues (Franklin & others, 2010)
- Added commentary that most perception is intermodal (Bahrick, 2010)

Chapter 5: Cognitive Development in Infancy

- Expanded conclusions about the themes of the current field of infant cognitive development to emphasize the substantial increase in interest in cognitive developmental neuroscience and links between brain processes and cognitive processes (Diamond, 2013; Morasch & others, 2013; Peltzer-Karpf, 2012)
- Description of a recent study indicating that joint attention enhanced the long-term memory of 9-month-old infants (Kopp & Lindenberger, 2011)
- Discussion of a recent study that found responding to joint attention at 1 month of age was linked to self-regulation skills at 3 years of age (Van Hecke & others, 2012)
- Updated coverage of concept formation, including a revised definition of concepts
- Addition of recent commentary about learning by infant researcher Alison Gopnik (2010) on the importance of putting things into the right categories
- Coverage of a recent longitudinal study on the stability of intelligence from 12 months to 4 years of age (Blaga & others, 2009)
- Modifications and updates of the discussion of language development based on comments by leading expert Catherine McBride-Chang
- Updated information about developmental aspects of the pointing gesture in the first two years of life (Colonessi & others, 2010)
- Discussion of recent research on differences in early gesture as explanations for SES disparities in child vocabulary at school entry (Rowe & Goldin-Meadow, 2009)
- New material on cross-linguistic differences in early word learning (Lieven & Stoll, 2010)
- Description of a recent study that revealed 6-month-old infants comprehend names of parts of their body, such as "feet" and "hands" (Tincoff & Jusczyk, 2012)

- Expanded material on why children in low-income families may have difficulty in language development
- Expanded and updated material on how parents can facilitate their infants' and toddlers' language development based on recent recommendations by Ellen Galinsky (2010)
- New discussion of cultural variations in language support (Ochs & Schieffelin, 2008; Schieffelin, 2005)

Chapter 6: Socioemotional Development in Infancy

- Revision and updating of the functions of emotion in infancy to include its role in behavioral organization (social responding and adaptive behavior) (Easterbrooks & others, 2013; Thompson, 2013a)
- Discussion of a recent study that revealed the newborns of depressed mothers showed less vocal distress at the cries of another infant, reflecting emotional and physiological dysregulation (Jones, 2012)
- Description of a recent study that found mothers' emotional reactions (anxiety and anger) increased the risk of subsequent attachment insecurity (Leerkes, Parade, & Gudmunson, 2011)
- Inclusion of recent research indicating a link between problems in infant soothability at 6 months of age and insecure attachment at 12 months of age (Mills-Koonce, Propper, & Barnett, 2012)
- Discussion of a recent study that revealed U.S. infants showed more temperamental fearfulness while Finnish infants engaged in more positive affect, especially effortful control (Gaias & others, 2012)
- Coverage of a recent study linking behavioral inhibition at 3 years of age with shyness 4 years later (Volbrecht & Goldsmith, 2010)
- Description of recent research that found being fearful in situations that are relatively low in threat at 24 months of age was related to higher levels of anxiety in kindergarten (Buss, 2012)
- Discussion of a recent longitudinal study linking shyness/inhibition in infancy/childhood to social anxiety at 21 years of age (Bohlin & Hagekull, 2009)
- New commentary suggesting that too often the biological foundations of temperament are interpreted as meaning that temperament can develop and change; however, key dimensions (such as adaptability and soothability) of the self-regulatory aspect of temperament do develop and change as neurobiological and experiential processes develop and change (Easterbrooks & others, 2013)
- Addition of information about research indicating that decreases in infants' negative emotionality are related to higher levels of parents' sensitivity, involvement, and responsivity (Bates, 2012a, b)
- Coverage of a longitudinal study that found changes in attachment security/insecurity from infancy to adulthood were linked to stresses and supports in socioemotional contexts (Van Ryzin, Carlson, & Sroufe, 2011)
- New description of the developmental cascade model that is increasingly being used to study connections across domains over time that influence developmental pathways and outcomes (Cicchetti, 2013; Masten, 2013)
- New section on Developmental Social Neuroscience and Attachment
- New coverage of the roles of oxytocin and vasopressin in attachment and maternal behavior (Feldman, 2012; Strathearn & others, 2012)
- Discussion of a recent meta-analysis that found strong links between levels or patterns of oxytocin and mother-infant attachment (Galbally & others, 2011)
- New Figure 6.8, Regions of the Brain Proposed as Likely to Be Important in Infant-Mother Attachment
- Inclusion of new information about the concept of transactions reflecting reciprocal socialization (Sameroff, 2009, 2012)

- Inclusion of recent research studies on the transition to parenthood that involve negative changes in relationships for both married and cohabiting women with their partners, and violated expectations (Biehle & Mickelson, 2012; Mortensen & others, 2012)
- New section on Managing and Guiding Infants' Behavior (Holden, Vittrup, & Rosen, 2011)
- New material on the percentage of parents who use various management and corrective methods in dealing with infants' undesirable behaviors, including new Figure 6.10 (Vittrup, Holden, & Buck, 2006)
- Description of a recent study that found marital intimacy and partner support during prenatal development were linked to father-infant attachment following childbirth (Yu & others, 2012)
- Discussion of recent research indicating that fathers with a college-level education engaged in more stimulating physical activities with their infants and that fathers in a conflicting couple relationship participated in less caregiving and physical play with their infants (Cabrera, Hofferth, & Chae, 2011)
- Coverage of recent research linking early higher quality of child care with higher cognitive-academic achievement and lower externalizing behavior at 15 years of age (Vandell & others, 2010)
- Inclusion of the following important point about the NICHD SECCYD research: findings consistently show that family factors are considerably stronger and more consistent predictors of a wide variety of child outcomes than are child care experiences (quality, quantity, type)
- Description of a recent study using the NICHD SECCYD data indicating that the worst socioemotional outcomes for children occurred when both home and child care settings conferred risk (Watamura & others, 2011)

Chapter 7: Physical and Cognitive Development in Early Childhood

- New discussion of unusually short children, including causes (Wit, Kiess, & Mullis, 2011)
- Coverage of a recent study indicating that growth hormone treatment of very short children was effective in partially reducing their height deficit as adults (Deodati & Cianfarani, 2011)
- Inclusion of recent research indicating that growth hormone treatment of very short children was linked with an increase in height as well as improvements in self-esteem and mood (Chaplin & others, 2012)
- Description of a recent study linking sleep problems in early childhood with subsequent attention problems that in some cases persist into early adolescence (O'Callaghan & others, 2010)
- Coverage of a recent study indicating that having trouble sleeping in childhood was related to alcohol use problems in adolescence and early adulthood (Wong & others, 2010)
- Coverage of a recent analysis indicating that chronic child sleep disorders that deprive children of adequate sleep may lead to impaired brain development (Jan & others, 2010)
- Inclusion of information from a recent research review that concluded a short sleep duration is linked to being overweight in childhood (Hart, Cairns, & Jelalian, 2011)
- Description of a recent study that found the most frequently consumed vegetable by 2- and 3-year-olds was French fries or other fried potatoes (Fox & others, 2010)
- Coverage of recent data on the increasing percentage of 2- to 5-year-old obese children in the United States, including trends from 1976–1980 through 2007–2010 (Ogden & others, 2012)

- Discussion of a recent study indicating that preschool children who were overweight had a significant risk of being overweight/obese at 11 years of age (Shankaran & others, 2011)
- Description of a recent study that found parental smoking was a risk factor for higher blood pressure in children (Simonetti & others, 2011)
- Description of a recent fMRI study identifying brain locations that were linked to 9- and 10-year-olds' conservation success in comparison with non-conserving 5- and 6-year-olds (Houde & others, 2011)
- Coverage of recent research linking television watching and video game playing to children's attention problems (Swing & others, 2010)
- New material on using computer exercises to improve children's attention, including a website (www.teach-the-brain.org/learn/attention/index.htm) about how to use the games with children) (Jaeggi, Berman, & Jonides, 2009; Tang & Posner, 2009)
- New discussion of the increasing interest in executive functioning, including the importance of its early development in the preschool years (Carlson & White, 2013; Zelazo & Muller, 2011)
- Inclusion of recent research by Stephanie Carlson (2010, 2011) on developmental changes in children's executive functioning, including a description and a photograph of a task used in her research
- Deletion of material on strategies and movement to their discussion to Chapter 12, Cognitive Development in Middle and Late Childhood
- New commentary that whether infants have a theory of mind continues to be debated (Rakoczy, 2012)
- New description of the poor performance in task sequencing of children with autism (Peterson, Wellman, & Slaughter, 2012)
- Expanded coverage of cognitive factors other than theory of mind that might be involved in autism, including eye gaze, face processing, memory, and language impairment (Boucher, 2012; Boucher, Mayes, & Bigham, 2012; Elsabbagh & others, 2012)
- New material on Kathy Hirsh-Pasek, Roberta Golinkoff, and Justin Harris' (Harris, Golinkoff, & Hirsch-Pasek, 2011; Hirsh-Pasek & Golinkoff, 2013) six principles for optimal word learning in young children
- New material on strategies for using books with preschoolers (Galinsky, 2010)
- Description of a recent study indicating that Early Head Start had a protective effect on the risks children might experience in parenting, language development, and self-control (Ayoub, Vallotton, & Mastergeorge, 2011)

Chapter 8: Socioemotional Development in Early Childhood

- Expanded and updated discussion of young children's optimistic self-conception to consider some young children's negative self-evaluations, especially when they experience stress and adverse family conditions (Goodvin & others, 2008; Thompson, 2011, 2013d)
- Expanded and updated material on the increasing belief that young children are more socially sensitive than was previously envisioned and that this means parents and teachers can help young children to better understand people's internal cognitive and emotional states (Thompson, 2013c, d)
- Description of the current debate about Ross Thompson's (2013c, d) view that young children are more socially sensitive and Susan Harter's (2012) view that they are more egocentric
- Coverage of a recent study that found fathers' emotion coaching was related to children's social competence (Baker, Fenning, & Crnic, 2011)
- Inclusion of recent research indicating that maternal emotional coping was linked to less oppositional behavior in children (Dunsmore, Booker, & Ollendick, 2012)

- Expanded material on the importance of emotion regulation in children's social competence, self-regulation, and executive functioning (Cole & Hall, 2012; Nelson & others, 2012; Thompson, 2013a, b)
- New description of recent research by Cybelle Raver and her colleagues (Raver & others, 2012; Zhai, Raver, & Jones, 2012) on links between increased caregiver emotional expression, self-regulation, and reduced behavior problems in Head Start families
- Discussion of research indicating that mothers' knowledge about what distresses and comforts their children predicts children's coping, empathy, and prosocial behavior (Vinik, Almas, & Grusec, 2011)
- Updated and expanded coverage of criticisms of Piaget's view of young children's moral development based on research indicating that young children often show a non-egocentric awareness of others' intentions and know when someone violates a moral prohibition (Thompson, 2012)
- Inclusion of recent research showing that 3-year-olds were less likely to offer assistance to an adult they previously had observed being harmful to another person (Vaish, Carpenter, & Tomasello, 2010)
- New description of research by Ross Thompson and his colleagues (2009) that linked young children's secure attachment with their mother and aspects of the mother's conversational dialogue with the children
- Inclusion of new information about the positive developmental outcomes for children when parents use behavioral and psychological control, thus directing children without being coercive or punitive (Baumrind, Larzelere, & Owens, 2010)
- New commentary about recent research on Asian American parents and Confucian goals (Russell, Crockett, & Chao, 2010)
- Description of a recent study in six countries linking physical punishment to high rates of aggression in children (Gershoff & others, 2010)
- Expanded and updated discussion of the effects of punishment on children's development, including longitudinal studies that have linked early physical punishment to later aggression (Lansford & others, 2011; Taylor & others, 2010), and cross-cultural studies indicating that in countries where physical punishment is considered normal and necessary for handling children's transgressions, the effects of punishment are less harmful (Lansford & others, 2005, 2012)
- Description of a recent study of father involvement and coparenting (Jia & Schoppe-Sullivan, 2011)
- Updated statistics on child maltreatment (U.S. Department of Health and Human Services, 2010)
- Expanded and updated coverage of family-related factors that can contribute to child maltreatment (Cicchetti, 2013; Laslett & others, 2012; Turner & others, 2012)
- Discussion of a study linking child maltreatment with financial and employment-related difficulties in adulthood (Zielinski, 2009)
- Coverage of a recent study that revealed a significant increase in suicide attempts before age 18 when repeated child maltreatment occurred (Jonson-Reid, Kohl, & Drake, 2012)
- Description of recent research studies that linked child maltreatment to risk for various diseases and physical health problems, sexual problems, and depression in adulthood (Lacelle & others, 2012; Nanni, Uher, & Danese, 2012; Widom & others, 2012)
- Added commentary about parental work's effect on children not being only a maternal employment issue but often involving the father as well (Parke & Clarke-Stewart, 2011)
- New discussion of E. Mark Cummings and his colleagues' (Cummings & Davies, 2010; Cummings, El-Sheikh, & Kouros, 2009) emotional security theory and its focus on the type of marital conflict that is negative for children's development

- Expanded and updated coverage of the relationship between divorced parents and its link to visitations by the non-custodial parent (Fabricius & others, 2010)
- Coverage of a recent study indicating that an intervention aimed at improving the mother-child relationship was linked to improvements in the coping skills of children in divorced families (Velez & others, 2011)
- Added comment about father involvement dropping off more than mother involvement following a divorce, especially for fathers of girls
- Inclusion of information about joint custody working best for children when the divorced parents can get along with each other (Parke & Clarke-Stewart, 2011)
- Coverage of recent information about child and adolescent outcomes for individuals conceived by new reproductive technologies, which are increasingly used by gay and lesbian adults (Golombok, 2011a, b; Golombok & Tasker, 2010)
- Discussion of a recent study linking early and persistent poverty to lower cognitive functioning in 5-year-old children (Schoon & others, 2012)
- Expanded and updated coverage of the stressful and difficult experiences that children in many immigrant families face, including children in undocumented families (Yoshikawa, 2011)
- Description of how many ethnic/immigrant families focus on issues associated with promoting children's ethnic pride, knowledge of their ethnic group, and discrimination (Rogers & others, 2012; Simpkins & others, 2012)
- New discussion of concerns expressed by Kathy Hirsh-Pasek, Roberta Golinkoff, & Dorothy Singer (Hirsh-Pasek & others, 2009; Singer, Golinkoff, & Hirsh-Pasek, 2006) about the decline of play in young children's lives and inclusion of the many positive cognitive and socioemotional outcomes that come from play
- Coverage of a recent study linking 3- to 5-year-olds' sleep problems to (1) watching TV after 7 p.m., and (2) watching violent TV shows (Garrison & others, 2011)

Chapter 9: Physical and Cognitive Development in Middle and Late Childhood

- Inclusion of recent research on 9-year-olds focused on the connection between physical activity level and risk for metabolic disease (Parrett & others, 2011)
- Description of recent research showing links between aerobic exercise and children's and adolescents' cognitive skills (Best, 2010; Davis & others, 2011; Monti, Hillman, & Cohen, 2012)
- Coverage of a recent research review that found school-based programs for increasing children's physical activity are effective (Kriemler & others, 2011)
- Description of recent data on the percentage of U.S. 6- to 11-year-olds that are overweight or obese, which in 2009–2010 was 50 percent higher than the percentage of 2- to 5-year-olds who were overweight (Ogden & others, 2012)
- Inclusion of recent research that found both peers and family members teased overweight children more than normal-weight children (McCormack & others, 2011)
- Inclusion of information about a recent successful behavior modification program that increased overweight and obese children's exercise and reduced their TV viewing time (Goldfield, 2012)
- Coverage of recent intervention studies that indicate modifying parents' eating habits and increasing children's exercise can help overweight and obese children to lose weight (Collins & others, 2011)
- Updated material on childhood cancer, including improving survival rates for some childhood cancers (National Cancer Institute, 2012; Wayne, 2011)

- Updated statistics on the percentage of students with various disabilities who receive special education services in U.S. schools (Aud & others, 2011)
- Expanded discussion of possible misdiagnosis of ADHD, including details of a recent experimental study that found clinicians overdiagnosed ADHD symptoms, especially in boys (Bruchmiller, Margraf, & Schneider, 2012)
- New description of some developmental outcomes of children with ADHD, including increased risks for dropping out of school, adolescent pregnancy, substance abuse problems, and antisocial behavior (Chang, Lichtenstein, & Larsson, 2012; Von Polier, Vioet, & Herpertz-Dahlmann, 2012)
- Coverage of a recent study indicating delayed development in the frontal lobes of children with ADHD, likely due to a delay or a decrease in myelination (Nagel & others, 2011)
- Description of a recent study that linked cigarette smoking during pregnancy to ADHD in 6- to 7-year-old children (Sciberras, Ukoumunne, & Efron, 2011)
- New coverage of executive functioning deficits in children with ADHD and their links to brain functioning (Supekar & Menon, 2012; Tomasi & Volkow, 2012)
- New material on deficits in theory of mind in children with ADHD (Buhler & others, 2011; Shuai, Chan, & Wang, 2011)
- Inclusion of recent estimates indicating that in 2008 1 in 88 children had an autistic spectrum disorder, a dramatic increase since 2002 estimates (Centers for Disease Control & Prevention, 2012)
- New discussion of the role that connectivity between different brain regions might play in the development of autism (Just & others, 2012; Philip & others, 2012)
- New Figure 9.10 that illustrates Baddeley's working memory model
- New coverage of three recent studies of working memory that indicate how important and wide-ranging working memory capacity is for children's cognitive development and achievement (Andersson, 2010; Aslan, Zellner, & Bauml, 2010; Welsh & others, 2010)
- Expanded discussion of children's creative thinking, including recent research indicating a decline in creative thinking by U.S. schoolchildren and increased interest in teaching creative thinking in Chinese schools (Kim, 2010; Plucker, 2010)
- New section, Executive Functioning, that highlights the increased interest in children's executive functioning, including Adele Diamond's (2013; Diamond & Lee, 2011) view on the key dimensions of executive functioning in 4- to 11-year-old children and interventions that have been shown to improve executive functioning
- Description of a recent research review that concluded more than 1,000 genes may influence an individual's intelligence (Davies & others, 2011)
- New information about the environment's role in intelligence that is reflected in the 12 to 18 point IQ gain children make when they are adopted from lower SES to middle SES homes (Nisbett & others, 2012)
- Coverage of recent research indicating that bilingual children have a lower vocabulary in each language than monolingual children (Bialystok, 2011)

Chapter 10: Socioemotional Development in Middle and Late Childhood

- Updated and expanded discussion of children's socioemotional development based on leading expert Ross Thompson's feedback
- New discussion of the role of executive functioning and children's perspective taking in socioemotional development (Galinsky, 2010)

- Discussion of a recent study focused on the positive aspects of perspective-taking skills in children who are emotionally reactive (Bengtsson & Arvidsson, 2011)
- New information indicating that the foundations of self-esteem in middle and late childhood occur through the quality of relationships with parents in infancy and early childhood (Thompson, 2011, 2013a, b, c, d)
- New material on dose/response effects in the study of how disasters and traumatic events affect children's adjustment and adaptation (Masten, 2013; Masten & Narayan, 2012)
- Substantial updates on moral development based on feedback from leading experts Darcia Narvaez and Daniel Lapsley
- Coverage of a recent study that revealed links between a higher level of multicultural experience and a lower level of closed mindedness, a growth mindset, and higher moral judgment (Narvaez & Hill, 2010)
- Expanded discussion of moral identity with an emphasis on Darcia Narvaez' (2010) recent view that moral metacognition, especially through self-monitoring and self-reflection, is linked to moral maturity
- Much expanded, revised, and updated material on the domain theory of moral development and social conventional reasoning (Helwig & Turiel, 2011; Smetana, 2011a, b)
- Coverage of a recent gender stereotyping study of 6- to 10-year-olds who reported that math is mainly for boys (Cvencek, Meltzoff, & Greenwald, 2011)
- Inclusion of information about a recent meta-analysis that revealed no gender differences in math skills for adolescents (Lindberg & others, 2010)
- Description of a recent research review focused on girls' negative attitudes about math and the negative expectations that parents and teachers have for girls' math competence (Gunderson & others, 2012)
- New main section on attachment in middle and late childhood
- New discussion of research by Kathryn Kerns and her colleagues (Brumariu, Kerns, & Seibert, 2012; Kerns & Seibert, 2012; Kerns, Siener, & Brumariu, 2011) that focuses on the role of secure attachment in internalizing symptoms, anxiety, depression, and emotion regulation
- Updated and expanded discussion of gender differences in emotion (Leaper & Bigler, 2011; Nolen-Hoeksema, 2012)
- Coverage of a recent study that found having supportive friends was linked to lower levels of bullying and victimization (Kendrick, Jutengren, & Stattin, 2012)
- New discussion of cyberbullying (Donnerstein, 2012; Kowalsky, Limber, & Agatston, 2012)
- Inclusion of recent research on links between children's cyber aggression and negative peer relations outcomes (Schoffstall & Cohen, 2012)
- Discussion of recent research on a higher level of depression and suicide in children who are the victims of bullying (Fisher & others, 2012; Lemstra & others, 2012)
- Description of a recent longitudinal study of more than 6,000 children that found a link between bullying/victimization and suicide ideation (Winsper & others, 2012)
- Coverage of a recent study found a link between victims of peer bullying and the development of borderline personality symptoms (Wolke & others, 2012)
- Description of a recent study linking bullying and moral disengagement (Obermann, 2011)
- Coverage of a recent study that found students who engaged in aggressive-disruptive classroom behavior were more likely to have aggressive friends (Powers & Bierman, 2012)
- Discussion of recent research on outcomes of 9- to 19-year-old African American boys after experiencing the New Hope antipoverty program (McLoyd & others, 2011)

- New commentary about the diversity of Asian American students' academic outcomes, with students from some cultural backgrounds being more successful than those from other backgrounds
- Updated coverage of Carol Dweck's (2013) concept of mindset, including new Figure 10.7 about her Brainology program
- New discussion of the importance of parental involvement in children's learning, including the research of Eva Pomerantz and her colleagues (Cheung & Pomerantz, 2012; Pomerantz, Cheung, & Qin, 2012; Pomerantz, Kim, & Cheung, 2012) that especially focuses on comparisons of U.S. and Chinese children and their parents

Chapter 11: Physical and Cognitive Development in Adolescence

- New discussion of changes needed in social policy regarding adolescents
- New material on the work of Peter Benson and his colleagues (2010; Benson & Scales, 2011; Scales, Benson, & Roehlkepartain, 2011)
- Inclusion of recent research indicating that college students from low-SES backgrounds were less likely to engage in healthy behavior patterns than their higher-SES counterparts (VanKim & Laska, 2012)
- Description of a recent cross-cultural study in 29 countries that found childhood obesity was linked to early puberty in girls (Currie & others, 2012)
- Coverage of a recent study that found a linear increase in having a positive body image for both boys and girls as they moved from the beginning to the end of adolescence (Holsen & others, 2012)
- Discussion of a recent study of gender differences in the aesthetic aspects of adolescents' body image (Abbott & Barber, 2010)
- Inclusion of information about a recent study of adolescents with the most positive body images, which was linked to their health-enhancing behaviors, especially regular exercise (Frisen & Holmqvist, 2010)
- Updated material on the negative outcomes of early maturation in girls (Negriff, Susman, & Trickett, 2011)
- Revised and updated data (Figure 11.5) on the percentage of adolescents who reported having had sexual intercourse, including a recent gender reversal among twelfth-graders, with a higher percentage of twelfth-grade girls reporting having had sex than twelfth-grade boys (Eaton & others, 2010)
- Updated information on the percentage of U.S. adolescents who report that they are currently sexually active (Eaton & others, 2010)
- Revised and updated data on the percentage of non-Latino White, African American, and Latino adolescents who report having had sexual intercourse (Eaton & others, 2010)
- Discussion of a recent study that revealed a link between neighborhood poverty concentration and 15- to 17-year old boys' and girls' sexual initiation (Cubbin & others, 2010)
- Description of the results from a recent research review of a number of aspects of connectedness, such as family connectedness and parent-adolescent communication about sexuality, and links to adolescent sexuality outcomes (Markham & others, 2010)
- Coverage of recent research in low-income neighborhoods that found caregiver hostility was linked to early sexual activity and sex with multiple partners, while caregiver warmth was related to later sexual initiation and a lower incidence of sex with multiple partners (Gardner, Martin, & Brooks-Gunn, 2012)
- Description of recent research linking deviant peer relations in early adolescence with an increase in multiple sexual partners at age 16 (Lansford & others, 2010)

- Coverage of a recent study that found a high level of impulsiveness was linked to early adolescent sexual risk-taking (Khurana & others, 2012)

- Updated information about trends in the percentage of sexually active adolescents who used a condom the last time they had sexual intercourse (Eaton & others, 2010)

- Discussion of recent research on U.S. 15- to 19-year-olds with unintended pregnancies resulting in live births: 50 percent of these adolescent girls were not using any type of birth control when they got pregnant and 34 percent believed they could not get pregnant at the time (Centers for Disease Control and Prevention, 2012)

- Coverage of the recent decline in births to adolescent girls to a record low in 2009, including new Figure 11.6 (Ventura & Hamilton, 2011)

- Inclusion of information about some sex education programs that are now abstinence-plus sexuality, promoting abstinence as well as contraceptive use (Realini & others, 2010)

- Updated data on trends in adolescent obesity from 1999–2000 to 2009–2010 with an increase in obesity among boys but not in girls during this time frame (Ogden & others, 2012)

- Inclusion of recent research linking obesity in adolescence with the development of severe obesity in emerging adulthood (The & others, 2010)

- Discussion of a recent longitudinal study of overweight and obesity involving individuals from 14 years of age to 24 years of age (Patton & others, 2011)

- New discussion of links between screen-based activity and physical exercise in adolescents, including recent research indicating that adolescents who combine low physical activity and high screen-based activity are nearly twice as likely to be overweight (Sisson & others, 2010)

- Updated data on developmental changes in adolescent sleep patterns (Eaton & others, 2010)

- Coverage of a longitudinal study that found sleep problems in adolescence were linked to subsequent suicidal thoughts and attempts in adolescence and early adulthood (Wong & Brower, 2012)

- Description of a recent study on delaying school start time for ninth- to twelfth-grade students and their improved sleep, alertness, mood, and health (Owens, Belon, & Moss, 2010).

- New content on a comparison of U.S. and Asian adolescents' sleep patterns (Gradisar, Gardner, & Dohnt, 2011)

- New coverage of sleep in emerging adulthood (Galambos, Howard, & Maggs, 2011)

- Discussion of a recent study of emerging adults' sleep patterns and indications that first-year college students have bedtimes and rise times that are later than seniors in high school but that bedtimes and rise times decline by the third and fourth year of college (Lund & others, 2010)

- Updated statistics on leading causes of death in adolescence (Eaton & others, 2010)

- Updated coverage of the Monitoring the Future study's assessment of drug use by secondary school students (Johnston & others, 2011)

- Description of research that found the onset of alcohol use before age 11 was linked to a higher risk of alcohol dependence in early adulthood (Guttmannova & others, 2012)

- Discussion of recent research that linked authoritative parenting with lower adolescent alcohol consumption (Piko & Balazs, 2012) and parent-adolescent conflict with higher consumption (Chaplin & others, 2012)

- Updated research on a confluence of peer factors that are linked to alcohol use in adolescence (Cruz, Emery, & Turkheimer, 2012; Patrick & Schulenberg, 2010)

- New commentary about links between anorexia nervosa, obsessive thinking about weight, and compulsive exercise (Hildebrant & others, 2012)

- New description of the perfectionistic tendencies of anorexics and bulimics (Lampard & others, 2012)

- New discussion of the likely brain changes in adolescents who are anorexic (Lock, 2012b)

- Coverage of recent research on a link between attachment insecurity and eating disorders in adolescence (Abbate-Daga & others, 2010)

- Extensively expanded and updated content on executive functioning in adolescence

- New section on the importance of controlling attention and reducing interfering thoughts

- New section on cognitive control, including new material on the roles of controlling attention, inhibiting distracting thoughts, and being cognitively flexible (Diamond, 2013; Galinsky, 2010)

- New Figure 11.12, which lets students evaluate their cognitive flexibility (Galinsky, 2010)

- New discussion of Robert Crosnoe's (2011) recent book, *Fitting In, Standing Out,* suggesting that the conformity demands of complex peer cultures in high school undermine students' academic achievement

- Updated coverage of school dropout rates, including new Figure 11.13 that shows dropout rates by gender and ethnicity, as well as the significant decrease of Latino dropouts in the first decade of the twenty-first century (National Center for Education Statistics, 2010)

- New discussion of the controversy in determining accurate school dropout rates

Chapter 12: Socioemotional Development in Adolescence

- Inclusion of recent research indicating that age differences are stronger than generational differences in narcissism (Roberts, Edmonds, & Grijalva, 2010)

- Coverage of a recent study indicating that between 12 and 20 years of age individuals explore their identity in greater depth (Klimstra & others, 2010)

- Revised and updated information about diversity, especially ethnic identity and immigration, based on feedback from leading expert Diane Hughes

- Coverage of a recent study that found a positive ethnic identity helped to buffer the negative effects of discrimination experienced by Mexican American adolescents (Umana-Taylor & others, 2012)

- Updated data on trends in the percentage of first-year college students who attend religious services (Pryor & others, 2011)

- Description of a recent study of religious identity and religious participation of adolescents from different ethnic groups (Lopez, Huynh, & Fuligni, 2011)

- Inclusion of a recent study that found parents' own religiousness during youths' adolescence was positively linked to youths' own religiousness during adolescence (Spilman & others, 2012)

- Updated and expanded section, Parental Management and Monitoring, that especially provides recent information about the increasing interest in studying adolescents' management of their parents' access to information (Laird & Marrero, 2010; Smetana, 2011a, b)

- Description of a recent analysis that concluded the most consistent outcomes of secure attachment in adolescence involve positive peer relations and the development of emotion regulation capacities (Allen & Miga, 2010)
- Discussion of a recent study of young adolescents' friendships and depression (Brendgen & others, 2010)
- Updated and expanded coverage of the positive outcomes of positive friendship relationships in adolescence (Kendrick, Jutengren, & Stattin, 2012; Tucker & others, 2012; Way & Silverman, 2012)
- Coverage of a recent study that found romantic activity was associated with depression in early adolescent girls (Starr & others, 2012)
- Description of recent research on the negative outcomes of adolescent girls having an older romantic partner (Haydon & Halpern, 2010)
- Expanded and updated material on immigrant families and their bicultural orientation, including recent research by Ross Parke and his colleagues (2011)
- New discussion of the role of immigrant adolescents as cultural brokers for their parents (Villanueva & Buriel, 2010)
- Substantial updating of media use rates based on the 2009 national survey of more than 2,000 U.S. adolescents, including comparisons with earlier national surveys to show trends in media use by adolescents (Rideout, Foehr, & Roberts, 2010)
- Description of a recent study of 8- to 12-year-old girls that found a higher level of media multitasking was linked to negative social well-being while a higher level of face-to-face communication was associated with a higher level of social well-being, such as social success, feeling normal, and having fewer friends whom parents perceived as a bad influence (Pea & others, 2012)
- Coverage of a recent national survey of trends in adolescents' use of social media, including dramatic increases in social networking and text messaging, and declines in tweeting and blogging (Lenhart & others, 2010)
- New commentary about text messaging now being the main way that adolescents prefer to connect with their friends (Lenhart & others, 2010)
- Inclusion of information that Facebook replaced Google as the most frequently visited Internet site in 2010
- Description of a recent study of parenting predictors of adolescent media use (Padilla-Walker & Coyne, 2011)
- Inclusion of recent research linking problematic relationships between mothers and early adolescents with negative peer relations on the Internet during emerging adulthood (Szwedo, Mikami, & Allen, 2011)
- Discussion of recent research on the role of parental monitoring and support during adolescence in reducing criminal behavior during emerging adulthood (Johnson & others, 2011)
- Description of a recent study that found repeated poverty was a high risk factor for delinquency (Najman & others, 2010)
- Discussion of a recent meta-analysis of five programs for reducing the recidivism of juvenile offenders, with family treatment being the only one that was effective (Schwalbe & others, 2012)
- Coverage of a recent study that revealed male Chinese adolescents and emerging adults experience more depression than their female counterparts (Sun & others, 2010)
- New discussion of the role of genes in adolescent depression and recent research that found the link between adolescent girls' perceived stress and depression occurred only when the girls had the short version of the serotonin-related gene—5HTTLPR (Beaver & others, 2012)
- Inclusion of recent research indicating that mother-daughter co-rumination was linked to increased anxiety and depression in adolescent daughters (Waller & Rose, 2010)
- Coverage of research indicating that exposure to maternal depression prior to age 12 predicted risk processes during development (difficulties in family relationships, for example), which set the course for the development of the adolescent's depression (Garber & Cole, 2010)
- Description of a recent study that found relational aggression was linked to depression in girls (Spieker & others, 2012)
- Discussion of recent research indicating that four types of bullying were all linked to adolescents' depression (Wang, Nansel, & Ianotti, 2011)
- Inclusion of recent research indicating that weight-related concerns increase adolescent girls' depressive symptoms (Vaughan & Halpern, 2010)
- Coverage of a recent research view that found the most effective treatment for adolescent depression was a combination of drug therapy and cognitive behavior therapy (Maalouf & Brent, 2012)
- Updated national data through 2011 on the percentage of adolescents who seriously think about committing suicide, attempt suicide, and require medical attention for suicide attempts (Youth Risk Behavior Survey, 2011)
- Coverage of a recent study that found increased family support, peer support, and community connectedness was linked to a lower risk of suicidal tendencies (Matlin, Molock, & Tebes, 2011)
- Description of a recent study that found that the most common link between adolescent suicide attempts and drug use was any lifetime use of tranquilizers or sedatives (Kokkevi & others, 2012)
- Inclusion of recent research on suicide attempts by young Latinas (Zayas & others, 2010)
- Discussion of a recent study linking sexual victimization to suicide attempts in adolescence (Plener, Singer, & Goldbeck, 2011)
- Updated coverage of outcomes for the Fast Track delinquency intervention study through age 19 that found the program was successful in reducing juvenile arrest rates (Conduct Problems Prevention Research Group, 2011; Miller & others, 2011)

Chapter 13: Physical and Cognitive Development in Early Adulthood

- Expanded discussion of emerging adulthood, including material on whether it is likely to be universal or not, and its occurrence in European countries and Australia, as well as the United States (Kins & Beyers, 2010; Sirsch & others, 2009)
- Coverage of a recent Belgian study indicating that continued co-residence with parents during emerging adulthood slows down the process of becoming a self-sufficient and independent adult (Kins & Beyers, 2010)
- Inclusion of recent research indicating that the majority of 18- to 26-year-olds in India felt that they had achieved adulthood (Seiter & Nelson, 2011)
- Inclusion of criticism of the concept of emerging adulthood (Cote & Bynner, 2008)
- Updated and expanded information about the increase in health problems in emerging adulthood compared with adolescence (Fatusi & Hindin, 2010)
- Updated statistics on the percentage of 20- to 39-year-olds who are obese in the United States (National Center for Health Statistics, 2011)

- Inclusion of a recent forecast that 42 percent of U.S. adults will be obese (Finkelstein & others, 2012)

- New coverage of the highest and lowest percentages of obese adults in 33 developed countries, including new Figure 13.3 (OECD, 2010)

- Discussion of a recent meta-analysis linking obesity with depression in women but not men (de Wit & others, 2010)

- New material on the National Weight Control Registry, including research indicating that individuals who have lost at least 30 pounds and kept it off for one year engage in a high level of physical activity (Catenacci & others, 2008; Ogden & others, 2012)

- Description of a recent study of gender differences in college students' motivation to exercise (Egli & others, 2011)

- Coverage of a recent study estimating the number of years lost in life expectancy because of heavy TV viewing (Veerman & others, 2012)

- Updated material on college students' drinking habits including new data on extreme binge drinking and the recent decline in college drinking (Johnston & others, 2011)

- Updated statistics on the continuing decline in smoking by U.S. adults (Centers for Disease Control and Prevention, 2012)

- Inclusion of recent data from a study of sexual activity by 25- to 44-year-olds in the United States (Chandra, Mosher, Copen, & Sioneau, 2011)

- Updated figures on the number of people in the United States who are living with an HIV infection (National Center for Health Statistics, 2011)

- Inclusion of information about the recent significant drop in the rate of new HIV infections globally (UNAIDS, 2011)

- Inclusion of a recent survey on knowledge regarding contraception and HIV infection in low- and middle-income countries (UNAIDS, 2011)

- New commentary about the increase in "hooking up" during college (Holman & Sillars, 2012)

- Description of a recent study on the significant underreporting of rape in college women (Wolitzky-Taylor & others, 2011)

- Coverage of a recent study that indicated sexual assault was more likely to occur if the offender was using substances, regardless of whether or not the victim was using them (Brecklin & Ullman, 2010)

- New discussion of the views of Labouvie-Vief and her colleagues (2010) on the role of developmental changes in the integration and complexity of cognition and emotion, as well as the presence of increasing internal reflection and less context-dependent thinking in middle-aged adults as compared with young adults

- Revision of the definition of postformal thought to include the view of Labouvie-Vief and her colleagues (2010) on the role of emotion in cognitive changes

- Inclusion of recent information about the assessment of postformal thinking, including new Figure 13.9 that gives students an opportunity to evaluate their postformal thinking (Cartwright & others, 2009)

- Discussion of a recent study indicating that college students with a higher number of cross-category friends have a higher level of postformal thinking than their counterparts with fewer cross-category friends (Galupo, Cartwright, & Savage, 2010)

- Coverage of a recent study indicating that discussing purpose in life benefitted college students' goal direction (Bundick, 2011)

- New commentary about the increasing trend in the U.S. workforce of the disappearing long-term career, with many young and older adults working at a series of jobs and/or short-term jobs (Hollister, 2011)

- Inclusion of recent information from the *Occupational Outlook Handbook* (2012) that includes job projections through 2020

- Updated statistics on the percentage of college students who work while going to college (National Center for Education Statistics, 2010)

- Description of a recent study of unemployment and mortality risk at different points in an individual's career (Roelfs & others, 2011)

Chapter 14: Socioemotional Development in Early Adulthood

- New description of a longitudinal study that linked undercontrolled temperament at age 3 with compulsive gambling in early adulthood (Slutske & others, 2012)

- Coverage of a longitudinal study that found individuals who were securely attached to their caregivers during infancy were in more stable romantic relationships in adulthood (Salvatore & others, 2011)

- Inclusion of recent research on emerging adults' attachment security and the quality of their romantic relationships (Holland & Roisman, 2010)

- Discussion of a recent study that revealed attachment-anxious individuals show strong ambivalence toward a romantic partner (Mikulincer & others, 2010)

- Description of a recent study indicating that anxiously attached adults were more ambivalent about relationship commitment than their securely attached counterparts (Joel, MacDonald, & Shiomotomai, 2011)

- Inclusion of recent research indicating that insecurely attached adults had higher levels of depressive and anxious symptoms than securely attached adults (Jinyao & others, 2012)

- New research indicating that adults with an avoidant attachment style are less resistant to the temptations of infidelity, which is linked to their lower level of relationship commitment (DeWall & others, 2011)

- Description of recent research that found insecurely attached adults had a lower level of sexual satisfaction than securely attached adults (Brassard & others, 2012)

- Coverage of a recent meta-analysis confirming that adults who are securely attached have better close relationships than adults who are characterized by avoidant or anxious attachment (Li & Chan, 2012)

- Discussion of recent research on links between anxious and avoidant attachment styles and various health problems (McWilliams & Bailey, 2010)

- Description of recent research confirming Erikson's theory that identity development in adolescence is a precursor of intimacy in romantic relationships in emerging adulthood (Beyers & Seiffge-Krenke, 2010)

- Coverage of a recent meta-analysis that found identity development was linked to intimacy with the connection being stronger for men than women (Arseth & others, 2009)

- Inclusion of information from a recent meta-analysis in which males showed higher avoidance and lower anxiety about romantic love than females (Del Giudice, 2011)

- Description of a recent study of relationship dissolution in 18- to 35-year-olds and its links to psychological stress and life satisfaction (Rhoades & others, 2011)

- New coverage of Andrew Cherlin's (2009) recent analysis of how Americans move in and out of relationship styles more than is the case than in other countries

- Updated data on single adults in the United States—for the first time, in 2009 the number of U.S. single adults from 25 to 34 years of age surpassed the number of married adults (U.S. Census Bureau, 2010)

- New coverage of Bella DePaulo's (2006, 2011) conclusion that there is widespread bias against unmarried adults

- Discussion of a recent large-scale study of U.S. singles that found women are now more likely than men to want their independence in relationships (Match.com, 2011)

- Coverage of another large-scale survey that found many singles reported that they were looking for love, but either were ambivalent about getting married or did not want to get married (Match.com, 2012)
- Updated data on the continuing increase in the number of U.S. adults who are cohabiting (U.S. Census Bureau, 2010)
- Coverage of recent research indicating that the link between premarital cohabitation and marital instability in first marriages has weakened in recent cohorts (Manning & Cohen, 2012; Reinhold, 2010)
- Description of a recent study that found cohabiting relationships were characterized by more commitment, lower satisfaction, more negative communication, and more physical aggression than dating (noncohabiting) relationships (Rhoades, Stanley, & Markman, 2012)
- Inclusion of information from a recent study on the motivation for cohabiting, including gender differences regarding drawbacks in cohabiting (Huang & others, 2011)
- Further clarification of factors involved in whether cohabiting results in negative marital outcomes (Cherlin, 2009)
- Updated coverage of the continuing decline in the rate of marriage in the United States from 2007 to 2010 (Pew Research Center, 2010)
- Updated information about the percentage of individuals in the United States who have ever been married by age 40 (Pew Research Center, 2011)
- Revised and updated analysis of marriage trends, including recent research on the percentage of U.S. adults under age 30 who think marriage is headed for extinction and the percentage of those young adults who still plan to get married (Pew Research Center, 2010)
- Discussion of a recent study of premarital education in first and second marriages (Doss & others, 2009)
- Expanded and updated discussion on the benefits of a good marriage, including a recent study indicating that a lower proportion of time spent in marriage was linked to a likelihood of earlier death (Henretta, 2010)
- Description of a recent large-scale analysis of a number of studies that concluded married individuals have a survival advantage over unmarried individuals, and that marriage gives men a longevity boost more than it does women (Rendall & others, 2011)
- Updated coverage on the resumption of a decline in the rate of divorce in the United States from 2007 to 2009 following an increase from 2005 to 2007 (National Center for Health Statistics, 2010)
- New discussion of remarried families suggesting that some of these families are more adult-focused and others more child-focused (Anderson & Greene, 2011)
- Description of a recent study of stigma and same-sex relationships (Frost, 2011)
- New Figure 14.10 that lets students evaluate how effective they are in making bids for improving a relationship, and how they respond to bids based on leading expert John Gottman's work
- Updated statistic on the age at which U.S. women give birth to a child for the first time (U.S. Census Bureau, 2011)

Chapter 15: Physical and Cognitive Development in Middle Adulthood

- Inclusion of recent ideas from Patricia Cohen's (2012) book, *In Our Prime: The Invention of Middle Age,* that traces the emergence of the concept of middle age in the nineteenth century
- New commentary about taking a balanced approach to middle age, acknowledging the physical declines that characterize middle age but also recognizing that in recent decades an increasing number of middle-aged adults have engaged in healthier lifestyles

- Updated data on the percentage of middle-aged adults in the United States who are classified as obese (National Center for Health Statistics, 2011)
- Description of a recent research review that concluded management of weight and resistance training were the best strategies for slowing down sarcopenia (Rolland & others, 2011)
- Coverage of a recent study linking low cognitive development in early adulthood to reduced lung functioning in middle age (Carroll & others, 2011)
- Recent analysis that indicates the link between reduced lung functioning and a decline in cognitive ability is likely related to the influence of lung functioning on brain structure and functioning (MacDonald, DeCarlo, & Dixon, 2011)
- Description of a recent research review indicating a link between chronic stress exposure and metabolic syndrome (Tamashiro & others, 2011)
- Inclusion of recent research results involving physical activity, metabolic syndrome, and cardiovascular disease (Broekuizen & others, 2011)
- Discussion of a recent study that found several factors in adolescence were related to the development of metabolic syndrome in middle-aged women and men (Gustaffson, Persson, & Hammerstrom, 2011)
- Description of a recent study that found middle-aged adults who slept less than six hours a night on average had an increased risk of developing stroke symptoms (Ruiter & others, 2012)
- Coverage of a recent study that found links between changes in the number of hours of sleep and cognitive functioning in middle-aged adults (Ferrie & others, 2011)
- New discussion of the increase in sleep-disordered breathing and restless legs syndrome in middle age (Polo-Kantola, 2011)
- Coverage of a recent study that found social support had a positive influence on reducing the link between cardiovascular disease and depression in aging African Americans (Heard & others, 2011)
- New description of the view of David Almeida and his colleagues (2011) regarding chronic stress and its potential damage to physiological functioning and health
- Discussion of a recent study indicating that aerobic exercise was related to the presence of a lower level of senescent T cells (Spielmann & others, 2011)
- New section on having a sense of control, which peaks in middle age, and its links to health and disease (Lachman, Neupert, & Agrigoroaei, 2011)
- Expanded and updated coverage of lifestyle factors during perimenopause and whether these factors are linked to the development of cardiovascular disease or chronic illnesses (ESHRE Capri Workshop Group, 2011)
- Updated statistics on mortality causes in middle age (Kochanek & others, 2011)
- Inclusion of information from a recent analysis indicating that diabetes has a higher mortality risk in Latinos than non-Latino Whites (Hunt & others, 2011)
- Description of a recent study indicating that increased estradiol and improved sleep but not hot flashes predicted enhanced mood during the menopausal transition (Joffe & others, 2011)
- Discussion of a recent research review indicating that there is no clear evidence that depressive disorders occur more frequently during menopause than at other times in a woman's reproductive life (Judd, Hickey, & Bryant, 2012)
- Description of the recent conclusion that reduction of cardiovascular disease occurs when HRT is initiated before 60 years of age and/or

within 10 years of menopause and continued for six years or more (Hodis & others, 2012)

- Updated coverage of recent research studies in a number of countries indicating that coinciding with the decreased use of HRT in recent years, research is mixed regarding effects on the incidence of breast cancer (Baber, 2011; Chlebowski & others, 2010: Gompel & Santen, 2012; Howell & Evans, 2011)
- Update on the percentage of aging men who experience erectile dysfunction (Berookhim & Bar-Charma, 2011)
- Description of recent research that found how often middle-aged adults engaged in sexual intercourse, the quality of their sexual life, and their interest in sex was linked to how healthy they were (Lindau & Gavrilova, 2010)
- Expanded and updated coverage of the causes of increases in intelligence during middle age in recent cohorts (Schaie, 2011)
- Updated and expanded evaluation of the lack of age differences in everyday cognition from 20 to 75 years of age, and why there is no decline (Allaire, 2012; Salthouse, 2012)
- New discussion of whether there are differences between the job performance of young adults and middle-aged adults (Salthouse, 2012)
- Description of a recent study in which task persistence in early adolescence predicted career success in middle age (Andersson & Bergman, 2011)
- New commentary about the premature retirement of some middle-aged adults because of the recent economic downturn and recession (Lusardi, Mitchell, & Curto, 2012)
- New discussion of an analysis of research studies indicating a strong link between spirituality/religion and mortality (Lucchetti, Lucchetti, & Koenig, 2011)
- New coverage of the distinctions between religion, religiousness, and spirituality based on a recent analysis by Pamela King and her colleagues (2011)
- New discussion of links between having an increased sense of meaning in life and clearer guidelines for living one's life, enhanced motivation to take care of oneself and reach goals, a higher level of psychological well-being, and better health (Park, 2012b)

Chapter 16: Socioemotional Development in Middle Adulthood

- New discussion of a recent study linking generativity with positive social engagement in such contexts as family life and community involvement (Cox & others, 2010)
- Description of a recent study of older adult women's daily stressors and negative affect (Charles & others, 2010)
- New discussion of the manner in which different stressors—chronic and daily—affect health events (Piazza & others, 2010)
- New section on stress and gender that focuses on how women and men differ in the way they experience and respond to stressors (Almeida & others, 2011)
- Coverage of a recent study on gender differences in depressive symptoms and the social contexts linked to those symptoms in middle-aged and older women (Lin & others, 2011)
- New discussion of Shelley Taylor and her colleagues' (2011a, b, c; Taylor & others, 2000) concept that women are more likely to respond to stress with "tend and befriend" behavior than with the "fight or flight" reaction that characterizes men
- Inclusion of a recent research study on the stability and change in the Big Five personality factors indicating that the positive aspects of four

of the five factors (such as emotional stability) peaked between 40 and 60 years of age, while being conscientious continued to increase from early through late adulthood (Specht, Egloff, & Schukle, 2011)

- New coverage of research on how the Big Five factors of personality are linked to important aspects of a person's life, such as health (Turiano & others, 2012), intelligence (Sharp & others, 2010), achievement and work (Zhao, Seibert, & Lumpkin, 2010), and relationships (Donnellan, Larson-Rife, & Conger, 2005)
- New discussion of research on how the Big Five factors are related to historical changes (George, Helson, & John, 2011)
- Updated research on the greatest change in personality occurring in early adulthood (Lucas & Donnellan, 2011)
- Description of two recent studies that found middle-aged parents provide more support for their children than for their aging parents (Fingerman & others, 2011a, 2012)
- Coverage of recent research that indicated affection and support, reflecting solidarity, were more prevalent in intergenerational relationships than ambivalence was (Hogerbrugge & Komter, 2012)
- New discussion of how more than 40 percent of middle-aged children (mainly daughters) provide care for their aging parents or parents-in-law (Blieszner & Roberto, 2012; National Alliance for Caregiving, 2009)
- New coverage of the concept of the middle generation more often functioning as a "pivot" generation than a "sandwich" generation (Fingerman & Birditt, 2011; Fingerman & others, 2011b)

Chapter 17: Physical Development in Late Adulthood

- Added commentary about increased longevity being due not only to improvements in the health and well-being of adults but also to the substantial reduction in infant deaths in recent decades
- Updated statistics on life expectancy around the world, with Monaco having the highest estimated life expectancy at birth in 2011 (90 years of age) (Central Intelligence Agency, 2012)
- Updated statistics on life expectancy at birth and at 65 and 100 years of age today (U.S. Census Bureau, 2011)
- New commentary suggesting that the sex difference in longevity favoring women is still present but less pronounced in late adulthood and is especially linked to the higher level of cardiovascular disease in men than women (Yang & Kosloski, 2011)
- Updated information about the number of centenarians in the United States (U.S. Census Bureau, 2011)
- Coverage of a recent study indicating that the older the age group of centenarians (110 to 119 compared with 100 to 104, for example), the later the onset of diseases such as cancer and cardiovascular disease, as well as delayed functional decline (Andersen & others, 2012)
- Discussion of a recent study that found telomere length was linked to the quality of middle-aged and older adults' social relationships (Uchino & others, 2012)
- Updated and expanded material on telomeres and telomerase, including the increasing role they might play in stem cell regeneration (Piper & others, 2012; Shay, Reddel, & Wright, 2012)
- Inclusion of information about recent research interest in the role that exercise might play in reducing oxidative damage in cells (Muthusamy & others, 2012)
- New material on the allostatic load view of stress in the coverage of the hormonal stress theory of aging (Almeida & others, 2011)
- Discussion of a recent study that found a decrease in total brain volume and volume in key brain structures, such as the frontal lobes and hippocampus, from 22 to 88 years of age (Sherwood & others, 2011)

- Recent analysis indicating that the decrease in brain volume in healthy aging is likely due primarily to neuron shrinkage, lower numbers of synapses, and reduced length of axons and only to a minor extent to neuron loss (Fjell & Walhovd, 2010)
- Updated coverage of neurogenesis and aging, including a recent study in which coping with stress stimulated hippocampal neurogenesis in adult monkeys (Lyons & others, 2010)
- New commentary about the increased interest in the role that neurogenesis might play in neurogenerative diseases such as Alzheimer disease, Parkinson disease, and Huntington disease (Walton & others, 2012)
- Discussion of recent research on variation in the link between cognitive processing and asymmetry in the prefrontal cortex in older adults (Manenti, Cotelli, & Miniussi, 2011)
- Updated information on links between unintended accidents and death in the elderly
- New main section on sleep in older adults
- New information about the percentage of older adults who have difficulty in sleeping (Neikrug & Ancoli-Israel, 2010)
- Discussion of recent research on sleep difficulties and lower cognitive functioning in older adults (Aly & Moscovitch, 2010; Pace-Schott & Spencer, 2011)
- Coverage of a recent study that found regular exercise improves the sleep profile of older adults (Lira & others, 2011)
- New commentary about reductions in the number of older adults, especially the young old, who have problems with erectile dysfunction because of the recent development of drugs such as Viagra (Lowe & Costabile, 2012; Rubio-Aurioles & others, 2012)
- Coverage of recent research on obesity and mobility restrictions in older adults, including the benefits of walking for obese older adults (Mullen & others, 2012; Vincent, Raiser, & Vincent, 2012)
- Inclusion of recent research indicating that a combined program of physical activity and weight loss were linked to preserving mobility in older, obese adults in poor cardiovascular health (Rejeski & others, 2011)
- Expanded coverage of factors involved in declining vision in elderly adults to include speed of visual processing and contrast sensitivity (Owsley, 2011; van Rijn & others, 2011)
- Description of recent research that found hearing decline was associated with a reduction in cognitive functioning in older adults (Lin, 2011)
- Description of a study linking macular degeneration to an increased risk of falls in older adults (Wood & others, 2011)
- Coverage of a recent national survey of the percentage of adults 70 years and older with hearing loss (Lin & others, 2011)
- Inclusion of recent research that found the severity of age-related hearing loss was linked to impaired activities in daily living (Gopinath & others, 2012)
- Coverage of a recent national study that found an increase in resistant hypertension in the United States in recent years, likely because of increases in obesity and the number of older adults (Roberie & Elliott, 2012)
- Description of a recent study of older adults that found total daily activity was linked to increased longevity across a four-year period (Buchman & others, 2012)
- Discussion of a recent study of postmenopausal women that found exercise buffered the effect of chronic stress on telomere length (Puterman & others, 2010)
- Description of two recent studies that revealed exercise training was linked to improvements in hippocampal functioning and memory

- in older adults (Erickson & others, 2011; Head, Singh, & Bugg, 2012)
- New data indicating that 28 percent of U.S. adults 60 years and age older were obese in 2011 (Centers for Disease Control and Prevention, 2012)
- New section on overweight and obesity and the current controversy regarding whether overweight adults live longer than normal-weight adults (Chang & others, 2012)
- Discussion of a recent study that found being overweight was consistently linked with the worst health profiles (Zajacova, Dowd, & Burgard, 2011)
- New coverage of the recent controversy about what the best measure of overweight/obesity is to predict longevity (de Hollander & others, 2012; Staiano & others, 2012)
- Description of recent research reviews indicating that taking antioxidant vitamin supplements does not reduce the risk of cancer and cardiovascular disease (Chen & others, 2012; Dolara, Bigagli, & Collins, 2012)
- Coverage of a recent meta-analysis that found dietary intake (not vitamin supplements) of antioxidants was associated with a reduced risk of Alzheimer disease (Li, Shen, & Ji, 2012)
- New Figure 17.16, Binge Drinking Through the Life Span, that provides recent data on developmental changes in binge drinking through the adult years (Centers for Disease Control and Prevention, 2012)

Chapter 18: Cognitive Development in Late Adulthood

- Update on 92-year-old Helen Small's cognitive fitness, including publication of her first book, *Why not? My seventy year plan for a college degree* (Small, 2011)
- Coverage of recent research indicating that especially as attentional demands increase, the greater distractibility of older adults is associated with less effective functioning in neural networks running through the frontal and parietal lobes of the brain that are involved in cognitive control (Campbell & others, 2012)
- Description of a recent study of sustained attention from early adulthood through late adulthood (Carriere & others, 2010)
- New discussion of a recent study of older adults that found the greater their variability in sustained attention the more likely they were to experience falls (O'Halloran & others, 2012)
- Discussion of a recent study showing a decline in executive attention in older adults (Mahoney & others, 2010)
- Description of a recent study that found the most common memory errors older adults reported having had in the last 24 hours were those involving tip-of-the-tongue (Ossher, Flegal, & Lustig, 2012)
- Coverage of a recent study indicating that working memory continued to decline from 65 to 89 years of age (Elliott & others, 2011)
- Discussion of research that found multitasking was especially disruptive to older adults' working memory, likely because of an interruption in retrieving information (Clapp & others, 2011)
- Description of a recent study that linked a reduction in decision-making quality in risky situations by older adults to declines in memory and processing speed (Henninger, Madden, & Huettel, 2010)
- Coverage of a recent study that found older adults who had a higher level of trans fat in their blood plasma showed a lower level of cognitive functioning (Bowman & others, 2012)
- Discussion of recent research across a 12-year period that found older adults who reduced their participation in lifestyle cognitive activities (using a computer and playing bridge, for example) showed subsequent

poorer cognitive functioning (semantic memory for example) (Small & others, 2012b). The poorer cognitive functioning was then linked to a lower level of engaging in social activities.

- New Figure 18.5 that shows an image of the prefrontal cortex
- Coverage of a recent study of older adults who engaged in a memory training program and how it affected their source memory and brain (Engvig & others, 2010)
- Discussion of two recent neuroimaging studies that found older adults' memory was better the less lateralized their brain activity was (Angel & others, 2011; Manenti, Cotelli, & Miniussi, 2011)
- New section on executive functioning in late adulthood and connections with discussions of executive functioning in earlier periods of development
- New coverage of Schaie's (2012) recent research regarding links between hippocampal and cognitive functioning from middle age to late adulthood
- Description of a recent study that found a higher level of cognitive stimulation at work and outside work was linked with improved cognitive functioning over a 10-year period for both young and older adults (Marquie & others, 2010)
- Coverage of a recent study that concluded cognitive change before death is more accurately described as terminal decline than as terminal drop (MacDonald, Hultsch, & Dixon, 2011)
- Description of a recent study of older adults that linked cardiorespiratory fitness to better performance on a cognitive task through recruitment of neural circuits in the prefrontal cortex and parietal regions of the brain that are involved in attentional control (Prakash & others, 2011)
- Expanded, updated, and revised content on interventions in cognitive aging to include the views of a consensus of leading experts at the Stanford Center for Longevity (2011)
- Discussion of a recent research review of dietary supplements and cognitive aging (Gorby, Brownawell, & Falk, 2010)
- Description of a recent study that found that when retelling a story older adults were less likely than younger adults to compress discourse and less likely to improve the cohesiveness of their narratives (Saling, Laroo, & Saling, 2012)
- New Figure 18.6: Percentage of 65- to 69-Year-Old Men and Women Working or Looking for Work in 1998 and 2008
- New Figure 18.7: Percentage of U.S. Adults 65 Years and Older in the Labor Force Who Are Working Full-Time or Part-Time
- Expanded commentary about older adults increasingly seeking a type of bridge employment that permits a gradual rather than a sudden movement out of the work context (Bowen, Noack, & Staudinger, 2011)
- New data on the average age of retirement for men (64 years) and women (62 years) in 2011 in the United States (Munnell, 2011)
- Discussion of a 2012 survey that indicated confidence regarding having enough money to live comfortably in retirement had dropped to 14 percent (Helman, Copeland, & VanDerhei, 2012)
- New commentary suggesting that the two main income concerns as individuals approach retirement are (1) drawing retirement income from savings, and (2) paying for health care expenses (Yakoboski, 2011)
- Coverage of a recent study that revealed different predictors for men's and women's psychological well-being after retirement (Kubicek & others, 2010)
- Description of a recent meta-analysis that found the following living conditions were associated with risk for depression in older adults:

living alone, in a nursing home, or in an institutionalized setting (Xiu-Ying & others, 2012)

- Expanded material on links between the ApoE4 gene and Alzheimer disease (Caselli, 2012; Ward & others, 2012)
- New discussion of K. Warner Schaie's (2012) recent research that found individuals who had the ApoE4 allele showed more cognitive decline beginning in middle age
- Coverage of a recent research study that found the ApoE4 gene creates a cascade of molecular signaling that causes blood vessels to become more porous and leak toxins into the brain and damage neurons (Bell & others, 2012)
- Description of recent research indicating that the presence of amyloid protein in the spinal fluid of individuals with mild cognitive impairment predicted whether they would develop Alzheimer disease within the next five years (De Meyer & others, 2010)
- New material indicating that one of the best strategies for preventing/intervening in the lives of people who are at risk for Alzheimer disease is to improve their cardiac functioning (Gelber, Launer, & White, 2012; Wagner & others, 2012)
- Coverage of a recent study that compared the family caregivers' perceptions of caring for someone with Alzheimer disease, cancer, or schizophrenia; the highest perceived burden was for Alzheimer disease (Papastavrou & others, 2012)
- Description of a Pew poll that found belief in God was higher in older adults than in any other age group (Pew Forum on Religion and Public Life, 2008)
- Inclusion of recent research that found a higher level of spirituality was linked to resilience in older women (Vahia & others, 2011a)
- Discussion of the religious interest of older African American adults (Williams, Keigher, & Williams, 2012)

Chapter 19: Socioemotional Development in Late Adulthood

- Expanded coverage of regrets in older adults, indicating that it is important not to dwell on them, especially since opportunities to undo earlier actions decline with age (Suri & Gross, 2012)
- Inclusion of recent research that revealed an important factor in older adults who showed a higher level of emotion regulation and successful aging was reduced responsiveness to regrets (Brassen & others, 2012)
- Discussion of a recent meta-analysis of 128 studies of reminiscence interventions in older adults with positive effects on a number of dimensions (Pinquart & Frostmeier, 2012)
- Description of a recent study that found older adults were happiest when they combined effortful social, physical, cognitive and, household activities with restful activities (Oerlemans, Bakker, & Veenhoven, 2011)
- Coverage of research by Laura Carstensen and her colleagues (2011) on links between aging and emotional well-being, emotional stability, and longevity
- Expanded discussion of emotion and aging indicating that compared to younger adults, older adults react less to negative circumstances, are better at ignoring irrelevant negative information, and remember more positive than negative information (Mather, 2012)
- Description of a recent study that found positive emotion increased from 50 years of age through the mid-eighties while anger was highest in the early twenties (Stone & others, 2011)
- Discussion of a recent study of younger and older adults' information-focus and emotion-focus in health-care decision making (Mikels & others, 2010)

- New coverage of the newly emerging field of developmental social neuroscience that involves connecting changes in the aging brain and older adults' emotion (Kaszniak & Menchola, 2012; Samanez-Larkin & Carstensen, 2011)

- Inclusion of information about a recent study that found conscientiousness predicted greater longevity in older adults (Hill & others, 2011)

- Discussion of a recent study that revealed higher neuroticism was linked to older adults' medication non-adherence across a six-year time frame (Jerant & others, 2011)

- Description of a recent study indicating that elevated neuroticism, lower conscientiousness, and lower openness were related to increased risk of developing Alzheimer disease across a six-year period in older adults (Duberstein & others, 2011)

- Coverage of a recent study that found older adults had higher self-esteem when they had a youthful identity and more positive personal experiences (Westerhof, Whitbourne, & Freeman, 2012)

- Updated information about the percent of older adults living in poverty (Administration on Aging, 2011)

- Discussion of recent research on links between frequency of computer use among older adults and their levels of cognitive functioning (Tun & Lachman, 2010)

- Description of a study in which a 40-hour video game training program improved older adults' attention and memory (Smith & others, 2009)

- Coverage of a recent study that revealed when older adults played a brain training game about 15 minutes a day for 4 weeks, the experience improved their executive functioning and speed of processing information (Nouchi & others, 2012)

- Updated data on the percentage of older adults living in poverty (U.S. Census Bureau, 2010)

- Updated statistics on the percentage of older adults who are married and divorced (U.S. Census Bureau, 2011)

- Coverage of a recent study that found cohabiting older adults were less likely to receive partner care than married older adults were (Noel-Miller, 2011)

- Description of research on marital satisfaction in octogenarians and its ability to protect their happiness from the effects of daily fluctuations in perceived health (Waldinger & Schulz, 2010)

- New material on how in late adulthood married individuals are more likely to find themselves having to care for a sick spouse with a limiting health condition (Blieszner & Roberto, 2012)

- Updated and expanded discussion of social support and aging, including recent research linking a higher level of social support with reduced cognitive decline (Dickinson & others, 2011)

- Coverage of a recent study in which loneliness predicted increased blood pressure four years later in middle-aged and older adults (Hawkley & others, 2010)

- Discussion of a recent study that linked social isolation in late adulthood to a greater risk of being inactive, smoking, and engaging in other health-risk behaviors (Shankar & others, 2011)

- Description of three recent longitudinal studies that found feelings of loneliness were linked with an earlier death (Luo & others, 2012; Perissinotto, Stijacic Cenzer, & Covinsky, 2012)

- Inclusion of information from a recent study that found older adults who volunteered for other-oriented reasons had a lower mortality risk but those who volunteered for self-oriented reasons had a mortality risk similar to that of nonvolunteers (Konrath & others, 2012)

- Discussion of a recent study that found the more older adults engaged in volunteering the happier they were (Dulin & others, 2012)

- New description of a research study that revealed maximizing one's psychological resources (self-efficacy and optimism) was linked to a higher quality of life in late adulthood (Bowling & Iliffe, 2011)

- Expanded discussion of successful aging, including information about the important agenda of continuing to improve our understanding of how people can live longer, healthier, more productive and satisfying lives (Beard & others, 2012)

Chapter 20: Death, Dying, and Grieving

- New discussion of Physician Orders for Life-Sustaining Treatment (POLST), a document that is more specific than other advanced directives in translating treatment preferences into medical orders (Fromme & others, 2012; Hammes & others, 2012)

- Inclusion of a recent Dutch study of passive and active euthanasia, including the percentage of dying persons who requested them and the percentage whose request was granted (Onwuteaka-Philipsen & others, 2010)

- Discussion of a recent Belgian sutdy that found approximately 50 percent of the requests for euthanasia were granted (Van Wesemael & others, 2011)

- Description of a recent study in the Netherlands indicating that approximately 75 percent of the euthanasia requests came from cancer patients and the main reason for the requests was pain (van Alphen, Donker, & Marquet, 2010)

- Expanded and updated coverage of complicated grief or prolonged grief disorder, including its recent proposal for inclusion in DSM-V (Shear, 2012a, b)

- Description of recent research on aspects of death most likely to be linked to prolonged grief (Fujisawa & others, 2010)

- Discussion of a recent study that found individuals who were depressed were more likely to have complicated grief (Sung & others, 2011)

- Inclusion of research that found complicated grief was more likely to be present in older adults when the grief occurred in response to the death of a child or spouse (Newsom & others, 2011)

- New information about the percentage of women and men 65 years of age and older who are widowed in the United States (U.S. Census Bureau, 2011)

- Coverage of a recent large-scale study that found a link between loss of a spouse and risk of psychiatric visits as well as earlier death in individuals 75 years of age and older (Moller & others, 2011)

- Updated statistics and projections on the percentage of corpses being cremated in the United States (Cremation Association of North America, 2011)

ACKNOWLEDGMENTS

I very much appreciate the support and guidance provided to me by many people at McGraw-Hill. Mike Sugarman, Publisher, has brought a wealth of publishing knowledge and vision to bear on improving my texts. Allison McNamara, Senior Editor, deserves mention for the work she has done as the editor for this book. Sarah Kiefer, Editorial Coordinator, has done a very competent job of obtaining reviewers and handling many editorial chores. Janet Tilden did a superb job as the book's copy editor. Sheila Frank did a terrific job in coordinating the book's production. And Jennifer Blankenship provided me with excellent choices of new photographs for this edition of the book.

I also want to thank my parents, John and Ruth Santrock, my wife, Mary Jo, our children, Tracy and Jennifer, and our grandchildren, Jordan, Alex, and Luke, for their wonderful contributions to my life and for helping me to better understand the marvels and mysteries of life-span development.

REVIEWERS

I owe a special debt of gratitude to the reviewers who provided detailed feedback on *Life-Span Development*.

Expert Consultants

Life-span development has become an enormous, complex field, and no single author can possibly be an expert in all areas of the field. To solve this problem, beginning with the sixth edition, I have sought the input of leading experts in many different areas of life-span development. This tradition continues in the fourteenth edition. These experts have provided me with detailed recommendations of new research to include in every period of the life span. The panel of experts is literally a *Who's Who* in the field of life-span development. The names of the expert consultants, their photographs, and biographies are on pages xiv–xvi.

Connect Life-Span Board of Advisors

Shirley Bass-Wright, *St. Phillip's College*

Brent Costleigh, *Brookdale Community College*

Andrea Garvey, *American River College*

Lisa Hagan, *Metropolitan State College of Denver*

Ericka Hamilton, *Moraine Valley Community College*

Alycia Hund, *Illinois State University*

Joan Brandt Jensen, *Central Piedmont Community College*

Amy Reesing, *Arizona State University*

Angela Tiru, *Naugatuck Valley Community College*

Martin Wolfger, *Ivy Tech Community College*

Expert Consultants for Previous Editions

Karen Adolph, *New York University*

Toni C. Antonucci, *University of Michigan, Ann Arbor*

Pamela Balls Organista, *University of California—San Francisco*

Paul Baltes, *Max Planck Institute for Human Development*

Diana Baumrind, *University of California—Berkeley*

Carol Beal, *University of Massachusetts, Amherst*

Jean Berko Gleason, *Boston University*

James Birren, *University of California—Los Angeles*

Marc H. Bornstein, *National Institute of Child Health and Development*

Sue Bredekamp, *National Association for the Education of Young Children*

Urie Bronfenbrenner, *Cornell University*

Joseph Campos, *University of California—Berkeley*

Deborah Carr, *Rutgers University*

Rosalind Charlesworth, *Weber State University*

Florence Denmark, *Pace University*

Joseph Durlack, *Loyola University*

Glen Elder, *University of North Carolina, Chapel Hill*

Tiffany Field, *University of Miami*

Karen Fingerman, *Purdue University*

Alan Fogel, *University of Utah*

James Garbarino, *Loyola University, Chicago*

Jean Berko Gleason, *Boston University*

Gilbert Gottlieb, *University of North Carolina*

Julia Graber, *Columbia University*

Sandra Graham, *University of California—Los Angeles*

Elena Grigorenko, *Yale University*

Jane Halonen, *Alverno College*

Yvette R. Harris, *Miami University, Ohio*

Algea O. Harrison-Hale, *Oakland University*

Craig Hart, *Brigham Young University*

Bert Hayslip, *University of North Texas*

Ravenna Helson, *University of California—Berkeley*

Maria Hernandez-Reif, *University of Alabama*

William Hoyer, *Syracuse University*

Diane Hughes, *New York University*

Cigdem Kagitcibasi, *Koc University (Turkey)*

Robert Kastenbaum, *Arizona State University*

Arthur Kramer, *University of Illinois*

Gisela Labouvie-Vief, *Wayne State University*

Margie Lachman, *Brandeis University*

Barry M. Lester, *Women and Infants' Hospital*

Jean M. Mandler, *University of California—San Diego*

James Marcia, *Simon Fraser University*

Linda Mayes, *Yale University*

Andrew Meltzoff, *University of Washington*

Phyllis Moen, *University of Minnesota*

Scott Miller, *University of Florida*

Candice Mills, *University of Texas at Dallas*

David Moore, *Pitzer College and Claremont Graduate University*

Phyllis Moen, *Cornell University*

David Moore, *Pitzer College and Claremont Graduate University*

Ross D. Parke, *University of California—Riverside*

James Reid, *Washington University*

Carolyn Saarni, *Sonoma State University*

Barba Patton, *University of Houston, Victoria*

K. Warner Schaie, *Pennsylvania State University*

John Schulenberg, *University of Michigan*

Jan Sinnott, *Towson State University*

Margaret Beale Spencer, *University of Pennsylvania*

Wolfgang Stroebe, *University of Utrecht, The Netherlands*

Elizabeth Susman, *Pennsylvania State University*

Ross A. Thompson, *University of Nebraska, Lincoln*

Marian Underwood, *University of Texas at Dallas*

Elisa Velásquez-Andrade, *Sonoma State University*

Elizabeth Vera, *Loyola University, Chicago*

L. Monique Ward, *University of Michigan*

Camille Wortman, *University of Michigan*

Susan Whitbourne, *University of Massachusetts, Amherst*

General Text Reviewers for Previous Editions

Patrick K. Ackles, *Michigan State University;* Berkeley Adams, *Jamestown Community College;* Jackie Adamson, *South Dakota School of Mines & Technology;* Pamela Adelmann, *Saint Paul Technical College;* Joanne M. Alegre, *Yavapai College;* Gary L. Allen, *University of South Carolina;* Kristy Allen, *Ozark Technical College;* Lilia Allen, *Charles County Community College;* Ryan Allen, *The Citadel;* Susan E. Allen, *Baylor University;* Paul Anderer Castillo, *SUNY Canton;* Doreen Arcus, *University of Massachusetts–Lowell;* Frank R. Ashbur, *Valdosta State College;* Leslie Ault, *Hostos Community College–CUNY;* Renee L. Babcock, *Central Michigan University;* John Bauer, *University of Dayton;* Diana Baumrind, *University of California–Berkeley;* Daniel R. Bellack, *Trident Technical College;* Helen E. Benedict, *Baylor University;* Alice D. Beyrent, *Hesser College;* John Biondo, *Community College of Allegheny County–Boyce Campus;* James A. Blackburn, *University of Wisconsin at Madison;* William Blackston, *Baltimore City Community College;* Stephanie Blecharczyk, *Keene State College;* Belinda Blevins-Knabe, *University of Arkansas–Little Rock;* Marc H. Bornstein, *National Institute of Child Health & Development;* Karyn Mitchell Boutlin, *Massasoit Community College;* Donald Bowers, *Community College of Philadelphia;* Saundra Y. Boyd, *Houston Community College;* Michelle Boyer-Pennington, *Middle Tennessee State University;* Ann Brandt-Williams, *Glendale Community College;* Julia Braungart-Rieke, *University of Notre Dame;* Gregory Braswell, *Illinois State University;* Kathy Brown, *California State University at Fullerton;* Jack Busky, *Harrisburg Area Community College;* Marion Cahill, *Our Lady of the Lake College;* Joan B. Cannon, *University of Lowell;* Jeri Carter, *Glendale Community College;* Vincent Castranovo, *Community College of Philadelphia;* Ginny Chappeleau, *Muskingum Area Technical College;* Dominique Charlotteaux, *Broward Community College;* Rosalind Charlesworth, *Weber State University;* Yiwei Chen, *Bowling Green State University;* Bill Cheney, *Crichton College;* M. A. Christenberry, *Augusta College;* Saundra Ciccarelli, *Florida Gulf University;* Kevin Clark, *Indiana University at Kokomo;* Andrea Clements, *East Tennessee State University;* Meredith Cohen, *University of Pittsburgh;* Diane Cook, *Gainesville College;* Pamela Costa, *Tacoma Community College;* Ava Craig, *Sacramento City College;* Kathleen Crowley-Long, *College of Saint Rose;* Cynthia Crown, *Xavier University;* Jennifer Dale, *Community College of Aurora;* Dana Davidson, *University of Hawaii at Manoa;* Diane Davis, *Bowie State University;* Karen Davis, *Chippewa Valley Technical College;* Tom L. Day, *Weber State University;* Mehgen Delaney, *College of the Canyons;* Doreen DeSantio, *West Chester University;* Jill De Villiers, *Smith College;* Darryl M. Dietrich, *College of St. Scholastica;* Alisa Diop, *The Community College of Baltimore County;* Bailey Drechsler, *Cuesta College;* Joseph Durlack, *Loyola University;* Mary B. Eberly, *Oakland University;* Margaret Sutton Edmonds, *University of Massachusetts–Boston;* Glen Elder, *University of North Carolina at Chapel Hill;* Martha M. Ellis, *Collin County Community College;* Lena Eriksen, *Western Washington University;* Richard Ewy, *Pennsylvania State University;* Dan Fawaz, *Georgia Perimeter College;* Shirley Feldman, *Stanford University;* Roberta Ferra, *University of Kentucky;* Tiffany Field, *University of Miami;* Alan Fogel, *University of Utah;* Linda E. Flickinger, *St. Claire Community College;* Lynne Andreozzi Fontaine, *Community College of Rhode Island;* Tom Frangicetto, *Northampton Community College;* Kathleen Corrigan Fuhs, *J. Sargeant Reynolds Community College;* J. Steven Fulks, *Utah State University;* Cathy Furlong, *Tulsa Junior College;* Duwayne Furman, *Western Illinois University;* John Gat, *Humboldt State University;* Marvin Gelman, *Montgomery County College;* G.R. Germo, *University of California—Irvine;* Rebecca J. Glare, *Weber State College;*

David Goldstein, *Temple University;* **Arthur Gonchar,** *University of LaVerne;* **Judy Goodell,** *National University;* **Mary Ann Goodwyn,** *Northeast Louisiana University;* **Caroline Gould,** *Eastern Michigan University;* **Julia Graber,** *Columbia University;* **Peter C. Gram,** *Pensacola Junior College;* **Dan Grangaard,** *Austin Community College;* **Tom Gray,** *Laredo Community College;* **Michele Gregoire,** *University of Florida at Gainesville;* **Michael Green,** *University of North Carolina;* **Rea Gubler,** *Southern Utah University;* **Gary Gute,** *University of Northern Iowa;* **Laura Hanish,** *Arizona State University;* **Ester Hanson,** *Prince George's Community College;* **Marian S. Harris,** *University of Illinois at Chicago;* **Yvette R. Harris,** *Miami University of Ohio;* **Amanda W. Harrist,** *Oklahoma State University;* **Robert Heavilin,** *Greater Hartford Community College;* **Donna Henderson,** *Wake Forest University;* **Debra Hollister,** *Valencia Community College;* **Heather Holmes-Lonergan,** *Metropolitan State College of Denver;* **Ramona O. Hopkins,** *Brigham Young University;* **Donna Horbury,** *Appalachian State University;* **Susan Horton,** *Mesa Community College;* **Sharon C. Hott,** *Allegany College of Maryland;* **John Hotz,** *Saint Cloud State University;* **Tasha Howe,** *Humboldt State University;* **Kimberley Howe-Norris,** *Cape Fear Community College;* **Stephen Hoyer,** *Pittsburgh State University;* **Charles H. Huber,** *New Mexico State University;* **Kathleen Day Hulbert,** *University of Massachusetts–Lowell;* **Derek Isaacowitz,** *Brandeis University;* **Kathryn French Iroz,** *Utah Valley State College;* **Terry Isbell,** *Northwestern State University of Louisiana;* **Erwin Janek,** *Henderson State University;* **James Jasper-Jacobsen,** *Indiana University at Purdue;* **Christina Jose-Kampfner,** *Eastern Michigan University;* **Ursula Joyce,** *St. Thomas Aquinas College;* **Barbara Kane,** *Indiana State University;* **Ulas Kaplan,** *Harvard University;* **Kevin Keating,** *Broward Community College;* **James L. Keeney,** *Middle Georgia College;* **Elinor Kinarthy,** *Rio Hondo College;* **Karen Kirkendall,** *Sangamon State University;* **A. Klingner,** *Northwest Community College;* **Steven J. Kohn,** *Nazareth College;* **Amanda Kowal,** *University of Missouri;* **Jane Krump,** *North Dakota State College of Science;* **Nadene L'Amoreaux,** *Indiana University of Pennsylvania;* **Gisela Labouvie-Vief,** *Wayne State University;* **Joseph C. LaVoie,** *University of Nebraska at Omaha;* **Kathy Lein,** *Community College of Denver;* **Jean Hill Macht,** *Montgomery County Community College;* **James Marcia,** *Simon Fraser University;* **Salvador Macias,** *University of South Carolina at Sumter;* **Karen Macrae,** *University of South Carolina;* **Christine Malecki,** *Northern Illinois University;* **Kathy Manuel,** *Bossier Parish Community College;* **Myra Marcus,** *Florida Gulf Coast University;* **Carrie Margolin,** *The Evergreen State College;* **Allan Mayotte,** *Riverland Community College;* **Susan McClure,** *Westmoreland Community College;* **Dorothy H. McDonald,** *Sandhills Community College;* **Robert C. McGinnis,** *Ancilla College;* **Clara McKinney,** *Barstow College;* **Robert McLaren,** *California State University at Fullerton;* **Deborah H. McMurtrie,** *University of South Carolina, Aiken;* **Sharon McNeeley,** *Northeastern Illinois University;* **Daysi Mejia,** *Florida Gulf Coast University;* **Kathleen Mentink,** *Chippewa Valley Technical College;* **James Messina,** *University of Phoenix;* **Heather E. Metcalfe,** *University of Windsor;* **Karla Miley,** *Black Hawk College;* **Jessica Miller,** *Mesa State College;* **Scott Miller,** *University of Florida;* **Teri M. Miller-Schwartz,** *Milwaukee Area Technical College;* **David B. Mitchell,** *Loyola University;* **Joann Montepare,** *Emerson College;* **Gary T. Montgomery,** *University of Texas—Pan American;* **Martin D. Murphy,** *University of Akron;* **Malinda Muzi,** *Community College of Philadelphia;* **Gordon K. Nelson,** *Pennsylvania State University;* **Michael Newton,** *Sam Houston State University;* **Charisse Nixon,** *Pennsylvania State University at Erie;* **Beatrice Norrie,** *Mount Royal College;* **Jean O'Neil,** *Boston College;* **Laura Overstreet,** *Tarrant County College-Northeast;* **Karla Parise,** *The Community College of Baltimore County at Essex;* **Jennifer Parker,** *University of South Carolina;* **Barba Patton,** *University of Houston–Victoria;* **Susan Perez,** *University of North Florida;* **Pete Peterson,** *Johnson County Community College;* **Richard Pierce,** *Pennsylvania State University-Altoona;* **David Pipes,** *Caldwell Community College;* **Leslee Pollina,** *Southeast Missouri State University;* **Robert Poresky,** *Kansas State University;* **Christopher Quarto,** *Middle Tennessee State University;* **Bob Rainey,** *Florida Community College;* **Nancy Rankin,** *University of New England;* **H. Ratner,** *Wayne State University;* **Cynthia Reed,** *Tarrant County College-Northeast;* **James Reid,** *Washington University;* **Amy Reesing,** *Arizona University;* **Russell Riley,** *Lord Fairfax Community College;* **Mark P. Rittman,** *Cuyahoga Community College;* **Cathie Robertson,** *Grossmont College;* **Clarence Romeno,** *Riverside Community College;* **Paul Roodin,** *SUNY-Oswego;* **Ron Rossac,** *University of North Florida;* **Julia Rux,** *Georgia Perimeter College;* **Carolyn Saarni,** *Sonoma State University;* **Karen Salekin,** *University of Alabama;* **Gayla Sanders,** *Community College of*

Baltimore County–Essex; **Toru Sato**, *Shippensburg University;* **Nancy Sauerman**, *Kirkwood Community College;* **Cynthia Scheibe**, *Ithaca College;* **Robert Schell**, *SUNY–Oswego;* **Rachel Schremp**, *Santa Fe Community College;* **Pamela Schuetze**, *Buffalo State College;* **Edythe Schwartz**, *California State University at Sacramento;* **Lisa Scott**, *University of Minnesota–Twin Cities;* **Owen Sharkey**, *University of Prince Edward Island;* **Elisabeth Shaw**, *Texarkana College;* **Susan Nakayama Siaw**, *California State Polytechnic University;* **Vicki Simmons**, *University of Victoria;* **Jessica Siebenbruner**, *Winona State College;* **Gregory Smith**, *University of Maryland;* **Jon Snodgrass**, *California State University–Los Angeles;* **Donald Stanley**, *North Dallas Community College;* **Jean A. Steitz**, *University of Memphis;* **Terre Sullivan**, *Chippewa Valley Technical College;* **Collier Summers**, *Florida Community College at Jacksonville;* **Barbara Thomas**, *National University;* **Stacy D. Thompson**, *Oklahoma State University;* **Debbie Tindell**, *Wilkes University;* **Stephen Truhon**, *Winston-Salem State University;* **James Turcott**, *Kalamazoo Valley Community College;* **Marian Underwood**, *University of Texas at Dallas;* **Dennis Valone**, *Pennsylvania State University at Erie;* **Gaby Vandergiessen**, *Fairmount State College;* **Elisa Velasquez**, *Sonoma State University;* **Stephen Werba**, *Community College of Baltimore County at Catonsville;* **B. D. Whetstone**, *Birmingham Southern College;* **Susan Whitbourne**, *University of Massachusetts at Amherst.* **Nancy C. White**, *Reynolds Community College;* **Lyn W. Wickelgren**, *Metropolitan State College;* **Ann M. Williams**, *Luzerne County Community College;* **Myron D. Williams**, *Great Lakes Bible College;* **Linda B. Wilson**, *Quincy College;* **Mark Winkel**, *University of Texas—Pan American;* **Mary Ann Wisniewski**, *Carroll College;*

Instructor Resources

The resources listed here may accompany *Life-Span Development*, 14th edition. Please contact your McGraw-Hill representative for details concerning policies, prices, and availability.

Online Resources   The instructor's side of the Online Learning Center at http://www.mhhe.com/santrockld14e contains the *Instructor's Manual,* Test Bank files, PowerPoint slides, Image Gallery, and other valuable material to help you design and enhance your course. Ask your local McGraw-Hill representative for your password.

Instructor's Manual   Each chapter of the *Instructor's Manual* is introduced by a Total Teaching Package Outline. This fully integrated tool helps instructors more easily locate and choose among the many resources available for the course by linking each element of the *Instructor's Manual* to a particular teaching topic within the chapter. These elements include chapter outlines, suggested lecture topics, classroom activities and demonstrations, suggested student research projects, essay questions, critical thinking questions, and implications for guidance.

Test Bank and Computerized Test Bank   This comprehensive Test Bank includes more than 1,500 multiple-choice and approximately 75 essay questions. Organized by chapter, the questions are designed to test factual, applied, and conceptual understanding. All test questions are compatible with EZ Test, McGraw-Hill's Computerized Test Bank program.

PowerPoint Slides   These presentations cover the key points of each chapter and include charts and graphs from the text. They can be used as is, or you may modify them to meet your specific needs.

McGraw-Hill's Visual Assets Database for Lifespan Development ("VAD")
McGraw-Hill's Visual Assets Database for Lifespan Development (VAD 2.0) at www.mhhe.com/vad is an online database of videos for use in the developmental psychology classroom, created specifically for instructors. You can customize classroom presentations by downloading the videos to your computer and showing the videos on their own or inserting them into your course cartridge or PowerPoint presentations. All of the videos are available with or without captions. Ask your McGraw-Hill representative for access information.

LIFE-SPAN
DEVELOPMENT

All the world's a stage,
And all the men and women merely players.
They have their exits and their entrances;
and one man in his time plays many parts.

—WILLIAM SHAKESPEARE
English Playwright, 17th Century

The Life-Span Perspective

This book is about human development—its universal features, its individual variations, its nature. Every life is distinct, a new biography in the world. Examining the shape of life-span development allows us to understand it better. *Life-Span Development* is about the rhythm and meaning of people's lives, about turning mystery into understanding, and about weaving a portrait of who each of us was, is, and will be. In Section 1, you will read "Introduction" (Chapter 1).

INTRODUCTION

chapter **outline**

1 The Life-Span Perspective

Learning Goal 1 Discuss the distinctive features of a life-span perspective on development.

The Importance of Studying Life-Span Development
Characteristics of the Life-Span Perspective
Some Contemporary Concerns

2 The Nature of Development

Learning Goal 2 Identify the most important processes, periods, and issues in development.

Biological, Cognitive, and Socioemotional Processes
Periods of Development
The Significance of Age
Developmental Issues

3 Theories of Development

Learning Goal 3 Describe the main theories of human development.

Psychoanalytic Theories
Cognitive Theories
Behavioral and Social Cognitive Theories
Ethological Theory
Ecological Theory
An Eclectic Theoretical Orientation

4 Research in Life-Span Development

Learning Goal 4 Explain how research on life-span development is conducted.

Methods for Collecting Data
Research Designs
Time Span of Research
Conducting Ethical Research
Minimizing Bias

Ted Kaczynski sprinted through high school, not bothering with his junior year and making only passing efforts at social contact. Off to Harvard at age 16, Kaczynski was a loner during his college years. One of his roommates at Harvard said that he avoided people by quickly shuffling by them and slamming the door behind him. After obtaining his Ph.D. in mathematics at the University of Michigan, Kaczynski became a professor at the University of California at Berkeley. His colleagues there remember him as hiding from social circumstances—no friends, no allies, no networking.

After several years at Berkeley, Kaczynski resigned and moved to a rural area of Montana where he lived as a hermit in a crude shack for 25 years. Town residents described him as a bearded eccentric. Kaczynski traced his own difficulties to growing up as a genius in a kid's body and sticking out like a sore thumb in his surroundings as a child. In 1996, he was arrested and charged as the notorious Unabomber, America's most wanted killer. Over the course of 17 years, Kaczynski had sent 16 mail bombs that left 23 people wounded or maimed and 3 people dead. In 1998, he pleaded guilty to the offenses and was sentenced to life in prison.

A decade before Kaczynski mailed his first bomb, Alice Walker spent her days battling racism in Mississippi. She had recently won her first writing fellowship, but rather than use the money to follow her dream of moving to Senegal, Africa, she put herself into the heart and heat of the civil rights movement. Walker had grown up knowing the brutal effects of poverty and racism. Born in 1944, she was the eighth child of Georgia sharecroppers who earned $300 a year. When Walker was 8, her brother accidentally shot her in the left eye with a BB gun. By the time her parents got her to the hospital a week later (they had no car), she was blind in that eye, and it had developed a disfiguring layer of scar tissue. Despite the counts against her, Walker overcame pain and anger and went on to win a Pulitzer Prize for her book *The Color Purple*. She became not only a novelist but also an essayist, a poet, a short-story writer, and a social activist.

Ted Kaczynski, the convicted Unabomber, traced his difficulties to growing up as a genius in a kid's body and not fitting in when he was a child.

Ted Kaczynski, about age 15–16.

Alice Walker won the Pulitzer Prize for her book *The Color Purple*. Like the characters in her book, Walker overcame pain and anger to triumph and celebrate the human spirit.

Alice Walker, about age 8.

preview

What leads one individual, so full of promise, to commit brutal acts of violence and another to turn poverty and trauma into a rich literary harvest? If you have ever wondered why people turn out the way they do, you have asked yourself the central question we will explore in this book. This book is a window into the journey of human development—your own and that of every other member of the human species. In this first chapter, we will explore what it means to take a life-span perspective on development, examine the nature of development, and outline how science helps us to understand it.

1 The Life-Span Perspective

LG1 Discuss the distinctive features of a life-span perspective on development.

The Importance of Studying Life-Span Development

Characteristics of the Life-Span Perspective

Some Contemporary Concerns

Each of us develops partly like all other individuals, partly like some other individuals, and partly like no other individual. Most of the time our attention is directed to an individual's uniqueness. But as humans, we have all traveled some common paths. Each of us—Leonardo da Vinci, Joan of Arc, George Washington, Martin Luther King, Jr., and you—walked at about 1 year, engaged in fantasy play as a young child, and became more independent as a youth. Each of us, if we live long enough, will experience hearing problems and the death of family members and friends. This is the general course of our **development,** the pattern of movement or change that begins at conception and continues through the human life span.

In this section, we will explore what is meant by the concept of development and why the study of life-span development is important. We will outline the main characteristics of the life-span perspective and discuss various sources of contextual influences. In addition, we will examine some contemporary concerns in life-span development.

> We reach backward to our parents and forward to our children, and through their children to a future we will never see, but about which we need to care.
>
> —CARL JUNG
> *Swiss Psychiatrist, 20th Century*

THE IMPORTANCE OF STUDYING LIFE-SPAN DEVELOPMENT

How might people benefit from examining life-span development? Perhaps you are, or will be, a parent or teacher. If so, responsibility for children is, or will be, a part of your everyday life. The more you learn about them, the better you can deal with them. Perhaps you hope to gain some insight about your own history—as an infant, a child, an adolescent, or a young adult. Perhaps you want to know more about what your life will be like as you grow through

development The pattern of change that begins at conception and continues through the life span. Most development involves growth, although it also includes decline brought on by aging and dying.

life-span perspective The perspective that development is lifelong, multidimensional, multidirectional, plastic, multidisciplinary, and contextual; involves growth, maintenance, and regulation; and is constructed through biological, sociocultural, and individual factors working together.

Peanuts : © United Features Syndicate, Inc.

the adult years—as a middle-aged adult, or as an adult in old age, for example. Or perhaps you just stumbled onto this course, thinking that it sounded intriguing and that the study of the human life span might raise some provocative issues. Whatever your reasons for taking this course, you will discover that the study of life-span development is intriguing and filled with information about who we are, how we came to be this way, and where our future will take us.

Most development involves growth, but it also includes decline (as in dying). In exploring development, we will examine the life span from the point of conception until the time when life (or at least life as we know it) ends. You will see yourself as an infant, as a child, and as an adolescent, and be stimulated to think about how those years influenced the kind of individual you are today. And you will see yourself as a young adult, as a middle-aged adult, and as an adult in old age, and be motivated to think about how your experiences today will influence your development through the remainder of your adult years.

CHARACTERISTICS OF THE LIFE-SPAN PERSPECTIVE

Although growth and development are dramatic during the first two decades of life, development is not something that happens only to children and adolescents. The traditional approach to the study of development emphasizes extensive change from birth to adolescence (especially during infancy), little or no change in adulthood, and decline in old age. But a great deal of change does occur in the five or six decades after adolescence. The life-span approach emphasizes developmental change throughout adulthood as well as childhood (Lerner, Easterbrooks & Mistry, 2013; Schaie, 2012; Whitbourne & Sliwinski, 2012).

Recent increases in human life expectancy contributed to the popularity of the life-span approach to development. The upper boundary of the human life span (based on the oldest age documented) is 122 years, as indicated in Figure 1.1; this maximum life span of humans has not changed since the beginning of recorded history. What has changed is life expectancy—the average number of years that a person born in a particular year can expect to live. In the twentieth century alone, life expectancy in the United States increased by 30 years, thanks to improvements in sanitation, nutrition, and medicine (see Figure 1.2). In the first half of the second decade of the twenty-first century, the life expectancy in the United States is 78 years of age (U.S. Census Bureau, 2011). Today, for most individuals in developed countries, childhood and adolescence represent only about one-fourth of their lives.

The belief that development occurs throughout life is central to the life-span perspective on human development, but this perspective has other characteristics as well. According to life-span development expert Paul Baltes (1939–2006), the **life-span perspective** views development as lifelong, multidimensional, multidirectional, plastic, multidisciplinary, and contextual, and as a process that involves growth, maintenance, and regulation of loss (Baltes, 1987, 2003; Baltes, Lindenberger, & Staudinger, 2006). In Baltes' view, it is important to understand that development is constructed through biological, sociocultural, and individual factors working together. Let's look at each of these components of the life-span perspective.

Development Is Lifelong In the life-span perspective, early adulthood is not the endpoint of development; rather, no age period dominates development. Researchers increasingly study the experiences and psychological orientations of adults at different points in their lives. Later in this chapter, we will describe the age periods of development and their characteristics.

Development Is Multidimensional No matter what your age might be, your body, mind, emotions, and relationships are changing and affecting each other. Consider the development of Ted Kaczynski, the Unabomber discussed at the beginning of this chapter. When he was 6 months old, he was

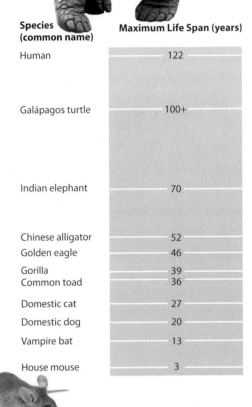

Species (common name)	Maximum Life Span (years)
Human	122
Galápagos turtle	100+
Indian elephant	70
Chinese alligator	52
Golden eagle	46
Gorilla	39
Common toad	36
Domestic cat	27
Domestic dog	20
Vampire bat	13
House mouse	3

FIGURE 1.1

MAXIMUM RECORDED LIFE SPAN FOR DIFFERENT SPECIES. Our only competitor for the maximum recorded life span is the Galápagos turtle.

Paul Baltes, a leading architect of the life-span perspective of development, conversing with one of the long-time research participants in the Berlin Aging Study that he directs. She joined the study in the early 1990s and has participated six times in extensive physical, medical, psychological, and social assessments. In her professional life, she was a practicing medical doctor.

Time Period	Average Life Expectancy (years)
2011, USA	78
1954, USA	70
1915, USA	54
1900, USA	47
19th century, England	41
1620, Massachusetts Bay Colony	35
Middle Ages, England	33
Ancient Greece	20
Prehistoric times	18

FIGURE **1.2**

HUMAN LIFE EXPECTANCY AT BIRTH FROM PREHISTORIC TO CONTEMPORARY TIMES. It took 5,000 years to extend human life expectancy from 18 to 41 years of age.

developmental **connection**

Exercise

What effect might exercise have on older adults' ability to process information? Chapter 17, p. 555

What characterizes the life-span perspective of development?

normative age-graded influences Influences that are similar for individuals in a particular age group.

hospitalized with a severe allergic reaction and his parents were rarely allowed to visit the baby. According to his mother, the previously happy baby was never the same after his hospitalization. The infant became withdrawn and unresponsive. As Ted grew up, he had periodic "shutdowns" accompanied by rage. In his mother's view, a biological event in infancy warped the development of her son's mind and emotions.

Development has biological, cognitive, and socioemotional dimensions. Even within a dimension, there are many components. For example, attention, memory, abstract thinking, speed of processing information, and social intelligence are just a few of the components of the cognitive dimension.

Development Is Multidirectional   Throughout life, some dimensions or components of a dimension expand and others shrink. For example, when one language (such as English) is acquired early in development, the capacity for acquiring second and third languages (such as Spanish and Chinese) decreases later in development, especially after early childhood (Levelt, 1989). During adolescence, as individuals establish romantic relationships, their time spent with friends may decrease. During late adulthood, older adults might become wiser because they have more experience than younger adults to draw upon to guide their decision making, but they perform more poorly on tasks that require speed in processing information (Ardelt, 2011; Bassett, 2012; Dirk & Schmiedek, 2012; Salthouse, 2012).

Development Is Plastic   Even at 10 years old, Ted Kaczynski was extraordinarily shy. Was he destined to remain forever uncomfortable with people? Developmentalists debate how much plasticity people have in various dimensions at different points in their development. Plasticity means the capacity for change. For example, can you still improve your intellectual skills when you are in your seventies or eighties? Or might these intellectual skills be fixed by the time you are in your thirties so that further improvement is impossible? Researchers have found that the cognitive skills of older adults can be improved through training and developing better strategies (Katzel & Steinbrenner, 2012; Schaie, 2012). However, possibly we possess less capacity for change as we grow older (Salthouse, 2010, 2012, 2013). The search for plasticity and its constraints is a key element on the contemporary agenda for developmental research (Depp, Vahia, & Jeste, 2012; Freund, Nikitin, & Riediger, 2013; Park & Bischof, 2011).

Developmental Science Is Multidisciplinary   Psychologists, sociologists, anthropologists, neuroscientists, and medical researchers all share an interest in unlocking the mysteries of development through the life span. How do your heredity and health limit your intelligence? Do intelligence and social relationships change with age in the same way around the world? How do families and schools influence intellectual development? These are examples of research questions that cut across disciplines.

Development Is Contextual   All development occurs within a context, or setting. Contexts include families, schools, peer groups, churches, cities, neighborhoods, university laboratories, countries, and so on. Each of these settings is influenced by historical, economic, social, and cultural factors (Gollnick & Chinn, 2013; Kitayama & Uskul, 2011).

Contexts, like individuals, change (Gauvain, 2013; Gerstorff & Ram, 2012). Thus, individuals are changing beings in a changing world. As a result of these changes, contexts exert three types of influences (Baltes, 2003): (1) normative age-graded influences, (2) normative history-graded influences, and (3) nonnormative or highly individualized life events. Each of these types can have a biological or environmental impact on development. **Normative age-graded influences** are similar for individuals in a particular age group. These influences include biological processes such as puberty and menopause. They also include sociocultural, environmental processes such as beginning formal education (usually at about age 6 in most cultures) and retirement from the workforce (which takes place during the fifties and sixties in most cultures).

Normative history-graded influences are common to people of a particular generation because of historical circumstances. For example, in their youth American baby boomers shared the experience of the Cuban missile crisis, the assassination of John F. Kennedy, and the Beatles invasion. Other examples of normative history-graded influences include economic, political, and social upheavals such as the Great Depression in the 1930s, World War II in the 1940s, the civil rights and women's rights movements of the 1960s and 1970s, the terrorist attacks of 9/11/2001, as well as the integration of computers and cell phones into everyday life during the 1990s (Schaie, 2010, 2012; Schaie & Zanjani, 2012). Long-term changes in the genetic and cultural makeup of a population (due to immigration or changes in fertility rates) are also part of normative historical change.

Nonnormative life events are unusual occurrences that have a major impact on the lives of individual people. These events do not happen to everyone, and when they do occur they can influence people in different ways. Examples include the death of a parent when a child is young, pregnancy in early adolescence, a fire that destroys a home, winning the lottery, or getting an unexpected career opportunity.

Nonnormative life events, such as Hurricane Katrina in August 2005, are unusual circumstances that have a major impact on a person's life.

Development Involves Growth, Maintenance, and Regulation of Loss   Baltes and his colleagues (2006) assert that the mastery of life often involves conflicts and competition among three goals of human development: growth, maintenance, and regulation of loss. As individuals age into middle and late adulthood, the maintenance and regulation of loss in their capacities takes center stage. Thus, a 75-year-old man might aim not to improve his memory or his golf swing but to maintain his independence and his ability to play golf at all. In Chapters 15 and 16, we will discuss these ideas about maintenance and regulation of loss in greater depth.

Development Is a Co-construction of Biology, Culture, and the Individual
Development is a co-construction of biological, cultural, and individual factors working together (Baltes, Reuter-Lorenz, & Rösler, 2006). For example, the brain shapes culture, but it is also shaped by culture and the experiences that individuals have or pursue. In terms of individual factors, we can go beyond what our genetic inheritance and environment give us. We can author a unique developmental path by actively choosing from the environment the things that optimize our lives (Rathunde & Csikszentmihalyi, 2006).

SOME CONTEMPORARY CONCERNS

Pick up a newspaper or magazine and you might see headlines like these: "Political Leanings May Be Written in the Genes," "Mother Accused of Tossing Children into Bay," "Gender Gap Widens," "FDA Warns About ADHD Drug," "Heart Attack Deaths Higher in African American Patients," "Test May Predict Alzheimer's Disease." Researchers using the life-span perspective are examining these and many other topics of contemporary concern. The roles that health and well-being, parenting, education, and sociocultural contexts play in life-span development, as well as how social policy is related to these issues, are a particular focus of this textbook.

Health and Well-Being   Health professionals today recognize the power of lifestyles and psychological states in health and well-being (Hahn, Payne, & Lucas, 2013; Insel & Roth, 2012; Marks, 2013). In every chapter of this book, issues of health and well-being are integrated into our discussion.

Clinical psychologists are among the health professionals who help people improve their well-being. Read about one clinical psychologist who helps adolescents who have become juvenile delinquents or substance abusers in *Connecting with Careers*.

developmental **connection**

Middle Age

Adults typically face more losses in middle age than earlier in life. Chapter 15, p. 485

How might growth versus maintenance and regulation be reflected in the development of this grandfather and his grandchild?

normative history-graded influences Influences that are common to people of a particular generation because of historical circumstances.

nonnormative life events Unusual occurrences that have a major impact on an individual's life.

Luis Vargas, Clinical Child Psychologist

Luis Vargas is Director of the Clinical Child Psychology Internship Program and a professor in the Department of Psychiatry at the University of New Mexico Health Sciences Center. He also is Director of Psychology at the University of New Mexico Children's Psychiatric Center.

Vargas obtained an undergraduate degree in psychology from St. Edward's University in Texas, a master's degree in psychology from Trinity University in Texas, and a Ph.D. in clinical psychology from the University of Nebraska-Lincoln.

Vargas' main interests are cultural issues and the assessment and treatment of children, adolescents, and families. He is motivated to find better ways to provide culturally responsive mental health services. One of his special interests is the treatment of Latino youth for delinquency and substance abuse.

Luis Vargas (*left*) conducting a child therapy session.

For more information about what clinical psychologists do, see page 44 in the Careers in Life-Span Development appendix immediately following this chapter.

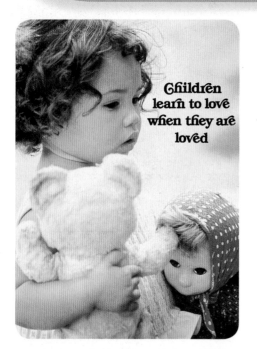

culture The behavior patterns, beliefs, and all other products of a group that are passed on from generation to generation.

cross-cultural studies Comparison of one culture with one or more other cultures. These provide information about the degree to which development is similar, or universal, across cultures, and the degree to which it is culture-specific.

ethnicity A characteristic based on cultural heritage, nationality characteristics, race, religion, and language.

Parenting and Education   Can two gay men raise a healthy family? Are children harmed if both parents work outside the home? Are U.S. schools failing to teach children how to read and write and calculate adequately? We hear many questions like these involving pressures on the contemporary family and the problems of U.S. schools (Lansford, 2012; McCombs, 2013; Powell, 2012). In later chapters, we will analyze child care, the effects of divorce, parenting styles, child maltreatment, intergenerational relationships, early childhood education, relationships between childhood poverty and education, bilingual education, new educational efforts to improve lifelong learning, and many other issues related to parenting and education (Bassett, 2012; Lessow-Hurley, 2013; Taylor & Fratto, 2012).

Sociocultural Contexts and Diversity   Health, parenting, and education—like development itself—are all shaped by their sociocultural context. To analyze this context, four concepts are especially useful: culture, ethnicity, socioeconomic status, and gender.

Culture encompasses the behavior patterns, beliefs, and all other products of a particular group of people that are passed on from generation to generation. Culture results from the interaction of people over many years (Mistry, Contreras, & Dutta, 2013). A cultural group can be as large as the United States or as small as an isolated Appalachian town. Whatever its size, the group's culture influences the behavior of its members (Matsumoto & Juang, 2012). **Cross-cultural studies** compare aspects of two or more cultures. The comparison provides information about the degree to which development is similar, or universal, across cultures, or is instead culture-specific (Gauvain, 2011, 2013; Postert & others, 2012).

Ethnicity (the word *ethnic* comes from the Greek word for "nation") is rooted in cultural heritage, nationality, race, religion, and language. African Americans, Latinos, Asian Americans, Native Americans, European Americans, and Arab Americans are a few examples of broad ethnic groups in the United States. Diversity exists within each ethnic group (Kottak & Kozaitis, 2012; Nieto & Bode, 2012).

Socioeconomic status (SES) refers to a person's position within society based on occupational, educational, and economic characteristics. Socioeconomic status implies

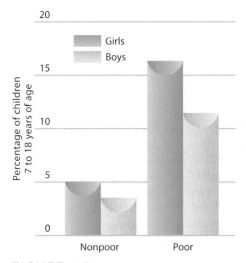

FIGURE **1.3**

PERCENTAGE OF CHILDREN 7 TO 18 YEARS OF AGE AROUND THE WORLD WHO HAVE NEVER BEEN TO SCHOOL OF ANY KIND. When UNICEF (2004) surveyed the education that children around the world are receiving, it found that far more girls than boys receive no formal schooling at all.

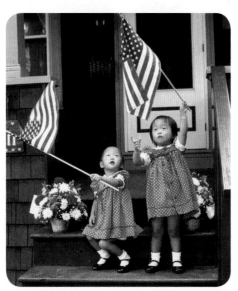

Two Korean-born children on the day they became United States citizens. Asian American and Latino children are the fastest-growing immigrant groups in the United States. *How diverse are the students in your life-span development class? How are their experiences in growing up likely to have been similar to or different from yours?*

Around the world women too often are treated as burdens rather than assets in the political process. *What can be done to strengthen women's roles in the political process?*

Doly Akter, age 17, lives in a slum in Dhaka, Bangladesh, where sewers overflow, garbage rots in the streets, and children are undernourished, Nearly two-thirds of young women in Bangladesh get married before they are 18. Doly recently organized a club supported by UNICEF in which girls go door-to-door to monitor the hygiene habits of households in their neighborhood. The monitoring has led to improved hygiene and health in the families. Also, her group has managed to stop several child marriages by meeting with parents and convincing them that it is not in their daughter's best interests. When talking with parents in their neighborhoods, the girls in the club emphasize the importance of staying in school and how this will improve their daughters' future. Doly says that the girls in her UNICEF group are far more aware of their rights than their mothers ever were. (UNICEF, 2007).

certain inequalities. Differences in the ability to control resources and to participate in society's rewards produce unequal opportunities (Moore, Murphey, & Bandy, 2012; Ortega & others, 2012).

Gender refers to the characteristics of people as males and females. Few aspects of our development are more central to our identity and social relationships than gender (Hyde & Quest, 2013; Leaper, 2013; Matlin, 2012).

In the United States, the sociocultural context has become increasingly diverse in recent years (Wright & others, 2012). The U.S. population includes a greater variety of cultures and ethnic groups than ever before. This changing demographic tapestry promises not only the richness that diversity produces but also difficult challenges in extending the American dream to all individuals (Hillemeier & others, 2012; McLoyd & others, 2011). We will discuss sociocultural contexts and diversity in each chapter.

A special cross-cultural concern is the educational and psychological conditions of women around the world (UNICEF, 2012). Inadequate educational opportunities, violence, and mental health issues are among the problems faced by many women.

One analysis found that a higher percentage of girls than boys around the world have never had any education (UNICEF, 2004) (see Figure 1.3). The countries with the fewest females being educated are in Africa, where in some areas, girls and women are receiving no education at all. Canada, the United States, and Russia have the highest percentages of educated women. In developing countries, 67 percent of women over the age of 25 (compared with 50 percent of men) have never been to school. At the beginning of the twenty-first century, 80 million more boys than girls were in primary and secondary educational settings around the world (United Nations, 2002).

Social Policy   **Social policy** is a government's course of action designed to promote the welfare of its citizens. Values, economics, and politics all shape a nation's social policy. Out of concern that policy makers are doing too little to protect the well-being of children and older adults, life-span researchers are increasingly undertaking studies that they hope will lead to effective social policy (Cross & others, 2012; Goodman, Evans, & DiPietro, 2012).

Statistics such as infant mortality rates, mortality among children under 5, and the percentage of children who are malnourished or living in poverty provide benchmarks for

socioeconomic status (SES) Refers to the grouping of people with similar occupational, educational, and economic characteristics.

gender The characteristics of people as males or females.

social policy A national government's course of action designed to promote the welfare of its citizens.

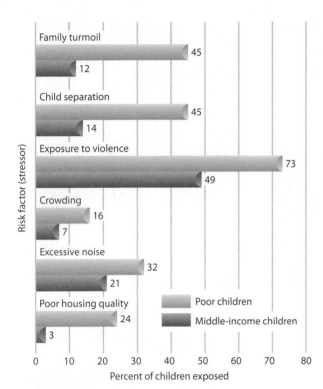

FIGURE 1.4

EXPOSURE TO SIX STRESSORS AMONG POOR AND MIDDLE-INCOME CHILDREN. One study analyzed the exposure to six stressors among poor children and middle-income children (Evans & English, 2002). Poor children were much more likely to face each of these stressors.

evaluating how well children are doing in a particular society (Britto & Ulkuer, 2012; Panter-Brick, Lende, & Kohrt, 2012; UNICEF, 2012). Marian Wright Edelman, a tireless advocate of children's rights, has pointed out that indicators like these place the United States at or near the lowest rank for industrialized nations in the treatment of children.

Children who grow up in poverty represent a special concern (Evans & others, 2012; Webb, 2012). In 2010, 22 percent of U.S. children were living in families with incomes below the poverty line (U.S. Census Bureau, 2012). This is an increase from 2001 (16.2 percent) and 2009 (20.7 percent) but a slight decrease from a peak of 22.7 percent in 1993. In 2010, poverty rates in the U.S. were much higher for African American (38.2 percent) and Latino (34.8 percent) children than for non-Latino White children (17 percent) (U.S. Census Bureau, 2012). As indicated in Figure 1.4, one study found that a higher percentage of U.S. children in poor families than in middle-income families were exposed to family turmoil, separation from a parent, violence, crowding, excessive noise, and poor housing (Evans & English, 2002). One study also revealed that the more years children spent living in poverty, the higher their physiological indices of stress (Evans & Kim, 2007).

The U.S. figure of 22 percent of children living in poverty is much higher than those of other industrialized nations. For example, Canada has a child poverty rate of 9 percent and Sweden has a rate of 2 percent.

Edelman says that parenting and nurturing the next generation of children is our society's most important function and that we need to take it more seriously than we have in the past. To read about efforts to improve the lives of children through social policies, see *Connecting Development to Life*.

Some children triumph over poverty or other adversities. They show *resilience* (Jackson & others, 2012; Masten, 2013). Think back to the chapter-opening story about Alice Walker. In spite of racism, poverty, her low socioeconomic status, and a disfiguring eye injury, she went on to become a successful author and champion for equality.

Are there certain characteristics that make children like Alice Walker resilient? Are there other characteristics that make children like Ted Kaczynski, who despite his intelligence and

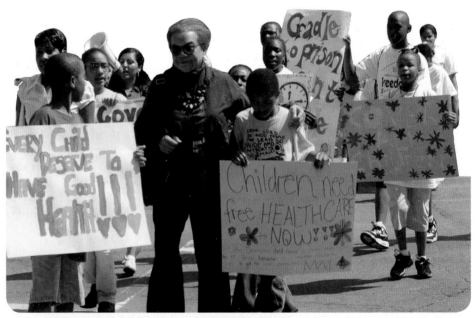

Marian Wright Edelman, president of the Children's Defense Fund (shown here advocating for health care), has been a tireless advocate of children's rights and has been instrumental in calling attention to the needs of children. *What are some of these needs?*

Improving Family Policy

In the United States, the actions of the national government, state governments, and city governments influence the well-being of children (Parish & others, 2012; Sum, 2012). When families seriously endanger a child's well-being, governments often step in to help. At the national and state levels, policy makers have debated for decades whether helping poor parents ends up helping their children as well. Researchers are providing some answers by examining the effects of specific policies (Duncan, 2012; Huston, 2012; Windsler & others, 2012).

For example, the Minnesota Family Investment Program (MFIP) was designed in the 1990s primarily to influence the behavior of adults—specifically, to move adults off the welfare rolls and into paid employment. A key element of the program was its guarantee that adults participating in the program would receive more income if they worked than if they did not. When the adults' income rose, how did that affect their children? A study of the effects of MFIP found that increases in the incomes of working poor parents were linked with

benefits for their children (Gennetian & Miller, 2002). The children's achievement in school improved, and their behavior problems decreased. A current MFIP study is examining the influence of specific services on low-income families at risk for child maltreatment and other negative outcomes for children (Minnesota Family Investment Program, 2009).

Developmental psychologists and other researchers have examined the effects of many other government policies. They are seeking ways to help families living in poverty improve their well-being, and they have offered many suggestions for improving government policies (Duncan, 2012; Hetzner & Brooks-Gunn, 2012; Waldfogel, 2012).

Earlier, we learned that children who live in poverty experience higher levels of physiological stress. How might a child's stress level be affected by the implementation of MFIP?

education, became a killer? After analyzing research on this topic, Ann Masten and her colleagues (Masten, 2006, 2009, 2011, 2013; Masten, Burt, & Coatsworth, 2006; Masten, Liebkind, & Hernandez, 2012; Masten & Narayan, 2012) concluded that a number of individual factors, such as good intellectual functioning, influence resiliency. In addition, as Figure 1.5 shows, the families and extrafamilial contexts of resilient individuals tend to share certain features. For example, resilient children are likely to have a close relationship to a caring parent figure and bonds to caring adults outside the family.

At the other end of the life span, the well-being of older adults also creates policy issues (Fisher & others, 2013; Johansson & Berg, 2012). Key concerns are escalating health care costs and the access of older adults to adequate health care (Dilworth-Anderson, Pierre, & Hilliard, 2012). One study found that the U.S. health care system fails older adults in many areas (Wenger & others, 2003). For example, older adults received the recommended care for general medical conditions such as heart disease only 52 percent of the time; they received appropriate care for undernutrition and Alzheimer disease only 31 percent of the time.

These concerns about the well-being of older adults are heightened by two facts. First, the number of older adults in the United States is growing dramatically, as Figure 1.6 shows. Second, many of these older Americans are likely to need society's help (Viachantoni, 2012). Compared with earlier decades, U.S. adults today are less likely to be married, more likely to be childless, and more likely to be living alone. As the older population continues to expand during the twenty-first century, an increasing number of older adults will be without either a spouse or children—traditionally the main sources of support for older adults (Ament & others, 2012). These individuals will need social relationships, networks, and other forms of support (Antonucci, Birditt, & Ajrouch, 2013).

Source	Characteristic
Individual	Good intellectual functioning Appealing, sociable, easygoing disposition Self-confidence, high self-esteem Talents Faith
Family	Close relationship to caring parent figure Authoritative parenting: warmth, structure, high expectations Socioeconomic advantages Connections to extended supportive family networks
Extrafamilial Context	Bonds to caring adults outside the family Connections to positive organizations Attending effective schools

FIGURE **1.5**
CHARACTERISTICS OF RESILIENT CHILDREN AND THEIR CONTEXTS

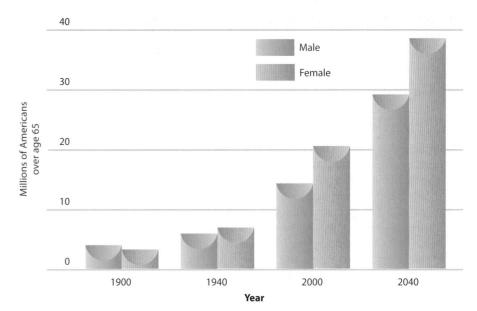

FIGURE 1.6

THE AGING OF AMERICA. The number of Americans over age 65 has grown dramatically since 1900 and is projected to increase further from the present to the year 2040. A significant increase will also occur in the number of individuals in the 85-and-over group. Centenarians—persons 100 years of age or older—are the fastest-growing age group in the United States, and their numbers are expected to swell in the coming decades.

Maggie Kuhn (1905–1995) was the founder of the Gray Panthers, an international advocacy group that began in 1970 with five older women committed to improving the social conditions of older adults.

Review *Connect* Reflect

LG1 Discuss the distinctive features of a life-span perspective on development.

Review

- What is meant by the concept of development? Why is the study of life-span development important?
- What are the main characteristics of the life-span perspective? What are three sources of contextual influences?
- What are some contemporary concerns in life-span development?

Connect

- Give your own example (not found in this chapter) of how biology, culture, and individual experience interact to affect development.

Reflect *Your Own Personal Journey of Life*

- Imagine what your development would have been like in a culture that offered fewer or distinctly different choices. How might your development have been different if your family had been significantly richer or poorer?

2 The Nature of Development

LG2 Identify the most important processes, periods, and issues in development.

| Biological, Cognitive, and Socioemotional Processes | Periods of Development | The Significance of Age | Developmental Issues |

In this section, we will explore what is meant by developmental processes and periods, as well as variations in the way age is conceptualized. We will examine key developmental issues and strategies we can use to evaluate them.

If you wanted to describe how and why Alice Walker or Ted Kaczynski developed during their lifetimes, how would you go about it? A chronicle of the events in any person's life can quickly become a confusing and tedious array of details. Two concepts help provide a framework for describing and understanding an individual's development: developmental processes and periods.

BIOLOGICAL, COGNITIVE, AND SOCIOEMOTIONAL PROCESSES

At the beginning of this chapter, we defined development as the pattern of change that begins at conception and continues through the life span. The pattern is complex because it is the product of biological, cognitive, and socioemotional processes (see Figure 1.7).

Biological Processes **Biological processes** produce changes in an individual's physical nature. Genes inherited from parents, the development of the brain, height and weight gains, changes in motor skills, nutrition, exercise, the hormonal changes of puberty, and cardiovascular decline are all examples of biological processes that affect development.

Cognitive Processes **Cognitive processes** refer to changes in the individual's thought, intelligence, and language. Watching a colorful mobile swinging above the crib, putting together a two-word sentence, memorizing a poem, imagining what it would be like to be a movie star, and solving a crossword puzzle all involve cognitive processes.

Socioemotional Processes **Socioemotional processes** involve changes in the individual's relationships with other people, changes in emotions, and changes in personality. An infant's smile in response to a parent's touch, a toddler's aggressive attack on a playmate, a school-age child's development of assertiveness, an adolescent's joy at the senior prom, and the affection of an elderly couple all reflect the role of socioemotional processes in development.

Connecting Biological, Cognitive, and Socioemotional Processes Biological, cognitive, and socioemotional processes are inextricably intertwined. Consider a baby smiling in response to a parent's touch. This response depends on biological processes (the physical nature of touch and responsiveness to it), cognitive processes (the ability to understand intentional acts), and socioemotional processes (the act of smiling that often reflects a positive emotional feeling and helps to connect us in positive ways with other human beings). Nowhere is the connection across biological, cognitive, and socioemotional processes more obvious than in two rapidly emerging fields:

- *developmental cognitive neuroscience*, which explores links between development, cognitive processes, and the brain (Diamond, 2013; Johnson & de Haan, 2012; Park & Bischof, 2011)
- *developmental social neuroscience*, which examines connections between socioemotional processes, development, and the brain (Bell & Calkins, 2012; Pfeifer & Blakemore, 2012; Samanez-Larkin & Carstensen, 2011)

In many instances, biological, cognitive, and socioemotional processes are bidirectional. For example, biological processes can influence cognitive processes and vice versa. Thus, although usually we will study the different processes of development (biological, cognitive, and socioemotional) in separate locations, keep in mind that we are talking about the development of an integrated individual with a mind and body that are interdependent. In many places throughout the book, we will call attention to these connections.

PERIODS OF DEVELOPMENT

The interplay of biological, cognitive, and socioemotional processes produces the periods of the human life span (see Figure 1.8). *A developmental period* refers to a time frame in a person's life that is characterized by certain features. For the purposes of organization and

FIGURE 1.7

PROCESSES INVOLVED IN DEVELOPMENTAL CHANGES. Biological, cognitive, and socioemotional processes interact as individuals develop.

developmental **connection**

Brain Development

Is there a link between changes in the adolescent's brain and their mood swings and increased risk taking? Chapter 11, p. 361

biological processes Changes in an individual's physical nature.

cognitive processes Changes in an individual's thought, intelligence, and language.

socioemotional processes Changes in an individual's relationships with other people, emotions, and personality.

Periods of Development

| Prenatal period (conception to birth) | Infancy (birth to 18–24 months) | Early childhood (3–5 years) | Middle and late childhood (6–10/11 years) | Adolescence (10–12 to 18–21 years) | Early adulthood (20s and 30s) | Middle adulthood (40s and 50s) | Late adulthood (60s–70s to death) |

Biological Processes

Cognitive Processes Socioemotional Processes

Processes of Development

FIGURE **1.8**

PROCESSES AND PERIODS OF DEVELOPMENT. The unfolding of life's periods of development is influenced by the interaction of biological, cognitive, and socioemotional processes.

understanding, we commonly describe development in terms of these periods. The most widely used classification of developmental periods involves the eight-period sequence shown in Figure 1.8. Approximate age ranges are listed for the periods to provide a general idea of when a period begins and ends.

The prenatal period is the time from conception to birth. It involves tremendous growth—from a single cell to an organism complete with brain and behavioral capabilities—and takes place in approximately a 9-month period.

Infancy is the developmental period from birth to 18 or 24 months. Infancy is a time of extreme dependence upon adults. During this period, many psychological activities—language, symbolic thought, sensorimotor coordination, and social learning, for example—are just beginning.

Early childhood is the developmental period from 3 through 5 years of age. This period is sometimes called the "preschool years." During this time, young children learn to become more self-sufficient and to care for themselves, develop school readiness skills (following instructions, identifying letters), and spend many hours playing with peers. First grade typically marks the end of early childhood.

Middle and late childhood is the developmental period from about 6 to 10 or 11 years of age, approximately corresponding to the elementary school years. During this period, children master the fundamental skills of reading, writing, and arithmetic, and they are formally exposed to the larger world and its culture. Achievement becomes a more central theme of the child's world, and self-control increases.

Adolescence is the developmental period of transition from childhood to early adulthood, entered at approximately 10 to 12 years of age and ending at 18 to 21 years of age. Adolescence begins with rapid physical changes—dramatic gains in height and weight, changes in body contour, and the development of sexual characteristics such as enlargement of the breasts, growth of pubic and facial hair, and deepening of the voice. At this point in development, the pursuit of independence and an identity are preeminent. Thought is more logical, abstract, and idealistic. More time is spent outside the family.

Early adulthood is the developmental period that begins in the early twenties and lasts through the thirties. It is a time of establishing personal and economic independence, advancing in a career, and for many, selecting a mate, learning to live with that person in an intimate way, starting a family, and rearing children.

Middle adulthood is the developmental period from approximately 40 to about 60 years of age. It is a time of expanding personal and social involvement and responsibility; of assisting the next generation in becoming competent, mature individuals; and of reaching and maintaining satisfaction in a career.

Late adulthood is the developmental period that begins in the sixties or seventies and lasts until death. It is a time of life review, retirement, and adjustment to new social roles and diminishing strength and health.

Late adulthood has the longest span of any period of development, and as noted earlier, the number of people in this age group has been increasing dramatically. As a result, life-span developmentalists have been paying more attention to differences within late adulthood (Corrada, Berlau, & Kawas, 2012; Zekry & others, 2012). Paul Baltes and Jacqui Smith (2003) argue that a major change takes place in older adults' lives as they become the "oldest-old," on average at about 85 years of age. For example, the "young-old" (classified as 65 through 84 in this analysis) have substantial potential for physical and cognitive fitness, retain much of their cognitive capacity, and can develop strategies to cope with the gains and losses of aging. In contrast, the oldest-old (85 and older) show considerable loss in cognitive skills, experience an increase in chronic stress, and are more frail.

Thus, Baltes and Smith concluded that considerable plasticity and adaptability characterize adults from their 60s until their mid-80s but that the oldest-old have reached the limits of their functional capacity, which makes interventions to improve their lives difficult. Nonetheless, as will be described in later chapters, considerable variation exists in how much the oldest-old retain their capabilities (Andersen & others, 2012; Conneely & others, 2012).

Four Ages   Life-span developmentalists who focus on adult development and aging increasingly describe life-span development in terms of four "ages" (Baltes, 2006; Willis & Schaie, 2006):

First age: Childhood and adolescence

Second age: Prime adulthood, ages 20 through 59

Third age: Approximately 60 to 79 years of age

Fourth age: Approximately 80 years and older

The major emphasis in this conceptualization is on the third and fourth ages, especially the increasing evidence that individuals in the third age are healthier and can lead more active, productive lives than their predecessors in earlier generations. However, when older adults reach their eighties (fourth age), especially 85 and over, health and well-being decline for many individuals.

Connections Across Periods of Development   A final important point needs to be made about the periods of the human life span. Just as there are many connections between biological, cognitive, and socioemotional processes, so are there many connections between the periods of the human life span. A key aspect in the study of life-span development is how development in one period is connected to development in another period. For example, when individuals reach adolescence, many developments and experiences have already taken place in their lives. If an adolescent girl becomes depressed, might her depression be linked to development early in her life, as well as recent and current development? Throughout the text we will call attention to such connections across periods of development through Developmental Connections inserts that guide you to earlier or later connections with the material you are currently reading.

THE SIGNIFICANCE OF AGE

In our description of developmental periods, we linked an approximate age range with each period. But we also have noted that there are variations in the capabilities of individuals of

"This is the path to adulthood. You're here."

© Robert Weber/The New Yorker Collection/
www.cartoonbank.com

One's children's children's children. Look back to us as we look to you; we are related by our imaginations. If we are able to touch, it is because we have imagined each other's existence, our dreams running back and forth along a cable from age to age.

—ROGER ROSENBLATT
American writer, 20th century

Which of these individuals is likely to be the happiest and to report the highest level of psychological well-being?

the same age, and we have seen how changes with age can be exaggerated. How important is age in understanding the characteristics of an individual?

Age and Happiness   Is there a best age to be? An increasing number of studies indicate that in the United States adults are happier as they age. For example, a recent study of more than 300,000 U.S. adults revealed that psychological well-being increased after the age of 50 years (Stone & others, 2010). In this study, specific aspects of negative affect showed different age trends. When individuals were asked about affect experienced yesterday, stress and anger declined sharply from the early twenties, worry was elevated during middle age and then declined, and sadness showed little change from 18 to 85 years of age.

Consider also a U.S. study of approximately 28,000 individuals from 18 to 88 that revealed happiness increased with age (Yang, 2008). About 33 percent were very happy at 88 years of age compared with only about 24 percent in their late teens and early twenties. Why might older people report being happier and more satisfied with their lives than younger people? Despite the increase in physical problems and losses older adults experience, they are more content with what they have in their lives, have better relationships with the people who matter to them, are less pressured to achieve, have more time for leisurely pursuits, and have many years of experience resulting in wisdom that may help them adapt better to their circumstances than younger adults do (Bassett, 2012; Carstensen & others, 2011; Choi & Landeros, 2011). Also in the study, baby boomers (those born between 1946 and 1964) reported being less happy than individuals born earlier—possibly because they are not lowering their aspirations and idealistic hopes as they age as did earlier generations. Because growing older is a certain outcome of living, it is good to know that we are likely to be happier as older adults than we were when we were younger.

Now that you have read about age variations in life satisfaction, think about how satisfied you are with your life. To help you answer this question, complete the items in Figure 1.9, which presents the most widely used measure in research on life satisfaction (Diener, 2012).

Conceptions of Age   According to some life-span experts, chronological age is not very relevant to understanding a person's psychological development (Botwinick, 1978). *Chronological age* is the number of years that have elapsed since birth. But time is a crude index of experience, and it does not cause anything. Chronological age, moreover, is not the only way of measuring age. Just as there are different domains of development, there are different ways of thinking about age.

Age has been conceptualized not just as chronological age but also as biological age, psychological age, and social age (Hoyer & Roodin, 2009). *Biological age* is a person's age in terms of biological health. Determining biological age involves knowing the functional capacities of a person's vital organs (Zekry & others, 2012). One person's vital capacities may be better or worse than those of others of comparable age (Feinglass & others, 2012). The younger the person's biological age, the longer the person is expected to live, regardless of chronological age.

Psychological age is an individual's adaptive capacities compared with those of other individuals of the same chronological age. Thus, older adults who continue to learn, are flexible, are motivated, have positive personality traits, control their emotions, and think clearly are engaging in more adaptive behaviors than their chronological age-mates who do not continue to learn, are rigid, are unmotivated, do not control their emotions, and do not think clearly (Depp, Vahia,

Below are five statements that you may agree or disagree with. Using the 1–7 scale below, indicate your agreement with each item by placing the appropriate number on the line preceding that item. Please be open and honest in your responding.

Response	Statement
_____	In most ways my life is close to my ideal.
_____	The conditions of my life are excellent.
_____	I am satisfied with my life.
_____	So far I have gotten the important things I want in life.
_____	If I could live my life over, I would change almost nothing.
_____	Total score

Scale
7 Strongly agree
6 Agree
5 Slightly agree
4 Neither agree nor disagree
3 Slightly disagree
2 Disagree
1 Strongly disagree

Scoring
31–35 Extremely satisfied
26–30 Satisfied
21–25 Slightly satisfied
   20 Neutral
15–19 Slightly dissatisfied
10–14 Dissatisfied
  5–9 Extremely dissatisfied

FIGURE **1.9**

HOW SATISFIED AM I WITH MY LIFE?

Source: E. Diener, R. A. Emmons, R. J. Larson, & S. Griffin (1985). The Satisfaction with Life Scale. *Journal of Personality Assessment, 48,* 71–75.

(*Left*) Dawn Russel, competing in the long jump in a Senior Olympics competition in Oregon; (*right*) a sedentary, overweight middle-aged man. *Even though Dawn Russel's chronological age is older, might her biological age be younger than the middle-aged man's?*

& Jeste, 2012; Schaie, 2012). A longitudinal study of more than 1,200 individuals across seven decades revealed that the personality trait of conscientiousness (being organized, careful, and disciplined, for example) predicted lower mortality (frequency of death) risk from childhood through late adulthood (Martin, Friedman, & Schwartz, 2007).

Social age refers to connectedness with others and the social roles individuals adopt. Individuals who have better social relationships with others are happier and more likely to live longer than individuals who are lonely (Carstensen & others, 2011).

Life-span expert Bernice Neugarten (1988) argues that in U.S. society chronological age is becoming irrelevant. The 28-year-old mayor, the 35-year-old grandmother, the 65-year-old father of a preschooler, the 55-year-old widow who starts a business, and the 70-year-old student illustrate that old assumptions about the proper timing of life events no longer govern our lives. We still have some expectations for when certain life events—such as getting married, having children, and retiring—should occur. However, chronological age has become a less accurate predictor of these life events in our society. Moreover, issues such as how to deal with intimacy and how to cope with success and failure appear and reappear throughout the life span.

From a life-span perspective, an overall age profile of an individual involves not just chronological age but also biological age, psychological age, and social age. For example, a 70-year-old man (chronological age) might be in good physical health (biological age), be experiencing memory problems and not be coping well with the demands placed on him by his wife's recent hospitalization (psychological age), and have a number of friends with whom he regularly plays golf (social age).

DEVELOPMENTAL ISSUES

Was Ted Kaczynski born a killer, or did his life turn him into one? Kaczynski himself thought that his childhood was the root of his troubles. He grew up as a genius in a boy's body and never fit in with other children. Did his early experiences determine his later life? Is your own journey through life marked out ahead of time, or can your experiences change your path? Are the experiences you have early in your journey more important than later ones? Is your journey more like taking an elevator up a skyscraper with distinct stops along the way or more like a cruise down a river with smoother ebbs and flows? These questions point to three issues about the nature of development: the roles played by nature and nurture, stability and change, and continuity and discontinuity.

Nature and Nurture The **nature-nurture issue** involves the extent to which development is influenced by nature and by nurture. Nature refers to an organism's biological inheritance, nurture to its environmental experiences.

> ## How old would you be if you didn't know how old you were?
>
> —**Satchel Paige**
> *American baseball pitcher, 20th century*

What are some key developmental issues?

nature-nurture issue Debate about whether development is primarily influenced by nature or nurture. Nature refers to an organism's biological inheritance, nurture to its environmental experiences.

developmental connection

Nature and Nurture

Can specific genes be linked to specific environmental experiences to influence development? Chapter 2, p. 71

developmental connection

Personality

How much does personality change as people go through the adult years? Chapter 16, p. 520

According to those who emphasize the role of nature, just as a sunflower grows in an orderly way—unless flattened by an unfriendly environment—so too the human grows in an orderly way. An evolutionary and genetic foundation produces commonalities in growth and development (Buss, 2012; Cosmides, 2012; Durrant & Ellis, 2013). We walk before we talk, speak one word before two words, grow rapidly in infancy and less so in early childhood, experience a rush of sex hormones in puberty, reach the peak of our physical strength in late adolescence and early adulthood, and then physically decline. Proponents of the importance of nature acknowledge that extreme environments—those that are psychologically barren or hostile—can depress development. However, they believe that basic growth tendencies are genetically programmed into humans (Mader, 2012).

By contrast, other psychologists emphasize the importance of nurture, or environmental experiences, in development (Blieszner & Roberto, 2012; Grusec & others, 2013; Maholmes & King, 2012). Experiences run the gamut from the individual's biological environment (nutrition, medical care, drugs, and physical accidents) to the social environment (family, peers, schools, community, media, and culture).

Stability and Change   Is the shy child who hides behind the sofa when visitors arrive destined to become a wallflower at college dances, or might the child become a sociable, talkative individual? Is the fun-loving, carefree adolescent bound to have difficulty holding down a 9-to-5 job as an adult? These questions reflect the **stability-change issue,** which involves the degree to which early traits and characteristics persist through life or change.

Many developmentalists who emphasize stability in development argue that stability is the result of heredity and possibly early experiences in life. For example, many argue that if an individual is shy throughout life (as Ted Kaczynski was), this stability is due to heredity and possibly early experiences in which the infant or young child encountered considerable stress when interacting with people.

Developmentalists who emphasize change take the more optimistic view that later experiences can produce change. Recall that in the life-span perspective, plasticity, the potential for change, exists throughout the life span. Experts such as Paul Baltes (2003) argue that older adults often show less capacity for learning new things than younger adults do. However, many older adults continue to be good at practicing what they have learned earlier in life.

The roles of early and later experience are an aspect of the stability-change issue that has long been hotly debated (Crosnoe, Wu, & Bonazzo, 2012; Schaie, 2012). Some argue that warm, nurturant caregiving during infancy and toddlerhood predicts optimal development later in life (Cassidy & others, 2011). The later-experience advocates see children as malleable throughout development and believe later sensitive caregiving is just as important as earlier sensitive caregiving (Antonucci & others, 2013; Blieszner & Roberto, 2012).

Continuity and Discontinuity   When developmental change occurs, is it gradual or abrupt? Think about your own development for a moment. Did you gradually become the person you are today? Or did you experience sudden, distinct changes in your growth? For the most part, developmentalists who emphasize nurture describe development as a gradual, continuous process. Those who emphasize nature often describe development as a series of distinct stages.

The **continuity-discontinuity issue** focuses on the degree to which development involves either gradual, cumulative change (continuity) or distinct stages (discontinuity). In terms of continuity, as the oak grows from seedling to giant oak, it becomes more of an oak—its development is continuous (see Figure 1.10). Similarly, a child's first word, though seemingly an abrupt, discontinuous event, is actually the result of weeks and months of growth and practice. Puberty might seem abrupt, but it is a gradual process that occurs over several years.

In terms of discontinuity, as an insect grows from a caterpillar to a chrysalis to a butterfly, it passes through a sequence of stages in which change is qualitatively rather than quantitatively different. Similarly, at some point a child moves from not being able to think abstractly about the world to being able to. This is a qualitative, discontinuous change in development rather than a quantitative, continuous change.

Continuity

Discontinuity

FIGURE **1.10**

CONTINUITY AND DISCONTINUITY IN DEVELOPMENT. Is our development like that of a seedling gradually growing into a giant oak? Or is it more like that of a caterpillar suddenly becoming a butterfly?

Evaluating the Developmental Issues   Most life-span developmentalists acknowledge that development is not all nature or all nurture, not all stability or all change, and not all continuity or all discontinuity. Nature and nurture, stability and change, continuity and discontinuity characterize development throughout the human life span.

Although most developmentalists do not take extreme positions on these three important issues, there is spirited debate regarding how strongly development is influenced by each of these factors (Buss, 2012; Easterbrooks & others, 2013; Rutter, 2013; Schaie, 2012).

stability-change issue Debate about whether we become older renditions of our early experience (stability) or whether we develop into someone different from who we were at an earlier point in development (change).

continuity-discontinuity issue Debate about the extent to which development involves gradual, cumulative change (continuity) or distinct stages (discontinuity).

Review Connect Reflect

LG2 Identify the most important processes, periods, and issues in development.

Review

- What are three key developmental processes?
- What are eight main developmental periods?
- How is age related to development?
- What are three main developmental issues?

Connect

- In the previous section, we discussed biological, cognitive, and socioemotional versus nurture also discussed in this section?

Reflect *Your Own Personal Journey of Life*

- Do you think there was/is/will be a best age for you to be? If so, what is it? Why?

---

3 Theories of Development   LG3 Describe the main theories of human development.

| Psychoanalytic Theories | Cognitive Theories | Behavioral and Social Cognitive Theories | Ethological Theory | Ecological Theory | An Eclectic Theoretical Orientation |

How can we answer questions about the roles of nature and nurture, stability and change, and continuity and discontinuity in development? How can we determine, for example, whether deterioration of memory in older adults can be prevented or whether special care can repair the harm inflicted by child neglect? The scientific method is the best tool we have to answer such questions.

The **scientific method** is essentially a four-step process: (1) conceptualize a process or problem to be studied, (2) collect research information (data), (3) analyze the data, and (4) draw conclusions.

In step 1, when researchers are formulating a problem to study, they often draw on theories and develop hypotheses. A **theory** is an interrelated, coherent set of ideas that helps to explain phenomena and facilitate predictions. It may suggest **hypotheses,** which are specific assertions and predictions that can be tested. For example, a theory on mentoring might state that sustained support and guidance from an adult makes a difference in the lives of children from impoverished backgrounds because the mentor gives the children opportunities to observe and imitate the behavior and strategies of the mentor.

This section outlines key aspects of five theoretical orientations to development: psychoanalytic, cognitive, behavioral and social cognitive, ethological, and ecological. Each contributes an important piece to the life-span development puzzle. Although the theories disagree about certain aspects of development, many of their ideas are complementary rather than contradictory. Together they let us see the total landscape of life-span development in all its richness.

PSYCHOANALYTIC THEORIES

Psychoanalytic theories describe development as primarily unconscious (beyond awareness) and heavily colored by emotion. Psychoanalytic theorists emphasize that behavior is merely a

> There is nothing quite so practical as a good theory.
>
> —KURT LEWIN
> *American social psychologist, 20th century*

scientific method An approach that can be used to obtain accurate information. It includes the following steps: (1) conceptualize the problem, (2) collect data, (3) draw conclusions, and (4) revise research conclusions and theory.

theory An interrelated, coherent set of ideas that helps to explain phenomena and facilitate predictions.

hypotheses Specific assumptions and predictions that can be tested to determine their accuracy.

psychoanalytic theories Theories that describe development as primarily unconscious and heavily colored by emotion. Behavior is merely a surface characteristic, and the symbolic workings of the mind have to be analyzed to understand behavior. Early experiences with parents are emphasized.

Oral Stage	Anal Stage	Phallic Stage	Latency Stage	Genital Stage
Infant's pleasure centers on the mouth.	Child's pleasure focuses on the anus.	Child's pleasure focuses on the genitals.	Child represses sexual interest and develops social and intellectual skills.	A time of sexual reawakening; source of sexual pleasure becomes someone outside the family.
Birth to 1½ Years	**1½ to 3 Years**	**3 to 6 Years**	**6 Years to Puberty**	**Puberty Onward**

FIGURE **1.11**

FREUDIAN STAGES. Because Freud emphasized sexual motivation, his stages of development are known as psychosexual stages. In his view, if the need for pleasure at any stage is either undergratified or overgratified, an individual may become fixated, or locked in, at that stage of development.

Sigmund Freud, the pioneering architect of psychoanalytic theory. *How did Freud portray the organization of an individual's personality?*

Erik Erikson with his wife, Joan, an artist. Erikson generated one of the most important developmental theories of the twentieth century. *Which stage of Erikson's theory are you in? Does Erikson's description of this stage characterize you?*

Erikson's theory Includes eight stages of human development. Each stage consists of a unique developmental task that confronts individuals with a crisis that must be resolved.

surface characteristic and that a true understanding of development requires analyzing the symbolic meanings of behavior and the deep inner workings of the mind. Psychoanalytic theorists also stress that early experiences with parents extensively shape development. These characteristics are highlighted in the main psychoanalytic theory, that of Sigmund Freud (1856–1939).

Freud's Theory As Freud listened to, probed, and analyzed his patients, he became convinced that their problems were the result of experiences early in life. He thought that as children grow up, their focus of pleasure and sexual impulses shifts from the mouth to the anus and eventually to the genitals. As a result, we go through five stages of psychosexual development: oral, anal, phallic, latency, and genital (see Figure 1.11). Our adult personality, Freud (1917) claimed, is determined by the way we resolve conflicts between sources of pleasure at each stage and the demands of reality.

Freud's theory has been significantly revised by a number of psychoanalytic theorists. Many of today's psychoanalytic theorists maintain that Freud overemphasized sexual instincts; they place more emphasis on cultural experiences as determinants of an individual's development. Unconscious thought remains a central theme, but conscious thought plays a greater role than Freud envisioned. One of the most influential revisionists of Freud's ideas was Erik Erikson.

Erikson's Psychosocial Theory Erik Erikson (1902–1994) recognized Freud's contributions but believed that Freud misjudged some important dimensions of human development. For one thing, Erikson (1950, 1968) said we develop in psychosocial stages, rather than in psychosexual stages as Freud maintained. According to Freud, the primary motivation for human behavior is sexual in nature; according to Erikson, it is social and reflects a desire to affiliate with other people. According to Freud, our basic personality is shaped during the first five years of life; according to Erikson, developmental change occurs throughout the life span. Thus, in terms of the early-versus-later-experience issue described earlier in the chapter, Freud viewed early experience as being far more important than later experiences, whereas Erikson emphasized the importance of both early and later experiences.

In **Erikson's theory,** eight stages of development unfold as we go through life (see Figure 1.12). At each stage, a unique developmental task confronts individuals with a crisis that must be resolved. According to Erikson, this crisis is not a catastrophe but a turning point marked by both increased vulnerability and enhanced potential. The more successfully an individual resolves each crisis, the healthier development will be.

Trust versus mistrust is Erikson's first psychosocial stage, which is experienced in the first year of life. The development of trust during infancy sets the stage for a lifelong expectation that the world will be a good and pleasant place to live.

Autonomy versus shame and doubt is Erikson's second stage. This stage occurs in late infancy and toddlerhood (1 to 3 years). After gaining trust in their caregivers, infants begin to discover that their behavior is their own. They start to assert their sense of independence or autonomy. They realize their will. If infants and toddlers are restrained too much or punished too harshly, they are likely to develop a sense of shame and doubt.

Initiative versus guilt, Erikson's third stage of development, occurs during the preschool years. As preschool children encounter a widening social world, they face new challenges that require active, purposeful, responsible behavior. Feelings of guilt may arise, though, if the child is irresponsible and is made to feel too anxious.

Industry versus inferiority is Erikson's fourth developmental stage, occurring approximately during the elementary school years. Children now need to direct their energy toward mastering knowledge and intellectual skills. The negative outcome is that the child may develop a sense of inferiority—feeling incompetent and unproductive.

During the adolescent years, individuals need to find out who they are, what they are all about, and where they are going in life. This is Erikson's fifth developmental stage, *identity versus identity confusion*. If adolescents explore roles in a healthy manner and arrive at a positive path to follow in life, then they achieve a positive identity; if they do not, identity confusion reigns.

Intimacy versus isolation is Erikson's sixth developmental stage, which individuals experience during early adulthood. At this time, individuals face the developmental task of forming intimate relationships. If young adults form healthy friendships and an intimate relationship with another, intimacy will be achieved; if not, isolation will result.

Generativity versus stagnation, Erikson's seventh developmental stage, occurs during middle adulthood. By generativity Erikson means primarily a concern for helping the younger generation to develop and lead useful lives. The feeling of having done nothing to help the next generation is stagnation.

Integrity versus despair is Erikson's eighth and final stage of development, which individuals experience in late adulthood. During this stage, a person reflects on the past. If the person's life review reveals a life well spent, integrity will be achieved; if not, the retrospective glances likely will yield doubt or gloom—the despair Erikson described.

Evaluating Psychoanalytic Theories   Contributions of psychoanalytic theories include an emphasis on a developmental framework, family relationships, and unconscious aspects of the mind. Criticisms include a lack of scientific support, too much emphasis on sexual underpinnings, and an image of people that is too negative.

COGNITIVE THEORIES

Whereas psychoanalytic theories stress the importance of the unconscious, cognitive theories emphasize conscious thoughts. Three important cognitive theories are Jean Piaget's cognitive developmental theory, Lev Vygotsky's sociocultural cognitive theory, and the information-processing theory.

Piaget's Cognitive Developmental Theory   Piaget's **theory** states that children go through four stages of cognitive development as they actively construct their understanding of the world. Two processes underlie this cognitive construction of the world: organization and adaptation. To make sense of our world, we organize our experiences. For example, we separate important ideas from less important ideas, and we connect one idea to another. In addition to organizing our observations and experiences, we adapt, adjusting to new environmental demands (Miller, 2011).

Piaget (1954) also held that we go through four stages in understanding the world (see Figure 1.13). Each stage is age-related and consists of a distinct way of thinking, a different way of understanding the world. Thus, according to Piaget (1896–1980), the child's cognition is qualitatively different from one stage to another. What are Piaget's four stages of cognitive development?

- The *sensorimotor stage*, which lasts from birth to about 2 years of age, is the first Piagetian stage. In this stage, infants construct an understanding of the

Jean Piaget, the famous Swiss developmental psychologist, changed the way we think about the development of children's minds. *What are some key ideas in Piaget's theory?*

Erikson's Stages	Developmental Period
Integrity versus despair	Late adulthood (60s onward)
Generativity versus stagnation	Middle adulthood (40s, 50s)
Intimacy versus isolation	Early adulthood (20s, 30s)
Identity versus identity confusion	Adolescence (10 to 20 years)
Industry versus inferiority	Middle and late childhood (elementary school years, 6 years to puberty)
Initiative versus guilt	Early childhood (preschool years, 3 to 5 years)
Autonomy versus shame and doubt	Infancy (1 to 3 years)
Trust versus mistrust	Infancy (first year)

FIGURE **1.12**

ERIKSON'S EIGHT LIFE-SPAN STAGES. Like Freud, Erikson proposed that individuals go through distinct, universal stages of development. Thus, in terms of the continuity-discontinuity issue discussed in this chapter, both favor the discontinuity side of the debate. Notice that the timing of Erikson's first four stages is similar to that of Freud's stages. *What are the implications of saying that people go through stages of development?*

Piaget's theory Theory stating that children actively construct their understanding of the world and go through four stages of cognitive development.

Sensorimotor Stage

The infant constructs an understanding of the world by coordinating sensory experiences with physical actions. An infant progresses from reflexive, instinctual action at birth to the beginning of symbolic thought toward the end of the stage.

Birth to 2 Years of Age

Preoperational Stage

The child begins to represent the world with words and images. These words and images reflect increased symbolic thinking and go beyond the connection of sensory information and physical action.

2 to 7 Years of Age

Concrete Operational Stage

The child can now reason logically about concrete events and classify objects into different sets.

7 to 11 Years of Age

Formal Operational Stage

The adolescent reasons in more abstract, idealistic, and logical ways.

11 Years of Age Through Adulthood

FIGURE **1.13**

PIAGET'S FOUR STAGES OF COGNITIVE DEVELOPMENT. According to Piaget, how a child thinks—not how much the child knows—determines the child's stage of cognitive development.

Lev Vygotsky was born the same year as Piaget, but he died much earlier, at the age of 37. There is considerable interest today in Vygotsky's sociocultural cognitive theory of child development. *What are some key characteristics of Vygotsky's theory?*

world by coordinating sensory experiences (such as seeing and hearing) with physical, motoric actions—hence the term *sensorimotor*.

- The *preoperational stage*, which lasts from approximately 2 to 7 years of age, is Piaget's second stage. In this stage, children begin to go beyond simply connecting sensory information with physical action and represent the world with words, images, and drawings. However, according to Piaget, preschool children still lack the ability to perform what he calls operations, which are internalized mental actions that allow children to do mentally what they previously could only do physically. For example, if you imagine putting two sticks together to see whether they would be as long as another stick, without actually moving the sticks, you are performing a concrete operation.

- The *concrete operational stage*, which lasts from approximately 7 to 11 years of age, is the third Piagetian stage. In this stage, children can perform operations that involve objects, and they can reason logically when the reasoning can be applied to specific or concrete examples. For instance, concrete operational thinkers cannot imagine the steps necessary to complete an algebraic equation, which is too abstract for thinking at this stage of development.

- The *formal operational stage*, which appears between the ages of 11 and 15 and continues through adulthood, is Piaget's fourth and final stage. In this stage, individuals move beyond concrete experiences and begin to think in abstract and more logical terms. As part of thinking more abstractly, adolescents develop images of ideal circumstances. They might think about what an ideal parent would be like and compare their parents to this ideal standard. They begin to entertain possibilities for the future and are fascinated with what they can be. In solving problems, they become more systematic, developing hypotheses about why something is happening the way it is and then testing these hypotheses. We will examine Piaget's cognitive developmental theory further in Chapters 5, 7, 9, and 11.

Vygotsky's Sociocultural Cognitive Theory Like Piaget, the Russian developmentalist Lev Vygotsky (1896–1934) argued that children actively construct their knowledge. However, Vygotsky (1962) gave social interaction and culture far more important roles in cognitive development than Piaget did. **Vygotsky's theory** is a sociocultural cognitive theory that emphasizes how culture and social interaction guide cognitive development.

Vygotsky portrayed the child's development as inseparable from social and cultural activities (Alexsandrova-Howell, Abramson, & Craig, 2012; Gauvain, 2011, 2013). He maintained that cognitive development involves learning to use the inventions of society, such as language, mathematical systems, and memory strategies. Thus in one culture, children might learn to count with the help of a computer; in another, they might learn by using beads. According to Vygotsky, children's social interaction with more-skilled adults and peers is indispensable to their cognitive development (Daniels, 2011). Through this interaction, they learn to use the tools that will help them adapt and be successful in their culture. (Mahn & John-Steiner, 2013). In Chapter 7, we examine ideas about learning and teaching that are based on Vygotsky's theory.

Early computers may be the best candidates for the title of "founding fathers" of information-processing theory. Although many factors stimulated the growth of this theory, none was more important than the computer. Psychologists began to wonder if the logical operations carried out by computers might tell us something about how the human mind works. They drew analogies between a computer's hardware and the brain and between computer software and cognition.

The Information-Processing Theory

Information-processing theory emphasizes that individuals manipulate information, monitor it, and strategize about it. Unlike Piaget's theory, but like Vygotsky's theory, information-processing theory does not describe development as stage-like. Instead, according to this theory, individuals develop a gradually increasing capacity for processing information, which allows them to acquire increasingly complex knowledge and skills (Siegler, 2012a, b; Sternberg, 2013a, b).

Robert Siegler (2006, 2007, 2012, 2013), a leading expert on children's information processing, states that thinking is information processing. In other words, when individuals perceive, encode, represent, store, and retrieve information, they are thinking. Siegler emphasizes that an important aspect of development is learning good strategies for processing information. For example, becoming a better reader might involve learning to monitor the key themes of the material being read.

Evaluating Cognitive Theories

Contributions of cognitive theories include a positive view of development and an emphasis on the active construction of understanding. Criticisms include skepticism about the pureness of Piaget's stages and too little attention to individual variations.

BEHAVIORAL AND SOCIAL COGNITIVE THEORIES

Behaviorism essentially holds that we can study scientifically only what can be directly observed and measured. Out of the behavioral tradition grew the belief that development is observable behavior that can be learned through experience with the environment (Miltenberger, 2012). In terms of the continuity-discontinuity issue discussed earlier in this chapter, the behavioral and social cognitive theories emphasize continuity in development and argue that development does not occur in stage-like fashion. Let's explore two versions of behaviorism: Skinner's operant conditioning and Bandura's social cognitive theory.

B. F. Skinner was a tinkerer who liked to make new gadgets. The younger of his two daughters, Deborah, was raised in Skinner's enclosed Air-Crib, which he invented because he wanted to control her environment completely. The Air-Crib was sound-proofed and temperature controlled. Debbie, shown here as a child with her parents, is currently a successful artist, is married, and lives in London. *What do you think about Skinner's Air-Crib?*

Skinner's Operant Conditioning

According to B. F. Skinner (1904–1990), through operant conditioning the consequences of a behavior produce changes in the probability of the behavior's occurrence. A behavior followed by a rewarding stimulus is more likely to recur, whereas a behavior followed by a punishing stimulus is less likely to recur. For example, when an adult smiles at a child after the child has done something, the child is more likely to engage in that behavior again than if the adult gives the child a disapproving look.

In Skinner's (1938) view, such rewards and punishments shape development. For Skinner the key aspect of development is behavior, not thoughts and feelings. He emphasized that development consists of the pattern of behavioral changes that are brought about by rewards and punishments. For example, Skinner would say that shy people learned to be shy as a result of experiences they had while growing up. It follows that modifications in an environment can help a shy person become more socially oriented.

Vygotsky's theory A sociocultural cognitive theory that emphasizes how culture and social interaction guide cognitive development.

information-processing theory Emphasizes that individuals manipulate information, monitor it, and strategize about it. Central to this theory are the processes of memory and thinking.

Albert Bandura has been one of the leading architects of social cognitive theory. *How does Bandura's theory differ from Skinner's?*

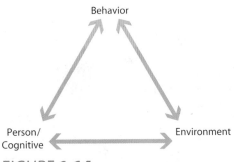

FIGURE **1.14**

BANDURA'S SOCIAL COGNITIVE MODEL.
The arrows illustrate how relations between behavior, person/cognitive, and environment are reciprocal rather than one way. Person/cognitive refers to cognitive processes (for example, thinking and planning) and personal characteristics (for example, believing that you can control your experiences).

developmental **connection**

Achievement

Bandura emphasizes that self-efficacy is a key person/cognitive factor in children's achievement. Chapter 10, p. 320

developmental **connection**

Attachment

Human babies go through a series of phases in developing an attachment to a caregiver. Chapter 6, p. 189

Bandura's Social Cognitive Theory   Some psychologists agree with the behaviorists' notion that development is learned and is influenced strongly by environmental interactions. However, unlike Skinner, they also see cognition as important in understanding development (Mischel, 2004; Mischel & others, 2011). **Social cognitive theory** holds that behavior, environment, and cognition are the key factors in development.

American psychologist Albert Bandura (1925–) is the leading architect of social cognitive theory. Bandura (1986, 2004, 2010a, b, 2012) emphasizes that cognitive processes have important links with the environment and behavior. His early research program focused heavily on observational learning (also called imitation or modeling), which is learning that occurs through observing what others do. For example, a young boy might observe his father yelling in anger and treating other people with hostility; with his peers, the young boy later acts very aggressively, showing the same characteristics as his father's behavior. Social cognitive theorists stress that people acquire a wide range of behaviors, thoughts, and feelings through observing others' behavior and that these observations form an important part of life-span development.

What is cognitive about observational learning in Bandura's view? He proposes that people cognitively represent the behavior of others and then sometimes adopt this behavior themselves.

Bandura's (2004, 2010a, b, 2012) most recent model of learning and development includes three elements: behavior, the person/cognition, and the environment. An individual's confidence that he or she can control his or her success is an example of a person factor; strategies are an example of a cognitive factor. As shown in Figure 1.14, behavior, person/cognitive, and environmental factors operate interactively.

Evaluating Behavioral and Social Cognitive Theories   Contributions of the behavioral and social cognitive theories include an emphasis on scientific research and environmental determinants of behavior. Criticisms include too little emphasis on cognition in Skinner's view and inadequate attention paid to developmental changes.

ETHOLOGICAL THEORY

Ethology stresses that behavior is strongly influenced by biology, is tied to evolution, and is characterized by critical or sensitive periods. These are specific time frames during which, according to ethologists, the presence or absence of certain experiences has a long-lasting influence on individuals.

European zoologist Konrad Lorenz (1903–1989) helped bring ethology to prominence. In his best-known research, Lorenz (1965) studied the behavior of greylag geese, which will follow their mothers as soon as they hatch. Lorenz separated the eggs laid by one goose into two groups. One group he returned to the goose to be hatched by her. The other group was hatched in an incubator. The goslings in the first group performed as predicted. They followed their mother as soon as they hatched. However, those in the second group, which saw Lorenz when they first hatched, followed him everywhere, as though he were their mother. Lorenz marked the goslings and then placed both groups under a box. Mother goose and "mother" Lorenz stood aside as the box lifted. Each group of goslings went directly to its "mother." Lorenz called this process imprinting—the rapid, innate learning that involves attachment to the first moving object seen.

John Bowlby (1969, 1989) illustrated an important application of ethological theory to human development. Bowlby stressed that attachment to a caregiver over the first year of life has important consequences throughout the life span. In his view, if this attachment is positive and secure, the individual will likely develop positively in childhood and adulthood. If the attachment is negative and insecure, life-span development will likely not be optimal. In Chapter 6, we will explore the concept of infant attachment in much greater detail.

In Lorenz's view, imprinting needs to take place at a certain, very early time in the life of the animal, or else it will not take place. This point in time is called a critical period. A related concept is that of a sensitive period, and an example of this is the time during infancy when, according to Bowlby, attachment should occur in order to promote optimal development of social relationships.

Konrad Lorenz, a pioneering student of animal behavior, is followed through the water by three imprinted greylag geese. Describe Lorenz's experiment with the geese. *Do you think his experiment would have had the same results with human babies? Explain.*

Another theory that emphasizes biological foundations of development—evolutionary psychology—will be presented in Chapter 2, along with views on the role of heredity in development. In addition, we will examine a number of biological theories of aging in Chapter 17.

Contributions of ethological theory include a focus on the biological and evolutionary basis of development, and the use of careful observations in naturalistic settings. Criticisms include too much emphasis on biological foundations and a belief that the critical and sensitive period concepts might be too rigid.

ECOLOGICAL THEORY

While ethological theory stresses biological factors, ecological theory emphasizes environmental factors. One ecological theory that has important implications for understanding life-span development was created by Urie Bronfenbrenner (1917–2005). **Bronfenbrenner's ecological theory** (Bronfenbrenner, 1986, 2004; Bronfenbrenner & Morris, 1998, 2006) holds that development reflects the influence of several environmental systems. The theory identifies five environmental systems: microsystem, mesosystem, exosystem, macrosystem, and chronosystem (see Figure 1.15).

The *microsystem* is the setting in which the individual lives. These contexts include the person's family, peers, school, and neighborhood. It is in the microsystem that the most direct interactions with social agents take place—with parents, peers, and teachers, for example. The individual is not a passive recipient of experiences in these settings, but someone who helps to construct the settings.

The *mesosystem* involves relations between microsystems or connections between contexts. Examples are the relation of family experiences to school experiences, school experiences to religious experiences, and family experiences to peer experiences. For example, children whose parents have rejected them may have difficulty developing positive relations with teachers.

The *exosystem* consists of links between a social setting in which the individual does not have an active role and the individual's immediate context. For example, a husband's or child's experience at home may be influenced by a mother's experiences at work. The mother might receive a promotion that requires more travel, which might increase conflict with the husband and change patterns of interaction with the child.

The *macrosystem* involves the culture in which individuals live. Remember from earlier in the chapter that culture refers to the behavior patterns, beliefs, and all other products of a group of people that are passed on from generation to generation. Remember also that cross-cultural studies—the comparison of one culture with one or more other cultures—provide information about the generality of development.

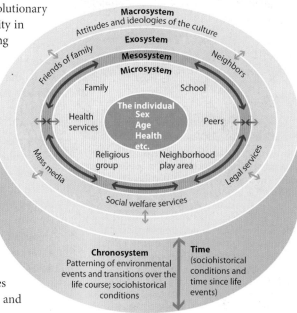

FIGURE **1.15**

BRONFENBRENNER'S ECOLOGICAL THEORY OF DEVELOPMENT. Bronfenbrenner's ecological theory consists of five environmental systems: microsystem, mesosystem, exosystem, macrosystem, and chronosystem.

social cognitive theory The view of psychologists who emphasize behavior, environment, and cognition as the key factors in development.

ethology Stresses that behavior is strongly influenced by biology, is tied to evolution, and is characterized by critical or sensitive periods.

Bronfenbrenner's ecological theory Bronfenbrenner's environmental systems theory that focuses on five environmental systems: microsystem, mesosystem, exosystem, macrosystem, and chronosystem.

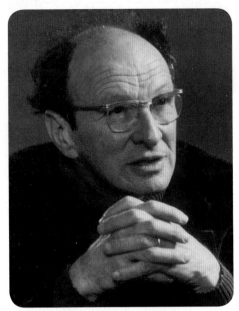

developmental **connection**

Parenting

How are parent-child relationships and children's peer relations linked? Chapter 8, p. 268

Urie Bronfenbrenner developed ecological theory, a perspective that is receiving increased attention today. His theory emphasizes the importance of both micro and macro dimensions of the environment in which the child lives.

eclectic theoretical orientation An orientation that does not follow any one theoretical approach but rather selects from each theory whatever is considered the best in it.

The *chronosystem* consists of the patterning of environmental events and transitions over the life course, as well as sociohistorical circumstances. For example, divorce is one transition. Researchers have found that the negative effects of divorce on children often peak in the first year after the divorce (Hetherington, 1993, 2006). By two years after the divorce, family interaction has become more stable. As an example of sociohistorical circumstances, consider how career opportunities for women have increased since the 1960s.

Bronfenbrenner (2004; Bronfenbrenner & Morris, 2006) subsequently added biological influences to his theory, describing it as a bioecological theory. Nonetheless, it is still dominated by ecological, environmental contexts.

Contributions of the theory include a systematic examination of macro and micro dimensions of environmental systems, and attention to connections between environmental systems. A further contribution of Bronfenbrenner's theory is an emphasis on a range of social contexts beyond the family, such as neighborhood, religion, school, and workplace, as influential in children's development (Gauvain & Parke, 2010). Criticisms include giving inadequate attention to biological factors, as well as too little emphasis on cognitive factors.

AN ECLECTIC THEORETICAL ORIENTATION

No single theory described in this chapter can explain entirely the rich complexity of life-span development, but each has contributed to our understanding of development. Psychoanalytic theory best explains the unconscious mind. Erikson's theory best describes the changes that occur during adult development. Piaget's, Vygotsky's, and the information-processing views provide the most complete description of cognitive development. The behavioral and social cognitive and ecological theories have been the most adept at examining the environmental determinants of development. The ethological theories have highlighted biology's role and the importance of sensitive periods in development.

In short, although theories are helpful guides, relying on a single theory to explain development is probably a mistake. This book instead takes an **eclectic theoretical orientation,** which does not follow any one theoretical approach but rather selects from each theory whatever is considered its best features. In this way, you can view the study of development as it actually exists—with different theorists making different assumptions, stressing different empirical problems, and using different strategies to discover information. Figure 1.16 compares the main theoretical perspectives in terms of how they view important issues in life-span development.

THEORY	ISSUES	
	Continuity/discontinuity, early versus later experiences	**Biological and environmental factors**
Psychoanalytic	Discontinuity between stages—continuity between early experiences and later development; early experiences very important; later changes in development emphasized in Erikson's theory	Freud's biological determination interacting with early family experiences; Erikson's more balanced biological-cultural interaction perspective
Cognitive	Discontinuity between stages in Piaget's theory; continuity between early experiences and later development in Piaget's and Vygotsky's theories; no stages in Vygotsky's theory or information-processing theory	Piaget's emphasis on interaction and adaptation; environment provides the setting for cognitive structures to develop; information-processing view has not addressed this issue extensively but mainly emphasizes biological-environmental interaction
Behavioral and social cognitive	Continuity (no stages); experience at all points of development important	Environment viewed as the cause of behavior in both views
Ethological	Discontinuity but no stages; critical or sensitive periods emphasized; early experiences very important	Strong biological view
Ecological	Little attention to continuity/discontinuity; change emphasized more than stability	Strong environmental view

FIGURE **1.16**

A COMPARISON OF THEORIES AND ISSUES IN LIFE-SPAN DEVELOPMENT

Review *Connect* Reflect

LG3 Describe the main theories of human development.

Review

- What are the four steps of the scientific method? How can theory and hypotheses be defined? What are two main psychoanalytic theories? What are some contributions and criticisms of the psychoanalytic theories?
- What are three main cognitive theories? What are some contributions and criticisms of the cognitive theories?
- What are two main behavioral and social cognitive theories? What are some contributions and criticisms of the behavioral and social cognitive theories?
- What is the nature of ethological theory? What are some contributions and criticisms of the theory?
- What characterizes ecological theory? What are some contributions and criticisms of the theory?
- What is an eclectic theoretical orientation?

Connect

- The beginning of this section started with a question about whether special care might be able to repair the harm inflicted by child neglect. How might this question be answered differently using the various theories outlined?

Reflect *Your Own Personal Journey of Life*

- Which of the life-span theories do you think best explains your own development? Why?

4 Research in Life-Span Development

LG4 Explain how research on life-span development is conducted.

Methods for Collecting Data · Research Designs · Time Span of Research · Conducting Ethical Research · Minimizing Bias

If they follow an eclectic orientation, how do scholars and researchers determine that one feature of a theory is somehow better than another? Through scientific research, the features of theories can be tested and refined (Cooper, 2012; Smith & Davis, 2013).

Generally, research in life-span development is designed to test hypotheses, which in some cases are derived from the theories just described. Through research, theories are modified to reflect new data, and occasionally new theories arise. How are data about life-span development collected? What types of research designs are used to study life-span development? And what are some ethical considerations in conducting research on life-span development?

> Science refines everyday thinking.
>
> —**Albert Einstein**
> *German-born American Physicist, 20th Century*

METHODS FOR COLLECTING DATA

Whether we are interested in studying attachment in infants, the cognitive skills of children, or social relationships in older adults, we can choose from several ways of collecting data (Graziano & Raulin, 2013). Here we outline the measures most often used, beginning with observation.

Observation Scientific observation requires an important set of skills (Bakeman & Quera, 2012; Gravetter & Forzano, 2012). For observations to be effective, they have to be systematic. We have to have some idea of what we are looking for. We have to know whom we are observing, when and where we will observe, how the observations will be made, and how they will be recorded.

Where should we make our observations? We have two choices: the laboratory and the everyday world.

When we observe scientifically, we often need to control certain factors that determine behavior but are not the focus of our inquiry (Beins, 2013). For this reason, some research in

What are some important strategies in conducting observational research with children?

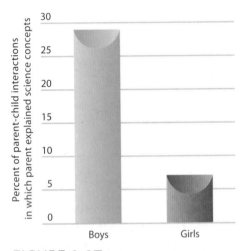

FIGURE **1.17**

PARENTS' EXPLANATIONS OF SCIENCE TO SONS AND DAUGHTERS AT A SCIENCE MUSEUM. In a naturalistic observation study at a children's science museum, parents were three times more likely to explain science to boys than to girls (Crowley & others, 2001). The gender difference occurred regardless of whether the father, the mother, or both parents were with the child, although the gender difference was greatest for fathers' science explanations to sons and daughters.

laboratory A controlled setting in which many of the complex factors of the "real world" are removed.

naturalistic observation Studies that involve observing behavior in real-world settings.

life-span development is conducted in a **laboratory,** a controlled setting where many of the complex factors of the "real world" are absent. For example, suppose you want to observe how children react when they see other people act aggressively. If you observe children in their homes or schools, you have no control over how much aggression the children observe, what kind of aggression they see, which people they see acting aggressively, or how other people treat the children. In contrast, if you observe the children in a laboratory, you can control these and other factors and therefore have more confidence about how to interpret your observations.

Laboratory research does have some drawbacks, however, including the following:

1. It is almost impossible to conduct research without the participants knowing they are being studied.

2. The laboratory setting is unnatural and therefore can cause the participants to behave unnaturally.

3. People who are willing to come to a university laboratory may not accurately represent groups from diverse cultural backgrounds.

4. People who are unfamiliar with university settings and with the idea of "helping science" may be intimidated by the laboratory setting.

Naturalistic observation provides insights that sometimes cannot be attained in the laboratory (Leedy & Ormrod, 2013). **Naturalistic observation** means observing behavior in real-world settings, making no effort to manipulate or control the situation. Life-span researchers conduct naturalistic observations at sporting events, child-care centers, work settings, malls, and other places people live in and frequent.

Naturalistic observation was used in one study that focused on conversations in a children's science museum (Crowley & others, 2001). When visiting exhibits at the science museum, parents were far more likely to engage boys than girls in explanatory talk. This finding suggests a gender bias that encourages boys more than girls to be interested in science (see Figure 1.17).

Survey and Interview Sometimes the best and quickest way to get information about people is to ask them for it. One technique is to interview them directly. A related method is the survey (sometimes referred to as a questionnaire), which is especially useful when information from many people is needed. A standard set of questions is used to obtain peoples' self-reported attitudes or beliefs about a particular topic. In a good survey, the questions are clear and unbiased, allowing respondents to answer unambiguously.

Surveys and interviews can be used to study topics ranging from religious beliefs to sexual habits to attitudes about gun control to beliefs about how to improve schools. Surveys and interviews may be conducted in person, over the telephone, and over the Internet.

One problem with surveys and interviews is the tendency of participants to answer questions in a way that they think is socially acceptable or desirable rather than to say what they truly think or feel (Madill, 2012). For example, on a survey or in an interview some individuals might say that they do not take drugs even though they do.

Standardized Test   A **standardized test** has uniform procedures for administration and scoring. Many standardized tests allow a person's performance to be compared with that of other individuals; thus they provide information about individual differences among people (Watson, 2012). One example is the Stanford-Binet intelligence test, which is described in Chapter 9. Your score on the Stanford-Binet test tells you how your performance compares with that of thousands of other people who have taken the test (Geisinger, 2012).

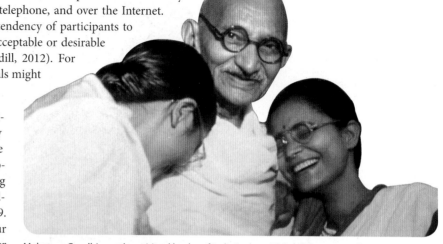

Mahatma Gandhi was the spiritual leader of India in the middle of the twentieth century. Erik Erikson conducted an extensive case study of Gandhi's life to determine what contributed to his identity development. *What are some limitations of the case study approach?*

One criticism of standardized tests is that they assume a person's behavior is consistent and stable, yet personality and intelligence—two primary targets of standardized testing—can vary with the situation. For example, a person may perform poorly on a standardized intelligence test in an office setting but score much higher at home, where he or she is less anxious.

Case Study   A **case study** is an in-depth look at a single individual. Case studies are performed mainly by mental health professionals when, for either practical or ethical reasons, the unique aspects of an individual's life cannot be duplicated and tested in other individuals. A case study provides information about one person's experiences; it may focus on nearly any aspect of the subject's life that helps the researcher understand the person's mind, behavior, or other attributes (Yin, 2012). A researcher may gather information for a case study from interviews and medical records. In later chapters, we discuss vivid case studies, such as that of Michael Rehbein, who had much of the left side of his brain removed at 7 years of age to end severe epileptic seizures.

A case study can provide a dramatic, in-depth portrayal of an individual's life, but we must be cautious when generalizing from this information. The subject of a case study is unique, with a genetic makeup and personal history that no one else shares. In addition, case studies involve judgments of unknown reliability. Researchers who conduct case studies rarely check to see if other professionals agree with their observations or findings.

Physiological Measures   Researchers are increasingly using physiological measures when they study development at different points in the life span. For example, as puberty unfolds, the blood levels of certain hormones increase. To determine the nature of these hormonal changes, researchers analyze blood samples from adolescent volunteers (Susman & Dorn, 2013).

Figure 1.18 compares the brain images of two adolescents—one a non-drinker and the other a heavy drinker—while they are engaged in a memory task. We have much more to say about neuroimaging and other physiological measures at various points in this book.

Another physiological measure that is increasingly used is neuroimaging, especially functional magnetic resonance imaging (fMRI), in which electromagnetic waves are used to construct images of a person's brain tissue and biochemical activity. The study of the brain through advances such as fMRI represents one of the main changes in improving our knowledge about human development in recent years (Bauer & Dunn, 2013; Morrison & Baxter, 2012). In many chapters of this book, you will read about recent research on changes in the brain during prenatal development, infancy, childhood, adolescence, and aging.

Yet another dramatic change in physiological methods is the advancement in methods to assess the actual units of hereditary information—genes—in studies of biological influences on development (van den Hoodakker & others, 2012). For example, in Chapter 17 you will read about the role of the ApoE4 gene in Alzheimer disease (Dafnis & others, 2012).

developmental **connection**

Cognitive Neuroscience and Aging

The cognitive neuroscience of aging involves the study of links between the brain's development in older adults and changes in their cognitive skills. Chapter 18, p. 578

developmental **connection**

Gene × Environment (G × E) Interaction

Increasingly, researchers are exploring how the interaction of a specific gene and a specific aspect of the environment affects development. Chapter 2, p. 71

standardized test A test with uniform procedures for administration and scoring. Many standardized tests allow a person's performance to be compared with the performance of other individuals.

case study An in-depth look at a single individual.

FIGURE **1.18**

BRAIN IMAGING OF 15-YEAR-OLD ADOLESCENTS. These two brain images indicate how alcohol can influence the functioning of an adolescent's brain. Notice the pink and red coloring (which indicates effective brain functioning involving memory) in the brain of the 15-year-old non-drinker (*left*) while engaging in a memory task, and compare it with the lack of those colors in the brain of the 15-year-old heavy drinker (*right*) under the influence of alcohol.

RESEARCH DESIGNS

When you are conducting research on life-span development, in addition to a method for collecting data, you also need a research design. There are three main types of research designs: descriptive, correlational, and experimental.

Descriptive Research   All of the data-collection methods that we have discussed can be used in **descriptive research,** which aims to observe and record behavior. For example, a researcher might observe the extent to which people are altruistic or aggressive toward each other. By itself, descriptive research cannot prove what causes some phenomena, but it can reveal important information about people's behavior (Pistrang & Barker, 2012).

Correlational Research   In contrast with descriptive research, correlational research goes beyond describing phenomena to provide information that will help us to predict how people will behave. In **correlational research,** the goal is to describe the strength of the relationship between two or more events or characteristics. The more strongly the two events are correlated (or related or associated), the more effectively we can predict one event from the other (Aron, Aron, & Coups, 2013; Heiman, 2012).

For example, to find out whether children of permissive parents have less self-control than other children, you would need to carefully record observations of parents' permissiveness and their children's self-control. You might observe that the higher a parent was in permissiveness, the lower the child was in self-control. You would then analyze these data statistically to yield a numerical measure, called a **correlation coefficient,** a number based on a statistical analysis that is used to describe the degree of association between two variables. The correlation coefficient ranges from +1.00 to –1.00. A negative number means an inverse relation. In this example, you might find an inverse correlation between permissive parenting and children's self-control with a coefficient of, say, –.30. By contrast, you might find a positive correlation of +.30 between parental monitoring of children and children's self-control.

The higher the correlation coefficient (whether positive or negative), the stronger the association between the two variables. A correlation of 0 means that there is no association between the variables. A correlation of –.40 is stronger than a correlation of +.20 because we disregard whether the correlation is positive or negative in determining the strength of the correlation.

A caution is in order, however. Correlation does not equal causation (Caldwell, 2013). The correlational finding just mentioned does not mean that permissive parenting necessarily causes low self-control in children. It could mean that, but it also could mean that a child's lack of self-control caused the parents to throw up their arms in despair and give up trying to control the child. It also could mean that other factors, such as heredity or poverty, caused

descriptive research Studies designed to observe and record behavior.

correlational research Studies in which the goal is to describe the strength of the relationship between two or more events or characteristics.

correlation coefficient A number based on statistical analysis that is used to describe the degree of association between two variables.

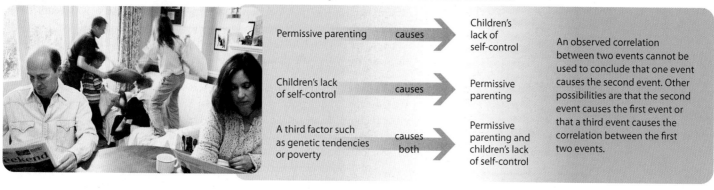

Observed Correlation: As permissive parenting increases, children's self-control decreases.

Possible explanations for this observed correlation

Permissive parenting **causes** → Children's lack of self-control

Children's lack of self-control **causes** → Permissive parenting

A third factor such as genetic tendencies or poverty **causes both** → Permissive parenting and children's lack of self-control

An observed correlation between two events cannot be used to conclude that one event causes the second event. Other possibilities are that the second event causes the first event or that a third event causes the correlation between the first two events.

FIGURE **1.19**
POSSIBLE EXPLANATIONS OF CORRELATIONAL DATA

the correlation between permissive parenting and low self-control in children. Figure 1.19 illustrates these possible interpretations of correlational data.

Experimental Research

To study causality, researchers turn to experimental research. An **experiment** is a carefully regulated procedure in which one or more factors believed to influence the behavior being studied are manipulated while all other factors are held constant. If the behavior under study changes when a factor is manipulated, we say that the manipulated factor has caused the behavior to change. In other words, the experiment has demonstrated cause and effect. The cause is the factor that was manipulated. The effect is the behavior that changed because of the manipulation. Nonexperimental research methods (descriptive and correlational research) cannot establish cause and effect because they do not involve manipulating factors in a controlled way.

Independent and Dependent Variables

Experiments include two types of changeable factors, or variables: independent and dependent. An independent variable is a manipulated, influential, experimental factor. It is a potential cause. The label "independent" is used because this variable can be manipulated independently of other factors to determine its effect. An experiment may include one independent variable or several of them.

A dependent variable is a factor that can change in an experiment, in response to changes in the independent variable. As researchers manipulate the independent variable, they measure the dependent variable for any resulting effect.

For example, suppose that you conducted a study to determine whether women could change the breathing and sleeping patterns of their newborn babies by meditating during pregnancy. You might require one group of pregnant women to engage in a certain amount and type of meditation each day while another group would not meditate; the meditation is thus the independent variable. When the infants are born, you would observe and measure their breathing and sleeping patterns. These patterns are the dependent variable, the factor that changes as the result of your manipulation.

Experimental and Control Groups

Experiments can involve one or more experimental groups and one or more control groups (Kirk, 2013). An experimental group is a group whose experience is manipulated. A control group is a comparison group that is as similar to the experimental group as possible and that is treated in every way like the experimental group except for the manipulated factor (independent variable). The control group serves as a baseline against which the effects of the manipulated condition can be compared.

Random assignment is an important principle for deciding whether each participant will be placed in the experimental group or in the control group. Random assignment means that researchers assign participants to experimental and control groups by chance. It reduces the likelihood that the experiment's results will be due to any preexisting differences between groups (Christensen, 2012). In the example of the effects of meditation by pregnant women on the breathing and sleeping patterns of their newborns, you would randomly assign half of the pregnant women to engage in meditation over a period of weeks (the experimental group) and the other half to not meditate over the same number of weeks (the control group). Figure 1.20 illustrates the nature of experimental research.

experiment A carefully regulated procedure in which one or more of the factors believed to influence the behavior being studied are manipulated while all other factors are held constant.

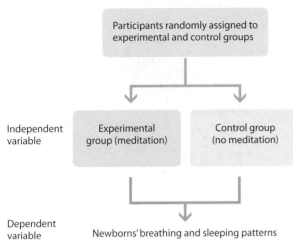

FIGURE **1.20**

PRINCIPLES OF EXPERIMENTAL RESEARCH. Imagine that you decide to conduct an experimental study of the effects of meditation by pregnant women on their newborns' breathing and sleeping patterns. You would randomly assign pregnant women to experimental and control groups. The experimental-group women would engage in meditation over a specified number of sessions and weeks. The control group would not. Then, when the infants are born, you would assess their breathing and sleeping patterns. If the breathing and sleeping patterns of newborns whose mothers were in the experimental group are more positive than those of the control group, you would conclude that meditation caused the positive effects.

developmental **connection**

Intelligence

Cohort effects help to explain differences in the intelligence of people born at different points in time. Chapter 15, p. 496

cross-sectional approach A research strategy in which individuals of different ages are compared at one time.

longitudinal approach A research strategy in which the same individuals are studied over a period of time, usually several years or more.

cohort effects Effects due to a person's time of birth, era, or generation rather than the person's actual age.

TIME SPAN OF RESEARCH

Researchers in life-span development have a special concern with studies that focus on the relation of age to some other variable. We have several options: Researchers can study different individuals of varying ages and compare them or they can study the same individuals as they age over time.

Cross-Sectional Approach   The **cross-sectional approach** is a research strategy that simultaneously compares individuals of different ages. A typical cross-sectional study might include three groups of children: 5-year-olds, 8-year-olds, and 11-year-olds. Another study might include groups of 15-year-olds, 25-year-olds, and 45-year-olds. The groups can be compared with respect to a variety of dependent variables: IQ, memory, peer relations, attachment to parents, hormonal changes, and so on. All of this can be accomplished in a short time. In some studies, data are collected in a single day. Even in large-scale cross-sectional studies with hundreds of subjects, data collection does not usually take longer than several months to complete.

The main advantage of the cross-sectional study is that the researcher does not have to wait for the individuals to grow up or become older. Despite its efficiency, though, the cross-sectional approach has its drawbacks. It gives no information about how individuals change or about the stability of their characteristics. It can obscure the increases and decreases of development—the hills and valleys of growth and development. For example, a cross-sectional study of life satisfaction might reveal average increases and decreases, but it would not show how the life satisfaction of individual adults waxed and waned over the years. It also would not tell us whether the same adults who had positive or negative perceptions of life satisfaction in early adulthood maintained their relative degree of life satisfaction as they became middle-aged or older adults.

Longitudinal Approach   The **longitudinal approach** is a research strategy in which the same individuals are studied over a period of time, usually several years or more. For example, in a longitudinal study of life satisfaction, the same adults might be assessed periodically over a 70-year time span—at the ages of 20, 35, 45, 65, and 90, for example.

Longitudinal studies provide a wealth of information about vital issues such as stability and change in development and the importance of early experience for later development, but they do have drawbacks (Sliwinski, 2011; Windle, 2012). They are expensive and time consuming. The longer the study lasts, the more participants drop out—they move, get sick, lose interest, and so forth. The participants who remain may be dissimilar to those who drop out, biasing the outcome of the study. Those individuals who remain in a longitudinal study over a number of years may be more responsible and conformity-oriented, for example, or they might lead more stable lives.

Cohort Effects   A *cohort* is a group of people who are born at a similar point in history and share similar experiences as a result, such as living through the Vietnam War or growing up in the same city around the same time. These shared experiences may produce a range of differences among cohorts (Schaie, 2012). For example, people who were teenagers during the Great Depression are likely to differ from people who were teenagers during the booming 1990s in their educational opportunities and economic status, in how they were raised, and in their attitudes toward sex and religion. In life-span development research, **cohort effects** are due to a person's time of birth, era, or generation but not to actual age.

Cohort effects are important because they can powerfully affect the dependent measures in a study ostensibly concerned with age. Researchers have shown that it is especially important to be aware of cohort effects when assessing adult intelligence (Schaie, 2009, 2012). Individuals born at different points in time—such as 1920, 1940, and 1960—have had varying opportunities for education. Individuals born in earlier years had less access to education, and this fact may have a significant effect on how this cohort performs on intelligence tests.

Cross-sectional studies can show how different cohorts respond, but they can confuse age changes and cohort effects. Longitudinal studies are effective in studying age changes but only within one cohort.

Cohort effects are due to a person's time of birth or generation but not actually to age. Think for a moment about growing up in (a) the Great Depression and (b) today. *How might your development differ depending on which of these time frames has dominated your life? your parents' lives? your grandparents' lives?*

Various generations have been given labels by the popular culture. Figure 1.21 describes the labels of various generations, their historical period, and the reasons for their labels. Consider the following description of the current generation of youth and think about how they differ from earlier youth generations:

> They are history's first "always connected" generation. Steeped in digital technology and social media, they treat their multi-tasking hand-held gadgets almost like a body part—for better or worse. More than 8-in-10 say they sleep with a cell phone glowing by the bed, poised to disgorge texts, phone calls, e-mails, songs, news, videos, games, and wake-up jingles. But sometimes convenience yields to temptation. Nearly two-thirds admit to texting while driving (Pew Research Center, 2010, p. 1).

So far we have discussed many aspects of research in life-span development, but where can you read about this research firsthand? Read *Connecting Through Research* to find out.

How are today's millennials experiencing youth differently from earlier generations?

Generation	Historical Period	Reasons for Label
Millennials	Individuals born in 1980 and later	First generation to come of age and enter emerging adulthood (18 to 25 years of age) in the twenty-first century (the new millennium). Two main characteristics: (1) connection to technology, and (2) ethnic diversity.
Generation 3	Individuals born between 1965 and 1980	Described as lacking an identity and savvy loners.
Baby Boomers	Individuals born between 1946 and 1964	Label used because this generation represents the spike in the number of babies born after World War II; the largest generation ever to enter late adulthood in the United States.
Silent Generation	Individuals born between 1928 and 1945	Children of the Great Depression and World War II; described as conformists and civic minded.

FIGURE **1.21**
GENERATIONS, THEIR HISTORICAL PERIODS, AND CHARACTERISTICS

connecting through research

Where Is Life-Span Research Published?

Regardless of whether you pursue a career in life-span development, psychology, or some related scientific field, you can benefit by learning about the journal process. As a student, you might be required to look up original research in journals. As a parent, teacher, or nurse you might want to consult journals to obtain information that will help you understand and work more effectively with people. And, as an inquiring person, you might look up information in journals after you have heard or read something that piqued your curiosity.

A journal publishes scholarly and academic information, usually in a specific domain—like physics, math, sociology, or our current interest, life-span development. Scholars in these fields publish most of their research in journals, which are the source of core information in virtually every academic discipline.

An increasing number of journals publish information about life-span development. Among the leading journals in life-span development are *Developmental Psychology, Child Development, Pediatrics, Pediatric Nursing, The Journals of Gerontology, Infant Behavior and Development, Journal of Research on Adolescence, Journal of Adult Development, Journal of Gerontological Nursing, Psychology and Aging, Human Development,* and many others. Also, a number of journals that do not focus solely on development publish articles on various aspects of human development. These journals include *Journal of Educational Psychology, Sex Roles, Journal of Cross-Cultural Research, Journal of Marriage and the Family,* and *Journal of Consulting and Clinical Psychology.*

Every journal has a board of experts who evaluate articles submitted for publication. Each submitted paper is accepted or rejected on the basis of such factors as its contribution to the field, methodological excellence, and clarity of writing. Some of the most prestigious journals reject as many as 80 to 90 percent of the articles submitted.

Journal articles are usually written by professionals for other professionals in the specialized field of the journal's focus; therefore, they often contain technical language and terms specific to the discipline that are difficult for nonprofessionals to understand. Their organization often takes this course: abstract, introduction, method, results, discussion, and references.

The *abstract* is a brief summary that appears at the beginning of the article. The abstract lets readers quickly determine whether the article is relevant to their interests. The *introduction* introduces the problem or

Research journals are the core of information in virtually every academic discipline. Those shown here are among the increasing number of research journals that publish information about life-span development. *What are the main parts of a research article that presents findings from original research?*

issue that is being studied. It includes a concise review of research relevant to the topic, theoretical ties, and one or more hypotheses to be tested. The *method* section consists of a clear description of the subjects evaluated in the study, the measures used, and the procedures that were followed. The method section should be sufficiently clear and detailed so that by reading it another researcher could repeat or replicate the study. The *results* section reports the analysis of the data collected. In most cases, the results section includes statistical analyses that are difficult for nonprofessionals to understand. The *discussion* section describes the author's conclusions, inferences, and interpretation of what was found. Statements are usually made about whether the hypotheses presented in the introduction were supported, limitations of the study, and suggestions for future research. The last part of the journal article, called *references,* includes bibliographic information for each source cited in the article. The references section is often a good source for finding other articles relevant to the topic that interests you.

Where do you find journals such as those described above? Your college or university library likely has some of them, and some public libraries also carry journals. Online resources such as PsycINFO and PubMed, which can facilitate the search for journal articles, are available to students on many campuses.

The research published in the journals mentioned above shapes our lives. It not only informs the research of other life-span development researchers, but it also informs the practices of law and policy makers, physicians, educators, parents, and many others. In fact, much of what you will find that is new in this edition of this textbook comes directly from the research that can be found in the journals mentioned above.

Research journals are the core of information in virtually every academic discipline. Those shown here are among the increasing number of research journals that publish information about life-span development.

What are the main parts of a research article that presents findings from original research?

CONDUCTING ETHICAL RESEARCH

Ethics in research may affect you personally if you ever serve as a participant in a study. In that event, you need to know your rights as a participant and the responsibilities of researchers to assure that these rights are safeguarded.

If you ever become a researcher in life-span development yourself, you will need an even deeper understanding of ethics. Even if you only carry out experimental projects in psychology courses, you must consider the rights of the participants in those projects (Rosnow & Rosenthal, 2013). A student might think, "I volunteer in a home for the mentally retarded several hours per week. I can use the residents of the home in my study to see if a particular treatment helps improve their memory for everyday tasks." But without proper permissions, the most well-meaning, kind, and considerate studies still violate the rights of the participants.

Today, proposed research at colleges and universities must pass the scrutiny of a research ethics committee before the research can be initiated. In addition, the American Psychological Association (APA) has developed ethics guidelines for its members. The code of ethics instructs psychologists to protect their participants from mental and physical harm. The participants' best interests need to be kept foremost in the researcher's mind (Fried, 2012). APA's guidelines address four important issues:

1. *Informed consent.* All participants must know what their research participation will involve and what risks might develop. Even after informed consent is given, participants must retain the right to withdraw from the study at any time and for any reason.

2. *Confidentiality.* Researchers are responsible for keeping all of the data they gather on individuals completely confidential and, when possible, completely anonymous.

3. *Debriefing.* After the study has been completed, participants should be informed of its purpose and the methods that were used. In most cases, the experimenter also can inform participants in a general manner beforehand about the purpose of the research without leading participants to behave in a way they think that the experimenter is expecting.

4. *Deception.* In some circumstances, telling the participants beforehand what the research study is about substantially alters the participants' behavior and invalidates the researcher's data. In all cases of deception, however, the psychologist must ensure that the deception will not harm the participants and that the participants will be debriefed (told the complete nature of the study) as soon as possible after the study is completed.

MINIMIZING BIAS

Studies of life-span development are most useful when they are conducted without bias or prejudice toward any particular group of people. Of special concern is bias based on gender and bias based on culture or ethnicity.

Gender Bias   For most of its existence, our society has had a strong gender bias, a preconceived notion about the abilities of women and men that prevented individuals from pursuing their own interests and achieving their potential (Hyde & Quest, 2013; Matlin, 2012). Gender bias also has had a less obvious effect within the field of life-span development. For example, it is not unusual for conclusions to be drawn about females' attitudes and behaviors from research conducted with males as the only participants.

Furthermore, when researchers find gender differences, their reports sometimes magnify those differences (Denmark & others, 1988). For example, a researcher might report that 74 percent of the men in a study had high achievement expectations versus only 67 percent of the women and go on to talk about the differences in some detail. In reality, this might be a rather small difference. It also might disappear if the study were repeated, or the study might have methodological problems that don't allow such strong interpretations.

Pam Reid is a leading researcher who studies gender and ethnic bias in development. You can read about Pam's interests in *Connecting with Careers.*

Pam Reid, Educational and Developmental Psychologist

When she was a child, Pam Reid liked to play with chemistry sets. Reid majored in chemistry during college and wanted to become a doctor. However, when some of her friends signed up for a psychology class as an elective, she decided to take the course. She was intrigued by learning about how people think, behave, and develop—so much so that she changed her major to psychology. Reid went on to obtain her Ph.D. in psychology (American Psychological Association, 2003, p. 16).

For a number of years, Reid was a professor of education and psychology at the University of Michigan, where she also was a research scientist at the Institute for Research on Women and Gender. Her main focus has been on how children and adolescents develop social skills, with a special interest in the development of African American girls (Reid & Zalk, 2001). She has been involved in numerous community activities, including the creation of a math and technology

Pam Reid (*Center*), with students at Saint Joseph College in Hartford, Connecticut, where she is the president of the college.

enrichment program for middle school girls. In 2004, Reid became provost and executive vice-president at Roosevelt University in Chicago, and in 2008 became president of Saint Joseph College in Hartford, Connecticut.

For more information about what educational psychologists do, see page 45 in the Careers in Life-Span Development appendix.

Cultural and Ethnic Bias   There is a growing realization that research on life-span development needs to include more people from diverse ethnic groups (Nagata, Kohn-Wood, & Suzuki, 2012). Historically, people from ethnic minority groups (African American, Latino, Asian American, and Native American) were excluded from most research in the United States and simply thought of as variations from the norm or average. If minority individuals were included in samples and their scores didn't fit the norm, they were viewed as confounds or "noise" in data and discounted. Given the fact that individuals from diverse ethnic groups were excluded from research on life-span development for so long, we might reasonably conclude that people's real lives are perhaps more varied than research data have indicated in the past.

Researchers also have tended to overgeneralize about ethnic groups (Wright & others, 2012). **Ethnic gloss** is using an ethnic label such as African American or Latino in a superficial way that portrays an ethnic group as being more homogeneous than it really is (Trimble, 1988). For example, a researcher might describe a research sample like this: "The participants were 60 Latinos." A more complete description of the Latino group might be something like this: "The 60 Latino participants were Mexican Americans from low-income neighborhoods in the southwestern area of Los Angeles. Thirty-six were from homes in which Spanish is the dominant language spoken, 24 from homes in which English is the main language spoken. Thirty were born in the United States, 30 in Mexico. Twenty-eight described themselves as Mexican American, 14 as Mexican, 9 as American, 6 as Chicano, and 3 as Latino." Ethnic gloss can cause researchers to obtain samples of ethnic groups that are not representative of the group's diversity, which can lead to overgeneralization and stereotyping.

Ross Parke and Raymond Buriel (2006) described how research on ethnic minority children and their families has not been given adequate attention, especially in light of their significant rate of growth. Until recently, ethnic minority families were combined in the category "minority," which masks important differences among ethnic groups as well as diversity

ethnic gloss Using an ethnic label such as African American or Latino in a superficial way that portrays an ethnic group as being more homogeneous than it really is.

Look at these two photographs, one of all non-Latino White males, the other of a diverse group of females and males from different ethnic groups, including some non-Latino White males. Consider a topic in life-span development, such as parenting, love, or cultural values. *If you were conducting research on this topic, might the results of the study differ depending on whether the participants in your study were the individuals in the photograph on the left or on the right?*

within an ethnic group. When research has been conducted on ethnic groups, most often they are compared to non–Latino Whites to identify group differences. An assumption in two-group studies is that ethnic minority children have not advanced far enough to be the same as non–Latino White children and that this developmental lag contributes to ethnic minority children's problems. Recently, some researchers have replaced two-group studies with more in-depth examination of variations within a single ethnic group. For example, a researcher might study how parents in an ethnic group adapt to the challenges they face as a minority in U.S. society and how these experiences contribute to the goals they have for their children.

The continued growth of minority families in the United States in approaching decades will mainly be due to the immigration of Latino and Asian families. Researchers need "to take into account their acculturation level and generational status of parents and children," and consider how these factors might influence family processes and child outcomes (Parke & Buriel, 2006, p. 487). More attention also needs to be given to biculturalism because the complexity of diversity means that some children of color identify with two or more ethnic groups (Phinney & Baldelomar, 2011). And language development research needs to focus more on second-language acquisition (usually English) and bilingualism and how they are linked to school achievement (Bialystok, 2011).

Review Connect Reflect

LG4 Explain how research on life-span development is conducted.

Review

- What methods do researchers use to collect data on life-span development?
- What research designs are used to study human development?
- How is research conducted on the time span of people's lives?
- What are researchers' ethical responsibilities to the people they study?
- How can gender, cultural, and ethnic bias affect the outcome of a research study?

Connect

- Earlier in the chapter, you read about normative age-graded influences, normative history-graded influences, and nonnormative life events. Describe how these influences relate to what you just read about cohort effects.

Reflect *Your Own Personal Journey of Life*

- You and your parents grew up at different points in time. Consider some ways that you are different from your parents. Do you think some of your differences might be due to cohort effects? Explain.

topical connections -------- looking forward ----➤

In Chapter 2, you will continue to learn about theory and research as you explore the biological underpinnings of life-span development. The influence of human evolution on development will be covered, including a discussion of natural selection and adaptive behavior. You will examine how the human genome works, the collaborative nature of genes, and how DNA plays a role in the person each of us becomes. You also will explore the challenges and choices people encounter when deciding to reproduce, including infertility treatments and adoption. And you will read in greater depth about the many sides of the age-old nature-nurture debate, focusing on the way heredity and environment interact.

reach your learning goals

Introduction

1 The Life-Span Perspective

The Importance of Studying Life-Span Development

Characteristics of the Life-Span Perspective

Some Contemporary Concerns

 LG1 Discuss the distinctive features of a life-span perspective on development.

- Development is the pattern of change that begins at conception and continues through the human life span. It includes both growth and decline. Studying life-span development helps prepare us to take responsibility for children, gives us insight about our own lives, and gives us knowledge about what our lives will be like as we age.

- The life-span perspective includes these basic conceptions: Development is lifelong, multidimensional, multidirectional, and plastic; its study is multidisciplinary; it is contextual; it involves growth, maintenance, and regulation of loss; and it is a co-construction of biological, cultural, and individual factors. Three important sources of contextual influences are (1) normative age-graded influences, (2) normative history-graded influences, and (3) nonnormative life events.

- Health and well-being, parenting, education, sociocultural contexts and diversity, and social policy are all areas of contemporary concern that are closely tied to life-span development. Important dimensions of the sociocultural context include culture, ethnicity, socioeconomic status, and gender. There is increasing interest in social policy issues related to children and to older adults.

2 The Nature of Development

Biological, Cognitive and Socioemotional Processes

Periods of Development

LG2 Identify the most important processes, periods, and issues in development.

- Three key developmental processes are biological, cognitive, and socioemotional. Throughout development, there are extensive connections between these processes.

- The life span is commonly divided into the following development periods: prenatal, infancy, early childhood, middle and late childhood, adolescence, early adulthood, middle adulthood, and late adulthood. Recently, life-span developmentalists have described the human life span in terms of four ages with a special focus on the third and fourth ages, as well as a distinction between the young-old and oldest-old. An important aspect of life-span development involves connections across periods of development.

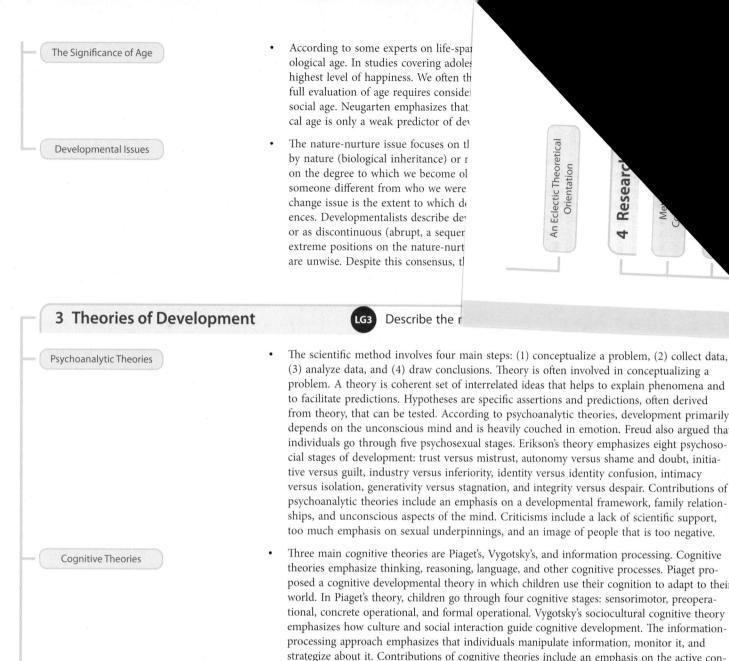

The Significance of Age

- According to some experts on life-span... ological age. In studies covering adoles... highest level of happiness. We often th... full evaluation of age requires conside... social age. Neugarten emphasizes that... cal age is only a weak predictor of dev...

Developmental Issues

- The nature-nurture issue focuses on tl... by nature (biological inheritance) or r... on the degree to which we become ol... someone different from who we were... change issue is the extent to which d... ences. Developmentalists describe dev... or as discontinuous (abrupt, a sequer... extreme positions on the nature-nurt... are unwise. Despite this consensus, tl...

An Eclectic Theoretical Orientation

4 Resear...

3 Theories of Development

LG3 Describe the r...

Psychoanalytic Theories

- The scientific method involves four main steps: (1) conceptualize a problem, (2) collect data, (3) analyze data, and (4) draw conclusions. Theory is often involved in conceptualizing a problem. A theory is coherent set of interrelated ideas that helps to explain phenomena and to facilitate predictions. Hypotheses are specific assertions and predictions, often derived from theory, that can be tested. According to psychoanalytic theories, development primarily depends on the unconscious mind and is heavily couched in emotion. Freud also argued that individuals go through five psychosexual stages. Erikson's theory emphasizes eight psychosocial stages of development: trust versus mistrust, autonomy versus shame and doubt, initiative versus guilt, industry versus inferiority, identity versus identity confusion, intimacy versus isolation, generativity versus stagnation, and integrity versus despair. Contributions of psychoanalytic theories include an emphasis on a developmental framework, family relationships, and unconscious aspects of the mind. Criticisms include a lack of scientific support, too much emphasis on sexual underpinnings, and an image of people that is too negative.

Cognitive Theories

- Three main cognitive theories are Piaget's, Vygotsky's, and information processing. Cognitive theories emphasize thinking, reasoning, language, and other cognitive processes. Piaget proposed a cognitive developmental theory in which children use their cognition to adapt to their world. In Piaget's theory, children go through four cognitive stages: sensorimotor, preoperational, concrete operational, and formal operational. Vygotsky's sociocultural cognitive theory emphasizes how culture and social interaction guide cognitive development. The information-processing approach emphasizes that individuals manipulate information, monitor it, and strategize about it. Contributions of cognitive theories include an emphasis on the active construction of understanding and a positive view of development. Criticisms include giving too little attention to individual variations and skepticism about the pureness of Piaget's stages.

Behavioral and Social Cognitive Theories

- Two main behavioral and social cognitive theories are Skinner's operant conditioning and Bandura's social cognitive theory. In Skinner's operant conditioning, the consequences of a behavior produce changes in the probability of the behavior's occurrence. In Bandura's social cognitive theory, observational learning is a key aspect of life-span development. Bandura emphasizes reciprocal interactions among person/cognition, behavior, and environment. Contributions of the behavioral and social cognitive theories include an emphasis on scientific research and a focus on environmental factors. Criticisms include inadequate attention to developmental changes and, in Skinner's view, too little attention to cognition.

Ethological Theory

- Ethology stresses that behavior is strongly influenced by biology, is tied to evolution, and is characterized by critical or sensitive periods. Contributions of ethological theory include a focus on the biological and evolutionary basis of development. Criticisms include a belief that the concepts of critical and sensitive periods may be too rigid.

Ecological Theory

- Ecological theory emphasizes environmental contexts. Bronfenbrenner's environmental systems view of development proposes five environmental systems: microsystem, mesosystem, exosystem, macrosystem, and chronosystem. Contributions of the theory include a systematic examination of macro and micro dimensions of environmental systems and attention to connections between them. Criticisms include giving inadequate attention to biological factors, as well as a lack of emphasis on cognitive factors.

- An eclectic theoretical orientation does not follow any one theoretical approach but rather selects from each theory whatever is considered the best in it.

in Life-Span Development **LG4** Explain how research in life-span development is conducted.

**thods for
llecting Data**

Research Designs

Time Span of Research

**Conducting Ethical
Research**

Minimizing Bias

- Methods for collecting data about life-span development include observation (in a laboratory or a naturalistic setting), survey (questionnaire) or interview, standardized test, case study, and physiological measures.

- Three main research designs are descriptive, correlational, and experimental. Descriptive research aims to observe and record behavior. In correlational research, the goal is to describe the strength of the relationship between two or more events or characteristics. Experimental research involves conducting an experiment, which can determine cause and effect. An independent variable is the manipulated, influential, experimental factor. A dependent variable is a factor that can change in an experiment, in response to changes in the independent variable. Experiments can involve one or more experimental groups and control groups. In random assignment, researchers assign participants to experimental and control groups by chance.

- When researchers decide about the time span of their research, they can conduct cross-sectional or longitudinal studies. Life-span researchers are especially concerned about cohort effects.

- Researchers' ethical responsibilities include seeking participants' informed consent, ensuring their confidentiality, debriefing them about the purpose and potential personal consequences of participating, and avoiding unnecessary deception of participants.

- Researchers need to guard against gender, cultural, and ethnic bias in research. Every effort should be made to make research equitable for both females and males. Individuals from varied ethnic backgrounds need to be included as participants in life-span research, and overgeneralization about diverse members within a group must be avoided.

key terms

key people

Chapter 1 | INTRODUCTION

Connecting with

Learning Objectives	Application Activities	Activity Type	Page Reference
Discuss developmental issues: nature/nurture, stability/change, continuity/discontinuity.	Continuity and Change	Video	pp. 19–21
Describe the psychoanalytic theories.	Erickson's Eight Lifespan Stages	Click & drag activity	pp. 21–23
Describe the cognitive theories.	Piaget's Stages of Development	Click & drag activity	pp. 23–26
	Piaget's Stages of Development	Interactive exercise	
Describe the ecological theory.	Bronfenbrenner's Ecological Theory	Click & drag activity	pp. 27–28
Explain research designs.	Research Methods for Studying Infants	Video	pp. 29–36
	Conducting Research on Adolescents	Video	
	Cross-Cultural Comparison of Adolescent Emotions	Video	
	Intelligence Research	Video	
	Designing an Experiment: Dependent and Independent Variables	Interactive exercise	
	The Scientific Method	Interactive exercise	
	Correlations	Interactive exercise	
	Naturalistic Observations	Interactive exercise	
Explain how to conduct ethical research.	Ethical Dilemmas	Interactive exercise	p. 37
Discuss minimizing bias.	Ethnic Identity Socialization	Video	pp. 38–39
	Ethical Issues in Studying Infants	Video	

appendix

Careers in Life-Span Development

The field of life-span development offers an amazing breadth of careers that can provide extremely satisfying work. College and university professors teach courses in many areas of life-span development. Teachers impart knowledge, understanding, and skills to children and adolescents. Counselors, clinical psychologists, nurses, and physicians help people of different ages to cope more effectively with their lives and improve their well-being.

These and many other careers related to life-span development offer many rewards. By working in the field of life-span development, you can help people to improve their lives, understand yourself and others better, possibly advance the state of knowledge in the field, and have an enjoyable time while you are doing these things. Many careers in life-span development pay reasonably well. For example, psychologists earn well above the median salary in the United States.

If you are considering a career in life-span development, would you prefer to work with infants? children? adolescents? older adults? As you go through this term, try to spend some time with people of different ages. Observe their behavior. Talk with them about their lives. Think about whether you would like to work with people of this age in your life's work.

In addition, to find out about careers in life-span development you might talk with people who work in various jobs. For example, if you have some interest in becoming a school counselor, call a school, ask to speak with a counselor, and set up an appointment to discuss the counselor's career and work. If you have an interest in becoming a nurse, call the nursing department at a hospital and set up an appointment to speak with the nursing coordinator about a nursing career.

Another way to explore careers in life-span development is to work in a related job while you are in college. Many colleges and universities offer internships or other work experiences for students who major in specific fields. Course credit or pay is given for some of these jobs. Take advantage of these opportunities. They can help you decide if this is the right career for you, and they can help you get into graduate school, if you decide you want to go.

An advanced degree is not absolutely necessary for some careers in life-span development, but usually you can considerably expand your opportunities (and income) by obtaining a graduate degree. If you think you might want to go to graduate school, talk with one or more professors about your interests, keep a high grade-point average, take appropriate courses, and realize that you likely will need to take the Graduate Record Examination at some point.

In the upcoming sections, we will profile a number of careers in four areas: education/research; clinical/counseling; medical/nursing/physical development; and families/relationships. These are not the only career options in life-span development, but the profiles should give you an idea of the range of opportunities available. For each career, we will describe the work and address the amount of education required and the nature of the training. We have provided page numbers after some entries telling you where within the text you can find *Connecting With Careers*, the career profiles of people who hold some of these positions. The Web site for this book gives more detailed information about these careers in life-span development.

Education/Research

Numerous careers in life-span development involve education or research. The opportunities range from college professor to preschool teacher to school psychologist.

College/University Professor

Professors teach courses in life-span development at many types of institutions, including research universities with master's or Ph.D. programs in life-span development, four-year colleges with no graduate programs, and community colleges. The courses in life-span development are offered in many different programs and schools, including psychology, education, nursing, child and family studies, social work, and medicine. In addition to teaching at the undergraduate or graduate level (or both), professors may conduct research, advise students or direct their research, and serve on college or university committees. Research is part of a professor's job description at most universities with master's and Ph.D. programs, but some college professors do not conduct research and focus instead on teaching.

Teaching life-span development at a college or university almost always requires a Ph.D. or master's degree. Obtaining a Ph.D. usually takes four to six years of graduate work; a master's degree requires approximately two years. The training involves taking graduate courses, learning to conduct research, and attending and presenting papers at professional meetings. Many graduate students work as teaching or research assistants for professors in an apprenticeship relationship that helps them to become competent teachers and researchers. **Read the profiles of professors on p. 528 and p. 614.**

Researcher

Some individuals in the field of life-span development work in research positions. They might work for a university, a government agency such as the National Institute of Mental Health, or private industry. They generate research ideas, plan studies, carry out the research, and usually attempt to publish the research in a scientific journal. A researcher often works in collaboration with other researchers. One researcher might spend much of his or her time in a laboratory; another researcher might work out in the field, such as in schools, hospitals, and so on. Most researchers in life-span development have either a master's or a Ph.D.

Elementary or Secondary School Teacher

Elementary and secondary school teachers teach one or more subject areas, preparing the curriculum, giving tests, assigning grades, monitoring students' progress, conducting parent-teacher conferences, and attending workshops. Becoming an elementary or secondary school teacher requires a minimum of an undergraduate degree. The training involves taking a wide range of courses with a major or concentration in education as well as completing supervised practice teaching.

Exceptional Children (Special Education) Teacher

Teachers of exceptional children spend concentrated time with children who have a disability such as ADHD, mental retardation, or cerebral palsy, or with children who are gifted. Usually some of their work occurs outside of the students' regular classroom and some of it inside the students' regular classroom. The exceptional children teacher works closely with the student's regular classroom teacher and parents to create the best educational program for the student. Teachers of exceptional children often continue their education after obtaining their undergraduate degree and attain a master's degree.

Early Childhood Educator

Early childhood educators work on college faculties and usually teach in community colleges that award an associate degree in early childhood education. They have a minimum of a master's degree in their field. In graduate school, they take courses in early childhood education and receive supervisory training in child-care or early childhood programs.

Preschool/Kindergarten Teacher

Preschool teachers teach mainly 4-year-old children, and kindergarten teachers primarily teach 5-year-old children. They usually have an undergraduate degree in education, specializing in early childhood education. State certification to become a preschool or kindergarten teacher usually is required.

Family and Consumer Science Educator

Family and consumer science educators may specialize in early childhood education or instruct middle and high school students about such matters as nutrition, interpersonal relationships, human sexuality, parenting, and human development. Hundreds of colleges and universities throughout the United States offer two- and four-year degree programs in family and consumer science. These programs usually require an internship. Additional education courses may be needed to obtain a teaching certificate. Some family and consumer educators go on to graduate school for further training, which provides a background for possible jobs in college teaching or research. **Read a profile of a family and consumer science educator on p. 365.**

Educational Psychologist

Educational psychologists most often teach in a college or university and conduct research in areas of educational psychology such as learning, motivation, classroom management, and assessment. They help train students for positions in educational psychology, school psychology, and teaching. Most educational psychologists have a doctorate in education, which takes four to six years of graduate work. **Read a profile of an educational psychologist on p. 38.**

School Psychologist

School psychologists focus on improving the psychological and intellectual well-being of elementary, middle, and high school students. They give psychological tests, interview students and their parents, consult with teachers, and may provide counseling to students and their families. They may work in a centralized office in a school district or in one or more schools.

School psychologists usually have a master's or doctoral degree in school psychology. In graduate school, they take courses in counseling, assessment, learning, and other areas of education and psychology.

Gerontologist

Gerontologists usually work in research in some branch of the federal or state government. They specialize in the study of aging with a particular focus on government programs for older adults, social policy, and delivery of services to older adults. In their research, gerontologists define problems to be studied, collect data, interpret the results, and make recommendations for social policy. Most gerontologists have a master's or doctoral degree and have taken a concentration of coursework in adult development and aging.

Clinical/Counseling

A wide variety of clinical and counseling jobs are linked with life-span development. These range from child clinical psychologist to adolescent drug counselor to geriatric psychiatrist.

Clinical Psychologist

Clinical psychologists seek to help people with psychological problems. They work in a variety of settings, including colleges and universities, clinics, medical schools, and private practice. Some clinical psychologists only conduct psychotherapy; others do psychological assessment and psychotherapy; some also do research. Clinical psychologists may specialize in a particular age group, such as children (child clinical psychologist) or older adults (often referred to as a geropsychologist).

Clinical psychologists have either a Ph.D. (which involves clinical and research training) or a Psy.D. degree (which only involves clinical training). This graduate training usually takes five to seven years and includes courses in clinical psychology and a one-year supervised internship in an accredited setting toward the end of the training. Many geropsychologists pursue a year or two of postdoctoral training. Most states require clinical psychologists to pass a test in order to become licensed in the state and to call themselves clinical psychologists. **Read a profile of a clinical psychologist on p. 10.**

Psychiatrist

Psychiatrists obtain a medical degree and then do a residency in psychiatry. Medical school takes approximately four years and the psychiatry residency another three to four years. Unlike most psychologists (who do not go to medical school), psychiatrists can administer drugs to clients. (Recently, several states gave clinical psychologists the right to prescribe drugs.)

Like clinical psychologists, psychiatrists might specialize in working with children (child psychiatry) or with older adults (geriatric psychiatry). Psychiatrists might work in medical schools in teaching and research roles, in a medical clinic or hospital, or in private practice. In addition to administering drugs to help improve the lives of people with psychological problems, psychiatrists also may conduct psychotherapy. **Read a profile of a child psychiatrist on p. 344.**

Counseling Psychologist

Counseling psychologists work in the same settings as clinical psychologists and may do psychotherapy, teach, or conduct research. Many counseling psychologists do not do therapy with individuals who have severe mental disorders, such as schizophrenia.

Counseling psychologists go through much the same training as clinical psychologists, although in a graduate program in counseling rather than clinical psychology. Counseling psychologists have either a master's degree or a doctoral degree. They also must go through a licensing procedure. One type of master's degree in counseling leads to the designation of licensed professional counselor.

School Counselor

School counselors help students to cope with adjustment problems, identify their abilities and interests, develop academic plans, and explore career options. The focus of the job depends on the age of the children. High school counselors advise students about vocational and technical training, college admission requirements, entrance exams, financial aid, and choosing a major. Elementary school counselors mainly counsel students about social and personal problems. They may observe children in the classroom and at play as part of their work. School counselors may work with students individually, in small groups, or even in a classroom. They often consult with parents, teachers, and school administrators when trying to help students. School counselors usually have a master's degree in counseling.

Career Counselor

Career counselors help individuals to identify their best career options and guide them in applying for jobs. They may work in private industry or at a college or university. They usually interview individuals and give them vocational and/or psychological tests to identify careers that fit their interests and abilities. Sometimes they help individuals to create résumés or conduct mock interviews to help them feel comfortable in a job interview. They might arrange and promote job fairs or other recruiting events to help individuals obtain jobs.

Rehabilitation Counselor

Rehabilitation counselors work with individuals to identify career options, develop adjustment and coping skills to maximize independence, and resolve problems created by a disability. A master's degree in rehabilitation counseling or guidance or counseling psychology is generally considered the minimum education requirement.

Social Worker

Many social workers are involved in helping people with social or economic problems. They may investigate, evaluate, and attempt to rectify reported cases of abuse, neglect, endangerment, or domestic disputes. They may intervene in families and provide counseling and referral services to individuals and families. Some social workers specialize in a certain area. For example, a medical social worker might coordinate support services to people with a long-term disability; family-care social workers often work with families with children or an older adult who needs support services. Social workers often work for publicly funded agencies at the city, state, or national level, although increasingly they work in the private sector in areas such as drug rehabilitation and family counseling.

Social workers have a minimum of an undergraduate degree from a school of social work that includes coursework in sociology and psychology. Some social workers also have a master's or doctoral degree. For example, medical social workers have a master's degree in social work (M.S.W.) and complete graduate coursework and supervised clinical experiences in medical settings.

Drug Counselor

Drug counselors provide counseling to individuals with drug-abuse problems. Some drug counselors specialize in working with adolescents or older adults. They may work on an individual basis with a substance abuser or conduct group therapy. They may work in private practice, with a state or federal government agency, with a company, or in a hospital.

At a minimum, drug counselors complete an associate's or certificate program. Many have an undergraduate degree in substance-abuse counseling, and some have master's and doctoral degrees. Most states provide a certification procedure for obtaining a license to practice drug counseling.

Medical/Nursing/Physical Development

This third main area of careers in life-span development includes a wide range of choices in the medical and nursing areas, as well as jobs pertaining to improving some aspect of a person's physical development.

Obstetrician/Gynecologist

An obstetrician/gynecologist prescribes prenatal and postnatal care, performs deliveries in maternity cases, and treats diseases and injuries of the female reproductive system. Becoming an obstetrician/gynecologist requires a medical degree plus three to five years of residency in obstetrics/gynecology. Obstetricians may work in private practice, a medical clinic, a hospital, or a medical school.

Pediatrician

A pediatrician monitors infants' and children's health, works to prevent disease or injury, helps children attain optimal health, and treats children with health problems. Pediatricians have earned a medical degree and completed a three- to five-year residency in pediatrics.

Pediatricians may work in private practice, a medical clinic, a hospital, or a medical school. Many pediatricians on the faculty of medical schools also teach and conduct research on children's health and diseases. **Read the profile of a pediatrician on p. 121.**

Geriatric Physician

Geriatric physicians diagnose medical problems of older adults, evaluate treatment options, and make recommendations for nursing care or other arrangements. They have a medical degree and a three- to five-year residency in geriatric medicine. Like other doctors, geriatric physicians may work in private practice, a medical clinic, a hospital, or a medical school. Those in medical school settings may not only treat older adults but also teach future physicians and conduct research.

Neonatal Nurse

Neonatal nurses deliver care to newborn infants. They may work with infants born under normal circumstances or premature and critically ill neonates. A minimum of an undergraduate degree in nursing with a specialization in the newborn is required. This training involves coursework in nursing and the biological sciences, as well as supervised clinical experiences.

Nurse-Midwife

A nurse-midwife formulates and provides comprehensive care to expectant mothers as they prepare to give birth, guides them through the birth process, and cares for them after the birth. The nurse-midwife also may provide care to the newborn, counsel parents on the infant's development and parenting, and provide guidance about health practices. Becoming a nurse-midwife generally requires an undergraduate degree from a school of nursing. A nurse-midwife most often works in a hospital setting. **Read the profile of a perinatal nurse on p. 93.**

Pediatric Nurse

Pediatric nurses monitor infants' and children's health, work to prevent disease or injury, and help children attain optimal health. They may work in hospitals, schools of nursing, or with pediatricians in private practice or at a medical clinic.

Pediatric nurses have a degree in nursing that takes two to five years to complete. They take courses in biological sciences, nursing care, and pediatrics, usually in a school of nursing. They also undergo supervised clinical experiences in medical settings. Some pediatric nurses go on to earn a master's or doctoral degree in pediatric nursing.

Geriatric Nurse

Geriatric nurses seek to prevent or intervene in the chronic or acute health problems of older adults. They may work in hospitals, nursing homes, schools of nursing, or with geriatric medical specialists or psychiatrists in a medical clinic or in private practice. Like pediatric nurses, geriatric nurses take courses in a school of nursing and obtain a degree in nursing, which takes from two to five years. They complete courses in biological sciences, nursing care, and mental health as well as supervised clinical training in geriatric settings. They also may obtain a

master's or doctoral degree in their specialty. **Read a profile of a geriatric nurse on p. 558.**

Physical Therapist

Physical therapists work with individuals who have a physical problem due to disease or injury to help them function as competently as possible. They may consult with other professionals and coordinate services for the individual. Many physical therapists work with people of all ages, although some specialize in working with a specific age group, such as children or older adults.

Physical therapists usually have an undergraduate degree in physical therapy and are licensed by a state. They take courses and undergo supervised training in physical therapy.

Occupational Therapist

Occupational therapists initiate the evaluation of clients with various impairments and manage their treatment. They help people regain, develop, and build skills that are important for independent functioning, health, well-being, security, and happiness. An "Occupational Therapist Registered" (OTR) must have a master's and/or doctoral degree with education ranging from two to six years. Training includes occupational therapy courses in a specialized program. National certification is mandatory, and licensing/registration is required in some states.

Therapeutic/Recreation Therapist

Therapeutic/recreation therapists maintain or improve the quality of life for people with special needs through intervention, leisure education, and recreation. They work in hospitals, rehabilitation centers, local government agencies, at-risk youth programs, as well as other settings. Becoming a therapeutic/recreation therapist requires an undergraduate degree with coursework in leisure studies and a concentration in therapeutic recreation. National certification is usually required. Coursework in anatomy, special education, and psychology is beneficial.

Audiologist

Audiologists assess and identify the presence and severity of hearing loss, as well as problems in balance. They may work in a medical clinic, with a physician in private practice, in a hospital, or in a medical school.

An audiologist completes coursework and supervised training to earn a minimum of an undergraduate degree in hearing science. Some audiologists also go on to obtain a master's or doctoral degree.

Speech Therapist

Speech therapists identify, assess, and treat speech and language problems. They may work with physicians, psychologists, social workers, and other health care professionals in a team approach to help individuals with physical or psychological problems that involve speech and language. Some speech therapists specialize in working with individuals of a particular age or people with a particular type of speech disorder. Speech therapists have a minimum of an undergraduate degree in speech and hearing science or in a specific type of communications disorder. They may work in private practice, hospitals and medical schools, and government agencies.

Genetic Counselor

Genetic counselors identify and counsel families at risk for genetic disorders. They work as members of a health care team, providing information and support to families who have members with genetic defects or disorders or are at risk for a variety of inherited conditions. They also serve as educators and resource people for other health care professionals and the public. Almost one-half work in university medical centers; one-fourth work in private hospital settings.

Genetic counselors have specialized graduate degrees and experience in medical genetics and counseling. Most enter the field after majoring in undergraduate disciplines as biology, genetics, psychology, nursing, public health, or social work. **Read a profile of a genetic counselor on p. 62.**

Families/Relationships

A number of careers and jobs related to life-span development focus on working with families and couples who have relationship problems. These range from home health aide to marriage and family therapist.

Home Health Aide

A home health aide provides in-home services to older adults, helping them with basic self-care tasks. No higher education is required for this position. There is brief training by an agency.

Child Welfare Worker

Child protective services in each state employ child welfare workers. They protect children's rights, evaluate any maltreatment, and may have children removed from their homes if necessary. A child social worker has a minimum of an undergraduate degree in social work.

Child Life Specialist

Child life specialists work with children and their families when the child needs to be hospitalized. They monitor the child's activities, seek to reduce the child's stress, and help the child to cope and to enjoy the hospital experience as much as possible. Child life specialists may provide parent education and develop individualized treatment plans based on an assessment of the child's development, temperament, medical plan, and available social supports. Child life specialists have an undergraduate degree. They have taken courses in child development and education and usually completed additional courses in a child life program. **Read a profile of a child life specialist on p. 286.**

Marriage and Family Therapist

Marriage and family therapists work on the principle that many individuals who have psychological problems benefit when psychotherapy is provided in the context of a marital or family relationship. Marriage and family therapists may provide marital therapy, couple therapy to individuals in a relationship who are not married, and family therapy to two or more members of a family.

Marriage and family therapists have a master's or a doctoral degree. They complete a training program in graduate school similar to a clinical psychologist's but with the focus on marital and family relationships. In most states, it is necessary to go through a licensing procedure to practice marital and family therapy.

Further Careers

These are only a handful of careers that require an understanding of developmental psychology. *Connecting With Careers* highlight additional careers, including an infant assessment specialist (p. 159), child care director (p. 198), toy designer (p. 227), health psychologist (p. 407), college/career counselor (p. 425), pastoral counselor (p. 503), and home hospice nurse (p. 629). *What other careers can you think of that require a knowledge of human development?*

There are one hundred and ninety-three living species of monkeys and apes. One hundred and ninety-two of them are covered with hair. The exception is the naked ape, self-named Homo sapiens.

—**DESMOND MORRIS**
British Zoologist, 20th Century

Beginnings

The rhythm and meaning of life involve beginnings. Questions are raised about how, from so simple a beginning, endless forms develop, grow, and mature. What was this organism, what is the organism, and what will this organism be? In Section 2, you will read two chapters: "Biological Beginnings" (Chapter 2) and "Prenatal Development and Birth" (Chapter 3).

chapter 2

BIOLOGICAL BEGINNINGS

chapter **outline**

1 The Evolutionary Perspective

Learning Goal 1 Discuss the evolutionary perspective on life-span development.

Natural Selection and Adaptive Behavior
Evolutionary Psychology

2 Genetic Foundations of Development

Learning Goal 2 Describe what genes are and how they influence human development.

The Collaborative Gene
Genes and Chromosomes
Genetic Principles
Chromosomal and Gene-Linked Abnormalities

3 Reproductive Challenges and Choices

Learning Goal 3 Identify some important reproductive challenges and choices.

Prenatal Diagnostic Tests
Infertility and Reproductive Technology
Adoption

4 Heredity-Environment Interaction: The Nature-Nurture Debate

Learning Goal 4 Explain some of the ways that heredity and environment interact to produce individual differences in development.

Behavior Genetics
Heredity-Environment Correlations
Shared and Nonshared Environmental Experiences
The Epigenetic View and Gene × Environment (G × E) Interaction
Conclusions About Heredity-Environment Interaction

Jim Springer and Jim Lewis are identical twins. They were separated at 4 weeks of age and did not see each other again until they were 39 years old. Both worked as part-time deputy sheriffs, vacationed in Florida, drove Chevrolets, had dogs named Toy, and married and divorced women named Betty. One twin named his son James Allan, and the other named his son James Alan. Both liked math but not spelling, enjoyed carpentry and mechanical drawing, chewed their fingernails down to the nubs, had almost identical drinking and smoking habits, had hemorrhoids, put on 10 pounds at about the same point in development, first suffered headaches at the age of 18, and had similar sleep patterns.

Jim and Jim do have some differences. One wears his hair over his forehead, the other slicks it back and has sideburns. One expresses himself best orally; the other is more proficient in writing. But, for the most part, their profiles are remarkably similar.

Another pair of identical twins, Daphne and Barbara, are called the "giggle sisters" because after being reunited they were always making each other laugh. A thorough search of their adoptive families' histories revealed no gigglers. The giggle sisters ignored stress, avoided conflict and controversy whenever possible, and showed no interest in politics.

Jim and Jim and the giggle sisters were part of the Minnesota Study of Twins Reared Apart, directed by Thomas Bouchard and his colleagues. The study brings identical twins (identical genetically because they come from the same fertilized egg) and fraternal twins (who come from different fertilized eggs) from all over the world to Minneapolis to investigate their lives. There the twins complete personality and intelligence tests, and they provide detailed medical histories, including information about diet and smoking, exercise habits, chest X-rays, heart stress tests, and EEGs. The twins are asked more than 15,000

Jim Lewis (*left*) and Jim Springer (*right*).

-topical **connections** ----

The previous chapter introduced the field of life-span development, including discussion of three key developmental processes: biological, cognitive, and socioemotional. In this chapter, we lay the foundation of the biological aspects of development. Biological processes, guided by genes, influence an individual's development in every period of the human life span. The forthcoming discussion of genetics and the previous discussion of theories (psychoanalytic, cognitive, behavioral and social cognitive, ethological, and ecological) in Chapter 1 provide a knowledge base from which to examine one of life-span development's major issues and debates—how strongly development is influenced by heredity (nature) and the environment (nurture).

◄--- *looking back* -----

questions about their family and childhood, personal interests, vocational orientation, values, and aesthetic judgments (Bouchard & others, 1990).

When genetically identical twins who were separated as infants show such striking similarities in their tastes and habits and choices, can we conclude that their genes must have caused the development of those tastes and habits and choices? Other possible causes need to be considered. The twins shared not only the same genes but also some experiences. Some of the separated twins lived together for several months prior to their adoption; some of the twins had been reunited prior to testing (in some cases, many years earlier); adoption agencies often place twins in similar homes; and even strangers who spend several hours together and start comparing their lives are likely to come up with some coincidental similarities (Joseph, 2006). The Minnesota study of identical twins points to both the importance of the genetic basis of human development and the need for further research on genetic and environmental factors (Lykken, 2001). We will discuss twin studies in more detail in the section on behavior genetics later in this chapter.

preview

The examples of Jim and Jim and the giggle sisters stimulate us to think about our genetic heritage and the biological foundations of our existence. However, organisms are not like billiard balls, moved by simple external forces to predictable positions on life's table. Environmental experiences and biological foundations work together to make us who we are. Our coverage of life's biological beginnings focuses on evolution, genetic foundations, challenges and choices regarding reproduction, and the interaction of heredity and environment.

1 The Evolutionary Perspective

LG1 Discuss the evolutionary perspective on life-span development.

> Natural Selection and Adaptive Behavior

> Evolutionary Psychology

How does the attachment of this Vietnamese baby to its mother reflect the evolutionary process of adaptive behavior?

In evolutionary time, humans are relative newcomers to Earth. As our earliest ancestors left the forest to feed on the savannahs and then to form hunting societies on the open plains, their minds and behaviors changed, and they eventually established humans as the dominant species on Earth. How did this evolution come about?

NATURAL SELECTION AND ADAPTIVE BEHAVIOR

Natural selection is the evolutionary process by which those individuals of a species that are best adapted are the ones that survive and reproduce. To understand what this means, let's return to the middle of the nineteenth century, when British naturalist Charles Darwin was traveling around the world, observing many different species of animals in their natural surroundings. Darwin, who published his observations and thoughts in *On the Origin of Species* (1859), noted that most organisms reproduce at rates that would cause enormous increases in the population of most species and yet populations remain nearly constant. He reasoned that an intense, constant struggle for food, water, and resources must occur among the many young born each generation, because many of the young do not survive. Those that do survive and reproduce pass on their characteristics to the next generation. Darwin argued that these survivors are better *adapted* to their world than are the nonsurvivors (Simon,

Dickey, & Reese, 2013). The best-adapted individuals survive to leave the most offspring. Over the course of many generations, organisms with the characteristics needed for survival make up an increasing percentage of the population. Over many, many generations, this could produce a gradual modification of the whole population. If environmental conditions change, however, other characteristics might become favored by natural selection, moving the species in a different direction (Mader & Windelspecht, 2013).

All organisms must adapt to particular places, climates, food sources, and ways of life (Hoefnagels, 2013). An eagle's claws are a physical adaptation that facilitates predation. *Adaptive behavior* is behavior that promotes an organism's survival in the natural habitat (Johnson, 2012). For example, attachment between a caregiver and a baby ensures the infant's closeness to a caregiver for feeding and protection from danger, thus increasing the infant's chances of survival.

EVOLUTIONARY PSYCHOLOGY

Although Darwin introduced the theory of evolution by natural selection in 1859, his ideas only recently have become a popular framework for explaining behavior. Psychology's newest approach, **evolutionary psychology,** emphasizes the importance of adaptation, reproduction, and "survival of the fittest" in shaping behavior. "Fit" in this sense refers to the ability to bear offspring that survive long enough to bear offspring of their own. In this view, natural selection favors behaviors that increase reproductive success—the ability to pass your genes to the next generation (Cosmides, 2013; Durrant & Ellis, 2013).

David Buss (1995, 2004, 2008, 2012) has been especially influential in stimulating new interest in how evolution can explain human behavior. He reasons that just as evolution has contributed to our physical features such as body shape and height, it also pervasively influences how we make decisions, how aggressive we are, our fears, and our mating patterns. For example, assume that our ancestors were hunters and gatherers on the plains and that men did most of the hunting and women stayed close to home gathering seeds and plants for food. If you have to travel some distance from your home to find and slay a fleeing animal, you need certain physical traits along with the capacity for certain types of spatial thinking. Men with these traits would be more likely than men without them to survive, to bring home lots of food, and to be considered attractive mates—and thus to reproduce and pass on these characteristics to their children. In other words, if their assumptions were correct, potentially these traits would provide a reproductive advantage for males—over many generations, men with good spatial thinking skills might become more numerous in the population. Critics point out that this scenario might or might not have actually happened.

Evolutionary Developmental Psychology Recently, interest has grown in using the concepts of evolutionary psychology to understand human development (Bjorklund, 2007, 2012; Brune & others, 2012; Schlomer & Belsky, 2012). Here we discuss some ideas proposed by evolutionary developmental psychologists (Bjorklund & Pellegrini, 2002).

An extended childhood period might have evolved because humans require time to develop a large brain and learn the complexity of human societies. Humans take longer to become reproductively mature than any other mammal (see Figure 2.1). During this extended childhood period, they develop a large brain and have the experiences needed to become competent adults in a complex society.

Many of our evolved psychological mechanisms are domain-specific. That is, the mechanisms apply only to a specific aspect of a person's psychological makeup. According to evolutionary psychology, the mind is not a general-purpose device that can be applied equally to a vast array of problems. Instead, as our ancestors dealt with certain recurring problems such as hunting and finding shelter, specialized modules evolved to process information related to those problems. For example, such specialized modules might include a module for physical

FIGURE **2.1**

THE BRAIN SIZES OF VARIOUS PRIMATES AND HUMANS IN RELATION TO THE LENGTH OF THE CHILDHOOD PERIOD. Compared with other primates, humans have both a larger brain and a longer childhood period. *What conclusions can you draw from the relationship indicated by this graph?*

What endless questions vex the thought, of whence and whither, when and how.

—Sir Richard Burton
British Explorer, 19th Century

evolutionary psychology Emphasizes the importance of adaptation, reproduction, and "survival of the fittest" in shaping behavior.

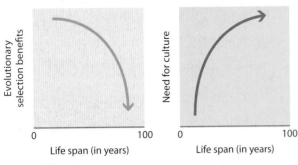

FIGURE 2.2

BALTES' VIEW OF EVOLUTION AND CULTURE ACROSS THE LIFE SPAN. Benefits derived from evolutionary selection decrease as we age, whereas the need for culture increases with age.

developmental **connection**

Life-Span Perspective

Baltes described eight main characteristics of the life-span perspective. Chapter 1, p. 7

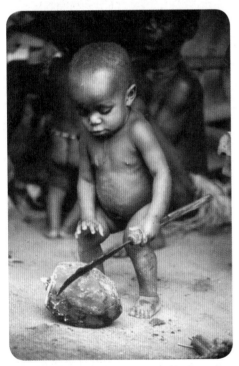

Children in all cultures are interested in the tools that adults in their cultures use. For example, this 11-month-old boy from the Efe culture in the Democratic Republic of the Congo in Africa is trying to cut a papaya with an apopau (a smaller version of a machete). *Might the infant's behavior be evolutionarily based or due to both biological and environmental conditions?*

knowledge for tracking animals, a module for mathematical knowledge for trading, and a module for language.

Evolved mechanisms are not always adaptive in contemporary society. Some behaviors that were adaptive for our prehistoric ancestors may not serve us well today. For example, the food-scarce environment of our ancestors likely led to humans' propensity to gorge when food is available and to crave high-caloric foods, a trait that might lead to an epidemic of obesity when food is plentiful.

Connecting Evolution and Life-Span Development   In evolutionary theory, what matters is that individuals live long enough to reproduce and pass on their characteristics (Starr & others, 2013). So why do humans live so long after reproduction? Perhaps evolution favored longevity because having older people around improves the survival rates of babies. Possibly having grandparents alive to care for the young while parents were out hunting and gathering food created an evolutionary advantage.

According to life-span developmentalist Paul Baltes (2003), the benefits conferred by evolutionary selection decrease with age. Natural selection has not weeded out many harmful conditions and nonadaptive characteristics that appear among older adults. Why? Natural selection operates primarily on characteristics that are tied to reproductive fitness, which extends through the earlier part of adulthood. Thus, says Baltes, selection primarily operates during the first half of life.

As an example, consider Alzheimer disease, an irreversible brain disorder characterized by gradual deterioration in thinking capacity. This disease typically does not appear until age 70 or later. If it were a disease that struck 20-year-olds, perhaps natural selection would have eliminated it eons ago.

Thus, unaided by evolutionary pressures against nonadaptive conditions, we suffer the aches, pains, and infirmities of aging. And as the benefits of evolutionary selection decrease with age, argues Baltes, the need for culture increases (see Figure 2.2). That is, as older adults weaken biologically, they need culture-based resources such as cognitive skills, literacy, medical technology, and social support. For example, older adults may need help and training from other people to maintain their cognitive skills (Hampstead & others, 2012a, b; Nouchi & others, 2012; Schaie, 2012).

Evaluating Evolutionary Psychology   Although the popular press gives a lot of attention to the ideas of evolutionary psychology, it remains just one theoretical approach among many. Like the theories described in Chapter 1, it has limitations, weaknesses, and critics (Hyde & Quest, 2013; Matlin, 2012). Albert Bandura (1998), whose social cognitive theory was described in Chapter 1, acknowledges the important influence of evolution on human adaptation. However, he rejects what he calls "one-sided evolutionism," which sees social behavior as strictly the product of evolved biology. An alternative is a bidirectional view in which environmental and biological conditions influence each other. In this view, evolutionary pressures created changes in biological structures that allowed the use of tools, which enabled our ancestors to manipulate the environment, constructing new environmental conditions. In turn, environmental innovations produced new selection pressures that led to the evolution of specialized biological systems for consciousness, thought, and language.

In other words, evolution gave us biological potentialities but it does not dictate behavior. People have used their biological capacities to produce diverse cultures—aggressive and peace-loving, egalitarian and autocratic. As American scientist Stephen Jay Gould (1981) concluded, in most domains of human functioning, biology allows a broad range of cultural possibilities.

The "big picture" idea of natural selection leading to the development of human traits and behaviors is difficult to refute or test because evolution occurs on a time scale that does not lend itself to empirical study. Thus, studying specific genes in humans and other species—and their links to traits and behaviors—may be the best approach for testing ideas coming out of evolutionary psychology.

Review

- How can natural selection and adaptive behavior be defined?
- What is evolutionary psychology? What are some basic ideas about human development proposed by evolutionary psychologists? How might evolutionary influences have different effects at different points in the life span? How can evolutionary psychology be evaluated?

Connect

- In the section on ethological theory in the previous chapter, you learned about critical time periods. How does the concept of critical period relate to what you learned about older adults and aging in this section?

Reflect *Your Own Personal Journey of Life*

- Which do you think is more persuasive in explaining your development: the views of evolutionary psychologists or their critics? Why?

---

2 Genetic Foundations of Development

LG2 Describe what genes are and how they influence human development.

The Collaborative Gene

Genes and Chromosomes

Genetic Principles

Chromosomal and Gene-Linked Abnormalities

Genetic influences on behavior evolved over time and across many species. The many traits and characteristics that are genetically influenced have a long evolutionary history that is retained in our DNA. Our DNA is not just inherited from our parents; it includes what we inherited as a species from other species that were our ancestors.

How are characteristics that suit a species for survival transmitted from one generation to the next? Darwin did not know the answer because genes and the principles of genetics had not yet been discovered. Each of us carries a "genetic code" that we inherited from our parents. Because a fertilized egg carries this human code, a fertilized human egg cannot grow into an egret, eagle, or elephant.

THE COLLABORATIVE GENE

Each of us began life as a single cell weighing about one twenty-millionth of an ounce! This tiny piece of matter housed our entire genetic code—information that helps us grow from that single cell to a person made of trillions of cells, each containing a replica of the original code. That code is carried by our genes. What are genes and what do they do? For the answer, we need to look into our cells.

The nucleus of each human cell contains **chromosomes,** which are threadlike structures made up of deoxyribonucleic acid (DNA). **DNA** is a complex molecule that has a double helix shape, like a spiral staircase (shown in Figure 2.3) and contains genetic information. **Genes,** the units of hereditary information, are short segments of DNA. They help cells to reproduce themselves and to assemble proteins. Proteins, in turn, are the building blocks of cells as well as the regulators that direct the body's processes (Belk & Maier, 2013; Tortora, Funke, & Case, 2013).

Each gene has its own location—its own designated place on a particular chromosome. Today, there is a great deal of enthusiasm about efforts to discover the specific locations of genes that are linked to certain functions and developmental outcomes (Plomin, 2012). An important step in this direction is the Human Genome Project's efforts to map the human

---

developmental **connection**

Biological Processes

A current biological theory of aging emphasizes that changes in the tips of chromosomes play a key role in aging. Chapter 17, p. 541

---

chromosomes Threadlike structures that come in 23 pairs, with one member of each pair coming from each parent. Chromosomes contain the genetic substance DNA.

DNA A complex molecule that contains genetic information.

genes Units of hereditary information composed of DNA. Genes help cells to reproduce themselves and help manufacture the proteins that maintain life.

FIGURE **2.3**

CELLS, CHROMOSOMES, DNA, AND GENES.
(*Top*) The body contains trillions of cells. Each cell
contains a central structure, the nucleus. (*Middle*)
Chromosomes are threadlike structures located in
the nucleus of the cell. Chromosomes are composed
of DNA. (*Bottom*) DNA has the structure of a spiral
staircase. A gene is a segment of DNA.

genome—the complete set of developmental information for creating proteins that initiate the making of a human organism (Hughes & Rosen, 2012).

Completion of the Human Genome Project has led to use of the *genome-wide association method* to identify genetic variations linked to a particular disease, such as cancer, cardiovascular disease, or Alzheimer disease (National Human Genome Research Institute, 2012). To conduct a genome-wide association study, researchers obtain DNA from individuals who have the disease and those who don't have it. Then, each participant's complete set of DNA, or genome, is purified from the blood or cells and scanned on machines to determine markers of genetic variation. If the genetic variations occur more frequently in people who have the disease, the variations point to the region in the human genome where the disease-causing problem exists. Genome-wide association studies have recently been conducted for child obesity (Early Growth Genetics Consortium & others, 2012), cardiovascular disease (Lusis, 2012), Alzheimer disease (Raj & others, 2012), and depression (Major Depressive Disorder Working Group of the Psychiatric GWAS Consortium, 2012).

One of the big surprises of the Human Genome Project was an early report indicating that humans have only about 30,000 genes (U.S. Department of Energy, 2001). More recently, the number of human genes has been revised further downward to approximately 20,500 (Ensembl Human, 2010; Science Daily, 2008). Scientists had thought that humans had as many as 100,000 or more genes. They had also maintained that each gene programmed just one protein. In fact, humans have far more proteins than they have genes, so there cannot be a one-to-one correspondence between genes and proteins (Commoner, 2002). Each gene is not translated, in automaton-like fashion, into one and only one protein (Moore, 2013). A gene does not act independently, as developmental psychologist David Moore (2001) emphasized by titling his book *The Dependent Gene*.

Rather than being a group of independent genes, the human genome consists of many genes that collaborate both with each other and with nongenetic factors inside and outside the body. The collaboration operates at many points. For example, the cellular machinery mixes, matches, and links small pieces of DNA to reproduce the genes—and that machinery is influenced by what is going on around it.

Whether a gene is turned "on"—working to assemble proteins—is also a matter of collaboration. The activity of genes (genetic expression) is affected by their environment (Gottlieb, 2007). For example, hormones that circulate in the blood make their way into the cell where they can turn genes "on" and "off." And the flow of hormones can be affected by environmental conditions such as light, day length, nutrition, and behavior. Numerous studies have shown that external events outside of the original cell and the person, as well as events inside the cell, can excite or inhibit gene expression (Gottlieb, Wahlsten, & Lickliter, 2006). Recent research has documented that factors such as stress, radiation, and temperature can influence gene expression (Georgakilas, 2011). For example, one study revealed that an increase in the concentration of stress hormones such as cortisol produced a fivefold increase in DNA damage (Flint & others, 2007). A recent study also found that exposure to radiation changed the rate of DNA synthesis in cells (Lee & others, 2011).

A positive result from the Human Genome Project.
Shortly after Andrew Gobea was born, his cells were
genetically altered to prevent his immune system
from failing.

GENES AND CHROMOSOMES

Genes are not only collaborative, they are enduring. How do the genes manage to get passed from generation to generation and end up in all of the trillion cells in the body? Three processes explain the heart of the story: mitosis, meiosis, and fertilization.

mitosis Cellular reproduction in which the cell's nucleus duplicates itself with two new cells being formed, each containing the same DNA as the parent cell, arranged in the same 23 pairs of chromosomes.

Calvin and Hobbes

by Bill Watterson

Mitosis, Meiosis, and Fertilization All cells in your body, except the sperm and egg, have 46 chromosomes arranged in 23 pairs. These cells reproduce through a process called **mitosis.** During mitosis, the cell's nucleus—including the chromosomes—duplicates itself and the cell divides. Two new cells are formed, each containing the same DNA as the original cell, arranged in the same 23 pairs of chromosomes.

However, a different type of cell division—**meiosis**—forms eggs and sperm (which also are called gametes). During meiosis, a cell of the testes (in men) or ovaries (in women) duplicates its chromosomes but then divides twice, thus forming four cells, each of which has only half of the genetic material of the parent cell (Johnson, 2012). By the end of meiosis, each egg or sperm has 23 unpaired chromosomes.

During **fertilization,** an egg and a sperm fuse to create a single cell, called a **zygote** (see Figure 2.4). In the zygote, the 23 unpaired chromosomes from the egg and the 23 unpaired chromosomes from the sperm combine to form one set of 23 paired chromosomes—one chromosome of each pair from the mother's egg and the other from the father's sperm. In this manner, each parent contributes half of the offspring's genetic material.

Figure 2.5 shows 23 paired chromosomes of a male and a female. The members of each pair of chromosomes are both similar and different: Each chromosome in the pair contains varying forms of the same genes, at the same location on the chromosome. A gene that influences hair color, for example, is located on both members of one pair of chromosomes, in the same location on each. However, one of those chromosomes might carry a gene associated with blond hair; the other chromosome in the pair might carry a gene associated with brown hair.

Do you notice any obvious differences between the chromosomes of the male and the chromosomes of the female in Figure 2.5? The difference lies in the 23rd pair. Ordinarily, in females this pair consists of two chromosomes called X chromosomes; in males, the 23rd pair consists of an X and a Y chromosome. The presence of a Y chromosome is one factor that makes a person male rather than female.

Sources of Variability Combining the genes of two parents in offspring increases genetic variability in the population, which is valuable for a species because it provides more

FIGURE **2.4**

A SINGLE SPERM PENETRATING AN EGG AT THE POINT OF FERTILIZATION

meiosis A specialized form of cell division that occurs to form eggs and sperm (also known as gametes).

fertilization A stage in reproduction when an egg and a sperm fuse to create a single cell, called a zygote.

zygote A single cell formed through fertilization.

FIGURE **2.5**

THE GENETIC DIFFERENCE BETWEEN MALES AND FEMALES. Set (*a*) shows the chromosome structure of a male, and set (*b*) shows the chromosome structure of a female. The last pair of 23 pairs of chromosomes is in the bottom right box of each set. Notice that the Y chromosome of the male is smaller than the X chromosome of the female. To obtain this kind of chromosomal picture, a cell is removed from a person's body, usually from the inside of the mouth. The chromosomes are stained by chemical treatment, magnified extensively, and then photographed.

(a)

(b)

characteristics for natural selection to operate on (Lewis, 2012). In fact, the human genetic process creates several important sources of variability.

First, the chromosomes in the zygote are not exact copies of those in the mother's ovaries or the father's testes. During the formation of the sperm and egg in meiosis, the members of each pair of chromosomes are separated, but which chromosome in the pair goes to the gamete is a matter of chance. In addition, before the pairs separate, pieces of the two chromosomes in each pair are exchanged, creating a new combination of genes on each chromosome (Mader & Windelspecht, 2013). Thus, when chromosomes from the mother's egg and the father's sperm are brought together in the zygote, the result is a truly unique combination of genes (Goodenough & McGuire, 2012).

If each zygote is unique, how do identical twins like those discussed in the opening of the chapter exist? *Identical twins* (also called monozygotic twins) develop from a single zygote that splits into two genetically identical replicas, each of which becomes a person. *Fraternal twins* (called dizygotic twins) develop when two eggs are fertilized by different sperm, creating two zygotes that are genetically no more similar than ordinary siblings.

Another source of variability comes from DNA (Brooker, 2012). Chance events, a mistake by cellular machinery, or damage from an environmental agent such as radiation may produce a *mutated gene*, which is a permanently altered segment of DNA.

There is increasing interest in studying *susceptibility genes*, those that make the individual more vulnerable to specific diseases or accelerated aging, and *longevity genes*, those that make the individual less vulnerable to certain diseases and more likely to live to an older age (Soerensen & others, 2012; Tabara, Kohara, & Miki, 2012). Even when their genes are identical, however, people vary. The difference between genotypes and phenotypes helps us to understand this source of variability. All of a person's genetic material makes up his or her **genotype.** However, not all of the genetic material is apparent in our observed and measurable characteristics. A **phenotype** consists of observable characteristics. Phenotypes include physical characteristics (such as height, weight, and hair color) and psychological characteristics (such as personality and intelligence).

For each genotype, a range of phenotypes can be expressed, providing another source of variability (Miller & Spoolman, 2012; Rende, 2012). An individual can inherit the genetic potential to grow very large, for example, but good nutrition, among other things, will be essential for achieving that potential.

GENETIC PRINCIPLES

What determines how a genotype is expressed to create a particular phenotype? Much is unknown about the answer to this question (Yashion & Cummings, 2012). However, a number of genetic principles have been discovered, among them those of dominant-recessive genes, sex-linked genes, genetic imprinting, and polygenically determined characteristics.

Dominant-Recessive Genes Principle   In some cases, one gene of a pair always exerts its effects; it is *dominant*, overriding the potential influence of the other gene, called the recessive gene. This is the *dominant-recessive genes principle*. A recessive gene exerts its influence only if the two genes of a pair are both recessive. If you inherit a recessive gene for a trait from each of your parents, you will show the trait. If you inherit a recessive gene from only one parent, you may never know you carry the gene. Brown hair, farsightedness, and dimples rule over blond hair, nearsightedness, and freckles in the world of dominant-recessive genes.

Can two brown-haired parents have a blond-haired child? Yes, they can. Suppose that each parent has a dominant gene for brown hair and a recessive gene for blond hair. Since dominant genes override recessive genes, the parents have brown hair, but both are carriers of blondness and pass on their recessive genes for blond hair. With no dominant gene to override them, the recessive genes can make the child's hair blond.

Sex-Linked Genes   Most mutated genes are recessive. When a mutated gene is carried on the X chromosome, the result is called *X-linked inheritance*. The implications for males may be very different from those for females (McClelland, Bowles, & Koopman, 2012). Remember that males have only one X chromosome. Thus, if there is an absent or altered, disease-relevant gene on the X chromosome, males have no "backup" copy to counter the harmful gene and therefore

genotype A person's genetic heritage; the actual genetic material.

phenotype The way an individual's genotype is expressed in observed and measurable characteristics.

may develop an X-linked disease. However, females have a second X chromosome, which is likely to be unchanged. As a result, they are not likely to have the X-linked disease. Thus, most individuals who have X-linked diseases are males. Females who have one abnormal copy of the gene on the X chromosome are known as "carriers," and they usually do not show any signs of the X-linked disease. Hemophilia and fragile-X syndrome, which we will discuss later in the chapter, are examples of X-linked inheritance diseases (Bartel, Weinstein, & Schaffer, 2012).

Genetic Imprinting   Genetic imprinting occurs when the expression of a gene has different effects depending on whether the mother or the father passed on the gene (Lambertini & others, 2012; Pidsley & others, 2012). A chemical process "silences" one member of the gene pair. For example, as a result of imprinting, only the maternally derived copy of the expressed gene might be active, while the paternally derived copy of the same expressed gene is silenced— or vice versa. Only a small percentage of human genes appear to undergo imprinting, but it is a normal and important aspect of development (Wakeling, 2011). When imprinting goes awry, development is disturbed, as in the case of Beckwith-Wiedemann syndrome (a growth disorder) and Wilms tumor (a type of cancer) (Mazzuco & others, 2012; Royer-Pokora, 2012).

Polygenic Inheritance   Genetic transmission is usually more complex than the simple examples we have examined thus far (Lewis, 2012; Moore, 2013). Few characteristics reflect the influence of only a single gene or pair of genes. Most are determined by the interaction of many different genes; they are said to be *polygenically determined* (Lu, Yu, & Deng, 2012). Even a simple characteristic such as height, for example, reflects the interaction of many genes as well as the influence of the environment. Most diseases, such as cancer and diabetes, develop as a consequence of complex gene interactions and environmental factors (Dastani & others, 2012; Philips & others, 2012).

The term *gene-gene interaction* is increasingly used to describe studies that focus on the interdependence of two or more genes in influencing characteristics, behavior, diseases, and development (Chen, Wang, & Chan, 2012). For example, recent studies have documented gene-gene interaction in children's immune system functioning (Reijmerink & others, 2011), asthma (Su & others, 2012), cancer (Bushel & others, 2012), cardiovascular disease (Xiao & others, 2012), and arthritis (Roninger & others, 2012).

CHROMOSOMAL AND GENE-LINKED ABNORMALITIES

Abnormalities characterize the genetic process in some individuals. Some of these abnormalities involve whole chromosomes that do not separate properly during meiosis. Other abnormalities are produced by harmful genes.

Chromosomal Abnormalities   Sometimes a gamete is formed in which the male's sperm and/or the female's ovum do not have their normal set of 23 chromosomes. The most notable examples involve Down syndrome and abnormalities of the sex chromosomes (see Figure 2.6).

Down Syndrome   An individual with **Down syndrome** has a round face, a flattened skull, an extra fold of skin over the eyelids, a protruding tongue, short limbs, and retardation of motor and mental abilities (Peters & Petrill, 2011). The syndrome is caused by the presence of an extra copy of chromosome 21. It is not known why the extra chromosome is present, but the health of the male sperm or female ovum may be involved.

Down syndrome appears approximately once in every 700 live births. Women between the ages of 16 and 34 are less likely to give birth to a child with Down syndrome than are younger or older women. African American children are rarely born with Down syndrome.

These athletes, who have Down syndrome, are participating in a Special Olympics competition. Notice the distinctive facial features of the individuals with Down syndrome, such as a round face and a flattened skull. *What causes Down syndrome?*

Sex-Linked Chromosomal Abnormalities   Recall that a newborn normally has either an X and a Y chromosome, or two X chromosomes. Human embryos must possess at least one X chromosome to be viable. The most common sex-linked chromosomal abnormalities involve the presence of an extra chromosome (either an X or Y) or the absence of one X chromosome in females.

Down syndrome A chromosomally transmitted form of mental retardation caused by the presence of an extra copy of chromosome 21.

Name	Description	Treatment	Incidence
Down syndrome	An extra chromosome causes mild to severe retardation and physical abnormalities.	Surgery, early intervention, infant stimulation, and special learning programs	1 in 1,900 births at age 20 1 in 300 births at age 35 1 in 30 births at age 45
Klinefelter syndrome (XXY)	An extra X chromosome causes physical abnormalities.	Hormone therapy can be effective	1 in 600 male births
Fragile X syndrome	An abnormality in the X chromosome can cause mental retardation, learning disabilities, or short attention span.	Special education, speech and language therapy	More common in males than in females
Turner syndrome (XO)	A missing X chromosome in females can cause mental retardation and sexual underdevelopment.	Hormone therapy in childhood and puberty	1 in 2,500 female births
XYY syndrome	An extra Y chromosome can cause above-average height.	No special treatment required	1 in 1,000 male births

FIGURE **2.6**

SOME CHROMOSOMAL ABNORMALITIES. The treatments for these abnormalities do not necessarily erase the problem but may improve the individual's adaptive behavior and quality of life.

A boy with fragile X syndrome.

Klinefelter syndrome A chromosomal disorder in which males have an extra X chromosome, making them XXY instead of XY.

fragile X syndrome A genetic disorder involving an abnormality in the X chromosome, which becomes constricted and often breaks.

Turner syndrome A chromosome disorder in females in which either an X chromosome is missing, making the person XO instead of XX, or the second X chromosome is partially deleted.

XYY syndrome A chromosomal disorder in which males have an extra Y chromosome.

phenylketonuria (PKU) A genetic disorder in which an individual cannot properly metabolize an amino acid called phenylalanine. PKU is now easily detected but, if left untreated, results in mental retardation and hyperactivity.

Klinefelter syndrome is a chromosomal disorder in which males have an extra X chromosome, making them XXY instead of XY. Males with this disorder have undeveloped testes, and they usually have enlarged breasts and become tall (Ross & others, 2012). Klinefelter syndrome occurs approximately once in every 600 live male births.

Fragile X syndrome is a genetic disorder that results from an abnormality in the X chromosome, which becomes constricted and often breaks (Estigarribia, Martin, & Roberts, 2012). Mental deficiency often is an outcome, but it may take the form of mental retardation, a learning disability, or a short attention span. One study revealed that boys with fragile X syndrome were characterized by cognitive deficits in inhibition, memory, and planning (Hooper & others, 2008). This disorder occurs more frequently in males than in females, possibly because the second X chromosome in females negates the effects of the abnormal X chromosome (Fung & others, 2012).

Turner syndrome is a chromosomal disorder in females in which either an X chromosome is missing, making the person XO instead of XX, or part of one X chromosome is deleted. Females with Turner syndrome are short in stature and have a webbed neck (Kaur & Phadke, 2012). They might be infertile and have difficulty in mathematics, but their verbal ability is often quite good (Lleo & others, 2012; Murphy & Mazzocco, 2008). Turner syndrome occurs in approximately 1 of every 2,500 live female births (Pinsker, 2012).

The **XYY syndrome** is a chromosomal disorder in which a male has an extra Y chromosome (Bishop & others, 2011; Stochholm & others, 2012). Early interest in this syndrome focused on the belief that the extra Y chromosome found in some males contributed to aggression and violence. However, researchers subsequently found that XYY males are no more likely to commit crimes than are normal XY males (Witkin & others, 1976).

Gene-Linked Abnormalities Abnormalities can be produced not only by an abnormal number of chromosomes but also by harmful genes. More than 7,000 such genetic disorders have been identified, although most of them are rare.

Phenylketonuria (PKU) is a genetic disorder in which the individual cannot properly metabolize phenylalanine, an amino acid. It results from a recessive gene and occurs about once in every 10,000 to 20,000 live births. Today, phenylketonuria is easily detected during infancy and it is treated by a diet that prevents an excess accumulation of phenylalanine (Giovannini & others, 2012). If phenylketonuria is left untreated, however, excess phenylalanine builds up in the child, producing mental retardation and hyperactivity. Phenylketonuria accounts for approximately 1 percent of institutionalized individuals who are mentally retarded, and it occurs primarily in Whites.

The story of phenylketonuria has important implications for the nature-nurture issue. Although phenylketonuria is a genetic disorder (nature), how or whether a gene's influence in phenylketonuria is played out depends on environmental influences since the disorder can be treated (nurture) using an environmental manipulation (Di Ciommo, Forcella, & Cotugno, 2012). That is, the presence of a genetic defect does not inevitably lead to the development of the disorder if the individual develops in the right environment (one free of phenylalanine). This is one example of the important principle of heredity-environment interaction. Under one environmental condition (phenylalanine in the diet), mental retardation results, but when other nutrients replace phenylalanine, intelligence develops in the normal range. The same genotype has different outcomes depending on the environment (in this case, the nutritional environment).

Sickle-cell anemia, which occurs most often in African Americans, is a genetic disorder that impairs the functioning of the body's red blood cells. Red blood cells carry oxygen to the body's other cells and are usually shaped like a disk. In sickle-cell anemia, a recessive gene causes the red blood cell to become a hook-shaped "sickle" that cannot carry oxygen properly and dies quickly. As a result, the body's cells do not receive adequate oxygen, causing anemia and early death (Mehari & others, 2012). About 1 in 400 African American babies is affected by sickle-cell anemia. One in 10 African Americans is a carrier, as is 1 in 20 Latin Americans. A National Institutes of Health (2008) panel concluded that the only FDA-approved drug (hydroxyurea) to treat sickle-cell anemia in adolescents and adults has been underutilized. Research is currently being conducted in a study named Baby HUG to determine whether the drug works with babies (Alvarez & others, 2012).

Other diseases that result from genetic abnormalities include cystic fibrosis, some forms of diabetes, hemophilia, Huntington's disease, spina bifida, and Tay-Sachs disease. Figure 2.7 provides further information about these diseases. Someday scientists may be able to identify why these and other genetic abnormalities occur and discover how to cure them.

During a physical examination for a college football tryout, Jerry Hubbard, 32, learned that he carried the gene for sickle-cell anemia. Daughter Sara is healthy but daughter Avery (in the print dress) has sickle-cell anemia. *If you were a genetic counselor, would you recommend that this family have more children? Explain.*

sickle-cell anemia A genetic disorder that affects the red blood cells and occurs most often in people of African descent.

Name	Description	Treatment	Incidence
Cystic fibrosis	Glandular dysfunction that interferes with mucus production; breathing and digestion are hampered, resulting in a shortened life span.	Physical and oxygen therapy, synthetic enzymes, and antibiotics; most individuals live to middle age.	1 in 2,000 births
Diabetes	Body does not produce enough insulin, which causes abnormal metabolism of sugar.	Early onset can be fatal unless treated with insulin.	1 in 2,500 births
Hemophilia	Delayed blood clotting causes internal and external bleeding.	Blood transfusions/injections can reduce or prevent damage due to internal bleeding.	1 in 10,000 males
Huntington's disease	Central nervous system deteriorates, producing problems in muscle coordination and mental deterioration.	Does not usually appear until age 35 or older; death likely 10 to 20 years after symptoms appear.	1 in 20,000 births
Phenylketonuria (PKU)	Metabolic disorder that, left untreated, causes mental retardation.	Special diet can result in average intelligence and normal life span.	1 in 10,000 to 1 in 20,000 births
Sickle-cell anemia	Blood disorder that limits the body's oxygen supply; it can cause joint swelling, as well as heart and kidney failure.	Penicillin, medication for pain, antibiotics, blood transfusions, and hydroxyurea.	1 in 400 African American children (lower among other groups)
Spina bifida	Neural tube disorder that causes brain and spine abnormalities.	Corrective surgery at birth, orthopedic devices, and physical/medical therapy.	2 in 1,000 births
Tay-Sachs disease	Deceleration of mental and physical development caused by an accumulation of lipids in the nervous system.	Medication and special diet are used, but death is likely by 5 years of age.	1 in 30 American Jews is a carrier.

FIGURE **2.7**
SOME GENE-LINKED ABNORMALITIES

Holly Ishmael, Genetic Counselor

Holly Ishmael is a genetic counselor at Children's Mercy Hospital in Kansas City. She obtained an undergraduate degree in psychology and a master's degree in genetic counseling from Sarah Lawrence College.

Genetic counselors like Ishmael work as members of a health care team, providing information and support to families with birth defects or genetic disorders. They identify families at risk by analyzing inheritance patterns and then explore options with the family. Some genetic counselors, like Ishmael, specialize in prenatal and pediatric genetics while others focus on cancer genetics or psychiatric genetic disorders.

Ishmael says, "Genetic counseling is a perfect combination for people who want to do something science-oriented, but need human contact and don't want to spend all of their time in a lab or have their nose in a book" (Rizzo, 1999, p. 3).

Genetic counselors have specialized graduate degrees in medical genetics and counseling. They enter graduate school from undergraduate programs in a variety of disciplines, including biology, genetics, psychol-

Holly Ishmael (*left*) in a genetic counseling session.

ogy, public health, and social work. There are approximately 30 graduate genetic counseling programs in the United States. If you are interested in this profession, you can obtain further information from the National Society of Genetic Counselors at www.nsgc.org.

For more information about what genetic counselors do, see page 47 in the Careers in Life-Span Development appendix.

The Human Genome Project has already linked specific DNA variations with increased risk of a number of diseases and conditions, including Huntington's disease (in which the central nervous system deteriorates), some forms of cancer, asthma, diabetes, hypertension, and Alzheimer disease (Tabara, Kohara, & Miki, 2012; Wu & others, 2012).

Dealing with Genetic Abnormalities   Every individual carries DNA variations that might predispose the person to serious physical disease or mental disorder. But not all individuals who carry a genetic disorder develop the disorder. Other genes or developmental events sometimes compensate for genetic abnormalities (Pessia & others, 2012). For example, recall the earlier example of phenylketonuria: Even though individuals might carry the genetic disorder associated with phenylketonuria, the phenotype does not develop when phenylalanine is replaced by other nutrients in their diet.

Thus, genes are not destiny, but genes that are missing, nonfunctional, or mutated can be associated with disorders (Moore, 2013; Solanas-Barkca & others, 2012). Identifying such genetic flaws could enable doctors to predict an individual's risks, recommend healthy practices, and prescribe the safest and most effective drugs (Cheng, Koch, & Wu, 2012; Couraud & others, 2012). A decade or two from now, parents of a newborn baby may be able to leave the hospital with a full genome analysis of their offspring that identifies disease risks.

However, this knowledge might bring important costs as well as benefits. Who would have access to a person's genetic profile? An individual's ability to land and hold jobs or obtain insurance might be threatened if she or he is known to be at risk for some disease. For example, should an airline pilot or a neurosurgeon who is predisposed to develop a disorder that makes one's hands shake be required to leave that job early?

Genetic counselors, usually physicians or biologists who are well-versed in the field of medical genetics, understand the kinds of problems just described, the odds of encountering them, and helpful strategies for offsetting some of their effects (Kingsmore & others, 2012; McGillivray & others, 2012). To read about the career and work of a genetic counselor, see *Connecting with Careers.*

Review *Connect* Reflect

LG2 Describe what genes are and how they influence human development.

Review

- What are genes?
- How are genes passed on?
- What basic principles describe how genes interact?
- What are some chromosomal and gene-linked abnormalities?

Connect

- Would you want to be able to access a full genome analysis of your offspring? Why or why not?

Reflect *Your Own Personal Journey of Life*

- Can you identify in yourself or a friend the likelihood of the influence of dominant and/or recessive genes? Explain.

3 Reproductive Challenges and Choices

LG3 Identify some important reproductive challenges and choices.

Prenatal Diagnostic Tests | Infertility and Reproductive Technology | Adoption

The facts and principles we have discussed regarding meiosis, genetics, and genetic abnormalities are a small part of the recent explosion of knowledge about human biology. This knowledge not only helps us understand human development but also opens up many new choices to prospective parents—choices that can also raise ethical questions.

PRENATAL DIAGNOSTIC TESTS

One choice open to prospective mothers is the extent to which they will undergo prenatal testing. A number of tests can indicate whether a fetus is developing normally, including ultrasound sonography, fetal MRI, chorionic villus sampling, amniocentesis, maternal blood screening, and noninvasive prenatal diagnosis.

Ultrasound Sonography An ultrasound test is often conducted seven weeks into a pregnancy and at various times later in pregnancy (Cignini & others, 2010). *Ultrasound sonography* is a prenatal medical procedure in which high-frequency sound waves are directed into the pregnant woman's abdomen. The echo from the sounds is transformed into a visual representation of the fetus's inner structures. This technique can detect many structural abnormalities in the fetus, including microencephaly, a form of mental retardation involving an abnormally small brain; it can also determine the number of fetuses and give clues to the baby's sex (Masselli & others, 2011). There is virtually no risk to the woman or fetus in this test.

Brain Imaging Techniques The development of brain-imaging techniques has led to increasing use of *fetal MRI* to diagnose fetal malformations (To, 2012) (see Figure 2.8). MRI, which stands for magnetic resonance imaging, uses a powerful magnet and radio images to generate detailed images of the body's organs and structures. Currently, ultrasound is still the first choice in fetal screening, but fetal MRI can provide more detailed images than ultrasound. In many instances, ultrasound will indicate a possible abnormality and then fetal MRI will be used to obtain a clearer, more detailed image

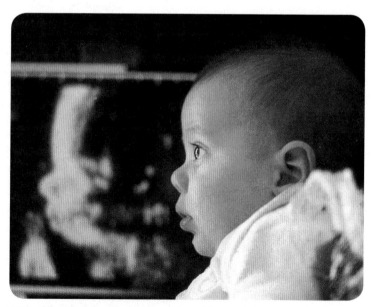

A 6-month-old infant poses with the ultrasound sonography record taken four months into the baby's prenatal development. *What is ultrasound sonography?*

FIGURE 2.8

A FETAL MRI, WHICH IS INCREASINGLY BEING USED IN PRENATAL DIAGNOSIS OF FETAL MALFORMATIONS

---

developmental connection

Biological Processes

Discover what the development of the fetus is like at the stages when chorionic villus sampling and amniocentesis can be used. Chapter 3, Figure 3.3, p. 81

(Mangione & others, 2011). Among the fetal malformations that fetal MRI may be able to detect better than ultrasound sonography are certain abnormalities of the central nervous system, chest, gastrointestinal, genital/urinary, and placental (Clouchoux & Limperopoulos, 2012; Panigraphy & others, 2012).

Chorionic Villus Sampling   At some point between the 10th and 12th weeks of pregnancy, chorionic villus sampling may be used to detect genetic defects and chromosomal abnormalities such as those discussed in the previous section (Basaran, Basaran, & Topatan, 2011). *Chorionic villus sampling (CVS)* is a prenatal medical procedure in which a small sample of the placenta (the vascular organ that links the fetus to the mother's uterus) is removed (Bauland & others, 2012). Diagnosis takes about 10 days. There is a small risk of limb deformity when CVS is used.

Amniocentesis   Between the 15th and 18th weeks of pregnancy, amniocentesis may be performed. *Amniocentesis* is a prenatal medical procedure in which a sample of amniotic fluid is withdrawn by syringe and tested for chromosomal or metabolic disorders (Athanasiadis & others, 2011). The amniotic fluid is found within the amnion, a thin sac in which the embryo is suspended. Ultrasound sonography is often used during amniocentesis so that the syringe can be placed precisely (Ajayi, 2011). The later amniocentesis is performed, the better its diagnostic potential. The earlier it is performed, the more useful it is in deciding how to handle a pregnancy. It may take two weeks for enough cells to grow to allow amniocentesis test results to be obtained. Amniocentesis brings a small risk of miscarriage: About 1 woman in every 200 to 300 miscarries after amniocentesis.

Both amniocentesis and chorionic villus sampling provide valuable information about the presence of birth defects, but they also raise difficult issues for parents about whether an abortion should be obtained if birth defects are present (Zhang & others, 2010). Chorionic villus sampling allows a decision to be made earlier, near the end of the first 12 weeks of pregnancy, when abortion is safer and less traumatic than later.

Maternal Blood Screening   During the 16th to 18th weeks of pregnancy, maternal blood screening may be performed. *Maternal blood screening* identifies pregnancies that have an elevated risk for birth defects such as spina bifida (a defect in the spinal cord) and Down syndrome (Ballard, 2011). The current blood test is called the *triple screen* because it measures three substances in the mother's blood. After an abnormal triple screen result, the next step is usually an ultrasound examination. If an ultrasound does not explain the abnormal triple screen results, amniocentesis is typically used.

Noninvasive Prenatal Diagnosis (NIPD)   *Noninvasive prenatal diagnosis (NIPD)* is increasingly being explored as an alternative to procedures such as chorionic villus sampling and amniocentesis (Avent, 2012; Chiu & Lo, 2012). At this point, NIPD has mainly focused on brain imaging techniques and the isolation and examination of fetal cells circulating in the mother's blood and analysis of cell-free fetal DNA in maternal plasma (Geaghan, 2012; Zugazaga Cortazar, & Martin Martinez, 2012).

Researchers already have used NIPD to successfully test for genes inherited from a father that cause cystic fibrosis and Huntington's disease. They also are exploring the potential for using NIPD very early in fetal development to diagnose a baby's sex and detect Down syndrome (Fernandez-Martinez & others, 2012; Miura & others, 2011).

Fetal Sex Determination   Chorionic villus sampling has often been used to determine the sex of the fetus at some point between 11 and 13 weeks of gestation. Recently, though, some noninvasive techniques have been able to detect the sex of the fetus at an earlier point (Kolialexi & others, 2012). A recent meta-analysis of studies confirmed that a baby's sex can be detected as early as 7 weeks into pregnancy (Devaney & others, 2011). Being able to detect an offspring's sex as well as the presence of various diseases and defects at such an early stage raises ethical concerns about couples' motivation to terminate a pregnancy (Lewis & others, 2012).

INFERTILITY AND REPRODUCTIVE TECHNOLOGY

Recent advances in biological knowledge have also opened up many choices for infertile individuals (Beall & Decherney, 2012; Ming & others, 2012). Approximately 10 to 15 percent of couples in the United States experience *infertility*, which is defined as the inability to conceive a child after 12 months of regular intercourse without contraception. The cause of infertility can rest with the woman or the man (Reindollar & Goldman, 2012). The woman may not be ovulating (releasing eggs to be fertilized), she may be producing abnormal ova, her fallopian tubes through which ova normally reach the womb may be blocked, or she may have a disease that prevents implantation of the embryo into the uterus. The man may produce too few sperm, the sperm may lack motility (the ability to move adequately), or he may have a blocked passageway (Kini & others, 2010).

In the United States, more than 2 million couples seek help for infertility every year. In some cases of infertility, surgery may correct the cause; in others, hormone-based drugs may improve the probability of having a child. Of the 2 million couples who seek help for infertility every year, about 40,000 try high-tech assisted reproduction. By far the most common technique used is *in vitro fertilization (IVF)*, in which eggs and sperm are combined in a laboratory dish. If any eggs are successfully fertilized, one or more of the resulting fertilized eggs is transferred into the woman's uterus. A national study in the United States by the Centers for Disease Control and Prevention (2006) found the success rate of IVF depends on the mother's age (see Figure 2.9).

The creation of families by means of the new reproductive technologies raises important questions about the physical and psychological consequences for children (Steel & Sutcliffe, 2010). One result of fertility treatments is an increase in multiple births. Twenty-five to 30 percent of pregnancies achieved by fertility treatments—including in vitro fertilization—now result in multiple births. A recent *meta-analysis* (a statistical technique that combines the results of multiple studies to determine the strength of the effect) revealed that twins conceived by in vitro fertilization have a slightly increased risk of low birth weight (McDonald & others, 2010) and another meta-analysis found that in vitro fertilization singletons have a significant risk of low birth weight (McDonald & others, 2009). To read about a study that addresses longer-term consequences of in vitro fertilization, see *Connecting Through Research*.

A technician using a micro-needle to inject human sperm into a human egg cell as part of an in vitro fertilization procedure. The injected sperm fertilizes the egg, and the resulting zygote is then grown in the laboratory until it reaches an early stage of embryonic development. Then it is implanted in the uterus.

ADOPTION

Although surgery and fertility drugs can sometimes solve infertility problems, another choice is to adopt a child (Grotevant & von Korff, 2011). Adoption is a social and legal process that establishes a parent-child relationship between persons unrelated at birth.

The Increased Diversity of Adopted Children and Adoptive Parents A number of changes have characterized adoptive children and adoptive parents during the last three to four decades (Brodzinsky & Pinderhughes, 2002). In the first half of the twentieth century, most U.S. adopted children were healthy, non–Latino White infants who were adopted at birth or soon after; however, in recent decades as abortion became legal and contraception increased, fewer of these infants became available for adoption. Increasingly, U.S. couples adopted a much wider diversity of children—from other countries, from other ethnic groups, children with physical and/or mental problems, and children who had been neglected or abused.

Changes also have characterized adoptive parents in the last three to four decades (Brodzinsky & Pinderhughes, 2002). In the first half of the twentieth century, most adoptive parents were from non–Latino White, middle or upper

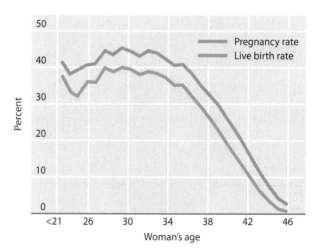

FIGURE **2.9**

SUCCESS RATES OF IN VITRO FERTILIZATION VARY ACCORDING TO THE WOMAN'S AGE

Do Children Conceived Through In Vitro Fertilization Show Significant Differences in Developmental Outcomes in Adolescence?

A longitudinal study examined 34 in vitro fertilization families, 49 adoptive families, and 38 families with a naturally conceived child (Golombok, MacCallum, & Goodman, 2001). Each type of family included a similar portion of boys and girls. Also, the ages of the young adolescents did not differ according to family type (mean age of 11 years, 11 months).

Children's socioemotional development was assessed by (1) interviewing the mother and obtaining detailed descriptions of any problems the child might have; (2) administering a strengths and difficulties questionnaire to the child's mother and teacher; and (3) administering the Social Adjustment Inventory for Children and Adolescents, which examines functioning in school, peer relationships, and self-esteem.

No significant differences between the children from the in vitro fertilization, adoptive, and naturally conceiving families were found. The results from the Social Adjustment Inventory for Children and Adolescents are shown in Figure 2.10. Recent reviews by leading researchers conclude that children and adolescents conceived through new reproductive technologies—such as in vitro fertilization—are as well adjusted as their counterparts conceived by natural means (Golombok, 2011a, b; Golombok & Tasker, 2010).

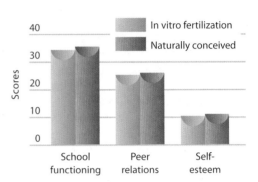

FIGURE **2.10**

SOCIOEMOTIONAL FUNCTIONING OF CHILDREN CONCEIVED THROUGH IN VITRO FERTILIZATION OR NATURALLY CONCEIVED. This graph shows the results of a study that compared the socioemotional functioning of young adolescents who had either been conceived through in vitro fertilization (IVF) or naturally conceived (Golombok, MacCallum, & Goodman, 2001). For each type of family, the study included a similar portion of boys and girls and children of similar age (mean age of 11 years, 11 months). Although the means for the naturally conceived group were slightly higher, this is likely due to chance: There were no significant differences between the groups.

socioeconomic status backgrounds who were married and did not have any type of disability. However, in recent decades, increased diversity has characterized adoptive parents. Many adoption agencies today have no income requirements for adoptive parents and now allow adults from a wide range of backgrounds to adopt children, including single adults, gay and lesbian adults, and older adults. Further, many adoptions involve other family members (aunts/uncles/grandparents); currently, 30 percent of U.S. adoptions are made by relatives (Ledesma, 2012). And slightly more than 50 percent of U.S. adoptions occur through the foster care system; recently, more than 100,000 children in the U.S. foster care system were waiting for someone to adopt them (Ledesma, 2012).

Outcomes for Adopted Children   How do adopted children fare after they are adopted? A majority of adopted children and adolescents (including those adopted at older ages, transracially, and across national borders) adjust effectively, and their parents report considerable satisfaction with their decision to adopt (Brodzinsky & Pinderhughes, 2002; Castle & others, 2010). A research review of 88 studies also revealed no difference in the self-esteem of adopted and nonadopted children and adolescents, as well as no differences between transracial and same-race adoptees (Juffer & van IJzendoorn, 2007).

Adopted children fare much better than children raised in long-term foster care or in an institutional environment (Bernard & Dozier, 2008). A recent study of infants in China revealed that their cognitive development improved two to six months following their adoption from foster homes and institutions (van den Dries & others, 2010).

An increasing number of Hollywood celebrities are adopting children from developing countries. Actress Angelina Jolie recently adopted a baby girl, Zahara (*above*), in Ethiopia.

Parenting Adopted Children

Many of the keys to effectively parenting adopted children are no different from those for effectively parenting biological children: Be supportive and caring, be involved and monitor the child's behavior and whereabouts, be a good communicator, and help the child learn to develop self-control. However, parents of adopted children face some unique circumstances (Fontenot, 2007; Von Korff & Grotevant, 2011). These parents need to recognize the differences involved in adoptive family life, communicate about these differences, show respect for the birth family, and support the child's search for self and identity.

Following are some of the problems parents face when their adopted children are at different points in development and some recommendations for how to handle these problems (Brodzinsky & Pinderhughes, 2002):

What are some strategies for parenting adopted children at different points in their development?

- **Infancy.** Researchers have found few differences in the attachment that adopted and nonadopted infants form with their parents. However, attachment can become problematic if parents have unresolved fertility issues or the child does not meet the parents' expectations. Counselors can help prospective adoptive parents develop realistic expectations.
- **Early childhood.** Because many children begin to ask where they came from when they are about 4 to 6 years old, this is a natural time to begin to talk in simple ways to children about their adoption status (Warshak, 2007). Some parents (although not as many as in the past) decide not to tell their children about the adoption. This secrecy may create psychological risks for the child if he or she later finds out about the adoption.
- **Middle and late childhood.** During the elementary school years, children begin to show more interest in their origins and may ask questions related to where they came from, what their birth parents looked like, and why their birth parents placed them for adoption.

As they grow older, children may develop mixed feelings about being adopted and question their adoptive parents' explanations. It is important for adoptive parents to recognize that this ambivalence is normal. Also, problems may arise from the desire of adoptive parents to make life too perfect for the adoptive child and to present a perfect image of themselves to the child. The result too often is that adopted children feel that they cannot release any angry feelings or openly discuss problems.

- **Adolescence.** Adolescents are likely to develop more abstract and logical thinking, to focus their attention on their bodies, and to search for an identity. These characteristics provide the foundation for adopted adolescents to reflect on their adoption status in more complex ways, such as focusing on how they look so different from their adoptive parents. As they explore their identity, adopted adolescents may have difficulty incorporating their adopted status in positive ways into their identity. It is important for adoptive parents to understand the complexity of the adopted adolescent's identity exploration and be patient with the adolescent's lengthy identity search.

According to the information presented here and in the preceding text, how can mental health professionals help both adopting parents and adopted children?

Children who are adopted very early in their lives are more likely to have positive outcomes than children adopted later in life (Bernard & Dozier, 2008). A recent Danish study indicated that being adopted was not a risk for juvenile delinquency if the individual was adopted at 12 months of age or earlier (Laubjerg & Petersson, 2011). However, those adopted after 12 months of age had a three to four times higher risk of becoming a juvenile delinquent than their nonadopted counterparts.

Also keep in mind that the changes in adoption practice over the last several decades make it difficult to generalize about the average adopted child or average adoptive parent. To read more about adoption, see *Connecting Development to Life*, in which we discuss effective parenting strategies with adopted children.

4 Heredity-Environment Interaction: The Nature-Nurture Debate

LG4 Explain some of the ways that heredity and environment interact to produce individual differences in development.

| Behavior Genetics | Heredity-Environment Correlations | Shared and Nonshared Environmental Experiences | The Epigenetic View and Gene × Environment (G × E) Interaction | Conclusions About Heredity-Environment Interaction |

Is it possible to untangle the influence of heredity from that of environment and discover the role of each in producing individual differences in development? When heredity and environment interact, how does heredity influence the environment and vice versa?

BEHAVIOR GENETICS

Twin studies compare identical twins with fraternal twins. Identical twins develop from a single fertilized egg that splits into two genetically identical organisms. Fraternal twins develop from separate eggs, making them genetically no more similar than nontwin siblings. *What is the nature of the twin study method?*

Behavior genetics is the field that seeks to discover the influence of heredity and environment on individual differences in human traits and development (Maxson, 2013). Note that behavior genetics does not identify the extent to which genetics or the environment affects an individual's traits. Instead, what behavior geneticists try to do is to figure out what is responsible for the differences among people—that is, to what extent people vary because of differences in genes, environment, or a combination of these factors (Archontaki, Lewis, & Bates, 2012; Rhemtulla & Tucker-Drob, 2012; Wang & others, 2012). To study the influence of heredity on behavior, behavior geneticists often use either twins or adoption situations (Kubarych & others, 2012).

In the most common **twin study,** the behavioral similarity of identical twins (who are genetically identical) is compared with the behavioral similarity of fraternal twins. Recall that although fraternal twins share the same womb, they are no more genetically alike than non-twin siblings. Thus, by comparing groups of identical and fraternal twins, behavior geneticists capitalize on the basic knowledge that identical twins are more similar genetically than are fraternal twins (Bell & Saffery, 2012). For example, one study found that conduct problems were more prevalent in identical twins than fraternal twins; the researchers concluded that the study demonstrated an important role for heredity in conduct problems (Scourfield & others, 2004).

However, several issues complicate interpretation of twin studies. For example, perhaps the environments of identical twins are more similar than the environments of fraternal twins. Adults might stress the similarities of identical twins more than those of fraternal twins, and identical twins might perceive themselves as a "set" and play

Heredity-Environment Correlation	Description	Examples
Passive	Children inherit genetic tendencies from their parents, and parents also provide an environment that matches their own genetic tendencies.	Musically inclined parents usually have musically inclined children and they are likely to provide an environment rich in music for their children.
Evocative	The child's genetic tendencies elicit stimulation from the environment that supports a particular trait. Thus genes evoke environmental support.	A happy, outgoing child elicits smiles and friendly responses from others.
Active (niche-picking)	Children actively seek out "niches" in their environment that reflect their own interests and talents and are thus in accord with their genotype.	Libraries, sports fields, and a store with musical instruments are examples of environmental niches children might seek out if they have intellectual interests in books, talent in sports, or musical talents, respectively.

FIGURE **2.11**
EXPLORING HEREDITY-ENVIRONMENT CORRELATIONS

together more than fraternal twins do. If so, the influence of the environment on the observed similarities between identical and fraternal twins might be very significant.

In an **adoption study,** investigators seek to discover whether the behavior and psychological characteristics of adopted children are more like those of their adoptive parents, who have provided a home environment, or more like those of their biological parents, who have contributed their heredity (Kendler & others, 2012). Another form of the adoption study compares adoptive and biological siblings.

HEREDITY-ENVIRONMENT CORRELATIONS

The difficulties that researchers encounter when they interpret the results of twin studies and adoption studies reflect the complexities of heredity-environment interaction. Some of these interactions are heredity-environment correlations, which means that individuals' genes may influence the types of environments to which they are exposed. In a sense, individuals "inherit" environments that may be related or linked to genetic "propensities." Behavior geneticist Sandra Scarr (1993) described three ways that heredity and environment are correlated (see Figure 2.11):

- **Passive genotype-environment correlations** occur because biological parents, who are genetically related to the child, provide a rearing environment for the child. For example, the parents might have a genetic predisposition to be intelligent and read skillfully. Because they read well and enjoy reading, they provide their children with books to read. The likely outcome is that their children, given their own inherited predispositions from their parents and their book-filled environment, will become skilled readers.

- **Evocative genotype-environment correlations** occur because a child's genetically influenced characteristics elicit certain types of environments. For example, active, smiling children receive more social stimulation than passive, quiet children do. Cooperative, attentive children evoke more pleasant and instructional responses from the adults around them than uncooperative, distractible children do.

- **Active (niche-picking) genotype-environment correlations** occur when children seek out environments that they find compatible and stimulating. *Niche-picking* refers to finding a setting that is suited to one's genetically influenced abilities. Children select from their surrounding environment certain aspects that they respond to, learn about, or ignore. Their active selections of environments are related to their particular genotype. For example, outgoing children tend to seek out social contexts in which to interact with people, whereas shy children don't. Children who are musically inclined are likely to select musical environments in which they can successfully perform their skills. How these "tendencies" come about will be discussed shortly under the topic of the epigenetic view.

Scarr observes that the relative importance of the three genotype-environment correlations changes as children develop from infancy through adolescence. In infancy, much of the

behavior genetics The field that seeks to discover the influence of heredity and environment on individual differences in human traits and development.

twin study A study in which the behavioral similarity of identical twins is compared with the behavioral similarity of fraternal twins.

adoption study A study in which investigators seek to discover whether, in behavior and psychological characteristics, adopted children are more like their adoptive parents, who provided a home environment, or more like their biological parents, who contributed their heredity. Another form of the adoption study compares adoptive and biological siblings.

passive genotype-environment correlations Correlations that exist when the natural parents, who are genetically related to the child, provide a rearing environment for the child.

evocative genotype-environment correlations Correlations that exist when the child's genetically influenced characteristics elicit certain types of environments.

active (niche-picking) genotype-environment correlations Correlations that exist when children seek out environments they find compatible and stimulating.

Tennis stars Venus and Serena Williams. *What might be some shared and nonshared environmental experiences they had while they were growing up that contributed to their tennis stardom?*

environment that children experience is provided by adults. Thus, passive genotype-environment correlations are more common in the lives of infants and young children than they are for older children and adolescents who can extend their experiences beyond the family's influence, create, and select their environments to a greater degree.

SHARED AND NONSHARED ENVIRONMENTAL EXPERIENCES

Behavior geneticists have argued that to understand the environment's role in differences between people, we should distinguish between shared and nonshared environments. That is, we should consider experiences that children share in common with other children living in the same home, and experiences that are not shared (Marceau & others, 2012; Plomin & Daniels, 2011).

Shared environmental experiences are siblings' common experiences, such as their parents' personalities or intellectual orientation, the family's socioeconomic status, and the neighborhood in which they live. By contrast, **nonshared environmental experiences** consist of a child's unique experiences, both within the family and outside the family, that are not shared with a sibling. Even experiences occurring within the family can be part of the "nonshared environment." For example, parents often interact differently with each sibling, and siblings interact differently with parents. Siblings often have different peer groups, different friends, and different teachers at school, all of which contribute to their nonshared environments.

Behavior geneticist Robert Plomin (2004) has found that shared environment accounts for little of the variation in children's personality or interests. In other words, even though two children live under the same roof with the same parents, their personalities are often very different. Further, Plomin argues that heredity influences the nonshared environments of siblings through the heredity-environment correlations we described earlier. For example, a child who has inherited a tendency to be athletic is likely to spend more time in environments related to sports, and a child who has inherited a tendency to be musically inclined is more likely to spend time in environments related to music.

What are the implications of Plomin's interpretation of the role of shared and nonshared environments in development? In *The Nurture Assumption,* Judith Harris (1998, 2009) argued that what parents do does not make a difference in their children's and adolescents' behavior. Yell at them. Hug them. Read to them. Ignore them. Harris says it won't influence how they turn out. She argues based on data like Plomin's that genes and peers are far more important than parents in children's and adolescents' development.

Genes and peers do matter, but Harris' descriptions of peer influences do not take into account the complexity of peer contexts and developmental trajectories (Hartup, 2009). In addition, Harris is wrong in saying that parents don't matter. For example, in the early childhood years parents play an important role in selecting children's peers and indirectly influencing children's development (Baumrind, 1999). A large volume of parenting literature with many research studies documents the importance of parents in children's development (Grusec & others, 2013; Rodrigo & others, 2012). We will discuss parents' important roles throughout this book.

THE EPIGENETIC VIEW AND GENE × ENVIRONMENT (G × E) INTERACTION

Critics argue that the concept of heredity-environment correlation gives heredity too much of a one-sided influence in determining development because it does not consider the role of prior environmental influences in shaping the correlation itself (Gottlieb, 2007). However, earlier in the chapter we discussed how genes are collaborative, not determining an individual's traits in an independent manner but rather in an interactive manner with the environment.

The Epigenetic View   In line with the concept of a collaborative gene, Gilbert Gottlieb (2007) emphasizes the **epigenetic view,** which states that development is the result of an ongoing,

- - - - - - - - - - - ➤

developmental **connection**

Parenting

Is quantity or quality more important in parenting? Chapter 8, p. 255

shared environmental experiences Siblings' common environmental experiences, such as their parents' personalities and intellectual orientation, the family's socioeconomic status, and the neighborhood in which they live.

nonshared environmental experiences The child's own unique experiences, both within the family and outside the family, that are not shared with another sibling. Thus, experiences occurring within the family can be part of the "nonshared environment."

epigenetic view Emphasizes that development is the result of an ongoing, bidirectional interchange between heredity and environment.

bidirectional interchange between heredity and the environment. Figure 2.12 compares the heredity-environment correlation and epigenetic views of development.

Let's look at an example that reflects the epigenetic view. A baby inherits genes from both parents at conception. During prenatal development, toxins, nutrition, and stress can influence some genes to stop functioning while others become more active or less active. During infancy, environmental experiences such as toxins, nutrition, stress, learning, and encouragement continue to modify genetic activity and the activity of the nervous system that directly underlies behavior. Heredity and environment operate together—or collaborate—to produce a person's intelligence, temperament, height, weight, ability to pitch a baseball, ability to read, and so on (Gottlieb, 2007).

Gene × Environment (G × E) Interaction   An increasing number of studies are exploring how the interaction between heredity and environment influences development, including interactions that involve specific DNA sequences (Bihagi & others, 2012; Moore, 2013; Slomko, Heo, & Einstein, 2012). The epigenetic mechanisms involve the actual molecular modification of the DNA strand as a result of environmental inputs in ways that alter gene functioning (Feil & Fraga, 2012; Meaney, 2010).

One study found that individuals who have a short version of a gene labeled 5-HTTLPR (a gene involving the neurotransmitter serotonin) have an elevated risk of developing depression only if they *also* lead stressful lives (Caspi & others, 2003). Thus, the specific gene did not directly cause the development of depression; rather, the gene interacted with a stressful environment in a way that allowed the researchers to predict whether individuals would develop depression. Recent studies also have found support for the interaction between the 5-HTTLPR gene and stress levels in predicting depression in adolescents and older adults (Petersen & others, 2012; Zannas & others, 2012).

Other research involving interaction between genes and environmental experiences has focused on attachment, parenting, and supportive child rearing environments (Berry & others, 2012). In one study, adults who experienced parental loss as young children were more likely to have unresolved attachment issues as adults only when they had the short version of the 5-HTTLPR gene (Caspers & others, 2009). The long version of the serotonin transporter gene apparently provided some protection and ability to cope better with parental loss. Other recent research has found that variations in dopamine-related genes interact with supportive or unsupportive rearing environments to influence children's development (Bakermans-Kranenburg & van IJzendoorn, 2011). The type of research just described is referred to as studies of **gene × environment (G × E) interaction**—the interaction of a specific measured variation in DNA and a specific measured aspect of the environment (Alexander & others, 2012; Karg & Sen, 2012).

CONCLUSIONS ABOUT HEREDITY-ENVIRONMENT INTERACTION

If an attractive, popular, intelligent girl is elected president of her senior class in high school, is her success due to heredity or to environment? Of course, the answer is both.

The relative contributions of heredity and environment are not additive. That is, we can't say that such-and-such a percentage of nature and such-and-such a percentage of experience make us who we are. Nor is it accurate to say that full genetic expression happens once, around conception or birth, after which we carry our genetic legacy into the world to see how far it takes us. Genes produce proteins throughout the life span, in many different environments. Or they don't produce these proteins, depending in part on how harsh or nourishing those environments are.

The emerging view is that complex behaviors are influenced by genes in a way that gives people a propensity for a particular developmental trajectory (Plomin, 2012; Tucker-Drob & Harden, 2012). However, the actual development requires more: an environment. And that environment is complex, just like the mixture of genes we inherit (Gahagan, 2012). Environmental influences range from the things we lump together under "nurture" (such as parenting, family dynamics, schooling, and neighborhood quality) to biological encounters (such as viruses, birth complications, and even biological events occurring at the cellular level).

FIGURE 2.12

COMPARISON OF THE HEREDITY-ENVIRONMENT CORRELATION AND EPIGENETIC VIEWS

developmental **connection**

Attachment

A recent study revealed links between infant attachment, responsive parenting, and the 5-HTTLPR gene. Chapter 6, p. 192

developmental **connection**

Nature Versus Nurture

The relative importance of nature and nurture is one of the main debates in the study of life-span development. Chapter 1, p. 19

gene × environment (G × E) interaction The interaction of a specific measured variation in the DNA and a specific measured aspect of the environment.

Imagine for a moment that there is a cluster of genes somehow associated with youth violence (this example is hypothetical because we don't know of any such combination). The adolescent who carries this genetic mixture might experience a world of loving parents, regular nutritious meals, lots of books, and a series of masterful teachers. Or the adolescent's world might include parental neglect, a neighborhood in which gunshots and crime are everyday occurrences, and inadequate schooling. In which of these environments are the adolescent's genes likely to manufacture the biological underpinnings of criminality?

If heredity and environment interact to determine the course of development, is that all there is to answering the question of what causes development? Are humans completely at the mercy of their genes and environment as they develop through the life span? Our genetic heritage and environmental experiences are pervasive influences on development (Eaton & others, 2012). But in thinking about what causes development, recall from Chapter 1 our discussion of development as the co-construction of biology, culture, *and* the individual. Not only are we the outcomes of our heredity and the environment we experience, but we also can author a unique developmental path by changing the environment. As one psychologist recently concluded:

> In reality, we are both the creatures and creators of our worlds. We are . . . the products of our genes and environments. Nevertheless, . . . the stream of causation that shapes the future runs through our present choices . . . Mind matters . . . Our hopes, goals, and expectations influence our future. (Myers, 2010, p. 168)

developmental **connection**

Life-Span Perspective

An important aspect of the life-span perspective is the co-construction of biology, environment, and the individual. Chapter 1, p. 9

Review *Connect* Reflect

 LG4 Explain some of the ways that heredity and environment interact to produce individual differences in development.

Review

- What is behavior genetics?
- What are three types of heredity-environment correlations?
- What is meant by the concepts of shared and nonshared environmental experiences?
- What is the epigenetic view of development? What characterizes gene × environment (G × E) interaction?
- What conclusions can be reached about heredity-environment interaction?

Connect

- Of passive, evocative, and active genotype-environment correlations, which is the best explanation for the similarities discovered between the twins discussed in the chapter-opening story?

Reflect *Your Own Personal Journey of Life*

- Someone tells you that she has analyzed your genetic background and environmental experiences and concluded that environment definitely has had little influence on your intelligence. What would you say about this analysis?

topical **connections**

In the following chapters, we will continue to explore biological influences on development, especially in the chapters on physical development, but also in the chapters on cognitive and socioemotional development. For instance, biology's influence on infants' gross and fine motor skills (Chapter 4) may be obvious, but we will also discuss such research questions as "Is there a biological basis for sexual orientation?" (Chapter 13). In addition, we will examine reproduction when we look at adolescents (Chapter 11) and young adults (Chapter 14) who become parents. Finally, we will touch on the dual influence of nature and nurture in every period of life-span development.

looking forward

Biological Beginnings

1 The Evolutionary Perspective

 Discuss the evolutionary perspective on life-span development.

Natural Selection and Adaptive Behavior

Evolutionary Psychology

- Natural selection is the process by which those individuals of a species that are best adapted survive and reproduce. Darwin proposed that natural selection fuels evolution. In evolutionary theory, adaptive behavior is behavior that promotes the organism's survival in a natural habitat.

- Evolutionary psychology holds that adaptation, reproduction, and "survival of the fittest" are important in shaping behavior. Ideas proposed by evolutionary developmental psychology include the view that an extended childhood period is needed to develop a large brain and learn the complexity of human social communities. According to Baltes, the benefits resulting from evolutionary selection decrease with age mainly because of a decline in reproductive fitness. At the same time, cultural needs increase. Like other theoretical approaches to development, evolutionary psychology has limitations. Bandura rejects "one-sided evolutionism" and argues for a bidirectional link between biology and environment. Biology allows for a broad range of cultural possibilities.

2 Genetic Foundations of Development

 Describe what genes are and how they influence human development.

The Collaborative Gene

Genes and Chromosomes

Genetic Principles

Chromosomal and Gene-Linked Abnormalities

- Short segments of DNA constitute genes, the units of hereditary information that help cells to reproduce and manufacture proteins. Genes act collaboratively, not independently.

- Genes are passed on to new cells when chromosomes are duplicated during the processes of mitosis and meiosis, which are two ways in which new cells are formed. When an egg and a sperm unite in the fertilization process, the resulting zygote contains the genes from the chromosomes in the father's sperm and the mother's egg. Despite this transmission of genes from generation to generation, variability is created in several ways, including through the exchange of chromosomal segments during meiosis, through mutations, and through environmental influences.

- Genetic principles include those involving dominant-recessive genes, sex-linked genes, genetic imprinting, and polygenic inheritance.

- Chromosomal abnormalities produce Down syndrome, which is caused by the presence of an extra copy of chromosome 21. Other sex-linked conditions include Klinefelter syndrome, fragile X syndrome, Turner syndrome, and XYY syndrome. Gene-linked abnormalities involve harmful or absent genes. Gene-linked disorders include phenylketonuria (PKU) and sickle-cell anemia. Genetic counseling offers couples information about their risk of having a child with inherited abnormalities.

3 Reproductive Challenges and Choices

LG3 Identify some important reproductive challenges and choices.

Prenatal Diagnostic Tests

Infertility and Reproductive Technology

- Ultrasound sonography, fetal MRI, chorionic villus sampling, amniocentesis, and maternal blood screening are used to determine whether a fetus is developing normally. Noninvasive prenatal diagnosis is increasingly being explored.

- Approximately 10 to 15 percent of U.S. couples have infertility problems, some of which can be corrected through surgery or fertility drugs. An additional option is in vitro fertilization.

- A majority of adopted children adapt effectively. When adoption occurs very early in development, the outcomes for the child are improved. Because of the dramatic changes that occurred in adoption in recent decades, it is difficult to generalize about the average adopted child or average adoptive family.

4 Heredity-Environment Interaction: The Nature-Nurture Debate

 LG4 Explain some of the ways that heredity and environment interact to produce individual differences in development.

Behavior Genetics

- Behavior genetics is the field concerned with the influence of heredity and environment on individual differences in human traits and development. Methods used by behavior geneticists include twin studies and adoption studies.

Heredity-Environment Correlations

- In Scarr's heredity-environment correlations view, heredity directs the types of environments that children experience. She describes three genotype-environment correlations: passive, evocative, and active (niche-picking). Scarr argues that the relative importance of these three genotype-environment correlations changes as children develop.

Shared and Nonshared Environmental Experiences

- Shared environmental experiences refer to siblings' common experiences, such as their parents' personalities and intellectual orientation, the family's socioeconomic status, and the neighborhood in which they live. Nonshared environmental experiences involve the child's unique experiences, both within the family and outside the family, that are not shared with a sibling. Many behavior geneticists argue that differences in the development of siblings are due to nonshared environmental experiences (and heredity) rather than shared environmental experiences.

The Epigenetic View and Gene × Environment (G × E) Interaction

- The epigenetic view emphasizes that development is the result of an ongoing, bidirectional interchange between heredity and environment. Gene × environment interaction involves the interaction of a specific measured variation in the DNA and a specific measured aspect of the environment. An increasing number of G × E studies are being conducted.

Conclusions About Heredity-Environment Interaction

- Behaviors are influenced by genes in a way that gives people a propensity for a particular developmental trajectory. However, actual development also requires an environment, and that environment is complex. The interaction of heredity and environment is extensive. Much remains to be discovered about the specific ways that heredity and environment interact to influence development. Although heredity and environment are pervasive influences on development, however, humans can author a unique developmental path by changing their environments.

key terms

evolutionary psychology 53
chromosomes 55
DNA 55
genes 55
mitosis 56
meiosis 57
fertilization 57
zygote 57
genotype 58

phenotype 58
Down syndrome 59
Klinefelter syndrome 60
fragile X syndrome 60
Turner syndrome 60
XYY syndrome 60
phenylketonuria (PKU) 60
sickle-cell anemia 61
behavior genetics 69

twin study 69
adoption study 69
passive genotype-environment correlations 69
evocative genotype-environment correlations 69
active (niche-picking) genotype-environment correlations 69

shared environmental experiences 70
nonshared environmental experiences 70
epigenetic view 70
gene × environment (G × E) interaction 71

key people

Thomas Bouchard 51
Charles Darwin 52
David Buss 53

Paul Baltes 54
Albert Bandura 54
Stephen Jay Gould 54

David Moore 56
Sandra Scarr 69
Robert Plomin 70

Judith Harris 70
Gilbert Gottlieb 70

Chapter 2 | BIOLOGICAL BEGINNINGS

Connecting with

Learning Objectives	Application Activities	Activity Type	Page Reference
Describe the collaborative gene.	The Gene	Click & drag activity	pp. 55–56
	Genes and Chromosomes	Click & drag activity	
Describe genes and chromosomes.	Sources of Variability: Twins	Click & drag activity	pp. 56–58
Describe genetic principles.	Genetic Principles	Click & drag activity	pp. 58–59

PRENATAL DEVELOPMENT AND BIRTH

chapter **outline**

1 Prenatal Development

Learning Goal 1 Describe prenatal development.

The Course of Prenatal Development
Teratology and Hazards to Prenatal Development
Prenatal Care
Normal Prenatal Development

2 Birth

Learning Goal 2 Describe the birth process.

The Birth Process
Assessing the Newborn
Preterm and Low Birth Weight Infants

3 The Postpartum Period

Learning Goal 3 Explain the changes that take place in the postpartum period.

Physical Adjustments
Emotional and Psychological Adjustments
Bonding

Diana and Roger married when he was 38 and she was 34. Both worked full-time and were excited when Diana became pregnant. Two months later, Diana began to have some unusual pains and bleeding. Just two months into her pregnancy she had lost the baby. Diana thought deeply about why she was unable to carry the baby to full term. It was about the time she became pregnant that the federal government began to warn that eating certain types of fish with a high mercury content during pregnancy on a regular basis can cause a miscarriage. Now she eliminated those fish from her diet.

Six months later, Diana became pregnant again. She and Roger read about pregnancy and signed up for birth preparation classes. Each Friday night for eight weeks they practiced simulated contractions. They talked about what kind of parents they wanted to be and discussed what changes in their lives the baby would make. When they found out that their offspring was going to be a boy, they gave him a name: Mr. Littles.

Alex, also known as "Mr. Littles."

This time, Diana's pregnancy went well, and Alex, also known as Mr. Littles, was born. During the birth, however, Diana's heart rate dropped precipitously, and she was given a stimulant to raise it. Apparently the stimulant also increased Alex's heart rate and breathing to a dangerous point, and he had to be placed in a neonatal intensive care unit (NICU).

Several times a day, Diana and Roger visited Alex in the NICU. A number of babies in the NICU with very low birth weights had been in intensive care for weeks, and some of the babies were not doing well. Fortunately, Alex was in better health. After he had spent several days in the NICU, his parents were permitted to take home a very healthy Alex.

topical connections ----------

Genes form the biological basis of our development. They are passed on through mitosis, meiosis, and, ultimately, fertilization. The impact of our genes involves the genetic principles of dominate-recessive genes, sex-linked genes, genetic imprinting, and polygenically determined characteristics. Approximately 10 to 15 percent of U.S. couples have problems with fertility. Some of these problems can be solved through surgery, drugs, or in vitro fertilization. Whether a pregnancy occurs naturally or with assistance, the resulting infant's development is shaped both by his or her genes (nature) and environment (nurture).

◄--- *looking back* -------------

preview

This chapter chronicles the truly remarkable developments from conception through birth. Imagine . . . at one time you were an organism floating in a sea of fluid in your mother's womb. Let's now explore what your development was like from the time you were conceived through the time you were born. We will explore normal development in the prenatal period, as well as the period's hazards (such as high levels of mercury that were mentioned in the preceding story). We also will study the birth process and tests used to assess the newborn; discuss parents' adjustment in the postpartum period; and evaluate parent-infant bonding.

1 Prenatal Development · **LG1** Describe prenatal development.

- The Course of Prenatal Development
- Teratology and Hazards to Prenatal Development
- Prenatal Care
- Normal Prenatal Development

Imagine how Alex ("Mr. Littles") came to be. Out of thousands of eggs and millions of sperm, one egg and one sperm united to produce him. Had the union of sperm and egg come a day or even an hour earlier or later, he might have been very different—maybe even of the opposite sex. Conception occurs when a single sperm cell from the male unites with an ovum (egg) in the female's fallopian tube in a process called fertilization. Over the next few months, the genetic code discussed in Chapter 2 directs a series of changes in the fertilized egg, but many events and hazards will influence how that egg develops and becomes tiny Alex.

THE COURSE OF PRENATAL DEVELOPMENT

Typical prenatal development, which begins with fertilization and ends with birth, takes between 266 and 280 days (38 to 40 weeks). It can be divided into three periods: germinal, embryonic, and fetal.

The Germinal Period   The **germinal period** is the period of prenatal development that takes place in the first two weeks after conception. It includes the creation of the fertilized egg, called a zygote, cell division, and the attachment of the zygote to the uterine wall.

Rapid cell division by the zygote continues throughout the germinal period (recall from Chapter 2 that this cell division occurs through a process called mitosis). By approximately one week after conception, the differentiation of these cells—their specialization to perform various tasks—has already begun. At this stage, the group of cells, now called the **blastocyst,** consists of an inner mass of cells that will eventually develop into the embryo, and the **trophoblast,** an outer layer of cells that later provides nutrition and support for the embryo. Implantation, the attachment of the zygote to the uterine wall, takes place about 11 to 15 days after conception. Figure 3.1 illustrates some of the most significant developments during the germinal period.

The Embryonic Period   The **embryonic period** is the period of prenatal development that occurs from two to eight weeks after conception. During the embryonic period, the rate of cell differentiation intensifies, support systems for cells form, and organs appear.

This period begins as the blastocyst attaches to the uterine wall. The mass of cells is now called an *embryo*, and three layers of cells form. The embryo's *endoderm* is the inner layer of cells, which will develop into the digestive and respiratory systems. The *mesoderm* is the middle layer, which will become the circulatory system, bones, muscles, excretory system, and reproductive system. The *ectoderm* is the outermost layer, which will become

germinal period The period of prenatal development that takes place in the first two weeks after conception. It includes the creation of the zygote, continued cell division, and the attachment of the zygote to the uterine wall.

blastocyst The inner layer of cells that develops during the germinal period. These cells later develop into the embryo.

trophoblast The outer layer of cells that develops in the germinal period. These cells provide nutrition and support for the embryo.

embryonic period The period of prenatal development that occurs two to eight weeks after conception. During the embryonic period, the rate of cell differentiation intensifies, support systems for the cells form, and organs appear.

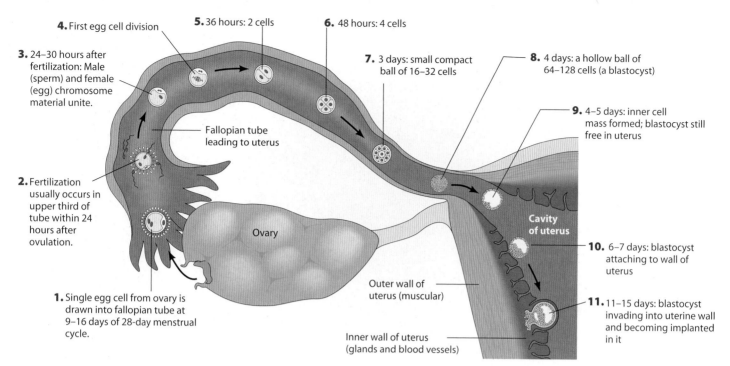

4. First egg cell division

5. 36 hours: 2 cells

6. 48 hours: 4 cells

3. 24–30 hours after fertilization: Male (sperm) and female (egg) chromosome material unite.

7. 3 days: small compact ball of 16–32 cells

8. 4 days: a hollow ball of 64–128 cells (a blastocyst)

9. 4–5 days: inner cell mass formed; blastocyst still free in uterus

Fallopian tube leading to uterus

2. Fertilization usually occurs in upper third of tube within 24 hours after ovulation.

Ovary

Cavity of uterus

10. 6–7 days: blastocyst attaching to wall of uterus

11. 11–15 days: blastocyst invading into uterine wall and becoming implanted in it

1. Single egg cell from ovary is drawn into fallopian tube at 9–16 days of 28-day menstrual cycle.

Outer wall of uterus (muscular)

Inner wall of uterus (glands and blood vessels)

FIGURE **3.1**

SIGNIFICANT DEVELOPMENTS IN THE GERMINAL PERIOD. Just one week after conception, cells of the blastocyst have already begun specializing. The germination period ends when the blastocyst attaches to the uterine wall. *Which of the steps shown in the drawing occur in the laboratory when IVF (described in Chapter 2) is used?*

the nervous system and brain, sensory receptors (ears, nose, and eyes, for example), and skin parts (hair and nails, for example). Every body part eventually develops from these three layers. The endoderm primarily produces internal body parts, the mesoderm primarily produces parts that surround the internal areas, and the ectoderm primarily produces surface parts.

As the embryo's three layers form, life-support systems for the embryo develop rapidly. These life-support systems include the amnion, the umbilical cord (both of which develop from the fertilized egg, not the mother's body), and the placenta. The **amnion** is like a bag or an envelope and contains a clear fluid in which the developing embryo floats. The amniotic fluid provides an environment that is temperature and humidity controlled, as well as shockproof. The **umbilical cord** contains two arteries and one vein, and connects the baby to the placenta. The **placenta** consists of a disk-shaped group of tissues in which small blood vessels from the mother and the offspring intertwine but do not join.

Figure 3.2 illustrates the placenta, the umbilical cord, and the blood flow in the expectant mother and developing organism. Very small molecules—oxygen, water, salt, food from the mother's blood, as well as carbon dioxide and digestive wastes from the offspring's blood—pass back and forth between the mother and embryo or fetus (Woolett, 2011). Virtually any drug or chemical substance the pregnant woman ingests can cross the placenta to some degree, unless it is metabolized or altered during passage, or is too large (Else & others, 2011; Iqbal & others, 2012). A recent study revealed that cigarette smoke weakened and increased the oxidative stress of fetal membranes, from which the placenta develops (Menon & others, 2011). Large molecules that cannot pass through the placental wall include red blood cells and harmful substances, such as most bacteria, maternal wastes, and hormones. The complex mechanisms that govern the transfer of substances across the placental barrier are still not entirely understood (Antonucci & others, 2012; Saunders, Liddelow, & Dziegielewska, 2012).

By the time most women know they are pregnant, the major organs have begun to form. **Organogenesis** is the name given to the process of organ formation during the first two

amnion The life-support system that is a bag or envelope that contains a clear fluid in which the developing embryo floats.

umbilical cord A life-support system containing two arteries and one vein that connects the baby to the placenta.

placenta A life-support system that consists of a disk-shaped group of tissues in which small blood vessels from the mother and offspring intertwine.

organogenesis Organ formation that takes place during the first two months of prenatal development.

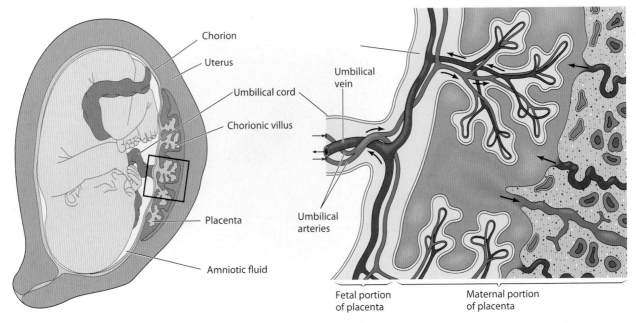

FIGURE **3.2**

THE PLACENTA AND THE UMBILICAL CORD. The area bound by the square is enlarged in the right half of the illustration. Arrows indicate the direction of blood flow. Maternal blood flows through the uterine arteries to the spaces housing the placenta, and it returns through the uterine veins to the maternal circulation. Fetal blood flows through the umbilical arteries into the capillaries of the placenta and returns through the umbilical vein to the fetal circulation. The exchange of materials takes place across the layer separating the maternal and fetal blood supplies, so the bloods never come into contact. *What is known about how the placental barrier works and its importance?*

months of prenatal development. While they are being formed, the organs are especially vulnerable to environmental changes (Rojas & others, 2010). In the third week after conception, the neural tube that eventually becomes the spinal cord forms. At about 21 days, eyes begin to appear, and at 24 days the cells for the heart begin to differentiate. During the fourth week, the urogenital system becomes apparent, and arm and leg buds emerge. Four chambers of the heart take shape, and blood vessels appear. From the fifth to the eighth week, arms and legs differentiate further; at this time, the face starts to form but still is not very recognizable. The intestinal tract develops and the facial structures fuse. At eight weeks, the developing organism weighs about 1/30 ounce and is just over 1 inch long.

The Fetal Period   The **fetal period,** lasting about seven months, is the prenatal period between two months after conception and birth in typical pregnancies. Growth and development continue their dramatic course during this time.

Three months after conception, the fetus is about 3 inches long and weighs about 3 ounces. It has become active, moving its arms and legs, opening and closing its mouth, and moving its head. The face, forehead, eyelids, nose, and chin are distinguishable, as are the upper arms, lower arms, hands, and lower limbs. In most cases, the genitals can be identified as male or female. By the end of the fourth month of pregnancy, the fetus has grown to 6 inches in length and weighs 4 to 7 ounces. At this time, a growth spurt occurs in the body's lower parts. For the first time, the mother can feel arm and leg movements.

By the end of the fifth month, the fetus is about 12 inches long and weighs close to a pound. Structures of the skin have formed—toenails and fingernails, for example. The fetus is more active, showing a preference for a particular position in the womb. By the end of the sixth month, the fetus is about 14 inches long and has gained another half pound to a pound. The eyes and eyelids are completely formed, and a fine layer of hair covers the head. A grasping reflex is present and irregular breathing movements occur.

As early as six months of pregnancy (about 24 to 25 weeks after conception), the fetus for the first time has a chance of surviving outside of the womb—that is, it is viable. Infants

The history of man for the nine months preceding his birth would, probably, be far more interesting, and contain events of greater moment, than all the three score and ten years that follow it.

—SAMUEL TAYLOR COLERIDGE
English Poet and Essayist, 19th Century

fetal period Lasting about seven months, the prenatal period between two months after conception and birth in typical pregnancies.

First trimester (first 3 months)

Conception to 4 weeks

- Is less than $\frac{1}{10}$ inch long
- Beginning development of spinal cord, nervous system, gastrointestinal system, heart, and lungs
- Amniotic sac envelopes the preliminary tissues of entire body
- Is called a "zygote"

8 weeks

- Is just over 1 inch long
- Face is forming with rudimentary eyes, ears, mouth, and tooth buds
- Arms and legs are moving
- Brain is forming
- Fetal heartbeat is detectable with ultrasound
- Is called an "embryo"

12 weeks

- Is about 3 inches long and weighs about 1 ounce
- Can move arms, legs, fingers, and toes
- Fingerprints are present
- Can smile, frown, suck, and swallow
- Sex is distinguishable
- Can urinate
- Is called a "fetus"

Second trimester (middle 3 months)

16 weeks

- Is about 6 inches long and weighs about 4 to 7 ounces
- Heartbeat is strong
- Skin is thin, transparent
- Downy hair (lanugo) covers body
- Fingernails and toenails are forming
- Has coordinated movements; is able to roll over in amniotic fluid

20 weeks

- Is about 12 inches long and weighs close to 1 pound
- Heartbeat is audible with ordinary stethoscope
- Sucks thumb
- Hiccups
- Hair, eyelashes, eyebrows are present

24 weeks

- Is about 14 inches long and weighs 1 to $1\frac{1}{2}$ pounds
- Skin is wrinkled and covered with protective coating (vernix caseosa)
- Eyes are open
- Waste matter is collected in bowel
- Has strong grip

Third trimester (last 3 months)

28 weeks

- Is about 16 inches long and weighs about 3 pounds
- Is adding body fat
- Is very active
- Rudimentary breathing movements are present

32 weeks

- Is $16\frac{1}{2}$ to 18 inches long and weighs 4 to 5 pounds
- Has periods of sleep and wakefulness
- Responds to sounds
- May assume the birth position
- Bones of head are soft and flexible
- Iron is being stored in liver

36 to 38 weeks

- Is 19 to 20 inches long and weighs 6 to $7\frac{1}{2}$ pounds
- Skin is less wrinkled
- Vernix caseosa is thick
- Lanugo is mostly gone
- Is less active
- Is gaining immunities from mother

FIGURE **3.3**

THE THREE TRIMESTERS OF PRENATAL DEVELOPMENT. Both the germinal and embryonic periods occur during the first trimester. The end of the first trimester as well as the second and third trimesters are part of the fetal period.

who are born early, or between 24 and 37 weeks of pregnancy, usually need help breathing because their lungs are not yet fully mature. By the end of the seventh month, the fetus is about 16 inches long and now weighs about 3 pounds.

During the last two months of prenatal development, fatty tissues develop, and the functioning of various organ systems—heart and kidneys, for example—steps up. During the eighth and ninth months, the fetus grows longer and gains substantial weight—about another 4 pounds. At birth, the average American baby weighs 7½ pounds and is about 20 inches long.

Figure 3.3 gives an overview of the main events during prenatal development. Notice that instead of describing development in terms of germinal, embryonic, and fetal periods, Figure 3.3 divides prenatal development into equal periods of three months, called trimesters. Remember that the three trimesters are not the same as the three prenatal periods we have discussed. The

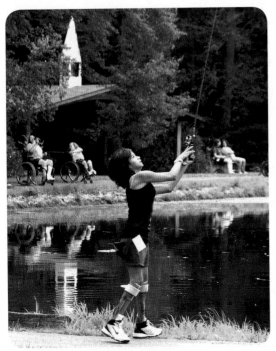

Yelyi Nordone, 12, of New York City, casts her line out into the pond during Camp Spifida at Camp Victory, near Millville, Pennsylvania, in July 2008. Camp Spifida is a week-long residential camp for children with spina bifida.

developmental **connection**

Brain Development

At birth, infants' brains weigh approximately 25 percent of what they will weigh in adulthood. Chapter 4, p. 112

FIGURE **3.4**

EARLY FORMATION OF THE NERVOUS SYSTEM. The photograph shows the primitive, tubular appearance of the nervous system at six weeks in the human embryo.

germinal and embryonic periods occur in the first trimester. The fetal period begins toward the end of the first trimester and continues through the second and third trimesters. Viability (the chances of surviving outside the womb) occurs at the very end of the second trimester.

The Brain   One of the most remarkable aspects of the prenatal period is the development of the brain (Nelson, 2012). By the time babies are born, they have approximately 100 billion **neurons,** or nerve cells, which handle information processing at the cellular level in the brain. During prenatal development, neurons spend time moving to the right locations and are starting to become connected. The basic architecture of the human brain is assembled during the first two trimesters of prenatal development. In typical development, the third trimester of prenatal development and the first two years of postnatal life are characterized by connectivity and functioning of neurons.

As the human embryo develops inside its mother's womb, the nervous system begins forming as a long, hollow tube located on the embryo's back. This pear-shaped neural tube, which forms at about 18 to 24 days after conception, develops out of the ectoderm. The tube closes at the top and bottom ends at about 24 days after conception. Figure 3.4 shows that the nervous system still has a tubular appearance six weeks after conception.

Two birth defects related to a failure of the neural tube to close are anencephaly and spina bifida. The highest regions of the brain fail to develop when fetuses have anencephaly or when the head end of the neural tube fails to close, and they die in the womb, during childbirth, or shortly after birth (Stoll & others, 2011). Spina bifida results in varying degrees of paralysis of the lower limbs. Individuals with spina bifida usually need assistive devices such as crutches, braces, or wheelchairs. Both maternal diabetes and obesity place the fetus at risk for developing neural tube defects (Stern & others, 2011). A strategy that can help to prevent neural tube defects is for women to take adequate amounts of the B vitamin folic acid, a topic we will further discuss later in the chapter (Collins & others, 2011).

In a normal pregnancy, once the neural tube has closed, a massive proliferation of new immature neurons begins to takes place about the fifth prenatal week and continues throughout the remainder of the prenatal period. The generation of new neurons is called *neurogenesis* (Kronenberg & others, 2010). At the peak of neurogenesis, it is estimated that as many as 200,000 neurons are being generated every minute.

At approximately 6 to 24 weeks after conception, *neuronal migration* occurs (Nelson, 2012). This involves cells moving outward from their point of origin to their appropriate locations and creating the different levels, structures, and regions of the brain (Zeisel, 2011). Once a cell has migrated to its target destination, it must mature and develop a more complex structure.

At about the 23rd prenatal week, connections between neurons begin to occur, a process that continues postnatally (Kostovic, Judas, & Sedmak, 2011). We will have much more to say about the structure of neurons, their connectivity, and the development of the infant brain in Chapter 4.

TERATOLOGY AND HAZARDS TO PRENATAL DEVELOPMENT

For Alex, the baby discussed at the opening of this chapter, the course of prenatal development went smoothly. His mother's womb protected him as he developed. Despite this protection, the environment can affect the embryo or fetus in many well-documented ways.

General Principles   A **teratogen** is any agent that can potentially cause a birth defect or negatively alter cognitive and behavioral outcomes. (The word comes from the Greek word *tera,* meaning "monster.") So many teratogens exist that practically every fetus is exposed to at least some teratogens. For this reason, it is difficult to determine which teratogen causes which problem. In addition, it may take a long time for the effects of a teratogen to show up. Only about half of all potential effects appear at birth.

The field of study that investigates the causes of birth defects is called teratology (Hyoun & others, 2012; Rasmussen, 2012). Some exposures to teratogens do not cause physical birth defects but can alter the developing brain and influence cognitive and behavioral functioning, in which case the field of study is called behavioral teratology.

The dose, genetic susceptibility, and the time of exposure to a particular teratogen influence both the severity of the damage to an embryo or fetus and the type of defect:

- *Dose.* The dose effect is rather obvious—the greater the dose of an agent, such as a drug, the greater the effect.

- *Genetic susceptibility.* The type or severity of abnormalities caused by a teratogen is linked to the genotype of the pregnant woman and the genotype of the embryo or fetus (Charlet & others, 2012; Schachter & Kohane, 2011). For example, how a mother metabolizes a particular drug can influence the degree to which the drug effects are transmitted to the embryo or fetus. The extent to which an embryo or fetus is vulnerable to a teratogen may also depend on its genotype (Dufour-Rainfray & others, 2011). Also, for unknown reasons, male fetuses are far more likely to be affected by teratogens than female fetuses.

- *Time of exposure.* Exposure to teratogens does more damage when it occurs at some points in development than at others (Holmes & Westgate, 2011). Damage during the germinal period may even prevent implantation. In general, the embryonic period is more vulnerable than the fetal period.

Figure 3.5 summarizes additional information about the effects of time of exposure to a teratogen. The probability of a structural defect is greatest early in the embryonic period, when organs are being formed (Holmes, 2011). Each body structure has its own critical period of formation. Recall from Chapter 1 that a critical period is a fixed time period very early in development during which certain experiences or events can have a long-lasting effect on development. The critical period for the nervous system (week 3) is earlier than for arms and legs (weeks 4 and 5).

After organogenesis is complete, teratogens are less likely to cause anatomical defects. Instead, exposure during the fetal period is more likely instead to stunt growth or to create problems in the way organs function. To examine some key teratogens and their effects, let's begin with drugs.

Prescription and Nonprescription Drugs   Many U.S. women are given prescriptions for drugs while they are pregnant—especially antibiotics, analgesics, and asthma medications. Prescription as well as nonprescription drugs, however, may have effects on the embryo or fetus that the women never imagine.

Prescription drugs that can function as teratogens include antibiotics, such as streptomycin and tetracycline; some antidepressants; certain hormones, such as progestin and synthetic estrogen; and Accutane (which often is prescribed for acne) (Crijns & others, 2012; Koren & Nordeng, 2012).

Nonprescription drugs that can be harmful include diet pills and high dosages of aspirin (Wojtowicz & others, 2011). However, recent studies indicated that low doses of aspirin pose no harm for the fetus but that high doses can contribute to maternal and fetal bleeding (Bennett, Bagot, & Arya, 2012; Marret & others, 2010).

Psychoactive Drugs   *Psychoactive drugs* are drugs that act on the nervous system to alter states of consciousness, modify perceptions, and change moods. Examples include caffeine, alcohol, and nicotine, as well as illicit drugs such as cocaine, methamphetamine, marijuana, and heroin.

Caffeine   People often consume caffeine when they drink coffee, tea, or colas, or when they eat chocolate. A recent research review found that high amounts of caffeine consumption by pregnant women do not increase the risk of miscarriage, congenital malformations, or growth retardation (Brent, Christian, & Diener, 2011). However, the U.S. Food and Drug

neurons Nerve cells, which handle information processing at the cellular level in the brain.

teratogen From the Greek word *tera,* meaning "monster." Any agent that causes a birth defect. The field of study that investigates the causes of birth defects is called teratology.

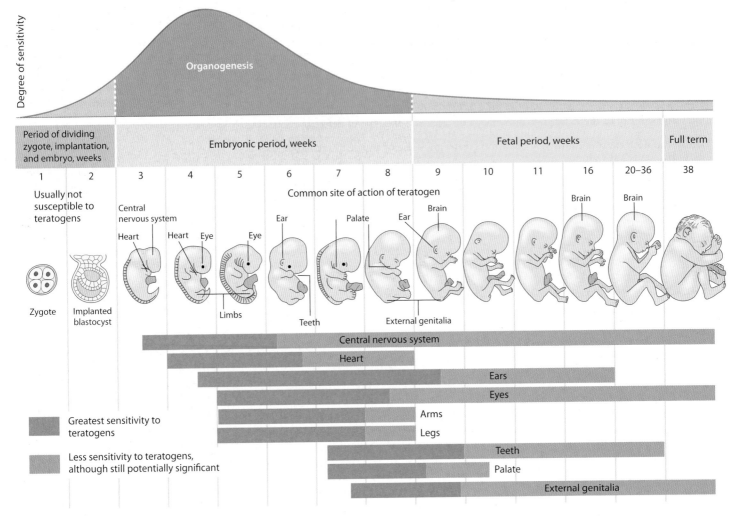

FIGURE **3.5**

TERATOGENS AND THE TIMING OF THEIR EFFECTS ON PRENATAL DEVELOPMENT. The danger of structural defects caused by teratogens is greatest early in embryonic development. The period of organogenesis (red color) lasts for about six weeks. Later assaults by teratogens (blue-green color) mainly occur in the fetal period and instead of causing structural damage are more likely to stunt growth or cause problems of organ function.

Fetal alcohol spectrum disorders (FASD) are characterized by a number of physical abnormalities and learning problems. Notice the wide-set eyes, flat cheekbones, and thin upper lip in this child with FASD.

Administration recommends that pregnant women either not consume caffeine or consume it only sparingly.

Alcohol Heavy drinking by pregnant women can be devastating to their offspring (Brocardo, Gil-Mohapel, & Christie, 2011). **Fetal alcohol spectrum disorders (FASD)** are a cluster of abnormalities and problems that appear in the offspring of mothers who drink alcohol heavily during pregnancy. The abnormalities include facial deformities and defective limbs, face, and heart (Painter, Williams, & Burd, 2012a, b). Most children with FASD have learning problems and many are below average in intelligence, with some that are mentally retarded (Painter, Williams, & Burd, 2012b). A recent study revealed that children with FASD have deficiencies in the brain pathways involved in working memory (Diwadkar & others, 2012). Although many mothers of FASD infants are heavy drinkers, many mothers who are heavy drinkers do not have children with FASD or have one child with FASD and other children who do not have it.

What are some guidelines for alcohol use during pregnancy? Even drinking just one or two servings of beer or wine or one serving of hard liquor a few days a week can have negative effects on the fetus, although it is generally agreed that this level of alcohol use will not cause fetal alcohol syndrome (Cheng & others, 2011; Valenzeula & others, 2012). The U.S.

Surgeon General recommends that no alcohol be consumed during pregnancy. And research suggests that it may not be wise to consume alcohol at the time of conception. One study revealed that intakes of alcohol by both men and women during the weeks of conception increased the risk of early pregnancy loss (Henriksen & others, 2004).

Nicotine   Cigarette smoking by pregnant women can also adversely influence prenatal development, birth, and postnatal development (Wehby & others, 2011). Preterm births and low birth weights, fetal and neonatal deaths, respiratory problems, and sudden infant death syndrome (SIDS, also known as crib death) are all more common among the offspring of mothers who smoked during pregnancy (Beyerlein & others, 2011; Burstyn & others, 2012).

Maternal smoking during pregnancy also has been identified as a risk factor for the development of attention deficit hyperactivity disorder in offspring (Abbott & Winzer-Serhan, 2012; Sagiv & others, 2012). Recent studies also indicate that environmental tobacco smoke is linked to an increased risk of low birth weight in offspring and to diminished ovarian functioning in female offspring (Leonardi-Bee & others, 2008; Kilic & others, 2012). Also, a recent meta-analysis indicated that maternal smoking during pregnancy predicted a modest increase in risk for childhood non-Hodgkin lymphoma (Antonopoulos & others, 2011).

What are some links between expectant mothers' alcohol and nicotine intake to outcomes for their offspring?

Cocaine   Does cocaine use during pregnancy harm the developing embryo and fetus? A recent research review concluded that that cocaine quickly crosses the placenta to reach the fetus (De Giovanni & Marchetti, 2012). The most consistent finding is that cocaine exposure during prenatal development is associated with reduced birth weight, length, and head circumference (Gouin & others, 2011). Also, in other studies, prenatal cocaine exposure has been linked to lower arousal, less effective self-regulation, higher excitability, and lower quality of reflexes at 1 month of age (Lester & others, 2002); to impaired motor development at 2 years of age and a slower rate of growth through 10 years of age (Richardson, Goldschmidt, & Willford, 2008); to deficits in behavioral self-regulation (Ackerman, Riggins, & Black, 2010); to elevated blood pressure at 9 years of age (Shankaran & others, 2010); to impaired language development and information processing (Beeghly & others, 2006), including attention deficits (especially impulsivity) (Accornero & others, 2006; Richardson & others, 2011); to learning disabilities at age 7 (Morrow & others, 2006); to increased likelihood of being in a special education program that involves support services (Levine & others, 2008); and to increased behavioral problems, especially externalizing problems such as high rates of aggression and delinquency (Minnes & others, 2010; Richardson & others, 2011).

Some researchers argue that these findings should be interpreted cautiously (Accornero & others, 2006). Why? Because other factors in the lives of pregnant women who use cocaine (such as poverty, malnutrition, and other substance abuse) often cannot be ruled out as possible contributors to the problems found in their children (Hurt & others, 2005; Messiah & others, 2011). For example, cocaine users are more likely than nonusers to smoke cigarettes, use marijuana, drink alcohol, and take amphetamines.

Despite these cautions, the weight of research evidence indicates that children born to mothers who use cocaine are likely to have neurological, medical, and cognitive deficits (Field, 2007; Mayer & Zhang, 2009; Richardson & others, 2011). Cocaine use by pregnant women is never recommended.

This baby was exposed to cocaine prenatally. *What are some of the possible effects on development of being exposed to cocaine prenatally?*

Methamphetamine   Methamphetamine, like cocaine, is a stimulant, speeding up an individual's nervous system. Babies born to mothers who use methamphetamine, or "meth," during pregnancy are at risk for a number of problems, including high infant mortality, low birth weight,

fetal alcohol spectrum disorders (FASD) A cluster of abnormalities that appear in the offspring of mothers who drink alcohol heavily during pregnancy.

and developmental and behavioral problems (Piper & others, 2011). A recent study revealed that prenatal meth exposure was associated with smaller head circumference, neonatal intensive care unit (NICU) admission, and referral to child protective services (Shah & others, 2012). Another study found that prenatal exposure to meth was linked to less brain activation in a number of areas, especially the frontal lobes, in 7- to 15-year-olds (Roussotte, 2011).

Marijuana   An increasing number of studies find that marijuana use by pregnant women also has negative outcomes for offspring. For example, researchers found that prenatal marijuana exposure was related to lower intelligence in children (Goldschmidt & others, 2008). Another study indicated that prenatal exposure to marijuana was linked to marijuana use at 14 years of age (Day, Goldschmidt, & Thomas, 2006). In sum, marijuana use is not recommended for pregnant women.

Heroin   It is well documented that infants whose mothers are addicted to heroin show several behavioral difficulties at birth (Ortigosa Gomez & others, 2011). The difficulties include withdrawal symptoms, such as tremors, irritability, abnormal crying, disturbed sleep, and impaired motor control. Many still show behavioral problems at their first birthday, and attention deficits may appear later in development. The most common treatment for heroin addiction, methadone, is associated with very severe withdrawal symptoms in newborns (Blandthorn, Forster, & Love, 2011).

Incompatible Blood Types   Incompatibility between the mother's and father's blood types poses another risk to prenatal development (Matsuda & others, 2011). Blood types are created by differences in the surface structure of red blood cells. One type of difference in the surface of red blood cells creates the familiar blood groups—A, B, O, and AB. A second difference creates what is called Rh-positive and Rh-negative blood. If a surface marker, called the Rh-factor, is present in an individual's red blood cells, the person is said to be Rh-positive; if the Rh-marker is not present, the person is said to be Rh-negative. If a pregnant woman is Rh-negative and her partner is Rh-positive, the fetus may be Rh-positive. If the fetus' blood is Rh-positive and the mother's is Rh-negative, the mother's immune system may produce antibodies that will attack the fetus. This can result in any number of problems, including miscarriage or stillbirth, anemia, jaundice, heart defects, brain damage, or death soon after birth (Li & others, 2010).

Generally, the first Rh-positive baby of an Rh-negative mother is not at risk, but with each subsequent pregnancy the risk increases. A vaccine (RhoGAM) may be given to the mother within three days of the first child's birth to prevent her body from making antibodies that will attack any future Rh-positive fetuses in subsequent pregnancies. Also, babies affected by Rh incompatibility can be given blood transfusions before or right after birth (Goodnough & others, 2011).

Environmental Hazards   Many aspects of our modern industrial world can endanger the embryo or fetus. Some specific hazards to the embryo or fetus include radiation, toxic wastes, and other chemical pollutants (Wiesel & others, 2011).

X-ray radiation can affect the developing embryo or fetus, especially in the first several weeks after conception, when women do not yet know they are pregnant. Women and their physicians should weigh the risk of an X-ray when an actual or potential pregnancy is involved (Rajaraman & others, 2011). However, a routine diagnostic X-ray of a body area other than the abdomen, with the woman's abdomen protected by a lead apron, is generally considered safe (Brent, 2009, 2011).

Environmental pollutants and toxic wastes are also sources of danger to unborn children. Among the dangerous pollutants are carbon monoxide, mercury, and lead, as well as certain fertilizers and pesticides.

Maternal Diseases   Maternal diseases and infections can produce defects in offspring by crossing the placental barrier, or they can cause damage during birth. Rubella (German measles) is one disease that can cause prenatal defects. Women who plan to have children should have a blood test before they become pregnant to determine whether they are immune to the disease (Rasmussen, 2012; Reef & others, 2011).

An explosion at the Chernobyl nuclear power plant in the Ukraine produced radioactive contamination that spread to surrounding areas. Thousands of infants were born with health problems and deformities as a result of the nuclear contamination, including this boy whose arm did not form. *Other than radioactive contamination, what are some other types of environmental hazards to prenatal development?*

Syphilis (a sexually transmitted infection) is more damaging later in prenatal development—four months or more after conception. Damage to offspring includes stillbirth, eye lesions (which can cause blindness), skin lesions, and congenital syphilis (Caddy & others, 2011; Ishaque & others, 2011).

Another infection that has received widespread attention is genital herpes. Newborns contract this virus when they are delivered through the birth canal of a mother with genital herpes (Li & others, 2011; Nigro & others, 2011). About one-third of babies delivered through an infected birth canal die; another one-fourth become brain damaged. If an active case of genital herpes is detected in a pregnant woman close to her delivery date, a cesarean section can be performed (in which the infant is delivered through an incision in the mother's abdomen) to keep the virus from infecting the newborn (Patel & others, 2011).

AIDS is a sexually transmitted infection that is caused by the human immunodeficiency virus (HIV), which destroys the body's immune system. A mother can infect her offspring with HIV/AIDS in three ways: (1) during gestation across the placenta, (2) during delivery through contact with maternal blood or fluids, and (3) postpartum (after birth) through breast feeding. The transmission of AIDS through breast feeding is especially a problem in many developing countries (UNICEF, 2013). Babies born to HIV-infected mothers can be (1) infected and symptomatic (show HIV symptoms), (2) infected but asymptomatic (not show HIV symptoms), or (3) not infected at all. An infant who is infected and asymptomatic may still develop HIV symptoms up until 15 months of age.

The more widespread disease of diabetes, characterized by high levels of sugar in the blood, also affects offspring. A research review indicated that when newborns have physical defects they are more likely to have diabetic mothers (Eriksson, 2009). Women who have gestational diabetes also may deliver very large infants (weighing 10 pounds or more), and the infants are at risk for diabetes themselves (Gluck & others, 2009). A recent large-scale study revealed that children whose mothers had diabetes during pregnancy had lower expressive language scores than those whose mothers who did not have diabetes during pregnancy (Krakowiak & others, 2012).

developmental **connection**

Conditions, Diseases, and Disorders

The greatest incidence of HIV/AIDS is in sub-Saharan Africa, where as many as 30 percent of mothers have HIV; many are unaware that they are infected with the virus. Chapter 4, p. 109

Because the fetus depends entirely on its mother for nutrition, it is important for pregnant women to have good nutritional habits. In Kenya, this government clinic provides pregnant women with information about how their diet can influence the health of their fetus and offspring. *What might the information about diet be like?*

Other Parental Factors   So far we have discussed a number of drugs, environmental hazards, maternal diseases, and incompatible blood types that can harm the embryo or fetus. Here we will explore other characteristics of the mother and father that can affect prenatal and child development, including nutrition, age, and emotional states and stress.

Maternal Diet and Nutrition   A developing embryo or fetus depends completely on its mother for nutrition, which comes from the mother's blood (Lowdermilk & Perry, 2012). The nutritional status of the embryo or fetus is determined by the mother's total caloric intake as well as her intake of proteins, vitamins, and minerals. Children born to malnourished mothers are more likely than other children to be malformed.

Maternal obesity adversely affects pregnancy outcomes through increased rates of hypertension, diabetes, respiratory complications, and infections in the mother (Nodine & Hastings-Tolsma, 2012). Also, pregnancies in obese women are characterized by a higher incidence of neural tube defects, preterm deliveries, and late fetal deaths (McKnight & others, 2011). Management of obesity including weight loss and increased exercise prior to pregnancy is likely to benefit the mother and the baby (Simmons, 2011; Vesco & others, 2012). Limiting gestational weight gain to 11 to 20 pounds among pregnant women is likely to improve outcomes for the mother and the child (Simmons, 2011).

One aspect of maternal nutrition that is important for normal prenatal development is folic acid, a B-complex vitamin (Talaulikar & Arulkumaran, 2011; Waddell, 2012). A study of more than 34,000 women taking folic acid either alone or as part of a multivitamin for at least one year prior to conceiving was linked with a 70 percent lower risk of delivering

developmental **connection**

Conditions, Diseases, and Disorders

What are some key factors that influence whether individuals will become obese? Chapter 13, p. 427

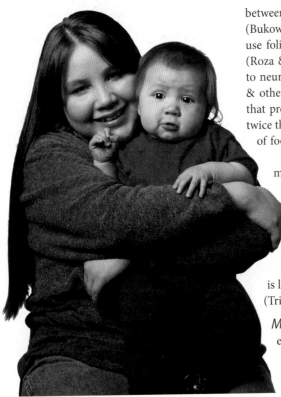

What are some of the risks for infants born to adolescent mothers?

How do pregnant women's emotional states and stress affect prenatal development and birth?

between 20 and 28 weeks and a 50 percent lower risk of delivering between 28 and 32 weeks (Bukowski & others, 2008). A recent study revealed that toddlers of mothers who did not use folic acid supplements in the first trimester of pregnancy had more behavior problems (Roza & others, 2010). Also, as indicated earlier in the chapter, a lack of folic acid is related to neural tube defects in offspring, such as spina bifida (a defect in the spinal cord) (Collins & others, 2011). The U.S. Department of Health and Human Services (2012) recommends that pregnant women consume a minimum of 400 micrograms of folic acid per day (about twice the amount the average woman gets in one day). Orange juice and spinach are examples of foods rich in folic acid.

Eating fish is often recommended as part of a healthy diet, but pollution has made many fish a risky choice for pregnant women. Some fish contain high levels of mercury, which is released into the air both naturally and by industrial pollution (Wells, 2011). When mercury falls into the water it can become toxic and accumulate in large fish, such as shark, swordfish, king mackerel, and some species of large tuna (American Pregnancy Association, 2012; Mayo Clinic, 2012). Mercury is easily transferred across the placenta, and the embryo's developing brain and nervous system are highly sensitive to the metal. Researchers have found that prenatal mercury exposure is linked to adverse outcomes, including miscarriage, preterm birth, and lower intelligence (Triche & Hossain, 2007; Xue & others, 2007).

Maternal Age   When possible harmful effects on the fetus and infant are considered, two maternal ages are of special interest: (1) adolescence, and (2) 35 years and older (Malizia, Hacker, & Penzias, 2009; Rudang & others, 2012). The mortality rate of infants born to adolescent mothers is double that of infants born to mothers in their twenties. Adequate prenatal care decreases the probability that a child born to an adolescent girl will have physical problems. However, adolescents are the least likely of women in all age groups to obtain prenatal assistance from clinics and health services.

Maternal age is also linked to the risk that a child will have Down syndrome (Ghosh & others, 2010). As discussed in Chapter 2, an individual with *Down syndrome* has distinctive facial characteristics, short limbs, and retardation of motor and mental abilities. A baby with Down syndrome rarely is born to a mother 16 to 34 years of age. However, when the mother reaches 40 years of age, the probability is slightly over 1 in 100 that a baby born to her will have Down syndrome, and by age 50 it is almost 1 in 10. When mothers are 35 years and older, risks also increase for low birth weight, preterm delivery, and fetal death (Koo & others, 2012; Mbugua Gitau & others, 2009).

We still have much to learn about the role of the mother's age in pregnancy and childbirth. As women remain active, exercise regularly, and are careful about their nutrition, their reproductive systems may remain healthier at older ages than was thought possible in the past.

Emotional States and Stress   When a pregnant woman experiences intense fears, anxieties, and other emotions or negative mood states, physiological changes occur that may affect her fetus (Brunton & Russell, 2011; Howerton & Bale, 2012). A mother's stress may also influence the fetus indirectly by increasing the likelihood that the mother will engage in unhealthy behaviors, such as taking drugs and receiving poor prenatal care.

High maternal anxiety and stress during pregnancy can have long-term consequences for the offspring (Dunkel Schetter, 2011; Monk, Fitelson, & Werner, 2011). A research review indicated that pregnant women with high levels of stress are at increased risk for having a child with emotional or cognitive problems, attention deficit hyperactivity disorder (ADHD), and language delay (Taige & others, 2007). A recent study of more than 30,000 offspring revealed that across the nine months of pregnancy, their risk of being born preterm was highest when maternal exposure to stress occurred during the fifth and sixth months of pregnancy (Class & others, 2011).

Might maternal depression also have an adverse effect on birth outcomes? A recent research review concluded that maternal depression during pregnancy is linked to preterm birth (Dunkel Schetter, 2011). Another recent research review indicated that untreated prenatal maternal depression is associated with negative outcomes for offspring, including reduced empathy in childhood (Davalos, Yadon, & Tregellas, 2012).

Paternal Factors   So far, we have discussed how characteristics of the mother—such as drug use, disease, diet and nutrition, age, and emotional states—can influence prenatal development and the development of the child. Might there also be some paternal risk factors? Indeed, there are several. Men's exposure to lead, radiation, certain pesticides, and petrochemicals may cause abnormalities in sperm that lead to miscarriage or diseases, such as childhood cancer (Cordier, 2008). The father's smoking during the mother's pregnancy also can cause problems for the offspring. In one study, heavy paternal smoking was associated with the risk of early pregnancy loss (Venners & others, 2004). This negative outcome may be related to secondhand smoke. And in a recent study, paternal smoking around the time of the child's conception was linked to an increased risk of the child developing leukemia (Milne & others, 2012). Also, a recent research review concluded that there is an increased risk of spontaneous abortion, autism, and schizophrenic disorders when the father is 40 years of age or older (Reproductive Endocrinology and Infertility Committee & others, 2012).

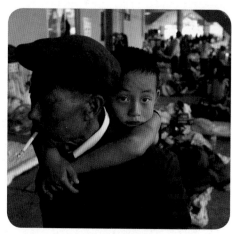

In a study in China, the longer fathers smoked, the greater the risk that their children would develop cancer (Ji & others, 1997). *What are some other paternal factors that can influence the development of the fetus and the child?*

PRENATAL CARE

Although prenatal care varies enormously, it usually involves a defined schedule of visits for medical care, which typically includes screening for manageable conditions and treatable diseases that can affect the baby or the mother (Gabbe & others, 2012; Lowdermilk & Perry, 2012). In addition to medical care, prenatal programs often include comprehensive educational, social, and nutritional services (Ickovics & others, 2011). A recent study revealed that group prenatal care provided pregnant women with a broad network of social support (McNeil & others, 2012).

Exercise increasingly is recommended as part of a comprehensive prenatal care program. Exercise during pregnancy helps prevent constipation, conditions the body, reduces excessive weight gain, and is associated with a more positive mental state, including a reduced level of depression (Robledo-Colonia & others, 2012; Ruchat & others, 2012; Streuling & others, 2011). Consider the positive outcomes of exercise during pregnancy in these recent studies:

- Pregnant women who completed a three-month supervised aerobic exercise program showed improved health-related quality of life, including better physical functioning and reduced bodily pain, compared with their counterparts who did not participate in the program (Montoya Arizabaleta & others, 2010).

- Exercise during pregnancy improved mothers' perception of their health (Barakat & others, 2011).

- Following 12 weeks of twice-weekly yoga or massage therapy, both therapy groups had a greater decrease in depression, anxiety, and back and leg pain than a control group (Field & others, 2012).

- A research review concluded that yoga during pregnancy was associated with a reduction in pregnancy discomforts, sleep disturbance, stress, and pain in mothers and a reduced incidence of low birth weight in offspring (Babbar & others, 2012).

However, it is important to remember not to overdo it. A recent study of almost 1,500 pregnant women found that the incidence of exercise-related injuries was low (Vladutiu, Evenson, & Marshall, 2010). Pregnant women should always consult their physician before starting any exercise program (Szymanski & Satin, 2012).

Does prenatal care matter? Information about pregnancy, labor, delivery, and caring for the newborn can be especially valuable for first-time mothers (Davidson & others, 2012). Prenatal care is also very important for women in poverty and immigrant women because it links them with other social services (Lyberg & others, 2012).

An innovative program that is rapidly expanding in the United States is CenteringPregnancy (Ickovics & others, 2011; Steming, 2008). This

How might a woman's exercise during pregnancy benefit her and her offspring?

A CenteringPregnancy program. This increasingly popular program alters routine prenatal care by bringing women out of exam rooms and into relationship-oriented groups.

program is relationship-centered and provides complete prenatal care in a group setting. CenteringPregnancy replaces traditional 15-minute physician visits with 90-minute peer group support settings and self-examination led by a physician or certified nurse-midwife. Groups of up to 10 women (and often their partners) meet regularly beginning at 12 to 16 weeks of pregnancy. The sessions emphasize empowering women to play an active role in experiencing a positive pregnancy. A recent study revealed that CenteringPregnancy groups made more prenatal visits, had higher breast feeding rates, and were more satisfied with their prenatal care than women in individual care (Klima & others, 2009). In another recent study, high-stress women were randomly assigned to a CenteringPregnancy Plus group, group prenatal care, or standard individual care from 18 weeks gestation to birth (Ickovics & others, 2011). The most stressed women in the CenteringPregnancy Plus group showed increased self-esteem and decreased stress and social conflict in their third trimester of pregnancy; their social conflict and depression also were lower at one-year postpartum.

Some prenatal programs for parents focus on home visitation (Eckenrode & others, 2010; Tandon & others, 2011). A recent research review concluded that prenatal home visits were linked to improved use of prenatal care, although there was less evidence that they improve newborns' birth weight (Issel & others, 2011). Research evaluations indicate that the Nurse Family Partnership created by David Olds and his colleagues (2004, 2007) is successful. The Nurse Family Partnership involves home visits by trained nurses beginning in the second or third trimester of prenatal development. The extensive program consists of approximately 50 home visits from the prenatal period through two years of age. The home visits focus on the mother's health, access to health care, parenting, and improvement of the mother's life by providing her with guidance in education, work, and relationships. Research revealed that the Nurse Family Partnership has numerous positive outcomes including fewer pregnancies, better work circumstances, and stability in relationship partners for the mother, and improved academic success and social development for the child (Olds & others, 2004, 2007).

NORMAL PRENATAL DEVELOPMENT

Much of our discussion so far in this chapter has focused on what can go wrong with prenatal development. Prospective parents should take steps to avoid the vulnerabilities to fetal development that we have described. But it is important to keep in mind that most of the time, prenatal development does not go awry, and development occurs along the positive path that we described at the beginning of the chapter.

Review *Connect* Reflect

 Describe prenatal development.

Review

- What is the course of prenatal development?
- What is teratology, and what are some of the main hazards to prenatal development?
- What are some good prenatal care strategies?
- Why is it important to take a positive approach to prenatal development?

Connect

- In Chapter 2, we discussed chromosomal and gene-linked abnormalities that can affect prenatal development. How are the symptoms of the related conditions or risks similar to or different from those caused by teratogens or other hazards?

Reflect *Your Own Personal Journey of Life*

- If you are a woman, imagine that you have just found out that you are pregnant. What health-enhancing strategies will you follow through the prenatal period? If you are not a woman, imagine that you are the partner of a woman who has just found out she is pregnant. What will be your role in increasing the likelihood that the prenatal period will go smoothly?

The Birth Process	Assessing the Newborn	Preterm and Low Birth Weight Infants

Nature writes the basic script for how birth occurs, but parents make important choices about conditions surrounding birth. We look first at the sequence of physical steps when a child is born.

THE BIRTH PROCESS

The birth process occurs in stages, occurs in different contexts, and in most cases involves one or more attendants.

Stages of Birth   The birth process occurs in three stages. The first stage is the longest of the three. Uterine contractions are 15 to 20 minutes apart at the beginning and last up to a minute. These contractions cause the woman's cervix to stretch and open. As the first stage progresses, the contractions come closer together, appearing every two to five minutes. Their intensity increases. By the end of the first birth stage, contractions dilate the cervix to an opening of about 10 centimeters (4 inches), so that the baby can move from the uterus to the birth canal. For a woman having her first child, the first stage lasts an average of 6 to 12 hours; for subsequent children, this stage typically is much shorter.

The second birth stage begins when the baby's head starts to move through the cervix and the birth canal. It terminates when the baby completely emerges from the mother's body. With each contraction, the mother bears down hard to push the baby out of her body. By the time the baby's head is out of the mother's body, the contractions come almost every minute and last for about a minute. This stage typically lasts approximately 45 minutes to an hour.

Afterbirth is the third stage, at which time the placenta, umbilical cord, and other membranes are detached and expelled. This final stage is the shortest of the three birth stages, lasting only minutes.

After the long journey of prenatal development, birth takes place. During birth the baby is on a threshold between two worlds. *What is the fetus/newborn transition like?*

> There was a star danced, and under that I was born.
>
> —**WILLIAM SHAKESPEARE**
> *English Playwright, 17th Century*

Childbirth Setting and Attendants   In the United States, 99 percent of births take place in hospitals (Martin & others, 2005). However, a 5 percent increase in home births occurred in 2005 and 2006 (Macdorman, Declercq, & Menacker, 2011). This increase in home births occurred mainly among non-Latino White women, especially those who were older and married. For these non-Latino White women, two-thirds of their home births were attended by a midwife.

The people who help a mother during birth vary across cultures. In U.S. hospitals, it has become the norm for fathers or birth coaches to remain with the mother throughout labor and delivery. In the East African Nigoni culture, men are completely excluded from the childbirth process. When a woman is ready to give birth, female relatives move into the woman's hut and the husband leaves, taking his belongings (clothes, tools, weapons, and so on) with him. He is not permitted to return until after the baby is born. In some cultures, childbirth is an open, community affair. For example, in the Pukapukan culture in the Pacific Islands, women give birth in a shelter that is open for villagers to observe.

Midwives   Midwifery is practiced in most countries throughout the world (Bryom & Symon, 2011; Kitzinger, 2011). In Holland, more than 40 percent of babies are delivered by midwives rather than doctors. However, in 2003, 91 percent of U.S. births were attended by physicians, and only 8 percent of women who delivered babies were attended by a midwife (Martin & others, 2005). Nonetheless, the 8 percent figure in 2003 represents a substantial increase from less than 1 percent of U.S. women attended by a midwife in 1975 (Martin &

afterbirth The third stage of birth, when the placenta, umbilical cord, and other membranes are detached and expelled.

In India, a midwife checks on the size, position, and heartbeat of a fetus. Midwives deliver babies in many countries around the world. *What are some cultural variations in prenatal care?*

others, 2005). Ninety-five percent of the midwives who delivered babies in the United States in 2003 were certified nurse-midwives. A recent research review concluded that for low-risk women, midwife-led care was characterized by a reduction in procedures during labor and increased satisfaction with care (Sutcliffe & others, 2012). Also, in this study no adverse outcomes were found for midwife-led care compared with physician-led care.

Doulas   In some countries, a doula attends a childbearing woman. Doula is a Greek word that means "a woman who helps." A **doula** is a caregiver who provides continuous physical, emotional, and educational support for the mother before, during, and after childbirth (Hansard, 2012). Doulas remain with the parents throughout labor, assessing and responding to the mother's needs. Researchers have found positive effects when a doula is present at the birth of a child (Akhavan & Lundgren, 2011; Dahlen, Jackson, & Stevens, 2011).

In the United States, most doulas work as independent providers hired by the expectant parents. Doulas typically function as part of a "birthing team," serving as an adjunct to the midwife or the hospital's obstetric staff.

Methods of Childbirth   U.S. hospitals often allow the mother and her obstetrician a range of options regarding the method of delivery. Key choices involve the use of medication, whether to use any of a number of nonmedicated techniques to reduce pain, and when to have a cesarean delivery.

Medication   Three basic kinds of drugs that are used for labor are analgesia, anesthesia, and oxytocin/pitocin.

Analgesia is used to relieve pain. Analgesics include tranquilizers, barbiturates, and narcotics (such as Demerol).

Anesthesia is used in late first-stage labor and during delivery to block sensation in an area of the body or to block consciousness. There is a trend toward not using general anesthesia, which blocks consciousness, in normal births because general anesthesia can be transmitted through the placenta to the fetus (Pennell & others, 2011). An *epidural block* is regional anesthesia that numbs the woman's body from the waist down. Researchers are continuing to explore safer drug mixtures for use at lower doses to improve the effectiveness and safety of epidural anesthesia (Balaji, Dhillon, & Russell, 2009; Jones & others, 2012).

Oxytocin is a synthetic hormone that is used to stimulate contractions; pitocin is the most widely used oxytocin. The relative benefits and risks of oxytocin as a part of childbirth continue to be debated (Buchanan & others, 2012).

Predicting how a drug will affect an individual woman and her fetus is difficult (Davidson & others, 2012). A particular drug might have only a minimal effect on one fetus yet have a much stronger effect on another. The drug's dosage also is a factor (Weiner & Buhimschi, 2009). Stronger doses of tranquilizers and narcotics given to decrease the mother's pain potentially have a more negative effect on the fetus than mild doses. It is important for the mother to assess her level of pain and have a voice in deciding whether she receives medication.

Natural and Prepared Childbirth   For a brief time not long ago, the idea of avoiding all medication during childbirth gained favor in the United States. Instead, many women chose to reduce the pain of childbirth through techniques known as natural childbirth and prepared childbirth. Today, at least some medication is used in the typical childbirth, but elements of natural childbirth and prepared childbirth remain popular (Oates & Abraham, 2010).

Natural childbirth is the method that aims to reduce the mother's pain by decreasing her fear through education about childbirth and by teaching her and her partner to use breathing methods and relaxation techniques during delivery.

French obstetrician Ferdinand Lamaze developed a method similar to natural childbirth that is known as **prepared childbirth,** or the Lamaze method. It includes a special breathing technique to control pushing in the final stages of labor, as well as more detailed education

A doula assisting a birth. *What types of support do doulas provide?*

doula A caregiver who provides continuous physical, emotional, and educational support for the mother before, during, and after childbirth.

natural childbirth This method attempts to reduce the mother's pain by decreasing her fear through education about childbirth and relaxation techniques during delivery.

Linda Pugh, Perinatal Nurse

Perinatal nurses work with childbearing women to support health and growth during the childbearing experience. Linda Pugh, Ph.D., R.N.C., is a perinatal nurse on the faculty at The Johns Hopkins University School of Nursing. She is certified as an inpatient obstetric nurse and specializes in the care of women during labor and delivery. She teaches undergraduate and graduate students, educates professional nurses, and conducts research. In addition, Pugh consults with hospitals and organizations about women's health issues and topics we discuss in this chapter. Her research interests include nursing interventions with low-income breast feeding women, ways to prevent and ameliorate fatigue during childbearing, and the use of breathing exercises during labor.

about anatomy and physiology. The Lamaze method has become very popular in the United States. The pregnant woman's partner usually serves as a coach who attends childbirth classes with her and helps her with her breathing and relaxation during delivery.

In sum, proponents of current prepared childbirth methods conclude that when information and support are provided, women know how to give birth. To read about one nurse whose research focuses on fatigue during childbearing and breathing exercises during labor, see the *Connecting with Careers* profile. And to read about the increased variety of techniques now being used to reduce stress and control pain during labor, see *Connecting Development to Life*.

An instructor conducting a Lamaze class. *What characterizes the Lamaze method?*

Cesarean Delivery Normally, the baby's head comes through the vagina first. But if the baby is in a **breech position,** the baby's buttocks are the first part to emerge from the vagina. In 1 of every 25 deliveries, the baby's head is still in the uterus when the rest of the body is out. Breech births can cause respiratory problems. As a result, if the baby is in a breech position, a surgical procedure known as a cesarean section, or a cesarean delivery, is usually performed. In a **cesarean delivery,** the baby is removed from the mother's uterus through an incision made in her abdomen.

The benefits and risks of cesarean sections continue to be debated (Bangdiwala & others, 2010; Minguez-Milio & others, 2011). Some critics believe that too many babies are delivered by cesarean section in the United States and around the world (Blakey, 2011; Gibbons & others, 2012). More cesarean sections are performed in the United States than in any other country in the world. In 2009, 33 percent of babies in the U.S. were cesarean deliveries (Solheim & others, 2011).

ASSESSING THE NEWBORN

Almost immediately after birth, after the baby and its parents have been introduced, a newborn is taken to be weighed, cleaned up, and tested for signs of developmental problems that might require urgent attention (Therrell & others, 2010). The **Apgar Scale** is widely used to assess the health of newborns at one and five minutes after birth. The Apgar Scale evaluates an infant's heart rate, respiratory effort, muscle tone, body color, and reflex irritability.

prepared childbirth Developed by French obstetrician Ferdinand Lamaze, this childbirth strategy is similar to natural childbirth but includes a special breathing technique to control pushing in the final stages of labor and a more detailed anatomy and physiology course.

breech position The baby's position in the uterus that causes the buttocks to be the first part to emerge from the vagina.

cesarean delivery Surgical procedure in which the baby is removed from the mother's uterus through an incision made in her abdomen.

Apgar Scale A widely used method of assessing the health of newborns at one and five minutes after birth. The Apgar Scale evaluates an infant's heart rate, respiratory effort, muscle tone, body color, and reflex irritability.

From Waterbirth to Music Therapy

The effort to reduce stress and control pain during labor has recently led to an increase in the use of some older and some newer nonmedicated techniques (Kalder & others, 2011; Simkin & Bolding, 2004). These include waterbirth, massage, acupuncture, hypnosis, and music therapy.

Waterbirth

Waterbirth involves giving birth in a tub of warm water. Some women go through labor in the water and get out for delivery; others remain in the water for delivery. The rationale for waterbirth is that the baby has been in an amniotic sac for many months and that delivery in a similar environment is likely to be less stressful for the baby and the mother (Meyer, Weible, & Woeber, 2010). Mothers get into the warm water when contractions become closer together and more intense. Getting into the water too soon can cause labor to slow or stop. Reviews of research have indicated mixed results for waterbirths (Cluett & Burns, 2009). A recent study did find that waterbirth was linked with a shorter second stage of labor (Cortes, Basra, & Kelleher, 2011). Waterbirth has been practiced more often in European countries such as Switzerland and Sweden in recent decades than in the United States but is increasingly being included in U.S. birth plans.

Massage

Massage is increasingly used prior to and during delivery (Field, 2007; Stager, 2009–2010). Two recent research reviews concluded that massage therapy reduces pain during labor (Jones & others, 2012; Smith & others, 2012). One study revealed that massage therapy reduced pain in pregnant women and alleviated prenatal depression in both parents and improved their relationship (Field & others, 2008).

Acupuncture

Acupuncture, the insertion of very fine needles into specific locations in the body, is used as a standard procedure to reduce the pain of childbirth in China, although it only recently has begun to be used in the United States for this purpose. Recent research indicates that acupuncture can have positive effects on labor and delivery (Borup & others, 2009; Citkovitz, Schnyer, & Hoskins, 2011; Smith & others, 2012).

What characterizes the use of waterbirth in delivering a baby?

Hypnosis

Hypnosis, the induction of a psychological state of altered attention and awareness in which the individual is unusually responsive to suggestions, is also increasingly being used during childbirth (Wilcox, 2009–2010). Some studies have indicated positive effects of hypnosis for reducing pain during childbirth (Abbasi & others, 2010), although a recent research review concluded that overall there is insufficient evidence to indicate that hypnosis reduces pain during labor (Smith & others, 2012).

Music Therapy

Music therapy during childbirth, which involves the use of music to reduce stress and manage pain, is becoming more common (Liu, Chang, & Chen, 2010). More research is needed to determine its effectiveness (Laopaiboon & others, 2009).

What are some reasons that natural childbirth methods such as these might be chosen instead of medication?

An obstetrician or a nurse does the evaluation and gives the newborn a score, or reading, of 0, 1, or 2 on each of these five health signs (see Figure 3.6). A total score of 7 to 10 indicates that the newborn's condition is good. A score of 5 indicates there may be developmental difficulties. A score of 3 or below signals an emergency and indicates that the baby might not survive.

Score	0	1	2
Heart rate	Absent	Slow—less than 100 beats per minute	Fast—100–140 beats per minute
Respiratory effort	No breathing for more than one minute	Irregular and slow	Good breathing with normal crying
Muscle tone	Limp and flaccid	Weak, inactive, but some flexion of extremities	Strong, active motion
Body color	Blue and pale	Body pink, but extremities blue	Entire body pink
Reflex irritability	No response	Grimace	Coughing, sneezing and crying

FIGURE 3.6

THE APGAR SCALE. A newborn's score on the Apgar Scale indicates whether the baby has urgent medical problems. *What are some trends in the Apgar scores of U.S. babies?*

The Apgar Scale is especially good at assessing the newborn's ability to cope with the stress of delivery and the new environment (Reynolds, 2010; Shehata & others, 2011). It also identifies high-risk infants who need resuscitation. A recent study revealed that compared with children who have a high Apgar score (9 to 10), the risk of developing attention deficit hyperactivity disorder (ADHD) in childhood was 75 percent higher for newborns with a low Apgar score (1 to 4) and 63 percent higher with an Apgar of 5 to 6 (Li & others, 2011). For a more thorough assessment of the newborn, the Brazelton Neonatal Behavioral Assessment Scale or the Neonatal Intensive Care Unit Network Neurobehavioral Scale may be used.

The **Brazelton Neonatal Behavioral Assessment Scale (NBAS)** is typically performed within 24 to 36 hours after birth. It is also used as a sensitive index of neurological competence up to one month after birth for typical infants and as a measure in many studies of infant development (Costa & Figueiredo, 2011; Jones, 2012). The NBAS assesses the newborn's neurological development, reflexes, and reactions to people and objects. Sixteen reflexes, such as sneezing, blinking, and rooting, are assessed, along with reactions to animate (such as a face and voice) and inanimate stimuli (such as a rattle). (We will have more to say about reflexes in Chapter 4, when we discuss motor development in infancy.)

The NBAS is designed to assess normal, healthy, full-term infants. An "offspring" of the NBAS, the **Neonatal Intensive Care Unit Network Neurobehavioral Scale (NNNS)** provides another assessment of the newborn's behavior, neurological and stress responses, and regulatory capacities (Brazelton, 2004; Lester & others, 2011). T. Berry Brazelton, along with Barry Lester and Edward Tronick, developed the NNNS specifically to assess the "at-risk" infant. It is especially useful for evaluating preterm infants (although it may not be appropriate for those less than 30 weeks' gestational age) and substance-exposed infants (El-Dib & others, 2012; Montirosso & others, 2012). A recent NNNS assessment (at one month of age) of preterm infants who were exposed to substance abuse prenatally revealed that the NNNS accurately predicted certain developmental outcomes, such as neurological difficulties, IQ, and school readiness at 4.5 years of age (Liu & others, 2010).

PRETERM AND LOW BIRTH WEIGHT INFANTS

Different conditions that pose threats for newborns have been given different labels. We will examine these conditions and discuss interventions for improving outcomes of preterm infants.

Preterm and Small for Date Infants Three related conditions pose threats to many newborns: low birth weight, being born preterm, and being small for date. **Low birth weight infants**

Brazelton Neonatal Behavioral Assessment Scale (NBAS) A measure that is used in the first month of life to assess the newborn's neurological development, reflexes, and reactions to people and objects.

Neonatal Intensive Care Unit Neurobehavioral Scale (NNNS) An "offspring" of the NBAS, the NNNS provides an assessment of the newborn's behavior, neurological and stress responses, and regulatory capacities.

low birth weight infants An infant that weighs less than 5½ pounds at birth.

A "kilogram kid," weighing less than 2.3 pounds at birth. *What are some long-term outcomes for weighing so little at birth?*

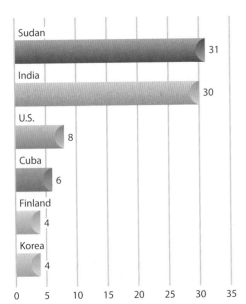

FIGURE **3.7**

PERCENTAGE OF INFANTS BORN WITH LOW BIRTH WEIGHT IN SELECTED COUNTRIES

developmental **connection**

Environment

Poverty continues to negatively affect development throughout childhood. Chapter 8, p. 267; Chapter 10, p. 342

weigh less than 5½ pounds at birth. *Very low birth weight* newborns weigh under 3½ pounds, and *extremely low birth weight* newborns weigh under 2 pounds. **Preterm infants** are those born three weeks or more before the pregnancy has reached its full term—in other words, before the completion of 37 weeks of gestation (the time between fertilization and birth). **Small for date infants** (also called *small for gestational age infants*) are those whose birth weight is below normal when the length of the pregnancy is considered. They weigh less than 90 percent of all babies of the same gestational age. Small for date infants may be preterm or full term. One study found that small for date infants had more than a fourfold increased risk of death (Regev & others, 2003).

In 2009, 12.2 percent of U.S. infants were born preterm—a 35 percent increase since the 1980s but 0.6 percent decrease since 2006 (National Center for Health Statistics, 2011). The increase in preterm birth since the 1980s is likely due to such factors as the increasing number of births to women 35 years and older, increasing rates of multiple births, increased management of maternal and fetal conditions (for example, inducing labor preterm if medical technology indicates it will increase the likelihood of survival), increased rates of substance abuse (tobacco, alcohol), and increased stress (Goldenberg & Culhane, 2007). Ethnic variations characterize preterm birth (Lhila & Long, 2011). For example, in 2009, the likelihood of being born preterm was 12.2 percent for all U.S. infants and 10.9 percent for non-Latino White infants, but the rate was 17.5 percent for African American infants (National Center for Health Statistics, 2009).

Recently, considerable attention has been directed to the role that progestin might play in reducing preterm births (Lucovnik & others, 2011). Recent research reviews indicate that progestin is most effective in reducing preterm births when it is administered to women with a history of a previous spontaneous birth at less than 37 weeks (da Fonseca & others, 2009), to women who have a short cervical length of 15 millimeters or less (da Fonseca & others, 2009), and to women with a singleton rather multiple offspring (Lucovnik & others, 2011).

Might exercise during pregnancy reduce the likelihood of preterm birth? One study found that compared with sedentary pregnant women, women who engaged in light leisure time physical activity had a 24 percent reduced likelihood of preterm delivery and those who participated in moderate to heavy leisure time physical activity had a 66 percent reduced risk of preterm delivery (Hegaard & others, 2008).

The incidence of low birth weight varies considerably from country to country. In some countries, such as India and Sudan, where poverty is rampant and the health and nutrition of mothers are poor, the percentage of low birth weight babies reaches as high as 31 percent (see Figure 3.7). In the United States, there has been an increase in low birth weight infants in the last two decades. The U.S. low birth weight rate of 8.2 percent in 2009 was considerably higher than that of many other developed countries (Centers for Disease Control & Prevention, 2012; Hoyert & others, 2006). For example, only 4 percent of the infants born in Sweden, Finland, Norway, and Korea are low birth weight, and only 5 percent of those born in New Zealand, Australia, and France are low birth weight.

In both developed and developing countries, adolescents who give birth when their bodies have not fully matured are at risk for having low birth weight babies (Pattanapisalsak, 2011; Shuaib & others, 2011). In the United States, the increase in the number of low birth weight infants is due to factors such as the use of drugs, poor nutrition, multiple births, reproductive technologies, and improved technology and prenatal care that result in more high-risk babies surviving (D'Angelo & others, 2011; National Center for Health Statistics, 2011). Nonetheless, poverty still is a major factor in preterm births in the United States. Women living in poverty conditions are more likely to be obese, have diabetes and hypertension, smoke cigarettes and use illicit drugs, and less likely to receive regular prenatal care (Timmermans & others, 2011).

Consequences of Preterm Birth and Low Birth Weight

Although most preterm and low birth weight infants are healthy, as a group they have more health and developmental problems than normal birth weight infants (Minde & Zelkowitz, 2008). For preterm birth, the terms *extremely preterm* and *very preterm* are increasingly used (Davidson & others, 2012). *Extremely preterm infants* are those born at less than 28 weeks gestation, and *very preterm infants* are those born less than 33 weeks of gestational age. Figure 3.8 shows the results of a recent Norwegian study indicating that the earlier preterm infants are born the more likely they are to drop out of school (Swamy, Ostbye, & Skjaerven, 2008).

The number and severity of these problems increase when infants are born very early and as their birth weight decreases (Baron & others, 2011; Duncan & others, 2011). Survival rates for infants who are born very early and very small have risen, but with this improved survival rate have come increases in rates of severe brain damage (Faroogi & others, 2011).

Children born low in birth weight are more likely than their normal birth weight counterparts to develop a learning disability, attention deficit hyperactivity disorder, or breathing problems such as asthma (Anderson & others, 2011). Approximately 50 percent of all low birth weight children are enrolled in special education programs.

Nurturing Low Birth Weight and Preterm Infants

Two increasingly used interventions in the neonatal intensive care unit (NICU) are kangaroo care and massage therapy. **Kangaroo care** involves skin-to-skin contact in which the baby, wearing only a diaper, is held upright against the parent's bare chest, much as a baby kangaroo is carried by its mother (Ludington-Hoe & others, 2006). Kangaroo care is typically practiced for two to three hours per day, skin-to-skin over an extended time in early infancy (Ahmed & others, 2011).

Why use kangaroo care with preterm infants? Preterm infants often have difficulty coordinating their breathing and heart rate, and the close physical contact with the parent provided by kangaroo care can help to stabilize the preterm infant's heartbeat, temperature, and breathing (Cong, Ludington-Hoe, & Walsh, 2011). Preterm infants who experience kangaroo care also gain more weight than their counterparts who are not given this care (Gathwala, Singh, & Singh, 2010). And a recent research review concluded the kangaroo care decreased the risk of mortality in low birth weight infants (Conde-Aguedelo, Belizan, & Diaz-Rossello, 2011).

Many adults will attest to the therapeutic effects of receiving a massage. In fact, many will pay a premium to receive one at a spa on a regular basis. But can massage play a role in improving the developmental outcomes for preterm infants? To find out, see *Connecting Through Research.*

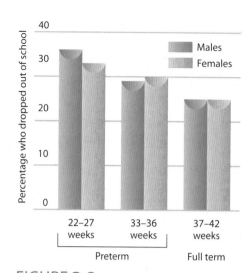

FIGURE 3.8

PERCENTAGE OF PRETERM AND FULL-TERM BIRTH INFANTS WHO DROPPED OUT OF SCHOOL

developmental **connection**

Attachment

A classic study with surrogate cloth and wire monkeys demonstrated the important role that touch plays in infant attachment. Chapter 6, p. 189

A new mother practicing kangaroo care. *What is kangaroo care?*

preterm infants Those born before the completion of 37 weeks of gestation (the time between fertilization and birth).

small for date infants Also called small for gestational age infants, these infants' birth weights are below normal when the length of pregnancy is considered. Small for date infants may be preterm or full term.

kangaroo care Treatment for preterm infants that involves skin-to-skin contact.

connecting through research

How Does Massage Therapy Affect the Mood and Behavior of Babies?

Throughout history and in many cultures, caregivers have massaged infants. In Africa and Asia, infants are routinely massaged by parents or other family members for several months after birth. In the United States, interest in using touch and massage to improve the growth, health, and well-being of infants has been stimulated by the research of Tiffany Field (2001, 2007, 2010a; Diego, Field, & Hernandez-Reif, 2008; Field, Diego, & Hernandez-Reif, 2008, 2010; Field & others, 2006, 2012; Hernandez-Reif, Diego, & Field, 2007), director of the Touch Research Institute at the University of Miami School of Medicine.

In one study, preterm infants in a neonatal intensive care unit (NICU) were randomly assigned to a massage therapy group or a control group (Hernandez-Reif, Diego, & Field, 2007). For five consecutive days, the preterm infants in the massage group were given three 15-minute moderate-pressure massages. Behavioral observations of the following stress behaviors were made on the first and last days of the study: crying, grimacing, yawning, sneezing, jerky arm and leg movements, startles, and finger flaring. The various stress behaviors were summarized in a composite stress behavior index. As indicated in Figure 3.9, massage had a stress-reducing effect on the preterm infants, which is especially important because they encounter numerous stressors while they are hospitalized.

In another study, Field and her colleagues (2004) tested a more cost-effective massage strategy. They taught mothers how to massage their full-term infants rather than having health care professionals do the massage. Beginning from day one of the newborn's life to the end of the first month, once a day before bedtime the mothers massaged the babies using either light or moderate pressure. Infants who were massaged with moderate pressure gained more weight, performed better on the orientation scale of the Brazelton, were less excitable and less depressed, and were less agitated during sleep.

Field has demonstrated the benefits of massage therapy for infants who face a variety of problems. For example, preterm infants exposed to cocaine in utero who received massage therapy gained weight and improved their scores on developmental tests (Wheeden & others, 1993). Another study investigated 1- to 3-month-old infants born to depressed adolescent mothers (Field & others, 1996). The infants of depressed mothers who received massage therapy had lower stress—as well as improved emotionality, sociability, and soothability—compared with the nonmassaged infants of depressed mothers.

Shown here is Tiffany Field massaging a newborn infant. *What types of infants has massage therapy been shown to help?*

In a research review of massage therapy with preterm infants, Field and her colleagues (2004) concluded that the most consistent findings involve two positive results: (1) increased weight gain and (2) discharge from the hospital from three to six days earlier. A recent study revealed that the mechanisms responsible for increased weight gain as a result of massage therapy were stimulation of the vagus nerve (one of 12 cranial nerves leading to the brain) and in turn the release of insulin (a food absorption hormone) (Field, Diego, & Hernandez-Reif, 2011).

Infants are not the only ones who may benefit from massage therapy (Field, 2007). In other studies, Field and her colleagues have demonstrated the benefits of massage therapy with women in reducing labor pain (Field, Hernandez-Reif, Taylor, & others, 1997), with children who have asthma (Field, Henteleff, & others, 1998), with autistic children's attentiveness (Field, Lasko, & others, 1997), and with adolescents who have attention deficit hyperactivity disorder (Field, Quintino, & others, 1998).

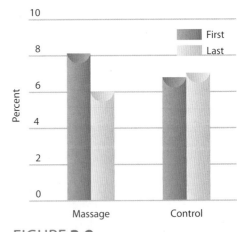

FIGURE **3.9**

PRETERM INFANTS SHOW REDUCED STRESS BEHAVIORS AND ACTIVITY AFTER FIVE DAYS OF MASSAGE THERAPY

Source: M. Hernandez-Reif, M. Diego, & T. Field (2007). Preterm infants show reduced stress behaviors and activity after 5 days of massage therapy. *Infant Behavior and Development, 30,* 557–561.

Review *Connect* Reflect

 LG2 Describe the birth process.

Review

- What are the three main stages of birth? What are some different birth strategies? What is the transition from fetus to newborn like for the infant?
- What are three measures of neonatal health and responsiveness?
- What are the outcomes for children if they are born preterm or with a low birth weight?

Connect

- What correlations have been found between birth weight and country of birth, and what might the causes be?

Reflect *Your Own Personal Journey of Life*

- If you are a female, which birth strategy do you prefer? Why? If you are a male, how involved would you want to be in helping your partner through the birth of your baby? Explain.

3 The Postpartum Period

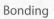 **LG3** Explain the changes that take place in the postpartum period.

Physical Adjustments   Emotional and Psychological Adjustments   Bonding

The weeks after childbirth present challenges for many new parents and their offspring. This is the **postpartum period,** the period after childbirth or delivery that lasts for about six weeks or until the mother's body has completed its adjustment and has returned to a nearly prepregnant state. It is a time when the woman adjusts, both physically and psychologically, to the process of childbearing.

The postpartum period involves a great deal of adjustment and adaptation. The adjustments needed are physical, emotional, and psychological.

PHYSICAL ADJUSTMENTS

A woman's body makes numerous physical adjustments in the first days and weeks after childbirth (Mattson & Smith, 2011). She may have a great deal of energy or feel exhausted and let down. Though these changes are normal, the fatigue can undermine the new mother's sense of well-being and confidence in her ability to cope with a new baby and a new family life (Runquist, 2007).

A concern is the loss of sleep that the primary caregiver experiences in the postpartum period (Kuo & others, 2012; Tsai & Thomas, 2012). In the 2007 Sleep in America survey, a substantial percentage of women reported loss of sleep during pregnancy and in the postpartum period (National Sleep Foundation, 2007) (see Figure 3.10). The loss of sleep can contribute to stress, marital conflict, and impaired decision making (Meerlo, Sgoifo, & Suchecki, 2008).

After delivery, a mother's body undergoes sudden and dramatic changes in hormone production. When the placenta is delivered, estrogen and progesterone levels drop steeply and remain low until the ovaries start producing hormones again.

EMOTIONAL AND PSYCHOLOGICAL ADJUSTMENTS

Emotional fluctuations are common for mothers in the postpartum period. For some women, emotional fluctuations decrease within several weeks after the delivery, but other women experience more long-lasting emotional swings.

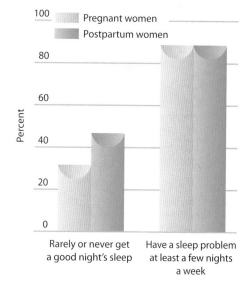

FIGURE 3.10

SLEEP DEPRIVATION IN PREGNANT AND POSTPARTUM WOMEN

postpartum period The period after childbirth when the mother adjusts, both physically and psychologically, to the process of childbirth. This period lasts for about six weeks or until her body has completed its adjustment and returned to a near prepregnant state.

Diane Sanford, Clinical Psychologist and Postpartum Expert

Diane Sanford has a doctorate in clinical psychology, and for many years she had a private practice that focused on marital and family relationships. But after she began collaborating with a psychiatrist whose clients included women with postpartum depression, Dr. Sanford, along with a women's health nurse, founded Women's Healthcare Partnership in St. Louis, Missouri, which specializes in women's adjustment during the postpartum period. Subsequently, they added a marriage and family relationships counselor and a social worker to their staff, and then later hired nurse educators, a dietician, and a fitness expert as consultants (Clay, 2001).

For more information about what clinical psychologists do, see page 45 in the Careers in Life-Span Development appendix.

Diane Sanford holding an infant of one of the mothers who comes to her for help in coping with postpartum issues.

Postpartum blues
Symptoms appear 2 to 3 days after delivery and usually subside within 1 to 2 weeks.

70%

10%

20%

Postpartum depression
Symptoms linger for weeks or months and interfere with daily functioning.

No symptoms

FIGURE **3.11**

POSTPARTUM BLUES AND POSTPARTUM DEPRESSION AMONG U.S. WOMEN. Some health professionals refer to the postpartum period as the "fourth trimester." Though the time span of the postpartum period does not necessarily cover three months, the term "fourth trimester" suggests continuity and the importance of the first several months after birth for the mother.

postpartum depression Characteristic of women who have such strong feelings of sadness, anxiety, or despair that they have trouble coping with daily tasks in the postpartum period.

As shown in Figure 3.11, about 70 percent of new mothers in the United States have what are called the postpartum blues. About two to three days after birth, they begin to feel depressed, anxious, and upset. These feelings may come and go for several months after the birth, often peaking about three to five days after birth. Even without treatment, these feelings usually go away after one or two weeks.

However, some women develop **postpartum depression,** which involves a major depressive episode that typically occurs about four weeks after delivery. Women with postpartum depression have such strong feelings of sadness, anxiety, or despair that for at least a two-week period they have trouble coping with their daily tasks. Without treatment, postpartum depression may become worse and last for many months (Nolen-Hoeksema, 2011; Stuart, 2012). And many women with postpartum depression don't seek help. For example, one recent study found that 15 percent of the women surveyed had postpartum depression symptoms but less than half sought help (McGarry & others, 2009). Estimates indicate that 10 to 14 percent of new mothers experience postpartum depression.

Several antidepressant drugs are effective in treating postpartum depression and appear to be safe for breast feeding women (Logsdon, Wisner, & Hanusa, 2009). Psychotherapy, especially cognitive therapy, is effective in easing postpartum depression for many women (Beck, 2006). Also, engaging in regular exercise may help in treating postpartum depression (Daley, Macarthur, & Winter, 2007).

Can a mother's postpartum depression affect the way she interacts with her infant? A recent research review concluded that the interaction difficulties of depressed mothers and their infants occur across cultures and socioeconomic status groups, and encompass less sensitivity of the mothers and less responsiveness on the part of their infants (Field, 2010b). Several caregiving activities also are compromised, including feeding (especially breast feeding), sleep routines, and safety practices. To read about one individual who specializes in women's adjustment during the postpartum period, see *Connecting with Careers.*

Fathers also undergo considerable adjustment in the postpartum period, even when they work away from home all day. When the mother develops postpartum depression, many fathers also experience elevated feelings of depression (Letourneau & others, 2012; Ramchandani & others, 2011). Many fathers feel that the baby comes first and gets all of the mother's attention; some feel that they have been replaced by the baby.

The father's support and caring can play a role in whether the mother develops postpartum depression (Persson & others, 2011). A recent study revealed that higher support by fathers was related to lower incidence of postpartum depression in women (Smith & Howard, 2008).

BONDING

A special component of the parent-infant relationship is **bonding,** the formation of a connection, especially a physical bond between parents and the newborn in the period shortly after birth. Sometimes hospitals seem determined to deter bonding. Drugs given to the mother to make her delivery less painful can make the mother drowsy, interfering with her ability to respond to and stimulate the newborn. Mothers and newborns are often separated shortly after delivery, and preterm infants are isolated from their mothers even more than full-term infants.

Do these practices do any harm? Some physicians believe that during the period shortly after birth, the parents and newborn need to form an emotional attachment as a foundation for optimal development in years to come (Kennell, 2006; Kennell & McGrath, 1999). Is there evidence that close contact between mothers in the first several days after birth is critical for optimal development later in life? Although some research supports this bonding hypothesis (Klaus & Kennell, 1976), a body of research challenges the significance of the first few days of life as a critical period (Bakeman & Brown, 1980; Rode & others, 1981). Indeed, the extreme form of the bonding hypothesis—that the newborn must have close contact with the mother in the first few days of life to develop optimally—simply is not true.

Nonetheless, the weakness of the bonding hypothesis should not be used as an excuse to keep motivated mothers from interacting with their newborns. Such contact brings pleasure to many mothers. In some mother-infant pairs—including preterm infants, adolescent mothers, and mothers from disadvantaged circumstances—early close contact may establish a climate for improved interaction after the mother and infant leave the hospital.

Many hospitals now offer a *rooming-in* arrangement, in which the baby remains in the mother's room most of the time during its hospital stay. However, if parents choose not to use this rooming-in arrangement, the weight of the research suggests that this decision will not harm the infant emotionally (Lamb, 1994).

The postpartum period is a time of considerable adjustment and adaptation for both the mother and the father. Fathers can provide an important support system for mothers, especially in helping mothers care for young infants. *What kinds of tasks might the father of a newborn do to support the mother?*

developmental **connection**

Attachment

Konrad Lorenz demonstrated the importance of early bonding in greylag geese, but the first few days of life are unlikely to be a critical period for bonding in human infants. Chapter 1, p. 27

bonding The formation of a close connection, especially a physical bond, between parents and their newborn in the period shortly after birth.

Review Connect Reflect

 Explain the changes that take place in the postpartum period.

Review

- What does the postpartum period involve? What physical adjustments does the woman's body make during this period?
- What emotional and psychological adjustments characterize the postpartum period?
- Is bonding critical for optimal development?

Connect

- Compare and contrast what you learned about kangaroo care and breast feeding

of preterm infants to what you learned about bonding and breast feeding when the mother is suffering from postpartum depression.

Reflect *Your Own Personal Journey of Life*

- If you are a female, what can you do to adjust effectively in the postpartum period? If you are a male, what can you do to help your partner in the postpartum period?

reach your learning goals

Prenatal Development and Birth

1 Prenatal Development

LG1 Describe prenatal development.

The Course of Prenatal Development

- Prenatal development is divided into three periods: germinal (conception until 10 to 14 days later), which ends when the zygote (a fertilized egg) attaches to the uterine wall; embryonic (two to eight weeks after conception), during which the embryo differentiates into three layers, life-support systems develop, and organ systems form (organogenesis); and fetal (from two months after conception until about nine months, or when the infant is born), a time when organ systems have matured to the point at which life can be sustained outside the womb. The growth of the brain during prenatal development is nothing short of remarkable. By the time babies are born, they have approximately 100 billion neurons, or nerve cells. Neurogenesis is the term for the formation of new neurons. The nervous system begins with the formation of a neural tube at 18 to 24 days after conception. Proliferation and migration are two processes that characterize brain development in the prenatal period. The basic architecture of the brain is formed in the first two trimesters of prenatal development.

Teratology and Hazards to Prenatal Development

- Teratology is the field that investigates the causes of congenital (birth) defects. Any agent that causes birth defects is called a teratogen. The dose, genetic susceptibility, and time of exposure influence the severity of the damage to an unborn child and the type of defect that occurs. Prescription drugs that can be harmful include antibiotics. Nonprescription drugs that can be harmful include diet pills, aspirin, and caffeine. Legal psychoactive drugs that are potentially harmful to prenatal development include alcohol and nicotine. Fetal alcohol spectrum disorders are a cluster of abnormalities that appear in offspring of mothers who drink heavily during pregnancy. Even when pregnant women drink moderately (one to two drinks a few days a week), negative effects on their offspring have been found. Cigarette smoking by pregnant women has serious adverse effects on prenatal and child development, including low birth weight. Illegal psychoactive drugs that are potentially harmful to offspring include methamphetamine, marijuana, cocaine, and heroin. Incompatibility of the mother's and the father's blood types can also be harmful to the fetus. Environmental hazards include radiation, environmental pollutants, and toxic wastes. Syphilis, rubella (German measles), genital herpes, and AIDS are infectious diseases that can harm the fetus. Other parental factors include maternal diet and nutrition, age, emotional states and stress, and paternal factors. A developing fetus depends entirely on its mother for nutrition. Maternal age can negatively affect the offspring's development if the mother is an adolescent or over 35. High stress in the mother is linked with less than optimal prenatal and birth outcomes. Paternal factors that can adversely affect prenatal development include exposure to lead, radiation, certain pesticides, and petrochemicals.

Prenatal Care

- Prenatal care varies extensively but usually involves health maintenance services with a defined schedule of visits.

Normal Prenatal Development

- It is important to remember that, although things can and do go wrong during pregnancy, most of the time pregnancy and prenatal development go well.

2 Birth

 LG2 Describe the birth process.

The Birth Process

- Childbirth occurs in three stages. The first stage, which lasts about 6 to 12 hours for a woman having her first child, is the longest stage. The cervix dilates to about 10 centimeters (4 inches) by the end of the first stage. The second stage begins when the baby's head starts to move through the cervix and ends with the baby's complete emergence. The third stage involves the delivery of the placenta after birth. Childbirth strategies involve the childbirth setting and attendants. In many countries, a doula attends a childbearing woman. Methods of delivery include medicated, natural or prepared, and cesarean.

Assessing the Newborn

- For many years, the Apgar Scale has been used to assess the newborn's health. The Brazelton Neonatal Behavioral Assessment Scale examines the newborn's neurological development, reflexes, and reactions to people. Recently, the Neonatal Intensive Care Unit Network Neurobehavioral Scale (NNNS) was created to assess the at-risk infants.

Preterm and Low Birth Weight Infants

- Low birth weight infants weigh less than 5½ pounds, and they may be preterm (born before the completion of 37 weeks of gestation) or small for date (also called small for gestational age, which refers to infants whose birth weight is below normal when the length of pregnancy is considered). Small for date infants may be preterm or full term. Although most low birth weight and preterm infants are normal and healthy, as a group they have more health and developmental problems than normal birth weight infants. Kangaroo care and massage therapy have been shown to have benefits for preterm infants.

3 The Postpartum Period

LG3 Explain the changes that take place in the postpartum period.

Physical Adjustments

- The postpartum period is the name given to the period after childbirth or delivery. The period lasts for about six weeks or until the woman's body has completed its adjustment. Physical adjustments in the postpartum period include fatigue, involution (the process by which the uterus returns to its prepregnant size five or six weeks after birth), and hormonal changes.

Emotional and Psychological Adjustments

- Emotional fluctuations on the part of the mother are common in this period, and they can vary a great deal from one mother to the next. Postpartum depression characterizes women who have such strong feelings of sadness, anxiety, or despair that they have trouble coping with daily tasks in the postpartum period. Postpartum depression occurs in about 10 percent of new mothers. The father also goes through a postpartum adjustment.

Bonding

- Bonding is the formation of a close connection, especially a physical bond between parents and the newborn shortly after birth. Early bonding has not been found to be critical in the development of a competent infant.

key **terms**

germinal period 78
blastocyst 78
trophoblast 78
embryonic period 78
amnion 79
umbilical cord 79
placenta 79
organogenesis 79
fetal period 80

neurons 83
teratogen 83
fetal alcohol spectrum disorders (FASD) 85
afterbirth 91
doula 92
natural childbirth 92
prepared childbirth 93
breech position 93

cesarean delivery 93
Apgar Scale 93
Brazelton Neonatal Behavioral Assessment Scale (NBAS) 95
Neonatal Intensive Care Unit Network Neurobehavioral Scale (NNNS) 95
low birth weight infants 95

preterm infants 97
small for date infants 97
kangaroo care 97
postpartum period 99
postpartum depression 100
bonding 101

key **people**

David Olds 90

Ferdinand Lamaze 92

T. Berry Brazelton 95

Tiffany Field 98

Chapter 3 | PRENATAL DEVELOPMENT AND BIRTH

Connecting with

Learning Objectives	Application Activities	Activity Type	Page Reference
Describe the course of prenatal development.	The Germinal Period	Click & drag activity	pp. 78–82
Describe the birth process.	The Birth Process	Click & drag activity	pp. 91–93
	Midwifery	Video	
	Midwives	Video	
Explain bonding between the parents and the infant.	Newborn Cry	Video	p. 101
	Crying at 2 Weeks	Video	

section **three**

Babies are such a nice way to start people.

—DON HEROLD
American Writer, 20th Century

Infancy

As newborns, we were not empty-headed organisms. We had some basic reflexes, among them crying, kicking, and coughing. We slept a lot, and occasionally we smiled, although the meaning of our first smiles was not entirely clear. We ate and we grew. We crawled and then we walked, a journey of a thousand miles beginning with a single step. Sometimes we conformed; sometimes others conformed to us. Our development was a continuous creation of more complex forms. We needed the meeting eyes of love. We juggled the necessity of curbing our will with becoming what we could will freely. Section 3 contains three chapters: "Physical Development in Infancy" (Chapter 4), "Cognitive Development in Infancy" (Chapter 5), and "Socioemotional Development in Infancy" (Chapter 6).

chapter 4

PHYSICAL DEVELOPMENT IN INFANCY

chapter **outline**

Latonya is a newborn baby in Ghana. During her first days of life, she has been kept apart from her mother and bottle fed. Manufacturers of infant formula provide the hospital where she was born with free or subsidized milk powder. Her mother has been persuaded to bottle feed rather than breast feed her. When her mother bottle feeds Latonya, she overdilutes the milk formula with unclean water. Latonya's feeding bottles have not been sterilized. Latonya becomes very sick. She dies before her first birthday.

Ramona was born in a Nigerian hospital with a "baby-friendly" program. In this program, babies are not separated from their mothers when they are born, and the mothers are encouraged to breast feed them. The mothers are told of the perils that bottle feeding can bring because of unsafe water and unsterilized bottles. They also are informed about the advantages of breast milk, which include its nutritious and hygienic qualities, its ability to immunize babies against common illnesses, and the role of breast feeding in reducing the mother's risk of breast and ovarian cancer. Ramona's mother is breast feeding her. At 1 year of age, Ramona is very healthy.

For many years, maternity units in hospitals favored bottle feeding and did not give mothers adequate information about the benefits of breast feeding. In recent years, the World Health Organization and UNICEF have tried to reverse the trend toward bottle feeding of infants in many impoverished countries. They instituted "baby-friendly" programs in many countries (Grant, 1993). They also persuaded the International Association of Infant Formula Manufacturers to stop marketing their baby formulas to hospitals in countries where the governments support the baby-friendly initiatives (Grant, 1993). For the hospitals themselves, costs actually were reduced as infant formula, feeding bottles, and separate nurseries became unnecessary. For example, baby-friendly Jose Fabella Memorial Hospital in the Philippines reported saving 8 percent of its annual budget. Still, there are many places in the world where the baby-friendly initiatives have not been implemented.

The advantages of breast feeding in impoverished countries are substantial (Coovadia & others, 2012; UNICEF, 2013). However, these advantages must be balanced against

(*Top*) An HIV-infected mother breast feeding her baby in Nairobi, Kenya. (*Bottom*) A Rwandan mother bottle feeding her baby. *What are some concerns about breast versus bottle feeding in impoverished African countries?*

topical connections

In the previous chapter, we followed the physical development that takes place from fertilization through the germinal, embryonic, and fetal periods of prenatal development. We learned that by the time the fetus has reached full gestational age (approximately 40 weeks), it has grown from a fertilized egg, barely visible to the human eye, to a fully formed human weighing approximately 7½ pounds measuring 20 inches in length. Also remarkable is the fact that by the end of the prenatal period the brain has developed approximately 100 billion neurons.

looking back

the risk of passing the human immunodeficiency virus (HIV) to babies through breast milk if the mothers have the virus (Goga & others, 2012; Muluye & others, 2012). In some areas of Africa, more than 30 percent of mothers have HIV, but the majority of these mothers don't know that they are infected (Mepham, Bland, and Newell, 2011). Later in the chapter, in the section on nutrition, we will look more closely at recent research on breast feeding in the United States, outlining the benefits for infants and mothers and discussing several life-threatening diseases that infants can contract as a result of malnutrition.

preview

It is very important for infants to get a healthy start. When they do, their first two years of life are likely to be a time of amazing development. In this chapter, we focus on the biological domain and the infant's physical development, exploring physical growth, motor development, and sensory and perceptual development.

1 Physical Growth and Development in Infancy

LG1 Discuss physical growth and development in infancy.

Patterns of Growth | Height and Weight | The Brain | Sleep | Nutrition

Infants' physical development in the first two years of life is extensive. Newborns' heads are quite large in comparison with the rest of their bodies. They have little strength in their necks and cannot hold their heads up, but they have some basic reflexes. In the span of 12 months, infants become capable of sitting anywhere, standing, stooping, climbing, and usually walking. During the second year, growth decelerates, but rapid increases in such activities as running and climbing take place. Let's now examine in greater detail the sequence of physical development in infancy.

PATTERNS OF GROWTH

An extraordinary proportion of the total body is occupied by the head during prenatal development and early infancy (see Figure 4.1). The **cephalocaudal pattern** is the sequence in which the earliest growth always occurs at the top—the head—with physical growth and differentiation of features gradually working their way down from top to bottom (for example, shoulders, middle trunk, and so on) (Pedroso, 2008). This same pattern occurs in the head area, because the top parts of the head—the eyes and brain—grow faster than the lower parts, such as the jaw.

Motor development generally proceeds according to the cephalocaudal principle. For example, infants see objects before they can control their torso, and they can use their hands long before they can crawl or walk. However, development does not follow a rigid blueprint. One study found that infants reached for toys with their feet prior to reaching with their hands (Galloway & Thelen, 2004). On average, infants first touched the toy with their feet when they were 12 weeks old and with their hands when they were 16 weeks old.

Growth also follows the **proximodistal pattern,** the sequence in which growth starts at the center of the body and moves toward the extremities. For example, infants control the muscles of their trunk and arms before they control their hands and fingers, and they use their whole hands before they can control several fingers.

A baby is the most complicated object made by unskilled labor.

—Anonymous

cephalocaudal pattern Developmental sequence in which the earliest growth always occurs at the top—the head—with physical growth in size, weight, and feature differentiation gradually working from top to bottom.

proximodistal pattern Developmental sequence in which growth starts at the center of the body and moves toward the extremities.

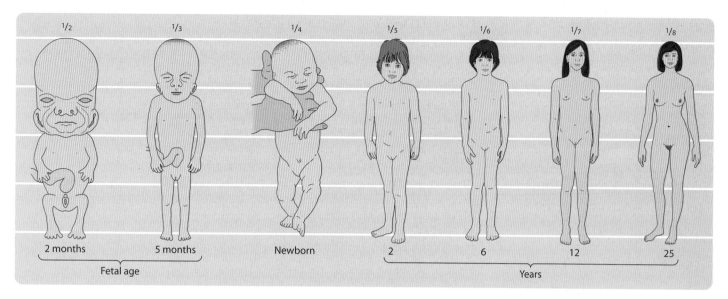

FIGURE **4.1**

CHANGES IN PROPORTIONS OF THE HUMAN BODY DURING GROWTH. As individuals develop from infancy through adulthood, one of the most noticeable physical changes is that the head becomes smaller in relation to the rest of the body. The fractions listed refer to head size as a proportion of total body length at different ages.

HEIGHT AND WEIGHT

The average North American newborn is 20 inches long and weighs 7 pounds. Ninety-five percent of full-term newborns are 18 to 22 inches long and weigh between 5 and 10 pounds.

In the first several days of life, most newborns lose 5 to 7 percent of their body weight before they adjust to feeding by sucking, swallowing, and digesting. Then they grow rapidly, gaining an average of 5 to 6 ounces per week during the first month. They have doubled their birth weight by the age of 4 months and have nearly tripled it by their first birthday. Infants grow about 1 inch per month during the first year, approximately doubling their birth length by their first birthday.

Growth slows considerably in the second year of life (Burns & others, 2013). By 2 years of age, infants weigh approximately 26 to 32 pounds, having gained a quarter to half a pound per month during the second year to reach about one-fifth of their adult weight. At 2 years of age, infants average 32 to 35 inches in height, which is nearly half of their adult height.

THE BRAIN

We described the amazing growth of the brain from conception to birth in Chapter 3. By the time it is born, the infant that began as a single cell is estimated to have a brain that contains approximately 100 billion nerve cells, or neurons. Extensive brain development continues after birth, through infancy and later (Diamond, 2013; Nelson, 2012). Because the brain is still developing so rapidly in infancy, the infant's head should be protected from falls or other injuries and the baby should never be shaken. *Shaken baby syndrome,* which includes brain swelling and hemorrhaging, affects hundreds of babies in the United States each year (Swaiman & others, 2012). A recent analysis found that fathers were the most frequent perpetrators of shaken baby syndrome, followed by child care providers and boyfriends of the victim's mother (National Center on Shaken Baby Syndrome, 2012).

Studying the brain's development in infancy is not as easy as it might seem. Even some of the latest brain-imaging technologies (described in

FIGURE **4.2**

MEASURING THE ACTIVITY OF AN INFANT'S BRAIN. By attaching up to 128 electrodes to a baby's scalp to measure the brain's activity, Charles Nelson and his colleagues (2006) have found that even newborns produce distinctive brain waves that reveal they can distinguish their mother's voice from another woman's, even while they are asleep. *Why is it so difficult to measure infants' brain activity?*

developmental **connection**

Brain Development

How does the brain change from conception to birth? Chapter 3, p. 82

Chapter 1) cannot make out fine details in adult brains and cannot be used with babies (Nelson, 2012). Positron-emission tomography (PET) scans pose a radiation risk to babies, and infants often wriggle too much for technicians to be able to capture accurate images using magnetic resonance imaging (MRI). However, researchers have been successful in using the electroencephalogram (EEG), a measure of the brain's electrical activity, to learn about the brain's development in infancy (Bell & Diaz, 2012; Cuevas & others, 2012). Among the researchers who are making strides in finding out more about the brain's development in infancy are Charles Nelson (Nelson, 2007, 2012, 2013) and John Richards and his colleagues (Mallin & Richards, 2012; Richards, 2009, 2010; Richards, Reynolds, & Courage, 2010) (see Figure 4.2).

The Brain's Development   At birth, the newborn's brain is about 25 percent of its adult weight. By the second birthday, the brain is about 75 percent of its adult weight. However, the brain's areas do not mature uniformly.

Mapping the Brain   Scientists analyze and categorize areas of the brain in numerous ways (Geng & others, 2012; South & Isaacs, 2013). The portion farthest from the spinal cord is known as the forebrain. This region includes the cerebral cortex and several structures beneath it. The cerebral cortex covers the forebrain like a wrinkled cap. The brain has two halves, or hemispheres (see Figure 4.3). Based on ridges and valleys in the cortex, scientists distinguish four main areas, called lobes, in each hemisphere. Although the lobes usually work together, each has a somewhat different primary function (see Figure 4.4):

FIGURE **4.3**

THE HUMAN BRAIN'S HEMISPHERES. The two hemispheres of the human brain are clearly seen in this photograph. It is a myth that the left hemisphere is the exclusive location of language and logical thinking and that the right hemisphere is the exclusive location of emotion and creative thinking.

- *Frontal lobes* are involved in voluntary movement, thinking, personality, and intentionality or purpose.
- *Occipital lobes* function in vision.
- *Temporal lobes* have an active role in hearing, language processing, and memory.
- *Parietal lobes* play important roles in registering spatial location, attention, and motor control.

To some extent, the type of information handled by neurons depends on whether they are in the left or right hemisphere of the cortex (Van der Haegen & others, 2011). Speech and grammar, for example, depend on activity in the left hemisphere in most people; humor and the use of metaphors depends on activity in the right hemisphere (Griffiths & others, 2012; Marinkovic & others, 2012; McGettigan & others, 2012). This specialization of function in one hemisphere of the cerebral cortex or the other is called **lateralization.** However, most neuroscientists agree that complex functions such as reading or performing music involve both hemispheres (Stroobant, Buijus, & Vingerhoets, 2009). Labeling people as "left-brained" because they are logical thinkers and "right-brained" because they are creative thinkers does not correspond to the way the brain's hemispheres work. Complex thinking in normal people is the outcome of communication between both hemispheres of the brain (Ibrahim & Eviatar, 2012).

At birth, the hemispheres of the cerebral cortex already have started to specialize: Newborns show greater electrical brain activity in the left hemisphere than the right hemisphere when they are listening to speech sounds (Telkemeyer & others, 2011). How are the areas of the brain different in the newborn and the infant from those in an adult, and why do the differences matter? Important differences have been documented at both the cellular and the structural levels.

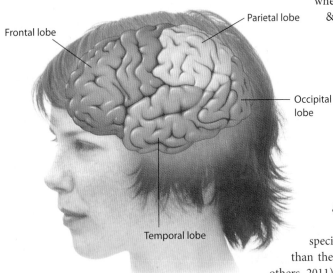

Parietal lobe

Frontal lobe

Occipital lobe

Temporal lobe

FIGURE **4.4**

THE BRAIN'S FOUR LOBES. Shown here are the locations of the brain's four lobes: frontal, occipital, temporal, and parietal.

lateralization Specialization of function in one hemisphere of the cerebral cortex or the other.

Changes in Neurons   Within the brain, the type of nerve cells called neurons send electrical and chemical signals, communicating with each other. As we indicated in Chapter 3, a *neuron* is a nerve cell that handles information processing (see Figure 4.5). Extending from the neuron's cell body are two types of fibers known as axons and dendrites. Generally, the axon carries signals away from the cell body and dendrites carry signals toward it. A *myelin sheath,* which is a layer of fat cells, encases many axons (see Figure 4.5). The myelin sheath insulates axons and helps electrical signals travel faster down the axon. Myelination also is involved in providing energy to neurons and in communication (Fancy & others, 2012; Harris & Attwell, 2012). At the end of the axon are terminal buttons, which release chemicals called *neurotransmitters* into *synapses*, which are tiny gaps between neurons' fibers. Chemical interactions in synapses connect axons and dendrites, allowing information to pass from neuron to neuron (Emes & Grant, 2013; Marzo, Gousset, & Zurzolo, 2012). Think of the synapse as a river that blocks a road. A grocery truck arrives at one bank of the river, crosses by ferry, and continues its journey to market. Similarly, a message in the brain is "ferried" across the synapse by a neurotransmitter, which pours out information contained in chemicals when it reaches the other side of the river.

Neurons change in two very significant ways during the first years of life. First, *myelination,* the process of encasing axons with fat cells, begins prenatally and continues after birth, even into adolescence (Lebel & others, 2012). Second, connectivity among neurons increases, creating new neural pathways, as Figure 4.6 illustrates. New dendrites grow, connections among dendrites increase, and synaptic connections between axons and dendrites proliferate. Whereas myelination speeds up neural transmissions, the expansion of dendritic connections facilitates the spreading of neural pathways in infant development.

Researchers have discovered an intriguing aspect of synaptic connections. Nearly twice as many of these connections are made as will ever be used (Huttenlocher & Dabholkar, 1997). The connections that are used become strengthened and survive, while the unused ones are replaced by other pathways or disappear. In the language of neuroscience, these connections will be "pruned" (Campbell & others, 2012; Ren, Zhang, & Zhao, 2012). For example, the more babies engage in physical activity or use language, the more those pathways will be strengthened.

Changes in Regions of the Brain

Figure 4.7 vividly illustrates the dramatic growth and later pruning of synapses in the visual, auditory, and prefrontal cortex (Huttenlocher & Dabholkar, 1997). Notice that "blooming and pruning" vary considerably by brain region. For example, the peak of synaptic overproduction in the visual cortex occurs at about the fourth postnatal month, followed by a gradual retraction until the middle to end of the preschool years. In areas of the brain involved in hearing and language, a similar, though somewhat later, course is detected. However, in the prefrontal cortex, the area of the brain where higher-level thinking and self-regulation occur, the peak of overproduction takes place at about 1 year of age; it is not until middle to late adolescence that the adult density of synapses is achieved. Both heredity and environment are thought to influence the timing and course of synaptic overproduction and subsequent retraction.

Meanwhile, the pace of myelination also varies in different areas of the brain (Gogtay & Thompson, 2010). Myelination for visual pathways occurs rapidly after birth and is completed in the first six months. Auditory myelination is not completed until 4 or 5 years of age.

In general, some areas of the brain, such as the primary motor areas, develop earlier than others, such as the primary sensory areas. The frontal lobes are immature in the newborn.

(a) Incoming information

Cell body

Nucleus

Axon

Dendrites

(b) Outgoing information

(c) Myelin sheath

(d) Terminal button

To next neuron

FIGURE **4.5**

THE NEURON. (*a*) The dendrites of the cell body receive information from other neurons, muscles, or glands through the axon. (*b*) Axons transmit information away from the cell body. (*c*) A myelin sheath covers most axons and speeds information transmission. (*d*) As the axon ends, it branches out into terminal buttons.

developmental **connection**

Brain Development

Changes in the prefrontal cortex in adolescents and older adults have important implications for their cognitive development. Chapter 11, p. 361; Chapter 17, p. 578

FIGURE **4.6**

THE DEVELOPMENT OF DENDRITIC SPREADING. Note the increase in connectedness between neurons over the course of the first two years of life. Reprinted by permission of the publisher from *The Postnatal Development of the Human Cerebral Cortex, Volumes I–VIII,* by J. LeRoy Conel, Cambridge, Mass.: Harvard University Press. Copyright © 1939, 1941, 1947, 1951, 1955, 1959, 1963, 1967 by the President and Fellows of Harvard College.

At birth   1 month   3 months   15 months   24 months

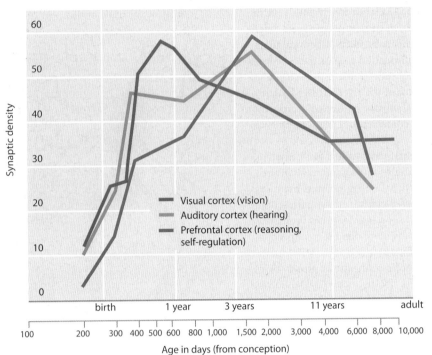

FIGURE 4.7

SYNAPTIC DENSITY IN THE HUMAN BRAIN FROM INFANCY TO ADULTHOOD. The graph shows the dramatic increase followed by pruning in synaptic density for three regions of the brain: visual cortex, auditory cortex, and prefrontal cortex. Synaptic density is believed to be an important indication of the extent of connectivity between neurons.

developmental **connection**

Nature and Nurture

In the epigenetic view, development is an ongoing, bidirectional interchange between heredity and the environment. Chapter 2, p. 70

FIGURE 4.8

EARLY DEPRIVATION AND BRAIN ACTIVITY.
These two photographs are PET (positron emission tomography) scans, which use radioactive tracers to image and analyze blood flow and metabolic activity in the body's organs. These scans show the brains of (a) a normal child and (b) an institutionalized Romanian orphan who experienced substantial deprivation since birth. In PET scans, the highest to lowest brain activity is reflected in the colors of red, yellow, green, blue, and black, respectively. As can be seen, red and yellow show up to a much greater degree in the PET scan of the normal child than the deprived Romanian orphan.

(a) (b)

However, as neurons in the frontal lobes become myelinated and interconnected during the first year of life, infants develop an ability to regulate their physiological states, such as sleep, and gain more control over their reflexes. Cognitive skills that require deliberate thinking do not emerge until later in the first year (Bell, 2012; Morasch & others, 2013). Indeed, the prefrontal region of the frontal lobe has the most prolonged development of any brain region, with changes detectable at least into emerging adulthood (Blakemore, 2012; Steinberg, 2012, 2013).

Early Experience and the Brain Children who grow up in a deprived environment may have depressed brain activity (McLaughlin & others, 2011; Roeber & others, 2012). As shown in Figure 4.8, a child who grew up in the unresponsive and unstimulating environment of a Romanian orphanage showed considerably depressed brain activity compared with a normal child.

Are the effects of deprived environments irreversible? There is reason to think the answer is no. The brain demonstrates both flexibility and resilience. Consider 14-year-old Michael Rehbein. At age 7, he began to experience uncontrollable seizures—as many as 400 a day. Doctors said the only solution was to remove the left hemisphere of his brain where the seizures were occurring. Recovery was slow, but his right hemisphere began to reorganize and take over functions that normally occur in the brain's left hemisphere, including speech (see Figure 4.9).

Neuroscientists believe that what wires the brain—or rewires it, in the case of Michael Rehbein—is repeated experience. Each time a baby tries to touch an attractive object or gazes intently at a face, tiny bursts of electricity shoot through the brain, knitting together neurons into circuits. The results are some of the behavioral milestones we discuss in this chapter.

The Neuroconstructivist View Not long ago, scientists thought that our genes determined how our brains were "wired" and that the cells in the brain responsible for processing information just maturationally unfolded with little or no input from environmental experiences. Whatever brain your heredity had dealt you, you were essentially stuck with. This view, however, turned out to be wrong. Instead, the brain has plasticity and its development depends on context (Diamond, 2013; Nelson, 2012).

The infant's brain depends on experiences to determine how connections are made (Diamond, 2013). Before birth, it appears that genes mainly direct basic wiring patterns. Neurons grow and travel to distant places awaiting further instructions (Nelson, 2012). After birth, the inflowing stream of sights, sounds, smells, touches, language, and eye contact help shape the brain's neural connections.

In the increasingly popular **neuroconstructivist view,** (a) biological processes (genes, for example) and environmental conditions (enriched or impoverished, for example) influence the brain's development; (b) the brain has plasticity and is context dependent; and (c) development of the brain and the child's cognitive development are closely linked. These factors constrain or advance the construction of cognitive skills (Miller & Kinsbourne, 2012; Nelson, 2013; Peltzer-Karpf, 2012; Westerman, Thomas, & Karmiloff-Smith, 2011). The neuroconstructivist view emphasizes the importance of considering interactions between experience and gene expression in the brain's development, much in the way the epigenetic view proposes (see Chapter 2, "Biological Beginnings").

SLEEP

When we were infants, sleep consumed more of our time than it does now. The typical newborn sleeps approximately 18 hours a day, but newborns vary a lot in how much they sleep (Sadeh, 2008). The range is from about 10 hours to about 21 hours a day.

Infants also vary in their preferred times for sleeping and their patterns of sleep. Although the total amount of time spent sleeping remains somewhat consistent, an infant may change from sleeping 7 or 8 hours several times a day to sleeping for only a few hours three or four times a day. By about 1 month of age, many American infants have begun to sleep longer at night. By 6 months of age, they usually have moved closer to adult-like sleep patterns, spending the most time sleeping at night and the most time awake during the day (Sadeh, 2008). A recent research review concluded that infants 0 to 2 years of age slept an average of 12.8 hours out of the 24, within a range of 9.7 to 15.9 hours (Galland & others, 2012). A recent study revealed that by 6 months of age the majority of infants slept through the night, awakening their mothers only once or twice a week (Weinraub & others, 2012).

The most common infant sleep-related problem reported by parents is nighttime waking (Hospital for Sick Children & others, 2010). Surveys indicate that 20 to 30 percent of infants have difficulty going to sleep at night and staying asleep until morning (Sadeh, 2008). A recent study found that nighttime wakings at 1 year of age predicted lower sleep efficiency at 4 years of age (Tikotzky & Shaashua, 2012). Also, a study revealed that the mother's emotional availability at bedtime was linked to fewer infant sleep problems, supporting the premise that parents' emotional availability to infants in sleep contexts increases feelings of safety and security, and consequently better-regulated infant sleep (Teti & others, 2010). Another study found that a higher involvement of fathers in overall infant care was related to fewer infant sleep problems (Tikotzky, Sadeh, & Glickman-Gavrieli, 2010). However, infant nighttime waking problems have consistently been linked to excessive parental involvement in sleep-related interactions with their infant (Sadeh, 2008). Further research found that maternal depression during pregnancy, early introduction of solid foods, infant TV viewing, and child care attendance were related to shorter duration of infant sleep (Nevarez & others, 2010).

Cultural variations influence infant sleeping patterns. For example, in the Kipsigis culture in Kenya, infants sleep with their mothers at night and are permitted to nurse on demand (Super & Harkness, 1997). During the day, they are strapped to their mothers' backs, accompanying them on daily rounds of chores and social activities. As a result, the Kipsigis infants do not sleep through the night until much later than American infants do. During the first eight months of postnatal life, Kipsigis infants rarely sleep longer than three hours at a stretch, even at night. This sleep pattern contrasts with that of American infants, many of whom begin to sleep up to eight hours a night by 8 months of age.

(a)

(b)

FIGURE **4.9**

PLASTICITY IN THE BRAIN'S HEMISPHERES. (*a*) Michael Rehbein at 14 years of age. (*b*) Michael's right hemisphere (*top*) has reorganized to take over the language functions normally carried out by corresponding areas in the left hemisphere of an intact brain (*bottom*). However, the right hemisphere is not as efficient as the left, and more areas of the brain are recruited to process speech.

Sleep that knits up the ravelled sleave of care . . . Balm of hurt minds, nature's second course. Chief nourisher in life's feast.

—**William Shakespeare**
English Playwright, 17th Century

neuroconstructivist view Perspective holding that biological processes and environmental conditions influence the brain's development; the brain has plasticity and is context dependent; and development of the brain and cognitive development are closely linked.

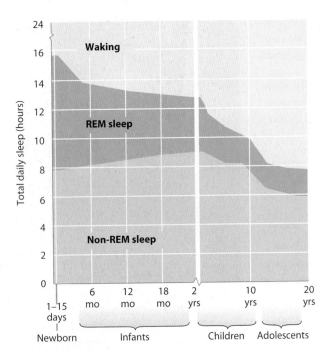

FIGURE 4.10
DEVELOPMENTAL CHANGES IN REM AND NON-REM SLEEP

- - - - - - - - - - ▶

developmental **connection**

Sleep

What are some sleep problems that children encounter in early childhood? Chapter 7, p. 212

- - - - - - - - - - ▶

developmental **connection**

Sleep

Sleep patterns change in adolescence and are linked to changes in the brain. Chapter 11, p. 368

sudden infant death syndrome (SIDS) A condition that occurs when an infant stops breathing, usually during the night, and suddenly dies without an apparent cause.

REM Sleep In REM sleep, the eyes flutter beneath closed lids; in non-REM sleep, this type of eye movement does not occur and sleep is more quiet (Sankupellay & others, 2011). Figure 4.10 shows developmental changes in the average number of total hours spent in REM and non-REM sleep. By the time they reach adulthood, individuals spend about one-fifth of their night in REM sleep, and REM sleep usually appears about one hour after non-REM sleep. However, about half of an infant's sleep is REM sleep, and infants often begin their sleep cycle with REM sleep rather than non-REM sleep. A much greater amount of time is taken up by REM sleep in infancy than at any other point in the life span. By the time infants reach 3 months of age, the percentage of time they spend in REM sleep falls to about 40 percent, and REM sleep no longer begins their sleep cycle.

Why do infants spend so much time in REM sleep? Researchers are not certain. The large amount of REM sleep may provide infants with added self-stimulation, since they spend less time awake than do older children. REM sleep also might promote the brain's development in infancy (Graven, 2006).

When adults are awakened during REM sleep, they frequently report that they have been dreaming, but when they are awakened during non-REM sleep, they are much less likely to report they have been dreaming (Cartwright & others, 2006). Since infants spend more time than adults in REM sleep, can we conclude that they dream a lot? We don't know whether infants dream or not, because they don't have any way of reporting dreams.

Shared Sleeping Sleeping arrangements for newborns vary from culture to culture (Mindell & others, 2010a, b). For example, sharing a bed with a mother is a common practice in many cultures, such as Guatemala and China, whereas in others, such as the United States and Great Britain, newborns sleep in a crib, either in the same room as the parents or in a separate room. In some cultures, infants sleep with the mother until they are weaned, after which they sleep with siblings until middle and late childhood (Walker, 2006). Whatever the sleeping arrangements, it is recommended that the infant's bedding provide firm support and that cribs should have side rails.

Shared sleeping remains a controversial issue, with some experts recommending it and others arguing against it, although recently the recommendation trend has been to avoid infant-parent bed sharing, especially until the infant is at least 6 months of age (McIntosh, Tonkin, & Gunn, 2010; Norton & Grellner, 2011). The American Academy of Pediatrics Task Force on Infant Positioning and SIDS (AAPTFIPS) (2000) recommends against shared sleeping. Its members argue that in some instances bed sharing might lead to sudden infant death syndrome (SIDS), as could be the case if a sleeping mother rolls over on her baby. Recent studies have found that bed sharing is linked with a higher incidence of SIDS, especially when parents smoke (Senter & others, 2010).

SIDS Sudden infant death syndrome (SIDS) is a condition that occurs when infants stop breathing, usually during the night, and die suddenly without any apparent reason. SIDS continues to be a leading cause of infant death in the United States, with nearly 3,000 infant deaths annually attributed to SIDS (Montagna & Chokroverty, 2011). Risk of SIDS is highest at 2 to 4 months of age (NICHD, 2011).

Since 1992, the American Academy of Pediatrics (AAP) has recommended that infants be placed to sleep on their backs (supine position) to reduce the risk of SIDS, and the frequency of prone sleeping (on the stomach) among U.S. infants has dropped dramatically (AAPTFIPS, 2000). Researchers have found that SIDS does indeed decrease when infants sleep on their backs rather than their stomachs or sides (Yiallourou & others, 2011). Among the reasons given for prone sleeping being a risk factor for SIDS are that it impairs the infant's arousal from sleep and restricts the infant's ability to swallow effectively (Franco & others, 2010). One study revealed that 26 percent of U.S. mothers of 3-month-old infants did not use the recommended supine position for their infants' nighttime sleep (Hauck & others, 2008).

In addition to sleeping in a prone position, researchers have found that the following factors are linked to SIDS:

- SIDS is less likely to occur in infants who use a pacifier when they go to sleep (Moon & others, 2012).

- Low birth weight infants are 5 to 10 times more likely to die of SIDS than are their normal-weight counterparts (Horne & others, 2002).

- Two recent reviews concluded that breast feeding is linked to a lower incidence of SIDS (Hauck & others, 2011; Zotter & Pichler, 2012)

- Infants whose siblings have died of SIDS are two to four times as likely to die of it (Lenoir, Mallet, & Calenda, 2000).

- Six percent of infants with *sleep apnea,* a temporary cessation of breathing in which the airway is completely blocked, (usually for 10 seconds or longer), die of SIDS (Katz, Mitchell, & D'Ambrosio, 2012; McNamara & Sullivan, 2000).

- African American and Eskimo infants are four to six times more likely than all others to die of SIDS (Ige & Shelton, 2004; Kitsantas & Gaffney, 2010).

- SIDS is more common in lower socioeconomic groups (Mitchell & others, 2000).

- SIDS is more common in infants who are passively exposed to cigarette smoke (Dietz & others, 2010).

- SIDS is more common when infants and parents share the same bed (Senter & others, 2010).

- SIDS is more common if infants sleep in soft bedding (Task Force on Sudden Infant Death Syndrome & Moon, 2011).

- SIDS is less common when infants sleep in a bedroom with a fan. One study revealed that sleeping in a bedroom with a fan lowers the risk of SIDS by 70 percent (Coleman-Phox, Odouli, & Li, 2008).

- SIDS occurs more often in infants with abnormal brain stem functioning involving the neurotransmitter serotonin (Broadbent & others, 2012; Duncan & others, 2010).

- Heart arrhythmias are estimated to occur in as many as 10 to 15 percent of SIDS cases, and two recent studies revealed that gene mutations are linked to the occurrence of these arrhythmias in SIDS cases (Brion & others, 2012; Van Norstrand & others, 2012).

Is this a good sleep position for infants? Why or why not?

NUTRITION

From birth to 1 year of age, human infants nearly triple their weight and increase their length by 50 percent. What do they need to sustain this growth?

Nutritional Needs and Eating Behavior   Individual differences among infants in terms of their nutrient reserves, body composition, growth rates, and activity patterns make defining actual nutrient needs difficult (Byrd-Bredbenner & others, 2013; Schiff, 2013). However, because parents need guidelines, nutritionists recommend that infants consume approximately 50 calories per day for each pound they weigh—more than twice an adult's requirement per pound.

A number of developmental changes involving eating characterize the infant's first year (Black & Hurley, 2007; Golley & others, 2012; Symon & Bammann, 2012). As infants' motor skills improve, they change from using suck-and-swallow movements with breast milk or formula to chew-and-swallow movements with semisolid and then more complex foods (van Dijk, Hunnius, & van Geert, 2012). As their fine motor control improves in the first year, they transition from being fed by others toward self-feeding. "By the end of the first year of life, children can sit independently, can chew and swallow a range of textures, are learning to feed themselves, and are making the transition to the family diet and meal patterns" (Black & Hurley, 2007, p. 1). At this point, infants need to have a diet that includes a variety of foods—especially fruits and vegetables.

Caregivers play very important roles in infants' early development of eating patterns (Lumeng & others, 2012). Caregivers who are not sensitive to developmental changes in infants' nutritional needs, neglectful caregivers, and conditions of poverty can contribute to the development of eating problems in infants (Black & Lozoff, 2008). A recent study found that low maternal sensitivity when infants were 15 and 24 months of age was linked to a higher risk of obesity in adolescence (Anderson & others, 2012).

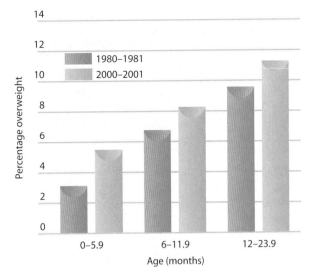

FIGURE **4.11**

PERCENTAGE OF OVERWEIGHT U.S. INFANTS IN 1980–1981 AND 2000–2001. *Note:* Infants above the 95th percentile for their age and gender on a weight-for-height index were categorized as overweight.

A national study of more than 3,000 randomly selected 4- to 24-month-olds documented that many U.S. parents aren't feeding their babies enough fruits and vegetables, but are feeding them too much junk food (Fox & others, 2004). Up to one-third of the babies ate no vegetables and fruit but frequently ate French fries, and almost half of the 7- to 8-month-old babies were fed desserts, sweets, or sweetened drinks. By 15 months, French fries were the most common vegetable the babies ate.

Such poor dietary patterns early in development can result in more infants being overweight (Dattilo & others, 2012; Gross & others, 2012). One analysis revealed that in 1980, 3.4 percent of U.S. babies less than 6 months old were overweight, a percentage that increased to almost 10 percent in 2004 (the latest U.S. government data reported) and is likely even higher today (Centers for Disease Control and Prevention, 2010; Kim & others, 2006). As shown in Figure 4.11, as younger infants become older infants, an even greater percentage are overweight.

In addition to consuming too many French fries, sweetened drinks, and desserts, are there other factors that might explain this increase in overweight U.S. infants? A mother's weight gain during pregnancy and a mother's own high weight before pregnancy may be factors (McKinney & Murray, 2013). One important factor likely is whether an infant is breast fed or bottle fed (Lawrence, 2012; Lewallen, 2012). Breast-fed infants have lower rates of weight gain than bottle-fed infants in childhood and adolescence, and it is estimated that breast feeding reduces the risk of obesity by approximately 20 percent (Li & others, 2007; Scott, Ng, & Cobiac, 2012). Also, a recent study found that the introduction of solid foods before 4 months of age was associated with an increased risk of obesity at 3 years of age (Huh & others, 2011).

Breast versus Bottle Feeding   For the first four to six months of life, human milk or an alternative formula is the baby's source of nutrients and energy. For years, debate has focused on whether breast feeding is better for the infant than bottle feeding. The growing consensus is that breast feeding is better for the baby's health (McKinney & Murray, 2013; Vasquez & Berg, 2012). Since the 1970s, breast feeding by U.S. mothers has soared (see Figure 4.12). In 2008 more than 75 percent of U.S. mothers breast fed their newborns, and 44 percent breast fed their 6-month-olds (Centers for Disease Control and Prevention, 2011). The American Academy of Pediatrics Section on Breastfeeding (2012) recently reconfirmed its recommendation of exclusive breast feeding in the first six months followed by continued breast feeding as complementary foods are introduced, and further breast feeding for one year or longer as mutually desired by the mother and infant.

What are some of the benefits of breast feeding? The following conclusions have been supported by research:

Outcomes for the Child

- *Gastrointestinal infections.* Breast-fed infants have fewer gastrointestinal infections (Garofalo, 2010).
- *Lower respiratory tract infections.* Breast-fed infants have fewer lower respiratory tract infections (Prameela, 2011).
- *Allergies.* A research review by the American Academy of Pediatrics indicated that there is no evidence that breast feeding reduces the risk of allergies in children (Greer & others, 2008).
- *Asthma.* The research review by the American Academy of Pediatrics concluded that exclusive breast feeding for three months protects against wheezing in babies, but whether it prevents asthma in older children is unclear (Greer & others, 2008).
- *Otitis media.* Breast-fed infants are less likely to develop this middle ear infection (Pelton & Leibovitz, 2009).
- *Overweight and obesity.* Consistent evidence indicates that breast-fed infants are less likely to become overweight or obese in childhood, adolescence, and adulthood (Scott, Ng, & Cobiac, 2012).

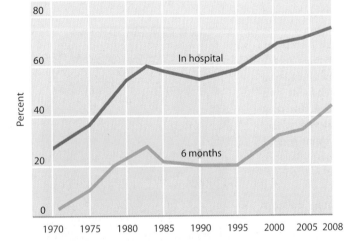

FIGURE **4.12**

TRENDS IN BREAST FEEDING IN THE UNITED STATES, 1970–2008

- *Diabetes.* Breast-fed infants are less likely to develop type 1 diabetes in childhood (Ping & Hagopian, 2006) and type 2 diabetes in adulthood (Villegas & others, 2008).
- *SIDS.* Breast-fed infants are less likely to experience SIDS (Zotter & Pichler, 2012).

In large-scale research reviews, no conclusive evidence for the benefits of breast feeding was found for children's cognitive development and cardiovascular health (Agency for Healthcare Research and Quality, 2007; Ip & others, 2009).

Outcomes for the Mother

- *Breast cancer.* Consistent evidence indicates a lower incidence of breast cancer in women who breast feed their infants (Akbari & others, 2011).
- *Ovarian cancer.* Evidence also reveals a reduction in ovarian cancer in women who breast feed their infants (Stuebe & Schwartz, 2010).
- *Type 2 diabetes.* Some evidence suggests a small reduction in type 2 diabetes in women who breast feed their infants (Stuebe & Schwartz, 2010).

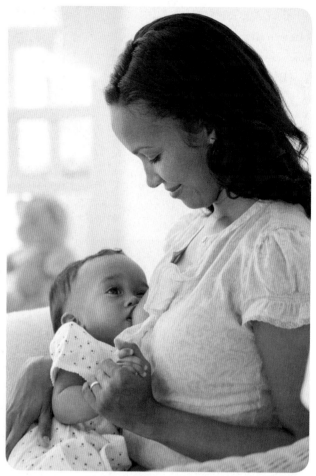

Human milk or an alternative formula is a baby's source of nutrients for the first four to six months. The growing consensus is that breast feeding is better for the baby's health, although controversy still swirls about the issue of breast feeding versus bottle feeding. *Why is breast feeding strongly recommended by pediatricians?*

In large-scale research reviews, no conclusive evidence could be found for the maternal benefits of breast feeding on return to prepregnancy weight, osteoporosis, and postpartum depression (Agency for Healthcare Research and Quality, 2007; Ip & others, 2009). However, one study revealed that women who breast fed their infants had a lower incidence of metabolic syndrome (a disorder characterized by obesity, hypertension, and insulin resistance) in midlife (Ram & others, 2008).

Many health professionals have argued that breast feeding facilitates the development of an attachment bond between the mother and infant (Britton, Britton, & Gronwaldt, 2006; Wittig & Spatz, 2008). However, a research review found that the positive role of breast feeding on the mother-infant relationship is not supported by research (Jansen, de Weerth, & Riksen-Walraven, 2008). The review concluded that recommending breast feeding should not be based on its role in improving the mother-infant relationship but rather on its positive effects on infant and maternal health.

Which women are least likely to breast feed? They include mothers who work full-time outside of the home, mothers under age 25, mothers without a high school education, African American mothers, and mothers in low-income circumstances (Merewood & others, 2007). In one study of low-income mothers in Georgia, interventions (such as counseling focused on the benefits of breast feeding and the free loan of a breast pump) increased the incidence of breast feeding (Ahluwalia & others, 2000). Increasingly, mothers who return to work in the infant's first year of life use a breast pump to extract breast milk that can be stored for later feeding of the infant when the mother is not present.

The American Academy of Pediatrics Section on Breastfeeding (2012) strongly endorses exclusive breast feeding through 6 months and further recommends breast feeding for another year. Are there circumstances when mothers should not breast feed? Yes, a mother should not breast feed (1) when she is infected with HIV or some other infectious disease that can be transmitted through her milk, (2) if she has active tuberculosis, or (3) if she is taking any drug that may not be safe for the infant (Goga & others, 2012).

Some women cannot breast feed their infants because of physical difficulties; others feel guilty if they terminate breast feeding early. Mothers may also worry that they are depriving their infants of important emotional and psychological benefits if they bottle feed rather than breast feed. Some researchers have found, however, that there are no psychological differences between breast fed and bottle fed infants (Ferguson, Harwood, & Shannon, 1987; Young, 1990).

A further issue in interpreting the benefits of breast feeding was underscored in large-scale research reviews (Agency for Healthcare Research and Quality, 2007; Ip & others,

developmental **connection**

Research Methods

How does a correlational study differ from an experimental study? Chapter 1, p. 32

2009). While highlighting a number of breast feeding benefits for children and mothers, the report issued a caution about breast feeding research: None of the findings imply causality. Breast versus bottle feeding studies are correlational not experimental, and women who breast feed are wealthier, older, more educated, and likely more health-conscious than their bottle feeding counterparts, which could explain why breast fed children are healthier.

Malnutrition in Infancy   Many infants around the world are malnourished (UNICEF, 2013). Early weaning of infants from breast milk to inadequate sources of nutrients, such as unsuitable and unsanitary cow's milk formula, can cause protein deficiency and malnutrition in infants. However, as we saw in the chapter opening story, a concern in developing countries is the increasing number of women who are HIV-positive and the fear that they will transmit this virus to their offspring (Muluye & others, 2012). Breast feeding is more optimal for mothers and infants in developing countries, except for mothers who have or are suspected of having HIV/AIDS.

A recent large-scale study that examined feeding practices in 28 developing countries found that the practices were far from optimal (Arabi & others, 2012). In this study, only 25 percent of infants 5 months of age and younger were breast fed. Also, feeding guidelines call for introducing complementary foods (solid and semisolid foods) beginning at 6 months. However, in this study, only 50 percent of the caregivers reported feeding their 6- to 8-month-olds complementary foods.

Two life-threatening conditions that can result from malnutrition are marasmus and kwashiorkor. **Marasmus** is caused by a severe protein-calorie deficiency and results in a wasting away of body tissues in the infant's first year. The infant becomes grossly underweight and his or her muscles atrophy. **Kwashiorkor,** caused by severe protein deficiency, usually appears between 1 and 3 years of age. Children with kwashiorkor sometimes appear to be well fed even though they are not because the disease can cause the child's abdomen and feet to swell with water. Kwashiorkor causes a child's vital organs to collect the nutrients that are present and deprive other parts of the body of them. The child's hair also becomes thin, brittle, and colorless, and the child's behavior often becomes listless.

Even if not fatal, severe and lengthy malnutrition is detrimental to physical, cognitive, and social development (Bentley, Wasser, & Creed-Kanashiro, 2011; Laus & others, 2011). One study found that Asian Indian children who had a history of chronic malnutrition performed more poorly on tests of attention and memory than their counterparts who were not malnourished (Kar, Rao, & Chandramouli, 2008). And a longitudinal study revealed that Barbadian infants who had experienced moderate to severe protein/energy malnutrition had persisting attention deficits when they were 40 years old (Galler & others, 2012). Researchers also have found that interventions can benefit individuals who have experienced malnutrition in infancy. Consider the following studies:

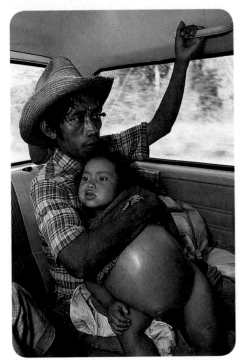

This Honduran child has kwashiorkor. Notice the telltale sign of kwashiorkor—a greatly expanded abdomen. *What are some other characteristics of kwashiorkor?*

- Standard nutritional care combined with a psychosocial intervention (group meetings with mothers and play sessions with infants, as well as six months of home visits) reduced the negative effects of malnutrition on severely malnourished Bangladesh 6- to 24-month-olds' cognitive development (Najar & others, 2008).

- Guatemalan infants whose mothers had been given nutritious supplements during pregnancy, and who themselves had been given more nutritious, high-calorie foods in their first two years of life, were more active, more involved, more helpful with their peers, less anxious, and happier than their counterparts who had not been given nutritional supplements at the time they entered elementary school (Barrett, Radke-Yarrow, & Klein, 1982).

To read further about providing nutritional supplements to improve infants' and young children's nutrition, see *Connecting Development to Life.*

Adequate early nutrition is an important aspect of healthy development (Schiff, 2013). In addition to sound nutrition, children need a nurturing, supportive environment (Anderson & others, 2012). One individual who has stood out as an advocate of caring for children is T. Berry Brazelton, who is featured in *Connecting with Careers.*

marasmus A wasting away of body tissues in the infant's first year, caused by severe protein-calorie deficiency.

kwashiorkor A condition caused by severe protein deficiency in which the child's abdomen and feet become swollen with water; usually appears between 1 and 3 years of age.

Improving the Nutrition of Infants and Young Children Living in Low-Income Families

Poor nutrition is a special concern in the lives of infants from low-income families. To address this problem in the United States, the WIC (Women, Infants, and Children) program provides federal grants to states for healthy supplemental foods, health care referrals, and nutrition education for women from low-income families beginning in pregnancy, and to infants and young children up to 5 years of age who are at nutritional risk (Hillier & others, 2012; WIC New York, 2011; Whaley & others, 2012). WIC serves approximately 7,500,000 participants in the United States.

Positive influences on infants' and young children's nutrition and health have been found for participants in WIC (Davis, Lazariu, & Sekhobo, 2010; Sekhobo & others, 2010). One study revealed that a WIC program that introduced peer counseling services for pregnant women increased breast feeding initiation by 27 percent (Olson & others, 2010a, b). Another study found that entry in the first trimester of pregnancy to the WIC program in Rhode Island reduced maternal cigarette smoking (Brodsky, Viner-Brown, & Handler, 2009). And a recent multiple-year literacy intervention with Spanish-speaking families in the WIC program in Los Angeles increased literacy resources and activities at home, which in turn led to a higher level of school readiness in children (Whaley & others, 2011).

Participants in the WIC program. *What are some changes the WIC program is trying to implement?*

Why would the WIC program provide lactation counseling as part of its services?

connecting with careers

T. Berry Brazelton, Pediatrician

T. Berry Brazelton is America's best-known pediatrician as a result of his numerous books, television appearances, and newspaper and magazine articles about parenting and children's health. He takes a family-centered approach to child development issues and communicates with parents in easy-to-understand ways.

Dr. Brazelton founded the Child Development Unit at Boston Children's Hospital and created the Brazelton Neonatal Behavioral Assessment Scale, a widely used measure of the newborn's health and well-being (which you read about in Chapter 3). He also has conducted a number of research studies on infants and children and has been president of the Society for Research in Child Development, a leading research organization.

For more information about what pediatricians do, see page 45 in the Careers in Life-Span Development appendix.

T. Berry Brazelton, pediatrician, with a young child.

Review *Connect* Reflect

LG1 Discuss physical growth and development in infancy.

Review

- What are cephalocaudal and proximodistal patterns?
- What changes in height and weight take place in infancy?
- What are some key features of the brain and its development in infancy?
- What changes occur in sleep during infancy?
- What are infants' nutritional needs?

Connect

- What types of brain research technology can be used to study infants that cannot be used to study them before they are born? Which can be used on adults but not infants? How might this affect our understanding of the human brain across the life span?

Reflect *Your Own Personal Journey of Life*

- What sleep and nutrition guidelines would you follow for enhancing the health and safety of your own infant?

2 Motor Development

LG2 Describe infants' motor development.

The Dynamic Systems View   Reflexes   Gross Motor Skills   Fine Motor Skills

Esther Thelen is shown conducting an experiment to discover how infants learn to control their arm movements to reach and grasp for objects. A computer device is used to monitor the infant's arm movements and to track muscle patterns. Thelen's research is conducted from a dynamic systems perspective. *What is the nature of this perspective?*

As a newborn, Ramona, whom you read about in the chapter opening, could suck, fling her arms, and tightly grip a finger placed in her tiny hand. Within just two years, she would be toddling around on her own, opening doors and jars as she explored her little world. Are her accomplishments inevitable? How do infants develop their motor skills, and which skills do they develop when?

THE DYNAMIC SYSTEMS VIEW

Developmentalist Arnold Gesell (1934) thought his painstaking observations had revealed how people develop their motor skills. He had discovered that infants and children develop rolling, sitting, standing, and other motor skills in a fixed order and within specific time frames. These observations, said Gesell, show that motor development comes about through the unfolding of a genetic plan, or *maturation.*

Later studies, however, demonstrated that the sequence of developmental milestones is not as fixed as Gesell indicated and not due as much to heredity as Gesell argued (Adolph & Berger, 2013; Adolph & Robinson, 2013). In the last two decades, the study of motor development experienced a renaissance as psychologists developed new insights about *how* motor skills develop (Thelen & Smith, 1998, 2006). One increasingly influential theory is dynamic systems theory, proposed by Esther Thelen.

According to **dynamic systems theory,** infants assemble motor skills for perceiving and acting. Notice that perception and action are coupled, according to this theory (Thelen & Smith, 2006). To develop motor skills, infants must perceive something in the environment that motivates them to act and use their perceptions to fine-tune their movements. Motor skills represent solutions to the infant's goals (Keen, 2011).

How is a motor skill developed, according to this theory? When infants are motivated to do something, they might create a new motor behavior. The new behavior is the result of many converging factors: the development of the nervous system, the body's physical properties and its possibilities for movement, the goal the child is motivated to reach, and the environmental support for the skill. For example, babies learn to walk only when maturation of the nervous system allows them to control certain leg muscles, when their legs have grown enough to support their weight, and when they want to move.

dynamic systems theory The perspective on motor development that seeks to explain how motor behaviors are assembled for perceiving and acting.

Mastering a motor skill requires the infant's active efforts to coordinate several components of the skill. Infants explore and select possible solutions to the demands of a new task; they assemble adaptive patterns by modifying their current movement patterns. The first step occurs when the infant is motivated by a new challenge—such as the desire to cross a room—and gets into the "ballpark" of the task demands by taking a couple of stumbling steps. Then, the infant "tunes" these movements to make them smoother and more effective. The tuning is achieved through repeated cycles of action and perception of the consequences of that action. According to the dynamic systems view, even universal milestones, such as crawling, reaching, and walking, are learned through this process of adaptation: Infants modulate their movement patterns to fit a new task by exploring and selecting possible configurations (Adolph & Robinson, 2013).

To see how dynamic systems theory explains motor behavior, imagine that you offer a new toy to a baby named Gabriel (Thelen & others, 1993). There is no exact program that can tell Gabriel ahead of time how to move his arm and hand and fingers to grasp the toy. Gabriel must adapt to his goal—grasping the toy—and the context. From his sitting position, he must make split-second adjustments to extend his arm, holding his body steady so that his arm and torso don't plow into the toy. Muscles in his arm and shoulder contract and stretch in a host of combinations, exerting a variety of forces. He improvises a way to reach out with one arm and wrap his fingers around the toy.

Thus, according to dynamic systems theory, motor development is not a passive process in which genes dictate the unfolding of a sequence of skills over time. Rather, the infant actively puts together a skill to achieve a goal within the constraints set by the infant's body and environment. Nature and nurture, the infant and the environment, are all working together as part of an ever-changing system.

As we examine the course of motor development, we will describe how dynamic systems theory applies to some specific skills. First, though, let's examine how the story of motor development begins with reflexes.

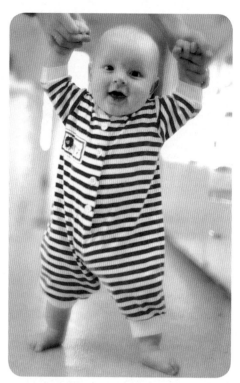

How might dynamic systems theory explain the development of learning to walk?

REFLEXES

The newborn is not completely helpless. Among other things, it has some basic reflexes. For example, when submerged in water, the newborn automatically holds its breath and contracts its throat to keep water out. **Reflexes** are built-in reactions to stimuli; they govern the newborn's movements, which are automatic and beyond the newborn's control. Reflexes are genetically carried survival mechanisms. They allow infants to respond adaptively to their environment before they have had the opportunity to learn.

The rooting and sucking reflexes are important examples. Both have survival value for newborn mammals, who must find a mother's breast to obtain nourishment. The **rooting reflex** occurs when the infant's cheek is stroked or the side of the mouth is touched. In response, the infant turns its head toward the side that was touched in an apparent effort to find something to suck. The **sucking reflex** occurs when newborns automatically suck an object placed in their mouth. This reflex enables newborns to get nourishment before they have associated a nipple with food and also serves as a self-soothing or self-regulating mechanism.

Another example is the **Moro reflex,** which occurs in response to a sudden, intense noise or movement (see Figure 4.13). When startled, the newborn arches its back, throws back its head, and flings out its arms and legs. Then the newborn rapidly closes its arms and legs. The Moro reflex is believed to be a way of grabbing for support while falling; it would have had survival value for our primate ancestors.

Some reflexes—coughing, sneezing, blinking, shivering, and yawning, for example—persist throughout life. They are as important for the adult as they are for the infant. Other reflexes, though, disappear several months following birth, as the infant's brain matures and voluntary control over many behaviors develops. The rooting and Moro reflexes, for example, tend to disappear when the infant is 3 to 4 months old.

The movements of some reflexes eventually become incorporated into more complex, voluntary actions. One important example is the **grasping reflex,** which occurs when something touches the infant's palms (see Figure 4.13). The infant responds by grasping tightly. By the end of the third month, the grasping reflex diminishes and the infant shows a more

reflexes Built-in reactions to stimuli that govern the newborn's movements, which are automatic and beyond the newborn's control.

rooting reflex A newborn's built-in reaction that occurs when the infant's cheek is stroked or the side of the mouth is touched. In response, the infant turns his or her head toward the side that was touched, in an apparent effort to find something to suck.

sucking reflex A newborn's built-in reaction to automatically suck an object placed in its mouth. The sucking reflex enables the infant to get nourishment before he or she has associated a nipple with food and also serves as a self-soothing or self-regulating mechanism.

Moro reflex A neonatal startle response that occurs in reaction to a sudden, intense noise or movement. When startled, the newborn arches its back, throws its head back, and flings out its arms and legs. Then the newborn rapidly pulls its arms and legs close to the center of the body.

grasping reflex A neonatal reflex that occurs when something touches the infant's palms. The infant responds by grasping tightly.

FIGURE 4.13
NEWBORN REFLEXES. Young infants have several reflexes, including the Moro reflex (*Top*) and grasping reflex (*Bottom*).

voluntary grasp. As its motor coordination becomes smoother, the infant will grasp objects, carefully manipulate them, and explore their qualities.

The old view of reflexes is that they were exclusively genetic, built-in mechanisms that govern the infant's movements. The new perspective on infant reflexes is that they are not automatic or completely beyond the infant's control. For example, infants can control such movements as alternating their legs to make a mobile jiggle or change their sucking rate to listen to a recording (Adolph & Berger, 2013).

GROSS MOTOR SKILLS

Ask any parents about their baby, and sooner or later you are likely to hear about one or more motor milestones, such as "Cassandra just learned to crawl," "Jesse is finally sitting alone," or "Angela took her first step last week." Parents proudly announce such milestones as their children transform themselves from babies unable to lift their heads to toddlers who grab things off the grocery store shelf, chase a cat, and participate actively in the family's social life (Thelen, 2000). These milestones are examples of **gross motor skills,** which are skills that involve large-muscle activities, such as moving one's arms and walking.

The Development of Posture　How do gross motor skills develop? As a foundation, these skills require postural control (Thelen & Smith, 2006). For example, to track moving objects, you must be able to control your head in order to stabilize your gaze; before you can walk, you must be able to balance on one leg.

Posture is more than just holding still and straight. Posture is a dynamic process that is linked with sensory information in the skin, joints, and muscles, which tell us where we are in space; in vestibular organs in the inner ear that regulate balance and equilibrium; and in vision and hearing (Thelen & Smith, 2006).

Newborn infants cannot voluntarily control their posture. Within a few weeks, though, they can hold their heads erect, and soon they can lift their heads while prone. By 2 months of age, babies can sit while supported on a lap or an infant seat, but they cannot sit independently until they are 6 or 7 months of age. Standing also develops gradually during the first year of life. By about 8 to 9 months of age, infants usually learn to pull themselves up and hold on to a chair, and they often can stand alone by about 10 to 12 months of age.

Learning to Walk　Locomotion and postural control are closely linked, especially in walking upright (Adolph & Berger, 2013; Adolph & Robinson, 2013). To walk upright, the baby must be able both to balance on one leg as the other is swung forward and to shift the weight from one leg to the other.

Even young infants can make the alternating leg movements that are needed for walking. The neural pathways that control leg alternation are in place from a very early age, even at birth or before. Indeed, researchers have found that alternating leg movements occur during the fetal period and at birth (Adolph & Robinson, 2013).

If infants can produce forward stepping movements so early, why does it take them so long to learn to walk? The key skills in learning to walk appear to be stabilizing balance on one leg long enough to swing the other forward and shifting the weight without falling. These are difficult biomechanical problems to solve, and it takes infants about a year to do it.

In learning to locomote, infants learn what kinds of places and surfaces are safe for locomotion (Adolph & others, 2012). Karen Adolph (1997) investigated how experienced and inexperienced crawling infants and walking infants go down steep slopes (see Figure 4.14). Newly crawling infants, who averaged about 8½ months in age, rather indiscriminately went down the steep slopes, often falling in the process (with their mothers next to the slope to

gross motor skills Motor skills that involve large-muscle activities, such as walking.

Newly crawling infant

Experienced walker

FIGURE **4.14**

THE ROLE OF EXPERIENCE IN CRAWLING AND WALKING INFANTS' JUDGMENTS OF WHETHER TO GO DOWN A SLOPE. Karen Adolph (1997) found that locomotor experience rather than age was the primary predictor of adaptive responding on slopes of varying steepness. Newly crawling and walking infants could not judge the safety of the various slopes. With experience, they learned to avoid slopes where they would fall. When expert crawlers began to walk, they again made mistakes and fell, even though they had judged the same slope accurately when crawling. Adolph referred to this as the specificity of learning because it does not transfer across crawling and walking.

catch them). After weeks of practice, the crawling babies became more adept at judging which slopes were too steep to crawl down and which ones they could navigate safely. New walkers also could not judge the safety of the slopes, but experienced walkers accurately matched their skills with the steepness of the slopes. They rarely fell downhill, either refusing to go down the steep slopes or going down backward in a cautious manner. Experienced walkers perceptually assessed the situation—looking, swaying, touching, and thinking before they moved down the slope. With experience, both the crawlers and the walkers learned to avoid the risky slopes where they would fall, integrating perceptual information with the development of a new motor behavior. In this research, we again see the importance of perceptual-motor coupling in the development of motor skills. Thus, practice is very important in the development of new motor skills (Adolph & others, 2012).

Practice is especially important in learning to walk (Adolph & Robinson, 2013). "Thousands of daily walking steps, each step slightly different from the last because of variations in the terrain and the continually varying biomechanical constraints on the body, may help infants to identify the relevant" combination of strength and balance required to improve their walking skills (Adolph, Vereijken, & Shrout, 2003, p. 495). In a recent study, Adolph and her colleagues (2012) observed 12- to 19-month-olds during free play. Locomotor experience was extensive, with the infants averaging 2,368 steps and 17 falls per hour.

The First Year: Motor Development Milestones and Variations Figure 4.15 summarizes the range in which infants accomplish various gross motor skills during the first year, culminating in the ability to walk easily. The timing of these milestones, especially the later ones, may vary by as much as two to four months, and experiences can modify the onset of these accomplishments (Adolph & Berger, 2013). For example, since 1992, when pediatricians began recommending that parents place their babies on their backs when they sleep, fewer babies crawled, and those who did crawled later (Davis & others, 1998). Also, some infants do not follow the standard sequence of motor accomplishments. For example, many American infants never crawl on their belly or on their hands and knees. They may discover an idiosyncratic form of locomotion before walking, such as rolling, or they might never locomote until they get upright (Adolph & Robinson, 2013). In the African Mali tribe, most infants do not crawl (Bril, 1999). And in Jamaica, approximately one-fourth of babies skip crawling (Hopkins, 1991).

According to Karen Adolph and Sarah Berger (2005), "the old-fashioned view that growth and motor development reflect merely the age-related output of maturation is, at best, incomplete. Rather, infants acquire new skills with the help of their caregivers in a real-world environment of objects, surfaces, and planes."

Development in the Second Year The motor accomplishments of the first year bring increasing independence, allowing infants to explore their environment more extensively and to initiate interaction with others more readily. In the second year of life, toddlers become more

A baby is an angel whose wings decrease as his legs increase.

—**French Proverb**

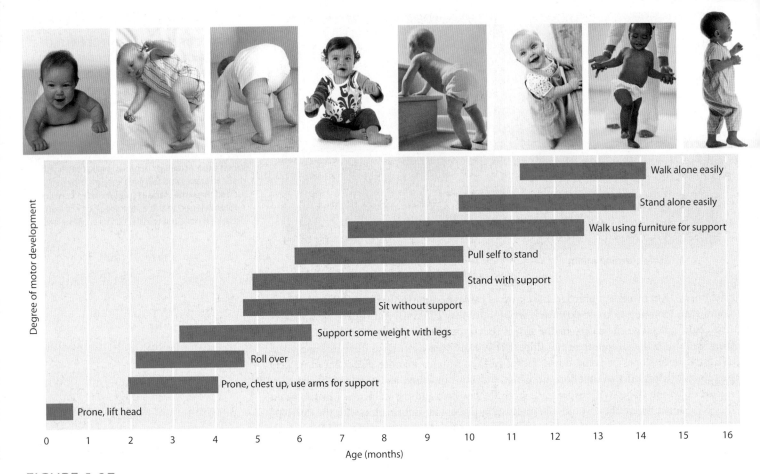

FIGURE **4.15**

MILESTONES IN GROSS MOTOR DEVELOPMENT. The horizontal red bars indicate the range in which most infants reach various milestones in gross motor development.

motorically skilled and mobile. Motor activity during the second year is vital to the child's competent development, and few restrictions, except for safety, should be placed on their adventures.

By 13 to 18 months, toddlers can pull a toy attached to a string and use their hands and legs to climb up a number of steps. By 18 to 24 months, toddlers can walk quickly or run stiffly for a short distance, balance on their feet in a squatting position while playing with objects on the floor, walk backward without losing their balance, stand and kick a ball without falling, stand and throw a ball, and jump in place.

Can parents give their babies a head start on becoming physically fit and physically talented through structured exercise classes? Most infancy experts recommend against structured exercise classes for babies. But there are other ways to guide infants' motor development.

Mothers in developing countries tend to stimulate their infants' motor skills more than mothers in more developed countries (Hopkins, 1991). In many African, Indian, and Caribbean cultures, mothers massage and stretch their infants during daily baths (Adolph, Karasik, & Tamis-LeMonda, 2010). Mothers in the Gusii culture of Kenya also encourage vigorous movement in their babies.

(*Left*) In the Algonquin culture in Quebec, Canada, babies are strapped to a cradle board for much of their infancy. (*Right*) In Jamaica, mothers massage and stretch their infants' arms and legs. *To what extent do cultural variations in the activity infants engage in influence the time at which they reach motor milestones?*

Do these cultural variations make a difference in the infant's motor development? When caregivers provide babies with physical guidance by physically handling them in special ways (such as stroking, massaging, or stretching) or by giving them opportunities for exercise, the infants often reach motor milestones earlier than infants whose caregivers have not provided these activities (Adolph, Karasik, & Tamis-LeMonda, 2010). For example, Jamaican mothers expect their infants to sit and walk alone two to three months earlier than English mothers do (Hopkins & Westra, 1990). And in sub-Saharan Africa, traditional practices in many villages involve mothers and siblings engaging babies in exercises, such as frequent exercise for trunk and pelvic muscles (Super & Harkness, 1997).

Many forms of restricted movement—such as Chinese sandbags, orphanage restrictions, and failure of caregivers to encourage movement in Budapest—have been found to produce substantial delays in motor development (Adolph, Karasik, & Tamis-LeMonda, 2010). In some rural Chinese provinces, for example, babies are placed in a bag of fine sand, which acts as a diaper and is changed once a day. The baby is left alone, face up, and is visited only when being fed by the mother (Xie & Young, 1999). Some studies of swaddling show slight delays in motor development, but other studies show no delays. Cultures that do swaddle infants usually do so early in the infant's development when the infant is not mobile; when the infant becomes more mobile, swaddling decreases.

A young girl using a pincer grip to pick up puzzle pieces.

FINE MOTOR SKILLS

Whereas gross motor skills involve large muscle activity, **fine motor skills** involve finely tuned movements. Grasping a toy, using a spoon, buttoning a shirt, or anything that requires finger dexterity demonstrates fine motor skills. Infants have hardly any control over fine motor skills at birth, but newborns do have many components of what will become finely coordinated arm, hand, and finger movements (McCormack, Hoerl, & Butterfill, 2012).

The onset of reaching and grasping marks a significant achievement in infants' ability to interact with their surroundings (Greif & Needham, 2012; Sgandurra & others, 2012; Ziemer, Plumert, & Pick, 2012). During the first two years of life, infants refine how they reach and grasp (Needham, 2009). Initially, infants reach by moving their shoulders and elbows crudely, swinging toward an object. Later, when infants reach for an object they move their wrists, rotate their hands, and coordinate their thumb and forefinger. Infants do not have to see their own hands in order to reach for an object (Clifton & others, 1993). Cues from muscles, tendons, and joints, not sight of the limb, guide reaching by 4-month-old infants.

Infants refine their ability to grasp objects by developing two types of grasps. Initially, infants grip with the whole hand, which is called the *palmer grasp*. Later, toward the end of the first year, infants also grasp small objects with their thumb and forefinger, which is called the *pincer grip*. Their grasping system is very flexible. They vary their grip on an object depending on its size, shape, and texture, as well as the size of their own hands relative to the object's size. Infants grip small objects with their thumb and forefinger (and sometimes their middle finger too), whereas they grip large objects with all of the fingers of one hand or both hands.

Perceptual-motor coupling is necessary for the infant to coordinate grasping (Barrett, Traupman, & Needham, 2008). Which perceptual system the infant is most likely to use to coordinate grasping varies with age. Four-month-old infants rely greatly on touch to determine how they will grip an object; 8-month-olds are more likely to use vision as a guide (Newell & others, 1989). This developmental change is efficient because vision lets infants preshape their hands as they reach for an object.

Experience plays a role in reaching and grasping. In one study, 3-month-old infants participated in play sessions wearing "sticky mittens"—"mittens with palms that stuck to the edges of toys and allowed the infants to pick up the toys" (Needham, Barrett, & Peterman, 2002, p. 279) (see Figure 4.16). Infants who participated in sessions with the mittens grasped and manipulated objects earlier in their development than a control group of infants who did not receive the "mitten" experience. The experienced infants looked at the objects longer, swatted at them more during visual contact, and were more likely to mouth the objects. In a recent study, 5-month-old infants whose parents trained them to use the sticky mittens for 10 minutes a day over a two-week period showed advances in their reaching behavior at the end of the two weeks (Libertus & Needham, 2010).

FIGURE **4.16**

INFANTS' USE OF "STICKY MITTENS" TO EXPLORE OBJECTS. Amy Needham and her colleagues (2002) found that "sticky mittens" enhanced young infants' object exploration skills.

fine motor skills Motor skills that involve more finely tuned movements, such as finger dexterity.

Just as infants need to exercise their gross motor skills, they also need to exercise their fine motor skills (Needham, 2009). Especially when they can manage a pincer grip, infants delight in picking up small objects. Many develop the pincer grip and begin to crawl at about the same time, and infants at this time pick up virtually everything in sight, especially on the floor, and put the objects in their mouth. Thus, parents need to be vigilant in regularly monitoring what objects are within the infant's reach (Keen, 2005).

Rachel Keen (2011) emphasizes that tool use is an excellent context for studying problem solving in infants because tool use provides information about how infants plan to reach a goal. Researchers in this area have studied infants' intentional actions, which range from picking up a spoon in different orientations to retrieving rakes from inside tubes.

Review *Connect* Reflect

 LG2 Describe infants' motor development.

Review

- What is the dynamic systems view?
- What are some reflexes that infants have?
- How do gross motor skills develop in infancy?
- How do fine motor skills develop in infancy?

Connect

- What are the differences between the grasping reflex present at birth and the fine

motor grasping skills an infant develops between 4 and 12 months of age?

Reflect *Your Own Personal Journey of Life*

- Think of a motor skill that you perform. How would dynamic systems theory explain your motor skill performance?

---

3 Sensory and Perceptual Development

 LG3 Summarize the course of sensory and perceptual development in infancy.

| What Are Sensation and Perception? | The Ecological View | Visual Perception | Other Senses | Intermodal Perception | Nature, Nurture, and Perceptual Development | Perceptual-Motor Coupling |

> The experiences of the first three years of life are almost entirely lost to us, and when we attempt to enter into a small child's world, we come as foreigners who have forgotten the landscape and no longer speak the native tongue.
>
> —SELMA FRAIBERG
> *Developmentalist and Child Advocate, 20th Century*

How do sensations and perceptions develop? Can a newborn see? If so, what can it perceive? What about the other senses—hearing, smell, taste, and touch? What are they like in the newborn, and how do they develop? Can an infant put together information from two modalities, such as sight and sound? These are among the intriguing questions that we will explore in this section.

WHAT ARE SENSATION AND PERCEPTION?

How does a newborn know that her mother's skin is soft rather than rough? How does a 5-year-old know what color his hair is? Infants and children "know" these things as a result of information that comes through the senses. Without vision, hearing, touch, taste, and smell, we would be isolated from the world; we would live in dark silence, a tasteless, colorless, feelingless void.

Sensation occurs when information interacts with sensory *receptors*—the eyes, ears, tongue, nostrils, and skin. The sensation of hearing occurs when waves of pulsating air are collected by the outer ear and transmitted through the bones of the inner ear to the auditory nerve. The sensation of vision occurs as rays of light contact the eyes, become focused on the retina, and are transmitted by the optic nerve to the visual centers of the brain.

Perception is the interpretation of what is sensed. The air waves that contact the ears might be interpreted as noise or as musical sounds, for example. The physical energy transmitted to

sensation The product of the interaction between information and the sensory receptors—the eyes, ears, tongue, nostrils, and skin.

perception The interpretation of what is sensed.

the retina of the eye might be interpreted as a particular color, pattern, or shape, depending on how it is perceived.

THE ECOLOGICAL VIEW

For the past several decades, much of the research on perceptual development in infancy has been guided by the ecological view of Eleanor and James J. Gibson (E. J. Gibson, 1969, 1989, 2001; J. J. Gibson, 1966, 1979). They argue that we do not have to take bits and pieces of data from sensations and build up representations of the world in our minds. Instead, our perceptual system can select from the rich information that the environment itself provides.

According to the Gibsons' **ecological view,** we directly perceive information that exists in the world around us. This view is called *ecological* "because it connects perceptual capabilities to information available in the world of the perceiver" (Kellman & Arterberry, 2006, p. 112). Thus, perception brings us into contact with the environment so we can interact with and adapt to it. Perception is designed for action. Perception gives people such information as when to duck, when to turn their bodies through a narrow passageway, and when to put their hands up to catch something.

In the Gibsons' view, objects have **affordances,** which are opportunities for interaction offered by objects that fit within our capabilities to perform activities. A pot may afford you something to cook with, and it may afford a toddler something to bang. Adults typically know when a chair is appropriate for sitting, when a surface is safe for walking, or when an object is within reach. We directly and accurately perceive these affordances by sensing information from the environment—the light or sound reflecting from the surfaces of the world—and from our own bodies through muscle receptors, joint receptors, and skin receptors, for example (Ziemer, Plumert, & Pick, 2012).

An important developmental question is: What affordances can infants or children detect and use? In one study, for example, when babies who could walk were faced with a squishy waterbed, they stopped and explored it, then chose to crawl rather than walk across it (Gibson & others, 1987). They combined perception and action to adapt to the demands of the task.

Similarly, as we described earlier in the section on motor development, infants who were just learning to crawl or just learning to walk were less cautious when confronted with a steep slope than experienced crawlers or walkers were (Adolph, 1997). The more experienced crawlers and walkers perceived that a slope *affords* the possibility for not only faster locomotion but also for falling. Again, infants coupled perception and action to make a decision about what do in their environment. Through perceptual development, children become more efficient at discovering and using affordances.

Studying infants' perceptions has not been an easy task. For instance, if newborns have limited communication abilities and are unable to verbalize what they are seeing, hearing, smelling, and so on, how can we study their perception? *Connecting Through Research* describes some of the ingenious ways researchers study infants' perceptions.

VISUAL PERCEPTION

What do newborns see? How does visual perception develop in infancy?

Visual Acuity and Human Faces   Psychologist William James (1890/1950) called the newborn's perceptual world a "blooming, buzzing confusion." More than a century later, we can safely say that he was wrong (Atkinson & Braddick, 2013; Johnson, 2012, 2013; Mauer & Lewis, 2013). Even the newborn perceives a world with some order. That world, however, is far different from the one perceived by the toddler or the adult.

Just how well can infants see? At birth, the nerves and muscles and lens of the eye are still developing. As a result, newborns cannot see small things that are far away. The newborn's vision is estimated to be 20/240 on the well-known Snellen chart used for eye examinations, which means that a newborn can see at 20 feet what a normal adult can see at 240 feet (Aslin & Lathrop, 2008). In other words, an object 20 feet away is only as clear to the newborn as it would be if it were 240 feet away from an adult with normal vision (20/20). By 6 months of age, though, on *average* vision is 20/40 (Aslin & Lathrop, 2008).

How would you use the Gibsons' ecological theory of perception and the concept of affordance to explain the role that perception is playing in this toddler's activity?

ecological view The view that perception functions to bring organisms in contact with the environment and to increase adaptation.

affordances Opportunities for interaction offered by objects that fit within our capabilities to perform functional activities.

How Can Newborns' Perception Be Studied?

The creature has poor motor coordination and can move itself only with great difficulty. Although it cries when uncomfortable, it uses few other vocalizations. In fact, it sleeps most of the time, about 16 to 17 hours a day. You are curious about this creature and want to know more about what it can do. You think to yourself, "I wonder if it can see. How could I find out?"

You obviously have a communication problem with the creature. You must devise a way that will allow the creature to "tell" you that it can see. While examining the creature one day, you make an interesting discovery. When you move an object horizontally in front of the creature, its eyes follow the object's movement.

The creature's head movement suggests that it has at least some vision. In case you haven't already guessed, the creature you have been reading about is the human infant, and the role you played is that of a researcher interested in devising techniques to learn about the infant's visual perception. After years of work, scientists have developed research methods and tools sophisticated enough to examine the subtle abilities of infants and to interpret their complex actions (Bendersky & Sullivan, 2007).

Visual Preference Method

Robert Fantz (1963) was a pioneer in this effort. Fantz made an important discovery that advanced the ability of researchers to investigate infants' visual perception: Infants look at different things for different lengths of time. Fantz placed an infant in a "looking chamber," which had two visual displays on the ceiling above the infant's head. An experimenter viewed the infant's eyes by looking through a peephole. If the infant was fixating on one of the displays, the experimenter could see the display's reflection in the infant's eyes. This allowed the experimenter to determine how long the infant looked at each display. Fantz (1963) found that infants only two days old look longer at patterned stimuli, such as

faces and concentric circles, than at red, white, or yellow discs. Infants 2 to 3 weeks old also preferred to look at patterns—a face, a piece of printed matter, or a bull's-eye—longer than at red, yellow, or white discs (see Figure 4.17). Fantz' research method—studying whether infants can distinguish one stimulus from another by measuring the length of time they attend to different stimuli—is referred to as the **visual preference method.**

Habituation and Dishabituation

Another way that researchers have studied infant perception is to present a stimulus (such as a sight or a sound) a number of times. If the infant decreases its response to the stimulus after several presentations, it indicates that the infant is no longer interested in looking at the stimulus. If the researcher now presents a new stimulus, the infant's response will recover—indicating the infant can discriminate between the old and new stimulus (Snyder & Torrence, 2008).

Habituation is the name given to decreased responsiveness to a stimulus after repeated presentations of the stimulus. **Dishabituation** is the recovery of a habituated response after a change in stimulation. Newborn infants can habituate to repeated sights, sounds, smells, or touches (Rovee-Collier, 2004). Among the measures researchers use in

visual preference method A method used to determine whether infants can distinguish one stimulus from another by measuring the length of time they attend to different stimuli.

habituation Decreased responsiveness to a stimulus after repeated presentations of the stimulus.

dishabituation Recovery of a habituated response after a change in stimulation.

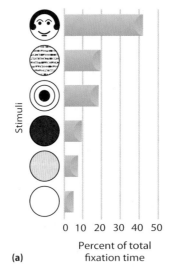

(a)

Stimuli

Percent of total fixation time

(b)

FIGURE **4.17**

FANTZ' EXPERIMENT ON INFANTS' VISUAL PERCEPTION. (*a*) Infants 2 to 3 weeks old preferred to look at some stimuli more than others. In Fantz' experiment, infants preferred to look at patterns rather than at color or brightness. For example, they looked longer at a face, a piece of printed matter, or a bull's-eye than at red, yellow, or white discs. (*b*) Fantz used a "looking chamber" to study infants' perception of stimuli.

(continued)

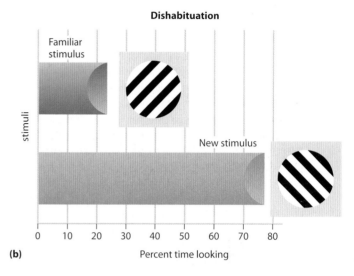

FIGURE **4.18**

HABITUATION AND DISHABITUATION. In the first part of one study, (*a*) 7-hour-old newborns were shown a stimulus. As indicated, the newborns looked at it an average of 41 seconds when it was first presented to them (Slater, Morison, & Somers, 1988). Over seven more presentations of the stimulus, they looked at it less and less. In the second part of the study, (*b*) infants were presented with both the familiar stimulus to which they had just become habituated and a new stimulus (which was rotated 90 degrees). The newborns looked at the new stimulus three times as long as the familiar stimulus.

habituation studies are sucking behavior (sucking stops when the young infant attends to a novel object), heart and respiration rates, and the length of time the infant looks at an object. Figure 4.18 shows the results of one study of habituation and dishabituation with newborns (Slater, Morison, & Somers, 1988).

High-Amplitude Sucking

To assess an infant's attention to sound, researchers often use a method called *high-amplitude sucking*. In this method, infants are given a nonnutritive nipple to suck, and the nipple is connected to a sound generating system. The researcher computes a baseline high-amplitude sucking rate in a one-minute silent period. Following the baseline, presentation of a sound is made contingent on the rate of high-amplitude sucking. Initially babies suck frequently so the sound occurs often. Gradually they lose interest in hearing the same sound, so they begin to suck less often. Then the researcher changes the sound that is being presented. If

FIGURE **4.19**

AN INFANT WEARING EYE-TRACKING HEADGEAR. Photo from Karen Adolph's laboratory at New York University.

the babies renew their vigorous sucking, the inference is that they have discriminated the sound change and are sucking more because they want to hear the interesting new sound (Menn & Stoel-Gammon, 2009).

The Orienting Response and Eye-Tracking

A technique that can be used to determine whether an infant can see or hear is the *orienting response*, which involves turning one's head toward a sight or sound. Another technique, *eye-tracking* consists of measuring eye movements that follow (*track*) a moving object and can be used to evaluate an infant's early visual ability, or a startle response can determine an infant's reaction to a noise (Bendersky & Sullivan, 2007). The most important recent advance in measuring infant perception is the development of sophisticated eye-tracking equipment (Franchak & others, 2011; Morgante, Zolfaghari, & Johnson, 2012; Navab & others, 2012). Figure 4.19 shows an infant wearing an

(continued)

eye-tracking headgear in a recent study on visually guided motor behavior and social interaction.

One of the main reasons that infant perception researchers are so enthusiastic about the recent availability of sophisticated eye-tracking equipment is that looking time is among the most important measures of infant perceptual and cognitive development (Aslin, 2012). The new eye-tracking equipment allows for far greater precision in assessing various aspects of infant looking and gaze than is possible with human observation (Oakes, 2012). Among the areas of infant perception in which eye-tracking equipment is being used are memory, joint attention, and face processing (Falck-Yttere & others, 2012; Richmond & Nelson, 2009; Wheeler & others, 2011). Further, eye-tracking equipment is improving our understanding of atypically developing infants, such as those with autism (Sasson & Elison, 2012), and infants at risk for atypical developmental outcomes, including infants at risk for developing autism and preterm infants (Bedford & others, 2012).

A recent eye-tracking study shed light on the effectiveness of TV programs and DVDs that claim to educate infants (Kirkorian, Anderson, & Keen, 2012). In this study, 1-year-olds, 4-year-olds, and adults watched *Sesame Street* and the eye-tracking equipment recorded precisely what they looked at on the screen. The 1-year-olds were far less likely to consistently look at the same part of the screen as their older counterparts, suggesting that the 1-year-olds showed little understanding of the *Sesame Street* video but instead were more likely to be attracted by what was salient than by what was relevant.

Equipment

Technology can facilitate the use of most methods for investigating the infant's perceptual abilities. Video-recording equipment allows researchers to investigate elusive behaviors. High-speed computers make it possible to perform complex data analysis in minutes. Other equipment records respiration, heart rate, body movement, visual fixation, and sucking behavior, which provide clues to what the infant is perceiving. For example, some researchers use equipment that detects whether a change in infants' respiration follows a change in the pitch of a sound. If so, it suggests that the infants heard the pitch change.

Scientists have had to be very creative when assessing the development of infants, discovering ways to "interview" them even though they cannot yet talk. Other segments of the population, such as adults who have suffered from a stroke, have difficulty communicating verbally. What kinds of methods or equipment do you think researchers might use to evaluate their perceptual abilities?

Infants show an interest in human faces soon after birth (Lee & others, 2013). Figure 4.20 shows a computer estimation of what a picture of a face looks like to an infant at different ages from a distance of about 6 inches. Infants spend more time looking at their mother's face than a stranger's face as early as 12 hours after being born (Bushnell, 2003). By 3 months of age, infants match voices to faces, distinguish between male and female faces, and discriminate between faces of their own ethnic group and those of other ethnic groups (Gaither & others, 2012; Kelly & others, 2005, 2007; Liu & others, 2011).

As infants develop, they change the way they gather information from the visual world, including human faces (Otsuka & others, 2012). One study recorded eye movements of 3-, 6-,

FIGURE **4.20**

VISUAL ACUITY DURING THE FIRST MONTHS OF LIFE. The four photographs represent a computer estimation of what a picture of a face looks like to a 1-month-old, 2-month-old, 3-month-old, and 1-year-old (which approximates the visual acuity of an adult).

and 9-month-old infants as they viewed clips from an animated film—*A Charlie Brown Christmas* (Frank, Vul, & Johnson, 2009). From 3 to 9 months of age, infants gradually began focusing their attention more on the faces in the animated film and less on salient background stimuli.

Also, as we discussed in the *Connecting Through Research* interlude, young infants can perceive certain patterns. With the help of his "looking chamber," Robert Fantz (1963) revealed that even 2- to 3-week-old infants prefer to look at patterned displays rather than nonpatterned displays. For example, they prefer to look at a normal human face rather than one with scrambled features, and prefer to look at a bull's-eye target or black-and-white stripes rather than a plain circle.

Color Vision The infant's color vision also improves (Aslin & Lathrop, 2008). By 8 weeks, and possibly as early as 4 weeks, infants can discriminate some colors (Kelly, Borchert, & Teller, 1997). By 4 months of age, they have color preferences that mirror adults' in some cases, preferring saturated colors such as royal blue over pale blue, for example (Bornstein, 1975).

A recent study of the reactions to blue, yellow, red, and green hues by 4- to 5-month-old infants revealed that they looked longest at reddish hues and shortest at greenish hues (Franklin & others, 2010). In part, the changes in vision described here reflect maturation. Experience, however, is also necessary for color vision to develop normally (Sugita, 2004).

Perceptual Constancy Some perceptual accomplishments are especially intriguing because they indicate that the infant's perception goes beyond the information provided by the senses (Johnson, 2012, 2013; Slater & others, 2011). This is the case in perceptual constancy, in which sensory stimulation is changing but perception of the physical world remains constant. If infants did not develop perceptual constancy, each time they saw an object at a different distance or in a different orientation, they would perceive it as a different object. Thus, the development of perceptual constancy allows infants to perceive their world as stable. Two types of perceptual constancy are size constancy and shape constancy.

Size constancy is the recognition that an object remains the same even though the retinal image of the object changes as you move toward or away from the object. The farther away from us an object is, the smaller its image is on our eyes. Thus, the size of an object on the retina is not sufficient to tell us its actual size. For example, you perceive a bicycle standing right in front of you as smaller than the car parked across the street, even though the bicycle casts a larger image on your eyes than the car does. When you move away from the bicycle, you do not perceive it to be shrinking even though its image on your retinas shrinks; you perceive its size as constant.

But what about babies? Do they have size constancy? Researchers have found that babies as young as 3 months of age show size constancy (Bower, 1966; Day & McKenzie, 1973). However, at 3 months of age, this ability is not full-blown. It continues to develop until 10 or 11 years of age (Kellman & Banks, 1998).

Shape constancy is the recognition that an object remains the same shape even though its orientation to us changes. Look around the room you are in right now. You likely see objects of varying shapes, such as tables and chairs. If you get up and walk around the room, you will see these objects from different sides and angles. Even though your retinal image of the objects changes as you walk and look, you will still perceive the objects as having the same shape.

Do babies have shape constancy? As with size constancy, researchers have found that babies as young as 3 months of age have shape constancy (Bower, 1966; Day & McKenzie, 1973). Three-month-old infants, however, do not have shape constancy for irregularly shaped objects such as tilted planes (Cook & Birch, 1984).

Perception of Occluded Objects Look around where you are now. You likely see that some objects are partly occluded by other objects that are in front of them—possibly a desk behind a chair, some books behind a computer, or a car parked behind a tree. Do infants perceive an object as complete when it is occluded by an object in front of it?

In the first two months of postnatal development, infants don't perceive occluded objects as complete; instead, they perceive only what is visible (Johnson, 2009). Beginning at about 2 months of age, infants develop the ability to perceive that occluded objects are whole (Slater, Field, & Hernandez-Reif, 2007). How does perceptual completion develop? In Scott Johnson's

size constancy The recognition that an object remains the same even though the retinal image of the object changes as you move toward or away from the object.

shape constancy The recognition that an object's shape remains the same even though its orientation to us changes.

(a) Gradual occlusion

(b) Abrupt occlusion

(c) Implosion

FIGURE **4.21**

INFANTS' PREDICTIVE TRACKING OF A BRIEFLY OCCLUDED MOVING BALL. The top photograph shows the visual scene that infants experienced. At the beginning of each event, a multicolored ball bounced up and down with an accompanying bouncing sound, and then rolled across the floor until it disappeared behind the partition. The bottom drawing shows the three stimulus events that the 5- to 9-month-old infants experienced: (*a*) Gradual occlusion—the ball gradually disappears behind the right side of the occluding partition located in the center of the display. (*b*) Abrupt occlusion—the ball abruptly disappears when it reaches the location of the white circle and then abruptly reappears two seconds later at the location of the second white circle on the other side of the occluding partition. (*c*) Implosion— the rolling ball quickly decreases in size as it approaches the occluding partition and rapidly increases in size as it reappears on the other side of the occluding partition.

research (2004, 2009, 2010, 2011, 2012, 2013; Johnson & others, 2000), learning, experience, and self-directed exploration via eye movements play key roles in the development of perceptual completion in young infants.

Many objects that are occluded appear and disappear behind closer objects, as when you are walking down the street and see cars appear and disappear behind buildings as they move or you move. Infants develop the ability to track briefly occluded moving objects at about 3 to 5 months of age (Bertenthal, 2008). One study explored the ability of 5- to 9-month-old infants to track moving objects that disappeared gradually behind an occluded partition, disappeared abruptly, or imploded (shrank quickly in size) (Bertenthal, Longo, & Kenny, 2007) (see Figure 4.21). In this study, the infants were more likely to accurately predict the moving object when it disappeared gradually rather than when it vanished abruptly or imploded.

Depth Perception   Might infants even perceive depth? To investigate this question, Eleanor Gibson and Richard Walk (1960) constructed a miniature cliff with a dropoff covered by glass in their laboratory. They placed infants on the edge of this visual cliff and had their mothers coax them to crawl onto the glass (see Figure 4.22). Most infants would not crawl out on the glass, choosing instead to remain on the shallow side, an indication that they could perceive depth.

The 6- to 12-month-old infants in the visual cliff experiment had extensive visual experience. Do younger infants without this experience still perceive depth? Since younger infants do not crawl, this question is difficult to answer. Two- to 4-month-old infants show differences in heart rate when they are placed directly on the deep side of the visual cliff instead of on the shallow side (Campos, Langer, & Krowitz, 1970). However, these differences might mean that young infants respond to differences in some visual characteristics of the deep and shallow cliffs, with no actual knowledge of depth (Adolph & Kretch, 2012). Although researchers do not know exactly how early in life infants can perceive depth, we do know that infants develop the ability to use binocular cues to depth by about 3 to 4 months of age.

OTHER SENSES

Other sensory systems besides vision also develop during infancy. We will explore development in hearing, touch and pain, smell, and taste.

Hearing   During the last two months of pregnancy, as the fetus nestles in its mother's womb, it can hear sounds such as the mother's voice, music, and so on (Kisilevsky & others, 2009). Two psychologists wanted to find out if a fetus who heard Dr. Seuss' classic story *The Cat in the Hat* while still in the mother's womb would prefer hearing the story after birth (DeCasper & Spence, 1986). During the last months of pregnancy, 16 women read *The Cat in the Hat* to their fetuses. Then shortly after the babies were born, their mothers read either *The Cat in the Hat* or a story with a different rhyme and pace, *The King, the Mice and the Cheese* (which was not read to them during prenatal development). The infants sucked on a nipple in a different way when the mothers read the two stories, suggesting that the infants recognized the pattern and tone of *The Cat in the Hat* (see Figure 4.23). This study illustrates not only that a fetus can hear but also that it has a remarkable ability to learn and remember even before birth. A recent fMRI study confirmed capacity of the fetus to hear at 33 to 34 weeks into the prenatal period by assessing fetal brain response to auditory stimuli (Jardri & others, 2012).

The fetus can also recognize the mother's voice, as one study demonstrated (Kisilevsky & others, 2003). Sixty term fetuses (mean gestational age, 38.4 weeks) were exposed to a tape recording either of their mother or of a female stranger reading a passage. The sounds of the tape were delivered through a loudspeaker held just above the mother's abdomen. Fetal heart rate increased in response to the mother's voice but decreased in response to the stranger's voice.

What kind of changes in hearing take place during infancy? They involve perception of a sound's loudness, pitch, and localization: ·

- *Loudness.* Immediately after birth, infants cannot hear soft sounds quite as well as adults can; a stimulus must be louder to be heard by a newborn than by an adult

(Trehub & others, 1991). For example, an adult can hear a whisper from about 4 to 5 feet away, but a newborn requires that sounds be closer to a normal conversational level to be heard at that distance.

- *Pitch.* Infants are also less sensitive to the pitch of a sound than adults are. *Pitch* is the perception of the frequency of a sound. A soprano voice sounds high-pitched, a bass voice low-pitched. Infants are less sensitive to low-pitched sounds and are more likely to hear high-pitched sounds (Aslin, Jusczyk, & Pisoni, 1998). A recent study revealed that by 7 months of age, infants can process simultaneous pitches when they hear voices but they are more likely to encode the higher-pitched voice (Marie & Trainor, 2012). By 2 years of age, infants have considerably improved their ability to distinguish sounds with different pitches.

- *Localization.* Even newborns can determine the general location from which a sound is coming, but by 6 months of age, they are more proficient at *localizing* sounds or detecting their origins. Their ability to localize sounds continues to improve during the second year (Burnham & Mattock, 2010).

Touch and Pain
Do newborns respond to touch? Can they feel pain?

Newborns do respond to touch. A touch to the cheek produces a turning of the head; a touch to the lips produces sucking movements.

Newborns can also feel pain (Field & Hernandez-Reif, 2008; Gunnar & Quevado, 2007). If and when you have a son and consider whether he should be circumcised, the issue of an infant's pain perception probably will become important to you. Circumcision is usually performed on young boys about the third day after birth. Will your young son experience pain if he is circumcised when he is 3 days old? An investigation by Megan Gunnar and her colleagues (1987) found that newborn infant males cried intensely during circumcision. The circumcised infant also displays amazing resiliency. Within several minutes after the surgery, they can nurse and interact in a normal manner with their mothers. And, if allowed to, the newly circumcised newborn drifts into a deep sleep, which seems to serve as a coping mechanism.

For many years, doctors performed operations on newborns without anesthesia. This practice was accepted because of the dangers of anesthesia and because of the supposition that newborns do not feel pain. As researchers demonstrated that newborns can feel pain, the practice of operating on newborns without anesthesia is being challenged. Anesthesia now is used in some circumcisions (Morris & others, 2012).

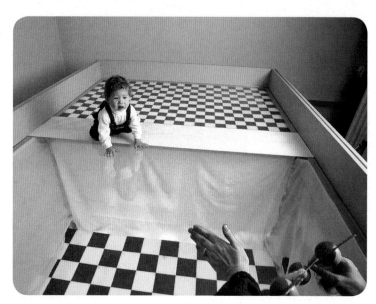

FIGURE **4.22**

EXAMINING INFANTS' DEPTH PERCEPTION ON THE VISUAL CLIFF.
Eleanor Gibson and Richard Walk (1960) found that most infants would not crawl out on the glass, which, according to Gibson and Walk, indicated that they had depth perception. However, some critics point out that the visual cliff is a better indication of the infant's social referencing and fear of heights than of the infant's perception of depth.

(a)   (b)

FIGURE **4.23**

HEARING IN THE WOMB. (*a*) Pregnant mothers read *The Cat in the Hat* to their fetuses during the last few months of pregnancy. (*b*) When they were born, the babies preferred listening to a recording of their mothers reading *The Cat in the Hat,* as evidenced by their sucking on a nipple that produced this recording, rather than another story, *The King, the Mice and the Cheese.*

FIGURE **4.24**

NEWBORNS' PREFERENCE FOR THE SMELL OF THEIR MOTHER'S BREAST PAD. In the experiment by MacFarlane (1975), 6-day-old infants preferred to smell their mother's breast pad rather than a clean one that had never been used, but 2-day-old infants did not show this preference, indicating that odor preference requires several days of experience to develop.

The important ability to connect information about vision with information about touch is evident during infancy. Coordination of vision and touch has been well documented in 6-month-olds (Rose, 1990) and in one study was demonstrated in 2- to 3-month-olds (Streri, 1987).

Smell   Newborns can differentiate odors (Doty & Shah, 2008). The expressions on their faces seem to indicate that they like the way vanilla and strawberry smell but do not like the way rotten eggs and fish smell (Steiner, 1979). In one investigation, 6-day-old infants who were breast fed showed a clear preference for smelling their mother's breast pad rather than a clean breast pad (MacFarlane, 1975) (see Figure 4.24). However, when they were 2 days old, they did not show this preference, indicating that they require several days of experience to recognize this odor.

Taste   Sensitivity to taste is present even before birth (Doty & Shah, 2008). Human newborns learn tastes prenatally through the amniotic fluid and in breast milk after birth (Beauchamp & Mennella, 2009; Mennella, 2009). In one study, even at only 2 hours of age, babies made different facial expressions when they tasted sweet, sour, and bitter solutions (Rosenstein & Oster, 1988) (see Figure 4.25). At about 4 months of age, infants begin to prefer salty tastes, which as newborns they had found to be aversive (Doty & Shah, 2008).

INTERMODAL PERCEPTION

Imagine yourself playing basketball or tennis. You are experiencing many visual inputs: the ball coming and going, other players moving around, and so on. However, you are experiencing many auditory inputs as well: the sound of the ball bouncing or being hit, the grunts and groans of other players, and so on. There is good correspondence between much of the visual and auditory information: When you see the ball bounce, you hear a bouncing sound; when a player stretches to hit a ball, you hear a groan. When you look at and listen to what is going on, you do not experience just the sounds or just the sights—you put all these things together. You experience a unitary episode. This is **intermodal perception,** which involves integrating information from two or more sensory modalities, such as vision and hearing (Bremner & others, 2012). Most perception is intermodal (Bahrick, 2010).

Early, exploratory forms of intermodal perception exist even in newborns (Bahrick & Hollich, 2008). For example, newborns turn their eyes and their head toward the sound of a voice or rattle when the sound is maintained for several seconds (Clifton & others, 1981), but the newborn can localize a sound and look at an object only in a crude way (Bechtold, Bushnell, & Salapatek, 1979). These early forms of intermodal perception become sharpened with experience in the first year of life (Kirkham & others, 2012). In one study, infants as young as 3 months old looked more at their mother when they also heard her voice and longer at their father when they also heard his voice (Spelke & Owsley, 1979). Thus, even young infants can coordinate visual-auditory information involving people.

FIGURE **4.25**

NEWBORNS' FACIAL RESPONSES TO BASIC TASTES. Facial expressions elicited by (a) a sweet solution, (b) a sour solution, and (c) a bitter solution.

Can young infants put vision and sound together as precisely as adults do? In the first six months, infants have difficulty connecting sensory input from different modes, but in the second half of the first year they show an increased ability to make this connection mentally.

NATURE, NURTURE, AND PERCEPTUAL DEVELOPMENT

Now that we have discussed many aspects of perceptual development, let's explore one of developmental psychology's key issues as it relates to perceptual development: the nature-nurture issue. There has been a longstanding interest in how strongly infants' perception is influenced by nature or nurture (Johnson, 2011, 2012, 2013; Slater & others, 2011). In the field of perceptual development, nature proponents are referred to as *nativists* and those who emphasize learning and experience are called *empiricists*.

In the nativist view, the ability to perceive the world in a competent, organized way is inborn or innate. At the beginning of our discussion of perceptual development, we examined the ecological view of the Gibsons because it has played such a pivotal role in guiding research in perceptual development. The Gibsons' ecological view leans toward a nativist explanation of perceptual development because it holds that perception is direct and evolved over time to allow the detection of size and shape constancy, a three-dimensional world, intermodal perception, and so on, early in infancy. However, the Gibsons' view is not entirely nativist because they emphasized that perceptual development involves distinctive features that are detected at different ages (Slater & others, 2011).

The Gibsons' ecological view is quite different from Piaget's constructivist view that reflects an empiricist approach to explaining perceptual development. According to Piaget, much of perceptual development in infancy must await the development of a sequence of cognitive stages for infants to construct more complex perceptual tasks. Thus, in Piaget's view the ability to perceive size and shape constancy, a three-dimensional world, intermodal perception, and so on, develops later in infancy than the Gibsons envision.

Much of early perception develops from innate (nature) foundations and the basic foundation of many perceptual abilities can be detected in newborns, whereas other abilities unfold maturationally (Bornstein, Arterberry, & Mash, 2011). However, as infants develop, environmental experiences (nurture) refine or calibrate many perceptual functions, and they may be the driving force behind some functions (Amso & Johnson, 2010). The accumulation of experience with and knowledge about their perceptual world contributes to infants' ability to process coherent perceptions of people and things (Johnson, 2012, 2013). Thus, a full portrait of perceptual development includes the influence of nature, nurture, and a developing sensitivity to information (Arterberry, 2008).

PERCEPTUAL-MOTOR COUPLING

As we come to the end of this chapter, we return to the important theme of perceptual-motor coupling. The distinction between perceiving and doing has been a time-honored tradition in psychology. However, a number of experts on perceptual and motor development question whether this distinction makes sense (Adolph & Robinson, 2013; Thelen & Smith, 2006). The main thrust of research in Esther Thelen's dynamic systems approach is to explore how people assemble motor behaviors for perceiving and acting. The main theme of the ecological approach of Eleanor and James J. Gibson is to discover how perception guides action. Action can guide perception, and perception can guide action. Only by moving one's eyes, head, hands, and arms and by moving from one location to another can an individual fully experience his or her environment and learn how to adapt to it. Perception and action are coupled (Kim & Johnson, 2010).

Babies, for example, continually coordinate their movements with perceptual information to learn how to maintain balance, reach for objects in space, and move across various surfaces and terrains (Adolph & Berger, 2013; Thelen & Smith, 2006). They are motivated to move by

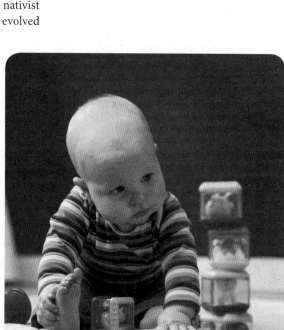

What is intermodal perception? Which senses is this infant using to integrate information about the toy?

What roles do nature and nurture play in the infant's perceptual development?

The infant is by no means as helpless as it looks and is quite capable of some very complex and important actions.

—HERB PICK
Contemporary Developmental Psychologist, University of Minnesota

intermodal perception The ability to relate and integrate information from two or more sensory modalities, such as vision and hearing.

what they perceive. Consider the sight of an attractive toy across the room. In this situation, infants must perceive the current state of their bodies and learn how to use their limbs to reach the toy. Although their movements at first are awkward and uncoordinated, babies soon learn to select patterns that are appropriate for reaching their goals.

Equally important is the other part of the perception-action coupling. That is, action educates perception (Adolph & Robinson, 2013). For example, watching an object while exploring it manually helps infants to discriminate its texture, size, and hardness. Locomoting in the environment teaches babies about how objects and people look from different perspectives, or whether various surfaces will support their weight.

How do infants develop new perceptual-motor couplings? Recall from our discussion earlier in this chapter that in the traditional view of Gesell, infants' perceptual-motor development is prescribed by a genetic plan to follow a fixed and sequential progression of stages in development. The genetic determination view has been replaced by the dynamic systems view that infants learn new perceptual-motor couplings by assembling skills for perceiving and acting. New perceptual-motor coupling is not passively accomplished; rather, the infant actively develops a skill to achieve a goal within the constraints set by the infant's body and the environment (Adolph & Robinson, 2013).

Children perceive in order to move and move in order to perceive. Perceptual and motor development do not occur in isolation from each other but instead are coupled.

How are perception and action coupled in children's development?

Review Connect Reflect

LG3 Summarize the course of sensory and perceptual development in infancy.

Review

- What are sensation and perception?
- What is the ecological view of perception?
- How does visual perception develop in infancy?
- How do hearing, touch and pain, smell, and taste develop in infancy?
- What is intermodal perception?
- What roles do nature and nurture play in perceptual development?
- How is perceptual-motor development coupled?

Connect

- Perceptual-motor coupling was discussed in the previous section as well as in this section. Describe how this concept could be linked to the concept of nature versus nurture (p. 33).

Reflect *Your Own Personal Journey of Life*

- How much sensory stimulation would you provide your own baby? A little? A lot? Could you overstimulate your baby? Explain.

topical connections --------

In the next chapter, you will read about the remarkable cognitive changes that characterize infant development and how early infants competently process information about their world. Advances in infants' cognitive development—together with the development of the brain and perceptual-motor advances discussed in this chapter—allow infants to adapt more effectively to their environment. In Chapter 7, we will further explore physical development when we examine how children progress through the early childhood years (ages 3 to 5). Young children's physical development continues to change and to become more coordinated in early childhood, although gains in height and weight are not as dramatic in early childhood as in infancy.

looking forward - - - - ➤

Physical Development in Infancy

1 Physical Growth and Development in Infancy

LG1 Discuss physical growth and development in infancy.

- Patterns of Growth
- Height and Weight
- The Brain
- Sleep
- Nutrition

- The cephalocaudal pattern is the sequence in which growth proceeds from top to bottom. The proximodistal pattern is the sequence in which growth starts at the center of the body and moves toward the extremities.

- The average North American newborn is 20 inches long and weighs 7 pounds. Infants grow about 1 inch per month in the first year and nearly triple their weight by their first birthday. The rate of growth slows in the second year.

- One of the most dramatic changes in the brain in the first two years of life is dendritic spreading, which increases the connections between neurons. Myelination, which speeds the conduction of nerve impulses, continues through infancy and even into adolescence. The cerebral cortex has two hemispheres (left and right). Lateralization refers to specialization of function in one hemisphere or the other. Early experiences play an important role in brain development. Neural connections are formed early in an infant's life. Before birth, genes mainly direct neurons to different locations. After birth, the inflowing stream of sights, sounds, smells, touches, language, and eye contact help shape the brain's neural connections, as does stimulation from caregivers and others. The neuroconstructivist view is an increasingly popular view of the brain's development.

- Newborns usually sleep about 18 hours a day. By 6 months of age, many American infants approach adult-like sleeping patterns. REM sleep—during which dreaming occurs—is present more in early infancy than in childhood and adulthood. Sleeping arrangements for infants vary across cultures. In America, infants are more likely to sleep alone than in many other cultures. Some experts believe shared sleeping can lead to sudden infant death syndrome (SIDS), a condition that occurs when a sleeping infant suddenly stops breathing and dies without an apparent cause.

- Infants need to consume about 50 calories per day for each pound they weigh. The growing consensus is that in most instances breast feeding is superior to bottle feeding for both the infant and the mother, although the correlational nature of studies must be considered. Severe infant malnutrition is still prevalent in many parts of the world. A special concern in impoverished countries is early weaning from breast milk and the misuse and hygiene problems associated with bottle feeding in these countries. The Women, Infants, and Children (WIC) program has produced positive benefits in low-income families.

2 Motor Development

LG2 Describe infants' motor development.

- The Dynamic Systems View
- Reflexes
- Gross Motor Skills
- Fine Motor Skills

- Thelen's dynamic systems theory seeks to explain how motor behaviors are assembled for perceiving and acting. Perception and action are coupled. According to this theory, motor skills are the result of many converging factors, such as the development of the nervous system, the body's physical properties and its movement possibilities, the goal the child is motivated to reach, and environmental support for the skill. In the dynamic systems view, motor development is far more complex than the result of a genetic blueprint.

- Reflexes—automatic movements—govern the newborn's behavior. They include the sucking, rooting, and Moro reflexes. The rooting and Moro reflexes disappear after three to four months. Permanent reflexes include coughing and blinking. For infants, sucking is an especially important reflex because it provides a means of obtaining nutrition.

- Gross motor skills involve large-muscle activities. Key skills developed during infancy include control of posture and walking. Although infants usually learn to walk by their first birthday, the neural pathways that allow walking begin to form earlier. The age at which infants reach milestones in the development of gross motor skills may vary by as much as two to four months, especially for milestones in late infancy.

- Fine motor skills involve finely tuned movements. The onset of reaching and grasping marks a significant accomplishment, and this becomes more refined during the first two years of life.

3 Sensory and Perceptual Development

 LG3 Summarize the course of sensory and perceptual development in infancy.

What Are Sensation and Perception?

- Sensation occurs when information interacts with sensory receptors. Perception is the interpretation of sensation.

The Ecological View

- Created by the Gibsons, the ecological view states that we directly perceive information that exists in the world around us. Perception brings people in contact with the environment to interact with and adapt to it. Affordances provide opportunities for interaction offered by objects that fit within our capabilities to perform activities.

Visual Perception

- Researchers have developed a number of methods to assess the infant's perception, including the visual preference method (which Fantz used to determine young infants' preference for looking at patterned over nonpatterned displays), habituation and dishabituation, and tracking. The infant's visual acuity increases dramatically in the first year of life. Infants' color vision improves as they develop. Young infants systematically scan human faces. As early as 3 months of age, infants show size and shape constancy. At approximately 2 months of age, infants develop the ability to perceive that occluded objects are complete. In Gibson and Walk's classic study, infants as young as 6 months of age indicated they could perceive depth.

Other Senses

- The fetus can hear during the last two months of pregnancy. Immediately after birth, newborns can hear, but their sensory threshold is higher than that of adults. Developmental changes in the perception of loudness, pitch, and localization of sound occur during infancy. Newborns can respond to touch and feel pain. Newborns can differentiate odors, and sensitivity to taste may be present before birth.

Intermodal Perception

- Early, exploratory forms of intermodal perception—the ability to relate and integrate information from two or more sensory modalities—are present in newborns and become sharpened over the first year of life.

Nature, Nurture, and Perceptual Development

- In perception, nature advocates are referred to as nativists and nurture proponents are called empiricists. The Gibsons' ecological view that has guided much of perceptual development research leans toward a nativist approach but still allows for developmental changes in distinctive features. Piaget's constructivist view leans toward an empiricist approach, emphasizing that many perceptual accomplishments must await the development of cognitive stages in infancy. A strong empiricist approach is unwarranted. A full account of perceptual development includes the roles of nature, nurture, and the developing sensitivity to information.

Perceptual-Motor Coupling

- Perception and action are often not isolated but rather are coupled. Individuals perceive in order to move and move in order to perceive.

key terms

key people

Chapter 4 | PHYSICAL DEVELOPMENT IN INFANCY

Connecting with

Learning Objectives	Application Activities	Activity Type	Page Reference
Discuss the patterns of physical growth and development in infancy.	Growth Pattern, Amalia and Krista, 2 weeks–5 yrs	Milestones	pp. 110–122
Discuss the brain during infancy.	Influences on Infant Brain Development	Video	pp. 111–115
	Structure of Neurons	Interactive exercise	
	The Neuron	Click & drag activity	
Discuss sleep and sleep habits during infancy.	REM Sleep at 2 Weeks	Video	pp. 115–117
	Sudden Infant Death Syndrome: Expert Interview	Video	
Discuss nutrition in infancy.	Breast vs. Bottle Feeding	Video	pp. 117–121
	Eating Habits, Atlas, 4–18 mos	Milestones	
Discuss gross motor skills in infancy.	Bi-Pedal Posture and Dynamic Systems Theory, Colin, 2 wks–14 mos	Milestones	pp. 124–127
	Range of Motor Development, Yovani, 2–16 mos	Milestones	
Discuss fine motor skills in infancy.	Second Year Fine Motor Development, Atlas, 20–32 mos	Milestones	pp. 127–128
Describe sensation and perception.	Sensation and Perception, Felana, 13–18 mos	Milestones	pp. 128–129
Describe the ecological view.	Affordances, Felana, 13 mos–2 yrs	Milestones	p. 129
	Ecological View of Perception, Felana, 6–9 mos	Milestones	
Describe visual perception.	Visual Acuity, Colin, 1 wk–12 mos	Milestones	pp. 129–134
Describe auditory, olfactory, and taste sense.	Sound Sensitivity, Yovani, 2 mos–2 yrs	Milestones	pp. 134–136

chapter 5

COGNITIVE DEVELOPMENT IN INFANCY

chapter **outline**

Jean Piaget, the famous Swiss psychologist, was a meticulous observer of his three children—Laurent, Lucienne, and Jacqueline. His books on cognitive development are filled with these observations. Here are a few of Piaget's observations of his children in infancy (Piaget, 1952):

- At 21 days of age, "Laurent found his thumb after three attempts: prolonged sucking begins each time. But, once he has been placed on his back, he does not know how to coordinate the movement of the arms with that of the mouth and his hands draw back even when his lips are seeking them" (p. 27).

- During the third month, thumb sucking becomes less important to Laurent because of new visual and auditory interests. But, when he cries, his thumb goes to the rescue.

- Toward the end of Lucienne's fourth month, while she is lying in her crib, Piaget hangs a doll above her feet. Lucienne thrusts her feet at the doll and makes it move. "Afterward, she looks at her motionless foot for a second, then recommences. There is no visual control of her foot, for the movements are the same when Lucienne only looks at the doll or when I place the doll over her head. On the other hand, the tactile control of the foot is apparent: after the first shakes, Lucienne makes slow foot movements as though to grasp and explore" (p. 159).

- At 11 months, "Jacqueline is seated and shakes a little bell. She then pauses abruptly in order to delicately place the bell in front of her right foot; then she kicks hard. Unable to recapture it, she grasps a ball which she then places at the same spot in order to give it another kick" (p. 225).

- At 1 year, 2 months, "Jacqueline holds in her hands an object which is new to her: a round, flat box which she turns all over, shakes, [and] rubs against the bassinet. . . . She lets it go and tries to pick it up. But she only succeeds in touching it with her index finger, without grasping it. She nevertheless makes an attempt and presses on the edge. The box then tilts up and falls again" (p. 273). Jacqueline shows an interest in this result and studies the fallen box.

- At 1 year, 8 months, "Jacqueline arrives at a closed door with a blade of grass in each hand. She stretches out her right hand toward the [door] knob but sees that she cannot turn it without letting go of the grass. She puts the grass on the floor, opens the door, picks up the grass again, and enters. But when she wants to leave the room, things become complicated. She puts the grass on the floor and grasps the doorknob. But then she perceives that in pulling the door toward her she will simultaneously chase away the grass which she placed between the door and the threshold. She therefore picks it up in order to put it outside the door's zone of movement" (p. 339).

For Piaget, these observations reflect important changes in the infant's cognitive development. Piaget maintained that infants go through six substages as they progress in less than two short years from Laurent's thumb sucking to Jacqueline's problem solving.

topical connections

In Chapter 4, you learned that impressive advances occur in the development of the brain during infancy. Engaging in various physical, cognitive, and socioemotional activities strengthens the baby's neural connections. Motor and perceptual development also are key aspects of the infant's development. An important part of this development is the coupling of perceptions and actions. The nature-nurture issue continues to be debated with regard to the infant's perceptual development. In this chapter, you will expand your understanding of the infant's brain, motor, and perceptual development by further examining how infants develop their competencies, focusing on how advances in their cognitive development help them adapt to their world, and how the nature-nurture issue is a key aspect of the infant's cognitive and language development.

◄ - - - *looking back* - - - - - - - - - - - - -

preview

Piaget's descriptions of infants are just the starting point for our exploration of cognitive development. Excitement and enthusiasm about the study of infant cognition have been fueled by an interest in what newborns and infants know, by continued fascination about innate and learned factors in the infant's cognitive development, and by controversies about whether infants construct their knowledge (Piaget's view) or know their world more directly. In this chapter, you will study not only Piaget's theory of infant development but also learning, remembering, and conceptualizing by infants; individual differences; and language development.

---

1 Piaget's Theory of Infant Development

 Summarize and evaluate Piaget's theory of infant development.

Cognitive Processes   The Sensorimotor Stage   Evaluating Piaget's Sensorimotor Stage

We are born capable of learning.

—JEAN-JACQUES ROUSSEAU
Swiss-Born French Philosopher, 18th Century

Poet Nora Perry asks, "Who knows the thoughts of a child?" As much as anyone, Piaget knew. Through careful observations of his own three children—Laurent, Lucienne, and Jacqueline—and observations of and interviews with other children, Piaget changed perceptions of the way children think about the world.

Piaget's theory is a general, unifying story of how biology and experience sculpt cognitive development. Piaget thought that, just as our physical bodies have structures that enable us to adapt to the world, we build mental structures that help us adjust to new environmental demands. Piaget stressed that children actively construct their own cognitive worlds; information is not just poured into their minds from the environment. He sought to discover how children at different points in their development think about the world and how systematic changes in their thinking occur.

COGNITIVE PROCESSES

schemes In Piaget's theory, actions or mental representations that organize knowledge.

assimilation Piagetian concept of using existing schemes to deal with new information or experiences.

What processes do children use as they construct their knowledge of the world? Piaget developed several concepts to answer this question; especially important are schemes, assimilation, accommodation, organization, equilibrium, and equilibration.

Schemes As the infant or child seeks to construct an understanding of the world, said Piaget (1954), the developing brain creates **schemes.** These are actions or mental representations that organize knowledge. In Piaget's theory, behavioral schemes (physical activities) characterize infancy, and mental schemes (cognitive activities) develop in childhood (Lamb, Bornstein, & Teti, 2002). A baby's schemes are structured by simple actions that can be performed on objects, such as sucking, looking, and grasping. Older children have schemes that include strategies and plans for solving problems. For example, in the descriptions at the opening of this chapter, Laurent displayed a scheme for sucking; Jacqueline displayed a problem-solving scheme when she was able to open the door without losing her blades of grass. By the time we have reached adulthood, we have constructed an enormous number of diverse schemes, ranging from driving a car to balancing a budget to understanding the concept of fairness.

Assimilation and Accommodation To explain how children use and adapt their schemes, Piaget offered two concepts: assimilation and accommodation. **Assimilation** occurs when children use their existing schemes to deal with new information or experiences. **Accommodation** occurs when children adjust their schemes to take new information and experiences into account.

Think about a toddler who has learned the word *car* to identify the family vehicle. The toddler might call all moving vehicles on roads "cars," including motorcycles and trucks; the child has assimilated these objects to his or her existing scheme. But the child soon learns that motorcycles and trucks are not cars and fine-tunes the category to exclude motorcycles and trucks, accommodating the scheme.

Assimilation and accommodation operate even in very young infants. Newborns reflexively suck everything that touches their lips; they assimilate all sorts of objects into their sucking scheme. By sucking different objects, they learn about their taste, texture, shape, and so on. After several months of experience, though, they construct their understanding of the world differently. Some objects, such as fingers and the mother's breast, can be sucked, and others, such as fuzzy blankets, should not be sucked. In other words, they accommodate their sucking scheme.

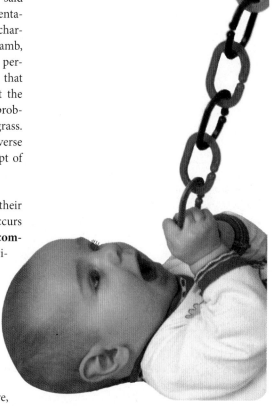

In Piaget's view, what is a scheme? What schemes might this young infant be displaying?

Organization To make sense out of their world, said Piaget, children cognitively organize their experiences. **Organization** in Piaget's theory is the grouping of isolated behaviors and thoughts into a higher-order system. Continual refinement of this organization is an inherent part of development. A boy who has only a vague idea about how to use a hammer may also have a vague idea about how to use other tools. After learning how to use each one, he relates these uses, organizing his knowledge.

Equilibration and Stages of Development Assimilation and accommodation always take the child to a higher ground, according to Piaget. In trying to understand the world, the child inevitably experiences cognitive conflict, or *disequilibrium.* That is, the child is constantly faced with counterexamples to his or her existing schemes and with inconsistencies. For example, if a child believes that pouring water from a short and wide container into a tall and narrow container changes the amount of water, then the child might be puzzled by where the "extra" water came from and whether there is actually more water to drink. The puzzle creates disequilibrium; for Piaget, an internal search for equilibrium creates motivation for change. The child assimilates and accommodates, adjusting old schemes, developing new schemes, and organizing and reorganizing the old and new schemes. Eventually, the new organization has become fundamentally different from the old organization; it is a new way of thinking.

In short, according to Piaget, children constantly assimilate and accommodate as they seek equilibrium. There is considerable movement between states of cognitive equilibrium and disequilibrium as assimilation and accommodation work in concert to produce cognitive

How might assimilation and accommodation be involved in infants' sucking?

accommodation Piagetian concept of adjusting schemes to fit new information and experiences.

organization Piaget's concept of grouping isolated behaviors and thoughts into a higher-order, more smoothly functioning cognitive system.

Substage	Age	Description	Example
1 Simple reflexes	Birth to 1 month	Coordination of sensation and action through reflexive behaviors.	Rooting, sucking, and grasping reflexes; newborns suck reflexively when their lips are touched.
2 First habits and primary circular reactions	1 to 4 months	Coordination of sensation and two types of schemes: habits (reflex) and primary circular reactions (reproduction of an event that initially occurred by chance). Main focus is still on the infant's body.	Repeating a body sensation first experienced by chance (sucking thumb, for example); then infants might accommodate actions by sucking their thumb differently from how they suck on a nipple.
3 Secondary circular reactions	4 to 8 months	Infants become more object-oriented, moving beyond self-preoccupation; repeat actions that bring interesting or pleasurable results.	An infant coos to make a person stay near; as the person starts to leave, the infant coos again.
4 Coordination of secondary circular reactions	8 to 12 months	Coordination of vision and touch—hand-eye coordination; coordination of schemes and intentionality.	Infant manipulates a stick in order to bring an attractive toy within reach.
5 Tertiary circular reactions, novelty, and curiosity	12 to 18 months	Infants become intrigued by the many properties of objects and by the many things they can make happen to objects; they experiment with new behavior.	A block can be made to fall, spin, hit another object, and slide across the ground.
6 Internalization of schemes	18 to 24 months	Infants develop the ability to use primitive symbols and form enduring mental representations.	An infant who has never thrown a temper tantrum before sees a playmate throw a tantrum; the infant retains a memory of the event, then throws one himself the next day.

FIGURE **5.1**
PIAGET'S SIX SUBSTAGES OF SENSORIMOTOR DEVELOPMENT

developmental **connection**

Cognitive Theory

Recall the main characteristics of Piaget's four stages of cognitive development. Chapter 1, p. 24

equilibrium A mechanism that Piaget proposed to explain how children shift from one stage of thought to the next.

sensorimotor stage The first of Piaget's stages, which lasts from birth to about 2 years of age; infants construct an understanding of the world by coordinating sensory experiences with motoric actions.

simple reflexes Piaget's first sensorimotor substage, which corresponds to the first month after birth. In this substage, sensation and action are coordinated primarily through reflexive behaviors.

change. **Equilibration** is the name Piaget gave to this mechanism by which children shift from one stage of thought to the next.

The result of these processes, according to Piaget, is that individuals go through four stages of development. A different way of understanding the world makes one stage more advanced than another. Cognition is *qualitatively* different in one stage compared with another. In other words, the way children reason at one stage is different from the way they reason at another stage. Here our focus is on Piaget's stage of infant cognitive development. In later chapters, when we study cognitive development in early childhood, middle and late childhood, and adolescence (Chapters 7, 9, and 11) we will explore the last three Piagetian stages.

THE SENSORIMOTOR STAGE

The **sensorimotor stage** lasts from birth to about 2 years of age. In this stage, infants construct an understanding of the world by coordinating sensory experiences (such as seeing and hearing) with physical, motoric actions—hence the term "sensorimotor." At the beginning of this stage, newborns have little more than reflexes with which to work. At the end of the sensorimotor stage, 2-year-olds can produce complex sensorimotor patterns and use primitive symbols. We first will summarize Piaget's descriptions of how infants develop. Later we will consider criticisms of his view.

Substages   Piaget divided the sensorimotor stage into six substages: (1) simple reflexes; (2) first habits and primary circular reactions; (3) secondary circular reactions; (4) coordination of secondary circular reactions; (5) tertiary circular reactions, novelty, and curiosity; and (6) internalization of schemes (see Figure 5.1).

Simple reflexes, the first sensorimotor substage, corresponds to the first month after birth. In this substage, sensation and action are coordinated primarily through reflexive behaviors, such as rooting and sucking. Soon the infant produces behaviors that resemble reflexes in the absence of the usual stimulus for the reflex. For example, a newborn will suck a nipple or bottle only when it is placed directly in the baby's mouth or touched to the lips. But soon the infant might suck when a bottle or nipple is only nearby. Even in the first month of life, the infant is initiating action and actively structuring experiences.

First habits and primary circular reactions is the second sensorimotor substage, which develops between 1 and 4 months of age. In this substage, the infant coordinates sensation and two types of schemes: habits and primary circular reactions. A *habit* is a scheme based on a reflex that has become completely separated from its eliciting stimulus. For example, infants in substage 1 suck when bottles are put to their lips or when they see a bottle. Infants in substage 2 might suck even when no bottle is present. A *circular reaction* is a repetitive action.

A **primary circular reaction** is a scheme based on the attempt to reproduce an event that initially occurred by chance. For example, suppose an infant accidentally sucks his fingers when they are placed near his mouth. Later, he searches for his fingers to suck them again, but the fingers do not cooperate because the infant cannot coordinate visual and manual actions.

Habits and circular reactions are stereotyped—that is, the infant repeats them the same way each time. During this substage, the infant's own body remains the infant's center of attention. There is no outward pull by environmental events.

Secondary circular reactions is the third sensorimotor substage, which develops between 4 and 8 months of age. In this substage, the infant becomes more object-oriented, moving beyond preoccupation with the self. The infant's schemes are not intentional or goal-directed, but they are repeated because of their consequences. By chance, an infant might shake a rattle. The infant repeats this action for the sake of its fascination. This is a *secondary circular reaction:* an action repeated because of its consequences. The infant also imitates some simple actions, such as the baby talk or burbling of adults, and some physical gestures. However, the baby imitates only actions that he or she is already able to produce.

Coordination of secondary circular reactions is Piaget's fourth sensorimotor substage, which develops between 8 and 12 months of age. To progress into this substage the infant must coordinate vision and touch, eye and hand. Actions become more outwardly directed. Significant changes during this substage involve the coordination of schemes and intentionality. Infants readily combine and recombine previously learned schemes in a coordinated way. They might look at an object and grasp it simultaneously, or they might visually inspect a toy, such as a rattle, and finger it simultaneously, exploring it tactilely. Actions are even more outwardly directed than before. Related to this coordination is the second achievement—the presence of intentionality. For example, infants might manipulate a stick in order to bring a desired toy within reach, or they might knock over one block to reach and play with another one. Similarly, when 11-month-old Jacqueline, as described in the chapter opening, placed the ball in front of her and kicked it, she was demonstrating intentionality.

Tertiary circular reactions, novelty, and curiosity is Piaget's fifth sensorimotor substage, which develops between 12 and 18 months of age. In this substage, infants become intrigued by the many properties of objects and by the many things that they can make happen to objects. A block can be made to fall, spin, hit another object, and slide across the ground. *Tertiary circular reactions* are schemes in which the infant purposely explores new possibilities with objects, continually doing new things to them and exploring the results. Piaget says that this stage marks the starting point for human curiosity and interest in novelty.

Internalization of schemes is Piaget's sixth and final sensorimotor substage, which develops between 18 and 24 months of age. In this substage, the infant develops the ability to use primitive symbols. For Piaget, a *symbol* is an internalized sensory image or word that represents an event. Primitive symbols permit the infant to think about concrete events without directly acting them out or perceiving them. Moreover, symbols allow the infant to manipulate and transform the represented events in simple ways. In a favorite Piagetian example, Piaget's young daughter saw a matchbox being opened and closed. Later, she mimicked the event by opening and closing her mouth. This was an obvious expression of her image of the event.

This 17-month-old is in Piaget's stage of tertiary circular reactions. *What might the infant do to suggest that she is in this stage?*

developmental **connection**

Cognitive Theory

What are some changes in symbolic thought in young children? Chapter 7, p. 216

first habits and primary circular reactions Piaget's second sensorimotor substage, which develops between 1 and 4 months of age. In this substage, the infant coordinates sensation and two types of schemes: habits and primary circular reactions.

primary circular reaction A scheme based on the attempt to reproduce an event that initially occurred by chance.

secondary circular reactions Piaget's third sensorimotor substage, which develops between 4 and 8 months of age. In this substage, the infant becomes more object-oriented, moving beyond preoccupation with the self.

coordination of secondary circular reactions Piaget's fourth sensorimotor substage, which develops between 8 and 12 months of age. Actions become more outwardly directed, and infants coordinate schemes and act with intentionality.

tertiary circular reactions, novelty, and curiosity Piaget's fifth sensorimotor substage, which develops between 12 and 18 months of age. In this substage, infants become intrigued by the many properties of objects and by the many things that they can make happen to objects.

internalization of schemes Piaget's sixth and final sensorimotor substage, which develops between 18 and 24 months of age. In this substage, the infant develops the ability to use primitive symbols.

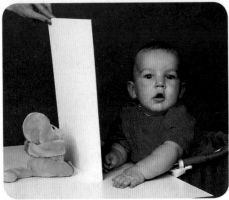

FIGURE 5.2

OBJECT PERMANENCE. Piaget argued that object permanence is one of infancy's landmark cognitive accomplishments. For this 5-month-old boy, "out-of-sight" is literally out of mind. The infant looks at the toy monkey (*top*), but, when his view of the toy is blocked (*bottom*), he does not search for it. Several months later, he will search for the hidden toy monkey, an action reflecting the presence of object permanence.

developmental **connection**

Perceptual Development

Eleanor Gibson was a pioneer in crafting the ecological perception view of development. Chapter 4, p. 129

object permanence The Piagetian term for understanding that objects and events continue to exist even when they cannot directly be seen, heard, or touched.

A-not-B error Error that occurs when infants make the mistake of selecting the familiar hiding place (A) rather than the new hiding place (B) as they progress into substage 4 in Piaget's sensorimotor stage; also called A$\overline{\text{B}}$ error.

Object Permanence   Imagine how chaotic and unpredictable your life would be if you could not distinguish between yourself and your world. This is what the life of a newborn must be like, according to Piaget. There is no differentiation between the self and world; objects have no separate, permanent existence.

By the end of the sensorimotor period, objects are both separate from the self and permanent. **Object permanence** is the understanding that objects continue to exist even when they cannot be seen, heard, or touched. Acquiring the sense of object permanence is one of the infant's most important accomplishments, according to Piaget.

How could anyone know whether an infant had a sense of object permanence or not? The principal way that object permanence is studied is by watching an infant's reaction when an interesting object disappears (see Figure 5.2). If infants search for the object, it is assumed that they believe it continues to exist.

Object permanence is just one of the basic concepts about the physical world developed by babies. To Piaget, children, even infants, are much like little scientists, examining the world to see how it works. But how can adult scientists determine what these "baby scientists" are finding out about the world and at what age they're finding it out? Read *Connecting Through Research* to find out.

EVALUATING PIAGET'S SENSORIMOTOR STAGE

Piaget opened up a new way of looking at infants with his view that their main task is to coordinate their sensory impressions with their motor activity. However, the infant's cognitive world is not as neatly packaged as Piaget portrayed it, and some of Piaget's explanations for the cause of change are debated. In the past several decades, sophisticated experimental techniques have been devised to study infants, and there have been a large number of research studies on infant development. Much of the new research suggests that Piaget's view of sensorimotor development needs to be modified (Baillargeon & Carey, 2012; Diamond, 2013; Johnson, 2012, 2013).

The A-not-B Error   One modification concerns Piaget's claim that certain processes are crucial in transitions from one stage to the next. The data do not always support his explanations. For example, in Piaget's theory, an important feature in the progression into substage 4, *coordination of secondary circular reactions*, is an infant's inclination to search for a hidden object in a familiar location rather than to look for the object in a new location. If a toy is hidden twice, initially at location A and subsequently at location B, 8- to 12-month-old infants search correctly at location A initially. But when the toy is subsequently hidden at location B, they make the mistake of continuing to search for it at location A. **A-not-B error** (also called A$\overline{\text{B}}$ error) is the term used to describe this common mistake. Older infants are less likely to make the A-not-B error because their concept of object permanence is more complete.

Researchers have found, however, that the A-not-B error does not show up consistently (Sophian, 1985). The evidence indicates that A-not-B errors are sensitive to the delay between hiding the object at B and the infant's attempt to find it (Diamond, 1985). Thus, the A-not-B error might be due to a failure in memory. Another explanation is that infants tend to repeat a previous motor behavior (Clearfield & others, 2006).

Perceptual Development and Expectations   A number of theorists, such as Eleanor Gibson (2001) and Elizabeth Spelke (1991, 2011; Spelke & Kinzler, 2009; Spelke & Lee, 2012), argue that infants' perceptual abilities are highly developed at a very early stage. Spelke concludes that young infants interpret the world as having predictable occurrences. For example, in Chapter 4 we discussed research that demonstrated the presence of intermodal perception— the ability to coordinate information from two or more sensory modalities, such as vision and hearing—by 3½ months of age, much earlier than Piaget would have predicted (Spelke & Owsley, 1979).

Research also suggests that infants develop the ability to understand how the world works at a very early age (Baillargeon & others, 2012; Hyde & Spelke, 2012). For example,

connecting through research

How Do Researchers Study Infants' Understanding of Object Permanence and Causality?

Two accomplishments of infants that Piaget examined were the development of object permanence and the child's understanding of causality. Let's examine two research studies that address these topics.

In both studies, Renée Baillargeon and her colleagues used a research method that involves *violation of expectations*. In this method, infants see an event happen as it normally would. Then, the event is changed, often in a way that creates a physically impossible event. That an infant looks longer at the changed event indicates he or she is surprised by it. In other words, the reaction is interpreted to indicate that the infant had certain expectations about the world that were violated.

In one study focused on object permanence, researchers showed infants a toy car that moved down an inclined track, disappeared behind a screen, and then reemerged at the other end, still on the track (Baillargeon & DeVos, 1991) (see Figure 5.3) (a). After this sequence was repeated several times, something different occurred: A toy mouse was

placed *behind* the tracks but was hidden by the screen while the car rolled by (b). This was the "possible" event. Then, the researchers created an "impossible event": The toy mouse was placed *on* the tracks but was secretly removed after the screen was lowered so that the car seemed to go through the mouse (c). In this study, infants as young as 3 months of age took a longer look at the impossible event than at the possible event, indicating that they were surprised by it. Their surprise suggested that they remembered not only that the toy mouse still existed (object permanence) but its location.

Another study focused on the infant's understanding of causality (Kotovsky & Baillargeon, 1994). In this research, a cylinder rolls down a ramp and hits a toy bug at the bottom of the ramp. By 5 and 6 months of age, after infants have seen how far the bug will be pushed by a medium-sized cylinder, their reactions indicate that they understand that the bug will roll farther if it is hit by a large cylinder than if it is hit by a small cylinder. Thus, by the middle of the first year of life these infants understood that the size of a moving object determines how far it will move a stationary object that it collides with.

In Baillargeon's (2008; Baillargeon & Carey, 2012; Baillargeon & others, 2011, 2012; Luo & Baillargeon, 2010) view, infants have a pre-adapted, innate bias called the *principle of persistence* that explains their assumption that objects don't change their properties—including how solid they are, their location, their color, and their form—unless some external factor (a person moves the object, for example) obviously intervenes. Shortly, we will revisit the extent to which nature and nurture are at work in the changes that take place in the infant's cognitive development.

The research findings discussed in this interlude and other research indicate that infants develop object permanence and causal reasoning much earlier than Piaget proposed (Baillargeon & others, 2011; Luo & Baillargeon, 2010). Indeed, as you will see in the next section, a major theme of infant cognitive development today is that infants are more cognitively competent than Piaget envisioned.

(a) Practice (No toy mouse)

(b) Possible event (Toy mouse behind the track)

(c) Impossible event (Toy mouse on the track)

FIGURE 5.3

USING THE VIOLATION OF EXPECTATIONS METHOD TO STUDY OBJECT PERMANENCE IN INFANTS. If infants looked longer at (*c*) than at (*b*), researchers reasoned that the impossible event in (*c*) violated the infants' expectations and that they remembered that the toy mouse existed.

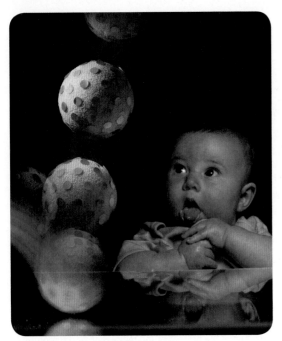

A 4-month-old in Elizabeth Spelke's infant perception laboratory is tested to determine whether she knows that an object in motion will not stop in midair. Spelke concluded that at 4 months babies don't expect objects like these balls to obey gravitational constraints, but that they do expect objects to be solid and continuous. Research by Spelke, Renée Baillargeon, and others suggest that infants develop an ability to understand how the world works earlier than Piaget envisioned. However, critics such as Andrew Meltzoff fault their research and conclude there is still controversy about how early some infant cognitive accomplishments occur.

by the time they are 3 months of age, infants develop expectations about future events. Marshall Haith and his colleagues (Canfield & Haith, 1991; Haith, Hazen, & Goodman, 1988) presented pictures to infants in either a regular alternating sequence (such as left, right, left, right) or an unpredictable sequence (such as right, right, left, right). When the sequence was predictable, the 3-month-old infants began to anticipate the location of the picture, looking at the side on which it was expected to appear. However, younger infants did not develop expectations about where a picture would be presented.

What kinds of expectations do infants form? Experiments by Spelke (1991, 2000; Spelke & Hespos, 2001) have addressed these questions. She placed babies before a puppet stage and showed them a series of actions that are unexpected if you know how the physical world works—for example, one ball seemed to roll through a solid barrier, another seemed to leap between two platforms, and a third appeared to hang in midair (Spelke, 1979). Spelke measured and compared the babies' looking times for unexpected and expected actions. She concluded that by 4 months of age, even though infants do not yet have the ability to talk about objects, move around objects, manipulate objects, or even see objects with high resolution, they expect objects to be solid and continuous. However, at 4 months of age, infants do not expect an object to obey gravitational constraints (Spelke & others, 1992). Similarly, research by Renée Baillargeon and her colleagues (1995, 2004) documents that infants as young as 3 to 4 months expect objects to be substantial (in the sense that other objects cannot move through them) and permanent (in the sense that objects continue to exist when they are hidden).

In sum, researchers conclude that infants see objects as bounded, unitary, solid, and separate from their background, possibly at birth or shortly thereafter, but definitely by 3 to 4 months of age—much earlier than Piaget envisioned. Young infants still have much to learn about objects, but the world appears both stable and orderly to them.

However, some critics, such as Andrew Meltzoff (2008; Meltzoff & Moore, 1998), argue that Spelke's and Baillargeon's research relies on how long infants look at unexpected events and thus assess infants' *perceptual expectations* about where and when objects will reappear rather than tapping their *knowledge* about where the objects are when they are out of sight. Meltzoff points out that whether infants act on their perception is an important aspect of assessing object permanence; he states that it does not appear that young infants can act on the information. Thus, Meltzoff (2008) concludes that whether longer looking time is a valid measure of object permanence and how early infants develop object permanence remains controversial.

By 6 to 8 months, infants have learned to perceive gravity and support—that an object hanging on the end of a table should fall, that ball-bearings will travel farther when rolled down a longer rather than a shorter ramp, and that cup handles will not fall when attached to a cup (Slater, Field, & Hernandez-Reif, 2007). As infants develop, their experiences and actions on objects help them to understand physical laws (Johnson, 2012, 2013).

The Nature-Nurture Issue In considering the big issue of whether nature or nurture plays the more important role in infant development, Elizabeth Spelke (Hyde & Spelke, 2012; Spelke, 2003, 2011) comes down clearly on the side of nature. Spelke endorses a **core knowledge approach,** which states that infants are born with domain-specific innate knowledge systems. Among these domain-specific knowledge systems are those involving space, number sense, object permanence, and language (which we will discuss later in this chapter). Strongly influenced by evolution, the core knowledge domains are theorized to be prewired to allow infants to make sense of their world (Spelke & Lee, 2012). After all, Spelke concludes, how could infants possibly grasp the complex world in which they live if they didn't come into the world equipped with core sets of knowledge? In this approach, the innate core knowledge domains form a foundation around which more mature cognitive functioning and learning develop (Baillargeon & Carey, 2012). The core knowledge approach argues that Piaget greatly underestimated the cognitive abilities of infants, especially young infants.

developmental **connection**

Nature Versus Nurture

The nature-nurture debate is one of developmental psychology's main issues. Chapter 1, p. 19

core knowledge approach States that infants are born with domain-specific innate knowledge systems.

Original event

1. Object placed in case   2. Screen comes up   3. Second object added   4. Hand leaves empty

(a)

Test events

Possible outcome

5. Screen drops...   revealing 2 objects

(b)

Impossible outcome

5. Screen drops...   revealing 1 object

(c)

FIGURE 5.4

INFANTS' NUMBER SENSE. Shown here is one of the sequences in Karen Wynn's (1992) study of 5-month-old infants' number sense. The experimenter was hidden behind the display and manipulated the objects through a trap door in the wall of the display. Five-month-old infants who saw the impossible event (only one Mickey Mouse doll) looked longer at the event than their 5-month-old counterparts who saw the possible event (two dolls).

An intriguing domain of core knowledge that has been investigated in young infants is whether they have a sense of number. Spelke and her colleagues conclude that they do (Hyde & Spelke, 2012; Izard & others, 2011; Spelke, 2011). Using the violation of expectations method discussed in this chapter's *Connecting Through Research*, Karen Wynn (1992) conducted an early experiment on infants' sense of number (see Figure 5.4). Five-month-old infants were shown one or two Mickey Mouse dolls on a puppet stage. Then the experimenter hid the doll(s) behind a screen and visibly removed or added one. Next, when the screen was lifted, the infants looked longer when they saw the incorrect number of dolls. Spelke and her colleagues (de Hevia & Spelke, 2010; Hyde & Spelke, 2012; Lipton & Spelke, 2004; Spelke & Kinzler, 2007; Xu, Spelke, & Goddard, 2005) have found that infants can distinguish between different numbers of objects, actions, and sounds. Efforts to find further support for infants' sense of number are extending to assessments of brain activity (Hyde & Spelke, 2012). For example, one study of 3-month-olds observing changes either in the identity of objects or in the number of objects revealed that changes in the type of objects activated a region of the brain's temporal lobe while changes in the number of objects activated an additional region of the parietal lobe (Izard, Dehaene-Lambertz, & Dehaene, 2008). In older children and adults, number sense activates the same region of the parietal lobe activated in the 3-month-old infants in this study.

Of course, not everyone agrees with Spelke's conclusions about young infants' math skills (Cohen, 2002). One criticism is that infants in the number experiments are merely responding to changes in the display that violated their expectations.

In criticizing the core knowledge approach, British developmental psychologist Mark Johnson (2008) says that the infants Spelke assesses in her research already have accumulated hundreds, and in some cases even thousands, of hours of experience in grasping what the world is about, which gives considerable room for the environment's role in the development of infant cognition (Highfield, 2008). According to Johnson (2008), infants likely come into the world with "soft biases to perceive and attend to different aspects of the environment, and to learn about the world in particular ways." Although debate about the cause and course of infant cognitive development continues, most developmentalists today agree that Piaget underestimated the early cognitive accomplishments of infants and that both nature and nurture are involved in infants' cognitive development.

What are some conclusions that can be reached about infant learning and cognition?

Conclusions   In sum, many researchers conclude that Piaget wasn't specific enough about how infants learn about their world and that infants, especially young infants, are more competent than Piaget thought (Baillargeon & others, 2012; Diamond, 2013; Johnson, 2012, 2013; Meltzoff & Williamson, 2103; Spelke, 2011). As they have examined the specific ways that infants learn, the field of infant cognition has become very specialized. There are many researchers working on different questions, with no general theory emerging that can connect all of the different findings (Nelson, 1999). Their theories often are local theories, focused on specific research questions, rather than grand theories like Piaget's (Kuhn, 1998). Among the unifying themes in the study of infant cognition are seeking to understand more precisely how developmental changes in cognition take place, the big issue of nature and nurture, and the brain's role in cognitive development (Aslin, 2012; Bornstein & Colombo, 2012; Mandler & DeLoache, 2012). Recall from Chapter 1 that exploring connections between brain, cognition, and development involves the recently emerging field of *developmental cognitive neuroscience* (Bell, 2012; Burack, Enns, & Fox, 2013; Cuevas & others, 2012; Diamond, 2013).

Review *Connect* Reflect

 LG1 Summarize and evaluate Piaget's theory of infant development.

Review

- What cognitive processes are important in Piaget's theory?
- What are some characteristics of Piaget's stage of sensorimotor development?
- What are some contributions and criticisms of Piaget's sensorimotor stage?

Connect

- You just read that by the age of 6 to 8 months infants have learned to perceive gravity and support. What physical developments occurring around this same time period (discussed in Chapter 4) might contribute to infants' exploration and understanding of these concepts?

Reflect *Your Own Personal Journey of Life*

- What are some implications of Piaget's theory for parenting your own baby?

2 Learning, Remembering, and Conceptualizing

 LG2 Describe how infants learn, remember, and conceptualize.

| Conditioning | Attention | Memory | Imitation | Concept Formation and Categorization |

When Piaget hung a doll above 4-month-old Lucienne's feet, as described in the chapter opening, did she remember the doll? If Piaget had rewarded her for moving the doll with her foot, would that have affected Lucienne's behavior? If he had shown her how to shake the doll's hand, could she have imitated him? If he had shown her a different doll, could she have formed the concept of a "doll"?

Questions like these might be examined by researchers taking the behavioral and social cognitive or information-processing approaches introduced in Chapter 1. In contrast with Piaget's theory, these approaches do not describe infant development in terms of stages. Instead, they document gradual changes in the infant's ability to understand and process information about the world (Diamond, 2013). In this section, we explore what researchers using these approaches can tell us about how infants learn, remember, and conceptualize.

developmental **connection**

Theories

The behavioral and social cognitive approaches emphasize continuity rather than discontinuity in development. Chapter 1, p. 25

CONDITIONING

In Chapter 1, we described Skinner's operant conditioning (in which the consequences of a behavior produce changes in the probability of the behavior's occurrence). For example, if an infant's behavior is followed by a rewarding stimulus, the behavior is likely to recur.

Operant conditioning has been especially helpful to researchers in their efforts to determine what infants perceive (Rovee-Collier & Barr, 2010). For example, infants will suck faster on a nipple when the sucking behavior is followed by a visual display, music, or a human voice (Rovee-Collier, 1987, 2007).

Carolyn Rovee-Collier (1987) has also demonstrated how infants can retain information from the experience of being conditioned. In a characteristic experiment, she places a 2½-month-old baby in a crib under an elaborate mobile (see Figure 5.5). She then ties one end of a ribbon to the baby's ankle and the other end to the mobile. Subsequently, she observes that the baby kicks and makes the mobile move. The movement of the mobile is the reinforcing stimulus (which increases the baby's kicking behavior) in this experiment. Weeks later, the baby is returned to the crib, but its foot is not tied to the mobile. The baby kicks, which suggests it has retained the information that if it kicks a leg, the mobile will move.

ATTENTION

Attention, the focusing of mental resources on select information, improves cognitive processing on many tasks. Even newborns can detect a contour and fix their attention on it. Older infants scan patterns more thoroughly. By 4 months, infants can selectively attend to an object. In adults, when individuals orient their attention to an object or event, the parietal lobes in the cerebral cortex are involved (Goldberg & others, 2012). It is likely that the parietal lobes are active when infants orient their attention, although research has not yet documented this. (Figure 4.4 in the previous chapter illustrates the location of the parietal lobes in the brain.)

Attention in the first year of life is dominated by an *orienting/investigative process* (Rothbart, 2011). This process involves directing attention to potentially important locations in the environment (that is, *where*) and recognizing objects and their features (such as color and form) (that is, *what*) (Richards, 2010). From 3 to 9 months of age, infants can deploy their attention more flexibly and quickly. Another important type of attention is *sustained attention,* also referred to as *focused attention* (Richards, 2010). New stimuli typically elicit an orienting response followed by sustained attention. It is sustained attention that allows infants to learn about and remember characteristics of a stimulus as it becomes familiar. Researchers have found that infants as young as 3 months of age engage in 5 to 10 seconds of sustained attention. From this age through the second year, the length of sustained attention increases (Courage & Richards, 2008).

Habituation and Dishabituation Closely linked with attention are the processes of habituation and dishabituation that we discussed in Chapter 4 (Colombo, Kapa, & Curtendale, 2011). If you say the same word or show the same toy to a baby several times in a row, the baby usually pays less attention to it each time. This is *habituation*—decreased responsiveness to a stimulus after repeated presentations of the stimulus. *Dishabituation* is the increase in responsiveness after a change in stimulation. Chapter 4 described some of the measures that researchers use to study whether habituation is occurring, such as sucking behavior (sucking stops when an infant attends to a novel object), heart rates, and the length of time the infant looks at an object.

Infants' attention is strongly governed by novelty and habituation (Courage & Richards, 2008; Richards, 2010). When an object becomes familiar, attention becomes shorter, and infants become more vulnerable to distraction (Oakes, Kannass, & Shaddy, 2002). One study found that 10-month-olds were more distractible than 26-month-olds (Ruff & Capozzoli, 2003).

Researchers study habituation to determine the extent to which infants can see, hear, smell, taste, and experience touch (Slater, Field, & Hernandez-Reif, 2007). Studies of habituation can also indicate whether infants recognize something they have previously experienced. Habituation provides a measure of an infant's maturity and well-being. Infants who have brain damage do not habituate well.

Knowing about habituation and dishabituation can help parents interact effectively with infants. Infants respond to changes in stimulation. Wise parents sense when an infant shows

FIGURE **5.5**

THE TECHNIQUE USED IN ROVEE-COLLIER'S INVESTIGATION OF INFANT MEMORY. In Rovee-Collier's experiment, operant conditioning was used to demonstrate that infants as young as 2½ months of age can retain information from the experience of being conditioned. *What did infants recall in Rovee-Collier's experiment?*

> developmental **connection**
>
> **Attention**
>
> In early childhood, children make significant advances in sustained attention. Chapter 7, p. 224

attention The focusing of mental resources on select information.

FIGURE **5.6**

GAZE FOLLOWING IN INFANCY. Researcher Rechele Brooks shifts her eyes from the infant to a toy in the foreground (*a*). The infant then follows her eye movement to the toy (*b*). Brooks and colleague Andrew Meltzoff (2005) found that infants begin to engage in this kind of behavior, called "gaze following," at 10 to 11 months of age. Why might gaze following be an important accomplishment for an infant?

(a)   (b)

an interest and realize that they may have to repeat something many times for the infant to process information. But if the stimulation is repeated often, the infant stops responding to the parent. In parent-infant interaction, it is important for parents to do novel things and to repeat them often until the infant stops responding. The parent stops or changes behaviors when the infant redirects his or her attention (Rosenblith, 1992).

Joint Attention Another aspect of attention that is an important aspect of infant development is **joint attention,** in which two or more individuals focus on the same object or event. Joint attention requires (1) an ability to track another's behavior, such as following the gaze of someone; (2) one person's directing another's attention, and (3) reciprocal interaction (Butterworth, 2004). Early in infancy, joint attention involves a caregiver pointing, turning the infant's head, snapping fingers, or using words to direct the infant's attention. Emerging forms of joint attention occur at about 7 to 8 months, but it is not until toward the end of the first year that joint attention skills are frequently observed (Heimann & others, 2006). In a study conducted by Andrew Meltzoff and Rechele Brooks (2006), at 10 to 11 months of age infants first began engaging in "gaze following," looking where another person has just looked (see Figure 5.6). And by their first birthday, infants have begun to direct adults' attention to objects that capture their interest (Heimann & others, 2006).

This young infant's attention is riveted on the blue frog. The young infant's attention to the toy will be strongly regulated by the processes of habituation and dishabituation. *What characterizes these processes?*

Joint attention plays important roles in many aspects of infant development and considerably increases infants' ability to learn from other people (Carpenter, 2011; Meltzoff, 2011). Nowhere is this more apparent than in observations of interchanges between caregivers and infants as infants are learning language (Tomasello, 2011; Tomasello & Hamann, 2012). When caregivers and infants frequently engage in joint attention, infants say their first word earlier and develop a larger vocabulary (Carpenter, Nagell, & Tomasello, 1998; Flom & Pick, 2003; Hirotani & others, 2009). Later in this chapter in our discussion of language, we further discuss joint attention as an early predictor of language development in older infants and toddlers (Tomasello, 2011; Tomasello & Hamann, 2012).

The following recent studies also document the role of joint attention in children's memory and self-regulation:

joint attention Process that occurs when individuals focus on the same object and an ability to track another's behavior is present, one individual directs another's attention, and reciprocal interaction takes place.

- The extent to which 9-month-old infants engaged in joint attention was linked to their long-term memory (a one-week

A mother and her infant daughter engaging in joint attention. *What about this photograph tells you that joint attention is occurring? Why is joint attention an important aspect of infant development?*

delay), possibly because joint attention enhances the relevance of attended items (Kopp & Lindenberger, 2011).

- Responding to joint attention at 12 months of age was linked to self-regulation skills at 3 years of age that involved delaying gratification for an attractive object (Van Hecke & others, 2012).

MEMORY

Memory involves the retention of information over time. Attention plays an important role in memory as part of a process called encoding, which is the process by which information is transferred to memory. What can infants remember, and when?

Some researchers such as Rovee-Collier (2008) have concluded that infants as young as 2 to 6 months of age can remember some experiences through 1½ to 2 years of age. However, critics such as Jean Mandler (2004), a leading expert on infant cognition, argue that the infants in Rovee-Collier's experiments were displaying only implicit memory. **Implicit memory** refers to memory without conscious recollection—memories of skills and routine procedures that are performed automatically. In contrast, **explicit memory** refers to conscious remembering of facts and experiences.

When people think about memory, they are usually referring to explicit memory. Most researchers find that babies do not show explicit memory until the second half of the first year (Bauer, 2013; Bauer & others, 2000). Then, explicit memory improves substantially during the second year of life (Bauer, Larkina, & Deocampo, 2011; Carver & Bauer, 2001). In one longitudinal study, infants were assessed several times during their second year (Bauer & others, 2000). Older infants showed more accurate memory and required fewer prompts to demonstrate their memory than younger infants. Figure 5.7 summarizes how long researchers have found infants of different ages can remember information (Bauer, 2009). As indicated in Figure 5.7, researchers have documented that 6-month-olds can remember information for 24 hours but by 20 months of age infants can remember information they encountered 12 months earlier.

What changes in the brain are linked to infants' memory development? From about 6 to 12 months of age, the maturation of the hippocampus and the surrounding cerebral cortex, especially the frontal lobes, makes explicit memory possible (Nelson, 2012; Nelson, Thomas, & de Haan, 2006) (see Figure 5.8). Explicit memory continues to improve in the second year as these brain structures further mature and connections between them increase. Less is known about the areas of the brain involved in implicit memory in infancy.

Let's examine another aspect of memory. Do you remember your third birthday party? Probably not. Most adults can remember little if anything from their first three years of life. This is called *infantile* or *childhood amnesia*. The few reported adult memories of life at age 2 or 3 are at best very sketchy (Fivush, 2011; Newcombe, 2008; Riggins, 2012). Elementary school children also do not remember much of their early childhood years (Lie & Newcombe, 1999).

What is the cause of infantile amnesia? One reason older children and adults have difficulty recalling events from their infancy and early childhood is that during these early years the prefrontal lobes of the brain are immature; this area of the brain is believed to play an important role in storing memories of events (Boyer & Diamond, 1992).

In sum, most of young infants' conscious memories appear to be rather fragile and short-lived, although their implicit memory of perceptual-motor actions can be substantial (Bauer, 2013; Ghetti & Bauer, 2012; Mandler, 2004). By the end of the second year, long-term memory is more substantial and reliable (Bauer, Larkina, & Deocampo, 2011).

IMITATION

Can infants imitate someone else's emotional expressions? If an adult smiles, for example, will the baby respond with a smile? If an adult protrudes her lower lip, wrinkles her forehead, and frowns, will the baby show a sad face?

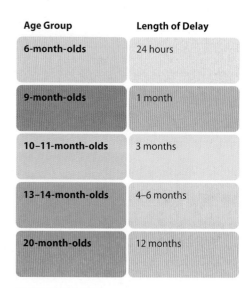

Age Group	Length of Delay
6-month-olds	24 hours
9-month-olds	1 month
10–11-month-olds	3 months
13–14-month-olds	4–6 months
20-month-olds	12 months

FIGURE **5.7**

AGE-RELATED CHANGES IN THE LENGTH OF TIME OVER WHICH MEMORY OCCURS

Cerebral cortex (tan-colored area with wrinkles and folds)

Frontal lobe

Hippocampus

FIGURE **5.8**

KEY BRAIN STRUCTURES INVOLVED IN EXPLICIT MEMORY DEVELOPMENT IN INFANCY

memory A central feature of cognitive development, pertaining to all situations in which an individual retains information over time.

implicit memory Memory without conscious recollection; involves skills and routine procedures that are automatically performed.

explicit memory Memory of facts and experiences that individuals consciously know and can state.

FIGURE **5.9**

INFANT IMITATION. Infant development researcher Andrew Meltzoff protrudes his tongue in an attempt to get the infant to imitate his behavior. *How do Meltzoff's findings about imitation compare with Piaget's descriptions of infants' abilities?*

I wish I could travel down by the road that crosses the baby's mind where reason makes kites of her laws and flies them....

—Rabindranath Tagore

Bengali Poet and Essayist, 20th Century

deferred imitation Imitation that occurs after a delay of hours or days.

concepts Cognitive groupings of similar objects, events, people, or ideas.

Infant development researcher Andrew Meltzoff (2004, 2005, 2011; Meltzoff & Moore, 1999; Meltzoff & Williamson, 2010, 2013) has conducted numerous studies of infants' imitative abilities. He sees infants' imitative abilities as biologically based, because infants can imitate a facial expression within the first few days after birth. He also emphasizes that the infant's imitative abilities do not resemble a hardwired response but rather involve flexibility and adaptability. In Meltzoff's observations of infants throughout their first 72 hours of life, the infants gradually displayed more complete imitation of an adult's facial expression, such as protruding the tongue or opening the mouth wide (see Figure 5.9).

Meltzoff (2007) concludes that infants don't blindly imitate everything they see and often make creative errors. He also argues that beginning at birth there is an interplay between learning by observing and learning by doing (Piaget emphasized learning by doing).

Not all experts on infant development accept Meltzoff's conclusions that newborns are capable of imitation. Some say that these babies were engaging in little more than automatic responses to a stimulus.

Meltzoff (2005, 2011) also has studied **deferred imitation,** which occurs after a time delay of hours or days. Piaget held that deferred imitation doesn't occur until about 18 months of age. Meltzoff's research suggested that it occurs much earlier. In one study, Meltzoff (1988) demonstrated that 9-month-old infants could imitate actions—such as pushing a recessed button in a box, which produced a beeping sound—that they had seen performed 24 hours earlier. Also, in a recent study, engagement in deferred imitation at 9 months of age was a strong predictor of more extensive production of communicative gestures at 14 months of age (Heimann & others, 2006). Two of the most common infant gestures are (1) extending the arm to show the caregiver something the infant is holding, and (2) pointing with the arm and index finger extended at some interesting object or event.

CONCEPT FORMATION AND CATEGORIZATION

Along with attention, memory, and imitation, concepts are key aspects of infants' cognitive development (Gelman, 2013; Mandler & DeLoache, 2012; Rakison & Lawson, 2013). **Concepts** are cognitive groupings of similar objects, events, people, or ideas. Without concepts, you would see each object and event as unique; you would not be able to make any generalizations.

Do infants have concepts? Yes, they do, although we do not know precisely how early concept formation begins (Mandler & DeLoach, 2012; Quinn, 2011).

Using habituation experiments like those described earlier in the chapter, some researchers have found that infants as young as 3 to 4 months of age can group together objects with similar appearances, such as animals. This research capitalizes on the knowledge that infants are more likely to look at a novel object than a familiar object. Jean Mandler (2004, 2009) argues that these early categorizations are best described as *perceptual categorization.* That is, the categorizations are based on similar perceptual features of objects, such as size, color, and movement, as well as parts of objects, such as legs for animals. Mandler (2004) concludes that it is not until about 7 to 9 months of age that infants form *conceptual* categories rather than just making perceptual discriminations between different categories. In one study of 9- to 11-month-olds, infants classified birds as animals and airplanes as vehicles even though the objects were perceptually similar—airplanes and birds with their wings spread (Mandler & McDonough, 1993) (see Figure 5.10).

Further advances in categorization occur in the second year of life (Booth, 2006). Many infants' "first concepts are broad and global in nature, such as 'animal' or 'indoor thing.' Gradually, over the first two years these broad concepts become more differentiated into concepts such as 'land animal,' then 'dog,' or to 'furniture,' then 'chair'" (Mandler, 2009, p. 1). Also in the second year, infants often categorize objects on the basis of their shape (Landau, Smith, & Jones, 1998).

Learning to put things into the correct categories—what makes something one kind of thing rather than another kind of thing, such as what makes a bird a bird, or a fish a

FIGURE **5.10**

CATEGORIZATION IN 9- TO 11-MONTH-OLDS. These are the stimuli used in the study that indicated 9- to 11-month-old infants categorized birds as animals and airplanes as vehicles even though the objects were perceptually similar (Mandler & McDonough, 1993).

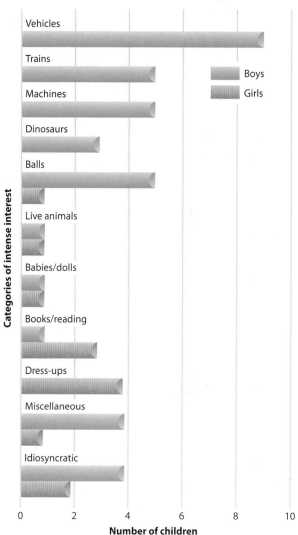

FIGURE **5.11**
CATEGORIZATION OF BOYS' AND GIRLS' INTENSE INTERESTS

fish—is an important aspect of learning (Pruden & others, 2012; Rakison & Lawson, 2013). As infant development researcher Alison Gopnik (2010, p. 159) recently pointed out, "If you can sort the world into the right categories—put things in the right boxes—then you've got a big advance on understanding the world."

Do some very young children develop an intense, passionate interest in a particular category of objects or activities? A recent study confirmed that they do (DeLoache, Simcock, & Macari, 2007). A striking finding was the large gender difference in categories, with an intense interest in particular categories stronger for boys than girls. Categorization of boys' intense interests focused on vehicles, trains, machines, dinosaurs, and balls; girls' intense interests were more likely to involve dress-ups and books/reading (See Figure 5.11). When your author's grandson Alex was 18 to 24 months old, he already had developed an intense, passionate interest in the category of vehicles. For example, at this age, he categorized vehicles into such subcategories as cars, trucks, earth-moving equipment, and buses. In addition to common classifications of cars into police cars, jeeps, taxis, and such, and trucks into fire trucks, dump trucks, and the like, his categorical knowledge of earth-moving equipment included bulldozers and excavators, and he categorized buses into school buses, London buses, and funky Malta buses (retro buses on the island of Malta). Later, at 3 years of age, Alex developed an intense, passionate interest in categorizing dinosaurs.

In sum, the infant's advances in processing information—through attention, memory, imitation, and concept formation—is much richer, more gradual and less stage-like, and occurs earlier than was envisioned by earlier theorists, such as Piaget (Diamond, 2013; Ghetti & Bower, 2012; Slater, 2012). As leading infant researcher Jean Mandler (2004) concluded, "The human infant shows a remarkable degree of learning power and complexity in what is being learned and in the way it is represented" (p. 304).

The author's grandson Alex at 2 years of age showing his intense, passionate interest in the category of vehicles while playing with a London taxi and a funky Malta bus.

Infants are creating concepts and organizing their world into conceptual domains that will form the backbone of their thought throughout life.

—**JEAN MANDLER**

Contemporary Psychologist, University of California–San Diego

3 Individual Differences and Assessment

 LG3 Discuss infant assessment measures and the prediction of intelligence.

Measures of Infant Development | Predicting Intelligence

So far, we have discussed how the cognitive development of infants generally progresses. We have emphasized what is typical of the largest number of infants or the average infant, but the results obtained for most infants do not apply to all infants. It is advantageous to know whether an infant is developing at a slow, normal, or advanced pace during the course of infancy. If an infant advances at an especially slow rate, then some form of enrichment may be necessary. If an infant develops at an advanced pace, parents may be advised to provide toys that stimulate cognitive growth in slightly older infants. How is an infant's cognitive development assessed?

MEASURES OF INFANT DEVELOPMENT

Individual differences in infant cognitive development have been studied primarily through the use of developmental scales or infant intelligence tests. For example, in Chapter 3 we discussed the Brazelton Neonatal Behavioral Assessment Scale (NBAS) and the Neonatal Intensive Care Unit Network Neurobehavioral Scale (NNNS), which are used to evaluate newborns. To read about the work of one infant assessment specialist, see *Connecting with Careers*.

The most important early contributor to the testing of infants was Arnold Gesell (1934). He developed a measure that helped sort out babies with normal functioning from ones with abnormal functioning. This was especially useful to adoption agencies, which had large numbers of babies awaiting placement. Gesell's examination was used widely for many years and still is frequently employed by pediatricians to distinguish normal and abnormal functioning in infants. The current version of the Gesell test has four categories of behavior: motor, language, adaptive, and personal-social. The **developmental quotient (DQ)** combines subscores in these categories to provide an overall score.

The widely used **Bayley Scales of Infant Development** were developed by Nancy Bayley (1969) to assess infant behavior and predict later development. The current version, Bayley-III, has five scales: cognitive, language, motor, socioemotional, and adaptive (Bayley, 2006). The first three scales are administered directly to the infant, while the latter two are questionnaires given to the caregiver. The Bayley-III also is more appropriate for use in clinical settings than were the two previous editions (Lennon & others, 2008).

---

developmental connection

Intelligence

Tests that assess older children's intelligence use more verbal items than do developmental assessments of infants. Chapter 9, p. 299

developmental quotient (DQ) An overall score that combines subscores in motor, language, adaptive, and personal-social domains in the Gesell assessment of infants.

Bayley Scales of Infant Development Scales developed by Nancy Bayley that are widely used to assess infant development. The current version has three components: a mental scale, a motor scale, and an infant behavior profile.

Toosje Thyssen Van Beveren, Infant Assessment Specialist

Toosje Thyssen Van Beveren is a developmental psychologist at the University of Texas Medical Center in Dallas. She has a master's degree in child clinical psychology and a Ph.D. in human development. Van Beveren has been involved for a number of years in a 12-week program called New Connections, which is a comprehensive intervention for infants who were affected by substance abuse prenatally and for their caregivers.

In the New Connections program, Van Beveren assesses infants' developmental status and progress. She might refer the infants to a speech, physical, or occupational therapist and monitor the infants' services and progress. Van Beveren trains the program staff and encourages them to use the exercises she recommends. She also discusses the child's problems with the primary

Toosje Thyssen Van Beveren conducting an infant assessment.

caregivers, suggests activities, and assists them in enrolling infants in appropriate programs.

During her graduate work at the University of Texas at Dallas, Van Beveren was author John Santrock's teaching assistant in his undergraduate course on life-span development for four years. As a teaching assistant, she attended classes, graded exams, counseled students, and occasionally gave lectures. Van Beveren returns periodically to give a lecture on prenatal development and infancy. She also teaches courses in infant development and in child development in the psychology department at UT–Dallas. In Van Beveren's words, "My days are busy and full. The work is often challenging. There are some disappointments but mostly the work is enormously gratifying."

How should a 6-month-old perform on the Bayley mental scale? The 6-month-old infant should be able to vocalize pleasure and displeasure, persistently search for objects that are just out of immediate reach, and approach a mirror that is placed in front of the infant by the examiner. By 12 months of age, the infant should be able to inhibit behavior when commanded to do so, imitate words the examiner says (such as "Mama"), and respond to simple requests (such as "Take a drink").

The explosion of interest in infant development has produced many new measures, especially tasks that evaluate the ways infants process information (Fogel, 2010). The Fagan Test of Infant Intelligence is increasingly being used (Fagan, 1992). This test focuses on the infant's ability to process information in such ways as encoding the attributes of objects, detecting similarities and differences between objects, forming mental representations, and retrieving these representations. For example, to estimate intelligence, it uses the amount of time babies look at a new object compared with the amount of time they spend looking at a familiar object.

Items in the Bayley-III Scales of Infant Development.

PREDICTING INTELLIGENCE

The infant-testing movement grew out of the tradition of IQ testing. However, IQ tests of older children pay more attention to verbal ability. Tests for infants contain far more items related to perceptual-motor development and include measures of social interaction.

One longitudinal study examined the intelligence of 200 children ranging from age 12 months (using the Bayley scales) to 4 years (using the Stanford Binet test) (Blaga & others, 2009). The results indicated considerable stability from late infancy through the preschool years. However, overall scores on such tests as the Gesell and the Bayley scales do not correlate highly with IQ scores obtained later in childhood. This result is not surprising because the components tested in infancy are not the same as the components assessed by IQ tests.

Unlike the Gesell and Bayley scales, the Fagan test is correlated with measures of intelligence in older children. In fact, evidence is accumulating that measures of habituation and dishabituation are linked to intelligence in childhood, adolescence, and even adulthood (Fagan, Holland, & Wheeler, 2007; Kavsek, 2004). One study revealed that habituation assessed at 3 or 6 months of age was linked to verbal skills and intelligence assessed at 32 months of age (Domsch, Lohaus, & Thomas, 2009). It is important, however, not to go too far and think that connections between cognitive development in early infancy and later cognitive development are so strong that no discontinuity takes place. Some important changes in cognitive development occur after infancy, changes that we will describe in later chapters.

Review *Connect* Reflect

 Discuss infant assessment measures and the prediction of intelligence.

Review

- What are some measures of infant development?
- Do tests of infants predict intelligence later in life?

Connect

- In this section, you learned that measures of habituation and dishabituation are linked to intelligence. In Section 2 of this chapter, what advice was given to parents regarding habituation and dishabituation?

Reflect *Your Own Personal Journey of Life*

- Imagine that you had your 1-year-old assessed with a developmental scale, and the baby did very well on it. How confident should you be that your baby is going to be a genius when he or she grows up?

4 Language Development

 Describe the nature of language and how it develops in infancy.

| Defining Language | Language's Rule Systems | How Language Develops | Biological and Environmental Influences | An Interactionist View |

In 1799, a nude boy was observed running through the woods in France. The boy was captured when he was 11 years old. He was called the Wild Boy of Aveyron and was believed to have lived in the woods alone for six years (Lane, 1976). When found, he made no effort to communicate. He never learned to communicate effectively. Sadly, a modern-day wild child named Genie was discovered in Los Angeles in 1970. Despite intensive intervention, Genie has never acquired more than a primitive form of language. Both cases—the Wild Boy of Aveyron and Genie—raise questions about the biological and environmental determinants of language, topics that we also will examine later in the chapter. First, though, we need to define language.

DEFINING LANGUAGE

Language is a form of communication—whether spoken, written, or signed—that is based on a system of symbols. Language consists of the words used by a community and the rules for varying and combining them.

Think how important language is in our everyday lives. We need language to speak with others, listen to others, read, and write. Our language enables us to describe past events in detail and to plan for the future. Language lets us pass down information from one generation to the next and create a rich cultural heritage.

language A form of communication, whether spoken, written, or signed, that is based on a system of symbols. Language consists of the words used by a community and the rules for varying and combining them.

All human languages have some common characteristics (Berko Gleason, 2009). These include infinite generativity and organizational rules. **Infinite generativity** is the ability to produce an endless number of meaningful sentences using a finite set of words and rules. Rules describe the way language works (Berko Gleason, 2009). Let's explore what these rules involve.

LANGUAGE'S RULE SYSTEMS

When nineteenth-century American writer Ralph Waldo Emerson said, "The world was built in order, and the atoms march in tune," he must have had language in mind. Language is highly ordered and organized (Song, 2013). The organization involves five systems of rules: phonology, morphology, syntax, semantics, and pragmatics.

Phonology   Every language is made up of basic sounds. **Phonology** is the sound system of the language, including the sounds that are used and how they may be combined (Kuhl & Damasio, 2012). For example, English has the initial consonant cluster *spr* as in *spring,* but no words begin with the cluster *rsp.*

Phonology provides a basis for constructing a large and expandable set of words out of two or three dozen phonemes. A *phoneme* is the basic unit of sound in a language; it is the smallest unit of sound that affects meaning. For example, in English the sound represented by the letter *p*, as in the words *pot* and *spot*, is a phoneme. The /p/ sound is slightly different in the two words, but this variation is not distinguished in English, and therefore the /p/ sound is a single phoneme. In some languages, such as Hindi, the variations of the /p/ sound represent separate phonemes.

Morphology   **Morphology** refers to the units of meaning involved in word formation. A *morpheme* is a minimal unit of meaning; it is a word or a part of a word that cannot be broken into smaller meaningful parts. Every word in the English language is made up of one or more morphemes. Some words consist of a single morpheme (for example, *help*), whereas others are made up of more than one morpheme (for example, *helper* has two morphemes, *help + er*, with the morpheme *-er* meaning "one who"—in this case, "one who helps"). Thus, not all morphemes are words by themselves; for example, *pre-, -tion,* and *-ing* are morphemes.

Just as the rules that govern phonology describe the sound sequences that can occur in a language, the rules of morphology describe the way meaningful units (morphemes) can be combined in words (Brown, 2013). Morphemes have many jobs in grammar, such as marking tense (for example, "she walks" versus "she walked") and number ("she walks" versus "they walk").

Syntax   **Syntax** involves the way words are combined to form acceptable phrases and sentences (de Villiers & de Villiers, 2013; Tallerman, 2013). If someone says to you, "Bob slugged Tom" or "Bob was slugged by Tom," you know who did the slugging and who was slugged in each case because you have a syntactic understanding of these sentence structures. You also understand that the sentence, "You didn't stay, did you?" is a grammatical sentence, but that "You didn't stay, didn't you?" is unacceptable and ambiguous.

If you learn another language, English syntax will not get you very far. For example, in English an adjective usually precedes a noun (as in *blue sky*), whereas in Spanish the adjective usually follows the noun *(cielo azul).* Despite the differences in their syntactic structures, however, syntactic systems in all of the world's languages have some common ground (Brown, Chumakina, & Corbett, 2013; Whaley, 2013). For example, no language we know of permits sentences like the following one:

The mouse the cat the farmer chased killed ate the cheese.

It appears that language users cannot process subjects and objects arranged in too complex a fashion in a sentence.

Semantics   **Semantics** refers to the meaning of words and sentences. Every word has a set of semantic features, which are required attributes related to meaning (Harris, Golinkoff, & Hirsh-Pasek, 2011). *Girl* and *woman*, for example, share many semantic features, but they differ semantically in regard to age.

Language allows us to communicate with others. *What are some important characteristics of language?*

infinite generativity The ability to produce an endless number of meaningful sentences using a finite set of words and rules.

phonology The sound system of the language, including the sounds that are used and how they may be combined.

morphology Units of meaning involved in word formation.

syntax The ways words are combined to form acceptable phrases and sentences.

semantics The meaning of words and sentences.

FRANK & ERNEST: © Thaves/Dist. by United Feature Syndicate, Inc.

Words have semantic restrictions on how they can be used in sentences (Mariscal & Gallego, 2012). The sentence *The bicycle talked the boy into buying a candy bar* is syntactically correct but semantically incorrect. The sentence violates our semantic knowledge that bicycles don't talk.

Pragmatics   A final set of language rules involves **pragmatics,** the appropriate use of language in different contexts. Pragmatics covers a lot of territory (Elbourne, 2012). When you take turns speaking in a discussion or use a question to convey a command ("Why is it so noisy in here? What is this, Grand Central Station?"), you are demonstrating knowledge of pragmatics. You also apply the pragmatics of English when you use polite language in appropriate situations (for example, when talking to your teacher) or tell stories that are interesting, jokes that are funny, and lies that convince. In each of these cases, you are demonstrating that you understand the rules of your culture for adjusting language to suit the context.

At this point, we have discussed five important rule systems involved in language. An overview of these rule systems is presented in Figure 5.12.

HOW LANGUAGE DEVELOPS

According to an ancient historian, in the thirteenth century the emperor of Germany, Frederick II, had a cruel idea. He wanted to know what language children would speak if no one talked to them. He selected several newborns and threatened their caregivers with death

pragmatics The appropriate use of language in different contexts.

Rule System	Description	Examples
Phonology	The sound system of a language. A phoneme is the smallest sound unit in a language.	The word *chat* has three phonemes or sounds: /ch/ /ă/ /t/. An example of phonological rule in the English language is while the phoneme /r/ can follow the phonemes /t/ or /d/ in an English consonant cluster (such as *track* or *drab*), the phoneme /l/ cannot follow these letters.
Morphology	The system of meaningful units involved in word formation.	The smallest sound units that have a meaning are called morphemes, or meaning units. The word *girl* is one morpheme, or meaning unit; it cannot be broken down any further and still have meaning. When the suffix *s* is added, the word becomes *girls* and has two morphemes because the *s* changed the meaning of the word, indicating that there is more than one girl.
Syntax	The system that involves the way words are combined to form acceptable phrases and sentences.	Word order is very important in determining meaning in the English language. For example, the sentence "Sebastian pushed the bike" has a different meaning than "The bike pushed Sebastian."
Semantics	The system that involves the meaning of words and sentences.	Knowing the meaning of individual words—that is, vocabulary. For example, semantics includes knowing the meaning of such words as *orange*, *transportation*, and *intelligent*.
Pragmatics	The system of using appropriate conversation and knowledge of how to effectively use language in context.	An example is using polite language in appropriate situations, such as being mannerly when talking with one's teacher. Taking turns in a conversation involves pragmatics.

FIGURE **5.12**
THE RULE SYSTEMS OF LANGUAGE

FIGURE **5.13**
FROM UNIVERSAL LINGUIST TO LANGUAGE-SPECIFIC LISTENER. In Patricia Kuhl's research laboratory babies listen to tape-recorded voices that repeat syllables. When the sounds of the syllables change, the babies quickly learn to look at the bear. Using this technique, Kuhl has demonstrated that babies are universal linguists until about 6 months of age, but in their next six months they become language-specific listeners. *Does Kuhl's research give support to the view that either "nature" or "nurture" is the source of language acquisition?*

if they ever talked to the infants. Frederick never found out what language the children spoke because they all died. Today, we are still curious about infants' development of language, although our experiments and observations are, to say the least, far more humane than the evil Frederick's.

Whatever language they learn, infants all over the world follow a similar path in language development. What are some key milestones in this development?

Recognizing Language Sounds

Long before they begin to learn words, infants can make fine distinctions among the sounds of the language. In Patricia Kuhl's (1993, 2000, 2007, 2009, 2011) research, phonemes from languages all over the world are piped through a speaker for infants to hear (see Figure 5.13). A box with a toy bear in it is placed where the infant can see it. A string of identical syllables is played; then the syllables are changed (for example, *ba ba ba ba*, and then *pa pa pa pa*). If the infant turns its head when the syllables change, the box lights up and the bear dances and drums, rewarding the infant for noticing the change.

Kuhl's (2007, 2009, 2011) research has demonstrated that from birth up to about 6 months of age, infants are "citizens of the world": They recognize when sounds change most of the time, no matter what language the syllables come from. But over the next six months, infants get even better at perceiving the changes in sounds from their "own" language (the one their parents speak) and gradually lose the ability to recognize differences that are not important in their own language (Kuhl & Damasio, 2012).

Babbling and Other Vocalizations

Long before infants speak recognizable words, they produce a number of vocalizations. The functions of these early vocalizations are to practice making sounds, to communicate, and to attract attention (Parish-Morris, Golinkoff & Hirsh-Pasek, 2013; Ransdell & others, 2012). Babies' sounds go through this sequence during the first year:

- *Crying.* Babies cry even at birth. Crying can signal distress, but, as we will discuss in Chapter 6, different types of cries signal different things.
- *Cooing.* Babies first coo at about 2 to 4 months (Menn & Stoel-Gannon, 2009). These are gurgling sounds that are made in the back of the throat and usually express pleasure during interaction with the caregiver.
- *Babbling.* In the middle of the first year, babies babble—that is, they produce strings of consonant-vowel combinations, such as "ba, ba, ba, ba."

Gestures

Infants start using gestures, such as showing and pointing, at about 7 to 15 months of age with a mean age of approximately 11 to 12 months (Colonnesi & others, 2010). They may wave bye-bye, nod to mean "yes," show an empty cup to ask for more milk, and point to a dog to draw attention to it. Some early gestures are symbolic, as

Long before infants speak recognizable words, they communicate by prod[ucing] a number of vocalizations and gestures. *At approximately what ages [do they] begin to produce different types of vocalizations and gestures?*

What characterizes the infant's early word learning?

FIGURE **5.14**

VARIATION IN LANGUAGE MILESTONES. *What are some possible explanations for variations in the timing of language milestones?*

…t is a difference in the way children learn …darin Chinese and English?

when an infant smacks her lips to indicate food/drink. Pointing is regarded by language experts as an important index of the social aspects of language, and it follows this developmental sequence: from pointing without checking on adult gaze to pointing while looking back and forth between an object and the adult (Goldin-Meadow, 2012; Goldin-Meadow & Alibali, 2013). Lack of pointing is a significant indicator of problems in the infant's communication system. For example, failure to engage in pointing characterizes many autistic children. The ability to use the pointing gesture effectively improves in the second year of life as advances in other aspects of language communication occur (Colonnesi & others, 2010).

One study found that parents in high socioeconomic status (SES) families were more likely to use gestures when communicating with their 14-month-old infants (Rowe & Goldin-Meadow, 2009). Further, the infants' use of gestures at 14 months of age in high SES families was linked to a larger vocabulary at 54 months of age.

First Words   Children understand their first words earlier than they speak them (Harris, Golinkoff, & Hirsh-Pasek, 2011; Pan & Uccelli, 2009). As early as 5 months of age, infants recognize their name when someone says it. On the average, infants understand about 50 words at about 13 months, but they can't say this many words until about 18 months (Menyuk, Liebergott, & Schultz, 1995). Thus, in infancy *receptive vocabulary* (words the child understands) considerably exceeds *spoken vocabulary* (words the child uses). A recent study revealed that 6-month-olds comprehend words that refer to body parts, such as "hand" and "feet," although of course they cannot yet speak these words (Tincoff & Jusczyk, 2012).

A child's first words include those that name important people (*dada*), familiar animals (*kitty*), vehicles (*car*), toys (*ball*), food (*milk*), body parts (*eye*), clothes (*hat*), household items (*clock*), and greeting terms (*bye*). These were the first words of babies 50 years ago, and they are the first words of babies today. Children often express various intentions with their single words, so that "cookie" might mean, "That's a cookie" or "I want a cookie."

The infant's spoken vocabulary rapidly increases once the first word is spoken (Waxman & Goswami, 2012). The average 18-month-old can speak about 50 words but by the age of 2 years can speak about 200 words. This rapid increase in vocabulary that begins at approximately 18 months is called the *vocabulary spurt* (Bloom, Lifter, & Broughton, 1985).

Like the timing of a child's first word, the timing of the vocabulary spurt varies (Lieven, 2008). Figure 5.14 shows the range for these two language milestones in 14 children. On average, these children said their first word at 13 months and had a vocabulary spurt at 19 months. However, the ages for the first spoken word of individual children varied from 10 to 17 months and for their vocabulary spurt from 13 to 25 months.

Cross-linguistic differences occur in word learning (Lieven & Stoll, 2010). Children learning Mandarin Chinese, Korean, and Japanese acquire more verbs earlier in their development than do children learning English. This cross-linguistic difference reflects the greater use of verbs in the language input to children in these Asian languages.

Children sometimes overextend or underextend the meanings of the words they use (Woodward & Markman, 1998). *Overextension* is the tendency to apply a word to objects that are inappropriate for the word's meaning. For example, children at first may say "dada" not only for "father" but also for other men, strangers, or boys. With time, overextensions decrease and eventually disappear. *Underextension* is the tendency to apply a word too narrowly; it occurs when children fail to use a word to name a relevant event or object. For example, a child might use the word *boy* to describe a 5-year-old neighbor but not apply the word to a male infant or to a 9-year-old male.

Two-Word Utterances   By the time children are 18 to 24 months of age, they usually speak in two-word utterances. To convey meaning with just two words, the child relies heavily on gesture, tone, and context. The wealth of meaning children can communicate with a two-word utterance includes the following (Slobin, 1972):

- Identification: "See doggie."
- Location: "Book there."
- Repetition: "More milk."
- Negation: "Not wolf."

- Possession: "My candy."
- Attribution: "Big car."
- Agent-action: "Mama walk."
- Action-direct object: "Hit you."
- Action-indirect object: "Give Papa."
- Action-instrument: "Cut knife."
- Question: "Where ball?"

These are examples from children whose first language is English, German, Russian, Finnish, Turkish, or Samoan.

Notice that the two-word utterances omit many parts of speech and are remarkably succinct. In fact, in every language, a child's first combinations of words have this economical quality; they are telegraphic. **Telegraphic speech** is the use of short and precise words without grammatical markers such as articles, auxiliary verbs, and other connectives. Telegraphic speech is not limited to two words. "Mommy give ice cream" and "Mommy give Tommy ice cream" also are examples of telegraphic speech.

Around the world, most young children learn to speak in two-word utterances at about 18 to 24 months of age. *What are some examples of these two-word utterances?*

BIOLOGICAL AND ENVIRONMENTAL INFLUENCES

We have discussed a number of language milestones in infancy; Figure 5.15 summarizes the approximate time at which infants typically reach these milestones. But what makes this amazing development possible? Everyone who uses language in some way "knows" its rules and has the ability to create an infinite number of words and sentences. Where does this knowledge come from? Is it the product of biology? Is language learned and influenced by experiences?

Biological Influences The ability to speak and understand language requires a certain vocal apparatus as well as a nervous system with certain capabilities. The nervous system and vocal apparatus of humanity's predecessors changed over hundreds of thousands or millions of years. With advances in the nervous system and vocal structures, *Homo sapiens* went beyond the grunting and shrieking of other animals to develop speech. Although estimates vary, many experts believe that humans acquired language about 100,000 years ago, which in evolutionary time represents a very recent acquisition. It gave humans an enormous edge over other animals and increased the chances of human survival (Arbib, 2012).

Some language scholars view the remarkable similarities in how children acquire language all over the world as strong evidence that language has a biological basis. There is evidence that particular regions of the brain are predisposed to be used for language (Lee & others, 2012). Two regions involved in language were first discovered in studies of brain-damaged individuals: **Broca's area**, an area in the left frontal lobe of the brain involved in producing

Typical Age	Language Milestones
Birth	Crying
2 to 4 months	Cooing begins
5 months	Understands first word
6 months	Babbling begins
7 to 11 months	Change from universal linguist to language-specific listener
8 to 12 months	Uses gestures, such as showing and pointing Comprehension of words appears
13 months	First word spoken
18 months	Vocabulary spurt starts
18 to 24 months	Uses two-word utterances Rapid expansion of understanding of words

FIGURE **5.15**

SOME LANGUAGE MILESTONES IN INFANCY. Despite great variations in the language input received by infants, around the world they follow a similar path in learning to speak.

telegraphic speech The use of short and precise words without grammatical markers such as articles, auxiliary verbs, and other connectives.

Broca's area An area in the brain's that is involved in speech product

In the wild, chimps communicate through calls, gestures, and expressions, which evolutionary psychologists believe might be the roots of true language. *How strong is biology's role in language?*

developmental **connection**

Language

Much of language is processed in the brain's left hemisphere. Chapter 4, p. 112

Broca's area

Wernicke's area

FIGURE **5.16**

BROCA'S AREA AND WERNICKE'S AREA. Broca's area is located in the frontal lobe of the brain's left hemisphere, and it is involved in the control of speech. Wernicke's area is a portion of the left hemisphere's temporal lobe that is involved in understanding language. *How does the role of these areas of the brain relate to lateralization, which was discussed in Chapter 4?*

Wernicke's area An area in the brain's left hemisphere that is involved in language comprehension.

aphasia A loss or impairment of language ability caused by brain damage.

language acquisition device (LAD) Chomsky's term that describes a biological endowment enabling the child to detect the features and rules of language, including phonology, syntax, and semantics.

words, and **Wernicke's area**, a region of the brain's left hemisphere involved in language comprehension (see Figure 5.16). Damage to either of these areas produces types of **aphasia**, which is a loss or impairment of language processing. Individuals with damage to Broca's area have difficulty producing words correctly; individuals with damage to Wernicke's area have poor comprehension and often produce fluent but incomprehensible speech.

Linguist Noam Chomsky (1957) proposed that humans are biologically prewired to learn language at a certain time and in a certain way. He said that children are born into the world with a **language acquisition device (LAD),** a biological endowment that enables the child to detect certain features and rules of language, including phonology, syntax, and semantics. Children are prepared by nature with the ability to detect the sounds of language, for example, and to follow rules such as how to form plurals and ask questions.

Chomsky's LAD is a theoretical construct, not a physical part of the brain. Is there evidence for the existence of a LAD? Supporters of the LAD concept cite the uniformity of language milestones across languages and cultures, evidence that children create language even in the absence of well-formed input, and biological substrates of language. But, as we will see, critics argue that even if infants have something like a LAD, it cannot explain the whole story of language acquisition.

Environmental Influences   Decades ago, behaviorists opposed Chomsky's hypothesis and argued that language represents nothing more than chains of responses acquired through reinforcement (Skinner, 1957). A baby happens to babble "Ma-ma"; Mama rewards the baby with hugs and smiles; the baby says "Mama" more and more. Bit by bit, said the behaviorists, the baby's language is built up. According to behaviorists, the use of language is a complex, learned skill, much like playing the piano or dancing.

The behaviorist view of language learning has several problems. First, it does not explain how people create novel sentences—sentences that people have never heard or spoken before. Second, children learn the syntax of their native language even if they are not reinforced for doing so. Social psychologist Roger Brown (1973) spent long hours observing parents and their young children. He found that parents did not directly or explicitly reward or correct the syntax of most children's utterances. That is, parents did not say "good," "correct," "right," "wrong," and so on. Also, parents did not offer direct corrections such as "You should say *two shoes,* not *two shoe.*" However, as we will see shortly, many parents do expand on their young children's grammatically incorrect utterances and recast many of those that have grammatical errors (Clark, 2009).

The behavioral view is no longer considered a viable explanation of how children acquire language. But a great deal of research describes ways in which children's environmental experiences influence their language skills (Harris, Golinkoff, & Hirsh-Pasek, 2011). Many language experts argue that a child's experiences, the particular language to be learned, and the context in which learning takes place can strongly influence language acquisition (Giorgis & Glazer, 2013).

Language is not learned in a social vacuum. Most children are bathed in language from a very early age (Kuhl, 2009, 2011), unlike the Wild Boy of Aveyron, who never learned to communicate effectively, having lived in social isolation for years. The support and involvement of caregivers and teachers greatly facilitate a child's language learning (Giorgis & Glazer, 2013). For example, one study found that when mothers immediately smiled and touched their 8-month-old infants after they babbled, the infants subsequently made more complex speechlike sounds than when mothers responded to their infants in a random manner (Goldstein, King, & West, 2003) (see Figure 5.17).

Michael Tomasello (2003, 2006, 2011; Tomasello & Hamann, 2012) stresses that young children are intensely interested in their social world and that early in their development they can understand the intentions of other people. His *interaction view* of language emphasizes that children learn language in specific contexts. For example, when a toddler and a father are jointly focused on a book, the father might say, "See the birdie." In this case, even a toddler understands that the father intends to name something and knows to look in the direction of the pointing. Through this kind of joint attention, early in their development children are able to use their social skills to acquire language (Carpenter, 2011; Tomasello, 2011; Tomasello & Hamann, 2012). One study revealed that joint attention at 12 and 18 months predicted language skills at 24 months of age (Mundy & others, 2007).

Researchers have also found that the child's vocabulary development is linked to the family's socioeconomic status and the type of talk that parents direct to their children. Betty Hart and Todd Risley (1995) observed the language environments of children whose parents were professionals and children whose parents were on welfare (public assistance). Compared with the professional parents, the parents on welfare talked much less to their young children, talked less about past events, and provided less elaboration. As indicated in Figure 5.18, the children of the professional parents had a much larger vocabulary at 36 months of age than the children of the welfare parents.

Other research has linked how much mothers speak to their infants with the size of the infants' vocabularies. For example, in one study by Janellen Huttenlocher and her colleagues (1991), infants whose mothers spoke more often to them had markedly higher vocabularies. By the second birthday, vocabulary differences were substantial.

However, a study of 1- to 3-year-old children living in low-income families found that the sheer amount of maternal talk was not the best predictor of a child's vocabulary growth (Pan & others, 2005). Rather, it was maternal language and literacy skills, and mothers' diversity of vocabulary use that best predicted children's vocabulary development. For example, when mothers used a more diverse vocabulary when talking with their children, their children's vocabulary benefited, but their children's vocabulary was not related to the total amount of their talkativeness with their children. Also, mothers who frequently used pointing gestures had children with a greater vocabulary. Pointing usually occurs in concert with speech, and it may enhance the meaning of mothers' verbal input to their children. These research studies and others (Hoff, 2012; NICHD Early Child Care Research Network, 2005) demonstrate the important effect that early speech input and poverty can have on the development of a child's language skills.

One intriguing component of the young child's linguistic environment is **child-directed speech,** language spoken in a higher pitch than normal with simple words and sentences (Naoi & others, 2012). It is hard to use child-directed speech when not in the presence of a baby, but parents shift into it when they start talking to a baby. Much of this is automatic and something most parents are not aware they are doing. Even 4-year-olds speak in simpler ways to 2-year-olds than to their 4-year-old friends. Child-directed speech has the important function of capturing the infant's attention and maintaining communication (Gauthier & Shi, 2011). Adults

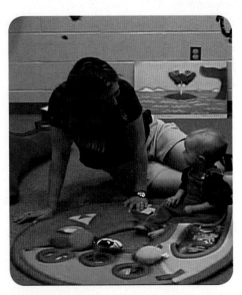

FIGURE **5.17**

SOCIAL INTERACTION AND BABBLING. One study focused on two groups of mothers and their 8-month-old infants (Goldstein, King, & West, 2003). One group of mothers was instructed to smile and touch their infants immediately after the babies cooed and babbled; the other group was also told to smile and touch their infants but in a random manner, unconnected to sounds the infants made. The infants whose mothers immediately responded in positive ways to their babbling subsequently made more complex, speechlike sounds, such as "da" and "gu." The research setting for this study, which underscores how important caregivers are in the early development of language, is shown above.

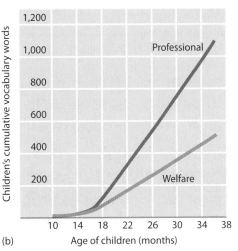

(a) Age of children (months)

(b) Age of children (months)

FIGURE **5.18**

LANGUAGE INPUT IN PROFESSIONAL AND WELFARE FAMILIES AND YOUNG CHILDREN'S VOCABULARY DEVELOPMENT. (*a*) In this study (Hart & Rísley, 1995), parents from professional families talked with their young children more than parents from welfare families. (*b*) All of the children learned to talk, but children from professional families developed vocabularies that were twice as large as those from welfare families. Thus, by the time children go to preschool, they already have experienced considerable differences in language input in their families and developed different levels of vocabulary that are linked to their socioeconomic context. *Does this study indicate that poverty caused deficiencies in vocabulary development?*

child-directed speech Language spoken in a higher pitch than normal, with simple words and sentences.

What characterizes shared reading in the lives of infants, toddlers, and young children?

often use strategies other than child-directed speech to enhance the child's acquisition of language, including recasting, expanding, and labeling:

- *Recasting* is rephrasing something the child has said, perhaps turning it into a question or restating the child's immature utterance in the form of a fully grammatical sentence. For example, if the child says, "The dog was barking," the adult can respond by asking, "When was the dog barking?" Effective recasting lets the child indicate an interest and then elaborates on that interest.

- *Expanding* is restating, in a linguistically sophisticated form, what a child has said. For example, a child says, "Doggie eat," and the parent replies, "Yes, the doggie is eating."

- *Labeling* is identifying the names of objects. Young children are forever being asked to identify the names of objects. Roger Brown (1958) called this "the original word game" and claimed that much of a child's early vocabulary is motivated by this adult pressure to identify the words associated with objects.

Parents use these strategies naturally and in meaningful conversations. Parents do not need to use a particular method to teach their children to talk, even for children who are slow in learning language. Children usually benefit when parents follow the child's lead, talking about things the child is interested in at the moment, and when parents provide information that children can process. If children are not ready to take in some information, they are likely to tell you (perhaps by turning away). Thus, giving the child more information is not always better.

Remember, the encouragement of language development, not drill and practice, is the key. Language development is not a simple matter of imitation and reinforcement.

Infants, toddlers, and young children benefit when adults read books to and with them (shared reading) (Khandekar & others, 2011; Piasta & others, 2012). Storybook reading especially benefits children when parents extend the meaning of the text by discussing it with children and encouraging them to ask and answer questions (Harris, Golinkoff, & Hirsh-Pasek, 2011; Houston & others, 2012). In one study, a majority of U.S. mothers in low-income families reported that they were reading to their infants and toddlers with some regularity (Raikes & others, 2006). In this study, non-Latino White, more highly educated mothers who were parenting a first-born child were more likely to read books to their infants and toddlers than were African American and Latino mothers who were parenting later-born children. Reading daily to children at 14 to 24 months of age was positively related to the children's language and cognitive development at 36 months of age. To read further about ways that parents can facilitate children's language development, see *Connecting Development to Life*.

AN INTERACTIONIST VIEW

If language acquisition depended only on biology, then the Wild Boy of Aveyron and Genie (discussed earlier in the chapter) should have talked without difficulty. A child's experiences influence language acquisition. But we have seen that language does have strong biological foundations. No matter how much you converse with a dog, it won't learn to talk. In contrast, children are biologically prepared to learn language. Children all over the world acquire language milestones at about the same time and in about the same order. However, there are cultural variations in the type of support given to children's language development. For example, caregivers in the Kaluli culture prompt young children to use a loud voice and particular morphemes that direct the speech act performed (calling out) and to refer to names, kinship relations, and places where there has been a shared past experience that indicates a closeness to the person being addressed (Ochs & Schieffelin, 2008; Schieffelin, 2005).

Environmental influences are also very important in developing competence in language (Hirsh-Pasek & Golinkoff, 2012a, b; Parish-Morris, Golinkoff & Hirsh-Pasek, 2013). Children whose parents provide them with a rich verbal environment show many positive benefits (Gunning, 2013; Vukelich, Christie, & Enz, 2012). Parents who pay attention to what their children are trying to say, expand their children's utterances, read to them, and label things in

How Parents Can Facilitate Infants' and Toddlers' Language Development

Linguist Naomi Baron (1992) in *Growing Up with Language,* and more recently Ellen Galinsky (2010) in *Mind in the Making,* provided ideas to help parents facilitate their infants' and toddlers' language development. A summary of their ideas follow:

- *Be an active conversational partner.* Talk to your baby from the time it is born. Initiate conversation with the baby. If the baby is in a day-long child-care program, ensure that the baby receives adequate language stimulation from adults.
- *Talk in a slowed-down pace and don't worry about how you sound to other adults when you talk to your baby.* Talking in a slowed-down pace will help your baby detect words in the sea of sounds they experience. Babies enjoy and attend to the high-pitched sound of child-directed speech.
- *Use parent-look and parent-gesture, and name what you are looking at.* When you want your child to pay attention to something, look at it and point to it. Then name it—for example, you might say, "Look, Alex, there's an airplane."
- *When you talk with infants and toddlers, be simple, concrete, and repetitive.* Don't try to talk to them in abstract, high-level ways and think you have to say something new or different all of the time. Using familiar words often will help them remember the words.
- *Play games.* Use word games like peek-a-boo and pat-a-cake to help infants learn words.
- *Remember to listen.* Since toddlers' speech is often slow and laborious, parents are often tempted to supply words and thoughts for them. Be patient and let toddlers express themselves, no matter how painstaking the process is or how great a hurry you are in.
- *Expand and elaborate language abilities and horizons with infants and toddlers.* Ask questions that encourage answers other than "yes" or "no." Actively repeat, expand, and recast the utterances. Your toddler might say, "Dada." You could follow with, "Where's Dada?" and then you might continue, "Let's go find him."
- *Adjust to your child's idiosyncrasies instead of working against them.* Many toddlers have difficulty pronouncing words and making themselves understood. Whenever possible, make toddlers feel that they are being understood.
- *Resist making normative comparisons.* Be aware of the ages at which your child reaches specific milestones (such as the first word,

It is a good idea for parents to begin talking to their babies at the start. The best language teaching occurs when the talking begins before the infant becomes capable of intelligible speech. *What are some other guidelines for parents to follow in helping their infants and toddlers develop their language skills?*

first 50 words), but do not measure this development rigidly against that of other children. Such comparisons can bring about unnecessary anxiety.

The first suggestion above to parents of infants is to "be an active conversational partner." What did you learn earlier in the chapter about the amount of conversation mothers have with their infants? Does the amount of conversation or the mother's literacy skills and vocabulary diversity have more of a positive effect on infants' vocabulary?

the environment, are providing valuable benefits for them (Berko Gleason, 2009; Parish-Morris, Golinkoff & Hirsh-Pasek, 2013).

An interactionist view emphasizes that both biology and experience contribute to language development (Schoenemann, 2012). How much of language acquisition is biologically determined and how much depends on interaction with others is a subject of debate among linguists and psychologists. However, all agree that both biological capacity and relevant experience are necessary (Berko Gleason, 2009; Kuhl, 2012; Tomasello & Hamann, 2012).

Review

- What is language?
- What are language's rule systems?
- How does language develop in infancy?
- What are some biological and environmental influences on language?
- To what extent do biological and environmental influences interact to produce language development?

Connect

- In Chapter 1, you learned that the more years children spend living in poverty, the more their physiological indices of stress are elevated. In this chapter, you learned about the effects of SES on children's language acquisition and vocabulary building. How might these effects influence children's school performance?

Reflect *Your Own Personal Journey of Life*

- Would it be a good idea for you as a parent to hold large flash cards of words in front of your baby for several hours each day to help the baby learn language and improve the baby's intelligence? Why or why not? What do you think Piaget would say about this activity?

---

topical **connections** — — — — — — — — — — — — — — — —

Advances in infants' cognitive development are linked to their socioemotional development. In Chapter 6 you will learn about the infant's developing social orientation and understanding, which involve perceiving people as engaging in intentional and goal-directed behavior, joint attention, and cooperation. In Chapter 7 you will read about two major theorists—Piaget and Vygotsky—and compare their views of how young children's thinking advances. You will see how young children become more capable of sustaining their attention; learn about the astonishing rate at which preschool children's vocabulary expands; and explore variations in early childhood education.

looking **forward** ---➤

---

reach your **learning goals**

Cognitive Development in Infancy

1 Piaget's Theory of Infant Development

 LG1 Summarize and evaluate Piaget's theory of infant development.

Cognitive Processes

- In Piaget's theory, children actively construct their own cognitive worlds, building mental structures to adapt to their world. Schemes are actions or mental representations that organize knowledge. Behavioral schemes (physical activities) characterize infancy, whereas mental schemes (cognitive activities) develop in childhood. Assimilation occurs when children use their existing schemes to deal with new information; accommodation refers to children's adjustment of their schemes in the face of new information. Through organization, children group isolated behaviors into a higher-order, more smoothly functioning cognitive system. Equilibration is a mechanism Piaget proposed to explain how children shift from one cognitive stage to the next. As children experience cognitive conflict in trying to understand the world, they use assimilation and accommodation to attain equilibrium. The result is a new stage of thought. According to Piaget, there are four qualitatively different stages of thought. The first of these, the sensorimotor stage, is described in this chapter. The other three stages are discussed in subsequent chapters.

The Sensorimotor Stage

- In sensorimotor thought, the first of Piaget's four stages, the infant organizes and coordinates sensations with physical movements. The stage lasts from birth to about 2 years of age. Sensorimotor thought has six substages: simple reflexes; first habits and primary circular reactions; secondary circular reactions; coordination of secondary circular reactions; tertiary circular reactions, novelty, and curiosity; and internalization of schemes. One key accomplishment of this stage is object permanence, the ability to understand that objects continue to exist even when the infant is no longer observing them. Another aspect involves infants' understanding of cause and effect.

Evaluating Piaget's Sensorimotor Stage

- Piaget opened up a whole new way of looking at infant development in terms of coordinating sensory input with motoric actions. In the past decades, revisions of Piaget's view have been proposed based on research. For example, researchers have found that a stable and differentiated perceptual world is established earlier than Piaget envisioned, and infants begin to develop concepts as well. The nature-nurture issue in regard to infant cognitive development continues to be debated. Spelke endorses a core knowledge approach, which states that infants are born with domain-specific innate knowledge systems. Critics argue that Spelke has not given adequate attention to early experiences that infants have.

2 Learning, Remembering, and Conceptualizing

 LG2 Describe how infants learn, remember, and conceptualize.

Conditioning

- Operant conditioning techniques have been especially useful to researchers in demonstrating infants' perception and retention of information about perceptual-motor actions.

Attention

- Attention is the focusing of mental resources on select information, and in infancy attention is closely linked with habituation. In the first year, much of attention is of the orienting/investigative type, but sustained attention also becomes important. Habituation is the repeated presentation of the same stimulus, causing reduced attention to the stimulus. If a different stimulus is presented, and the infant pays increased attention to it, dishabituation is occurring. Joint attention plays an important role in infant development, especially in the infant's acquisition of language.

Memory

- Memory is the retention of information over time. Infants as young as 2 to 6 months of age can retain information about perceptual-motor actions. However, many experts argue that what we commonly think of as memory (consciously remembering the past) does not occur until the second half of the first year of life. By the end of the second year, long-term memory is more substantial and reliable. The hippocampus and frontal lobes of the brain are involved in development of explicit memory in infancy. The phenomenon of not being able to remember events that occurred before the age of 3—known as infantile or childhood amnesia—may be due to the immaturity of the prefrontal lobes of the brain at that age.

Imitation

- Meltzoff has shown that newborns can match their behaviors (such as protruding their tongue) to a model. His research also shows that deferred imitation occurs as early as 9 months of age.

Concept Formation and Categorization

- Mandler argues that it is not until about 7 to 9 months of age that infants form conceptual categories, although we do not know precisely when concept formation begins. Infants' first concepts are broad. Over the first two years of life, these broad concepts gradually become more differentiated.

3 Individual Differences and Assessment

 Discuss infant assessment measures and the prediction of intelligence.

Measures of Infant Development

- Gesell's scale is still widely used by pediatricians to distinguish normal and abnormal infants; it provides a developmental quotient (DQ). The Bayley Scales of Infant Development, developed by Nancy Bayley, continue to be widely used to assess infant development. The current version, the Bayley-III, consists of five scales: cognitive, language, motor, socioemotional, and adaptive. Increasingly used, the Fagan Test of Infant Intelligence assesses how effectively the infant processes information.

Predicting Intelligence

- Developmental scales for infants grew out of the tradition of IQ testing of older children. These scales are less verbally oriented than IQ tests. Global scores on the Gesell and Bayley scales are not good predictors of IQ scores in later childhood. However, measures of information processing such as speed of habituation and degree of dishabituation do correlate with intelligence later in childhood. There is both continuity and discontinuity between infant cognitive development and cognitive development later in childhood.

4 Language Development

 Describe the nature of language and how it develops in infancy.

Defining Language

- Language is a form of communication, whether spontaneous, written, or signed, that is based on a system of symbols. Language consists of the words used by a community and the rules for varying and combining them. Language is characterized by infinite generativity.

Language's Rule Systems

- Phonology is the sound system of the language, including the sounds that are used and how they may be combined. Morphology refers to the units of meaning involved in word formation. Syntax is the way words are combined to form acceptable phrases and sentences. Semantics involves the meaning of words and sentences. Pragmatics is the appropriate use of language in different contexts.

How Language Develops

- Among the milestones in infant language development are crying (birth), cooing (1 to 2 months), babbling (6 months), making the transition from universal linguist to language-specific listener (6 to 12 months), using gestures (8 to 12 months), comprehending words (8 to 12 months), speaking one's first word (13 months), undergoing a vocabulary spurt (19 months), rapidly expanding one's understanding of words (18 to 24 months), and producing two-word utterances (18 to 24 months).

Biological and Environmental Influences

- In evolution, language clearly gave humans an enormous advantage over other animals and increased their chance of survival. Broca's area and Wernicke's area are important locations for language processing in the brain's left hemisphere. Chomsky argues that children are born with the ability to detect basic features and rules of language. In other words, they are biologically prepared to learn language with a prewired language acquisition device (LAD). The behavioral view—that children acquire language as a result of reinforcement—has not been supported. Adults help children acquire language through engaging in child-directed speech, recasting, expanding, and labeling. Environmental influences are demonstrated by differences in the language development of children as a consequence of being exposed to different language environments in the home. Parents should talk extensively with an infant, especially about what the baby is attending to.

An Interactionist View

- Today, most language researchers believe that children everywhere arrive in the world with special social and linguistic capacities that make language acquisition not just likely but inevitable for virtually all children. How much of the language is biologically determined, and how much depends on interaction with others, is a subject of debate among linguists and psychologists. However, all agree that both biological capacity and relevant experience are necessary.

key **terms**

schemes 144
assimilation 144
accommodation 145
organization 145
equilibration 146
sensorimotor stage 146
simple reflexes 146
first habits and primary circular
    reactions 147
primary circular reaction 147
secondary circular reactions 147

coordination of secondary
    circular reactions 147
tertiary circular reactions,
    novelty, and curiosity 147
internalization of schemes 147
object permanence 148
A-not-B error 148
core knowledge approach 150
attention 153
joint attention 154
memory 155

implicit memory 155
explicit memory 155
deferred imitation 156
concepts 156
developmental quotient
    (DQ) 158
Bayley Scales of Infant
    Development 158
language 160
infinite generativity 161
phonology 161

morphology 161
syntax 161
semantics 161
pragmatics 162
telegraphic speech 165
Broca's area 165
Wernicke's area 166
aphasia 166
language acquisition device
    (LAD) 166
child-directed speech 167

key **people**

Jean Piaget 143
Eleanor Gibson 148
Elizabeth Spelke 148
Renée Baillargeon 149
Andrew Meltzoff 150

Karen Wynn 151
Carolyn Rovee-Collier 153
Jean Mandler 155
Arnold Gesell 158

Nancy Bayley 158
Patricia Kuhl 163
Noam Chomsky 166
Roger Brown 166

Michael Tomasello 166
Betty Hart and Todd Risley 167
Janellen Huttenlocher 167
Naomi Baron 169

Chapter 5 | COGNITIVE DEVELOPMENT IN INFANCY

Connecting with McGraw Hill **connect**®

Learning Objectives	Application Activities	Activity Type	Page Reference
Summarize the cognitive processes in infancy.	Brain Development and Cognition-1	Video	pp. 144–146
	Brain Development and Cognition-2	Video	
	Schemes and Organization, Colin, 2 wks–10 mos	Milestones	
	Assimilation and Accommodation, Atlas, 2 wks–10 mos	Milestones	
	Piaget's Substages, 2 wks–20 mos	Milestones	

(continued)

Learning Objectives	Application Activities	Activity Type	Page Reference
Summarize the sensorimotor stage of infancy.	Object Permanence 4–16 Months	Milestones	pp. 146–148
	Lacking Object Permanence at 4 Months	Video	
	Object Permanence at Age 1	Video	
Evaluate Piaget's sensorimotor stage of infancy.	Piaget's Stages of Sensorimotor Development	Click & drag activity	pp. 148–152
Describe attention in infancy.	Joint Attention, Atlas, 4–13 mos	Milestones	pp. 153–155
Discuss assessment measures of infant development.	Bayley Scale, Del, 6–12 mos	Milestones	pp. 158–159
Describe language's rule systems.	Language Rule Systems Part 1	Click & drag activity	pp. 161–162
	Language Rule Systems Part 2	Click & drag activity	
	Rule Systems of Language, Amalia, 3 mos–5 yrs	Milestones	
Describe how language develops in infancy.	Major Language Milestones in Infancy	Click & drag activity	pp. 162–165
	Cry Differentiation 2–22 Weeks	Milestones	
	Emergence of Language 10–15 Months	Milestones	
	Emergence of Language 16–20 Months	Milestones	
	Receptive Language	Video	
	Motherese with a 4-month-old-1	Video	
	Motherese with a 4-month-old-2	Video	
	First Words at 18 Months	Video	
	Language Ability at Age 2	Video	
Describe the biological and environmental influences on language.	Bilingual Household, Yovani, 4–22 mos	Milestones	pp. 165–168

chapter 6

SOCIOEMOTIONAL DEVELOPMENT IN INFANCY

chapter outline

Many fathers are spending more time with their infants today than in the past.

An increasing number of fathers are staying home to care for their children (Lamb, 2010; O'Brien & Moss, 2010). Consider 17-month-old Darius. On weekdays, Darius' father, a writer, cares for him during the day while his mother works full-time as a landscape architect. Darius' father is doing a great job of caring for him. He keeps Darius nearby while he is writing and spends lots of time talking to him and playing with him. From their interactions, it is clear that they genuinely enjoy each other.

Last month, Darius began spending one day a week at a child-care center. His parents carefully selected the center after observing a number of centers and interviewing teachers and center directors. His parents placed him in the center one day a week because they wanted to help Darius get some experience with peers and to give his father some time out from his caregiving.

Darius' father looks to the future and imagines the Little League games Darius will play in and the many other activities he can enjoy with Darius. Remembering how little time his own father spent with him, he is dedicated to making sure that Darius has an involved, nurturing experience with his father.

When Darius' mother comes home in the evenings, she spends considerable time with him. Darius has a secure attachment with both his mother and his father.

topical connections

Until now, we have only discussed the social situations and emotions of parents before and after the arrival of their infants, focusing on such topics as parents' feelings of joy, anticipation, anxiety, and stress during pregnancy; how a mother's optimism may lead to better outcomes for her fetus; and parents' emotional and psychological adjustments during the postpartum period. In this chapter, we will explore the infant's socioemotional development.

◄- - - *looking back* - - - - - - -

preview

In Chapters 4 and 5, you read about how the infant perceives, learns, and remembers. Infants also are socioemotional beings, capable of displaying emotions and initiating social interaction with people close to them. The main topics that we will explore in this chapter are emotional and personality development, social understanding and attachment, and the social contexts of the family and child care.

1 Emotional and Personality Development

 LG1 Discuss the development of emotions and personality in infancy.

Emotional Development   Temperament   Personality Development

Anyone who has been around infants for even a brief time detects that they are emotional beings. Not only do infants express emotions, but they also vary in their temperaments. Some are shy and others are outgoing. Some are active and others much less so. In this section, we will explore these and other aspects of emotional and personality development in infants.

EMOTIONAL DEVELOPMENT

Imagine your life without emotion. Emotion is the color and music of life, as well as the tie that binds people together. How do psychologists define and classify emotions, and why are they important to development? How do emotions develop during the first two years of life?

What Are Emotions?   For our purposes, we will define **emotion** as feeling, or affect, that occurs when a person is in a state or an interaction that is important to him or her, especially to his or her well-being. Especially in infancy, emotions play important roles in (1) communication with others, and (2) behavioral organization. Through emotions, infants communicate important aspects of their lives such as joy, sadness, interest, and fear (Witherington & others, 2010). In terms of behavioral organization, emotions influence infants' social responses and adaptive behavior as they interact with others in their world (Easterbrooks & others, 2013; Thompson, 2013d).

Psychologists classify the broad range of emotions in many ways, but almost all classifications designate an emotion as either positive or negative (Izard, 2009). Positive emotions include enthusiasm, joy, and love. Negative emotions include anxiety, anger, guilt, and sadness.

Biological and Environmental Influences   Emotions are influenced both by biological foundations and by a person's experience (Calkins, 2012; Thompson, 2013c, d; Easterbrooks & others, 2013). Biology's importance to emotion is apparent in the changes in a baby's emotional capacities (Kagan, 2010). Certain regions of the brain that develop early in life (such as the brain stem, hippocampus, and amygdala) play a role in distress, excitement, and rage, and even infants display these emotions (de Haan & Matheson, 2009). But, as we discuss later in the chapter, infants only gradually develop the ability to regulate their emotions, and this ability seems tied to the gradual maturation of the frontal regions of the cerebral cortex (discussed in Chapter 4) that can exert control over other areas of the brain (Cuevas & others, 2012; Morasch & Bell, 2012).

These biological factors, however, are only part of the story of emotion. Emotions serve important functions in our relationships (Duncombe & others, 2012; Slatcher & Trentacosta, 2012). As we discuss later in this section, emotions are the first language with which parents and infants communicate. Emotion-linked interchanges, as when Darius cries and his father sensitively responds, provide the foundation for the infant's developing attachment to the parent.

Social relationships, in turn, provide the setting for the development of a rich variety of emotions (Easterbrooks & others, 2013; Thompson, 2013c, d). When toddlers hear their

> Blossoms are scattered by the wind
> And the wind cares nothing, but
> The blossoms of the heart
> No wind can touch.
>
> —**YOSHIDA KENKO**
> *Buddhist Monk, 14th Century*

How do biological and environmental factors influence the infant's emotional development?

emotion Feeling, or affect, that occurs when a person is in a state or interaction that is important to him or her. Emotion is characterized by behavior that reflects (expresses) the pleasantness or unpleasantness of the state a person is in or the transactions being experienced.

Joy

Sadness

Fear

Surprise

FIGURE **6.1**
EXPRESSION OF DIFFERENT EMOTIONS IN INFANTS

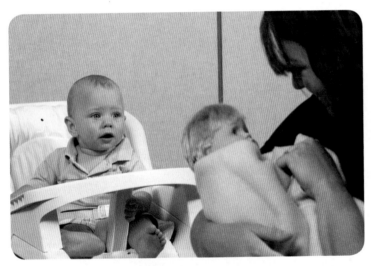

FIGURE **6.2**

IS THIS THE EARLY EXPRESSION OF JEALOUSY? In the study by Hart and Carrington (2002), the researchers concluded that the 6-month-old infants who observed their mothers giving attention to a baby doll displayed negative emotions— such as anger and sadness—which may indicate the early appearance of jealousy. However, experts on emotional development, such as Michael Lewis (2007) and Jerome Kagan (2010), argue that it is unlikely emotions such as jealousy appear in the first year. *Why do they conclude that it is unlikely jealousy occurs in the first year?*

primary emotions Emotions that are present in humans and other animals and emerge early in life; examples are joy, anger, sadness, fear, and disgust.

self-conscious emotions Emotions that require self-awareness, especially consciousness and a sense of "me"; examples include jealousy, empathy, and embarrassment.

parents quarreling, they often react with distress and inhibit their play. Well-functioning families make each other laugh and may develop a light mood to defuse conflicts. A recent study of 18- to 24-month-olds found that parents' elicitation of talk about emotions was associated with their toddlers' sharing and helping (Brownell & others, 2012).

Biological evolution has endowed human beings to be emotional, but embeddedness in relationships and culture with others provides diversity in emotional experiences (Tamis-LeMonda & Song, 2013; Thompson & Virmani, 2010). For example, researchers have found that East Asian infants display less frequent and less positive and negative emotions than non-Latino White infants (Cole & Tan, 2007). Further, Japanese parents try to prevent their children from experiencing negative emotions, whereas non-Latino White mothers are more likely to respond after their children become distressed and then help them cope (Cole & Tan, 2007).

Early Emotions   A leading expert on infant emotional development, Michael Lewis (2007, 2008, 2010) distinguishes between primary emotions and self-conscious emotions. **Primary emotions** are present in humans and other animals; these emotions appear in the first 6 months of the human infant's development. Primary emotions include surprise, interest, joy, anger, sadness, fear, and disgust (see Figure 6.1 for infants' facial expressions of some of these early emotions). In Lewis' classification, **self-conscious emotions** require self-awareness that involves consciousness and a sense of "me." Self-conscious emotions include jealousy, empathy, embarrassment, pride, shame, and guilt, most of these occurring for the first time at some point in the second half of the first year through the second year. Some experts on emotion call self-conscious emotions such as embarrassment, shame, guilt, and pride *other-conscious emotions* because they involve the emotional reactions of others when they are generated (Saarni & others, 2006). For example, approval from parents is linked to toddlers beginning to show pride when they successfully complete a task.

Researchers such as Joseph Campos (2005) and Michael Lewis (2007) debate how early in the infant and toddler years the emotions that we have described first appear and in what sequence. As an indication of the controversy regarding when certain emotions first are displayed by infants, consider jealousy. Some researchers argue that jealousy does not emerge until approximately 15 to 18 months of age (Lewis, 2007), whereas others emphasize that it is displayed much earlier (Draghi-Lorenz, 2007; Draghi-Lorenz, Reddy, & Costall, 2001). Consider a research study in which 6-month-old infants observed their mothers either giving attention to a life-like baby doll (hugging or gently rocking it, for example) or to a book (Hart & Carrington, 2002). When mothers directed their attention to the doll, the infants were more likely to display negative emotions, such as anger and sadness, which may have indicated their jealousy (see Figure 6.2). On the other hand, their expressions of anger and sadness may have reflected frustration in not being able to have the novel doll to play with. Debate about the onset of an emotion such as jealousy illustrates the complexity and difficulty in indexing early emotions. That said, some experts on infant socioemotional development, such as Jerome Kagan (2010), conclude that the structural immaturity of the infant brain make it unlikely that emotions which require thought—such as guilt, pride, despair, shame, empathy, and jealousy—can be experienced in the first year.

Emotional Expression and Social Relationships   Emotional expressions are involved in infants' first relationships. The ability of infants to communicate emotions permits coordinated interactions with their caregivers and the beginning of an emotional bond between them (Easterbrooks & others, 2013; Thompson, 2013b). Not only do parents change their emotional expressions in response to infants' emotional expressions, but infants also modify their emotional expressions in response to their parents' emotional expressions (Slatcher & Trentacosta, 2012). In other words, these interactions are mutually regulated. Because of this coordination, the interactions are described as reciprocal, or synchronous, when all is going well. Sensitive, responsive parents help their infants grow emotionally, whether the infants respond in distressed or happy ways (Wilson, Havighurst, & Harley, 2012).

Cries and smiles are two emotional expressions that infants display when interacting with parents. These are babies' first forms of emotional communication.

Crying   Crying is the most important mechanism newborns have for communicating with their world. The first cry verifies that the baby's lungs have filled with air. Cries also may provide information about the health of the newborn's central nervous system. Newborns even tend to respond with cries and negative facial expressions when they hear other newborns cry (Dondi, Simion, & Caltran, 1999). However, a recent study revealed that newborns of depressed mothers showed less vocal distress when another infant cried, reflecting emotional and physiological dysregulation (Jones, 2012).

What are some different types of cries?

Babies have at least three types of cries:

- **Basic cry.** A rhythmic pattern that usually consists of a cry, followed by a briefer silence, then a shorter whistle that is somewhat higher in pitch than the main cry, then another brief rest before the next cry. Some infancy experts believe that hunger is one of the conditions that incites the basic cry.
- **Anger cry.** A variation of the basic cry in which more excess air is forced through the vocal cords.
- **Pain cry.** A sudden long, initial loud cry followed by breath holding; no preliminary moaning is present. The pain cry is stimulated by a high-intensity stimulus.

Most adults can determine whether an infant's cries signify anger or pain (Zeskind, Klein, & Marshall, 1992). Parents can distinguish the cries of their own baby better than those of another baby.

Smiling   Smiling is critical as a means of developing a new social skill and is a key social signal (Witherington & others, 2010). The power of the infant's smiles was appropriately captured by British theorist John Bowlby (1969): "Can we doubt that the more and better an infant smiles the better he is loved and cared for? It is fortunate for their survival that babies are so designed by nature that they beguile and enslave mothers." Two types of smiling can be distinguished in infants:

- **Reflexive smile.** A smile that does not occur in response to external stimuli and appears during the first month after birth, usually during sleep.
- **Social smile.** A smile that occurs in response to an external stimulus, typically a face in the case of the young infant. Social smiling occurs as early as 2 months of age.

Fear   One of a baby's earliest emotions is fear, which typically first appears at about 6 months of age and peaks at about 18 months. However, abused and neglected infants can show fear as early as 3 months (Witherington & others, 2010). Researchers have found that infant fear is linked to guilt, empathy, and low aggression at 6 to 7 years of age (Rothbart, 2007).

The most frequent expression of an infant's fear involves **stranger anxiety,** in which an infant shows a fear and wariness of strangers. Stranger anxiety usually emerges gradually. It first appears at about 6 months of age in the form of wary reactions. By age 9 months, the fear of strangers is often more intense, reaching a peak toward the end of the first year of life and then decreasing thereafter (Scher & Harel, 2008).

Not all infants show distress when they encounter a stranger. Besides individual variations, whether an infant shows stranger anxiety also depends on the social context and the characteristics of the stranger.

basic cry A rhythmic pattern usually consisting of a cry, a briefer silence, a shorter inspiratory whistle that is higher pitched than the main cry, and then a brief rest before the next cry.

anger cry A variation of the basic cry, with more excess air forced through the vocal cords.

pain cry A sudden appearance of a long, initial loud cry without preliminary moaning, followed by breath holding.

reflexive smile A smile that does not occur in response to external stimuli. It happens during the month after birth, usually during sleep.

social smile A smile in response to an external stimulus, which early in development is typically a face.

stranger anxiety An infant's fear and wariness of strangers; it tends to appear in the second half of the first year of life.

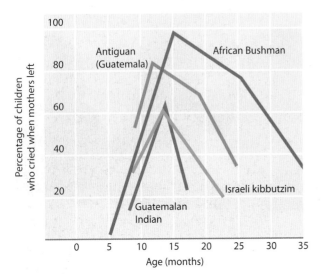

FIGURE **6.3**

SEPARATION PROTEST IN FOUR CULTURES. Note that separation protest peaked at about the same age in all four cultures in this study (13 to 15 months) (Kagan, Kearsley, & Zelazo, 1978). However, a higher percentage (100 percent) of infants in an African Bushman culture engaged in separation protest compared with only about 60 percent of infants in Guatemalan Indian and Israeli kibbutzim cultures. *What might explain the fact that separation protest peaks at about the same time in different cultures?* Reprinted by permission of the publisher from *Infancy: Its Place in Human Development* by Jerome Kagan, Richard B. Kearsley, and Philip R. Zelazo, p. 107, Cambridge, Mass.: Harvard University Press. Copyright © 1978 by the President and Fellows of Harvard College.

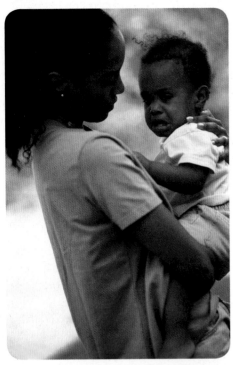

Should a crying baby be given attention and soothed, or does this spoil the infant? Should the infant's age, the type of cry, and the circumstances be considered?

separation protest An infant's distressed crying when the caregiver leaves.

Infants show less stranger anxiety when they are in familiar settings. For example, in one study 10-month-olds showed little stranger anxiety when they met a stranger in their own home but much greater fear when they encountered a stranger in a research laboratory (Sroufe, Waters, & Matas, 1974). Thus, it appears that, when infants feel secure, they are less likely to show stranger anxiety.

Who the stranger is and how the stranger behaves also influence stranger anxiety in infants. Infants are less fearful of child strangers than adult strangers. They also are less fearful of friendly, outgoing, smiling strangers than of passive, unsmiling strangers (Bretherton, Stolberg, & Kreye, 1981).

In addition to stranger anxiety, infants experience fear of being separated from their caregivers. The result is **separation protest**—crying when the caregiver leaves. Separation protest is initially displayed by infants at approximately 7 to 8 months and peaks at about 15 months among U.S. infants (Kagan, 2008). In fact, one study found that separation protest peaked at about 13 to 15 months in four different cultures (Kagan, Kearsley, & Zelazo, 1978). As indicated in Figure 6.3, the percentage of infants who engaged in separation protest varied across cultures, but the infants reached a peak of protest at about the same age—just before the middle of the second year of life.

Emotional Regulation and Coping During the first year of life, the infant gradually develops an ability to inhibit, or minimize, the intensity and duration of emotional reactions (Calkins, 2012; Bell & Cuevas, 2012; Morasch & Bell, 2012). From early in infancy, babies put their thumbs in their mouths to soothe themselves. But at first, infants mainly depend on caregivers to help them soothe their emotions, as when a caregiver rocks an infant to sleep, sings lullabyes to the infant, gently strokes the infant, and so on.

The caregivers' actions influence the infant's neurobiological regulation of emotions (Easterbrooks & others, 2013; Thompson, 2013c, d). By soothing the infant, caregivers help infants to modulate their emotion and reduce the level of stress hormones. Many developmentalists stress that it is a good strategy for a caregiver to soothe an infant before the infant gets into an intense, agitated, uncontrolled state (McElwain & Booth-LaForce, 2006).

Later in infancy, when they become aroused, infants sometimes redirect their attention or distract themselves in order to reduce their arousal. By 2 years of age, toddlers can use language to define their feeling states and the context that is upsetting them. A toddler might say, "Doggy scary." This type of communication may help caregivers to assist the child in regulating emotion.

Contexts can influence emotional regulation (Easterbrooks & others, 2013; Thompson, 2011, 2013d). Infants are often affected by fatigue, hunger, time of day, which people are around them, and where they are. Infants must learn to adapt to different contexts that require emotional regulation. Further, new demands appear as the infant becomes older and parents modify their expectations. For example, a parent may take it in stride if a 6-month-old infant screams in a restaurant but may react very differently if a 6-year-old starts screaming.

To soothe or not to soothe—should a crying baby be given attention and soothed, or does this spoil the infant? Many years ago, the behaviorist John Watson (1928) argued that parents spend too much time responding to infant crying. As a consequence, he said, parents reward crying and increase its incidence. More recently, behaviorist Jacob Gewirtz (1977) found that a caregiver's quick, soothing response to crying increased crying. In contrast, infancy experts Mary Ainsworth (1979) and John Bowlby (1989) stress that you can't respond too much to infant crying in the first year of life. They believe that a quick, comforting response to the infant's cries is an important ingredient in developing a strong bond between the infant and caregiver. In one of Ainsworth's studies, infants whose mothers responded quickly when they cried at 3 months of age cried less later in the first year of life (Bell & Ainsworth, 1972).

Controversy still characterizes the question of whether or how parents should respond to an infant's cries. However, developmentalists increasingly argue that an infant cannot be spoiled in the first year of life, which suggests that parents should soothe a crying infant. This reaction should help infants develop a sense of trust and secure attachment to the caregiver. A recent study revealed that mothers' emotional reactions (anger and anxiety) to crying increased the risk of subsequent attachment insecurity (Leerkes, Parade, & Gudmundson, 2011). And another recent study found that problems in infant soothability at 6 months of age were linked to insecure attachment at 12 months of age (Mills-Koonce, Propper, & Barnette, 2012).

TEMPERAMENT

Do you get upset a lot? Does it take much to get you angry, or to make you laugh? Even at birth, babies seem to have different emotional styles. One infant is cheerful and happy much of the time; another baby seems to cry constantly. These tendencies reflect **temperament,** which involves individual differences in behavioral styles, emotions, and characteristic ways of responding. With regard to its link to emotion, temperament refers to individual differences in how quickly the emotion is shown, how strong it is, how long it lasts, and how quickly it fades away.

"Oh, he's cute, all right, but he's got the temperament of a car alarm." © Barbara Smaller/The New Yorker Collection/www.cartoonbank.com

Describing and Classifying Temperament How would you describe your temperament or the temperament of a friend? Researchers have described and classified the temperament of individuals in different ways. Here we will examine three of those ways.

Chess and Thomas' Classification Psychiatrists Alexander Chess and Stella Thomas (Chess & Thomas, 1977; Thomas & Chess, 1991) identified three basic types, or clusters, of temperament:

- An **easy child** is generally in a positive mood, quickly establishes regular routines in infancy, and adapts easily to new experiences.
- A **difficult child** reacts negatively and cries frequently, engages in irregular daily routines, and is slow to accept change.
- A **slow-to-warm-up child** has a low activity level, is somewhat negative, and displays a low intensity of mood.

In their longitudinal investigation, Chess and Thomas found that 40 percent of the children they studied could be classified as easy, 10 percent as difficult, and 15 percent as slow to warm up. Notice that 35 percent did not fit any of the three patterns. Researchers have found that these three basic clusters of temperament are moderately stable across the childhood years.

Kagan's Behavioral Inhibition Another way of classifying temperament focuses on the differences between a shy, subdued, timid child and a sociable, extraverted, bold child. Jerome Kagan (2002, 2008, 2010, 2013) regards shyness with strangers (peers or adults) as one feature of a broad temperament category called inhibition to the unfamiliar. Inhibited children react to many aspects of unfamiliarity with initial avoidance, distress, or subdued affect, beginning about 7 to 9 months of age.

Kagan has found that inhibition shows considerable stability from infancy through early childhood. One study classified toddlers into extremely inhibited, extremely uninhibited, and intermediate groups (Pfeifer & others, 2002). Follow-up assessments occurred at 4 and 7 years of age. Continuity was demonstrated for both inhibition and lack of inhibition, although a substantial number of the inhibited children moved into the intermediate groups at 7 years of age. One study revealed that behavioral inhibition at 3 years of age was linked to shyness four years later (Volbrecht & Goldsmith, 2010). Another study found that 24-month-olds who were fearful in situations relatively low in threat were likely to experience higher than average anxiety levels in kindergarten (Buss, 2011). And in another study, shyness/inhibition in infancy/childhood was linked to social anxiety at 21 years of age (Bohlin & Hagekull, 2009).

Rothbart and Bates' Classification New classifications of temperament continue to be forged. Mary Rothbart and John Bates (2006) argue that three broad dimensions best represent what researchers have found to characterize the structure of temperament: extraversion/surgency, negative affectivity, and effortful control (self-regulation):

- *Extraversion/surgency* includes "positive anticipation, impulsivity, activity level, and sensation seeking" (Rothbart, 2004, p. 495). Kagan's uninhibited children fit into this category.

What are some characteristics of an inhibited temperament?

temperament Involves individual differences in behavioral styles, emotions, and characteristic ways of responding.

easy child A child who is generally in a positive mood, quickly establishes regular routines in infancy, and adapts easily to new experiences.

difficult child A child who tends to react negatively and cry frequently, engages in irregular daily routines, and is slow to accept change.

slow-to-warm-up child A child who has a low activity level, is somewhat negative, and displays a low intensity of mood.

- *Negative affectivity* includes "fear, frustration, sadness, and discomfort" (Rothbart, 2004, p. 495). These children are easily distressed; they may fret and cry often. Kagan's inhibited children fit this category.
- *Effortful control (self-regulation)* includes "attentional focusing and shifting, inhibitory control, perceptual sensitivity, and low-intensity pleasure" (Rothbart, 2004, p. 495). Infants who are high on effortful control show an ability to keep their arousal from getting too high and have strategies for soothing themselves. By contrast, children low on effortful control are often unable to control their arousal; they become easily agitated and intensely emotional.

In Rothbart's (2004, p. 497) view, "early theoretical models of temperament stressed the way we are moved by our positive and negative emotions or level of arousal, with our actions driven by these tendencies." The more recent focus on effortful control, however, emphasizes that individuals can engage in a more cognitive, flexible approach to stressful circumstances.

An important point about temperament classifications such as those of Chess and Thomas or Rothbart and Bates is that children should not be pigeonholed as having only one temperament dimension, such as "difficult" or "negative affectivity." A good strategy when attempting to classify a child's temperament is to think of temperament as consisting of multiple dimensions (Bates, 2012a, b). For example, a child might be extraverted, show little emotional negativity, and have good self-regulation. Another child might be introverted, show little emotional negativity, and have a low level of self-regulation.

The development of temperament capabilities such as effortful control allows individual differences to emerge. For example, although maturation of the brain's prefrontal lobes must occur for any child's attention to improve and the child to achieve effortful control, some children develop effortful control while others do not. And it is these individual differences in children that are at the heart of what temperament is (Bates, 2012a, b).

Biological Foundations and Experience   How does a child acquire a certain temperament? Kagan (2002, 2010, 2013) argues that children inherit a physiology that biases them to have a particular type of temperament. However, through experience they may learn to modify their temperament to some degree. For example, children may inherit a physiology that biases them to be fearful and inhibited, but they can learn to reduce their fear and inhibition to some degree.

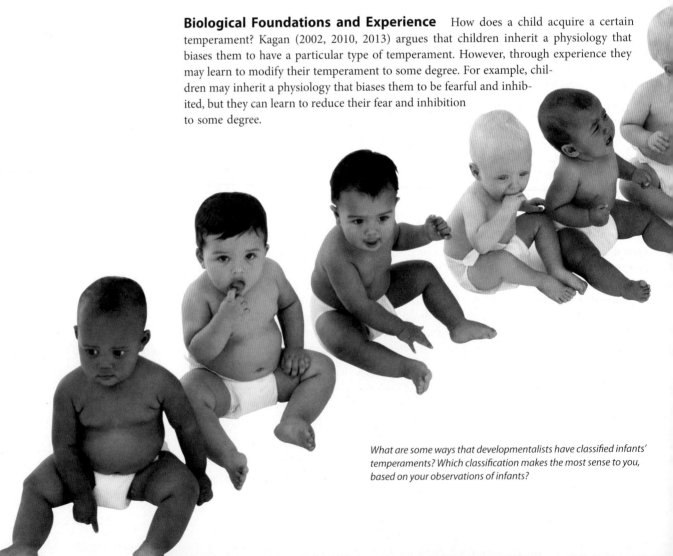

What are some ways that developmentalists have classified infants' temperaments? Which classification makes the most sense to you, based on your observations of infants?

Biological Influences Physiological characteristics have been linked with different temperaments (Bates, 2012a, b; Frodl & O'Keane, 2012; Kagan, 2013; Mize & Jones, 2012). In particular, an inhibited temperament is associated with a unique physiological pattern that includes high and stable heart rate, high level of the hormone cortisol, and high activity in the right frontal lobe of the brain (Kagan, 2008, 2010). This pattern may be tied to the excitability of the amygdala, a structure of the brain that plays an important role in fear and inhibition.

What is heredity's role in the biological foundations of temperament? Twin and adoption studies suggest that heredity has a moderate influence on differences in temperament within a group of people (Plomin & others, 2009). The contemporary view is that temperament is a biologically based but evolving aspect of behavior; it evolves as the child's experiences are incorporated into a network of self-perceptions and behavioral preferences that characterize the child's personality (Thompson, Winer, & Goodvin, 2011).

Too often the biological foundations of temperament are interpreted to mean that temperament cannot develop or change. However, important self-regulatory dimensions of temperament such as adaptability, soothability, and persistence look very different in a 1-year-old and a 5-year-old (Easterbrooks & others, 2013). These temperament dimensions develop and change with the growth of the neurobiological foundations of self-regulation.

Gender, Culture, and Temperament Gender may be an important factor shaping the environmental context that influences temperament (Gaias & others, 2012). Parents might

react differently to an infant's temperament depending on whether the baby is a boy or a girl. For example, in one study, mothers were more responsive to the crying of irritable girls than to the crying of irritable boys (Crockenberg, 1986).

Similarly, the caregiver's reaction to an infant's temperament may depend in part on culture (Chen & others, 2011; Rothbart, 2011). For example, behavioral inhibition is more highly valued in China than in North America, and researchers have found that Chinese children are more inhibited than Canadian infants are (Chen & others, 1998). The cultural differences in temperament were linked to parent attitude and behaviors. Canadian mothers of inhibited 2-year-olds were less accepting of their infants' inhibited temperament, whereas Chinese mothers were more accepting. Also, a recent study revealed that U.S infants showed more temperamental fearfulness while Finnish infants engaged in more positive affect, such as effortful control (Gaias & others, 2012).

In short, many aspects of a child's environment can encourage or discourage the persistence of temperament characteristics (Bates, 2012a, b; Rothbart, 2011). One useful way of thinking about these relationships applies the concept of goodness of fit, which we examine next.

developmental **connection**

Community and Culture

Cross-cultural studies seek to determine culture-universal and culture-specific aspects of development. Chapter 1, p. 11

Parenting and the Child's Temperament

What are the implications of temperamental variations for parenting? Although answers to this question necessarily are speculative, these conclusions regarding the best parenting strategies to use in relation to children's temperament were reached by temperament experts Ann Sanson and Mary Rothbart (1995):

- *Attention to and respect for individuality.* Good parenting involves sensitivity to the child's individual characteristics. A goal might be accomplished in one way with one child and in another way with another child, depending on the child's temperament.
- *Structuring the child's environment.* Crowded, noisy environments can pose greater problems for some children (such as a "difficult child") than others (such as an "easy child"). We might also expect that a fearful, withdrawing child would benefit from slower entry into new contexts.
- *The "difficult child" and packaged parenting programs.* Programs for parents often focus on dealing with children who have "difficult" temperaments. In some cases, "difficult child" refers to Thomas and Chess' description of a child who reacts negatively, cries frequently, engages in irregular daily routines, and is slow to accept change. In others, the concept might be used to describe a child who is irritable,

displays anger frequently, does not follow directions well, or some other negative characteristic. Acknowledging that some children are harder than others to parent is often helpful, and advice on how to handle particular difficult characteristics can be useful. However, whether a particular characteristic is difficult depends on its fit with the environment. To label a child "difficult" has the danger of becoming a self-fulfilling prophecy. If a child is identified as "difficult," people may treat the child in a way that actually elicits "difficult" behavior.

Too often, we pigeonhole children into categories without examining the context (Bates, 2012a, b; Rothbart, 2011). Nonetheless, caregivers need to take children's temperament into account. Research does not yet allow for many highly specific recommendations, but, in general, caregivers should (1) be sensitive to the individual characteristics of the child, (2) be flexible in responding to these characteristics, and (3) avoid applying negative labels to the child.

How does the advice to "structure the child's environment" relate to what you learned about the concept of "goodness of fit"?

An infant's temperament can vary across cultures. *What do parents need to know about a child's temperament?*

goodness of fit Refers to the match between a child's temperament and the environmental demands with which the child must cope.

Goodness of Fit and Parenting   Goodness of fit refers to the match between a child's temperament and the environmental demands the child must cope with. Suppose Jason is an active toddler who is made to sit still for long periods of time, and Jack is a slow-to-warm-up toddler who is abruptly pushed into new situations on a regular basis. Both Jason and Jack face a lack of fit between their temperament and environmental demands. Lack of fit can produce adjustment problems (Rothbart, 2011).

Some temperament characteristics pose more parenting challenges than others, at least in modern Western societies (Rothbart, 2011). When children are prone to distress, as exhibited by frequent crying and irritability, their parents may eventually respond by ignoring the child's distress or trying to force the child to "behave." In one research study, though, extra support and training for mothers of distress-prone infants improved the quality of mother-infant interaction (van den Boom, 1989). The training led the mothers to alter their demands on the child, improving the fit between the child and the environment. Researchers also have found that decreases in infants' negative emotionality are linked to higher levels of parental sensitivity, involvement, and responsiveness (Bates, 2012a, b; Penela & others, 2012; Wachs & Bates, 2010). To read further about some positive strategies for parenting that take into account the child's temperament, see the *Connecting Development to Life* interlude.

PERSONALITY DEVELOPMENT

Emotions and temperament form key aspects of personality, the enduring personal characteristics of individuals. Let's now examine characteristics that often are thought of as central to personality development during infancy: trust and the development of self and independence.

Trust   According to Erik Erikson (1968), the first year of life is characterized by the trust-versus-mistrust stage of development. Following a life of regularity, warmth, and protection in the mother's womb, the infant faces a world that is less secure. Erikson proposed that infants learn trust when they are cared for in a consistent, warm manner. If the infant is not well fed and kept warm on a consistent basis, a sense of mistrust is likely to develop.

Trust versus mistrust is not resolved once and for all in the first year of life. It arises again at each successive stage of development, which can have positive or negative outcomes. For example, children who leave infancy with a sense of trust can still have their sense of mistrust activated at a later stage, perhaps if their parents are separated or divorced under conflictual circumstances.

The Developing Sense of Self   When does the individual begin to sense a separate existence from others? Studying the self in infancy is difficult mainly because infants cannot verbally express their thoughts and impressions. They also cannot understand complex instructions from researchers.

One ingenious strategy to test infants' visual self-recognition is the use of a mirror technique, in which an infant's mother first puts a dot of rouge on the infant's nose. Then an observer watches to see how often the infant touches its nose. Next, the infant is placed in front of a mirror, and observers detect whether nose touching increases. Why does this matter? The idea is that increased nose touching indicates that the infant recognizes the self in the mirror and is trying to touch or rub off the rouge because the rouge violates the infant's view of the self. Increased touching indicates that the infant realizes that it is the self in the mirror but that something is not right since the real self does not have a dot of rouge on it.

Figure 6.4 displays the results of two investigations that used the mirror technique. The researchers found that before they were 1 year old, infants did not recognize themselves in the mirror (Amsterdam, 1968; Lewis & Brooks-Gunn, 1979). Signs of self-recognition began to appear among some infants when they were 15 to 18 months old. By the time they were

developmental **connection**

Personality

Erikson proposed that individuals go through eight stages in the course of human development. Chapter 1, p. 22

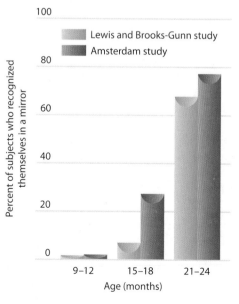

FIGURE **6.4**

THE DEVELOPMENT OF SELF-RECOGNITION IN INFANCY. The graph shows the findings of two studies in which infants less than 1 year of age did not recognize themselves in a mirror. A slight increase in the percentage of infant self-recognition occurred around 15 to 18 months of age. By 2 years of age, a majority of children recognized themselves. *Why do researchers study whether infants recognize themselves in a mirror?*

Erikson believed that autonomy versus shame and doubt is the key developmental theme of the toddler years. *What are some good strategies for parents to use with their toddlers?*

2 years old, most children recognized themselves in the mirror. In sum, infants begin to develop a self-understanding called self-recognition at approximately 18 months of age (Hart & Karmel, 1996; Lewis, 2005).

However, mirrors are not familiar to infants in all cultures (Rogoff, 2003). Thus, physical self-recognition may be a more important marker of self-recognition in Western than non–Western cultures (Thompson & Virmani, 2010). Supporting this cultural variation view, one study revealed that 18- to 20-month-old toddlers from urban middle SES German families were more likely to recognize their mirror images than were toddlers from rural Cameroon farming families (Keller & others, 2005).

Late in the second year and early in the third year, toddlers show other emerging forms of self-awareness that reflect a sense of "me" (Thompson, Winer, & Goodvin, 2011). For example, they refer to themselves such as by saying "me big"; they label their internal experiences such as emotions; they monitor themselves, as when a toddler says, "do it myself"; and they declare that things are theirs (Bates, 1990; Fasig, 2000).

Independence Erik Erikson (1968) stressed that independence is an important issue in the second year of life. Erikson describes the second stage of development as the stage of autonomy versus shame and doubt. Autonomy builds as the infant's mental and motor abilities develop. At this point in development, not only can infants walk, but they can also climb, open and close, drop, push and pull, and hold and let go. Infants feel pride in these new accomplishments and want to do everything themselves, whether the activity is flushing a toilet, pulling the wrapping off a package, or deciding what to eat. It is important for parents to recognize the motivation of toddlers to do what they are capable of doing at their own pace. Then they can learn to control their muscles and their impulses themselves. But when caregivers are impatient and do for toddlers what they are capable of doing themselves, shame and doubt develop. Every parent has rushed a child from time to time. It is only when parents consistently overprotect toddlers or criticize accidents (wetting, soiling, spilling, or breaking, for example) that children develop an excessive sense of shame and doubt about their ability to control themselves and their world. As we discuss in later chapters, Erikson emphasized that the stage of autonomy versus shame and doubt has important implications for the individual's future development.

developmental **connection**

Personality

Two key points in development when there is a strong push for independence are the second year of life and early adolescence. Chapter 12, p. 395

Review Connect Reflect

LG1 Discuss the development of emotions and personality in infancy.

Review

- What are emotions? What is the nature of an infant's emotions and how do they change?
- What is temperament, and how does it develop in infancy?
- What are some important aspects of personality in infancy, and how do they develop?

Connect

- Earlier in this section, you read that twin and adoption studies have been used to sort out the influence of heredity and environment on temperament. In Chapter 2, you learned how twin and adoption studies are conducted. Discuss the characteristics of twin and adoption studies.

Reflect *Your Own Personal Journey of Life*

- How would you describe your temperament? Does it fit one of Chess and Thomas' three styles—easy, slow to warm up, or difficult? If you have siblings, is your temperament similar to or different from theirs?

| Social Orientation/ Understanding | Attachment and Its Development | Individual Differences in Attachment | Caregiving Styles and Attachment | Developmental Social Neuroscience and Attachment |

So far, we have discussed how emotions and emotional competence change as children develop. We have also examined the role of emotional style; in effect, we have seen how emotions set the tone of our experiences in life. But emotions also write the lyrics because they are at the core of our relationships with others.

SOCIAL ORIENTATION/UNDERSTANDING

In Ross Thompson's (2006, 2011, 2013c, d) view, infants are socioemotional beings who show a strong interest in the social world and are motivated to orient to it and understand it. In previous chapters, we described many of the biological and cognitive foundations that contribute to the infant's development of social orientation and understanding. In this chapter, we will call attention to relevant biological and cognitive factors as we explore social orientation; locomotion; intention and goal-directed behavior; social referencing; and social sophistication and insight. Discussing biological, cognitive, and social processes together reminds us of an important aspect of development that was pointed out in Chapter 1: These processes are intricately intertwined (Diamond, 2013).

Social Orientation   From early in their development, infants are captivated by the social world. As we discussed in our coverage of infant perception in Chapter 4, young infants stare intently at faces and are attuned to the sounds of human voices, especially their caregiver's (Gaither, Pauker, & Johnson, 2012; Lowe & others, 2012). Later, they become adept at interpreting the meaning of facial expressions.

Face-to-face play often begins to characterize caregiver-infant interactions when the infant is about 2 to 3 months of age. The focused social interaction of face-to-face play may include vocalizations, touch, and gestures (Leppanen & others, 2007). Such play is part of many mothers' motivation to create a positive emotional state in their infants (Thompson, 2013c, d).

In part because of such positive social interchanges between caregivers and infants, by 2 to 3 months of age, infants respond in different ways to people and objects, showing more positive emotion to people than to inanimate objects such as puppets (Legerstee, 1997). At this age, most infants expect people to react positively when the infants initiate a behavior, such as a smile or a vocalization. This finding has been discovered using a method called the still-face paradigm, in which the caregiver alternates between engaging in face-to-face interaction with the infant and remaining still and unresponsive (Bigelow & Power, 2012). As early as 2 to 3 months of age, infants show more withdrawal, negative emotions, and self-directed behavior when their caregivers are still and unresponsive (Adamson & Frick, 2003). The frequency of face-to-face play decreases after 7 months of age as infants become more mobile (Thompson, 2006). A meta-analysis revealed that infants' higher positive affect and lower negative affect as displayed during the still-face paradigm were linked to secure attachment at one year of age (Mesman, van IJzendoorn, & Bakersman-Kranenburg, 2009).

Infants also learn about the social world through contexts other than face-to-face play with a caregiver (Thompson, 2013b). Even though infants as young as 6 months of age show an interest in each other, their interaction with peers increases considerably in the last half of the second year. Between 18 and 24 months of age, children markedly increase their imitative and reciprocal play, such as imitating nonverbal actions like jumping and running

developmental **connection**

Life-Span Perspective

Biological, cognitive, and socioemotional processes are often linked as individuals go through the life span. Chapter 1, p. 15

A mother and her baby engaging in face-to-face play. *At what age does face-to-face play usually begin, and when does it typically start decreasing in frequency?*

FIGURE **6.5**

THE COOPERATION TASK. The cooperation task consisted of two handles on a box, atop which was an animated musical toy, surreptitiously activated by remote control when both handles were pulled. The handles were placed far enough apart that one child could not pull both handles. The experimenter demonstrated the task, saying, "Watch! If you pull the handles, the doggie will sing" (Brownell, Ramani, & Zerwas, 2006).

What is social referencing? What are some developmental changes in social referencing?

social referencing "Reading" emotional cues in others to help determine how to act in a particular situation.

(Eckerman & Whitehead, 1999). One study involved presenting 1- and 2-year-olds with a simple cooperative task that consisted of pulling a lever to get an attractive toy (Brownell, Ramani, & Zerwas, 2006) (see Figure 6.5). Any coordinated actions of the 1-year-olds appeared to be more coincidental rather than cooperative, whereas the 2-year-olds' behavior was characterized as more active cooperation to reach a goal.

Locomotion   Recall from earlier in the chapter the growing importance of independence for infants, especially in the second year of life. As infants develop the ability to crawl, walk, and run, they are able to explore and expand their social world. These newly developed, self-produced locomotion skills allow the infant to independently initiate social interchanges on a more frequent basis (Laible & Thompson, 2007). Remember from Chapter 4 that the development of these gross motor skills results from factors such as the development of the nervous system, the goal the infant is motivated to reach, and environmental support for the skill (Adolph & Berger, 2013; Adolph & Robinson, 2013).

The infant's and toddler's push for independence also is likely paced by the development of locomotion skills. Of further importance is locomotion's motivational implications. Once infants have the ability to move in goal-directed pursuits, the reward from these pursuits leads to further efforts to explore and develop skills.

Intention and Goal-Directed Behavior   Perceiving people as engaging in intentional and goal-directed behavior is an important social cognitive accomplishment, and this initially occurs toward the end of the first year (Thompson, 2010). Joint attention and gaze-following help the infant to understand that other people have intentions (Bedford & others, 2012; Tomasello & Hamann, 2012). Recall from Chapter 5 that *joint attention* occurs when the caregiver and infant focus on the same object or event. We indicated that emerging aspects of joint attention occur at about 7 to 8 months, but at about 10 to 11 months of age joint attention intensifies and infants begin to follow the caregiver's gaze. By their first birthday, infants have begun to direct the caregiver's attention to objects that capture their interest (Heimann & others, 2006).

Social Referencing   Another important social cognitive accomplishment in infancy is developing the ability to "read" the emotions of other people (Cornew & others, 2012). **Social referencing** is the term used to describe "reading" emotional cues in others to help determine how to act in a particular situation. The development of social referencing helps infants to interpret ambiguous situations more accurately, as when they encounter a stranger and need to know whether to fear the person (Pelaez, Virues-Ortega, & Gewirtz, 2012). By the end of the first year, a mother's facial expression—either smiling or fearful—influences whether an infant will explore an unfamiliar environment.

Infants become better at social referencing in the second year of life. At this age, they tend to "check" with their mother before they act; they look at her to see if she is happy, angry, or fearful. For example, in one study 14- to 22-month-old infants were more likely to look at their mother's face as a source of information for how to act in a situation than were 6- to 9-month-old infants (Walden, 1991).

Infants' Social Sophistication and Insight   In sum, researchers are discovering that infants are more socially sophisticated and insightful at younger ages than was previously envisioned (Thompson, 2013c, d). This sophistication and insight is reflected in infants' perceptions of others' actions as intentionally motivated and goal-directed and their motivation to share and participate in that intentionality by their first birthday. The more advanced social cognitive skills of infants likely influence their understanding and awareness of attachment to a caregiver.

ATTACHMENT AND ITS DEVELOPMENT

Attachment is a close emotional bond between two people. There is no shortage of theories about infant attachment. Three theorists discussed in Chapter 1—Freud, Erikson, and Bowlby—proposed influential views.

Freud emphasized that infants become attached to the person or object that provides oral satisfaction. For most infants, this is the mother, since she is most likely to feed the infant. Is feeding as important as Freud thought? A classic study by Harry Harlow (1958) reveals that the answer is no (see Figure 6.6).

Harlow removed infant monkeys from their mothers at birth; for six months they were reared by surrogate (substitute) "mothers." One surrogate mother was made of wire, the other of cloth. Half of the infant monkeys were fed by the wire mother, half by the cloth mother. Periodically, the amount of time the infant monkeys spent with either the wire or the cloth mother was computed. Regardless of which mother fed them, the infant monkeys spent far more time with the cloth mother. Even if the wire mother, but not the cloth mother, provided nourishment, the infant monkeys spent more time with the cloth mother. And when Harlow frightened the monkeys, those "raised" by the cloth mother ran to the mother and clung to it; those raised by the wire mother did not. Whether the mother provided comfort seemed to determine whether the monkeys associated the mother with security. This study clearly demonstrated that feeding is not the crucial element in the attachment process and that contact comfort is important.

Physical comfort also plays a role in Erik Erikson's (1968) view of the infant's development. Recall Erikson's proposal that the first year of life represents the stage of trust versus mistrust. Physical comfort and sensitive care, according to Erikson (1968), are key to establishing a basic trust in infants. The infant's sense of trust, in turn, is the foundation for attachment and sets the stage for a lifelong expectation that the world will be a good and pleasant place to be.

The ethological perspective of British psychiatrist John Bowlby (1969, 1989) also stresses the importance of attachment in the first year of life and the responsiveness of the caregiver. Bowlby maintains both infants and their primary caregivers are biologically predisposed to form attachments. He argues that the newborn is biologically equipped to elicit attachment behavior. The baby cries, clings, coos, and smiles. Later, the infant crawls, walks, and follows the mother. The immediate result is to keep the primary caregiver nearby; the long-term effect is to increase the infant's chances of survival.

Attachment does not emerge suddenly but rather develops in a series of phases, moving from a baby's general preference for human beings to a partnership with primary caregivers. Following are four such phases based on Bowlby's conceptualization of attachment (Schaffer, 1996):

- *Phase 1: From birth to 2 months.* Infants instinctively direct their attachment to human figures. Strangers, siblings, and parents are equally likely to elicit smiling or crying from the infant.
- *Phase 2: From 2 to 7 months.* Attachment becomes focused on one figure, usually the primary caregiver, as the baby gradually learns to distinguish familiar from unfamiliar people.
- *Phase 3: From 7 to 24 months.* Specific attachments develop. With increased locomotor skills, babies actively seek contact with regular caregivers, such as the mother or father.
- *Phase 4: From 24 months on.* Children become aware of others' feelings, goals, and plans and begin to take these into account in forming their own actions.

Bowlby argued that infants develop an *internal working model* of attachment, a simple mental model of the caregiver, their relationship, and the self as deserving of nurturant care. The infant's internal working model of attachment with the caregiver influences the infant's and later the child's subsequent responses to other people (Roisman & Groh, 2011). The internal model of attachment also has played a pivotal role in the discovery of links between attachment and subsequent emotional understanding, conscience development, and self-concept (Thompson, 2012).

INDIVIDUAL DIFFERENCES IN ATTACHMENT

Although attachment to a caregiver intensifies midway through the first year, isn't it likely that the quality of babies' attachment experiences varies? Mary Ainsworth (1979) thought so.

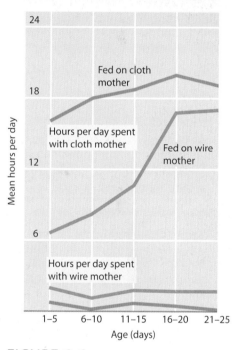

FIGURE 6.6

CONTACT TIME WITH WIRE AND CLOTH SURROGATE MOTHERS. Regardless of whether the infant monkeys were fed by a wire or a cloth mother, they overwhelmingly preferred to spend contact time with the cloth mother. *How do these results compare with what Freud's theory and Erikson's theory would predict about human infants?*

attachment A close emotional bond between two people.

In Bowlby's model, what are the four stages of infant attachment?

Ainsworth created the **Strange Situation,** an observational measure of infant attachment that takes about 20 minutes in which the infant experiences a series of introductions, separations, and reunions with the caregiver and an adult stranger in a prescribed order. In using the Strange Situation, researchers hope that their observations will provide information about the infant's motivation to be near the caregiver and the degree to which the caregiver's presence provides the infant with security and confidence.

Based on how babies respond in the Strange Situation, they are described as being securely attached or insecurely attached (in one of three ways) to the caregiver:

- **Securely attached babies** use the caregiver as a secure base from which to explore the environment. When in the presence of their caregiver, securely attached infants explore the room and examine toys that have been placed in it. When the caregiver departs, securely attached infants might protest mildly, and when the caregiver returns these infants reestablish positive interaction with her, perhaps by smiling or climbing onto her lap. Subsequently, they often resume playing with the toys in the room.

- **Insecure avoidant babies** show insecurity by avoiding the caregiver. In the Strange Situation, these babies engage in little interaction with the caregiver, are not distressed when she leaves the room, usually do not reestablish contact when she returns, and may even turn their back on her. If contact is established, the infant usually leans away or looks away.

- **Insecure resistant babies** often cling to the caregiver and then resist her by fighting against the closeness, perhaps by kicking or pushing away. In the Strange Situation, these babies often cling anxiously to the caregiver and don't explore the playroom. When the caregiver leaves, they often cry loudly and push away if she tries to comfort them on her return.

- **Insecure disorganized babies** appear disoriented. In the Strange Situation, these babies might seem dazed, confused, and fearful. To be classified as disorganized, babies must show strong patterns of avoidance and resistance or display certain specified behaviors, such as extreme fearfulness around the caregiver.

Evaluating the Strange Situation Does the Strange Situation capture important differences among infants? As a measure of attachment, it may be culturally biased. For example, German and Japanese babies often show patterns of attachment different from those of American infants. As illustrated in Figure 6.7, German infants are more likely to show an avoidant attachment pattern and Japanese infants are less likely to display this pattern than U.S. infants (van IJzendoorn & Kroonenberg, 1988). The avoidant pattern in German babies likely occurs because their caregivers encourage them to be independent (Grossmann & others, 1985). Also as shown in Figure 6.7, Japanese babies are more likely than American babies to be categorized as resistant. This may have more to do with the Strange Situation as a measure of attachment than with attachment insecurity itself. Japanese mothers rarely let anyone unfamiliar with their babies care for them. Thus, the Strange Situation might create considerably more stress for Japanese infants than for American infants, who are more accustomed to separation from their mothers (Miyake, Chen, & Campos, 1985). Even though there are cultural variations in attachment classification, the most frequent classification in every culture studied so far is secure attachment (Thompson, 2006; Jin & others, 2012; van IJzendoorn & Kroonenberg, 1988).

Interpreting Differences in Attachment Do individual differences in attachment matter? Ainsworth argues that secure attachment in the first year of life provides an important foundation for psychological development later in life. The securely attached infant moves freely away from the mother but keeps track of where

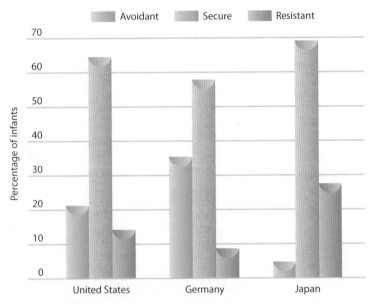

FIGURE **6.7**

CROSS-CULTURAL COMPARISON OF ATTACHMENT. In one study, infant attachment in three countries—the United States, Germany, and Japan—was measured in the Ainsworth Strange Situation (van IJzendoorn & Kroonenberg, 1988). The dominant attachment pattern in all three countries was secure attachment. However, German infants were more avoidant and Japanese infants were less avoidant and more resistant than U.S. infants. *What are some explanations for differences in how German, Japanese, and American infants respond to the Strange Situation?*

she is through periodic glances. The securely attached infant responds positively to being picked up by others, and when put back down, freely moves away to play. An insecurely attached infant, by contrast, avoids the mother or is ambivalent toward her, fears strangers, and is upset by minor, everyday separations.

If early attachment to a caregiver is important, it should be linked to a child's social behavior later in development. For some children, early attachments seem to foreshadow later functioning (Bretherton, 2012; Brisch, 2012; Kok & others, 2012). Consider the following studies:

- In the extensive longitudinal study conducted by Alan Sroufe and his colleagues (2005), early secure attachment (assessed by the Strange Situation at 12 and 18 months) was linked with positive emotional health, high self-esteem, self-confidence, and socially competent interaction with peers, teachers, camp counselors, and romantic partners through adolescence.

- Being classified as insecure resistant in infancy was a negative predictor of cognitive development in elementary school (O'Connor & McCartney, 2007).

- Yet another study found that attachment security at 24 and 36 months was linked to the child's enhanced social problem-solving skills at 54 months (Raikes & Thompson, 2009).

An important issue regarding attachment is whether infancy is a critical or sensitive period for development. The three studies just described show continuity, with secure attachment in infancy predicting subsequent positive development in childhood and adolescence. For some children, though, there is little continuity. Not all research reveals the power of infant attachment to predict subsequent development (Roisman & Groh, 2011; Thompson, 2013a). In one longitudinal study, attachment classification in infancy did not predict attachment classification at 18 years of age (Lewis, Feiring, & Rosenthal, 2000). In this study, the best predictor of an insecure attachment classification at 18 was the occurrence of parental divorce in the intervening years. Consistently positive caregiving over a number of years is likely an important factor in connecting early attachment with the child's functioning later in development. Indeed, researchers have found that early secure attachment and subsequent experiences, especially maternal care and life stresses, are linked with children's later behavior and adjustment (Thompson, 2013a). For example, a longitudinal study revealed that changes in attachment security/insecurity from infancy to adulthood were linked to stresses and supports in socioemotional contexts (Van Ryzin, Carlson, & Sroufe, 2011). These results suggest that attachment continuity may be a reflection of stable social contexts as much as early working models. The study just described (Van Ryzin, Carlson, & Sroufe, 2011) reflects an increasingly accepted view of the development of attachment and its influence on development. That is, it is important to recognize that attachment security in infancy does not always by itself produce long-term positive outcomes, but rather is linked to later outcomes through connections with the way children and adolescents subsequently experience various social contexts as they develop.

The Van Ryzin, Carlson, and Sroufe (2011) study reflects a **developmental cascade model,** which involves connections across domains over time that influence developmental pathways

What is the nature of secure and insecure attachment?

developmental connection

Attachment

How might secure and insecure attachment be reflected in the relationships of young adults? Chapter 14, p. 454

Strange Situation An observational measure of infant attachment that requires the infant to move through a series of introductions, separations, and reunions with the caregiver and an adult stranger in a prescribed order.

securely attached babies Babies who use the caregiver as a secure base from which to explore the environment.

insecure avoidant babies Babies who show insecurity by avoiding the caregiver.

insecure resistant babies Babies who often cling to the caregiver, then resist the caregiver by fighting against the closeness, perhaps by kicking or pushing away.

insecure disorganized babies Babies who show insecurity by being disorganized and disoriented.

developmental cascade model Involves connections across domains over time that influence developmental pathways and outcomes.

To what extent might this adolescent girl's development be linked to how securely or insecurely attached she was during infancy?

developmental **connection**

Nature Versus Nurture

What is involved in gene × environment (G × E) interaction? Chapter 2, p. 71

◀‑ ‑ ‑ ‑ ‑ ‑ ‑ ‑ ‑ ‑ ‑

In the Hausa culture, siblings and grandmothers provide a significant amount of care for infants. *How might these variations in care affect attachment?*

and outcomes (Cicchetti, 2013; Masten, 2013). Developmental cascades can include connections between a wide range of biological, cognitive, and socioemotional processes (attachment, for example), and also can involve social contexts such as families, peers, schools, and culture. Further, links can produce positive or negative outcomes at different points in development, such as infancy, early childhood, middle and late childhood, adolescence, and adulthood.

In addition to challenging whether secure attachment in infancy serves as a critical or sensitive period, some developmentalists argue that the secure attachment concept does not adequately consider certain biological factors in development, such as genes and temperament.

For example, Jerome Kagan (1987, 2002) points out that infants are highly resilient and adaptive; he argues that they are evolutionarily equipped to stay on a positive developmental course, even in the face of wide variations in parenting. Kagan and others stress that genetic characteristics and temperament play more important roles in a child's social competence than the attachment theorists, such as Bowlby and Ainsworth, are willing to acknowledge (Bakermans-Kranenburg & van IJzendoorn, 2011). For example, if some infants inherit a low tolerance for stress, this, rather than an insecure attachment bond, may be responsible for an inability to get along with peers. One study found links between disorganized attachment in infancy, a specific gene, and levels of maternal responsiveness (Spangler & others, 2009). In this study, infants with the short version of the gene—serotonin transporter gene, 5-HTTLPR—developed a disorganized attachment style only when mothers were slow in responding to them.

A third criticism of attachment theory (in addition to the critical/sensitive period issue and inadequate attention to biological-based factors) is that it ignores the diversity of socializing agents and contexts that exists in an infant's world. A culture's value system can influence the nature of attachment. In some cultures, infants show attachments to many people. Among the Hausa (who live in Nigeria), both grandmothers and siblings provide a significant amount of care for infants (Harkness & Super, 1995). Infants in agricultural societies tend to form attachments to older siblings, who are assigned a major responsibility for younger siblings' care. Researchers recognize the importance of competent, nurturant caregivers in an infant's development (Grusec, 2011b; Roisman & Groh, 2011); at issue, though, is whether or not secure attachment, especially to a single caregiver, is critical (Lamb, 2010; Thompson, 2013a).

Despite such criticisms, there is ample evidence that secure attachment is important in development (Thompson, 2013a; Sroufe, Coffino, & Carlson, 2010). Is secure attachment the sole predictor of positive developmental outcomes for infants? No, and neither is any other single factor, but secure attachment in infancy is important because it reflects a positive parent-infant relationship and provides the foundation that supports healthy socioemotional development in the years that follow.

CAREGIVING STYLES AND ATTACHMENT

Is the style of caregiving linked with the quality of the infant's attachment? Securely attached babies have caregivers who are sensitive to their signals and are consistently available to respond to their infants' needs (Bigelow & others, 2010; Jin & others, 2012). These caregivers often let their babies have an active part in determining the onset and pacing of interaction in the first year of life. One study revealed that maternal sensitive responding was linked to infant attachment security (Finger & others, 2009). Another study found that maternal sensitivity—but not infants' temperament—when infants were 6 months old was linked to subsequent attachment security (Leerkes, 2011).

How do the caregivers of insecurely attached babies interact with them? Caregivers of avoidant babies tend to be unavailable or rejecting (Posada & Kaloustian, 2010). They often don't respond to their babies' signals and have little physical contact with them. When they do interact with their babies, they may behave in an angry and irritable way. Caregivers of resistant babies tend to be inconsistent; sometimes they respond to their babies' needs and sometimes they don't. In general, they tend not to be very affectionate with their babies and show little synchrony when interacting with them. Caregivers of disorganized babies often neglect or physically abuse them (Bernard & others, 2012; Bohlin & others, 2012; Groh & others, 2012). In some cases, these caregivers are depressed.

DEVELOPMENTAL SOCIAL NEUROSCIENCE AND ATTACHMENT

In Chapter 1, we described the emerging field of developmental social neuroscience that examines connections between socioemotional processes, development, and the brain (Pfeifer & Blakemore, 2012; Singer, 2012). Attachment is one of the main areas in which theory and research on developmental social neuroscience has focused. These connections of attachment and the brain involve the neuroanatomy of the brain, neurotransmitters, and hormones.

Theory and research on the role of the brain's regions in mother-infant attachment is just emerging (De Haan & Gunnar, 2009; Parsons & others, 2010). One theoretical view proposed that the prefrontal cortex likely has an important role in maternal attachment behavior, as do the subcortical (areas of the brain lower than the cortex) regions of the amygdala (which is strongly involved in emotion) and the hypothalamus (Gonzalez, Atkinson, & Fleming, 2009).

Research on the role of hormones and neurotransmitters in attachment has emphasized the importance of two neuropeptide hormones—oxytocin and vasopressin—in the formation of the maternal-infant bond (Strathearn & others, 2012; Bisceglia & others, 2012). Oxytocin, a mammalian hormone that also acts as a neurotransmitter in the brain, is released during breast feeding and by contact and warmth (Ebstein & others, 2012). Oxytocin is especially thought to be a likely candidate in the formation of infant-mother attachment (Feldman, 2012; Nagasawa & others, 2012). A recent research review indicated strong links between levels or patterns of oxytocin and aspects of mother-infant attachment (Galbally & others, 2011). The influence of these neuropeptides on the neurotransmitter dopamine in the nucleus accumbens (a collection of neurons in the forebrain that are involved in pleasure) likely is important in motivating approach to the attachment object (de Haan & Gunnar, 2009). Figure 6.8 shows the regions of the brain we have described that have been proposed as important in infant-mother attachment.

FIGURE 6.8

REGIONS OF THE BRAIN PROPOSED AS LIKELY TO BE IMPORTANT IN INFANT-MOTHER ATTACHMENT

Review Connect Reflect

 LG2 Describe social orientation/understanding and the development of attachment in infancy.

Review

- How do infants orient to the social world?
- What is attachment, and how is it conceptualized?
- What are some individual variations in attachment? What are some criticisms of attachment theory?
- How are caregiving styles related to attachment?

Connect

- Do the different theories of attachment you just read about complement or contradict each other? Describe how the concept of nature versus nurture is involved.

Reflect Your Own Personal Journey of Life

- What can you do as a parent to improve the likelihood that your baby will have a secure attachment with you?

3 Social Contexts

 LG3 Explain how social contexts influence the infant's development.

The Family   Child Care

Now that we have explored the infant's emotional and personality development and attachment, let's examine the social contexts in which these occur. We will begin by studying a number of aspects of the family and then turn to a social context in which infants increasingly spend time—child care.

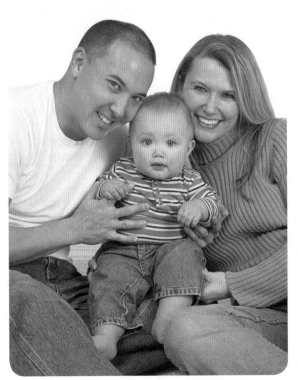

What characterizes the transition to parenting?

- - - - - - - - - ➤

developmental **connection**

Cognitive Theory

A version of scaffolding is an important aspect of Lev Vygotksy's sociocultural cognitive theory of development. Chapter 7, p. 220

reciprocal socialization Socialization that is bidirectional; children socialize parents, just as parents socialize children.

scaffolding Practice in which parents time interactions so that infants experience turn taking with the parents.

THE FAMILY

The family can be thought of as a constellation of subsystems—a complex whole made up of interrelated, interacting parts—defined in terms of generation, gender, and role. Each family member participates in several subsystems (Parke & Clarke-Stewart, 2011). The father and child represent one subsystem, the mother and father another; the mother-father-child yet another; and so on.

These subsystems have reciprocal influences on each other, as Figure 6.9 highlights. For example, Jay Belsky (1981) emphasizes that marital relations, parenting, and infant behavior and development can have both direct and indirect effects on each other. An example of a direct effect is the influence of the parents' behavior on the child. An indirect effect is how the relationship between the spouses mediates the way a parent acts toward the child (Cummings, Papp, & Kouros, 2012; Cummings & Schatz, 2012). For example, marital conflict might reduce the efficiency of parenting, in which case marital conflict would indirectly affect the child's behavior. The simple fact that two people are becoming parents may have profound effects on their relationship.

The Transition to Parenthood   When people become parents through pregnancy, adoption, or stepparenting, they face disequilibrium and must adapt. Parents want to develop a strong attachment with their infant, but they still want to maintain strong attachments to their spouse and friends, and possibly continue their careers. Parents ask themselves how this new being will change their lives. A baby places new restrictions on partners; no longer will they be able to rush out to a movie on a moment's notice, and money may not be readily available for vacations and other luxuries. Dual-career parents ask, "Will it harm the baby to place her in child care? Will we be able to find responsible babysitters?"

In a longitudinal investigation of couples from late pregnancy until 3½ years after the baby was born, couples enjoyed more positive marital relations before the baby was born than after (Cowan & Cowan, 2000; Cowan & others, 2005). Still, almost one-third showed an increase in marital satisfaction. Some couples said that the baby had both brought them closer together and moved them farther apart; being parents enhanced their sense of themselves and also gave them a new, more stable identity as a couple. Babies opened men up to a concern with intimate relationships, and the demands of juggling work and family roles stimulated women to manage family tasks more efficiently and to pay attention to their own personal growth.

Other recent studies have explored the transition to parenthood (Brown, Feinberg, & Kan, 2012; Menendez & others, 2011). One study found similar negative change in relationship satisfaction for married and cohabiting women during the transition to parenthood (Mortensen & others, 2012). Another study revealed that mothers experienced unmet expectations in the transition to parenting, with fathers doing less than they had anticipated (Biehle & Mickelson, 2012).

The Bringing Home Baby project is a workshop that helps new parents to strengthen their relationship, understand and become acquainted with their baby, resolve conflict, and develop parenting skills (Gottman, 2012). Evaluations of the project revealed that parents who participated improved their ability to work together as parents; fathers became more involved with their baby and sensitive to the baby's behavior; mothers had a lower incidence of postpartum depression symptoms; and babies showed better overall development than infants whose parents were part of a control group (Gottman, Shapiro, & Parthemer, 2004; Shapiro & Gottman, 2005).

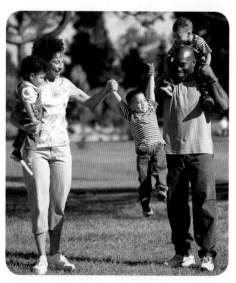

Children socialize parents, just as parents socialize children.

Reciprocal Socialization

The mutual influence that parents and children exert on each other goes beyond specific interactions in games such as peek-a-boo; it extends to the whole process of socialization (Manongdo & Garcia, 2011). Socialization between parents and children is not a one-way process. Parents do socialize children, but socialization in families is reciprocal (Grusec, 2011; Parke & Clarke-Stewart, 2011). **Reciprocal socialization** is socialization that is bidirectional; children socialize parents just as parents socialize children. These reciprocal interchanges and mutual influence processes are sometimes referred to as *transactional* (Sameroff, 2009, 2012).

When reciprocal socialization has been studied in infancy, mutual gaze or eye contact plays an important role in early social interaction (Stern, 2010). In one investigation, the mother and infant engaged in a variety of behaviors while they looked at each other (Stern & others, 1977). By contrast, when they looked away from each other, the rate of such behaviors dropped considerably. In sum, the behaviors of mothers and infants involve substantial interconnection, mutual regulation, and synchronization (Laurent, Ablow, & Measelle, 2012; Tronick, 2010). One study revealed that *parent-infant synchrony*—the temporal coordination of social behavior—played an important role in children's development (Feldman, 2007). In this study, parent-infant synchrony at 3 and 9 months of age were positively linked to children's self-regulation from 2 to 6 years of age.

An important form of reciprocal socialization is **scaffolding,** in which parents time interactions in such a way that the infant experiences turn taking with the parents. Scaffolding involves parental behavior that supports children's efforts, allowing them to be more skillful than they would be if they had to rely only on their own abilities (Bigelow & others, 2010). In using scaffolding, caregivers provide a positive, reciprocal framework in which they and their children interact. For example, in the game peek-a-boo, the mother initially covers the baby. Then she removes the cover and registers "surprise" at the infant's reappearance. As infants become more skilled at peek-a-boo, pat-a-cake, and so on, there are other caregiver games that exemplify scaffolding and turn-taking sequences. Engaging in turn taking and games like peek-a-boo reflect the development of joint attention by the caregiver and infant, which we discussed in Chapter 5 (Melzi, Schick, & Kennedy, 2011).

Managing and Guiding Infants' Behavior

In addition to sensitive parenting that involves warmth and caring that can help babies become securely attached to their parents, other important aspects of parenting infants involve managing and guiding their behavior in an attempt to reduce or eliminate undesirable behaviors (Holden, Vittrup, & Rosen, 2011). This management process includes (1) being proactive and childproofing the environment so infants won't encounter potentially dangerous objects or situations, and (2) engaging in corrective methods when infants engage in undesirable behaviors such as excessive fussing and crying, throwing objects, and so on.

One study assessed results of discipline and corrective methods that parents had used by the time infants were 12 and 24 months old (Vittrup, Holden, & Buck, 2006). As indicated in Figure 6.10, the main method parents used by the time infants were 12 months old was diverting the infants' attention, followed by reasoning, ignoring, and negotiating. Also note in Figure 6.10 that more than one-third of parents had yelled at their infant, about one-fifth had slapped the infant's hands or threatened the infant, and approximately one-sixth had spanked the infant before his or her first birthday.

As infants move into the second year of life and become more mobile and capable of exploring a wider range of environments, parental management of the toddler's behavior often triggers even more corrective feedback and discipline (Holden, Vittrup, & Rosen, 2011). As indicated in

Caregivers often play games such as peek-a-boo and pat-a-cake. *How is scaffolding involved in these games?*

Method	12 Months	24 Months
Spank with hand	14	45
Slap infant's hand	21	31
Yell in anger	36	81
Threaten	19	63
Withdraw privileges	18	52
Time-out	12	60
Reason	85	100
Divert attention	100	100
Negotiate	50	90
Ignore	64	90

FIGURE **6.10**

PARENTS' METHODS FOR MANAGING AND CORRECTING INFANTS' UNDESIRABLE BEHAVIOR. Shown here are the percentage of parents who had used various corrective methods by the time the infants were 12 and 24 months old. *Source:* After data presented by Vittrup, Holden & Buck, 2006, Table 1.

- - - - - - - - - - - ➤

developmental **connection**

Parenting

Psychologists give a number of reasons why harsh physical punishment can be harmful to children's development. Chapter 8, p. 257

An Aka pygmy father with his infant son. In the Aka culture, fathers were observed to be holding or near their infants 47 percent of the time (Hewlett, 1991).

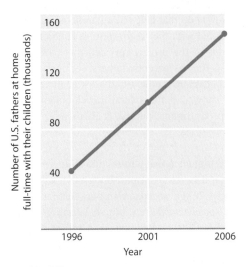

FIGURE **6.11**

THE INCREASE IN THE NUMBER OF U.S. FATHERS STAYING AT HOME FULL-TIME WITH THEIR CHILDREN

Figure 6.10, in the study just described, yelling increased from 36 percent at 1 year of age to 81 percent at 2 years of age, slapping the infant's hands increased from 21 percent at 1 year to 31 percent at age 2, and spanking increased from 14 percent at 1 year to 45 percent at age 2 (Vittrup, Holden, & Buck, 2006).

A special concern is that such corrective discipline tactics not become abusive. Too often what starts out as mild to moderately intense discipline on the part of parents can move into highly intense anger. In Chapter 8, you will read more extensively about the use of punishment with children and child abuse.

Maternal and Paternal Caregiving

An increasing number of U.S. fathers stay home full-time with their children (Lamb, 2010). As indicated in Figure 6.11, there was a 300-plus percent increase in stay-at-home fathers in the United States from 1996 to 2006. A large portion of the full-time fathers have career-focused wives who provide most of the family income. One study revealed that the stay-at-home fathers were as satisfied with their marriage as traditional parents, although they indicated that they missed their daily life in the workplace (Rochlen & others, 2008). In this study, the stay-at-home fathers reported that they tended to be ostracized when they took their children to playgrounds and often were excluded from parent groups.

Can fathers take care of infants as competently as mothers can? Observations of fathers and their infants suggest that fathers have the ability to act as sensitively and responsively as mothers with their infants (Lamb, 2010). Consider the Aka pygmy culture in Africa where fathers spend as much time interacting with their infants as do their mothers (Hewlett, 1991, 2000; Hewlett & MacFarlan, 2010). A recent study also found that marital intimacy and partner support during prenatal development were linked to father-infant attachment following childbirth (Yu & others, 2012). And another recent study revealed that fathers with a college-level education engaged in more stimulating physical activities with their infants and that fathers in a conflicting couple relationship participated in less caregiving and physical play with their infants (Cabrera, Hofferth, & Chae, 2011).

Remember, however, that although fathers can be active, nurturing, involved caregivers with their infants, as Aka pygmy fathers are, in many cultures men have not chosen to follow this pattern (Parkinson, 2010). Also, if fathers have mental health problems, they may not interact as effectively with their infants. A recent study revealed that depressed fathers focused more on their own needs than their infants' needs, directing more negative and critical speech toward infants (Sethna, Murray, & Ramchandani, 2012).

Do fathers and mothers interact with their infants in different ways? Maternal interactions usually center on child-care activities such as feeding, changing diapers, or bathing. Paternal interactions are more likely to include play (Parke & Clarke-Stewart, 2011). Fathers engage in more rough-and-tumble play than mothers do. They bounce infants, throw them up in the air, tickle them, and so on (Lamb, 2000). Mothers do play with infants, but their play is less physical and arousing than that of fathers.

In one study, fathers were interviewed about their caregiving responsibilities when their children were 6, 15, 24, and 36 months of age (NICHD Early Child Care Research Network, 2000). Some of the fathers were videotaped while playing with their children at 6 and 36 months. Fathers were more involved in caregiving—bathing, feeding, dressing the child, taking the child to child care, and so on—when they worked fewer hours and mothers worked more hours, when mothers and fathers were younger, when mothers reported greater marital intimacy, and when the children were boys.

CHILD CARE

Many U.S. children today experience multiple caregivers. Most do not have a parent staying home to care for them; instead, the children have some type of care provided by others—"child care." Many parents worry that child care will reduce their infants' emotional attachment to them, harm the infants' cognitive development, fail to teach them how to control anger, and allow them to become unduly influenced by their peers. How extensively is child care used by families? Are the worries of these parents justified?

Parental Leave   Today far more young children are in child care than at any other time in history. About 2 million children in the United States currently receive formal, licensed child care, and uncounted millions of children are cared for by unlicensed babysitters. In part, these numbers reflect the fact that U.S. adults do not receive paid leave from their jobs to care for their young children.

Child-care policies around the world vary (O'Brien & Moss, 2010; Tolani & Brooks-Gunn, 2008). Europe led the way in creating new standards of parental leave: The European Union (EU) mandated a paid 14-week maternity leave in 1992. In most European countries today, working parents on leave receive from 70 to 100 percent of their prior wage, and paid leave averages about 16 weeks (Tolani & Brooks-Gunn, 2008). The United States currently allows up to 12 weeks of unpaid leave to workers caring for a newborn.

Most countries provide parental benefits only to women who have been employed for a minimum time prior to childbirth. In Denmark, however, even unemployed mothers are eligible for extended parental leave related to childbirth. In Germany, child-rearing leave is available to almost all parents. The Nordic countries (Denmark, Norway, and Sweden) have extensive gender-equity family leave policies for childbirth that emphasize the contributions of both women and men (O'Brien & Moss, 2010; Tolani & Brooks-Gunn, 2008). For example, in Sweden, parents can take an 18-month job-protected parental leave with benefits that can be shared by parents and applied to full-time or part-time work.

How do most fathers and mothers interact differently with infants?

Variations in Child Care   Because the United States does not have a policy of paid leave for child care, child care in the United States has become a major national concern (Berlin, 2012; Lamb, 2012; Phillips & Lowenstein, 2011). Many factors influence the effects of child care, including the age of the child, the type of child care, and the quality of the program.

In the United States, approximately 15 percent of children 5 years of age and younger attend more than one child-care arrangement. One study of 2- and 3-year-old children revealed that an increase in the number of child-care arrangements the children experienced was linked to an increase in behavioral problems and a decrease in prosocial behavior (Morrissey, 2009).

The type of child care varies extensively (Berlin, 2012; Hillemeier & others, 2012; Lamb, 2012). Child care is provided in large centers with elaborate facilities and in private homes. Some child-care centers are commercial operations; others are nonprofit centers run by churches, civic groups, and employers. Some child-care providers are professionals; others are mothers who want to earn extra money. Figure 6.12 presents the primary care arrangements for children under 5 years of age with employed mothers (Clarke-Stewart & Miner, 2008).

Child-care quality makes a difference (Berlin, 2012; Lamb, 2012). What constitutes a high-quality child-care program for infants? In high-quality child care (Clarke-Stewart & Miner, 2008, p. 273):

> Caregivers encourage the children to be actively engaged in a variety of activities, have frequent, positive interactions that include smiling, touching, holding, and speaking at the child's eye level, respond properly to the child's questions or requests, and encourage children to talk about their experiences, feelings, and ideas.

How are child-care policies in many European countries, such as Sweden, different from those in the United States?

Wanda Mitchell, Child-Care Director

Wanda Mitchell is the Center Director at the Hattie Daniels Day Care Center in Wilson, North Carolina. Her responsibilities include directing the operation of the center, which involves creating and maintaining an environment in which young children can learn effectively, and ensuring that the center meets state licensing requirements. Wanda obtained her undergraduate degree from North Carolina A & T University, majoring in Child Development. Prior to her current position, she was an education coordinator for Head Start and an instructor at Wilson Technical Community College. Describing her work, Wanda says, "I really enjoy working in my field. This is my passion. After graduating from college, my goal was to advance in my field."

For more information about what early childhood educators do, see page 44 in the Careers in Life-Span Development appendix.

Wanda Mitchell, child-care director, working with some of the children at her center.

FIGURE **6.12**

PRIMARY CARE ARRANGEMENTS IN THE UNITED STATES FOR CHILDREN UNDER 5 YEARS OF AGE WITH EMPLOYED MOTHERS

We have all the knowledge necessary to provide absolutely first-rate child care in the United States. What is missing is the commitment and the will.

—EDWARD ZIGLER

Contemporary Developmental Psychologist, Yale University

High-quality child care also involves providing children with a safe environment, access to age-appropriate toys and participation in age-appropriate activities, and a low caregiver-child ratio that allows caregivers to spend considerable time with children on an individual basis.

Children are more likely to experience poor-quality child care if they come from families with few resources (psychological, social, and economic) (Berlin, 2012; Carta & others, 2012). Many researchers have examined the role of poverty in the quality of child care (Hillemeier & others, 2012). One study found that extensive child care was harmful to low-income children only when the care was of low quality (Votruba-Drzal, Coley, & Chase-Lansdale, 2004). Even if the child was in child care more than 45 hours a week, high-quality care was linked with fewer internalizing problems (anxiety, for example) and externalizing problems (aggressive and destructive behaviors, for example). Another study revealed that children from low-income families benefited in terms of school readiness and language development when their parents selected higher-quality child care (McCartney & others, 2007).

To read about one individual who provides quality child care to individuals from impoverished backgrounds, see *Connecting with Careers.* Do children in low-income families usually get quality care at day care? To answer that question and to learn more about the effects of child care, read *Connecting Through Research.*

What are some strategies parents can follow in regard to child care? Child-care expert Kathleen McCartney (2003, p. 4) offered this advice:

- *Recognize that the quality of your parenting is a key factor in your child's development.*
- *Monitor your child's development.* "Parents should observe for themselves whether their children seem to be having behavior problems." They need to talk with their child-care providers and pediatricians about their child's behavior.
- *Take some time to find the best child care.* Observe different child-care facilities and be certain that you like what you see. "Quality child care costs money, and not all parents can afford the child care they want. However, state subsidies, and other programs like Head Start, are available for families in need."

How Does the Quality and Quantity of Child Care Affect Children?

In 1991, the National Institute of Child Health and Human Development (NICHD) began a comprehensive, longitudinal study of child-care experiences. Data were collected on a diverse sample of almost 1,400 children and their families at 10 locations across the United States over a period of seven years. Researchers used multiple methods (trained observers, interviews, questionnaires, and testing) and measured many facets of children's development, including physical health, cognitive development, and socioemotional development. Following are some of the results of what is now referred to as the NICHD Study of Early Child Care and Youth Development or NICHD SECCYD (NICHD Early Child Care Research Network, 2001, 2002, 2003, 2004, 2005, 2006).

- *Patterns of use.* Many families placed their infants in child care very soon after the child's birth, and there was considerable instability in the child-care arrangements. By 4 months of age, nearly three-fourths of the infants had entered some form of nonmaternal child care. Almost half of the infants were cared for by a relative when they first entered care; only 12 percent were enrolled in child-care centers.

  Socioeconomic factors were linked to the amount and type of care. For example, mothers with higher incomes and families that were more dependent on the mother's income placed their infants in child care at an earlier age. Mothers who believed that maternal employment has positive effects on children were more likely than other mothers to place their infant in nonmaternal care for more hours. Low-income families were more likely than more affluent families to use child care, but infants from low-income families who were in child care averaged as many hours as other income groups. In the preschool years, mothers who were single, those with more education, and families with higher incomes used more hours of center care than other families. Minority families and mothers with less education used more hours of care by relatives.

- *Quality of care.* Evaluations of quality of care were based on characteristics such as group size, child-adult ratio, physical environment, caregiver characteristics (such as formal education, specialized training, and child-care experience), and caregiver behavior (such as sensitivity to children). An alarming conclusion is that a majority of

What are some important findings from the national longitudinal study of child care conducted by the National Institute of Child Health and Human Development?

the child care in the first three years of life was of unacceptably low quality. Positive caregiving by nonparents in child-care settings was infrequent—only 12 percent of the children studied experienced positive nonparental child care (such as positive talk, lack of detachment and flat affect, and language stimulation). Further, infants from low-income families experienced lower-quality child care than infants from higher-income families. When quality of caregivers' care was high, children performed better on cognitive and language tasks, were more cooperative with their mothers during play, showed more positive and skilled interaction with peers, and had fewer behavior problems. Caregiver training and good child-staff ratios were linked with higher cognitive and social competence when children were 54 months of age. Using data collected as part of the NICHD early child care longitudinal study, a recent analysis indicated that higher-quality early childhood care, especially at 27 months of age, was linked to children's higher vocabulary scores in the fifth grade (Belsky & others, 2007).

  Higher-quality child care was also related to higher-quality mother-child interaction among the families that used nonmaternal care. Further, poor-quality care was related to an increase of insecure attachment to the mother among infants who were 15 months of age, but only when the mother was low in sensitivity and responsiveness. However, child-care quality was not linked to attachment security at 36 months of age. A recent study revealed that higher-quality child care from birth to 4½ years of age was linked to higher cognitive-academic achievement at 15 years of age (Vandell & others, 2010). In this study, early higher-quality care also was related to youth reports of less externalizing behavior (lower rates of delinquency, for example).

- *Amount of child care.* In general, when children spent 30 hours or more per week in child care, their development was less than optimal (Ramey, 2005). In a recent study, more hours of early non-relative child care was related to higher levels of risk taking and impulsivity at 15 years of age (Vandell & others, 2010).

- *Family and parenting influences.* The influence of families and parenting was not weakened by extensive child care. Parents played a

(continued)

(continued)

significant role in helping children to regulate their emotions. Especially important parenting influences were being sensitive to children's needs, being involved with children, and cognitively stimulating them. Indeed, parental sensitivity has been the most consistent predictor of a secure attachment, with child-care experiences being relevant in many cases only when mothers engage in insensitive parenting (Friedman, Melhuish, & Hill, 2010).

An important point about the extensive NICHD research is that findings show that family factors are considerably stronger and more consistent predictors of a wide variety of child outcomes than are child-care experiences (such as quality, quantity, type). The worst outcomes for children occur when both home and child care settings are of poor quality. For example, a recent study involving the NICHD SECCYD data revealed that worse socioemotional outcomes (more problem behavior, low level of prosocial behavior) for children occurred when they experienced both home and child care environments that conferred risk (Watamura & others, 2011).

This study reinforces the conclusions of other researchers cited earlier in this section of the chapter—it is not the *quantity* so much as the *quality* of child care a child receives that is important. What is also significant to note is the emphasis on the positive effect families and parents can have on children's child-care experiences.

Review *Connect* Reflect

LG3 Explain how social contexts influence the infant's development.

Review

- What are some important family processes in infant development?
- How does child care influence infant development?

Connect

- In Chapter 4, you learned about a fine motor skills experiment involving 3-month-olds and grasping. What concept in this last section of this chapter is related to the use of "sticky gloves" in the experiment in Chapter 4?

Reflect *Your Own Personal Journey of Life*

- Imagine that a friend of yours is getting ready to put her baby in child care. What advice would you give to her? Do you think she should stay home with the baby? Why or why not? What type of child care would you recommend?

topical **connections**

In Chapter 8 we will discuss socioemotional development in early childhood. Babies no more, young children make considerable progress in the development of their self, their emotions, and their social interactions. In early childhood, they show increased self-understanding and understanding of others, as well as an increased capacity to regulate their emotions. Many of the advances in young children's socioemotional development become possible because of the remarkable changes in their brain and cognitive development, which you will read about in Chapter 7. In early childhood, relationships and interactions with parents and peers expand their knowledge of and connections with the social world. Additionally, play becomes something they not only enjoy doing on a daily basis but also a wonderful context for advancing both their socioemotional and cognitive development.

looking forward

Socioemotional Development in Infancy

1 Emotional and Personality Development

 LG1 Discuss the development of emotions and personality in infancy.

Emotional Development

- Emotion is feeling, or affect, that occurs when a person is in a state or an interaction that is important to him or her. The broad range of emotions includes enthusiasm, joy, and love (positive emotions) and anxiety, anger, and sadness (negative emotions). Psychologists stress that emotions, especially facial expressions of emotions, have a biological foundation. Biological evolution endowed humans to be emotional, but embeddedness in culture and relationships provides diversity in emotional experiences. Emotions are the first language with which parents and infants communicate, and emotions play key roles in parent-child relationships. Infants display a number of emotions early in their development, although researchers debate the onset and sequence of these emotions. Lewis distinguishes between primary emotions and self-conscious emotions. Crying is the most important mechanism newborns have for communicating with their world. Babies have at least three types of cries—basic, anger, and pain cries. Controversy swirls about whether babies should be soothed when they cry, although increasingly experts recommend immediately responding in a caring way in the first year. Social smiling occurs as early as 2 months of age. Two fears that infants develop are stranger anxiety and separation from a caregiver (which is reflected in separation protest). As infants develop, it is important for them to engage in emotional regulation.

Temperament

- Temperament involves individual differences in behavioral styles, emotions, and characteristic ways of responding. Chess and Thomas classified infants as (1) easy, (2) difficult, or (3) slow to warm up. Kagan proposed that inhibition to the unfamiliar is an important temperament category. Rothbart and Bates' view of temperament emphasizes this classification: (1) extraversion/surgency, (2) negative affectivity, and (3) effortful control (self-regulation). Physiological characteristics are associated with different temperaments. Children inherit a physiology that biases them to have a particular type of temperament, but through experience they learn to modify their temperament style to some degree. Goodness of fit refers to the match between a child's temperament and the environmental demands the child must cope with. Goodness of fit can be an important aspect of a child's adjustment. Although research evidence is sketchy at this point, some general recommendations are that caregivers should (1) be sensitive to the individual characteristics of the child, (2) be flexible in responding to these characteristics, and (3) avoid negatively labeling the child.

Personality Development

- Erikson argued that an infant's first year is characterized by the stage of trust versus mistrust. The infant begins to develop a self-understanding called self-recognition at about 18 months of age. Independence becomes a central theme in the second year of life. Erikson stressed that the second year of life is characterized by the stage of autonomy versus shame and doubt.

2 Social Orientation/Understanding and Attachment

 LG2 Describe social orientation/understanding and the development of attachment in infancy.

Social Orientation/ Understanding

- Infants show a strong interest in the social world and are motivated to understand it. Infants orient to the social world early in their development. Face-to-face play with a caregiver begins to occur at about 2 to 3 months of age. Newly developed self-produced locomotion skills significantly expand the infant's ability to initiate social interchanges and explore their social world more independently. Perceiving people as engaging in intentional and goal-directed behavior is an important social cognitive accomplishment that occurs toward the end of the first year. Social referencing increases in the second year of life.

| Attachment and Its Development | • Attachment is a close emotional bond between two people. In infancy, contact comfort and trust are important in the development of attachment. Bowlby's ethological theory stresses that the caregiver and the infant are biologically predisposed to form an attachment. Attachment develops in four phases during infancy. |

| Individual Differences in Attachment | • Securely attached babies use the caregiver, usually the mother, as a secure base from which to explore the environment. Three types of insecure attachment are avoidant, resistant, and disorganized. Ainsworth created the Strange Situation, an observational measure of attachment. Ainsworth points out that secure attachment in the first year of life provides an important foundation for psychological development later in life. The strength of the link between early attachment and later development has varied somewhat across studies. Three criticisms of the concept of secure attachment in infancy are (1) there is insufficient support for the assertion that infancy serves as a critical/sensitive period for later development; (2) biologically based factors such as genes and temperament have not been given adequate consideration; and (3) diversity of social agents and contexts have received insufficient attention. A current trend in attachment research reflects the developmental cascade model by considering not only attachment but also stability and change in stresses and social contexts as children and adolescents develop. Despite these criticisms, there is ample evidence that attachment is an important aspect of human development. Cultural variations in attachment have been found, but in all cultures studied to date secure attachment is the most common classification. |

| Caregiving Styles and Attachment | • Caregivers of secure babies are sensitive to the babies' signals and are consistently available to meet their needs. Caregivers of avoidant babies tend to be unavailable or rejecting. Caregivers of resistant babies tend to be inconsistently available to their babies and usually are not very affectionate. Caregivers of disorganized babies often neglect or physically abuse their babies. |

| Developmental Social Neuroscience and Attachment | • Increased interest has been directed toward the role of the brain in the development of attachment. The hormone oxytocin is a key candidate for influencing the development of maternal-infant attachment. |

3 Social Contexts

LG3 Explain how social contexts influence the infant's development.

| The Family | • The transition to parenthood requires considerable adaptation and adjustment on the part of parents. Children socialize parents, just as parents socialize children. Parent-infant synchrony and scaffolding are important aspects of reciprocal socialization. Belsky's model describes direct and indirect effects. Parents use a wide range of methods to manage and guide infants' behavior. The mother's primary role when interacting with the infant is caregiving; the father's is playful interaction. |

| Child Care | • More U.S. children are in child care now than at any earlier point in history. The quality of child care is uneven, and child care remains a controversial topic. Quality child care can be achieved and seems to have few adverse effects on children. In the NICHD child-care study, infants from low-income families were more likely to receive the lowest quality of care. Also, higher-quality child care was linked with fewer problems in children. |

key terms

emotion 177	social smile 179	goodness of fit 184	insecure disorganized babies 191
primary emotions 178	stranger anxiety 179	social referencing 188	developmental cascade
self-conscious emotions 178	separation protest 180	attachment 189	model 191
basic cry 179	temperament 181	Strange Situation 191	reciprocal socialization 194
anger cry 179	easy child 181	securely attached babies 191	scaffolding 194
pain cry 179	difficult child 181	insecure avoidant babies 191	
reflexive smile 179	slow-to-warm-up child 181	insecure resistant babies 191	

Chapter 6 | SOCIOEMOTIONAL DEVELOPMENT IN INFANCY

Connecting with

Learning Objectives	Application Activities	Activity Type	Page Reference
Discuss emotional development in infancy.	Social Smile 2–9 Weeks	Milestones	pp. 177–181
	Emotional Expression 2 Weeks–3 Years	Milestones	
	Emotional Expression Between 8 and 36 Weeks	Milestones	
Discuss temperament.	Temperament, Esme, 10–15 mos	Milestones	pp. 181–184
Discuss personality development in infancy.	Development of Autonomy 13–15 Months	Milestones	pp. 185–187
	Rouge Test at Age 2	Video	
	Self-Awareness	Video	
	Telling a Story at Age 2	Video	
	Trust and Mistrust, Atlas, 4 mos–2 yrs	Milestones	
	Autonomy and Self-Doubt, Felana, 18–39 mos	Milestones	
Describe social orientation/ understanding in infancy.	Interactional Synchrony	Milestones	pp. 187–188
	Goal-Oriented Behaviors, Yovani, 6–26 mos	Milestones	

(continued)

Learning Objectives	Application Activities	Activity Type	Page Reference
Describe attachment and its development.	Development of Attachment Between Child and Caregiver 2 Weeks–17 Months	Milestones	pp. 189–193
	Bowlby's Stages of Attachment	Click & drag activity	
	Attachment Theory	Video	
	Emotions and Attachment, Esme, 13–32 mos	Milestones	
Explain the role of the family in relation to the infant.	Parent-Infant Interaction With An 18-Month-Old	Video	pp. 194–197
	History of Father Role	Video	
	Paternal Caregivers, 4–12 mos	Milestones	
Explain child care.	Daycare Environment at 3 Years	Video	pp. 197–200
	Preschool Teacher Interaction with 4-Year-Olds	Video	
	Quality Child Care Indicators	Video	

section **four**

You are troubled at seeing him spend his early years doing nothing. What! Is it nothing to be happy? Is it nothing to skip, to play, to run about all day long? Never in his life will he be so busy as now.

—JEAN JACQUES ROUSSEAU
Swiss-Born French Philosopher, 18th Century

Early Childhood

In early childhood, our greatest untold poem was being only 4 years old. We skipped and ran and played all the sun long, never in our lives so busy, busy being something we had not quite grasped yet. Who knew our thoughts, which we worked up into small mythologies all our own? Our thoughts and images and drawings took wings. The blossoms of our heart, no wind could touch. Our small world widened as we discovered new refuges and new people. When we said, "I," we meant something totally unique, not to be confused with any other. Section 4 consists of two chapters: "Physical and Cognitive Development in Early Childhood" (Chapter 7) and "Socioemotional Development in Early Childhood" (Chapter 8).

PHYSICAL AND COGNITIVE DEVELOPMENT IN EARLY CHILDHOOD

chapter outline

1 Physical Changes

Learning Goal 1 Identify physical changes in early childhood.

Body Growth and Change
Motor Development
Sleep
Nutrition and Exercise
Illness and Death

2 Cognitive Changes

Learning Goal 2 Describe three views of the cognitive changes that occur in early childhood.

Piaget's Preoperational Stage
Vygotsky's Theory
Information Processing

3 Language Development

Learning Goal 3 Summarize how language develops in early childhood.

Understanding Phonology and Morphology
Changes in Syntax and Semantics
Advances in Pragmatics
Young Children's Literacy

4 Early Childhood Education

Learning Goal 4 Evaluate different approaches to early childhood education.

Variations in Early Childhood Education
Education for Young Children Who Are Disadvantaged
Controversies in Early Childhood Education

The Reggio Emilia approach is an educational program for young children that was developed in the northern Italian city of Reggio Emilia. Children of single parents and children with disabilities have priority in admission; other children are admitted according to a scale of needs. Parents pay on a sliding scale based on income.

The children are encouraged to learn by investigating and exploring topics that interest them. A wide range of stimulating media and materials is available for children to use as they learn music, movement, drawing, painting, sculpting, collages, puppets and disguises, and photography, for example (Freeman, 2011).

In this program, children often explore topics in a group, which fosters a sense of community, respect for diversity, and a collaborative approach to problem solving. Two co-teachers are present to serve as guides for children. The Reggio Emilia teachers consider a project as an adventure, which can start from an adult's suggestion, from a child's idea, or from an event, such as a snowfall or something else unexpected. The teachers allow children enough time to think and craft a project.

At the core of the Reggio Emilia approach is the image of children who are competent and have rights, especially the right to outstanding care and education. Parent participation is considered essential, and cooperation is a major theme in the schools. Many early childhood education experts believe the Reggio Emilia approach provides a supportive, stimulating context in which children are motivated to explore their world in a competent and confident manner (Martin & Evaldsson, 2012).

A Reggio Emilia classroom in which young children explore topics that interest them.

topical connections

Physical growth in infancy is dramatic. Even though physical growth in early childhood slows, it is not difficult to distinguish young children from infants when you look at them. Most young children lose their "baby fat," and their legs and trunks become longer. In addition to what you can see with the naked eye, much development also continues below the surface in the brain. In infancy, myelination of axons in the brain paved the way for development of such functions as full visual capacity. Continued myelination in early childhood provides children with much better hand-eye coordination. In terms of cognitive development, you learned that infants make amazing progress in their attentional, memory, concept formation, and language skills. In this chapter, you will discover that these information-processing skills continue to show remarkable advances in early childhood.

looking back

preview

Parents and educators who clearly understand how young children develop can play an active role in creating programs that foster their natural interest in learning, rather than stifling it. In this chapter, we will explore the physical, cognitive, and language changes that typically occur as the toddler develops into the preschooler, and then examine different approaches to early childhood education.

1 Physical Changes   **LG1**   Identify physical changes in early childhood.

Body Growth and Change   Motor Development   Sleep   Nutrition and Exercise   Illness and Death

Remember from Chapter 4 that an infant's growth in the first year is rapid and follows cephalocaudal and proximodistal patterns. Improvement in fine motor skills—such as being able to turn the pages of a book one at a time—also contributes to the infant's sense of mastery in the second year. The growth rate continues to slow down in early childhood. If it did not, we would be a species of giants.

BODY GROWTH AND CHANGE

Growth in height and weight is the obvious physical change that characterizes early childhood. Unseen changes in the brain and nervous system are no less significant, however, in preparing children for advances in cognition and language.

Height and Weight   The average child grows 2½ inches in height and gains between 5 and 7 pounds a year during early childhood. As the preschool child grows older, the percentage of increase in height and weight decreases with each additional year (Wilson & Hockenberry, 2012). Girls are only slightly smaller and lighter than boys during these years, a difference that continues until puberty. During the preschool years, both boys and girls slim down as the trunks of their bodies lengthen. Although their heads are still somewhat large for their bodies, by the end of the preschool years most children have lost their top-heavy look. Body fat also shows a slow, steady decline during the preschool years. The chubby baby often looks much leaner by the end of early childhood. Girls have more fatty tissue than boys; boys have more muscle tissue.

Growth patterns vary individually (Burns & others, 2013). Think back to your preschool years. This was probably the first time you noticed that some children were taller than you, some shorter; some were fatter, some thinner; some were stronger, some weaker. Much of the variation was due to heredity, but environmental experiences were also involved. A review of the height and weight of children around the world concluded that the two most important contributors to height differences are ethnic origin and nutrition (Meredith, 1978). Urban, middle-socioeconomic-status, and firstborn children were taller than rural, lower-socioeconomic-status, and later-born children. In the United States, African American children are taller than non-Latino White children.

Why are some children unusually short? The primary contributing influences are congenital factors (genetic or prenatal problems), growth hormone deficiency, a physical problem that develops in childhood, maternal smoking during pregnancy, or an emotional difficulty (Wit, Kiess, & Mullis, 2011).

Growth hormone deficiency is the absence or deficiency of growth hormone produced by the pituitary gland to stimulate the body to grow. Growth hormone deficiency may occur during infancy or later in childhood (Savendahl & others, 2012). As many as 10,000 to 15,000 U.S. children may have growth hormone deficiency (Stanford University Medical Center,

The bodies of 5-year-olds and 2-year-olds are different. Notice that the 5-year-old not only is taller and weighs more, but also has a longer trunk and legs than the 2-year-old. *Can you think of some other physical differences between 2- and 5-year-olds?*

growth hormone deficiency Absence or deficiency of growth hormone produced by the pituitary gland to stimulate the body to grow.

2012). Without treatment, most children with growth hormone deficiency will not reach a height of five feet. Twice as many boys as girls are treated with growth hormone, likely because there is a greater stigma attached to boys being short. A recent research review concluded that growth hormone therapy with children of short stature was partially effective in reducing the deficit in height as adults (Deodati & Cianfarani, 2011). A recent study also revealed that growth hormone treatment of children very short in stature was linked to an increase in height as well as improvements in self-esteem and mood (Chaplin & others, 2012).

The Brain One of the most important physical developments during early childhood is the continuing development of the brain and nervous system (Diamond, 2013; Nelson, 2012). Although the brain continues to grow in early childhood, it does not grow as rapidly as it did in infancy. By the time children reach 3 years of age, the brain is three-quarters of its adult size. By age 6, the brain has reached about 95 percent of its adult size (Lenroot & Giedd, 2006). Thus, the brain of a 5-year-old is nearly the size it will be when the child reaches adulthood, but as we will see in later chapters, the development that occurs inside the brain continues through the remaining years of childhood and adolescence.

Some of the brain's interior changes involve increases in dendritic connections as well as **myelination,** in which nerve cells are covered and insulated with a layer of fat cells (see Figure 7.1). Myelination has the effect of increasing the speed and efficiency of information traveling through the nervous system. Myelination is important in the development of a number of abilities during childhood (Diamond, 2013; Lebel & others, 2012). For example, myelination in the areas of the brain related to hand-eye coordination is not complete until about 4 years of age.

Researchers also have discovered that children's brains undergo dramatic anatomical changes between the ages of 3 and 15 (Gogtay & Thompson, 2010; Posner, 2011; Steinberg, 2012). By repeatedly obtaining brain scans of the same children for up to four years, they have found that children's brains experience rapid, distinct spurts of growth. The amount of brain material in some areas can nearly double within as little as a year, followed by a drastic loss of tissue as unneeded cells are purged and the brain continues to reorganize itself. The scientists have revealed that the overall size of the brain does not show dramatic growth in the 3- to 15-year age range. However, what does dramatically change are local patterns within the brain. Researchers have found that in children from 3 to 6 years of age the most rapid growth takes place in the frontal lobe areas involved in planning and organizing new actions, and in maintaining attention to tasks (Diamond, Casey, & Munakata, 2011; Gogtay & Thompson, 2010).

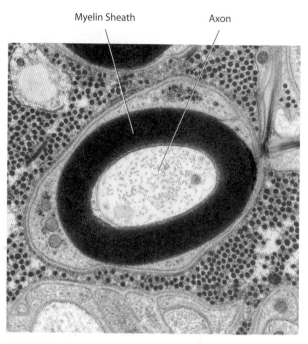

Myelin Sheath   Axon

FIGURE **7.1**

A MYELINATED NERVE FIBER. The myelin sheath, shown in brown, encases the axon (white). This image was produced by an electron microscope that magnified the nerve fiber 12,000 times. *What role does myelination play in the brain's development and children's cognition?*

developmental **connection**

Brain Development

In middle and late childhood, cortical thickening occurs in the frontal lobes, which may be linked to improvements in language abilities such as reading. Chapter 9, p. 283

MOTOR DEVELOPMENT

Most preschool children are as active as they will ever be in the life span. Let's explore what this activity involves in young children's lives.

Gross Motor Skills The preschool child no longer has to make an effort simply to stay upright and to move around. As children move their legs with more confidence and carry themselves more purposefully, moving around in the environment becomes more automatic (Burns & others, 2013). However, there are large individual differences in young children's gross motor skills (Legear & others, 2012).

At 3 years of age, children enjoy simple movements, such as hopping, jumping, and running back and forth, just for the sheer delight of performing these activities. They take considerable pride in showing how they can run across a room and jump all of 6 inches. The run-and-jump will win no Olympic gold medals, but for the 3-year-old the activity is a source of considerable pride and accomplishment.

At 4 years of age, children are still enjoying the same kind of activities, but they have become more adventurous. They scramble over low jungle gyms as they display their athletic prowess.

myelination The process by which the nerve cells are covered and insulated with a layer of fat cells, which increases the speed at which information travels through the nervous system.

At 5 years of age, children are even more adventuresome than when they were 4. It is not unusual for self-assured 5-year-olds to perform hair-raising stunts on practically any climbing object. Five-year-olds run hard and enjoy races with each other and their parents.

Fine Motor Skills At 3 years of age, although children have had the ability to pick up the tiniest objects between their thumb and forefinger for some time, they are still somewhat clumsy at it. Three-year-olds can build surprisingly high block towers, placing each block with intense concentration but often not in a completely straight line. When 3-year-olds play with a simple jigsaw puzzle, they are rather rough in placing the pieces. Even when they recognize the hole a piece fits into, they are not very precise in positioning the piece. They often try to force the piece into the hole or pat it vigorously.

By 4 years of age, children's fine motor coordination has improved substantially and become much more precise. Sometimes 4-year-old children have trouble building high towers with blocks because, in their desire to place each of the blocks perfectly, they may upset those already stacked. By age 5, children's fine motor coordination has improved further. Hand, arm, and body all move together under better command of the eye.

SLEEP

Experts recommend that young children get 11 to 13 hours of sleep each night (National Sleep Foundation, 2012). Most young children sleep through the night and have one daytime nap. Not only is the amount of sleep children get important, but so is uninterrupted sleep (Owens & Mindell, 2011). However, it sometimes is difficult to get young children to go to sleep as they drag out their bedtime routine. Studies often report that young children don't get adequate sleep (Aishworiya & others, 2012).

Children can experience a number of sleep problems, including narcolepsy (extreme daytime sleepiness), insomnia (difficulty getting to sleep or staying asleep), and nightmares (Moore, 2012). One estimate indicates that more than 40 percent of children experience a sleep problem at some point in their development (Boyle & Cropley, 2004). The following research studies indicate links between children's sleep problems and negative developmental outcomes:

- Children who had trouble sleeping in childhood were more likely to have alcohol use problems in adolescence and early adulthood (Wong & others, 2010).
- Sleep problems in early childhood were a subsequent indicator of attention problems that in some cases persisted into early adolescence (O'Callaghan & others, 2010).
- A recent analysis concluded that chronic sleep disorders that deprive children of adequate sleep may result in impaired brain development (Jan & others, 2010).
- A recent research review concluded that short sleep duration in children is linked with being overweight (Hart, Cairns, & Jelalian, 2011).

What characterizes young children's sleep problems?

developmental **connection**

Sleep

What sleep disorder in infancy leads to the most infant deaths and at what age is the infant most at risk for this disorder? Chapter 4, p. 116

NUTRITION AND EXERCISE

Eating habits are important aspects of development during early childhood (Schiff, 2013; Wardlaw & Smith, 2012). What children eat affects their skeletal growth, body shape, and susceptibility to disease. Exercise and physical activity also are very important aspects of young children's lives (Graham, Holt/Hale, & Parker, 2013).

Overweight Young Children Being overweight has become a serious health problem in early childhood (Thompson & Manore, 2013). A national study revealed that 45 percent of children's meals exceed recommendations for saturated and trans fats, which can raise cholesterol levels and increase the risk of heart disease (Center for Science in the Public Interest, 2008). The same study found that one-third of children's daily caloric intake comes from restaurants—twice the percentage consumed away from home in the 1980s. Further, 93 percent of almost 1,500 possible choices at 13 major fast-food chains exceeded 430 calories—one-third of what the National Institute of Medicine recommends that 4- to 8-year-old children consume in a day. Nearly all of the children's meal options at KFC, Taco Bell, Sonic, Jack in the Box, and Chick-fil-A were too high in calories. One study of U.S. 2- and 3-year-olds found that French fries and other fried potatoes were the vegetable they were most likely to consume (Fox & others, 2010).

Young children's eating behavior is strongly influenced by their caregivers' behavior (Black & Hurley, 2007; Farrow, 2012; Gibson & others, 2012). Young children's eating behavior improves when caregivers eat with children on a predictable schedule, model eating healthy food, make mealtimes pleasant occasions, and engage in certain feeding styles. Distractions from television, family arguments, and competing activities should be minimized so that children can focus on eating. A sensitive/responsive caregiver feeding style, in which the caregiver is nurturant, provides clear information about what is expected, and appropriately responds to children's cues, is recommended (Black & Lozoff, 2008). Forceful and restrictive caregiver behaviors are not recommended (Riesch & others, 2012).

The Centers for Disease Control and Prevention (2012) has categories for obesity, overweight, and at risk for being overweight. These categories are determined by body mass index (BMI), which is computed using a formula that takes into account height and weight. Only children and adolescents at or above the 97th percentile are classified as obese; those at the 95th or 96th percentile as overweight; and those from the 85th to the 94th percentile as at risk of being overweight.

The percentages of young children who are overweight or at risk of being overweight in the United States have increased dramatically in recent decades, and these percentages are likely to climb further unless changes occur in children's lifestyles (Summerbell & others, 2012). In 2009–2010, 12.1 percent of U.S. 2- to 5-year-olds were classified as obese, compared with 5 percent in 1976–1980 and 10.4 percent in 2007–2008 (Ogden & others, 2012).

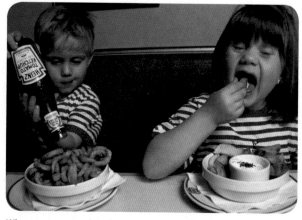

What are some trends in the eating habits and weight of young children?

The risk that overweight children will continue to be overweight when they are older was documented in a study in which 80 percent of the children who were at risk for being overweight at age 3 were also at risk for being overweight or were overweight at age 12 (Nader & others, 2006). A recent study likewise revealed that preschool children who were overweight were at significant risk for being overweight or obese in adolescence (Shankaran & others, 2011).

One comparison of 34 countries revealed that the United States had the second highest rate of child obesity (Janssen & others, 2005). Childhood obesity contributes to a number of health problems in young children (Anspaugh & Ezell, 2013). For example, physicians are now seeing type 2 (adult-onset) diabetes (a condition directly linked with obesity and a low level of fitness) and hypertension in children as young as 5 years of age (Riley & Bluhm, 2012; Trasande & Elbel, 2012). We will have much more to consider about children's eating behavior and weight status in Chapter 9.

Exercise Routine physical activity should be a daily occurrence for young children (Wuest & Fisette, 2012). Guidelines recommend that preschool children engage in two hours

How much physical activity should preschool children engage in per day?

developmental **connection**

Health

As boys and girls reach and progress through adolescence, they exercise less. Chapter 11, p. 368

of physical activity per day, divided into one hour of structured activity and one hour of unstructured free play (National Association for Sport and Physical Education, 2002). The child's life should be centered around activities, not meals (Graber & Woods, 2013; Willis & others, 2012). Following are some recent research studies that examine young children's exercise and activities:

- Observations of 3- to 5-year-old children during outdoor play at preschools revealed that the preschool children were mainly sedentary even when participating in outdoor play (Brown & others, 2009). In this study, throughout the day the preschoolers were sedentary 89 percent of the time, engaged in light activity 8 percent of the time, and participated in moderate to vigorous physical activity only 3 percent of the time.

- Preschool children's physical activity was enhanced by family members engaging in sports together and by parents' perception that it was safe for their children to play outside (Beets & Foley, 2008).

- Incorporation of a "move and learn" physical activity curriculum increased the activity level of 3- to 5-year-old children in a half-day preschool program (Trost, Fees, & Dzewaltowski, 2008).

Malnutrition in Young Children From Low-Income Families

Malnutrition is a problem for many U.S. children, with approximately 11 million preschool children experiencing malnutrition that places their health at risk. One of the most common nutritional problems in early childhood is iron deficiency anemia, which results in chronic fatigue. This problem results from the failure to eat adequate amounts of quality meats and dark green vegetables. Young children from low-income families are the most likely to develop iron deficiency anemia (Shamah & Villalpando, 2006).

ILLNESS AND DEATH

What are the greatest risks to the health of young children in the United States? How pervasive is death among young children around the world?

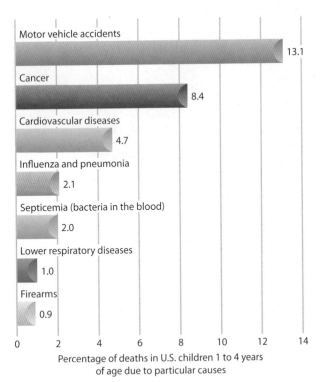

FIGURE **7.2**

MAIN CAUSES OF DEATH IN CHILDREN 1 THROUGH 4 YEARS OF AGE. These figures show the percentage of deaths in U.S. children 1 to 4 years of age due to particular causes in 2002 (National Vital Statistics Reports, 2004).

The United States Young children's active and exploratory nature, coupled with their unawareness of danger in many instances, often puts them in situations in which they are at risk for injuries (Durbin, 2011). In the United States, motor vehicle accidents are the leading cause of death in young children, followed by cancer and cardiovascular disease (National Vital Statistics Report, 2004) (see Figure 7.2). In addition to motor vehicle accidents, other accidental deaths in children involve drowning, falls, burns, and poisoning (Duke & others, 2011; Zielinski, Rochette, & Smith, 2012).

Children's Safety   Children's safety is influenced not only by their own skills and safety behaviors but also by characteristics of their family and home, school and peers, and the community's actions (Lindqvist & Dalal, 2012). Figure 7.3 describes steps that can be taken in each of these contexts to enhance children's safety and prevent injury (Sleet & Mercy, 2003). Children in poverty have higher rates of accidents, death, and asthma than children from higher-income families (Green, Muir, & Maher, 2011).

Environmental Tobacco Smoke   Estimates indicate that approximately 22 percent of children and adolescents in the United States are exposed to tobacco smoke in the home. An increasing number of studies reach the conclusion that children are at risk for health problems when they live in homes in which a parent smokes (Hwang & others, 2012). Children exposed to tobacco smoke in the home are more likely to develop wheezing symptoms and asthma than children in nonsmoking homes (Yi & others, 2012). A recent study found that parental smoking was a risk factor for higher blood pressure in children (Simonetti & others, 2011). And another recent study revealed that exposure to secondhand smoke was related to young children's sleep problems, including sleep-disordered breathing (Yolton & others, 2010).

The State of Illness and Health of the World's Children
Devastating effects on the health of young children occur in countries where poverty rates are high (UNICEF, 2013). The poor are the majority in nearly one of every five nations in the world. They often experience lives of hunger, malnutrition, illness, inadequate access to health care, unsafe water, and a lack of protection from harm (Gaiha & others, 2012).

In the last decade, there has been a dramatic increase in the number of young children who have died because of HIV/AIDS transmitted to them by their parents (UNICEF, 2013). Deaths in young children due to HIV/AIDS especially occur in countries with high rates of poverty and low levels of education (Toure & others, 2012).

Many of the deaths of young children around the world could be prevented by a reduction in poverty and improvements in nutrition, sanitation, education, and health services (UNICEF, 2013).

Individual

Development of social skills and ability to regulate emotions

Impulse control (such as not darting out into a street to retrieve a ball)

Frequent use of personal protection (such as bike helmets and safety seats)

Family/Home

High awareness and knowledge of child management and parenting skills

Frequent parent protective behaviors (such as use of child safety seats)

Presence of home safety equipment (such as smoke alarms and cabinet locks)

School/Peers

Promotion of home/school partnerships

Absence of playground hazards

Injury prevention and safety promotion policies and programs

Community

Availability of positive activities for children and their parents

Active surveillance of environmental hazards

Effective prevention policies in place (such as pool fencing)

FIGURE 7.3

CHARACTERISTICS THAT ENHANCE YOUNG CHILDREN'S SAFETY. In each context of a child's life, steps can be taken to create conditions that enhance the child's safety and reduce the likelihood of injury. *How are the contexts listed in the figure related to Bronfenbrenner's theory (described in Chapter 1)?*

Many children in impoverished countries die before reaching the age of 5 from dehydration and malnutrition brought about by diarrhea. *What are some of the other main causes of death in young children around the world?*

Review Connect Reflect

LG1 Identify physical changes in early childhood.

Review

- How does the body grow and change during early childhood?
- What changes take place in motor development during early childhood?
- What are some problems associated with sleep in young children?
- What roles do nutrition and exercise play in early childhood?
- What are some major causes of illness and death among young children in the United States and around the world?

Connect

- In this section you learned that experts recommend that children get 11 to 13 hours of sleep a night during early childhood. How does that compare with what you learned about the sleep patterns of infants in Chapter 4?

Reflect *Your Own Personal Journey of Life*

- What were your eating habits like as a young child? In what ways are they similar or different from your current eating habits? Did your early eating habits predict whether or not you have weight problems today?

---

2 Cognitive Changes

LG2 Describe three views of the cognitive changes that occur in early childhood.

Piaget's Preoperational Stage   Vygotsky's Theory   Information Processing

The cognitive world of the preschool child is creative, free, and fanciful. Preschool children's imaginations work overtime, and their mental grasp of the world improves. Our coverage of cognitive development in early childhood focuses on three theories: Piaget's, Vygotsky's, and information processing.

PIAGET'S PREOPERATIONAL STAGE

Remember from Chapter 5 that, during Piaget's first stage of development, the sensorimotor stage, the infant progresses in the ability to organize and coordinate sensations and perceptions with physical movements and actions. The **preoperational stage,** which lasts from approximately 2 to 7 years of age, is the second Piagetian stage. In this stage, children begin to represent the world with words, images, and drawings. They form stable concepts and begin to reason. At the same time, the young child's cognitive world is dominated by egocentrism and magical beliefs.

Because Piaget called this stage "preoperational," it might sound like an unimportant waiting period. Not so. Instead, the label *preoperational* emphasizes that the child does not yet perform **operations,** which are reversible mental actions that allow children to do mentally what before they could do only physically. Adding and subtracting numbers mentally are examples of operations. *Preoperational thought* is the beginning of the ability to reconstruct in thought what has been established in behavior. This developmental stage can be divided into two substages: the symbolic function substage and the intuitive thought substage.

The Symbolic Function Substage   The **symbolic function substage** is the first substage of preoperational thought, occurring roughly between the ages of 2 and 4. In this substage, the young child gains the ability to mentally represent an object that is not present. This ability vastly expands the child's mental world (Callaghan, 2013; DeLoache, 2011; Mandler & DeLoache, 2012). Young children use scribble designs to represent people, houses, cars, clouds, and so on; they begin to use language and engage in pretend play. However, although young children make distinct progress during this substage, their thought still has important limitations, two of which are egocentrism and animism.

---

developmental **connection**

Cognitive Theory

Object permanence is an important accomplishment in the sensorimotor stage. Chapter 5, p. 148

preoperational stage Piaget's second stage, lasting from about 2 to 7 years of age, during which children begin to represent the world with words, images, and drawings, and symbolic thought goes beyond simple connections of sensory information and physical action; stable concepts are formed, mental reasoning emerges, egocentrism is present, and magical beliefs are constructed.

operations In Piaget's theory, these are reversible mental actions that allow children to do mentally what they formerly did physically.

symbolic function substage Piaget's first substage of preoperational thought, in which the child gains the ability to mentally represent an object that is not present (between about 2 and 4 years of age).

Model of Mountains

Photo 1
(View from A)

Photo 2
(View from B)

Photo 3
(View from C)

Photo 4
(View from D)

FIGURE **7.4**

THE THREE MOUNTAINS TASK. View 1 shows the child's perspective from where he or she is sitting. View 2 is an example of one of the photographs the child would be shown, along with other photographs taken from different perspectives. It shows what the mountains look like to a person sitting at spot B. When asked what a view of the mountains looks like from position B, the preoperational child selects a photograph taken from location A, the child's view at the time. A child who thinks in a preoperational way cannot take the perspective of a person sitting at another spot.

Egocentrism is the inability to distinguish between one's own perspective and someone else's perspective. Piaget and Barbel Inhelder (1969) initially studied young children's egocentrism by devising the three mountains task (see Figure 7.4). The child walks around the model of the mountains and becomes familiar with what the mountains look like from different perspectives, and she can see that there are different objects on the mountains. The child is then seated on one side of the table on which the mountains are placed. The experimenter moves a doll to different locations around the table, at each location asking the child to select from a series of photos the one photo that most accurately reflects the view that the doll is seeing. Children in the preoperational stage often pick their own view rather than the doll's view. Preschool children frequently show the ability to take another's perspective on some tasks but not others.

Animism, another limitation of preoperational thought, is the belief that inanimate objects have lifelike qualities and are capable of action. A young child might show animism by saying, "That tree pushed the leaf off, and it fell down," or "The sidewalk made me mad; it made me fall down." A young child who uses animism fails to distinguish the appropriate occasions for using human and nonhuman perspectives (Opfer & Gelman, 2011).

Possibly because young children are not very concerned about reality, their drawings are fanciful and inventive. Suns are blue, skies are yellow, and cars float on clouds in their symbolic, imaginative world. One 3½-year-old looked at a scribble he had just drawn and described it as a pelican kissing a seal (see Figure 7.5a). The symbolism is simple but strong, like abstractions

(a)

(b)

FIGURE **7.5**

THE SYMBOLIC DRAWINGS OF YOUNG CHILDREN. (*a*) A 3½-year-old's symbolic drawing. Halfway into his drawing, the 3½-year-old artist said it was a "pelican kissing a seal." (*b*) This 11-year-old's drawing is neater and more realistic but also less inventive.

egocentrism The inability to distinguish between one's own perspective and someone else's (salient feature of the first substage of preoperational thought).

animism The belief that inanimate objects have lifelike qualities and are capable of action.

"I still don't have all the answers, but I'm beginning to ask the right questions."
© Lee Lorenz/The New Yorker Collection/www.cartoon.bank.

found in some modern art. Twentieth-century Spanish artist Pablo Picasso commented, "I used to draw like Raphael but it has taken me a lifetime to draw like young children." During the elementary school years, a child's drawings become more realistic, neat, and precise (see Figure 7.5b) (Winner, 1986).

The Intuitive Thought Substage   The **intuitive thought substage** is the second substage of preoperational thought, occurring between approximately 4 and 7 years of age. In this substage, children begin to use primitive reasoning and want to know the answers to all sorts of questions. Consider 4-year-old Tommy, who is at the beginning of the intuitive thought substage. Although he is starting to develop his own ideas about the world he lives in, his ideas are still simple, and he is not very good at thinking things out. He has difficulty understanding events that he knows are taking place but that he cannot see. His fantasized thoughts bear little resemblance to reality. He cannot yet answer the question "What if?" in any reliable way. For example, he has only a vague idea of what would happen if a car were to hit him. He also has difficulty negotiating traffic because he cannot do the mental calculations necessary to estimate whether an approaching car will hit him when he crosses the road.

By the age of 5, children have just about exhausted the adults around them with "why" questions. The child's questions signal the emergence of interest in reasoning and in figuring out why things are the way they are. Following are some samples of the questions children ask during the questioning period of 4 to 6 years of age (Elkind, 1976): "What makes you grow up?" "Who was the mother when everybody was a baby?" "Why do leaves fall?" "Why does the sun shine?" Piaget called this substage intuitive because young children seem so sure about their knowledge and understanding yet are unaware of how they know what they know. That is, they know something but know it without the use of rational thinking.

Centration and the Limits of Preoperational Thought   One limitation of preoperational thought is **centration,** a centering of attention on one characteristic to the exclusion of all others. Centration is most clearly evidenced in young children's lack of **conservation,** the awareness that altering an object's or a substance's appearance does not change its basic properties. For example, to adults, it is obvious that a certain amount of liquid stays the same, regardless of a container's shape. But this is not at all obvious to young children. Instead, they are struck by the height of the liquid in the container; they focus on that characteristic to the exclusion of others.

The situation that Piaget devised to study conservation is his most famous task. In the conservation task, children are presented with two identical beakers, each filled to the same level with liquid (see Figure 7.6). They are asked if these beakers have the same amount of

intuitive thought substage Piaget's second substage of preoperational thought, in which children begin to use primitive reasoning and want to know the answers to all sorts of questions (between 4 and 7 years of age).

centration Focusing attention on one characteristic to the exclusion of all others.

conservation In Piaget's theory, awareness that altering an object's or a substance's appearance does not change its basic properties.

FIGURE **7.6**

PIAGET'S CONSERVATION TASK. The beaker test is a well-known Piagetian test to determine whether a child can think operationally—that is, can mentally reverse actions and show conservation of the substance. (*a*) Two identical beakers are presented to the child. Then the experimenter pours the liquid from B into C, which is taller and thinner than A or B. (*b*) The child is asked if these beakers (A and C) have the same amount of liquid. The preoperational child says "no." When asked to point to the beaker that has more liquid, the preoperational child points to the tall, thin beaker.

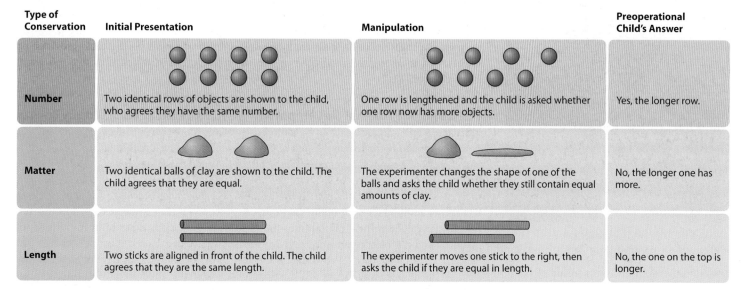

Type of Conservation	Initial Presentation	Manipulation	Preoperational Child's Answer
Number	Two identical rows of objects are shown to the child, who agrees they have the same number.	One row is lengthened and the child is asked whether one row now has more objects.	Yes, the longer row.
Matter	Two identical balls of clay are shown to the child. The child agrees that they are equal.	The experimenter changes the shape of one of the balls and asks the child whether they still contain equal amounts of clay.	No, the longer one has more.
Length	Two sticks are aligned in front of the child. The child agrees that they are the same length.	The experimenter moves one stick to the right, then asks the child if they are equal in length.	No, the one on the top is longer.

FIGURE **7.7**

SOME DIMENSIONS OF CONSERVATION: NUMBER, MATTER, AND LENGTH. *What characteristics of preoperational thought do children demonstrate when they fail these conservation tasks?*

liquid, and they usually say yes. Then the liquid from one beaker is poured into a third beaker, which is taller and thinner than the first two. The children are then asked if the amount of liquid in the tall, thin beaker is equal to that which remains in one of the original beakers. Children who are less than 7 or 8 years old usually say no and justify their answers in terms of the differing height or width of the beakers. Older children usually answer yes and justify their answers appropriately ("If you poured the water back, the amount would still be the same").

In Piaget's theory, failing the conservation-of-liquid task is a sign that children are at the preoperational stage of cognitive development. The failure demonstrates not only centration but also an inability to mentally reverse actions. For example, in the conservation of matter example shown in Figure 7.7, preoperational children say that the longer shape has more clay because they assume that "longer is more." Preoperational children cannot mentally reverse the clay-rolling process to see that the amount of clay is the same in both the shorter ball shape and the longer stick shape.

In addition to failing to conserve volume, preoperational children also fail to conserve number, matter, length, and area. However, children often vary in their performance on different conservation tasks. Thus, a child might be able to conserve volume but not number. A recent fMRI brain imaging study of conservation of number revealed that advances in a network in the parietal and frontal lobes were linked to 9- and 10-year-olds' conservation success when compared to non-conserving 5- and 6-year-olds (Houde & others, 2011).

Some developmentalists disagree with Piaget's estimate of when children's conservation skills emerge. For example, Rochel Gelman (1969) showed that when the child's attention to relevant aspects of the conservation task is improved, the child is more likely to conserve. Gelman has also demonstrated that attentional training on one dimension, such as number, improves the preschool child's performance on another dimension, such as mass. Thus, Gelman argues that conservation appears earlier than Piaget thought and that attention is especially important in explaining conservation.

VYGOTSKY'S THEORY

Piaget's theory is a major developmental theory. Another developmental theory that focuses on children's cognition is Vygotsky's theory. Like Piaget, Vygotsky (1962) emphasized that children actively construct their knowledge and understanding. In Piaget's theory, children develop ways of thinking and understanding by their actions and interactions with the

Upper limit

Level of additional responsibility
child can accept with assistance
of an able instructor

**Zone of proximal
development (ZPD)**

Lower limit

Level of problem solving
reached on these tasks by
child working alone

FIGURE **7.8**

**VYGOTSKY'S ZONE OF PROXIMAL
DEVELOPMENT.** Vygotsky's zone of proximal
development has a lower limit and an upper limit.
Tasks in the ZPD are too difficult for the child to
perform alone. They require assistance from an adult
or a more-skilled child. As children experience the
verbal instruction or demonstration, they organize
the information in their existing mental structures, so
they can eventually perform the skill or task alone.

---

developmental **connection**

Parenting

Scaffolding also is an effective strategy for
parents to adopt in interacting with their
infants. Chapter 6, p. 195

---

zone of proximal development (ZPD) Vygotsky's
term for tasks that are too difficult for children to
master alone but can be mastered with the
assistance of adults or more-skilled children.

physical world. In Vygotsky's theory, children are more often described as social creatures
than in Piaget's theory. They develop their ways of thinking and understanding primarily
through social interaction. Their cognitive development depends on the tools provided by
society, and their minds are shaped by the cultural context in which they live (Gauvain,
2013; Gredler, 2012).

The Zone of Proximal Development   Vygotsky's belief in the importance of social
influences, especially instruction, on children's cognitive development is reflected in his concept of the zone of proximal development. **Zone of proximal development (ZPD)** is Vygotsky's
term for the range of tasks that are too difficult for the child to master alone but can be learned
with guidance and assistance from adults or more-skilled children. Thus, the lower limit of
the ZPD is the level of skill reached by the child working independently. The upper limit is
the level of additional responsibility the child can accept with the assistance of an able instructor (see Figure 7.8). The ZPD captures the child's cognitive skills that are in the process of
maturing and can be accomplished only with the assistance of a more-skilled person (Petrick-
Steward, 2012). Vygotsky (1962) called these the "buds" or "flowers" of development, to distinguish them from the "fruits" of development, which the child already can accomplish
independently.

Scaffolding   Closely linked to the idea of the ZPD is the concept of scaffolding. *Scaffolding* means changing the level of support. Over the course of a teaching session, a more-
skilled person (a teacher or advanced peer) adjusts the amount of guidance to fit the child's
current performance (Daniels, 2011). When the student is learning a new task, the skilled
person may use direct instruction. As the student's competence increases, less guidance is
given.

Language and Thought   The use of dialogue as a tool for scaffolding is only one example of the important role of language in a child's development. According to Vygotsky, children
use speech not only to communicate socially but also to help them solve tasks. Vygotsky (1962)
further believed that young children use language to plan, guide, and monitor their behavior.
This use of language for self-regulation is called *private speech*. For Piaget, private speech is
egocentric and immature, but for Vygotsky it is an important tool of thought during the early
childhood years (John-Steiner, 2007).

Vygotsky said that language and thought initially develop independently of each other
and then merge. He emphasized that all mental functions have external, or social, origins.
Children must use language to communicate with others before they can focus inward on their
own thoughts. Children also must communicate externally and use language for a long period
of time before they can make the transition from external to internal speech. This transition
period occurs between 3 and 7 years of age and involves talking to oneself. After a while, the
self-talk becomes second nature to children, and they can act without verbalizing. When they
gain this skill, children have internalized their egocentric speech in the form of *inner speech*,
which becomes their thoughts.

Vygotsky reasoned that children who use a lot of private speech are more socially competent than those who don't. He argued that private speech represents an early transition in
becoming more socially communicative. For Vygotsky, when young children talk to themselves, they are using language to govern their behavior and guide themselves. For example, a
child working on a puzzle might say to herself, "Which pieces should I put together first? I'll
try those green ones first. Now I need some blue ones. No, that blue one doesn't fit there. I'll
try it over here."

Piaget maintained that self-talk is egocentric and reflects immaturity. However, researchers have found support for Vygotsky's view that private speech plays a positive role in children's
development (Winsler, Carlton, & Barry, 2000). Researchers have found that children use
private speech more often when tasks are difficult, after they have made errors, and when they
are not sure how to proceed (Berk, 1994). They also have revealed that children who use
private speech are more attentive and improve their performance more than children who do
not use private speech (Berk & Spuhl, 1995).

Teaching Strategies   Vygotsky's theory has been embraced by many teachers and has been successfully applied to education (Costley, 2012). Here are some ways Vygotsky's theory can be incorporated in classrooms:

1. *Assess the child's ZPD.* Like Piaget, Vygotsky did not recommend formal, standardized tests as the best way to assess children's learning. Rather, Vygotsky argued that assessment should focus on determining the child's zone of proximal development. The skilled helper presents the child with tasks of varying difficulty to determine the best level at which to begin instruction.

2. *Use the child's ZPD in teaching.* Teaching should begin toward the zone's upper limit, so that the child can reach the goal with help and move to a higher level of skill and knowledge. Offer just enough assistance. You might ask, "What can I do to help you?" Or simply observe the child's intentions and attempts and provide support when it is needed. When the child hesitates, offer encouragement. And encourage the child to practice the skill. You may watch and appreciate the child's practice or offer support when the child forgets what to do.

3. *Use more-skilled peers as teachers.* Remember that it is not just adults who are important in helping children learn. Children also benefit from the support and guidance of more-skilled children.

4. *Place instruction in a meaningful context.* Educators today are moving away from abstract presentations of material; instead, they provide students with opportunities to experience learning in real-world settings. For example, rather than just memorizing math formulas, students work on math problems with real-world implications.

5. *Transform the classroom with Vygotskian ideas.* What does a Vygotskian classroom look like? The Kamehameha Elementary Education Program (KEEP) in Hawaii is based on Vygotsky's theory (Tharp, 1994). The ZPD is the key element of instruction in this program. Children might read a story and then interpret its meaning. Many of the learning activities take place in small groups. All children spend at least 20 minutes each morning in a setting called "Center One." In this context, scaffolding is used to improve children's literary skills. The instructor asks questions, responds to students' queries, and builds on the ideas that students generate.

Connecting Development to Life further explores the implications of Vygotsky's theory for children's education.

Evaluating Vygotsky's Theory   Even though their theories were proposed at about the same time, most of the world learned about Vygotsky's theory later than they learned about Piaget's theory. Thus, Vygotsky's theory has not yet been evaluated as thoroughly. However, Vygotsky's view of the importance of sociocultural influences on children's development fits with the current belief that it is important to evaluate the contextual factors in learning (Gredler, 2012).

We already have compared several aspects of Vygotsky's and Piaget's theories, such as Vygotsky's emphasis on the importance of inner speech in development and Piaget's view that such speech is immature. Although both theories are constructivist, Vygotsky's takes a **social constructivist approach,** which emphasizes the social contexts of learning and the construction of knowledge through social interaction (O'Donnell, 2011).

In moving from Piaget to Vygotsky, the conceptual shift is one from the individual to collaboration, social interaction, and sociocultural activity (Gauvain, 2013). The endpoint of cognitive development for Piaget is formal operational thought. For Vygotsky, the endpoint can differ depending on which skills are considered to be the most important in a particular culture. In Piaget's, children construct knowledge by transforming, organizing, and reorganizing previous knowledge. From Vygotsky's perspective, children construct knowledge through social interaction (Costley, 2012; Gauvain, 2013; Goncu & Gauvain, 2011). The implication of

Lev Vygotsky (1896–1934), shown here with his daughter, reasoned that children's cognitive development is advanced through social interaction with more-skilled individuals embedded in a sociocultural backdrop. *How is Vygotsky's theory different from Piaget's?*

How can Vygotsky's ideas be applied to educating children?

social constructivist approach An approach that emphasizes the social contexts of learning and asserts that knowledge is mutually built and constructed. Vygotsky's theory reflects this approach.

connecting development to life

Tools of the Mind

Tools of the Mind is an early childhood education curriculum that emphasizes children's development of self-regulation and the cognitive foundations of literacy. The curriculum was created by Elena Bodrova and Deborah Leong (2007) and has been implemented in more than 200 classrooms. Most of the children in the Tools of the Mind programs are at risk because of their living circumstances, which in many instances involve poverty and other difficult conditions such as being homeless and having parents with drug problems.

Tools of the Mind is grounded in Vygotsky's (1962) theory with special attention given to cultural tools and developing self-regulation, the zone of proximal development, scaffolding, private speech, shared activity, and play as important activity. In a Tools of the Mind classroom, dramatic play has a central role. Teachers guide children in creating themes that are based on the children's interests, such as treasure hunt, store, hospital, and restaurant. Teachers also incorporate field trips, visitor presentations, videos, and books in the development of children's play. They help children develop a play plan, which increases the maturity of their play. Play plans describe what the children expect to do in the play period, including the imaginary context, roles, and props to be used. The play plans increase the quality of their play and self-regulation.

Scaffolding writing is another important theme in the Tools of the Mind classroom. Teachers guide children in planning their own message by drawing a line to stand for each word the child says. Children then repeat the message, pointing to each line as they say the word. Then, the child writes on the lines, trying to represent each word with some letters or symbols. Figure 7.9 shows how the scaffolding writing process improved a 5-year-old child's writing over the course of two months.

Research assessments of children's writing in Tools of the Mind classrooms revealed that they have more advanced writing skills than children in other early childhood programs (Bodrova & Leong, 2007) (see Figure 7.9). For example, they write more complex messages, use more words, spell more accurately, show better letter recognition, and have a better understanding of the concept of a sentence.

One study assessed the effects of the Tools of the Mind curriculum on at-risk preschool children (Diamond & others, 2007). The results indicated that the Tools of the Mind curriculum improved the self-regulatory and cognitive control skills (such as resisting distractions and temptations) of the at-risk children. Other research on the Tools of the Mind curriculum also has found that it improves young children's cognitive skills (Barnett & others, 2006; Bodrova, Leong, & Akhutina, 2011; Saifer, 2007).

How does the Reggio Emilia approach to education that you read about in the story that opened this chapter compare with the Tools of the Mind approach described here?

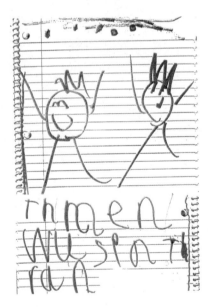

(*a*) Five-year-old Aaron's independent journal writing prior to using the scaffolded writing technique.

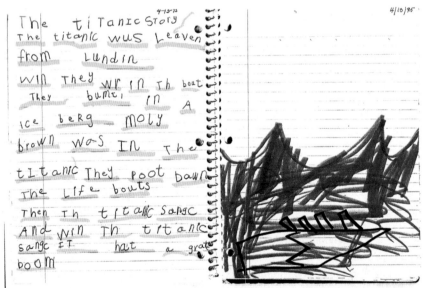

(*b*) Aaron's journal two months after using the scaffolded writing technique.

FIGURE **7.9**

WRITING PROGRESS OF A 5-YEAR-OLD BOY OVER TWO MONTHS USING THE SCAFFOLDING WRITING PROCESS IN TOOLS OF THE MIND

	Vygotsky	Piaget
Sociocultural Context	Strong emphasis	Little emphasis
Constructivism	Social constructivist	Cognitive constructivist
Stages	No general stages of development proposed	Strong emphasis on stages (sensorimotor, preoperational, concrete operational, and formal operational)
Key Processes	Zone of proximal development, language, dialogue, tools of the culture	Schema, assimilation, accommodation, operations, conservation, classification
Role of Language	A major role; language plays a powerful role in shaping thought	Language has a minimal role; cognition primarily directs language
View on Education	Education plays a central role, helping children learn the tools of the culture	Education merely refines the child's cognitive skills that have already emerged
Teaching Implications	Teacher is a facilitator and guide, not a director; establish many opportunities for children to learn with the teacher and more-skilled peers	Also views teacher as a facilitator and guide, not a director; provide support for children to explore their world and discover knowledge

FIGURE **7.10**
COMPARISON OF VYGOTSKY'S AND PIAGET'S THEORIES

Piaget's theory for teaching is that children need support to explore their world and discover knowledge. The main implication of Vygotsky's theory for teaching is that students need many opportunities to learn with the teacher and more-skilled peers. In both Piaget's and Vygotsky's theories, teachers serve as facilitators and guides, rather than as directors and molders of learning. Figure 7.10 compares Vygotsky's and Piaget's theories.

Criticisms of Vygotsky's theory also have surfaced. Some critics point out that Vygotsky was not specific enough about age-related changes (Goncu & Gauvain, 2011). Another criticism is that Vygotsky did not adequately describe how changes in socioemotional capabilities contribute to cognitive development (Gauvain, 2008). Yet another criticism is that he overemphasized the role of language in thinking. Also, his emphasis on collaboration and guidance has potential pitfalls. Might facilitators be too helpful in some cases, as when a parent becomes too overbearing and controlling? Further, some children might become lazy and expect help when they might have done something on their own.

INFORMATION PROCESSING

Piaget's and Vygotsky's theories provided important ideas about how young children think and how their thinking changes. More recently, the information-processing approach has generated research that illuminates how children process information during the preschool years (Bjorklund, 2013; Cohen, 2012; Feldman, 2013; Twardosz & Bell, 2012). What are the limitations and advances in the young child's ability to pay attention to the environment, to remember, to develop strategies and solve problems, and to understand their own mental processes and those of others?

Attention   Recall from Chapter 6, "Cognitive Development in Infancy," that *attention* was defined as the focusing of mental resources on select information. The child's ability to pay attention improves significantly during the preschool years (Bell & Cuevas, 2013; Rothbart, 2011). Toddlers wander around, shift attention from one activity to another, and seem to spend little time focused on any one object or event. By comparison, the preschool child might be observed watching television for a half hour or longer. A recent research study revealed that watching television and playing video games were both linked to attention problems in children (Swing & others, 2010).

What are some advances in children's attention in early childhood?

(a)

(b)

FIGURE **7.11**

THE PLANFULNESS OF ATTENTION. In one study, children were given pairs of houses to examine, like the ones shown here (Vurpillot, 1968). For three pairs of houses, what was in the windows was identical (*a*). For the other three pairs, the windows had different items in them (*b*). By filming the reflection in the children's eyes, it could be determined what they were looking at, how long they looked, and the sequence of their eye movements. Children under 6 examined only a fragmentary portion of each display and made their judgments on the basis of insufficient information. By contrast, older children scanned the windows in more detailed ways and were more accurate in their judgments of which windows were identical.

Young children especially make advances in two aspects of attention—executive attention and sustained attention (Bell & Cuevas, 2013; Rothbart, 2011). **Executive attention** involves action planning, allocating attention to goals, error detection and compensation, monitoring progress on tasks, and dealing with novel or difficult circumstances. **Sustained attention** is focused and extended engagement with an object, task, event, or other aspect of the environment.

Mary Rothbart and Maria Gartstein (2008, p. 332) recently described why advances in executive and sustained attention are so important in early childhood:

> The development of the . . . executive attention system supports the rapid increases in effortful control in the toddler and preschool years. Increases in attention are due, in part, to advances in comprehension and language development. As children are better able to understand their environment, this increased appreciation of their surroundings helps them to sustain attention for longer periods of time.

In at least two ways, however, the preschool child's control of attention is still deficient:

- *Salient versus relevant dimensions.* Preschool children are likely to pay attention to stimuli that stand out, or are *salient,* even when those stimuli are not relevant to solving a problem or performing a task. For example, if a flashy, attractive clown presents the directions for solving a problem, preschool children are likely to pay more attention to the clown than to the directions. After the age of 6 or 7, children attend more efficiently to the dimensions of the task that are relevant, such as the directions for solving a problem. This change reflects a shift to cognitive control of attention, so that children act less impulsively and reflect more.

- *Planfulness.* When experimenters ask children to judge whether two complex pictures are the same, preschool children tend to use a haphazard comparison strategy, not examining all of the details before making a judgment. By comparison, elementary school age children are more likely to systematically compare the details across the pictures, one detail at a time (Vurpillot, 1968) (see Figure 7.11).

In Central European countries, such as Hungary, kindergarten children participate in exercises designed to improve their attention (Mills & Mills, 2000; Posner & Rothbart, 2007). For example, in one eye-contact exercise, the teacher sits in the center of a circle of children and each child is required to catch the teacher's eye before being permitted to leave the group. In other exercises created to improve attention, teachers have children participate in stop-go activities during which they have to listen for a specific signal, such as a drumbeat or an exact number of rhythmic beats, before stopping the activity.

Computer exercises recently have been developed to improve children's attention (Jaeggi, Berman, & Jonides, 2009; Tang & Posner, 2009). For example, one study revealed that five days of computer exercises that involved learning how to use a joystick, working memory, and the resolution of conflict improved the attention of 4- to 6-year-old children (Rueda & others, 2005). Although not commercially available, further information about computer exercises for improving children's attention is available at www.teach-the-brain.org/learn/attention/index.

The ability of preschool children to control and sustain their attention is related to school readiness (Posner & Rothbart, 2007). For example, a study of more than 1,000 children revealed that their ability to sustain their attention at 54 months of age was linked to their school readiness (which included achievement and language skills) (NICHD Early Child Care Research Network, 2005). And in another study children whose parents and teachers rated them higher on a scale of having attention problems at 54 months of age had a lower level of social skills in peer relations in the first and third grades than their counterparts who were rated lower on the attention problems scale at 54 months of age (NICHD Early Child Care Research Network, 2009).

Memory *Memory*—the retention of information over time—is a central process in children's cognitive development. In Chapter 5, we saw that most of a young infant's memories are fragile and, for the most part, short-lived—except for the memory of perceptual-motor actions, which can be substantial (Bauer, 2013; Bauer & Fivush, 2013). Thus, we saw that to understand the infant's capacity to remember we need to distinguish *implicit memory* from *explicit memory*. Explicit memory itself, however, comes in many forms. One distinction occurs between relatively permanent or long-term memory and short-term memory.

Short-Term Memory   In **short-term memory,** individuals retain information for up to 30 seconds if there is no rehearsal of the information. Using rehearsal (repeating information after it has been presented), we can keep information in short-term memory for a much longer period. One method of assessing short-term memory is the memory-span task. You hear a short list of stimuli—usually digits—presented at a rapid pace (one per second, for example). Then you are asked to repeat the digits.

Research with the memory-span task suggests that short-term memory increases during early childhood. For example, in one investigation memory span increased from about 2 digits in 2- to 3-year-old children to about 5 digits in 7-year-old children, yet between 7 and 13 years of age memory span increased only by 2 more digits (Dempster, 1981) (see Figure 7.12). Keep in mind, though, that memory span varies from one individual to another.

Why does memory span change with age? Rehearsal of information is important; older children rehearse the digits more than younger children do. Speed—especially the speed with which memory items can be identified—and efficiency of processing information are important, too (Schneider, 2011).

The speed-of-processing explanation highlights a key point in the information-processing perspective: The speed with which a child processes information is an important aspect of the child's cognitive abilities, and there is abundant evidence that the speed with which many cognitive tasks are completed improves dramatically across the childhood years (Kail, 2007).

How Accurate Are Young Children's Long-Term Memories?   While toddlers' short-term memory span increases during the early childhood years, their memory also becomes more accurate. Young children can remember a great deal of information if they are given appropriate cues and prompts (Ghetti & Bauer, 2012; Riggins, 2012). Increasingly, young children are even being allowed to testify in court, especially if they are the sole witnesses to abuse, a crime, and so forth (Bruck & Ceci, 2012). Several factors can influence the accuracy of a young child's memory (Bruck & Ceci, 1999):

- *There are age differences in children's susceptibility to suggestion.* Preschoolers are the most suggestible age group in comparison with older children and adults (Lehman & others, 2010). For example, preschool children are more susceptible to believing misleading or incorrect information given after an event (Ghetti & Alexander, 2004). Despite these age differences, there is still concern about the reaction of older children when they are subjected to suggestive interviews (Bruck & Ceci, 2012).
- *There are individual differences in susceptibility.* Some preschoolers are highly resistant to interviewers' suggestions, whereas others immediately succumb to the slightest suggestion (Ceci & Klemfuss, 2010). One study revealed that preschool children's ability to produce a high-quality narrative was linked to their resistance to suggestion (Kulkofsky & Klemfuss, 2008).
- *Interviewing techniques can produce substantial distortions in children's reports about highly salient events.* Children are suggestible not just about peripheral details but also about the central aspects of an event (Bruck & Ceci, 2012; Malloy & others, 2012). In some cases, children's false reports can be tinged with sexual connotations. In laboratory studies, young children have made false claims about "silly events" that involved body contact (such as "Did the nurse lick your knee?" or "Did she blow in your ear?"). A significant number of preschool children have falsely reported that someone touched their private parts, kissed them, and hugged them, when these events clearly did not happen in the research. Nonetheless, young children are capable of recalling much that is relevant about an event (Fivush, 1993). When young children do accurately recall information about an event, the interviewer often has a neutral tone, there is limited use of misleading questions, and there is an absence of any motivation for the child to make a false report (Bruck & Ceci, 2012).

In sum, whether a young child's eyewitness testimony is accurate or not may depend on a number of factors such as the type, number, and intensity of the suggestive techniques the

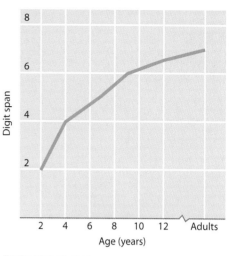

FIGURE **7.12**

DEVELOPMENTAL CHANGES IN MEMORY SPAN. In one study, from 2 years of age to 7 years of age children's memory span increased about 2 digits to 5 digits (Dempster, 1981). Between 7 and 13 years of age, memory span had increased on average only another 2 digits, to 7 digits. *What factors might contribute to the increase in memory span during childhood?*

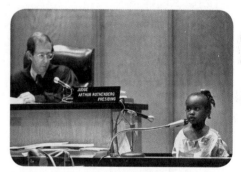

Four-year-old Jennifer Royal was the only eyewitness to one of her playmates' being shot to death. She was allowed to testify in open court, and the clarity of her statements helped to convict the gunman. *What are some issues involved in deciding whether young children should be allowed to testify in court?*

executive attention Involves action planning, allocating attention to goals, error detection and compensation, monitoring progress on tasks, and dealing with novel or difficult circumstances.

sustained attention Focused and extended engagement with an object, task, event, or other aspect of the environment.

short-term memory The memory component in which individuals retain information for up to 30 seconds, assuming there is no rehearsal of the information.

child has experienced (Lamb & Malloy, 2013; La Rooy, Malloy, & Lamb, 2012; Orbach & others, 2012). It appears that the reliability of young children's reports has as much to do with the skills and motivation of the interviewer as with any natural limitations on young children's memory (Bruck & Ceci, 2012).

Executive Function   Recently, increasing attention has been given to the development of children's **executive functioning,** an umbrella-like concept that consists of a number of higher-level cognitive processes linked to the development of the brain's prefrontal cortex. Executive functioning involves managing one's thoughts to engage in goal-directed behavior and self control. Earlier in this chapter, we described the recent interest in *executive attention*, which comes under the umbrella of executive functioning.

In early childhood, executive functioning especially involves developmental advances in cognitive inhibition (such as inhibiting a strong tendency that is incorrect), cognitive flexibility (such as shifting attention to another item or topic), goal-setting (such as sharing a toy or mastering a skill like catching a ball), and delay of gratification (waiting longer to get a more attractive reward, for example) (Beck & others, 2011; Carlson, 2010, 2011; Carlson & White, 2013; Carlson, Zelazo, & Faja, 2013; Conway & Stifter, 2012; Zelazo & Muller, 2011). During early childhood, the relatively stimulus-driven toddler is transformed into a child capable of flexible, goal-directed problem solving that characterizes executive functioning (Zelazo & Muller, 2011).

Stephanie Carlson (2010, 2011) has conducted a number of research studies on young children's executive functioning. In one study, Carlson and her colleagues (2005) gave young children a task called Less Is More, in which they are shown two trays of candy—one with five pieces, the other with two—and they are told that the tray they pick will be given to a stuffed animal seated at the table (see Figure 7.13). Three-year-olds consistently selected the tray with five pieces of candy, thus giving away more candy than they kept for themselves. However, 4-year-olds were far more likely to give away the tray with only two pieces of candy, keeping five pieces for themselves, and thus inhibiting their impulsiveness far better than the 3-year-olds. In another study, young children were read either *Planet Opposite*—a fantasy book in which everything is turned upside down—or *Fun Town*—a reality-oriented fiction book (Carlson & White, 2011). After being read one of the books, the young children completed the Less Is More Task. Sixty percent of the 3-year-olds who heard the *Planet Opposite* story gave away the five pieces of candy compared with only 20 percent of their counterparts who heard the more straightforward story. The results indicated that learning about a topsy-turvy imaginary world likely helped the young children become more flexible in their thinking.

Researchers have found that advances in executive functioning during the preschool years are linked with school readiness (Bierman & others, 2008). Significant advances in the development of executive functioning occur in middle and late childhood (Diamond, 2013). Adult-level executive functioning emerges in early adolescence on many tasks, but on some tasks executive functioning continues to improve during the adult years (Zelazo & Muller, 2011).

Some developmental psychologists use their training in areas such as cognitive development to pursue careers in applied areas. To read about the work of Helen Hadani, an individual who has followed this path, see the *Connecting with Careers* profile.

The Child's Theory of Mind   Even young children are curious about the nature of the human mind (Apperly, 2012; Astington & Hughes, 2013; Wellman, 2011). They have a **theory of mind,** which refers to awareness of one's own mental processes and the mental processes of others. Studies of theory of mind view the child as "a thinker who is trying to explain, predict, and understand people's thoughts, feelings, and utterances" (Harris, 2006, p. 847).

Developmental Changes   Children's theory of mind changes as they develop through childhood (Gelman, 2013; Miller, 2012; Wellman, 2011). Although whether infants have a theory of mind continues to be questioned by some (Rakoczy, 2012), the consensus is that some changes occur quite early in development, as we see next.

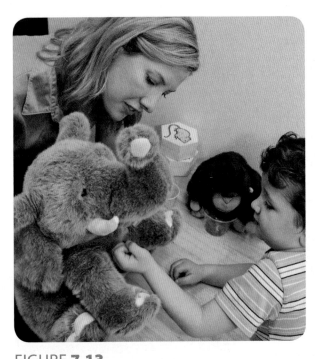

FIGURE **7.13**
STUDYING EXECUTIVE FUNCTIONING IN YOUNG CHILDREN.
Researcher Stephanie Carlson administers the Less Is More task to a 4-year-old boy. *What were the results of Carlson's research?*

executive functioning An umbrella-like concept that consists of a number of higher-level cognitive processes linked to the development of the brain's prefrontal cortex. Executive functioning involves managing one's thoughts to engage in goal-directed behavior and self-control.

theory of mind Awareness of one's own mental processes and the mental processes of others.

Helen Hadani, Developmental Psychologist, Toy Designer, and LANGO Regional Director

Helen Hadani obtained a Ph.D. from Stanford University in developmental psychology. As a graduate student at Stanford, she worked part-time for Hasbro Toys testing its children's software on preschoolers. Her first job after graduate school was with Zowie Entertainment, which was subsequently bought by LEGO. In her work as a toy designer there, Helen conducted experiments and focus groups at different stages of a toy's development, as well as studying the age-effectiveness of the toy. In Helen's words, "Even in a toy's most primitive stage of development . . . you see children's creativity in responding to challenges, their satisfaction when a problem is solved or simply their delight in having fun" (Schlegel, 2000, p. 50).

More recently, she began working for LANGO, a company established on the premise that every American child should learn a foreign language. LANGO uses music, games, and art to help children learn a second language. Helen is currently a regional director for LANGO.

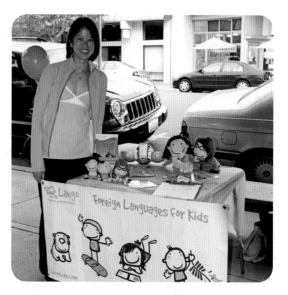

Helen Hadani, a developmental psychologist, with some of the toys and materials for guiding children in learning a second language.

From 18 months to 3 years of age, children begin to understand three mental states:

- *Perceptions.* By 2 years of age, a child recognizes that another person will see what's in front of her own eyes instead of what's in front of the child's eyes (Lempers, Flavell, & Flavell, 1977), and by 3 years of age, the child realizes that looking leads to knowing what's inside a container (Pratt & Bryant, 1990).

- *Emotions.* The child can distinguish between positive (for example, happy) and negative (sad, for example) emotions. A child might say, "Tommy feels bad."

- *Desires.* All humans have some sort of desires. But when do children begin to recognize that someone else's desires may differ from their own? Toddlers recognize that if people want something, they will try to get it. For instance, a child might say, "I want my mommy."

Two- to three-year-olds understand the way that desires are related to actions and to simple emotions. For example, they understand that people will search for what they want and that if they obtain it, they are likely to feel happy, but if they don't, they will keep searching for it and are likely to feel sad or angry (Wellman & Woolley, 1990). Children also refer to desires earlier and more frequently than they refer to cognitive states such as thinking and knowing (Bartsch & Wellman, 1995).

One of the landmark developments in understanding others' desires is recognizing that someone else may have different desires from one's own (Doherty, 2008). Eighteen-month-olds understand that their own food preferences may not match the preferences of others—they will give an adult the food to which she says "Yummy!" even if the food is something that the infants detest (Repacholi & Gopnik, 1997). As they get older, they can verbalize that they themselves do not like something but an adult might (Flavell & others, 1992).

Between the ages of 3 and 5, children come to understand that the mind can represent objects and events accurately or inaccurately (Low & Simpson, 2012). The realization that people can have *false beliefs*—beliefs that are not true—develops in a majority of children by the time they are 5 years old (Wellman, Cross, & Watson, 2001) (see Figure 7.14). This point

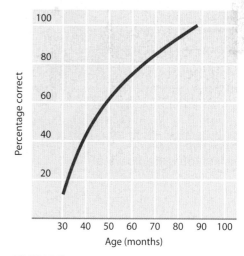

FIGURE **7.14**

DEVELOPMENTAL CHANGES IN FALSE-BELIEF PERFORMANCE. False-belief performance—the child's understanding that a person has a false belief that contradicts reality—dramatically increases from 2½ years of age through the middle of the elementary school years. In a summary of the results of many studies, 2½-year-olds gave incorrect responses about 80 percent of the time (Wellman, Cross, & Watson, 2001). At 3 years, 8 months, they were correct about 50 percent of the time, and after that, they gave increasingly correct responses.

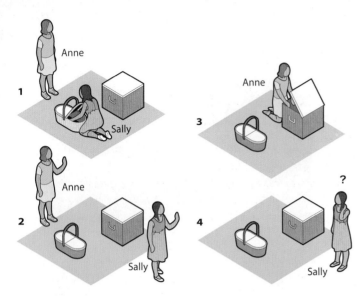

FIGURE 7.15

THE SALLY AND ANNE FALSE-BELIEF TASK. In the false-belief task, the skit above in which Sally has a basket and Anne has a box is shown to children. Sally places a toy in her basket and then leaves. While Sally is gone and can't watch, Anne removes the toy from Sally's basket and places it in her box. Sally then comes back and the children are asked where they think Sally will look for her toy. Children are said to "pass" the false-belief task if they understand that Sally looks in her basket first before realizing the toy isn't there.

FIGURE 7.16

AMBIGUOUS LINE DRAWING

is often described as a pivotal one in understanding the mind—recognizing that beliefs are not just mapped directly into the mind from the surrounding world, but that different people can also have different, and sometimes incorrect, beliefs (Gelman, 2009). In a classic false-belief task, young children were shown a Band-Aids box and asked what was inside (Jenkins & Astington, 1996). To the children's surprise, the box actually contained pencils. When asked what a child who had never seen the box would think was inside, 3-year-olds typically responded, "Pencils." However, the 4- and 5-year-olds, grinning at the anticipation of the false beliefs of other children who had not seen what was inside the box, were more likely to say "Band-Aids."

In a similar task, children are told a story about Sally and Anne: Sally places a toy in a basket and then leaves the room (see Figure 7.15). In her absence, Anne takes the toy from the basket and places it in a box. Children are asked where Sally will look for the toy when she returns. The major finding is that 3-year-olds tend to fail false-belief tasks, saying that Sally will look in the box (even though Sally could not have known that the toy has moved to this new location). Four-year-olds and older children tend to perform the task correctly, saying that Sally will have a "false belief"—she will think the object is in the basket, even though that belief is now false. The conclusion from these studies is that children younger than 4 years old do not understand that it is possible to have a false belief.

However, there are many reasons to question the focus on this one supposedly pivotal moment in the development of a theory of mind. For example, the false-belief task is a complicated one that involves a number of factors such as the characters in the story and all of their individual actions (Bloom & German, 2000).

It is only beyond the preschool years—at approximately 5 to 7 years of age—that children have a deepening appreciation of the mind itself rather than just an understanding of mental states. For example, they begin to recognize that people's behaviors do not necessarily reflect their thoughts and feelings (Flavell, Green, & Flavell, 1993). Not until middle and late childhood do children see the mind as an active constructor of knowledge or processing center (Flavell, Green, & Flavell, 1998) and move from understanding that beliefs can be false to realizing that the same event can be open to multiple interpretations (Carpendale & Chandler, 1996). For example, in one study, children saw an ambiguous line drawing (for example, a drawing that could be seen as either a duck or a rabbit); one puppet told the child she believed the drawing was a duck while another puppet told the child he believed the drawing was a rabbit (see Figure 7.16). Before the age of 7, children said that there was one right answer, and it was not okay for both puppets to have different opinions.

Although most research on children's theory of mind focuses on children around or before their preschool years, at 7 years of age and beyond there are important developments in the ability to understand the beliefs and thoughts of others (Apperly, 2012; Miller, 2012). While understanding that people may have different interpretations is important, it is also necessary to recognize that some interpretations and beliefs may still be evaluated on the basis of the merits of arguments and evidence (Kuhn, Cheney, & Weinstock, 2000). In early adolescence, children begin to understand that people can have ambivalent feelings (Flavell & Miller, 1998). They start to recognize that the same person can feel both happy and sad about the same event. They also engage in more recursive thinking: thinking about what other people are thinking about.

Individual Differences As in other developmental research, there are individual differences in the ages when children reach certain milestones in their theory of mind (Pellicano, 2010). For example, children who talk with their parents about feelings frequently as 2-year-olds show better performance on theory of mind tasks (Ruffman, Slade, & Crowe, 2002), as do children who frequently engage in pretend play (Harris, 2000).

connecting through research

How Does Theory of Mind Differ in Children with Autism?

Approximately 1 in 150 children is estimated to have some sort of autism spectrum disorder (National Autism Association, 2011). Autism can usually be diagnosed by the age of 3 years, and sometimes earlier. Children with autism show a number of behaviors different from typically developing children their age, including deficits in social interaction and communication as well as repetitive behaviors or interests. They often show indifference toward others, in many instances preferring to be alone and showing more interest in objects than people.

What causes the autism spectrum disorders? The current consensus is that autism is a brain dysfunction with abnormalities in brain structure and neurotransmitters (Bosl & others, 2011; Shukla & others, 2011). Genetic factors likely play a role in the development of the autism spectrum disorders (Ronald & Hoekstra, 2011).

Children and adults with autism have difficulty in social interactions (Scheeren, Koot, & Begeer, 2012). These deficits are generally greater than deficits in children of the same mental age with mental retardation (Baron-Cohen, 2011). Researchers have found that children with autism have difficulty in developing a theory of mind, especially in understanding others' beliefs and emotions (Boucher, 2012a). Although children with autism tend to do poorly when reasoning about false-belief tasks and task sequencing (Peterson, 2005; Peterson, Wellman, & Slaughter, 2012), they can perform much

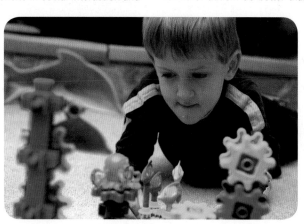

A young boy with autism. *What are some characteristics of autistic children? What are some deficits in autistic children's theory of mind?*

better on reasoning tasks that require an understanding of physical causality.

However, it is important to consider individual variations in children with autism and particular aspects of theory of mind (Harris, 2006; Matthews & others, 2012). Children with autism are not a homogeneous group and some have less severe social and communication problems than others. Thus, it is not surprising that children who have less severe forms of autism do better than those who have more severe forms of the disorder on some theory of mind tasks. For example, higher-functioning children with autism show reasonable progress in understanding others' desires (Harris, 2006).

A further important consideration in thinking about autism and theory of mind is that children with autism might have difficulty in understanding others' beliefs and emotions not solely due to theory of mind deficits but to other aspects of cognition such as problems in focusing attention, eye gaze, face recognition, memory, language impairment, or some general intellectual impairment (Boucher, 2012b; Boucher, Mayes, & Bigham, 2012; Elsabbagh & others, 2012).

Some recent theories of autism suggest that weaknesses in executive functioning are linked to autism and may relate to the problems those with autism have on theory of mind tasks (Just & others, 2012). Other theories have pointed out that typically developing individuals process information by extracting the big picture, whereas those with autism process information in a very detailed, almost obsessive way (Wang & others, 2012). It may be that in autism, a number of different but related deficits lead to social cognitive deficits.

Executive function, which describes several functions (such as inhibition and planning) that are important for flexible, future-oriented behavior, also may be connected to theory of mind development (Carroll & others, 2012; Ford & others, 2012; Muller & others, 2012). For example, in one executive function task, children are asked to say the word "night" when they see a picture of a sun, and the word "day" when they see a picture of a moon and stars. Children who perform better at executive function tasks seem also to have a better understanding of theory of mind (Sabbagh & others, 2006).

Another individual difference in understanding the mind involves autism. To learn how theory of mind differs in children with autism, see *Connecting Through Research*.

Review

- What characterizes Piaget's stage of preoperational thought?
- What does Vygotsky's theory suggest about how preschool children construct knowledge?
- What are some important ways in which information processing changes during early childhood? What characterizes children's theory of mind?

Connect

- In this section, you learned that children who frequently engage in pretend play

perform better on theory of mind tasks. During which substage of Piaget's preoperational stage do children begin to engage in pretend play? What mental ability does it signify?

Reflect *Your Own Personal Journey of Life*

- If you were the parent of a 4-year-old child, would you try to train the child to develop conservation skills? Explain.

3 Language Development

LG3 Summarize how language develops in early childhood.

| Understanding Phonology and Morphology | Changes in Syntax and Semantics | Advances in Pragmatics | Young Children's Literacy |

The greatest poem ever known
Is one all poets have outgrown;
The poetry, innate, untold,
Of being only four years old.

—**Christopher Morley**
American Novelist, 20th Century

Toddlers move rather quickly from producing two-word utterances to creating three-, four-, and five-word combinations. Between 2 and 3 years of age, they begin the transition from saying simple sentences that express a single proposition to saying complex sentences.

As young children learn the special features of their own language, there are extensive regularities in how they acquire that particular language (Berko Gleason, 2009; Wagner & Hoff, 2013; Waxman & Goswami, 2012). For example, all children learn the prepositions *on* and *in* before other prepositions. Children learning other languages, such as Russian or Chinese, also acquire the particular features of those languages in a consistent order.

UNDERSTANDING PHONOLOGY AND MORPHOLOGY

During the preschool years, most children gradually become more sensitive to the sounds of spoken words and become increasingly capable of producing all the sounds of their language (Zhou & others, 2012). By the time children are 3 years of age, they can produce all the vowel sounds and most of the consonant sounds (Menn & Stoel-Gammon, 2009).

As children move beyond two-word utterances, they demonstrate a knowledge of morphology rules (Park & others, 2012). Children begin using the plural and possessive forms of nouns (such as *dogs* and *dog's*). They put appropriate endings on verbs (such as *-s* when the subject is third-person singular and *-ed* for the past tense). They use prepositions (such as *in* and *on*), articles (such as *a* and *the*), and various forms of the verb *to be* (such as "I *was* going to the store"). Some of the best evidence for changes in children's use of morphological rules occurs in their overgeneralization of the rules, as when a preschool child says "foots" instead of "feet," or "goed" instead of "went."

In a classic experiment that was designed to study children's knowledge of morphological rules, such as how to make a plural, Jean Berko (1958) presented preschool children and first-grade children with cards such as the one shown in Figure 7.17. Children were asked to look at the card while the experimenter read aloud the words on the card. Then the children were asked to supply the missing word. This might sound easy, but Berko was interested in the children's ability to apply the appropriate morphological rule, in this case to say "wugs" with the *z* sound that indicates the plural.

Although the children's answers were not perfect, they were much better than chance. What makes Berko's study impressive is that most of the words were made up for the experiment. Thus, the children could not base their responses on remembering past instances of hearing the words. That they could make the plurals or past tenses of words they had never heard before was proof that they knew the morphological rules.

CHANGES IN SYNTAX AND SEMANTICS

Preschool children also learn and apply rules of syntax (de Villiers & de Villiers, 2013; Gertner & Fisher, 2012; Kidd, 2012). They show a growing mastery of complex rules for how words should be ordered. Consider *wh-* questions, such as "Where is Daddy going?" or "What is that boy doing?" To ask these questions properly, the child must know two important differences between *wh-* questions and affirmative statements (for instance, "Daddy is going to work" and "That boy is waiting on the school bus"). First, a *wh-* word must be added at the beginning of the sentence. Second, the auxiliary verb must be inverted—that is, exchanged with the subject of the sentence. Young children learn quite early where to put the *wh-* word, but they take much longer to learn the auxiliary-inversion rule. Thus, preschool children might ask, "Where Daddy is going?" and "What that boy is doing?"

Gains in semantics also characterize early childhood. Vocabulary development is dramatic (Pan & Uccelli, 2009). Some experts have concluded that between 18 months and 6 years of age, young children learn about one new word every waking hour (Gelman & Kalish, 2006). By the time they enter first grade, it is estimated that children know about 14,000 words (Clark, 1993).

What are some important aspects of how word learning optimally occurs? Kathy Hirsh-Pasek, Robert Golinkoff, and Justin Harris (Harris, Golinkoff, & Hirsh-Pasek, 2011; Hirsh-Pasek & Golinkoff, 2013) emphasize six key principles in young children's vocabulary development:

1. *Children learn the words they hear most often.* They learn the words that they encounter when interacting with parents, teachers, siblings, peers, as well as words that they hear when books are read aloud to them. They especially benefit from encountering words that they do not know.

2. *Children learn words for things and events that interest them.* Parents and teachers can direct young children to experience words in contexts that interest the children; playful peer interactions are especially helpful in this regard.

3. *Children learn words better in responsive and interactive contexts than in passive contexts.* Children who experience turn-taking opportunities, joint focusing experiences, and positive, sensitive socializing contexts with adults encounter the scaffolding necessary for optimal word learning. They learn words less effectively when they are passive learners.

4. *Children learn words best in contexts that are meaningful.* Young children learn new words more effectively when new words are encountered in integrated contexts rather than as isolated facts.

5. *Children learn words best when they access clear information about word meaning.* Children whose parents and teachers are sensitive to words the children might not understand and provide support and elaboration with hints about word meaning learn words better than those whose parents and teachers quickly state a new word and don't monitor whether children understand its meaning.

6. *Children learn words best when grammar and vocabulary are considered.* Children who experience a large number of words and diversity in verbal stimulation develop a richer vocabulary and better understanding of grammar. In many cases, vocabulary and grammar development are connected.

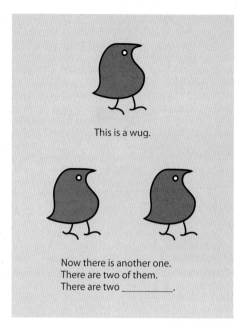

This is a wug.

Now there is another one.
There are two of them.
There are two _____.

FIGURE **7.17**

STIMULI IN BERKO'S STUDY OF YOUNG CHILDREN'S UNDERSTANDING OF MORPHOLOGICAL RULES. In Jean Berko's (1958) study, young children were presented cards, such as this one with a "wug" on it. Then the children were asked to supply the missing word; in supplying the missing word, they had to say it correctly, too. "Wugs" is the correct response here.

developmental **connection**

Language

The average 2-year-old can speak about 200 words. Chapter 5, p. 164

ADVANCES IN PRAGMATICS

Changes in pragmatics also characterize young children's language development (Crain & Zhou, 2012). A 6-year-old is simply a much better conversationalist than a 2-year-old is. What are some of the improvements in pragmatics during the preschool years?

Young children begin to engage in extended discourse (Akhtar & Herold, 2008, p. 581). For example, they learn culturally specific rules of conversation and politeness and become sensitive to the need to adapt their speech in different settings. Their developing linguistic skills and increasing ability to take the perspective of others contribute to their generation of more competent narratives.

As children get older, they become increasingly able to talk about things that are not here (grandma's house, for example) and not now (what happened to them yesterday or might happen tomorrow, for example). A preschool child can tell you what she wants for lunch tomorrow, something that would not have been possible at the two-word stage of language development.

What characterizes young children's advances in pragmatics?

Around 4 to 5 years of age, children learn to change their speech style to suit the situation. For example, even 4-year-old children speak to a 2-year-old differently from the way they speak to a same-aged peer; they use shorter sentences with the 2-year-old. They also speak differently to an adult and to a same-aged peer, using more polite and formal language with the adult (Shatz & Gelman, 1973).

YOUNG CHILDREN'S LITERACY

The concern about the ability of U.S. children to read and write has led to a careful examination of preschool and kindergarten children's experiences, with the hope that a positive orientation toward reading and writing can be developed early in life (Giorgis & Glazer, 2013). Parents and teachers need to provide young children with a supportive environment for developing literacy skills (Morrow, 2012; Tamis-LeMonda & Song, 2013). Children should be active participants and be immersed in a wide range of interesting listening, talking, writing, and reading experiences (Gunning, 2013). One study revealed that children whose mothers had more education had more advanced emergent literacy levels than children whose mothers had less education (Korat, 2009). Another study found that literacy experiences (such as how often the child was read to), the quality of the mother's engagement with her child (such as attempts to cognitively stimulate the child), and provision of learning materials (such as age-appropriate books) were important home literacy experiences in low-income families that were linked to the children's language development in positive ways (Rodriguez & others, 2009). Instruction should be built on what children already know about oral language, reading, and writing. Further, early precursors of literacy and academic success include language skills, phonological and syntactic knowledge, letter identification, and conceptual knowledge about print and its conventions and functions (Gunning, 2013; McGee & Richgels, 2012).

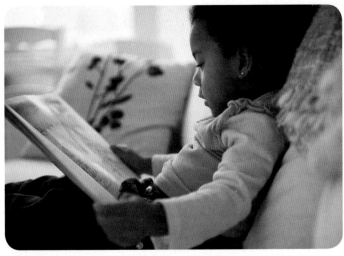

What are positive strategies for improving young children's literacy?

The following three longitudinal studies indicate the importance of early language skills and children's school readiness:

- Phonological awareness, letter name and sound knowledge, and naming speed in kindergarten were linked to reading success in the first and second grade (Schattschneider & others, 2004).
- Children's early home environment influenced their early language skills, which in turn predicted their readiness for school (Forget-Dubois & others, 2009).
- The number of letters children knew in kindergarten was highly correlated (.52) with their reading achievement in high school (Stevenson & Newman, 1986).

So far, our discussion of early literacy has focused on U.S. children. These findings may not apply to children in other countries. For example, the extent to which phonological awareness is linked to learning to read effectively varies across language to some degree (McBride-Chang, 2004). Rates of dyslexia (severe reading disability) differ across countries and are linked with the spelling and phonetic rules that characterize the language (McCardle, Lee, & Tzeng, 2011). English is one of the more difficult languages to learn because of its irregular spellings and pronunciations. In countries where English is spoken, the rate of dyslexia is higher than in countries where the alphabet script is more phonetically pronounced.

Books can be valuable in enhancing children's communication skills (Vukelich, Christie, & Enz, 2012). What are some strategies for using books effectively with preschool children? Ellen Galinsky (2010) recently emphasized these strategies:

- *Use books to initiate conversation with young children.* Ask them to put themselves in the book characters' places and imagine what they might be thinking or feeling.
- *Use what and why questions.* Ask young children what they think is going to happen next in a story and then see if it occurs.
- *Encourage children to ask questions about stories.*
- *Choose some books that play with language.* Creative books on the alphabet, including those with rhymes, often interest young children.

The advances in language that take place in early childhood lay the foundation for later development in the elementary school years, as we will discuss in Chapter 9.

Review *Connect* Reflect

 LG3 Summarize how language develops in early childhood.

Review

- How do phonology and morphology change during early childhood?
- What characterizes young children's understanding of syntax and semantics in early childhood?
- What advances in pragmatics occur in early childhood?
- What are some effective ways to guide young children's literacy?

Connect

- In this section, you learned that children can sometimes overgeneralize the rules for morphology. How is this different from or similar to the concept of overextension as it relates to infants' speech (covered in Chapter 5)?

Reflect *Your Own Personal Journey of Life*

- As a parent, what could you to do to improve the likelihood that your child would enter first grade with excellent literacy skills?

4 Early Childhood Education

 LG4 Evaluate different approaches to early childhood education.

| Variations in Early Childhood Education | Education for Young Children Who Are Disadvantaged | Controversies in Early Childhood Education |

To the teachers in a Reggio Emilia program (described in the chapter opening), preschool children are active learners who are engaged in exploring the world with their peers, constructing their knowledge of the world in collaboration with their community, and aided but not directed by the teachers. In many ways, the Reggio Emilia approach applies ideas consistent with the views of Piaget and Vygotsky that were discussed earlier in this chapter. Our exploration of early childhood education focuses on variations in programs, education for young children who are disadvantaged, and some controversies in early childhood education.

What are some characteristics of the child-centered kindergarten?

VARIATIONS IN EARLY CHILDHOOD EDUCATION

Attending preschool is rapidly becoming the norm for U.S. children. There are many variations in the way young children are educated (Feeney, Moravcik, & Nolte, 2013; Henninger, 2013). The foundation of early childhood education has been the child-centered kindergarten.

The Child-Centered Kindergarten   Nurturing is a key aspect of the **child-centered kindergarten,** which emphasizes the education of the whole child and concern for his or her physical, cognitive, and socioemotional development (Frost, Wortham, & Reifel, 2012). Instruction is organized around the child's needs, interests, and learning styles. Emphasis is on the process of learning, rather than what is learned (Moravcik, Nolte, & Feeney, 2012). The child-centered kindergarten honors three principles: Each child follows a unique developmental pattern; young children learn best through first-hand experiences with people and materials; and play is extremely important in the child's total development. *Experimenting, exploring, discovering, trying out, restructuring, speaking,* and *listening* are frequent activities in excellent kindergarten programs. Such programs are closely attuned to the developmental status of 4- and 5-year-old children.

The Montessori Approach   Montessori schools are patterned after the educational philosophy of Maria Montessori (1870–1952), an Italian physician-turned-educator who at the beginning of the twentieth century crafted a revolutionary approach to young children's education. The **Montessori approach** is a philosophy of education in which children are given considerable freedom and spontaneity in choosing activities. They are allowed to move from one activity to another as they desire. The teacher acts as a facilitator rather than a director. The teacher shows the child how to perform intellectual activities, demonstrates interesting ways to explore curriculum materials, and offers help when the child requests it (Isaacs, 2012; Murray, 2011). "By encouraging children to make decisions from an early age, Montessori programs seek to develop self-regulated problem solvers who can make choices and manage their time effectively" (Hyson, Copple, & Jones, 2006, p. 14). The number of Montessori schools in the United

Larry Page and Sergey Brin, founders of the highly successful Internet search engine Google said that their early years at Montessori schools were a major factor in their success (International Montessori Council, 2006). During an interview with Barbara Walters, they said they learned how to be self-directed and self-starters at Montessori (ABC News, 2005). They commented that Montessori experiences encouraged them to think for themselves and allowed them the freedom to develop their own interests.

States has expanded dramatically in recent years, from 1 school in 1959 to 355 schools in 1970 to more than 4,000 today.

Some developmentalists favor the Montessori approach, but others believe that it neglects children's socioemotional development. For example, although Montessori fosters independence and the development of cognitive skills, it deemphasizes verbal interaction between the teacher and child and between peers. Montessori's critics also argue that it restricts imaginative play and that its heavy reliance on self-corrective materials may not adequately allow for creativity and for a variety of learning styles.

What are some differences in developmentally appropriate and inappropriate practice?

Developmentally Appropriate and Inappropriate Education

Many educators and psychologists conclude that preschool and young elementary school children learn best through active, hands-on teaching methods such as games and dramatic play. They know that children develop at varying rates and that schools need to allow for these individual differences. They also argue that schools should focus on supporting children's socioemotional development as well as their cognitive development. Educators refer to this type of schooling as **developmentally appropriate practice (DAP),** which is based on knowledge of the typical development of children within an age span (age-appropriateness), as well as the uniqueness of the child (individual-appropriateness). DAP emphasizes the importance of creating settings that encourage active learning and reflect children's interests and capabilities (Bredekamp, 2011; Morrison, 2012). Desired outcomes for DAP include thinking critically, working cooperatively, solving problems, developing self-regulatory skills, and enjoying learning. The emphasis in DAP is on the process of learning rather than its content (Bredekamp, 2011). The most recent developmentally appropriate guidelines provided by the National Association for the Education of Young Children (NAEYC, 2009) are summarized in Figure 7.18.

Do developmentally appropriate educational practices improve young children's development? Some researchers have found that young children in developmentally appropriate classrooms are likely to have less stress, be more motivated, be more skilled socially, have better work habits, be more creative, have better language skills, and demonstrate better math skills than children in developmentally inappropriate classrooms (Hart & others, 2003). However, not all studies show significant positive benefits for developmentally appropriate education (Hyson, Copple, & Jones, 2006). Among the reasons it is difficult to generalize about research on developmentally appropriate education is that individual programs often vary, and developmentally appropriate education is an evolving concept. Recent changes in the concept have given more attention to sociocultural factors, to the teacher's active involvement and implementation of systematic intentions, and to how strong academic skills should be emphasized and how they should be taught.

EDUCATION FOR YOUNG CHILDREN WHO ARE DISADVANTAGED

For many years, U.S. children from low-income families did not receive any education before they entered the first grade. Often, they began first grade already several steps behind their classmates in their readiness to learn. In the summer of 1965, the federal government began an effort to break the cycle of poverty and poor education for young children in the United States through **Project Head Start.** It is a compensatory program designed to provide children from low-income families the opportunity to acquire the skills and experiences important for success in school (Hustedt, Friedman, & Barnett, 2012; Zigler & Styfco, 2010). After almost half a century, Head Start continues to be the largest federally funded program for U.S. children with almost 1 million U.S. children enrolled annually (Hagen & Lamb-Parker, 2008). In 2007, 3 percent of Head Start children were 5 years old, 51 percent were 4 years old, 36 percent were 3 years old, and 10 percent were under 3 years of age (Administration for Children & Families, 2008).

Early Head Start was established in 1995 to serve children from birth to 3 years of age. In 2007, half of all new funds appropriated for Head Start programs were used for the expansion of Early Head Start. Researchers have found positive effects for Early Head Start (Hoffman & Ewen, 2007). A recent study revealed that Early Head Start had a protective effect on risks

child-centered kindergarten Education that involves the whole child by considering both the child's physical, cognitive, and socioemotional development and the child's needs, interests, and learning styles.

Montessori approach An educational philosophy in which children are given considerable freedom and spontaneity in choosing activities and are allowed to move from one activity to another as they desire.

developmentally appropriate practice Education that focuses on the typical developmental patterns of children (age-appropriateness) and the uniqueness of each child (individual-appropriateness).

Project Head Start A government-funded program that is designed to provide children from low-income families with the opportunity to acquire the skills and experiences important for school success.

Core Considerations in Developmentally Appropriate Practice

1 Knowledge to Consider in Making Decisions

In all aspects of working with children, early childhood practitioners need to consider these three areas of knowledge: 1) What is known about child development and learning, especially age-related characteristics; 2) What is known about each child as an individual; and 3) What is known about the social and cultural contexts in which children live.

2 Challenging and Achievable Goals

Keeping in mind desired goals and what is known about the children as a group and individually, teachers plan experiences to promote children's learning and development.

Principles of Child Development and Learning That Inform Practice

1 All the domains of development and learning—physical, cognitive, and social—are important, and they are linked.

2 Many aspects of children's learning and development follow well-documented sequences, with later abilities, skills, and knowledge building on those already acquired.

3 Development and learning proceed at varying rates from child to child, and at uneven rates across different areas of a child's individual functioning.

4 Development and learning result from the interaction of biology and experience.

5 Early experiences have strong effects—both cumulative and delayed—on children's development and learning; optimal periods exist for certain types of development and learning.

6 Development proceeds toward greater complexity, self-regulation, and symbolic or representational capacities.

7 Children develop best when they have secure, consistent relationships with responsive adults and opportunities for positive peer relations.

8 Development and learning occur in and are influenced by multiple social and cultural contexts.

9 Always mentally active in seeking to understand the world around them, children learn in a variety of ways; a wide range of teaching strategies can be effective in guiding children's learning.

10 Play is an important context for developing self-regulation and for promoting language, cognition, and competence.

11 Development and learning advance when children are challenged to achieve at a level just beyond their current mastery and when they are given opportunities to practice newly acquired skills.

12 Children's experiences shape their motivation and approaches to learning, such as persistence, initiative, and flexibility; in turn, these characteristics influence their learning and development.

Guidelines for Developmentally Appropriate Practice

1 Creating a Caring Community of Learners

Each member of the community should be valued by the others; relationships are an important context through which children learn; practitioners ensure that members of the community feel psychologically safe.

2 Teaching to Enhance Development and Learning

The teacher takes responsibility for stimulating, directing, and supporting children's learning by providing the experiences that each child needs.

3 Planning Curriculum to Achieve Important Goals

The curriculum is planned to help children achieve goals that are developmentally appropriate and educationally significant.

4 Assessing Children's Development and Learning

In developmentally appropriate practice, assessments are linked to the program's goals for children.

5 Establishing Reciprocal Relationships with Families

A positive partnership between teachers and families benefits children's learning and development.

FIGURE **7.18**

RECOMMENDATIONS BY NAEYC FOR DEVELOPMENTALLY APPROPRIATE PRACTICE IN EARLY CHILDHOOD PROGRAMS SERVING CHILDREN FROM BIRTH THROUGH AGE 8

Source: NAEYC (2009). Developmentally appropriate practice in early childhood programs serving children from birth through age 8. Washington, DC: NAEYC

young children might experience in parenting stress, language development, and self-control (Ayoub, Vallotton, & Mastergeorge, 2011).

Head Start programs are not all created equal. One estimate is that 40 percent of the 1,400 Head Start programs are of questionable quality (Zigler & Styfco, 1994). More attention needs to be given to developing consistently high-quality Head Start programs (Hillemeier & others, 2012). One individual who is strongly motivated to make Head Start a valuable learning experience for young children from disadvantaged backgrounds is Yolanda Garcia. To read about her work, see *Connecting with Careers*.

Evaluations support the positive influence of quality early childhood programs on both the cognitive and social worlds of disadvantaged young children (Lamy, 2012; Ryan, Fauth, & Brooks-Gunn, 2006). A recent national evaluation of Head Start revealed that the program had a positive influence on language and cognitive development (Puma & others, 2010). By the end of the first grade there were some lasting outcomes—better vocabulary for those who

Yolanda Garcia, Director of Children's Services/Head Start

Yolanda Garcia has been the Director of the Children's Services Department for the Santa Clara, California, County Office of Education since 1980. As director, she is responsible for managing child development programs for 2,500 3- to 5-year-old children in 127 classrooms. Her training includes two master's degrees, one in public policy and child welfare from the University of Chicago and another in education administration from San Jose State University.

Garcia has served on many national advisory committees that have resulted in improvements in the staffing of Head Start programs. Most notably, she served on the Head Start Quality Committee that recommended the development of Early Head Start and revised performance standards for Head Start programs. Garcia currently is a member of the American Academy of Science Committee on the Integration of Science and Early Childhood Education.

Yolanda Garcia, Director of Children's Services/Head Start, working with a Head Start child in Santa Clara, California.

went to Head Start as 4-year-olds, and better oral comprehension for those who went to Head Start as 3-year-olds. Another recent study found that when young children initially began Head Start, they were well below their more academically advantaged peers in literacy and math (Hindman & others, 2010). However, by the end of first grade the Head Start children were on par with national averages in literacy and math.

One high-quality early childhood education program (although not a Head Start program) is the Perry Preschool program in Ypsilanti, Michigan, a two-year preschool program that includes weekly home visits from program personnel. In analyses of the long-term effects of the program, adults who had been in the Perry Preschool program were compared with a control group of adults from the same background who had not received the enriched early childhood education (Schweinhart & others, 2005; Weikert, 1993). Those who had been in the Perry Preschool program had fewer teen pregnancies and higher high school graduation rates, and at age 40 more were in the workforce, owned their own homes, had a savings account, and had fewer arrests than adults in the control group.

CONTROVERSIES IN EARLY CHILDHOOD EDUCATION

Two current controversies in early childhood education involve (1) what the curriculum for early childhood education should be (Epstein & Barnette, 2012; Moravcik, Nolte, & Feeney, 2012), and (2) whether preschool education should be universal in the United States (Zigler, Gilliam, & Barnett, 2011).

Curriculum Controversy A current controversy in early childhood education involves what the curriculum for early childhood education should be (Moravcik, Nolte, & Feeney, 2012). On one side are those who advocate a child-centered, constructivist approach much like that emphasized by the National Association for the Education of Young Children (NAEYC), along the lines of developmentally appropriate practice. On the other side are those who advocate an academic, direct-instruction approach.

In reality, many high-quality early childhood education programs include both academic and constructivist approaches. Many education experts like Lilian Katz (1999), though, worry about academic approaches that place too much pressure on young children to achieve and don't provide any opportunities to actively construct knowledge. Competent early childhood programs

What is the curriculum controversy in early childhood education?

also should focus on cognitive development *and* socioemotional development, not exclusively on cognitive development (NAEYC, 2009).

Universal Preschool Education   Another early childhood education controversy focuses on whether preschool education should be instituted for all U.S. 4-year-old children. Edward Zigler and his colleagues (2011) recently have argued that the United States should have universal preschool education. They emphasize that quality preschools prepare children for school readiness and academic success. Zigler and his colleagues (2006) cite research that shows quality preschool programs decrease the likelihood that once children go to elementary and secondary school they will be retained in a grade or drop out of school. They also point to analyses indicating that universal preschool would bring cost savings on the order of billions of dollars because of a diminished need for remedial and justice services (Karoly & Bigelow, 2005).

Critics of universal preschool education argue that the gains attributed to preschool and kindergarten education are often overstated. They especially stress that research has not proven that nondisadvantaged children benefit from attending a preschool. Thus, the critics say it is more important to improve preschool education for young children who are disadvantaged rather than funding preschool education for all 4-year-old children. Some critics, especially homeschooling advocates, emphasize that young children should be educated by their parents, not by schools. Thus, controversy continues to surround questions about whether universal preschool education should be implemented.

Review *Connect* Reflect

LG4 Evaluate different approaches to early childhood education.

Review

- What are some variations in early childhood education?
- What are the main efforts to educate young children who are disadvantaged?
- What are two controversies about early childhood education?

Connect

- In Chapter 1 you learned about cross-sectional and longitudinal research designs.

Which type of research design is the Perry Preschool program?

Reflect *Your Own Personal Journey of Life*

- What type of early childhood education program would you want your child to attend? Why?
- What is the curriculum controversy in early childhood education?

topical connections

In the next chapter, you will read about the many advances that take place during the socioemotional development of young children. The cognitive advances we discussed in this chapter, combined with the socioemotional experiences young children have in interacting with others, pave the way for social cognitive advances in understanding the self and others. Then, in Chapter 9 you will read about the continuing changes in children's physical and cognitive development in middle and late childhood. In terms of physical development, their motor skills become smoother and more coordinated. The development of their brain—especially in the prefrontal cortex—provides the foundation for a number of cognitive advances, including the development of learning strategies and reading skills.

looking forward

Physical and Cognitive Development in Early Childhood

1 Physical Changes

LG1 Identify physical changes in early childhood.

Body Growth and Change

Motor Development

Sleep

Nutrition and Exercise

Illness and Death

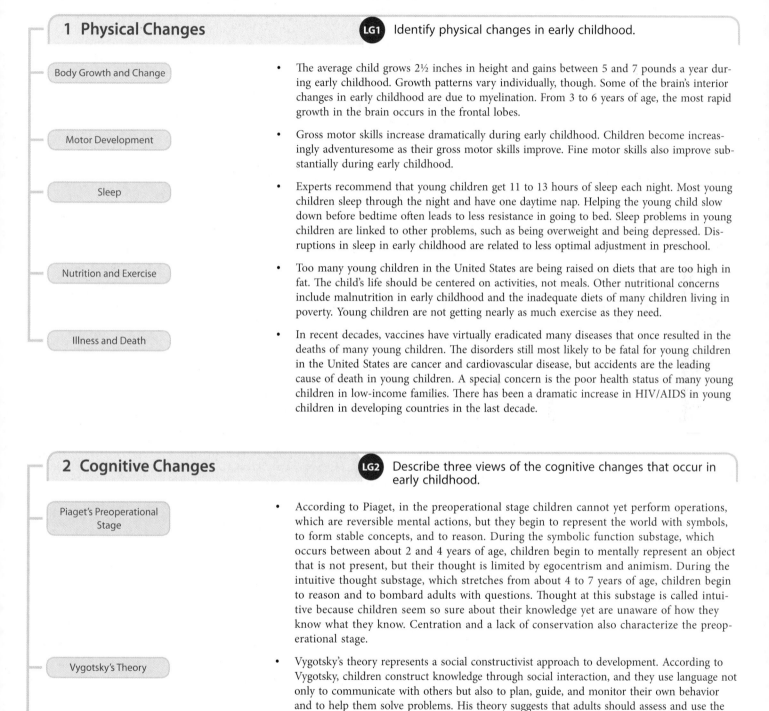

- The average child grows 2½ inches in height and gains between 5 and 7 pounds a year during early childhood. Growth patterns vary individually, though. Some of the brain's interior changes in early childhood are due to myelination. From 3 to 6 years of age, the most rapid growth in the brain occurs in the frontal lobes.

- Gross motor skills increase dramatically during early childhood. Children become increasingly adventuresome as their gross motor skills improve. Fine motor skills also improve substantially during early childhood.

- Experts recommend that young children get 11 to 13 hours of sleep each night. Most young children sleep through the night and have one daytime nap. Helping the young child slow down before bedtime often leads to less resistance in going to bed. Sleep problems in young children are linked to other problems, such as being overweight and being depressed. Disruptions in sleep in early childhood are related to less optimal adjustment in preschool.

- Too many young children in the United States are being raised on diets that are too high in fat. The child's life should be centered on activities, not meals. Other nutritional concerns include malnutrition in early childhood and the inadequate diets of many children living in poverty. Young children are not getting nearly as much exercise as they need.

- In recent decades, vaccines have virtually eradicated many diseases that once resulted in the deaths of many young children. The disorders still most likely to be fatal for young children in the United States are cancer and cardiovascular disease, but accidents are the leading cause of death in young children. A special concern is the poor health status of many young children in low-income families. There has been a dramatic increase in HIV/AIDS in young children in developing countries in the last decade.

2 Cognitive Changes

LG2 Describe three views of the cognitive changes that occur in early childhood.

Piaget's Preoperational Stage

Vygotsky's Theory

- According to Piaget, in the preoperational stage children cannot yet perform operations, which are reversible mental actions, but they begin to represent the world with symbols, to form stable concepts, and to reason. During the symbolic function substage, which occurs between about 2 and 4 years of age, children begin to mentally represent an object that is not present, but their thought is limited by egocentrism and animism. During the intuitive thought substage, which stretches from about 4 to 7 years of age, children begin to reason and to bombard adults with questions. Thought at this substage is called intuitive because children seem so sure about their knowledge yet are unaware of how they know what they know. Centration and a lack of conservation also characterize the preoperational stage.

- Vygotsky's theory represents a social constructivist approach to development. According to Vygotsky, children construct knowledge through social interaction, and they use language not only to communicate with others but also to plan, guide, and monitor their own behavior and to help them solve problems. His theory suggests that adults should assess and use the child's zone of proximal development (ZPD), which is the range of tasks that are too difficult for children to master alone but that can be learned with the guidance and assistance of adults or more-skilled children. The theory also suggests that adults and peers should teach through scaffolding, which involves changing the level of support over the course of a teaching session, with the more-skilled person adjusting guidance to fit the student's current performance level.

- The child's ability to attend to stimuli dramatically improves during early childhood. Advances in executive attention and sustained attention are especially important in early childhood, but the young child still attends to the salient rather than the relevant features of a task. Significant improvement in short-term memory occurs during early childhood. With good prompts, young children's long-term memories can be accurate, although young children can be led into developing false memories. Advances in executive functioning, an umbrella-like concept that consists of a number of higher-level cognitive processes linked to the development of the prefrontal cortex, occur in early childhood. Executive functioning involves managing one's thoughts to engage in goal-directed behavior and self-control. Young children express curiosity about the human mind, and this has been studied under the topic of theory of mind. A number of developmental changes characterize children's theory of mind, including those involved in false beliefs. Individual variations also are involved in theory of mind. For example, autistic children have difficulty developing such a theory.

3 Language Development

 LG3 Summarize how language develops in early childhood.

Understanding Phonology and Morphology

Changes in Syntax and Semantics

Advances in Pragmatics

Young Children's Literacy

- Young children increase their grasp of language's rule systems. In terms of phonology, most young children become more sensitive to the sounds of spoken language. Berko's classic experiment demonstrated that young children understand morphological rules.

- Preschool children learn and apply rules of syntax and of how words should be ordered. In terms of semantics, vocabulary development increases dramatically during early childhood.

- Young children's conversational skills improve, they increase their sensitivity to the needs of others in conversation, and they learn to change their speech style to suit the situation.

- Parents and teachers need to provide young children a supportive environment for them to develop literacy skills. Children should be active participants and be immersed in a wide range of interesting listening, talking, writing, and reading experiences.

4 Early Childhood Education

LG4 Evaluate different approaches to early childhood education.

Variations in Early Childhood Education

Education for Young Children Who Are Disadvantaged

Controversies in Early Childhood Education

- The child-centered kindergarten emphasizes the education of the whole child, with particular attention to individual variation, the process of learning, and the importance of play in development. The Montessori approach allows children to choose from a range of activities while teachers serve as facilitators. Developmentally appropriate practice focuses on the typical patterns of children (age-appropriateness) and the uniqueness of each child (individual-appropriateness). Such practice contrasts with developmentally inappropriate practice, which ignores the concrete, hands-on approach to learning.

- The U.S. government has tried to break the poverty cycle with programs such as Head Start. The Early Head Start program began in 1995. Model programs have been shown to have positive effects on children who live in poverty.

- Controversy characterizes early childhood education curricula. On the one side are the child-centered, constructivist advocates; on the other are those who advocate an instructivist, academic approach. Another controversy focuses on whether preschool education makes a difference, especially for children who are not disadvantaged.

key terms

growth hormone deficiency 210
myelination 211
preoperational stage 216
operations 216
symbolic function substage 216
egocentrism 217

animism 217
intuitive thought substage 218
centration 218
conservation 218
zone of proximal development (ZPD) 220

social constructivist approach 221
executive attention 225
sustained attention 225
short-term memory 225
executive functioning 226

theory of mind 226
child-centered kindergarten 235
Montessori approach 235
developmentally appropriate practice 235
Project Head Start 235

key people

Chapter 7 | PHYSICAL AND COGNITIVE DEVELOPMENT IN EARLY CHILDHOOD

Connecting with

Learning Objectives	Application Activities	Activity Type	Page Reference
Identify motor development in early childhood.	Advanced Gross Motor Skills	Milestones	pp. 211–212
	Advanced Fine Motor Skills	Milestones	
	Copying Shapes at Age 3–1	Video	
	Copying Shapes at Age 3–2	Video	
	Copying Shapes at Age 4–1	Video	
	Copying Shapes at Age 4–2	Video	
	Copying Shapes at Age 5	Video	
	Copying Shapes at Age 7	Video	
	Fine Motor Skills at Age 3	Video	
	Drawing Pictures at Age 4	Video	
	Fine Motor Skills at Age 5	Video	
	Drawing Pictures at Age 6	Video	
Describe nutrition in early childhood	Children and Nutrition	Video	pp. 212–214
Characterize Piaget's preoperational stage.	Lacking Concept of Conservation (Liquid) at Age 3	Video	pp. 216–219
	Lacking Concept of Conservation (Mass, Liquid, Number) at Age 4	Video	
	Development of Concept of Conservation	Video	

(continued)

Learning Objectives	Application Activities	Activity Type	Page Reference
Discuss Vygotsky's theory.	Scaffolding 18–47 Months	Milestones	pp. 219–223
	Comparing Vygotsky's and Piaget's Theories	Click & drag activity	
Discuss information processing views.	Understanding Numbers and Logic 40–47 Months	Milestones	pp. 223–229
	Learning to Follow Instructions 28–32 Months	Milestones	
	Imitative Learning 6–15 Months	Milestones	
	Comparing Piaget's Theory and Information Processing Theory	Click & drag activity	
	Theory of Mind 6 months–3 years	Milestones	
	Limits to Memory at Age 3	Video	
	Memory Ability at Age 3	Video	
	Memory Ability at Age 4	Video	
	Memory Ability at Age 5	Video	
	Levels of Processes	Interactive exercise	
Summarize phonology and morphology in early childhood.	Language Challenges, Jasmine, 2–4 yrs	Milestones	pp. 230–231
Summarize young children's literacy.	Pre-Literacy: Learning about Words and Books 3 Months–3 Years	Milestones	pp. 232–233
Evaluate variations in early childhood education.	What Makes a Successful Preschool Teacher	Video	pp. 234–235
	Preschool Environment with 4-Year-Olds	Video	
	Preschool Teacher's Philosophy of Teaching	Video	
Characterize education for young children who are disadvantaged.	Working with Children Who Are Abused and Neglected	Video	pp. 235–237
Evaluate controversies in early childhood education.	Children and Public Policy	Video	pp. 237–238

SOCIOEMOTIONAL DEVELOPMENT IN EARLY CHILDHOOD

chapter **outline**

1 Emotional and Personality Development

Learning Goal 1 Discuss emotional and personality development in early childhood.

The Self
Emotional Development
Moral Development
Gender

2 Families

Learning Goal 2 Explain how families can influence young children's development.

Parenting
Child Maltreatment
Sibling Relationships and Birth Order
The Changing Family in a Changing Society

3 Peer Relations, Play, and Media/Screen Time

Learning Goal 3 Describe the roles of peers, play, and media/screen time in young children's development.

Peer Relations
Play
Media and Screen Time

In his memoir, *Burning Fence: A Western Memoir of Fatherhood,* award-winning novelist Craig Lesley describes one memory from his early childhood:

> Lifting me high above his head, my father placed me in the crotch of the Bing cherry tree growing beside my mother's parents' house in The Dalles. A little frightened at the dizzying height, I pressed my palms into the tree's rough, peeling bark. My father stood close, reassuring. I could see his olive skin, dazzling smile, and sharp-creased army uniform.
>
> "Rudell, don't let him fall." My mother watched, her arms held out halfway, as if to catch me. . . .
>
> The cherries were ripe and robins flittered through the green leaves, pecking at the Bings. Tipping my head back I could see blue sky beyond the extended branches.
>
> "That's enough. Bring him down now." My mother's arms reached out farther.
>
> Laughing, my father grabbed me under the arms, twirled me around, and plunked me into the grass. I wobbled a little. Imprinted on my palms was the pattern of the tree bark, and I brushed off the little bark pieces on my dungarees.
>
> In a moment, my grandmother gave me a small glass of lemonade. . . .
>
> This first childhood memory of my father remains etched in my mind. . . .
>
> When I grew older, I realized that my father had never lifted me into the cherry tree. After Rudell left, I never saw him until I was fifteen. My grandfather had put me in the tree. Still, the memory of my father lifting me into the tree persists. Even today, I remain half-convinced by the details, the press of bark against my palms, the taste of lemonade, the texture of my father's serge uniform. Apparently, my mind has cross-wired the photographs of my handsome father in his army uniform with the logical reality that my grandfather set me in the crotch of the tree.
>
> Why can I remember the event so vividly? I guess because I wanted so much for my father to be there. I have no easy answers. (Lesley, 2005, pp. 8–10)

Like millions of children, Lesley experienced a family torn by divorce; he would also experience abuse by a stepfather. When his father left, Lesley was an infant, but even as a preschooler, he felt his father's absence. Once he planned to win a gift for his father so that his grandmother "could take it to him and then he'd come to see me" (Lesley, 2005, p. 16). In just a few years, the infant had become a child with a complicated emotional and social life.

-topical **connections** -

During infancy, children's socioemotional development makes considerable progress as their caregivers (especially their parents) socialize them and they develop more sophisticated ways of initiating social interactions with others. Development of a secure attachment is a key aspect of infant development, and the development of autonomy in the second year of life also signals an important accomplishment. As children move through infancy, it is important for caregivers to guide them in regulating their emotions. Temperament also is a central characteristic of the infant's profile, and some temperament styles are more adaptive than others. The use of child care has become increasingly common in recent years, and the quality of this care varies considerably. Parents continue to play key roles in children's development in the early childhood period, but peers begin to play more important roles as well.

◄ - - - *looking back* - - - - - - - - - - - - - - -

preview

In early childhood, children's emotional lives and personalities develop in significant ways, and their small worlds widen. In addition to the continuing influence of family relationships, peers take on a more significant role in children's development, and play as well as media and screen time fill the days of many young children's lives.

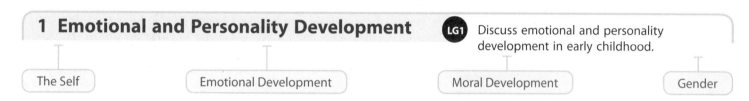

1 Emotional and Personality Development **LG1** Discuss emotional and personality development in early childhood.

The Self   Emotional Development   Moral Development   Gender

Many changes characterize young children's socioemotional development in early childhood. Their developing minds and social experiences produce remarkable advances in the development of their self, emotional maturity, moral understanding, and gender awareness.

THE SELF

We learned in Chapter 6 that during the second year of life children make considerable progress in self-recognition. In the early childhood years, young children develop in many ways that enable them to enhance their self-understanding.

Initiative Versus Guilt   In Chapter 1, you read about Erik Erikson's (1968) eight developmental stages that are encountered during certain time periods in the human life span. As you learned in Chapter 6, Erikson's first two stages—trust versus mistrust and autonomy versus shame and doubt—describe what he considers to be the main developmental tasks of infancy. Erikson's psychosocial stage associated with early childhood is initiative versus guilt. By now, children have become convinced that they are persons in their own right; during early childhood, they begin to discover what kind of person they will become. They identify intensely with their parents, who most of the time appear to them to be powerful and beautiful, although often unreasonable, disagreeable, and sometimes even dangerous. During early childhood, children use their perceptual, motor, cognitive, and language skills to make things happen. They have a surplus of energy that permits them to forget failures quickly and to approach new areas that seem desirable—even if dangerous—with undiminished zest and some increased sense of direction. On their own initiative, then, children at this stage exuberantly move out into a wider social world.

The great governor of initiative is conscience. Their initiative and enthusiasm may bring them not only rewards but also guilt, which lowers self-esteem.

Self-Understanding and Understanding Others   Recent research studies have revealed that young children are more psychologically aware—of themselves and others—than used to be thought (Easterbrooks & others, 2013; Thompson, 2013c). This psychological awareness reflects young children's expanding psychological sophistication.

Self-Understanding   In Erikson's portrait of early childhood, the young child clearly has begun to develop **self-understanding,** which is the representation of self, the substance and content of self-conceptions (Harter, 2012). Though not the whole of personal identity, self-understanding provides its rational underpinnings. Mainly through interviews, researchers have probed children's conceptions of many aspects of self-understanding.

As we saw in Chapter 6, "Socioemotional Development in Infancy," early self-understanding involves self-recognition. In early childhood, young children think that the self can be described by many material characteristics, such as size, shape, and color. They distinguish themselves from others through physical and material attributes. Says 4-year-old Sandra, "I'm

self-understanding The child's cognitive representation of self, the substance and content of the child's self-conceptions.

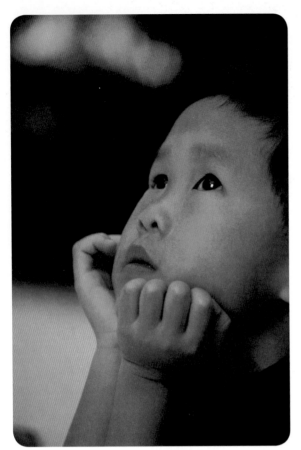

What characterizes young children's self-understanding?

different from Jennifer because I have brown hair and she has blond hair." Says 4-year-old Ralph, "I am different from Hank because I am taller and I am different from my sister because I have a bicycle." Physical activities are also a central component of the self in early childhood (Keller, Ford, & Meacham, 1978). For example, preschool children often describe themselves in terms of activities such as play. In sum, during early childhood, children often provide self-descriptions that involve body attributes, material possessions, and physical activities.

Although young children mainly describe themselves in terms of concrete, observable features and action tendencies, at about 4 to 5 years of age as they hear others use words describing psychological traits and emotions, they begin to include these in their own self-descriptions (Marsh, Ellis, & Craven, 2002). Thus, in a self-description, a 4-year-old might say, "I'm not scared. I'm always happy." Young children's self-descriptions are typically unrealistically positive, as reflected in the comment of this 4-year-old who says he is always happy, which he is not (Harter, 2012). They express this optimism because they don't yet distinguish between their desired competence and their actual competence, tend to confuse ability and effort (thinking that differences in ability can be changed as easily as can differences in effort), don't engage in spontaneous social comparison of their abilities with those of others, and tend to compare their present abilities with what they could do at an earlier age (which usually makes their abilities look quite good). This overestimation of their attributes helps to protect young children from negative self-evaluations.

However, as in virtually all areas of human development, there are individual variations in young children's self-conceptions, and there is increasing evidence that some children are vulnerable to negative self-attributions (Thompson, 2011, 2013a). For example, one study revealed that insecurely attached preschool children whose mothers reported a high level of parenting stress and depressive symptoms had a lower self-concept than other young children in more positive family circumstances (Goodvin & others, 2008). This research indicates that young children's generally optimistic self-ascriptions do not buffer them from adverse, stressful family conditions (Thompson, 2013a).

Understanding Others   Children also make advances in their understanding of others and learn from others in early childhood (Harter, 2012; Mills & others, 2012). As we saw in Chapter 7, "Physical and Cognitive Development in Early Childhood," young children's theory of mind includes understanding that other people have emotions and desires. And, at about 4 to 5 years, children not only start describing themselves in terms of psychological traits, but they also begin to perceive others in terms of psychological traits. Thus, a 4-year-old might say, "My teacher is nice."

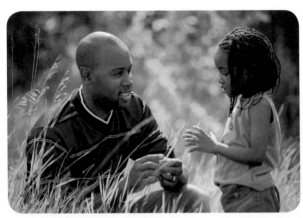

Young children are more psychologically aware of themselves and others than used to be thought. Some children are better than others at understanding people's feelings and desires—and, to some degree, these individual differences are influenced by conversations caregivers have with young children about feelings and desires.

Something important for children to develop is an understanding that people don't always give accurate reports of their beliefs (Mills, Elashi, & Archacki, 2011). Researchers have found that even 4-year-olds understand that people may make statements that aren't true to obtain what they want or to avoid trouble (Lee & others, 2002). For example, one study revealed that 4- and 5-year-olds were increasingly skeptical of another child's claim to be sick when the children were informed that the child was motivated to avoid having to go to camp (Gee & Heyman, 2007). Another study found that at 3 years of age, children mistrusted people who made a single error, but it wasn't until 4 years of age that in deciding whom to trust, children took into account the relative frequency of errors informants made (Pasquini & others, 2007).

Another important aspect of understanding others involves understanding joint commitments. As children approach their third birthday, their collaborative interactions with others increasingly involve obligations to the partner (Tomasello & Hamann, 2012). A recent study revealed that 3-year-olds, but not 2-year-olds, recognized when an adult is committed and when they themselves are committed to joint activity that involves obligation to a partner (Grafenhain & others, 2009).

Both the extensive theory of mind research and the recent research on young children's social understanding underscore that young children are not as egocentric as Piaget envisioned (Sokol, Snjezana, & Muller, 2010; Thompson, 2012). Piaget's concept of egocentrism has become so ingrained in people's thinking about young children that too often the current research on social awareness in infancy and early childhood has been overlooked. Research increasingly shows that young children are more socially sensitive and perceptive than was previously envisioned, suggesting that parents and teachers can help them to better understand and interact in the social world by how they interact with them (Thompson 2013b, d). If young children are seeking to better understand various mental and emotional states (intentions, goals, feelings, desires) that they know underlie people's actions, then talking with them about these internal states can improve young children's understanding of them (Thompson, 2011, 2013c, d).

However, debate continues to surround the question of whether young children are socially sensitive or basically egocentric. Ross Thompson (2012, 2013a, b) comes down on the side of viewing young children as socially sensitive, while Susan Harter (2012) argues that there is still evidence to support the conclusion that young children are essentially egocentric.

EMOTIONAL DEVELOPMENT

The young child's growing awareness of self is linked to the ability to feel an expanding range of emotions. Young children, like adults, experience many emotions during the course of a day. Their emotional development in early childhood allows them to try to make sense of other people's emotional reactions and to begin to control their own emotions (Cummings, Braungart-Rieker, & Du Rocher-Schudlich, 2013; Thompson, 2011, 2013d).

Expressing Emotions   Recall from Chapter 6 that even young infants experience emotions such as joy and fear, but to experience *self-conscious emotions* children must be able to refer to themselves and be aware of themselves as distinct from others (Lewis, 2010). Pride, shame, embarrassment, and guilt are examples of self-conscious emotions. Self-conscious emotions do not appear to develop until self-awareness appears at approximately 15 to 18 months of age.

During the early childhood years, emotions such as pride and guilt become more common. They are especially influenced by parents' responses to children's behavior. For example, a young child may experience shame when a parent says, "You should feel bad about biting your sister."

Understanding Emotions   One of the most important advances in emotional development in early childhood is an increased understanding of emotion (Bassett & others, 2012; Denham & others, 2012). During early childhood, young children increasingly understand that certain situations are likely to evoke particular emotions, facial expressions indicate specific emotions, emotions affect behavior, and emotions can be used to influence others' emotions (Cole & others, 2009). A recent study also found that young children's understanding of emotions was linked to their prosocial behavior (Ensor, Spencer, & Hughes, 2011).

Between 2 and 4 years of age, children considerably increase the number of terms they use to describe emotions. During this time, they are also learning about the causes and consequences of feelings (Denham & others, 2011).

When they are 4 to 5 years of age, children show an increased ability to reflect on emotions. They also begin to understand that the same event can elicit different feelings in different people. Moreover, they show a growing awareness that they need to manage their emotions to meet social standards.

Regulating Emotions   As we saw in Chapter 6, "Socioemotional Development in Infancy," emotion regulation is an important aspect of development. Emotion regulation especially plays a key role in children's ability to manage the demands and conflicts they face in interacting with others (Lewis, 2013; Thompson, 2011, 2013c, d).

Many researchers consider the growth of emotion regulation in children as fundamental to becoming socially competent (Cole & Hall, 2012; Nelson & others, 2012; Perry & others, 2012; Thompson, 2013c, d). Emotion regulation can be conceptualized as an important

A young child expressing the emotion of shame, which occurs when a child evaluates his or her actions as not living up to standards. A child experiencing shame wishes to hide or disappear. *Why is shame called a self-conscious emotion?*

developmental **connection**

Executive Functioning

In early childhood, executive functioning especially involves developmental advances in cognitive inhibition, cognitive flexibility, goal-setting, and delay of gratification. Chapter 7, p. 226

component of self-regulation or of executive functioning. Recall from Chapter 7 that executive functioning is increasingly thought to be a key concept in describing the young child's higher-level cognitive functioning (Carlson & White, 2013; Conway & Stifter, 2012). Cybele Raver and her colleagues (Blair & Raver, 2012; McCoy & Raver, 2012; Raver & others, 2011, 2012; Zhai, Raver, & Jones, 2012) are using interventions, such as increasing caregiver emotional expressiveness, to improve young children's emotion regulation and reduce behavior problems in Head Start families.

Emotion-Coaching and Emotion-Dismissing Parents Parents can play an important role in helping young children regulate their emotions. Depending on how they talk with their children about emotion, parents can be described as taking an *emotion-coaching* or an *emotion-dismissing* approach (Gottman, 2012). The distinction between these approaches is most evident in the way the parent deals with the child's negative emotions (anger, frustration, sadness, and so on). *Emotion-coaching parents* monitor their children's emotions, view their children's negative emotions as opportunities for teaching, assist them in labeling emotions, and coach them in how to deal effectively with emotions. In contrast, *emotion-dismissing parents* view their role as to deny, ignore, or change negative emotions. Emotion-coaching parents interact with their children in a less rejecting manner, use more scaffolding and praise, and are more nurturant than are emotion-dismissing parents. Moreover, the children of emotion-coaching parents are better at soothing themselves when they get upset, more effective in regulating their negative affect, focus their attention better, and have fewer behavior problems than the children of emotion-dismissing parents (Gottman, 2012). Recent researcher studies found that fathers' emotion coaching was related to children's social competence (Baker, Fenning, & Crnic, 2011) and that mothers' emotion coaching was linked to less oppositional behavior (Dunsmore, Booker, & Ollendick, 2012).

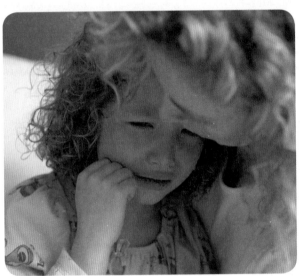

An emotion-coaching parent. *What are some differences in emotion-coaching and emotion-dismissing parents?*

Parents' knowledge of their children's emotional world can help them to guide their children's emotional development and to teach them how to cope effectively with problems. A recent study found that mothers' knowledge about what distresses and comforts their children predicts the children's coping, empathy, and prosocial behavior (Vinik, Almas, & Grusec, 2011).

A problem that parents face is that young children typically don't want to talk about difficult emotional topics, such as being distressed or engaging in negative behaviors. Among the strategies young children use to avoid these conversations is to not talk at all, change the topic, push away, or run away. In a recent study, Ross Thompson and his colleagues (2009) found that young children were more likely to openly discuss difficult emotional circumstances when they were securely attached to their mother and when their mother conversed with them in a way that validated and accepted the child's views. Links between parenting and children's emotional development are further explored in *Connecting Through Research*.

What role does emotion regulation play in peer relations?

Regulation of Emotion and Peer Relations Emotions play a strong role in determining the success of a child's peer relationships (Denham & others, 2011). Specifically, the ability to modulate one's emotions is an important skill that benefits children in their relationships with peers. Moody and emotionally negative children are more likely to experience rejection by their peers, whereas emotionally positive children are more popular. One study revealed that 4-year-olds recognized and generated strategies for controlling their anger more than did 3-year-olds (Cole & others, 2009).

MORAL DEVELOPMENT

moral development Development that involves thoughts, feelings, and behaviors regarding rules and conventions about what people should do in their interactions with other people.

Moral development involves the development of thoughts, feelings, and behaviors regarding rules and conventions about what people should do in their interactions with other people. Major developmental theories have focused on different aspects of moral development.

Are Specific Components of Parenting Linked to Specific Emotions in Children?

In one study, Maayan Davidov and Joan Grusec (2006) found some specific outcomes for children's emotional development depending on which aspect of parenting was expressed. In the study, parents' responses to children's distress (such as responding with empathy), but not parents' warmth, were linked to children's capacity to regulate their negative emotions (such as expressing appropriate affect in response to aggression by peers); in contrast, the mother's warmth, but not her response to her child's distress, was related to children's regulation of positive emotions (such as being cheerful) (Davidov & Grusec, 2006). This study underscores an important point about parenting. Many studies take a global approach to parenting, rather than examining specific components. For example, parents' responses to a child's distress and parents' warmth are often lumped together in a broad positive parenting category. However, in the Davidov and Grusec study, parents' responses to a child's distress and parents' warmth predicted different outcomes for children.

Developmentalists also argue that in many cases distinctive parenting responses should be activated depending on the domain involved (Beaulieu & Bugental, 2007; Grusec & Davidov, 2010). For example, if a child becomes distressed, a sensitive parent soothes the child, whereas an insensitive parent might try to distract the child's attention or might become power assertive; however, when a child is angrily defiant, a more assertive response, rather than soothing, might be required by the parent.

Moral Feelings Feelings of anxiety and guilt are central to the account of moral development provided by Freud's psychoanalytic theory (introduced in Chapter 1). According to Freud, to reduce anxiety, avoid punishment, and maintain parental affection, children identify with parents and internalize their standards of right and wrong, thus forming the superego—the moral element of personality.

Freud's ideas are not backed by research, but guilt certainly can motivate moral behavior. Other emotions, however, also contribute to the child's moral development, including positive feelings. One important example is empathy, which involves responding to another person's feelings with an emotion that echoes the other's feelings (Denham & others, 2011).

Infants have the capacity for some purely empathic responses, but empathy often requires the ability to discern another's inner psychological states, or what is called perspective taking. Learning how to identify a wide range of emotional states in others and to anticipate what kinds of action will improve another person's emotional state help to advance children's moral development (Thompson, 2011, 2012).

Moral Reasoning Interest in how children think about moral issues was stimulated by Piaget (1932), who extensively observed and interviewed children from the ages of 4 through 12. Piaget watched children play marbles to learn how they applied and thought about the game's rules. He also asked children about ethical issues—theft, lies, punishment, and justice, for example. Piaget concluded that children go through two distinct stages in how they think about morality.

- From about 4 to 7 years of age, children display **heteronomous morality,** the first stage of moral development in Piaget's theory. Children think of justice and rules as unchangeable properties of the world, removed from the control of people.

- From 7 to 10 years of age, children are in a transition showing some features of the first stage of moral reasoning and some stages of the second stage, autonomous morality.

- At about 10 years of age and older, children show **autonomous morality.** They become aware that rules and laws are created by people, and in judging an action they consider the actor's intentions as well as the consequences.

Because young children are heteronomous moralists, they judge the rightness or goodness of behavior by considering its consequences, not the intentions of the actor. For example, to

developmental **connection**

Theories

Freud theorized that individuals go through five psychosexual stages. Chapter 1, p. 22

heteronomous morality The first stage of moral development in Piaget's theory, occurring from approximately 4 to 7 years of age. Justice and rules are conceived of as unchangeable properties of the world, removed from the control of people.

autonomous morality In Piaget's theory, older children (about 10 years of age and older) become aware that rules and laws are created by people and that in judging an action one should consider the actor's intentions as well as the consequences.

How will this child's moral thinking about stealing a cookie differ whether he is in Piaget's heteronomous or autonomous stage?

the heteronomous moralist, breaking 12 cups accidentally is worse than breaking one cup intentionally. As children develop into moral autonomists, intentions become more important than consequences.

The heteronomous thinker also believes that rules are unchangeable and are handed down by all-powerful authorities. When Piaget suggested to young children that they use new rules in a game of marbles, they resisted. By contrast, older children—moral autonomists—accept change and recognize that rules are merely convenient conventions, subject to change.

The heteronomous thinker also believes in **immanent justice,** the concept that if a rule is broken, punishment will be meted out immediately. The young child believes that a violation is connected automatically to its punishment. Immanent justice also implies that if something unfortunate happens to someone, the person must have transgressed earlier. Older children, who are moral autonomists, recognize that punishment occurs only if someone witnesses the wrongdoing and that even then, punishment is not inevitable.

How do these changes in moral reasoning occur? Piaget concluded that the changes come about through the mutual give-and-take of peer relations. In the peer group, where others have power and status similar to the child's, plans are negotiated and coordinated, and disagreements are reasoned about and eventually settled. Parent-child relations, in which parents have the power and children do not, are less likely to advance moral reasoning, because rules are often handed down in an authoritarian way.

Earlier in this chapter you read about Ross Thompson's view that young children are not as egocentric as Piaget envisioned. Thompson (2012) recently further elaborated on this view, arguing that recent research indicates that young children often show a nonegocentric awareness of others' goals, feelings, and desires and how such internal states are influenced by the actions of others. Theory of mind research indicates that young children possess cognitive resources that allow them to be aware of others' intentions and to recognize when someone violates a moral prohibition. One study of 3-year-olds found that they were less likely to offer assistance to an adult they had previously observed being harmful to another person (Vaish, Carpenter, & Tomasello, 2010). However, because of limitations in their self-control skills, social understanding, and cognitive flexibility, young children's moral advancements often are inconsistent and vary across situations. They still have a long way to go before they have the capacity for developing a consistent moral character and making ethical judgments.

Moral Behavior   The behavioral and social cognitive approaches, initially described in Chapter 1, focus on moral behavior rather than moral reasoning. It holds that the processes of reinforcement, punishment, and imitation explain the development of moral behavior. When children are rewarded for behavior that is consistent with laws and social conventions, they are likely to repeat that behavior. When models who behave morally are provided, children are likely to adopt their actions. And, when children are punished for immoral behavior, those behaviors are likely to be reduced or eliminated. However, because punishment may have adverse side effects, as discussed later in this chapter, it should be used judiciously and cautiously.

In the moral behavior view, the situation also influences behavior. More than a half century ago, a comprehensive study of thousands of children in many situations—at home, at school, and at church, for example—found that the totally honest child was virtually nonexistent; so was the child who cheated in all situations (Hartshorne & May, 1928–1930). Behavioral and social cognitive researchers emphasize that what children do in one situation is often only weakly related to what they do in other situations. A child might cheat in class but not in a game; a child might steal a piece of candy when alone but not steal it when others are present.

Social cognitive theorists also stress that the ability to resist temptation is closely tied to the development of self-control. To achieve this self-control, children must learn to delay gratification. According to social cognitive theorists, cognitive factors are important in the child's development of self-control (Bandura, 2009, 2010a, b, 2012).

Conscience   Conscience refers to an internal regulation of standards of right and wrong that involves an integration of all three components of moral development we have described so

developmental connection

Development

Kohlberg's theory, like Piaget's, emphasizes that peers play more important roles in children's moral development than parents do. Chapter 10, p. 325

immanent justice The concept that if a rule is broken, punishment will be meted out immediately.

conscience An internal regulation of standards of right and wrong that involves integrating moral thought, feeling, and behavior.

far—moral thought, feeling, and behavior (Kochanska & others, 2010). Reflecting the presence of a conscience in young children, researchers have found that young children are aware of right and wrong, have the capacity to show empathy toward others, experience guilt, indicate discomfort following a transgression, and are sensitive to violating rules (Kochanska & Aksan, 2007; Kochanska & others, 2009).

A major interest in young children's conscience focuses on children's relationship with their caregivers (Kochanska & Kim, 2012a, b; Thompson, 2012). Especially important in this regard is the emergence of young children's willingness to embrace the values of their parents, an orientation that flows from a positive, close relationship (Kochanska & Aksan, 2007). For example, children who are securely attached are more likely to internalize their parents' values and rules (Kochanska & Kim, 2012a, b; Thompson, 2013a).

Parenting and Young Children's Moral Development   In Ross Thompson's (2006, 2009, 2012) view, young children are moral apprentices, striving to understand what is moral. Among the most important aspects of the relationship between parents and children that contribute to children's moral development are relational quality, parental discipline, proactive strategies, and conversational dialogue.

Parent-child relationships introduce children to the mutual obligations of close relationships (Kochanska & Kim, 2012a, b). Parents' obligations include engaging in positive caregiving and guiding children to become competent human beings. Children's obligations include responding appropriately to parents' initiatives and maintaining a positive relationship with parents.

An important parenting strategy involves proactively averting potential misbehavior by children before it takes place (Thompson, 2009). With younger children, being proactive means using diversion, such as distracting their attention or moving them to alternative activities. With older children, being proactive may involve talking with them about values that the parents deem important.

Conversations related to moral development can benefit children, regardless of whether they occur as part of a discipline encounter or outside the encounter in the everyday stream of parent-child interaction (Thompson, Meyer, & McGinley, 2006). The conversations can be planned or spontaneous and can focus on topics such as past events (for example, a child's prior misbehavior or positive moral conduct), shared future events (for example, going somewhere that may involve a temptation and requires positive moral behavior), and immediate events (for example, talking with the child about a sibling's tantrums).

What are some aspects of relationships between parents and children that contribute to children's moral development?

GENDER

Recall from Chapter 1 that *gender* refers to the characteristics of people as males and females. **Gender identity** involves a sense of one's own gender, including knowledge, understanding, and acceptance of being male or female (Egan & Perry, 2001; Perry, 2012). One aspect of gender identity involves knowing whether you are a girl or boy, an awareness that most children develop by about 2½ years of age (Blakemore, Berenbaum, & Liben, 2009). **Gender roles** are sets of expectations that prescribe how females or males should think, act, and feel. During the preschool years, most children increasingly act in ways that match their culture's gender roles. **Gender typing** refers to acquisition of a traditional masculine or feminine role. For example, fighting is more characteristic of a traditional masculine role and crying is more characteristic of a traditional feminine role. One study revealed that sex-typed behavior (boys playing with cars and girls with jewelry, for example) increased during the preschool years and that children who engaged in the most sex-typed behavior during the preschool years still did so at 8 years of age (Golombok & others, 2008).

How is gender influenced by biology? by children's social experiences? by cognitive factors?

Biological Influences   Biology clearly plays a role in gender development (Arnold, 2012; Hines, 2013). Among the possible biological influences are chromosomes, hormones, and evolution.

gender identity The sense of being male or female, which most children acquire by the time they are 3 years old.

gender role A set of expectations that prescribes how females or males should think, act, and feel.

gender typing Acquisition of a traditional masculine or feminine role.

Chromosomes and Hormones   Biologists have learned a great deal about how sex differences develop. Recall that humans normally have 46 chromosomes arranged in pairs (see Chapter 2). The 23rd pair consists of a combination of X and Y chromosomes, usually two X chromosomes in a female and an X and a Y in a male. In the first few weeks of gestation, however, female and male embryos look alike.

Males start to differ from females when genes on the Y chromosome in the male embryo trigger the development of testes rather than ovaries; the testes secrete copious amounts of the class of hormones known as androgens. Low levels of androgens in the female embryo allow the normal development of female sex organs.

Thus, hormones play a key role in the development of sex differences (Hines, 2011). The two main classes of sex hormones, estrogens and androgens, are secreted by the *gonads* (ovaries in females, testes in males). *Estrogens,* such as estradiol, influence the development of female physical sex characteristics. *Androgens,* such as testosterone, promote the development of male physical sex characteristics. Sex hormones also can influence children's socioemotional development.

The Evolutionary Psychology View   How might physical differences between the sexes give rise to psychological differences between males and females? Evolutionary psychology (introduced in Chapter 2) offers one answer. According to evolutionary psychology, adaptation during human evolution produced psychological differences between males and females (Buss, 2012; Mader, 2013). Because of their differing roles in reproduction, males and females faced differing pressures when the human species was evolving. In particular, because having multiple sexual liaisons improves the likelihood that males will pass on their genes, natural selection favored males who adopted short-term mating strategies. These are strategies that allow a male to win the competition with other males for sexual access to females. Therefore, say evolutionary psychologists, males evolved dispositions that favor violence, competition, and risk taking.

In contrast, according to evolutionary psychologists, females' contributions to the gene pool were improved when they secured resources that ensured that their offspring would survive. As a consequence, natural selection favored females who devoted effort to parenting and chose successful, ambitious mates who could provide their offspring with resources and protection.

Critics of evolutionary psychology argue that its hypotheses are backed by speculations about prehistory, not evidence, and that in any event people are not locked into behavior that was adaptive in the evolutionary past. Critics also claim that the evolutionary view pays little attention to cultural and individual variations in gender differences (Hyde & Else-Quest, 2013; Matlin, 2012).

Social Influences   Many social scientists do not locate the cause of psychological gender differences in biological dispositions. Rather, they argue that these differences reflect social experiences. Explanations for how gender differences come about through experience include both social and cognitive theories.

Social Theories of Gender   Three main social theories of gender have been proposed—social role theory, psychoanalytic theory, and social cognitive theory. Alice Eagly (2001, 2010, 2012; Eagly & Wood, 2012) proposed **social role theory,** which states that gender differences result from the contrasting roles of women and men. In most cultures around the world, women have less power and status than men, and they control fewer resources (UNICEF, 2011). Compared with men, women perform more domestic work, spend fewer hours in paid employment, receive lower pay, and are more thinly represented in the highest levels of organizations. In Eagly's view, as women adapted to roles with less power and less status in society, they showed more cooperative, less dominant profiles than men. Thus, the social hierarchy and division of labor are important causes of gender differences in power, assertiveness, and nurturing.

The **psychoanalytic theory of gender** stems from Freud's view that the preschool child develops a sexual attraction to the opposite-sex parent. This is the process known as the Oedipus (for boys) or Electra (for girls) complex. At 5 or 6 years of age, the child renounces this attraction because of anxious feelings. Subsequently, the child identifies with the same-sex

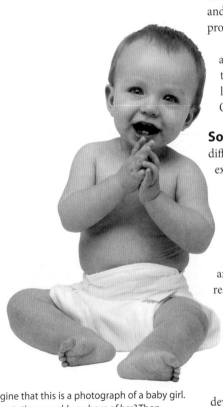

First imagine that this is a photograph of a baby girl. *What expectations would you have of her?* Then imagine that this is a photograph of a baby boy. *What expectations would you have of him?*

parent, unconsciously adopting the same-sex parent's characteristics. However, developmentalists have observed that gender development does not proceed as Freud proposed. Children become gender-typed much earlier than 5 or 6 years of age, and they become masculine or feminine even when the same-sex parent is not present in the family.

The social cognitive approach discussed in Chapter 1 provides an alternative explanation of how children develop gender-typed behavior. According to the **social cognitive theory of gender,** children's gender development occurs through observing and imitating what other people say and do, and through being rewarded and punished for gender-appropriate and gender-inappropriate behavior (Bussey & Bandura, 1999). From birth onward, males and females are treated differently from one another. When infants and toddlers show gender differences, adults tend to reward them. Parents often use rewards and punishments to teach their daughters to be feminine ("Karen, you are being a good girl when you play gently with your doll") and their sons to be masculine ("Keith, a boy as big as you is not supposed to cry"). Parents, however, are only one of many sources through which children learn gender roles (Leaper, 2013; Leaper & Bigler, 2011). Culture, schools, peers, the media, and other family members also provide gender role models. For example, children also learn about gender by observing the behavior of other adults in the neighborhood and on television (Bugental & Grusec, 2006). As children get older, peers become increasingly important. Let's take a closer look at the influence of parents and peers.

Parental Influences   Parents, by action and by example, influence their children's gender development (Cookston & McHale, 2012; Hilliard & Liben, 2012; Leaper, 2013). Both mothers and fathers are psychologically important to their children's gender development (Hyde & Else-Quest, 2013; Leaper, 2013). Cultures around the world, however, tend to give mothers and fathers different roles (Chen & others, 2011). A research review yielded the following conclusions (Bronstein, 2006):

- *Mothers' socialization strategies.* In many cultures, mothers socialize their daughters to be more obedient and responsible than their sons. They also place more restrictions on daughters' autonomy.
- *Fathers' socialization strategies.* Fathers show more attention to sons than daughters, engage in more activities with sons, and put forth more effort to promote sons' intellectual development.

Thus, according to Bronstein (2006, pp. 269–270), "Despite an increased awareness in the United States and other Western cultures of the detrimental effects of gender stereotyping, many parents continue to foster behaviors and perceptions that are consonant with traditional gender role norms."

Peer Influences   Parents provide the earliest discrimination of gender roles, but before long peers join the process of responding to and modeling masculine and feminine behavior (Bukowski, Ittel, & Juang, 2012; Goble & others, 2012). In fact, peers become so important to gender development that the playground has been called "gender school" (Luria & Herzog, 1985).

Peers extensively reward and punish gender behavior (Leaper, 2013; Leaper & Bigler, 2011). For example, when children play in ways that the culture says are sex-appropriate, their peers tend to reward them. But peers often reject children who act in a manner that is considered more characteristic of the other gender (Handrinos & others, 2012; Matlin, 2012). A little girl who brings a doll to the park may find herself surrounded by new friends; a little boy might be jeered at. However, there is greater pressure for boys to conform to a traditional male role than for girls to conform to a traditional female role (Fagot, Rogers, & Leinbach, 2000). For example, a preschool girl who wants to wear boys' clothing receives considerably more approval than a boy who wants to wear a dress. The very term "tomboy" implies broad social acceptance of girls' adopting traditional male behaviors.

Gender molds important aspects of peer relations (Field & others, 2012; Zozuls & others, 2012). It influences the composition of children's groups, the size of groups, and interactions within a group (Maccoby, 1998, 2002):

- *Gender composition of children's groups.* Around the age of 3, children already show a preference to spend time with same-sex playmates. From 4 to 12 years of age, this

"How is it gendered?"
© Edward Koren/The New Yorker Collection/
www.cartoonbank.com

developmental **connection**

Theories

What are the main themes of Bandura's social cognitive theory? Chapter 1, p. 26

social role theory A theory that gender differences result from the contrasting roles of men and women.

psychoanalytic theory of gender A theory deriving from Freud's view that the preschool child develops a sexual attraction to the opposite-sex parent, by approximately 5 or 6 years of age renounces this attraction because of anxious feelings, and subsequently identifies with the same-sex parent, unconsciously adopting the same-sex parent's characteristics.

social cognitive theory of gender A theory emphasizing that children's gender development occurs through the observation and imitation of gender behavior and through the rewards and punishments children experience for gender-appropriate and gender-inappropriate behavior.

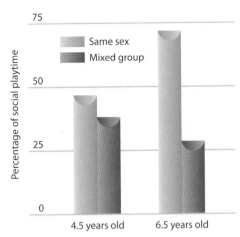

FIGURE 8.1

DEVELOPMENTAL CHANGES IN PERCENTAGE OF TIME SPENT IN SAME-SEX AND MIXED-GROUP SETTINGS. Observations of children show that they are more likely to play in same-sex than mixed-sex groups. This tendency increases between 4 and 6 years of age.

What role does gender play in children's peer relations?

preference for playing in same-sex groups increases, and during the elementary school years children spend a large majority of their free time with children of their own sex (see Figure 8.1).

- *Group size.* From about 5 years of age onward, boys are more likely to associate together in larger clusters than girls are. Boys are also more likely to participate in organized group games than girls are. In one study, same-sex groups of six children were permitted to use play materials in any way they wished (Benenson, Apostolaris, & Parnass, 1997). Girls were more likely than boys to play in dyads or triads, while boys were more likely to interact in larger groups and seek to attain a group goal.

- *Interaction in same-sex groups.* Boys are more likely than girls to engage in rough-and-tumble play, competition, conflict, ego displays, risk taking, and seeking dominance. By contrast, girls are more likely to engage in "collaborative discourse," in which they talk and act in a more reciprocal manner.

Cognitive Influences One influential cognitive theory is **gender schema theory,** which states that gender typing emerges as children gradually develop gender schemas of what is gender-appropriate and gender-inappropriate in their culture (Blakemore, Berenbaum, & Liben, 2009). A *schema* is a cognitive structure, a network of associations that guide an individual's perceptions. A *gender schema* organizes the world in terms of female and male. Children are internally motivated to perceive the world and to act in accordance with their developing schemas. Bit by bit, children pick up what is gender-appropriate and gender-inappropriate in their culture, and develop gender schemas that shape how they perceive the world and what they remember (Conry-Murray, Kim, & Turiel, 2012). Children are motivated to act in ways that conform to these gender schemas. Thus, gender schemas fuel gender typing.

gender schema theory The theory that gender typing emerges as children develop gender schemas of their culture's gender-appropriate and gender-inappropriate behavior.

Review Connect Reflect

LG1 Discuss emotional and personality development in early childhood.

Review

- What changes in the self occur during early childhood?
- What changes take place in emotional development in early childhood?
- What are some key aspects of moral development in young children?
- How does gender develop in young children?

Connect

- In the previous section, you read about the influence of parents on children's gender development. How does this compare with what you learned about parental influences on children's temperament in Chapter 6?

Reflect *Your Own Personal Journey of Life*

- Imagine that you are the parent of a 4-year-old child. What strategies would you use to increase your child's understanding of others?

2 Families   **LG2**   Explain how families can influence young children's development.

Parenting   Child Maltreatment   Sibling Relationships and Birth Order   The Changing Family in a Changing Society

Attachment to a caregiver is a key social relationship during infancy, but we saw in Chapter 6 that some experts maintain that secure attachment and the infant years have been overdramatized as determinants of life-span development. Social and emotional development is also shaped by other relationships and by temperament, contexts, and social experiences during the early childhood years and later. In this section, we will discuss social relationships in early childhood beyond attachment. We will explore different types of parenting, sibling relationships, and variations in family structures.

PARENTING

Good parenting takes time and effort (Grusec & others, 2013). You can't do it in a minute here and a minute there. You can't do it with CDs or DVDs. Of course, it's not just the quantity of time parents spend with children that is important for children's development—the quality of the parenting is clearly important (Huberman & Mendelsohn, 2012; Iruka, Laforett, & Odom, 2012; Widom & Nikulina, 2012). To understand variations in parenting, let's consider the styles parents use when they interact with their children, how they discipline their children, and coparenting.

Baumrind's Parenting Styles   Diana Baumrind (1971) argues that parents should be neither punitive nor aloof. Rather, they should develop rules for their children and be affectionate with them. She has described four types of parenting styles:

- **Authoritarian parenting** is a restrictive, punitive style in which parents exhort the child to follow their directions and respect their work and effort. The authoritarian parent places firm limits and controls on the child and allows little verbal exchange. For example, an authoritarian parent might say, "You do it my way or else." Authoritarian parents also might spank the child frequently, enforce rules rigidly but not explain them, and show rage toward the child. Children of authoritarian parents are often unhappy, fearful, and anxious about comparing themselves with others, fail to initiate activity, and have weak communication skills.

- **Authoritative parenting** encourages children to be independent but still places limits and controls on their actions. Extensive verbal give-and-take is allowed, and parents are warm and nurturing toward the child. An authoritative parent might put his arm around the child in a comforting way and say, "You know you should not have done

> Parenting is a very important profession, but no test of fitness for it is ever imposed in the interest of children.
>
> —**GEORGE BERNARD SHAW**
> *Irish Playwright, 20th Century*

Calvin and Hobbes

WHAT ASSURANCE DO I HAVE THAT YOUR PARENTING ISN'T SCREWING ME UP?

authoritarian parenting A restrictive, punitive style in which parents exhort the child to follow their directions and to respect their work and effort. The authoritarian parent places firm limits and controls on the child and allows little verbal exchange. Authoritarian parenting is associated with children's social incompetence.

authoritative parenting A parenting style in which parents encourage their children to be independent but still place limits and controls on their actions. Extensive verbal give-and-take is allowed, and parents are warm and nurturing toward the child. Authoritative parenting is associated with children's social competence.

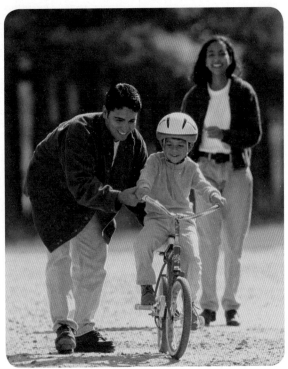

	Accepting, responsive	Rejecting, unresponsive
Demanding, controlling	Authoritative	Authoritarian
Undemanding, uncontrolling	Indulgent	Neglectful

FIGURE **8.2**

CLASSIFICATION OF PARENTING STYLES. The four types of parenting styles (authoritative, authoritarian, indulgent, and neglectful) involve the dimensions of acceptance and responsiveness, on the one hand, and demand and control on the other. For example, authoritative parenting involves being both accepting/responsive and demanding/controlling.

neglectful parenting A style of parenting in which the parent is uninvolved in the child's life; it is associated with children's social incompetence, especially a lack of self-control.

indulgent parenting A style of parenting in which parents are highly involved with their children but place few demands or controls on them. Indulgent parenting is associated with children's social incompetence, especially a lack of self-control.

that. Let's talk about how you can handle the situation better next time." Authoritative parents show pleasure and support in response to children's constructive behavior. They also expect mature, independent, and age-appropriate behavior from their children. Children whose parents are authoritative are often cheerful, self-controlled and self-reliant, and achievement-oriented; they tend to maintain friendly relations with peers, cooperate with adults, and cope well with stress.

As was just indicated, authoritative parents do exercise some direction and control over their children. The children of authoritative parents who engage in behavioral or psychological control without being coercive or punitive often show positive developmental outcomes (Baumrind, Larzelere, & Owens, 2010).

- **Neglectful parenting** is a style in which the parent is uninvolved in the child's life. Children whose parents are neglectful develop the sense that other aspects of the parents' lives are more important than they are. These children tend to be socially incompetent. Many have poor self-control and don't handle independence well. They frequently have low self-esteem, are immature, and may be alienated from the family. In adolescence, they may show patterns of truancy and delinquency.

- **Indulgent parenting** is a style in which parents are highly involved with their children but place few demands or controls on them. Such parents let their children do what they want. As a result, the children never learn to control their own behavior and always expect to get their way. Some parents deliberately rear their children in this way because they believe the combination of warm involvement and few restraints will produce a creative, confident child. However, children whose parents are indulgent rarely learn respect for others and have difficulty controlling their behavior. They might be domineering, egocentric, noncompliant, and have difficulties in peer relations.

These four classifications of parenting involve combinations of acceptance and responsiveness on the one hand and demand and control on the other (Maccoby & Martin, 1983). How these dimensions combine to produce authoritarian, authoritative, neglectful, and indulgent parenting is shown in Figure 8.2.

Keep in mind that research on parenting styles and children's development is *correlational*, not causal, in nature. Thus, if a study reveals that authoritarian parenting is linked to higher levels of children's aggression, the possibility that aggressive children elicited authoritarian parenting is just as likely as the possibility that authoritarian parenting produced aggressive children. Also recall from Chapter 1 that, in correlational studies, a third factor may influence the correlation between two factors. Thus, in the example of the correlation between authoritarian parenting and children's aggression, possibly authoritarian parents (first factor) and aggressive children (second factor) share genes (third factor) that predispose them to behave in ways that produced the correlation.

Parenting Styles in Context   Do the benefits of authoritative parenting transcend the boundaries of ethnicity, socioeconomic status (SES), and household composition? Although occasional exceptions have been found, evidence linking authoritative parenting with competence on the part of the child occurs in research across a wide range of ethnic groups, social strata, cultures, and family structures (Steinberg & Silk, 2002).

Nonetheless, researchers have found that in some ethnic groups, aspects of the authoritarian style may be associated with more positive child outcomes than Baumrind predicts (Parke & Clarke-Stewart, 2011). Elements of the authoritarian style may take on different meanings and have different effects depending on the context. For example, Asian American parents often continue aspects of traditional Asian child-rearing practices that have sometimes been described as authoritarian. The parents exert considerable control over their children's lives. However, Ruth Chao (2001, 2005, 2007; Chao & Otsuki-Clutter, 2011; Chao & Tseng, 2002) argues that the style of parenting used by many Asian American parents is distinct from the domineering control of the authoritarian style. Instead, Chao argues that this type of parental control reflects concern and involvement in their children's lives and is best conceptualized as a type of training. The high academic achievement of Asian American children may be a consequence of their "training" parents (Stevenson & Zusho, 2002). In recent research involving Chinese American adolescents and their parents, parental control was endorsed, as were the Confucian parental goals of perseverance, working hard in school, obedience, and being sensitive to parents' wishes (Russell, Crockett, & Chao, 2010).

An emphasis on requiring respect and obedience is also associated with the authoritarian style, but in Latino child rearing this focus may be positive rather than punitive. Rather than suppressing the child's development, it may encourage the development of a self and an identity that are embedded in the family and require respect and obedience (Dixon, Graber, & Brooks-Gunn, 2008).

Even physical punishment, another characteristic of the authoritarian style, may have varying effects in different contexts. African American parents are more likely than non-Latino White parents to use physical punishment (Deater-Deckard & Dodge, 1997). However, the use of physical punishment has been linked with increased externalized child problems (such as acting out and high levels of aggression) in non-Latino White families but not in African American families. One explanation of this finding points to the need for African American parents to enforce rules in the dangerous environments in which they are more likely to live (Harrison-Hale, McLoyd, & Smedley, 2004). As we see next, though, overall the use of physical punishment in disciplining children raises many concerns.

Punishment For centuries, corporal (physical) punishment, such as spanking, has been considered a necessary and even desirable method of disciplining children. Use of corporal punishment is legal in every state in America. A national survey of U.S. parents with 3- and 4-year-old children found that 26 percent of parents reported spanking their children frequently, and 67 percent of the parents reported yelling at their children frequently (Regalado & others, 2004). A cross-cultural comparison found that individuals in the United States were among those with the most favorable attitudes toward corporal punishment and were the most likely to remember it being used by their parents (Curran & others, 2001) (see Figure 8.3).

An increasing number of studies have examined the outcomes of physically punishing children, although those that have been conducted are correlational (Lansford & Deater-Deckard, 2012; Lansford & others, 2012). Clearly, it would be highly unethical to randomly assign parents to either spank or not spank their children in an experimental study. Recall that cause and effect cannot be determined in a correlational study. In one correlational study, spanking by parents was linked with children's antisocial behavior, including cheating, telling lies, being mean to others, bullying, getting into fights, and being disobedient (Strauss, Sugarman, & Giles-Sims, 1997).

A research review concluded that corporal punishment by parents is associated with higher levels of immediate compliance and aggression by the children (Gershoff, 2002). The review also found that corporal punishment is linked to lower levels of moral internalization and mental health (Gershoff, 2002). A study in six countries revealed that mothers' use of physical punishment was linked to the highest rates of aggression in their children (Gershoff & others, 2010). And several recent longitudinal studies also have found that physical punishment of young children is associated with higher levels of aggression later in childhood and adolescence (Berlin & others, 2009; Gershoff & others, 2012; Lansford & others, 2011; Taylor & others, 2010).

What are some reasons for avoiding spanking or similar punishments? The reasons include the following:

- When adults punish a child by yelling, screaming, or spanking, they are presenting children with out-of-control models for handling stressful situations. Children may imitate this aggressive, out-of-control behavior.
- Punishment can instill fear, rage, or avoidance. For example, spanking the child may cause the child to avoid being around the parent and to fear the parent.

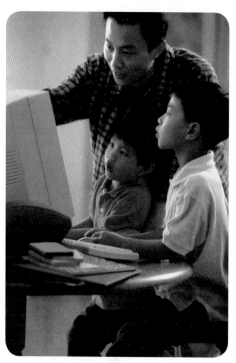

According to Ruth Chao, which type of parenting style do many Asian American parents use?

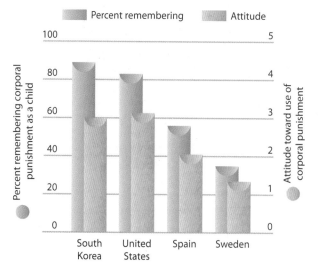

FIGURE **8.3**

CORPORAL PUNISHMENT IN DIFFERENT COUNTRIES.
A five-point scale was used to assess attitudes toward corporal punishment, with scores closer to 1 indicating an attitude against its use and scores closer to 5 suggesting an attitude favoring its use. *Why are studies of corporal punishment correlational studies, and how does that affect their usefulness?*

- Punishment tells children what not to do rather than what to do. Children should be given feedback, such as "Why don't you try this?"
- Punishment can be abusive. Parents might unintentionally become so aroused when they are punishing the child that they become abusive (Knox, 2010).

Most child psychologists recommend handling misbehavior by reasoning with the child, especially explaining the consequences of the child's actions for others. Time out, in which the child is removed from a setting that offers positive reinforcement, can also be effective. For example, when the child has misbehaved, a parent might take away TV viewing for a specified time.

Another point about the use of punishment with children is that debate about its effects on children's development continues (Gershoff & others, 2012; Grusec, 2011; Grusec & others, 2013). Some experts (including Diana Baumrind) argue that much of the evidence for the negative effects of physical punishment is based on studies in which parents acted in an abusive manner (Baumrind, Larzelere, & Cowan, 2002). She concludes from her research that when parents use punishment in a calm, reasoned manner (which she says characterized most of the authoritative parents in her studies), children's development benefits. Thus, she emphasizes that physical punishment does not need to present children with an out-of-control adult who is yelling and screaming, as well as spanking. A research review of 26 studies concluded that only severe or predominant use of spanking, not mild spanking, compared unfavorably with alternative discipline practices with children (Larzelere & Kuhn, 2005).

In addition to considering whether physical punishment is mild or out-of-control, another factor in evaluating effects on children's development involves cultural contexts. Recent research has indicated that in countries such as Kenya where physical punishment is considered normal and necessary for handling children's transgressions, the effects of physical punishment are less harmful than in countries such as Thailand where physical punishment is perceived as more harmful to children's development (Lansford & others, 2005, 2012).

In the view of some experts, based on the research evidence available, it is still difficult to tell whether the effects of physical punishment are always harmful to children's development, although such a view might be distasteful to some individuals (Grusec, 2011). One thing that is clear regarding research on punishment of children is that if physical punishment is used it needs to be mild, infrequent, age-appropriate, and used in the context of a positive parent-child relationship (Grusec, 2011). It is also clear that when physical punishment involves abuse, it can be very harmful to children's development (Cicchetti, 2013).

Coparenting   The support that parents provide one another in jointly raising a child is called **coparenting**. Poor coordination between parents, undermining of the other parent, lack of cooperation and warmth, and disconnection by one parent are conditions that place children at risk for problems (McHale & Sullivan, 2008; Solmeyer & others, 2011). For example, one study revealed that coparenting influenced young children's effortful control above and beyond maternal and paternal parenting by themselves (Karreman & others, 2008). And a recent study found that greater father involvement in young children's play was linked to an increase in supportive coparenting (Jia & Schoppe-Sullivan, 2011).

Parents who do not spend enough time with their children or who have problems in child rearing can benefit from counseling and therapy. To read about the work of marriage and family counselor Darla Botkin, see *Connecting with Careers*.

What characterizes coparenting?

CHILD MALTREATMENT

Unfortunately, punishment sometimes leads to the abuse of infants and children (Cicchetti, 2011, 2013). In 2009, approximately 702,000 U.S. children were found to be victims of child abuse at least once during that year (U.S. Department of Health and Human Services, 2010). Eighty-one percent of these children were abused by a parent or parents. Laws in many states now require physicians and teachers to report suspected cases of child abuse, yet many cases go unreported, especially those involving battered infants.

Whereas the public and many professionals use the term *child abuse* to refer to both abuse and neglect, developmentalists increasingly use the term *child maltreatment* (Cicchetti, 2011,

coparenting Support parents provide for each other in jointly raising their children.

Darla Botkin, Marriage and Family Therapist

Darla Botkin is a marriage and family therapist who teaches, conducts research, and engages in marriage and family therapy. She is on the faculty of the University of Kentucky. Botkin obtained a bachelor's degree in elementary education with a concentration in special education and then went on to receive a master's degree in early childhood education. She spent the next six years working with children and their families in a variety of settings, including child care, elementary school, and Head Start. These experiences led Botkin to recognize the interdependence of the developmental settings that children and their parents experience (such as home, school, and work). She returned to graduate school and obtained a Ph.D. in family studies from the University of Tennessee. She then became a faculty member in the Family Studies program at the University of Kentucky. Completing further coursework and clinical training in marriage and family therapy, she became certified as a marriage and family therapist.

Botkin's current interests include working with young children in family therapy, addressing gender and ethnic issues in family therapy, and exploring the role of spirituality in family wellness.

Darla Botkin (*left*) conducting a family therapy session.

For more information about what marriage and family therapists do, see page 47 in the Careers in Life-Span Development appendix.

2013; Cicchetti & others, 2012). This term does not have quite the emotional impact of the term *abuse* and acknowledges that maltreatment includes diverse conditions.

Types of Child Maltreatment   The four main types of child maltreatment are physical abuse, child neglect, sexual abuse, and emotional abuse (National Clearinghouse on Child Abuse and Neglect, 2004):

- *Physical abuse* is characterized by the infliction of physical injury as a result of punching, beating, kicking, biting, burning, shaking, or otherwise harming a child. The parent or other person may not have intended to hurt the child; the injury may have resulted from excessive physical punishment (Hornor, 2012).

- *Child neglect* is characterized by failure to provide for the child's basic needs. Neglect can be physical (abandonment, for example), educational (allowing chronic truancy, for example), or emotional (marked inattention to the child's needs, for example). Child neglect is by far the most common form of child maltreatment. In every country where relevant data have been collected, neglect occurs up to three times as often as abuse (Benoit, Coolbear, & Crawford, 2008).

- *Sexual abuse* includes fondling a child's genitals, intercourse, incest, rape, sodomy, exhibitionism, and commercial exploitation through prostitution or the production of pornographic materials (Preer, Sorrentino, & Newton, 2012).

- *Emotional abuse (psychological/verbal abuse/mental injury)* includes acts or omissions by parents or other caregivers that have caused, or could cause, serious behavioral, cognitive, or emotional problems (van Harmelen & others, 2010).

> Child maltreatment involves grossly inadequate and destructive aspects of parenting.
>
> —DANTE CICCHETTI
> *Contemporary Developmental Psychologist, University of Minnesota*

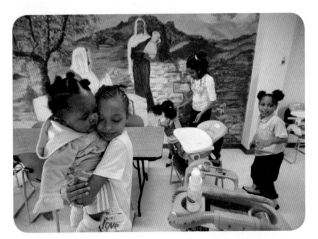

Eight-year-old Donnique Hein lovingly holds her younger sister, 6-month-old Maria Paschel, after a meal at Laura's Home, a crisis shelter in Westpark run by the City Mission, in March 2010.

Although any of these forms of child maltreatment may be found separately, they often occur in combination. Emotional abuse is almost always present when other forms are identified.

The Contexts of Abuse   No single factor causes child maltreatment (Cicchetti, 2011, 2013; Cicchetti & Rogosch, 2012). A combination of factors, including the culture, family, and developmental characteristics of the child, likely contribute to child maltreatment.

The extensive violence that takes place in American culture, including TV violence, is reflected in the occurrence of violence in the family (Durrant, 2008). The family itself is obviously a key part of the context of abuse (Cicchetti, 2013; Trickett & Negriff, 2011). Among the family and family-associated characteristics that may contribute to child maltreatment are parenting stress, substance abuse, social isolation, single parenting, and socioeconomic difficulties (especially poverty) (Cicchetti, 2013; Laslett & others, 2012; Turner & others, 2012). The interactions of all family members need to be considered, regardless of who performs the violent acts against the child. For example, even though the father may be the one who physically abuses the child, the behavior of the mother, the child, and siblings also should be evaluated.

Were parents who abuse children abused by their own parents? About one-third of parents who were abused themselves when they were young go on to abuse their own children (Cicchetti & Toth, 2006). Thus, some, but not a majority, of parents are involved in an intergenerational transmission of abuse.

Developmental Consequences of Abuse   Among the consequences of child maltreatment in childhood and adolescence are poor emotion regulation, attachment problems, problems in peer relations, difficulty in adapting to school, and other psychological problems such as depression and delinquency (Cicchetti, 2011, 2013; Cicchetti & Rogosch, 2012). As shown in Figure 8.4, maltreated young children in foster care were more likely to show abnormal stress hormone levels than middle-SES young children living with their birth family (Gunnar, Fisher, & The Early Experience, Stress, and Prevention Network, 2006). In this study, the abnormal stress hormone levels were mainly present in the foster children who were neglected, best described as "institutional neglect" (Fisher, 2005). Abuse also may have this effect on young children (Gunnar & others, 2006). Adolescents who experienced abuse or neglect as children are more likely than adolescents who were not maltreated as children to engage in violent romantic relationships, delinquency, sexual risk taking, and substance abuse (Shin, Hong, & Hazen, 2010; Trickett, Negriff, & Peckins, 2011). And a recent study revealed that a significant increase in suicide attempts before age 18 occurred with repeated child maltreatment (Jonson-Reid, Kohl, & Drake, 2012).

Later, during the adult years, individuals who were maltreated as children are more likely to experience physical ailments, mental illness, and sexual problems (Lacelle & others, 2012). A 30-year longitudinal study found that middle-aged adults who had experienced maltreatment in childhood were at increased risk for diabetes, lung disease, malnutrition, and vision problems (Widom & others, 2012). Another study revealed that child maltreatment was linked to depression in adulthood and to unfavorable outcomes for treatment of depression (Nanni, Uher, & Danese, 2012). Further, adults who were maltreated as children often have difficulty establishing and maintaining healthy intimate relationships (Dozier, Stovall-McClough, & Albus, 2009). As adults, maltreated children are also at higher risk for violent behavior toward other adults—especially dating partners and marital partners—as well as substance abuse, anxiety, and depression (Miller-Perrin, Perrin, & Kocur, 2009). One study also revealed that adults who had experienced child maltreatment were at increased risk for financial and employment-related difficulties (Zielinski, 2009).

An important research agenda is to discover how to prevent child maltreatment or to intervene in children's lives when they have been maltreated (Cicchetti & others, 2012; Preer, Sorrentino, & Newton, 2012; Shapiro, Prinz, & Sanders, 2012). In one study of maltreating mothers and their 1-year-olds, two treatments were effective in reducing child maltreatment:

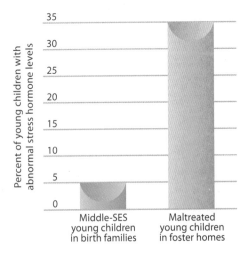

FIGURE **8.4**

ABNORMAL STRESS HORMONE LEVELS IN YOUNG CHILDREN IN DIFFERENT TYPES OF REARING CONDITIONS

(1) home visitation that emphasized improved parenting, coping with stress, and increasing support for the mother; and (2) parent-infant psychotherapy that focused on improving maternal-infant attachment (Cicchetti, Toth, & Rogusch, 2005).

SIBLING RELATIONSHIPS AND BIRTH ORDER

How do developmentalists characterize sibling relationships? How extensively does birth order influence behavior?

Sibling Relationships Approximately 80 percent of American children have one or more siblings—that is, sisters and brothers (Dunn, 2007). If you grew up with siblings, you probably have a rich memory of aggressive, hostile interchanges. Siblings in the presence of each other when they are 2 to 4 years of age, on average, have a conflict once every 10 minutes and then the conflicts go down somewhat from 5 to 7 years of age (Kramer, 2006). What do parents do when they encounter siblings having a verbal or physical confrontation? One study revealed that they do one of three things: (1) intervene and try to help them resolve the conflict, (2) admonish or threaten them, or (3) do nothing at all (Kramer & Perozynski, 1999). Of interest is that in families with two siblings 2 to 5 years of age, the most frequent parental reaction is to do nothing at all.

Laurie Kramer (2006), who has conducted a number of research studies on siblings, says that not intervening and letting sibling conflict escalate are not good strategies. She developed a program titled "More Fun with Sisters and Brothers" that teaches 4- to 8-year-old siblings social skills for developing positive interactions (Kramer & Radey, 1997). Among the social skills taught in the program are how to appropriately initiate play, how to accept and refuse invitations to play, how to take another person's perspective, how to deal with angry feelings, and how to manage conflict.

However, conflict is only one of the many dimensions of sibling relations (Howe, Ross, & Recchia, 2011). Sibling relations include helping, sharing, teaching, fighting, and playing, and siblings can act as emotional supports, rivals, and communication partners.

Judy Dunn (2007), a leading expert on sibling relationships, recently described three important characteristics of sibling relationships:

- *Emotional quality of the relationship.* Intense positive and negative emotions are often expressed by siblings toward each other. Many children and adolescents have mixed feelings toward their siblings.

- *Familiarity and intimacy of the relationship.* Siblings typically know each other very well, and this intimacy suggests that they can either provide support or tease and undermine each other, depending on the situation.

- *Variation in sibling relationships.* Some siblings describe their relationships more positively than others. Thus, there is considerable variation in sibling relationships. We just discussed that many siblings have mixed feelings about each other, but some children and adolescents mainly describe their siblings in warm, affectionate ways, whereas others primarily talk about how irritating and mean a sibling is. Research indicates that a high level of sibling conflict is linked to negative developmental outcomes (Fosco & others, 2012).

What characterizes children's sibling relationships?

Birth Order Whether a child has older or younger siblings has been linked to development of certain personality characteristics. For example, a recent review concluded that "firstborns are the most intelligent, achieving, and conscientious, while later-borns are the most rebellious, liberal, and agreeable" (Paulhus, 2008, p. 210). Compared with later-born children, firstborn children have also been described as more adult-oriented, helpful, conforming, and self-controlled. However, when such birth-order differences are reported, they often are small.

What accounts for differences related to birth order? Proposed explanations usually point to variations in interactions with parents and siblings associated with being in a particular position

developmental **connection**

Family

Siblings who are psychologically close to each other in adulthood tended to be that way in childhood. Chapter 16, p. 523

The one-child family is becoming much more common in China because of the strong motivation to limit the population growth in the People's Republic of China. The policy is still relatively new, and its effects on children have not been fully examined. *In general, though, what have researchers found the only child to be like?*

How does work affect parenting?

in the family. In one study, mothers became more negative, coercive, and restraining and played less with the firstborn following the birth of a second child (Dunn & Kendrick, 1982).

What is the only child like? The popular conception is that the only child is a "spoiled brat," with such undesirable characteristics as dependency, lack of self-control, and self-centered behavior. But researchers present a more positive portrayal of the only child. Only children often are achievement-oriented and display a desirable personality, especially in comparison with later-borns and children from large families (Falbo & Poston, 1993; Jiao, Ji, & Jing, 1996).

So far, our discussion suggests that birth order might be a strong predictor of behavior. However, an increasing number of family researchers stress that when all of the factors that influence behavior are considered, birth order by itself shows limited ability to predict behavior. Think about some of the other important factors beyond birth order in children's lives that influence their behavior. They include heredity, models of competency or incompetency that parents present to children on a daily basis, peer influences, school influences, socioeconomic factors, sociohistorical factors, and cultural variations. When someone says firstborns are always like this but last-borns are always like that, the person is making overly simplistic statements that do not adequately take into account the complexity of influences on a child's development.

THE CHANGING FAMILY IN A CHANGING SOCIETY

Beyond variations in the number of siblings, the families that children experience differ in many important ways. The number of children growing up in single-parent families is staggering. As shown in Figure 8.5, the United States has one of the highest percentages of single-parent families in the world. Among two-parent families, there are those in which both parents work outside the home, one or both parents had a previous marriage that ended in divorce, or the parents are gay or lesbian. Differences in culture and socioeconomic status (SES) also influence families. How do these variations in families affect children?

Working Parents   More than one of every two U.S. mothers with a child under the age of 5 is in the labor force; more than two of every three with a child from 6 to 17 years of age is employed. Maternal employment is a part of modern life, but its effects continue to be debated.

Most research on parental work has focused on the role of maternal employment on young children's development (Brooks-Gunn, Han, & Waldfogel, 2010). However, the effects of working parents involve the father as well as the mother when such matters as work schedules and work-family stress are considered (O'Brien & Moss, 2010; Parke & Clarke-Stewart, 2011). Recent research indicates that the nature of parents' work has more influence on children's development than the fact that one parent works outside the home (Han, 2009; Parke & Clarke-Stewart, 2011). Work can produce positive and negative effects on parenting

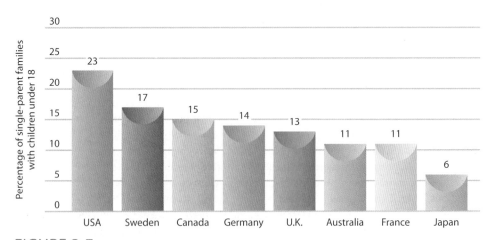

FIGURE **8.5**
SINGLE-PARENT FAMILIES IN DIFFERENT COUNTRIES

(Crouter & McHale, 2005). Ann Crouter (2006) described how parents bring their experiences at work into their homes. She concluded that parents who face poor working conditions such as long hours, overtime work, stressful work, and lack of autonomy on the job are likely to be more irritable at home and to engage in less effective parenting than their counterparts with better working conditions. A consistent finding is that children (especially girls) of working mothers engage in less gender stereotyping and have more egalitarian views of gender than children whose mothers are not employed outside the home (Goldberg & Lucas-Thompson, 2008).

Children in Divorced Families

Divorce rates changed rather dramatically in the United States and many countries around the world in the late twentieth century (Amato & Dorius, 2010). The U.S. divorce rate increased dramatically in the 1960s and 1970s but has declined since the 1980s. However, the divorce rate in the United States remains much higher than it is in most other countries.

It is estimated that 40 percent of children born to married parents in the United States will experience their parents' divorce (Hetherington & Stanley-Hagan, 2002). Let's examine some important questions about children in divorced families.

Are children better adjusted in intact, never-divorced families than in divorced families? Most researchers agree that children from divorced families show poorer adjustment than their counterparts in nondivorced families (Amato & Dorius, 2010; Hetherington, 2006; Lansford, 2012; Robbers & others, 2012; Wallerstein, 2008) (see Figure 8.6). Those who have experienced multiple divorces are at greater risk. Children in divorced families are more likely than children in nondivorced families to have academic problems, to show externalized problems (such as acting out and delinquency) and internalized problems (such as anxiety and depression), to be less socially responsible, to have less competent intimate relationships, to drop out of school, to become sexually active at an early age, to take drugs, to associate with antisocial peers, to have low self-esteem, and to be less securely attached as young adults (Conger & Chao, 1996). Nonetheless, keep in mind that a majority of children in divorced families do not have significant adjustment problems (Ahrons, 2007). One study found that 20 years after their parents had divorced when they were children, approximately 80 percent of adults concluded that their parents' decision to divorce was a wise one (Ahrons, 2004).

Should parents stay together for the sake of the children? Whether parents should stay in an unhappy marriage for the sake of their children is one of the most commonly asked questions about divorce (Hetherington, 2006). If the stresses and disruptions in family relationships associated with an unhappy, conflictual marriage that erode the well-being of children are reduced by the move to a divorced, single-parent family, divorce can be advantageous. However, if the diminished resources and increased risks associated with divorce also are accompanied by inept parenting and sustained or increased conflict, not only between the divorced couple but also among the parents, children, and siblings, the best choice for the children would be that an unhappy marriage is retained (Hetherington & Stanley-Hagan, 2002). It is difficult to determine how these "ifs" will play out when parents either remain together in an acrimonious marriage or become divorced.

Note that marital conflict may have negative consequences for children in the context of marriage or divorce (El-Sheikh & others, 2012). And many of the problems that children from divorced homes experience begin during the predivorce period, a time when parents are often in active conflict with each other. Thus, when children from divorced homes show problems, the problems may not be due only to the divorce but also to the marital conflict that led to it.

E. Mark Cummings and his colleagues (Cummings & Davies, 2010; Cummings, El-Sheikh, & Kouros, 2009; Cummings & Schatz, 2012; Koss & others, 2011, 2012) have proposed *emotion security theory*, which has its roots in attachment theory and states that children appraise marital conflict in terms of their sense of security and safety in the family. They make a distinction between marital conflict that is negative for children (such as hostile emotional displays and destructive conflict tactics) and marital conflict that can be positive for children (such as marital disagreement that involves calmly discussing each person's perspective and then working together to reach a solution).

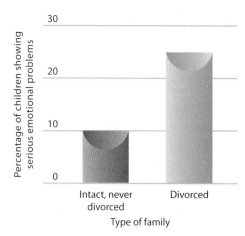

FIGURE **8.6**

DIVORCE AND CHILDREN'S EMOTIONAL PROBLEMS. In Hetherington's research, 25 percent of children from divorced families showed serious emotional problems compared with only 10 percent of children from intact, never-divorced families. However, keep in mind that a substantial majority (75 percent) of the children from divorced families did not show serious emotional problems.

What concerns are involved in whether parents should stay together for the sake of the children or become divorced?

How much do family processes matter in divorced families? Family processes matter a great deal (Lansford, 2012; Sigal & others, 2011; Sutherland, Altenhofen, & Biringen, 2012). For example, when divorced parents' relationship with each other is harmonious and when they use authoritative parenting, the adjustment of children improves (Hetherington, 2006). When the divorced parents can agree on childrearing strategies and can maintain a cordial relationship with each other, frequent visits by the noncustodial parent usually benefit the child (Fabricius & others, 2010). Following a divorce, father involvement with children drops off more than mother involvement, especially for fathers of girls. Also, a recent study in divorced families revealed that an intervention focused on improving the mother-child relationship was linked to improvements in relationship quality that increased children's coping skills over the short term (6 months) and long term (6 years) (Velez & others, 2011).

What factors influence an individual child's vulnerability to suffering negative consequences from living in a divorced family? Among the factors involved in the child's risk and vulnerability is the child's adjustment prior to the divorce, as well as the child's personality and temperament, gender, and custody situation (Hetherington, 2006). Children whose parents later divorce show poorer adjustment before the breakup (Amato & Booth, 1996). Children who are socially mature and responsible, who show few behavioral problems, and who have an easy temperament are better able to cope with their parents' divorce. Children with a difficult temperament often have problems coping with their parents' divorce (Hetherington, 2000).

Earlier studies reported gender differences in response to divorce, with divorce being more negative for boys than girls in mother-custody families. However, more recent studies have shown that gender differences are less pronounced and consistent than was previously believed. Some of the inconsistency may be due to the increase in father custody, joint custody, and increased involvement of noncustodial fathers, especially in their sons' lives (Ziol-Guest, 2009).

Research on whether different types of custodial arrangements are better for children in divorced families has yielded inconsistent results (Spruijt & Duindam, 2010). An analysis of studies found that children in joint-custody families were better adjusted than children in sole-custody families (Bauserman, 2002). However, joint custody works best for children when the parents can get along with each other (Parke & Clarke-Stewart, 2011). What role does socioeconomic status play in the lives of children in divorced families? Custodial mothers experience the loss of about one-fourth to one-half of their predivorce income, in comparison with a loss of only one-tenth by custodial fathers. This income loss for divorced mothers is accompanied by increased workloads, high rates of job instability, and residential moves to less desirable neighborhoods with inferior schools (Sayer, 2006).

In sum, many factors are involved in determining how divorce influences a child's development (Hetherington, 2006; Lansford, 2012). To read about some strategies for helping children cope with the divorce of their parents, see *Connecting Development to Life.*

developmental connection

Family

Early marriage, low educational level, low income, not having a religious affiliation, having parents who are divorced, and having a baby before marriage are factors linked to an increased probability of divorce. Chapter 14, p. 465

What are the research findings regarding the development and psychological well-being of children raised by gay and lesbian couples?

Gay and Lesbian Parents   Increasingly, gay and lesbian couples are creating families that include children (Patterson & D'Augelli, 2013). Approximately 20 percent of lesbians and 10 percent of gays are parents. There may be more than 1 million gay and lesbian parents in the United States today.

Like heterosexual couples, gay and lesbian parents vary greatly. They may be single or they may have same-gender partners. Many lesbian mothers and gay fathers are noncustodial parents because they lost custody of their children to heterosexual spouses after a divorce. In addition, gays and lesbians are increasingly choosing parenthood through donor insemination or adoption. Researchers have found that the children created through new reproductive technologies—such as in vitro fertilization—are as well adjusted as their counterparts conceived by natural means (Golombok, 2011a, b; Golombok & Tasker, 2010).

Parenthood among lesbians and gays is controversial. Opponents claim that being raised by gay or lesbian parents harms the child's development. But researchers have found few differences between children growing up with lesbian mothers or gay fathers on the one hand, and children growing up with heterosexual parents on the other (Golombok & Tasker, 2010; Patterson, 2012; Patterson & Farr, 2012). For example, children growing up in gay or lesbian families are just as popular with their peers, and no differences are found in the adjustment

connecting development to life

Communicating with Children About Divorce

Ellen Galinsky and Judy David (1988) developed a number of guidelines for communicating with children about divorce.

- *Explain the separation.* As soon as daily activities in the home make it obvious that one parent is leaving, tell the children. If possible, both parents should be present when children are told about the separation to come. The reasons for the separation are very difficult for young children to understand. No matter what parents tell children, children can find reasons to argue against the separation. It is extremely important for parents to tell the children who will take care of them and to describe the specific arrangements for seeing the other parent.

- *Explain that the separation is not the child's fault.* Young children often believe their parents' separation or divorce is their own fault. Therefore, it is important to tell children that they are not the cause of the separation. Parents need to repeat this statement a number of times.

- *Explain that it may take time to feel better.* Tell young children that it's normal to not feel good about what is happening and that many other children feel this way when their parents become separated. It is also okay for divorced parents to share some of their emotions with children, by saying something like "I'm having a hard time since the separation just like you, but I know it's going to get better after a while." Such statements are best kept brief and should not criticize the other parent.

- ***Keep the door open for further discussion.*** Tell your children to come to you anytime they want to talk about the separation. It is healthy for children to express their pent-up emotions in discussions with their parents and to learn that the parents are willing to listen to their feelings and fears.

- ***Provide as much continuity as possible.*** The less children's worlds are disrupted by the separation, the easier their transition to a single-parent family will be. Thus, parents should maintain the rules already in place as much as possible. Children need parents who care enough not only to give them warmth and nurturance but also to set reasonable limits.

- ***Provide support for your children and yourself.*** After a divorce or separation, parents are as important to children as before the divorce or separation. Divorced parents need to provide children with as much support as possible. Parents function best when other people are available to give them support as adults and as parents. Divorced parents can find people who provide practical help and with whom they can talk about their problems.

How does the third bullet point above ("Explain that it may take time to feel better.") relate to what you learned earlier in this chapter about emotion coaching?

---

and mental health of children living in these families when they are compared with children in heterosexual families (Hyde, & Else-Quest, 2013). Contrary to the once-popular expectation that being raised by a gay or lesbian parent would result in the child growing up to be gay or lesbian, in reality the overwhelming majority of children from gay or lesbian families have a heterosexual orientation (Golombok & Tasker, 2010; Tasker & Golombok, 1997).

Cultural, Ethnic, and Socioeconomic Variations Parenting can be influenced by culture, ethnicity, and socioeconomic status (Parra Cardona & others, 2012; Taylor & others, 2012; Widom & Nikulina, 2012). Recall from Bronfenbrenner's ecological theory (see Chapter 1) that a number of social contexts influence the child's development. In Bronfenbrenner's theory, culture, ethnicity, and socioeconomic status are classified as part of the macrosystem because they represent broader, societal contexts.

Cross-Cultural Studies Different cultures often give different answers to basic questions such as what the father's role in the family should be, what support systems are available to families, and how children should be disciplined (Bekman & Aksu-Koc, 2012). There are important cross-cultural variations in parenting and the value placed on children (Trommsdorff, 2012). In some cultures, such as rural areas of many countries, authoritarian parenting is widespread.

Cultural change, brought about by factors such as increasingly frequent international travel, the Internet and electronic communications, and economic globalization, is coming to families in many countries around the world. There are trends toward greater family mobility, migration to urban areas, separation as some family members work in cities or countries far from their homes, smaller families, fewer extended-family households, and increases in maternal employment (Brown & Larson, 2002). These trends can change the resources that are available to children. For example, when several generations no longer live near each other, children may lose support and guidance from grandparents, aunts, and uncles. On the positive side, smaller families may produce more openness and communication between parents and children.

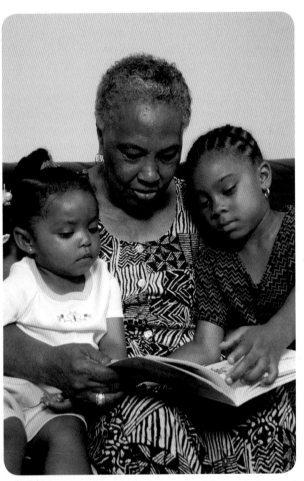

What are some characteristics of families within different ethnic groups?

Ethnicity Families within different ethnic groups in the United States differ in their typical size, structure, composition, reliance on kinship networks, and levels of income and education (Conger & others, 2012; Gonzales & others, 2012). Large and extended families are more common among minority groups than among the non-Latino White majority. For example, 19 percent of Latino families have three or more children, compared with 14 percent of African American and 10 percent of White families. African American and Latino children interact more with grandparents, aunts, uncles, cousins, and more distant relatives than do White children.

Single-parent families are more common among African Americans and Latinos than among White Americans (Zeiders, Roosa, & Tein, 2011). In comparison with two-parent households, single parents often have more limited resources of time, money, and energy (Wright & others, 2012). Ethnic minority parents also are less educated and more likely to live in low-income circumstances than their White counterparts. Still, many impoverished ethnic minority families manage to find ways to raise competent children (Hattery & Smith, 2007). Of course, individual families vary, and how ethnic minority families deal with stress depends on many factors (Nieto & Bode, 2012). Whether the parents are native-born or immigrants, how long the family has been in this country, its socioeconomic status, and its national origin all make a difference (Gonzales & others, 2012). The characteristics of the family's social context also influence its adaptation. What are the attitudes toward the family's ethnic group within its neighborhood or city? Can the family's children attend good schools? Are there community groups that welcome people from the family's ethnic group? Do members of the family's ethnic group form community groups of their own?

Recently immigrated families may face special problems. Many individuals in immigrant families are dealing with problems associated with being undocumented. Living in an undocumented family can affect children's developmental outcomes because of parents' unwillingness to sign up for services for which they may be eligible, conditions linked to low-wage work and lack of benefits, stress, and a lack of cognitive stimulation in the home (Yoshikawa, 2011).

Ethnic minority/immigrant children and their parents are expected to move beyond their own cultural background and identify with aspects of the dominant culture. They undergo varying degrees of acculturation, which refers to cultural changes that occur when one culture comes in contact with another. Asian American parents, for example, may feel pressed to modify the traditional training style of parental control discussed earlier as they encounter the more permissive parenting typical of the dominant culture.

Recent research indicates that many members of families that have recently immigrated to the United States adopt a bicultural orientation, selecting characteristics of the U.S. culture that help them to survive and advance, while still retaining aspects of their culture of origin (Mok & Morris, 2012). In adopting characteristics of the U.S. culture, Latino families are increasingly embracing its emphasis on education (Cooper, 2011). Although their school dropout rates have remained higher than those of other ethnic groups, toward the end of the first decade of the twenty-first century they declined considerably (National Center for Education Statistics, 2011). However, while many ethnic/immigrant families adopt a bicultural orientation, parenting in many ethnic minority families also focuses on issues associated with promoting children's ethnic pride, knowledge of their ethnic group, and awareness of discrimination (Ho & others, 2012; Hughes & others, 2009; Rogers & others, 2012; Simpkins & others, 2012).

Socioeconomic Status   Low-income families have less access to resources than higher-income families do (Conger & others, 2012; Duncan, 2012; Evans & others, 2012). The differential in access to resources encompasses nutrition, health care, protection from danger, and enriching educational and socialization opportunities such as tutoring and lessons in various activities (Glick & Clark, 2012; Huston, 2012). These differences are compounded in low-income families characterized by long-term poverty (Maholmes & King, 2012; Widom & Nikulina, 2012). A recent study found that persistent economic hardship and very early poverty were linked to lower cognitive functioning in children at 5 years of age (Schoon & others, 2012).

In the United States and most Western cultures, differences have been found in child rearing among families with different socioeconomic statuses (SES) (Hoff, Laursen, & Tardif, 2002, p. 246):

- "Lower-SES parents (1) are more concerned that their children conform to society's expectations, (2) create a home atmosphere in which it is clear that parents have authority over children," (3) use physical punishment more in disciplining their children, and (4) are more directive and less conversational with their children.

- "Higher-SES parents (1) are more concerned with developing children's initiative" and delay of gratification, "(2) create a home atmosphere in which children are more nearly equal participants and in which rules are discussed as opposed to being laid down" in an authoritarian manner, (3) are less likely to use physical punishment, and (4) "are less directive and more conversational" with their children.

Review Connect Reflect

LG2 Explain how families can influence young children's development.

Review

- What are the four main parenting styles, and what aspects of parenting are linked with young children's development?
- What are the types and consequences of child maltreatment?
- How are sibling relationships and birth order related to young children's development?
- How is young children's development affected by having two wage-earning parents, having divorced parents, having gay or lesbian parents, and being part of a particular cultural, ethnic, and socioeconomic group?

Connect

- In Chapter 4, you learned that fathers were most often the perpetrators in shaken baby syndrome. Given what you learned in this chapter, which family interactions would a researcher or marriage and family therapist be likely to explore in such a case of child maltreatment?

Reflect *Your Own Personal Journey of Life*

- Which style or styles of parenting did your mother and father use in rearing you? What effects do you think their parenting styles have had on your development?

3 Peer Relations, Play, and Media/Screen Time

LG3 Describe the roles of peers, play, and media/screen time in young children's development.

Peer Relations | Play | Media and Screen Time

The family is an important social context for children's development. However, children's development also is strongly influenced by what goes on in other social contexts, such as in peer groups and when children are playing or spending time with the media, computers, and other electronic devices.

What are some characteristics of peer relations in early childhood?

developmental **connection**

Peers

Children's peer relations have been classified in terms of five peer statuses. Chapter 10, p. 336

How do relationships with parents influence children's peer relationships?

PEER RELATIONS

As children grow older, they spend an increasing amount of time with their *peers*—children of about the same age or maturity level.

Peer Group Functions   What are the functions of a child's peer group? One of its most important functions is to provide a source of information and comparison about the world outside the family. Children receive feedback about their abilities from their peer group. Children evaluate what they do in terms of whether it is better than, as good as, or worse than what other children do. It is hard to make these judgments at home because siblings are usually older or younger.

Good peer relations can be necessary for normal socioemotional development (Ladd & others, 2012; Ryan & Ladd, 2012). Special concerns in peer relations focus on children who are withdrawn or aggressive (Roll, Koglin, & Petermann, 2012; Rubin & others, 2011, 2013). Withdrawn children who are rejected by peers or are victimized and feel lonely are at risk for depression. Children who are aggressive with their peers are at risk for developing a number of problems, including delinquency and dropping out of school (Bukowski, Buhrmester, & Underwood, 2011).

Developmental Changes   Recall from our discussion of gender that, by about the age of 3, children already prefer to spend time with same-sex rather than opposite-sex playmates, and this preference increases in early childhood. During these same years the frequency of peer interaction, both positive and negative, picks up considerably (Cillessen & Bellmore, 2011). Many preschool children spend considerable time in peer interaction conversing with playmates about such matters as "negotiating roles and rules in play, arguing, and agreeing" (Rubin, Bukowski, & Parker, 2006). And during early childhood children's interactions with peers become more coordinated and involve longer turns and sequences (Coplan & Arbeau, 2009).

Friends   In early childhood, children distinguish between friends and nonfriends (Howes, 2009). For most young children, a friend is someone to play with. Young preschool children are more likely than older children to have friends who are of different gender and ethnicity (Howes, 2009).

The Connected Worlds of Parent-Child and Peer Relations   Parents may influence their children's peer relations in many ways, both directly and indirectly (Reich & Vandell, 2011). Parents affect such relations through their interactions with their children, how they manage their children's lives, and the opportunities they provide to their children (Brown & Bakken, 2011).

Basic lifestyle decisions by parents—their choices of neighborhoods, churches, schools, and their own friends—largely determine the pool from which their children select possible friends. These choices in turn affect which children their children meet, their purpose in interacting, and eventually which children become their friends.

Researchers also have found that children's peer relations are linked to attachment security and parents' marital quality (Booth-LaForce & Kerns, 2009). Early attachments to caregivers provide a connection to children's peer relations not only by creating a secure base from which children can explore social relationships beyond the family but also by conveying a working model of relationships (Hartup, 2009).

Do these results indicate that children's peer relations always are wedded to parent-child relationships? Although parent-child relationships influence children's subsequent peer relations, children also learn other modes of relating through their relationships with peers. For example, rough-and-tumble play occurs mainly with other children, not in parent-child interaction. In times of stress, children often turn to parents rather than peers for support. In parent-child relationships, children learn how to relate to authority figures. With their peers, children are likely to interact on a much more equal basis and to learn a mode of relating based on mutual influence. We will have much more to say about peer relations in Chapter 10, "Socioemotional Development in Middle and Late Childhood."

PLAY

An extensive amount of peer interaction during childhood involves play, but social play is only one type of play. Play is a pleasurable activity in which children engage for its own sake, and its functions and forms vary.

Play's Functions   Play makes important contributions to young children's cognitive and socioemotional development (Coplan & Arbeau, 2009; Pellegrini, 2013). Theorists have focused on different aspects of play and highlighted a long list of functions.

According to Freud and Erikson, play helps children master anxieties and conflicts. Because tensions are relieved in play, children can cope with life's problems. Play permits children to work off excess physical energy and to release pent-up tensions. Therapists use *play therapy* both to allow children to work off frustrations and to analyze children's conflicts and ways of coping with them (Sanders, 2008). Children may feel less threatened and be more likely to express their true feelings in the context of play.

Play also is an important context for cognitive development (Power, 2011). Both Piaget and Vygotsky concluded that play is a child's work. Piaget (1962) maintained that play advances children's cognitive development. At the same time, he said that children's cognitive development *constrains* the way they play. Play permits children to practice their competencies and acquired skills in a relaxed, pleasurable way. Piaget thought that cognitive structures need to be exercised, and play provides the perfect setting for this exercise.

Vygotsky (1962) also considered play to be an excellent setting for cognitive development. He was especially interested in the symbolic and make-believe aspects of play, as when a child substitutes a stick for a horse and rides the stick as if it were a horse. For young children, the imaginary situation is real. Parents should encourage such imaginary play, because it advances the child's cognitive development, especially creative thought.

Daniel Berlyne (1960) described play as exciting and pleasurable in itself because it satisfies our exploratory drive. This drive involves curiosity and a desire for information about something new or unusual. Play encourages exploratory behavior by offering children the possibilities of novelty, complexity, uncertainty, surprise, and incongruity.

More recently, play has been described as an important context for the development of language and communication skills (Harris, Golinkoff, & Hirsh-Pasek, 2011; Hirsh-Pasek & Golinkoff, 2013). Language and communication skills may be enhanced through discussions and negotiations regarding roles and rules in play as young children practice various words and phrases. These types of social interactions during play can benefit young children's literacy skills (Gunning, 2013; Morrow, 2012). And, as we saw in Chapter 7, play is a central focus of the child-centered kindergarten and is thought to be an essential aspect of early childhood education (Feeney, Moravcik, & Nolte, 2013; Henninger, 2013).

Types of Play   The contemporary perspective on play emphasizes both the cognitive and the social aspects of play (Fung & Cheng, 2012; Vong, 2012). Among the most widely studied types of children's play today are sensorimotor and practice play, pretense/symbolic play, social play, constructive play, and games (Bergen, 1988).

Sensorimotor and Practice Play   **Sensorimotor play** is behavior by infants that lets them derive pleasure from exercising their sensorimotor schemes. The development of sensorimotor play follows Piaget's description of sensorimotor thought, which we discussed in Chapter 5. Infants initially engage in exploratory and playful visual and motor transactions in the second quarter of the first year of life. At about 9 months of age, infants begin to select novel objects for exploration and play, especially responsive objects such as toys that make noise or bounce.

Practice play involves the repetition of behavior when new skills are being learned or when physical or mental mastery and coordination of skills are required for games or sports. Sensorimotor play, which often involves practice play, is primarily confined to infancy, whereas

> Let us play, for it is yet day
> And we cannot go to sleep;
> Besides, in the sky the little birds fly
> And the hills are all covered with sheep.
>
> —**WILLIAM BLAKE**
> *English Poet, 19th Century*

developmental **connection**

Sociocultural Cognitive Theory

Vygotsky emphasized that children develop their ways of thinking and understanding mainly through social interaction. Chapter 7, p. 221

sensorimotor play Behavior engaged in by infants that lets them derive pleasure from exercising their existing sensorimotor schemas.

practice play Play that involves repetition of behavior when new skills are being learned or when physical or mental mastery and coordination of skills are required for games or sports.

practice play can be engaged in throughout life. During the preschool years, children often engage in practice play.

Pretense/Symbolic Play **Pretense/symbolic play** occurs when the child transforms the physical environment into a symbol. Between 9 and 30 months of age, children increase their use of objects in symbolic play. They learn to transform objects—substituting them for other objects and acting toward them as if they were those other objects. For example, a preschool child treats a table as if it were a car and says, "I'm fixing the car," as he grabs a leg of the table.

Many experts on play consider the preschool years the "golden age" of symbolic/pretense play that is dramatic or sociodramatic in nature. This type of make-believe play often appears at about 18 months of age and reaches a peak at 4 to 5 years of age, then gradually declines.

Some child psychologists conclude that pretend play is an important aspect of young children's development and often reflects advances in their cognitive development, especially as an indication of symbolic understanding. For example, Catherine Garvey (2000) and Angeline Lillard (2006) emphasize that hidden in young children's pretend play narratives are remarkable capacities for role-taking, balancing of social roles, metacognition (thinking about thinking), testing of the reality-pretense distinction, and numerous nonegocentric capacities that reveal the remarkable cognitive skills of young children. In one recent analysis, a major accomplishment in early childhood is the development of children's ability to share their pretend play with peers (Coplan & Arbeau, 2009). And researchers have found that pretend play contributes to young children's self-regulation, mainly because of the self-monitoring and social sensitivity that is required in creating and enacting a sociodramatic narrative in cooperation with other children (Diamond & others, 2007).

Social Play **Social play** involves interaction with peers. Social play increases dramatically during the preschool years. For many children, social play is the main context for young children's social interactions with peers (Power, 2011).

Constructive Play **Constructive play** combines sensorimotor/practice play with symbolic representation. It occurs when children engage in the self-regulated creation of a product or a solution. Constructive play increases in the preschool years as symbolic play increases and sensorimotor play decreases. It also becomes a frequent form of play in the elementary school years, both in and out of the classroom.

And that park grew up with me; that small world widened as I learned its secrets and boundaries, as I discovered new refuges in its woods and jungles: hidden homes and lairs for the multitudes of imagination, for cowboys and Indians. . . . I used to dawdle on half holidays along the bent and Devon-facing seashore, hoping for gold watches or the skull of a sheep or a message in a bottle to be washed up with the tide.

—**Dylan Thomas**
Welsh Poet, 20th Century

A preschool "superhero" at play.

What characterizes social play?

Trends in Play Kathy Hirsh-Pasek, Roberta Golinkoff, and Dorothy Singer (Hirsh-Pasek & others, 2009; Singer, Golinkoff, & Hirsh-Pasek, 2006) are concerned about the amount of time for free play that young children have, reporting that it has declined considerably in recent decades. They especially are worried about young children's playtime being restricted at home and school so they can spend more time on academic subjects. They also point out that many schools have eliminated recess. And it is not just the declining time for free play that bothers them. They underscore that learning in playful contexts captivates children's minds in ways that enhance their cognitive and socioemotional development—Singer, Golinkoff, and Hirsh-Pasek's (2006) first book on play was titled: *Play = Learning*. Among the cognitive benefits of play they described are skills in the following areas: creativity; abstract thinking; imagination; attention, concentration, and persistence; problem-solving; social cognition, empathy, and perspective taking; language; and mastery of new concepts. Among the socioemotional experiences and development they believe play promotes are enjoyment, relaxation, and self-expression; cooperation, sharing, and turn-taking; anxiety reduction; and self-confidence. With so many positive cognitive and socioemotional outcomes of play, clearly it is important that we find more time for play in young children's lives.

Kathy Hirsh-Pasek interacting with a young child in a play context. *What are some of the benefits of play for children according to Hirsh-Pasek and her colleagues?*

Games **Games** are activities that children engage in for pleasure and that have rules. Often they involve competition. Preschool children may begin to participate in social games that involve simple rules of reciprocity and turn taking. However, games take on a much stronger role in the lives of elementary school children. In one study, the highest incidence of game playing occurred between 10 and 12 years of age (Eiferman, 1971). After age 12, games decline in popularity (Bergen, 1988).

MEDIA AND SCREEN TIME

Few developments in society in the second half of the twentieth century had a greater impact on children than television (Brown & Bobkowski, 2011; Zimmerman & others, 2012). Television continues to have a strong influence on children's development, but children's use of other media and information/communication devices has led to the use of the term *screen time*, which includes how much time individuals spend with television, DVDs, computers, video games, and mobile media such as iPhones (De Decker & others, 2012; Schmidt & others, 2012). Television is still the elephant in young children's media lives, with 2- to 4-year-old children watching TV approximately 2 to 4 hours per day (Roberts & Foehr, 2008). However, a recent study revealed that 12 percent of 2- to 4-year-old U.S. children use computers every day and 22 percent of 5- to 8-year-olds use computers daily (Common Sense Media, 2011). A recent recommendation stated that for children 2 to 4 years of age, screen time should be limited to no more than 1 hour per day (Tremblay & others, 2012). Many children spend more time with various screen media than they do interacting with their parents and peers.

What are some concerns about the increase in children's media and screen time?

Screen time can have a negative influence on children by making them passive learners, distracting them from doing homework, teaching them stereotypes, providing them with violent models of aggression, and presenting them with unrealistic views of the world.

Among other concerns about young children having so much screen time are decreasing time spent in play, less time interacting with peers, decreasing physical activity, an increased tendency to become overweight or obese, poor sleep habits, and higher rates of aggression. A research review concluded that a higher level of screen time at 4 to 6 years of age was linked to increased obesity and lower physical activity from preschool through adolescence (te Velde & others, 2012). Another study found that sleep problems were more common in 3- to 5-year-old children who (1) watched TV after 7 p.m. and (2) watched TV shows with violence (Garrison, Liekweg, & Christakis, 2011). Next, let's take a closer look at the effects of television on children's aggression.

pretense/symbolic play Play in which the child transforms the physical environment into a symbol.

social play Play that involves social interactions with peers.

constructive play Play that combines sensorimotor and repetitive activity with symbolic representation of ideas. Constructive play occurs when children engage in self-regulated creation or construction of a product or a solution.

games Activities engaged in for pleasure that include rules and often involve competition with one or more individuals.

Effects of Television on Children's Aggression The extent to which children are exposed to violence and aggression on television raises special concerns (Matos, Ferreira, & Haase, 2012). For example, Saturday morning cartoon shows average more than 25 violent acts

How is television violence linked to children's aggression?

per hour. In one experiment, preschool children were randomly assigned to one of two groups: One group watched television shows taken directly from violent Saturday morning cartoons on 11 days; the second group watched television cartoon shows with all of the violence removed (Steur, Applefield, & Smith, 1971). The children were then observed during play at their preschool. The preschool children who had seen the TV cartoon shows with violence kicked, choked, and pushed their playmates more than did the preschool children who watched nonviolent TV cartoon shows. Because the children were randomly assigned to the two conditions (TV cartoons with violence versus nonviolent TV cartoons), we can conclude that exposure to TV violence caused the increased aggression in the children in this investigation.

Other research has found links between watching television violence as a child and acting aggressively years later. For example, in one study, exposure to media violence at 6 to 10 years of age was linked with young adult aggressive behavior (Huesmann & others, 2003).

In addition to television violence, there is increased concern about children who play violent video games, especially those that are highly realistic (Escobar-Chaves & Anderson, 2008). Recent research reviews have concluded that playing violent video games is linked to aggression in both males and females (Gentile, 2011; Holtz & Appel, 2011).

Effects of Television on Children's Prosocial Behavior   Television can have a positive influence on children's development by presenting motivating educational programs, providing information about the world beyond their immediate environment, and displaying models of prosocial behavior (Wilson, 2008). Researchers have found that when children watch positive social interchanges in which children are taught how to use social skills on the TV show *Sesame Street*, they subsequently are likely to imitate these positive social behaviors (Bryant, 2007).

Review Connect Reflect

 Describe the roles of peers, play, and media/screen time in young children's development.

Review

- How do peers affect young children's development?
- What are some theories and types of play?
- How does television influence young children's development?

Connect

- Earlier in this chapter, you learned about Laurie Kramer's program for teaching

siblings social skills to develop positive interactions. Do you think her recommendations would be relevant or irrelevant to peer relationships? Why?

Reflect *Your Own Personal Journey of Life*

- What guidelines would you adopt for your own children's television viewing?

topical connections

The middle and late childhood years bring further changes in children's socioemotional development. Development of self-understanding and understanding of others becomes more sophisticated, emotional understanding improves, and moral reasoning advances. Children now spend less time with parents, but parents still play very important roles in children's lives, especially in guiding their academic achievement and managing their opportunities. Peer status and friendship become more important in children's peer relations and school takes on a stronger academic focus.

looking forward ---->

Socioemotional Development in Early Childhood

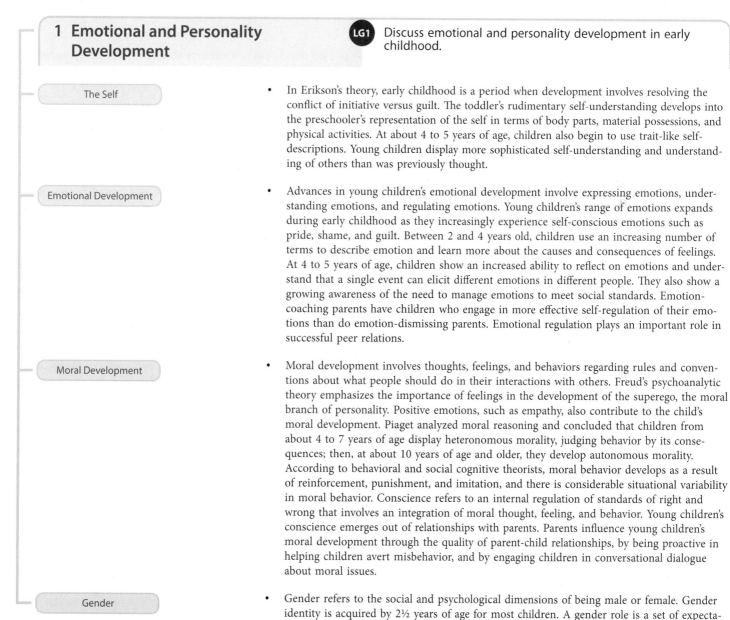

1 Emotional and Personality Development

LG1 Discuss emotional and personality development in early childhood.

The Self

- In Erikson's theory, early childhood is a period when development involves resolving the conflict of initiative versus guilt. The toddler's rudimentary self-understanding develops into the preschooler's representation of the self in terms of body parts, material possessions, and physical activities. At about 4 to 5 years of age, children also begin to use trait-like self-descriptions. Young children display more sophisticated self-understanding and understanding of others than was previously thought.

Emotional Development

- Advances in young children's emotional development involve expressing emotions, understanding emotions, and regulating emotions. Young children's range of emotions expands during early childhood as they increasingly experience self-conscious emotions such as pride, shame, and guilt. Between 2 and 4 years old, children use an increasing number of terms to describe emotion and learn more about the causes and consequences of feelings. At 4 to 5 years of age, children show an increased ability to reflect on emotions and understand that a single event can elicit different emotions in different people. They also show a growing awareness of the need to manage emotions to meet social standards. Emotion-coaching parents have children who engage in more effective self-regulation of their emotions than do emotion-dismissing parents. Emotional regulation plays an important role in successful peer relations.

Moral Development

- Moral development involves thoughts, feelings, and behaviors regarding rules and conventions about what people should do in their interactions with others. Freud's psychoanalytic theory emphasizes the importance of feelings in the development of the superego, the moral branch of personality. Positive emotions, such as empathy, also contribute to the child's moral development. Piaget analyzed moral reasoning and concluded that children from about 4 to 7 years of age display heteronomous morality, judging behavior by its consequences; then, at about 10 years of age and older, they develop autonomous morality. According to behavioral and social cognitive theorists, moral behavior develops as a result of reinforcement, punishment, and imitation, and there is considerable situational variability in moral behavior. Conscience refers to an internal regulation of standards of right and wrong that involves an integration of moral thought, feeling, and behavior. Young children's conscience emerges out of relationships with parents. Parents influence young children's moral development through the quality of parent-child relationships, by being proactive in helping children avert misbehavior, and by engaging children in conversational dialogue about moral issues.

Gender

- Gender refers to the social and psychological dimensions of being male or female. Gender identity is acquired by 2½ years of age for most children. A gender role is a set of expectations that prescribes how females or males should think, act, and feel. Gender typing refers to the acquisition of a traditional masculine or feminine role. Biological influences on gender development include chromosomes and hormones. However, biology does not completely dictate destiny in gender development; children's socialization experiences matter a great deal. Social role theory, psychoanalytic theory, and social cognitive theory emphasize various aspects of social experiences in the development of gender characteristics. Parents influence children's gender development, and peers are especially adept at rewarding gender-appropriate behavior. Gender schema theory emphasizes the role of cognition in gender development.

2 Families

 Explain how families can influence young children's development.

Parenting

- Authoritarian, authoritative, neglectful, and indulgent are four main parenting styles. Authoritative parenting is the most widely used style around the world and is the style most often associated with children's social competence. However, ethnic variations in parenting styles suggest that in Asian American families, some aspects of control may benefit children. Physical punishment is widely used by U.S. parents, but some experts conclude that there are a number of reasons it should not be used with children. However, there currently is controversy about the effects of physical punishment on children, with few studies making a distinction between abusive and mild physical punishment. Coparenting has positive effects on children's development.

Child Maltreatment

- Child maltreatment may take the form of physical abuse, child neglect, sexual abuse, and emotional abuse. Child maltreatment places the child at risk for academic, emotional, and social problems. Adults who suffered child maltreatment are also vulnerable to a range of problems.

Sibling Relationships and Birth Order

- Siblings interact with each other in positive and negative ways. Birth order is related in certain ways to personality characteristics—for example, firstborns are more adult-oriented and self-controlled than later-born children. Only children often are achievement-oriented. By itself, however, birth order is not a good predictor of behavior.

The Changing Family in a Changing Society

- In general, having both parents employed full-time outside the home has not been shown to have negative effects on children. However, the nature of parents' work can affect their parenting quality. Divorce can have negative effects on children's adjustment, but so can an acrimonious relationship between parents who stay together for their children's sake. If divorced parents develop a harmonious relationship and practice authoritative parenting, children's adjustment improves. Researchers have found few differences between children growing up in gay or lesbian families and children growing up in heterosexual families. Cultures vary on a number of issues regarding families. African American and Latino children are more likely than White American children to live in single-parent families and larger families and to have extended family connections. Low-income families have less access to resources than higher-income families do. Lower-SES parents create a home atmosphere with more parental authority and greater use of physical punishment, while higher-SES parents are more concerned about developing children's initiative and ability to delay gratification.

3 Peer Relations, Play, and Media/Screen Time

 Describe the roles of peers, play, and media/screen time in young children's development.

Peer Relations

- Peers are powerful socialization agents. Peers provide a source of information and comparison about the world outside the family. In early childhood, children distinguish between friends and nonfriends, with a friend often described as someone to play with. Parent-child and peer relationships are often connected. Parents influence their children's peer relations by how they manage children's lives and the opportunities they provide for interacting with peers. Rough-and-tumble play is more likely to occur in peer relations, whereas in times of stress children often turn to parents rather than peers for support.

Play

- Play's functions include affiliation with peers, tension release, advances in cognitive development, exploration, and provision of a safe haven. The contemporary perspective on play emphasizes both the cognitive and the social aspects of play. Among the most widely studied types of children's play are sensorimotor play, practice play, pretense/symbolic play, social play, constructive play, and games. There is concern about the decreasing number of hours children spend in free play and in recess at school. Because play is a powerful positive context for the development of children's cognitive and socioemotional skills, it is important that we find more time for play in children's lives.

Media and Screen Time

- Young children watch 2 to 4 hours of TV per day on average, but experts recommend that they watch 1 hour or less. Young children increasingly are spending time with other media and information/communication devices such as computers, DVDs, video games, and iPhones, which has given rise to the term *screen time*. Screen time can have both negative influences (such as turning children into passive learners, presenting them with aggressive models, and decreasing time spent with peers and in play and physical activity) and positive influences (such as providing models of prosocial behavior) on children's development. Both watching TV violence and playing violent video games have been linked to children's aggressive behavior. Watching prosocial behavior on TV can teach children positive behavior.

key **terms**

key **people**

Chapter 8 | SOCIOEMOTIONAL DEVELOPMENT IN EARLY CHILDHOOD

Connecting with

Learning Objectives	Application Activities	Activity Type	Page Reference
Discuss the self in early childhood.	Self Care 33–41 Months	Milestones	pp. 245–247
	Self Care, Felana, 7–39 mos	Milestones	
Describe gender, gender identity, and gender roles in early childhood.	Gender Constancy at Age 4	Video	pp. 251–255
	Sex-Typed Play	Video	
	Male Sex-Typed Play	Video	

(continued)

Learning Objectives	Application Activities	Activity Type	Page Reference
	Girls Engaging in Non Sex-Typed Play	Video	
	Boys Engaging in Sex-Typed Play	Video	
	Gender Stereotype Beliefs at Age 6	Video	
	If My Son Wore a Dress	Video	
	Sex Differences	Video	
	Sex Differences in Bullying Behavior	Video	
	Gender, Amalia, 2–5 yrs	Milestones	
Characterize parenting styles.	Parenting Styles	Click & drag activity	pp. 255–258
Explain sibling relationships and birth order.	Only Children	Video	pp. 261–262
	When Second Baby Comes Along	Video	
	Sibling Differential Treatment	Video	
	Sibling Conflicts and Parent Intervention	Video	
	Sibling Jealousy	Video	
Discuss the changing family in a changing society.	Children and Divorce	Video	pp. 262–267
Describe peer relations in early childhood.	Social Interactions	Milestones	pp. 268–269
	Friendship 1–4 Years	Milestones	
	Children's Social Networks	Video	
	Describing A Best Friend at Age 2	Video	
Characterize play during this period of children's development.	Types of Play 12 Months–4 Years	Milestones	pp. 269–271
	Types of Play	Click & drag activity	
	Siblings at Play	Video	
	Parallel Play in the Sandbox	Video	
Summarize television's influence on children in early childhood.	Children and Television	Video	pp. 271–272

Every forward step we take we leave some phantom of ourselves behind.

—John Lancaster Spalding
American Educator, 19th Century

Middle and Late Childhood

In middle and late childhood, children are on a different plane, belonging to a generation and feeling all their own. It is the wisdom of the human life span that at no time are children more ready to learn than during the period of expansive imagination at the end of early childhood. Children develop a sense of wanting to make things—and not just to make them, but to make them well and even perfectly. They seek to know and to understand. They are remarkable for their intelligence and for their curiosity. Their parents continue to be important influences in their lives, but their growth also is shaped by peers and friends. They don't think much about the future or about the past, but they enjoy the present moment. Section 5 consists of two chapters: "Physical and Cognitive Development in Middle and Late Childhood" (Chapter 9) and "Socioemotional Development in Middle and Late Childhood" (Chapter 10).

chapter 9

PHYSICAL AND COGNITIVE DEVELOPMENT IN MIDDLE AND LATE CHILDHOOD

chapter **outline**

The following comments were made by Angie, an elementary-school-aged girl:

When I was 8 years old, I weighed 125 pounds. My clothes were the size that large teenage girls wear. I hated my body, and my classmates teased me all the time. I was so overweight and out of shape that when I took a P.E. class my face would get red and I had trouble breathing. I was jealous of the kids who played sports and weren't overweight like I was.

I'm 9 years old now and I've lost 30 pounds. I'm much happier and proud of myself. How did I lose the weight? My mom said she had finally decided enough was enough. She took me to a pediatrician who specializes in helping children lose weight and keep it off. The pediatrician counseled my mom about my eating and exercise habits, then had us join a group that he had created for overweight children and their parents. My mom and I go to the group once a week and we've now been participating in the program for 6 months. I no longer eat fast food meals and my mom is cooking more healthy meals. Now that I've lost weight, exercise is not as hard for me and I don't get teased by the kids at school. My mom's pretty happy too because she's lost 15 pounds herself since we've been in the counseling program.

Not all overweight children are as successful as Angie at reducing their weight. Indeed, being overweight or obese in childhood has become a major national concern in the United States. Later in this chapter, we will further explore being overweight and obese in childhood, including obesity's causes and outcomes.

-topical **connections** - - - - - - - - - - - - - -

Children grow more slowly in early childhood than in infancy, but they still grow an average of 2.5 inches and gain 4 to 7 pounds a year. In early childhood, the most rapid growth in the brain occurs in the prefrontal cortex. The gross and fine motor skills of children also become smoother and more coordinated. In terms of cognitive development, early childhood is a period in which young children increasingly engage in symbolic thought. Young children's information-processing skills also improve considerably—executive and sustained attention advance, short-term memory gets better, and their understanding of the human mind makes considerable progress. Young children also increase their knowledge of language's rule systems and their literacy benefits from being active participants in a wide range of language experiences. Most young children attend an early childhood education program, and there are many variations in these programs.

◄ - - - - *looking back* - - - - - - - - - - - - - - - -

preview

During the middle and late childhood years, children grow taller, heavier, and stronger. They become more adept at using their physical skills, and they develop new cognitive skills. This chapter is about physical and cognitive development in middle and late childhood. To begin, we will explore some changes in physical development.

1 Physical Changes and Health ⟨LG1⟩ Describe physical changes and health in middle and late childhood.

Body Growth and Change | The Brain | Motor Development | Exercise | Health, Illness, and Disease

Continued change characterizes children's bodies during middle and late childhood, and their motor skills improve. As children move through the elementary school years, they gain greater control over their bodies and can sit and keep their attention focused for longer periods of time. Regular exercise is one key to making these years a time of healthy growth and development.

BODY GROWTH AND CHANGE

The period of middle and late childhood involves slow, consistent growth (Burns & others, 2013). This is a period of calm before the rapid growth spurt of adolescence. During the elementary school years, children grow an average of 2 to 3 inches a year until, at the age of 11, the average girl is 4 feet, 10 inches tall, and the average boy is 4 feet, 9 inches tall. During the middle and late childhood years, children gain about 5 to 7 pounds a year. The weight increase is due mainly to increases in the size of the skeletal and muscular systems, as well as the size of some body organs.

Proportional changes are among the most pronounced physical changes in middle and late childhood. Head circumference and waist circumference decrease in relation to body height (Kliegman & others, 2012). A less noticeable physical change is that bones continue to ossify during middle and late childhood but yield to pressure and pull more than mature bones.

THE BRAIN

The development of brain-imaging techniques, such as magnetic resonance imaging (MRI), has led to increased research on changes in the brain during middle and late childhood and links between these brain changes and cognitive development (Diamond, 2013). Total brain volume stabilizes by the end of late childhood, but significant changes in various structures and regions of the brain continue to occur. In particular, the brain pathways and circuitry involving the prefrontal cortex, the highest level in the brain, continue to increase during middle and late childhood (see Figure 9.1). These advances in the prefrontal cortex are linked to children's improved attention, reasoning, and cognitive control (Crone & others, 2009).

Leading developmental neuroscientist Mark Johnson and his colleagues (2009) proposed that the prefrontal cortex likely orchestrates the functions of many other brain regions during development. As part of this neural leadership role, the prefrontal cortex may provide an advantage to neural networks and connections that include

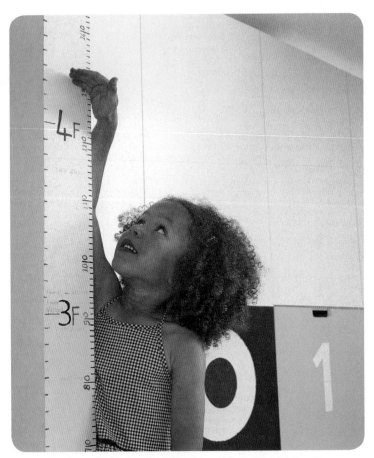

What characterizes children's physical growth in middle and late childhood?

the prefrontal cortex. In their view, the prefrontal cortex coordinates the best neural connections for solving a problem at hand.

Changes also occur in the thickness of the cerebral cortex (cortical thickness) in middle and late childhood (Thomason & Thompson, 2011). One study used brain scans to assess cortical thickness in 5- to 11-year-old children (Sowell & others, 2004). Cortical thickening across a two-year time period was observed in the temporal and frontal lobe areas that function in language, which may reflect improvements in language abilities such as reading. Figure 4.4 in Chapter 4 shows the locations of the temporal and frontal lobes in the brain.

As children develop, some brain areas become more active while others become less so (Diamond, 2013; Nelson, 2012). One shift in activation that occurs as children develop is from diffuse, larger areas to more focal, smaller areas (Turkeltaub & others, 2003). This shift is characterized by synaptic pruning, a process in which areas of the brain not being used lose synaptic connections and those being used show an increase in connections. In one study, researchers found less diffusion and more focal activation in the prefrontal cortex from 7 to 30 years of age (Durston & others, 2006).

MOTOR DEVELOPMENT

During middle and late childhood, children's motor skills become much smoother and more coordinated than they were in early childhood. For example, only one child in a thousand can hit a tennis ball over the net at the age of 3, yet by the age of 10 or 11 most children can learn to play the sport. Running, climbing, skipping rope, swimming, bicycle riding, and skating are just a few of the many physical skills elementary school children can master. In gross motor skills involving large muscle activity, boys usually outperform girls.

Increased myelination of the central nervous system is reflected in the improvement of fine motor skills during middle and late childhood. Children can more adroitly use their hands as tools. Six-year-olds can hammer, paste, tie shoes, and fasten clothes. By 7 years of age, children's hands have become steadier. At this age, children prefer a pencil to a crayon for printing, and reversal of letters is less common. Printing becomes smaller. At 8 to 10 years of age, the hands can be used independently with more ease and precision. Fine motor coordination develops to the point at which children can write rather than print words. Cursive letter size becomes smaller and more even. At 10 to 12 years of age, children begin to show manipulative skills similar to the abilities of adults. They can master the complex, intricate, and rapid movements needed to produce fine-quality crafts or to play a difficult piece on a musical instrument. Girls usually outperform boys in their use of fine motor skills.

EXERCISE

American children and adolescents are not getting enough exercise (Gao, 2012; Goldfield, 2012; Graber & Woods, 2013). Increasing children's exercise levels has positive outcomes (Graham, Holt/Hale, & Parker, 2013; Wuest & Fisette, 2012). One study found that 45 minutes of moderate physical activity and 15 minutes of vigorous physical activity daily were related to decreased odds of children being overweight (Wittmeier, Mollard, & Kriellaars, 2008). And a recent study of 9-year-olds revealed that a higher level of physical activity was linked to a lower level of metabolic disease risk based on measures such as cholesterol, waist circumference, and insulin levels (Parrett & others, 2011).

A recent research review concluded that aerobic exercise also is linked to children's cognitive skills (Best, 2010). Researchers have found that aerobic exercise benefits children's attention, memory, effortful and goal-directed thinking and behavior, and creativity (Davis & Cooper, 2011; Davis & others, 2007, 2011; Hinkle, Tuckman, & Sampson, 1993; Monti, Hillman, & Cohen, 2012; Pesce & others, 2009).

Parents and schools play important roles in determining children's exercise levels (Cong & others, 2012; Graber & Woods, 2013). Growing up with parents who exercise regularly provides positive models of exercise for children (Crawford & others, 2010). A recent study revealed that mothers were more likely than fathers to limit sedentary behavior in boys and girls (Edwardson & Gorely, 2010). In this study, fathers did have an influence on their sons' physical activity, but primarily through explicit modeling of physical activity, such as showing

Prefrontal cortex

FIGURE **9.1**

THE PREFRONTAL CORTEX. The brain pathways and circuitry involving the prefrontal cortex (shaded in purple) show significant advances in development during middle and late childhood. *What cognitive processes are linked to these changes in the prefrontal cortex?*

developmental **connection**

Brain Development

Synaptic pruning is an important aspect of the brain's development, and the pruning varies by brain region across children's development. Chapter 4, p. 113

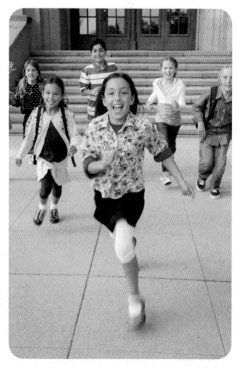

What are some good strategies for increasing children's exercise?

their sons how to shoot a basketball. Another recent research review found that school-based physical activity was successful in improving children's fitness and lowering their fat levels (Kriemler & others, 2011).

Screen time also is linked with low activity and obesity in children. Recall from Chapter 8 that a research review concluded that a higher level of screen time at 4 to 6 years of age was linked to increased obesity and lower physical activity from preschool through adolescence (te Velde & others, 2012).

Here are some ways to get children to exercise more:

- Offer more physical activity programs run by volunteers at school facilities.
- Improve physical fitness activities in schools.
- Have children plan community and school activities that interest them.
- Encourage families to focus more on physical activity, and encourage parents to exercise more.

HEALTH, ILLNESS, AND DISEASE

For the most part, middle and late childhood is a time of excellent health. Disease and death are less prevalent at this time than during other periods in childhood and in adolescence. However, many children in middle and late childhood face health problems that harm their development.

Accidents and Injuries   Injuries are the leading cause of death during middle and late childhood, and the most common cause of severe injury and death in this period is motor vehicle accidents, either as a pedestrian or as a passenger (Committee on Injury, Violence, and Poison Prevention, 2011). For this reason, safety advocates recommend the use of safety-belt restraints in vehicles because they can greatly reduce the severity of motor vehicle injuries. Other serious injuries involve bicycles, skateboards, roller skates, and other sports equipment.

Overweight Children   Being overweight is an increasingly prevalent health problem in children (Schiff, 2013; Summerbell & others, 2012). Recall from Chapter 7, "Physical and Cognitive Development in Early Childhood," that being overweight is defined in terms of body mass index (BMI), which is computed by a formula that takes into account height and weight—children at or above the 97th percentile are included in the obesity category, at or above the 95th percentile in the overweight category, and children at or above the 85th percentile are described as at risk for being overweight (Centers for Disease Control and Prevention, 2012a). Over the last three decades, the percentage of U.S. children who are at risk for being overweight has doubled from 15 percent in the 1970s to almost 30 percent today, and the percentage of children who are overweight has tripled during this time frame (Orsi, Hale, & Lynch, 2011). In Chapter 7, we indicated that 12.1 percent of 2- to 5-year-old U.S. children are obese. That figure is 50 percent higher for 6- to 11-year-old U.S. children—in 2009–2010, 18 percent of U.S. 6- to 11-year-olds were classified as obese (Ogden & others, 2012).

The levels of child obesity, overweight, and risk for being overweight remain far too high and are expected to increase in the future (Wardlaw & Smith, 2012).

Causes of Children Being Overweight   Heredity and environmental contexts are related to being overweight in childhood (Dubois & others, 2012). Recent genetic analysis indicates that heredity is an important factor in children becoming overweight (Freitag, Asherson, & Hebebrand, 2012). Overweight parents tend to have overweight children (Pufal & others, 2012). For example, one study found that the greatest risk factor for being overweight at 9 years of age was having an overweight parent (Agras & others, 2004). Parents and

What are some concerns about the increase in overweight and obese children?

their children often have similar body types, height, body fat composition, and metabolism (Pereira-Lancha & others, 2012). Environmental factors that influence whether children become overweight include the greater availability of food (especially food high in fat content), energy-saving devices, declining physical activity, parents' eating habits and monitoring of children's eating habits, the context in which a child eats, and heavy screen time (Faith & others, 2012; Riesch & others, 2012; te Velde & others, 2012). A recent behavior modification study of overweight and obese children made watching TV contingent on their engagement in exercise (Goldfield, 2012). The intervention markedly increased their exercise and reduced their TV viewing time.

Consequences of Being Overweight   The increase in overweight children in recent decades is cause for great concern because being overweight raises the risk for many medical and psychological problems (Schiff, 2013). Diabetes, hypertension (high blood pressure), and elevated blood cholesterol levels are common in children who are overweight (Lytle, 2012; Trasande & Ebel, 2012). A recent research review concluded that obesity was linked with low self-esteem in children (Gomes & others, 2011). And in one recent study, overweight children were more likely than normal-weight children to report being teased by their peers and family members (McCormack & others, 2011).

Intervention Programs   A combination of diet, exercise, and behavior modification is often recommended to help children lose weight (Cronk & others, 2011). Intervention programs that emphasize getting parents to engage in healthier life styles themselves, as well as to feed their children healthier food and get them to exercise more, can produce weight reduction in overweight and obese children (Brotman & others, 2012; Magarey & others, 2011). For example, a recent study found that a combination of a child-centered activity program and a parent-centered dietary modification program were successful in helping overweight children lose pounds over a two-year period (Collins & others, 2011).

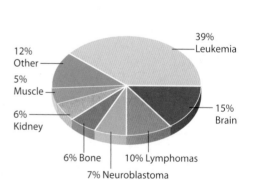

Cardiovascular Disease   Cardiovascular disease is uncommon in children. Nonetheless, environmental experiences and behavior in the childhood years can sow the seeds for cardiovascular disease in adulthood. Many elementary-school-aged children already possess one or more of the risk factors for cardiovascular disease, such as hypertension and obesity (Assadi, 2012; Dencker & others, 2012). A national study found that an increasing percentage of U.S. children and adolescents had elevated blood pressure from 1988 to 2006 (Ostchega & others, 2009). In this study, children who were obese were more likely to have elevated blood pressure. Another study revealed that high blood pressure goes undiagnosed in 75 percent of children with the disease (Hansen, Gunn, & Kaelber, 2007). Yet another study found that children with a high body mass index and waist circumference are at risk for *metabolic syndrome*—a constellation of factors, including obesity, high blood pressure, and type 2 diabetes—placing individuals at risk for developing cardiovascular disease in adulthood (Sun & others, 2008).

Cancer   Cancer is the second leading cause of death in U.S. children 5 to 14 years of age. One in every 330 children in the United States develops cancer before the age of 19. The incidence of cancer in children has increased slightly in recent years (National Cancer Institute, 2012).

Childhood cancers mainly attack the white blood cells (leukemia), brain, bone, lymph system, muscles, kidneys, and nervous system. All are characterized by an uncontrolled proliferation of abnormal cells (Fabbri & others, 2012). As indicated in Figure 9.2, the most common cancer in children is leukemia, a cancer in which bone marrow manufactures an abundance of abnormal white blood cells, which crowd out normal cells, making the child highly susceptible to bruising and infection (Lund & others, 2011).

Because of advancements in cancer treatment, children with cancer are surviving longer than in the past (National Cancer Institute, 2012). Approximately 80 percent of children with acute lymphoblastic leukemia are cured with current chemotherapy treatment (Wayne, 2011).

Child life specialists are among the health professionals who work to make the lives of children with diseases less stressful. To read about the work of child life specialist Sharon McLeod, see *Connecting with Careers.*

developmental **connection**

Conditions, Diseases, and Disorders

Metabolic syndrome has increased in middle-aged adults in recent years and is linked to early death. Chapter 15, p. 488

39% Leukemia

12% Other

5% Muscle

6% Kidney

15% Brain

6% Bone   10% Lymphomas

7% Neuroblastoma

FIGURE **9.2**

TYPES OF CANCER IN CHILDREN. Cancers in children have a different profile from adult cancers, which attack mainly the lungs, colon, breast, prostate, and pancreas.

connecting with careers

Sharon McLeod, Child Life Specialist

Sharon McLeod is a child life specialist who is senior clinical director in the Division of Child Life and Division of Integrative Care at the Children's Hospital Medical Center in Cincinnati.

Under McLeod's direction, the goals of her department are to promote children's optimal growth and development, reduce the stress of health care experiences, and provide support to child patients and their families. These goals are accomplished through therapeutic play and developmentally appropriate activities, educating and psychologically preparing children for medical procedures, and serving as a resource for parents and other professionals regarding children's development and health care issues.

McLeod says that human growth and development provides the foundation for her profession as a child life specialist. She also says her best times as a student were when she conducted fieldwork, had an internship, and experienced hands-on theories and concepts that she learned in her courses.

Sharon McLeod, child life specialist, working with a child at Children's Hospital Medical Center in Cincinnati.

For more information about what child life specialists do, see page 47 in the Careers in Life-Span Development appendix.

Review *Connect* Reflect

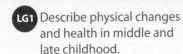 **LG1** Describe physical changes and health in middle and late childhood.

Review

- What are some changes in body growth and proportions in middle and late childhood?
- What characterizes the development of the brain in middle and late childhood?
- How do children's motor skills develop in middle and late childhood?
- What role does exercise play in children's lives?
- What are some characteristics of health, illness, and disease in middle and late childhood?

Connect

- In this section, you learned that increased myelination of the central nervous system is reflected in the improvement of fine motor skills during middle and late childhood. What developmental advances were connected with increased myelination in infancy and early childhood?

Reflect *Your Own Personal Journey of Life*

- One way that children get exercise is to play a sport. If you played a sport as a child, was it a positive or negative experience? Do you think that playing a sport as a child likely made a difference in whether you continue to exercise on a regular basis today? Explain. If you did not play a sport, do you wish you had? Explain.

2 Children with Disabilities

 LG2 Identify children with different types of disabilities and discuss issues in educating them.

The Scope of Disabilities   Educational Issues

What are some of the disabilities that children have? What characterizes the education of children with disabilities?

THE SCOPE OF DISABILITIES

Of all children from 3 to 21 years of age in the United States, 14 percent received special education or related services in 2008–2009 (Aud & others, 2011). Figure 9.3 shows the four largest groups of students with a disability who were served by federal programs in the 2008–2009 school year (Aud & others, 2011). As indicated in Figure 9.3, students with a learning disability were by far the largest group of students with a disability to be given special education, followed by children with speech or language impairments, intellectual disability, and emotional disturbance.

Learning Disabilities   The U.S. government created a definition of learning disabilities in 1997 and then reauthorized the definition with a few minor changes in 2004. Following is a summary of the government's definition of what determined whether a child should be classified as having a learning disability. A child with a **learning disability** has difficulty in learning that involves understanding or using spoken or written language, and the difficulty can appear in listening, thinking, reading, writing, and spelling. A learning disability also may involve difficulty in doing mathematics (Jitendra & Montague, 2013). To be classified as a learning disability, the learning problem is not primarily the result of visual, hearing, or motor disabilities; mental retardation; emotional disorders; or environmental, cultural, or economic disadvantage.

About three times as many boys as girls are classified as having a learning disability. Among the explanations for this gender difference are a greater biological vulnerability among boys and *referral bias.* That is, boys are more likely to be referred by teachers for treatment because of troublesome behavior.

Approximately 80 percent of children with a learning disability have a reading problem (Shaywitz, Gruen, & Shaywitz, 2007). Three types of learning disabilities are dyslexia, dysgraphia, and dyscalculia:

- **Dyslexia** is a category reserved for individuals who have a severe impairment in their ability to read and spell (Allor & Al Otaiba, 2013; Ramus & Ahissar, 2012).
- **Dysgraphia** is a learning disability that involves difficulty in handwriting (Mason, Harris, & Graham, 2013). Children with dysgraphia may write very slowly, their writing products may be virtually illegible, and they may make numerous spelling errors because of their inability to match up sounds and letters (Arfe, Dockrell, & Berninger, 2013; Hayes & Berninger, 2013).
- **Dyscalculia,** also known as developmental arithmetic disorder, is a learning disability that involves difficulty in math computation (Bryant & others, 2013).

The precise causes of learning disabilities have not yet been determined (Hallahan, Kauffman, & Pullen, 2012; Vaughn & Bos, 2012). Researchers also use brain-imaging techniques, such as magnetic resonance imaging, to reveal any regions of the brain that might be involved in learning disabilities (Shaywitz, Lyon, & Shaywitz, 2006) (see Figure 9.4). This research indicates that it is unlikely learning disabilities reside in a single, specific brain location. More likely, learning disabilities are due to problems in integrating information from multiple brain regions or subtle difficulties in brain structures and functions.

Interventions with children who have a learning disability often focus on improving reading ability (Carlisle, Kenney, & Vereb, 2013; Hern & Chard, 2013; Lerner & Johns, 2012).

Disability	Percentage of All Children in Public Schools
Learning disabilities	5.0
Speech or hearing impairments	2.9
Intellectual disability	1.0
Emotional disturbance	0.9

FIGURE **9.3**

U.S. CHILDREN WITH A DISABILITY WHO RECEIVE SPECIAL EDUCATION SERVICES. Figures are for the 2008–2009 school year and represent the four categories with the highest numbers and percentages of children. Both learning disability and attention deficit hyperactivity disorder are combined in the learning disabilities category (Aud & others, 2011).

learning disability Difficulty in understanding or using spoken or written language or in doing mathematics. To be classified as a learning disability, the learning problem is not primarily the result of visual, hearing, or motor disabilities; mental retardation; emotional disorders; or due to environmental, cultural, or economic disadvantage.

dyslexia A category of learning disabilities involving a severe impairment in the ability to read and spell.

dysgraphia A learning disability that involves difficulty in handwriting.

dyscalculia Also known as developmental arithmetic disorder; a learning disability that involves difficulty in math computation.

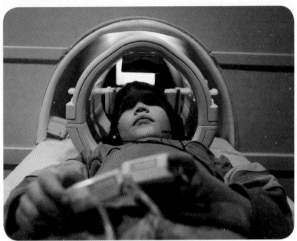

FIGURE **9.4**

BRAIN SCANS AND LEARNING DISABILITIES. An increasing number of studies are using MRI brain scans to examine the brain pathways involved in learning disabilities. Shown here is 9-year-old Patrick Price, who has dyslexia. Patrick is going through an MRI scanner disguised by drapes to look like a child-friendly castle. Inside the scanner, children must lie virtually motionless as words and symbols flash on a screen, and they are asked to identify them by clicking different buttons.

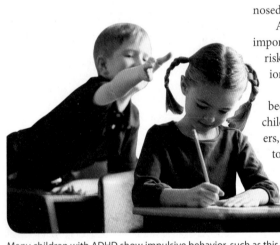

Many children with ADHD show impulsive behavior, such as this boy reaching to pull a girl's hair. *How would you handle this situation if you were a teacher and this were to happen in your classroom?*

attention deficit hyperactivity disorder (ADHD) A disability in which children consistently show one or more of the following characteristics: (1) inattention, (2) hyperactivity, and (3) impulsivity.

Intensive instruction over a period of time by a competent teacher can help many children (Berninger & Dunn, 2012).

Attention Deficit Hyperactivity Disorder (ADHD) **Attention deficit hyperactivity disorder (ADHD)** is a disability in which children consistently show one or more of the following characteristics over a period of time: (1) inattention, (2) hyperactivity, and (3) impulsivity. Children who are inattentive have such difficulty focusing on any one thing that they may get bored with a task after only a few minutes—or even seconds. Children who are hyperactive show high levels of physical activity, seeming to be almost constantly in motion. Children who are impulsive have difficulty curbing their reactions; they do not do a good job of thinking before they act. Depending on the characteristics that children with ADHD display, they can be diagnosed as having (1) ADHD with predominantly inattention, (2) ADHD with predominantly hyperactivity/impulsivity, or (3) ADHD with both inattention and hyperactivity/impulsivity.

The number of children diagnosed and treated for ADHD has increased substantially in recent decades. The disorder occurs as much as four to nine times more frequently in boys than in girls. There is controversy, however, about the increased diagnosis of ADHD (Friend, 2011). Some experts attribute the increase mainly to heightened awareness of the disorder; others are concerned that many children are being incorrectly diagnosed (Parens & Johnston, 2009).

A recent study examined the possible misdiagnosis of ADHD (Bruchmiller, Margraf, & Schneider, 2012). In this study, child psychologists, psychiatrists, and social workers were given vignettes of children with ADHD. Some vignettes matched the diagnostic criteria for the disorder, while others did not. The child in each vignette was sometimes identified as male and sometimes as female. The researchers assessed whether the mental health professionals gave a diagnosis of ADHD to the child described in the vignette. The professionals overdiagnosed ADHD almost 20 percent of the time, and regardless of the symptoms described boys were twice as likely as girls to be diagnosed as having ADHD.

Adjustment and optimal development are difficult for children who have ADHD, so it is important that the diagnosis be accurate. Children diagnosed with ADHD have an increased risk of school dropout, adolescent pregnancy, substance use problems, and antisocial behavior (Chang, Lichtenstein, & Larsson, 2012; Von Polier, Vioet, & Herpertz-Dahlmann, 2012).

Definitive causes of ADHD have not been found. However, a number of causes have been proposed (American Academy of Pediatrics & Reiff, 2011; Sonuga-Barke, 2013). Some children likely inherit a tendency to develop ADHD from their parents (Stergiakouli & others, 2012; Williams & others, 2012). Other children likely develop ADHD because of damage to their brain during prenatal or postnatal development (Lindblad & Hjern, 2010). Among early possible contributors to ADHD are cigarette and alcohol exposure, as well as a high level of maternal stress during prenatal development and low birth weight (Choudhry & others, 2012; Knopik, 2009). For example, a recent study revealed that cigarette smoking during pregnancy was linked to ADHD in 6- to 7-year-old children (Sciberras, Ukoumunne, & Efron, 2011).

As with learning disabilities, the development of brain-imaging techniques is leading to a better understanding of ADHD (Almeida Montes & others, 2012; Cubillo & others, 2012; Qui & others, 2011). One study revealed that peak thickness of the cerebral cortex occurred three years later (10.5 years) in children with ADHD than in children without ADHD (peak at 7.5 years) (Shaw & others, 2007). The delay was more prominent in the prefrontal regions of the brain that especially are important in attention and planning (see Figure 9.5). Another recent study also found delayed development of the brain's frontal lobes in children with ADHD, likely due to delayed or decreased myelination (Nagel & others, 2011). Researchers also are exploring the roles that various neurotransmitters, such as serotonin and dopamine, might play in ADHD (Dalley & Roiser, 2012; Shen, Liao, & Tseng, 2012).

The delays in brain development just described are in areas linked to executive functioning (Supekar & Menon, 2012; Tomasi & Volkow, 2012). An increasing interest in the study of children with ADHD is their difficulty on executive functioning tasks, such as inhibiting behavior when necessary, using working memory, and effective planning (Miller, Ho, & Hinshaw, 2012). Researchers also have found deficits in theory of mind in children with ADHD (Buhler & others, 2011; Shuai, Chan, & Wang, 2011).

Stimulant medication such as Ritalin or Adderall (which has fewer side effects than Ritalin) is effective in improving the attention of many children with ADHD, but it usually does not improve their attention to the same level as children who do not have ADHD (Sclar & others, 2012; Wong & Stevens, 2012). A meta-analysis concluded that behavior management treatments are useful in reducing the effects of ADHD (Fabiano & others, 2009). Researchers have often found that a combination of medication (such as Ritalin) and behavior management improves the behavior of some but not all children with ADHD better than medication alone or behavior management alone (Parens & Johnston, 2009).

Emotional and Behavioral Disorders   Most children have minor emotional difficulties at some point during their school years. A small percentage have problems so serious and persistent that they are classified as having an emotional or behavioral disorder (Jolivette, 2013). These problems may include internalized disorders, such as depression, or externalized disorders, such as aggression (Kern, Hilt-Panehon, & Mukherjee, 2013; Lane & others, 2013).

What are some characteristics of children with an emotional or behavioral disorder?

Emotional and behavioral disorders consist of serious, persistent problems that involve relationships, aggression, depression, and fears associated with personal or school matters, as well as other inappropriate socioemotional characteristics. Approximately 8 percent of children who have a disability and require an individualized education plan fall into this classification. Boys are three times as likely as girls to have these disorders.

Autism Spectrum Disorders   **Autism spectrum disorders (ASD),** also called pervasive developmental disorders, range from the severe disorder labeled autistic disorder to the milder disorder called Asperger syndrome. Autism spectrum disorders are characterized by problems in social interaction, problems in verbal and nonverbal communication, and repetitive behaviors (Hall, 2013). Children with these disorders may also show atypical responses to sensory experiences (National Institute of Mental Health, 2012). Mental retardation is present in some children with autism; others show average or above-average intelligence (Memari & others, 2012). Autism spectrum disorders can often be detected in children as early as 1 to 3 years of age.

Recent estimates of autism spectrum disorders indicate that they are dramatically increasing in occurrence (or are increasingly being detected). Once thought to affect only 1 in 2,500 children decades ago, they were estimated to be present in about 1 in 150 children in 2002 (Centers for Disease Control and Prevention, 2007). However, the most recent estimate is that 1 in 88 children had an autism spectrum disorder in 2008 (Centers for Disease Control & Prevention, 2012b). In the most recent survey, autism spectrum disorders were identified five times more in boys than in girls.

Autistic disorder is a severe developmental autism spectrum disorder that has its onset during the first three years of life and includes deficiencies in social relationships, abnormalities in communication, and restricted, repetitive, and stereotyped patterns of behavior.

Asperger syndrome is a relatively mild autism spectrum disorder in which the child has relatively good verbal language, milder nonverbal language problems, and a restricted range of interests and relationships (Soares & Patel, 2012). Children with Asperger syndrome often

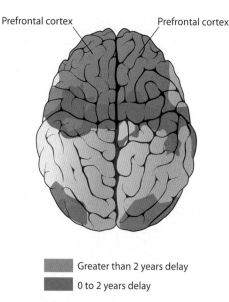

Prefrontal cortex   Prefrontal cortex

■ Greater than 2 years delay
■ 0 to 2 years delay

FIGURE **9.5**
REGIONS OF THE BRAIN IN WHICH CHILDREN WITH ADHD HAD A DELAYED PEAK IN THE THICKNESS OF THE CEREBRAL CORTEX.
Note: The greatest delays occurred in the prefrontal cortex.

developmental **connection**

Conditions, Diseases, and Disorders

Autistic children have difficulty in developing a theory of mind, especially in understanding others' beliefs and emotions. Chapter 7, p. 229

emotional and behavioral disorders Serious, persistent problems that involve relationships, aggression, depression, fears associated with personal or school matters, as well as other inappropriate socioemotional characteristics.

autism spectrum disorders (ASD) Also called pervasive developmental disorders, they range from the severe disorder labeled autistic disorder to the milder disorder called Asperger syndrome. Children with these disorders are characterized by problems in social interaction, verbal and nonverbal communication, and repetitive behaviors.

autistic disorder A severe autism spectrum disorder that has its onset in the first three years of life and includes deficiencies in social relationships, abnormalities in communication, and restricted, repetitive, and stereotyped patterns of behavior.

Asperger syndrome A relatively mild autism spectrum disorder in which the child has relatively good verbal language skills, milder nonverbal language problems, and a restricted range of interests and relationships.

What characterizes children with autism?

engage in obsessive, repetitive routines and preoccupations with a particular subject. For example, a child may be obsessed with baseball scores or railroad timetables.

What causes the autism spectrum disorders? The current consensus is that autism is a brain dysfunction characterized by abnormalities in brain structure and neurotransmitters (Mendez & others, 2012; Toma & others, 2012). Recent interest has focused on a lack of connectivity between brain regions as a key factor in autism (Just & others, 2012; Philip & others, 2012).

Genetic factors also are likely to play a role in the development of the autism spectrum disorders (Chahrour & others, 2012; Yates, 2012). One study revealed that mutations—missing or duplicated pieces of DNA on chromosome 16—can raise a child's risk of developing autism 100-fold (Weiss & others, 2008). There is no evidence that family socialization causes autism.

Boys are estimated to be five times more likely to have autism spectrum disorders than girls are (Centers for Disease Control and Prevention, 2012b). Expanding on autism's male linkage, Simon Baron-Cohen (2008, 2011) recently argued that autism reflects an extreme male brain, especially indicative of males' less effective ability to show empathy and read facial expressions and gestures than girls. In an attempt to improve these skills in 4- to 8-year-old autistic boys, Baron-Cohen and his colleagues (2007) produced a number of animations on a DVD that place faces with different emotions on toy trains and tractor characters in a boy's bedroom (see Figure 9.6). (See www.thetransporters.com for a look at a number of the facial expression animations in addition to the one shown in Figure 9.6.) After the autistic children watch the animations 15 minutes every weekday for one month, their ability to interpret expressions on real faces in a different context equaled that of children without autism.

Children with autism benefit from a well-structured classroom, individualized teaching, and small-group instruction. Behavior modification techniques are sometimes effective in helping autistic children learn (Boutot & Myles, 2011; Iovannone, 2013).

FIGURE **9.6**

A SCENE FROM THE DVD ANIMATIONS USED IN A STUDY BY BARON-COHEN AND OTHERS (2007). *What did they do to improve autistic children's ability to read facial expressions?*
© Crown copyright MMVI, www.thetransporters.com, courtesy of Changing Media Development.

individualized education plan (IEP) A written statement that spells out a program specifically tailored to a child with a disability.

least restrictive environment (LRE) A setting that is as similar as possible to the one in which children who do not have a disability are educated.

inclusion Educating a child with special education needs full-time in the regular classroom.

EDUCATIONAL ISSUES

Until the 1970s most U.S. public schools either refused enrollment to children with disabilities or inadequately served them. This changed in 1975 when Public Law 94-142, the Education for All Handicapped Children Act, required that all students with disabilities be given a free, appropriate public education. In 1990, Public Law 94-142 was recast as the Individuals with Disabilities Education Act (IDEA). IDEA was amended in 1997 and then reauthorized in 2004 and renamed the Individuals with Disabilities Education Improvement Act.

IDEA spells out broad mandates for services to children with disabilities of all kinds (Turnbull & others, 2013). These services include evaluation and eligibility determination, appropriate education and an individualized education plan (IEP), and education in the least restrictive environment (LRE) (Yudof & others, 2012).

An **individualized education plan (IEP)** is a written statement that spells out a program that is specifically tailored for the student with a disability. The **least restrictive environment (LRE)** is a setting that is as similar as possible to the one in which children who do not have a disability are educated. This provision of the IDEA has given a legal basis to efforts to educate children with a disability in the regular classroom. The term **inclusion** describes educating a child with special educational needs full-time in the regular classroom (McLeskey, Rosenberg, & Westling, 2013). Figure 9.7 indicates that in a recent school year slightly more than 50 percent of U.S. students with a disability spent more than 80 percent of their school day in a general classroom.

The outcomes of many legal changes regarding children with disabilities have been extremely positive (Smith & others, 2012). Compared with several decades ago, far more children today are receiving competent, specialized services. For many children, inclusion in the regular classroom, with modifications or supplemental services, is appropriate. However, some leading experts on special education argue that in some cases the effort to educate

FIGURE **9.7**

PERCENTAGE OF U.S. STUDENTS WITH DISABILITIES 6 TO 21 YEARS OF AGE RECEIVING SPECIAL SERVICES IN THE GENERAL CLASSROOM. Data for 2004–2005 school year.
Source: National Center for Education Statistics, 2007.

children with disabilities in the regular classroom has become too extreme. For example, James Kauffman and his colleagues (Kauffman, McGee, & Brigham, 2004) state that inclusion too often has meant making accommodations in the regular classroom that do not always benefit children with disabilities. They advocate a more individualized approach that does not always involve full inclusion but allows options such as special education outside the regular classroom. Kauffman and his colleagues (2004, p. 620) acknowledge that children with disabilities "*do* need the services of specially trained professionals" and "*do* sometimes need altered curricula or adaptations to make their learning possible." However, they believe "we sell students with disabilities short when we pretend that they are not different from typical students. We make the same error when we pretend that they must *not* be expected to put forth extra effort if they are to learn to do some things—or learn to do something in a different way." Like general education, special education should challenge students with disabilities "to become all they can be."

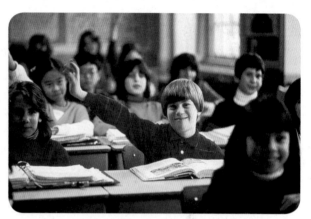

IDEA mandates free, appropriate education for all children. *What services does IDEA mandate for children with disabilities?*

Review *Connect* Reflect

LG2 Identify children with different types of disabilities and discuss issues in educating them.

Review

- Who are children with disabilities? What characterizes children with learning disabilities?
- How would you describe children with attention deficit hyperactivity disorder?
- What are autism spectrum disorders, what are they caused by, and how are they characterized?
- What are some issues in educating children with disabilities?

Connect

- In Chapters 5 and 7, you learned about the development of attention in infancy and early childhood. How might ADHD be linked to earlier attention difficulties in infancy and early childhood?

Reflect *Your Own Personal Journey of Life*

- Think about your own schooling and how children with learning disabilities or ADHD either were or were not diagnosed. Were you aware of such individuals in your classes? Were they helped by specialists? You may know one or more individuals with a learning disability or ADHD. Ask them about their educational experiences and whether they think schools could have done a better job of helping them.

Do children enter a new stage of cognitive development in middle and late childhood? How do children process information during this age period? What is the nature of children's intelligence? Let's explore some answers to these questions.

PIAGET'S COGNITIVE DEVELOPMENTAL THEORY

According to Piaget (1952), the preschool child's thought is preoperational. Preschool children can form stable concepts, and they have begun to reason, but their thinking is flawed by egocentrism and magical belief systems. As we discussed in Chapter 7, however, Piaget may have underestimated the cognitive skills of preschool children. Some researchers argue that under the right conditions, young children may display abilities that are characteristic of Piaget's next stage of cognitive development, the stage of concrete operational thought (Gelman, 1969). Here we will cover the characteristics of concrete operational thought and evaluate Piaget's portrait of this stage.

The Concrete Operational Stage Piaget proposed that the *concrete operational stage* lasts from approximately 7 to 11 years of age. In this stage, children can perform concrete operations, and they can reason logically as long as reasoning can be applied to specific or concrete examples. Remember that *operations* are mental actions that are reversible, and *concrete operations* are operations that are applied to real, concrete objects.

The conservation tasks described in Chapter 7 indicate whether children are capable of concrete operations. For example, recall that in one task involving conservation of matter, the child is presented with two identical balls of clay. The experimenter rolls one ball into a long, thin shape; the other remains in its original ball shape. The child is then asked if there is more clay in the ball or in the long, thin piece of clay. By the time children reach the age of 7 or 8, most answer that the amount of clay is the same. To answer this problem correctly, children have to imagine the clay rolling back into a ball. This type of imagination involves a reversible mental action applied to a real, concrete object. Concrete operations allow the child to consider several characteristics rather than to focus on a single property of an object. In the clay example, the preoperational child is likely to focus on height *or* width. The concrete operational child coordinates information about both dimensions.

What other abilities are characteristic of children who have reached the concrete operational stage? One important skill is the ability to classify or divide things into different sets or subsets and to consider their interrelationships. Consider the family tree of four generations that is shown in Figure 9.8 (Furth & Wachs, 1975). This family tree suggests that the grandfather (A) has three children (B, C, and D), each of whom has two children (E through J), and that one of these children (J) has three children (K, L, and M). A child who comprehends the classification system can move up and down a level, across a level, and up and down and across within the system. The concrete operational child understands that person J can at the same time be father, brother, and grandson, for example.

Children who have reached the concrete operational stage are also capable of **seriation,** which is the ability to order stimuli along a quantitative dimension (such as length). To see if students can serialize, a teacher might haphazardly place eight sticks of different lengths on a table. The teacher then asks the students to order the sticks by length. Many young children end up with two or three small groups of "big" sticks or "little" sticks, rather than a correct ordering of all eight sticks. Another mistaken strategy they use is to evenly line up the tops of the sticks but ignore the bottoms. The concrete operational thinker simultaneously understands that each stick must be longer than the one that precedes it and shorter than the one that follows it.

Another aspect of reasoning about the relations between classes is **transitivity,** which is the ability to logically combine relations to understand certain conclusions. In this case, consider

---

developmental **connection**

Centration

Centration, a centering of attention on one characteristic to the exclusion of all others, is present in young children's lack of conservation. Chapter 7, p. 218

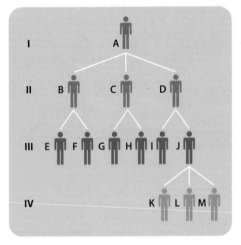

FIGURE **9.8**

CLASSIFICATION: AN IMPORTANT ABILITY IN CONCRETE OPERATIONAL THOUGHT. A family tree of four generations (I to IV): The preoperational child has trouble classifying the members of the four generations, while the concrete operational child can classify the members vertically, horizontally, and obliquely (up and down and across). For example, the concrete operational child understands that a family member can be a son, a brother, and a father, all at the same time.

seriation The concrete operation that involves ordering stimuli along a quantitative dimension (such as length).

transitivity The ability to logically combine relations to understand certain conclusions.

three sticks (A, B, and C) of differing lengths. A is the longest, B is intermediate in length, and C is the shortest. Does the child understand that if A is longer than B and B is longer than C, then A is longer than C? In Piaget's theory, concrete operational thinkers do, while preoperational thinkers do not.

Evaluating Piaget's Concrete Operational Stage   Has Piaget's portrait of the concrete operational child stood the test of research? According to Piaget, various aspects of a stage should emerge at the same time. In fact, however, some concrete operational abilities do not appear in synchrony. For example, children do not learn to conserve at the same time they learn to cross-classify.

Furthermore, education and culture exert stronger influences on children's development than Piaget reasoned (Cole & Packer, 2011). Some preoperational children can be trained to reason at a concrete operational stage. And the age at which children acquire conservation skills is related to how much practice their culture provides in these skills.

Thus, although Piaget was a giant in the field of developmental psychology, his conclusions about the concrete operational stage have been challenged. In Chapter 11, after examining the final stage in his theory of cognitive development, we will further evaluate Piaget's contributions and the criticisms of his theory.

Neo-Piagetians argue that Piaget got some things right but that his theory needs considerable revision. They give more emphasis to how children use attention, memory, and strategies to process information (Case & Mueller, 2001). They especially believe that a more accurate portrayal of children's thinking requires attention to children's strategies, the speed at which children process information, the particular task involved, and the division of problems into smaller, more precise steps (Morra & others, 2008). These are issues addressed by the information-processing approach, and we discuss some of them later in this chapter.

INFORMATION PROCESSING

If instead of describing children's stage of thinking we were to examine how they process information during middle and late childhood, what would we find? During these years, most children dramatically improve their ability to sustain and control attention (Siegler, 2012). As we discussed in Chapter 7, they pay more attention to task-relevant stimuli than to salient stimuli. Other changes in information processing during middle and late childhood involve memory, thinking, metacognition, and executive functioning (Diamond, 2013; McCormick, Dimmitt, & Sullivan, 2013).

Memory   In Chapter 7, we concluded that short-term memory increases considerably during early childhood but after the age of 7 does not show as much increase. **Long-term memory,** a relatively permanent and unlimited type of memory, increases with age during middle and late childhood. In part, improvements in memory reflect children's increased knowledge and their increased use of strategies. Keep in mind that it is important not to view memory in terms of how children add something to it but rather to underscore how children actively construct their memory (Bjorklund, 2013; Cohen, 2012; Willoughby & others, 2012).

Working Memory   Short-term memory is like a passive storehouse with shelves to store information until it is moved to long-term memory. Alan Baddeley (1990, 2001, 2007, 2010, 2012) defines **working memory** as a kind of mental "workbench," where individuals manipulate and assemble information when they make decisions, solve problems, and comprehend written and spoken language (see Figure 9.9). Working memory is described as more active and powerful in modifying information than short-term memory. Working memory involves bringing information to mind and mentally working with or updating it, as when you link one idea to another and relate what you are reading now to something you read earlier (Diamond, 2010).

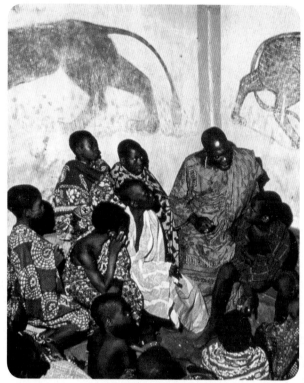

An outstanding teacher and instruction in the logic of science and mathematics are important cultural experiences that promote the development of operational thought. *Might Piaget have underestimated the roles of culture and schooling in children's cognitive development?*

> We owe to Piaget the present field of cognitive development with its image of the developing child, who through its own active and creative commerce with its environment, builds an orderly succession of cognitive structures en route to intellectual maturity.

—JOHN FLAVELL

Contemporary Developmental Psychologist, Stanford University

neo-Piagetians Developmentalists who argue that Piaget got some things right but that his theory needs considerable revision. They have elaborated on Piaget's theory, giving more emphasis to information processing, strategies, and precise cognitive steps.

long-term memory A relatively permanent type of memory that holds huge amounts of information for a long period of time.

working memory A mental "workbench" where individuals manipulate and assemble information when making decisions, solving problems, and comprehending written and spoken language.

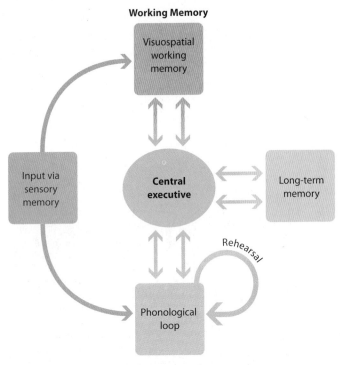

Working Memory

Visuospatial working memory

Input via sensory memory

Central executive

Long-term memory

Rehearsal

Phonological loop

FIGURE **9.9**

WORKING MEMORY. In Baddeley's working memory model, working memory is like a mental workbench where a great deal of information processing is carried out. Working memory consists of three main components: the phonological loop and visuospatial working memory serve as assistants, helping the central executive do its work. Input from sensory memory goes to the phonological loop, where information about speech is stored and rehearsal takes place, and visuospatial working memory, where visual and spatial information, including imagery, are stored. Working memory is a limited-capacity system, and information is stored there for only a brief time. Working memory interacts with long-term memory, using information from long-term memory in its work and transmitting information to long-term memory for longer storage.

developmental **connection**

Cognitive Processes

In early childhood, executive functioning especially involves advances in cognitive inhibition, cognitive flexibility, and goal-setting. Chapter 7, p. 226

strategies Deliberate mental activities that improve the processing of information.

elaboration An important strategy for remembering that involves engaging in more extensive processing of information.

Note in Figure 9.9 that a key component of working memory is the *central executive*, which supervises and controls the flow of information. The central executive is especially at work in selective attention and inhibition, planning and decision making, and trouble shooting. Recall from Chapter 7 our description of *executive functioning* as an umbrella-like concept that encompasses a number of higher-level cognitive processes. One of those cognitive processes is working memory, especially its central executive dimension.

Working memory is linked to many aspects of children's development (Baddeley, 2010, 2012; Caviola & others, 2012). The following three recent studies illustrate the importance of working memory to children's cognitive and language development:

- Working memory and control of attention predicted growth in emergent literacy and number skills in young children in low-income families (Welsh & others, 2010).
- Working memory capacity at 9 to 10 years of age predicted foreign language comprehension two years later at 11 to 12 years of age (Andersson, 2010).
- Working memory capacity predicted how many items on a to-be-remembered list that fourth-grade children forgot (Aslan, Zellner, & Bauml, 2010).

Knowledge and Expertise   Much of the research on the role of knowledge in memory has compared experts and novices. Experts have acquired extensive knowledge about a particular content area; this knowledge influences what they notice and how they organize, represent, and interpret information (Siegler, 2013). These aspects in turn affect their ability to remember, reason, and solve problems. When individuals have expertise about a particular subject, their memory also tends to be good regarding material related to that subject (Staszewski, 2013).

For example, one study found that 10- and 11-year-olds who were experienced chess players ("experts") were able to remember more information about the location of chess pieces on a chess board than college students who were not chess players ("novices") (Chi, 1978) (see Figure 9.10). In contrast, when the college students were presented with other stimuli, they were able to remember them better than the children were. Thus, the children's expertise in chess gave them superior memories, but only in chess.

There are developmental changes in expertise (Blair & Somerville, 2009). Older children usually have more expertise about a subject than younger children do, which can contribute to their better memory for the subject.

Strategies   If we know anything at all about long-term memory, it is that long-term memory depends on the learning activities individuals engage in when learning and remembering information (Robinson-Riegler & Robinson-Riegler, 2012). A key learning activity involves **strategies,** which consist of deliberate mental activities to improve the processing of information. For example, organizing is a strategy that older children, adolescents, and adults use to remember more effectively. Strategies do not occur automatically; they require effort and work.

Following are some effective strategies for adults to use when attempting to improve children's memory skills:

- *Advise children to elaborate on what is to be remembered.* **Elaboration** is an important strategy that involves engaging in more extensive processing of information. When individuals engage in elaboration, their memory benefits (Schneider, 2011). Thinking of examples and relating information to one's own self and experiences are good ways to elaborate information. Forming personal associations with information makes the information more meaningful and helps children to remember it. For example, if the word *win* is on a list of words a child is asked to remember, the child might think of the last time he won a bicycle race with a friend.

- *Encourage children to engage in mental imagery.* Mental imagery can help even young schoolchildren to remember pictures. However, for remembering verbal information, mental imagery works better for older children than for younger children (Schneider, 2011).

- *Motivate children to remember material by understanding it rather than by memorizing it.* Children will remember information better over the long term if they understand the information rather than just rehearse and memorize it. Rehearsal works well for encoding information into short-term memory, but when children need to retrieve the information from long-term memory, it is much less efficient. For most information, encourage children to understand it, give it meaning, elaborate it, and personalize it. Give children concepts and ideas to remember and then ask them how they can relate the concepts and ideas to their own personal experiences and meanings. Give them practice on elaborating a concept so they will process the information more deeply.

- *Repeat with variation on the instructional information and link early and often.* These are memory development research expert Patricia Bauer's (2009) recommendations to improve children's consolidation and reconsolidation of the information they are learning. Variations on a lesson theme increase the number of associations in memory storage, and linking expands the network of associations in memory storage; both strategies expand the routes for retrieving information from storage.

- *Embed memory-relevant language when instructing children.* Teachers vary considerably in how much they use memory-relevant language that encourages students to remember information. In research that involved extensive observations of a number of first-grade teachers in the classroom, Peter Ornstein & his colleagues (Ornstein, Coffman, & Grammer, 2007, 2009; Ornstein & others, 2010) found that for the time segments observed the teachers rarely used strategy suggestions or metacognitive (thinking about thinking) questions. In this research, when lower-achieving students were placed in classrooms in which teachers were categorized as "high-mnemonic teachers" who frequently embedded memory-relevant information in their teaching, their achievement increased (Ornstein, Coffman, & Grammer, 2007).

Fuzzy Trace Theory   Might something other than knowledge and strategies be responsible for the improvement in memory during the elementary school years? Charles Brainerd and Valerie Reyna (1993; Reyna, 2004) argue that fuzzy traces account for much of this improvement. Their **fuzzy trace theory** states that memory is best understood by considering two types of memory representations: (1) verbatim memory trace, and (2) gist. The *verbatim memory trace* consists of the precise details of the information, whereas *gist* refers to the central idea of the information. When gist is used, fuzzy traces are built up. Although individuals of all ages extract gist, young children tend to store and retrieve verbatim traces. At some point during the early elementary school years, children begin to use gist more and, according to the theory, this contributes to the improved memory and reasoning of older children because fuzzy traces are more enduring and less likely to be forgotten than verbatim traces.

Thinking   Three important aspects of thinking are being able to think critically, creatively, and scientifically.

Critical Thinking   Currently, there is considerable interest among psychologists and educators in critical thinking (Barnett & Francis, 2012; Choy & Oo, 2012). **Critical thinking** involves thinking reflectively and productively and evaluating evidence. In this book, the second and third parts of the *Review, Connect, Reflect* sections of each chapter challenge you to think critically about a topic or an issue related to the discussion.

According to Ellen Langer (2005), **mindfulness**—being alert, mentally present, and cognitively flexible while going through life's everyday activities and tasks—is an important aspect

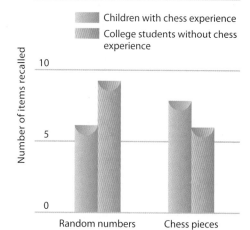

FIGURE 9.10

THE ROLE OF EXPERTISE IN MEMORY. Notice that when 10- to 11-year-old children and college students were asked to remember a string of random numbers that had been presented to them, the college students fared better. However, the 10- to 11-year-olds who had experience playing chess ("experts") had better memory for the location of chess pieces on a chess board than college students with no chess experience ("novices") (Chi, 1978).

fuzzy trace theory States that memory is best understood by considering two types of memory representations: (1) verbatim memory trace, and (2) gist. In this theory, older children's better memory is attributed to the fuzzy traces created by extracting the gist of information.

critical thinking Thinking reflectively and productively, as well as evaluating the evidence.

mindfulness Being alert, mentally present, and cognitively flexible while going through life's everyday activities and tasks.

"For God's sake, think! Why is he being so nice to you?"
© Sam Gross/The New Yorker Collection/www.cartoonbank.com

developmental **connection**

Creativity

How can you cultivate your curiosity and interest to live a more creative life? Chapter 13, p. 440

What do you mean, "What is it?" It's the spontaneous, unfettered expression of a young mind not yet bound by the restraints of narrative or pictorial representation.
Science Cartoons Plus.com

creative thinking The ability to think in novel and unusual ways and to come up with unique solutions to problems.

convergent thinking Thinking that produces one correct answer and is characteristic of the kind of thinking tested by standardized intelligence tests.

divergent thinking Thinking that produces many answers to the same question and is characteristic of creativity.

of thinking critically. Mindful children and adults maintain an active awareness of the circumstances in their life and are motivated to find the best solutions to tasks. Mindful individuals create new ideas, are open to new information, and explore multiple strategies and perspectives. By contrast, mindless individuals are entrapped in old ideas, engage in automatic behavior, and often use a single strategy or adopt a single perspective.

Jacqueline and Martin Brooks (2001) lament that few schools really teach students to think critically and develop a deep understanding of concepts. Deep understanding occurs when students are stimulated to rethink previously held ideas. In Brooks and Brooks' view, schools spend too much time getting students to give a single correct answer in an imitative way, rather than encouraging them to expand their thinking by coming up with new ideas and rethinking earlier conclusions. They observe that too often teachers ask students to recite, define, describe, state, and list, rather than to analyze, infer, connect, synthesize, criticize, create, evaluate, think, and rethink. Many successful students complete their assignments, do well on tests and get good grades, yet they don't ever learn to think critically and deeply. They think superficially, staying on the surface of problems rather than stretching their minds and becoming deeply engaged in meaningful thinking.

Creative Thinking   Cognitively competent children not only think critically, but also creatively (Runco & Spritzker, 2011). **Creative thinking** is the ability to think in novel and unusual ways and to come up with unique solutions to problems. Thus, intelligence and creativity are not the same thing. This difference was recognized by J. P. Guilford (1967), who distinguished between **convergent thinking,** which produces one correct answer and characterizes the kind of thinking that is required on conventional tests of intelligence, and **divergent thinking,** which produces many different answers to the same question and characterizes creativity. For example, a typical item on a conventional intelligence test is "How many quarters will you get in return for 60 dimes?" In contrast, the following question has many possible answers: "What image comes to mind when you hear the phrase 'sitting alone in a dark room' or 'some unique uses for a paper clip'?"

A special concern is that children's creative thinking appears to be declining. A study of approximately 300,000 U.S. children and adults found that creativity scores rose until 1990, but since then have been steadily declining (Kim, 2010). Among the likely causes of the creativity decline are the number of hours U.S. children watch TV and play video games instead of engaging in creative activities, as well as the lack of emphasis on creative thinking skills in schools (Gregorson, Kaufman, & Snyder, 2013; Kaufman & Sternberg, 2013; Sternberg, 2012c) Some countries, though, are placing increasing emphasis on creative thinking in schools. For example, historically, creative thinking has typically been discouraged in Chinese schools. However, Chinese educators are now encouraging teachers to spend more classroom time on creative activities (Plucker, 2010).

It is important to recognize that children will show more creativity in some domains than others (Sternberg, 2012a; Sternberg & Sternberg, 2012). A child who shows creative thinking skills in mathematics may not exhibit these skills in art, for example. An important goal is to help children become more creative. The *Connecting Development to Life* interlude examines some recommendations for ways to accomplish this goal.

Scientific Thinking   Like scientists, children ask fundamental questions about reality and seek answers to problems that may seem utterly trivial or unanswerable to many adults (such as "Why is the sky blue?"). Do children generate hypotheses, perform experiments, and reach conclusions about their data in ways resembling those of scientists?

Scientific reasoning often is aimed at identifying causal relations. Like scientists, children place a great deal of emphasis on causal mechanisms. Their understanding of how events are caused weighs more heavily in their causal inferences than even such strong influences as whether the cause happened immediately before the effect.

There also are important differences between the reasoning of children and the reasoning of scientists (Kuhn, 2011). For example, children have difficulty designing experiments that can distinguish among alternative causes. Instead, they tend to bias the experiments in favor of whatever hypothesis they began with. Sometimes they see the results as supporting their original hypothesis even when the results directly contradict it.

Strategies for Increasing Children's Creative Thinking

Below are some strategies for increasing children's creative thinking.

Encourage Brainstorming

Brainstorming is a technique in which people are encouraged to come up with creative ideas in a group, play off each other's ideas, and say practically whatever comes to mind that seems relevant to a particular issue. Facilitators usually tell participants to hold off from criticizing others' ideas at least until the end of the brainstorming session.

Provide Environments That Stimulate Creativity

Some environments nourish creativity, while others inhibit it. Parents and teachers who encourage creativity often rely on children's natural curiosity. They provide exercises and activities that stimulate children to find insightful solutions to problems, rather than ask a lot of questions that require rote answers (Baer & Kaufman, 2013). Teachers also encourage creativity by taking students on field trips to locations where creativity is valued. Science, discovery, and children's museums offer rich opportunities to stimulate creativity.

Don't Overcontrol Children

Teresa Amabile (1993) says that telling children exactly how to do things leaves them feeling that originality is a mistake and exploration is a waste of time. Instead of dictating which activities they should engage in, teachers and parents who let children select their interests and who support their inclinations are less likely to stifle their natural curiosity (Hennessey, 2011).

Encourage Internal Motivation

Parents and teachers should avoid excessive use of prizes, such as gold stars, money, or toys, which can stifle creativity by undermining the intrinsic pleasure students derive from creative activities (Hennessey, 2011). Creative children's motivation is the satisfaction generated by the work itself.

Build Children's Confidence

To expand children's creativity, teachers and parents should encourage children to believe in their own ability to create something innovative and worthwhile. Building children's confidence in their creative skills aligns with Bandura's (2010a, 2012) concept of *self-efficacy*, the belief that one can master a situation and produce positive outcomes.

What are some good strategies for guiding children in thinking more creatively?

Guide Children to Be Persistent and Delay Gratification

Parents and teachers need to be patient and understand that most highly successful creative products take years to develop. Most creative individuals work on ideas and projects for months and years without being rewarded for their efforts.

Encourage Children to Take Intellectual Risks

Parents and teachers should encourage children to take intellectual risks. Creative individuals take intellectual risks and seek to discover or invent something never before discovered or invented. Creative people are not afraid of failing or getting something wrong (Baer & Kaufman, 2013).

Introduce Children to Creative People

Teachers can invite creative people to their classrooms and ask them to describe what helps them become creative or to demonstrate their creative skills. A writer, poet, musician, scientist, and many others can bring their props and productions to the classroom, turning it into a forum for stimulating students' creativity.

You learned that it is important to recognize that children will show more creativity in some domains than others. Choose one of the strategies mentioned above and describe how you would implement it differently to encourage creativity in writing, science, math, and art in children in middle and late childhood.

Too often, the skills scientists use, such as careful observation, graphing, self-regulatory thinking, and knowing when and how to apply one's knowledge to solve problems, are not routinely taught in schools. Children have many concepts that are incompatible with science and reality. Good teachers perceive and understand a child's underlying scientific concepts, then use the concepts as a scaffold for learning (McNeill & Krajcik, 2012; Seefeldt, Galper, &

brainstorming A technique in which individuals are encouraged to come up with creative ideas in a group, play off each other's ideas, and say almost anything that comes to mind.

Luis Recalde holds up a seaweed specimen in one of the hands-on, high-interest learning contexts he creates for students. Recalde, a fourth- and fifth-grade science teacher in New Haven, Connecticut, uses every opportunity to make science fascinating for students to learn. To help students get a better sense of what it is like to be a scientist, he brings lab coats to the classroom for students to wear. He often gives up his vacation time to help students with science projects.

developmental **connection**

Cognitive Theory

Theory of mind—awareness of one's own mental processes and the mental processes of others—involves metacognition. Chapter 7, p. 227

Cognitive developmentalist John Flavell is a pioneer in providing insights about children's thinking. Among his many contributions are establishing the field of metacognition and conducting numerous studies in this area, including metamemory and theory of mind studies.

metacognition Cognition about cognition, or knowing about knowing.

Jones, 2012). Effective science teaching helps children distinguish between fruitful errors and misconceptions and detect plainly wrong ideas that need to be replaced by more accurate conceptions (Zembal-Saul, McNeill, & Hershberger, 2013).

Metacognition   Metacognition is cognition about cognition, or knowing about knowing (Flavell, 2004). Many studies classified as "metacognitive" have focused on *metamemory*, or knowledge about memory. This includes general knowledge about memory, such as knowing that recognition tests are easier than recall tests. It also encompasses knowledge about one's own memory, such as a student's ability to monitor whether she has studied enough for a test that is coming up next week.

Young children do have some general knowledge about memory (Harris & others, 2010). By 5 or 6 years of age, children usually already know that familiar items are easier to learn than unfamiliar ones, that short lists are easier than long ones, that recognition is easier than recall, and that forgetting is more likely to occur over time (Lyon & Flavell, 1993). However, in other ways young children's metamemory is limited. They don't understand that related items are easier to remember than unrelated ones and that remembering the gist of a story is easier than remembering information verbatim (Kreutzer, Leonard, & Flavell, 1975). By the fifth grade, students understand that gist recall is easier than verbatim recall.

Young children also have only limited knowledge about their own memory. They have an inflated opinion of their memory abilities. For example, in one study a majority of young children predicted that they would be able to recall all 10 items on a list of 10 items. When tested for this, none of the young children managed this feat (Flavell, Friedrichs, & Hoyt, 1970). As they move through the elementary school years, children give more realistic evaluations of their memory skills (Schneider, 2011).

In addition to metamemory, metacognition includes knowledge about strategies (McCormick, Dimmitt, & Sullivan, 2013; Sperling & others, 2012). In the view of Michael Pressley (2003), the key to education is helping students learn a rich repertoire of strategies that result in solutions to problems. Good thinkers routinely use strategies and effective planning to solve problems. Good thinkers also know when and where to use strategies. Understanding when and where to use strategies often results from monitoring the learning situation (Serra & Metcalfe, 2010).

Pressley and his colleagues (Pressley & others, 2003, 2004, 2007) spent considerable time in recent years observing strategy instruction by teachers and strategy use by students in elementary and secondary school classrooms. They conclude that strategy instruction is far less complete and intense than what students need in order to learn how to use strategies effectively. They argue that education needs to be restructured so that students are provided with more opportunities to become competent strategic learners.

Executive Functioning   In Chapter 7, you read about executive functioning and its characteristics in early childhood (Carlson & White, 2013; Conway & Stifter, 2012). Some of the cognitive topics we already have discussed in this chapter—working memory, critical thinking, creative thinking, and metacognition—can be considered under the umbrella of executive functioning and linked to the development of the brain's prefrontal cortex. Also, earlier in the chapter in the coverage of brain development in middle and late childhood, you read about the increase in cognitive control, which involves flexible and effective control in a number of areas such as focusing attention, reducing interfering thoughts, inhibiting motor actions, and exercising flexibility in deciding between competing choices.

Adele Diamond and Kathleen Lee (2011) recently highlighted the following dimensions of executive functioning that they conclude are the most important for 4- to 11-year-old children's cognitive development and school success:

• *Self-control/inhibition.* Children need to develop self-control that will allow them to concentrate and persist on learning tasks, to inhibit their tendencies to repeat incorrect responses, and to resist the impulse to do something now that they later would regret.

- *Working memory.* Children need an effective working memory to mentally work with the masses of information they will encounter as they go through school and beyond.
- *Flexibility.* Children need to be flexible in their thinking to consider different strategies and perspectives.

Researchers have found that executive functioning is a better predictor of school readiness than general IQ (Blair & Razza, 2007). A number of diverse activities have been found to increase children's executive functioning, such as computerized training that uses games to improve working memory (CogMed, 2013), aerobic exercise (Chang & others, 2012), mindfulness (the Tools of the Mind program discussed in Chapter 7, for example) (Bodrova, Leong, & Akhutina, 2011), and some types of school curricula (the Montessori curriculum, for example) (Diamond, 2013; Diamond & Lee, 2011).

What are some key dimensions of executive functioning that are linked to children's cognitive development and school success?

INTELLIGENCE

How can intelligence be defined? **Intelligence** is the ability to solve problems and to adapt and learn from experiences. Interest in intelligence has often focused on individual differences and assessment. **Individual differences** are the stable, consistent ways in which people are different from each other. We can talk about individual differences in personality or any other domain, but it is in the domain of intelligence that the most attention has been directed at individual differences. For example, an intelligence test purports to inform us about whether a student can reason better than others who have taken the test. Let's go back in history and see what the first intelligence test was like.

> The thirst to know and understand. . . .
> These are the good in life's rich hand.
>
> —SIR WILLIAM WATSON
> *English Poet, 20th Century*

The Binet Tests In 1904, the French Ministry of Education asked psychologist Alfred Binet to devise a method of identifying children who were unable to learn in school. School officials wanted to reduce crowding by placing students who did not benefit from regular classroom teaching in special schools. Binet and his student Theophile Simon developed an intelligence test to meet this request. The test is called the 1905 Scale. It consisted of 30 questions on topics ranging from the ability to touch one's ear to the ability to draw designs from memory and define abstract concepts.

Binet developed the concept of **mental age (MA)**, an individual's level of mental development relative to others. Not much later, in 1912, William Stern created the concept of **intelligence quotient (IQ)**, a person's mental age divided by chronological age (CA), multiplied by 100. That is: IQ = MA/CA × 100. If mental age is the same as chronological age, then the person's IQ is 100. If mental age is above chronological age, then IQ is more than 100. If mental age is below chronological age, then IQ is less than 100.

Alfred Binet constructed the first intelligence test after being asked to create a measure to determine which children could benefit from instruction in France's schools and which could not.

developmental **connection**

Intelligence

Does intelligence decrease when individuals become middle-aged? Chapter 15, p. 496

The Binet test has been revised many times to incorporate advances in the understanding of intelligence and intelligence tests. These revisions are called the *Stanford-Binet tests* (Stanford University is where the revisions have been done). In 2004, the test—now called the Stanford-Binet 5—was revised to analyze an individual's response in five content areas: fluid reasoning, knowledge, quantitative reasoning, visual-spatial reasoning, and working memory. A general composite score also is still obtained.

By administering the test to large numbers of people of different ages (from preschool through late adulthood) from different backgrounds, researchers have found that scores on the Stanford-Binet approximate a normal distribution (see Figure 9.11). A **normal distribution** is symmetrical, with a majority of the scores falling in the middle of the possible range of scores and few scores appearing toward the extremes of the range.

intelligence Problem-solving skills and the ability to learn from and adapt to the experiences of everyday life.

individual differences The stable, consistent ways in which people differ from each other.

mental age (MA) Binet's measure of an individual's level of mental development, compared with that of others.

intelligence quotient (IQ) A person's mental age divided by chronological age, multiplied by 100.

normal distribution A symmetrical distribution with most scores falling in the middle of the possible range of scores and a few scores appearing toward the extremes of the range.

FIGURE **9.11**

THE NORMAL CURVE AND STANFORD-BINET IQ SCORES. The distribution of IQ scores approximates a normal curve. Most of the population falls in the middle range of scores. Notice that extremely high and extremely low scores are very rare. Slightly more than two-thirds of the scores fall between 85 and 115. Only about 1 in 50 individuals has an IQ of more than 130, and only about 1 in 50 individuals has an IQ of less than 70.

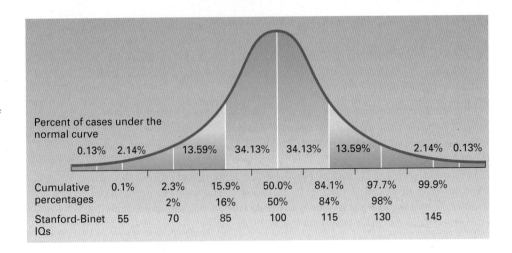

Percent of cases under the normal curve								
0.13%	2.14%		13.59%	34.13%	34.13%	13.59%	2.14%	0.13%
Cumulative percentages	0.1%	2.3%	15.9%	50.0%	84.1%	97.7%	99.9%	
		2%	16%	50%	84%	98%		
Stanford-Binet IQs	55	70	85	100	115	130	145	

Verbal Subscales

Similarities

A child must think logically and abstractly to answer a number of questions about how things might be similar.

Example: "In what way are a lion and a tiger alike?"

Comprehension

This subscale is designed to measure an individual's judgment and common sense.

Example: "What is the advantage of keeping money in a bank?"

Nonverbal Subscales

Block Design

A child must assemble a set of multicolored blocks to match designs that the examiner shows.
Visual-motor coordination, perceptual organization, and the ability to visualize spatially are assessed.

Example: "Use the four blocks on the left to make the pattern on the right."

FIGURE **9.12**

SAMPLE SUBSCALES OF THE WECHSLER INTELLIGENCE SCALE FOR CHILDREN—FOURTH EDITION (WISC-IV). The Wechsler includes 11 subscales—6 verbal and 5 nonverbal. Three of the subscales are shown here. Simulated items similar to those found in the Wechsler Intelligence Scale for Children—Fourth Edition. Copyright © 2004 by NCS Pearson, Inc. Reproduced by permission. All rights reserved. "Wechsler Intelligence Scale for Children" and "WISC" are trademarks of Harcourt Assessment, Inc. registered in the United States of America and/or other jurisdictions.

triarchic theory of intelligence Sternberg's theory that intelligence consists of analytical intelligence, creative intelligence, and practical intelligence.

The Wechsler Scales   Another set of tests widely used to assess students' intelligence is called the Wechsler scales, developed by psychologist David Wechsler. They include the Wechsler Preschool and Primary Scale of Intelligence—Third Edition (WPPSI-III) to test children from 2.5 years to 7.25 years of age; the Wechsler Intelligence Scale for Children—Fourth Edition (WISC-IV) for children and adolescents 6 to 16 years of age; and the Wechsler Adult Intelligence Scale—Third Edition (WAIS-III).

The Wechsler scales not only provide an overall IQ score, but they also yield several composite indexes (for example, the Verbal Comprehension Index, the Working Memory Index, and the Processing Speed Index) that allow the examiner to quickly determine the areas in which the child is strong or weak. Three of the Wechsler subscales are shown in Figure 9.12.

Types of Intelligence   Is it more appropriate to think of a child's intelligence as a general ability or as a number of specific abilities? Robert Sternberg and Howard Gardner have proposed influential theories oriented to this second viewpoint.

Sternberg's Triarchic Theory   Robert J. Sternberg (1986, 2004, 2010, 2011, 2012b; 2013a, b) developed the **triarchic theory of intelligence,** which states that intelligence comes in three forms: (1) *analytical intelligence,* which refers to the ability to analyze, judge, evaluate, compare, and contrast; (2) *creative intelligence,* which consists of the ability to create, design, invent, originate, and imagine; and (3) *practical intelligence,* which involves the ability to use, apply, implement, and put ideas into practice.

Sternberg (2010, 2011, 2012b, 2013a, b) says that children with different triarchic patterns "look different" in school. Students with high analytic ability tend to be favored in conventional schooling. They often do well under direct instruction, in which the teacher lectures and gives students objective tests. They often are considered to be "smart" students who get good grades, show up in high-level tracks, do well on traditional tests of intelligence and the SAT, and later get admitted to competitive colleges.

In contrast, children who are high in creative intelligence often are not on the top rung of their class. Many teachers have specific expectations about how assignments should be done, and creatively intelligent students may not conform to those expectations. Instead of giving conformist

Robert J. Sternberg, who developed the triarchic theory of intelligence.

answers, they give unique answers, for which they might get reprimanded or marked down. No teacher wants to discourage creativity, but Sternberg stresses that too often a teacher's desire to improve students' knowledge suppresses creative thinking.

Like children high in creative intelligence, children who are practically intelligent often do not relate well to the demands of school. However, many of these children do well outside of the classroom's walls. They may have excellent social skills and good common sense. As adults, some become successful managers, entrepreneurs, or politicians in spite of having undistinguished school records.

Gardner's Eight Frames of Mind

Howard Gardner (1983, 1993, 2002) suggests there are eight types of intelligence, or "frames of mind." These are described here, with examples of the types of vocations in which they are reflected as strengths (Campbell, Campbell, & Dickinson, 2004):

"You're wise, but you lack tree smarts."
© Donald Reilly/The New Yorker Collection/
www.cartoonbank.com

Verbal: The ability to think in words and use language to express meaning. Occupations: authors, journalists, speakers.

Mathematical: The ability to carry out mathematical operations. Occupations: scientists, engineers, accountants.

Spatial: The ability to think three-dimensionally. Occupations: architects, artists, sailors.

Bodily-kinesthetic: The ability to manipulate objects and be physically adept. Occupations: surgeons, craftspeople, dancers, athletes.

Musical: A sensitivity to pitch, melody, rhythm, and tone. Occupations: composers and musicians.

Interpersonal: The ability to understand and interact effectively with others. Occupations: successful teachers, mental health professionals.

Intrapersonal: The ability to understand oneself. Occupations: theologians, psychologists.

Naturalist: The ability to observe patterns in nature and understand natural and human-made systems. Occupations: farmers, botanists, ecologists, landscapers.

According to Gardner, everyone has all of these intelligences to varying degrees. As a result, we prefer to learn and process information in different ways. People learn best when they can do so in a way that uses their stronger intelligences.

Evaluating the Multiple-Intelligence Approaches

Sternberg's and Gardner's approaches have much to offer. They have stimulated teachers to think more broadly about what makes up children's competencies. And they have motivated educators to develop programs that instruct students in multiple domains. These approaches have also contributed to interest in assessing intelligence and classroom learning in innovative ways, such as by evaluating student portfolios (Moran & Gardner, 2006, 2007).

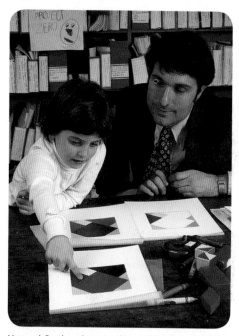

Howard Gardner, here working with a young child, developed the view that intelligence comes in the forms of eight kinds of skills: verbal, mathematical, spatial, bodily-kinesthetic, musical, intrapersonal, interpersonal, and naturalist.

However, doubts about multiple-intelligence approaches persist. A number of psychologists think that the multiple-intelligence views have taken the concept of specific intelligences too far (Reeve & Charles, 2008). Some argue that a research base to support the three intelligences of Sternberg or the eight intelligences of Gardner has not yet emerged. One expert on intelligence, Nathan Brody (2007), observes that people who excel at one type of intellectual task are likely to excel in others. Thus, individuals who do well at memorizing lists of digits are also likely to be good at solving verbal problems and spatial layout problems. If musical skill reflects a distinct type of intelligence, ask other critics, why not label the skills of outstanding chess players, prizefighters, painters, and poets as types of intelligence?

The argument between those who support the concept of general intelligence and those who advocate the multiple-intelligence view is ongoing (Brody, 2007; Sternberg, 2012, 2013a, b). Sternberg (2012, 2013b) actually accepts that there is a general intelligence for the kinds of analytical tasks that traditional IQ tests assess but thinks that the range of tasks those tests measure is far too narrow.

Culture and Intelligence

Differences in conceptions of intelligence occur not only among psychologists but also among cultures (Sternberg, 2012c). What is viewed as intelligent in one culture may not be thought of as intelligent in

Children in the Key School form "pods," in which they pursue activities of special interest to them. Every day, each child can choose from activities that draw on Gardner's eight intelligences. The school has pods that range from gardening to architecture to gliding to dancing.

"You can't build a hut, you don't know how to find edible roots and you know nothing about predicting the weather. In other words, you do terribly on our I.Q. test."
ScienceCartoonsPlus.com

developmental **connection**

Intelligence

Polygenic inheritance is the term used to describe the effects of multiple genes on a particular characteristic. Chapter 2, p. 59

developmental **connection**

Nature Versus Nurture

The epigenetic view emphasizes that development is an ongoing, bidirectional interchange between heredity and environment. Chapter 2, p. 71

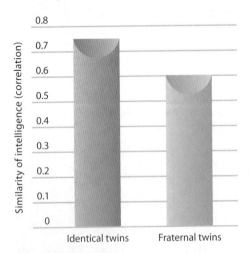

FIGURE **9.13**

CORRELATION BETWEEN INTELLIGENCE TEST SCORES AND TWIN STATUS. The graph represents a summary of research findings that have compared the intelligence test scores of identical and fraternal twins. An approximate .15 difference has been found, with a higher correlation for identical twins (.75) and a lower correlation for fraternal twins (.60).

another. For example, people in Western cultures tend to view intelligence in terms of reasoning and thinking skills, whereas people in Eastern cultures see intelligence as a way for members of a community to engage successfully in social roles (Nisbett, 2003).

Interpreting Differences in IQ Scores   The IQ scores that result from tests such as the Stanford-Binet and Wechsler scales provide information about children's mental abilities. However, interpreting what performance on an intelligence test means is a subject of debate among researchers.

The Influence of Genetics   How strong is the effect of genetics on intelligence? This question is difficult to answer because (as we discussed in Chapter 2) making clear-cut distinctions between the influences of heredity and environment is virtually impossible. Also, most research on heredity and environment does not include environments that differ radically. Thus, it is not surprising that many genetic studies show environment to be a fairly weak influence on intelligence.

Have scientists been able to pinpoint specific genes that are linked to intelligence? A recent research review concluded that there may be more than 1,000 genes that affect intelligence, each possibly having a small influence on an individual's intelligence (Davies & others, 2011). However, researchers have not been able to identify the specific genes that contribute to intelligence (Deary, 2012).

One strategy for examining the role of heredity in intelligence is to compare the IQs of identical and fraternal twins, which we initially discussed in Chapter 2. Recall that identical twins have exactly the same genetic makeup but fraternal twins do not. If intelligence is genetically determined, say some investigators, identical twins' IQs should be more similar than the intelligence of fraternal twins. A research review of many studies found that the difference in the average correlation of intelligence between identical and fraternal twins was .15, a relatively low correlation (Grigorenko, 2000) (see Figure 9.13).

Today, most researchers agree that genetics and environment interact to influence intelligence (Cooper, 2012). For most people, this means that modifications in environment can change their IQ scores considerably. Although genetic endowment may always influence a person's intellectual ability, the environmental influences and opportunities we provide to children and adults do make a difference (Sternberg, 2013a, b).

Environmental Influences   In Chapter 5 we described one study that demonstrated the influence of parents on cognitive abilities. Researchers went into homes and observed how extensively parents from welfare and middle-income professional families talked and communicated with their young children (Hart & Risley, 1995). They found that the middle-income professional parents were much more likely to communicate with their young children than the welfare parents were. How much the parents communicated with their children in the first three years of their lives was correlated with the children's Stanford-Binet IQ scores at age 3. The more parents communicated with their children, the higher the children's IQs were.

The environment's role in intelligence is reflected in the 12- to 18-point increase in IQ that occurs when children are adopted from lower SES to middle SES homes (Nisbett & others, 2012). Environmental influences on intelligence also involve schooling (Gustafsson, 2007). The biggest effects have been found when large groups of children have been deprived of formal education for an extended period, resulting in lower intelligence (Ceci & Gilstrap, 2000). Another possible effect of education can be seen in rapidly increasing IQ test scores around the world (Flynn, 1999, 2007, 2011, 2012). IQ scores have been increasing so fast that a high percentage of people regarded as having average intelligence at the turn of the century would be considered below average in intelligence today (see Figure 9.14). If a representative sample of people today took the Stanford-Binet test version used in 1932, about 25 percent would be defined as having very superior intelligence, a label usually accorded to fewer than 3 percent of the population. Because the increase has taken place in a relatively short time, it can't be due to heredity, but rather may be due to increasing levels of education attained by a much greater percentage of the world's population, or to other environmental factors such as the explosion of information to which people are exposed. The worldwide increase in intelligence test scores that has occurred over a short time frame has been called the *Flynn effect* after the researcher who discovered it, James Flynn.

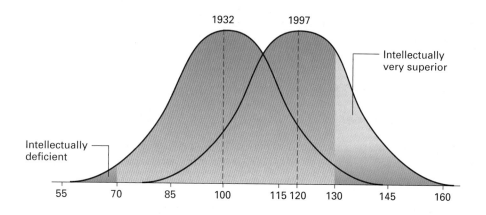

FIGURE **9.14**

INCREASING IQ SCORES FROM 1932 TO 1997.
As measured by the Stanford-Binet intelligence test,
American children seem to be getting smarter. Scores
of a group tested in 1932 fell along a bell-shaped
curve with half below 100 and half above. Studies
show that if children took that same test today, half
would score above 120 on the 1932 scale. Very few of
them would score in the "intellectually deficient" end
on the left side, and about one-fourth would rank in
the "very superior" range on the right side.

Researchers are increasingly concerned about improving the early environment of children who are at risk for impoverished intelligence and poor developmental outcomes (Bagnato & Macy, 2012; Huberman & Mendelsohn, 2012). For various reasons, many low-income parents have difficulty providing an intellectually stimulating environment for their children. Programs that educate parents to be more sensitive caregivers and better teachers, as well as support services such as quality child care and early childhood education programs, can make a difference in a child's intellectual development (Johnson & Brooks-Gunn, 2012; Morrison, 2012; Squires & others, 2013). Thus, the efforts to counteract a deprived early environment's effect on intelligence emphasize prevention rather than remediation.

A review of the research on early interventions concluded that (1) high-quality interventions based in child-care centers are associated with increases in children's intelligence and school achievement; (2) the interventions are most successful with poor children and children whose parents have little education; (3) the positive benefits continue through adolescence but are not as strong as in early childhood or the beginning of elementary school; and (4) the programs that continue into middle and late childhood have the best long-term results (Brooks-Gunn, 2003). To read further about environmental influences on intelligence, see *Connecting Through Research.*

In sum, there is a consensus among psychologists that both heredity and environment influence intelligence (Grigorenko & Takanishi, 2012). This consensus reflects the nature-nurture issue that was highlighted in Chapter 1. Recall that the nature-nurture issue focuses on the extent to which development is influenced by nature (heredity) and nurture (environment). Although psychologists agree that intelligence is the product of both nature and nurture, there is still disagreement about how strongly each influences intelligence.

Group Differences   On the average, African American schoolchildren in the United States score 10 to 15 points lower on standardized intelligence tests than non–Latino White American schoolchildren do (Brody, 2000). Children from Latino families also score lower than non–Latino White children. These are average scores, however; there is significant overlap in the distribution of scores. About 15 to 25 percent of African American schoolchildren score higher than half of White schoolchildren do, and many White schoolchildren score lower than most African American schoolchildren. As African Americans have gained social, economic, and educational opportunities, the gap between African Americans and Whites on standardized intelligence tests has narrowed (Nisbett & others, 2012). This gap especially narrows in college, where African American and White students often experience more similar environments than in the elementary and high school years (Myerson & others, 1998).

Creating Culture-Fair Tests   **Culture-fair tests** are tests of intelligence that are intended to be free of cultural bias. Two types of culture-fair tests have been devised. The first includes items that are familiar to children from all socioeconomic and ethnic backgrounds, or items that at least are familiar to the children taking the test. For example, a child might be asked how a bird and a dog are different, on the assumption that all children have been exposed to birds and dogs. The second type of culture-fair test has no verbal questions. Figure 9.15 shows a sample question from the Raven's Progressive Matrices Test. Even though tests such as the

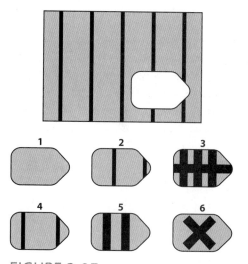

FIGURE **9.15**

SAMPLE ITEM FROM THE RAVEN'S PROGRESSIVE MATRICES TEST. Individuals are presented with a matrix arrangement of symbols, such as the one at the top of this figure, and must then complete the matrix by selecting the appropriate missing symbol from a group of symbols, such as the ones at the bottom. These symbols and the matrix are similar to those found in the Raven's Progressive Matrices. Copyright © 1998 by NCS Pearson, Inc. Reproduced with permission. All rights reserved.

culture-fair tests Tests of intelligence that are designed to be free of cultural bias.

How Much Does Environment Affect Intelligence?

Each morning a young mother waited with her child for the bus that would take the child to school. The child was only 2 months old, and "school" was an experimental program at the University of North Carolina at Chapel Hill. There the child experienced a number of interventions designed to improve her intellectual development—everything from bright objects dangled in front of her eyes while she was a baby to language instruction and counting activities when she was a toddler (Wickelgren, 1999). The child's mother had an IQ of 40 and could not read signs or determine how much change she should receive from a cashier. Her grandmother had a similarly low IQ.

Today, at age 20, the child's IQ measures 80 points higher than her mother's did when the child was 2 months old. Not everyone agrees that IQ can be affected this extensively, but environment can make a substantial difference in a child's intelligence. As behavior geneticist Robert Plomin (1999) says, even something that is highly heritable (like intelligence) may be malleable through interventions.

The child we just described was part of the Abecedarian Intervention program at the University of North Carolina at Chapel Hill conducted by Craig Ramey and his associates (Ramey & Campbell, 1984; Ramey & Ramey, 1998; Ramey, Ramey, & Lanzi, 2001). They randomly assigned 111 young children from low-income, poorly educated families to either an intervention group, which received full-time, year-round child care along with medical and social work services, or

to a control group, which received medical and social benefits but no child care. The child-care program included game-like learning activities aimed at improving language, motor, social, and cognitive skills.

The success of the program in improving IQ was evident by the time the children were 3 years old. At that age, the experimental group showed normal IQs averaging 101, a 17-point advantage over the control group. Recent follow-up results suggest that the effects are long-lasting. More than a decade later at age 15, children from the intervention group still maintained an IQ advantage of 5 points over the control-group children (97.7 to 92.6) (Campbell & others, 2001; Ramey, Ramey, & Lanzi, 2001). They also did better on standardized tests of reading and math, and were less likely to be held back a year in school. Also, the greatest IQ gains were made by the children whose mothers had especially low IQs—below 70. At age 15, these children showed a 10-point IQ advantage over a group of children whose mothers' IQs were below 70 but who had not experienced the child-care intervention.

This research reinforces the research mentioned earlier that found prevention rather than remediation is important in counteracting a deprived early environment's effect on intelligence. It also supports the conclusion that modifications in environment can change IQ scores considerably. Therefore, it is important to consider the types of environments we provide for children—both those in the general population and those with disabilities (Waber, 2010).

Raven's Progressive Matrices are designed to be culture-fair, people with more education still score higher on them than do those with less education.

Why is it so hard to create culture-fair tests? Most tests tend to reflect what the dominant culture thinks is important. If tests have time limits, that will bias the test against groups not concerned with time. If languages differ, the same words might have different meanings for different language groups. Even pictures can produce bias because some cultures have less experience with drawings and photographs. Because of such difficulties in creating culture-fair tests, Robert Sternberg (2012c) concludes that there are no culture-fair tests, only *culture-reduced tests*.

Using Intelligence Tests   Here are some cautions about IQ that can help you avoid the pitfalls of using information about a child's intelligence in negative ways:

- *Avoid stereotyping and expectations.* A special concern is that the scores on an IQ test easily can lead to stereotypes and expectations about students. Sweeping generalizations are too often made on the basis of an IQ score. An IQ test should always be considered a measure of current performance. It is not a measure of fixed potential. Maturational changes and enriched environmental experiences can advance a student's intelligence.

- *Know that IQ is not a sole indicator of competence.* Another concern about IQ tests occurs when they are used as the main or sole assessment of competence. A high IQ is not the ultimate human value. As we have seen in this chapter, it is important to consider not only students' intellectual competence in such areas as verbal skills but also their creative and practical skills.

mental retardation A condition of limited mental ability in which an individual has a low IQ, usually below 70 on a traditional test of intelligence, and has difficulty adapting to everyday life.

organic retardation Mental retardation that is caused by a genetic disorder or brain damage.

cultural-familial retardation Retardation in which there is no evidence of organic brain damage, but the individual's IQ is generally between 50 and 70.

gifted Having above-average intelligence (an IQ of 130 or higher) and/or superior talent for something.

- *Use caution in interpreting an overall IQ score.* In evaluating a child's intelligence, it is wiser to think of intelligence as consisting of a number of domains. Keep in mind the different types of intelligence described by Sternberg and Gardner. Remember that by considering the different domains of intelligence you can find that every child has at least one or more strengths.

EXTREMES OF INTELLIGENCE

Intelligence tests have been used to discover indications of mental retardation or intellectual giftedness, the extremes of intelligence. At times, intelligence tests have been misused for this purpose. Keeping in mind the theme that an intelligence test should not be used as the sole indicator of mental retardation or giftedness, we will explore the nature of these intellectual extremes.

Mental Retardation   **Mental retardation** is a condition of limited mental ability in which an individual has a low IQ, usually below 70 on a traditional intelligence test, and has difficulty adapting to everyday life. About 5 million Americans fit this definition of mental retardation.

There are several classifications of mental retardation (Hallahan, Kaufmann, & Pullen, 2012). About 89 percent of those with mental retardation fall into the mild category, with IQs of 55 to 70; most of them are able to live independently as adults and work at a variety of jobs. About 6 percent are classified as having moderate mental retardation, with IQs of 40 to 54; these people can attain a second-grade level of skills and may be able to support themselves as adults through some types of labor. About 3.5 percent of those with mental retardation are in the severe category, with IQs of 25 to 39; these individuals learn to talk and accomplish very simple tasks but require extensive supervision. Less than 1 percent have IQs below 25; they fall into the profoundly mentally retarded classification and need constant supervision.

Mental retardation can have an organic cause, or it can be social and cultural in origin:

- **Organic retardation** is mental retardation that is caused by a genetic disorder or by brain damage; the word organic refers to the tissues or organs of the body, indicating physical damage. Most people who suffer from organic retardation have IQs that range between 0 and 50. However, children with Down syndrome have an average IQ of approximately 50. As discussed in Chapter 2, Down syndrome is caused by an extra copy of chromosome 21.
- **Cultural-familial retardation** is a mental deficit in which no evidence of organic brain damage can be found; individuals' IQs generally range from 50 to 70. Psychologists suspect that such mental deficits result from the normal variation that distributes people along the range of intelligence scores combined with growing up in a below-average intellectual environment.

Giftedness   There have always been people whose abilities and accomplishments outshine others'—the whiz kid in class, the star athlete, the natural musician. People who are **gifted** have above-average intelligence (an IQ of 130 or higher) and/or superior talent for something. When it comes to programs for the gifted, most school systems select children who have intellectual superiority and academic aptitude, whereas children who are talented in the visual and performing arts (arts, drama, dance), athletics, or who have other special aptitudes tend to be overlooked.

Characteristics   What are the characteristics of children who are gifted? Despite speculation that giftedness is linked with having a mental disorder, no relation between giftedness and mental disorder has been found. Similarly, the idea that gifted children are maladjusted is a myth, as Lewis Terman (1925) found when he conducted an extensive study of 1,500 children whose Stanford-Binet IQs averaged 150. The children in Terman's study were socially well adjusted, and many went on to become successful doctors, lawyers, professors, and scientists. Studies support the conclusion that gifted people tend to be more mature than others, have fewer emotional problems than others, and grow up in a positive family climate (Davidson, 2000).

A child with Down syndrome. *What causes a child to develop Down syndrome? In which major classification of mental retardation does the condition fall?*

At 2 years of age, art prodigy Alexandra Nechita colored in coloring books for hours and also took up pen and ink. She had no interest in dolls or friends. By age 5 she was using watercolors. Once she started school, she would start painting as soon as she got home. At the age of 8, in 1994, she saw the first public exhibit of her work. In succeeding years, working quickly and impulsively on canvases as large as 5 feet by 9 feet, she has completed hundreds of paintings, some of which sell for close to $100,000 apiece. As a teenager, she continues to paint—relentlessly and passionately. It is, she says, what she loves to do. *What are some characteristics of children who are gifted?*

Ellen Winner (1996) described three criteria that characterize gifted children, whether in art, music, or academic domains:

1. *Precocity.* Gifted children are precocious. They begin to master an area earlier than their peers. Learning in their domain is more effortless for them than for ordinary children. In most instances, these gifted children are precocious because they have an inborn high ability in a particular domain or domains.

2. *Marching to their own drummer.* Gifted children learn in a qualitatively different way from ordinary children. One way that they march to a different drummer is that they need minimal help, or scaffolding, from adults to learn. In many instances, they resist any kind of explicit instruction. They often make discoveries on their own and solve problems in unique ways.

3. *A passion to master.* Gifted children are driven to understand the domain in which they have high ability. They display an intense, obsessive interest and an ability to focus. They motivate themselves, says Winner, and do not need to be "pushed" by their parents.

Nature-Nurture   Is giftedness a product of heredity or environment? Likely both (Sternberg & Sternberg, 2012). Individuals who are gifted recall that they had signs of high ability in a particular area at a very young age, prior to or at the beginning of formal training. This suggests the importance of innate ability in giftedness. However, researchers have also found that individuals with world-class status in the arts, mathematics, science, and sports all report strong family support and years of training and practice (Bloom, 1985). Deliberate practice is an important characteristic of individuals who become experts in a particular domain. For example, in one study the best musicians engaged in twice as much deliberate practice over their lives as did the least successful ones (Ericsson, Krampe, & Tesch-Romer, 1993).

Domain-Specific Giftedness and Development   Individuals who are highly gifted are typically not gifted in many domains, and research on giftedness is increasingly focused on domain-specific developmental trajectories (Sternberg & Sternberg, 2012; Winner, 2009). During the childhood years, the domain(s) in which individuals are gifted usually emerges. Thus, at some point in the childhood years the child who is to become a gifted artist or the child who is to become a gifted mathematician begins to show expertise in that domain. Regarding domain-specific giftedness, software genius Bill Gates (1998), the founder of Microsoft and one of the world's richest persons, commented that sometimes you have to be careful when you are good at something and resist the urge to think that you will be good at everything. Gates says that because he has been so successful at software development, people expect him to be brilliant about other domains in which he is far from being a genius.

Identifying an individual's domain-specific talent and providing individually appropriate and optional educational opportunities need to be accomplished at the very latest by adolescence (Keating, 2009). During adolescence, individuals who are talented become less reliant on parental support and increasingly pursue their own interests.

Education of Children Who Are Gifted   An increasing number of experts argue that the education of children who are gifted in the United States requires a significant overhaul (Ambrose, Sternberg, & Sriraman, 2012). Ellen Winner (1996, 2006) argues that too often children who are gifted are socially isolated and underchallenged in the classroom. It is not unusual for them to be ostracized and labeled "nerds" or "geeks." Many eminent adults report that school was a negative experience for them, that they were bored and sometimes knew more than their teachers (Bloom, 1985). Winner argues that American education will benefit when standards are raised for all children. When some children are still underchallenged, she recommends that they be allowed to attend advanced classes in their domain of exceptional ability. For example, some especially precocious middle school students may take college classes in their area of expertise. For example, Bill Gates took college math classes at 13; Yo-Yo Ma, a famous cellist, graduated from high school at 15 and attended Juilliard School of Music in New York City.

A young Bill Gates, founder of Microsoft and now one of the world's richest people. Like many highly gifted students, Gates was not especially fond of school. He hacked a computer security system when he was 13, and as a high school student he was allowed to take some college math classes. He dropped out of Harvard University and began developing a plan for what was to become Microsoft Corporation. *What are some ways that schools can enrich the education of such highly talented students as Gates to make it a more challenging, interesting, and meaningful experience?*

Review

- What characterizes Piaget's stage of concrete operational thought? What are some contributions and criticisms of Piaget?
- How do children process information in the middle and late childhood years?
- What is intelligence, and how is it assessed? What characterizes links between neuroscience and intelligence? What determines individual and group differences in IQ scores?
- What are the key characteristics of mental retardation and giftedness?

Connect

- In discussing memory, thinking, and intelligence, the topic of recommended educational strategies often came up. Compare these recommendations to those you learned about in the "Early Childhood Education" section of Chapter 7.

Reflect *Your Own Personal Journey of Life*

- A CD-ROM, *Children's IQ and Achievement Test*, now lets parents test their child's IQ and identify how well the child is performing in relation to his or her grade in school. Would you want to personally test your own child's IQ? What might be some problems with parents giving their children an IQ test?

---

4 Language Development

LG4 Discuss language development in middle and late childhood.

| Vocabulary, Grammar, and Metalinguistic Awareness | Reading | Writing | Bilingualism and Second-Language Learning |

Children gain new skills as they enter school that make it possible for them to learn to read and write: These include increased use of language to talk about things that are not physically present, learning what a word is, and learning how to recognize and talk about sounds. They also learn the *alphabetic principle*—that the letters of the alphabet represent sounds of the language.

VOCABULARY, GRAMMAR, AND METALINGUISTIC AWARENESS

During middle and late childhood, changes occur in the way children's mental vocabulary is organized. When asked to say the first word that comes to mind when they hear a word, preschool children typically provide a word that often follows the word in a sentence. For example, when asked to respond to *dog* the young child may say "barks," or to the word *eat* respond with "lunch." At about 7 years of age, children begin to respond with a word that is the same part of speech as the stimulus word. For example, a child may now respond to the word *dog* with "cat" or "horse." To *eat*, they now might say "drink." This is evidence that children now have begun to categorize their vocabulary by parts of speech.

The process of categorizing becomes easier as children increase their vocabulary (Clark, 2012). Children's vocabulary increases from an average of about 14,000 words at age 6 to an average of about 40,000 words by age 11.

Children make similar advances in grammar (Behrens, 2012). During the elementary school years, children's improvement in logical reasoning and analytical skills helps them understand such constructions as the appropriate use of comparatives *(shorter, deeper)* and subjectives ("If you were president . . ."). During the elementary school years, children become

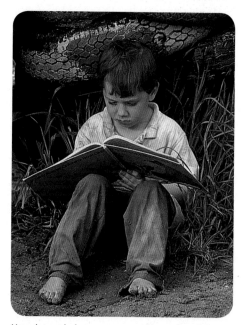

How do vocabulary, grammar, and metalinguistic awareness change in middle and late childhood?

increasingly able to understand and use complex grammar, such as the following sentence: *The boy who kissed his mother wore a hat.* They also learn to use language in a more connected way, producing connected discourse. They become able to relate sentences to one another to produce descriptions, definitions, and narratives that make sense. Children must be able to do these things orally before they can be expected to deal with them in written assignments.

These advances in vocabulary and grammar during the elementary school years are accompanied by the development of **metalinguistic awareness,** which is knowledge about language, such as understanding what a preposition is or being able to discuss the sounds of a language. Metalinguistic awareness allows children "to think about their language, understand what words are, and even define them" (Berko Gleason, 2009, p. 4). It improves considerably during the elementary school years (Pan & Uccelli, 2009). Defining words becomes a regular part of classroom discourse, and children increase their knowledge of syntax as they study and talk about the components of sentences such as subjects and verbs (Crain, 2012; Meltzi & Ely, 2009).

Children also make progress in understanding how to use language in culturally appropriate ways—a process called pragmatics (Bryant, 2012). By the time they enter adolescence, most children know the rules for the use of language in everyday contexts—that is, what is appropriate and inappropriate to say.

READING

Before learning to read, children learn to use language to talk about things that are not present; they learn what a word is; and they learn how to recognize sounds and talk about them. Children who begin elementary school with a robust vocabulary have an advantage when it comes to learning to read (Vacca & others, 2012).

How should children be taught to read? Currently, debate focuses on the whole-language approach versus the phonics approach (Reutzel & Cooter, 2012, 2013; Vacca & others, 2012).

The **whole-language approach** stresses that reading instruction should parallel children's natural language learning. In some whole-language classes, beginning readers are taught to recognize whole words or even entire sentences, and to use the context of what they are reading to guess at the meaning of words. Reading materials that support the whole-language approach are whole and meaningful—that is, children are given material in its complete form, such as stories and poems, so that they learn to understand language's communicative function. Reading is connected with listening and writing skills. Although there are variations in whole-language programs, most share the premise that reading should be integrated with other skills and subjects, such as science and social studies, and that it should focus on real-world material. Thus, a class might read newspapers, magazines, or books, and then write about and discuss them.

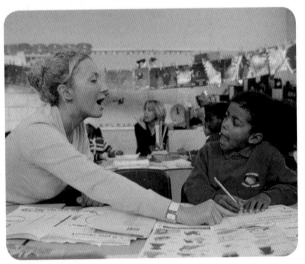

This teacher is helping a student sound out words. Researchers have found that phonics instruction is a key aspect of teaching students to read, especially beginning readers and students with weak reading skills.

In contrast, the **phonics approach** emphasizes that reading instruction should teach basic rules for translating written symbols into sounds. Early phonics-centered reading instruction should involve simplified materials. Only after children have learned correspondence rules that relate spoken phonemes to the alphabet letters that are used to represent them should they be given complex reading materials, such as books and poems (Fox, 2012).

Which approach is better? Research suggests that children can benefit from both approaches, but instruction in phonics needs to be emphasized (Tompkins, 2013). An increasing number of experts in the field of reading now conclude that direct instruction in phonics is a key aspect of learning to read (Cunningham, 2013; Dow & Baer, 2013; Fox, 2012).

metalinguistic awareness Refers to knowledge about language, such as understanding what a preposition is or being able to discuss the sounds of a language.

whole-language approach An approach to reading instruction based on the idea that instruction should parallel children's natural language learning. Reading materials should be whole and meaningful.

phonics approach The idea that reading instruction should teach the basic rules for translating written symbols into sounds.

PEANUTS © United Features Syndicate, Inc.

Beyond the phonics/whole language issue in learning to read, becoming a good reader includes learning to read fluently (Gunning, 2013; Vacca & others, 2012). Many beginning or poor readers do not recognize words automatically. Their processing capacity is consumed by the demands of word recognition, so they have less capacity to devote to comprehension of groupings of words as phrases or sentences. As their processing of words and passages becomes more automatic, it is said that their reading becomes more *fluent* (Fox, 2012). Metacognitive strategies, such as learning to monitor one's reading progress, getting the gist of what is being read, and summarizing also are important in becoming a good reader (Nash-Ditzel, 2010).

WRITING

As they begin to write, children often invent spellings. Parents and teachers should encourage children's early writing but not be overly concerned about the formation of letters or spelling. Corrections of spelling and printing should be selective and made in positive ways that do not discourage the child's writing and spontaneity.

Like becoming a good reader, becoming a good writer takes many years and lots of practice (Temple, Nathan, & Temple, 2013; Tompkins, 2013). Children should be given many writing opportunities. As their language and cognitive skills improve with good instruction, so will their writing skills. For example, developing a more sophisticated understanding of syntax and grammar serves as an underpinning for better writing. So do such cognitive skills as organization and logical reasoning. Through the course of the school years, students develop increasingly sophisticated methods of organizing their ideas.

Major concerns about students' writing competence are increasingly being voiced (Soter, 2013). One study revealed that 70 to 75 percent of U.S. students in grades 4 through 12 are low-achieving writers (Persky, Dane, & Jin, 2003). College instructors report that 50 percent of high school graduates are not prepared for college-level writing (Achieve, Inc., 2005).

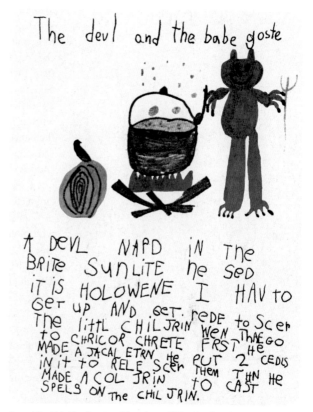

Anna Mudd is the 6-year-old author of "The Devil and the Babe Goste." Anna has been writing stories for at least two years. Her story includes poetic images, sophisticated syntax, and vocabulary that reflect advances in language development.

BILINGUALISM AND SECOND-LANGUAGE LEARNING

Are there sensitive periods in learning a second language? That is, if individuals want to learn a second language, how important is the age at which they begin to learn it? What is the best way to teach children who come from homes in which English is not the primary language?

Second-Language Learning   For many years, it was claimed that if individuals did not learn a second language prior to puberty they would never reach native-language learners' proficiency in the second language (Johnson & Newport, 1991). However, recent research indicates a more complex conclusion: Sensitive periods likely vary across different language systems (Thomas & Johnson, 2008). Thus, for late language learners, such as adolescents and adults, new vocabulary is easier to learn than new sounds or new grammar (Neville, 2006). For example, children's ability to pronounce words with a native-like accent in a second language typically decreases with age, with an especially sharp drop occurring after the age of about 10 to 12. Also, adults tend to learn a second language faster than children, but their final level of second-language attainment is not as high as children's. And the way children and adults learn a second language differs somewhat. Compared with adults, children are less sensitive to feedback, less likely to use explicit strategies, and more likely to learn a second language from large amounts of input (Thomas & Johnson, 2008).

Students in the United States are far behind their counterparts in many developed countries in learning a second language. For example, in Russia, schools have 10 grades, called forms, which roughly correspond to the 12 grades in American schools. Russian children begin school at age 7 and begin learning English in the third form. Because of this emphasis on teaching English, most Russian citizens under the age of 40 today are able to speak at least some English. The United States is the only technologically advanced Western nation that does not have a national foreign language requirement at the high school level, even for students in rigorous academic programs.

U.S. students who do not learn a second language may be missing more than the chance to acquire a skill. Bilingualism—the ability to speak two languages—has a positive effect on children's cognitive development. Children who are fluent in two languages perform better than their single-language counterparts on tests of control of attention, concept formation, analytical reasoning, cognitive flexibility, and cognitive complexity (Bialystok, 2001, 2007, 2011; Bialystok & Craik, 2010). They also are more conscious of the structure of spoken and written language and better at noticing errors of grammar and meaning, skills that benefit their reading ability (Bialystok, 1997; Kuo & Anderson, 2012). However, recent research indicates that bilingual children have a smaller vocabulary in each language than monolingual children (Bialystok, 2011).

In the United States, many immigrant children go from being monolingual in their home language to bilingual in that language and in English, only to end up as monolingual speakers of English. This is called *subtractive bilingualism,* and it can have negative effects on children, who often become ashamed of their home language.

Bilingual Education   A current controversy related to bilingualism involves the millions of U.S. children who come from homes in which English is not the primary language (Echevarria, Vogt, & Short, 2013; Lessow-Hurley, 2013). The controversy concerns questions about the best way to teach these children.

For the last two decades, the preferred strategy has been *bilingual education,* which teaches academic subjects to immigrant children in their native language while slowly teaching English (Diaz-Rico, 2012; Horowitz, 2013). Advocates of bilingual education programs argue that if children who do not know English are taught only in English, they will fall behind in academic subjects. How, they ask, can 7-year-olds learn arithmetic or history taught only in English when they do not speak the language?

Some critics of bilingual programs argue that too often it is thought that immigrant children need only one year of bilingual education. However, most immigrant children take approximately three to five years to develop speaking proficiency and seven years to develop reading proficiency in English (Hakuta, Butler, & Witt, 2000). Also, immigrant children vary in their ability to learn English (Horowitz, 2013). Children who come from lower socioeconomic backgrounds have more difficulty than those from higher socioeconomic backgrounds (Hakuta, 2001). Thus, especially for immigrant children from low socioeconomic backgrounds, more years of bilingual education may be needed than they currently are receiving.

Critics who oppose bilingual education argue that as a result of these programs, the children of immigrants are not learning English, which puts them at a permanent disadvantage in U.S. society. What have researchers found regarding outcomes of bilingual education programs? Drawing conclusions about the effectiveness of bilingual education programs is difficult because of variations across programs in the number of years they are in effect, type of instruction, qualities of schooling other than bilingual education, teachers, children, and other factors. Further, no experiments that compare bilingual

A first- and second-grade bilingual English-Cantonese teacher instructing students in Chinese in Oakland, California. *What have researchers found about the effectiveness of bilingual education?*

Salvador Tamayo, Bilingual Education Teacher

Salvador Tamayo teaches bilingual education in the fifth grade at Turner Elementary School in West Chicago. He recently was given a National Educator Award by the Milken Family Foundation for his work in bilingual education classes. He and his students have created several award-winning Web sites about the West Chicago City Museum, the local Latino community, and the history of West Chicago. His students also developed an "I Want to Be an American Citizen" Web site to assist family and community members in preparing for the U.S. citizenship test. Tamayo also teaches a bilingual education class at Wheaton College.

For more information about what elementary school teachers do, see page 44 in the Careers in Life-Span Development appendix.

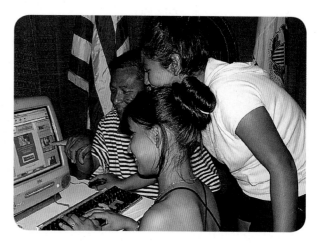

Salvador Tamayo working with bilingual education students.

education with English-only education in the United States have been effectively conducted (Snow & Kang, 2006).

Research supports bilingual education in that (1) children have difficulty learning a subject when it is taught in a language they do not understand, and (2) when both languages are integrated in the classroom, children learn the second language more readily and participate more actively (Gonzales, Yawkey, & Minaya-Rowe, 2006; Hakuta, 2001, 2005). To read about the work of one bilingual education teacher, see *Connecting with Careers*.

Review *Connect* Reflect

 Discuss language development in middle and late childhood.

Review

- What are some changes in vocabulary and grammar in the middle and late childhood years?
- What controversy characterizes how to teach children to read?
- What characterizes children's writing skills and their development?
- What is bilingual education? What issues are involved in bilingual education?

Connect

- Earlier in the chapter you learned about metacognition. Compare that with metalinguistic awareness.

Reflect *Your Own Personal Journey of Life*

- Did you learn a second language as a child? If you did, do you think it was beneficial to you? If so, how? If you did not learn a second language as a child, do you wish you had? Why or why not?

topical **connections** ---------------

The slow physical growth of middle and late childhood gives way to the dramatic changes of puberty in early adolescence. Significant changes also occur in the adolescent's brain in which earlier maturation of the amygdala (emotion processing) and later maturation of the prefrontal cortex (decision making, self-regulation) are likely linked to increases in risk-taking and sensation seeking. Sexual development is a normal aspect of adolescence, but having sexual intercourse early in adolescence is associated with a number of problems. Adolescence is a critical juncture in health because many poor health habits begin in adolescence. Despite recent declines, the United States has one of the highest rates of illicit drug use of any developed nation. Adolescent thought is more abstract, idealistic, and logical than children's. The transition from elementary school to middle school or junior high is difficult for many individuals because it coincides with so many physical, cognitive, and socioemotional changes in development.

looking forward ---- ➤

reach your **learning goals**

Physical and Cognitive Development in Middle and Late Childhood

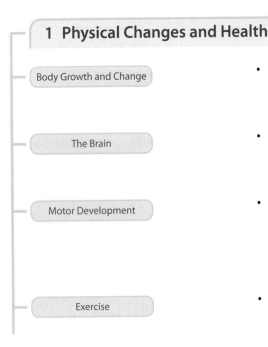

1 Physical Changes and Health

 LG1 Discuss physical changes and health in middle and late childhood.

Body Growth and Change

- The period of middle and late childhood involves slow, consistent growth. During this period, children grow an average of 2 to 3 inches a year. Muscle mass and strength gradually increase. Among the most pronounced changes in body growth and proportion are decreases in head circumference and waist circumference in relation to body height.

The Brain

- Changes in the brain in middle and late childhood include advances in functioning in the prefrontal cortex, which are reflected in improved attention, reasoning, and cognitive control. During middle and late childhood, less diffusion and more focal activation occurs in the prefrontal cortex, a change that is associated with an increase in cognitive control.

Motor Development

- During the middle and late childhood years, motor development becomes much smoother and more coordinated. Children gain greater control over their bodies and can sit and attend for longer periods of time. However, their lives should include abundant physical activity. Increased myelination of the central nervous system is reflected in improved motor skills. Improved fine motor skills appear in the form of handwriting development. Boys are usually better at gross motor skills, girls at fine motor skills.

Exercise

- Most American children do not get nearly enough exercise. Parents play an especially important role in guiding children to increase their exercise. Heavy television and computer use are linked to lower activity levels in children.

| Health, Illness, and Disease | • | For the most part, middle and late childhood is a time of excellent health. The most common cause of severe injury and death in childhood is motor vehicle accidents. Being overweight or obese is an increasing child health problem, raising the risk for many medical and psychological problems. Cardiovascular disease is uncommon in children, but the precursors to adult cardiovascular disease are often already apparent during childhood. Cancer is the second leading cause of death in children (after accidents). Leukemia is the most common childhood cancer. |

2 Children with Disabilities

 Identify children with different types of disabilities and discuss issues in educating them.

| The Scope of Disabilities | • | Approximately 14 percent of U.S. children from 3 to 21 years of age receive special education or related services. A child with a learning disability has difficulty in learning that involves understanding or using spoken or written language, and the difficulty can appear in listening, thinking, reading, writing, and spelling. A learning disability also may involve difficulty in doing mathematics. To be classified as a learning disability, the learning problem is not primarily the result of visual, hearing, or motor disabilities; mental retardation; emotional disorders; or due to environmental, cultural, or economic disadvantage. Dyslexia is a category of learning disabilities that involves a severe impairment in the ability to read and spell. Dysgraphia is a learning disability that involves having difficulty in handwriting. Dyscalculia is a learning disability that involves difficulties in math computation. Attention deficit hyperactivity disorder (ADHD) is a disability in which individuals consistently show problems in one or more of these areas: (1) inattention, (2) hyperactivity, and (3) impulsivity. ADHD has been increasingly diagnosed. Emotional and behavioral disorders consist of serious, persistent problems that involve relationships, aggression, depression, fears associated with personal or school matters, as well as other inappropriate socioemotional characteristics. Autism spectrum disorders (ASD), also called pervasive developmental disorders, range from autistic disorder, a severe developmental disorder, to Asperger syndrome, a relatively mild autism spectrum disorder. The current consensus is that autism is a brain dysfunction with abnormalities in brain structure and neurotransmitters. Children with autism spectrum disorders are characterized by problems in social interaction, verbal and nonverbal communication, and repetitive behaviors. |

| Educational Issues | • | In 1975, Public Law 94-142, the Education for All Handicapped Children Act, required that all children with disabilities be given a free, appropriate public education. This law was renamed the Individuals with Disabilities Education Act (IDEA) in 1990 and updated in 2004. IDEA includes requirements that children with disabilities receive an individualized education plan (IEP), which is a written plan that spells out a program tailored to the child and requires that they be educated in the least restrictive environment (LRE), which is a setting that is as similar as possible to the one in which children without disabilities are educated. The term *inclusion* means educating children with disabilities full-time in the regular classroom. |

3 Cognitive Changes

 Explain cognitive changes in middle and late childhood.

| Piaget's Cognitive Developmental Theory | • | Piaget said that the stage of concrete operational thought characterizes children from about 7 to 11 years of age. During this stage, children are capable of concrete operations, conservation, classification, seriation, and transitivity. Critics argue that some abilities emerge earlier than Piaget thought, that elements of a stage do not appear at the same time, and that education and culture have more influence on development than Piaget predicted. Neo-Piagetians place more emphasis on how children process information, their use of strategies, speed of information processing, and division of cognitive problems into more precise steps. |

| Information Processing | • | Long-term memory increases in middle and late childhood. Working memory is an important memory process. Knowledge and expertise influence memory. Strategies can be used by children to improve their memory, and it is important for adults who instruct children to encourage children's strategy use. Fuzzy trace theory has been proposed to explain developmental changes in memory. Critical thinking involves thinking reflectively and productively, as well as evaluating available evidence. Mindfulness is an important aspect of critical thinking. A special concern is the lack of emphasis on critical thinking in many schools. |

Creative thinking is the ability to think in novel and unusual ways and to come up with unique solutions to problems. Guilford distinguished between convergent and divergent thinking. A number of strategies can be used to encourage children's creative thinking, including brainstorming. Children think like scientists in some ways, but in others they don't. Metacognition is knowing about knowing. Many metacognitive studies have focused on metamemory. Pressley views the key to education as helping students learn a rich repertoire of strategies for problem solving. Among the key dimensions of executive functioning that are important in cognitive development and school success are self-control/inhibition, working memory, and flexibility.

Intelligence

- Intelligence consists of problem-solving skills and the ability to adapt to and learn from life's everyday experiences. Interest in intelligence often focuses on individual differences and assessment. Widely used intelligence tests today include the Stanford-Binet tests and Wechsler scales. Results on these tests may be reported in terms of an overall IQ or in terms of performance on specific areas of the tests. Sternberg proposed that intelligence comes in three main forms: analytical, creative, and practical. Gardner proposes that there are eight types of intelligence: verbal, mathematical, spatial, bodily-kinesthetic, interpersonal, intrapersonal, musical, and naturalist. The multiple-intelligence approaches have expanded our conception of intelligence, but critics argue that the research base for these approaches is not well established. IQ scores are influenced by both genetics and characteristics of the environment. Parents, home environments, schools, and intervention programs can influence these scores. Intelligence test scores have risen considerably around the world in recent decades. This phenomenon is called the Flynn effect, and it supports the role of environment in intelligence. Group differences in IQ scores may reflect many influences, including cultural bias. Tests may be biased against certain groups that are not familiar with a standard form of English, with the content tested, or with the testing situation. Tests are likely to reflect the values and experience of the dominant culture.

Extremes of Intelligence

- Mental retardation involves low IQ and problems in adapting to everyday life. One classification of mental retardation distinguishes between organic and cultural-familial retardation. Individuals who are gifted have above-average intelligence (an IQ of 130 or higher) and/or superior talent for something. Three characteristics of gifted children are precocity, marching to their own drummer, and a passion to master their domain. Giftedness is likely a consequence of both heredity and environment. Developmental changes characterize giftedness, and increasingly the domain-specific aspect of giftedness is emphasized. Concerns exist about the education of children who are gifted.

4 Language Development

LG4 Discuss language development in middle and late childhood.

Vocabulary, Grammar, and Metalinguistic Awareness

- Children gradually become more analytical and logical in their approach to words and grammar. In terms of grammar, children now better understand comparatives and subjectives. They become increasingly able to use complex grammar and produce narratives that make sense. Improvements in metalinguistic awareness—knowledge about language—are evident during the elementary school years as children increasingly define words, expand their knowledge of syntax, and understand better how to use language in culturally appropriate ways.

Reading

- A current debate in reading focuses on the phonics approach versus the whole-language approach. The phonics approach advocates phonetics instruction and giving children simplified materials. The whole-language approach stresses that reading instruction should parallel children's natural language learning and that children should be given whole-language materials such as books and poems. Three key processes in learning to read a printed word are being aware of sound units in words, decoding words, and accessing word meaning.

Writing

- Advances in children's language and cognitive development provide the underpinnings for improved writing. Major concerns are increasingly being voiced about children's writing competence. Teachers play a key role in improving children's writing skills.

Bilingualism and Second-Language Learning

- Recent research indicates the complexity of determining whether there are sensitive periods in learning a second language. Bilingual education aims to teach academic subjects to immigrant children in their native languages while gradually adding English instruction. Researchers have found that bilingualism does not interfere with performance in either language.

key **terms**

key **people**

Chapter 9 | PHYSICAL AND COGNITIVE DEVELOPMENT IN MIDDLE AND LATE CHILDHOOD

Connecting with

Learning Objectives	Application Activities	Activity Type	Page Reference
Explain Piaget's cognitive developmental theory.	Concrete Operational Stage	Click & drag activity	pp. 292–293
Discuss intelligence during middle and late childhood.	Gardner's Eight Frames of Mind	Click & drag activity	pp. 299–305

SOCIOEMOTIONAL DEVELOPMENT IN MIDDLE AND LATE CHILDHOOD

chapter **outline**

In *The Shame of the Nation,* Jonathan Kozol (2005) described his visits to 60 U.S. schools in urban low-income areas in 11 states. He saw many schools in which minorities totaled 80 to 90 percent of the student population. Kozol observed numerous inequities—unkempt classrooms, hallways, and restrooms; inadequate textbooks and supplies; and lack of resources. He also saw teachers mainly instructing students to memorize material by rote, especially as preparation for mandated tests, rather than stimulating them to engage in higher-level thinking. Kozol also frequently observed teachers using threatening disciplinary tactics to control the classroom.

However, some teachers Kozol observed were effective in educating children in these undesirable conditions. At P.S. 30 in the South Bronx, Mr. Bedrock teaches fifth grade. One student in his class, Serafina, recently lost her mother to AIDS. When author Jonathan Kozol visited the class, he was told that two other children had taken the role of "allies in the child's struggle for emotional survival" (Kozol, 2005, p. 291). Textbooks are in short supply for the class, and the social studies text is so out of date it claims that Ronald Reagan is the country's president. But Mr. Bedrock told Kozol that it's a "wonderful" class this year. About their teacher, 56-year-old Mr. Bedrock, one student said, "'He's getting old, . . . but we love him anyway'" (p. 292). Kozol observed the students in Mr. Bedrock's class to be orderly, interested, and engaged.

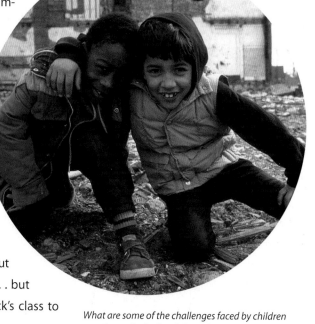

What are some of the challenges faced by children growing up in the South Bronx?

topical **connections**

In early childhood, according to Erikson, young children are in the stage of initiative versus guilt. Parents continue to play an important role in their development, and an authoritative parenting style is most likely to have positive outcomes for children. In early childhood, peer relations begin to take on a more significant role as children's social worlds widen. Play has a special place in young children's lives and is an important context for both cognitive and socioemotional development.

looking back

preview

The years of middle and late childhood bring many changes to children's social and emotional lives. Transformations in their relationships with parents and peers occur, and schooling takes on a more academic flavor. The development of their self-conceptions, moral reasoning, and moral behavior is also significant.

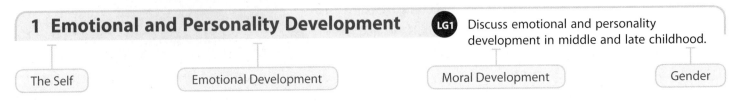

1 Emotional and Personality Development

LG1 Discuss emotional and personality development in middle and late childhood.

The Self | Emotional Development | Moral Development | Gender

In this section, we will explore how the self continues to develop during middle and late childhood and the emotional changes that take place during these years. We will also discuss children's moral development and many aspects of the role that gender plays in their development in middle and late childhood.

THE SELF

What is the nature of the child's self-understanding, understanding of others, and self-esteem during the elementary school years? What roles do self-efficacy and self-regulation play in children's achievement?

The Development of Self-Understanding   In middle and late childhood, especially from 8 to 11 years of age, children increasingly describe themselves in terms of psychological characteristics and traits, in contrast with the more concrete self-descriptions of younger children. For example, older children are more likely to describe themselves using adjectives such as "*popular, nice, helpful, mean, smart,* and *dumb*" (Harter, 2006, p. 526).

In addition, during the elementary school years, children become more likely to recognize social aspects of the self (Harter, 2012). They include references to social groups in their self-descriptions, such as referring to themselves as Girl Scouts, as Catholics, or as someone who has two close friends (Livesly & Bromley, 1973).

Children's self-understanding in the elementary school years also includes increasing reference to social comparison (Harter, 2012). At this point in development, children are more likely to distinguish themselves from others in comparative rather than in absolute terms. That is, elementary-school-age children are no longer as likely to think about what they do or do not do, but are more likely to think about what they can do in comparison with others.

Consider a series of studies in which Diane Ruble (1983) investigated children's use of social comparison in their self-evaluations. Children were given a difficult task and then offered feedback on their performance, as well as information about the performances of other children their age. The children were then asked for self-evaluations. Children younger than 7 made virtually no reference to the information about other children's performances. However, many children older than 7 included socially comparative information in their self-descriptions.

In sum, in middle and late childhood, self-description increasingly involves psychological and social characteristics, including social comparison.

Understanding Others   In Chapter 8, we described the advances and limitations of young children's social understanding. In middle and late childhood, **perspective taking,** the social cognitive process involved in assuming the perspective of others and understanding their thoughts and feelings, improves. Executive functioning, discussed in Chapter 7, "Physical and Cognitive Development in Early Childhood," is at work in perspective taking (Galinsky, 2010). Among the executive functions called on when children engage in perspective taking

---

Children are busy becoming something they have not quite grasped yet, something which keeps changing.

—ALASTAIR REID
American Poet, 20th Century

---

developmental **connection**

Identity

In adolescence, individuals become more introspective and reflective in their self-understanding as they search for an identity. Chapter 12, p. 389

---

perspective taking The social cognitive process involved in assuming the perspective of others and understanding their thoughts and feelings.

are cognitive inhibition (controlling one's own thoughts to consider the perspective of others) and cognitive flexibility (seeing situations in different ways).

In Robert Selman's (1980) view, at about 6 to 8 years of age, children begin to understand that others may have a different perspective because some people have more access to information. Then, he says, in the next several years, children begin to realize that each individual is aware of the other's perspective and that putting oneself in the other's place is a way of judging the other person's intentions, purposes, and actions.

Perspective taking is thought to be especially important in determining whether children develop prosocial or antisocial attitudes and behavior. In terms of prosocial behavior, taking another's perspective improves children's likelihood of understanding and sympathizing with others when they are distressed or in need. A recent study revealed that in children characterized as being emotionally reactive, good perspective-taking skills were linked to being able to regain a neutral emotional state after being emotionally aroused (Bengtsson & Arvidsson, 2011). In this study, children who made gains in perspective-taking skills reduced their emotional reactivity over a two-year period.

In middle and late childhood, children also become more skeptical of others' claims (Mills, Elashi, & Archacki, 2011). In Chapter 8, we indicated that even 4-year-old children show some skepticism of others' claims. In middle and late childhood, children become increasingly skeptical of some sources of information about psychological traits. For example, in one study, 10- to 11-year-olds were more likely to reject other children's self-reports that they were *smart* and *honest* than were 6- to 7-year-olds (Heyman & Legare, 2005). The more psychologically sophisticated 10- to 11-year-olds also showed a better understanding that others' self-reports may involve socially desirable tendencies than the 6- to 7-year-olds did.

What are some changes in children's understanding of others in middle and late childhood?

Self-Esteem and Self-Concept
High self-esteem and a positive self-concept are important characteristics of children's well-being (Marsh, Martin, & Xu, 2012; Rochat, 2013). Investigators sometimes use the terms *self-esteem* and *self-concept* interchangeably or do not precisely define them, but there is a meaningful difference between them. **Self-esteem** refers to global evaluations of the self; it is also called *self-worth* or *self-image*. For example, a child may perceive that she is not merely a person but a *good* person. **Self-concept** refers to domain-specific evaluations of the self. Children can make self-evaluations in many domains of their lives—academic, athletic, appearance, and so on. In sum, *self-esteem* refers to global self-evaluations, *self-concept* to domain-specific evaluations.

The foundations of self-esteem and self-concept emerge from the quality of parent-child interaction in infancy and early childhood. Thus, if children have low self-esteem in middle and late childhood, they may have experienced neglect or abuse in relationships with their parents earlier in development. Children with high self-esteem are more likely to be securely attached to parents and have parents who engage in sensitive caregiving (Thompson, 2011, 2013a, b, c, d).

Self-esteem reflects perceptions that do not always match reality (Baumeister & others, 2003; Pauletti & others, 2012). A child's self-esteem might reflect a belief about whether he or she is intelligent and attractive, for example, but that belief is not necessarily accurate. Thus, high self-esteem may refer to accurate, justified perceptions of one's worth as a person and one's successes and accomplishments, but it can also refer to an arrogant, grandiose, unwarranted sense of superiority over others (Krueger, Vohs, & Baumeister, 2008). In the same manner, low self-esteem may reflect either an accurate perception of one's shortcomings or a distorted, even pathological insecurity and inferiority.

Variations in self-esteem have been linked with many aspects of children's development. However, much of the research is *correlational* rather than *experimental*. Recall from Chapter 1 that correlation does not equal causation. Thus, if a correlational study finds an association between children's low self-esteem and low academic achievement, low academic achievement could cause the low self-esteem as much as low self-esteem causes low academic achievement.

In fact, there are only moderate correlations between school performance and self-esteem, and these correlations do not suggest that high self-esteem produces better school performance (Baumeister & others, 2003). Efforts to increase students' self-esteem have not always led to improved school performance (Davies & Brember, 1999).

What are some issues involved in understanding children's self-esteem in school?

self-esteem The global evaluative dimension of the self. Self-esteem is also referred to as self-worth or self-image.

self-concept Domain-specific evaluations of the self.

Increasing Children's Self-Esteem

Ways to improve children's self-esteem include identifying the causes of low self-esteem, providing emotional support and social approval, helping children achieve, and helping children cope (Bednar, Wells, & Peterson, 1995; Harter, 2006, 2012).

- *Identify the causes of low self-esteem.* Intervention should target the causes of low self-esteem. Children have the highest self-esteem when they perform competently in domains that are important to them. Therefore, children should be encouraged to identify and value areas of competence. These areas might include academic skills, athletic skills, physical attractiveness, and social acceptance.

- *Provide emotional support and social approval.* Some children with low self-esteem come from conflicted families or conditions in which they experienced abuse or neglect—situations in which support was not available. In some cases, alternative sources of support can be arranged either informally through the encouragement of a teacher, a coach, or

How can parents help children develop higher self-esteem?

another significant adult, or more formally, through programs such as Big Brothers and Big Sisters.

- *Help children achieve.* Achievement also can improve children's self-esteem. For example, the straightforward teaching of real skills to children often results in increased achievement and, thus, in enhanced self-esteem. Children develop higher self-esteem because they know the important tasks that will achieve their goals, and they have performed them or similar behaviors in the past.

- *Help children cope.* Self-esteem often increases when children face a problem and try to cope with it, rather than avoid it. If coping rather than avoidance prevails, children face problems realistically, honestly, and nondefensively. This produces favorable self-evaluative thoughts, which lead to the self-generated approval that raises self-esteem.

As discussed in the "Emotional Development" section of Chapter 8, which parenting approach might help accomplish the last goal mentioned here? How?

Children with high self-esteem have greater initiative, but this can produce positive or negative outcomes (Baumeister & others, 2003). Childen with high-self-esteem are prone to both prosocial and antisocial actions (Krueger, Vohs, & Baumeister, 2008).

In addition, a current concern is that too many of today's children grow up receiving praise for mediocre or even poor performance and as a consequence have inflated self-esteem (Graham, 2005; Stipek, 2005). They may have difficulty handling competition and criticism. This theme is vividly captured by the title of a book, *Dumbing Down Our Kids: Why American Children Feel Good About Themselves But Can't Read, Write, or Add* (Sykes, 1995).

What are some good strategies for effectively increasing children's self-esteem? See the *Connecting Development to Life* interlude for some answers to this question.

Self-Efficacy   The belief that one can master a situation and produce favorable outcomes is called **self-efficacy.** Albert Bandura (2001, 2008, 2010a, 2012), whose social cognitive theory we described in Chapter 1, states that self-efficacy is a critical factor in whether or not students achieve. Self-efficacy is the belief that "I can"; helplessness is the belief that "I cannot". Students with high self-efficacy endorse such statements as "I know that I will be able to learn the material in this class" and "I expect to be able to do well at this activity."

Dale Schunk (2012) has applied the concept of self-efficacy to many aspects of students' achievement. In his view, self-efficacy influences a student's choice of activities. Students with low self-efficacy for learning may avoid many learning tasks, especially those that are challenging. By contrast, high-self-efficacy counterparts eagerly work at learning tasks (Schunk,

self-efficacy The belief that one can master a situation and produce favorable outcomes.

2012). Students with high-efficacy are more likely to expend effort and persist longer at a learning task than students with low self-efficacy.

Self-Regulation One of the most important aspects of the self in middle and late childhood is the increased capacity for self-regulation. This increased capacity is characterized by deliberate efforts to manage one's behavior, emotions, and thoughts, leading to increased social competence and achievement (Thompson, 2013c, d). A recent study found that self-control increased from 4 years to 10 years of age and that high self-control was linked to lower levels of deviant behavior (Vazsonyi & Huang, 2010). In this study, parenting characterized by warmth and positive affect predicted the developmental increase in self-control. Another recent study revealed that children from low-income families who had a higher level of self-regulation earned better grades in school than their counterparts who had a lower level of self-regulation (Buckner, Mezzacappa, & Beardslee, 2009).

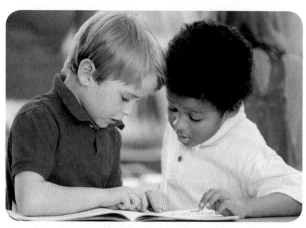

What characterizes Erikson's stage of industry versus inferiority?

The increased capacity for self-regulation is linked to developmental advances in the brain's prefrontal cortex, as discussed in Chapter 9, "Physical and Cognitive Development in Middle and Late Childhood." Recall our discussion there of the increased focal activation in the prefrontal cortex that is linked to improved cognitive control, which includes self-regulation (Diamond, 2013).

Industry Versus Inferiority In Chapter 1, we described Erik Erikson's (1968) eight stages of human development. His fourth stage, industry versus inferiority, appears during middle and late childhood. The term *industry* expresses a dominant theme of this period: Children become interested in how things are made and how they work. When children are encouraged in their efforts to make, build, and work—whether building a model airplane, constructing a tree house, fixing a bicycle, solving an addition problem, or cooking—their sense of industry increases. However, parents who see their children's efforts at making things as "mischief" or "making a mess" encourage children's development of a sense of inferiority.

Children's social worlds beyond their families also contribute to a sense of industry. School becomes especially important in this regard. Consider children who are slightly below average in intelligence. They are too bright to be in special classes but not bright enough to be in gifted classes. They fail frequently in their academic efforts, developing a sense of inferiority. By contrast, consider children whose sense of industry is derogated at home. A series of sensitive and committed teachers may revitalize their sense of industry (Elkind, 1970).

developmental **connection**

Erikson's Theory

Initiative versus guilt is Erikson's early childhood stage and identity versus identity confusion is his adolescence stage. Chapter 1, p. 23

EMOTIONAL DEVELOPMENT

In Chapter 8, we saw that preschoolers become more adept at talking about their own and others' emotions. They also show a growing awareness of the need to control and manage their emotions to meet social standards. In middle and late childhood, children further develop their understanding and self-regulation of emotion (McRae & others, 2012; Thompson, 2013c, d).

Developmental Changes Developmental changes in emotions during the middle and late childhood years include the following (Denham, Bassett, & Wyatt, 2007; Denham & others, 2011; Kuebli, 1994; Thompson, 2013c, d):

- *Improved emotional understanding.* For example, children in elementary school develop an increased ability to understand such complex emotions as pride and shame. These emotions become less tied to the reactions of other people; they become more self-generated and integrated with a sense of personal responsibility.

- *Increased understanding that more than one emotion can be experienced in a particular situation.* A third-grader, for example, may realize that achieving something might involve both anxiety and joy.

What are some changes in emotion during the middle and late childhood years?

- *Increased tendency to be aware of the events leading to emotional reactions.* A fourth-grader may become aware that her sadness today is influenced by her friend moving to another town last week.
- *Ability to suppress or conceal negative emotional reactions.* A fifth-grader has learned to tone down his anger better than he used to when one of his classmates irritates him.
- *The use of self-initiated strategies for redirecting feelings.* In the elementary school years, children become more reflective about their emotional lives and increasingly use strategies to control their emotions. They become more effective at cognitively managing their emotions, such as soothing themselves after an upset.
- *A capacity for genuine empathy.* For example, a fourth-grader feels sympathy for a distressed person and experiences vicariously the sadness the distressed person is feeling.

Coping with Stress　An important aspect of children's emotional lives is learning how to cope with stress (Masten, 2013). As children get older, they are able to more accurately appraise a stressful situation and determine how much control they have over it. Older children generate more coping alternatives to stressful conditions and use more cognitive coping strategies (Saarni & others, 2006). They are better than younger children at intentionally shifting their thoughts to something that is less stressful and at reframing, or changing their perception of a stressful situation. For example, younger children may be very disappointed that their teacher did not say hello to them when they arrived at school. Older children may reframe this type of situation and think, "She may have been busy with other things and just forgot to say hello."

By 10 years of age, most children are able to use these cognitive strategies to cope with stress (Saarni, 1999). However, in families that have not been supportive and are characterized by turmoil or trauma, children may be so overwhelmed by stress that they do not use such strategies.

Disasters can especially harm children's development and produce adjustment problems (Franks, 2011; McDermott & Cobham, 2012). Among the outcomes for children who experience disasters are acute stress reactions, depression, panic disorder, and post-traumatic stress disorder (Salloum & Overstreet, 2012). The likelihood that a child will face these problems following a disaster depends on factors such as the nature and severity of the disaster and the type of support available to the child.

In research on disasters/trauma, the term *dose-response effects* is often used. A widely supported finding in this research area is that the more severe the disaster/trauma (dose), the worse the adaptation and adjustment (response) following the disaster/trauma (Masten, 2013; Masten & Narayan, 2012).

developmental **connection**

Biological Processes

In older adults, stress hormones stay elevated in the bloodstream longer, which can accelerate aging and harm immune system functioning. Chapter 17, p. 542

What are some effective strategies to help children cope with traumatic events such as the terrorist attacks on the United States on 9/11/2001 and the destruction caused by Hurricane Katrina in September 2005?

The terrorist attacks on the World Trade Center in New York City and the Pentagon in Washington, D.C., on September 11, 2001, and hurricanes Katrina and Rita in September 2005 raised special concerns about how to help children cope with such stressful events.

Researchers have offered the following recommendations for parents, teachers, and other adults caring for children after a disaster (Gurwitch & others, 2001, pp. 4–11):

- Reassure children (numerous times, if necessary) of their safety and security.
- Allow children to retell events and be patient in listening to them.
- Encourage children to talk about any disturbing or confusing feelings, reassuring them that such feelings are normal after a stressful event.
- Protect children from re-exposure to frightening situations and reminders of the trauma—for example, by limiting discussion of the event in front of the children.
- Help children make sense of what happened, keeping in mind that children may misunderstand what took place. For example, young children "may blame themselves, believe things happened that did not happen, believe that terrorists are in the school, etc. Gently help children develop a realistic understanding of the event" (p. 10).

Traumatic events may cause individuals to think about the moral aspects of life. Hopelessness and despair may short-circuit moral development when a child is confronted by the violence of war zones and impoverished inner cities (Nader, 2001). Let's further explore children's moral development.

MORAL DEVELOPMENT

Remember from Chapter 8 our description of Piaget's view of moral development. Piaget proposed that younger children are characterized by heteronomous morality—but that by 10 years of age they have moved into a higher stage called autonomous morality. According to Piaget, older children consider the intentions of the individual, believe that rules are subject to change, and are aware that punishment does not always follow wrongdoing.

A second major perspective on moral development was proposed by Lawrence Kohlberg (1958, 1986). Piaget's cognitive stages of development serve as the underpinnings for Kohlberg's theory, but Kohlberg suggested that there are six stages of moral development. These stages, he argued, are universal. Development from one stage to another, said Kohlberg, is fostered by opportunities to take the perspective of others and to experience conflict between one's current stage of moral thinking and the reasoning of someone at a higher stage.

Kohlberg arrived at his view after 20 years of using a unique interview with children. In the interview, children are presented with a series of stories in which characters face moral dilemmas. The following is the most popular Kohlberg dilemma:

Lawrence Kohlberg, the architect of a provocative cognitive developmental theory of moral development. *What is the nature of his theory?*

> In Europe a woman was near death from a special kind of cancer. There was one drug that the doctors thought might save her. It was a form of radium that a druggist in the same town had recently discovered. The drug was expensive to make, but the druggist was charging ten times what the drug cost him to make. He paid $200 for the radium and charged $2,000 for a small dose of the drug. The sick woman's husband, Heinz, went to everyone he knew to borrow the money, but he could only get together $1,000 which is half of what it cost. He told the druggist that his wife was dying and asked him to sell it cheaper or let him pay later. But the druggist said, "No, I discovered the drug, and I am going to make money from it." So Heinz got desperate and broke into the man's store to steal the drug for his wife. (Kohlberg, 1969, p. 379)

This story is one of 11 that Kohlberg devised to investigate the nature of moral thought. After reading the story, the interviewee answers a series of questions about the moral dilemma. Should Heinz have stolen the drug? Was stealing it right or wrong? Why? Is it a husband's duty to steal the drug for his wife if he can get it no other way? Would a good husband steal? Did the druggist have the right to charge that much when there was no law setting a limit on the price? Why or why not?

The Kohlberg Stages   Based on the answers interviewees gave for this and other moral dilemmas, Kohlberg described three levels of moral thinking, each of which is characterized by two stages (see Figure 10.1). A key concept in understanding progression through the

LEVEL 1	LEVEL 2	LEVEL 3
Preconventional Level **No Internalization**	**Conventional Level** **Intermediate Internalization**	**Postconventional Level** **Full Internalization**
Stage 1 Heteronomous Morality	**Stage 3** Mutual Interpersonal Expectations, Relationships, and Interpersonal Conformity	**Stage 5** Social Contract or Utility and Individual Rights
Children obey because adults tell them to obey. People base their moral decisions on fear of punishment.	*Individuals value trust, caring, and loyalty to others as a basis for moral judgments.*	*Individuals reason that values, rights, and principles undergird or transcend the law.*
Stage 2 Individualism, Purpose, and Exchange	**Stage 4** Social System Morality	**Stage 6** Universal Ethical Principles
Individuals pursue their own interests but let others do the same. What is right involves equal exchange.	*Moral judgments are based on understanding and the social order, law, justice, and duty.*	*The person has developed moral judgments that are based on universal human rights. When faced with a dilemma between law and conscience, a personal, individualized conscience is followed.*

FIGURE 10.1

KOHLBERG'S THREE LEVELS AND SIX STATES OF MORAL DEVELOPMENT. Kohlberg argued that people everywhere develop their moral reasoning by passing through these age-based stages. *Where does Kohlberg's theory stand on the nature-nurture and continuity-discontinuity issues discussed in Chapter 1?*

preconventional reasoning The lowest level in Kohlberg's theory of moral development. The individual's moral reasoning is controlled primarily by external rewards and punishment.

heteronomous morality Kohlberg's first stage of preconventional reasoning in which moral thinking is tied to punishment.

individualism, instrumental purpose, and exchange Kohlberg's second stage of preconventional reasoning, in which individuals pursue their own interests but also let others do the same.

conventional reasoning The second, or intermediate, level in Kohlberg's theory of moral development. At this level, individuals abide by certain standards, but these are the standards of others such as parents or society.

mutual interpersonal expectations, relationships, and interpersonal conformity Kohlberg's third stage of moral development. At this stage, individuals value trust, caring, and loyalty to others as a basis of moral judgments.

social systems morality The fourth stage in Kohlberg's theory of moral development, in which moral judgments are based on understanding the social order, law, justice, and duty.

postconventional reasoning The highest level in Kohlberg's theory of moral development. At this level, the individual recognizes alternative moral courses, explores the options, and then decides on a personal moral code.

levels and stages is that the person's morality gradually becomes more internal or mature. That is, their reasons for moral decisions or values begin to go beyond the external or superficial reasons they gave when they were younger. Let's further examine Kohlberg's stages.

Kohlberg's Level 1: Preconventional Reasoning   Preconventional reasoning is the lowest level of moral reasoning in Kohlberg's theory and consists of two stages: punishment and obedience orientation (stage 1) and individualism, instrumental purpose, and exchange (stage 2).

- Stage 1. **Heteronomous morality** is the first Kohlberg stage of moral development. At this stage, moral thinking is often tied to punishment. For example, children and adolescents obey adults because adults tell them to obey.
- Stage 2. **Individualism, instrumental purpose, and exchange** is the second stage of Kohlberg's theory. At this stage, individuals pursue their own interests but also let others do the same. Thus, what is right involves an equal exchange. People are nice to others so that others will be nice to them in return.

Kohlberg's Level 2: Conventional Reasoning   Conventional reasoning is the second, or intermediate, level in Kohlberg's theory of moral development. Individuals abide by certain standards (internal), but they are the standards of others, such as parents or the laws of society. The conventional reasoning level consists of two stages: mutual interpersonal expectations, relationships, and interpersonal conformity (stage 3) and social systems morality (stage 4).

- *Stage 3.* **Mutual interpersonal expectations, relationships, and interpersonal conformity** is Kohlberg's third stage of moral development. At this stage, individuals value trust, caring, and loyalty to others as a basis of moral judgments. Children and adolescents often adopt their parents' moral standards at this stage, seeking to be thought of by their parents as a "good girl" or a "good boy."
- *Stage 4.* **Social systems morality** is the fourth stage in Kohlberg's theory of moral development. At this stage, moral judgments are based on understanding the social order, law, justice, and duty. For example, adolescents may reason that in order for a community to work effectively, it needs to be protected by laws that are adhered to by its members.

Kohlberg's Level 3: Postconventional Reasoning   Postconventional reasoning is the third and highest level in Kohlberg's theory. At this level, morality is more internal. The postconventional level of morality consists of two stages: social contract or utility and individual rights (stage 5) and universal ethical principles (stage 6).

- *Stage 5.* **Social contract or utility and individual rights** is the fifth Kohlberg stage. At this stage, individuals reason that values, rights, and principles undergird or transcend the law. A person evaluates the validity of actual laws and examines social systems in terms of the degree to which they preserve and protect fundamental human rights and values.

- *Stage 6.* **Universal ethical principles** is the sixth and highest stage in Kohlberg's theory of moral development. At this stage, the person has developed a moral standard based on universal human rights. When faced with a conflict between law and conscience, the person will follow conscience, even though the decision might involve personal risk.

Kohlberg maintained that these levels and stages occur in a sequence and are age-related: Before age 9, most children use level 1, preconventional reasoning based on external rewards and punishments, when they consider moral choices. By early adolescence, their moral reasoning is increasingly based on the application of standards set by others. Most adolescents reason at stage 3, with some signs of stages 2 and 4. By early adulthood, a small number of individuals reason in postconventional ways.

What evidence supports this description of development? A 20-year longitudinal investigation found that use of stages 1 and 2 decreased with age (Colby & others, 1983) (see Figure 10.2). Stage 4, which did not appear at all in the moral reasoning of 10-year-olds, was reflected in the moral thinking of 62 percent of the 36-year-olds. Stage 5 did not appear until age 20 to 22 and never characterized more than 10 percent of the individuals.

Thus, the moral stages appeared somewhat later than Kohlberg initially envisioned, and reasoning at the higher stages, especially stage 6, was rare. Although stage 6 has been removed from the Kohlberg moral judgment scoring manual, it still is considered to be theoretically important in the Kohlberg scheme of moral development.

Influences on the Kohlberg Stages

What factors influence movement through Kohlberg's stages? Although moral reasoning at each stage presupposes a certain level of cognitive development, Kohlberg argued that advances in children's cognitive development did not ensure development of moral reasoning. Instead, moral reasoning also reflects children's experiences in dealing with moral questions and moral conflict.

Several investigators have tried to advance individuals' levels of moral development by having a model present arguments that reflect moral thinking one stage above each individual's established level. This approach applies the concepts of equilibrium and conflict that Piaget used to explain cognitive development. By presenting arguments slightly beyond the children's level of moral reasoning, the researchers created a disequilibrium that motivated the children to restructure their moral thought. The upshot of studies using this approach is that virtually any plus-stage discussion, for any length of time, seems to promote more advanced moral reasoning (Walker, 1982).

Kohlberg emphasized that peer interaction and perspective taking are critical aspects of the social stimulation that challenges children to change their moral reasoning. Whereas adults characteristically impose rules and regulations on children, the give-and-take among peers gives children an opportunity to take the perspective of another person and to generate rules democratically. Kohlberg stressed that in principle, encounters with any peers can produce perspective-taking opportunities that may advance a child's moral reasoning. A recent research review of cross-cultural studies involving Kohlberg's theory revealed strong support for a link between perspective-taking skills and more advanced moral judgments (Gibbs & others, 2007).

Kohlberg's Critics

Kohlberg's theory has provoked debate, research, and criticism (Berkowitz, 2012; Helwig & Turiel, 2011; Narvaez & others, 2012; Walker & Frimer, 2011). Key criticisms involve the link between moral thought and moral behavior, the roles of culture and the family in moral development, and the significance of concern for others.

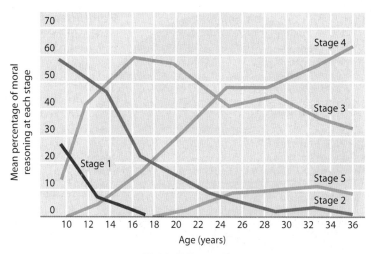

FIGURE **10.2**

AGE AND THE PERCENTAGE OF INDIVIDUALS AT EACH KOHLBERG STAGE. In one longitudinal study of males from 10 to 36 years of age, at age 10 most moral reasoning was at stage 2 (Colby & others, 1983). At 16 to 18 years of age, stage 3 became the most frequent type of moral reasoning, and it was not until the mid-twenties that stage 4 became the most frequent. Stage 5 did not appear until 20 to 22 years of age, and it never characterized more than 10 percent of the individuals. In this study, the moral stages appeared somewhat later than Kohlberg envisioned and stage 6 was absent. *Do you think it matters that all of the participants in this study were males? Why or why not?*

developmental **connection**

Peers

Piaget argued that the mutual give-and-take of peer relations is more important than parenting in enhancing children's moral reasoning. Chapter 8, p. 250

social contract or utility and individual rights The fifth Kohlberg stage. At this stage, individuals reason that values, rights, and principles undergird or transcend the law.

universal ethical principles The sixth and highest stage in Kohlberg's theory of moral development, in which individuals develop a moral standard based on universal human rights.

This 14-year-old boy in Nepal is thought to be the sixth-holiest Buddhist in the world. In one study of 20 adolescent male Buddhist monks in Nepal, the issue of justice, a basic theme in Kohlberg's theory, was not a central focus in the monks' moral views (Huebner & Garrod, 1993). Also, the monks' concerns about prevention of suffering and the importance of compassion are not captured in Kohlberg's theory.

Moral Thought and Moral Behavior   Kohlberg's theory has been criticized for placing too much emphasis on moral thought and not enough emphasis on moral behavior (Walker, 2004). Moral reasons can sometimes be a shelter for immoral behavior. Corrupt CEOs and politicians endorse the loftiest of moral virtues in public before their own behavior is exposed. Whatever the latest public scandal, you will probably find that the culprits displayed virtuous thoughts but engaged in immoral behavior. No one wants a nation of cheaters and thieves who can reason at the postconventional level. The cheaters and thieves may know what is right yet still do what is wrong. Heinous actions can be cloaked in a mantle of moral virtue.

Culture and Moral Reasoning   Kohlberg emphasized that his stages of moral reasoning are universal, but some critics claim his theory is culturally biased (Gibbs, 2010; Miller, 2007). Both Kohlberg and his critics may be partially correct. One review of 45 studies in 27 cultures around the world, mostly non-European, provided support for the universality of Kohlberg's first four stages (Snarey, 1987). Individuals in diverse cultures developed through these four stages in sequence as Kohlberg predicted. Stages 5 and 6, however, have not been found in all cultures (Gibbs & others, 2007; Snarey, 1987). Furthermore, Kohlberg's scoring system does not recognize the higher-level moral reasoning of certain cultures and thus that level of moral reasoning is more culture-specific than Kohlberg envisioned (Snarey, 1987). In sum, although Kohlberg's approach does capture much of the moral reasoning voiced in various cultures around the world, his approach misses or misconstrues some important moral concepts in particular cultures (Gibbs, 2010).

A recent study explored links between culture, mindset, and moral judgment (Narváez & Hill, 2010). In this study, a higher level of multicultural experience was linked to closed mind-edness (being cognitively inflexible), a growth mindset (perceiving that one's qualities can change and improve through effort), and higher moral judgment.

Families and Moral Development   Kohlberg argued that family processes are essentially unimportant in children's moral development. As noted earlier, he argued that parent-child relationships usually provide children with little opportunity for give-and-take or perspective taking. Rather, Kohlberg said that such opportunities are more likely to be provided by children's peer relationships.

Did Kohlberg underestimate the contribution of family relationships to moral development? Most experts on children's moral development conclude that parents' moral values and actions influence children's development of moral reasoning (Laible & Thompson, 2007). Nonetheless, most developmentalists agree with Kohlberg and Piaget that peers play an important role in the development of moral reasoning.

Gender and the Care Perspective   The most publicized criticism of Kohlberg's theory has come from Carol Gilligan (1982, 1992, 1996), who argues that Kohlberg's theory reflects a gender bias. According to Gilligan, Kohlberg's theory is based on a male norm that puts abstract principles above relationships and concern for others and sees the individual as standing alone and independently making moral decisions. It puts justice at the heart of morality. In contrast with Kohlberg's **justice perspective,** Gilligan argues for a **care perspective,** which is a moral perspective that views people in terms of their connectedness with others and emphasizes interpersonal communication, relationships with others, and concern for others. According to Gilligan, Kohlberg greatly underplayed the care perspective, perhaps because he was a male, because most of his research was with males rather than females, and because he used male responses as a model for his theory.

However, questions have been raised about Gilligan's gender conclusions (Walker & Frimer, 2009a). For example, a meta-analysis (a statistical analysis that combines the results of many different studies) casts doubt on Gilligan's claim of substantial gender differences in moral judgment (Jaffee & Hyde, 2000). And a research review concluded that girls' moral orientations are "somewhat more likely to focus on care for others than on abstract principles of justice, but they can use both moral orientations when needed (as can boys . . .)" (Blakemore, Berenbaum, & Liben, 2009, p. 132).

Carol Gilligan. *What is Gilligan's view of moral development?*

Domain Theory: Moral, Social Conventional, Personal Reasoning

The **domain theory of moral development** states that there are different domains of social knowledge and reasoning, including moral, social conventional, and personal domains. In domain theory, children's and adolescents' moral, social conventional, and personal knowledge and reasoning emerge from their attempts to understand and deal with different forms of social experience (Smetana, 2011a, b).

Some theorists and researchers argue that Kohlberg did not adequately distinguish between moral reasoning and social conventional reasoning (Helwig & Turiel, 2011; Smetana, 2011a, b). **Social conventional reasoning** focuses on conventional rules that have been established by social consensus in order to control behavior and maintain the social system. The rules themselves are arbitrary, such as raising your hand in class before speaking, using one staircase at school to go up and the other to go down, not cutting in front of someone standing in line to buy movie tickets, and stopping at a stop sign when driving. There are sanctions if we violate these conventions, although they can be changed by consensus.

In contrast, moral reasoning focuses on ethical issues and rules of morality. Unlike conventional rules, moral rules are not arbitrary. They are obligatory, widely accepted, and somewhat impersonal (Helwig & Turiel, 2011). Rules pertaining to lying, cheating, stealing, and physically harming another person are moral rules because violation of these rules affronts ethical standards that exist apart from social consensus and convention. Moral judgments involve concepts of justice, whereas social conventional judgments are concepts of social organization. Violating moral rules is usually more serious than violating conventional rules.

The social conventional approach is a serious challenge to Kohlberg's approach because Kohlberg argued that social conventions are a stop-over on the road to higher moral sophistication. For social conventional reasoning advocates, social conventional reasoning is not lower than postconventional reasoning but rather something that needs to be disentangled from the moral thread (Helwig & Turiel, 2011; Smetana, 2011a, b).

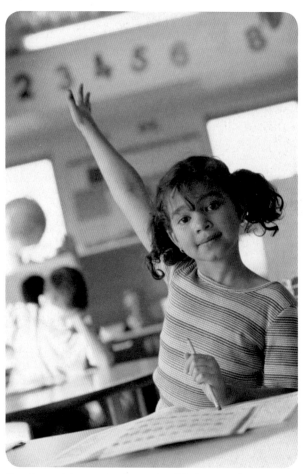

How does social conventional reasoning differ from moral reasoning? What are some examples of social conventional reasoning?

Recently, a distinction also has been made between moral and conventional issues, which are viewed as legitimately subject to adult social regulation, and personal issues, which are more likely subject to the child's or adolescent's independent decision making and personal discretion (Helwig & Turiel, 2011; Smetana, 2011a, b). Personal issues include control over one's body, privacy, and choice of friends and activities. Thus, some actions belong to a *personal* domain and are not governed by moral reasoning or social norms.

Moral, conventional, and personal domains of reasoning arise in families. Moral issues include such areas as lying to parents about engaging in a deviant behavior and stealing money from a sibling. Conventional issues involve such matters as obeying curfews and deciding who takes out the garbage. Personal issues involve such things as musical preferences, styles of dress, what to put on the walls of one's bedroom, and which friends to choose.

In domain theory, boundaries are developed regarding adult authority, which can produce parent-adolescent conflict. Adolescents have a large personal domain and most parents can live with that; however, parents have a larger moral domain than adolescents think is reasonable (Smetana, 2011a, b).

Prosocial Behavior

Whereas Kohlberg's and Gilligan's theories have focused primarily on the development of moral reasoning, the study of prosocial moral behavior has placed more emphasis on the behavioral aspects of moral development (Eisenberg, Spinrad, & Morris, 2013; Grusec & Sherman, 2011; Poorthuis & others, 2012). Children engage in immoral, antisocial acts such as lying and cheating and also display prosocial moral behavior such as showing empathy or acting altruistically. Even during the preschool years, children may care for others or comfort others in distress, but prosocial behavior occurs more often in adolescence than in childhood (Eisenberg & others, 2009).

William Damon (1988) described how sharing develops. During their first years, when children share, it is usually not for reasons of empathy but for the fun of the social play

justice perspective A moral perspective that focuses on the rights of the individual and in which individuals independently make moral decisions.

care perspective The moral perspective of Carol Gilligan, which views people in terms of their connectedness with others and emphasizes interpersonal communication, relationships with others, and concern for others.

domain theory of moral development States that there are different domains of social knowledge and reasoning, including moral, social conventional, and personal domains. These domains arise from children's and adolescents' attempts to understand and deal with different forms of social experience.

social conventional reasoning Thoughts about social consensus and convention, in contrast with moral reasoning, which stresses ethical issues.

How does children's sharing change from the preschool to the elementary school years?

ritual or out of imitation. Then, at about 4 years of age, a combination of empathic awareness and adult encouragement produces a sense of obligation on the part of the child to share with others. Most 4-year-olds are not selfless saints, however. Children believe they have an obligation to share but do not necessarily think they should be as generous to others as they are to themselves.

Children's sharing comes to reflect a more complex sense of what is just and right during middle and late childhood. By the start of the elementary school years, children begin to express objective ideas about fairness. It is common to hear 6-year-old children use the word *fair* as synonymous with *equal* or *same*. By the mid- to late elementary school years, children believe that equity can sometimes mean that people with special merit or special needs deserve special treatment.

Moral Personality   Beyond the development of moral reasoning and specific moral feelings and prosocial behaviors, do children also develop a pattern of moral characteristics that is distinctively their own? In other words, do children develop a *moral personality*, and if so, what are its components? Researchers have focused attention on three possible components (Walker & Frimer, 2011): (1) moral identity, (2) moral character, and (3) moral exemplars:

- *Moral identity*. Individuals have a moral identity when moral notions and moral commitments are central to their lives (Hardy & others, 2012). They construct the self with reference to moral categories. Violating their moral commitment would place the integrity of their self at risk. Recently, Darcia Narváez (2010) concluded that a mature moral individual cares about morality and being a moral person. For these individuals, moral responsibility is central to their identity. Mature moral individuals engage in moral metacognition, including moral self-monitoring and moral self-reflection. Moral self-monitoring involves monitoring one's thoughts and actions related to moral situations, and engaging in self-control when it is needed. Moral self-reflection encompasses critical evaluations of one's self-judgments and efforts to minimize bias and self-deception.

- *Moral character*. A person with moral character has the willpower, desires, and integrity to stand up to pressure, overcome distractions and disappointments, and behave morally. A person of good moral character displays moral virtues such as "honesty, truthfulness, and trustworthiness, as well as those of care, compassion, thoughtfulness, and considerateness. Other salient traits revolve around virtues of dependability, loyalty, and conscientiousness" (Walker, 2002, p. 74).

- *Moral exemplars*. Moral exemplars are people who have lived exemplary moral lives. Their moral personality, identity, character, and set of virtues reflect moral excellence and commitment (Walker & Frimer, 2008).

In sum, moral development is a multifaceted, complex concept. Included in this complexity are an individual's thoughts, feelings, behaviors, and personality.

GENDER

Gilligan's claim that Kohlberg's theory of moral development reflects gender bias reminds us of the pervasive influence of gender on development. Long before elementary school, boys and girls show preferences for different toys and activities. As we discussed in Chapter 8, preschool children display a gender identity and gender-typed behavior that reflects biological, cognitive, and social influences. Here we will examine gender stereotypes, gender similarities and differences, and gender-role classification.

Gender Stereotypes   According to the old ditty, boys are made of "frogs and snails" and girls are made of "sugar and spice and all that is nice." In the past, a well-adjusted boy was supposed to be independent, aggressive, and powerful. A well-adjusted girl was supposed to be dependent, nurturing, and uninterested in power. These notions reflect **gender stereotypes,** which are broad categories that reflect general impressions and beliefs about females and males.

What are little boys made of?
Frogs and snails
And puppy-dogs' tails.
What are little girls made of?
Sugar and spice
And all that is nice.

—J. O. HALLIWELL
English Author, 19th Century

gender stereotypes Broad categories that reflect our impressions and beliefs about females and males.

Recent research has found that gender stereotypes are, to a great extent, still present in today's world, both in the lives of children and adults (Leaper & Bigler, 2011; Matlin, 2012). Gender stereotyping continues to change during middle and late childhood and adolescence (Blakemore, Berenbaum, & Liben, 2009). By the time children enter elementary school, they have considerable knowledge about which activities are linked with being male or female. Until about 7 to 8 years of age, gender stereotyping is extensive because young children don't recognize individual variations in masculinity and femininity. By 5 years of age, both boys and girls stereotype boys as powerful and in more negative terms, such as mean, and girls in more positive terms, such as nice (Martin & Ruble, 2010). Across the elementary school years, children become more flexible in their gender attitudes (Trautner & others, 2005).

A study of 3- to 10-year-old U.S. children revealed that girls and older children used a higher percentage of gender stereotypes (Miller & others, 2009). In this study, appearance stereotypes were more prevalent on the part of girls while activity (sports, for example) and trait (aggressive, for example) stereotyping was more commonly engaged in by boys. Another recent study of 6- to 10-year-olds found that both boys and girls indicated math is for boys (Cvencek, Meltzoff, & Greenwald, 2011). Researchers also have found that boys' gender stereotypes are more rigid than girls' (Blakemore, Berenbaum, & Liben, 2009).

Gender Similarities and Differences   What is the reality behind gender stereotypes? Let's examine some of the similarities and differences between the sexes, keeping in mind that (1) the differences are averages—not all females versus all males; (2) even when differences are reported, there is considerable overlap between the sexes; and (3) the differences may be due primarily to biological factors, sociocultural factors, or both. First, we will examine physical similarities and differences, and then we will turn to cognitive and socioemotional similarities and differences.

Physical Development   Women have about twice the body fat of men, most of it concentrated around their breasts and hips. In males, fat is more likely to go to the abdomen. On the average, males grow to be 10 percent taller than females. Other physical differences are less obvious. From conception on, females have a longer life expectancy than males, and females are less likely than males to develop physical or mental disorders. Males have twice the risk of coronary disease as females.

Does gender matter when it comes to brain structure and function? Human brains are much alike, whether the brain belongs to a male or a female (Halpern & others, 2007). However, researchers have found some differences in the brains of males and females (Hofer & others, 2007). For example, female brains are smaller than male brains, but female brains have more folds; the larger folds (called convolutions) allow more surface brain tissue within the skulls of females than males (Luders & others, 2004). An area of the parietal lobe that functions in visuospatial skills is larger in males than females (Frederikse & others, 2000). And the areas of the brain involved in emotional expression show more metabolic activity in females than males (Gur & others, 1995).

Although some differences in brain structure and function have been found, many of these differences are small or research is inconsistent regarding the differences. Also, when sex differences in the brain have been revealed, in many cases they have not been directly linked to psychological differences (Blakemore, Berenbaum, & Liben, 2009). Although research on sex differences in the brain is still in its infancy, it is likely that there are far more similarities than differences in the brains of females and males. A further point is worth noting: Anatomical sex differences in the brain may be due to the biological origins of these differences, behavioral experiences (which underscores the brain's continuing plasticity), or a combination of these factors.

Cognitive Development   No gender differences in general intelligence have been revealed, but some gender differences have been found in some cognitive areas (Blakemore, Berenbaum, & Liben, 2009). Research has shown that in general girls and women have slightly better verbal skills than boys and men, although in some verbal skill areas the differences are substantial (Blakemore, Berenbaum, & Liben, 2009). For example, in recent national assessments,

"So according to the stereotype, you can put two and two together, but I can read the handwriting on the wall."
© Joel Pett. Author rights reserved.

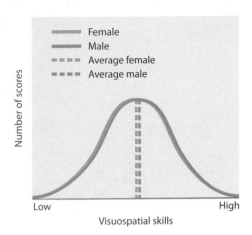

FIGURE **10.3**

VISUOSPATIAL SKILLS OF MALES AND FEMALES. Notice that although an average male's visuospatial skills are higher than an average female's, the scores for the two sexes almost entirely overlap. Not all males have better visuospatial skills than all females—the overlap indicates that although the average male score is higher, many females outperform most males on such tasks.

developmental **connection**

Gender

The nature and extent of gender differences in communication in relationships is controversial. Chapter 14, p. 473

girls were significantly better than boys in reading and writing (National Assessment of Educational Progress, 2005, 2007).

Are there gender differences in math skills? A recent very large-scale study of more than 7 million U.S. students in grades 2 through 11 revealed no differences in math test scores for boys and girls (Hyde & others, 2008). And a recent meta-analysis found no gender differences in math for adolescents (Lindberg & others, 2010). A recent research review concluded that girls have more negative math attitudes and that parents' and teachers' expectancies for children's math competence are often gender-biased in favor of boys (Gunderson & others, 2012).

One area of math that has been examined for possible gender differences is visuospatial skills, which include being able to rotate objects mentally and to determine what they would look like when rotated (Halpern, 2012). These types of skills are important in courses such as plane and solid geometry and geography. A recent research review revealed that boys have better visuospatial skills than girls (Halpern & others, 2007). For example, despite equal participation in the National Geography Bee, in most years all 10 finalists are boys (Liben, 1995). However, some experts argue that the gender difference in visuospatial skills is small (Hyde, 2007; Hyde & Else-Quest, 2013) (see Figure 10.3).

Socioemotional Development Three areas of socioemotional development in which gender similarities and differences have been studied extensively are aggression, emotion, and prosocial behavior.

One of the most consistent gender differences is that boys are more physically aggressive than girls are (Coyne, Nelson, & Underwood, 2011). The difference occurs in all cultures and appears very early in children's development (White, 2001). The physical aggression difference is especially pronounced when children are provoked. Both biological and environmental factors have been proposed to account for gender differences in aggression. Biological factors include heredity and hormones. Environmental factors include cultural expectations, adult and peer models, and social agents that reward aggression in boys and punish aggression in girls.

Although boys are consistently more physically aggressive than girls, might girls show levels of verbal aggression, such as yelling, that equal or exceed the levels shown by boys? When verbal aggression is considered, gender differences often disappear, although sometimes verbal aggression is more pronounced in girls (Eagly & Steffen, 1986).

Recently, increased attention has been directed to *relational aggression*, which involves harming someone by manipulating a relationship. Relational aggression includes such behaviors as spreading malicious rumors about someone in order to make others dislike that person (Kawabata & others, 2012; Underwood, 2004, 2011). Relational aggression increases in middle and late childhood (Dishion & Piehler, 2009). Mixed findings have characterized research on whether girls show more relational aggression than boys, but one consistent finding is that relational aggression comprises a greater percentage of girls' overall aggression than is the case

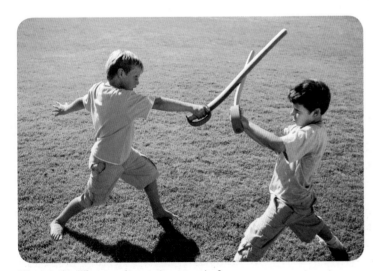

What gender differences characterize aggression?

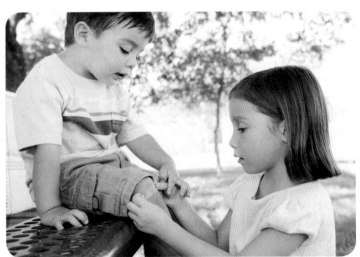

What gender differences characterize children's prosocial behavior?

for boys (Putallaz & others, 2007). And a recent research review revealed that girls engage in more relational aggression than boys in adolescence but not in childhood (Smith, Rose, & Schwartz-Mette, 2010).

Gender differences occur in some aspects of emotion (Leaper & Bigler, 2011; Nolen-Hoeksema, 2012). Females express emotion more than do males, are better than males at decoding emotion, smile more, cry more, and are happier (Gross, Fredrickson, & Levenson, 1994; LaFrance, Hecht, & Paluck, 2003). Males report experiencing and expressing more anger than do females (Kring, 2000).

An important skill is to be able to regulate and control one's emotions and behavior (Thompson, Winer, & Goodvin, 2011). Boys usually show less self-regulation than girls (Eisenberg, Spinrad, & Eggum, 2010). This low self-control can translate into behavior problems.

Are there gender differences in prosocial behavior? Females view themselves as more prosocial and empathic (Eisenberg & Morris, 2004). Across childhood and adolescence, females engage in more prosocial behavior (Hastings, Utendale, & Sullivan, 2007). The biggest gender difference occurs for kind and considerate behavior, with a smaller difference in sharing.

Earlier in the chapter, we discussed Carol Gilligan's theory that many females are more sensitive about relationships and have better relationship skills than males do. In Chapter 14, "Socioemotional Development in Early Adulthood," we will further explore this aspect of gender.

Gender-Role Classification
Not long ago, it was accepted that boys should grow up to be masculine and girls to be feminine. In the 1970s, however, as both females and males became dissatisfied with the burdens imposed by their stereotypical roles, alternatives to femininity and masculinity were proposed. Instead of describing masculinity and femininity based on a continuum in which more of one means less of the other, it was proposed that individuals could have both masculine and feminine traits.

This thinking led to the development of the concept of **androgyny,** the presence of positive masculine and feminine characteristics in the same person (Bem, 1977; Spence & Helmreich, 1978). The androgynous boy might be assertive (masculine) and nurturant (feminine). The androgynous girl might be powerful (masculine) and sensitive to others' feelings (feminine). Measures have been developed to assess androgyny (see Figure 10.4).

Gender experts such as Sandra Bem argue that androgynous individuals are more flexible, competent, and mentally healthy than their masculine or feminine counterparts. To some degree, though, which gender-role classification is best depends on the context involved. For example, in close relationships, feminine and androgynous orientations might be more desirable. One study found that girls and individuals high in femininity showed a stronger interest in caring than did boys and individuals high in masculinity (Karniol, Grosz, & Schorr, 2003). However, masculine and androgynous orientations might be more desirable in traditional academic and work settings because of the achievement demands in these contexts.

Despite talk about the "sensitive male," William Pollack (1999) argues that little has been done to change traditional ways of raising boys. He says that the "boy code" tells boys that they should show little if any emotion and should act tough. Boys learn the boy code in many contexts—sandboxes, playgrounds, schoolrooms, camps, hangouts. The result, according to Pollack, is a "national crisis of boyhood." Pollack and others suggest that boys would benefit from being socialized to express their anxieties and concerns and to better regulate their aggression.

Gender in Context
Both the concept of androgyny and gender stereotypes describe people in terms of personality traits such as "aggressive" or "caring." However, the traits people display may vary with the situation (Leaper & Bigler, 2011). Thus, the nature and extent of gender differences may depend on the context (Blakemore, Berenbaum, & Liben, 2009).

Consider helping behavior. The stereotype is that females are better than males at helping. But it depends on the situation. Females are more likely than males to volunteer their time to help children with personal problems and to engage in caregiving behavior. However, in situations in which males feel a sense of competence and circumstances that involve danger, males are more likely than females to help (Eagly & Crowley, 1986). For example,

---

Examples of masculine items

Defends open beliefs
Forceful
Willing to take risks
Dominant
Aggressive

Examples of feminine items

Does not use harsh language
Affectionate
Loves children
Understanding
Gentle

FIGURE 10.4

THE BEM SEX-ROLE INVENTORY. These items are from the Bem Sex-Role Inventory (BSRI). When taking the BSRI, an individual is asked to indicate on a 7-point scale how well each of the 60 characteristics describes herself or himself. The scale ranges from 1 (never or almost never true) to 7 (always or almost always true). The items are scored on independent dimensions of masculinity and femininity. Individuals who score high on the masculine items and low on the feminine items are categorized as masculine; those who score high on the feminine items and low on the masculine items are categorized as feminine; and those who score high on both the masculine and feminine items are categorized as androgynous.

developmental **connection**

Community and Culture

Bronfenbrenner's ecological theory emphasizes the importance of contexts; in his theory the macrosystem includes cross-cultural comparisons. Chapter 1, p. 27

androgyny The presence of positive masculine and feminine characteristics in the same individual.

In China, females and males are usually socialized to behave, feel, and think differently. The old patriarchal traditions of male supremacy have not been completely uprooted. Chinese women still make considerably less money than Chinese men do, and in rural China (such as here in the Lixian Village of Sichuan) male supremacy still governs many women's lives.

a male is more likely than a female to stop and help a person stranded by the roadside with a flat tire. Indeed, one study documented that males are more likely to help when the context is masculine in nature (MacGeorge, 2003).

The importance of considering gender in context is nowhere more apparent than when examining what is culturally prescribed behavior for females and males in different countries around the world (Matlin, 2012). Although there has been greater acceptance of androgyny and similarities in male and female behavior in the United States in recent years, in many countries gender roles have remained gender-specific. For example, in many Middle Eastern countries, the division of labor between males and females is dramatic. Males are socialized and schooled to work in the public sphere, females in the private world of home and child rearing. Also, in Iran the dominant view is that the man's duty is to provide for his family and the woman's is to care for her family and household. China also has been a male-dominant culture. Although women have made some strides in China, especially in urban areas, the male role is still dominant. Most males in China do not accept androgynous behavior or gender equity.

Review *Connect* Reflect

 Discuss emotional and personality development in middle and late childhood.

Review

- What changes take place in the self during the middle and late childhood years?
- How does emotional expression change during middle and late childhood?
- What characterizes moral development in middle and late childhood? What are gender stereotypes, and what some important gender differences?

Connect

- In Chapter 5, you learned about the concept of joint attention. How is that similar to or different from the concept of perspective taking you learned about here?

Reflect *Your Own Personal Journey of Life*

- A young man who had been sentenced to serve 10 years for selling a small amount of marijuana escaped from a prison six months after he was sent there. He is now in his fifties and has been a model citizen. Should he be sent back to prison? Why or why not? At which Kohlberg stage should your response be placed? Do you think the stage at which you placed your response accurately captures the level of your moral thinking? Explain.

2 Families
LG2 Describe developmental changes in parent-child relationships, parents as managers, attachment, and stepfamilies.

Developmental Changes in Parent-Child Relationships   Parents as Managers   Attachment   Stepfamilies

Our discussion of parenting and families in this section focuses on how parent-child interactions typically change in middle and late childhood, the importance of parents being effective managers of children's lives, attachment, and how children are affected by living with stepparents.

DEVELOPMENTAL CHANGES IN PARENT-CHILD RELATIONSHIPS

As children move into the middle and late childhood years, parents spend considerably less time with them (Grusec & others, 2013). In one study, parents spent less than half as much time with their children aged 5 to 12 in caregiving, instruction, reading, talking, and playing as when the children were younger (Hill & Stafford, 1980). Although parents spend less time with their children in middle and late childhood than in early childhood, parents continue to be extremely important in their children's lives. In a recent analysis of the contributions of parents in middle and late childhood, the following conclusion was reached: "Parents serve as gatekeepers and provide scaffolding as children assume more responsibility for themselves and . . . regulate their own lives" (Huston & Ripke, 2006, p. 422).

Parents especially play an important role in supporting and stimulating children's academic achievement in middle and late childhood (Huston & Ripke, 2006; Pomerantz, Cheung, & Qin, 2012). The value parents place on education can determine whether children do well in school. Parents not only influence children's in-school achievement, but they also make decisions about children's out-of-school activities. Whether children participate in sports, music, and other activities is heavily influenced by the extent to which parents sign up children for such activities and encourage their participation (Simpkins & others, 2006).

Elementary school children tend to receive less physical discipline than they did as preschoolers. Instead of spanking or coercive holding, their parents are more likely to use deprivation of privileges, appeals to the child's self-esteem, comments designed to increase the child's sense of guilt, and statements that the child is responsible for his or her actions.

During middle and late childhood, some control is transferred from parent to child. The process is gradual, and it produces coregulation rather than control by either the child or the parent alone. Parents continue to exercise general supervision and control, while children are allowed to engage in moment-to-moment self-regulation. The major shift to autonomy does not occur until about the age of 12 or later. A key developmental task as children move toward autonomy is learning to relate to adults outside the family on a regular basis—adults such as teachers who interact with children much differently from their parents.

What are some changes in the focus of parent-child relationships in middle and late childhood?

PARENTS AS MANAGERS

Parents can play important roles as managers of children's opportunities, as monitors of their behavior, and as social initiators and arrangers (Grusec & others, 2013; Parke & Clarke-Stewart, 2011). Mothers are more likely than fathers to engage in a managerial role in parenting.

Researchers have found that family management practices are positively related to students' grades and self-responsibility, and negatively to school-related problems (Eccles, 2007; Taylor & Lopez, 2005). Among the most important family management practices in this regard are maintaining a structured and organized family environment, such as establishing routines for homework, chores, bedtime, and so on, and effectively monitoring the child's behavior. A research review of the role of family functioning in determining African American students' academic achievement found that when African American parents monitored their son's academic achievement by ensuring that homework was completed, restricted time spent on nonproductive distractions (such as video games and TV), and participated in a consistent, positive dialogue with teachers and school officials, their son's academic achievement benefited (Mandara, 2006).

ATTACHMENT

In Chapter 6, you read about the importance of secure attachment in infancy and the role of sensitive parenting in attachment (Berlin, 2012; Bretherton, 2012; Thompson, 2013a). The attachment process continues to be an important aspect of children's development in the childhood years. In middle and late childhood, attachment becomes more sophisticated and as children's social worlds expand to include peers, teachers, and others, they typically spend less time with parents.

Kathryn Kerns and her colleagues (Brumariu, Kerns, & Siebert, 2012; Kerns & Siebert, 2012; Kerns, Siener, & Brumariu, 2011; Siener & Kerns, 2012) have studied links between attachment to parents and various child outcomes in the middle and late childhood years. They have found that during this period of development, secure attachment is associated with a lower level of internalized symptoms, anxiety, and depression in children (Brumariu

& Kerns, 2010). For example, a recent study revealed that children who were less securely attached to their mother reported having more anxiety (Brumariu, Kerns, & Seibert, 2012). Also in this study, secure attachment was linked to a higher level of children's emotion regulation and less difficulty in identifying emotions.

STEPFAMILIES

Not only has divorce become commonplace in the United States, so has remarriage. It takes time for parents to marry, have children, get divorced, and then remarry. Consequently, there are far more elementary and secondary school children than infant or preschool children living in stepfamilies.

The number of remarriages involving children has grown steadily in recent years. Also, divorces occur at a 10 percent higher rate in remarriages than in first marriages (Cherlin & Furstenberg, 1994). About half of all children whose parents divorce will have a stepparent within four years of the separation.

Remarried parents face some unique tasks. The couple must define and strengthen their marriage and at the same time renegotiate the biological parent-child relationships and establish stepparent-stepchild and stepsibling relationships (Coleman, Ganong, & Fine, 2004). The complex histories and multiple relationships make adjustment difficult in a stepfamily (Higginbotham & others, 2012). Only one-third of stepfamily couples stay remarried.

In some cases, the stepfamily may have been preceded by the death of a spouse. However, by far the largest number of stepfamilies are preceded by divorce rather than death (Pasley & Moorefield, 2004). Three common types of stepfamily structure are (1) stepfather, (2) stepmother, and (3) blended or complex. In stepfather families, the mother typically had custody of the children and remarried, introducing a stepfather into her children's lives. In stepmother families, the father usually had custody and remarried, introducing a stepmother into his children's lives. In a blended or complex stepfamily, both parents bring children from previous marriages to live in the newly formed stepfamily.

- - - - - - - - - ➤

developmental **connection**

Family

Approximately 50 percent of remarried women bear children within their newly formed union. Chapter 14, p. 466

How does living in a stepfamily influence a child's development?

In E. Mavis Hetherington's (2006) most recent longitudinal analyses, children and adolescents who had been in a simple stepfamily (stepfather or stepmother) for a number of years were adjusting better than in the early years of the remarried family and were functioning well in comparison with children and adolescents in conflictual nondivorced families and children and adolescents in complex (blended) stepfamilies. More than 75 percent of the adolescents in long-established simple stepfamilies described their relationships with their stepparents as "close" or "very close." Hetherington (2006) concluded that in long-established simple stepfamilies adolescents seem to eventually benefit from the presence of a stepparent and the resources provided by the stepparent.

Children often have better relationships with their custodial parents (mothers in stepfather families, fathers in stepmother families) than with stepparents (Santrock, Sitterle, & Warshak, 1988). Also, children in simple stepfamilies (stepmother, stepfather) often show better adjustment than their counterparts in complex (blended) families (Hetherington & Kelly, 2002). As in divorced families, children in stepfamilies show more adjustment problems than children in nondivorced families (Hetherington & Kelly, 2002). The adjustment problems are similar to those found among children of divorced parents—academic problems and lower self-esteem, for example (Anderson & others, 1999). However, it is important to recognize that a majority of children in stepfamilies do not have such problems. In one analysis, 25 percent of children from stepfamilies showed adjustment problems compared with 10 percent in intact, never-divorced families (Hetherington & Kelly, 2002).

Adolescence is an especially difficult time for the formation of a stepfamily (Gosselin, 2010). This difficulty may occur because becoming part of a stepfamily exacerbates normal adolescent concerns about identity, sexuality, and autonomy.

3 Peers
LG3 Identify changes in peer relationships in middle and late childhood.

Developmental Changes | Peer Status | Social Cognition | Bullying | Friends

Having positive relationships with peers is especially important in middle and late childhood (Hymel & others, 2011; Ladd & others, 2012; Rodkin & Ryan, 2012; Wentzel, Donlan, & Morrison, 2012). Engaging in positive interactions with peers, resolving conflicts with peers in nonaggressive ways, and maintaining quality friendships in middle and late childhood not only have positive outcomes at this time in children's lives, but also are linked to more positive relationship outcomes in adolescence and adulthood (Huston & Ripke, 2006). For example, in one longitudinal study, being popular with peers and engaging in low levels of aggression at 8 years of age were related to higher levels of occupational status at 48 years of age (Huesmann & others, 2006). Another study found that peer competence (a composite measure that included social contact with peers, popularity with peers, friendship, and social skills) in middle and late childhood was linked to having better relationships with coworkers in early adulthood (Collins & van Dulmen, 2006).

DEVELOPMENTAL CHANGES

As children enter the elementary school years, reciprocity becomes especially important in peer interchanges. Researchers estimate that the percentage of time spent in social interaction with peers increases from approximately 10 percent at 2 years of age to more than 30 percent in middle and late childhood (Rubin, Bukowski, & Parker, 2006). In an early classic study, a typical day in elementary school included approximately 300 episodes with peers (Barker & Wright, 1951). As children move through middle and late childhood, the size of their peer group increases, and peer interaction is less closely supervised by adults. Until about 12 years of age, children's preference for same-sex peer groups increases.

PEER STATUS

Which children are likely to be popular with their peers and which ones tend to be disliked? Developmentalists address this and similar questions by examining *sociometric status,* a term that describes the extent to which children are liked or disliked by their peer group (Cillessen, Schwartz, & Mayeux, 2011; Cillessen & van den Berg, 2012). Sociometric status is typically assessed by asking children to rate how much they like or dislike each of their classmates. Or it may be assessed by asking children to name the children they like the most and those they like the least.

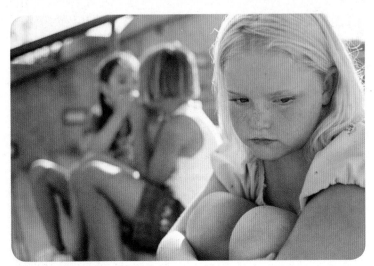

What are some statuses that children have with their peers?

Developmentalists have distinguished five peer statuses (Wentzel & Asher, 1995):

- **Popular children** are frequently nominated as a best friend and are rarely disliked by their peers.
- **Average children** receive an average number of both positive and negative nominations from their peers.
- **Neglected children** are infrequently nominated as a best friend but are not disliked by their peers.
- **Rejected children** are infrequently nominated as someone's best friend and are actively disliked by their peers.
- **Controversial children** are frequently nominated both as someone's best friend and as being disliked.

Popular children have a number of social skills that contribute to their being well liked. They give out reinforcements, listen carefully, maintain open lines of communication with peers, are happy, control their negative emotions, act like themselves, show enthusiasm and concern for others, and are self-confident without being conceited (Hartup, 1983; Rubin, Bukowski, & Parker, 1998). Rejected children often have serious adjustment problems (White & Kistner, 2011). One study evaluated 112 fifth-grade boys over a period of seven years until the end of high school (Kupersmidt & Coie, 1990). The best predictor of whether rejected children would engage in delinquent behavior or drop out of school later during adolescence was aggression toward peers in elementary school.

John Coie (2004, pp. 252–253) provided three reasons why aggressive, peer-rejected boys have problems in social relationships:

- "First, the rejected, aggressive boys are more impulsive and have problems sustaining attention. As a result, they are more likely to be disruptive of ongoing activities in the classroom and in focused group play.
- Second, rejected, aggressive boys are more emotionally reactive. They are aroused to anger more easily and probably have more difficulty calming down once aroused. Because of this they are more prone to become angry at peers and attack them verbally and physically. . . .
- Third, rejected children have fewer social skills in making friends and maintaining positive relationships with peers."

Not all rejected children are aggressive (Hymel & others, 2011). Although aggression and its related characteristics of impulsiveness and disruptiveness underlie rejection about half the time, approximately 10 to 20 percent of rejected children are shy.

How can rejected children be trained to interact more effectively with their peers? Rejected children may be taught to more accurately assess whether the intentions of their peers are negative (Bierman & Powers, 2009). They may be asked to engage in role playing or to discuss hypothetical situations involving negative encounters with peers, such as when a peer cuts into a line ahead of them. In some programs, children are shown videotapes of appropriate peer interaction and asked to draw lessons from what they have seen (Ladd, Buhs, & Troop, 2004).

SOCIAL COGNITION

A boy accidentally trips and knocks another boy's soft drink out of his hand. That boy misinterprets the encounter as hostile, which leads him to retaliate aggressively against the boy who tripped. Through repeated encounters of this kind, the aggressive boy's classmates come to perceive him as habitually acting in inappropriate ways.

This encounter demonstrates the importance of *social cognition*—thoughts about social matters, such as the aggressive boy's interpretation of an encounter as hostile and his classmates' perception of his behavior as inappropriate (Dodge, 2011a, b). Children's social cognition about their peers becomes increasingly important for understanding peer relationships in middle and

popular children Children who are frequently nominated as a best friend and are rarely disliked by their peers.

average children Children who receive an average number of both positive and negative nominations from peers.

neglected children Children who are infrequently nominated as a best friend but are not disliked by their peers.

rejected children Children who are infrequently nominated as a best friend and are actively disliked by their peers.

controversial children Children who are frequently nominated both as a best friend and as being disliked by their peers.

late childhood. Of special interest are the ways in which children process information about peer relations and their social knowledge (Dodge, 2011b; White & Kistner, 2011).

Kenneth Dodge (1983, 2011b) argues that children go through six steps in processing information about their social world: they selectively attend to social cues, attribute intent, generate goals, access behavioral scripts from memory, make decisions, and enact behavior. Dodge has found that aggressive boys are more likely to perceive another child's actions as hostile when the child's intention is ambiguous. And when aggressive boys search for cues to determine a peer's intention, they respond more rapidly, less efficiently, and less reflectively than do nonaggressive children. These are among the social cognitive factors believed to be involved in children's conflicts.

Social knowledge also is involved in children's ability to get along with peers. They need to know what goals to pursue in poorly defined or ambiguous situations, how to initiate and maintain a social bond, and what scripts to follow to get other children to be their friends. For example, as part of the script for getting friends, it helps to know that saying nice things, regardless of what the peer does or says, will make the peer like the child more.

How might the way that children process information influence how much aggressive behavior they display?

BULLYING

Significant numbers of students are victimized by bullies (Lemstra & others, 2012). In a national survey of more than 15,000 sixth- through tenth-grade students, nearly one of every three students said that they had experienced occasional or frequent involvement as a victim or perpetrator in bullying (Nansel & others, 2001). In this study, bullying was defined as verbal or physical behavior intended to disturb someone less powerful. As shown in Figure 10.5, being belittled about looks or speech was the most frequent type of bullying. A recent study revealed that bullying decreased as students went from the fall of the sixth grade (20 percent were bullied extensively) through the spring of the eighth grade (6 percent were bullied extensively) (Nylund & others, 2007). Boys are more likely to be bullies than girls, but gender differences regarding victims of bullies is less clear (Peets, Hodges, & Salmivalli, 2011).

Who is likely to be bullied? In the study just described, boys and younger middle school students were most likely to be affected (Nansel & others, 2001). Children who said they were bullied reported more loneliness and difficulty in making friends, while those who did the bullying were more likely to have low grades and to smoke and drink alcohol. Researchers have found that anxious, socially withdrawn, and aggressive children are often the victims of bullying (Hanish & Guerra, 2004). Anxious and socially withdrawn children may be victimized because they are nonthreatening and unlikely to retaliate if bullied, whereas aggressive children may be the targets of bullying because their behavior is irritating to bullies (Rubin & others, 2011). A recent study revealed that having supportive friends was linked to a lower level of bullying and victimization (Kendrick, Jutengren, & Stattin, 2012).

An increasing concern is peer bullying and harassment on the Internet (called *cyberbullying*) (Donnerstein, 2012; Kowalsky, Limber, & Agatston, 2012; Valkenburg & Peter, 2011). A recent study of third- to sixth-graders revealed that engaging in cyber aggression was related to loneliness, lower self-esteem, fewer mutual friendships, and lower peer popularity (Schoffstall & Cohen, 2012). Information about preventing cyberbullying can be found at www.stopcyberbullying.org/.

Social contexts also influence bullying (Schwartz & others, 2010). Recent research indicates that 70 to 80 percent of victims and their bullies are in the same school classroom (Salmivalli & Peets, 2009). Classmates are often aware of bullying incidents and in many cases witness bullying. The larger social context of the peer group plays an important role in bullying (Salmivalli, Peets, & Hodges, 2011). In many cases, bullies torment victims to gain higher status in the peer group and bullies need others to witness their power displays.

What are the outcomes of bullying? Researchers have found that children who are bullied are more likely to experience depression and engage in suicide ideation and attempt suicide than their counterparts who have not been the victims of bullying (Fisher & others, 2012;

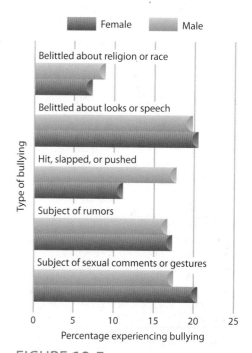

FIGURE 10.5

BULLYING BEHAVIORS AMONG U.S. YOUTH.
This graph shows the type of bullying most often experienced by U.S. youth. The percentages reflect the extent to which bullied students said that they had experienced a particular type of bullying. In terms of gender, note that when they were bullied, boys were more likely to be hit, slapped, or pushed than girls were.

What Are the Perspective Taking and Moral Motivation Skill Levels of Bullies, Bully-Victims, Victims, and Prosocial Children?

A recent study explored the roles that perspective taking and moral motivation play in the lives of bullies, bully-victims, victims, and prosocial children (Gasser & Keller, 2009):

- *Bullies* are highly aggressive toward other children but are not victims of bullying.
- *Bully-victims* are not only highly aggressive toward other children but also are the recipients of other children's bullying.
- *Victims* are passive, nonaggressive respondents to bullying.
- *Prosocial children* engage in positive behaviors such as sharing, helping, comforting, and empathizing.

Teacher and peer ratings in 34 classrooms were used to classify 212 boys and girls 7 or 8 years of age into the aforementioned four categories. On a 5-point scale (from never to several times a week), teachers rated (1) how often the child bullied others and (2) how often the child was bullied. The ratings focused on three types of bullying and being victimized: physical, verbal, and excluding others. On a 4-point scale (from not applicable to very clearly applicable), teachers also rated children's prosocial behavior on three items: "willingly shares with others," "comforts others if necessary," and "empathizes with others." Peer ratings assessed children's nominations of which children in the classroom acted as bullies, were victimized by bullies, and engaged in prosocial behavior. Combining the teacher and peer ratings after eliminating those that did not agree on which children were bullies, victims, or prosocial children, the final sample consisted of 49 bullies, 80 bully-victims, 33 victims, and 50 prosocial children.

Children's perspective-taking skills were assessed using theory of mind tasks, and moral motivation was examined by interviewing children about aspects of right and wrong in stories about children's transgressions. In one theory of mind task, children were tested to see if they understood that people may have false beliefs about another individual. In another theory of mind task, children were assessed to determine whether they understood that people sometimes hide their emotions by showing an emotion different from their true feelings. A moral interview also was conducted in which children were told four moral transgression stories (with content about being unwilling to share with a classmate, stealing sweets from a classmate, hiding a victim's shoes, and verbally bullying a victim) and then asked to judge whether the acts were right or wrong and how the participants in the stories likely felt.

The results of the study indicated that only bully-victims—but not bullies—were deficient in perspective taking. Further analysis revealed that both aggressive groups of children—bullies and bully-victims—had a deficiency in moral motivation. The analyses were consistent with a portrait of bullies as socially competent and knowledgeable in terms of perspective-taking skills and capable of effectively interacting with peers. However, bullies use this social knowledge for their own manipulative purposes. The analysis also confirmed the picture of the bully as being morally insensitive. Another recent study also found that bullying was linked to moral disengagement (Obermann, 2011).

How can researchers ensure that results that might help prevent bullying are properly applied in school settings (and not, for instance, used to label potential bullies or segregate potential victims)?

Who is likely to be bullied? What are some outcomes of bullying?

Lemstra & others, 2012). A recent longitudinal study of more than 6,000 children found that children who were the victims of peer bullying from 4 to 10 years of age were more likely to engage in suicide ideation at 11½ years of age (Winsper & others, 2012). Consider these three recent cases in which bullying was linked to suicide: An 8-year-old jumped out of a two-story building in Houston; a 13-year-old hanged himself in Houston; and teenagers harassed a girl so mercilessly that she killed herself in Massachusetts (Meyers, 2010). A recent study also revealed that 11-year-olds who were victims of peer bullying were more likely to have a heightened risk of developing borderline personality disorder symptoms (a pervasive pattern of unstable interpersonal relationships, low self-image, and emotional difficulties) (Wolke & others, 2012).

What kinds of perspective taking and moral motivation skills do bullies, bully-victims, and prosocial children tend to exhibit? To find out, see the *Connecting Through Research* interlude.

Extensive interest is developing in preventing and treating bullying and victimization (Salmivalli, Garandeau, & Veenstra, 2012; Waasdrop, Bradshaw, & Leaf, 2012). A research review of school-based interventions yielded mixed results (Vreeman & Carroll, 2007).

School-based interventions vary greatly, ranging from involving the whole school in an antibullying campaign to providing individualized social skills training (Alsaker & Valanover, 2012; Roland & Midthassel, 2012; Strohmeier & Noam, 2012). One of the most promising bullying intervention programs has been created by Dan Olweus. This program focuses on 6- to 15-year-olds with the goal of decreasing opportunities and rewards for bullying. School staff are instructed in ways to improve peer relations and make schools safer. When properly implemented, the program reduces bullying by 30 to 70 percent (Ericson, 2001; Olweus, 2003). Information on how to implement the program can be obtained from the Center for the Prevention of Violence at the University of Colorado (www.colorado.edu/espv/blueprints).

FRIENDS

Friendship is an important aspect of children's development (MacEvoy & Asher, 2012; Numsoo, Einav, & Hood, 2012; Piehler, Veronneau, & Dishion, 2012; Rose & others, 2012). Like adult friendships, children's friendships are typically characterized by similarity (Brechwald & Prinstein, 2011). Throughout childhood, friends are more similar than dissimilar in terms of age, sex, race, and many other factors. Friends often have similar attitudes toward school, similar educational aspirations, and closely aligned achievement orientations.

Why are children's friendships important? Willard Hartup (1983, 1996, 2009) has studied peer relations and friendship for more than three decades. He recently concluded that friends can provide cognitive and emotional resources from childhood through old age. For example, friends can foster self-esteem and a sense of well-being.

More specifically, children's friendships can serve six functions (Gottman & Parker, 1987):

- *Companionship*. Friendship provides children with a familiar partner and playmate, someone who is willing to spend time with them and join in collaborative activities.
- *Stimulation*. Friendship provides children with interesting information, excitement, and amusement.
- *Physical support*. Friendship provides time, resources, and assistance.
- *Ego support*. Friendship provides the expectation of support, encouragement, and feedback, which helps children maintain an impression of themselves as competent, attractive, and worthwhile individuals.
- *Social comparison*. Friendship provides information about where the child stands vis-à-vis others and whether the child is doing okay.
- *Affection and intimacy*. Friendship provides children with a warm, close, trusting relationship with another individual. **Intimacy in friendships** is characterized by self disclosure and the sharing of private thoughts. Research reveals that intimate friendships may not appear until early adolescence (Berndt & Perry, 1990).

Although having friends can be a developmental advantage, not all friendships are alike (Vitaro, Boivin, & Bukowski, 2009; Wentzel, 2013). People differ in the company they keep—that is, who their friends are. Developmental advantages occur when children have friends who are socially skilled and supportive. However, it is not developmentally advantageous to have coercive and conflict-ridden friendships (Laursen & Pursell, 2009). A recent study found that students who engaged in classroom aggressive-disruptive behavior were more likely to have aggressive friends (Powers & Bierman, 2012).

Friendship also plays an important role in children's emotional well-being and academic success. Students with friends who are academically oriented are more likely to achieve success in school themselves (Wentzel, 2013). In one study, sixth-grade students who did not have a friend engaged in less prosocial behavior (cooperation, sharing, helping others), had lower grades, and were more emotionally distressed (depression, lower levels of well-being) than their counterparts who had one or more friends (Wentzel, Barry, & Caldwell, 2004). In this study, two years later, in the eighth grade, the students who did not have a friend in the sixth grade continued to be more emotionally distressed.

developmental **connection**

Peers

Beginning in early adolescence, teenagers typically prefer to have a smaller number of friendships that are more intense and intimate. Chapter 12, p. 397

What are some characteristics of children's friendships?

intimacy in friendships Self-disclosure and the sharing of private thoughts.

Review *Connect* Reflect

 LG3 Identify changes in peer relationships in middle and late childhood.

Review

- What developmental changes characterize peer relations in middle and late childhood?
- How does children's peer status influence their development?
- How is social cognition involved in children's peer relations?
- What is the nature of bullying?
- What are children's friendships like?

Connect

- Earlier in the chapter, you read that most developmentalists agree that peers play an important role in the development of moral reasoning. Of the five peer status groups you learned about in this section of the chapter, in which group do you think children would have the least opportunity to fully develop their moral reasoning capacities and why?

Reflect *Your Own Personal Journey of Life*

- Which of the five peer statuses characterized you as a child? Did your peer status change in adolescence? How do you think your peer status as a child has influenced your development?

4 Schools   **LG4**   Characterize aspects of schooling in children's development in middle and late childhood.

Contemporary Approaches to Student Learning	Socioeconomic Status, Ethnicity, and Culture

For most children, entering the first grade signals new obligations. They develop new relationships and adopt new standards by which to judge themselves. School provides children with a rich source of new ideas to shape their sense of self. They will spend many years in schools as members of small societies in which there are tasks to be accomplished, people to socialize with and be socialized by, and rules that define and limit behavior, feelings, and attitudes. By the time students graduate from high school, they have spent 12,000 hours in the classroom.

Is this classroom more likely constructivist or direct instruction? Explain.

constructivist approach A learner-centered approach that emphasizes the importance of individuals actively constructing their knowledge and understanding with guidance from the teacher.

CONTEMPORARY APPROACHES TO STUDENT LEARNING

Controversy swirls about the best way to teach children and how to hold schools and teachers accountable for whether children are learning (Mayer, 2012; Paris & others, 2012; Paas, van Merrienboer, & van Gog, 2012).

Constructivist and Direct Instruction Approaches The **constructivist approach** to instruction is a learner-centered approach that emphasizes the importance of individuals actively constructing their knowledge and understanding with guidance from the teacher. In the constructivist view, teachers should not attempt to simply pour information into children's minds. Rather, children should be encouraged to explore their world, discover knowledge, reflect, and think critically with careful monitoring and meaningful guidance from the teacher (O'Donnell, 2012; Slavin, 2012). Constructivists believe that for too long in American education children have been required to sit still, be passive learners, and rotely memorize irrelevant as well as relevant information (Loyens, Kirschner, & Paas, 2012).

Today, constructivism may include an emphasis on collaboration—children working with each other in their efforts to know and understand (Slavin, 2012). A teacher with a constructivist instructional philosophy would not have children memorize information rotely but would give them opportunities to meaningfully construct the knowledge and understand the material while guiding their learning (O'Donnell, 2012).

By contrast, the **direct instruction approach** is a structured, teacher-centered approach that is characterized by teacher direction and control, high teacher expectations for students' progress, maximum time spent by students on academic tasks, and efforts by the teacher to keep negative affect to a minimum. An important goal in the direct instruction approach is maximizing student learning time.

Advocates of the constructivist approach argue that the direct instruction approach turns children into passive learners and does not adequately challenge them to think in critical and creative ways (Webb, Metha, & Jordan, 2013). Direct instruction enthusiasts say that the constructivist approaches do not give enough attention to the content of a discipline, such as history or science. They also believe that the constructivist approaches are too relativistic and vague.

Some experts in educational psychology believe that many effective teachers use both a constructivist *and* a direct instruction approach rather than relying exclusively on one or the other (Bransford & others, 2006; Parkay, 2013). Further, some circumstances may call more for a constructivist approach, others for a direct instruction approach. For example, experts increasingly recommend an explicit, intellectually engaging direct instruction approach when teaching students who have a reading or a writing disability (Berninger & O'Malley, 2011).

Accountability   Since the 1990s, the U.S. public and governments at every level have demanded increased accountability from schools. One result was the spread of state-mandated testing to measure just what students had or had not learned (Elliott, Kurz, & Neergaard, 2012; Russell & Airasian, 2012). Many states identified objectives for students in their state and created tests to measure whether students were meeting those objectives. This approach became national policy in 2002 when the No Child Left Behind (NCLB) legislation was signed into law.

Advocates argue that statewide standardized testing will have a number of positive effects. These include improved student performance; more time spent teaching the subjects that are tested; high expectations for all students; identification of poorly performing schools, teachers, and administrators; and improved confidence in schools as test scores rise.

Critics argue that the NCLB legislation is doing more harm than good (Noddings, 2007; Sadker & Zittleman, 2012). One criticism stresses that using a single test as the sole indicator of students' progress and competence presents a very narrow view of students' skills (Lewis, 2007). This criticism is similar to the one leveled at IQ tests, which we described in Chapter 9. To assess student progress and achievement, many psychologists and educators emphasize that a number of measures should be used, including tests, quizzes, projects, portfolios, classroom observations, and so on. Also, the tests used as part of NCLB don't measure creativity, motivation, persistence, flexible thinking, and social skills (Stiggins, 2008). Critics point out that teachers end up spending far too much class time "teaching to the test" by drilling students and having them memorize isolated facts at the expense of teaching that focuses on thinking skills, which students need for success in life (Pressley, 2007). Also, recall from Chapter 9 that some individuals are concerned that in the era of No Child Left Behind policy there is a neglect of gifted students in the effort to raise the achievement level of students who are not doing well (Clark, 2008).

Consider also the following: Each state is allowed to have different criteria for what constitutes passing or failing grades on tests designated for NCLB inclusion. An analysis of NCLB data indicated that almost every fourth-grade student in Mississippi knows how to read but only half of Massachusetts' students do (Birman & others, 2007). Because state standards are so varied, state-by-state comparisons of success on NCLB tests are likely to be unreliable. In

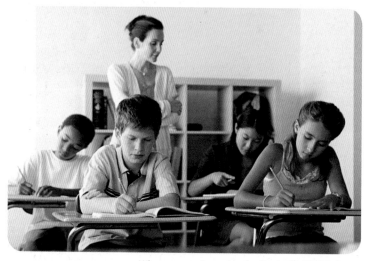

What are some issues involved in the No Child Left Behind legislation?

direct instruction approach A structured, teacher-centered approach that is characterized by teacher direction and control, mastery of academic skills, high expectations for students' progress, maximum time spent on learning tasks, and efforts to keep negative affect to a minimum.

the analysis of state-by-state comparisons, many states have taken the safe route and kept the standard for passing low. Thus, while one of NCLB's goals is to raise standards for achievement in U.S. schools, apparently allowing states to set their own standards has lowered achievement standards.

Despite such criticisms, the U.S. Department of Education is committed to implementing No Child Left Behind, and schools are making accommodations to meet the requirements of this law. Indeed, most educators support the importance of establishing high expectations and high standards of excellence for students and teachers. At issue, however, is whether the tests and procedures mandated by NCLB are the best ones for achieving these high standards (Witte, 2012; Waugh & Gronlund, 2013).

SOCIOECONOMIC STATUS, ETHNICITY, AND CULTURE

Children from low-income, ethnic minority backgrounds have more difficulties in school than do their middle-socioeconomic-status, White counterparts. Why? Critics argue that schools have not done a good job of educating low-income, ethnic minority students to overcome the barriers to their achievement (Golnick & Chinn, 2013; Spring, 2013). And recent comparisons of student achievement indicate that U.S. students have lower achievement in math and science than those in a number of other countries, especially those in east Asia (OECD, 2010). Let's further explore the roles of socioeconomic status, ethnicity, and culture in schools.

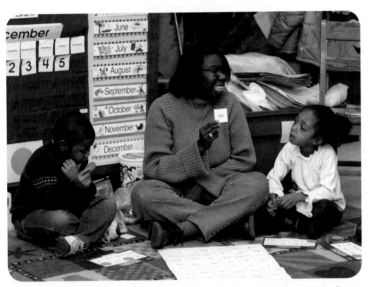

In *The Shame of a Nation,* Jonathan Kozol (2005) criticized the inadequate quality and lack of resources in many U.S. schools, especially those in the poverty areas of inner cities that have high concentrations of ethnic minority children. Kozol praises teachers like Angela Lively (*above*), who keeps a box of shoes in her Indianapolis classroom for students in need.

The Education of Students from Low-Income Backgrounds Many children living in poverty face problems that present barriers to their learning (Chen & Brooks-Gunn, 2012; Rowley, Kurtz-Costes, & Cooper, 2011). They might have parents who don't set high educational standards for them, who are incapable of reading to them, or who don't have enough money to pay for educational materials and experiences, such as books and trips to zoos and museums. They may be malnourished or live in areas where crime and violence are a way of life. One study revealed that neighborhood disadvantage (involving such characteristics as low neighborhood income and high unemployment) was linked to less consistent, less stimulating, and more punitive parenting, and ultimately to negative child outcomes such as behavioral problems and low verbal ability (Kohen & others, 2008). Another study revealed that the longer children experienced poverty, the more detrimental the poverty was to their cognitive development (Najman & others, 2009).

Compared with schools in higher-income areas, schools in low-income areas are more likely to have more students with low achievement test scores, low graduation rates, and smaller percentages of students going to college; they are more likely to have young teachers with less experience; and they are more likely to encourage rote learning (Nelson, Palonsky, & McCarthy, 2013). Many of the schools' buildings and classrooms are old and crumbling. These are the types of undesirable conditions Jonathan Kozol (2005) observed in many inner-city schools, including the South Bronx in New York City, as described at the beginning of the chapter. In sum, far too many schools in low-income neighborhoods provide students with environments that are not conducive to effective learning (Chen & Brooks-Gunn, 2012; Duncan, 2012; Duncan & others, 2013).

Might intervention with families of children living in poverty improve children's school performance? In a recent experimental study, Aletha Huston and her colleagues (2006; Gupta, Thornton, & Huston, 2008) evaluated the effects of New Hope—a program designed to increase parental employment and reduce family poverty—on adolescent development. They randomly assigned families with 6- to 10-year-old children living in poverty to the New Hope program or a control group. New Hope offered adults living in poverty who were employed 30 or more hours a week benefits that were designed to increase family income (a wage supplement which ensured that net income increased as parents earned more) and provide work supports through subsidized child care (for any child under age 13) and health insurance. Management services were provided to New Hope participants to assist them in job searches and other needs. The New Hope program was available to the experimental group families for three years (until the children were 9 to 13 years old). Five years after the program began and two years after it had ended, the program's effects on the children were examined when they were 11 to 16 years old. Compared with adolescents in the control group, New Hope adolescents were more competent at reading, had better school performance, were less likely to be in special education classes, had more positive social skills, and were more likely to be in formal after-school arrangements. New Hope parents reported better psychological well-being and a greater sense of self-efficacy in managing their adolescents than control-group parents did.

In further assessment, the influence of the New Hope program on 9- to 19-year-olds after they left the program was evaluated (McLoyd & others, 2011). Positive outcomes especially occurred for African American boys, who became more optimistic about their future employment and career prospects after experiencing the New Hope program.

Ethnicity in Schools More than one-third of all African American and almost one-third of all Latino students attend schools in the 47 largest city school districts in the United States, compared with only 5 percent of all White and 22 percent of all Asian American students. Many of these inner-city schools continue to be racially segregated, are grossly underfunded, and do not provide adequate opportunities for children to learn effectively. Thus, the effects of SES and the effects of ethnicity are often intertwined (Golnick & Chinn, 2013).

The school experiences of students from different ethnic groups vary considerably (Nieto & Bode, 2012; Urdan, 2012). African American and Latino students are much less likely than non-Latino White or Asian American students to be enrolled in academic, college preparatory programs and are much more likely to be enrolled in remedial and special education programs. Asian American students are far more likely than other ethnic minority groups to take advanced math and science courses in high school. African American students are twice as likely as Latinos, Native Americans, or non-Latino Whites to be suspended from school.

However, it is very important to note that diversity characterizes every ethnic group (Spring, 2013). For example, the higher percentage of Asian American students in advanced classes is mainly true for students with Chinese, Taiwanese, Japanese, Korean, and East Indian cultural backgrounds, but students with Hmong and Vietnamese cultural backgrounds have had less academic success.

Following are some strategies for improving relationships among ethnically diverse students:

- *Turn the class into a jigsaw classroom.* When Eliot Aronson was a professor at the University of Texas at Austin, the school system contacted him for ideas on how to reduce the increasing racial tension in classrooms. Aronson (1986) developed the concept of a "jigsaw classroom" in which students from different cultural backgrounds are placed in a cooperative group in which they have to construct different parts of a project to reach a common goal. Aronson used the term *jigsaw* because he saw the technique as much like a group of students cooperating to put different pieces together to complete a jigsaw puzzle. How might this work? Team sports, drama productions, and music performances are examples of contexts in which students participate cooperatively to reach a common goal; however, the jigsaw technique also lends itself to group science projects, history reports, and other learning experiences with a variety of subject matter.

- *Encourage students to have positive personal contact with diverse other students.* Mere contact does not do the job of improving relationships with diverse others. For example, busing ethnic minority students to predominantly White schools, or vice versa, has not reduced prejudice or improved interethnic relations. What matters is what happens after children get to school. Especially beneficial in improving interethnic relations is sharing one's worries, successes, failures, coping strategies, interests, and other personal information with people of other ethnicities. When this happens, people tend to look at others as individuals rather than as members of a homogeneous group.

- *Reduce bias.* Teachers can reduce bias by displaying images of children from diverse ethnic and cultural groups, selecting play materials and classroom activities that

James Comer, Child Psychiatrist

James Comer grew up in a low-income neighborhood in East Chicago, Indiana, and credits his parents with leaving him with no doubt about the importance of education. He earned a BA degree from Indiana University and went on to obtain a medical degree from Howard University College of Medicine, a Master of Public Health degree from the University of Michigan School of Public Health, and psychiatry training at the Yale University School of Medicine's Child Study Center. He currently is the Maurice Falk professor of Child Psychiatry at the Yale University Child Study Center and an associate dean at the Yale University Medical School. During his years at Yale, Comer has concentrated his career on promoting a focus on child development as a way of improving schools. His efforts in support of healthy development of young people have received international recognition.

Comer is, perhaps, best known for founding the School Development Program in 1968, which promotes the collaboration of parents, educators, and communities to improve social, emotional, and academic outcomes for children.

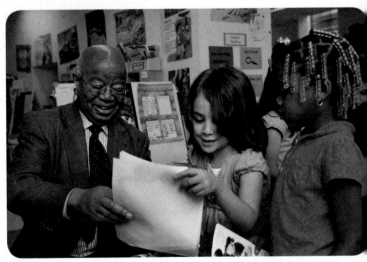

James Comer is shown with some of the inner-city children who attend a school that became a better learning environment because of Comer's intervention.

For more information about what child psychiatrists do, see page 45 in the Careers in Life-Span Development appendix.

encourage cultural understanding, helping students resist stereotyping, and working with parents to reduce children's exposure to bias and prejudice at home.

- *View the school and community as a team.* James Comer (1988, 2004, 2006, 2010) advocates a community-based, team approach as the best way to educate children. Three important aspects of the Comer Project for Change are (1) a governance and management team that develops a comprehensive school plan, assessment strategy, and staff development plan; (2) a mental health or school support team; and (3) a parents' program. Comer believes that the entire school community should have a cooperative rather than an adversarial attitude. The Comer program is currently operating in more than 600 schools in 26 states. Read further about James Comer's work in the *Connecting with Careers* profile.

- *Be a competent cultural mediator.* Teachers can play a powerful role as cultural mediators by being sensitive to biased content in materials and classroom interactions, learning more about different ethnic groups, being aware of children's ethnic attitudes, viewing students of color positively, and thinking of positive ways to get parents of color more involved as partners with teachers in educating children.

Cross-Cultural Comparisons   In the past three decades, the poor performance of American children in math and science has become well publicized (Educational Testing Service, 1992). In a large-scale comparison of math and science achievement by fourth-grade students in 2007, the average fourth-grade math score for the United States was higher than for 23 of the 35 countries and lower than for 8 countries (all in Asia and Europe) (National Center for Education Statistics, 2009). Fourth-graders from Hong Kong had the highest math score. The average fourth-grade U.S. math score did improve slightly (11 points) from the same assessment in 1995, but some Asian countries improved their scores considerably more—the Hong Kong score was 50 points higher and the Slovenia score 40 points higher in 2007 than in 1995, for example.

In 2007, the fourth-grade U.S. science score was higher than those in 25 countries and lower than those in 4 countries (all in Asia). However, the average U.S. fourth-grade science score decreased 3 points from 1995 to 2007 while the science scores for some countries increased dramatically—63 points for Singapore, 56 points for Latvia, and 55 points for Iran, for example.

Harold Stevenson's (1995, 2000; Stevenson, Hofer, & Randel, 1999; Stevenson & others, 1990) research explores possible reasons for the poor performance of American students compared with students in selected Asian countries. Stevenson and his colleagues have completed five cross-cultural comparisons of students in the United States, China, Taiwan, and Japan. In these studies, Asian students consistently outperform American students. And, the longer the students are in school, the wider the gap becomes between Asian and American students—the lowest difference is in the first grade, the highest in the eleventh grade (the highest grade studied).

To learn more about the reasons for these large cross-cultural differences, Stevenson and his colleagues spent thousands of hours observing in classrooms, as well as interviewing and surveying teachers, students, and parents. They found that the Asian teachers spent more of their time teaching math than did the American teachers. For example, more than one-fourth of total classroom time in the first grade was spent on math instruction in Japan, compared with only one-tenth of the time in the U.S. first-grade classrooms. Also, the Asian students were in school an average of 240 days a year, compared with 178 days in the United States.

In addition to the substantially greater time spent on math instruction in the Asian schools than the American schools, differences were found between the Asian and American parents. The American parents had much lower expectations for their children's education and achievement than did the Asian parents. Also, the American parents were more likely to believe that their children's math achievement was due to innate ability; the Asian parents were more likely to say that their children's math achievement was the consequence of effort and training (see Figure 10.6). The Asian students were more likely to do math homework than were the American students, and the Asian parents were far more likely to help their children with their math homework than were the American parents (Chen & Stevenson, 1989).

Related to the differences between Asian and U.S. parents in explaining effort and ability, Carol Dweck (2006, 2013) described the importance of children's **mindset,** which she defines as the cognitive view individuals develop for themselves. She concludes that individuals have one of two mindsets: (1) a *fixed mindset,* in which they believe that their qualities are carved in stone and cannot change; or (2) a *growth mindset,* in which they believe their qualities can change and improve through their effort.

Dweck (2006, 2013) argued that individuals' mindsets influence whether they will be optimistic or pessimistic, what their goals will be and how hard they will strive to reach those goals, and what they will achieve. Dweck says that mindsets begin to be shaped in childhood as children interact with parents, teachers, and coaches, who themselves have either a fixed mindset or a growth mindset. She described the growth mindset of Chicago second-grade teacher Marva Collins, a masterful teacher. Collins' goal is to change apathetic, fixed-mindset children into growth-mindset children. On the first day of school, she tells her students, many of whom are repeating the second grade,

> Well, goodbye to failure, children. Welcome to success. You will read hard books in here and understand what you read. You will write every day . . . But you must help me to help you. If you don't give anything, don't expect anything. Success is not coming to you, you must come to it. (Dweck, 2006, pp. 188–189)

Marva Collins' second-grade students usually have to start off with the lowest level of reader available, but by the end of the school year, most of the students are reading at the fifth-grade level.

How do U.S. students fare against Asian students in math and science achievement? What were some findings in Stevenson's research that might explain the results of those international comparisons?

FIGURE **10.6**

MOTHERS' BELIEFS ABOUT THE FACTORS RESPONSIBLE FOR CHILDREN'S MATH ACHIEVEMENT IN THREE COUNTRIES. In one study, mothers in Japan and Taiwan were more likely to believe that their children's math achievement was due to effort rather than innate ability, while U.S. mothers were more likely to believe their children's math achievement was due to innate ability (Stevenson, Lee, & Stigler, 1986). If parents believe that their children's math achievement is due to innate ability and their children are not doing well in math, the implication is that they are less likely to think their children will benefit from putting forth more effort.

mindset The cognitive view, either fixed or growth, that individuals develop for themselves.

Marva Collins, challenging a child to achieve.

Related to her emphasis on encouraging students to develop a growth mindset, Dweck and her colleagues (Blackwell & Dweck, 2008; Blackwell & others, 2007; Dweck, 2013; Dweck & Master, 2009) have recently incorporated information about the brain's plasticity into their effort to improve students' motivation to achieve and succeed. In one study, they assigned two groups of students to eight sessions of either (1) study skills instruction or (2) study skills instruction plus information about the importance of developing a growth mindset (called incremental theory in the research) (Blackwell & others, 2007). One of the exercises in the growth mindset group was titled "You Can Grow Your Brain" and emphasized that the brain is like a muscle that can change and grow as it is exercised and develops new connections. Students were informed that the more you challenge your brain to learn, the more your brain cells grow. Both groups had a pattern of declining math scores prior to the intervention. Following the intervention, the group who only received the study skills instruction continued to decline, but the group that received the combination of study skills instruction plus the growth mindset emphasis reversed the downward trend and improved their math achievement.

In other work, Dweck has been creating a computer-based workshop, "Brainology," to teach students that their intelligence can change (Blackwell & Dweck, 2008; Dweck, 2013). Students experience six modules about how the brain works and how they can make their brain improve (see Figure 10.7). After the program was tested in 20 New York City schools, students strongly endorsed the value of the computer-based brain modules. Said one student, "I will try harder because I know that the more you try the more your brain knows" (Dweck & Master, 2009, p. 137).

Other research by Eva Pomerantz and her colleagues (Pomerantz, Cheung, & Qin, 2012; Pomerantz, Kim, & Cheung, 2012) indicates that the more involved parents are in children's learning, the higher the level of achievement children will attain. As indicated earlier, East Asian parents spend considerably more time helping their children with homework than do U.S. parents (Chen & Stevenson, 1989). This higher level of East Asian parental involvement in children's learning is present as early as the preschool years and continues in the elementary school years (Cheung & Pomerantz, 2012; Siegler & Mu, 2008). In East Asia, children's learning is considered to be a far greater responsibility of parents than in the United States (Pomerantz, Kim, & Cheung, 2012). However, a recent study revealed that when U.S. parents are more involved in their children's learning, the children's achievement benefits (Cheung & Pomerantz, 2012). In this study, for both U.S. and Chinese children, the more parents were involved in their children's learning, the more motivated the children were to achieve in school for parent-oriented reasons and this was linked to enhanced self-regulated learning and higher grades.

FIGURE **10.7**

DWECK'S BRAINOLOGY PROGRAM. A screen from Carol Dweck's Brainology program, which is designed to cultivate children's growth mindset.

topical **connections**

In adolescence, children begin spending more time thinking about their identity—who they are, what they are all about, and where they are going in life. Time spent with peers increases in adolescence and friendships become more intense and intimate. Dating and romantic relationships also become more central to the lives of most adolescents. Parents continue to have an important influence on adolescent development. Having good relationships with parents provides support for adolescents as they seek more autonomy and explore a widening social world. Problems that adolescents can develop include juvenile delinquency and depression.

looking forward ----➤

reach your **learning goals**

Socioemotional Development in Middle and Late Childhood

1 Emotional and Personality Development

LG1 Discuss emotional and personality development in middle and late childhood.

The Self

- In middle and late childhood, self-understanding increasingly involves social and psychological characteristics, including social comparison. Children increase their perspective taking in middle and late childhood, and their social understanding shows increasing psychological sophistication as well. Self-concept refers to domain-specific evaluations of the self. Self-esteem refers to global evaluations of the self and is also referred to as self-worth or self-image. Self-esteem is only moderately related to school performance but is more strongly linked to initiative. Four ways to increase self-esteem are to (1) identify the causes of low self-esteem, (2) provide emotional support and social approval, (3) help children achieve, and (4) help children cope. Self-efficacy is the belief that one can master a situation and produce positive outcomes. Bandura believes that self-efficacy is a critical factor in whether students will achieve. Schunk argues that self-efficacy influences a student's choice of tasks, with low-efficacy students avoiding many learning tasks. The development of self-regulation is an important aspect of children's development. Erikson's fourth stage of development, industry versus inferiority, characterizes the middle and late childhood years.

Emotional Development

- Developmental changes in emotion include increased understanding of complex emotions such as pride and shame, detecting that more than one emotion can be experienced in a particular situation, taking into account the circumstances that led up to an emotional reaction, improvements in the ability to suppress and conceal negative emotions, and the use of self-initiated strategies to redirect feelings. As children get older, they use a greater variety of coping strategies and more cognitive strategies.

Moral Development

- Kohlberg argued that moral development occurs on three levels—preconventional, conventional, and postconventional—and six stages (two at each level). Kohlberg maintained that these stages were age-related. Influences on movement through the stages include cognitive development, imitation and cognitive conflict, peer relations, and perspective taking. Criticisms of Kohlberg's theory have been made, especially by Gilligan, who advocates a stronger care perspective. Other criticisms focus on the inadequacy of moral reasoning to predict moral behavior, culture, and family influences. The domain theory of moral development states that there are different domains of social knowledge and reasoning, including moral, social conventional, and personal. Prosocial behavior involves positive moral behaviors such as sharing. Most sharing in the first three years is not done for empathy, but at about 4 years of age empathy contributes to sharing. By the start of the elementary school years, children express objective ideas about fairness. By the mid- to late elementary school years, children believe equity can mean that others with special needs/merit deserve special treatment. Recently, there has been a surge of interest in moral personality.

Gender

- Gender stereotypes are prevalent around the world. A number of physical differences exist between males and females. Some experts argue that cognitive differences between males and females have been exaggerated. In terms of socioemotional differences, males are more physically aggressive than females, whereas females regulate their emotions better and engage in more prosocial behavior than males. Gender-role classification focuses on the degree to which individuals are masculine, feminine, or androgynous. Androgyny means having positive feminine and masculine characteristics. It is important to think about gender in terms of context.

2 Families

LG2 Describe developmental changes in parent-child relationships, parents as managers, attachment, and stepfamilies.

Developmental Changes in Parent-Child Relationships

- Parents spend less time with children during middle and late childhood than in early childhood. Parents especially play an important role in supporting and stimulating children's academic achievement. Discipline changes, and control becomes more coregulatory.

Parents as Managers

- Parents have important roles as managers of children's opportunities, as monitors of their behavior, and as social initiators and arrangers. Mothers are more likely to function in these parental management roles than fathers are.

Attachment

- Secure attachment to parents is linked a lower level of internalized symptoms, anxiety, and depression in children during middle and late childhood.

Stepfamilies

- As in divorced families, children living in stepparent families face more adjustment problems than their counterparts in nondivorced families. However, a majority of children in stepfamilies do not have adjustment problems. Children in complex (blended) stepfamilies have more problems than children in simple stepfamilies or nondivorced families.

3 Peers

LG3 Identify changes in peer relationships in middle and late childhood.

Developmental Changes

- Among the developmental changes in peer relations in middle and late childhood are increased preference for same-sex groups, increased time spent in peer interaction and the size of the peer group, and less supervision of the peer group by adults.

Peer Status	• Popular children are frequently named as a best friend and are rarely disliked by their peers. Average children receive an average number of both positive and negative nominations from their peers. Neglected children are infrequently named as a best friend but are not disliked by their peers. Rejected children are infrequently named as a best friend and are actively disliked by their peers. Controversial children are frequently named both as a best friend and as being disliked by peers. Rejected children are especially at risk for a number of problems.
Social Cognition	• Social information-processing skills and social knowledge are two important dimensions of social cognition in peer relations.
Bullying	• Significant numbers of children are bullied, and this can result in short-term and long-term negative effects for both the victims and bullies.
Friends	• Like adult friends, children who are friends tend to be similar to each other. Children's friendships serve six functions: companionship, stimulation, physical support, ego support, social comparison, and intimacy/affection.

4 Schools

LG4 Characterize aspects of schooling in children's development in middle and late childhood.

Contemporary Approaches to Student Learning

• Two contemporary issues involve whether it is best to educate students by using a constructivist approach (a learner-centered approach) or a direct instruction approach (a teacher-centered approach) and how to hold teachers accountable for whether children are learning. In the United States, standardized testing of elementary school students has been mandated by many state governments and by the No Child Left Behind federal legislation. Numerous criticisms of NCLB have been made.

Socioeconomic Status, Ethnicity, and Culture

• Children in poverty face many barriers to learning at school as well as at home. The effects of SES and ethnicity on schools are intertwined, and many U.S. schools are segregated. Low expectations for ethnic minority children represent one of the barriers to their learning. American children are more achievement-oriented than children in many countries but are less achievement-oriented than many children in Asian countries such as China, Taiwan, and Japan. Mindset is the cognitive view, either fixed or growth, that individuals develop for themselves. Dweck argues that a key aspect of supporting children's development is to guide them in developing a growth mindset. Pomerantz emphasizes that parental involvment is a key aspect of children's achievement.

key terms

perspective taking 318
self-esteem 319
self-concept 319
self-efficacy 320
preconventional reasoning 324
heteronomous morality 324
individualism, instrumental purpose, and exchange 324
conventional reasoning 324

mutual interpersonal expectations, relationships, and interpersonal conformity 324
social systems morality 324
postconventional reasoning 324
social contract or utility and individual rights 325

universal ethical principles 325
justice perspective 327
care perspective 327
domain theory of moral development 327
social conventional reasoning 327
gender stereotypes 328
androgyny 331

popular children 336
average children 336
neglected children 336
rejected children 336
controversial children 336
intimacy in friendships 339
constructivist approach 340
direct instruction approach 341
mindset 345

key people

Diane Ruble 318
Albert Bandura 320
Dale Schunk 320
Jonathan Kozol 317
Erik Erikson 321
Lawrence Kohlberg 323

Carol Gilligan 326
William Damon 327
Sandra Bem 331
William Pollack 331
Kathryn Kerns 333
E. Mavis Hetherington 334

John Coie 336
Kenneth Dodge 337
Dan Olweus 339
Willard Hartup 339
Eliot Aronson 343
James Comer 344

Harold Stevenson 345
Carol Dweck 345
Eva Pomerantz 346

Chapter 10 | SOCIOEMOTIONAL DEVELOPMENT IN MIDDLE AND LATE CHILDHOOD

Connecting with

Learning Objectives	Application Activities	Activity Type	Page Reference
Discuss the self during middle and late childhood.	Self-Perception at 10 Years and 8 Years of Age	Video	pp. 318–321
Characterize moral development during middle and late childhood.	Kohlberg's Moral Reasoning, Part 1	Click & drag activity	pp. 323–328
	Kohlberg's Moral Reasoning, Part 2	Click & drag activity	
	Stages of Moral Development	Interactive exercise	
	Kohlberg's Moral Reasoning	Interactive exercise	
Describe developmental changes in parent-child relationships during middle and late childhood.	Relationships with Parents at Age 11	Video	pp. 332–334
Summarize bullying during middle and late childhood.	Characteristics of Children Who Bully	Video	pp. 337–339
	Characteristics of School Shooters	Video	
	Developmental Changes in Bullying	Video	
Discuss the role of friends during middle and late childhood.	Describing Friendships at Age 8	Video	pp. 339–340
	Describing a Best Friend at Age 10	Video	
	Describing a Best Friend at Age 11	Video	

section **six**

In no order of things is adolescence the simple time of life.

—JEAN ERSKINE STEWART
American Writer, 20th Century

Adolescence

Adolescents try on one face after another, seeking to find a face of their own. Their generation of young people is the fragile cable by which the best and the worst of their parents' generation is transmitted to the present. In the end, there are only two lasting bequests parents can leave youth—one is roots, the other wings. Section 6 contains two chapters: "Physical and Cognitive Development in Adolescence" (Chapter 11) and "Socioemotional Development in Adolescence" (Chapter 12).

chapter 11

PHYSICAL AND COGNITIVE DEVELOPMENT IN ADOLESCENCE

chapter outline

1 The Nature of Adolescence

Learning Goal 1 Discuss the nature of adolescence.

2 Physical Changes

Learning Goal 2 Describe the changes involved in puberty, as well as the changes in the brain and sexuality during adolescence.

Puberty
The Brain
Adolescent Sexuality

3 Issues in Adolescent Health

Learning Goal 3 Identify adolescent problems related to health, substance use and abuse, and eating disorders.

Adolescent Health
Substance Use and Abuse
Eating Disorders

4 Adolescent Cognition

Learning Goal 4 Explain cognitive changes in adolescence.

Piaget's Theory
Adolescent Egocentrism
Information Processing

5 Schools

Learning Goal 5 Summarize some key aspects of how schools influence adolescent development.

The Transition to Middle or Junior High School
Effective Schools for Young Adolescents
High School
Extracurricular Activities
Service Learning

Fifteen-year-old Latisha developed a drinking problem, and she was kicked off the cheerleading squad for missing practice so often—but that didn't stop her drinking. She and her friends began skipping school regularly so they could drink.

Fourteen-year-old Arnie is a juvenile delinquent. Last week he stole a TV set, struck his mother and bloodied her face, broke some streetlights in the neighborhood, and threatened a boy with a wrench and hammer.

Twelve-year-old Katie, more than just about anything else, wanted a playground in her town. She knew that the other kids also wanted one, so she put together a group that generated funding ideas for the playground. They presented their ideas to the town council. Her group involved more youth, and they raised money by selling candy and sandwiches door-to-door. The playground became a reality, a place where, as Katie says, "People have picnics and make friends." Katie's advice: "You won't get anywhere if you don't try."

Adolescents like Latisha and Arnie are the ones we hear about the most. But there are many adolescents like Katie who contribute in positive ways to their community and competently make the transition through adolescence. Indeed, for most adolescents, adolescence is not a time of rebellion, crisis, pathology, and deviance. A far more accurate vision of adolescence is that it is a time of evaluation, decision making, commitment, and carving out a place in the world. Most of the problems of today's youth are not with the youth themselves, but with needs that go unmet. To reach their full potential, adolescents need a range of legitimate opportunities as well as long-term support from adults who care deeply about them (Balsano, Theokas, & Bobek, 2009; Lerner & others, 2012; Swanson, Edwards, & Spencer, 2010).

Katie Bell (*front*) and some of her volunteers.

·-topical **connections** ----------------------

In middle and late childhood, physical growth continues but at a slower pace than in infancy and early childhood. Gross motor skills become much smoother and more coordinated, and fine motor skills also improve. Significant advances in the development of the prefrontal cortex occur. Cognitive and language skills also improve considerably. In terms of cognitive development, most children become concrete operational thinkers, long-term memory increases, and metacognitive skills improve, especially if children learn a rich repertoire of strategies. In terms of language development, children's understanding of grammar and syntax increases, and learning to read becomes an important achievement.

◄ - - - *looking **back*** -

preview

Adolescence is a transitional period in the human life span, linking childhood and adulthood. We begin the chapter by examining some general characteristics of adolescence and then explore the major physical changes and health issues of adolescence. Next, we consider the significant cognitive changes that characterize adolescence and conclude the chapter by describing various aspects of schools for adolescents.

1 The Nature of Adolescence

LG1 Discuss the nature of adolescence.

As in development during childhood, genetic/biological and environmental/social factors influence adolescent development. During their childhood years, adolescents experienced thousands of hours of interactions with parents, peers, and teachers, but now they face dramatic biological changes, new experiences, and new developmental tasks. Relationships with parents take a different form, moments with peers become more intimate, and dating occurs for the first time, as do sexual exploration and possibly intercourse. The adolescent's thoughts become more abstract and idealistic. Biological changes trigger a heightened interest in body image. Adolescence has both continuity and discontinuity with childhood.

There is a long history of worrying about how adolescents will "turn out." In 1904, G. Stanley Hall proposed the "storm-and-stress" view that adolescence is a turbulent time charged with conflict and mood swings. However, when Daniel Offer and his colleagues (1988) studied the self-images of adolescents in the United States, Australia, Bangladesh, Hungary, Israel, Italy, Japan, Taiwan, Turkey, and West Germany, at least 73 percent of the adolescents displayed a healthy self-image. Although there were differences among them, the adolescents were happy most of the time, they enjoyed life, they perceived themselves as able to exercise self-control, they valued work and school, they felt confident about their sexual selves, they expressed positive feelings toward their families, and they felt they had the capability to cope with life's stresses—not exactly a storm-and-stress portrayal of adolescence.

Public attitudes about adolescence emerge from a combination of personal experience and media portrayals, neither of which produces an objective picture of how normal adolescents develop (Feldman & Elliott, 1990). Some of the readiness to assume the worst about adolescents likely involves the short memories of adults. Many adults measure their current perceptions of adolescents by their memories of their own adolescence. Adults may portray

Growing up has never been easy. However, adolescence is not best viewed as a time of rebellion, crisis, pathology, and deviance. A far more accurate vision of adolescence describes it as a time of evaluation, of decision making, of commitment, and of carving out a place in the world. Most of the problems of today's youth are not with the youth themselves. What adolescents need is access to a range of legitimate opportunities and to long-term support from adults who care deeply about them. *What might be some examples of such support and caring?*

today's adolescents as more troubled, less respectful, more self-centered, more assertive, and more adventurous than they were.

However, in matters of taste and manners, the young people of every generation have seemed unnervingly radical and different from adults—different in how they look, in how they behave, in the music they enjoy, in their hairstyles, and in the clothing they choose. It would be an enormous error, though, to confuse adolescents' enthusiasm for trying on new identities and enjoying moderate amounts of outrageous behavior with hostility toward parental and societal standards. Acting out and boundary testing are time-honored ways in which adolescents move toward accepting, rather than rejecting, parental values.

Most adolescents negotiate the lengthy path to adult maturity successfully, but too large a group does not. Ethnic, cultural, gender, socioeconomic, age, and lifestyle differences influence the actual life trajectory of each adolescent (Astell-Burt & others, 2012; Chen & Brooks-Gunn, 2012; Soenens & Beyers, 2012). Different portrayals of adolescence emerge, depending on the particular group of adolescents being described. Today's adolescents are exposed to a complex menu of lifestyle options through the media, and many face the temptations of drug use and sexual activity at increasingly young ages. Too many adolescents are not provided with adequate opportunities and support to become competent adults (Jackson & others, 2012; Lerner & others, 2012).

Recall from Chapter 1 that *social policy* is the course of action designed by the national government to influence the welfare of its citizens. Currently, many researchers in adolescent development are designing studies that they hope will lead to wise and effective social policy decision making (Eccles & Roeser, 2013; Feinstein, Richter, & Foster, 2012; Lerner & others, 2012).

Peter Benson and his colleagues (Benson, 2010; Benson, Roehlkepartain, & Scales, 2012; Benson & Scales, 2009, 2011; Scales, Benson, & Roehlkepartain, 2011) argue that the United States has a fragmented social policy for youth that too often has focused only on the negative developmental deficits of adolescents, especially health-compromising behaviors such as drug use and delinquency, and not enough on positive, strength-based approaches. According to Benson and his colleagues (2004, p. 783), a strength-based approach to social policy for youth

> adopts more of a wellness perspective, places particular emphasis on the existence of healthy conditions, and expands the concept of health to include the skills and competencies needed to succeed in employment, education, and life. It moves beyond the eradication of risk and deliberately argues for the promotion of well-being.

Research indicates that youth benefit enormously when they have caring adults in their lives in addition to parents or guardians (Gardner, Martin, & Brooks-Gunn, 2012). Caring adults—such as coaches, neighbors, teachers, mentors, and after-school leaders—can serve as role models, confidants, advocates, and resources. Relationships with caring adults are powerful when youth know they are respected, that they matter to the adult, and that the adult wants to be a resource in their lives. However, in a recent survey, only 20 percent of U.S. 15-year-olds reported having meaningful relationships with adults outside their family that are helping them to succeed in life (Search Institute, 2010).

Review *Connect* Reflect

 LG1 Discuss the nature of adolescence.

Review

- What characterizes adolescent development? What especially needs to be done to improve the lives of adolescents?

Connect

- In this section you read about how important it is for adolescents to have caring adults in their lives. In previous chapters, what did you learn about the role parents play in their children's lives *leading up to* adolescence that might influence adolescents' development?

Reflect *Your Own Personal Journey of Life*

- Was your adolescence better described as a stormy and stressful time or as one of trying out new identities as you sought to find an identity of your own? Explain.

2 Physical Changes LG2 Describe the changes involved in puberty, as well as the changes in the brain and sexuality during adolescence.

Puberty   The Brain   Adolescent Sexuality

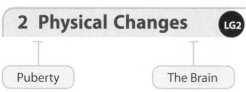

One father remarked that the problem with his teenage son was not that he grew, but that he did not know when to stop growing. As we will see, there is considerable variation in the timing of the adolescent growth spurt. In addition to pubertal changes, other physical changes we will explore involve sexuality and the brain.

PUBERTY

Puberty is not the same as adolescence. For most of us, puberty ends long before adolescence does, although puberty is the most important marker of the beginning of adolescence. **Puberty** is a period of rapid physical maturation involving hormonal and bodily changes that occurs primarily during early adolescence. Puberty is not a single, sudden event. We know whether a young boy or girl is going through puberty, but pinpointing puberty's beginning and end is difficult (Dorn & Biro, 2011; Susman & Dorn, 2013). Among the most noticeable changes are signs of sexual maturation and increases in height and weight.

Sexual Maturation, Height, and Weight   Think back to the onset of your puberty. Of the striking changes that were taking place in your body, what was the first to occur? Researchers have found that male pubertal characteristics typically develop in this order: increase in penis and testicle size, appearance of straight pubic hair, minor voice change, first ejaculation (which usually occurs through masturbation or a wet dream), appearance of kinky pubic hair, onset of maximum growth in height and weight, growth of hair in armpits, more detectable voice changes, and, finally, growth of facial hair.

What is the order of appearance of physical changes in females? First, either the breasts enlarge or pubic hair appears. Later, hair appears in the armpits. As these changes occur, the female grows in height and her hips become wider than her shoulders. **Menarche**—a girl's first menstruation—comes rather late in the pubertal cycle. Initially, her menstrual cycles may be highly irregular. For the first several years, she may not ovulate every menstrual cycle; some girls do not ovulate at all until a year or two after menstruation begins. No voice changes comparable to those in pubertal males occur in pubertal females. By the end of puberty, the female's breasts have become more fully rounded.

Marked weight gains coincide with the onset of puberty. During early adolescence, girls tend to outweigh boys, but by about age 14 boys begin to surpass girls. Similarly, at the beginning of

ZITS By Jerry Scott and Jim Borgman

ZITS © ZITS Partnership. King Features Syndicate.

puberty A period of rapid physical maturation, occurring primarily in early adolescence, that involves hormonal and bodily changes.

menarche A girl's first menstruation.

the adolescent period, girls tend to be as tall as or taller than boys of their age, but by the end of the middle school years most boys have caught up or, in many cases, surpassed girls in height.

As indicated in Figure 11.1, the growth spurt occurs approximately two years earlier for girls than for boys. The mean age at the beginning of the growth spurt in girls is 9; for boys, it is 11. The peak rate of pubertal change occurs at 11½ years for girls and 13½ years for boys. During their growth spurt, girls increase in height about 3½ inches per year, boys about 4 inches. Boys and girls who are shorter or taller than their peers before adolescence are likely to remain so during adolescence; however, as much as 30 percent of an individual's height in late adolescence is unexplained by his or her height in the elementary school years.

Hormonal Changes   Behind the first whisker in boys and the widening of hips in girls is a flood of **hormones,** powerful chemical substances secreted by the endocrine glands and carried through the body by the bloodstream.

The concentrations of certain hormones increase dramatically during adolescence (Nguyen & others, 2012). *Testosterone* is a hormone associated in boys with genital development, increased height, and deepening of the voice. *Estradiol* is a type of estrogen that in girls is associated with breast, uterine, and skeletal development. In one study, testosterone levels increased eighteen-fold in boys but only twofold in girls during puberty; estradiol increased eightfold in girls but only twofold in boys (Nottelmann & others, 1987). Thus, both testosterone and estradiol are present in the hormonal makeup of both boys and girls, but testosterone dominates in male pubertal development, estradiol in female pubertal development.

The same influx of hormones that grows hair on a male's chest and increases the fatty tissue in a female's breasts may also contribute to psychological development in adolescence (Dorn & Biro, 2011; Susman & Dorn, 2013; Tyrka & others, 2012). In one study of boys and girls ranging in age from 9 to 14, a higher concentration of testosterone was present in boys who rated themselves as more socially competent (Nottelmann & others, 1987). However, hormonal effects by themselves do not account for adolescent development (Susman & Dorn, 2013). For example, in one study, social factors were much better predictors of young adolescent girls' depression and anger than hormonal factors (Brooks-Gunn & Warren, 1989). Behavior and moods also can affect hormones (DeRose & Brooks-Gunn, 2008). Stress, eating patterns, exercise, sexual activity, tension, and depression can activate or suppress various aspects of the hormonal system (Marceau, Dorn, & Susman, 2012). In sum, the hormone-behavior link is complex (Susman & Dorn, 2013).

Timing and Variations in Puberty   In the United States—where children mature up to a year earlier than children in European countries—the average age of menarche has declined significantly since the mid-nineteenth century (see Figure 11.2). Fortunately, however, we are unlikely to see pubescent toddlers, since what has happened in the past century is likely the result of improved nutrition and health.

Why do the changes of puberty occur when they do, and how can variations in their timing be explained? The basic genetic program for puberty is wired into the species (Dvornyk & Waqar-ul-Haq, 2012), but nutrition, health, family stress, and other environmental factors also affect puberty's timing and makeup (James & others, 2012). A recent cross-cultural study in 29 countries found that childhood obesity was linked to early puberty in girls (Currie & others, 2012).

For most boys, the pubertal sequence may begin as early as age 10 or as late as 13½, and it may end as early as age 13 or as late as 17. Thus, the normal range is wide enough that, given two boys of the same chronological age, one might complete the pubertal sequence before the other one has begun it. For girls, menarche is considered within the normal range if it appears between the ages of 9 and 15. An increasing number of U.S. girls are beginning puberty at 8 and 9 years of age, with African American girls developing earlier than non-Latino White girls (Herman-Giddens, 2007; Sorensen & others, 2012).

Body Image   One psychological aspect of physical change in puberty is universal: Adolescents are preoccupied with their bodies and develop images of what their bodies are like (Holsen, Carolson Jones, & Skogbrott Birkeland, 2012). Preoccupation with body image is

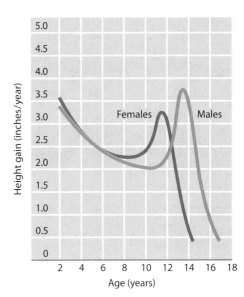

FIGURE 11.1

PUBERTAL GROWTH SPURT. On average, the peak of the growth spurt during puberty occurs two years earlier for girls (11½) than for boys (13½). *How are hormones related to the growth spurt and to the difference between the average height of adolescent boys and that of girls?*

What are some of the differences in the ways girls and boys experience pubertal growth?

hormones Powerful chemical substances secreted by the endocrine glands and carried through the body by the bloodstream.

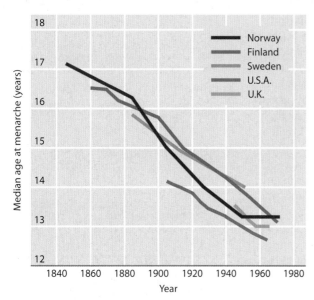

FIGURE **11.2**

AGE AT MENARCHE IN NORTHERN EUROPEAN COUNTRIES AND THE UNITED STATES IN THE NINETEENTH AND TWENTIETH CENTURIES. Notice the steep decline in the age at which girls experienced menarche in four northern European countries and the United States from 1845 to 1969. Recently the age at which girls experience menarche has been leveling off.

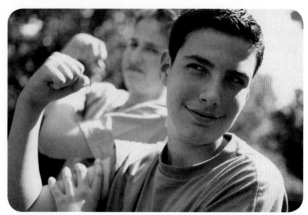

Adolescents show a strong preoccupation with their changing bodies and develop images of what their bodies are like. *Why might adolescent males have more positive body images than adolescent females?*

strong throughout adolescence but is especially acute during early adolescence, a time when adolescents are more dissatisfied with their bodies than in late adolescence.

Gender differences characterize adolescents' perceptions of their bodies. In general, girls are less happy with their bodies and have more negative body images than boys throughout puberty (Bearman & others, 2006). Girls' more negative body images may be due to media portrayals of the attractiveness of being thin and the increase in body fat in girls during puberty (Benowitz-Fredericks & others, 2012). A recent study found that both boys' and girls' body images became more positive as they moved from the beginning to the end of adolescence (Holsen, Carlson Jones, & Skogbrott Birkeland, 2012).

Two recent studies shed further light on gender differences in body image during adolescence:

- Adolescent girls place a higher aesthetic value on body image but have a lower aesthetic satisfaction with their bodies than do adolescent boys (Abbott & Barber, 2010).
- The profile of adolescents with the most positive body images is characterized by health-enhancing behaviors, especially regular exercise (Frisen & Holmqvist, 2010).

Early and Late Maturation You may have entered puberty earlier or later than average, or perhaps you were right on schedule. Adolescents who mature earlier or later than their peers perceive themselves differently (Susman & Dorn, 2013). In the Berkeley Longitudinal Study some years ago, early-maturing boys perceived themselves more positively and had more successful peer relations than did their late-maturing counterparts (Jones, 1965). When the late-maturing boys were in their thirties, however, they had developed a stronger sense of identity than the early-maturing boys had (Peskin, 1967). This identity development may have occurred because the late-maturing boys had more time to explore life's options, or because the early-maturing boys continued to focus on their advantageous physical status instead of on career development and achievement. More recent research confirms, though, that at least during adolescence it is advantageous to be an early-maturing rather than a late-maturing boy (Graber, Brooks-Gunn, & Warren, 2006).

For girls, early and late maturation have been linked with body image. In the sixth grade, early-maturing girls show greater satisfaction with their figures than do late-maturing girls, but by the tenth grade late-maturing girls are more satisfied (Simmons & Blyth, 1987) (see Figure 11.3). One possible reason for this is that in late adolescence early-maturing girls are shorter and stockier, whereas late-maturing girls are taller and thinner. Thus, late-maturing girls in late adolescence have bodies that more closely approximate the current American ideal of feminine beauty—tall and thin.

An increasing number of researchers have found that early maturation increases girls' vulnerability to a number of problems (Bralic & others, 2012; DeRose & others, 2011). Early-maturing girls are more likely to smoke, drink, be depressed, have an eating disorder, engage

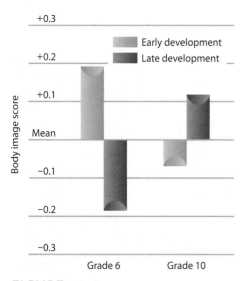

FIGURE **11.3**

EARLY- AND LATE-MATURING ADOLESCENT GIRLS' PERCEPTIONS OF BODY IMAGE IN EARLY AND LATE ADOLESCENCE. The sixth-grade girls in this study had positive body image scores if they were early maturers but negative body image scores if they were late maturers (Simmons & Blyth, 1987). Positive body image scores indicated satisfaction with their figures. By the tenth grade, however, it was the late maturers who had positive body image scores.

in delinquency, struggle for earlier independence from their parents, and have older friends; and their bodies are likely to elicit responses from males that lead to earlier dating and earlier sexual experiences (Baker & others, 2012; Negriff, Susman, & Trickett, 2011). And early-maturing girls are less likely to graduate from high school and tend to cohabit and marry earlier (Cavanagh, 2009). Apparently as a result of their social and cognitive immaturity, combined with early physical development, early-maturing girls are easily lured into problem behaviors, not recognizing the possible long-term negative effects on their development.

THE BRAIN

Along with the rest of the body, the brain changes during adolescence, but the study of adolescent brain development is still in its infancy. As advances in technology take place, significant strides will also likely be made in charting developmental changes in the adolescent brain (Brynes, 2012; Reyna & others, 2012). What do we know now?

Recall from our discussion of brain development in Chapter 4 that researchers have discovered that nearly twice as many synaptic connections are made as will ever be used (Huttenlocher & Dabholkar, 1997). The connections that are used are strengthened and survive, while the unused ones are replaced by other pathways or disappear. That is, in the language of neuroscience, these connections will be "pruned." As a result of this pruning, by the end of adolescence individuals have "fewer, more selective, more effective neuronal connections than they did as children" (Kuhn, 2009, p. 153). And this pruning indicates that the activities adolescents choose to engage in and not to engage in influence which neural connections will be strengthened and which will disappear.

Using fMRI brain scans, scientists have recently discovered that adolescents' brains undergo significant structural changes (Giedd & others, 2012). The **corpus callosum,** where fibers connect the brain's left and right hemispheres, thickens in adolescence, and this improves adolescents' ability to process information (Gilliam & others, 2011). We described advances in the development of the prefrontal cortex—the highest level of the frontal lobes involved in reasoning, decision making, and self-control—in Chapter 9. However, the prefrontal cortex doesn't finish maturing until the emerging adult years, approximately 18 to 25 years of age, or later, whereas the **amygdala**—the seat of emotions such as anger—matures earlier than the prefrontal cortex (Chick & Reyna, 2012; Giedd & others, 2012). Figure 11.4 shows the locations of the corpus callosum, prefrontal cortex, and amygdala.

Many of the changes in the adolescent brain that have been described involve the rapidly emerging field of *social developmental neuroscience,* which focuses on connections between development, the brain, and socioemotional processes (Pfeifer & Blakemore, 2012). For example, consider leading researcher Charles Nelson's (2003) view that, although adolescents are capable of very strong emotions, their prefrontal cortex hasn't adequately developed to the point at which they can control these passions. It is as if their brain doesn't have the brakes to slow down their emotions. Or consider this interpretation of the development of emotion and cognition in adolescents: "early activation of strong 'turbo-charged' feelings with a relatively unskilled set of 'driving skills' or cognitive abilities to modulate strong emotions and motivations" (Dahl, 2004, p. 18).

Of course, a major question is which comes first, biological changes in the brain or experiences that stimulate these changes (Lerner, Boyd, & Du, 2008; Steinberg, 2012, 2013). Consider a study in which the prefrontal cortex thickened and more brain connections formed when adolescents resisted peer pressure (Paus & others, 2007). Scientists have yet to determine whether the brain changes come first or whether they result from experiences with peers, parents, and others. Once again, we encounter the nature-nurture issue that is so prominent in an examination of development through the life span.

Prefrontal cortex
This "judgment" region reins in intense emotions but doesn't finish developing until at least emerging adulthood.

Corpus callosum
These nerve fibers connect the brain's two hemispheres; they thicken in adolescence to process information more effectively.

Amygdala
The seat of emotions such as anger; this area develops quickly before other regions that help to control it.

FIGURE **11.4**
CHANGES IN THE ADOLESCENT BRAIN

developmental **connection**

Brain Development

Although the prefrontal cortex shows considerable development in childhood, it is still not fully mature in adolescence. Chapter 9, p. 283

corpus callosum The location where fibers connect the brain's left and right hemispheres.

amygdala The region of the brain that is the seat of emotions.

ADOLESCENT SEXUALITY

Not only is adolescence characterized by substantial changes in physical growth and the development of the brain, but adolescence also is a bridge between the asexual child and the sexual adult (Tolman & McClelland, 2011). Adolescence is a time of sexual exploration and experimentation, of sexual fantasies and realities, of incorporating sexuality into one's identity. Adolescents have an almost insatiable curiosity about sexuality. They are concerned about whether they are sexually attractive, how to do sex, and what the future holds for their sexual lives. Although most adolescents experience times of vulnerability and confusion, the majority will eventually develop a mature sexual identity. In the United States, information about sexuality is widely available to adolescents. They learn a great deal about sex from television, videos, magazines, the lyrics of popular music, and Web sites (Epstein & Ward, 2008; Ward & others, 2011; Welch, 2011).

Developing a Sexual Identity   Mastering emerging sexual feelings and forming a sense of sexual identity are multifaceted and lengthy processes (Allen & Diamond, 2012; Diamond, 2013). They involve learning to manage sexual feelings (such as sexual arousal and attraction), developing new forms of intimacy, and learning how to regulate sexual behavior to avoid undesirable consequences. Developing a sexual identity also involves more than just sexual behavior. Sexual identities emerge in the context of physical factors, social factors, and cultural factors, with most societies placing constraints on the sexual behavior of adolescents.

An adolescent's sexual identity involves activities, interests, styles of behavior, and an indication of sexual orientation (whether an individual has same-sex or other-sex attractions, or both) (Buzwell & Rosenthal, 1996). For example, some adolescents have a high anxiety level about sex, others a low level. Some adolescents are strongly aroused sexually, others less so. Some adolescents are very active sexually, others not at all (Haydon & others, 2012). Some adolescents are sexually inactive in response to their strong religious upbringing; others go to church regularly and yet their religious training does not inhibit their sexual activity (Thorton & Camburn, 1989).

It is commonly thought that most gays and lesbians quietly struggle with same-sex attractions in childhood, do not engage in heterosexual dating, and gradually recognize that they are a gay or lesbian in mid- to late adolescence. Many youth do follow this developmental pathway, but others do not (Cohen & Savin-Williams, 2013; Diamond, 2013). For example, many youth have no recollection of early same-sex attractions and experience a more abrupt sense of their same-sex attraction in late adolescence. The majority of adolescents with same-sex attractions also experience some degree of other-sex attractions (Hock, 2012). Even though some adolescents who are attracted to individuals of their same sex fall in love with these individuals, others claim that their same-sex attractions are purely physical (Diamond & Savin-Willlams, 2013; Savin-Williams, 2013).

In sum, gay and lesbian youth have diverse patterns of initial attraction, often have bisexual attractions, and may have physical or emotional attraction to same-sex individuals but do not always fall in love with them (Diamond, 2013; Savin-Williams, 2011, 2013). In Chapter 13, "Physical and Cognitive Development in Early Adulthood," we will further explore same-sex and heterosexual attraction.

The Timing of Adolescent Sexual Behaviors   What is the current profile of sexual activity of adolescents? In a U.S. national survey conducted in 2009, 62 percent of twelfth-graders reported that they had experienced sexual intercourse, compared with 32 percent of ninth-graders (Eaton & others, 2010). By age 20, 77 percent of U.S. youth have engaged in sexual intercourse (Dworkin & Santelli, 2007). Nationally, 49 percent of twelfth-graders, 40 percent of eleventh-graders, 29 percent of tenth-graders, and 21 percent of ninth-graders reported being sexually active (Eaton & others, 2010).

What trends in adolescent sexual activity have occurred in the last two decades? From 1991 to 2009, fewer adolescents reported ever having had sexual intercourse, currently being sexually active, having had sexual intercourse

Adolescents are exposed to sex virtually everywhere in the American culture, and sex is used to sell just about everything.

before the age of 13, and having had sexual intercourse with four or more persons during their lifetime (Eaton & others, 2010).

Until very recently, at all grade levels, adolescent males were more likely than adolescent females to report having had sexual intercourse and being sexually active (MMWR, 2006). However, in the 2009 national survey, a higher percentage of twelfth-grade females (65 percent) reported having had sexual intercourse than twelfth-grade males (60 percent); a higher percentage of ninth-grade males (34 percent) still reported having had sexual intercourse than ninth-grade females (29 percent) (Eaton & others, 2010). (See Figure 11.5.) Adolescent males are more likely than their female counterparts to describe sexual intercourse as an enjoyable experience.

Sexual initiation varies by ethnic group in the United States (Tolman & McClelland, 2011). In a recent national U.S. survey of ninth- to twelfth-graders, 67 percent of African Americans, 51 percent of Latinos, and 43 percent of non-Latino Whites said they had experienced sexual intercourse (Eaton & others, 2010). In this study, 15 percent of African Americans (compared with 7 percent of Latinos and 3 percent of non-Latino Whites) reported having had their first sexual experience before 13 years of age. Other research indicates that Asian American adolescents engage in sexual intercourse later than non-Latino Whites and adolescents from other ethnic groups (Feldman, Turner, & Araujo, 1999).

Recent research indicates that oral sex is now a common occurrence among U.S. adolescents (Fava & Bay-Cheng, 2012; Song & Halpern-Felsher, 2010). In a national survey, 55 percent of U.S. 15- to 19-year-old boys and 54 percent of girls said they had engaged in oral sex (National Center for Health Statistics, 2002).

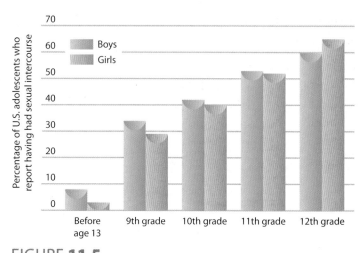

FIGURE **11.5**

TIMING OF SEXUAL INTERCOURSE IN U.S. ADOLESCENTS

Risk Factors in Adolescent Sexual Behavior   Many adolescents are not emotionally prepared to handle sexual experiences, especially in early adolescence. Early sexual activity is linked with risky behaviors such as drug use, delinquency, and school-related problems (Sales & others, 2012; Yi & others, 2010). Other risk factors for sexual problems in adolescence include contextual factors such as socioeconomic status (SES) and poverty, family/parenting and peer factors (Van Ryzin & others, 2011). A recent study revealed that neighborhood poverty concentrations predicted 15- to 17-year-old girls' and boys' sexual initiation (Cubbin & others, 2010).

A number of family factors are linked to sexuality outcomes for adolescents (Morales-Campos & others, 2012). A research review indicated that the following aspects of connectedness predicted sexual and reproductive health outcomes for youth: family connectedness, parent-adolescent communication about sexuality, parental monitoring, and partner connectedness (Markham & others, 2010). A recent study in low-income neighborhoods found that caregiver hostility was linked to early sexual activity and sex with multiple partners while caregiver warmth was related to later sexual initiation and a lower incidence of sex with multiple partners (Gardner, Martin, & Brooks-Gunn, 2012). Also, having older sexually active siblings or pregnant/parenting teenage sisters placed adolescent girls at increased risk for pregnancy (Miller, Benson, & Galbraith, 2001). Further, recent research indicated that associating with more deviant peers in early adolescence was related to having more sexual partners at age 16 (Lansford & others, 2010). And a recent research review found that school connectedness was linked to positive sexuality outcomes (Markham & others, 2010). A recent study also found that a high level of impulsiveness was linked to early adolescent sexual risk-taking (Khurana & others, 2012).

Contraceptive Use   Are adolescents increasingly using condoms? A recent national study revealed a substantial increase in the use of contraceptives (61 percent in 2009 compared with 46 percent in 1991) by U.S. high school students the last time they had sexual intercourse (Eaton & others, 2010). However, in this study, condom use by U.S. adolescents did not significantly change from 2003 through 2009.

Many sexually active adolescents still do not use contraceptives, or they use them inconsistently (Tschann & others, 2010). In 2009, 34 percent of sexually active adolescents did not use a condom the last time they had sexual intercourse (Eaton & others, 2010). Younger adolescents are less likely than older adolescents to take contraceptive precautions. A recent

<hr />

developmental **connection**

Sexuality

What characterizes the sexual activity of emerging adults (18 to 25 years of age)? Chapter 13, p. 432

What are some risks associated with early initiation of sexual intercourse?

Psychologists are exploring ways to encourage adolescents to make less risky sexual decisions. Here an adolescent participates in an interactive video session developed by Julie Downs and her colleagues at the Department of Social and Decision Making Sciences at Carnegie Mellon University. The videos help adolescents evaluate their responses and decisions in high-risk sexual contexts.

FIGURE 11.6

CROSS-CULTURAL COMPARISONS OF ADOLESCENT PREGNANCY RATES. Pregnancy rates among U.S. adolescents are among the highest in the industrialized world.

- - - - - - - - - ⟫

developmental **connection**

Conditions, Diseases, and Disorders

What are some good strategies for protecting against HIV and other sexually transmitted infections? Chapter 13, p. 434

What are some consequences of adolescent pregnancy?

sexually transmitted infections (STIs) Infections that are contracted primarily through sexual contact, including oral-genital and anal-genital contact.

study also found that 50 percent of U.S. 15- to 19-year-old girls with unintended pregnancies ending in live births were not using any birth control method when they got pregnant and 34 percent believed they could not get pregnant at the time (Centers for Disease Control and Prevention, 2012a).

Sexually Transmitted Infections   Some forms of contraception, such as birth control pills or implants, do not protect against sexually transmitted infections, or STIs. **Sexually transmitted infections (STIs)** are contracted primarily through sexual contact, including oral-genital and anal-genital contact. Every year more than 3 million American adolescents (about one-fourth of those who are sexually experienced) acquire an STI (Centers for Disease Control and Prevention, 2012b). In a single act of unprotected sex with an infected partner, a teenage girl has a 1 percent risk of getting HIV, a 30 percent risk of acquiring genital herpes, and a 50 percent chance of contracting gonorrhea (Glei, 1999). Yet another very widespread STI is chlamydia. In Chapter 13, we will consider these and other sexually transmitted infections.

Adolescent Pregnancy   In cross-cultural comparisons, the United States continues to have one of the highest adolescent pregnancy and childbearing rates in the industrialized world, despite a considerable decline in the 1990s. (See Figure 11.6.) The U.S. adolescent pregnancy rate is eight times as high as that in the Netherlands. Although U.S. adolescents are no more sexually active than their counterparts in the Netherlands, their adolescent pregnancy rate is dramatically higher.

Despite the negative comparisons of the United States with many other developed countries, there have been some encouraging trends in U.S. adolescent pregnancy rates. In 2009, births to adolescent girls fell to a record low (Ventura & Hamilton, 2011). The U.S. adolescent birth rate decreased by 8 percent from 2007 to 2009 (Ventura & Hamilton, 2011). Fear of sexually transmitted infections, especially AIDS; school/community health classes; and higher hopes for the future are the likely reasons for declining pregnancy rates in U.S. adolescents in recent decades.

Ethnic variations characterize birth rates for U.S. adolescents (Centers for Disease Control and Prevention, 2012a) (see Figure 11.7). Latina adolescents are more likely than African American and non-Latina White adolescents to have a child (Ventura & Hamilton, 2011). Latina and African American adolescent girls who have a child are also more likely to have a second child than are non-Latina White adolescent girls (Rosengard, 2009). And daughters of teenage mothers are at increased risk for teenage childbearing, thus perpetuating an intergenerational cycle (Meade, Kershaw, & Ickovics, 2008).

Adolescent pregnancy creates health risks for both the baby and the mother. Infants born to adolescent mothers are more likely to have low birth weights—a prominent factor in infant mortality—as well as neurological problems and childhood illness (Khashan, Baker, & Kenny, 2010). Adolescent mothers also are more likely than their peers to drop out of school. Although

Lynn Blankenship, Family and Consumer Science Educator

Lynn Blankenship is a family and consumer science educator with an undergraduate degree in this field from the University of Arizona. She has taught for more than 20 years, the last 14 at Tucson High Magnet School.

Blankenship was honored as the Tucson Federation of Teachers Educator of the Year for 1999–2000 and the Arizona Teacher of the Year in 1999. Blankenship especially enjoys teaching life skills to adolescents. One of her favorite activities is having students care for an automated baby that imitates the needs of real babies. She says that this program has a profound impact on students because the baby must be cared for around the clock for the duration of the assignment. Blankenship also coordinates real-world work experiences and training for students in several child-care facilities in the Tucson area.

Lynn Blankenship (*center*) teaching life skills to students.

For more information about what family and consumer science educators do, see page 45 in the Careers in Life-Span Development appendix.

many adolescent mothers resume their education later in life, they generally never catch up economically with women who postpone childbearing until their twenties. One longitudinal study found that the children of women who had their first birth during their teens had lower achievement test scores and more behavioral problems than did children whose mothers had their first birth as adults (Hofferth & Reid, 2002).

Although the consequences of America's high adolescent pregnancy rate are cause for great concern, it often is not pregnancy alone that leads to negative consequences for an adolescent mother and her offspring. Adolescent mothers are more likely to come from low-SES backgrounds (Molina & others, 2010). Many adolescent mothers also were not good students before they became pregnant (Malamitsi-Puchner & Boutsikou, 2006). However, not every adolescent female who bears a child lives a life of poverty and low achievement. Thus, although adolescent pregnancy is a high-risk circumstance, and adolescents who do not become pregnant generally fare better than those who do, some adolescent mothers do well in school and have positive outcomes (Schaffer & others, 2012).

Serious, extensive efforts are needed to help pregnant adolescents and young mothers enhance their educational and occupational opportunities (Gruber, 2012). Adolescent mothers also need help obtaining competent child care and planning for the future.

Adolescents can benefit from age-appropriate family-life education. Family and consumer science educators teach life skills, such as effective decision making, to adolescents. To read about the work of one family and consumer science educator, see *Connecting with Careers*. And to learn more about ways to reduce adolescent pregnancy, see *Connecting Development to Life*.

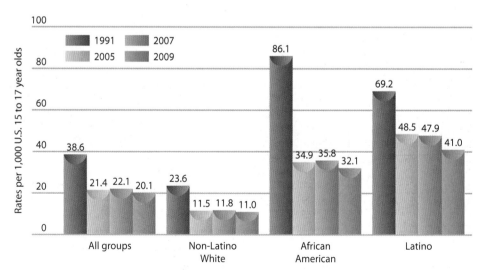

FIGURE 11.7

BIRTH RATES FOR U.S. 15- TO 17-YEAR-OLDS FROM 1991 TO 2009

Reducing Adolescent Pregnancy

One strategy for reducing adolescent pregnancy, called the Teen Outreach Program (TOP), focuses on engaging adolescents in volunteer community service and stimulates discussions that help adolescents appreciate the lessons they learn through volunteerism. In one study, 695 adolescents in grades 9 to 12 were randomly assigned to either a Teen Outreach group or a control group (Allen & others, 1997). They were assessed at program entry and at program exit nine months later. The rate of pregnancy was substantially lower for the Teen Outreach adolescents. These adolescents also had lower rates of school failure and academic suspension.

Girls, Inc., has four programs that are intended to increase adolescent girls' motivation to avoid pregnancy until they are mature enough to make responsible decisions about motherhood (Roth & others, 1998). Growing Together, a series of five two-hour workshops for mothers and adolescents, and Will Power/Won't Power, a series of six two-hour sessions that focus on assertiveness training, are for 12- to 14-year-old girls. For older adolescent girls, Taking Care of Business provides nine sessions that emphasize career planning as well as information about sexuality, reproduction, and contraception. Health Bridge coordinates health and education services—girls can participate in this program as one of their club activities. Girls who participated in these programs were less likely to get pregnant than girls who did not participate (Girls, Inc., 1991).

The sources and the accuracy of adolescents' sexual information are linked to adolescent pregnancy. Adolescents can get information about sex from many sources, including parents, siblings, schools, peers, magazines, television, and the Internet. A special concern is the accuracy of sexual information to which adolescents have access on the Internet.

Currently, a major controversy in sex education is whether schools should have an abstinence-only program or a program that emphasizes contraceptive knowledge (Kraft & others, 2012; Stidham-Hall, Moreau, & Trussell, 2012).

A number of leading experts on adolescent sexuality now conclude that sex education programs that emphasize contraceptive knowledge do not increase the incidence of sexual intercourse and are more likely to reduce the risk of adolescent pregnancy and sexually transmitted infections than abstinence-only programs (Carroll, 2013; Eisenberg & others, 2008; Hyde & DeLamater, 2011). Some sex education programs are starting to include abstinence-plus sexuality by promoting abstinence while also providing instructions on contraceptive use (Nixon & others, 2011; Realini & others, 2010).

These are not adolescent mothers, but rather adolescents who are participating in the Teen Outreach Program (TOP), which engages adolescents in volunteer community service. These adolescent girls are serving as volunteers in a child-care center for babies born addicted to crack. Researchers have found that such volunteer experiences can reduce the rate of adolescent pregnancy.

Based on the information you read earlier about risk factors in adolescent sexual behavior, which segments of the adolescent population would benefit most from the types of sex education programs described here?

3 Issues in Adolescent Health

LG3 Identify adolescent problems related to health, substance use and abuse, and eating disorders.

Adolescent Health   Substance Use and Abuse   Eating Disorders

Many health experts argue that whether adolescents are healthy depends primarily on their own behavior. To improve adolescent health, adults should aim to (1) increase adolescents' *health-enhancing* behaviors, such as eating nutritiously, exercising, wearing seat belts, and getting adequate sleep; and (2) reduce adolescents' *health-compromising* behaviors, such as drug abuse, violence, unprotected sexual intercourse, and dangerous driving.

ADOLESCENT HEALTH

Adolescence is a critical juncture in the adoption of behaviors that are relevant to health (Catalano & others, 2012; Feinstein & others, 2012). Many of the behaviors that are linked to poor health habits and early death in adults begin during adolescence. Conversely, the early formation of healthy behavior patterns, such as regular exercise and a preference for foods low in fat and cholesterol, not only has immediate health benefits but helps in adulthood to delay or prevent disability and mortality from heart disease, stroke, diabetes, and cancer (Insel & Roth, 2012; Okosun & others, 2012).

Nutrition and Exercise   Concerns are growing about adolescents' nutrition and exercise habits (Alberga & others, 2012; Dowdy & others, 2012). National data indicated that the percentage of overweight U.S. 12- to 19-year-olds increased from 11 to 17 percent from the early 1990s to 2009-2010 (Ogden & others, 2012). During this time frame, the prevalence of obesity in adolescent boys increased from 14 to 19 percent, but there was no significant change in obesity in adolescent girls.

A special concern in American culture is the amount of fat we consume (Nabhan & Hannon, 2012). Many of today's adolescents virtually live on fast-food meals, which are high in fat. A comparison of adolescents in 28 countries found that U.S. and British adolescents were more likely to eat fried food and less likely to eat fruits and vegetables than adolescents in most other countries that were studied (World Health Organization, 2000). One study found that eating regular family meals during early adolescence was linked to healthy eating habits five years later (Burgess-Champoux & others, 2009).

Being obese in adolescence predicts obesity in emerging adulthood. For example, a longitudinal study of more than 8,000 adolescents found that obese adolescents were more likely to develop severe obesity in emerging adulthood than were overweight or normal-weight adolescents (The & others, 2010). In another longitudinal study, the percentage of overweight individuals increased from 20 percent at 14 years of age to 33 percent at 24 years of age (Patton & others, 2011).

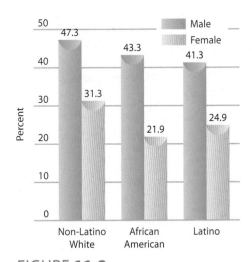

FIGURE 11.8

EXERCISE RATES OF U.S. HIGH SCHOOL STUDENTS, BY GENDER AND ETHNICITY.
Note: Data are for high school students who did any kind of physical activity that increased their heart rate and made them breathe hard some of the time for a total of at least 60 minutes per day on five or more of the seven days preceding the survey.

What are some characteristics of adolescents' exercise patterns?

Researchers have found that individuals become less active as they reach and progress through adolescence (Alberga & others, 2012; Kwan & others, 2012; Pienaar & others, 2012). A national study revealed that only 31 percent of U.S. 15-year-olds met the federal government's exercise recommendations (a minimum of 60 minutes of moderate to vigorous exercise per day) on weekdays and only 17 percent met the recommendations on weekends (Nader & others, 2008). In this study, adolescent boys were more likely to engage in moderate to vigorous exercise than girls were. Another national study of U.S. adolescents revealed that physical activity increased until 13 years of age in boys and girls but then declined through 18 years of age (Kahn & others, 2008).

Ethnic differences in exercise participation rates of U.S. adolescents also occur, and these rates vary by gender. As indicated in Figure 11.8, in the National Youth Risk Survey, non-Latino White boys exercised the most, African American girls the least (Eaton & others, 2010).

Exercise is linked to a number of positive physical outcomes in adolescence. One outcome is that regular exercise has a positive effect on adolescents' weight status (Alberga & others, 2012). Other positive outcomes of exercise in adolescence are reduced triglyceride levels, lower blood pressure, and a lower incidence of type II diabetes (Shi, de Groh, & Morrison, 2012). Low levels of exercise are related to depressive symptoms in young adolescents (Raudsepp & Neissaar, 2012; Sund, Larsson, & Wichstrom, 2011). A recent study found that eighth-, tenth-, and twelfth-grade students who engaged in higher levels of exercise had lower levels of alcohol, cigarette, and marijuana use (Teery-McElrath, O'Malley, & Johnston, 2011).

Screen-based activity (watching television, using computers, talking on the phone, texting, and instant messaging for long hours) may be involved in lower levels of physical fitness in adolescence (Leatherdale, 2010; Wang & others, 2012). A recent study revealed that children and adolescents who engaged in the highest amount of daily screen-based activity (TV/video/video game in this study) were less likely than their peers to exercise daily (Sisson & others, 2010). In this study, children and adolescents who engaged in low physical activity and high screen-based activity were almost twice as likely to be overweight as their more active, less sedentary counterparts.

Sleep Patterns   Like nutrition and exercise, sleep is an important influence on well-being. Might changing sleep patterns in adolescence contribute to adolescents' health-compromising behaviors? Recently there has been a surge of interest in adolescent sleep patterns (Beebe, 2011; Colrain & Baker, 2011).

In a national survey of youth, only 31 percent of U.S. adolescents got eight or more hours of sleep on an average school night (Eaton & others, 2010). In this study, the percentage of adolescents getting this much sleep on an average school night decreased as they got older (see Figure 11.9).

The National Sleep Foundation (2006) conducted a U.S. survey of 1,602 caregivers and their 11- to 17-year-olds. Forty-five percent of the adolescents got less than eight hours of sleep on school nights. Older adolescents (ninth- to twelfth-graders) got markedly less sleep on school nights than younger adolescents (sixth- to eighth-graders)—62 percent of the older adolescents got inadequate sleep compared with 21 percent of the younger adolescents. Adolescents who got inadequate sleep (eight hours or less) on school nights were more likely to feel more tired or sleepy, to be more cranky and irritable, to fall asleep in school, to be in a depressed mood, and to drink caffeinated beverages than their counterparts who got optimal

FIGURE 11.9

DEVELOPMENTAL CHANGES IN U.S. ADOLESCENTS' SLEEP PATTERNS ON AN AVERAGE SCHOOL NIGHT

sleep (nine or more hours). Also, a longitudinal study of more than 6,000 adolescents found that sleep problems were linked to subsequent suicidal thoughts and attempts in adolescence and early adulthood (Wong & Brower, 2012).

Mary Carskadon and her colleagues (2004, 2005, 2011a, b; Crowley & Carskadon, 2010; Tarokh & Carskadon, 2010) have conducted a number of research studies on adolescent sleep patterns. They found that when given the opportunity adolescents will sleep an average of 9 hours and 25 minutes a night. Most get considerably less than nine hours of sleep, however, especially during the week. This shortfall creates a sleep deficit, which adolescents often attempt to make up on the weekend. The researchers also found that older adolescents tend to be sleepier during the day than younger adolescents. They theorized that this sleepiness was not due to academic work or social pressures. Rather, their research suggests that adolescents' biological clocks undergo a shift as they get older, delaying their period of sleepiness by about one hour. A delay in the nightly release of the sleep-inducing hormone melatonin, which is produced in the brain's pineal gland, seems to underlie this shift. Melatonin is secreted at about 9:30 p.m. in younger adolescents and approximately an hour later in older adolescents.

In Mary Carskadon's sleep laboratory at Brown University, an adolescent girl's brain activity is being monitored. Carskadon (2005) says that in the morning, sleep-deprived adolescents' "brains are telling them it's night time . . . and the rest of the world is saying it's time to go to school" (p. 19).

Carskadon concludes that early school starting times may cause grogginess, inattention in class, and poor performance on tests. Based on her research, school officials in Edina, Minnesota, decided to start classes at 8:30 a.m. rather than the usual 7:25 a.m. Since then there have been fewer referrals for discipline problems, and the number of students who report being ill or depressed has decreased. The school system reports that test scores have improved for high school students, but not for middle school students. This finding supports Carskadon's suspicion that early start times are likely to be more stressful for older than for younger adolescents. Also, a recent study found that just a 30-minute delay in school start time was linked to improvements in adolescents' sleep, alertness, mood, and health (Owens, Belon, & Moss, 2010). And a recent research review found that Asian adolescents' bedtimes were even later than those of their peers in North America and Europe, resulting in less total sleep on school nights and more daytime sleepiness for the Asian adolescents (Gradisar, Gardner, & Dohnt, 2011).

Do sleep patterns change in emerging adulthood? Research indicates that they do (Galambos, Howard, & Maggs, 2011). A recent study revealed that more than 60 percent of college students were categorized as poor-quality sleepers (Lund & others, 2010). In this study, the weekday bedtimes and rise times of first-year college students were approximately 1 hour and 15 minutes later than those of seniors in high school (Lund & others, 2010). However, the first-year college students had later bedtimes and rise times than third- and fourth-year college students, indicating that at about 20 to 22 years of age, a reverse in the timing of bedtimes and rise times occurs.

Leading Causes of Death in Adolescence   The three leading causes of death in adolescence are unintentional injuries, homicide, and suicide (Eaton & others, 2010). Almost half of all deaths from 15 to 24 years of age are due to unintentional injuries, the majority of them involving motor vehicle accidents. Risky driving habits, such as speeding, tailgating, and driving under the influence of alcohol or other drugs, may be more important contributors to these accidents than lack of driving experience (Marcotte & others, 2012; Mirman & others, 2012). In about 50 percent of motor vehicle fatalities involving adolescents, the driver has a blood alcohol level of 0.10 percent—twice the level needed to be designated as "under the influence" in some states. A high rate of intoxication is also found in adolescents who die as pedestrians or while using vehicles other than automobiles.

Homicide is the second leading cause of death in adolescence (Eaton & others, 2010), especially among African American males. Also notable is the adolescent suicide rate, which has tripled since the 1950s. Suicide accounts for 6 percent of the deaths in the 10-to-14 age

Students comfort each other in Canisteo, New York, at a memorial on the bridge where four adolescents from Jasper, New York, were killed in a car crash in 2007.

FIGURE **11.10**

TRENDS IN DRUG USE BY U.S. EIGHTH-, TENTH-, AND TWELFTH-GRADE STUDENTS.
This graph shows the percentage of U.S. eighth-, tenth-, and twelfth-grade students who reported having taken an illicit drug in the last 12 months from 1991 to 2011, for eighth- and tenth-graders, and from 1975 to 2011, for twelfth-graders (Johnston & others, 2012).

- - - - - - - - - ▶

developmental **connection**

Substance Abuse

Does substance abuse increase or decrease in emerging adulthood? Chapter 13, p. 426

What are some trends in alcohol use by U.S. adolescents?

What are some risk factors that predict whether adolescents will become regular smokers?

group and 12 percent of deaths in the 15-to-19 age group. We will discuss suicide further in Chapter 12.

SUBSTANCE USE AND ABUSE

Each year since 1975, Lloyd Johnston and his colleagues at the Institute of Social Research at the University of Michigan have monitored the drug use of America's high school seniors in a wide range of public and private high schools. Since 1991, they also have surveyed drug use by eighth- and tenth-graders. In 2011, the study surveyed 47,000 secondary school students (Johnston & others, 2012).

According to this study, the proportions of eighth-, tenth-, and twelfth-grade U.S. students who used any illicit drug declined in the late 1990s and the first decade of the twenty-first century (Johnston & others, 2012) (see Figure 11.10). Marijuana is the illicit drug most widely used in the United States, and its use by adolescents increased from 2008 to 2011 (Johnston & others, 2012). As shown in Figure 11.10, in which marijuana is included, an increase in illicit drug use by U.S. adolescents occurred from 2008 to 2011. However, when marijuana use is subtracted from the illicit drug index, no increase in illicit drug use by adolescents occurred in this time frame (Johnston & others, 2012). The United States still has one of the highest rates of adolescent drug use of any industrialized nation.

How extensive is alcohol use by U.S. adolescents? Sizeable declines in adolescent alcohol use have occurred in recent years (Johnston & others, 2012). The percentage of U.S. eighth-graders reporting having had any alcohol to drink in the past 30 days fell from a 1996 high of 26 percent to 13 percent in 2011. The 30-day prevalence fell among tenth-graders from 39 percent in 2001 to 27 percent in 2011 and among high school seniors from 72 percent in 1980 to 40 percent in 2011. Binge drinking (defined in the University of Michigan surveys as having five or more drinks in a row in the last two weeks) by high school seniors declined from 41 percent in 1980 to 25 percent in 2011. Binge drinking by eighth- and tenth-graders also has dropped in recent years. A consistent sex difference occurs in binge drinking, with males engaging in this behavior more than females.

A special concern is adolescents who drive while they are under the influence of alcohol or other substances (Catalano & others, 2012; Marcotte & others, 2012). In the University of Michigan Monitoring the Future Study, 30 percent of high school seniors said they had been in a vehicle with a drugged or drinking driver in the past two weeks (Johnston & others, 2008).

Cigarette smoking among U.S. adolescents peaked in 1996 and has gradually declined since then (Johnston & others, 2012). Following peak use in 1996, smoking rates for U.S. eighth-graders have fallen by 50 percent. In 2011, the percentages of adolescents who said they had smoked cigarettes in the last 30 days were 19 percent (twelfth grade), 12 percent (tenth grade), and 6 percent (eighth grade).

The Roles of Development, Parents, Peers, and Education   There are serious consequences when adolescents begin to use drugs early in adolescence or even in childhood (Kenney, 2012). A longitudinal study of individuals from 8 to 42 years of age found that early onset of drinking was linked to increased risk of heavy drinking in middle age (Pitkänen, Lyyra, & Pulkkinen, 2005). And a recent study revealed that the onset of alcohol use before age 11 was linked to a higher risk for alcohol dependence in early adulthood (Guttmannova & others, 2012).

Parents play an important role in preventing adolescent drug abuse (Feinstein, Richter, & Foster, 2012; Wang, Kviz, & Miller, 2012). Positive relationships with parents and others can reduce adolescents' drug use (Cleveland & others, 2012). Researchers have found that parental monitoring is linked with a lower incidence of drug use (Tobler & Komro, 2010). A recent research review concluded that the more frequently adolescents ate dinner with their family, the less likely they were to have substance abuse problems (Sen, 2010). And recent research revealed that authoritative parenting was linked to lower adolescent alcohol consumption (Piko & Balazs, 2012), while parent-adolescent conflict was related to a higher level of adolescent alcohol use (Chaplin & others, 2012).

Along with parents, peers play a very important role in adolescent substance use (Tucker & others, 2012). A recent large-scale study of eighth- and tenth-graders found that of various risk factors the strongest predictors of substance use involved peer relations (Patrick & Schulenberg, 2010). In this study, spending more evenings out with peers, having friends who get drunk, feeling pressure to drink, and perceived availability of alcohol were linked to heavy episodic drinking. Another recent study found that peer network drinking increased adolescents' alcohol use (Cruz, Emery, & Turkheimer, 2012).

Educational success is also a strong buffer for the emergence of drug problems in adolescence (Balsa, Giuliano, & French, 2011). An analysis by Jerald Bachman and his colleagues (2008) revealed that early educational achievement considerably reduced the likelihood that adolescents would develop drug problems, including alcohol abuse, smoking, and abuse of various illicit drugs. But what can families do to educate themselves and their children and reduce adolescent drinking and smoking behavior? To find out, see *Connecting Through Research*.

What are some of the ways that parents influence whether their adolescents take drugs?

EATING DISORDERS

Let's now examine two eating problems—anorexia nervosa and bulimia nervosa—that are far more common in adolescent girls than boys.

Anorexia Nervosa   Although most U.S. girls have been on a diet at some point, slightly less than 1 percent ever develop anorexia nervosa. **Anorexia nervosa** is an eating disorder that involves the relentless pursuit of thinness through starvation. It is a serious disorder that can lead to death. Four main characteristics apply to people suffering from anorexia nervosa: (1) weight less than 85 percent of what is considered normal for their age and height; (2) an intense fear of gaining weight that does not decrease with weight loss; (3) a distorted image of their body shape (Stewart & others, 2012), and (4) *amenorrhea* (lack of menstruation) in girls who have reached puberty. Obsessive thinking about weight and compulsive exercise also are linked to anorexia nervosa (Hildebrandt & others, 2012). Even when they are extremely thin, they see themselves as too fat. They never think they are thin enough, especially in the abdomen, buttocks, and thighs. They usually weigh themselves frequently, often take their body measurements, and gaze critically at themselves in mirrors.

Anorexia nervosa typically begins in the early to middle adolescent years, often following an episode of dieting and some type of life stress (Fitzpatrick, 2012; Smink, van Hoeken, & Hoek, 2012). It is about 10 times more likely to occur in females than males. When anorexia nervosa does occur in males, the symptoms and other characteristics (such as a distorted body image and family conflict) are usually similar to those reported by females who have the disorder (Ariceli & others, 2005).

Anorexia nervosa has become an increasing problem for adolescent girls and young adult women. *What are some possible causes of anorexia nervosa?*

anorexia nervosa An eating disorder that involves the relentless pursuit of thinness through starvation.

connecting through research

What Can Families Do to Reduce Drinking and Smoking in Young Adolescents?

Experimental studies have been conducted to determine whether family programs can reduce drinking and smoking in young adolescents. In one experimental study, 1,326 families with 12- to 14-year-old adolescents living in various parts of the United States were interviewed (Bauman & others, 2002). After the baseline interviews, participants were randomly assigned either to go through the Family Matters program (experimental group) or not to experience the program (control group) (Bauman & others, 2002).

The families assigned to the Family Matters program received four mailings of booklets. Each mailing was followed by a telephone call from a health educator to "encourage participation by all family members, answer any questions, and record information" (Bauman & others, 2002, pp. 36–37). The first booklet focused on the negative consequences of adolescent substance abuse to the family. The second emphasized "supervision, support, communication skills, attachment, time spent together, educational achievement, conflict reduction, and how well adolescence is understood." The third booklet asked parents to list things that they do that might inadvertently encourage their child's use of tobacco or alcohol, identify rules that might influence the child's use, and consider ways to monitor use. Then adult family members and the child met "to agree upon rules and sanctions related to adolescent use." Booklet four dealt with "what the child can do to resist peer and media pressures for use."

Two follow-up interviews with the parents and adolescents were conducted three months and one year after the experimental group had completed the program. Adolescents in the Family Matters program reported lower alcohol and cigarette use at three months and at one year after the program had been completed. Figure 11.11 shows the results for alcohol.

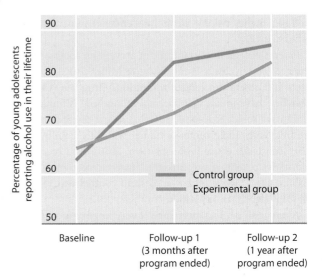

FIGURE **11.11**

YOUNG ADOLESCENTS' REPORTS OF ALCOHOL USE IN THE FAMILY MATTERS PROGRAM. Note that at baseline (before the program started) the young adolescents in the Family Matters program (experimental group) and their counterparts who did not go through the program (control group) reported approximately the same lifetime use of alcohol (slightly higher use by the experimental group). However, three months after the program ended, the experimental group reported lower alcohol use, and this reduction was still present one year after the program had ended, although at a reduced level.

The topics covered in the second booklet underscore the importance of parental influence earlier in development. For instance, staying actively involved and establishing an authoritative, as opposed to a neglectful, parenting style early in children's lives will better ensure that children have a clear understanding of the parents' level of support and expectations when the children reach adolescence.

Most anorexics are non-Latina White adolescent or young adult females from well-educated middle- and upper-income families and are competitive and high-achieving (Darcy, 2012; Dodge, 2012). They set high standards, become stressed about not being able to reach the standards, and are intensely concerned about how others perceive them. Unable to meet these high expectations, they turn to something they can control: their weight. Offspring of mothers with anorexia nervosa are at risk for becoming anorexic themselves (Striegel-Moore & Bulik, 2007). Problems in family functioning are increasingly being found to be linked to the appearance of anorexia nervosa in adolescent girls (Stiles-Shields & others, 2012), and a research review concluded that family therapy is often the most effective treatment of adolescent girls with anorexia nervosa (Bulik & others, 2007).

Biology and culture are involved in anorexia nervosa. Genes play an important role in anorexia nervosa (Lock, 2012a). Also, the physical effects of dieting may change neural networks and thus sustain the disordered pattern (Lock, 2012b). The fashion image in U.S. culture likely contributes to the incidence of anorexia nervosa (Benowitz-Fredericks & others, 2012; Carr & Peebles, 2012). The media portray thin as beautiful in their choice of fashion models,

bulimia nervosa An eating disorder in which the individual consistently follows a binge-and-purge pattern.

whom many adolescent girls strive to emulate. And many adolescent girls who strive to be thin hang out together.

Bulimia Nervosa   Whereas anorexics control their weight by restricting food intake, most bulimics cannot. **Bulimia nervosa** is an eating disorder in which the individual consistently follows a binge-and-purge pattern. The bulimic goes on an eating binge and then purges by self-inducing vomiting or using a laxative. Although many people binge and purge occasionally and some experiment with it, a person is considered to have a serious bulimic disorder only if the episodes occur at least twice a week for three months (Uher & Rutter, 2012).

As with anorexics, most bulimics are preoccupied with food, have a strong fear of becoming overweight, are depressed or anxious, and have a distorted body image. Like adolescents who are anorexic, bulimics are highly perfectionistic (Lampard & others, 2012). Unlike anorexics, individuals who binge and purge typically fall within a normal weight range, which makes bulimia more difficult to detect.

Approximately 1 to 2 percent of U.S. women are estimated to develop bulimia nervosa, and about 90 percent of bulimics are women. Bulimia nervosa typically begins in late adolescence or early adulthood. Many women who develop bulimia nervosa were somewhat overweight before the onset of the disorder, and the binge eating often began during an episode of dieting. A recent study of individuals with anorexia nervosa or bulimia nervosa revealed that attachment insecurity was linked with body dissatisfaction, which was a key aspect of predicting and perpetuating these eating disorders (Abbate-Daga & others, 2010). In this study, need for approval was an important predictor of bulimia nervosa. As with anorexia nervosa, about 70 percent of individuals who develop bulimia nervosa eventually recover from the disorder (Agras & others, 2004). Drug therapy and psychotherapy have been effective in treating anorexia nervosa and bulimia nervosa (Hagman & Frank, 2012; Wilson & Zandberg, 2012).

Review *Connect* Reflect

LG3 Identify adolescent problems related to health, substance use and abuse, and eating disorders.

Review

- What are key concerns about the health of adolescents?
- What are some characteristics of adolescents' substance use and abuse?
- What are the characteristics of the major eating disorders?

Connect

- In *Connecting Through Research*, you learned that attachment was one of the things that the Family Matters program

emphasized as important in reducing drinking and smoking behavior in adolescents. Do the research findings discussed in Chapter 6 support or contradict this emphasis on early attachment's affect on development and behavior later in life?

Reflect *Your Own Personal Journey of Life*

- How health-enhancing and health-compromising were your patterns of behavior in adolescence? Explain.

4 Adolescent Cognition   **LG4** Explain cognitive changes in adolescence.

Piaget's Theory   Adolescent Egocentrism   Information Processing

Adolescents' developing power of thought opens up new cognitive and social horizons. Let's examine some explanations of how their power of thought develops, beginning with Piaget's theory (1952).

Might adolescents' ability to reason hypothetically and to evaluate what is ideal versus what is real lead them to engage in demonstrations such as this protest related to improving education? What other causes might be attractive to adolescents' newfound cognitive abilities of hypothetical-deductive reasoning and idealistic thinking?

"Ben is in his first year of high school, and he's questioning all the right things."

© Edward Koren/The New Yorker Collection/www.cartoonbank.com.

developmental **connection**

Cognitive Theory

Is there a fifth, postformal stage of cognitive development that characterizes young adults? Chapter 13, p. 439

hypothetical-deductive reasoning Piaget's formal operational concept that adolescents have the cognitive ability to develop hypotheses, or best guesses, about ways to solve problems.

PIAGET'S THEORY

As we discussed in Chapter 9, Jean Piaget proposed that around 7 years of age children enter the *concrete operational stage* of cognitive development. They can reason logically about concrete events and objects, and they make gains in their ability to classify objects and to reason about the relationships between classes of objects. Around age 11, according to Piaget, the fourth and final stage of cognitive development—the formal operational stage—begins.

The Formal Operational Stage What are the characteristics of the formal operational stage? Formal operational thought is more abstract than concrete operational thought. Adolescents are no longer limited to actual, concrete experiences as anchors for thought. They can conjure up make-believe situations, abstract propositions, and events that are purely hypothetical, and can try to reason logically about them.

The abstract quality of thinking during the formal operational stage is evident in the adolescent's verbal problem-solving ability. Whereas the concrete operational thinker needs to see the concrete elements A, B, and C to be able to make the logical inference that if A = B and B = C, then A = C, the formal operational thinker can solve this problem merely through verbal presentation.

Another indication of the abstract quality of adolescents' thought is their increased tendency to think about thought itself. One adolescent commented, "I began thinking about why I was thinking what I was. Then I began thinking about why I was thinking about what I was thinking about what I was." If this sounds abstract, it is, and it characterizes the adolescent's enhanced focus on thought and its abstract qualities.

Accompanying the abstract nature of formal operational thought is thought full of idealism and possibilities, especially during the beginning of the formal operational stage, when assimilation dominates. Adolescents engage in extended speculation about ideal characteristics—qualities they desire in themselves and in others. Such thoughts often lead adolescents to compare themselves with others in regard to such ideal standards. And their thoughts are often fantasy flights into future possibilities.

At the same time that adolescents think more abstractly and idealistically, they also think more logically. Children are likely to solve problems through trial and error; adolescents begin to think more as a scientist thinks, devising plans to solve problems and systematically testing solutions. This type of problem solving requires **hypothetical-deductive reasoning,** which involves creating a hypothesis and deducing its implications, steps that provide ways to test the hypothesis. Thus, formal operational thinkers develop hypotheses about ways to solve problems and then systematically deduce the best path to follow to solve the problem.

Evaluating Piaget's Theory Researchers have challenged some of Piaget's ideas about the formal operational stage (Brynes, 2012; Diamond, 2013; Kuhn, 2011). Among their findings is that there is much more individual variation than Piaget envisioned: Only about one in three young adolescents is a formal operational thinker, and many American adults (and adults in other cultures) never become formal operational thinkers.

Furthermore, education in the logic of science and mathematics promotes the development of formal operational thinking. This point recalls a criticism of Piaget's theory that we discussed in Chapter 9: Culture and education exert stronger influences on cognitive development than Piaget maintained (Goncu & Gauvain, 2012; Harris, Graham, & Urdan, 2012).

Piaget's theory of cognitive development has been challenged on other points as well (Diamond, 2013; Hyde & Spelke, 2012). As we noted in Chapter 9, Piaget conceived of stages as unitary structures of thought, with various aspects of a stage emerging at the same time. However, most contemporary developmentalists agree that cognitive development is not as stage-like as Piaget thought (Siegler, 2012a, b). Furthermore, children can be trained to reason at a higher cognitive stage, and some cognitive abilities emerge earlier than Piaget thought (Baillargeon & Carey, 2012; Johnson, 2012, 2013). Some understanding of the conservation of number has been demonstrated as early as age 3, although Piaget did not think it emerged until age 7. Other cognitive abilities can emerge later than Piaget thought (Brynes, 2012). As we just noted, many adolescents still think in concrete operational ways or are just beginning to master formal operations, and even many adults are not formal operational thinkers.

Despite these challenges to Piaget's ideas, we owe him a tremendous debt (Miller, 2011). Piaget was the founder of the present field of cognitive development, and he developed a long list of masterful concepts of enduring power and fascination: assimilation, accommodation, object permanence, egocentrism, conservation, and others. Psychologists also owe him the current vision of children as active, constructive thinkers. And they are indebted to him for creating a theory that has generated a huge volume of research on children's cognitive development.

Piaget also was a genius when it came to observing children. His careful observations demonstrated inventive ways to discover how children act on and adapt to their world. He also showed us how children need to make their experiences fit their schemes yet simultaneously adapt their schemes to accommodate their experiences. Piaget also revealed how cognitive change is likely to occur if the context is structured to allow gradual movement to the next higher level. Concepts do not emerge suddenly, full-blown, but instead develop through a series of partial accomplishments that lead to increasingly comprehensive understanding (Mandler & DeLoache, 2012).

ADOLESCENT EGOCENTRISM

Adolescent egocentrism is the heightened self-consciousness of adolescents. David Elkind (1976) points out that adolescent egocentrism has two key components—the imaginary audience and personal fable. The **imaginary audience** consists of adolescents' belief that others are as interested in them as they themselves are, as well as attention-getting behavior—attempts to be noticed, visible, and "on stage." For example, an eighth-grade boy might walk into a classroom and think that all eyes are riveted on his spotty complexion. Adolescents sense that they are "on stage" in early adolescence, believing they are the main actors and all others are the audience.

According to Elkind, the **personal fable** is the part of adolescent egocentrism involving a sense of uniqueness and invincibility (or invulnerability). For example, 13-year-old Adrienne says this about herself: "No one understands me, particularly my parents. They have no idea of what I am feeling." Adolescents' sense of personal uniqueness makes them believe that no one can understand how they really feel. As part of their effort to retain a sense of personal uniqueness, adolescents might craft a story about the self that is filled with fantasy, immersing themselves in a world that is far removed from reality. Personal fables frequently show up in adolescent diaries.

Adolescents often have been portrayed as having a sense of invincibility or invulnerability. For example, during a conversation with a girl who is the same age, 14-year-old Margaret says, "Are you kidding? I won't get pregnant." This sense of invincibility may lead adolescents to believe that they themselves are invulnerable to dangers and catastrophes (such as deadly car wrecks) that happen to other people. As a result, some adolescents engage in risky behaviors such as drag racing, drug use, suicide attempts, and having sexual intercourse without using contraceptives or barriers against STIs (Alberts, Elkind, & Ginsberg, 2007).

However, an increasing number of research studies suggest that rather than perceiving themselves to be invulnerable, adolescents tend to portray themselves as vulnerable to experiencing a premature death (Reyna & Rivers, 2008). For example, in a recent study, 12- to 18-year-olds were asked about their chances of dying in the next year and prior to age 20 (Fischhoff & others, 2010). The adolescents greatly overestimated their chance of dying prematurely.

INFORMATION PROCESSING

Deanna Kuhn (2009) identified some important characteristics of adolescents' information processing and thinking. In her view, in the later years of childhood and continuing in adolescence, individuals approach cognitive levels that may or may not be achieved, in contrast to the largely universal cognitive levels that young children attain. By adolescence, considerable variation in cognitive functioning is present across individuals. This variability supports the argument that adolescents are producers of their own development to a greater extent than are children.

Many adolescent girls spend long hours in front of the mirror, depleting cans of hairspray, tubes of lipstick, and jars of cosmetics. *How might this behavior be related to changes in adolescent cognitive and physical development?*

developmental **connection**

Cognitive Theory

Piaget described a form of egocentrism that characterizes young children. Chapter 7, p. 217

adolescent egocentrism The heightened self-consciousness of adolescents.

imaginary audience Adolescents' belief that others are as interested in them as they themselves are, as well as attention-getting behavior motivated by a desire to be noticed, visible, and "on stage."

personal fable The part of adolescent egocentrism that involves an adolescent's sense of uniqueness and invincibility (or invulnerability).

developmental **connection**

The Brain

The prefrontal cortex is the location in the brain where much of executive functioning occurs. Chapter 7, p. 226

Kuhn (2009) further argues that the most important cognitive change in adolescence is improvement in *executive functioning,* which we discussed earlier in Chapters 7 and 9. Recall from Chapters 7 and 9 the description of *executive functioning* as an umbrella-like concept that consists of a number of higher-level cognitive processes linked to the development of the prefrontal cortex. Executive functioning involves managing one's thoughts to engage in goal-directed behavior and to exercise self-control. Our further coverage of executive functioning in adolescence focuses on cognitive control, decision making, and critical thinking.

Cognitive Control   In Chapter 9, you read about the increase in cognitive control that occurs in middle and late childhood. Recall that **cognitive control** involves effective control in a number of areas, including controlling attention, reducing interfering thoughts, and being cognitively flexible (Diamond, 2013). Cognitive control continues to increase in adolescence and emerging adulthood (Casey, Jones, & Somerville, 2011).

Think about all the times adolescents need to engage in cognitive control, such as the following situations (Galinsky, 2010):

- making a real effort to stick with a task, avoiding interfering thoughts or environmental events, and instead doing what is most effective.
- stopping and thinking before acting to avoid blurting out something that a minute or two later they wished they hadn't said.
- continuing to work on something that is important but boring when there is something a lot more fun to do, inhibiting their behavior and doing the boring but important task, saying to themselves, "I have to show the self-discipline to finish this."

Control Attention and Reduce Interfering Thoughts   Controlling attention is a key aspect of learning and thinking in adolescence and emerging adulthood (Bjorklund, 2012). Distractions that can interfere with attention in adolescence and emerging adulthood come from the external environment (other students talking while the student is trying to listen to a lecture, or the student turning on a laptop or tablet PC during a lecture and looking at a new friend request on Facebook, for example) or intrusive distractions from competing thoughts in the individual's mind. Self-oriented thoughts, such as worrying, self-doubt, and intense emotionally laden thoughts may especially interfere with focusing attention on thinking tasks (Gillig & Sanders, 2011; Walsh, 2011).

Be Cognitively Flexible   *Cognitive flexibility* involves being aware that options and alternatives are available and adapting to the situation. Before adolescents and emerging adults adapt their behavior in a situation, they must be aware that they need to change their way of thinking and be motivated to do. Having confidence in their ability to adapt their thinking to a particular situation, an aspect of *self-efficacy,* also is important in being cognitively flexible (Bandura, 2012). To evaluate how cognitively flexible you are, see Figure 11.12 (Galinsky, 2010).

Circle the number that best reflects how you think for each of the four items:

	Exactly Like You	Very Much Like You	Somewhat Like You	Not Too Much Like You	Not At All Like You
1. When I try something that doesn't work, it's hard for me to give it up and try another solution.	1	2	3	4	5
2. I adapt to change pretty easily.	5	4	3	4	5
3. When I can't convince someone of my point of view, I can usually understand why not.	5	4	3	4	5
4. I am not very quick to take on new ideas.	1	2	3	4	5

Add your numbers for each of the four items: Total Score: _____
If your overall score is between 20 and 15, then you rate high on cognitive flexibility. If you scored between 9 and 14, you are in the middle category, and if you scored 8 or below, you likely could improve your cognitive flexibility considerably.

FIGURE **11.12**
HOW COGNITIVELY FLEXIBLE ARE YOU?

Decision Making   Adolescence is a time of increased decision making—which friends to choose; which person to date; whether to have sex, buy a car, go to college, and so on (Chick & Reyna, 2012; Stanovich, West, & Toplak, 2012; Steinberg, 2012). How competent are adolescents at making decisions? Older adolescents are described as more competent than younger adolescents, who in turn are more competent than children (Keating, 1990). Compared with children, young adolescents are more likely to generate different options, examine a situation from a variety of perspectives, anticipate the consequences of decisions, and consider the credibility of sources.

Most people make better decisions when they are calm than when they are emotionally aroused. That may especially be true for adolescents, who have a tendency to be emotionally intense. The same adolescent who makes a wise decision when calm may make an unwise decision when emotionally aroused (Albert & Steinberg, 2011a, b). In the heat of the moment, emotions may overwhelm decision-making ability.

The social context plays a key role in adolescent decision making. For example, adolescents' willingness to make risky decisions is more likely to occur in contexts where substances and other temptations are readily available (Reyna & Rivers, 2008). Recent research reveals that the presence of peers in risk-taking situations increases the likelihood that adolescents will make risky decisions (Albert & Steinberg, 2011a, b).

One proposal to explain adolescent decision making is the **dual-process model,** which states that decision making is influenced by two cognitive systems—one analytical and one experiential—which compete with each other (Chick & Reyna, 2012; Klaczynski, 2001; Reyna & Farley, 2006). The dual-process model emphasizes that it is the experiential system—monitoring and managing actual experiences—that benefits adolescents' decision making, not the analytical system. In this view, adolescents don't benefit from engaging in reflective, detailed, higher-level cognitive analysis about a decision, especially in high-risk, real-world contexts. In such contexts, adolescents just need to know that there are some circumstances that are so dangerous that they need to be avoided at all costs (Mills, Reyna, & Estrada, 2008). However, some experts on adolescent cognition argue that in many cases adolescents benefit from both analytical and experiential systems (Kuhn, 2009).

Adolescents need more opportunities to practice and discuss realistic decision making. Many real-world decisions on matters such as sex, drugs, and daredevil driving occur in an atmosphere of stress that includes time constraints and emotional involvement. One strategy for improving adolescent decision making is to provide more opportunities for them to engage in role playing and peer group problem solving.

Critical Thinking   Adolescence is an important transitional period in the development of critical thinking (Keating, 1990). In one study of fifth-, eighth-, and eleventh-graders, critical thinking increased with age but still occurred in only 43 percent of even the eleventh-graders, and many adolescents showed self-serving biases in their reasoning.

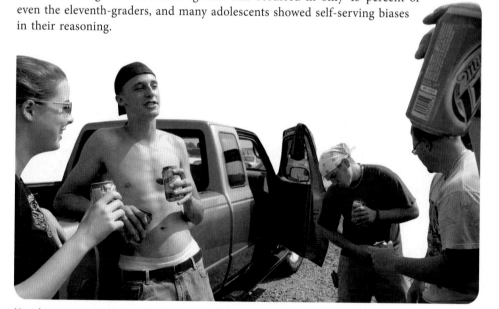

How do emotions and social contexts influence adolescents' decision making?

cognitive control Effective control of thinking in a number of areas, including controlling attention, reducing interfering thoughts, and being cognitively flexible.

dual-process model A view of thinking in which decision making is influenced by two systems—one analytical and one experiential—that compete with each other.

If fundamental skills (such as literacy and math skills) are not developed during childhood, critical-thinking skills are unlikely to mature in adolescence. For the subset of adolescents who lack such fundamental skills, potential gains in adolescent thinking are unlikely. For other adolescents, however, cognitive changes that allow improved critical thinking in adolescence include the following: (1) increased speed, automaticity, and capacity of information processing, which free cognitive resources for other purposes; (2) more breadth of content knowledge in a variety of domains; (3) increased ability to construct new combinations of knowledge; and (4) a greater range and more spontaneous use of strategies or procedures for applying or obtaining knowledge, such as planning, considering alternatives, and cognitive monitoring.

Review *Connect* Reflect

LG4 Explain cognitive changes in adolescence.

Review

- What is Piaget's theory of adolescent cognitive development?
- What is adolescent egocentrism?
- What are some important aspects of information processing in adolescence?

Connect

- Egocentrism was also mentioned in Chapter 7 in the context of early childhood cognitive development. How is adolescent egocentrism similar to or different from egocentrism in early childhood?

Reflect *Your Own Personal Journey of Life*

- Evaluate the level of your thinking as you made the transition to adolescence and through adolescence. Does Piaget's stage of formal operational thinking accurately describe the changes that occurred in your thinking? Explain.

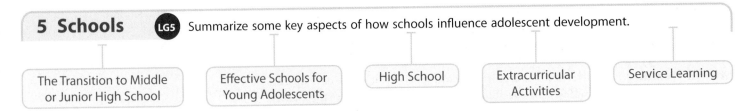

5 Schools

LG5 Summarize some key aspects of how schools influence adolescent development.

The Transition to Middle or Junior High School   Effective Schools for Young Adolescents   High School   Extracurricular Activities   Service Learning

What is the transition from elementary to middle or junior high school like? What are the characteristics of effective schools for adolescents? How can adolescents benefit from service learning?

THE TRANSITION TO MIDDLE OR JUNIOR HIGH SCHOOL

The first year of middle school or junior high school can be difficult for many students (Anderman, 2012). For example, in one study of the transition from sixth grade in an elementary school to the seventh grade in a junior high school, adolescents' perceptions of the quality of their school life plunged in the seventh grade (Hirsch & Rapkin, 1987). Compared with their earlier feelings as sixth-graders, the seventh-graders were less satisfied with school, were less committed to school, and liked their teachers less. The drop in school satisfaction occurred regardless of how academically successful the students were. The transition to middle or junior high school is less stressful when students have positive relationships with friends and go through the transition in team-oriented schools where 20 to 30 students take the same classes together (Hawkins & Berndt, 1985).

The transition to middle or junior high school takes place at a time when many changes— in the individual, in the family, and in school—are occurring simultaneously (Eccles & Roeser,

2012). These changes include puberty and related concerns about body image; the emergence of at least some aspects of formal operational thought, including accompanying changes in social cognition; increased responsibility and decreased dependency on parents; change to a larger, more impersonal school structure; change from one teacher to many teachers and from a small, homogeneous set of peers to a larger, more heterogeneous set of peers; and an increased focus on achievement and performance. Moreover, when students make the transition to middle or junior high school, they experience the **top-dog phenomenon,** moving from being the oldest, biggest, and most powerful students in the elementary school to being the youngest, smallest, and least powerful students in the middle or junior high school.

The transition to middle or junior high school also can have positive aspects. Students are more likely to feel grown up, have more subjects from which to select, have more opportunities to spend time with peers and locate compatible friends, and enjoy increased independence from direct parental monitoring. They also may be more challenged intellectually by academic work.

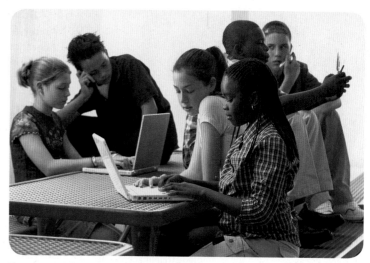

The transition from elementary to middle or junior high school occurs at the same time as a number of other developmental changes. *What are some of these other developmental changes?*

EFFECTIVE SCHOOLS FOR YOUNG ADOLESCENTS

Critics argue that middle and junior high schools should offer activities that reflect a wide range of individual differences in biological and psychological development among young adolescents. In 1989 the Carnegie Corporation issued an extremely negative evaluation of our nation's middle schools. It concluded that most young adolescents attended massive, impersonal schools; were taught from irrelevant curricula; trusted few adults in school; and lacked access to health care and counseling. It recommended that the nation develop smaller "communities" or "houses" to lessen the impersonal nature of large middle schools, have lower student-to-counselor ratios (10 to 1 instead of several hundred to 1), involve parents and community leaders in schools, develop new curricula, have teachers team teach in more flexibly designed curriculum blocks that integrate several disciplines, boost students' health and fitness with more in-school programs, and help students who need public health care to get it. Twenty years later, experts are still finding that middle schools throughout the nation need a major redesign if they are to be effective in educating adolescents (Anderman, 2012; Eccles & Roeser, 2012).

HIGH SCHOOL

Just as there are concerns about U.S. middle school education, so are there concerns about U.S. high school education (Bill and Melinda Gates Foundation, 2011). Critics stress that in many high schools expectations for success and standards for learning are too low. Critics also argue that too often high schools foster passivity and that schools should create a variety of pathways for students to achieve an identity. Many students graduate from high school with inadequate reading, writing, and mathematical skills—including many who go on to college and must enroll in remediation classes there. Other students drop out of high school and do not have skills that will allow them to obtain decent jobs, much less to be informed citizens.

Robert Crosnoe's (2011) recent book, *Fitting In, Standing Out,* highlighted another major problem with U.S. high schools: How the negative social aspects of adolescents' lives undermine their academic achievement. In his view, adolescents become immersed in complex peer group cultures that demand conformity. High school is supposed to be about getting an education, but for many youth it is about navigating the social worlds of peer relations that may or may not value education and academic achievement. Adolescents who fail to fit in, especially those who are obese or gay, become stigmatized. Crosnoe recommends increased school counseling services, expanded extracurricular activities, and improved parental monitoring to reduce such problems.

top-dog phenomenon The circumstance of moving from the top position in elementary school to the lowest position in middle or junior high school.

Students are shown using the technology training center at Wellpinit Elementary/High School located on the Spokane Indian Reservation in the state of Washington. An important educational goal is to increase the high school graduation rate of Native American adolescents.

In the last half of the twentieth century and the first several years of the twenty-first century, U.S. high school dropout rates declined (National Center for Education Statistics, 2010). In the 1940s, more than half of U.S. 16- to 24-year-olds had dropped out of school; by 2008, this figure had decreased to 8 percent. The dropout rate among Latino adolescents remains high, although it has been decreasing in the twenty-first century (from 28 percent in 2000 to 18 percent in 2008). The lowest dropout rate in 2008 occurred for Asian American adolescents (3.2 percent), followed by non-Latino White adolescents (6.2 percent), African American adolescents (10.4 percent), then Latino adolescents (18 percent). Native American adolescents likely have the highest dropout rate. Although government statistics for this ethnic group have not been adequately assessed, some estimates indicate that their dropout rate is higher than 50 percent.

Gender differences characterize U.S. dropout rates, with males more likely to drop out than females (10.4 versus 7.9 percent) (data for 2008) (National Center for Education Statistics, 2010). The gender gap in dropout rates is especially large for Latino adolescents (21.9 versus 15 percent). Figure 11.13 shows the dropout rates of 16- to 24-year-olds by ethnicity and gender in 2008.

The average U.S. high school dropout rates just described mask some very high dropout rates in low-income areas of inner cities. For example, in cities such as Detroit, Cleveland, and Chicago, dropout rates are above 50 percent. Also, the percentages cited in Figure 11.13 are for 16- to 24-year-olds. When dropout rates are calculated in terms of students who graduate from high school in four years, the percentage of students is also much higher. Thus, in considering high school dropout rates, it is important to examine age, the number of years it takes to complete high school, and various contexts including ethnicity, gender, and school location.

Students drop out of school for many reasons (Fall & Roberts, 2012; Schoeneberger, 2012). In one study, almost 50 percent of the dropouts cited school-related reasons for leaving school, such as not liking school or being expelled or suspended (Rumberger, 1983). Twenty percent of the dropouts (but 40 percent of the Latino students) cited economic reasons for leaving school. One-third of the female students dropped out for personal reasons such as pregnancy or marriage.

According to a research review, the most effective programs to discourage dropping out of high school provide early intervention for reading problems, tutoring, counseling, and mentoring (Lehr & others, 2003). Clearly, then, early detection of children's school-related difficulties and getting children engaged with school in positive ways are important strategies for reducing the dropout rate (Fall & Roberts, 2012).

Also, the Bill and Melinda Gates Foundation (2008, 2011) has funded efforts to reduce the dropout rate in schools where dropout rates are high. One strategy that is being emphasized in the Gates' funding is making sure that students who are at risk for dropping out of school remain with the same teachers throughout their high school years. The hope is that the teachers will get to know these students much better, their relationships with the students will improve, and they will be able to monitor and guide the students toward graduating from high school.

One program that has been very effective in reducing school dropout rates is "I Have a Dream" (IHAD), an innovative, comprehensive, long-term dropout prevention program administered by the National "I Have a Dream" Foundation in New York ("I Have A Dream" Foundation, 2012). Local IHAD projects around the country "adopt" entire grades (usually the third or fourth) from public elementary schools, or corresponding age cohorts from public housing developments. These children—"Dreamers"—are then provided with a program of academic, social, cultural, and recreational activities throughout their elementary, middle school, and high school years.

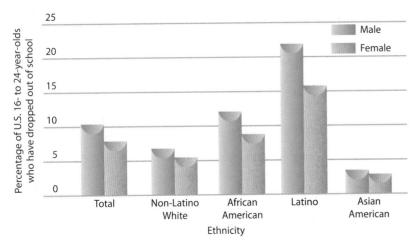

FIGURE **11.13**

SCHOOL DROPOUT RATES OF U.S. 16- TO 24-YEAR-OLDS BY GENDER AND ETHNICITY

Evaluations of IHAD programs have found dramatic improvements in grades, test scores, and school attendance, as well as a reduction in behavioral problems among Dreamers. For example, in Portland, Oregon, twice as many Dreamers as control-group students had reached a math standard, and the Dreamers were less likely to be referred to the juvenile justice system (Davis, Hyatt, & Arrasmith, 1998).

EXTRACURRICULAR ACTIVITIES

Adolescents in U.S. schools usually can choose from a wide array of extracurricular activities in addition to their academic courses. These adult-sanctioned activities typically occur in the after-school hours and can be sponsored either by the school or by the community. They include such diverse activities as sports, academic clubs, band, drama, and math clubs. Researchers have found that participation in extracurricular activities is linked to higher grades, greater school engagement, less likelihood of dropping out of school, improved probability of going to college, higher self-esteem, and lower rates of depression, delinquency, and substance abuse (Eccles & Roeser, 2012; Fredricks & Eccles, 2010). Adolescents gain more benefit from a breadth of extracurricular activities than from focusing on a single extracurricular activity.

Of course, the quality of the extracurricular activities matters (Eccles & Roeser, 2012). High-quality extracurricular activities that are likely to promote positive adolescent development provide competent, supportive adult mentors; opportunities for increasing school connectedness; challenging and meaningful activities; and opportunities for improving skills.

These adolescents are participating in the "I Have a Dream" (IHAD) Program, a comprehensive, long-term dropout prevention program that has been very successful. *What are some other strategies for reducing high school dropout rates?*

developmental **connection**

Gender

Females are more likely to engage in prosocial behavior than males. Chapter 10, p. 331

SERVICE LEARNING

Service learning is a form of education that promotes social responsibility and service to the community. In service learning, adolescents engage in activities such as tutoring, helping older adults, working in a hospital, assisting at a child-care center, or cleaning up a vacant lot to make a play area. An important goal of service learning is that adolescents become less self-centered and more strongly motivated to help others (Davidson & others, 2010). Service learning is often more effective when two conditions are met (Nucci, 2006): (1) giving students some degree of choice in the service activities in which they participate, and (2) providing students opportunities to reflect about their participation.

Service learning takes education out into the community (Zaff & others, 2010). One eleventh-grade student worked as a reading tutor for students from low-income backgrounds with reading skills well below their grade levels. She commented that until she did the tutoring, she did not realize how many students had not experienced the same opportunities that she had when she was growing up. An especially rewarding moment was when one young girl told her, "I want to learn to read like you so I can go to college when I grow up." Thus, a key feature of service learning is that it benefits not only adolescents but also the recipients of their help.

Researchers have found that service learning benefits adolescents in a number of ways (Gonsalves, 2011; Kielsmeier, 2011). Improvements in adolescent development related to service learning include higher grades in school, increased goal setting, higher self-esteem, a greater sense of being able to make a difference for others, and an increased willingness to serve as volunteers in the future (Hart, Matsuba, & Atkins, 2008). One study found that adolescent girls participated in service learning more than did adolescent boys (Webster & Worrell, 2008).

What are some of the positive effects of service learning?

service learning A form of education that promotes social responsibility and service to the community.

Review *Connect* Reflect

LG5 Summarize some key aspects of how schools influence adolescent development.

Review

- What is the transition to middle or junior high school like?
- What are some characteristics of effective schools for young adolescents?
- What are some important things to know about high school dropouts and improving high schools?
- How does participation in extracurricular activities influence adolescent development?
- What is service learning, and how does it affect adolescent development?

Connect

- Compare the optimal school learning environments for adolescents described in this chapter with those described for younger children in previous chapters. Aside from age-appropriate curricula, what else is similar or different?

Reflect *Your Own Personal Journey of Life*

- What was your middle or junior high school like? How did it measure up to the Carnegie Corporation's recommendations?

topical **connections**

From 18 to 25 years of age, individuals make a transition from adolescence to adulthood. This transitional period, called emerging adulthood, is characterized by identity exploration, instability, and awareness of possibilities. Individuals often reach the peak of their physical skills between 19 and 26 years of age, followed by declining physical development during the early thirties. Cognitive development becomes more pragmatic and realistic, as well as more reflective and relativistic. Work becomes a more central aspect of individuals' lives.

looking forward - - - ->

reach your **learning goals**

Physical and Cognitive Development in Adolescence

1 The Nature of Adolescence

 LG1 Discuss the nature of adolescence.

- Many stereotypes of adolescents are too negative. Most adolescents today successfully negotiate the path from childhood to adulthood. However, too many of today's adolescents are not provided with adequate opportunities and support to become competent adults. It is important to view adolescents as a heterogeneous group because different portraits of adolescents emerge, depending on the particular set of adolescents being described. Social policy regarding adolescents too often has focused on health-compromising behaviors and not enough on strength-based approaches. Adolescents need more caring adults in their lives.

2 Physical Changes

 LG2 Describe the changes involved in puberty, as well as changes in the brain and sexuality during adolescence.

Puberty

- Puberty is a period of rapid physical maturation involving hormonal and bodily changes that occur primarily during early adolescence. Puberty's determinants include nutrition, health, and heredity. The initial onset of the pubertal growth spurt occurs on the average at 9 years for girls and 11 for boys, reaching a peak change for girls at 11½ and for boys at 13½. Individual variation in pubertal changes is substantial. Adolescents show considerable interest in their body image, with girls having more negative body images than boys do. For boys, early maturation brings benefits, at least during early adolescence. Early-maturing girls are vulnerable to a number of risks.

The Brain

- Changes in the brain during adolescence involve the thickening of the corpus callosum and a gap in maturation between the amygdala and the prefrontal cortex, which functions in reasoning and self-regulation.

Adolescent Sexuality

- Adolescence is a time of sexual exploration and sexual experimentation. Having sexual intercourse in early adolescence is associated with negative developmental outcomes. Contraceptive use by adolescents is increasing. About one in four sexually experienced adolescents acquires a sexually transmitted infection (STI). America's adolescent pregnancy rate is higher than in other industrialized nations but has been decreasing in recent years.

3 Issues in Adolescent Health

LG3 Identify adolescent problems related to health, substance use and abuse, and eating disorders.

Adolescent Health

- Adolescence is a critical juncture in health because many of the factors related to poor health habits and early death in the adult years begin during adolescence. Poor nutrition, lack of exercise, and inadequate sleep are concerns. The three leading causes of death in adolescence are unintentional injuries, homicide, and suicide.

Substance Use and Abuse

- Despite recent declines, the United States has one of the highest rates of adolescent illicit drug use of any industrialized nation. Alcohol abuse is a major adolescent problem, although its rate has been dropping in recent years, as has the rate of cigarette smoking. Parents, peers, social support, and educational success play important roles in whether adolescents take drugs.

Eating Disorders

- Eating disorders have increased in adolescence, along with the percentage of adolescents who are overweight. Two eating disorders that may emerge in adolescence are anorexia nervosa and bulimia nervosa. Anorexia nervosa typically starts in the early to middle adolescent years following a dieting episode, and involves the relentless pursuit of thinness through starvation. Bulimia nervosa involves a binge-and-purge pattern, but—unlike anorexics—bulimics typically fall within a normal weight range.

4 Adolescent Cognition

LG4 Explain cognitive changes in adolescence.

Piaget's Theory

- During the formal operational stage, Piaget's fourth stage of cognitive development, thinking becomes more abstract, idealistic, and logical than during the concrete operational stage. However, many adolescents are not formal operational thinkers but are consolidating their concrete operational thought.

Adolescent Egocentrism

- Elkind describes adolescent egocentrism as the heightened self-consciousness of adolescents that consists of two parts: the imaginary audience and the personal fable. Recent research questions whether adolescents perceive themselves to be invulnerable.

Information Processing

- Adolescence is characterized by a number of advances in executive functioning. Cognitive control involves effective control and flexible thinking in a number of areas, including controlling attention, reducing interfering thoughts, remaining cognitively flexible, making decisions, and thinking critically.

5 Schools

LG5 Summarize some key aspects of how schools influence adolescent development.

The Transition to Middle or Junior High School

- The transition to middle or junior high school coincides with many social, familial, and individual changes in the adolescent's life, and this transition is often stressful. One source of stress is the move from the top-dog position to the lowest position in school.

Effective Schools for Young Adolescents

- Some critics argue that a major redesign of U.S. middle schools is needed. Critics say that U.S. high schools foster passivity and do not develop students' academic skills adequately. Characteristics of effective schools include lower student-to-counselor ratios, involvement of parents and community leaders in schools, team teaching, and efforts to boost students' health and fitness.

- A number of strategies have been proposed for improving U.S. high schools, including raising expectations and providing better support. The overall high school dropout rate declined considerably in the last half of the twentieth century, but the dropout rates among Latino and Native American youth remain very high.

- Participation in extracurricular activities is associated with positive academic and psychological outcomes. Adolescents benefit from participating in a variety of extracurricular activities; the quality of the activities also matters.

- Service learning, a form of education that promotes social responsibility and service to the community, has been linked with positive benefits for adolescents such as higher grades, increased goal setting, and improved self-esteem.

key terms

puberty 358
menarche 358
hormones 359
corpus callosum 361
amygdala 361

sexually transmitted
  infections
  (STIs) 364
anorexia nervosa 371
bulimia nervosa 372

hypothetical-deductive
  reasoning 374
adolescent egocentrism 375
imaginary audience 375
personal fable 375

cognitive control 377
dual-process model 377
top-dog phenomenon 379
service learning 381

key people

Peter Benson 357
Lloyd Johnston 370

Jean Piaget 374

David Elkind 375

Deanna Kuhn 375

Chapter 11 | PHYSICAL AND COGNITIVE DEVELOPMENT IN ADOLESCENCE

Connecting with

Learning Objectives	Application Activities	Activity Type	Page Reference
Describe body growth and change during middle and late childhood.	Adolescent Perspectives on Body Image	Milestones: Transitions	pp. 358–361
Discuss the changes involved in the brain during adolescence.	Changes in the Adolescent Brain	Click & drag activity	p. 361
	Influence of Brain Development on Puberty	Video	

(continued)

Learning Objectives	Application Activities	Activity Type	Page Reference
Characterize adolescent sexuality.	Adolescent Perspectives on Sexuality	Milestones: Transitions	pp. 362–366
	Awareness of Sex	Milestones: Transitions	
	Talking About Teen Sex at Age 14	Video	
	Adolescent Sexual Activity	Video	
	Sexual Activity Among GLBT Youth	Video	
	Sexual Activity and Risk in Adolescence	Video	
	Sexual Identity Development	Video	
Explain adolescent health.	Obesity	Video	pp. 367–370
	Overscheduling Our Adolescents	Video	
	Adolescent Stress Over Time	Video	
Summarize substance use and abuse during adolescence.	Attitude about Smoking	Milestones: Transitions	pp. 370–371
	Attitude about Drinking	Milestones: Transitions	
	Awareness of Substance Abuse	Milestones: Transitions	
	Talking about Drugs at Age 15	Video	
	Marijuana Use Among Young Adults: Expert Interview	Video	
Discuss eating disorders.	Girls' View on Body Image	Video	pp. 371–373
	Eating Disorders: Anorexia Specific	Video	
Explain adolescent egocentrism.	Self-Perception at 14 Years of Age	Video	p. 375
	Personal Fable	Milestones: Transition	
Describe information processing during adolescence.	Adolescent Perspectives on Thinking and Memory	Milestones: Transitions	pp. 375–378
Identify key aspects of how high school influences adolescent development.	Thoughts on School	Video	pp. 379–381
	School and Public Policy	Video	

chapter 12

SOCIOEMOTIONAL DEVELOPMENT IN ADOLESCENCE

chapter outline

1 The Self, Identity, and Religious/Spiritual Development

Learning Goal 1 Discuss self, identity, and religious/spiritual development in adolescence.

Self-Esteem
Identity
Religious/Spiritual Development

2 Families

Learning Goal 2 Describe changes that take place in adolescents' relationships with their parents.

Parental Monitoring and Information Management
Autonomy and Attachment
Parent-Adolescent Conflict

3 Peers

Learning Goal 3 Characterize the changes that occur in peer relationships during adolescence.

Friendships
Peer Groups
Dating and Romantic Relationships

4 Culture and Adolescent Development

Learning Goal 4 Explain how culture influences adolescent development.

Cross-Cultural Comparisons
Ethnicity
The Media

5 Adolescent Problems

Learning Goal 5 Identify adolescent problems in socioemotional development and strategies for helping adolescents with problems.

Juvenile Delinquency
Depression and Suicide
The Interrelation of Problems and Successful Prevention/Intervention Programs

The mayor of the city says she is "everywhere." She recently persuaded the city's school committee to consider ending the practice of locking tardy students out of their classrooms. She also swayed a neighborhood group to support her proposal for a winter jobs program. According to one city councilman, "People are just impressed with the power of her arguments and the sophistication of the argument" (Silva, 2005, pp. B1, B4). She is Jewel E. Cash, and she is only 16 years old.

A junior at Boston Latin Academy, Jewel was raised in one of Boston's housing projects by her mother, a single parent. Today she belongs to the Boston Student Advisory Council, mentors children, volunteers at a women's shelter, manages and dances in two troupes, and participates in a neighborhood watch group—among other activities. Jewel is far from typical, but her activities illustrate that cognitive and socioemotional development allows adolescents to be capable, effective individuals.

Jewel Cash seated next to her mother participating in a crime watch meeting at a community center.

-topical **connections** - - - - - - - - -

In middle and late childhood, development of self-understanding and understanding others becomes more sophisticated, emotional understanding improves, and moral reasoning advances. In Erikson's view, children now are in the industry versus inferiority stage, with their industry expressed as an interest in building things and figuring out how things work. Children now spend more time with peers, but parents continue to play important roles in their development, especially in guiding their academic achievement and managing their opportunities. Peer status and friendship become more important in children's peer relations, and school takes on a stronger academic focus.

◄- - - *looking **back*** - - - - - - - - - - - - - - - -

Significant changes characterize socioemotional development in adolescence. These changes include increased efforts to understand themselves and to find their identity. Changes also occur in the social contexts of adolescents' lives, with transformations occurring in relationships with families and peers in cultural contexts. Adolescents also may develop socioemotional problems such as delinquency and depression.

1 The Self, Identity, and Religious/ Spiritual Development

LG1 Discuss self, identity, and religious/spiritual development in adolescence.

Self-Esteem   Identity   Religious/Spiritual Development

Jewel Cash told an interviewer from the Boston Globe, "I see a problem and I say, 'How can I make a difference?' . . . I can't take on the world, even though I can try. . . . I'm moving forward but I want to make sure I'm bringing people with me" (Silva, 2005, pp. B1, B4). Jewel's confidence and positive identity sound at least as impressive as her activities. This section examines how adolescents develop characteristics like these. How much did you understand yourself during adolescence, and how did you acquire the stamp of your identity? Is your identity still developing?

SELF-ESTEEM

Recall from Chapter 10 that self-esteem is the overall way we evaluate ourselves. Controversy characterizes the extent to which self-esteem changes during adolescence and whether there are gender differences in adolescents' self-esteem (Harter, 2006). In one study, both boys and girls had particularly high self-esteem in childhood, but their self-esteem dropped considerably during adolescence (Robins & others, 2002). The self-esteem of girls declined more than the self-esteem of boys during adolescence in this study.

Does self-esteem in adolescence foreshadow adjustment and competence in adulthood? A New Zealand longitudinal study assessed the self-esteem of adolescents at 11, 13, and 15 years of age and then assessed the adjustment and competence of the same individuals when they were 26 years old (Trzesniewski & others, 2006). The results revealed that adults with poorer mental and physical health, worse economic prospects, and higher levels of criminal behavior were more likely to have had low self-esteem in adolescence than their better adjusted, more competent adult counterparts.

Some critics argue that developmental changes and gender differences in self-esteem during adolescence have been exaggerated (Harter, 2006). Despite the differing results and interpretations, the self-esteem of girls is likely to decline at least somewhat during early adolescence.

Why would the self-esteem of girls decline during early adolescence? One explanation points to girls' negative body images during pubertal change. Another explanation involves the greater interest young adolescent girls take in social relationships and society's failure to reward that interest (Impett & others, 2008).

Self-esteem reflects perceptions that do not always match reality (Krueger, Vohs, & Baumeister, 2008). An adolescent's self-esteem might indicate a perception about whether he or she is intelligent and attractive, for example, but that perception may not be accurate. Thus, high self-esteem may refer to accurate, justified perceptions of one's worth as a person and one's successes and accomplishments, but it can also indicate an arrogant, grandiose, unwarranted sense of superiority over others. In the same manner, low self-esteem may suggest either an accurate perception of one's shortcomings or a distorted, even pathological insecurity and inferiority.

Narcissism refers to a self-centered and self-concerned approach toward others. Typically, narcissists are unaware of their actual self and how others perceive them. This lack of awareness

narcissism A self-centered and self-concerned approach toward others.

contributes to their adjustment problems. Narcissists are excessively self-centered and self-congratulatory, viewing their own needs and desires as paramount.

Are today's adolescents and emerging adults more self-centered and narcissistic than their counterparts in earlier generations? Research by Jean Twenge and her colleagues (2008a, b) indicated that compared with Baby Boomers who were surveyed in 1975, twelfth-graders surveyed in 2006 were more self-satisfied overall and far more confident that they would be very good employees, mates, and parents. However, other recent large-scale analyses have revealed no increase in high school and college students' narcissism from the 1980s through the first generation of the twenty-first century (Roberts, Edmonds, & Grijalva, 2010; Trzesniewski & Donnellan, 2010; Trzesniewski, Donnellan, & Robins, 2008a, b).

In one recent analysis, age changes in narcissism were much stronger than generation changes (Roberts, Edmonds, & Grijalva, 2010). In this study, across three generations, college students were the most narcissistic, followed by their parents, and then students' grandparents were the least narcissistic. These researchers say that is more accurate to label today's adolescents and emerging adults *developmental me* rather than *generational me*.

What characterizes narcissistic adolescents? Are today's adolescents more narcissistic than their counterparts in earlier generations?

IDENTITY

Who am I? What am I all about? What am I going to do with my life? What is different about me? How can I make it on my own? These questions reflect the search for an identity. By far the most comprehensive and provocative theory of identity development is Erik Erikson's. In this section, we examine his views on identity. We also discuss contemporary research on how identity develops and how social contexts influence that development.

What Is Identity?   Identity is a self-portrait composed of many pieces, including these:

- The career and work path the person wants to follow (vocational/career identity)
- Whether the person is conservative, liberal, or middle-of-the-road (political identity)
- The person's spiritual beliefs (religious identity)
- Whether the person is single, married, divorced, and so on (relationship identity)
- The extent to which the person is motivated to achieve and is intellectually oriented (achievement, intellectual identity)
- Whether the person is heterosexual, homosexual, or bisexual (sexual identity)
- Which part of the world or country a person is from and how intensely the person identifies with his or her cultural heritage (cultural/ethnic identity)
- The kind of things a person likes to do, which can include sports, music, hobbies, and so on (interests)
- The individual's personality characteristics, such as being introverted or extroverted, anxious or calm, friendly or hostile, and so on (personality)
- The individual's body image (physical identity)

Synthesizing the identity components can be a long and drawn-out process, with many negations and affirmations of various roles and faces (Kroger, 2012). Identity development gets done in bits and pieces. Decisions are not made once and for all, but have to be made again and again. Identity development does not happen neatly, and it does not happen cataclysmically (Duriez & others, 2012; Schwartz & others, 2011, 2013).

Erikson's View   It was Erik Erikson (1950, 1968) who first understood how central questions about identity are to understanding adolescent development.

Recall from Chapter 1 that Erikson's fifth developmental stage, which individuals experience during adolescence, is *identity versus identity confusion*. During this time, said Erikson, adolescents are faced with deciding who they are, what they are all about, and where they are going in life.

The search for an identity during adolescence is aided by a *psychosocial moratorium*, which is Erikson's term for the gap between childhood security and adult autonomy. During

"Who are you?" said the Caterpillar. Alice replied, rather shyly, "I—I hardly know, Sir, just at present—at least I know who I was when I got up this morning, but I must have changed several times since then."

—LEWIS CARROLL
English Writer, 19th Century

developmental **connection**

Cognitive Theory

Erikson's stage for middle and late childhood is industry versus inferiority and for early adulthood is intimacy versus isolation. Chapter 10, p. 321; Chapter 14, p. 457

What are some important dimensions of identity?

Once formed, an identity furnishes individuals with a historical sense of who they have been, a meaningful sense of who they are now, and a sense of who they might become in the future.

—James Marcia
Contemporary Psychologist, Simon Fraser University

crisis Marcia's term for a period of identity development during which the adolescent is exploring alternatives.

commitment Marcia's term for the part of identity development in which adolescents show a personal investment in identity.

identity diffusion Marcia's term for the status of individuals who have not yet experienced a crisis (explored meaningful alternatives) or made any commitments.

identity foreclosure Marcia's term for the status of individuals who have made a commitment but have not experienced a crisis.

identity moratorium Marcia's term for the status of individuals who are in the midst of a crisis, but their commitments are either absent or vaguely defined.

identity achievement Marcia's term for the status of individuals who have undergone a crisis and have made a commitment.

this period, society leaves adolescents relatively free of responsibilities and able to try out different identities. Adolescents experiment with different roles and personalities. They may want to pursue one career one month (lawyer, for example) and another career the next month (doctor, actor, teacher, social worker, or astronaut, for example). They may dress neatly one day, sloppily the next. This experimentation is a deliberate effort on the part of adolescents to find out where they fit in the world. Most adolescents eventually discard undesirable roles.

Youth who successfully cope with conflicting identities emerge with a new sense of self that is both refreshing and acceptable. Adolescents who do not successfully resolve this identity crisis suffer what Erikson calls identity confusion. The confusion takes one of two courses: Individuals withdraw, isolating themselves from peers and family, or they immerse themselves in the world of peers and lose their identity in the crowd.

Developmental Changes Although questions about identity may be especially important during adolescence, identity formation neither begins nor ends during these years. What is important about identity development in adolescence, especially late adolescence, is that for the first time, physical development, cognitive development, and socioemotional development advance to the point at which the individual can sort through and synthesize childhood identities and identifications to construct a viable path toward adult maturity.

How do individual adolescents go about the process of forming an identity? Eriksonian researcher James Marcia (1980, 1994) reasons that Erikson's theory of identity development contains four statuses of identity, or ways of resolving the identity crisis: identity diffusion, identity foreclosure, identity moratorium, and identity achievement. What determines an individual's identity status? Marcia classifies individuals based on the existence or extent of their crisis or commitment (see Figure 12.1). **Crisis** is defined as a period of identity development during which the individual is exploring alternatives. Most researchers use the term *exploration* rather than *crisis*. **Commitment** is personal investment in identity.

The four statuses of identity are described below:

- **Identity diffusion** is the status of individuals who have not yet experienced a crisis or made any commitments. Not only are they undecided about occupational and ideological choices, they are also likely to show little interest in such matters.
- **Identity foreclosure** is the status of individuals who have made a commitment but not experienced a crisis. This occurs most often when parents hand down commitments to their adolescents, usually in an authoritarian way, before adolescents have had a chance to explore different approaches, ideologies, and vocations on their own.
- **Identity moratorium** is the status of individuals who are in the midst of a crisis but whose commitments are either absent or are only vaguely defined.
- **Identity achievement** is the status of individuals who have undergone a crisis and made a commitment.

Earlier in this chapter we described a number of dimensions of identity. To explore your identity status on a number of dimensions, see Figure 12.1.

	Identity Status			
Position on Occupation and Ideology	**Identity Diffusion**	**Identity Foreclosure**	**Identity Moratorium**	**Identity Achievement**
Crisis	Absent	Absent	Present	Present
Commitment	Absent	Present	Absent	Present

FIGURE **12.1**

MARCIA'S FOUR STATUSES OF IDENTITY. According to Marcia, an individual's status in developing an identity can be categorized as identity diffusion, identity foreclosure, identity moratorium, or identity achievement. The status depends on the presence or absence of (1) a crisis or exploration of alternatives and (2) a commitment to an identity. *What is the identity status of most young adolescents?*

Emerging Adulthood and Beyond   A recent study found that as individuals matured from early adolescence to emerging adulthood, they increasingly pursued in-depth exploration of their identity (Klimstra & others, 2010). And a recent meta-analysis of 124 studies by Jane Kroger and her colleagues (2010) revealed that during adolescence and emerging adulthood, identity moratorium status rose steadily to age 19 and then declined; identity achievement rose across late adolescence and emerging adulthood; and foreclosure and diffusion statuses declined across the high school years but fluctuated in the late teens and emerging adulthood. The studies also found that a large portion of individuals were not identity achieved by the time they reached their twenties.

Indeed, a consensus is developing that the key changes in identity are more likely to take place in emerging adulthood (18 to 25 years of age) or later than during adolescence (Moshman, 2011; Schwartz & others, 2013; Syed, 2010, 2013). For example, Alan Waterman (1985, 1999) has found that from the years preceding high school through the last few years of college, the number of individuals who are identity achieved increases, while the number who are identity diffused decreases. College upperclassmen are more likely to be identity achieved than college freshmen or high school students. Many young adolescents, on the other hand, are identity diffused. These developmental changes are especially true for vocational choice. In terms of religious beliefs and political ideology, fewer college students reach the identity-achieved status; a substantial number are characterized by foreclosure and diffusion. Thus, the timing of identity development may depend on the particular dimension.

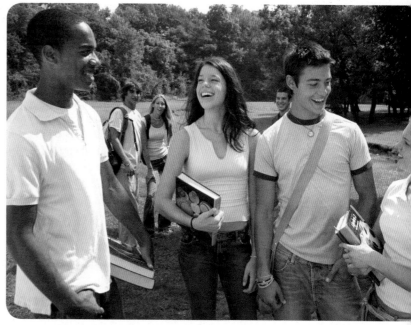

How does identity change in emerging adulthood?

Why might college produce some key changes in identity? Increased complexity in the reasoning skills of college students combined with a wide range of new experiences that highlight contrasts between home and college and between themselves and others stimulates them to reach a higher level of integrating various dimensions of their identity (Phinney, 2008).

Resolution of the identity issue during adolescence and emerging adulthood does not mean that identity will be stable throughout the remainder of life. Many individuals who develop positive identities follow what are called "MAMA" cycles; that is, their identity status changes from moratorium to achievement to moratorium to achievement (Marcia, 1994). These cycles may be repeated throughout life (Francis, Fraser, & Marcia, 1989). Marcia (2002) points out that the first identity is just that—it is not, and should not be expected to be, the final product.

Ethnic Identity   Throughout the world, ethnic minority groups have struggled to maintain their ethnic identities while blending in with the dominant culture (Erikson, 1968). **Ethnic identity** is an enduring aspect of the self that includes a sense of membership in an ethnic group, along with the attitudes and feelings related to that membership (Hudley & Irving, 2012). Most adolescents from ethnic minority groups develop a *bicultural identity*. That is, they identify in some ways with their ethnic group and in other ways with the majority culture.

For ethnic minority individuals, adolescence and emerging adulthood are often special junctures in their development (Syed, 2010, 2013). Although children are aware of some ethnic and cultural differences, individuals consciously confront their ethnicity for the first time in adolescence or emerging adulthood. Unlike children, adolescents and emerging adults have the ability to interpret ethnic and cultural information, to reflect on the past, and to speculate about the future. With their advancing cognitive skills of abstract thinking and self-reflection, adolescents (especially older adolescents) increasingly consider the meaning of their ethnicity and also have more ethnic-related experiences (O'Hara & others, 2012; Seaton & others, 2011). Because adolescents are more mobile and independent from their parents, they are more likely to experience ethnic stereotyping and discrimination as they interact with diverse individuals in school contexts and other public settings (Brody, Kogan, & Chen, 2012; Potochnick, Perreira, & Fuligni, 2012). Researchers have found that many ethnic minority groups experience stereotyping and discrimination, including African American, Latino, and Asian

ethnic identity An enduring, basic aspect of the self that includes a sense of membership in an ethnic group and the attitudes and feelings related to that membership.

American adolescents (Hughes, Way, and Rivas-Drake, 2011; Roberts & others, 2012; Umana Taylor & others, 2012).

The indicators of identity change often differ for each succeeding generation (Phinney & Ong, 2007). First-generation immigrants are likely to be secure in their identities and unlikely to change much; they may or may not develop a new identity. The degree to which they begin to feel "American" appears to be related to whether or not they learn English, develop social networks beyond their ethnic group, and become culturally competent in their new country. Second-generation immigrants are more likely to think of themselves as "American," possibly because citizenship is granted at birth. Their ethnic identity is likely to be linked to retention of their ethnic language and social networks. In the third and later generations, the issues become more complex. Historical, contextual, and political factors that are unrelated to acculturation may affect the extent to which members of this generation retain their ethnic identities. For non-European ethnic groups, racism and discrimination influence whether ethnic identity is retained.

Researchers are also increasingly finding that a positive ethnic identity is related to positive outcomes for ethnic minority adolescents (Umana-Taylor, Updegraff, & Gonzales-Bracken, 2011). A recent study revealed that a positive ethnic identity helped to buffer some of the negative effects of discrimination experienced by Mexican American adolescents (Umana-Taylor & others, 2012). Another study indicated that Navajo adolescents' positive ethnic heritage was linked to higher self-esteem, school connectedness, and social functioning (Jones & Galliher, 2007).

RELIGIOUS/SPIRITUAL DEVELOPMENT

In Chapter 11, we described the many positive benefits of service learning. A number of studies have found that adolescents who are involved in religious institutions are more likely to engage in service learning than their counterparts who don't participate in religious institutions (Lerner, Roeser, & Phelps, 2009; Lerner & others, 2013; Saroglou, 2013). Let's explore adolescents' religious and spiritual experiences.

Religious issues are important to many adolescents, but during the twenty-first century religious interest among adolescents has declined. In a 2010 national study of American college freshmen, 73 percent said they had attended religious services frequently or occasionally during their senior year in high school, down from a high of 85 percent in 1997 (Pryor & others, 2011).

A developmental study revealed that religiousness declined from 14 to 20 years of age in the United States (Koenig, McGue, & Iacono, 2008) (see Figure 12.2). In this study, religiousness was assessed with items such as frequency of prayer, frequency of discussing religious teachings, frequency of deciding moral actions for religious reasons, and the overall importance of religion in everyday life. As indicated in Figure 12.2, more change in religiousness occurred from 14 to 18 years of age than from 20 to 24 years of age. Also in this study, attending religious services declined from 14 to 18 years of age and then began to increase at 20 years of age.

Researchers have found that adolescent girls are more religious than are adolescent boys (King & Roeser, 2009). One study of 13- to 17-year-olds revealed that girls are more likely to attend religious services frequently, to perceive that religion shapes their daily lives, to participate in religious youth groups, to pray alone, and to feel closer to God (Smith & Denton, 2005).

Analysis of the World Values Survey of 18- to 24-year-olds revealed that emerging adults in less developed countries were more likely to be religious than their counterparts in more developed countries (Lippman & Keith, 2006). For example, emerging adults' reports that religion was very important in their lives ranged from a low of 0 in Japan to 93 percent in Nigeria, and belief in God ranged from a low of 40 percent in Sweden to a high of 100 percent in Pakistan.

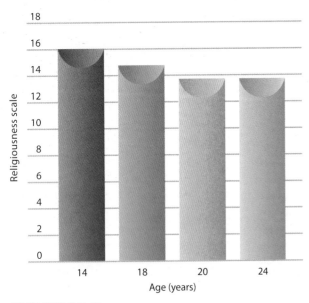

FIGURE **12.2**

DEVELOPMENTAL CHANGES IN RELIGIOUSNESS FROM 14 TO 24 YEARS OF AGE. *Note:* The religiousness scale ranged from 0 to 32, with higher scores indicating stronger religiousness.

Religion and Identity Development   As we saw earlier in this chapter, identity development becomes a central focus during adolescence and emerging adulthood (Schwartz & others, 2013; Syed, 2013). As part of their search for identity, adolescents and emerging adults begin to grapple in more sophisticated,

Many children and adolescents show an interest in religion, and many religious institutions created by adults (such as this Muslim school in Malaysia) are designed to introduce them to religious benefits and ensure that they will carry on a religious tradition.

logical ways with such questions as "Why am I on this planet?" "Is there really a God or higher spiritual being, or have I just been believing what my parents and the church imprinted in my mind?" "What really are my religious views?"

A recent study of Latino, African American, Asian, and non-Latino White adolescents revealed that their religious identity remained stable across high school grades but that religious participation declined (Lopez, Huynh, & Fuligni, 2011). In this study, Latino and Asian adolescents had the highest levels of religious identity, while Latino adolescents had the highest level of religious participation.

Cognitive Development and Religion in Adolescence Many of the cognitive changes thought to influence religious development involve Piaget's cognitive developmental theory. More so than in childhood, adolescents think abstractly, idealistically, and logically. The increase in abstract thinking lets adolescents consider various ideas about religious and spiritual concepts. For example, an adolescent might ask how a loving God can possibly exist given the extensive suffering of many people in the world (Good & Willoughby, 2008). Adolescents' increased idealistic thinking provides a foundation for thinking about whether religion provides the best route to a better world. And adolescents' increased logical reasoning gives them the ability to develop hypotheses and systematically sort through different answers to spiritual questions (Good & Willoughby, 2008).

The Positive Role of Religion in Adolescents' Lives Researchers have found that various aspects of religion are linked with positive outcomes for adolescents (Harakeh & others, 2012; Shek, 2012). A recent study revealed that parents' religiousness during youths' adolescence was positively related to youths' own religiousness during adolescence (Spilman & others, 2012). Religion plays a role in adolescents' health and influences whether they engage in problem behaviors (King, Ramos, & Clardy, 2013). For example, in a recent national random sample of more than 2,000 11- to 18-year-olds, those who had a stronger interest in

What are some positive roles of religion in adolescents' lives?

developmental **connection**

Religion

Religion plays an important role in the lives of many individuals in adulthood and is linked to their health and coping. Chapter 15, p. 502; Chapter 18, p. 590

religion were less likely to smoke, drink alcohol, use marijuana, be truant from school, engage in delinquent activities, and be depressed than their low-religiosity counterparts (Sinha, Cnaan, & Gelles, 2006).

Many religious adolescents also adopt their religion's message about caring and concern for people (Lerner & others, 2013; Saroglou, 2013; Shek, 2012). For example, in one survey religious youth were almost three times as likely to engage in community service as nonreligious youth (Youniss, McLellan, & Yates, 1999).

Review *Connect* Reflect

  LG1 Discuss self, identity, and religious/spiritual development in adolescence.

Review

- What are some changes in self-esteem that take place during adolescence?
- How does identity develop in adolescence?
- What characterizes religious and spiritual development in adolescence?

Connect

- Compare what is said about inflated self-esteem in middle and late childhood in Chapter 10 to what is said in this section about potential narcissism in adolescence. What are your conclusions?

Reflect *Your Own Personal Journey of Life*

- What role did religion/spiritual development play in your life during adolescence? Has your religious/spiritual thinking changed since you were an adolescent? If so, how?

2 Families

LG2 Describe changes that take place in adolescents' relationships with their parents.

| Parental Monitoring and Information Management | Autonomy and Attachment | Parent-Adolescent Conflict |

Adolescence typically alters the relationship between parents and their children. Among the most important aspects of family relationships in adolescence are those that involve parental monitoring and information management, autonomy and attachment, and parent-adolescent conflict.

PARENTAL MONITORING AND INFORMATION MANAGEMENT

In Chapter 10, we discussed the importance of parents as managers of children's development. A key aspect of the managerial role of parenting is effective monitoring, which is especially important as children move into the adolescent years (Smetana, 2010, 2011a, b). Monitoring includes supervising adolescents' choice of social settings, activities, and friends, as well as their academic efforts. Later in this chapter, we will describe lack of adequate parental monitoring as the parental factor most likely to be linked to juvenile delinquency.

A current interest involving parental monitoring focuses on adolescents' management of their parents' access to information, especially disclosing or concealing strategies about their activities (Amsel & Smetana, 2011; Rote & others, 2012). When parents engage in positive parenting practices, adolescents are more likely to disclose information (Rote & others, 2012). For example, disclosure increases when parents ask adolescents questions and when adolescents' relationship with parents is characterized by a high level of trust, acceptance, and quality (Keijsers & Laird, 2010). Researchers have found that adolescents' disclosure to parents about their whereabouts, activities, and friends is linked to positive adolescent adjustment (Laird & Marrero, 2010; Rote & others, 2012; Smetana, 2011a, b).

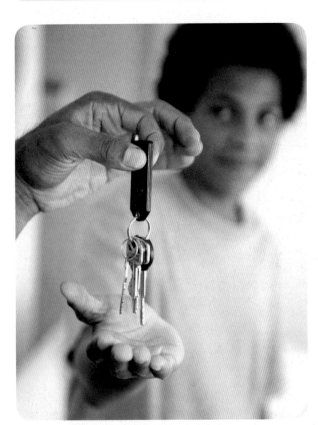

What role does parental monitoring and information management play in adolescent development?

AUTONOMY AND ATTACHMENT

With most adolescents, parents are likely to find themselves engaged in a delicate balancing act, weighing competing needs for autonomy and control, for independence and connection.

The typical adolescent's push for autonomy and responsibility puzzles and angers many parents. Most parents anticipate that their teenager will have some difficulty adjusting to the changes that adolescence brings, but few parents imagine and predict just how strong an adolescent's desires will be to spend time with peers or how intensely adolescents will want to show that it is they—not their parents—who are responsible for their successes and failures.

Adolescents' ability to attain autonomy and gain control over their behavior is acquired through appropriate adult reactions to their desire for control (McElhaney & Allen, 2012; Steinberg & Collins, 2011). At the onset of adolescence, the average individual does not have the knowledge to make appropriate or mature decisions in all areas of life. As the adolescent pushes for autonomy, the wise adult relinquishes control in those areas where the adolescent can make reasonable decisions, but continues to guide the adolescent to make reasonable decisions in areas where the adolescent's knowledge is more limited. Gradually, adolescents acquire the ability to make mature decisions on their own.

Gender differences characterize autonomy-granting in adolescence. Boys are given more independence than girls. In one study, this was especially true in U.S. families with a traditional gender-role orientation (Bumpus, Crouter, & McHale, 2001). Also, Latino parents protect and monitor their daughters more closely than is the case for non-Latino White parents (Allen & others, 2008; Updegraff & others, 2010).

The Role of Attachment   Recall from Chapter 6 that one of the most widely discussed aspects of socioemotional development in infancy is secure attachment to caregivers (Brisch, 2012; Easterbrooks & others, 2013; Kok & others, 2012). In the past decade, researchers have explored whether secure attachment also might be an important concept in adolescents' relationships with their parents (Gorrese & Ruggieri, 2012; Schwarz, Stutz, & Ledermann, 2012). Researchers have found that securely attached adolescents are less likely than those who are insecurely attached to have emotional difficulties and to engage in problem behaviors such as juvenile delinquency and drug abuse (Dykes & Cassidy, 2011; Hoeve & others, 2012). In a longitudinal study, Joseph Allen and colleagues (2009) found that secure attachment at 14 years of age was linked to a number of positive outcomes at 21 years of age, including relationship competence, financial/career competence, and fewer problematic behaviors. In a recent analysis, it was concluded that the most consistent outcomes of secure attachment in adolescence involve positive peer relations and development of the adolescent's capacity to regulate emotions (Allen & Miga, 2010).

Balancing Freedom and Control   We have seen that parents play very important roles in adolescent development (Morris, Cui, & Steinberg, 2013). Although adolescents are moving toward independence, they still need to stay connected with their family (Schwarz, Stutz, & Ledermann, 2012). For example, the National Longitudinal Study on Adolescent Health of more than 12,000 adolescents found that those who did not eat dinner with a parent five or more days a week had dramatically higher rates of smoking, drinking, using marijuana, getting into fights, and initiating sexual activity (Council of Economic Advisors, 2000).

PARENT-ADOLESCENT CONFLICT

Although parent-adolescent conflict increases in early adolescence, it does not reach the tumultuous proportions G. Stanley Hall envisioned at the beginning of the twentieth century (Bornstein, Jager, & Steinberg, 2013). Rather, much of the conflict involves the everyday events of family life, such as keeping a bedroom clean, dressing neatly, getting home by a certain time, and not talking endlessly on the phone. The conflicts rarely involve major dilemmas such as drugs or delinquency.

Conflict with parents often escalates during early adolescence, remains somewhat stable during the high school years, and then lessens as the adolescent reaches 17 to 20 years of age.

developmental **connection**

Parenting

In authoritative parenting, parents encourage children and adolescents to be independent but still place limits and controls on their actions. Extensive verbal give-and-take is allowed, and parents are warm and nurturant. Chapter 8, p. 255

When I was a boy of 14, my father was so ignorant I could hardly stand to have the man around. But when I got to be 21, I was astonished at how much he had learnt in 7 years.

—**MARK TWAIN**
American Writer and Humorist, 19th Century

Stacey Christensen, age 16: "I am lucky enough to have open communication with my parents. Whenever I am in need or just need to talk, my parents are there for me. My advice to parents is to let your teens grow at their own pace, be open with them so that you can be there for them. We need guidance; our parents need to help but not be too overwhelming."

developmental **connection**

Attachment

In secure attachment in infancy, babies use the caregiver as a secure base from which to explore the environment. Chapter 6, p. 190

Old Model	New Model
Autonomy, detachment from parents; parent and peer worlds are isolated	Attachment and autonomy; parents are important support systems and attachment figures; adolescent-parent and adolescent-peer worlds have some important connections
Intense, stressful conflict throughout adolescence; parent-adolescent relationships are filled with storm and stress on virtually a daily basis	Moderate parent-adolescent conflict is common and can serve a positive developmental function; conflict greater in early adolescence

FIGURE 12.3

OLD AND NEW MODELS OF PARENT-ADOLESCENT RELATIONSHIPS

Conflict with parents increases in early adolescence. *What is the nature of this conflict in a majority of American families?*

Parent-adolescent relationships become more positive if adolescents go away to college than if they attend college while living at home (Sullivan & Sullivan, 1980).

The everyday conflicts that characterize parent-adolescent relationships may actually serve a positive developmental function. These minor disputes and negotiations facilitate the adolescent's transition from being dependent on parents to becoming an autonomous individual. Recognizing that conflict and negotiation can serve a positive developmental function can tone down parental hostility.

The old model of parent-adolescent relationships suggested that as adolescents mature they detach themselves from parents and move into a world of autonomy apart from parents. The old model also suggested that parent-adolescent conflict is intense and stressful throughout adolescence. The new model emphasizes that parents serve as important attachment figures and support systems while adolescents explore a wider, more complex social world. The new model also emphasizes that in most families parent-adolescent conflict is moderate rather than severe and that the everyday negotiations and minor disputes not only are normal but also can serve the positive developmental function of helping the adolescent make the transition from childhood dependency to adult independence (see Figure 12.3).

Still, a high degree of conflict characterizes some parent-adolescent relationships (Schwarz, Stutz, & Ledermann, 2012). And this prolonged, intense conflict is associated with various adolescent problems: movement out of the home, juvenile delinquency, school dropout, pregnancy and early marriage, membership in religious cults, and drug abuse (Brook & others, 1990).

Review Connect Reflect

LG2 Describe changes that take place in adolescents' relationships with their parents.

Review

- What roles do parental managing and monitoring play in adolescent development?
- How do needs for autonomy and attachment develop in adolescence?
- What characterizes parent-adolescent conflict?

Connect

- Adolescence is identified as the second time in an individual's life when the quest for independence is especially strong.

When is the other time, and what characterizes that stage of development?

Reflect *Your Own Personal Journey of Life*

- How much autonomy did your parents give you in adolescence? Too much? Too little? How intense was your conflict with your parents during adolescence? What were the conflicts mainly about? Would you interact differently with your own adolescents than the way your parents did with you? If so, how?

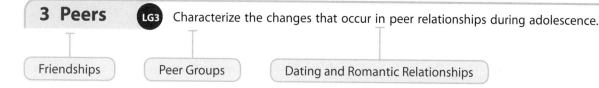

3 Peers (LG3) Characterize the changes that occur in peer relationships during adolescence.

Friendships   Peer Groups   Dating and Romantic Relationships

Peers play powerful roles in the lives of adolescents (Bornstein, Jager, & Steinberg, 2013; Way & Silverman, 2012; Wentzel, 2013). Peer relations undergo important changes in adolescence, including changes in friendships and in peer groups, as well as the beginning of romantic relationships.

FRIENDSHIPS

For most children, being popular with their peers is a strong motivator. Beginning in early adolescence, however, teenagers typically prefer to have a smaller number of friendships that are more intense and intimate than those of young children.

Harry Stack Sullivan (1953) was the most influential theorist to discuss the importance of adolescent friendships. During adolescence, said Sullivan, friends become increasingly important in meeting social needs. In particular, Sullivan argued that the need for intimacy intensifies during early adolescence, motivating teenagers to seek out close friends. If adolescents fail to develop such close friendships, they experience loneliness and a reduced sense of self-worth.

Many of Sullivan's ideas have withstood the test of time. For example, adolescents report disclosing intimate and personal information to their friends more often than do younger children (Buhrmester, 1998) (see Figure 12.4). Adolescents also say they depend more on friends than on parents to satisfy their needs for companionship, reassurance of worth, and intimacy. The ups and downs of experiences with friends shape adolescents' well-being (Cook, Buehler, & Blair, 2012). Adolescent girls are more likely to disclose information about problems to a friend than are adolescent boys (Rose & others, 2012).

Although having friends can be a developmental advantage, not all friendships are alike and the quality of friendship matters. People differ in the company they keep—that is, who their friends are. It is a developmental disadvantage to have coercive, conflict-ridden, and poor-quality friendships (Ali & Dwyer, 2011; Poulin & others, 2011). Developmental advantages occur when adolescents have friends who are socially skilled, supportive, and oriented toward academic achievement (Rodkin & Ryan, 2012; Ryan, 2011). Positive friendship relationships in adolescence are associated with a host of positive outcomes, including lower rates of delinquency, substance abuse, risky sexual behavior, and bullying victimization, and a higher level of academic achievement (Kendrick, Jutengren, & Stattin, 2012; Tucker & others, 2012; Way & Silverman, 2012; Wentzel, 2013).

Although most adolescents develop friendships with individuals who are close to their own age, some adolescents become best friends with younger or older individuals. Do older friends encourage adolescents to engage in delinquent behavior or early sexual behavior? Adolescents who interact with older youth do engage in more problem behaviors, such as delinquency and early sexual behavior (Poulin & Pedersen, 2007).

To read about strategies for helping adolescents develop friendships, see *Connecting Development to Life.*

PEER GROUPS

How extensive is peer pressure in adolescence? What roles do cliques and crowds play in adolescents' lives? As we see next, researchers have found that the standards of peer groups and the influence of crowds and cliques become increasingly important during adolescence.

Peer Pressure   Young adolescents conform more to peer standards than children do. Around the eighth and ninth grades, conformity to peers—especially to their antisocial

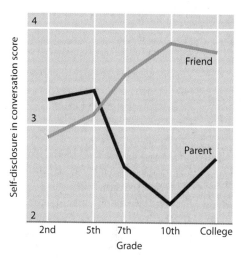

FIGURE **12.4**

DEVELOPMENTAL CHANGES IN SELF-DISCLOSING CONVERSATIONS. Self-disclosing conversations with friends increased dramatically in adolescence while declining in an equally dramatic fashion with parents. However, self-disclosing conversations with parents began to pick up somewhat during the college years. The measure of self-disclosure involved a 5-point rating scale completed by the children and youth, with a higher score representing greater self-disclosure. The data shown represent the means for each age group.

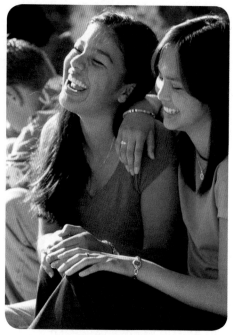

How do characteristics of an adolescent's friends influence whether the friends have a positive or negative influence on the adolescent?

Effective and Ineffective Strategies for Making Friends

Here are some strategies for making friends that adults can recommend to adolescents (Wentzel, 1997):

- *Initiate interaction.* Learn about a friend: Ask for his or her name, age, favorite activities. Use these prosocial overtures: introduce yourself, start a conversation, and invite him or her to do things.
- *Be nice.* Show kindness, be considerate, and compliment the other person.
- *Engage in prosocial behavior.* Be honest and trustworthy: Tell the truth, keep promises. Be generous, share, and be cooperative.
- *Show respect for yourself and others.* Have good manners, be polite and courteous, and listen to what others have to say. Have a positive attitude and personality.
- *Provide social support.* Show you care.

What are some effective and ineffective strategies for making friends?

And here are some inappropriate strategies for making friends that adults can recommend that adolescents avoid using (Wentzel, 1997):

- *Be psychologically aggressive.* Show disrespect and have bad manners. Use others, be uncooperative, don't share, ignore others, gossip, and spread rumors.
- *Present yourself negatively.* Be self-centered, snobby, conceited, and jealous; show off; care only about yourself. Be mean, have a bad attitude, be angry, throw temper tantrums, and start trouble.
- *Behave antisocially.* Be physically aggressive, yell at others, pick on them, make fun of them, be dishonest, tell secrets, and break promises.

Based on what you read earlier in this chapter, what else might you recommend to an adolescent about whom to approach as a potential friend?

What characterizes peer pressure in adolescence?

clique A small group of about 5 or 6 individuals that may form among adolescents who engage in similar activities.

standards—peaks (Brown & Larson, 2009; Brown & others, 2008). At this point, adolescents are most likely to go along with a peer to steal hubcaps off a car, draw graffiti on a wall, or steal cosmetics from a store counter. One study found that U.S. adolescents are more likely than Japanese adolescents to put pressure on their peers to resist parental influence (Rothbaum & others, 2000).

Which adolescents are most likely to conform to peers? Mitchell Prinstein and his colleagues (Cohen & Prinstein, 2006; Prinstein, 2007; Prinstein & Dodge, 2008) have recently conducted research suggesting that adolescents who feel uncertain about their social identity, which may be evident in low self-esteem and high social anxiety, are most likely to conform to peers. This uncertainty often increases during times of transition, such as changing circumstances in school and family life. Also, adolescents are more likely to conform to peers whom they perceive to have higher status than they do.

Cliques and Crowds Cliques and crowds assume more important roles during adolescence than during childhood (Brown, 2011). **Cliques** are small groups that range from 2 to about 12 individuals and average about 5 or 6 individuals. The clique members are usually of the same sex and about the same age.

Cliques can form because adolescents engage in similar activities, such as belonging to a club or playing on a sports team. Some cliques also form because of friendship. Several adolescents may form a clique because they have spent time with each other, share mutual interests, and enjoy each other's company.

Crowds are larger than cliques and less personal. Adolescents are usually members of a crowd based on reputation, and they may or may not spend much time together. Many crowds are defined by the activities adolescents engage in (such as "jocks" who are good at sports or "druggies" who take drugs) (Brown, 2011).

DATING AND ROMANTIC RELATIONSHIPS

Adolescents spend considerable time either dating or thinking about dating (Shulman, Davila, & Shachar-Shapira, 2011). Dating can be a form of recreation, a source of status, or a setting for learning about close relationships, as well as a way of finding a mate.

Developmental Changes in Dating and Romantic Relationships   Three stages characterize the development of romantic relationships in adolescence (Connolly & McIsaac, 2009):

1. *Entry into romantic attractions and affiliations at about 11 to 13 years of age.* This initial stage is triggered by puberty. From 11 to 13, adolescents become intensely interested in romance and it dominates many conversations with same-sex friends. Developing a crush on someone is common and the crush often is shared with a same-sex friend. Young adolescents may or may not interact with the individual who is the object of their infatuation. When dating occurs, it usually occurs in a group setting.

2. *Exploring romantic relationships at approximately 14 to 16 years of age.* At this point in adolescence, two types of romantic involvement occur: (a) Casual dating emerges between individuals who are mutually attracted. These dating experiences are often short-lived, lasting a few months at best, and usually endure for only a few weeks. (b) Dating in groups is common and reflects embeddedness in the peer context. Friends often act as third-party facilitators of a potential dating relationship by communicating their friend's romantic interest and confirming whether this attraction is reciprocated.

What are some developmental changes in romantic relationships in adolescence?

3. *Consolidating dyadic romantic bonds at about 17 to 19 years of age.* At the end of the high school years, more serious romantic relationships develop. This is characterized by strong emotional bonds more closely resembling those in adult romantic relationships. These bonds often are more stable and enduring than earlier bonds, typically lasting one year or more.

Two variations on these stages in the development of romantic relationships in adolescence involve early and late bloomers (Connolly & McIsaac, 2009). *Early bloomers* include 15 to 20 percent of 11- to 13-year-olds who say that they currently are in a romantic relationship and 35 percent who indicate that they have had some prior experience in romantic relationships. *Late bloomers* comprise approximately 10 percent of 17- to 19-year-olds who say that they have had no experience with romantic relationships and another 15 percent who report that they have not engaged in any romantic relationships that lasted more than four months.

Dating in Gay and Lesbian Youth   Recently, researchers have begun to study romantic relationships among gay and lesbian youth (Diamond & Savin-Williams, 2011; Savin-Williams, 2013). Many sexual minority youth date other-sex peers, which can help them to clarify their sexual orientation or disguise it from others (Cohen & Savin-Williams, 2013). Most gay and lesbian youth have had some same-sex sexual experience, often with peers who are "experimenting." Some gay and lesbian youth continue to have a same-sex orientation while others have a primarily heterosexual orientation (Diamond & Savin-Williams, 2011; Vrangalova & Savin-Williams, 2013). In one study, gay and lesbian youth rated the breakup of a

> Teenagers are people who express a burning desire to be different by dressing exactly alike.
>
> —**ANONYMOUS**

crowd A larger group structure than a clique that is usually based on reputation; members may or may not spend much time together.

current romance as their second most stressful problem, second only to disclosure of their sexual orientation to their parents (D'Augelli, 1991).

Sociocultural Contexts and Dating

The sociocultural context exerts a powerful influence on adolescents' dating patterns (Cheng & others, 2012; Holloway & others, 2012). This influence may be seen in differences in dating patterns among ethnic groups within the United States. For example, one study found that Asian American adolescents were less likely to have been involved in a romantic relationship in the past 18 months than African American or Latino adolescents were (Carver, Joyner, & Udry, 2003).

Values, religious beliefs, and traditions often dictate the age at which dating begins, how much freedom in dating is allowed, whether dates must be chaperoned by adults or parents, and the roles of males and females in dating. For example, Latino and Asian American cultures have more conservative standards regarding adolescent dating than does the Anglo-American culture. Dating may become a source of conflict within a family if the parents grew up in cultures where dating begins at a late age, little freedom in dating is allowed, dates are chaperoned, and dating by adolescent girls is especially restricted. When immigrant adolescents choose to adopt the ways of the dominant U.S. culture (such as unchaperoned dating), they often clash with parents and extended-family members who have more traditional values.

What are some ethnic variations in dating during adolescence?

Dating and Adjustment

Researchers have linked dating and romantic relationships with various measures of how well adjusted adolescents are (Collins, Welsh, & Furman, 2009). For example, a study of tenth-graders revealed that the more romantic experiences they had experienced, the more likely they were to report high levels of social acceptance, friendship competence, and romantic competence; however, having more romantic experience also was linked with a higher level of substance use, delinquency, and sexual behavior (Furman, Low, & Ho, 2009). In another study conducted among adolescent girls but not adolescent males, having an older romantic partner was linked with an increase in depressive symptoms, largely influenced by an increase in substance use (Haydon & Halpern, 2010).

Dating and romantic relationships at an early age can be especially problematic (Connolly & McIsaac, 2009). A recent study found that romantic activity was linked to depression in early adolescent girls (Starr & others, 2012). Researchers also have found that early dating and "going with" someone are linked with adolescent pregnancy and problems at home and school (Florsheim, Moore, & Edgington, 2003).

How are romantic relationships linked to adolescent adjustment?

Review Connect Reflect

 LG3 Characterize the changes that occur in peer relationships during adolescence.

Review
- What changes take place in friendship during adolescence?
- What are adolescents' peer groups like?
- What is the nature of adolescent dating and romantic relationships?

Connect
- Relational aggression was discussed here and in Chapter 10. In one of the studies in Chapter 10, what connection was made between parents and the relational aggression of their children?

Reflect *Your Own Personal Journey of Life*
- What were your peer relationships like during adolescence? What peer groups were you involved in? How did they influence your development? What were your dating and romantic relationships like in adolescence? If you could change anything about the way you experienced peer relations in adolescence, what would it be?

LG4 Explain how culture influences adolescent development.

In this section, we will discuss cross-cultural variations in a number of aspects of adolescent development. We also will examine how ethnicity affects U.S. adolescents and influences their development. And we will explore an important aspect of the cultural worlds of adolescents—the media.

CROSS-CULTURAL COMPARISONS

What traditions remain for adolescents around the globe? What circumstances are changing adolescents' lives? Depending on the culture, adolescence may involve many different experiences (Arnett, 2012).

Health   Adolescent health and well-being have improved in some respects but not in others. Overall, fewer adolescents around the world die from infectious diseases and malnutrition now than in the past (UNICEF, 2012). However, a number of adolescent health-compromising behaviors (especially illicit drug use and unprotected sex) are increasing in frequency. Extensive increases in the rates of HIV in adolescents have occurred in many sub-Saharan countries (UNICEF, 2012).

Gender   Around the world, the experiences of male and female adolescents continue to be quite different (Brown & Larson, 2002; Larson, Wilson, & Rickman, 2009). Except in a few regions, such as Japan, the Philippines, and Western countries, males have far greater access to educational opportunities than females do (UNICEF, 2012). In many countries, adolescent females have less freedom than males to pursue a variety of careers and engage in various leisure activities. Gender differences in sexual expression are widespread, especially in India, Southeast Asia, Latin America, and Arab countries where far more restrictions are placed on the sexual activity of adolescent females than on males. These gender differences do appear to be narrowing over time, however. In some countries, educational and career opportunities for women are expanding, and control over adolescent girls' romantic and sexual relationships is weakening.

Muslim school in Middle East with boys only.

Family   In some countries, adolescents grow up in closely knit families with extensive kin networks that retain a traditional way of life. For example, in Arab countries "adolescents are taught strict codes of conduct and loyalty" (Brown & Larson, 2002, p. 6). However, in Western countries such as the United States, parenting is less authoritarian than in the past, and much larger numbers of adolescents are growing up in divorced families and stepfamilies.

In many countries around the world, current trends "include greater family mobility, migration to urban areas, family members working in distant cities or countries, smaller families, fewer extended-family households, and increases in mothers' employment" (Brown & Larson, 2002, p. 7). Unfortunately, many of these changes may reduce the ability of families to spend time with their adolescents.

Peers   Some cultures give peers a stronger role in adolescence than other cultures do (Brown & others, 2008). In most Western nations, peers figure prominently in adolescents' lives, in some cases taking on roles that in other cultures are assumed by parents. Among street youth in South America, the peer network serves as a surrogate family that supports survival in dangerous and stressful settings. In other regions of the world, such as in Arab countries, peer relations are restricted, especially for girls (Booth, 2002).

Time Allocation to Different Activities   Reed Larson and his colleagues (Larson, 2001; Larson & Angus, 2011; Larson & Dawes, 2013; Larson & Verma, 1999; Larson & Walker, 2010; Larson & others, 2009; Larson, Wilson, & Rickman, 2009) have examined how adolescents spend their time in work, play, and developmental activities such as

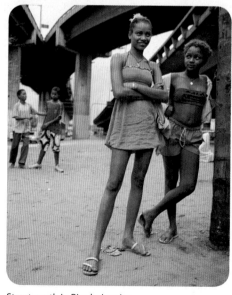

Street youth in Rio de Janeiro.

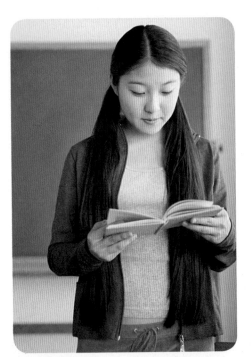

How do East Asian and U.S. adolescents spend their time differently?

school. U.S. adolescents spend about 60 percent as much time on schoolwork as East Asian adolescents do, which is mainly due to U.S. adolescents doing less homework (Larson & Verma, 1999).

What U.S. adolescents have in greater quantities than adolescents in other industrialized countries is discretionary time (Larson & Wilson, 2004; Larson, Wilson, & Rickman, 2009). About 40 to 50 percent of U.S. adolescents' waking hours (not counting summer vacations) is spent in discretionary activities, compared with 25 to 35 percent in East Asia and 35 to 45 percent in Europe. Whether this additional discretionary time is a liability or an asset for U.S. adolescents, of course, depends on how they use it.

According to Larson (2001), U.S. adolescents may have too much unstructured time because when they are given a choice they typically engage in unchallenging activities such as hanging out and watching TV. Although relaxation and social interaction are important aspects of adolescence, it seems unlikely that spending large numbers of hours per week in unchallenging activities would foster development. Structured voluntary activities may provide more promise for adolescent development than unstructured time, especially if adults give responsibility to adolescents, challenge them, and provide competent guidance in these activities (Larson & Walker, 2010; Larson & others, 2009).

In sum, adolescents' lives are characterized by a combination of change and tradition. Researchers have found both similarities and differences in the experiences of adolescents in different countries (Larson, Wilson, & Rickman, 2009; Schlegel, 2009).

Rites of Passage   Another variation in the experiences of adolescents in different cultures is whether the adolescents go through a rite of passage. Some societies have elaborate ceremonies that signal the adolescent's move to maturity and achievement of adult status (Kottak, 2009). A **rite of passage** is a ceremony or ritual that marks an individual's transition from one status to another. Most rites of passage focus on the transition to adult status. In some traditional cultures, rites of passage are the avenue through which adolescents gain access to sacred adult practices, to knowledge, and to sexuality. These rites often involve dramatic practices intended to facilitate the adolescent's separation from the immediate family, especially the mother. The transformation is usually characterized by some form of ritual death and rebirth, or by means of contact with the spiritual world. Bonds are forged between the adolescent and the adult instructors through shared rituals, hazards, and secrets to allow the adolescent to enter the adult world. This kind of ritual provides a forceful and discontinuous entry into the adult world at a time when the adolescent is perceived to be ready for the change.

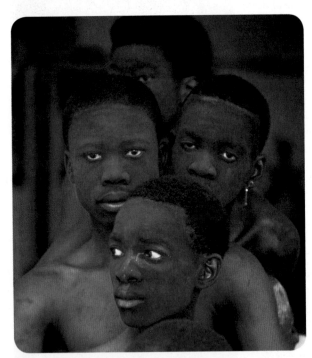

These Congolese Kota boys painted their faces as part of a rite of passage to adulthood. *What rites of passage do American adolescents have?*

An especially rich tradition of rites of passage for adolescents has prevailed in African cultures, especially sub-Saharan Africa. Under the influence of Western industrialized culture, many of these rites are disappearing today, although they are still prevalent in locations where formal education is not readily available.

Do we have such rites of passage for American adolescents? We certainly do not have universal formal ceremonies that mark the passage from adolescence to adulthood. Certain religious and social groups do, however, have initiation ceremonies that indicate that an advance in maturity has been reached: the Jewish bar and bat mitzvah, the Catholic confirmation, and social debuts, for example. School graduation ceremonies come the closest to being culture-wide rites of passage in the United States. The high school graduation ceremony has become nearly universal for middle-class adolescents and increasing numbers of adolescents from low-income backgrounds.

ETHNICITY

Earlier in this chapter, we explored the identity development of ethnic minority adolescents. Here we will further examine immigration and the relationship between ethnicity and socioeconomic status.

rite of passage A ceremony or ritual that marks an individual's transition from one status to another. Most rites of passage focus on the transition to adult status.

Immigration Relatively high rates of immigration are contributing to the growth of ethnic minorities in the United States. Immigrants often experience stressors uncommon to or less prominent among longtime residents, such as language barriers, dislocations and separations from support networks, changes in SES status, and the dual struggle to preserve identity and to acculturate (Urdan, 2012).

Recent research indicates that many members of families that have recently immigrated to the United States adopt a bicultural orientation, selecting characteristics of the U.S. culture that help them to survive and advance, while retaining aspects of their culture of origin. Immigration also involves cultural brokering, which has increasingly occurred in the United States as children and adolescents serve as mediators (cultural and linguistic) for their immigrant parents (Villanueva & Buriel, 2010).

In adopting characteristics of the U.S. culture, Latino families are increasingly embracing the importance of education. Although their school dropout rates have remained higher than those of other ethnic groups, toward the end of the first decade of the twenty-first century they declined considerably (National Center for Education Statistics, 2010). In retaining positive aspects of their culture of origin, as research by Ross Parke and his colleagues (2011) indicates, Latino families maintain a strong commitment to family that sustains them emotionally when they immigrate to the United States, even in the face of often having low-paying jobs and challenges in advancing economically. For example, divorce rates for Latino families are lower than for non-Latino White families of similar socioeconomic status.

Ethnicity and Socioeconomic Status Much of the research on ethnic minority adolescents has failed to tease apart the influences of ethnicity and socioeconomic status. Ethnicity and socioeconomic status can interact in ways that exaggerate the influence of ethnicity because ethnic minority individuals are overrepresented in the lower socioeconomic levels of American society (Chen & Brooks-Gunn, 2012; Wright & others, 2012). Consequently, researchers too often have given ethnic explanations for aspects of adolescent development that were largely due instead to socioeconomic status.

Not all ethnic minority families are poor. However, poverty contributes to the stressful life experiences of many ethnic minority adolescents (McLoyd & others, 2011; Way & Silverman, 2012). Thus, many ethnic minority adolescents experience a double disadvantage: (1) prejudice, discrimination, and bias because of their ethnic minority status; and (2) the stressful effects of poverty.

Although some ethnic minority youth have middle-income backgrounds, economic advantage does not entirely enable them to escape the prejudice, discrimination, and bias associated with being a member of an ethnic minority group (Duncan, 2012; Duncan & others, 2013; McLoyd & others, 2011). In one study, discrimination experienced by seventh- to tenth-grade African American students was related to their lower level of psychological functioning, including perceived stress, symptoms of depression, and lower perceived well-being; more positive treatment of African Americans was associated with more positive psychological functioning in adolescents (Sellers & others, 2006).

THE MEDIA

The culture adolescents experience not only involves values, socioeconomic status, and ethnicity, but also media influences. First, we will explore adolescents' use of various media and then we will discuss the role of digital media in adolescents' lives.

Media Use If the amount of time spent in an activity is any indication of its importance, there is no doubt that media play important roles in adolescents' lives (Hogan, 2012; Strasburger, Jordan, & Donnerstein, 2012). To better understand various aspects of U.S. adolescents' media use, the Kaiser Family Foundation has funded three national surveys in 1999, 2004, and 2009. The 2009 survey included more than 2,000 8- to 18-year-olds and documented that adolescent media use has increased dramatically in the last decade (Rideout, Foehr, & Roberts,

developmental **connection**

Environment

Poverty is linked to family turmoil, separation from a parent, violence, crowding, excessive noise, and poor housing. Chapter 1, p. 12

What are some cultural adaptations these Mexican American girls likely will have to make as immigrants to the United States?

How much time do adolescents spend using different types of media?

2010). Today's youth live in a world in which they are encapsulated by media. In this survey, in 2009, 8- to 11-year-olds used media 5 hours and 29 minutes a day, 11- to 14-year-olds used media an average of 8 hours and 40 minutes a day, and 15- to 18-year-olds an average of 7 hours and 58 minutes a day (see Figure 12.5). Thus, media use jumps more than 3 hours in early adolescence! The largest increases in media use in early adolescence are for TV and video games. TV use by youth increasingly has involved watching TV on the Internet, an iPod/MP3 player, and on a cell phone. As indicated in Figure 12.5, listening to music and using computers also increase considerably among 11- to 14-year-old adolescents. And based on the 2009 survey adding up the daily media use figures to obtain weekly media use leads to the staggering levels of more than 60 hours a week of media use by 11- to 14-year-olds and almost 56 hours a week by 15- to 18-year-olds!

A major trend in the use of technology is the dramatic increase in media multitasking (Pea & others, 2012). In the 2009 survey, when the amount of time spent multitasking was included in computing media use, 11- to 14-year-olds spent nearly 12 hours a day (compared with almost 9 hours a day when multitasking was not included) exposed to media (Rideout, Foehr, & Roberts, 2010)! In this survey, 39 percent of seventh- to twelfth-graders said "most of the time" they use two or more media concurrently, such as surfing the Web while listening to music. In some cases, media multitasking—such as text messaging, listening to an iPod, and updating a YouTube site—is engaged in while doing homework. It is hard to imagine that this allows a student to do homework efficiently, although there is little research on media multitasking. A study that compared heavy and light media multitaskers revealed that heavy media multitaskers were more susceptible to interference from irrelevant information (Ophir, Nass, & Wagner, 2009). A recent study of 8- to 12-year-old girls also found that a higher level of media multitasking was linked to negative social well-being while a higher level of face-to-face communication was associated with positive social-well-being indicators such as greater social success, feeling more normal, and having fewer friends whom parents thought were a bad influence (Pea & others, 2012).

Mobile media, such as cell phones and iPods, are mainly driving the increased media use by adolescents. For example, in the 2004 survey, only 18 percent of youth owned an iPod or MP3 player; In 2009, 76 percent owned them; in 2004, 39 percent owned a cell phone, a figure that jumped to 66 percent in 2009 (Rideout, Foehr, & Roberts, 2010).

Technology and Digitally Mediated Communication Culture involves change, and nowhere is that change greater than in the technological revolution individuals are experiencing with increased use of computers and the Internet (Gross, 2013; Levinson, 2013). Society still relies on some basic nontechnological competencies—for example, good communication skills, positive attitudes, and the ability to solve problems and to think deeply and creatively. But how people pursue these competencies is changing in ways and at speeds that few people had to cope with in previous eras. For youth to be adequately prepared for tomorrow's jobs, technology needs to become an integral part of their lives (Jackson & others, 2012).

The digitally mediated social environment of adolescents and emerging adults includes e-mail, instant messaging, social networking sites such as Facebook, chat rooms, video sharing and photo sharing, multiplayer online computer games, and virtual worlds. The remarkable increase in the popularity of Facebook was reflected in 2010 when it surpassed Google as the most frequently visited Internet site. Most of these digitally mediated social interactions began on computers but more recently have also shifted to cell phones,

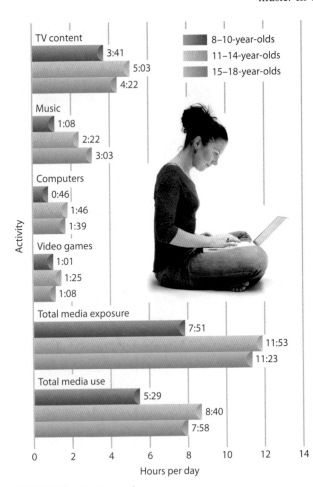

FIGURE **12.5**

DEVELOPMENTAL CHANGES IN THE AMOUNT OF TIME U.S. 8- TO 18-YEAR-OLDS SPEND WITH DIFFERENT TYPES OF MEDIA

especially smartphones (Underwood & others, 2012; Valkenburg & Peter, 2011).

A national survey revealed dramatic increases in adolescents' use of social media and text messaging (Lenhart & others, 2010). In 2009, nearly three-fourths of U.S. 12- to 17-year-olds reported that they used social networking sites. Eighty-one percent of 18- to 24-year-olds had created a profile on a social networking site and 31 percent of them visited a social networking site at least several times a day. More emerging adult women visit a social networking site several times a day (33 percent) than do their male counterparts (24 percent).

Text messaging has become the main way that adolescents connect with their friends, surpassing face-to-face contact, e-mail, instant messaging, and voice calling (Lenhart & others, 2010). However, voice mailing is the primary way that most adolescents connect with parents.

Two recent studies yielded the following information about the role of parents in guiding adolescents' use of the Internet and other media:

What characterizes the online social environment of adolescents and emerging adults?

- Both maternal and paternal authoritative parenting predicted proactive monitoring of adolescent media use, including restriction of certain media from adolescent use and parent-adolescent discussion of exposure to questionable media content (Padilla-Walker & Coyne, 2011).
- Problematic mother-adolescent (age 13) relationships that involved undermining attachment and autonomy predicted emerging adults' preference for online communication and greater probability of forming a low-quality relationship with someone they met online (Szwedo, Mikami, & Allen, 2011).

Review *Connect* Reflect

LG4 Explain how culture influences adolescent development.

Review

- What are some comparisons of adolescents in different cultures? How do adolescents around the world spend their time? What is the purpose of rites of passage?
- How does ethnicity influence adolescent development?
- What characterizes media use by adolescents?

Connect

- How might what you learned about school dropout rates and extracurricular activities

in Chapter 11 be linked to Reed Larson and his colleagues' view on adolescents' lacking adequate self-initiative?

Reflect *Your Own Personal Journey of Life*

- What is your ethnicity? Have you ever been stereotyped because of your ethnicity? How different is your identity from the mainstream culture?

5 Adolescent Problems

LG5 Identify adolescent problems in socioemotional development and strategies for helping adolescents with problems.

Juvenile Delinquency

Depression and Suicide

The Interrelation of Problems and Successful Prevention/Intervention Programs

In Chapter 11, we described several adolescent problems: substance abuse, sexually transmitted infections, and eating disorders. In this chapter, we will examine the problems of juvenile delinquency, depression, and suicide. We will also explore interrelationships among adolescent problems and describe how such problems can be prevented or remedied.

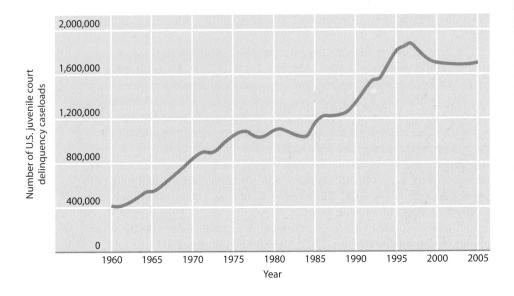

JUVENILE DELINQUENCY

The label **juvenile delinquent** is applied to an adolescent who breaks the law or engages in behavior that is considered illegal. Like other categories of disorders, juvenile delinquency is a broad concept, encompassing legal infractions that range from littering to murder.

Delinquency Rates   The number of juvenile court delinquency caseloads in the United States increased dramatically from 1960 to 1996 but has decreased slightly since 1996 (see Figure 12.6) (Puzzanchera & Sickmund, 2008). Note that this figure reflects only adolescents who have been arrested and assigned to juvenile court delinquency caseloads and does not include those who were arrested but not assigned to the delinquency caseloads, nor does the figure include youth who committed offenses but were not apprehended.

Males are more likely to engage in delinquency than are females. However, U.S. government statistics revealed that the percentage of delinquency caseloads involving females increased from 19 percent in 1985 to 27 percent in 2005 (Puzzanchera & Sickmund, 2008).

Delinquency rates among minority groups and lower-socioeconomic-status youth are especially high in proportion to the overall population of these groups. However, such groups have less influence over the judicial decision-making process in the United States and therefore may be judged delinquent more readily than their White, middle-socioeconomic-status counterparts.

A distinction is made between early-onset—before age 11—and late-onset—after 11—antisocial behavior. Early-onset antisocial behavior is associated with more negative developmental outcomes than late-onset antisocial behavior (Schulenberg & Zarrett, 2006). Not only is it more likely to persist into emerging adulthood but it is also associated with more mental health and relationship problems (Burke, 2011; Loeber & Burke, 2011).

Causes of Delinquency   Although delinquency is less exclusively a phenomenon of lower socioeconomic status than it was in the past, some characteristics of lower-SES culture might promote delinquency (Thio, 2010). The norms of many lower-SES peer groups and gangs are antisocial, or counterproductive, to the goals and norms of society at large. Getting into and staying out of trouble are prominent features of life for some adolescents in low-income neighborhoods. Being "tough" and "masculine" are high-status traits for lower-SES boys, and these traits are often measured by the adolescent's success in performing and getting away with delinquent acts. And adolescents in communities with high crime rates observe many models who engage in criminal activities. These communities

juvenile delinquent An adolescent who breaks the law or engages in behavior that is considered illegal.

Rodney Hammond, Health Psychologist

Rodney Hammond described how his college experiences led to his career choice:

> When I started as an undergraduate at the University of Illinois, Champaign-Urbana, I hadn't decided on my major. But to help finance my education, I took a part-time job in a child development research program sponsored by the psychology department. There, I observed inner-city children in settings designed to enhance their learning. I saw firsthand the contribution psychology can make, and I knew I wanted to be a psychologist (American Psychological Association, 2003, p. 26).

Rodney Hammond went on to obtain a doctorate in school and community psychology with a focus on children's development. For a number of years, he trained clinical psychologists at Wright State University in Ohio and directed a program to reduce violence in ethnic minority youth. There, he and his associates taught at-risk youth how to use social skills to effectively manage conflict and to recognize situations that could lead to violence. Today, Hammond is Director of Violence Prevention at the Centers for Disease Control and Prevention

Rodney Hammond, counseling an adolescent girl about the risks of adolescence and how to effectively cope with them.

in Atlanta. Hammond says that if you are interested in people and problem solving, psychology is a wonderful way to put these topics together.

---

may be characterized by poverty, unemployment, and feelings of alienation toward the middle class (Leventhal & Brooks-Gunn, 2012). Quality schooling, educational funding, and organized neighborhood activities may be lacking in these communities. A recent study found that youth whose families had experienced repeated poverty were more than twice as likely to be delinquent at 14 and 21 years of age (Najman & others, 2010).

Certain characteristics of families are also associated with delinquency (Connell, Dishion, & Klostermann, 2012; Tolou-Shams & others, 2012; Van Ryzin & Dishion, 2012). Parents of delinquents are less skilled in discouraging antisocial behavior and in encouraging skilled behavior than are parents of nondelinquents. Parental monitoring of adolescents is especially important in determining whether an adolescent becomes a delinquent (Fosco & others, 2012). A recent study found that early parental monitoring in adolescence and ongoing parental support were linked to a lower incidence of criminal behavior in emerging adulthood (Johnson & others, 2011). A study of families living in high-risk neighborhoods revealed that parents' lack of knowledge of their young adolescents' whereabouts was linked to whether the adolescents engaged in delinquency later in adolescence (Lahey & others, 2008). Family discord and inconsistent and inappropriate discipline are also associated with delinquency (Bor, McGee, & Fagan, 2004). Further, recent research indicates that family therapy is often effective in reducing delinquency (Baldwin & others, 2012; Henggeler & Sheidow, 2012). A recent meta-analysis found that of five program types (case management, individual treatment, youth court, restorative justice, and family treatment), family treatment was the only one that was linked to a reduction in recidivism for juvenile offenders (Schwalbe & others, 2012).

An increasing number of studies have found that siblings can have a strong influence on delinquency (Bank, Burraston, & Snyder, 2004). Finally, having delinquent peers greatly increases the risk of becoming delinquent (Fosco, Frank, & Dishion, 2012).

One individual whose goal is to help at-risk adolescents, such as juvenile delinquents, cope more effectively with their lives is Rodney Hammond. Read about his work in *Connecting with Careers*.

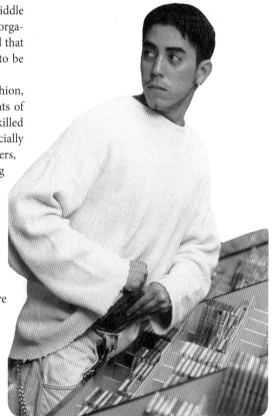

What are some factors that are linked to whether adolescents engage in delinquent acts?

DEPRESSION AND SUICIDE

What is the nature of depression in adolescence? What causes an adolescent to commit suicide?

Depression   How extensive is depression in adolescence? Rates of ever experiencing major depressive disorder range from 15 to 20 percent for adolescents (Graber & Sontag, 2009). By about age 15, adolescent females have a rate of depression that is twice that of adolescent males. Among the reasons for this gender difference are that females tend to ruminate on their depressed mood and amplify it; females' self-images, especially their body images, are more negative than those of males; females face more discrimination than males do; and puberty occurs earlier for girls than for boys (Nolen-Hoeksema, 2011). As a result, girls experience a piling up of changes and life experiences in the middle school years that can increase depression (Hammen, 2009).

Do gender differences in adolescent depression hold for other cultures? In many cultures the gender difference of females experiencing more depression does hold, but a recent study of more than 17,000 Chinese 11- to 22-year-olds revealed that the male adolescents and emerging adults experienced more depression than their female counterparts did (Sun & others, 2010). Explanation of the higher rates of depression among males in China focused on stressful life events and a less positive coping style.

Genes are linked to adolescent depression (Hansell & others, 2012). A recent study found that certain dopamine-related genes were associated with depressive symptoms in adolescents (Adkins & others, 2012). And another recent study revealed that the link between adolescent girls' perceived stress and depression occurred only when the girls had the short version of the serotonin-related gene—5HTTLPR (Beaver & others, 2012).

Certain family factors place adolescents at risk for developing depression (Kitts & Goldman, 2012). These include having a depressed parent, emotionally unavailable parents, parents who have high marital conflict, and parents with financial problems. A recent study revealed that mother-daughter co-rumination (extensively discussing, rehashing, and speculating about problems) was linked to an increase in anxiety and depression in adolescent girls (Waller & Rose, 2010). Another study found that exposure to maternal depression by age 12 predicted risk processes during development (higher stress and difficulties in family relationships), which set the course for the development of the adolescent's depression (Garber & Cole, 2010).

Poor peer relationships also are associated with adolescent depression (Vanhalst & others, 2012). Not having a close relationship with a best friend, having less contact with friends, and being rejected by peers increase depressive tendencies in adolescents (Kistner & others, 2006). A recent study revealed that four types of bullying—in person among bullies, victims, and bully-victims, as well as victims of cyberbullying—were all linked to adolescents' depression (Wang, Nansel, & Iannotti, 2011). Another recent study found that relational aggression was linked to depression for girls (Spieker & others, 2012). And as indicated earlier in this chapter, problems in adolescent romantic relationships can also trigger depression (Starr & others, 2012).

Friendship often provides social support. However, whether friendship is linked with a lower level of depression among girls and boys depends on the type of friendship. For example, in a recent study young adolescents with nondepressed friends were less likely to be depressed than young adolescents without friends, whereas young adolescents with depressed friends were more likely to be depressed (Brendgen & others, 2010). And a study of third-through ninth-graders revealed that girls' co-rumination predicted not only an increase in the positive quality of the friendship, but also an increase in further co-rumination and in depressive and anxiety symptoms (Rose, Carlson, & Waller, 2007).

Being stressed about weight-related concerns is increasingly thought to contribute to the greater incidence of depression in adolescent girls than in adolescent boys (Alberga & others, 2012). A recent study revealed that one explanation for adolescent girls' higher level of depressive symptoms is a heightened tendency to perceive oneself as overweight and to diet (Vaughan & Halpern, 2010).

What type of treatment is most likely to reduce depression in adolescence? A recent research review concluded that drug therapy using serotonin reuptake inhibitors, cognitive

developmental **connection**

The epigenetic approach

The epigenetic approach states that development is an ongoing, bidirectional interaction between heredity and the environment. Chapter 2, p. 71

What are some characteristics of adolescents who become depressed?

behavior therapy, and interpersonal therapy are effective in treating adolescent depression (Maalouf & Brent, 2012). However, in this review, the most effective treatment was a combination of drug therapy and cognitive behavior therapy.

Suicide Suicide behavior is rare in childhood but escalates in adolescence and then increases further in emerging adulthood (Park & others, 2006). Suicide is the third-leading cause of death in 10- to 19-year-olds today in the United States (National Center for Health Statistics, 2012). Approximately 4,400 adolescents commit suicide each year (Eaton & others, 2010).

Although a suicide threat should always be taken seriously, far more adolescents contemplate or attempt it unsuccessfully than actually commit it. As indicated in Figure 12.7, in the last two decades there has been a considerable decline in the percentage of adolescents who think about committing suicide, although from 2009 to 2011 this percentage increased from 14 to 16 percent (Youth Risk Behavior Survey, 2011). In this national study, in 2011, 8 percent attempted suicide and 2 percent engaged in suicide attempts that required medical attention.

Females are more likely to attempt suicide than males, but males are more likely to succeed in committing suicide. Males use more lethal means, such as guns, in their suicide attempts, whereas adolescent females are more likely to cut their wrists or take an overdose of sleeping pills—methods less likely to result in death.

Distal, or earlier, experiences often are involved in suicide attempts as well. The adolescent may have a long-standing history of family instability and unhappiness (Wan & Leung, 2010). Just as a lack of affection and emotional support, high control, and pressure for achievement by parents during childhood are related to adolescent depression, such combinations of family experiences also are likely to show up as distal factors in adolescents' suicide attempts.

Adolescents' peer relations also are linked to suicide attempts. A recent research review revealed that prior suicide attempts by a member of an adolescent's social groups were linked to the probability that the adolescent also would attempt suicide (de Leo & Heller, 2008). Adolescents who attempt suicide may lack supportive friendships. And a recent study revealed that peer victimization was linked to suicide thoughts and attempts (Klomek & others, 2008).

Adolescent suicide attempts also vary across ethnic groups in the United States (Wong & others, 2012). As indicated in Figure 12.8, more than 20 percent of American Indian/Alaska Native (AI/AN) female adolescents reported that they had attempted suicide in the previous year, and suicide accounts for almost 20 percent of AI/AN deaths in 15- to 19-year-olds (Goldston & others, 2008). As indicated in Figure 12.8, African American and non-Latino White males reported the lowest incidence of suicide attempts. A major risk factor in the high rate of suicide attempts by AI/AN adolescents is their elevated rate of alcohol abuse. A recent study revealed that continuous, escalating stress, especially at home, was linked with suicide attempts in young Latinas (Zayas & others, 2010). Results of this study reflected the cultural discontinuity experienced by young Latinas, who struggle to reconcile traditional Latina gender socialization with the gender expectations of modern Western society.

Just as genetic factors are associated with depression, they also are associated with suicide (Kapornai & Vetro, 2008). The closer a person's genetic relationship to someone who has committed suicide, the more likely that person is to also commit suicide.

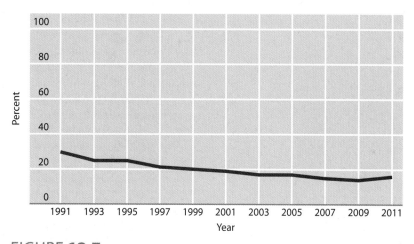

FIGURE 12.7

PERCENTAGE OF U.S. NINTH- TO TWELFTH-GRADE STUDENTS WHO SERIOUSLY CONSIDERED ATTEMPTING SUICIDE IN THE PREVIOUS 12 MONTHS FROM 1991 TO 2011

> developmental **connection**
>
> **Conditions, Diseases, and Disorders**
>
> What characterizes depression and suicide in older adults? Chapter 18, p. 584

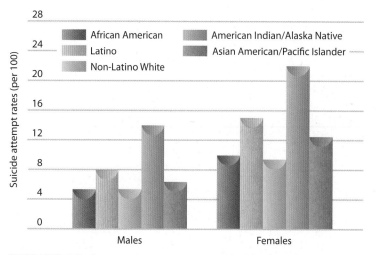

FIGURE 12.8

SUICIDE ATTEMPTS BY U.S. ADOLESCENTS FROM DIFFERENT ETHNIC GROUPS. *Note:* Data shown are for one-year rates of self-reported suicide attempts.

What is the psychological profile of the suicidal adolescent? Suicidal adolescents often have depressive symptoms (Woolgar & Tranah, 2010). Although not all depressed adolescents are suicidal, depression is the most frequently cited factor associated with adolescent suicide (Thapar & others, 2012). Further, one study indicated that adolescents' use of alcohol while they were sad or depressed was linked with risk for making a suicide attempt (Schilling & others, 2009). A recent study also found that the strong link between self-reported adolescent suicide attempts and drug use was any lifetime use of tranquilizers or sedatives (Kokkevi & others, 2012). And the National Longitudinal Study of Adolescent Health identified the following indicators of suicide risk: depressive symptoms, a sense of hopelessness, engaging in suicide ideation, having a family background of suicidal behavior, and having friends with a history of suicidal behavior (Thompson, Kuruwita, & Foster, 2009). A recent study revealed that family support, peer support, and community connectedness was linked to a lower risk of suicidal tendencies in African American adolescents (Matlin, Molock, & Tebes, 2011). And in yet another study, sexual victimization was linked to a risk for suicide attempts in adolescence (Plener, Singer, & Goldbeck, 2011). Further, as discussed in Chapter 10, bullying victimization is associated with suicide-related thoughts and behavior (McMahon & others, 2012).

THE INTERRELATION OF PROBLEMS AND SUCCESSFUL PREVENTION/INTERVENTION PROGRAMS

We have described some of the major adolescent problems in this chapter and in Chapter 11: substance abuse; juvenile delinquency; school-related problems such as dropping out of school; adolescent pregnancy and sexually transmitted infections; eating disorders; depression; and suicide.

The four problems that affect the most adolescents are (1) drug abuse, (2) juvenile delinquency, (3) sexual problems, and (4) school-related problems (Dryfoos, 1990; Dryfoos & Barkin, 2006). The adolescents most at risk have more than one of these problems. Researchers are increasingly finding that problem behaviors in adolescence are interrelated (Milburn & others, 2012; Passini, 2012). For example, heavy substance abuse is related to early sexual activity, lower grades, dropping out of school, and delinquency (Marti, Stice, & Springer, 2010; Tull & others, 2012). Early initiation of sexual activity is associated with the use of cigarettes and alcohol, the use of marijuana and other illicit drugs, lower grades, dropping out of school, and delinquency (Harden & Mendle, 2011). Delinquency is related to early sexual activity, early pregnancy, substance abuse, and dropping out of school (Pedersen & Mastekaasa, 2011). As many as 10 percent of adolescents in the United States have been estimated to engage in all four of these problem behaviors (for example, adolescents who have dropped out of school are behind in their grade level, are users of heavy drugs, regularly use cigarettes and marijuana, and are sexually active but do not use contraception). In 1990, it was estimated that another 15 percent of high-risk youth engage in two or three of the four main problem behaviors (Dryfoos, 1990). Recently, this figure increased to 20 percent of all U.S. adolescents (Dryfoos & Barkin, 2006).

A review of the programs that have been successful in preventing or reducing adolescent problems found these common components (Dryfoos, 1990; Dryfoos & Barkin, 2006):

1. *Intensive individualized attention.* In successful programs, high-risk adolescents are attached to a responsible adult who gives the adolescent attention and deals with the adolescent's specific needs. This theme occurs in a number of programs. In a successful substance-abuse program, a student assistance counselor is available full-time for individual counseling and referral for treatment.

2. *Community-wide multiagency collaborative approaches.* The basic philosophy of community-wide programs is that a number of different programs

How are problems interrelated in adolescence? Which components of programs have been successful in preventing or reducing adolescent problems?

Which Children Are Most Likely to Benefit From Early Intervention?

Fast Track is an intervention that attempts to lower the risk of juvenile delinquency and other problems (Conduct Problems Prevention Research Group, 2010, 2011; Dodge & McCourt, 2010; Jones & others, 2010; Miller & others, 2011). Schools in four areas (Durham, North Carolina; Nashville, Tennessee; Seattle, Washington; and rural central Pennsylvania) were identified as high-risk based on neighborhood crime and poverty data. Researchers screened more than 9,000 kindergarten children in the four schools and randomly assigned 891 of the highest-risk and moderate-risk children to intervention or control groups. The average age of the children when the intervention began was 6.5 years.

The 10-year intervention consisted of parent behavior management training, child social cognitive skills training, reading tutoring, home visitations, mentoring, and a revised classroom curriculum that was designed to increase socioemotional competence and decrease aggression. Outcomes were assessed in the third, sixth, and ninth grades for conduct disorder (multiple instances of behaviors such as truancy, running away, fire setting, cruelty to animals, breaking and entering, and excessive fighting across a six-month period), oppositional defiant disorder (an ongoing pattern of disobedient, hostile, and defiant behavior toward authority figures), attention deficit hyperactivity disorder (as described in Chapter 9, being characterized by one or more of these characteristics over a period of time: inattention, hyperactivity, and impulsivity), any externalizing disorder (presence of any of the three disorders previously described), and self-reported antisocial behavior (a list of 34 behaviors, such as skipping school, stealing, and attacking someone with an intent to hurt them).

The extensive intervention was successful only for children and adolescents who were identified as having the highest risk in kindergarten, lowering their incidence of conduct disorder, attention deficit hyperactivity disorder, any externalized disorder, and antisocial behavior (Dodge & McCourt, 2010). Positive outcomes for the intervention occurred as early as the third grade and continued through the ninth grade. For example, in the ninth grade the intervention reduced the likelihood that the highest-risk kindergarten children would develop conduct disorder by 75 percent, attention deficit hyperactivity disorder by 53 percent, and any externalized disorder by 43 percent. Recently, data have been reported through age 19 (Miller & others, 2011). Findings indicate that the comprehensive Fast Track intervention was successful in reducing youth arrest rates (Conduct Problems Prevention Research Group, 2011).

and services have to be in place. In one successful substance-abuse program, a community-wide health promotion campaign has been implemented that uses local media and community education, in concert with a substance-abuse curriculum in the schools.

3. *Early identification and intervention.* Reaching younger children and their families before children develop problems or at the onset of their problems is a successful strategy. One preschool program serves as an excellent model for the prevention of delinquency, pregnancy, substance abuse, and dropping out of school. Operated by the High/Scope Foundation in Ypsilanti, Michigan, the Perry Preschool has had a long-term positive impact on its students. This enrichment program, directed by David Weikart, serves disadvantaged African American children. They attend a high-quality two-year preschool program and receive weekly home visits from program personnel. Based on official police records, by age 19, individuals who had attended the Perry Preschool program were less likely to have been arrested and reported fewer adult offenses than a control group did. The Perry Preschool students also were less likely to drop out of school, and teachers rated their social behavior as more competent than that of a control group who had not received the enriched preschool experience (High/Scope Resource, 2005). To read further about which children are most likely to benefit from an early intervention, see *Connecting Through Research.*

What are some strategies for preventing and intervening in adolescent problems?

Review *Connect* **Reflect**

LG5 Identify adolescent problems in socioemotional development and strategies for helping adolescents with problems.

Review

- What is juvenile delinquency? What causes it?
- What is the nature of depression and suicide in adolescence?
- How are adolescent problems interrelated? What are some components of successful prevention/intervention programs for adolescents?

Connect

- In Chapter 10, what did you learn about the connection between bullying in middle and late childhood and problems in adolescence?

Reflect *Your Own Personal Journey of Life*

- Did you have any of the problems during adolescence discussed in this chapter or Chapter 11—such as substance abuse, eating disorders, juvenile delinquency, depression, and attempted suicide? If you had one or more of the problems, why do you think you developed the problem? If you did not have one of the problems, why do you think you didn't develop one or more of them?

topical **connections** ----

Adolescents enter emerging adulthood at approximately 18 to 25 years of age, during which time they more intensely explore their identity and experience instability in different contexts. As adults, they benefit from a secure attachment style in close relationships. Love and possibly marriage become central aspects of many young adults' socioemotional development. Many young adults not only are marrying later or not at all but also are having children later than in past decades. Many young adults also cohabit with a romantic partner.

looking forward ---->

reach your **learning goals**

Socioemotional Development in Adolescence

1 The Self, Identity, and Religious/ Spiritual Development

LG1 Discuss self, identity, and religious/spiritual development in adolescence.

Self-Esteem

- Some researchers have found that self-esteem declines in early adolescence for both boys and girls, but the drop for girls is greater. Other researchers caution that these declines are often exaggerated and actually are small. Self-esteem reflects perceptions that do not always match reality. Thus, high self-esteem may be justified or it might reflect an arrogant, grandiose self-image that is not warranted. Controversy surrounds the question of whether today's adolescents and emerging adults are more narcissistic than their counterparts in earlier generations.

Identity

- Identity development is complex and takes place in bits and pieces. Erikson argues that identity versus identity confusion is the fifth stage of the human life span, which individuals experience during adolescence. A psychosocial moratorium during adolescence allows the personality and role experimentation that are important aspects of identity development. James Marcia proposed four identity statuses—identity diffusion, foreclosure, moratorium, and achievement—that are based on crisis (exploration) and commitment. Increasingly, experts argue the main changes in identity occur in emerging adulthood rather than adolescence. Individuals often follow moratorium-achievement-moratorium-achievement (MAMA) cycles in their lives. Throughout the world, ethnic minority groups have struggled to maintain their identities while blending into the majority culture.

Religious/Spiritual Development

- Many adolescents show an interest in religious and spiritual development. As part of their search for identity, many adolescents and emerging adults begin to grapple with more complex aspects of religion. Various aspects of religion are linked with positive outcomes in adolescent development.

2 Families

LG2 Describe changes that take place in adolescents' relationships with their parents.

Parental Monitoring and Information Management

- A key aspect of parenting in adolescence is effectively monitoring the adolescent's development. Monitoring includes supervising adolescents' choice of social settings, activities, friends, and academic efforts. Adolescents' management of information involves the extent to which adolescents disclose information to parents about their whereabouts. This disclosure, which is more likely when parents engage in positive parenting practices, is linked to positive adolescent adjustment.

Autonomy and Attachment

- Many parents have a difficult time handling the adolescent's push for autonomy, even though the push is one of the hallmarks of adolescence. Adolescents do not simply move into a world isolated from parents; attachment to parents increases the probability that an adolescent will be socially competent.

Parent-Adolescent Conflict

- Parent-adolescent conflict increases in adolescence. The conflict is usually moderate rather than severe, and the increased conflict may serve the positive developmental function of promoting autonomy and identity. A subset of adolescents experiences high parent-adolescent conflict, which is linked with negative outcomes.

3 Peers

LG3 Characterize the changes that occur in peer relationships during adolescence.

Friendships

- Harry Stack Sullivan was the most influential theorist to discuss the importance of adolescent friendships. He argued that there is a dramatic increase in the psychological importance and intimacy of close friends in early adolescence. Friends become increasingly important in meeting social needs.

Peer Groups

- The pressure to conform to peers is strong during adolescence, especially during the eighth and ninth grades. Cliques and crowds assume more importance in the lives of adolescents than in the lives of children.

Dating and Romantic Relationships

- Dating can have many functions. Three stages characterize the development of romantic relationships in adolescence: (1) entry into romantic attractions and affiliations at about 11 to 13 years of age; (2) exploring romantic relationships at approximately 14 to 16 years of age; and (3) consolidating dyadic romantic bonds at about 17 to 19 years of age. Many gay and lesbian youth date other-sex peers, which can help them to clarify their sexual orientation or disguise it from others. Culture can exert a powerful influence on adolescent dating. Dating shows mixed connections with adjustment during adolescence. Early dating is linked with developmental problems.

4 Culture and Adolescent Development

 LG4 Explain how culture influences adolescent development.

Cross-Cultural Comparisons

- There are both similarities and differences in adolescents across different countries. In some countries, traditions are being continued in the socialization of adolescents, whereas in others, substantial changes in the experiences of adolescents are taking place. Adolescents often fill their time with different activities, depending on the culture in which they live. A rite of passage is a ceremony or ritual that marks an individual's transition from one status to another, especially into adulthood. In primitive cultures, rites of passage are often well defined. In contemporary America, rites of passage to adulthood are ill-defined.

Ethnicity

- Many of the families that have immigrated to the United States in recent decades come from collectivist cultures in which there is a strong sense of family obligation. Much of the research on ethnic minority adolescents has not teased apart the influences of ethnicity and socioeconomic status. Because of this failure, too often researchers have given ethnic explanations for characteristics that were largely due to socioeconomic factors. Although not all ethnic minority families are poor, poverty contributes to the stress experienced by many ethnic minority adolescents.

The Media

- In terms of exposure, the average U.S. 8- to 18-year-old spends 6½ hours a day using electronic media. If media multitasking is taken into account, adolescents use electronic media 8 hours a day. Adolescents are rapidly increasing the time they spend online. Older adolescents reduce their TV viewing and video game playing and increase their music listening and computer use. Large numbers of adolescents and college students engage in social networking.

5 Adolescent Problems

 LG5 Identify adolescent problems in socioemotional development and strategies for helping adolescents with problems.

Juvenile Delinquency

- A juvenile delinquent is an adolescent who breaks the law or engages in conduct that is considered illegal. Low socioeconomic status, negative family experiences (especially a low level of parental monitoring and having a sibling who is a delinquent), and negative peer influences have been linked to juvenile delinquency.

Depression and Suicide

- Adolescents and emerging adults have higher rates of depression than children do. Female adolescents and emerging adults are more likely to have mood and depressive disorders than their male counterparts. Adolescent suicide is the third-leading cause of death in U.S. adolescents.

The Interrelation of Problems and Successful Prevention/Intervention Programs

- Researchers are increasingly finding that problem behaviors in adolescence are interrelated, and at-risk adolescents have one or more of these problems: (1) drug abuse, (2) juvenile delinquency, (3) sexual problems, and (4) school-related problems. Dryfoos found a number of common components in successful programs designed to prevent or reduce adolescent problems: These programs provide individual attention to high-risk adolescents, they develop community-wide intervention, and they include early identification and intervention.

key terms

key people

Chapter 12 | SOCIOEMOTIONAL DEVELOPMENT IN ADOLESCENCE

Connecting with

Learning Objectives	Application Activities	Activity Type	Page Reference
Discuss changes in self-esteem in adolescence.	Girls' Views on Self-Esteem at Age 14	Video	pp. 388–389
	Adolescent Self-Esteem	Video	
Identify the changes in identity during adolescence.	Adolescent Perspectives on Emotions	Milestones: Transitions	pp. 389–392
	Marcia's Four Statuses of Identity	Click & drag activity	
	Ethnic and Racial Identity	Video	
	Ethnic and Racial Identity in Adolescence	Video	
	Defining Ethnic Identity	Video	
	Coming Out	Video	
	Sexual Minority Youth	Video	
	Girls and Body Image	Video	
Describe religious and spiritual development during adolescence.	Religious identity	Milestones: Transitions	pp. 392–394
Describe autonomy and attachment during adolescence.	Adolescent Loneliness	Video	p. 395
Summarize parent-adolescent conflict during adolescence.	Relationships with Parents at Age 14	Video	pp. 395–396
	Relationships with Parents at Age 15	Video	
	Relationships with Parents at Age 16	Video	
	Adolescent-Parent Conflict	Video	
	Adolescent and Parent Emotions	Video	
	Conflicts with Parents	Milestones: Transitions	
	Lying	Milestones: Transitions	
	Motiviation Orientation	Milestones: Transitions	

(continued)

Learning Objectives	Application Activities	Activity Type	Page Reference
Characterize the changes in friendships during adolescence.	Importance of Peers	Video	p. 397
	Friendship in Adolescence	Video	
	Views on Family and Peers at Age 15	Video	
	Friendship in Adolescence at Age 15	Video	
Identify changes in peer groups during adolescence.	Talking About Cliques at 15 Years of Age	Video	pp. 397–399
	15-Year-Old Girls Describe Friendships with Boys	Video	
	Social Networking	Milestones: Transitions	
	Cliques and Crowds	Milestones: Transitions	
	Gender Differences in Peer Relationships	Milestones: Transitions	
Describe dating and adolescence relationships during adolescences	Dating	Milestones: Transitions	pp. 399–400
Describe juvenile delinquency.	Juvenile Offenders	Video	pp. 406–407
	Impulsive Behavior	Milestones: Transitions	
Discuss depression and suicide during adolescence.	Suicide Risk Factors	Interactive exercise	pp. 408–410

How many roads must a man walk down before you call him a man?

—BOB DYLAN
American Folk Singer, 20th Century

Early Adulthood

Early adulthood is a time for work and a time for love, sometimes leaving little time for anything else. For some of us, finding our place in adult society and committing to a more stable life take longer than we imagine. We still ask ourselves who we are and wonder if it isn't enough just to be. Our dreams continue and our thoughts are bold, but at some point we become more pragmatic. Sex and love are powerful passions in our lives—at time angels of light, at others fiends of torment. And we possibly will never fully know the love of our parents until we become parents ourselves. Section 7 contains two chapters: "Physical and Cognitive Development in Early Adulthood" (Chapter 13) and "Socioemotional Development in Early Adulthood" (Chapter 14).

chapter 13

PHYSICAL AND COGNITIVE DEVELOPMENT IN EARLY ADULTHOOD

chapter outline

He was a senior in college when both of his parents died of cancer within five weeks of each other. What would he do? He and his 8-year-old brother left Chicago to live in California where their older sister was entering law school. Dave would take care of his younger brother, but he needed a job. That first summer, he took a class in furniture painting; then he worked for a geological surveying company, re-creating maps on a computer. Soon, though, he did something very different: with friends from high school, Dave Eggers started *Might,* a satirical magazine for twenty-somethings. It was an edgy, highly acclaimed publication, but not a moneymaker. After a few years, Eggers had to shut down the magazine, and he abandoned California for New York.

Dave Eggers, talented and insightful author.

This does not sound like a promising start for a career. But within a decade after his parents' death, Eggers had not only raised his young brother but had also founded a quarterly journal and Web site, *McSweeney's,* and had written a best-seller, *A Heartbreaking Work of Staggering Genius*, which received the National Book Critics Circle Award and was nominated for a Pulitzer Prize. It is a slightly fictionalized account of Eggers' life as he helped care for his dying mother, raised his brother, and searched for his own place in the world. Despite the pain of his loss and the responsibility for his brother, Eggers quickly built a record of achievement as a young adult.

topical connections

Early adolescence is a time of dramatic physical change as puberty unfolds. Pubertal change also brings considerable interest in one's body image. And pubertal change ushers in an intense interest in sexuality. Although most adolescents develop a positive sexual identity, many encounter sexual risk factors that can lead to negative developmental outcomes. Adolescence also is a critical time in the development of behaviors related to health, such as good nutrition and regular exercise, which are health enhancing, and drug abuse, which is health compromising. Significant changes occur in the adolescent's brain—the early development of the amygdala and the delayed development of the prefrontal cortex—that may contribute to risk taking and sensation seeking. Adolescent thinking becomes more abstract, idealistic, and logical—which Piaget described as the key aspects of formal operational thought. The brain's development and social contexts influence adolescents' decision making.

looking back

preview

In this chapter we will explore many aspects of physical and cognitive development in early adulthood. These include some of the areas that were so important in Dave Eggers' life, such as using his creative talents and pursuing a career. We also will examine changes in physical development, sexuality, and cognitive development. We will begin where we left off in Section 6, "Adolescence," and address the transition from adolescence to adulthood, a time during which Dave Eggers displayed resilience in the face of intense stress.

1 The Transition from Adolescence to Adulthood

 LG1 Describe the transition from adolescence to adulthood.

> Becoming an Adult

> The Transition from High School to College

When does an adolescent become an adult? In Chapter 11, we saw that it is not easy to tell when a girl or a boy enters adolescence. The task of determining when an individual becomes an adult is even more difficult.

BECOMING AN ADULT

For most individuals, becoming an adult involves a lengthy transition period. Recently, the transition from adolescence to adulthood has been referred to as **emerging adulthood,** which occurs from approximately 18 to 25 years of age (Arnett, 2006, 2007, 2010, 2012). Experimentation and exploration characterize the emerging adult. At this point in their development, many individuals are still exploring which career path they want to follow, what they want their identity to be, and which lifestyle they want to adopt (for example, single, cohabiting, or married).

Key Features Jeffrey Arnett (2006) concluded that five key features characterize emerging adulthood:

- *Identity exploration, especially in love and work.* Emerging adulthood is the time during which key changes in identity take place for many individuals (Kroger, 2012; Schwarz & others, 2013).
- *Instability.* Residential changes peak during early adulthood, a time during which there also is often instability in love, work, and education.
- *Self-focused.* According to Arnett (2006, p. 10), emerging adults "are self-focused in the sense that they have little in the way of social obligations, little in the way of duties and commitments to others, which leaves them with a great deal of autonomy in running their own lives."
- *Feeling in-between.* Many emerging adults don't consider themselves adolescents or full-fledged adults.
- *The age of possibilities, a time when individuals have an opportunity to transform their lives.* Arnett (2006) describes two ways in which emerging adulthood is the age of possibilities: (1) many emerging adults are optimistic about their future; and (2) for emerging adults who have experienced difficult times while growing up, emerging adulthood presents an opportunity to chart their life course in a more positive direction.

Recent research indicates that these five aspects characterize not only individuals in the United States as they make the transition from adolescence to early adulthood, but also their counterparts in European countries and Australia

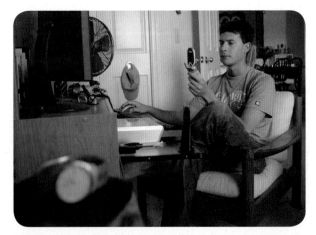

Chris Barnard, 24-year-old emerging adult, in the apartment he shares with two roommates. While in college, he changed dorms three years in a row; then as a senior, he moved to an off-campus apartment. After college, Chris moved back home, then to another apartment, and currently to yet another apartment.

(Arnett, 2012; Buhl & Lanz, 2007; Sirsch & others, 2009). Although emerging adulthood does not characterize development in all cultures, it does appear to occur in cultures that postpone assuming adult roles and responsibilities (Kins & Beyers, 2010). Criticism of the concept of emerging adulthood is that it applies mainly to privileged adolescents and is not always a self-determined choice for many young people, especially those in limiting socioeconomic conditions (Cote & Bynner, 2008).

An important aspect of emerging adulthood is the resilience that some individuals have and their ability to change their life in a positive direction following a troubled adolescence (Burt & Paysnick, 2011; Masten, 2013; Masten & Tellegen, 2012). Consider the changing life of Michael Maddaus (Broderick, 2003; Masten, Obradovic, & Burt, 2006). During Michael's childhood and adolescence in Minneapolis, his mother drank heavily and his stepfather abused him. He coped by spending increasing time on the streets, being arrested more than 20 times for his delinquency, frequently being placed in detention centers, and rarely going to school. At 17, he joined the Navy and the experience helped him to gain self-discipline and hope. After his brief stint in the Navy, he completed a GED and began taking community college classes. However, he continued to have some setbacks with drugs and alcohol. A defining moment during his emerging adulthood came when he delivered furniture to a surgeon's home. The surgeon became interested in helping Michael, and his mentorship led to Michael volunteering at a reha- bilitation center, then to his taking a job with a neurosurgeon. Eventually, he obtained his undergraduate degree, went to medical school, got married, and started a family. Today, Michael Maddaus is a successful surgeon. One of his most gratifying volunteer activities is telling his story to troubled youth.

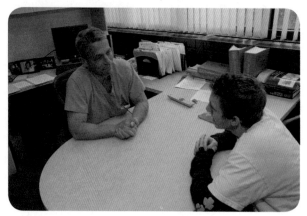

Dr. Michael Maddaus, counseling a troubled youth.

In a longitudinal study, Ann Masten and her colleagues (2006) found that emerging adults who became competent after experiencing difficulties while growing up were more intelligent, experienced higher parenting quality, and were less likely to grow up in poverty or low-income circumstances than their coun- terparts who did not become competent as emerging adults. A further analysis focused on individuals who were still showing maladaptive patterns in emerging adulthood but had gotten their lives together by the time they were in the late twenties and early thirties. The three characteristics shared by these "late-bloomers" were support by adults, being planful, and showing positive aspects of autonomy.

Markers of Becoming an Adult

In the United States, the most widely recognized marker of entry into adulthood is holding a more or less permanent, full-time job, which usually happens when an individual finishes school—high school for some, college for others, graduate or professional school for still others. However, other criteria are far from clear. Economic independence is one marker of adult status, but achieving it is often a long process. College graduates are increasingly returning to live with their parents as they attempt to establish themselves economically. A longitudinal study found that at age 25 only slightly more than half of the participants were fully financially independent of their family of origin (Cohen & others, 2003). The most dramatic findings in this study, though, involved the extensive variability in the individual trajectories of adult roles from 17 to 27 years of age; many of the participants moved back and forth between increasing and decreasing economic dependency. A recent study revealed that continued co-residence with parents during emerg- ing adulthood slowed down the process of becoming a self-sufficient and independent adult (Kins & Beyers, 2010).

Other studies suggest that taking responsibility for oneself may be an important marker of adult status for many individuals. In one study, both parents and college students agreed that taking responsibility for one's actions and developing emotional control are important aspects of becoming an adult (Nelson & others, 2007).

What we have identified as markers of adult status mainly characterize individuals in industrialized societies, especially Americans. Are the criteria for adulthood the same in devel- oping countries as they are in the United States? In developing countries, marriage is more often a significant marker for entry into adulthood, and this usually occurs much earlier than the adulthood markers in the United States (Arnett, 2004). In a recent study, the majority of 18- to 26-year-olds in India felt that they had achieved adulthood (Seiter & Nelson, 2011).

emerging adulthood The transition from adolescence to adulthood (occurring from approximately 18 to 25 years of age), which is characterized by experimentation and exploration.

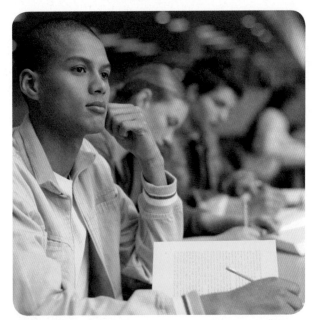

The transition from high school to college often involves positive as well as negative features. In college, students are likely to feel grown up, be able to spend more time with peers, have more opportunities to explore different lifestyles and values, and enjoy greater freedom from parental monitoring. However, college involves a larger, more impersonal school structure and an increased focus on achievement and its assessment. *What was your transition to college like?*

Mental Health Difficulty	1–4 Times	5–8 Times	9 or More Times
Felt things were hopeless	39	11	13
Felt overwhelmed with all I had to do	32	25	36
Felt mentally exhausted	32	24	35
Felt so depressed it was difficult to function	18	7	10
Seriously contemplated suicide	8	1	1
Attempted suicide	1.2	0.2	0.2

FIGURE **13.1**

COLLEGE STUDENTS' MENTAL HEALTH DIFFICULTIES IN THE PAST YEAR. *Note:* Figure shows the percentage of college students who responded to the question: "Within the last school year, how many times have you . . . ?"

THE TRANSITION FROM HIGH SCHOOL TO COLLEGE

For many individuals in developed countries, graduating from high school and going to college is an important aspect of the transition to adulthood (Bowman, 2010). Just as the transition from elementary school to middle or junior high school involves change and possible stress, so does the transition from high school to college. The two transitions have many parallels. Going from being a senior in high school to being a freshman in college replays the top-dog phenomenon of transferring from the oldest and most powerful group of students to the youngest and least powerful group of students that occurred as adolescence began. For many students, the transition from high school to college involves movement to a larger, more impersonal school structure; interaction with peers from more diverse geographical and sometimes more diverse ethnic backgrounds; and increased focus on achievement and its assessment. And like the transition from elementary to middle or junior high school, the transition from high school to college can involve positive features. Students are more likely to feel grown up, have more subjects from which to select, have more time to spend with peers, have more opportunities to explore different lifestyles and values, enjoy greater independence from parental monitoring, and be challenged intellectually by academic work (Halonen & Santrock, 2013).

Today's college students experience more stress and are more depressed than students in previous generations, according to a national study of more than 200,000 freshmen at more than 400 colleges and universities (Pryor, DeAngelo, & Blake, 2011). And a national survey conducted by the American College Health Association (2008) of more than 90,000 students on 177 campuses revealed that feeling things are hopeless, feeling overwhelmed with all they have to do, feeling mentally exhausted, feeling sad, and feeling depressed are not uncommon among college students. Figure 13.1 indicates the percentage of students who had these feelings and how many times a year they experienced them.

Most college campuses have a counseling center that provides access to mental health professionals who can help students learn effective ways to cope with stress. Counselors can provide good information about coping with stress and dealing with academic challenges. To read about the work of college counselor Grace Leaf, see *Connecting with Careers.*

connecting with careers

Grace Leaf, College/Career Counselor

Grace Leaf is a counselor at Spokane Community College in Washington. She has a master's degree in educational leadership and is working toward a doctoral degree in educational leadership at Gonzaga University in Washington. Her job involves providing orientation sessions for international students, advising individuals and groups, and facilitating individual and group career planning. Leaf tries to connect students with their own goals and values and help them design an educational program that fits their needs and visions.

For more information about what career counselors do, see page 45 in the Careers in Life-Span Development appendix.

Grace Leaf, counseling college students at Spokane Community College about careers.

Review *Connect* Reflect

LG1 Describe the transition from adolescence to adulthood.

Review

- What is the nature of emerging adulthood? What are two main criteria for becoming an adult?
- What are some positive and negative aspects of the transition from high school to college?

Connect

- In Chapter 12, you learned about some strategies for preventing or reducing adolescent problems. What strategy played a role in this section's story of Michael Maddaus?

Reflect *Your Own Personal Journey of Life*

- What do you think is the most important criterion for becoming an adult? Does it make sense to describe becoming an adult in terms of "emerging adulthood" over a period of years, or is there a specific age at which someone becomes an adult? Explain.

---

2 Physical Development

LG2 Identify the changes in physical development in young adults.

| Physical Performance and Development | Health | Eating and Weight | Regular Exercise | Substance Abuse |

As more information becomes available about healthy lifestyles and how they contribute to a longer life span, emerging and young adults are increasingly interested in learning about physical performance, health, nutrition, exercise, and addiction.

PHYSICAL PERFORMANCE AND DEVELOPMENT

Most of us reach our peak levels of physical performance before the age of 30, often between the ages of 19 and 26. This peak of physical performance occurs not only for the average young

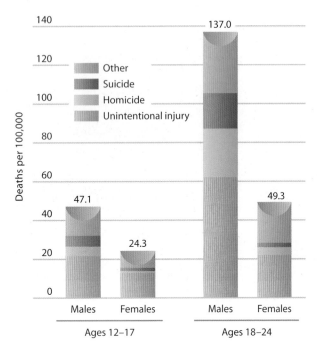

FIGURE **13.2**

MORTALITY RATES OF U.S. ADOLESCENTS AND EMERGING ADULTS

adult, but for outstanding athletes as well. Different types of athletes, however, reach their peak performances at different ages. Most swimmers and gymnasts peak in their late teens. Golfers and marathon runners tend to peak in their late twenties. In other areas of athletics, peak performance often occurs in the early to mid-twenties. However, in recent years, some highly conditioned athletes—such as Dana Torres (Olympic swimming), Lance Armstrong (cycling), and Tom Watson (golf)—have stretched the upper age limits of award-winning performances.

Not only do we reach our peak in physical performance during early adulthood, but it is also during this age period that we begin to decline in physical performance. Muscle tone and strength usually begin to show signs of decline around the age of 30. Sagging chins and protruding abdomens also may begin to appear for the first time. The lessening of physical abilities is a common complaint among the just-turned thirties.

HEALTH

Emerging adults have more than twice the mortality rate of adolescents (Park & others, 2006) (see Figure 13.2). As indicated in Figure 13.2, males are mainly responsible for the higher mortality rate of emerging adults.

Although emerging adults have a higher death rate than adolescents, emerging adults have few chronic health problems, and they have fewer colds and respiratory problems than when they were children (Rimsza & Kirk, 2005). Although most college students know what it takes to prevent illness and promote health, they don't fare very well when it comes to applying this information to themselves (Murphy-Hoefer, Alder, & Higbee, 2004). In many cases, emerging adults are not as healthy as they seem (Fatusi & Hindin, 2010). A recent study revealed that college students from low-SES backgrounds engaged in lower levels of physical activity, ate more fast food and less fruits/vegetables, and showed unhealthy weight control than their higher-SES counterparts (VanKim & Laska, 2012).

A longitudinal study revealed that most bad health habits that were engaged in during adolescence increased in emerging adulthood (Harris & others, 2006). Inactivity, diet, obesity, substance abuse, reproductive health care, and health care access worsened in emerging adulthood. For example, when they were 12 to 18 years of age, only 5 percent reported no weekly exercise, but when they became 19 to 26 years of age, 46 percent said they did not exercise during a week.

In emerging and early adulthood, few individuals stop to think about how their personal lifestyles will affect their health later in their adult lives. As emerging adults, many of us develop a pattern of not eating breakfast, not eating regular meals, and relying on snacks as our main food source during the day, overeating to the point where we exceed the normal weight for our age, smoking moderately or excessively, drinking moderately or excessively, failing to exercise, and getting by with only a few hours of sleep at night (Cousineau, Goldstein, & Franco, 2005). These lifestyles are associated with poor health, which in turn diminishes life satisfaction. In the Berkeley Longitudinal Study—in which individuals were evaluated over a period of 40 years—physical health at age 30 predicted life satisfaction at age 70, more so for men than for women (Mussen, Honzik, & Eichorn, 1982).

One study explored links between health behavior and life satisfaction in more than 17,000 individuals 17 to 30 years of age in 21 countries (Grant, Wardle, & Steptoe, 2009). The young adults' life satisfaction was positively related to not smoking, exercising regularly, using sun protection, eating fruit, and limiting fat intake, but was not related to alcohol consumption and fiber intake.

The health profile of emerging and young adults can be improved by reducing the incidence of certain health-impairing lifestyles, such as overeating, and by engaging in health-improving lifestyles that

Why might it be easy to develop bad health habits in emerging and early adulthood?

include good eating habits, regular exercise, abstaining from drugs, and getting adequate sleep (Cheng & others, 2012; Lachausse, 2012; Monahan & others, 2012).

EATING AND WEIGHT

In Chapters 7 and 9, we discussed aspects of overweight children's lives, and in Chapter 11 we examined the eating disorders of anorexia nervosa and bulimia nervosa in adolescence. Now we will turn our attention to obesity and the extensive preoccupation that many young adults have with dieting.

© www.CartoonStock.com

Obesity   Obesity is not only a problem for many children and adolescents but also a serious and pervasive problem for many adults (Corsica & Perri, 2013; Donatelle, 2013). A recent national survey found that 27 percent of U.S. 20- to 39-year-olds were obese (National Center for Health Statistics, 2011a). A recent analysis predicted that 42 percent of U.S. adults will be obese in 2030 (Finkelstein & others, 2012).

A recent international comparison of 33 developed countries revealed that the United States had the highest percentage of obese adults (OECD, 2010). Figure 13.3 shows the developed countries with the highest and lowest percentages of obese adults.

Being overweight or obese is linked to increased risk of hypertension, diabetes, and cardiovascular disease (Insel & Roth, 2012; O'Callahan & others, 2013). Overweight and obesity also are associated with mental health problems. For example, a recent meta-analysis revealed that overweight women were more likely to be depressed than women who were not overweight, but no significant difference was found for men (de Wit & others, 2010).

What factors are involved in obesity? The possible culprits include heredity, leptin, set point, metabolism, environmental factors, and dieting.

Heredity   Until recently, the genetic component of obesity was underestimated by scientists. Some individuals inherit a tendency to be overweight (Loos, 2012). Researchers have documented that animals can be inbred to have a propensity for obesity (Brown & others, 2011). Further, identical human twins have similar weights, even when they are reared apart (Collaku & others, 2004).

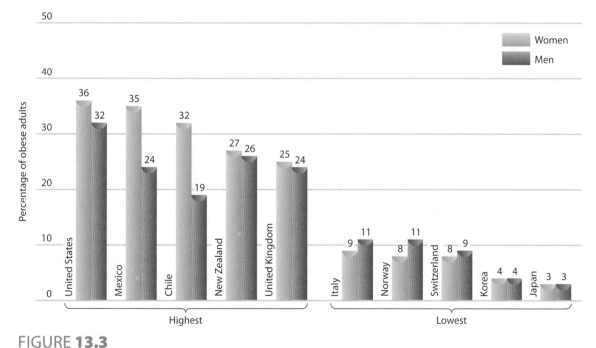

FIGURE **13.3**

COUNTRIES WITH THE HIGHEST AND LOWEST PERCENTAGE OF OBESE ADULTS IN 33 DEVELOPED COUNTRIES.
Source: OECD (2010), *Obesity and the Economics of Prevention—Fit Not Fat.* Paris: OECD.

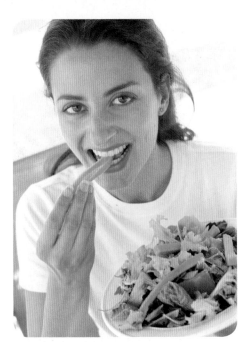

What factors influence an individual's weight? How effective are diet programs?

Leptin　*Leptin* (from the Greek word *leptos,* which means "thin") is a protein that is involved in satiety (the condition of being full to satisfaction) and released by fat cells, resulting in decreased food intake and increased energy expenditure. Leptin acts as an antiobesity hormone. In humans, leptin concentrations have been linked with weight, percentage of body fat, weight loss in a single diet episode, and cumulative percentage of weight loss (Rider & others, 2010). Some scientists are interested in the possibility that leptin might help obese individuals lose weight (Dubern & Clement, 2012; Williams & Schwartz, 2011). A recent study found that when obese individuals engaged in regular exercise, they lost weight, which was associated with changes in leptin levels (Rider & others, 2010).

Set Point　The amount of stored fat in your body is an important factor in your set point, the weight you maintain when you make no effort to gain or lose weight. Fat is stored in what are called adipose cells. When these cells are filled, you do not get hungry. When people gain weight, the number of their fat cells increases. A normal-weight individual has 30 to 40 billion fat cells. An obese individual has 80 to 120 billion fat cells. Some scientists have proposed that these fat cells can shrink but might not go away.

Environmental Factors　Environmental factors play an important role in obesity (Thompson & Manore, 2013; Veerman & others, 2012; Willett, 2013). The human genome has not changed markedly in the last century, yet obesity has noticeably increased. The obesity rate has doubled in the United States since 1900. This dramatic increase in obesity likely is due to greater availability of food (especially food high in fat), greater reliance on energy-saving devices, and declining physical activity. One study found that in 2000, U.S. women ate 335 more calories a day and men 168 more calories a day than they did in the early 1970s (National Center for Health Statistics, 2004).

Sociocultural factors are involved in obesity, which is six times more prevalent among women with low incomes than among women with high incomes. Americans also are more obese than Europeans and people in many other areas of the world (OECD, 2010).

Dieting　Ironically, although obesity is on the rise, dieting has become an obsession with many Americans (Schiff, 2013). Although many Americans regularly embark on a diet, few are successful in keeping weight off over the long term and many dieters risk becoming fatter (Dulloo, Jacquet, & Montani, 2012; Pietilainen & others, 2012). A research review of the long-term outcomes of calorie-restricting diets revealed that overall one-third to two-thirds of dieters regain more weight than they lost on their diets (Mann & others, 2007). However, some individuals do lose weight and maintain the loss (Chambers & Swanson, 2012; Cooper & others, 2012). How often this occurs and whether some diet programs work better than others are still open questions.

What we *do* know about losing weight is that the most effective programs include exercise (Palu, West, & Jensen, 2011; Snel & others, 2012). A recent research review concluded that adults who engaged in diet-plus-exercise programs lost more weight than those who relied on diet-only programs (Wu & others, 2009). A study of approximately 2,000 U.S. adults found that exercising 30 minutes a day, planning meals, and weighing themselves daily were the main strategies used by successful dieters as compared with unsuccessful dieters (Kruger, Blanck, & Gillespie, 2006) (see Figure 13.4). Another study also revealed that daily weigh-ins are linked to maintaining weight loss (Wing & others, 2007).

The National Weight Control Registry is an ongoing examination of individuals who have lost 30 pounds and kept it off for at least one year. Research on these successful dieters provides important information about losing weight and maintaining the weight loss (Ogden & others, 2012). One of the most consistent findings is that these successful dieters engage in a high level of physical activity (Catenacci & others, 2008).

REGULAR EXERCISE

One of the main reasons that health experts want people to exercise is that it helps to prevent chronic disorders such as heart disease and diabetes (Fahey, Insel, & Roth, 2013). Many health experts recommend that young adults engage in 30 minutes or

FIGURE 13.4

COMPARISON OF STRATEGIES IN SUCCESSFUL AND UNSUCCESSFUL DIETERS

(Chart legend)
■ Successful　■ Unsuccessful

Exercised 30 minutes a day — 47 / 38
Planned meals — 36 / 25
Weighed themselves daily — 20 / 11

Percent (50 40 30 20 10 0)

more of aerobic exercise a day, preferably every day. **Aerobic exercise** is sustained exercise—jogging, swimming, or cycling, for example—that stimulates heart and lung activity. Most health experts recommend that you raise your heart rate to at least 60 percent of your maximum heart rate. Only about one-fifth of adults, however, achieve these recommended levels of physical activity.

Researchers have found that exercise benefits not only physical health, but mental health as well. In particular, exercise improves self-concept and reduces anxiety and depression (Jazaieri & others, 2012; Sturm & others, 2012; Villaverde Guitierrez & others, 2012). Meta-analyses have shown that exercise can be as effective in reducing depression as psychotherapy (Richardson & others, 2005).

Research on the benefits of exercise suggests that both moderate and intense activities produce important physical and psychological gains. The enjoyment and pleasure we derive from exercise, added to its aerobic benefits, make exercise one of life's most important activities (Donatelle, 2013; Fahey, Insel, & Roth, 2013). A recent study of college students revealed that males' motivation to exercise involved strength, challenge, and competition, whereas females' motivation focused more on weight management and appearance (Egli & others, 2011).

Here are some helpful strategies for making exercise part of your life:

- **Reduce TV time.** Heavy TV viewing is linked to poor health and obesity. A recent study revealed that compared with individuals who watch no TV, watching TV 6 hours a day reduces life expectancy by 4.8 years (Veerman & others, 2012). Replace some of your TV time with exercise.

- **Chart your progress.** Systematically recording your exercise workouts will help you to chart your progress. This strategy is especially helpful over the long term.

- **Get rid of excuses.** People make up all kinds of excuses for not exercising. A typical excuse is "I don't have enough time." You likely do have enough time.

- **Imagine the alternative.** Ask yourself whether you are too busy to take care of your own health. What will your life be like if you lose your health?

SUBSTANCE ABUSE

In Chapter 11, we explored substance abuse in adolescence. Fortunately, by the time individuals reach their mid-twenties, many have reduced their use of alcohol and drugs. That is the conclusion reached by Jerald Bachman and his colleagues (2002) in a longitudinal analysis of more than 38,000 individuals who were evaluated from the time they were high school seniors through their twenties. As in adolescence, male college students and young adults are more likely to take drugs than their female counterparts (Johnston & others, 2008). One study revealed that only 20 percent of college students reported abstaining from alcohol (Huang & others, 2009).

Let's take a closer look at alcohol consumption and nicotine use by young adults and at the nature of **addiction,** which is a behavior pattern characterized by an overwhelming involvement with a drug and a preoccupation with securing its supply.

Alcohol   Let's examine two problems associated with drinking: binge drinking and alcoholism.

Binge Drinking   Heavy binge drinking often increases in college, and it can take its toll on students (Kinney, 2012). Chronic binge drinking is more common among college men than women and students living away from home, especially in fraternity houses (Chen & Jacobson, 2012; Schulenberg & others, 2000).

In 2010, 37 percent of U.S. college students reported having had 5 or more drinks in a row at least once in the last two weeks (Johnston & others, 2011). In the most recent survey, the Institute of Social Research introduced the term *extreme binge drinking* to describe individuals who had 10 or more drinks in a row. In 2010 approximately 13 percent of college students reported drinking this heavily (Johnston & others, 2011). While still at a very high rate, college

developmental **connection**

Health

Do adolescents exercise more or less than children do? Chapter 11, p. 368

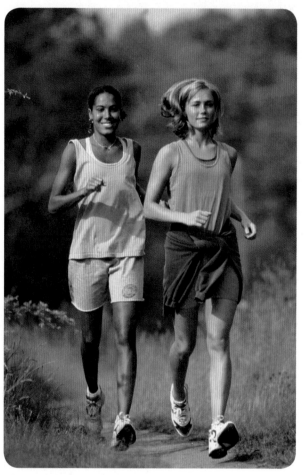

What are your exercise goals? What are some strategies for incorporating exercise into your life?

aerobic exercise Sustained exercise (such as jogging, swimming, or cycling) that stimulates heart and lung activity.

addiction A pattern of behavior characterized by an overwhelming involvement with using a drug and a preoccupation with securing its supply.

What kinds of problems are associated with binge drinking in college?

student drinking, including binge drinking, has declined in recent years. For example, binge drinking declined 4 percent from 2007 to 2010 (Johnston & others, 2011).

In a national survey of drinking patterns on 140 campuses, almost half of the binge drinkers reported problems that included absence from classes, physical injuries, troubles with police, and unprotected sex (Wechsler & others, 2002). For example, binge-drinking college students were 11 times as likely to fall behind in school, 10 times as likely to drive after drinking, and twice as likely to have unprotected sex as college students who did not engage in binge drinking.

Drinking alcohol before going out—called *pregaming*—has become common among college students (Bachrach & others, 2012; LaBrie & others, 2011). A recent study revealed that almost two-thirds of students on one campus had pregamed at least once during a two-week period (DeJong, DeRicco, & Schneider, 2010). Another recent study found that two-thirds of 18- to 24-year-old women on one college pregamed (Read, Merrill, & Bytschkow, 2010). Drinking games, in which the goal is to become intoxicated, also have become common on college campuses (Cameron & others, 2010). Higher levels of alcohol use have been consistently linked to higher rates of sexual risk taking, such as engaging in casual sex, sex without using contraception, and sexual assaults (Gilmore, Granato, & Lewis, 2012; Khan & others, 2012).

When does binge drinking peak during development? A longitudinal study revealed that binge drinking peaks at about 21 to 22 years of age and then declines through the remainder of the twenties (Bachman & others, 2002) (see Figure 13.5).

Alcoholism   *Alcoholism* is a disorder that involves long-term, repeated, uncontrolled, compulsive, and excessive use of alcoholic beverages and impairs the drinker's health and social relationships. One in nine individuals who drink will become an alcoholic. Those who do are disproportionately related to alcoholics (Gordh, Brkic, & Soderpalm, 2011). Family studies consistently reveal a high frequency of alcoholism in the first-degree relatives of alcoholics (Kramer & others, 2008). An estimated 50 to 60 percent of individuals who become alcoholics are believed to have a genetic predisposition for it.

Although studies reveal a genetic influence on alcoholism (Li, Zhao, & Gelenter, 2012; Nunez & Mayfield, 2012), they also show that environmental factors play a role. For example, family studies indicate that many individuals who suffer from alcoholism do not have close relatives who are addicted to alcohol (McCutcheon & others, 2012). Large cultural variations in alcohol use also underscore the environment's role in alcoholism. For example, Orthodox Jews and Mormons have especially low rates of alcohol use and alcoholism.

About one-third of alcoholics recover, whether or not they are ever in a treatment program. This figure was found in a long-term study of 700 individuals over 50 years and has consistently been found by other researchers as well (Vaillant, 1992). There is a "one-third rule" for alcoholism: By age 65, one-third are dead or in terrible shape, one-third are abstinent or drinking socially, and one-third are still trying to beat their addiction. A positive outcome and recovery from alcoholism are predicted by certain factors: (1) a strong negative experience related to drinking, such as a serious medical emergency or condition; (2) finding a substitute

FIGURE **13.5**

BINGE DRINKING IN THE ADOLESCENCE— EARLY ADULTHOOD TRANSITION. Note that the percentage of individuals engaging in binge drinking peaked at 21 or 22 years of age and then began to gradually decline through the remainder of the twenties. Binge drinking was defined as having five or more alcoholic drinks in a row in the past two weeks.

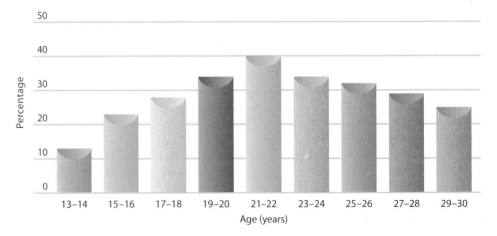

dependency to compete with alcohol abuse, such as meditation, exercise, or overeating (which of course has its own negative health consequences); (3) having new social supports (such as a concerned, helpful employer or a new marriage); and (4) joining an inspirational group, such as a religious organization or Alcoholics Anonymous (Vaillant, 1992).

Cigarette Smoking and Nicotine Converging evidence from a number of studies underscores the dangers of smoking or being around those who do (American Cancer Society, 2012). For example, smoking is linked to 30 percent of cancer deaths, 21 percent of heart disease deaths, and 82 percent of chronic pulmonary disease deaths. Secondhand smoke is implicated in as many as 9,000 lung cancer deaths a year. Children of smokers are at special risk for respiratory and middle-ear diseases (Hwang & others, 2012; Stosic & others, 2012).

Fewer people smoke today than in the past, and almost half of all living adults who ever smoked have quit. In the United States, the prevalence of smoking in individuals 18 years and older has dropped from 42 percent in 1965 to 19 percent in 2010 (Centers for Disease Control and Prevention, 2012). However, more than 50 million Americans still smoke cigarettes today. Cigarette smoking accounts for approximately 450,000 deaths, or 1 in 5 deaths, annually in the United States (Centers for Disease Control and Prevention, 2012).

Most adult smokers would like to quit, but their addiction to nicotine often makes quitting a challenge (Baimel, Borgland, & Corrigall, 2012; Verdejo-Garcia, Clark, & Dunn, 2012). Nicotine, the active drug in cigarettes, is a stimulant that increases the smoker's energy and alertness, a pleasurable and reinforcing experience (Swan & others, 2013). Nicotine also stimulates neurotransmitters (especially dopamine) that have a calming or pain-reducing effect (Cahill, Stead, & Lancaster, 2012).

"There's no shooting—we just make you keep smoking."
© Michael Shaw/The New Yorker Collection/www.cartoonbank.com

developmental **connection**

Health

Many individuals who smoke in emerging adulthood and early adulthood began smoking during adolescence. Chapter 11, p. 370

Review *Connect* Reflect

LG2 Identify the changes in physical development in young adults.

Review

- When does physical performance peak and then slow down in adulthood?
- What characterizes health in emerging and early adulthood?
- What are some important things to know about eating and weight?
- What are the benefits of exercise?
- How extensive is substance abuse in young adults? What effects does it have on their lives?

Connect

- Problems with weight in adulthood can often be preceded by problems with

weight earlier in life. What are some of the influences on children's eating and exercise behavior in early childhood that you learned about in Chapter 7?

Reflect *Your Own Personal Journey of Life*

- What is (or was) your life like from age 18 to 25? Do Arnett's five characteristics of emerging adulthood accurately describe your own experience during this period?

---

3 Sexuality **LG3** Discuss sexuality in young adults.

| Sexual Activity in Emerging Adulthood | Sexual Orientation and Behavior | Sexually Transmitted Infections | Forcible Sexual Behavior and Sexual Harassment |

We do not need sex for everyday survival the way we need food and water, but we do need it for the survival of the species. In Chapter 11, we looked at how adolescents develop a sexual identity and become sexually active. What happens to their sexuality during adulthood? Let's examine the sexual activity of Americans and their sexual orientation, as well as some of the problems that can be associated with sexual activity.

Noncohabiting

Men

Women

Cohabiting (married)

Men

Women

- Never
- A few times a year
- A few times a month
- 2–3 times a week
- 4 or more times a week

FIGURE **13.6**

THE SEX IN AMERICA SURVEY. The percentages show noncohabiting and cohabiting (married) males' and females' responses to the survey question "How often have you had sex in the past year?" (Michael & others, 1994). *What was one feature of the Sex in America survey that made it superior to most surveys of sexual behavior?*

developmental **connection**

Sexuality

Having intercourse in early adolescence is a risk factor in development. Chapter 11, p. 363

What are some characteristics of the sexual activity of emerging adults?

SEXUAL ACTIVITY IN EMERGING ADULTHOOD

At the beginning of emerging adulthood (age 18), surveys indicate that slightly more than 60 percent of individuals have experienced sexual intercourse, but by the end of emerging adulthood (age 25), most individuals have had sexual intercourse (Lefkowitz & Gillen, 2006). Also, the average age of marriage in the United States is currently 28 for males and 26 for females (Copen & others, 2012). Thus, emerging adulthood is a time frame during which most individuals are both sexually active and unmarried (Lefkowitz & Gillen, 2006).

Patterns of heterosexual behavior for males and females in emerging adulthood include the following (Lefkowitz & Gillen, 2006):

- Males have more casual sexual partners, and females report being more selective about their choice of a sexual partner.
- Approximately 60 percent of emerging adults have had sexual intercourse with only one individual in the past year, but compared with young adults in their late twenties and thirties, emerging adults are more likely to have had sexual intercourse with two or more individuals.
- Although emerging adults have sexual intercourse with more individuals than young adults, they have sex less frequently. Approximately 25 percent of emerging adults report having sexual intercourse only a couple of times a year or not at all (Michael & others, 1994).
- Casual sex is more common in emerging adulthood than in young adulthood. A recent trend has involved "hooking up" to have non-relationship sex (from kissing to intercourse) (Holman & Sillars, 2012; Olmstead, Pasley, & Fincham, 2012).

SEXUAL ORIENTATION AND BEHAVIOR

A recent national study of sexual behavior in the United States among adults 25 to 44 years of age found that 98 percent of the women and 97 percent of the men said that they had ever engaged in vaginal intercourse (Chandra & others, 2011). Also in this study, 89 percent of the women and 90 percent of the men reported that they had ever had oral sex with an opposite-sex partner, and 36 percent of the women and 44 percent of the men stated that they had ever had anal sex with an opposite-sex partner.

Detailed information about various aspects of sexual activity in adults of different ages comes from the 1994 Sex in America survey. In this study Robert Michael and his colleagues (1994) interviewed more than 3,000 people from 18 to 59 years of age who were randomly selected, in sharp contrast with earlier samples that were based on unrepresentative groups of volunteers.

Heterosexual Attitudes and Behavior Here are some of the key findings from the 1994 Sex in America survey:

- Americans tend to fall into three categories: One-third have sex twice a week or more, one-third a few times a month, and one-third a few times a year or not at all.
- Married (and cohabiting) couples have sex more often than noncohabiting couples (see Figure 13.6).
- Most Americans do not engage in kinky sexual acts. When asked about their favorite sexual acts, the vast majority (96 percent) said that vaginal sex was "very" or "somewhat" appealing. Oral sex was in third place, after an activity that many have not labeled a sexual act—watching a partner undress.

- Adultery is clearly the exception rather than the rule. Nearly 75 percent of the married men and 85 percent of the married women indicated that they have never been unfaithful.
- Men think about sex far more often than women do—54 percent of the men said they think about it every day or several times a day, whereas 67 percent of the women said they think about it only a few times a week or a few times a month.

In sum, one of the most powerful messages in the 1994 survey was that Americans' sexual lives are more conservative than was previously believed. Although 17 percent of the men and 3 percent of the women said they have had sex with at least 21 partners, the overall impression from the survey was that sexual behavior is ruled by marriage and monogamy for most Americans.

How extensive are gender differences in sexuality? A recent meta-analysis revealed that men reported having slightly more sexual experience and more permissive attitudes than women for most aspects of sexuality (Petersen & Hyde, 2010). For the following factors, stronger differences were found: Men indicated that they engaged more in masturbation, pornography use, and casual sex, and they held more permissive attitudes about casual sex than their female counterparts.

Given all of the media and public attention to the negative aspects of sexuality—such as adolescent pregnancy, sexually transmitted infections, rape, and so on—it is important to underscore that research has strongly supported the role of sexual activity in well-being (Brody, 2010). For example, in a recent Swedish study frequency of sexual intercourse was strongly related to life satisfaction for both men and women (Brody & Costa, 2009).

Sources of Sexual Orientation

In the Sex in America survey, 2.7 percent of the men and 1.3 percent of the women reported having had same-sex relations in the past year (Michael & others, 1994). Why are some individuals lesbian, gay, or bisexual (LGB) and others heterosexual? Speculation about this question has been extensive (Crooks & Baur, 2011).

Until the end of the nineteenth century, it was generally believed that people were either heterosexual or homosexual. Today, sexual orientation is generally seen not as an either/or proposition but as a continuum ranging from exclusive male-female relations to exclusive same-sex relations (King, 2013). Some individuals are bisexual, being sexually attracted to people of both sexes.

All people, regardless of their sexual orientation, have similar physiological responses during sexual arousal and seem to be aroused by the same types of tactile stimulation. Investigators typically find no differences between LGBs and heterosexuals in a wide range of attitudes, behaviors, and adjustments (Fingerhut & Peplau, 2013).

Recently, researchers have explored the possible biological basis of same-sex relations. The results of hormone studies have been inconsistent. If gays are given male sex hormones (androgens), their sexual orientation doesn't change. Their sexual desire merely increases. A very early prenatal critical period might influence sexual orientation (Berenbaum & Beltz, 2011). If this critical-period hypothesis turns out to be correct, it would explain why clinicians have found that sexual orientation is difficult, if not impossible, to modify.

An individual's sexual orientation—same-sex, heterosexual, or bisexual—is most likely determined by a combination of genetic, hormonal, cognitive, and environmental factors (King, 2013; Yarber, Sayad, & Strong, 2013). Most experts on same-sex relations point out that no single factor alone causes sexual orientation and that the relative weight of each factor can vary from one individual to the next.

Researchers have examined the role of genes in sexual orientation by using twins to estimate the genetic and environmental contributions to sexual orientation. A recent Swedish study of almost 4,000 twins demonstrated that only about 35 percent of the variation in homosexual behavior in men and 19 percent in women were explained by genetic differences (Langstrom & others, 2010). This result indicates that although genes likely play a role in sexual orientation, their influence is not as strong in explaining sexuality as it is for other characteristics such as intelligence (King, 2013).

Attitudes and Behavior of Lesbians and Gays

Many gender differences that appear in heterosexual relationships also occur in same-sex relationships (Diamond & Savin-Williams, 2013; Savin-Williams, 2013). For example, like heterosexual women, lesbians have

What likely determines an individual's sexual orientation?

developmental **connection**

Research Methods

A twin study compares the behavioral similarity of identical twins with that of fraternal twins. Chapter 2, p. 68

STI	Description/cause	Incidence	Treatment
Gonorrhea	Commonly called the "drip" or "clap." Caused by the bacterium *Neisseria gonorrhoeae*. Spread by contact between infected moist membranes (genital, oral-genital, or anal-genital) of two individuals. Characterized by discharge from penis or vagina and painful urination. Can lead to infertility.	500,000 cases annually in U.S.	Penicillin, other antibiotics
Syphilis	Caused by the bacterium *Treponema pallidum*. Characterized by the appearance of a sore where syphilis entered the body. The sore can be on the external genitals, vagina, or anus. Later, a skin rash breaks out on palms of hands and bottom of feet. If not treated, can eventually lead to paralysis or even death.	100,000 cases annually in U.S.	Penicillin
Chlamydia	A common STI named for the bacterium *Chlamydia trachomatis*, an organism that spreads by sexual contact and infects the genital organs of both sexes. A special concern is that females with chlamydia may become infertile. It is recommended that adolescent and young adult females have an annual screening for this STI.	About 3 million people in U.S. annually.	Antibiotics
Genital herpes	Caused by a family of viruses with different strains. Involves an eruption of sores and blisters. Spread by sexual contact.	One of five U.S. adults	No known cure but antiviral medications can shorten outbreaks
AIDS	Caused by a virus, the human immunodeficiency virus (HIV), which destroys the body's immune system. Semen and blood are the main vehicles of transmission. Common symptoms include fevers, night sweats, weight loss, chronic fatigue, and swollen lymph nodes.	More than 300,000 cumulative cases of HIV virus in U.S. 25–34-year-olds; epidemic incidence in sub-Saharan countries	New treatments have slowed the progression from HIV to AIDS; no cure
Genital warts	Caused by the human papillomavirus (HPV), which does not always produce symptoms. Usually appear as small, hard painless bumps in the vaginal area, or around the anus. Very contagious. Certain high-risk types of this virus cause cervical cancer and other genital cancers. May recur despite treatment. A new HPV preventive vaccine, Gardasil, has been approved for girls and women 9–26 years of age.	About 5.5 million new cases annually; considered the most common STI in the U.S.	A topical drug, freezing, or surgery

FIGURE **13.7**
SEXUALLY TRANSMITTED INFECTIONS

fewer sexual partners than gay men, and lesbians have less permissive attitudes about casual sex outside a primary relationship than gay men do (Fingerhut & Peplau, 2013).

How do lesbians and gays adapt to a world in which they are a minority? According to psychologist Laura Brown (1989), lesbians and gays experience life as a minority in a dominant, majority culture. For lesbians and gays, developing a bicultural identity creates new ways of defining themselves. Brown maintains that lesbians and gays adapt best when they don't define themselves in polarities, such as trying to live in an encapsulated lesbian or gay world completely divorced from the majority culture or completely accepting the dictates and biases of the majority culture. Balancing the demands of the two cultures—the minority lesbian/gay culture and the majority heterosexual culture—can often lead to more effective coping for lesbians and gays, says Brown.

A special concern involving sexual minority individuals are the hate crimes and stigma-related experiences they encounter (Lewis, Kholodkov, & Derlega, 2012). In one study, approximately 20 percent of sexual minority adults reported having experienced a person or property crime related to their sexual orientation, and about 50 percent said they had experienced verbal harassment (Herek, 2009).

SEXUALLY TRANSMITTED INFECTIONS

Sexually transmitted infections (STIs) are diseases that are primarily spread through sexual contact—intercourse as well as oral-genital and anal-genital sex. STIs affect about one in six U.S. adults (National Center for Health Statistics, 2011b). Among the most prevalent STIs are bacterial infections (such as gonorrhea, syphilis, and chlamydia) and STIs caused by viruses—genital herpes, genital warts, and HIV, which can lead to AIDS. Figure 13.7 describes several sexually transmitted infections.

sexually transmitted infections (STIs) Diseases that are contracted primarily through sexual activity.

Pat Hawkins, Community Psychologist and Director of an HIV/AIDS Clinic

Pat Hawkins is the associate executive director for policy and external affairs of the Whitman-Walker Clinic in Washington, DC, helping HIV and AIDS patients. She came to the clinic as a volunteer in 1983, just after HIV/AIDS exploded into an epidemic. Hawkins says that she would not do anything else but community work. "Nothing gets you engaged so fast as getting involved," she comments. "We often keep the academic world separate from the real world, and we desperately need psychologists' skills in the real world." Hawkins had a double major in psychology and sociology as an undergraduate and then went on to obtain her Ph.D. in community psychology.

Pat Hawkins counseling an AIDS patient.

No single STI has had a greater impact on sexual behavior, or created more public fear in the last several decades, than infection with the human immunodeficiency virus (HIV). HIV is a sexually transmitted infection that destroys the body's immune system. Once a person is infected with HIV, the virus breaks down and overpowers the immune system, which leads to acquired immune deficiency syndrome (AIDS). An individual sick with AIDS has such a weakened immune system that a common cold can be life threatening.

In 2010, 1.2 million people in the United States were living with an HIV infection (National Center for Health Statistics, 2012). In 2010, male-male sexual contact continued to be the most frequent AIDS transmission category. Because of education and the development of more effective drug treatments, deaths due to HIV/AIDS have begun to decline in the United States (National Center for Health Statistics, 2012). To read about the background and work of one individual who counsels HIV/AIDS patients, see *Connecting with Careers*.

Globally, the total number of individuals living with HIV was 34 million at the end of 2010, with 22 million of these individuals with HIV living in sub-Saharan Africa. Approximately half of all new HIV infections around the world occur in the 15- to 24-year-old age category. The good news is that global rates of HIV infection fell nearly 25 percent from 2001 to 2009 with substantial decreases in India and South Africa (UNAIDS, 2011). In a recent study, only 49 percent of 15- to 24-year-old females in low- and middle-income countries knew that using a condom helps to prevent HIV infection, compared with 74 percent of young males (UNAIDS, 2011).

What are some effective strategies for protecting against HIV and other sexually transmitted infections? They include the following:

- *Know your risk status and that of your partner.* Anyone who has had previous sexual activity with another person might have contracted an STI without being aware of it. Spend time getting to know a prospective partner before you have sex. Use this time to inform the other person of your STI status and inquire about your partner's. Remember that many people lie about their STI status.

- *Obtain medical examinations.* Many experts recommend that couples who want to begin a sexual relationship have a medical checkup to rule out STIs before they engage in sex. If cost is an issue, contact your campus health service or a public health clinic.

- *Have protected, not unprotected, sex.* When used correctly, latex condoms help to prevent many STIs from being transmitted. Condoms are most effective in preventing gonorrhea, syphilis, chlamydia, and HIV. They are less effective against the spread of herpes.

What are some good strategies for protecting against HIV and other sexually transmitted infections? How effectively have you practiced these strategies?

- *Do not have sex with multiple partners.* One of the best predictors of getting an STI is having sex with multiple partners. Having more than one sex partner elevates the likelihood that you will encounter an infected partner.

FORCIBLE SEXUAL BEHAVIOR AND SEXUAL HARASSMENT

Too often, sex involves the exercise of power. Here, we will briefly look at three of the problems that may result: two types of rape and sexual harassment.

Rape   **Rape** is forcible sexual intercourse with a person who does not give consent. Legal definitions of rape differ from state to state. For example, in some states husbands are not prohibited from forcing their wives to have intercourse, although this has been challenged in several of those states.

Because victims may be reluctant to suffer the consequences of reporting rape, the actual incidence is not easily determined (Spohn & Tellis, 2012; Willoughby & others, 2012). Nearly 200,000 rapes are reported each year in the United States. A recent study of college women who had been raped revealed that only 11.5 percent of them reported the rape to authorities and of those for which the rape involved drugs and/or alcohol, only 2.7 percent of the rapes were reported (Wolitzky-Taylor & others, 2011).

Although most victims of rape are women, rape of men does occur (Bullock & Beckson, 2011). Men in prisons are especially vulnerable to rape, usually by heterosexual males who use rape as a means of establishing their dominance and power (Barth, 2012).

Why does rape of women occur so often in the United States? Among the causes given are that males are socialized to be sexually aggressive, to regard women as inferior beings, and to view their own pleasure as the most important objective in sexual relations (Beech, Ward, & Fisher, 2006; Davies, Gilston, & Rogers, 2012). Researchers have found that male rapists share the following characteristics: aggression enhances their sense of power or masculinity; they are angry at women in general; and they want to hurt and humiliate their victims (Yarber, Sayad, & Strong, 2013). A recent study revealed that a higher level of men's sexual narcissism (assessed by these factors: sexual exploitation, sexual entitlement, low sexual empathy, and sexual skill) was linked to a greater likelihood that they would engage in sexual aggression (Widman & McNulty, 2010). A recent study also revealed that regardless of whether or not the victim was using substances, sexual assault was more likely to occur when the offender was using substances (Brecklin & Ullman, 2010).

Rape is a traumatic experience for the victims and those close to them (Jozkowski & Sanders, 2012). As victims strive to get their lives back to normal, they may experience depression, fear, anxiety, and increased substance use for months or years (Amstadter & others, 2011). Many victims make changes in their lives—such as moving to a new apartment or refusing to go out at night. Recovery depends on the victim's coping abilities, psychological adjustment prior to the assault, and social support. Parents, a partner, and others close to the victim can provide important support for recovery, as can mental health professionals (Ahrens & Aldana, 2012; Resick & others, 2012).

An increasing concern is **date or acquaintance rape,** which is coercive sexual activity directed at someone with whom the perpetrator is at least casually acquainted (Albright, Stevens, & Beussman, 2012; Angelone, Mitchell, & Lucente, 2012). In one survey, two-thirds of female college freshmen reported having been date raped or having experienced an attempted date rape at least once (Watts & Zimmerman, 2002). About two-thirds of college men admit that they fondle women against their will, and half admit to forcing sexual activity.

A number of colleges and universities describe the red zone as a period of time early in the first year of college when women are at especially high risk for unwanted sexual experiences. One study revealed that first-year women were more at risk for unwanted sexual experiences, especially early in the fall term, than second-year women (Kimble & others, 2008). Exactly how prevalent are sexual assaults on college campuses? To find out, see *Connecting Through Research.*

Sexual Harassment   Sexual harassment is a manifestation of power of one person over another. It takes many forms, ranging from inappropriate sexual remarks and physical contact

What are some characteristics of acquaintance rape in colleges and universities?

rape Forcible sexual intercourse with a person who does not consent to it.

date or acquaintance rape Coercive sexual activity directed at someone with whom the perpetrator is at least casually acquainted.

How Prevalent Are Sexual Assaults on College Campuses?

A major study that focused on campus sexual assault involved a phone survey of 4,446 women attending two- or four-year colleges (Fisher, Cullen, & Turner, 2000). Sexual victimization was measured in a two-stage process. First, a series of screening questions were asked to determine whether the respondent had experienced an act that might possibly be a victimization. Second, if the respondent answered "yes," the respondent was asked detailed questions about the incident, such as the type of unwanted contact and the means of coercion. In addition, respondents were asked about other aspects of their lives, including their lifestyles, routine activities, living arrangements, and prior sexual victimization.

Slightly less than 3 percent said that they had experienced either a rape or an attempted rape during the current academic year. About 1 of 10 college women said that they had experienced rape in their lifetime. Unwanted or uninvited sexual contacts were widespread, with more than one-third of the college women reporting these incidents. As shown in Figure 13.8, in this study, most women (about 9 out of 10) knew the person who had sexually victimized them. Most of the women attempted to take protective actions against their assailants but were reluctant to report the victimization to the police for a number of reasons (such as embarrassment, not clearly understanding the legal definition of rape, or not wanting to define someone they knew who had victimized them as a rapist). Several factors were associated with sexual victimization: living on campus, being unmarried, getting drunk frequently, and experiencing prior sexual victimization. The majority of rapes occurred in living quarters.

In addition, the researchers in this study examined a form of sexual victimization that has been studied infrequently: stalking. Thirteen percent of the female students said they had been stalked since the school year began. As with other sexual victimizations, 80 percent knew their stalkers, who most often were boyfriends (42 percent) or classmates (24 percent). Stalking incidents lasted an average of 60 days.

Given the prevalence of sexual assault on college campuses and the frequency with which those assaults involve perpetrators the victims know, it is clear that more research needs to be dedicated to effective intervention strategies for young men and women. In the past, too often the responsibility of prevention was placed on the would-be victim's behavior. While those sorts of strategies are not unhelpful, prevention strategies that target the behavior of the would-be rapist might get closer to the root of the problem.

FIGURE **13.8**

RELATIONSHIP BETWEEN VICTIM AND OFFENDER IN COMPLETED AND ATTEMPTED RAPES OF COLLEGE WOMEN. In a phone survey of college women, slightly less than 3 percent of the women said they had experienced a rape or attempted rape during the academic year (Fisher, Cullen, & Turner, 2000). The percentages shown here indicate the relationship between the victim and the offender. *What were some possible advantages and disadvantages of using a phone survey rather than face-to-face interviews to conduct this study?*

(patting, brushing against another person's body) to blatant propositions and sexual assaults. Millions of women experience sexual harassment each year in work and educational settings (Snyder, Scherer, & Fisher, 2012). Sexual harassment of men by women also occurs but to a far lesser extent than sexual harassment of women by men.

In a recent survey of 2,000 college women, 62 percent reported having experienced sexual harassment while attending college (American Association of University Women, 2006). Most of the college women said that the sexual harassment involved noncontact forms such as crude jokes, remarks, and gestures. However, almost one-third said that the sexual harassment was physical in nature. Sexual harassment can result in serious psychological consequences for the victim. The elimination of this type of exploitation requires the establishment of work and academic environments that provide women and men with equal opportunities to develop a career and obtain an education in a climate free of sexual harassment (Nielsen & Einarsen, 2012).

Review

- What characterizes the sexual activity of emerging adults?
- What is the nature of heterosexuality and same-sex sexual orientation?
- What are sexually transmitted infections? What are some important things to know about AIDS?
- What is rape? What is date or acquaintance rape? What are the effects of forcible sexual behavior and sexual harassment?

Connect

- As you learned in this section, sexual assault is connected with aggression in

males. In Chapter 8, what was identified as one way in which children learn to behave aggressively?

Reflect *Your Own Personal Journey of Life*

- How would you describe your sexual experiences during emerging adulthood? How similar or dissimilar are they to the way sexuality in emerging adulthood was described in this section?

---

4 Cognitive Development

LG4 Characterize cognitive changes in early adulthood.

Cognitive Stages   Creativity

developmental **connection**

Cognitive Theory

Adolescent cognition also includes adolescent egocentrism. Chapter 11, p. 375

Are there changes in cognitive performance during early adulthood? To explore the nature of cognition during this period of development, we will focus on issues related to cognitive stages and creative thinking.

COGNITIVE STAGES

Are young adults more advanced in their thinking than adolescents are? Let's examine how Jean Piaget and others have answered this intriguing question.

Piaget's View   Piaget concluded that an adolescent and an adult think qualitatively in the same way. That is, Piaget argued that at approximately 11 to 15 years of age, adolescents enter the formal operational stage, which is characterized by more logical, abstract, and idealistic thinking than the concrete operational thinking of 7- to 11-year-olds. Piaget did stress that young adults are more quantitatively advanced in their thinking in the sense that they have more knowledge than adolescents. He also reasoned, as do information-processing psychologists, that adults especially increase their knowledge in a specific area, such as a physicist's understanding of physics or a financial analyst's knowledge about finance. According to Piaget, however, formal operational thought is the final stage in cognitive development, and it characterizes adults as well as adolescents.

Some developmentalists theorize it is not until adulthood that many individuals consolidate their formal operational thinking. That is, they may begin to plan and hypothesize about intellectual problems in adolescence, but they become more systematic and sophisticated at this process as young adults. Nonetheless, even many adults do not think in formal operational ways (Keating, 2004).

What are some ways that young adults might think differently from adolescents?

Is There a Fifth, Postformal Stage?   Some theorists have pieced together these descriptions of adult thinking and have proposed that young adults move into a new

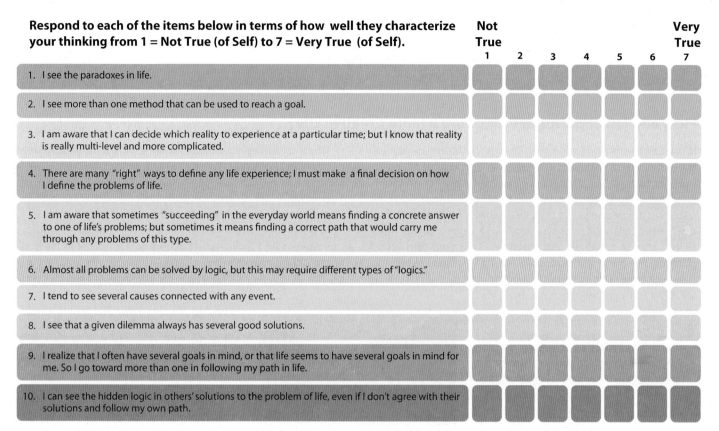

Respond to each of the items below in terms of how well they characterize your thinking from 1 = Not True (of Self) to 7 = Very True (of Self).

	Not True 1	2	3	4	5	6	Very True 7
1. I see the paradoxes in life.							
2. I see more than one method that can be used to reach a goal.							
3. I am aware that I can decide which reality to experience at a particular time; but I know that reality is really multi-level and more complicated.							
4. There are many "right" ways to define any life experience; I must make a final decision on how I define the problems of life.							
5. I am aware that sometimes "succeeding" in the everyday world means finding a concrete answer to one of life's problems; but sometimes it means finding a correct path that would carry me through any problems of this type.							
6. Almost all problems can be solved by logic, but this may require different types of "logics."							
7. I tend to see several causes connected with any event.							
8. I see that a given dilemma always has several good solutions.							
9. I realize that I often have several goals in mind, or that life seems to have several goals in mind for me. So I go toward more than one in following my path in life.							
10. I can see the hidden logic in others' solutions to the problem of life, even if I don't agree with their solutions and follow my own path.							

FIGURE 13.9

COMPLEX POSTFORMAL THOUGHT QUESTIONNAIRE. After you have responded to the items, total your score, which can range from 10 to 70. The higher your score, the more likely you are to engage in postformal thinking.

qualitative stage of cognitive development, postformal thought (Sinnott, 2003). **Postformal thought** is:

- *Reflective, relativistic, and contextual.* As young adults engage in solving problems, they might think deeply about many aspects of work, politics, relationships, and other areas of life (Labouvie-Vief, 1986). They find that what might be the best solution to a problem at work (with a boss or co-worker) might not be the best solution at home (with a romantic partner). Thus, postformal thought holds that the correct answer to a problem requires reflective thinking and may vary from one situation to another. Some psychologists argue that reflective thinking continues to increase and becomes more internal and less contextual in middle age (Mascalo & Fischer, 2010; Labouvie-Vief, Gruhn, & Studer, 2010).
- *Provisional.* Many young adults also become more skeptical about the truth and seem unwilling to accept an answer as final. Thus, they come to see the search for truth as an ongoing and perhaps never-ending process.
- *Realistic.* Young adults understand that thinking can't always be abstract. In many instances, it must be realistic and pragmatic.
- *Recognized as being influenced by emotion.* Emerging and young adults are more likely than adolescents to understand that their thinking is influenced by emotions (Labouvie-Vief, 2009; Labouvie-Vief, Gruhn, & Studer, 2010). However, too often negative emotions produce thinking that is distorted and self-serving at this point in development.

One effort to assess postformal thinking is the 10-item Complex Postformal Thought Questionnaire (Sinnott & Johnson, 1997). Figure 13.9 presents the questionnaire and gives you an opportunity to evaluate your thinking at the postformal level. A recent study found that the questionnaire items reflect three main categories of postformal thinking: (1) Taking into account multiple aspects of a problem or situation; (2) Making a subjective choice in a particular problem situation; and (3) Perceiving underlying complexities in a situation (Cartwright & others, 2009).

A study using the Complex Postformal Thought Questionnaire revealed that college students who had more cross-category friends (based on categories of gender, age, ethnicity, socioeconomic status, and sexual orientation) scored higher on the postformal thought measure than

developmental **connection**

Cognitive Theory

Some developmental psychologists believe that wisdom advances through adulthood. Chapter 18, p. 573

developmental **connection**

Cognitive Theory

Links between cognition and emotion are increasingly being studied. Chapter 1, p. 15

postformal thought Thinking that is reflective, relativistic, contextual, provisional, realistic, and influenced by emotions.

Flow and Other Strategies for Living a More Creative Life

Mihaly Csikszentmihalyi (pronounced ME-high CHICK-sent-me-high-ee) has recommended a number of strategies for becoming more creative. Csikszentmihalyi (1995) interviewed 90 leading figures in art, business, government, education, and science to learn how creativity works. He discovered that creative people regularly experience a state he calls *flow,* a heightened state of pleasure experienced when we are engaged in mental and physical challenges that absorb us. Csikszentmihalyi (2000) points out that everyone is capable of achieving flow. Based on his interviews with some of the most creative people in the world, the first step toward a more creative life is cultivating your curiosity and interest. How can you do this?

- *Try to be surprised by something every day.* Maybe it is something you see, hear, or read about. Become absorbed in a lecture or a book. Be open to what the world is telling you. Life is a stream of experiences. Swim widely and deeply in it, and your life will be richer.
- *Try to surprise at least one person every day.* In a lot of things you do, you have to be predictable and patterned. Do something different for a change. Ask a question you normally would not ask. Invite someone to go to a show or a museum you never have visited.
- *Write down each day what surprised you and how you surprised others.* Most creative people keep a diary, notes, or lab records to ensure that their experience is not fleeting or forgotten. Start with a specific task. Each evening record the most surprising event that occurred that day and your most surprising action. After a few days, reread your notes and reflect on your past experiences. After a few weeks, you might see a pattern of interest emerging in your notes, one that might suggest an area you can explore in greater depth.

- *When something sparks your interest, follow it.* Usually when something captures your attention, it is short-lived—an idea, a song, a flower. Too often we are too busy to explore the idea, song, or flower further. Or we think these areas are none of our business because we are not experts about them. Yet the world is our business. We can't know which part of it is best suited to our interests until we make a serious effort to learn as much about as many aspects of it as possible.
- *Wake up in the morning with a specific goal to look forward to.* Creative people wake up eager to start the day. Why? Not necessarily because they are cheerful, enthusiastic types but because they know that there is something meaningful to accomplish each day, and they can't wait to get started.
- *Spend time in settings that stimulate your creativity.* In Csikszentmihalyi's (1995) research, he gave people an electronic pager and beeped them randomly at different times of the day. When he asked them how they felt, they reported the highest levels of creativity when walking, driving, or swimming. I (your author) do my most creative thinking when I'm jogging. These activities are semiautomatic in that they take a certain amount of attention while leaving some time free to make connections among ideas.

Mihaly Csikszentmihalyi, in the setting where he gets his most creative ideas. *When and where do you get your most creative thoughts?*

Can the strategies for stimulating creative thinking in children found in the Connecting Development to Life interlude in Chapter 9 also be used by adults? How do the strategies discussed in Chapter 9 compare with those discussed here?

their counterparts who had fewer cross-category friends (Galupo, Cartwright, & Savage, 2010). Cross-category friendships likely stimulate individuals to move beyond either/or thinking, critically evaluate stereotypical thinking, and consider alternative explanations.

How strong is the evidence for a fifth, postformal stage of cognitive development? Researchers have found that young adults are more likely to engage in postformal thinking than adolescents are (Commons & Bresette, 2006). But critics argue that research has yet to document that postformal thought is a qualitatively more advanced stage than formal operational thought.

CREATIVITY

Early adulthood is a time of great creativity for some people. At the age of 30, Thomas Edison invented the phonograph, Hans Christian Andersen wrote his first volume of fairy tales, and

Mozart composed *The Marriage of Figaro*. One early study of creativity found that individuals' most creative products were generated in their thirties and that 80 percent of the most important creative contributions were completed by age 50 (Lehman, 1960).

More recently, researchers have found that creativity does peak in adulthood and then decline, but that the peak often occurs in the forties. However, qualifying any conclusion about age and creative accomplishments are (1) the magnitude of the decline in productivity, (2) contrasts across creative domains, and (3) individual differences in lifetime output (Simonton, 1996).

Even though a decline in creative contributions is often found in the fifties and later, the decline is not as great as is commonly thought. An impressive array of creative accomplishments occur in late adulthood. One of the most remarkable examples of creative accomplishment in late adulthood can be found in the life of Henri Chevreul. After a distinguished career as a physicist, Chevreul switched fields in his nineties to become a pioneer in gerontological research. He published his last research paper just a year prior to his death at the age of 103!

Any consideration of decline in creativity with age requires attention to the field of creativity involved. In such fields as philosophy and history, older adults often show as much creativity as they did when they were in their thirties and forties. By contrast, in such fields as lyric poetry, abstract math, and theoretical physics, the peak of creativity is often reached in the twenties or thirties.

There also is extensive individual variation in the lifetime output of creative individuals. Typically, the most productive creators in any field are far more prolific than their least productive counterparts. The contrast is so extreme that the top 10 percent of creative producers frequently account for 50 percent of the creative output in a particular field. For instance, only 16 composers account for half of the music regularly performed in the classical repertoire.

Can you make yourself more creative? To read about strategies for becoming more creative, see *Connecting Development to Life* on page 440.

developmental **connection**

Creativity

What strategies are likely to enhance children's creative thinking? Chapter 9, p. 297

Review *Connect* Reflect

 LG4 Characterize cognitive changes in early adulthood.

Review

- What changes in cognitive development in young adults have been proposed?
- Does creativity decline in adulthood? How can people lead more creative lives?

Connect

- In this section, postformal thought was characterized in part by a belief that emotions and subjective factors influence thinking. Why are adolescents not typically capable of this kind of thought?

Reflect *Your Own Personal Journey of Life*

- If you are in emerging adulthood, what do you think are the most important cognitive changes that have taken place so far in the transition period? If you are older, reflect on your emerging adult years and describe some of the cognitive changes that occurred during this time.

5 Careers and Work

LG5 Explain the key dimensions of career and work in early adulthood.

| Developmental Changes | Finding a Path to Purpose | Monitoring the Occupational Outlook | The Impact of Work | Diversity in the Workplace |

Earning a living, choosing an occupation, establishing a career, and developing in a career—these are important themes of early adulthood. What are some of the factors that go into choosing a job or career, and how does work typically affect the lives of young adults?

DEVELOPMENTAL CHANGES

Many children have idealistic fantasies about what they want to be when they grow up. For example, many young children want to be superheroes, sports stars, or movie actors. In the high school years, they often have begun to think about careers from a somewhat less idealistic perspective. In their late teens and early twenties, their career decision making has usually turned more serious as they explore different career possibilities and zero in on the career they want to enter. In college, this often means choosing a major or specialization that is designed to lead to work in a particular field. By their early and mid-twenties, many individuals have completed their education or training and started to enter a full-time occupation. From the mid-twenties through the remainder of early adulthood, individuals often seek to establish their emerging career in a particular field. They may work hard to move up the career ladder and improve their financial standing.

Phyllis Moen (2009a) recently described the career mystique—an ingrained cultural belief that engaging in hard work for long hours through adulthood will lead to status, security, and happiness. That is, many individuals envision a career path that will enable them to fulfill the American dream of upward mobility by climbing occupational ladders. However, the lockstep career mystique has never been a reality for many individuals, especially ethnic minority individuals, women, and poorly educated adults. Further, the career mystique has increasingly become a myth for many individuals in middle-income occupations as global outsourcing of jobs and the 2007–2009 recession have threatened the job security of millions of Americans.

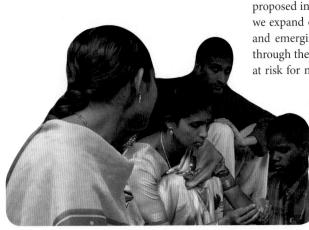

"Did you think the ladder of success would be straight up?"
© Joseph Farris/The New Yorker Collection/www.cartoonbank.com

FINDING A PATH TO PURPOSE

In Chapter 11 we described a perspective on identity development that William Damon (2008) proposed in his book *The Path to Purpose: Helping Our Children Find Their Calling in Life*. Here we expand on his view and explore how purpose is a missing ingredient in many adolescents' and emerging adults' achievement and career development. Too many youth drift aimlessly through their high school and college years, Damon says, engaging in behavior that places them at risk for not fulfilling their potential and not finding a life pursuit that energizes them.

In interviews with 12- to 22-year-olds, Damon found that only about 20 percent had a clear vision of where they wanted to go in life, what they wanted to achieve, and why. The largest percentage—about 60 percent—had engaged in some potentially purposeful activities, such as service learning or fruitful discussions with a career counselor—but they still did not have a real commitment or any reasonable plans for reaching their goals. And slightly more than 20 percent expressed no aspirations and in some instances said they didn't see any reason to have aspirations.

Damon concludes that most teachers and parents communicate the importance of studying hard and getting good grades, but rarely discuss the purpose of academic achievement. Damon emphasizes that too often students focus only on short-term goals and don't explore the big, long-term picture of what they want to do in life. These interview questions that Damon (2008, p. 135) has used in his research are good springboards for getting individuals to reflect on their purpose:

- What's most important to you in your life?
- Why do you care about those things?
- Do you have any long-term goals?
- Why are these goals important to you?
- What does it mean to have a good life?
- What does it mean to be a good person?
- If you were looking back on your life now, how would you like to be remembered?

Hari Prabhakar (*in rear*) at a screening camp in India that he created as part of his Tribal India Health Foundation. Hari reflects William Damon's concept of finding a path to purpose. His ambition is to become an international health expert. Hari graduated from Johns Hopkins University in 2006 with a double major in public health and writing. A top student (3.9 GPA), he took the initiative to pursue a number of activities outside the classroom, in the health field. As he made the transition from high school to college, Hari created the Tribal India Health Foundation (www.tihf.org), which provides assistance in bringing low-cost health care to rural areas in India. Juggling his roles as a student and as the foundation's director, Hari spent about 15 hours a week leading Tribal India Health throughout his four undergraduate years. In describing his work, Hari said (Johns Hopkins University, 2006):

"I have found it very challenging to coordinate the international operation.... It takes a lot of work, and there's not a lot of free time. But it's worth it when I visit our patients and see how they and the community are getting better."

Sources: Johns Hopkins University (2006); Prabhakar (2007).

A recent study found that discussing such questions involving their values and life goals improved college students' goal direction (Bundick, 2011).

MONITORING THE OCCUPATIONAL OUTLOOK

As you explore the type of work you are likely to enjoy and in which you can succeed, it is important to be knowledgeable about different fields and companies. Occupations may have many job openings one year but few in another year as economic conditions change. Thus, it is critical to keep up with the occupational outlook in various fields. An excellent source for doing this is the U.S. government's *Occupational Outlook Handbook,* which is revised every two years.

According to the 2012–2013 handbook, service industries, especially health services, professional and business services, and education, are projected to account for the greatest numbers of new jobs in the next decade (Occupational Outlook Handbook, 2012). Projected job growth varies widely by educational requirements. Jobs that require a college degree are expected to grow the fastest. Most of the highest-paying occupations require a college degree.

THE IMPACT OF WORK

Work defines people in fundamental ways (Highhouse & Schmitt, 2013; Motowidlo & Kell, 2013). It is an important influence on their financial standing, housing, the way they spend their time, where they live, their friendships, and their health (Allen, 2013; Shirom & others, 2011). Some people define their identity through their work. Work also creates a structure and rhythm to life that is often missed when individuals do not work for an extended period. During periods when they are unable to work, many individuals experience emotional distress and low self-esteem.

Most individuals spend about one-third of their time at work. In one survey, 35 percent of Americans worked 40 hours a week, but 18 percent worked 51 hours or more per week (Center for Survey Research at the University of Connecticut, 2000). Only 10 percent worked less than 30 hours a week.

A trend in the U.S. workforce is the disappearing long-term career for an increasing number of adults, especially men in private-sector jobs (Hollister, 2011). Among the reasons for this disappearance of many long-term jobs is the dramatic increase in technology and cheaper labor in other countries. Many young and older adults are working at a series of jobs, and many work in short-term jobs (Greenhaus, 2013).

An important consideration regarding work is how stressful it is (Jex, Swanson, & Grubb, 2013; Sonnentag & Frese, 2013). A national survey of U.S. adults revealed that 55 percent indicated they were less productive because of stress (American Psychological Association, 2007). In this study, 52 percent reported that they considered or made a career decision, such as looking for a new job, declining a promotion, or quitting a job, because of stress in the workplace (American Psychological Association, 2007). In this survey, main sources of stress included low salaries (44 percent), lack of advancement opportunities (42 percent), uncertain job expectations (40 percent), and long hours (39 percent).

Many adults have changing expectations about work, yet employers often aren't meeting their expectations (Lavoie-Tremblay & others, 2010; Moen, 2009a, b). For example, current policies and practices were designed for male breadwinners and an industrial economy, making these policies and practices out of step with a workforce of women and men, and of single-parent and dual earners. Many workers today want flexibility and greater control over their work schedules, and yet most employers offer little flexibility, even though policies like flextime may be "on the books."

Work During College The percentage of full-time U.S. college students who also held jobs increased from 34 percent in 1970 to 47 percent in 2008 (down from a peak of 52 percent in 2000) (National Center for Education Statistics, 2010). In this recent survey, 81 percent of part-time U.S. college students were employed.

developmental **connection**

Work

The middle-aged worker faces a number of challenges in the twenty-first century. Chapter 15, p. 500

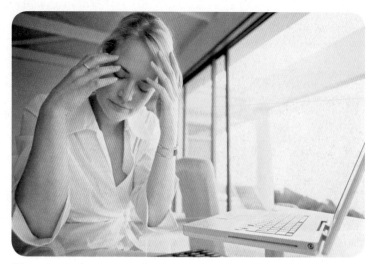

What are some characteristics of work settings linked with employees' stress?

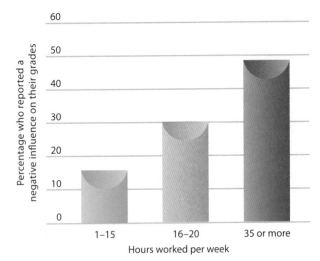

FIGURE **13.10**

THE RELATION OF HOURS WORKED PER WEEK IN COLLEGE TO GRADES. Among students working to pay for school expenses, 16 percent of those working 1 to 15 hours per week reported that working negatively influenced their grades (National Center for Education Statistics, 2002). Thirty percent of college students who worked 16 to 20 hours a week said the same, as did 48 percent who worked 35 hours or more per week.

Working can help offset some of the costs of schooling, but working also can restrict students' opportunities to learn. For those who identified themselves primarily as students, one national study found that as the number of hours worked per week increased, their grades suffered (National Center for Education Statistics, 2002) (see Figure 13.10). Thus, college students need to carefully examine whether the number of hours they work is having a negative impact on their college success.

Of course, jobs also can contribute to your education. More than 1,000 colleges in the United States offer *cooperative (co-op) programs,* which are paid apprenticeships in a field that you are interested in pursuing. (You may not be permitted to participate in a co-op program until your junior year.) Other useful opportunities for working while going to college include internships and part-time or summer jobs relevant to your field of study. Participating in these work experiences can help you land the job you want after you graduate.

Unemployment Unemployment rates in the United States have remained high in recent years, and global unemployment is increasing. Unemployment produces stress regardless of whether the job loss is temporary, cyclical, or permanent (Lundin, Backhans, & Hemmingsson, 2012; Romans, Cohen, & Forte, 2011). Economic problems that led to the recession at the end of the first decade of the twenty-first century produced unusually high unemployment rates. Researchers have found that unemployment is related to physical problems (such as heart attack and stroke), mental problems (such as depression and anxiety), marital difficulties, and homicide (Backhans & Hemmingsson, 2012; Freyer-Adam & others, 2011). A 15-year longitudinal study of more than 24,000 adults found that life satisfaction dropped considerably following unemployment and increased after becoming reemployed but did not completely return to the life satisfaction level previous to being unemployed (Lucas & others, 2004). A recent research review concluded that unemployment was associated with an increased mortality risk for individuals in the early and middle stages of their careers, but the increase was less pronounced for those who became unemployed late in their careers (Roelfs & others, 2011).

Stress caused by unemployment comes not only from a loss of income and the resulting financial hardships but also from decreased self-esteem (Howe & others, 2012). Individuals who cope best with unemployment have financial resources to rely on, often savings or the earnings of other family members. The support of understanding, adaptable family members also helps individuals cope with unemployment. Job counseling and self-help groups can provide emotional support during the job search as well as practical advice on finding job opportunities, writing résumés, and answering questions in job interviews.

Dual-Earner Couples Dual-earner couples may face special challenges finding a balance between work and family life (Demorouti, 2012; Moen, 2009b). If both partners are working, who cleans up the house or calls the repairman or takes care of the other endless details involved in maintaining a home? If the couple has children, who is responsible for making sure that the children get to school or to piano practice on time, who writes the notes to approve field trips or meets the teacher or makes the dental appointments?

Although single-earner married families still make up a sizeable minority of families, the proportion of two-earner couples has increased considerably in recent decades. As more U.S. women took jobs outside the home, the division

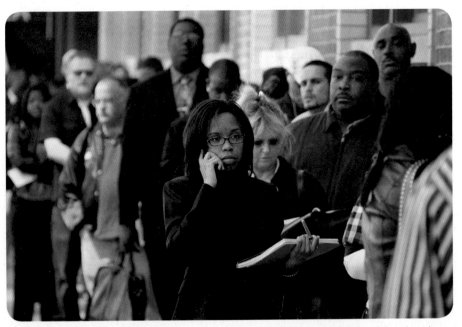

The economic recession that hit in 2007 resulted in millions of Americans losing their jobs, such as the individuals in line here waiting to apply for unemployment benefits in June 2009 in Chicago. *What are some of the potential negative outcomes of the stress caused by job loss?*

of responsibility for work and family changed in three ways: (1) U.S. husbands are taking increased responsibility for maintaining the home; (2) U.S. women are taking increased responsibility for breadwinning; (3) U.S. men are showing greater interest in their families and parenting.

Many jobs have been designed for single earners, usually male breadwinners, without regard to family responsibilities or the realities of people's lives. Consequently, many dual-earner couples engage in a range of adaptive strategies to coordinate their work and manage the family side of the work-family equation (Moen, 2009b). Researchers have found that even though couples may strive for gender equality in dual-earner families, gender inequalities persist (Cunningham, 2009). For example, women still do not earn as much as men in the same jobs, and this inequity means that gender divisions in how much time each partner spends in paid work, homemaking, and caring for children continue. Thus, dual-earner career decisions often are made in favor of men's greater earning power, with women spending more time than men taking care of the home and caring for children (Moen, 2009b).

DIVERSITY IN THE WORKPLACE

The workplace is becoming increasingly diverse (Hebl & Avery, 2013). Whereas at one time few women were employed outside the home, in developed countries women have increasingly entered the labor force. A recent projection indicates that women's share of the U.S. labor force will increase faster than men's share through 2020 (Occupational Outlook Handbook, 2012). In the United States, more than one-fourth of today's lawyers, physicians, computer scientists, and chemists are women.

Ethnic diversity also is increasing in the workplace in every developed country except France. In the United States, between 1980 and 2004 the percentage of Latinos and Asian Americans more than doubled in the workplace, a trend that is continuing (Occupational Outlook Handbook, 2012). Latinos are projected to constitute a larger percentage of the labor force than African Americans by 2020, growing from 13 percent in 2006 to 18.6 percent in 2020 (Occupational Outlook Handbook, 2012). The increasing diversity in the workplace requires a sensitivity to cultural differences and an appreciation of the cultural values that workers bring to a job (Hebl & Avery, 2013).

Despite the increasing diversity in the workplace, women and ethnic minorities experience difficulty in breaking through the glass ceiling that prevents them from being promoted to higher rungs on the corporate ladder. This invisible barrier to career advancement prevents women and ethnic minorities from holding managerial or executive jobs regardless of their accomplishments and merits (Schueller-Weidekamm & Kautzky-Willer, 2012).

How has the diversity of the workplace increased in recent years?

Review *Connect* Reflect

LG5 Explain the key dimensions of careers and work in early adulthood.

Review

- What are some developmental changes in careers and work?
- What does Damon argue is missing in many individuals' career pursuits?
- Which occupational areas are likely to offer the greatest increase in jobs in the next decade?
- What are some important things to know about work?
- What characterizes diversity in the workplace?

Connect

- How might what you learned about gender in Chapter 10 relate to what you learned in this section about how gender affects work opportunities and work environments?

Reflect *Your Own Personal Journey of Life*

- If you are an emerging adult, what careers do you want to pursue? How much education will they require? If you are older, how satisfied are you with your career choices as an emerging adult and young adult? Explain.

topical **connections**

At some point in middle age, more time stretches behind us than ahead of us. Midlife is changing—entered later and lasting longer—for many people. Middle adulthood is a time of declining physical skills and expanding responsibility, as well as balancing work and relationships. For many individuals, cognitive abilities peak in middle age, although some aspects of information processing, such as perceptual speed and memory, decline. Work continues to be central to people's lives in middle adulthood. Middle age also is when individuals become more interested in understanding the meaning of life.

looking forward - - - →

reach your **learning goals**

Physical and Cognitive Development in Early Adulthood

1 The Transition from Adolescence to Adulthood

LG1 Describe the transition from adolescence to adulthood.

Becoming an Adult

- Emerging adulthood is the term given to the transition from adolescence to adulthood. This period ranges from about 18 to 25 years of age, and it is characterized by experimentation and exploration. There is both continuity and change in the transition from adolescence to adulthood. Two criteria for adult status are economic independence and taking responsibility for the consequences of one's actions.

The Transition from High School to College

- The transition from high school to college can have both positive and negative aspects. Although students may feel more grown up and be intellectually challenged by academic work, for many the transition involves a focus on the stressful move from being the oldest and most powerful group of students to being the youngest and least powerful group. U.S. college students today report experiencing more stress and depression than college students in the past.

2 Physical Development

LG2 Identify the changes in physical development in young adults.

Physical Performance and Development

- Peak physical performance is often reached between 19 and 26 years of age. Toward the latter part of early adulthood, a detectable slowdown in physical performance is apparent for most individuals.

Health

- Emerging adults have more than twice the mortality rate of adolescents, with males being mainly responsible for the increase. Despite their higher mortality rate, emerging adults in general have few chronic health problems. Many emerging adults develop bad health habits that can impair their health later in life.

Eating and Weight

- Obesity is a serious problem, with about 33 percent of Americans overweight enough to be at increased health risk. Heredity, leptin, set point, and environmental factors are involved in obesity. Most diets don't work over the long term. For those that do, exercise is usually an important component.

| Regular Exercise | • Both moderate and intense exercise produce important physical and psychological gains. |
| Substance Abuse | • By the mid-twenties, a reduction in alcohol and drug use often takes place. Binge drinking among college students is still a major concern and can cause students to miss classes, have trouble with police, and engage in unprotected sex. Alcoholism is a disorder that impairs an individual's health and social relationships. Fewer young adults are smoking cigarettes now than in past decades. Most adult smokers would like to quit but their addiction to nicotine makes quitting a challenge. |

3 Sexuality

 Discuss sexuality in young adults.

Sexual Activity in Emerging Adulthood

- Emerging adulthood is a time during which most individuals are sexually active and become married. Emerging adults have sexual intercourse with more individuals than young adults, but they have sex less frequently. Also, casual sex is more common in emerging adulthood than young adulthood.

Sexual Orientation and Behavior

- In the 1994 Sex in America survey, American adults' sexual lives were portrayed as more conservative than was previously believed. An individual's sexual preference likely is the result of a combination of genetic, hormonal, cognitive, and environmental factors.

Sexually Transmitted Infections

- Also called STIs, sexually transmitted infections are contracted primarily through sexual contact. The STI that has received the most attention in the last several decades is infection with HIV, which can lead to AIDS (acquired immune deficiency syndrome). A person with AIDS has a weakened immune system—even a cold can be life threatening.

Forcible Sexual Behavior and Sexual Harassment

- Rape is forcible sexual intercourse with a person who does not give consent. Date or acquaintance rape involves coercive sexual activity directed at someone with whom the perpetrator is at least casually acquainted. Sexual harassment occurs when one person uses his or her power over another individual in a sexual manner, which can result in serious psychological consequences for the victim.

4 Cognitive Development

 Characterize cognitive changes in early adulthood.

Cognitive Stages

- Formal operational thought is Piaget's final cognitive stage, beginning at about age 11 to 15. According to Piaget, although adults are quantitatively more knowledgeable than adolescents, adults do not enter a new, qualitatively different stage. However, some have proposed that young adults move into a qualitatively higher stage of postformal thought that is more reflective, relativistic, and contextual; provisional; realistic; and recognized as being influenced by emotion.

Creativity

- Creativity peaks in adulthood, often in the forties, and then declines. However, there is extensive individual variation in lifetime creative output. Csikszentmihalyi proposed that the first step toward living a creative life is to cultivate curiosity and interest.

5 Careers and Work

Explain the key dimensions of career and work in early adulthood.

Developmental Changes

- Many young children have idealistic fantasies about a career. In the late teens and early twenties, their career thinking has usually turned more serious. By their early to mid-twenties, many individuals have completed their education or training and started in a career. In the remainder of early adulthood, they seek to establish their emerging career and start moving up the career ladder. Many individuals believe in the career mystique but recently this has become a myth for increasing numbers of Americans.

Finding a Path to Purpose

- Damon argues that too many individuals have not found a path to purpose in their career development. He concludes that too often individuals focus on short-term goals and don't explore the big, long-term picture of what they want to do with their lives.

Monitoring the Occupational Outlook

- Jobs that require a college education are expected to be the fastest-growing and highest-paying occupational sector in the United States over the next decade. Education, health care, business, and professional services are projected to account for most of the new jobs.

key terms

emerging adulthood 423	sexually transmitted	rape 436	postformal thought 439
aerobic exercise 429	infections	date or acquaintance	
addiction 429	(STIs) 434	rape 436	

key people

Jeffrey Arnett 422	Robert Michael 432	Jean Piaget 438	Phyllis Moen 442
Ann Masten 423	Laura Brown 434	Mihaly Csikszentmihalyi 440	William Damon 442
Jerald Bachman 429			

Chapter 13 | PHYSICAL AND COGNITIVE DEVELOPMENT IN EARLY ADULTHOOD

Connecting with **Mc Graw Hill** **connect**®

Learning Objectives	Application Activities	Activity Type	Page Reference
Describe the transition from high school to college.	Non College-Bound Adolescents	Video	pp. 424–425
	Balancing Work and School	Video	
Identify the changes in physical performance and development during early adulthood.	Early Adulthood Perspectives on Body Image	Milestones: Transitions	pp. 425–426

(continued)

Learning Objectives	Application Activities	Activity Type	Page Reference
Characterize the changes in substance abuse during early adulthood.	Marijuana Use Among Young Adults: Expert Interview	Video	pp. 429–431
Discuss sexuality in emerging adulthood.	Early Adulthood Perspectives on Sexuality	Milestones: Transitions	pp. 431–432
Describe sexual orientation and behavior during early adulthood.	Heterosexism	Video	pp. 432–434
Summarize cognitive changes during early adulthood.	Early Adulthood Perspectives on Thinking and Memory	Milestones: Transitions	pp. 438–440
	Cognitive Development in Early Adulthood	Click & drag activity	
Discuss the impact of work during early adulthood.	On Being a Working Mom	Video	pp. 443–445
	Dividing the Household Tasks	Video	
	The Work-Family Balance	Video	
	Making Dual Careers Work	Video	
	Working Mothers	Video	

SOCIOEMOTIONAL DEVELOPMENT IN EARLY ADULTHOOD

chapter **outline**

Commitment is an important issue in a romantic relationship for most individuals. Consider Gwenna, who decides that it is time to have a talk with Greg about his commitment to their relationship (Lerner, 1989, pp. 44–45):

She shared her perspective on both the strengths and weaknesses of their relationship and what her hopes were for the future. She asked Greg to do the same. Unlike earlier conversations, this one was conducted without her pursuing him, pressuring him, or diagnosing his problems with women. At the same time, she asked Greg some clear questions, which exposed his vagueness.

"How will you know when you are ready to make a commitment? What specifically would you need to change or be different than it is today?"

"I don't know," was Greg's response. When questioned further, the best he could come up with was that he'd just feel it.

"How much more time do you need to make a decision one way or another?"

"I'm not sure," Greg replied. "Maybe a couple of years, but I really can't answer a question like that. I can't predict my feelings."

And so it went.

Gwenna really loved this man, but two years (and maybe longer) was longer than she could comfortably wait. So, after much thought she told Greg that she would wait till fall (about ten months), and that she would move on if he couldn't commit himself to marriage by then. She was open about her wish to marry and have a family with him, but she was equally clear that her first priority was a mutually committed relationship. If Greg was not at that point by fall, then she would end the relationship—painful though it would be.

During the waiting period, Gwenna was able to not pursue him and not get distant or otherwise reactive to his expressions of ambivalence and doubt. In this way she gave Greg emotional space to struggle with his dilemma and the relationship had its best chance of succeeding. Her bottom-line position ("a decision by fall") was not a threat or an attempt to rope Greg in, but rather a clear statement of what was acceptable to her.

When fall arrived, Greg told Gwenna he needed another six months to make up his mind. Gwenna deliberated a while and decided she could live with that. But when the six months were up, Greg was uncertain and asked for more time. It was then that Gwenna took the painful but ultimately empowering step of ending their relationship.

-topical **connections**

A key aspect of socioemotional development in adolescence is an increased interest in identity; many of the key changes in identity, though, take place in emerging adulthood. Seeking autonomy in healthy ways while still being securely attached to parents are important aspects of parent-adolescent relationships. Adolescents also are motivated to spend more time with peers, friendships become more intimate, and romantic relationships begin to take a more central role in adolescents' lives.

◄- - - *looking back* - - - - - - - - - - - - - - -

preview

Love is of central importance in each of our lives, as it is in Gwenna and Greg's lives. Shortly, we will discuss the many faces of love, as well as marriage and the family, the diversity of adult lifestyles, and the role of gender in relationships. To begin, though, we will return to an issue we initially considered in Chapter 1: stability and change.

1 Stability and Change from Childhood to Adulthood

 LG1 Describe stability and change in temperament, and summarize adult attachment styles.

Temperament | Attachment

For adults, socioemotional development revolves around adaptively integrating our emotional experiences into enjoyable relationships with others on a daily basis (Duck, 2011). Young adults like Gwenna and Greg face choices and challenges in adopting lifestyles that will be emotionally satisfying, predictable, and manageable for them. They do not come to these tasks as blank slates, but do their decisions and actions simply reflect the persons they had become by the end of adolescence?

Current research shows that the first 20 years of life are not meaningless in predicting an adult's socioemotional landscape (Cicchetti, 2013; Easterbrooks & others, 2013). And there is also every reason to believe that experiences in the early adult years are important in determining what the individual is like later in adulthood. A common finding is that the smaller the time intervals over which we measure socioemotional characteristics, the more similar an individual will look from one measurement to the next. Thus, if we measure an individual's self-esteem at the age of 20 and then again at the age of 30, we will probably find more stability than if we measured the individual's self-esteem at the age of 10 and then again at the age of 30.

In trying to understand the young adult's socioemotional development, it would be misleading to look at an adult's life only in the present tense, ignoring the unfolding of social relationships and emotions. So, too, it would be a mistake to search only through a 30-year-old's first 5 to 10 years of life in trying to understand why he or she is having difficulty in a close relationship.

TEMPERAMENT

How stable is temperament? Recall that *temperament* is an individual's behavioral style and characteristic emotional responses. In early adulthood, most individuals show fewer emotional mood swings than they did in adolescence, and they become more responsible and engage in less risk-taking behavior (Charles & Luong, 2011). Along with these signs of a general change in temperament, researchers also find links between some dimensions of childhood temperament and adult personality (Zentner & Shiner, 2012; Zuckerman, 2012). For example, in one longitudinal study, children who were highly active at age 4 were likely to be very outgoing at age 23 (Franz, 1996).

Are other aspects of temperament in childhood linked with adjustment in adulthood? In Chapter 6, we saw that researchers have proposed various ways of describing and classifying types and dimensions of personality. Research has linked several of these types and dimensions during childhood with characteristics of adult personality (Zenter & Shiner, 2012). For example:

- *Easy and difficult temperaments.* In one longitudinal study, children who had an easy temperament at 3 to 5 years of age were likely to be well adjusted as young adults (Chess & Thomas, 1987). In contrast, many children who had a difficult temperament at 3 to 5 years of age were not well adjusted as young adults. Also, other researchers have found that boys with a difficult temperament in childhood are less likely as adults to continue their formal education, and girls with a difficult temperament in childhood are more likely to experience marital conflict as adults (Wachs, 2000).

To what extent is temperament in childhood linked to temperament in adulthood?

developmental **connection**

Personality

Among the main temperament categories are Chess and Thomas' easy and difficult; Kagan's inhibition; and Rothbart and Bates' effortful control (self-regulation). Chapter 6, p. 181

	Child A	Child B
Intervening Context		
Caregivers	Caregivers (parents) who are sensitive and accepting, and let child set his or her own pace.	Caregivers who use inappropriate "low-level control" and attempt to force the child into new situations.
Physical Environment	Presence of "stimulus shelters" or "defensible spaces" that the children can retreat to when there is too much stimulation.	Child continually encounters noisy, chaotic environments that allow no escape from stimulation.
Peers	Peer groups with other inhibited children with common interests, so the child feels accepted.	Peer groups consist of athletic extroverts, so the child feels rejected.
Schools	School is "undermanned," so inhibited children are more likely to be tolerated and feel they can make a contribution.	School is "overmanned," so inhibited children are less likely to be tolerated and more likely to feel undervalued.
Personality Outcomes		
	As an adult, individual is closer to extraversion (outgoing, sociable) and is emotionally stable.	As an adult, individual is closer to introversion and has more emotional problems.

FIGURE 14.1

TEMPERAMENT IN CHILDHOOD, PERSONALITY IN ADULTHOOD, AND INTERVENING CONTEXTS. Varying experiences with caregivers, the physical environment, peers, and schools can modify links between temperament in childhood and personality in adulthood. The example given here is for inhibition.

- *Inhibition.* Individuals who had an inhibited temperament in childhood are less likely than other adults to be assertive or experience social support, and more likely to delay entering a stable job track (Wachs, 2000). A longitudinal study revealed that the 15 percent most inhibited boys and girls at 4 to 6 years of age were rated as inhibited by their parents and delayed having a stable partnership and finding a first full-time job at 23 years of age (Asendorph, Denissen, & van Aken, 2008). And in the Uppsala (Sweden) Longitudinal Study, shyness/inhibition in infancy/childhood was linked to social anxiety at 21 years of age (Bohlin & Hagekull, 2009).

- *Ability to control one's emotions.* In one longitudinal study, when 3-year-old children showed good control of their emotions and were resilient in the face of stress, they were likely to continue to handle emotions effectively as adults (Block, 1993). By contrast, when 3-year-olds had low emotional control and were not very resilient, they were likely to show problems in these areas as young adults. And another longitudinal study revealed that an undercontrolled (behavioral and emotional) temperament at age 3 was linked to compulsive gambling in early adulthood (Slutske & others, 2012).

In sum, these studies reveal some continuity between certain aspects of temperament in childhood and adjustment in early adulthood (Rothbart, 2011). However, keep in mind that these connections between childhood temperament and adult adjustment are based on only a small number of studies, and more research is needed to verify these linkages. Indeed, Theodore Wachs (1994, 2000) proposed ways that linkages between temperament in childhood and personality in adulthood might vary depending on the intervening contexts in individuals' experience. For example, Figure 14.1 describes contexts in which an infant who displayed an inhibited temperament might develop a relatively sociable adult personality. As discussed in Chapter 6, many aspects of the environment—including gender, culture, parenting, and goodness of fit generally—may influence the persistence of aspects of a child's temperament through life.

ATTACHMENT

Like temperament, attachment appears during infancy and plays an important part in socioemotional development (Easterbrooks & others, 2013; Sroufe, Coffino, & Carlson, 2010). We discussed its role in infancy and adolescence (see Chapters 6 and 12). How do these earlier patterns of attachment and adults' attachment styles influence the lives of adults?

Although relationships with romantic partners differ from those with parents, romantic partners fulfill some of the same needs for adults as parents do for their children. Recall from Chapter 6 that *securely attached* infants are defined as those who use the caregiver as a secure base from which to explore the environment. Similarly, adults may count on their romantic

developmental **connection**

Attachment

Secure and insecure attachment have been proposed as important aspects of infants' and adolescents' socioemotional development. Chapter 6, p. 191; Chapter 12, p. 395

How might adult attachment patterns be linked to childhood attachment patterns with parents?

partners to be a secure base to which they can return and obtain comfort and security in stressful times (Mikulincer & others, 2010).

Do adult attachment patterns with partners reflect childhood attachment patterns with parents? In a retrospective study, Cindy Hazan and Phillip Shaver (1987) revealed that young adults who were securely attached in their romantic relationships were more likely to describe their early relationship with their parents as securely attached. In a longitudinal study, infants who were securely attached at 1 year of age were securely attached 20 years later in their adult romantic relationships (Steele & others, 1998). Also, a longitudinal study revealed that securely attached infants were in more stable romantic relationships in adulthood than their insecurely attached counterparts (Salvatore & others, 2011). However, in another longitudinal study links between early attachment styles and later attachment styles were lessened by stressful and disruptive experiences such as the death of a parent or instability of caregiving (Lewis, Feiring, & Rosenthal, 2000).

Hazan and Shaver (1987, p. 515) measured attachment styles using the following brief assessment.

Read each paragraph and then place a check mark next to the description that best describes you:

_____ 1. I find it relatively easy to get close to others and I am comfortable depending on them and having them depend on me. I don't worry about being abandoned or about someone getting too close to me.

_____ 2. I am somewhat uncomfortable being close to others. I find it difficult to trust them completely and to allow myself to depend on them. I get nervous when anyone gets too close to me and it bothers me when someone tries to be more intimate with me than I feel comfortable with.

_____ 3. I find that others are reluctant to get as close as I would like. I often worry that my partner doesn't really love me or won't want to stay with me. I want to get very close to my partner, and this sometimes scares people away.

These items correspond to three attachment styles—secure attachment (option 1 above) and two insecure attachment styles (avoidant—option 2 above, and anxious—option 3 above):

- **Secure attachment style.** Securely attached adults have positive views of relationships, find it easy to get close to others, and are not overly concerned with or stressed out about their romantic relationships. These adults tend to enjoy sexuality in the context of a committed relationship and are less likely than others to have one-night stands.
- **Avoidant attachment style.** Avoidant individuals are hesitant about getting involved in romantic relationships and once in a relationship tend to distance themselves from their partner.
- **Anxious attachment style.** These individuals demand closeness, are less trusting, and are more emotional, jealous, and possessive.

The majority of adults (about 60 to 80 percent) describe themselves as securely attached, and not surprisingly adults prefer having a securely attached partner (Zeifman & Hazan, 2008).

Researchers are studying links between adults' current attachment styles and many aspects of their lives (Mikulincer & Shaver, 2012; Tran & Simpson, 2012). For example, securely attached adults are more satisfied with their close relationships than insecurely attached adults, and the relationships of securely attached adults are more likely to be characterized by trust, commitment, and longevity.

The following recent studies confirmed the importance of adult attachment styles in people's lives:

- Attachment security predicted more positive romantic relationships (Holland & Roisman, 2010).
- Attachment-anxious individuals showed strong ambivalence toward a romantic partner (Mikulincer & others, 2010).

secure attachment style An attachment style that describes adults who have positive views of relationships, find it easy to get close to others, and are not overly concerned or stressed out about their romantic relationships.

avoidant attachment style An attachment style that describes adults who are hesitant about getting involved in romantic relationships and once in a relationship tend to distance themselves from their partner.

anxious attachment style An attachment style that describes adults who demand closeness, are less trusting, and are more emotional, jealous, and possessive.

- Anxiously attached adults were more ambivalent about relationship commitment than their securely attached counterparts (Joel, MacDonald, & Shimotomai, 2011).
- A national survey indicated that insecure attachment in adults was associated with the development of disease and chronic illness, especially cardiovascular system problems such as high blood pressure, heart attack, and stroke (McWilliams & Bailey, 2010).
- Attachment-anxious and attachment-avoidant adults had higher levels of depressive and anxious symptoms than attachment-secure adults (Jinyao & others, 2012).
- Individuals with an avoidant attachment style were less resistant to the temptations of infidelity, which was linked to their lower level of relationship commitment (Dewall & others, 2011).
- Adults with avoidant and anxious attachment patterns had a lower level of sexual satisfaction than their counterparts with a secure attachment pattern (Brassard & others, 2012).

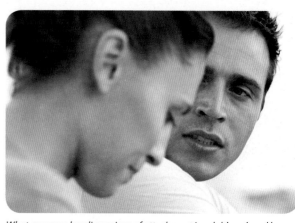

What are some key dimensions of attachment in adulthood, and how are they related to relationship patterns and well-being?

Recent interest also focuses on ways that genes might influence adult attachment. For example, one study examined the link between the serotonin transporter gene (5-HTTLPR) and adult unresolved attachment (Caspers & others, 2009). Unresolved attachment was assessed in an attachment interview and involved such speech patterns as indicating that the deceased parent was still playing a major role in the adult's life and giving excessive detail about the death. In this study, parental loss in early childhood was more likely to result in unresolved attachment in adulthood only for individuals who had the short version of the gene; the long version of the gene apparently provided some protection from the negative psychological effects of parental loss. Recall from Chapter 2 that this type of research is called gene x environment (G x E) interaction.

Leading experts Mario Mikulincer and Phillip Shaver (2007, 2012) reached the following conclusions about the benefits of secure attachment. Individuals who are securely attached have a well-integrated sense of self-acceptance, self-esteem, and self-efficacy. They have the ability to control their emotions, are optimistic, and are resilient. Facing stress and adversity, they activate cognitive representations of security, are mindful of what is happening around them, and mobilize effective coping strategies. A recent meta-analysis concluded that securely attached individuals have better relationships with their partner than those characterized by avoidant or anxious attachment (Li & Chan, 2012).

If you have an insecure attachment style, are you stuck with it and does it doom you to have problematic relationships? Attachment categories are somewhat stable in adulthood, but adults do have the capacity to change their attachment thinking and behavior. Although attachment insecurities are linked to relationship problems, attachment style makes only a moderate-size contribution to relationship functioning because other factors contribute to relationship satisfaction and success. Later in the chapter, we will discuss such factors in our coverage of marital relationships.

Review *Connect* Reflect

 LG1 Describe stability and change in temperament, and summarize adult attachment styles.

Review

- How stable is temperament from childhood to adulthood?
- What attachment styles characterize adults, and how are they linked to relationship outcomes?

Connect

- In Chapter 12, what behaviors were linked to insecure attachment in adolescence?

Reflect *Your Own Personal Journey of Life*

- What is your attachment style? How do you think it affects your relationships?

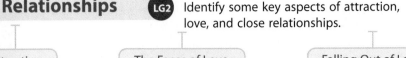

2 Attraction, Love, and Close Relationships

LG2 Identify some key aspects of attraction, love, and close relationships.

Attraction   The Faces of Love   Falling Out of Love

These are the themes of our exploration of close relationships: how these relationships get started, the faces of love, and falling out of love.

ATTRACTION

What attracts people like Gwenna and Greg to each other and motivates them to spend more time together? How important are personality traits and physical attraction in determining the relationships we form?

Familiarity and Similarity   Familiarity may breed contempt, as the old saying goes, but social psychologists have found that familiarity is a necessary condition for a close relationship to develop. For the most part, friends and lovers are people who have been around each other for a long time; they may have grown up together, gone to high school or college together, worked together, or gone to the same social events (Anderson & Sabatelli, 2011).

Another old saying, "Birds of a feather flock together," also helps to explain attraction. Overall, our friends and lovers are much more like us than unlike us (Guerrero, Andersen, & Afifi, 2011). Friends and lovers tend to have similar attitudes, values, lifestyles, and physical attractiveness. For some characteristics, though, opposites may attract. An introvert may wish to be with an extravert, or someone with little money may wish to associate with someone who is wealthy, for example.

Why are people attracted to others who have similar attitudes, values, and lifestyles? **Consensual validation** is one reason. Our own attitudes and values are supported when someone else's attitudes and values are similar to ours—their attitudes and values validate ours. Another reason similarity matters is that people tend to shy away from the unknown. We often prefer to be around people whose attitudes and values we can predict. And similarity implies that we will enjoy doing things with another person who likes the same things and has similar attitudes.

Recently, attraction has not only taken place in person but also over the Internet (Bateson & others, 2012). More than 16 million individuals in the United States and 14 million in China have tried online matchmaking (Masters, 2008). Some critics argue that online romantic relationships lose the interpersonal connection while others emphasize that the Internet may benefit shy or anxious individuals who find it difficult to meet potential partners in person (Holmes, Little, & Welsh, 2009). One problem with online matchmaking is that many individuals misrepresent their characteristics, such as how old they are, how attractive they are, and their occupation. Despite such dishonesty, researchers have found that romantic relationships

DILBERT © Scott Adams/Dist. by United Feature Syndicate, Inc.

initiated on the Internet are more likely than relationships established in person to last for more than two years (Bargh & McKenna, 2004).

Physical Attractiveness   As important as familiarity and similarity may be, they do not explain the spark that often ignites a romantic relationship: physical attractiveness. How important is physical attractiveness in relationships? Psychologists do not consider the link between physical beauty and attraction to be as clear-cut as many advertising agencies would like us to believe. For example, psychologists have determined that men and women differ on the importance of good looks when they seek an intimate partner. Women tend to rate as most important such traits as considerateness, honesty, dependability, kindness, understanding, and earning prospects; men prefer good looks, cooking skills, and frugality (Buss & Barnes, 1986; Eastwick & Finkel, 2008).

Complicating research about the role of physical attraction is changing standards of what is deemed attractive. The criteria for beauty can differ, not just across cultures, but over time within cultures as well. In the 1950s, the ideal of female beauty in the United States was typified by the well-rounded figure of Marilyn Monroe. Today, Monroe's 135-pound, 5-foot, 5-inch physique might be regarded as a bit overweight. The current ideal physique for both men and women is neither pleasingly plump nor extremely slender.

The force of similarity also operates at a physical level. We usually seek out someone at our own level of attractiveness in physical characteristics as well as social attributes. Research validates the **matching hypothesis,** which states that although we may prefer a more attractive person in the abstract, in the real world we end up choosing someone who is close to our own level of attractiveness. However, one study revealed that the matching hypothesis did not hold for couples once they became married (McNulty, Karney, & Neff, 2008). In the first six months of the marriage, the only link between levels of attractiveness and various aspects of the marital relationship was that attractive husbands were less satisfied. Also, rather than similarity, it was the difference between marital partners' attractiveness that best predicted their behavior toward each other: Both spouses behaved more positively when the wife was more attractive and behaved more negatively when the husband was more attractive. Thus, although matched attractiveness plays a powerful role early in relationships, it may have less influence in marriage.

This is DEFINATELY the last time I arrange a date over the internet...

© Fran Orford, www.francartoons.com

THE FACES OF LOVE

Once we are initially attracted to another person, other opportunities exist that may deepen the relationship to love. Love refers to a vast and complex territory of human behavior, spanning a range of relationships that includes friendship, romantic love, affectionate love, and consummate love (Berscheid, 2010). In most of these types of love, one recurring theme is intimacy (Sternberg & Sternberg, 2013).

Intimacy   Self-disclosure and the sharing of private thoughts are hallmarks of intimacy (Miller, 2012). As we discussed in Chapter 12, adolescents have an increased need for intimacy. At the same time, they are engaged in the essential tasks of developing an identity and establishing their independence from their parents. Juggling the competing demands of intimacy, identity, and independence also becomes a central task of adulthood.

Erikson's Stage: Intimacy Versus Isolation   Recall from our discussion in Chapter 12 that Erik Erikson (1968) argues that identity versus identity confusion—pursuing who we are, what we are all about, and where we are going in life—is the most important issue to be negotiated in adolescence. In early adulthood, according to Erikson, after individuals are well on their way to establishing stable and successful identities, they enter the sixth developmental stage, which is intimacy versus isolation. Erikson describes intimacy as finding oneself while losing oneself in another person, and it requires a commitment to another person. If a person fails to develop an intimate relationship in early adulthood, according to Erikson, isolation results.

A recent study confirmed Erikson's theory that identity development in adolescence is a precursor to intimacy in romantic relationships during emerging adulthood (Beyers &

> Love is a canvas furnished by nature and embroidered by imagination.
>
> —**VOLTAIRE**
> *French Essayist, 18th Century*

Why is intimacy an important aspect of early adulthood?

consensual validation An explanation of why individuals are attracted to people who are similar to them. Our own attitudes and behavior are supported and validated when someone else's attitudes and behavior are similar to our own.

matching hypothesis States that although we prefer a more attractive person in the abstract, in the real world we end up choosing someone who is close to our own level of attractiveness.

developmental **connection**

Erikson's Theory

Erikson's adolescence stage is identity versus identity confusion and his middle adulthood stage is generativity versus stagnation. Chapter 12, p. 389; Chapter 16, p. 510

developmental **connection**

Personality

Independence is an important aspect of the second year of life and adolescence. Chapter 6, p. 186; Chapter 12, p. 395

Seiffge-Krenke, 2010). And a meta-analysis revealed a positive link between identity development and intimacy, with the connection being stronger for men than women (Arseth & others, 2009).

An inability to develop meaningful relationships with others can harm an individual's personality. It may lead individuals to repudiate, ignore, or attack those who frustrate them. Such circumstances account for the shallow, almost pathetic attempts of youth to merge themselves with a leader. Many youth want to be apprentices or disciples of leaders and adults who will shelter them from the harm of the "out-group" world. If this fails—and Erikson points out that it must—sooner or later the individuals recoil into a self-search to discover where they went wrong. This introspection sometimes leads to painful depression and isolation. It also may contribute to a mistrust of others.

Intimacy and Independence   Development in early adulthood often involves balancing intimacy and commitment on the one hand with independence and freedom on the other. At the same time that individuals are trying to establish an identity, they face the challenges of increasing their independence from their parents, developing an intimate relationship with another individual, and continuing their friendship commitments. They also face the task of making decisions for themselves without always relying on what others say or do.

The extent to which young adults develop autonomy has important implications for them. For example, young adults who have not sufficiently moved away from parental ties may have difficulty in both interpersonal relationships and a career.

There is a delicate balance between intimacy and commitment on the one hand and independence and freedom on the other. Some individuals are able to experience a healthy independence and freedom along with an intimate relationship. Keep in mind that intimacy and commitment, and independence and freedom, are not just concerns of early adulthood. They are important themes of development that are worked and reworked throughout the adult years.

Friendship   Increasingly researchers are finding that friendship plays an important role in development throughout the human life span (Blieszner & Roberto, 2012). Most U.S. men and women have a best friend—92 percent of women and 88 percent of men have a best friend of the same sex (Blieszner, 2009). Many friendships are long-lasting, as 65 percent of U.S. adults have known their best friend for at least 10 years and only 15 percent have known their best friend for less than 5 years. Adulthood brings opportunities for new friendships as individuals move to new locations and may establish new friendships in their neighborhood or at work (Blieszner, 2009).

Gender Differences in Friendships   As in the childhood and adolescent years, there are gender differences in adult friendship (Blieszner & Roberto, 2012). Compared with men, women have more close friends and their friendships involve more self-disclosure and exchange of mutual support (Dow & Wood, 2006). Women are more likely to listen at length to what a friend has to say and be sympathetic, and women have been labeled as "talking companions" because talk is so central to their relationship (Gouldner & Strong, 1987). Women's friendships tend to be characterized not only by depth but also by breadth: Women share many aspects of their experiences, thoughts, and feelings (Helgeson, 2012). When female friends get together, they like to talk, but male friends are more likely to engage in activities, especially outdoors. Thus, the adult male pattern of friendship often involves keeping one's distance while sharing useful information. Men are less likely than women to talk about their weaknesses with their friends, and men seek practical solutions to their problems rather than sympathy (Tannen, 1990). Also, adult male friendships are more competitive than those of women (Helgeson, 2012).

Friendships Between Women and Men   What about female-male friendship? Cross-gender friendships are more common among adults than children but less common than same-gender friendships in adulthood (Blieszner, 2009). Cross-gender friendships can provide both opportunities and problems (Helgeson, 2012). The opportunities involve learning more about common feelings and interests and shared characteristics, as well as acquiring knowledge and understanding of beliefs and activities that historically have been typical of the other gender.

How is adult friendship different among female friends, male friends, and cross-gender friends?

romantic love Also called passionate love, or eros, romantic love has strong sexual and infatuation components and often predominates early in a love relationship.

affectionate love In this type of love, also called companionate love, an individual desires to have the other person near and has a deep, caring affection for the other person.

Problems can arise in cross-gender friendships because of different expectations. One problem that can plague an adult cross-gender friendship is unclear sexual boundaries, which can produce tension and confusion.

Romantic Love Some friendships evolve into **romantic love,** which is also called passionate love, or eros. Romantic love has strong components of sexuality and infatuation, and it often predominates in the early part of a love relationship (Berscheid, 2010). A recent meta-analysis found that males show higher avoidance and lower anxiety about romantic love than females (Del Giudice, 2011).

A complex intermingling of different emotions goes into romantic love—including such emotions as passion, fear, anger, sexual desire, joy, and jealousy (Del Giudice, 2011). Well-known love researcher Ellen Berscheid (1988) says that sexual desire is the most important ingredient of romantic love. Obviously, some of these emotions are a source of anguish, which can lead to other issues such as depression.

Affectionate Love Love is more than just passion (Berscheid, 2010). **Affectionate love,** also called *companionate love,* is the type of love that occurs when someone desires to have the other person near and has a deep, caring affection for the person. The early stages of love have more romantic love ingredients—but as love matures, passion tends to give way to affection.

Consummate Love So far we have discussed two forms of love: romantic (or passionate) and affectionate (or companionate). According to Robert J. Sternberg (1988), these are not the only forms of love. Sternberg proposed a triarchic theory of love in which love can be thought of as a triangle with three main dimensions—passion, intimacy, and commitment. Passion, as described earlier in the romantic love section, is physical and sexual attraction to another. Intimacy relates to the emotional feelings of warmth, closeness, and sharing in a relationship. Commitment is the cognitive appraisal of the relationship and the intent to maintain the relationship even in the face of problems.

In Sternberg's theory, the strongest, fullest form of love is *consummate love,* which involves all three dimensions (see Figure 14.2). If passion is the only ingredient in a relationship (with intimacy and commitment low or absent), we are merely *infatuated.* An affair or a fling in which there is little intimacy and even less commitment is an example. A relationship marked by intimacy and commitment but low or lacking in passion is called *affectionate love,* a pattern often found among couples who have been married for many years. If passion and commitment are present but intimacy is not, Sternberg calls the relationship *fatuous love,* as when one person worships another from a distance. But if couples share all three dimensions—passion, intimacy, and commitment—they experience consummate love (Sternberg & Sternberg, 2013).

FALLING OUT OF LOVE

The collapse of a close relationship may feel tragic. In the long run, however, as was the case for Gwenna, our happiness and personal development may benefit from ending a close relationship.

In particular, ending a relationship may be wise if you are obsessed with someone who repeatedly betrays your trust; if you are involved with someone who is draining you emotionally or financially or both; or if you are desperately in love with someone who does not return your feelings.

Being in love when love is not returned can lead to depression, obsessive thoughts, sexual dysfunction, health problems, inability to work effectively, difficulty in making new friends, and self-condemnation (Sbarra, 2012). Thinking clearly in such relationships is often difficult because our thoughts are so colored by arousing emotions (Guerrero, Andersen, & Afifi, 2011). A recent study of unmarried relationship dissolution in 18- to 35-year-olds revealed that experiencing a breakup was linked to an increase in psychological stress and a decrease in life satisfaction (Rhoades & others, 2011). In this study, having cohabited and

> We are what we love.
>
> —ERIK ERIKSON
>
> *Danish-Born American Psychoanalyst and Author, 20th Century*

Types of Love	Passion	Intimacy	Commitment
Infatuation	Present	Absent or low	Absent or low
Affectionate love	Absent or low	Present	Present
Fatuous love	Present	Absent or low	Present
Consummate love	Present	Present	Present

Present   Absent or low

FIGURE **14.2**

STERNBERG'S TRIANGLE OF LOVE. Sternberg identified three dimensions of love: passion, intimacy, and commitment. Various combinations of these dimensions result in infatuation, affectionate love, fatuous love, and consummate love.

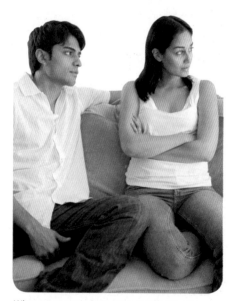

What are some negative aspects of being in love when love is not returned?

What Are the Positive Outcomes to a Romantic Relationship Breakup?

Studies of romantic breakups have mainly focused on their negative aspects (Kato, 2005; Moreau & others, 2011; Simon & Barrett, 2010). Few studies have examined the possibility that a romantic breakup might lead to positive changes.

One study assessed the personal growth that can follow the breakup of a romantic relationship (Tashiro & Frazier, 2003). The participants were 92 undergraduate students who had experienced a relationship breakup in the past nine months. They were asked to describe "what positive changes, if any, have happened as a result of your breakup that might serve to improve your future romantic relationships" (p. 118).

Self-reported positive growth was common following a romantic breakup. Changes were categorized as personal, relational, and environmental. The most commonly reported types of growth were personal changes, which included feeling stronger and more self-confident, more independent, and better off emotionally. Relational positive changes included gaining relational wisdom, and environmental positive changes included having better friendships because of the breakup. Figure 14.3 provides examples of these positive changes. Women were more likely to report positive growth than men were.

Change category	Exemplars of frequently mentioned responses
Person positives	1. "I am more self-confident." 2. "Through breaking up I found I could handle more on my own." 3. "I didn't always have to be the strong one, it's okay to cry or be upset without having to take care of him."
Relational positives	1. "Better communication." 2. "I learned many relationship skills that I can apply in the future (for example, the importance of saying you're sorry)." 3. "I know not to jump into a relationship too quickly."
Environmental positives	1. "I rely on my friends more. I forgot how important friends are when I was with him." 2. "Concentrate on school more: I can put so much more time and effort toward school." 3. "I believe friends' and family's opinions count—will seek them out in future relationships."

FIGURE **14.3**

EXAMPLES OF POSITIVE CHANGES IN THE AFTERMATH OF A ROMANTIC BREAKUP

having made plans for marriage were related to larger declines in life satisfaction following the breakup. Also, when relationship quality was higher, the decline in life satisfaction was smaller following the breakup.

Are there any positive outcomes to a romantic relationship breakup? To find out, see *Connecting Through Research.*

Review *Connect* Reflect

 Identify some key aspects of attraction, love, and close relationships.

Review

- What attracts someone to another person?
- What are some different types of love?
- What characterizes falling out of love?

Connect

- Describe how dating in adolescence differs from dating in early adulthood.

Reflect *Your Own Personal Journey of Life*

- Think about your own experiences with love. Based on those experiences, what advice about love would you give to someone else?

3 Adult Lifestyles **LG3** Characterize adult lifestyles.

Single Adults | Cohabiting Adults | Married Adults | Divorced Adults | Remarried Adults | Gay and Lesbian Adults

A striking social change in recent decades has been the decreased stigma attached to individuals who do not maintain what were long considered conventional families. Adults today choose many lifestyles and form many types of families (Benokraitis, 2012; Klinenberg, 2012). They live alone, cohabit, marry, divorce, or live with someone of the same sex.

In his book, *The Marriage-Go-Round*, sociologist Andrew Cherlin (2009) concluded that the United States has more marriages and remarriages, more divorces, and more short-term cohabiting (living together) relationships than most countries. Combined, these lifestyles create more turnover and movement in and out of relationships in the United States than in virtually any other country. Let's explore these varying relationship lifestyles.

SINGLE ADULTS

Recent decades have seen a dramatic rise in the percentage of single adults. Data from 2009 indicate that for the first time in history the proportion of individuals 25 to 34 years of age who have never been married (46 percent) exceeded those who were married (45 percent) (U.S. Census Bureau, 2010). The increasing number of single adults is the result of rising rates of cohabitation and a trend toward postponing marriage.

Even when single adults enjoy their lifestyles and are highly competent individuals, they often are stereotyped (Koropeckyj-Cox, 2009; Schwartz & Scott, 2012). Stereotypes associated with being single range from the "swinging single" to the "desperately lonely, suicidal" single. Of course, most single adults are somewhere between these extremes.

Common challenges faced by single adults may include forming intimate relationships with other adults, confronting loneliness, and finding a niche in a society that is marriage-oriented. Bella DePaulo (2006, 2011) argues that society has a widespread bias against unmarried adults that is seen in everything from missed perks in jobs to deep social and financial prejudices.

Advantages of being single include having time to make decisions about one's life course, time to develop personal resources to meet goals, freedom to make autonomous decisions and pursue one's own schedule and interests, opportunities to explore new places and try out new things, and privacy.

A recent nationally representative U.S. survey of more than 5,000 single adults 21 years and older not in a committed relationship revealed that men are more interested in love, marriage, and children than their counterparts were in earlier generations (Match.com, 2011). In this study, today's women desire more independence in their relationships than their mothers did. Across every age group, more women than men reported wanting to pursue their own interests, have personal space, have their own bank account, have regular nights out with girlfriends, and take vacations on their own. In a second national survey, many single adults reported that they were looking for love but not marriage (Match.com, 2012). In this survey, almost 40 percent of the single adults were uncertain about whether they wanted to get married, 34 percent said they did want to marry, and 27 percent said they didn't want to get married.

COHABITING ADULTS

Cohabitation refers to living together in a sexual relationship without being married. Cohabitation has undergone considerable changes in recent years (Benokraitis, 2012; Musick & Bumpass, 2012). As indicated in Figure 14.4, there has been a dramatic increase in the number of cohabiting U.S. couples since 1970, with more than 60 percent cohabiting prior to getting married (The National Marriage Project, 2011). And the upward trend shows no sign of letting up, having risen from 3.8 million cohabiting couples in 2000 to 7.5 million cohabiting couples in 2010 (U.S. Census Bureau, 2010). Cohabitation rates are even higher in some countries—in

FIGURE 14.4

THE INCREASE IN COHABITATION IN THE UNITED STATES. Since 1970, there has been a dramatic increase in the number of unmarried adults living together in the United States.

Sweden, for example, cohabitation before marriage is virtually universal (Stokes & Raley, 2009).

Some couples view their cohabitation not as a precursor to marriage but as an ongoing lifestyle (Klinenberg, 2012; Schwartz & Scott, 2012). These couples do not want the official aspects of marriage. In the United States, cohabiting arrangements tend to be short-lived, with one-third lasting less than a year (Hyde & DeLamater, 2011). Fewer than 1 out of 10 lasts five years. Of course, it is easier to dissolve a cohabitation relationship than to divorce.

A recent study revealed that young adults' main reasons for cohabiting are to spend time together, share expenses, and evaluate compatibility (Huang & others, 2011). In this study, gender differences emerged regarding drawbacks in cohabiting: men were more concerned about their loss of freedom while women were more concerned about delays in getting married.

Couples who cohabit face certain problems (Rhoades, Stanley, & Markman, 2009). Disapproval by parents and other family members can place emotional strain on the cohabiting couple. Some cohabiting couples have difficulty owning property jointly. Legal rights involving the dissolution of the relationship are less clear than in a divorce. A recent study also found that cohabiting relationships were characterized by more commitment, lower satisfaction, more negative communication, and more physical aggression than dating (noncohabiting) relationships (Rhoades, Stanley, & Markham, 2012).

If a couple lives together before they marry, does cohabiting help or harm their chances of later having a stable and happy marriage? The majority of studies have found lower rates of marital satisfaction and higher rates of divorce in couples who lived together before getting married (Copen & others, 2012; Whitehead & Popenoe, 2003). However, recent research indicates that the link between premarital cohabitation and marital instability in first marriages has weakened in recent cohorts (Manning & Cohen, 2012; Reinhold , 2010).

What might explain the possibility that cohabiting is linked with divorce more than not cohabiting? The most frequently given explanation is that the less traditional lifestyle of cohabitation may attract less conventional individuals who are not great believers in marriage in the first place. An alternative explanation is that the experience of cohabiting changes people's attitudes and habits in ways that increase their likelihood of divorce.

Recent research has provided clarification of cohabitation outcomes. One meta-analysis found the negative link between cohabitation and marital instability did not hold up when only cohabitation with the eventual marital partner was examined, indicating that these cohabitors may attach more long-term positive meaning to living together (Jose, O'Leary, & Moyer, 2010). Another study also revealed that for first marriages, cohabiting with the spouse without first being engaged was linked to more negative interaction and a higher probability of divorce than cohabiting after engagement (Stanley & others, 2006). In contrast, premarital cohabitation prior to a second marriage placed couples at risk for divorce regardless of whether they were engaged. Another analysis indicated that cohabiting does not have a negative effect on marriage if the couple did not have any previous live-in lovers and did not have children prior to the marriage (Cherlin, 2009).

What are some potential advantages and disadvantages of cohabitation?

MARRIED ADULTS

Until about 1930, stable marriage was widely accepted as the endpoint of adult development. In the last 70 to 80 years, however, personal fulfillment both inside and outside marriage has emerged as a goal that competes with marital stability. The changing norm of male-female equality in marriage and increasingly high expectations for what a marital relationship should be has produced marital relationships that are more fragile and intense than they were for earlier generations (Lavner & Bradbury, 2012).

Marital Trends   In recent years, marriage rates in the United States have declined. From 2007 to 2010, the marriage rate continued to drop. In 2010, 51 percent of Americans were married, down from 72 percent in 1960 (Pew Research Center, 2010).

More adults are remaining single longer, with 27 percent of U.S. adults currently having never married (Pew Research Center, 2010). In 2011, the U.S. average age for a first marriage climbed to 28.7 years for men and 26.5 years for women, higher than at any other point in history (Pew Research Center, 2011). In 1980, the average age for a first marriage in the United States was 24 years for men and 21 years for women. In addition, the increase in cohabitation and a slight decline in the percentage of divorced individuals who remarry contribute to the decline in marriage rates in the United States (Copen & others, 2012).

Despite the decline in marriage rates, the United States is still a marrying society (Popenoe, 2009). In 2010, by 40 years of age, 77 percent of individuals had ever been married, although this figure is substantially below the figure of 93 percent in the 1960s (Pew Research Center, 2011). In a recent national poll, more than 40 percent of Americans under 30 think marriage is headed for extinction, yet only 5 percent of those young adults said they didn't want to get married (Pew Research Center, 2010). These findings may reflect marriage's role as a way to show friends and family that you have a successful social life (Cherlin, 2009).

Is there a best age to get married? Marriages in adolescence are more likely to end in divorce than marriages in adulthood (Copen & others, 2012). However, researchers have not been able to pin down a specific age or age span for getting married in adulthood that is most likely to result in a successful marriage (Furstenberg, 2007).

How happy are people who do marry? The average duration of a marriage in the United States is currently just over nine years. As indicated in Figure 14.5, the percentage of married individuals in the United States who said their marriages were "very happy" declined from the 1970s through the early 1990s, but recently has begun to flatten out (Popenoe, 2009). Notice in Figure 14.5 that married men consistently report being happier than married women.

Cross-Cultural Comparisons Many aspects of marriage vary across cultures. For example, as part of China's efforts to control population growth, a 1981 law sets the minimum age for marriage at 22 years for males, 20 for females.

The traits that people look for in a marriage partner vary around the world. In one large-scale study of 9,474 adults from 37 cultures on six continents and five islands, people varied most regarding how much they valued chastity—desiring a marital partner with no previous experience in sexual intercourse (Buss & others, 1990). Chastity was the most important characteristic in selecting a marital partner in China, India, Indonesia, Iran, Taiwan, and the Palestinian Arab culture. Adults from Ireland and Japan placed moderate importance on chastity. In contrast, adults in Sweden, Finland, Norway, the Netherlands, and Germany generally said that chastity was not important in selecting a marital partner.

Domesticity is also valued in some cultures and not in others. In this study, adults from the Zulu culture in South Africa, Estonia, and Colombia placed a high value on housekeeping skills in their marital preference. By contrast, adults in the United States, Canada, and all western European countries except Spain said that housekeeping skill was not an important trait in their partner.

Religion plays an important role in marriage in many cultures. For example, Islam stresses the honor of the male and the purity of the female. It also emphasizes the woman's role in

> When two people are under the influence of the most violent, most insane, most delusive, and most transient of passions, they are required to swear that they will remain in that excited, abnormal, and exhausting condition continuously until death do them part.
>
> —GEORGE BERNARD SHAW
> *Irish Playwright, 20th Century*

FIGURE **14.5**

PERCENTAGE OF MARRIED PERSONS AGE 18 AND OLDER WITH "VERY HAPPY" MARRIAGES

(a)

(b)

(c)

(*a*) In Scandinavian countries, cohabitation is popular; only a small percentage of 20- to 24-year-olds are married. (*b*) Islam stresses male honor and female purity. (*c*) Japanese young adults live at home longer with their parents before marrying than young adults in most other countries.

childbearing, child rearing, educating children, and instilling the Islamic faith in their children. In India, more than 70 percent of marriages continue to be arranged. However, as more women have entered the workforce in India and moved from rural areas to cities, these Indian women increasingly resist an arranged marriage.

International comparisons of marriage also reveal that individuals in Scandinavian countries marry later than Americans, whereas their counterparts in many African, Asian, and Latin American countries marry younger (Waite, 2009). In Denmark, for example, almost 80 percent of the women and 90 percent of the men aged 20 to 24 have never been married. In Hungary, less than 40 percent of the women and 70 percent of the men the same age have never been married. In Scandinavian countries, cohabitation is popular among young adults; however, most Scandinavians eventually marry. In Sweden, women delay marriage until they are about 31, men until they are 33. Some countries, such as Hungary, encourage early marriage and childbearing to offset declines in the population. Like Scandinavian countries, Japan has a high proportion of unmarried young people. However, rather than cohabiting as the Scandinavians do, unmarried Japanese young adults live at home longer with their parents before marrying.

Premarital Education   Premarital education occurs in a group and focuses on relationship advice. Might premarital education improve the quality of a marriage and possibly reduce the chances that the marriage will end in divorce? Researchers have found that it can (Halford, Markman, & Stanley, 2008; Owen & others, 2011). For example, a survey of more than 3,000 adults revealed that premarital education was linked to a higher level of marital satisfaction and commitment to a spouse, a lower level of destructive marital conflict, and a 31 percent lower likelihood of divorce (Stanley & others, 2006). The premarital education programs in the study ranged from several hours to 20 hours, with a median of 8 hours. It is recommended that premarital education begin approximately six months to a year before the wedding. A recent study revealed that individuals in second marriages are less likely to get premarital education than those in first marriages (Doss & others, 2009). In this study, for both first and second marriages, individuals who received premarital education had a lower risk of subsequent marital distress and divorce.

The Benefits of a Good Marriage   Are there any benefits to having a good marriage? Yes. Individuals who are happily married live longer, healthier lives than those who are either divorced or unhappily married (Choi & Marks, 2011; Lee & others, 2011; Shor & others, 2012). One study indicated that the longer women were married, the less likely they were to develop a chronic health condition and that the longer men were married, the lower their risk of developing a disease (Dupre & Meadows, 2007). A recent study of U.S. adults 50 years and older also revealed that a lower portion of adult life spent in marriage was linked to an increased likelihood of dying at an earlier age (Henretta, 2010). And a recent large-scale

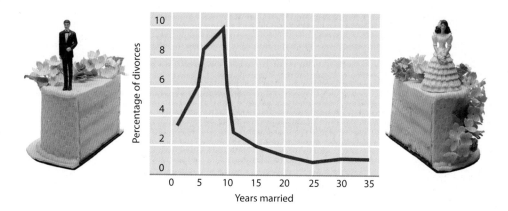

FIGURE **14.6**

THE DIVORCE RATE IN RELATION TO NUMBER OF YEARS MARRIED. Shown here is the percentage of divorces as a function of how long couples have been married. Notice that most divorces occur in the early years of marriage, peaking in the fifth to tenth years of marriage.

analysis of data from a number of studies indicated that being married benefitted the longevity of men more than women (Rendall & others, 2011). Further, an unhappy marriage can shorten a person's life by an average of four years (Gove, Style, & Hughes, 1990).

What are the reasons for these benefits of a happy marriage? People in happy marriages likely feel less physically and emotionally stressed, which puts less wear and tear on a person's body. Such wear and tear can lead to physical ailments such as high blood pressure and heart disease, as well as psychological problems such as anxiety, depression, and substance abuse.

DIVORCED ADULTS

Divorce has become an epidemic in the United States (Welch, 2012). However, the divorce rate declined in recent decades after peaking at 5.1 divorces per 1,000 people in 1981 and had declined by 2009 to 3.6 divorces per 1,000 people (National Center for Vital Statistics, 2010). Still, the United States has one of the highest divorce rates in the world.

Although divorce rates have increased in all socioeconomic groups, those in some groups have a higher incidence of divorce (Amato, 2010; Repetti, Flook, & Sperling, 2011). Youthful marriage, low educational level, low income, not having a religious affiliation, having parents who are divorced, and having a baby before marriage are factors that are associated with increases in divorce (Hoelter, 2009). And the following characteristics of one's partner increase the likelihood of divorce: alcoholism, psychological problems, domestic violence, infidelity, and inadequate division of household labor (Hoelter, 2009).

Earlier, we indicated that researchers have not been able to pin down a specific age that is the best time to marry so that the marriage is unlikely to end in a divorce. However, if a divorce is going to occur, it usually takes place early in a marriage; most occur in the fifth to tenth year of marriage (National Center for Health Statistics, 2000) (see Figure 14.6). This timing may reflect an effort by partners in troubled marriages to stay in the marriage and try to work things out. If after several years these efforts don't improve the relationship, they may then seek a divorce.

Both partners experience challenges after a marriage dissolves (Breslau & others, 2011; Lee & others, 2011; Olson, DeFrain, & Skogrand, 2011). Both divorced women and divorced men complain of loneliness, diminished self-esteem, anxiety about the unknowns in their lives, and difficulty in forming satisfactory new intimate relationships (Hetherington, 2006). One study revealed that following marital dissolution, both men and women were more likely to experience an episode of depression than individuals who remained with a spouse over a two-year period (Rotermann, 2007). And a recent Swedish study found that divorced adults were more likely to smoke daily than married or cohabiting adults (Lindstrom, 2010).

Despite all of these stresses and challenges, many people do cope effectively with divorce. Later in this chapter, we consider the varied paths people take after a divorce and suggested strategies for coping.

developmental **connection**

Family and Peers

Children in divorced families have more adjustment problems than children in never-divorced, intact families, but a majority of children in divorced families do not have adjustment problems. Chapter 8, p. 263

REMARRIED ADULTS

A wedding ceremony of remarried adults with their children. *What are some of the challenges that remarried adults face?*

Adults who remarry usually do so rather quickly, with approximately 50 percent remarrying within three years after their divorce (Sweeney, 2009, 2010). Men remarry sooner than women. Men with higher incomes are more likely to remarry than their counterparts with lower incomes. Remarriage occurs sooner for partners who initiate a divorce (especially in the first several years after divorce and for older women) than those who do not (Sweeney, 2009, 2010).

Evidence regarding the benefits of remarriage on adults is mixed. Remarried families are more likely to be unstable than first marriages, with divorce more likely to occur, especially in the first several years of the remarried family, than in first marriages (Waite, 2009). Adults who remarry have a lower level of mental health (higher rates of depression, for example) than adults in first marriages, but remarriage often improves the financial status of remarried adults, especially women (Waite, 2009). Researchers have found that remarried adults' marital relationship is more egalitarian and more likely to be characterized by shared decision making than first marriages (Waite, 2009). Remarried wives also report that they have more influence on financial matters in their new family than do wives in first marriages (Waite, 2009).

Stepfamilies come in many sizes and forms (DeGenova & others, 2011; Seccombe, 2012). The custodial and noncustodial parents and stepparent all might have been married and divorced, in some cases more than once. These parents might be caring for children from prior marriages and have a large network of grandparents and other relatives. Approximately 50 percent of remarried women bear children within their newly formed union, although the presence of stepchildren from a prior marriage reduces the likelihood of childbearing with the new husband (Waite, 2009). And some remarried individuals are more adult-focused, responding more to the concerns of their partner, while others are more child-focused, responding more to the concerns of the children (Anderson & Greene, 2011).

As indicated earlier, remarried adults often find it difficult to stay remarried. Why? For one thing, many remarry not for love but for financial reasons, for help in rearing children, and to reduce loneliness. They also might carry into the stepfamily negative patterns that produced failure in an earlier marriage. Remarried couples also experience more stress in rearing children than parents in never-divorced families (Ganong, Coleman, & Hans, 2006).

GAY AND LESBIAN ADULTS

The legal and social context of marriage creates barriers to breaking up that do not usually exist for same-sex partners (Brown & Henriquez, 2011). But in other ways, researchers have found that gay and lesbian relationships are similar—in their satisfactions, loves, joys, and conflicts—to heterosexual relationships (Fingerhut & Peplau, 2013). For example, like heterosexual couples, gay and lesbian couples need to find the balance of romantic love, affection, autonomy, and equality that is acceptable to both partners (Kurdek, 2006). An increasing number of gay and lesbian couples are creating families that include children (see Figure 14.7).

Lesbian couples especially place a high priority on equality in their relationships (Fingerhut & Peplau, 2013). One study of couples revealed that over the course of 10 years of cohabitation, partners in gay and lesbian relationships showed a higher average level of relationship quality than heterosexual couples (Kurdek, 2007).

There are numerous misconceptions about gay and lesbian couples (Fingerhut & Peplau, 2013). Contrary to stereotypes, one partner is masculine and the other feminine in only a small percentage of gay and lesbian couples. Only a small segment of the gay population has a large number of sexual partners, and this is uncommon among lesbians. Furthermore, researchers have found that gays and lesbians prefer long-term, committed relationships

FIGURE **14.7**

PERCENTAGE OF GAY AND LESBIAN COUPLES WITH CHILDREN: 1990 AND 2000. *Why do you think more lesbian couples have children than gay couples?*

developmental **connection**

Parenting

Researchers have found few differences between children who are being raised by gay and lesbian parents and children who are being raised by heterosexual parents. Chapter 8, p. 264

(Fingerhut & Peplau, 2013). About half of committed gay couples do have an open relationship that allows the possibility of sex (but not affectionate love) outside the relationship. Lesbian couples usually do not have this open relationship.

A special concern is the stigma, prejudice, and discrimination that lesbian, gay, and bisexual individuals experience because of widespread social devaluation of same-sex relationships (Balsam & Hughes, 2013). However, a recent study indicated that many individuals in these relationships saw stigma as bringing them closer together and strengthening their relationship (Frost, 2011).

Review Connect Reflect

LG3 Characterize adult lifestyles.

Review

- What are characteristics of the lives of single adults?
- What are key features of the lives of cohabiting adults?
- What are current marital trends?
- How does divorce affect adults?
- What are the lives of remarried parents like?
- How are gay and lesbian couples like or unlike heterosexual couples?

Connect

- What did you learn in Chapter 8 about the effects of divorce and remarriage on the children in those families?

Reflect *Your Own Personal Journey of Life*

- Which type of lifestyle are you living today? What do you think are the advantages and disadvantages of this lifestyle for you? If you could have a different lifestyle, which one would it be? Why?

4 Marriage and the Family

LG4 Discuss making marriage work, parenting, and divorce.

Making Marriage Work   Becoming a Parent   Dealing with Divorce

Whatever lifestyles young adults choose, they will bring certain challenges. Because many choose the lifestyle of marriage, we'll consider some of the challenges in marriage and how to make it work. We also examine some challenges in parenting and trends in childbearing. Given the statistics about divorce rates in the previous section, we'll then consider how to deal with divorce.

MAKING MARRIAGE WORK

John Gottman (1994, 2006, 2011; Gottman & Silver, 1999) has been studying married couples' lives since the early 1970s. He uses many methods to analyze what makes marriages work. Gottman interviews couples about the history of their marriage, their philosophy about marriage, and how they view their parents' marriages. He videotapes them talking to each other about how their day went and evaluates what they say about the good and bad times in their marriages. Gottman also uses physiological measures to measure their heart rate, blood flow, blood pressure, and immune functioning moment by moment. He also checks back with the couples every year to see how their marriage is faring. Gottman's research represents the most extensive assessment of marital relationships available. Currently, he and his colleagues are following 700 couples in seven studies.

John Gottman, who has conducted extensive research on what makes marriages work.

> Unlike most approaches to helping couples, mine is based on knowing what makes marriages succeed rather than fail.
>
> —**JOHN GOTTMAN**
> *Contemporary Psychologist, University of Washington*

What makes marriages work? What are the benefits of having a good marriage?

Gottman argues that it is important to realize that love is not something magical and that through knowledge and effort couples can improve their relationship. In his research, Gottman has found that seven main principles determine whether a marriage will work:

- *Establish love maps.* Individuals in successful marriages have personal insights and detailed maps of each other's life and world. They aren't psychological strangers. In good marriages, partners are willing to share their feelings with each other. They use these "love maps" to express not only their understanding of each other but also their fondness and admiration.

- *Nurture fondness and admiration.* In successful marriages, partners sing each other's praises. More than 90 percent of the time, when couples put a positive spin on their marriage's history, the marriage is likely to have a positive future.

- *Turn toward each other instead of away.* In good marriages, spouses are adept at turning toward each other regularly. They see each other as friends. This friendship doesn't keep arguments from occurring, but it can prevent differences from overwhelming the relationship. In these good marriages, spouses respect each other and appreciate each other's point of view despite disagreements.

- *Let your partner influence you.* Bad marriages often involve one spouse who is unwilling to share power with the other. Although power-mongering is more common in husbands, some wives also show this trait. A willingness to share power and to respect the other person's view is a prerequisite to compromising. One study revealed that equality in decision making was one of the main factors that predicted positive marriage quality (Amato, 2007).

- *Solve solvable conflicts.* Two types of problems occur in marriage: (1) perpetual and (2) solvable. Perpetual problems are the type that do not go away and may include differences about whether to have children and how often to have sex. Solvable problems can be worked out and may include such things as not helping each other reduce daily stresses and not being verbally affectionate. Unfortunately, more than two-thirds of marital problems fall into the perpetual category. Fortunately, marital therapists have found that couples often don't have to solve their perpetual problems for the marriage to work.

  In his research, Gottman has found that to resolve conflicts, couples should start out with a soft rather than a harsh approach, try to make and receive "repair attempts," regulate their emotions, compromise, and be tolerant of each other's faults. Conflict resolution is not about one person making changes; it is about negotiating and accommodating each other.

- *Overcome gridlock.* One partner wants the other to attend church; the other is an atheist. One partner is a homebody; the other wants to go out and socialize a lot. Such problems often produce gridlock. Gottman believes the key to ending gridlock is not to solve the problem but to move from gridlock to dialogue and be patient.

- *Create shared meaning.* The more partners can speak candidly and respectfully with each other, the more likely it is that they will create shared meaning in their marriage. This also includes sharing goals with one's spouse and working together to achieve each other's goals.

Gottman emphasizes that establishing a positive emotional connection is an important aspect of a successful close relationship. To evaluate your success in keeping a relationship going forward and moving in a positive direction, see Figure 14.8.

In addition to Gottman's view, other experts on marriage argue that such factors as forgiveness and commitment are important aspects of a successful marriage (Fincham, Stanley, & Beach, 2007). These factors function as self-repair processes in healthy relationships. For example, spouses may have a heated argument that has the potential to harm their relationship (Amato, 2007). After calming down, they may forgive each other and repair the damage.

Spouses who have a strong commitment to each other may in times of conflict sacrifice their personal self-interest for the benefit of the marriage. Commitment especially becomes

To take this quiz, think about a person who is important to you. Complete each item by indicating how much you agree or disagree with the statement.

1. I sometimes get ignored when I need attention the most.
   ○ strongly disagree
   ○ disagree
   ○ neutral
   ○ agree
   ○ strongly agree

2. This person usually doesn't have a clue as to what I am feeling.
   ○ strongly disagree
   ○ disagree
   ○ neutral
   ○ agree
   ○ strongly agree

3. I often have difficulty getting a meaningful conversation going with this person.
   ○ strongly disagree
   ○ disagree
   ○ neutral
   ○ agree
   ○ strongly agree

4. I get mad when I don't get the attention I need from this person.
   ○ strongly disagree
   ○ disagree
   ○ neutral
   ○ agree
   ○ strongly agree

5. I often find myself becoming irritable with this person.
   ○ strongly disagree
   ○ disagree
   ○ neutral
   ○ agree
   ○ strongly agree

6. I often feel irritated that this person isn't on my side.
   ○ strongly disagree
   ○ disagree
   ○ neutral
   ○ agree
   ○ strongly agree

7. I have trouble getting this person to listen to me.
   ○ strongly disagree
   ○ disagree
   ○ neutral
   ○ agree
   ○ strongly agree

8. I find it difficult to get this person to open up to me.
   ○ strongly disagree
   ○ disagree
   ○ neutral
   ○ agree
   ○ strongly agree

9. I have trouble getting this person to talk to me.
   ○ strongly disagree
   ○ disagree
   ○ neutral
   ○ agree
   ○ strongly agree

SCORING

Scoring For Each Item
Strongly disagree: 0
Disagree: 1
Neutral: 2
Agree: 3
Strongly agree: 4

Total Your score for questions 1–3:
Scores below 8 mean that you are direct in your relationship. This is great news for your relationship, because you have the ability to state clearly what you need from this person. If your score is 8 or higher, you may be too reticent in bidding. The other person in your relationship may feel as if they have to be a mind reader to understand what you need.

Total score for questions 4–6:
Scores below 8 mean that you are not overly forceful in expressing what you need from this person. Your relationship benefits from this quality of yours because it's easier for the other person to hear and understand what you need. If your score is 8 or higher, you may be expressing so much anger in your bidding that you are turning this person away. Maybe this is because of past frustrations, or maybe it is the way your personality is.

Total Your score for questions 7–9:
If your score is below 8, this means you have a high level of trust in your relationship. If your score is 8 or higher, this reflects a problem with the level of trust in your relationship. You may need to do more to win this person's trust. Some people accomplish this by concentrating more on responding to the other person's bids, rather than trying to get the other person to respond to you.

FIGURE **14.8**

BIDS FOR CONNECTION: THE BUILDING BLOCKS OF EMOTIONAL CONNECTION. In John Gottman's (2002) view, bids for connection can be verbal or non-verbal, physical or intellectual, sexual or non-sexual. The key is that the bid for connection is an attempt to create a connection between two people. The function of the bids is to keep the relationship moving forward and in a positive direction. Bids are important aspect of emotional connection. How individuals make bids for connection and how they are responded to influence how the relationship is going to fare over time. By answering the questions here, you can evaluate your style of relationship bidding and possibly discover ways to improve your emotional connections.
Source: Gottman, J. (2002), *The Relationship Cure.* New York: Three Rivers Press.

important when a couple is not happily married and can help them get through hard times with the hope that the future will involve positive changes in the relationship.

For remarried couples, strategies for coping with the stress of living in a stepfamily include the following (Visher & Visher, 1989):

- *Have realistic expectations.* Allow time for loving relationships to develop, and look at the complexity of the stepfamily as a challenge to overcome.

- *Develop new positive relationships within the family.* Create new traditions and ways of dealing with difficult circumstances. Allocation of time is especially important because so many people are involved. The remarried couple needs to allot time alone for each other.

> We never know the love of our parents until we have become parents.
>
> —Henry Ward Beecher
> *American Clergyman, 19th Century*

What are some parenting myths?

developmental **connection**

Parenting

For most families, an authoritative parenting style is linked to more positive behavior on the part of children than authoritarian, indulgent, and neglectful styles. Chapter 8, p. 256

BECOMING A PARENT

For many young adults, parental roles are well planned, coordinated with other roles in life, and developed with the individual's economic situation in mind. For others, the discovery that they are about to become parents is a startling surprise. In either event, the prospective parents may have mixed emotions and romantic illusions about having a child (Carl, 2012).

Parenting Myths and Reality   The needs and expectations of parents have stimulated many myths about parenting (Eibach & Mock, 2011; Williams, Sawyer, & Wahlstrom, 2012). These parenting myths include:

- The birth of a child will save a failing marriage.
- As a possession or extension of the parent, the child will think, feel, and behave as the parent did in his or her childhood.
- Having a child gives the parents a "second chance" to achieve what they should have achieved.
- Parenting is instinctual and requires no training.

Parenting requires a number of interpersonal skills and imposes emotional demands, yet there is little in the way of formal education for this task. Most parents learn parenting practices from their own parents—some they accept, some they discard. Unfortunately, when methods of parents are passed on from one generation to the next, both desirable and undesirable practices are perpetuated. Adding to the reality of the task of parenting, husbands and wives may bring different parenting practices to the marriage. The parents, then, may struggle with each other about who has a better way to interact with a child. Parent educators seek to help individuals to become better parents. To read about the work of one parent educator, see *Connecting with Careers.*

Trends in Childbearing   Like marriage, the age at which individuals have children has been increasing (Lauer & Lauer, 2012). In 2008, the average age at which women gave birth for the first time was 25 years of age, up from 21 years of age in 2001 (U.S. Census Bureau, 2011).

As the use of birth control has become common, many individuals consciously choose when they will have children and how many children they will rear. The number of one-child families is increasing, for example, and U.S. women overall are having fewer children. These childbearing trends are creating several trends:

- By giving birth to fewer children and reducing the demands of child care, women free up a significant portion of their life spans for other endeavors.
- Men are apt to invest a greater amount of time in fathering.
- Parental care is often supplemented by institutional care (child care, for example).

As more women show an increased interest in developing a career, they are not only marrying later but also having fewer children and having them later in life. What are some of the advantages of having children early or late? Some of the advantages of having children early (in the twenties) are that the parents are likely to have more physical energy (for example, they can cope better with such matters as getting up in the middle of the night with infants and waiting up until adolescents come home at night); the mother is likely to have fewer medical problems with pregnancy and childbirth; and the parents may be less likely to build up expectations for their children, as do many couples who have waited many years to have children.

Janis Keyser, Parent Educator

Janis Keyser is a parent educator who teaches in the Department of Early Childhood Education at Cabrillo College in California. In addition to teaching college classes and conducting parenting workshops, she also has coauthored a book with Laura Davis (1997): *Becoming the Parent You Want to Be: A Source-Book of Strategies for the First Five Years.*

Keyser also writes as an expert on the iVillage Web site (www. parentsplace.com), and she co-authors a nationally syndicated parenting column, "Growing Up, Growing Together." Keyser is the mother of three, stepmother of five, grandmother of twelve, and great-grandmother of six.

Janis Keyser (*right*), conducting a parenting workshop.

There are also advantages to having children later (in the thirties): The parents will have had more time to consider their goals in life, such as what they want from their family and career roles; the parents will be more mature and will be able to benefit from their life experiences to engage in more competent parenting; and the parents will be better established in their careers and have more income for child-rearing expenses.

DEALING WITH DIVORCE

If a marriage doesn't work, what happens after divorce? Psychologically, one of the most common characteristics of divorced adults is difficulty in trusting someone else in a romantic relationship. Following a divorce, though, people's lives can take diverse turns (Ben-Zur, 2012; Smith & others, 2012). In E. Mavis Hetherington's research, men and women took six common pathways in exiting divorce (Hetherington & Kelly, 2002, pp. 98–108):

- *The enhancers.* Accounting for 20 percent of the divorced group, most were females who "grew more competent, well-adjusted, and self-fulfilled" following their divorce (p. 98). They were competent in multiple areas of life, showing a remarkable ability to bounce back from stressful circumstances and to create something meaningful out of problems.

- *The good-enoughs.* The largest group of divorced individuals, they were described as average people coping with divorce. They showed some strengths and some weaknesses, some successes and some failures. When they experienced a problem, they tried to solve it. Many of them attended night classes, found new friends, developed active social lives, and were motivated to get higher-paying jobs. However, they were not as good at planning and were less persistent than the enhancers. Good-enough women usually married men who educationally and economically were similar to their first husbands, often going into a new marriage that was not much of an improvement over the first one.

- *The seekers.* These individuals were motivated to find new mates as soon as possible. "At one year post-divorce, 40 percent of the men and 38 percent of women had been

What are some diverse pathways individuals' lives can take following a divorce?

Coping and Adapting in the Aftermath of Divorce

Hetherington recommends these strategies for divorced adults (Hetherington & Kelly, 2002):

- Think of divorce as a chance to grow personally and to develop more positive relationships.
- Make decisions carefully. The consequences of your decision making regarding work, lovers, and children may last a lifetime.
- Focus more on the future than the past. Think about what is most important for you going forward in your life, set some challenging goals, and plan how to reach them.
- Use your strengths and resources to cope with difficulties.

- Don't expect to be successful and happy in everything you do. "The road to a more satisfying life is bumpy and will have many detours" (p. 109).
- Remember that "you are never trapped by one pathway. Most of those who were categorized as defeated immediately after divorce gradually moved on to a better life, but moving onward usually requires some effort" (p. 109).

Look back again at the six common pathways for exiting divorce that Hetherington proposes. Consider how someone on each of those pathways might particularly benefit from employing one or another of these strategies.

classified as seekers. But as people found new partners or remarried, or became more secure or satisfied in their single life, this category shrank and came to be predominated by men" (p. 102).

- *The libertines.* People in this category often spent more time in singles bars and had more casual sex than their counterparts in the other divorce categories. However, by the end of the first year post-divorce, they often grew disillusioned with their sensation-seeking lifestyle and wanted a stable relationship.
- *The competent loners.* These individuals, who made up only about 10 percent of the divorced group, were "well-adjusted, self-sufficient, and socially skilled." They had a successful career, an active social life, and a wide range of interests. However, "unlike enhancers, competent loners had little interest in sharing their lives with anyone else" (p. 105).
- *The defeated.* Some of these individuals had problems before their divorce, and these problems increased after the breakup when "the added stress of a failed marriage was more than they could handle. Others had difficulty coping because divorce cost them a spouse who had supported them, or in the case of a drinking problem, restricted them" (p. 106).

To read about some guidelines for coping and adapting in the aftermath of divorce, see *Connecting Development to Life.*

Review *Connect* Reflect

 LG4 Discuss making marriages work, parenting, and divorce.

Review

- What makes a marriage work?
- What are some current trends in childbearing?
- What paths do people take after a divorce?

Connect

- In this section you read about some of the advantages of having children early or late

in one's life. What did you learn about maternal age in Chapter 3?

Reflect *Your Own Personal Journey of Life*

- What do you think would be the best age to have children? Why?

Gender and Communication   Women's Development   Men's Development

Stereotypes about differences in men's and women's attitudes toward communication and about differences in how they communicate with each other have spawned countless cartoons and jokes. Are the supposed differences real? In this section, we will explore the answer to this question and also consider some aspects of both the woman's role and the man's role in relationships.

GENDER AND COMMUNICATION

When Deborah Tannen (1990) analyzed the talk of women and men, she found that many wives complain about their husbands, saying that "He doesn't listen to me anymore" and "He doesn't talk to me anymore." Lack of communication, though high on women's lists of reasons for divorce, is mentioned much less often by men.

Communication problems between men and women may come in part from differences in their preferred ways of communicating (Gamble & Gamble, 2008). Tannen distinguishes two ways of communicating: rapport talk and report talk. **Rapport talk** is the language of conversation; it is a way of establishing connections and negotiating relationships. **Report talk** is designed to give information and may include public speaking. According to Tannen, women enjoy rapport talk more than report talk, and men's lack of interest in rapport talk bothers many women. In contrast, men prefer to engage in report talk. Men hold center stage through such verbal performances as telling stories and jokes. They learn to use talk as a way of getting and keeping attention.

How extensive are gender differences in communication? Research has yielded somewhat mixed results. Several studies do reveal some gender differences. One study of a sampling of students' e-mails found that people could guess the writer's gender two-thirds of the time (Thompson & Murachver, 2001). Another study revealed that women make 63 percent of phone calls and when talking to another woman stay on the phone longer (7.2 minutes) than men do when talking with other men (4.6 minutes) (Smoreda & Licoppe, 2000). However, meta-analyses suggest that overall gender differences in communication are small for both children and adults (Hyde, 2005, 2007; Leaper & Smith, 2004). Further, a recent analysis revealed no gender differences in the average number of total words spoken by seven different samples of college men and women over 17 waking hours (Mehl & others, 2007).

A thorough study documented some gender differences in specific aspects of communication (Newman & others, 2008). In this study, women used words more for discussing people and what they were doing, as well as for communicating internal processes to others, including expression of doubts. By contrast, men used words more for external events, objects, and processes, including occupation, money, sports, and swearing. Contrary to popular stereotypes, men and women could not be distinguished in their reference to sexuality and anger. Thus, while gender similarity likely characterizes communication in general, as just indicated, there do seem to be some gender differences in certain aspects of communication (Helgeson, 2012).

"You have no idea how nice it is to have someone to talk to."
Copyright © Don Orehek. Reprinted by permission.

Understanding the other's ways of talking is a giant leap across the communication gap between women and men, and a giant step toward opening lines of communication.

—**Deborah Tannen**
Contemporary Sociologist, Georgetown University

WOMEN'S DEVELOPMENT

Tannen's analysis of women's preference for rapport talk suggests that women place a high value on relationships and focus on nurturing their connections with others. This view echoes some ideas of Jean Baker Miller (1986), who has been an important voice in stimulating the examination of psychological issues from a female perspective. Miller argues that when

rapport talk The language of conversation; it is a way of establishing connections and negotiating relationships.

report talk Talk that is designed to give information; includes public speaking.

"Sex brought us together, but gender drove us apart."
© Barbara Smaller/The New Yorker Collection/www.cartoonbank.com

researchers examine what women have been doing in life, a large part of it is active participation in the development of others. In Miller's view, women often try to interact with others in ways that will foster the other person's development along many dimensions—emotionally, intellectually, and socially.

Most experts believe it is important for women to not only maintain their competency in relationships but also to be self-motivated (Helgeson, 2012; Matlin, 2012). As Harriet Lerner (1989) concludes in her book *The Dance of Intimacy,* it is important for women to bring to their relationships nothing less than a strong, assertive, independent, and authentic self. She emphasizes that competent relationships are those in which the separate "I-ness" of both persons can be appreciated and enhanced while still staying emotionally connected to each other.

In sum, Miller, Tannen, and other gender experts such as Carol Gilligan, whose ideas you read about in Chapter 10, believe that women are more relationship-oriented than men—and that this relationship orientation should be prized as a skill in our culture more than it currently is. Critics of this view of gender differences in relationships contend that it is too stereotypical (Dindia, 2005; Hyde & Else-Quest, 2013). They argue that there is greater individual variation in the relationship styles of men and women than this view acknowledges.

MEN'S DEVELOPMENT

The male of the species—what is he really like? What are his concerns? According to Joseph Pleck's (1995) *role-strain view,* male roles are contradictory and inconsistent. Men not only experience stress when they violate men's roles, they also are harmed when they do act in accord with men's roles. Here are some of the areas where men's roles can cause considerable strain (Levant, 2002):

- *Health.* On average, men die about five years younger than women do. They have higher rates of stress-related disorders, alcoholism, car accidents, and suicide. Men are more likely than women to be the victims of homicide. In sum, the male role is hazardous to men's health.

- *Male-female relationships.* Too often, the male role involves expectations that men should be dominant, powerful, and aggressive and should control women. "Real men," according to many traditional definitions of masculinity, look at women in terms of their bodies, not their minds and feelings, have little interest in rapport talk and relationships, and do not consider women equal to men in work or many other aspects of life. Thus the traditional view of the male role encourages men to disparage women, be violent toward women, and refuse to have equal relationships with women.

- *Male-male relationships.* Too many men have had too little interaction with their fathers, especially fathers who are positive role models. Nurturing and being sensitive to others have been regarded as aspects of the female role, not the male role. And the male role emphasizes competition rather than cooperation. All of these aspects of the male role have left men with inadequate positive, emotional connections with other males.

In advising men on how to reconstruct their masculinity in more positive ways, Ron Levant (2002) suggests that every man should (1) reexamine his beliefs about manhood, (2) separate out the valuable aspects of the male role, and (3) get rid of those parts of the masculine role that are destructive. All of this involves becoming more "emotionally intelligent"—that is, becoming more emotionally self-aware, managing emotions more effectively, reading emotions better (one's own emotions and those of others), and being motivated to improve close relationships.

developmental **connection**

Gender

Many fathers interact with infants differently from the way mothers do. Chapter 6, p. 196

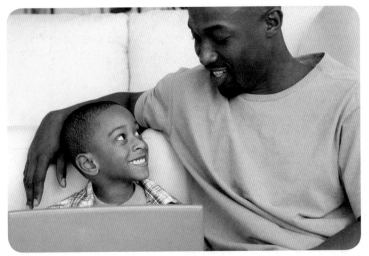

How might men be able to reconstruct their masculinity in positive ways?

Review

- What are some differences in how men and women communicate?
- What are some important aspects of the woman's role in relationships?
- What are some important aspects of the man's role in relationships?

Connect

- In this section you read about some of the gender role expectations men face in their lives. How does this relate to Pollack's "boy code" concept, which you read about in Chapter 10?

Reflect *Your Own Personal Journey of Life*

- If you are a woman, how would you like the men in your relationships today to change? If you are a man, how would you like the women in your relationships today to change?

topical **connections**

Middle adulthood is a time when individuals experience Erikson's seventh life-span stage, generativity versus stagnation. In this stage, it is important for middle-aged adults to contribute in meaningful ways to the next generation. In Levinson's theory, one of the key conflicts of middle age involves coping with the young-old polarity in life. Midlife crises are not as common as believed by many; however, when they occur, negative life events usually are involved. A number of longitudinal studies of stability and change in adult development have been conducted, and recently it has been argued that stability peaks in middle adulthood. Affectionate love increases in middle age. Many middle-aged adults become grandparents. Middle-aged women especially play an important role in connecting generations.

looking forward --->

reach your **learning goals**

Socioemotional Development in Early Adulthood

1 Stability and Change from Childhood to Adulthood

LG1 Describe stability and change in temperament, and summarize adult attachment styles.

Temperament

Attachment

- Links between childhood temperament and adult personality can vary, depending on contexts in an individual's experience. A high activity level in early childhood is linked with being an outgoing young adult. Young adults show fewer mood swings, are more responsible, and engage in less risk taking than adolescents. In some cases, certain dimensions of temperament in childhood are linked with adjustment problems in early adulthood.

- Three adult attachment styles are secure attachment, avoidant attachment, and anxious attachment. Attachment styles in early adulthood are linked with a number of relationship patterns and developmental outcomes. For example, securely attached adults often show more positive relationship patterns than insecurely attached adults. Also, adults with avoidant and anxious attachment styles tend to be more depressed and have more relationship problems than securely attached adults.

2 Attraction, Love, and Close Relationships

LG2 Identify some key aspects of attraction, love, and close relationships.

Attraction

- Familiarity precedes a close relationship. We like to associate with people who are similar to us. The principles of consensual validation and matching can explain this. Similarity in personality attributes may be especially important in a relationship's success. The criteria for physical attractiveness vary across cultures and historical time.

The Faces of Love

- The different types of love include friendship, romantic love, affectionate love, and consummate love. Friendship plays an important role in adult development, especially in providing emotional support. Romantic love, also called passionate love, includes passion, sexuality, and a mixture of emotions, not all of which are positive. Affectionate love, also called companionate love, usually becomes more important as relationships mature. Shaver proposed a developmental model of love and Sternberg a triarchic model of love (with dimensions of passion, intimacy, and commitment).

Falling Out of Love

- The collapse of a close relationship can be traumatic, but for some individuals it results in happiness and personal development. For most individuals, falling out of love is painful and emotionally intense.

3 Adult Lifestyles

LG3 Characterize adult lifestyles.

Single Adults

- Being single has become an increasingly prominent lifestyle. Autonomy is one of its advantages. Intimacy, loneliness, and finding a positive identity in a marriage-oriented society are challenges faced by single adults.

Cohabiting Adults

- Cohabitation is an increasingly popular lifestyle, but researchers have found it is often linked to negative marital outcomes, although this link depends on the timing of cohabitation. Negative marital outcomes are more likely when cohabitation occurs prior to becoming engaged.

Married Adults

- The age at which individuals marry in the United States is increasing. Despite a decline in marriage rates, a large percentage of Americans still marry. The benefits of marriage include better physical and mental health and a longer life.

Divorced Adults

- The U.S. divorce rate increased dramatically in the middle of the twentieth century but began to decline in the 1980s. Divorce is complex and emotional. Both divorced men and women can experience loneliness, anxiety, and difficulty in forming new relationships.

Remarried Adults

- When adults remarry, they tend to do so rather quickly, with men remarrying sooner than women. Remarriage confers some benefits on adults but also some problems. Remarried families are less stable than families in first marriages, and remarried adults have a lower level of mental health than adults in first marriages, although remarriage improves adults' (especially women's) financial status. Stepfamilies come in many sizes and forms.

Gay and Lesbian Adults

- One of the most striking findings about gay and lesbian couples is how similar their relationships are to heterosexual couples' relationships.

4 Marriage and the Family

LG4 Discuss making marriages work, parenting, and divorce.

Making Marriage Work

- Gottman's research indicates that happily married couples establish love maps, nurture fondness and admiration, turn toward each other, accept the influence of the partner, solve solvable conflicts, overcome gridlock, and create shared meaning.

Becoming a Parent

- Families are becoming smaller, and many women are delaying childbirth until they have become well established in a career. There are some advantages to having children earlier in adulthood and some advantages to having them later.

Dealing with Divorce

- Hetherington identified six pathways taken by people after divorce: enhancers, good-enoughs, seekers, libertines, competent loners, and the defeated. About 20 percent became better adjusted and more competent after the divorce.

5 Gender, Relationships, and Self-Development

LG5 Summarize the role of gender in relationships.

Gender and Communication

- Tannen distinguishes between rapport talk, which many women prefer, and report talk, which many men prefer. Meta-analyses have found small gender differences in overall communication, but recent research suggests some gender differences in specific aspects of communication, such as the way men and women use words.

Women's Development

- Some gender experts contend that women are more relationship-oriented than men and that their interactions focus on fostering the development of other people. Critics argue that there is more individual variation in women's and men's relationship styles than this view acknowledges. Many experts believe that it is important for women to retain their competence in relationships but also to be self-motivated.

Men's Development

- The traditional male role involves considerable strain, which takes a toll on men's health. The role also discourages equal relationships with women and discourages positive emotional connections with other men.

key terms

secure attachment style 454	consensual validation 457	romantic love 458	rapport talk 473
avoidant attachment style 454	matching hypothesis 457	affectionate love 458	report talk 473
anxious attachment style 454			

key people

Theodore Wachs 452	Erik Erikson 457	Bella DePaulo 461	Jean Baker Miller 473
Cindy Hazan 453	Ellen Berscheid 459	John Gottman 467	Harriet Lerner 474
Phillip Shaver 453	Robert J. Sternberg 459	E. Mavis Hetherington 471	Joseph Pleck 474
Mario Mikulincer 455	Andrew Cherlin 461	Deborah Tannen 473	

Chapter 14 | SOCIOEMOTIONAL DEVELOPMENT IN EARLY ADULTHOOD

Connecting with

Learning Objectives	Application Activities	Activity Type	Page Reference
Describe stability and change in temperament.	Early Adulthood Perspectives on Emotion	Milestones: Transitions	pp. 452–453

(continued)

Learning Objectives	Application Activities	Activity Type	Page Reference
Identify key aspects of attraction.	First Impressions and Attraction	Interactive exercise	pp. 456–457
	Mate Selection	Interactive exercise	
Summarize the faces of love.	Who I Love	Video	pp. 457–459
	Who I Love at Age 19	Video	
	Falling in Love—1	Video	
	Falling in Love—2	Video	
	Falling in Love—3	Video	
	What is Love? (Age 20)	Video	
	What is Love? (Age 21)—1	Video	
	What is Love? (Age 21)—2	Video	
	Interracial Couples and Discrimination	Video	
	Interracial Dating	Video	
	Interracial Relationships	Video	
	Interracial Relationships: Between Two Couples (1)	Video	
	Interracial Relationships	Video	
Characterize married adult lifestyles.	Interracial Marriage	Video	pp. 462–465
	Family Reaction to Interracial Marriage	Video	
	Nontraditional Weddings	Video	
	The Cost of Weddings Today: Lesbian Couple	Video	
	Transition to Marriage: Lesbian Couple	Video	
	Mate Selection	Interactive exercise	
Discuss divorced adult lifestyles.	Divorce Trends	Video	pp. 465–466
Describe gay male and lesbian adult lifestyles.	Cohabitation Among a Lesbian Couple	Video	pp. 466–467
	Heterosexism and the Wedding Ritual	Video	

(continued)

Learning Objectives	Application Activities	Activity Type	Page Reference
Discuss making marriage work.	Sharing Household Tasks	Video	pp. 467–469
Describe becoming a parent and parenting.	Transition to Parenting: Heterosexual Married Couple	Video	pp. 470–471
	Transition to Parenting: Lesbian Couple	Video	
	Interview with Adoptive Parents	Video	
	Sharing Tasks After the Birth of First Baby	Video	
	Division of Household Tasks	Video	
	Sharing Childcare Responsibilities	Video	
	Balancing Work and Family	Video	
	On Balancing Work and Family	Video	
	Working Parents: The Daily Routine	Video	
	Children's Reaction to Working Moms	Video	
	Children's Feelings About Work and Family	Video	
	Interview with Stay-Home Dad	Video	
	Fathers and the Transition to Parenting	Video	
	Having a Baby After 40	Video	

Generations will depend on the ability of every procreating individual to face his children.

—ERIK ERIKSON
American Psychologist, 20th Century

Middle Adulthood

In middle adulthood, what we have been forms what we will be. For some of us, middle age is a foggy place, a time when we need to discover what we are running from and to and why. We compare our life with what we vowed to make it. In middle age, more time stretches behind us than before us, and some evaluations, however reluctant, have to be made. As the young-old polarity greets us with a special force, we need to join the daring of youth with the discipline of age in a way that does justice to both. As middle-aged adults, we come to sense that the generations of living things pass in a short while and, like runners, hand on the torch of life. Section 8 consists of two chapters: "Physical and Cognitive Development in Middle Adulthood" (Chapter 15) and "Socioemotional Development in Middle Adulthood" (Chapter 16).

chapter 15

PHYSICAL AND COGNITIVE DEVELOPMENT IN MIDDLE ADULTHOOD

chapter outline

Our perception of time depends on where we are in the life span. We are more concerned about time at some points in life than others. Jim Croce's song "Time in a Bottle" reflects a time perspective that develops in the adult years:

If I could save time in a bottle
The first thing that I'd like to do
Is to save every day
'Til Eternity passes away
Just to spend them with you . . .
But there never seems to be enough time
To do the things you want to do
Once you find them
I've looked around enough to know
That you're the one I want to go
Through time with . . .
—Jim Croce, "Time in a Bottle"

Jim Croce's song connects time with love and the hope of going through time with someone we love. Love and intimacy are important themes of adult development. So is time. In middle adulthood as well as late adulthood, individuals increasingly think about time-left-to-live instead of time-since-birth (Kotter-Gruhn & Smith, 2011; Setterson, 2009). Middle-aged adults begin to look back to where they have been, reflecting on what they have done with the time they have had. They look toward the future more in terms of how much time remains to accomplish what they hope to do with their lives.

topical **connections**

Emerging adulthood, which occurs at approximately 18 to 25 years of age, is characterized by experimentation and exploration. Peak physical performance often occurs from about 19 to 26 years of age, but toward the latter part of early adulthood, a slowdown in physical performance is often apparent. Emerging adults have sexual intercourse with more individuals than young adults, but have sex less frequently. Thinking becomes more pragmatic and reflective in early adulthood than adolescence. Career development is an important aspect of early adulthood, and work becomes a more central aspect of most young adults' lives.

← - - - *looking back* -

preview

When young adults look forward in time to what their lives might be like as middle-aged adults, too often they anticipate that things will go downhill. However, like all periods of the human life span, for most individuals there usually are positive and negative features of middle age. In this first chapter on middle adulthood, we will discuss physical changes; cognitive changes; changes in careers, work, and leisure; as well as the importance of religion and meaning in life during middle adulthood. To begin, though, we will explore how middle age is changing.

1 The Nature of Middle Adulthood

 LG1 Explain how midlife is changing, and define middle adulthood.

Changing Midlife

Defining Middle Adulthood

Is midlife experienced the same way today as it was 100 years ago? Is it different from what it was like just 25 years ago? How can middle adulthood be defined, and what are some of its main characteristics?

CHANGING MIDLIFE

Many of today's 50-year-olds are in better shape, more alert, and more productive than their 40-year-old counterparts from a generation or two earlier. As more people lead healthier lifestyles and medical discoveries help to stave off the aging process, the boundaries of middle age are being pushed upward. It looks like middle age is starting later and lasting longer for increasing numbers of active, healthy, and productive people. A current saying is "60 is the new 40," implying that many 60-year-olds today are living a life that is as active, productive, and healthy as earlier generations did in their forties.

Questions such as, "To which age group do you belong?" and "How old do you feel?" reflect the concept of age identity. A consistent finding is that as adults become older their age identity is younger than their chronological age (Setterson & Trauten, 2009; Westerhof, 2009). One study found that almost half of the individuals 65 to 69 years of age considered themselves middle-aged (National Council on Aging, 2000), and another study found a similar pattern: Half of the 60- to 75-year-olds viewed themselves as being middle-aged (Lachman, Maier, & Budner, 2000). Also, some individuals consider the upper boundary of midlife as the age at which they make the transition from work to retirement.

When Carl Jung studied midlife transitions early in the twentieth century, he referred to midlife as the afternoon of life (Jung, 1933). Midlife serves as an important preparation for late adulthood, "the evening of life" (Lachman, 2004, p. 306). But "midlife" came much earlier in Jung's time. In 1900 the average life expectancy was only 47 years of age; only 3 percent of the population lived past 65. Today, the average life expectancy is 78, and 12 percent of the U.S. population is older than 65. As a much greater percentage of the population lives to an older age, the midpoint of life and what constitutes middle age or middle adulthood are getting harder to pin down (Cohen, 2012).

In a recent book, *In Our Prime: The Invention of Middle Age*, Patricia Cohen (2012) describes how middle age wasn't thought of as a separate developmental period until the mid-1800s and the term *midlife* wasn't in a dictionary until 1895. In Cohen's analysis, advances in health and more people living to older ages especially fueled the emergence of thinking about middle age. People today take longer to grow up and longer to die than in past centuries.

How is midlife changing?

Compared with previous decades and centuries, an increasing percentage of the population is made up of middle-aged and older adults. In the past, the age structure of the population could be represented by a pyramid, with the largest percentage of the population in the childhood years. Today, the percentages of people at different ages in the life span are more similar, creating what is called the "rectangularization" of the age distribution (a vertical rectangle) (Himes, 2009). The rectangularization has been created by health advances that promote longevity, low fertility rates, and the aging of the baby-boom cohort (Moen, 2007).

The portrait of midlife described so far here suggests that for too long the negative aspects of this developmental period have been overdrawn. However, as will be seen in the following sections, it is important not to go too far in describing midlife positively. Many physical aspects decline in middle adulthood, and increased rates of health problems such as obesity need to be considered in taking a balanced approach to this age period.

DEFINING MIDDLE ADULTHOOD

Although the age boundaries are not set in stone, we will consider **middle adulthood** to be the developmental period that begins at approximately 40 to 45 years of age and extends to about 60 to 65 years of age. For many people, middle adulthood is a time of declining physical skills and expanding responsibility; a period in which people become more conscious of the young-old polarity and the shrinking amount of time left in life; a point when individuals seek to transmit something meaningful to the next generation; and a time when people reach and maintain satisfaction in their careers. In sum, middle adulthood involves "balancing work and relationship responsibilities in the midst of the physical and psychological changes associated with aging" (Lachman, 2004, p. 305).

In midlife, as in other age periods, individuals make choices—selecting what to do, deciding how to invest time and resources, and evaluating what aspects of their lives they need to change. In midlife, "a serious accident, loss, or illness" may be a "wake-up call" and produce "a major restructuring of time and a reassessment" of life's priorities (Lachman, 2004, p. 310). And with an absence of seniority protections, many middle-aged adults experience unexpected job loss and/or are strongly encouraged to take early retirement packages (Sweet, Moen, & Meiksins, 2007).

The concept of gains (growth) and losses (decline) is an important one in life-span development. Middle adulthood is the age period in which gains and losses as well as biological and sociocultural factors balance each other (Baltes, Lindenberger, & Staudinger, 2006). Although biological functioning declines in middle adulthood, sociocultural supports such as education, career, and relationships may peak in middle adulthood (Willis & Schaie, 2005). Thus, middle adulthood may be a unique developmental period in which growth and loss balance each other for many individuals.

Remember from our discussion in Chapter 1 that individuals have not only a chronological age but also biological, psychological, and social ages. Some experts conclude that compared with earlier and later periods, middle age is influenced more heavily by sociocultural factors (Willis & Martin, 2005).

For many healthy adults, middle age is lasting longer than it did in the past. Indeed, an increasing number of experts on middle adulthood describe the age period of 55 to 65 as *late midlife* (Deeg, 2005). Compared with earlier midlife, late midlife is more likely to be characterized by "the death of a parent, the last child leaving the parental home, becoming a grandparent, the preparation for retirement, and in most cases actual retirement. Many people in this age range experience their first confrontation with health problems" (Deeg, 2005, p. 211). Overall, then, although gains and losses may balance each other in early midlife, losses may begin to outnumber gains for many individuals in late midlife (Baltes, Lindenberger, & Staudinger, 2006).

Keep in mind, though, that midlife is characterized by individual variations (Ailshire & Burgard, 2012; Wallin & others, 2012). As life-span expert Gilbert Brim (1992) commented, middle adulthood is full of changes, twists, and turns; the path is not fixed. People move in and out of states of success and failure.

Middle age is a mix of new opportunities and expanding resources accompanied by declines in physical abilities.

—Lois Verbrugge
Research Professor, Institute of Gerontology, University of Michigan

developmental **connection**

Life-Span Perspective

There are four types of age: chronological, biological, psychological, and social. Chapter 1, p. 17

middle adulthood The developmental period that begins at approximately 40 to 45 years of age and extends to about 60 to 65 years of age.

2 Physical Development

LG2 Discuss physical changes in middle adulthood.

| Physical Changes | Health, Disease, Stress, and Control | Mortality Rates | Sexuality |

What physical changes characterize middle adulthood? How healthy are middle-aged adults? What are the main causes of death in middle age? How sexually active are individuals in middle adulthood?

PHYSICAL CHANGES

Unlike the rather dramatic physical changes that occur in early adolescence and the sometimes abrupt decline in old age, midlife physical changes are usually more gradual. Although everyone experiences some physical change due to aging in the middle adulthood years, the rates of this aging vary considerably from one individual to another. Genetic makeup and lifestyle factors play important roles in whether chronic disease will appear and when. Middle age is a window through which we can glimpse later life while there is still time to engage in prevention and to influence some of the course of aging (Bertrand, Graham, & Lachman, 2013; Lachman, 2004). Let's now explore some of the physical changes of middle age.

Visible Signs   The most visible signs of physical changes in middle adulthood involve physical appearance. The first outwardly noticeable signs of aging usually are apparent by the forties or fifties. The skin begins to wrinkle and sag because of a loss of fat and collagen in underlying tissues (Stone & others, 2011). Small, localized areas of pigmentation in the skin produce age spots, especially in areas that are exposed to sunlight, such as the hands and face. Hair becomes thinner and grayer due to a lower replacement rate and a decline in melanin production. Fingernails and toenails develop ridges and become thicker and more brittle.

Since a youthful appearance is stressed in many cultures, individuals whose hair is graying, whose skin is wrinkling, whose body is sagging, and whose teeth are yellowing strive to make themselves look younger. Undergoing cosmetic surgery, dyeing hair, purchasing wigs, enrolling in weight reduction programs, participating in exercise regimens, and taking heavy doses of vitamins are common in middle age. Baby boomers have shown a strong interest in plastic surgery and Botox, which may reflect their desire to slow down the aging process (Brun & Brock-Utne, 2012).

Height and Weight   Individuals lose height in middle age, and many gain weight (Onwudiwe & others, 2011). On average, from 30 to 50 years of age, men lose about one inch in height, then may lose another inch from 50 to 70 years of age (Hoyer & Roodin, 2009). The height loss for women can be as much as 2 inches from 25 to 75 years of age. Note that there are large variations in the extent to which individuals become shorter with aging. The decrease in height is due to

Middle age is when your age starts to show around your middle.

—BOB HOPE
American Comedian, 20th Century

bone loss in the vertebrae. On average, body fat accounts for about 10 percent of body weight in adolescence; it makes up 20 percent or more in middle age.

Obesity increases from early to middle adulthood. In a national survey, 38 percent of U.S. adults 40 to 59 years of age were classified as obese (National Center for Health Statistics, 2011). In Chapter 13, we saw that 27 percent of U.S. adults age 20 to 39 were classified as obese. Being overweight is a critical health problem in middle adulthood (Simon & others, 2011). For example, obesity increases the probability that an individual will suffer a number of other ailments, among them hypertension (abnormally high blood pressure), diabetes, and digestive disorders (Cheong & others, 2012; Dorresteijn, Visseren, & Spiering, 2012; Nezu & others, 2013). A large-scale study found that being overweight or obese in middle age increases an individual's risk of dying earlier (Adams & others, 2006). More than 500,000 50- to 71-year-olds completed surveys about their height and weight, and the researchers examined the participants' death records across a 10-year period. Those who were overweight (defined as a body mass index, which takes into account height and weight, of 25 or more) at 50 had a 20 to 40 percent higher risk of earlier death, whereas those who were obese (a body mass index of 30 or more) had a 100 to 200 percent higher risk of premature death.

Strength, Joints, and Bones   As we saw in Chapter 13, maximum physical strength often is attained in the twenties. The term *sarcopenia* is given to age-related loss of muscle mass and strength (Doria & others, 2012; Drey & others, 2012). Muscle loss with age occurs at a rate of approximately 1 to 2 percent per year after age 50 (Marcell, 2003). A loss of strength especially occurs in the back and legs. Researchers are seeking to identify genes that are linked to the development of sarcopenia (Tan & others, 2012). Obesity is a risk factor for sarcopenia (Li & Heber, 2012). A recent research review concluded that management of weight loss and resistance training were the best strategies to slow down the decline of muscle mass and muscle strength (Rolland & others, 2011).

Peak functioning of the body's joints also usually occurs in the twenties. The cushions for the movement of bones (such as tendons and ligaments) become less efficient in the middle-adult years, a time when many individuals experience joint stiffness and more difficulty in movement.

Maximum bone density occurs by the mid- to late thirties, after which there is a progressive loss of bone. The rate of this bone loss begins slowly but accelerates with further aging (Baron, 2012). Women lose bone mass twice as fast as men do. By the end of midlife, bones break more easily and heal more slowly (Rachner, Khosia, & Hofbauer, 2011).

Famous actor Sean Connery as a young adult in his twenties (*top*) and as a middle-aged adult in his fifties (*bottom*). *What are some of the most outwardly noticeable signs of aging in the middle adulthood years?*

Vision and Hearing   *Accommodation* of the eye—the ability to focus and maintain an image on the retina—experiences its sharpest decline between 40 and 59 years of age. In particular, middle-aged individuals begin to have difficulty viewing close objects.

The eye's blood supply also diminishes, although usually not until the fifties or sixties. The reduced blood supply may decrease the visual field's size and account for an increase in the eye's blind spot. At 60 years of age, the retina receives only one-third as much light as it did at 20 years of age, much of which is due to a decrease in the size of the pupil (Scialfa & Kline, 2007).

Hearing also can start to decline by age 40. Auditory assessments indicate that hearing loss occurs in up to 50 percent of individuals 50 years and older (Fowler & Leigh-Paffenroth, 2007). Sensitivity to high pitches usually declines first. The ability to hear low-pitched sounds does not seem to decline much in middle adulthood, though. Men usually lose their sensitivity to high-pitched sounds sooner than women do. However, this gender difference might be due to men's greater exposure to noise in occupations such as mining, automobile work, and so on.

Researchers are identifying new possibilities for improving the vision and hearing of people as they age. One way this is being carried out is through better control of glare or background noise (Natalizia & others, 2010). Laser surgery and implantation of intraocular lenses have become routine procedures for correcting vision in middle-aged adults (Ang, Evans, & Mehta, 2012; Pasquali & Krueger, 2012). In addition, recent advances in hearing aids have dramatically improved hearing for many individuals (Banerjee, 2011).

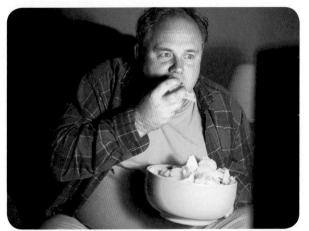

What characterizes the metabolic syndrome?

Members of the Masai tribe in Kenya, Africa, can stay on a treadmill for a long time because of their active lives. The extremely low incidence of heart disease in the Masai tribe is likely linked to their energetic lifestyle.

metabolic syndrome A condition characterized by hypertension, obesity, and insulin resistance. Metabolic syndrome often leads to the onset of diabetes and cardiovascular disease.

Cardiovascular System Midlife is the time when high blood pressure and high cholesterol often take adults by surprise (Lachman, 2004). Cardiovascular disease increases considerably in middle age (Chantler & Lakatta, 2012; Emery, Anderson, & Goodwin, 2013).

The level of cholesterol in the blood increases through the adult years and in midlife begins to accumulate on the artery walls, increasing the risk of cardiovascular disease (Emery & others, 2013). The type of cholesterol in the blood, however, influences its effect (Gadi, Amanullah, & Figueredo, 2012). Cholesterol comes in two forms: LDL (low-density lipoprotein) and HDL (high-density lipoprotein). LDL is often referred to as "bad" cholesterol because when the level of LDL is too high, it sticks to the lining of blood vessels, which can lead to atherosclerosis (hardening of the arteries). HDL is often referred to as "good" cholesterol because when it is high and LDL is low, the risk of cardiovascular disease is lessened (Sakuma, 2012).

High blood pressure (hypertension), too, often begins to appear for many individuals in their forties and fifties (Roberie & Elliott, 2012). At menopause, a woman's blood pressure rises sharply and usually remains above that of a man through life's later years (Taler, 2009). The health benefits of cholesterol-lowering and hypertension-lowering drugs are a major factor in improving the health of many middle-aged adults and increasing their life expectancy (de la Sierra & Barrios, 2012; Gadi & others, 2012).

An increasing problem in middle and late adulthood is **metabolic syndrome,** a condition characterized by hypertension, obesity, and insulin resistance. A recent research review concluded that chronic stress exposure is linked to metabolic syndrome (Tamashiro, 2011). Metabolic syndrome often leads to the development of diabetes and cardiovascular disease (Friese & others, 2012). Several recent studies have provided information about risk factors for metabolic syndrome:

- A meta-analysis revealed that metabolic syndrome was an important risk factor for any cause of death (Wu, Liu, & Ho, 2010).
- Individuals with metabolic syndrome who were physically active reduced their risk of developing cardiovascular disease (Broekhuizen & others, 2011).
- In one life course pathway, a high level of BMI in adolescence was related to metabolic syndrome in middle-aged men and women; in a second pathway, socioeconomic disadvantage in adolescence was linked to metabolic syndrome in middle-aged women (Gustafsson, Persson, & Hammarstrom, 2011).

Exercise, weight control, and a diet rich in fruits, vegetables, and whole grains can often help to stave off many cardiovascular problems in middle age (Currie, McKelvie, & MacDonald, 2012). For example, although cholesterol levels are influenced by heredity, LDL can be reduced and HDL increased by eating food that is low in saturated fat and cholesterol and by exercising regularly (Logan, 2011). One study of postmenopausal women revealed that 12 weeks of aerobic exercise training improved their cardiovascular functioning (O'Donnell, Kirwan, & Goodman, 2009).

The good news is that deaths due to cardiovascular disease have been decreasing in the United States since the 1970s. Why the decrease? Advances in drug medication to lower blood pressure and cholesterol, diet, and exercise in high-risk individuals have led to the reduction in deaths due to cardiovascular disease (Emery & others, 2013).

Does your fitness level in your young adult years have much impact on your risk of cardiovascular disease in middle age? To find out, see *Connecting Through Research.*

Lungs There is little change in lung capacity through most of middle adulthood for many individuals. However, at about age 55, the proteins in lung tissue become less elastic. This change, combined with a gradual stiffening of the chest wall, decreases the lungs' capacity to shuttle oxygen from the air people breathe to the blood in their veins. The lung capacity of individuals who are smokers drops precipitously in middle age, but if the individuals quit smoking, their lung capacity improves, although not to the level of individuals who have never smoked. Recent research also has found that low cognitive

How Does Physical Fitness in Young Adults Connect with Cardiovascular Health in Middle Age?

One longitudinal study was the first large-scale observational study to examine the role of physical fitness on healthy young adults' development of risk factors for heart disease (Carnethon & others, 2003). Previous studies had focused on the relation between fitness and death from heart disease and stroke.

The study involved 4,487 men and women in four cities (Birmingham, Alabama; Chicago, Illinois; Minneapolis, Minnesota; and Oakland, California). Initial assessments were made when the participants were 18 to 30 years of age and follow-up assessments conducted 2, 5, 7, 10, and 15 years later. Cardiorespiratory fitness was measured with an exercise treadmill test, which consisted of up to nine two-minute stages of progressive difficulty.

How might physical fitness in early adulthood be linked to health in middle adulthood?

Poor cardiorespiratory fitness in young men and women, determined by the duration of their treadmill exercise test, was associated with the risk of developing hypertension, diabetes, and metabolic syndrome in middle age. Improved fitness over seven years was related to a reduced risk of developing diabetes and metabolic syndrome.

This research reinforces the importance of establishing good health habits early in life. Staying fit when you are younger not only improves your health at that point in your life but also increases the likelihood that you will remain healthy as you get older.

ability in early adulthood is linked to reduced lung functioning in middle age (Carroll & others, 2011). And reduced lung functioning is related to lower cognitive ability later in development (Shipley & others, 2007). Such links between reduced lung functioning and cognitive ability are likely related to the influence of pulmonary functioning on brain structure and function, which in turn affects cognition (MacDonald, DeCarlo, & Dixon, 2011).

Sleep Some aspects of sleep become more problematic in middle age (Green & others, 2012; Polo-Kantola, 2011). The total number of hours slept usually remains the same as in early adulthood, but beginning in the forties, wakeful periods are more frequent and there is less of the deepest type of sleep (stage 4). The amount of time spent lying awake in bed at night begins to increase in middle age, and this can produce a feeling of being less rested in the morning. Sleep-disordered breathing and restless legs syndrome become more prevalent in middle age (Polo-Kantola, 2011). A recent study also found that middle-aged adults who sleep less than six hours a night on average had an increased risk of developing stroke symptoms (Ruiter & others, 2012). And a recent study found that change in sleep duration across five years in middle age was linked to cognitive functioning (Ferrie & others, 2011). In this study, a decrease from 6, 7, or 8 hours of sleep and an increase from 7 or 8 hours were related to lower scores on most assessments of cognitive functioning. Also, sleep problems in midlife are more common among individuals who use a higher number of prescription and nonprescription drugs, are obese, have cardiovascular disease, or are depressed (Loponen & others, 2010).

HEALTH, DISEASE, STRESS, AND CONTROL

In middle adulthood, the frequency of accidents declines and individuals are less susceptible to colds and allergies than in childhood, adolescence, or early adulthood. Indeed, many individuals live through middle adulthood without having a disease or persistent health problem.

developmental **connection**

Stress

Recently, a variation of hormonal stress theory has emphasized a decline in immune system functioning as an important contributor to lower resistance to stress in older adults. Chapter 17, p. 542

FIGURE **15.1**

NK CELLS AND CANCER. Two natural killer (NK) cells (*yellow*) are shown attacking a leukemia cell (*red*). Notice the blisters that the leukemia cell has developed to defend itself. Nonetheless, the NK cells are surrounding the leukemia cell and are about to destroy it.

chronic disorders Disorders that are characterized by slow onset and long duration. They are rare in early adulthood, increase during middle adulthood, and become common in late adulthood.

However, disease and persistent health problems become more common in middle adulthood for other individuals.

Chronic disorders are characterized by a slow onset and a long duration (Hoyt & Stanton, 2012). Chronic disorders are rare in early adulthood, increase in middle adulthood, and become common in late adulthood. Overall, arthritis is the leading chronic disorder in middle age, followed by hypertension, but the frequency of chronic disorders in middle age varies by gender. Men have a higher incidence of fatal chronic conditions (such as coronary heart disease, cancer, and stroke); women have a higher incidence of nonfatal ones (such as arthritis, varicose veins, and bursitis).

Stress and Disease   Stress is increasingly identified as a factor in many diseases (Dougall & Baum, 2012; Schwarzer & Luszczynska, 2013). The cumulative effect of stress often takes a toll on the health of individuals by the time they reach middle age. David Almeida and his colleagues (2011) recently described how chronic stress or prolonged exposure to stressors can have damaging effects on physical functioning, including an unhealthy overproduction of corticosteroids such as cortisol. Chronic stress can interfere with immune functioning, and this stress is linked to disease not only through the immune system but also through cardiovascular factors (Emery & others, 2013; Stowell, Robles, & Kane, 2013).

The Immune System and Stress   The immune system keeps us healthy by recognizing foreign materials such as bacteria, viruses, and tumors and then destroying them (Jennings & Egizio, 2012; Stowell, Robles, & Kane, 2013). Immune system functioning decreases with normal aging (Cavanaugh, Weyland, & Goronzky, 2012; Dougall & others, 2013).

The immune system's machinery consists of billions of white blood cells located in the circulatory system. The number of white blood cells and their effectiveness in killing foreign viruses or bacteria are related to stress levels. When a person is under stress, viruses and bacteria are more likely to multiply and cause disease. One study in young and middle-aged adults revealed that persistently unemployed individuals had lower natural killer (NK) cell levels than their previously unemployed counterparts who became reemployed (Cohen & others, 2007). NK cells are a type of white blood cell that is more likely to be present in low-stress circumstances (see Figure 15.1). Lower levels of NK cells in stressful situations indicate a weakened immune system. A recent study indicated aerobic fitness was related to the presence of a lower level of senescent T cells (prematurely aging cells that result from persistent immune activation) (Spielmann & others, 2011).

Stress and the Cardiovascular System   Stress and negative emotions can affect the development and course of cardiovascular disease by altering underlying physiological processes (Dougall & Baum, 2012). Sometimes, though, the link between stress and cardiovascular disease is indirect. For example, people who live in a chronically stressed condition, such as persistent poverty, are more likely to take up smoking, start overeating, and avoid exercising (Wilcox & others, 2011). All of these stress-related behaviors are linked with the development of cardiovascular disease (Dorresteijn, Visseren, & Spiering, 2011).

Culture and Health   Culture plays an important role in coronary disease. Cross-cultural psychologists maintain that studies of immigrants shed light on the role culture plays in health (Harris, 2012; Noymer & Lee, 2012). When people migrate to another culture, their health practices are likely to change while their genetic predispositions to certain disorders remain constant.

There also are differences within ethnic groups as well as among them. The living conditions and lifestyles of individuals within an ethnic group are influenced by their socioeconomic status, immigrant status, social and language skills, occupational opportunities, and such social resources as the availability of meaningful support networks—all of which play a role in health (Whitfield, Thorpe, & Szanton, 2011).

Despite these variations within ethnic groups, it is useful to know about differences among ethnic groups (Cichy, Stawski, & Almeida, 2012). Aging African Americans, for example, have above-average rates of high blood pressure and stroke (Delgado & others, 2012). A recent study revealed that social support had a positive influence on reducing the link between cardiovascular disease and depression in aging African Americans (Heard & others, 2011). Diabetes occurs at an above-average rate among Latinos, and a recent analysis indicated that diabetes poses a greater mortality risk for Latinos than non-Latino Whites (Hunt & others, 2011).

Prejudice and racial segregation are the historical underpinnings for the chronic stress of discrimination and poverty that adversely affects the health of many African Americans and Latinos (Berensen & others, 2012; Bhutta & Reddy, 2012). Support systems, such as an extended family network, may be especially important resources to improve the health of ethnic minorities and help them cope with stress.

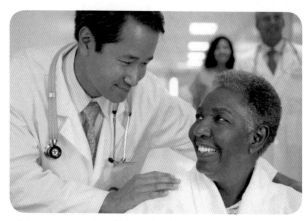

What are some ethnic variations in health?

Control   Although many diseases increase in middle age, having a sense of control is linked to many aspects of health and well-being (Scheier, Carver, & Armstrong, 2012; Lachman, Neuport, & Agrigoraei, 2011). Researchers have found that having a sense of control peaks in midlife then declines in late adulthood (Lachman, 2006; Lachman, Rosnick, & Rocke, 2009). However, in any adult age period, there is a wide range of individual differences in beliefs about control. Margie Lachman and her colleagues (2011) argue that having a sense of control in middle age is one of the most important modifiable factors in delaying the onset of diseases in middle adulthood and reducing the frequency of diseases in late adulthood.

MORTALITY RATES

Infectious disease was the main cause of death until the middle of the twentieth century. As infectious disease rates declined and more individuals lived through middle age, rates of chronic disorders increased (Keiley-Moore, 2009). Chronic diseases are now the main causes of death for individuals in middle adulthood.

In middle age, many deaths are caused by a single, readily identifiable condition, whereas in old age, death is more likely to result from the combined effects of several chronic conditions (Pizza & others, 2011). For many years heart disease was the leading cause of death in middle adulthood, followed by cancer; however, since 2005 more individuals 45 to 64 years of age in the United States died of cancer, followed by cardiovascular disease (Kochanek & others, 2011). The gap between cancer and the second leading cause of death widens as individuals age from 45 to 54 and 55 to 64 years of age (National Center for Health Statistics, 2008). Men have higher mortality rates than women for all of the leading causes of death (Kochanek & others, 2011).

SEXUALITY

What kinds of changes characterize the sexuality of women and men as they go through middle age? **Climacteric** is a term that is used to describe the midlife transition in which fertility declines. Let's explore the substantial differences in the climacteric experienced by women and men.

Menopause   Menopause is the time in middle age, usually during the late forties or early fifties, when a woman's menstrual periods cease. The average age at which U.S. women have their last period is 51 (Wise, 2006). However, there is a large variation in the age at which menopause occurs—from 39 to 59 years of age. Later menopause is linked with increased risk of breast cancer (Mishra & others, 2009).

Recall from Chapter 11, "Physical and Cognitive Development in Adolescence," that the timing of menarche, a girl's first menstruation, has significantly decreased since the mid-nineteenth century, occurring as much as four years earlier in some countries (Susman & Dorn, 2013). Has there been a similar earlier onset in the occurrence of menopause? No, there hasn't been a similar earlier corresponding change in menopause, and there is little or no correlation between ages at menarche and the onset of menopause (Gosden, 2007).

climacteric The midlife transition during which fertility declines.

menopause Cessation of a woman's menstrual periods, usually during the late forties or early fifties.

Researchers have found that almost 50 percent of Canadian and American women have occasional hot flashes, but only one in seven Japanese women do (Lock, 1998). *What factors might account for these variations?*

Perimenopause is the transitional period from normal menstrual periods to no menstrual periods at all, which often takes up to 10 years. Perimenopause usually occurs during the forties but can occur in the thirties (Derry & Derry, 2012; Prior & Hitchcock, 2011). One study of 30- to 50-year-old women found that depressed feelings, headaches, moodiness, and palpitations were the perimenopausal symptoms that these women most frequently discussed with health-care providers (Lyndaker & Hulton, 2004). Lifestyle factors such as whether women are overweight, smoke, drink heavily, or exercise regularly during perimenopause influence aspects of their future health such as whether they develop cardiovascular disease or chronic illnesses (ESHRE Capri Workshop Group, 2011).

In menopause, production of estrogen by the ovaries declines dramatically, and this decline produces uncomfortable symptoms in some women—"hot flashes," nausea, fatigue, and rapid heartbeat, for example. A recent study revealed that increased estradiol and improved sleep, but not hot flashes, predicted enhanced mood in women during their menopausal transition (Joffe & others, 2011).

Cross-cultural studies also reveal variations in the menopause experience (Lerner-Geva & others, 2010; Sievert & Obermeyer, 2012). For example, hot flashes are uncommon in Mayan women (Beyene, 1986). Asian women report fewer hot flashes than women in Western societies (Payer, 1991). It is difficult to determine the extent to which these cross-cultural variations are due to genetic, dietary, reproductive, or cultural factors.

Menopause overall is not the negative experience for most women that it was once thought to be (Henderson, 2011). Most women do not have severe physical or psychological problems related to menopause. For example, a recent research review concluded that there is no clear evidence that depressive disorders occur more often during menopause than at other times in a woman's reproductive life (Judd, Hickey, & Bryant, 2012).

However, the loss of fertility is an important marker for women—it means that they have to make final decisions about having children. Women in their thirties who have never had children sometimes speak about being "up against the biological clock" because they cannot postpone choices about having children much longer.

Until recently, hormone replacement therapy was often prescribed as treatment for unpleasant side effects of menopause. *Hormone replacement therapy (HRT)* augments the declining levels of reproductive hormone production by the ovaries (Yang & Reckelhoff, 2011). HRT can consist of various forms of estrogen, usually in combination with a progestin. A study of HRT's effects was halted as evidence emerged that participants who were receiving HRT faced an increased risk of stroke (National Institutes of Health, 2004). Since the link between HRT and increased risk of stroke was reported, there has been a 50 percent or more reduction in the use of HRT (Pines, Sturdee, & Maclennan, 2012). However, recent research has found a reduction of cardiovascular disease and minimal risks with HRT when it is initiated before 60 years of age and/or within 10 years of menopause and continued for six years or more (Hodis & others, 2012). Recent research studies on HRT have revealed that coinciding with the decreased use of HRT, research is mixed regarding changes in the incidence of breast cancer (Baber, 2011; Chlebowski & others, 2010; Gompel & Santen, 2012; Howell & Evans, 2011).

The National Institutes of Health recommends that women who have not had a hysterectomy who are currently taking hormones should consult with their doctor to determine whether they should continue the treatment. If they are taking HRT for short-term relief of symptoms, the benefits may outweigh the risks. Many middle-aged women are seeking alternatives to HRT such as regular exercise, dietary supplements, herbal remedies, relaxation therapy, acupuncture, and nonsteroidal medications (Holloway, 2010).

Hormonal Changes in Middle-Aged Men Do men go through anything like the menopause that women experience? That is, is there a male menopause? During middle adulthood, most men do not lose their capacity to father children, although there usually is a modest decline in their sexual hormone level and activity (Yassin & others, 2011). They experience hormonal changes in their fifties and sixties, but nothing like the dramatic drop in estrogen that women experience. Testosterone production begins to decline about 1 percent a year during middle adulthood, and sperm count usually shows a slow decline, but men do not lose their fertility in middle age. What has been referred to as "male menopause," then, probably

Age Groups	Not at all	A few times per year	A few times per month	2–3 times a week	4 or more times a week
Men					
18–24	15	21	24	28	12
25–29	7	15	31	36	11
30–39	8	15	37	23	6
40–49	9	18	40	27	6
50–59	11	22	43	20	3
Women					
18–24	11	16	2	9	12
25–29	5	10	38	37	10
30–39	9	16	6	33	6
40–49	15	16	44	20	5
50–59	30	22	35	12	2

FIGURE 15.2

THE SEX IN AMERICA SURVEY: FREQUENCY OF SEX AT DIFFERENT POINTS IN ADULT DEVELOPMENT. *Why do you think the frequency of sex declines as men and women get older?*

has less to do with hormonal change than with the psychological adjustment men must make when they are faced with declining physical energy and with family and work pressures. Testosterone therapy has not been found to relieve such symptoms, suggesting that they are not induced by hormonal change.

The gradual decline in men's testosterone levels in middle age can reduce their sexual drive (O'Connor & others, 2011). Their erections are less full and less frequent, and men require more stimulation to achieve them. Researchers once attributed these changes to psychological factors, but increasingly they find that as many as 75 percent of the erectile dysfunctions in middle-aged men stem from physiological problems. Smoking, diabetes, hypertension, elevated cholesterol levels, obesity, and lack of exercise are at fault in many erectile problems in middle-aged men (Javaroni & Neves, 2012; Kolotkin, Zunker, & Ostbye, 2012).

Erectile dysfunction (ED) (difficulty attaining or maintaining penile erection) affects approximately 50 percent of men 40 to 70 years of age (Berookhim & Bar-Charma, 2011). Treatment for men with erectile dysfunction has focused on Viagra and similar drugs such as Levitra and Cialis (Lowe & Costabile, 2012; Rubio-Aurioles & others, 2012). Viagra works by allowing increased blood flow into the penis, which produces an erection. Its success rate is in the 60 to 85 percent range (Claes & others, 2010).

Sexual Attitudes and Behavior

Although the ability of men and women to function sexually shows little biological decline in middle adulthood, sexual activity usually occurs less frequently in midlife than in early adulthood (Waite, Das, & Laumann, 2009). Figure 15.2 shows the age trends in frequency of sex from the Sex in America survey (described in Chapter 13). The frequency of having sex was greatest for individuals aged 25 to 29 years old (47 percent had sex twice a week or more) and dropped off for individuals in their fifties (23 percent of 50- to 59-year-old males said they had sex twice a week or more, and only 14 percent of the females in this age group reported this frequency) (Michael & others, 1994). Note, though, that the Sex in America survey may underestimate the frequency of sexual activity of middle-aged adults because the data were collected prior to the widespread use of erectile dysfunction drugs such as Viagra. Other research indicates that middle-aged men want sex, think about it more, and masturbate more often than middle-aged women (Stones & Stones, 2007). For many other forms of sexual behavior, such as kissing and hugging, sexual touching, and oral sex, male and female middle-aged adults report similar frequency of engagement (Stones & Stones, 2007). A large-scale longitudinal study of women

erectile dysfunction (ED) The inability to adequately achieve and maintain an erection to attain satisfactory sexual performance.

revealed that masturbation increased in early perimenopause but declined postmenopause (Avis & others, 2009). Also in this study, women's sexual desire decreased by late perimenopause. However, the menopausal transition was not linked to changes in the importance of sex, sexual arousal, frequency of sexual intercourse, emotional satisfaction with a partner, or physical pleasure.

If middle-aged adults have sex less frequently than they did when they were younger adults, does it mean they are less satisfied with their sex life? In a Canadian study of 40- to 64-year-olds, only 30 percent reported that their sexual life was less satisfying than when they were in their twenties (Wright, 2006).

Living with a spouse or partner makes all the difference in whether people engage in sexual activity, especially for women over 40 years of age. In one study conducted as part of the Midlife in the United States Study (MIDUS), 95 percent of women in their forties with partners said that they had been sexually active in the last six months, compared with only 53 percent of those without partners (Brim, 1999). By their fifties, 88 percent of women living with a partner have been sexually active in the last six months, but only 37 percent of those who are neither married nor living with someone say they have had sex in the last six months.

A large-scale study of U.S. adults 40 to 80 years of age found that premature ejaculation (26 percent) and erectile difficulties (22 percent) were the most common sexual problems of older men while lack of sexual interest (33 percent) and lubrication difficulties (21 percent) were the most common sexual problems of older women (Laumann & others, 2009).

A person's health in middle age is a key factor in sexual activity. A recent study found that how often individuals have sexual intercourse, the quality of their sexual life, and their interest in sex were linked to how healthy they were (Lindau & Gavrilova, 2010).

How does the pattern of sexual activity change when individuals become middle-aged?

Review *Connect* Reflect

LG2 Discuss physical changes in middle adulthood.

Review

- What are some key physical changes in middle adulthood?
- How would you characterize health and disease in middle adulthood?
- What are the main causes of death in middle age?
- What are the sexual lives of middle-aged adults like?

Connect

- In this section, you read that the production of estrogen by the ovaries declines dramatically in menopause. What did you learn about estrogen's role in puberty in Chapter 11?

Reflect *Your Own Personal Journey of Life*

- If you are a young or middle-aged adult, what can you do at this point in your life to optimize your health in middle age? If you are an older adult, what could you have done differently to optimize your health in middle age?

---

3 Cognitive Development

LG3 Identify cognitive changes in middle adulthood.

Intelligence   Information Processing

We have seen that middle-aged adults may not see as well, run as fast, or be as healthy as they were in their twenties and thirties. But what about their cognitive skills? Do these skills decline as we enter and move through middle adulthood? To answer this question, we will explore the possibility of cognitive changes in intelligence and information processing.

INTELLIGENCE

Our exploration of possible changes in intelligence in middle adulthood focuses on the concepts of fluid and crystallized intelligence, the Seattle Longitudinal Study, and cohort effects.

Fluid and Crystallized Intelligence

John Horn argues that some abilities begin to decline in middle age while others increase (Horn & Donaldson, 1980). Horn maintains that **crystallized intelligence,** an individual's accumulated information and verbal skills, continues to increase in middle adulthood, whereas **fluid intelligence,** one's ability to reason abstractly, begins to decline in middle adulthood (see Figure 15.3).

Horn's data were collected in a cross-sectional manner. Remember from Chapter 1 that a cross-sectional study assesses individuals of different ages at the same point in time. For example, a cross-sectional study might assess the intelligence of different groups of 40-, 50-, and 60-year-olds in a single evaluation, such as in 1980. The 40-year-olds in the study would have been born in 1940 and the 60-year-olds in 1920—different eras that offered different economic and educational opportunities. The 60-year-olds likely had fewer educational opportunities as they grew up. Thus, if we find differences between 40- and 60-year-olds on intelligence tests when they are assessed cross-sectionally, these differences might be due to cohort effects related to educational differences rather than to age.

By contrast, remember from Chapter 1 that in a longitudinal study, the same individuals are studied over a period of time. Thus, a longitudinal study of intelligence in middle adulthood might consist of giving the same intelligence test to the same individuals when they are 40, 50, and 60 years of age. As we see next, whether data on intelligence are collected cross-sectionally or longitudinally can make a difference in what is found about changes in crystallized and fluid intelligence and about intellectual decline (Abrams, 2009; Schaie, 2011a, b, 2012).

The Seattle Longitudinal Study

The Seattle Longitudinal Study that involves extensive evaluation of intellectual abilities during adulthood was initiated by K. Warner Schaie (1994, 1996, 2005, 2010, 2011a, b, 2012). Participants have been assessed in seven-year intervals since 1956: 1963, 1970, 1977, 1984, 1991, 1998, 2005, and 2012. Five hundred individuals initially were tested in 1956. New waves of participants are added periodically. The main focus in the Seattle Longitudinal Study has been on individual change and stability in intelligence, and the study is considered to be one of the most thorough examinations of how people develop and change as they go through adulthood.

The main mental abilities tested are:

- Verbal comprehension (ability to understand ideas expressed in words)
- Verbal memory (ability to encode and recall meaningful language units, such as a list of words)
- Number (ability to perform simple mathematical computations such as addition, subtraction, and multiplication)
- Spatial orientation (ability to visualize and mentally rotate stimuli in two- and three-dimensional space)
- Inductive reasoning (ability to recognize and understand patterns and relationships in a problem and use this understanding to solve other instances of the problem)
- Perceptual speed (ability to quickly and accurately make simple discriminations in visual stimuli)

As shown in Figure 15.4, the highest level of functioning for four of the six intellectual abilities occurred in the middle adulthood years (Schaie, 2012). For both women and men, peak performance on verbal ability, verbal memory, inductive reasoning, and spatial orientation was attained in middle age. For only two of the six abilities—number and perceptual

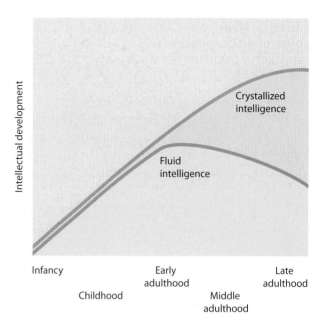

FIGURE **15.3**

FLUID AND CRYSTALLIZED INTELLECTUAL DEVELOPMENT ACROSS THE LIFE SPAN. According to Horn, crystallized intelligence (based on cumulative learning experiences) increases throughout the life span, but fluid intelligence (the ability to perceive and manipulate information) steadily declines from middle adulthood onward.

developmental **connection**

Cognitive Theory

A fifth, postformal stage of cognitive development has been proposed to describe cognitive advances in early adulthood. Chapter 13, p. 439

crystallized intelligence Accumulated information and verbal skills, which increase in middle adulthood, according to Horn.

fluid intelligence The ability to reason abstractly, which begins to decline from middle adulthood onward, according to Horn.

FIGURE 15.4

LONGITUDINAL CHANGES IN SIX INTELLECTUAL ABILITIES FROM AGE 25 TO AGE 95

Source: Adapted from Schaie, K.W. (2012). Developmental Influences on Adult Intelligence: The Seattle Longitudinal Study (2nd ed.), Fig. 5.8. New York: Oxford University Press.

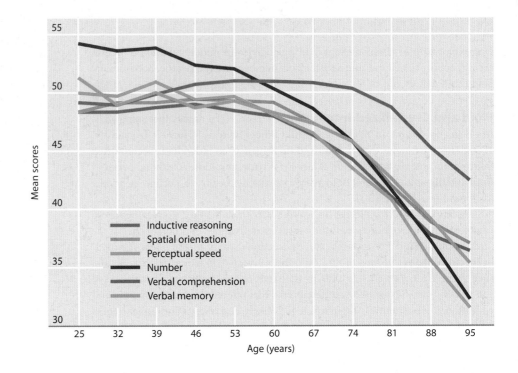

speed—were there declines in middle age. Perceptual speed showed the earliest decline, actually beginning in early adulthood. Interestingly, in terms of John Horn's ideas that were discussed earlier, for the participants in the Seattle Longitudinal Study, middle age was a time of peak performance for some aspects of both crystallized intelligence (verbal ability) and fluid intelligence (spatial orientation and inductive reasoning).

When Schaie (1994) assessed intellectual abilities both cross-sectionally and longitudinally, he found decline more likely in the cross-sectional than in the longitudinal assessments. For example, as shown in Figure 15.5, when assessed cross-sectionally, inductive reasoning showed a consistent decline during middle adulthood. In contrast, when assessed longitudinally, inductive reasoning increased until toward the end of middle adulthood when it began to show a slight decline. In Schaie's (2008, 2009, 2010, 2011a, b, 2012) view, it is in middle adulthood, not early adulthood, that people reach a peak in many intellectual skills.

In further analysis, Schaie (2007) examined generational differences in parents and their children over a seven-year time frame from 60 to 67 years of age. That is, parents were assessed when they were 60 to 67 years of age; and when their children reached 60 to 67 years of age, they also were assessed. Higher levels of cognitive functioning occurred for the second generation in inductive reasoning, verbal memory, and spatial orientation, whereas the first generation scored higher on numeric ability. Noteworthy was the finding that the parent generation showed cognitive decline from 60 to 67 years of age, but their offspring showed stability or modest increases in cognitive functioning across the same age range.

Such differences across generations involve cohort effects. In a recent analysis, Schaie (2011b) concluded that the advances in cognitive functioning in middle age that have occurred in recent decades are likely due to factors such as educational attainment, occupational structures (increases of workers in professional occupations and work complexity), health care and lifestyles, immigration, and social interventions in poverty. The impressive gains in cognitive functioning in recent cohorts have been documented more clearly for fluid intelligence than for crystallized intelligence (Schaie, 2011b).

The results from Schaie's study that have been described so far focus on average cognitive stability or change for all participants across the middle adulthood years. Schaie and Sherry Willis (Schaie, 2005; Willis & Schaie, 2005) examined individual differences for the participants in the Seattle study and found substantial individual variations. They classified participants as "decliners," "stable,"

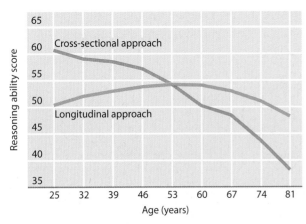

FIGURE 15.5

CROSS-SECTIONAL AND LONGITUDINAL COMPARISONS OF INTELLECTUAL CHANGE IN MIDDLE ADULTHOOD. *Why do you think reasoning ability peaks during middle adulthood?*

or "gainers" for three categories—number ability, delayed recall (a verbal memory task), and word fluency—from 46 to 60 years of age. The largest percentage of decline (31 percent) or gain (16 percent) occurred for delayed recall; the largest percentage with stable scores (79 percent) occurred for numerical ability. Word fluency declined for 20 percent of the individuals from 46 to 60 years of age.

Might the individual variations in cognitive trajectories in midlife be linked to cognitive impairment in late adulthood? In Willis and Schaie's analysis, cognitively normal and impaired older adults did not differ on measures of vocabulary, spatial orientation, and numerical ability in middle adulthood. However, declines in memory (immediate recall and delayed recall), word fluency, and perceptual speed in middle adulthood were linked to neuropsychologists' ratings of the individuals' cognitive impairment in late adulthood.

Some researchers disagree with Schaie that middle adulthood is the time when the level of functioning in a number of cognitive domains is maintained or even increases (Finch, 2009). For example, Timothy Salthouse (2009, 2012) recently has argued that cross-sectional research on aging and cognitive functioning should not be dismissed and that this research indicates reasoning, memory, spatial visualization, and processing speed begin declining in early adulthood and show further decline in the fifties. Salthouse (2009, 2012) does agree that cognitive functioning involving accumulated knowledge, such as vocabulary and general information, does not show early age-related decline but rather continues to increase at least until 60 years of age.

K. Warner Schaie (*right*) is one of the leading pioneers in the field of life-span development. He is shown here with two older adults who are actively using their cognitive skills. Schaie's research represents one of the most thorough examinations of how individuals develop and change as they go through the adult years.

Salthouse (2009, 2012) has emphasized that a lower level of cognitive functioning in early and middle adulthood is likely due to age-related neurobiological decline. Cross-sectional studies have shown that the following neurobiological factors decline during the twenties and thirties: regional brain volume, cortical thickness, synaptic density, some aspects of myelination, the functioning of some aspects of neurotransmitters such as dopamine and serotonin, blood flow in the cerebral cortex, and the accumulation of tangles in neurons (Del Tredici & Braak, 2008; Erixon-Lindroth & others, 2005; Finch, 2009; Hsu & others, 2008; Pieperhoff & others, 2008; Salat & others, 2004).

Schaie (2009, 2010, 2011a, b, 2012) continues to emphasize that longitudinal studies hold the key to determining age-related changes in cognitive functioning and that middle age is the time during which many cognitive skills actually peak. In the next decade, expanding research on age-related neurobiological changes and their possible links to cognitive skills should further refine our knowledge about age-related cognitive functioning in the adult years (Fletcher & Rapp, 2013; Merrill & others, 2012; Schlee & others, 2012).

INFORMATION PROCESSING

As we saw in our discussion of theories of development (Chapter 1) and of cognitive development from infancy through adolescence (Chapters 5, 7, 9, and 11), the information-processing approach provides another way of examining cognitive abilities. Among the information-processing changes that take place in middle adulthood are those involved in speed of processing information, memory, expertise, and practical problem-solving skills.

Speed of Information Processing   As we saw in Schaie's (1994, 1996, 2011a, b, 2012) Seattle Longitudinal Study, perceptual speed begins declining in early adulthood and continues to decline in middle adulthood. A common way to assess speed of information is through a reaction-time task, in which individuals simply press a button as soon as they see a light appear. Middle-aged adults are slower to push the button when the light appears than young adults are. However, keep in mind that the decline is not dramatic—under 1 second in most investigations.

A current interest focuses on possible causes for the decline in speed of processing information in adults (Salthouse, 2009, 2012). The causes may occur at different levels of analysis, such as cognitive ("maintaining goals, switching between tasks, or preserving internal representations despite distraction"), neuroanatomical ("changes in specific brain regions, such as

developmental **connection**

Memory

Some types of memory decline more than others in older adults. Chapter 18, p. 569

developmental **connection**

Memory

Working memory plays an important role in many aspects of children's cognitive and language development. Chapter 9, p. 293

developmental **connection**

Intelligence

One study found that 10- and 11-year-old children who were experienced chess players ("experts") remembered more about chess pieces than college students who were not chess players ("novices"). Chapter 9, p. 294

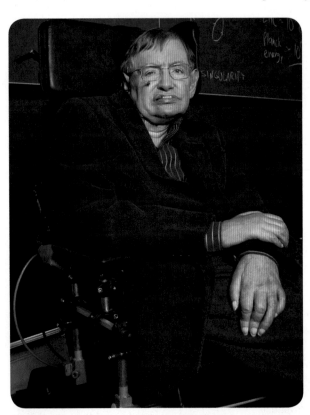

Stephen J. Hawking is a world-renowned expert in physics. Hawking authored the best-selling book, *A Brief History of Time*. Hawking has a neurological disorder that prevents him from walking or talking. He communicates with the aid of a voice-equipped computer. *What distinguishes experts from novices?*

the prefrontal cortex"), and neurochemical ("changes in neurotransmitter systems" such as dopamine) (Hartley, 2006, p. 201).

Memory   In Schaie's (1994, 1996) Seattle Longitudinal Study, verbal memory peaked in the fifties. However, in some other studies verbal memory has shown a decline in middle age, especially when assessed in cross-sectional studies (Salthouse, 2009, 2012). For example, in several studies in which people were asked to remember lists of words, numbers, or meaningful prose, younger adults outperformed middle-aged adults (Salthouse & Skovronek, 1992). Although there still is some controversy about whether memory declines during middle adulthood, most experts conclude that it does decline at some point during this period of adult development (Hoyer & Roodin, 2009; McCabe & Loaiza, 2012; Salthouse, 2012). However, some experts argue that studies that have concluded there is a decline in memory during middle age often have compared young adults in their twenties with older middle-aged adults in their late fifties and even have included some individuals in their sixties (Schaie, 2000). In this view, memory decline is either nonexistent or minimal in the early part of middle age but does occur in the latter part of middle age or in late adulthood.

Cognitive aging expert Denise Park (2001) argues that starting in late middle age, more time is needed to learn new information. The slowdown in learning new information has been linked to changes in *working memory*, the mental "workbench" where individuals manipulate and assemble information when making decisions, solving problems, and comprehending written and spoken language (Baddeley, 2007, 2012). In this view, in late middle age working memory capacity becomes more limited. Think of this situation as an overcrowded desk with many items in disarray. As a result of the overcrowding and disarray, long-term memory becomes less reliable, more time is needed to enter new information into long-term storage, and more time is required to retrieve the information. Thus, Park concludes that much of the blame for declining memory in late middle age is a result of information overload that builds up as we go through the adult years.

Memory decline is more likely to occur when individuals don't use effective memory strategies, such as organization and imagery (Small & others, 2012). By organizing lists of phone numbers into different categories, or imagining the phone numbers as representing different objects around the house, many individuals can improve their memory in middle adulthood.

Expertise   Because it takes so long to attain, expertise often shows up more in middle adulthood than in early adulthood (Charness & Krampe, 2008). Recall from Chapter 9 that expertise involves having extensive, highly organized knowledge and understanding of a particular domain. Developing expertise and becoming an "expert" in a field usually is the result of many years of experience, learning, and effort.

Strategies that distinguish experts from novices include these:

- Experts are more likely to rely on their accumulated experience to solve problems.
- Experts often process information automatically and analyze it more efficiently when solving a problem in their domain than novices do.
- Experts have better strategies and shortcuts to solving problems in their domain than novices do.
- Experts are more creative and flexible in solving problems in their domain than novices are.

Practical Problem Solving   Everyday problem solving is another important aspect of cognition (Allaire, 2012; Margrett & Deshpande-Kamat, 2009). Nancy Denney (1986, 1990) observed circumstances such as how young and middle-aged adults handled a landlord who would not fix their stove and what they did if a bank failed to deposit a check. She found that the ability to solve such practical problems improved through the forties and fifties as individuals accumulated practical experience.

However, since Denney's research other studies on everyday problem-solving and decision-making effectiveness across the adult years have been conducted (Allaire, 2012; Margrett & Deshpande-Kamat, 2009). A recent analysis of research found no evidence for significant changes in everyday cognition from 20 to 75 years of age (Salthouse, 2012). One possible explanation for the lack of any decline in everyday cognition is the increase in accumulated knowledge individuals possess as they grow older (Allaire, 2012).

Review Connect Reflect

LG3 Identify cognitive changes in middle adulthood.

Review

- How does intelligence develop in middle adulthood?
- What changes take place in processing information during middle age?

Connect

- In this section you read about longitudinal and cross-sectional studies of intelligence. What were the pros and cons that you learned about these two research approaches in Chapter 1?

Reflect *Your Own Personal Journey of Life*

- Think about your life and the lives of your parents and grandparents. Are there experiences that you are likely to have, are having, or have had that will enhance your intelligence in middle age more than the experiences they had or are having?

4 Careers, Work, and Leisure

LG4 Characterize career development, work, and leisure in middle adulthood.

Work in Midlife   Career Challenges and Changes   Leisure

What are some issues that workers face in midlife? What role does leisure play in the lives of middle-aged adults?

WORK IN MIDLIFE

The role of work, whether one works in a full-time career, a part-time job, as a volunteer, or a homemaker, is central during middle adulthood. Many middle-aged adults reach their peak in position and earnings. However, they may also be saddled with multiple financial burdens including rent or mortgage, child care, medical bills, home repairs, college tuition, loans to family members, or bills from nursing homes.

In the United States, approximately 80 percent of individuals 40 to 59 years of age are employed. In the 51-to-59 age group, slightly less than 25 percent do not work. More than half of this age group say that a health condition or an impairment limits the type of paid work that they do (Sterns & Huyck, 2001).

Do middle-aged workers perform their work as competently as younger adults? Age-related declines occur in some occupations, such as air traffic controllers and professional athletes, but for most jobs, no differences have been found in the work performance of young adults and middle-aged adults (Sturman, 2003; Salthouse, 2012).

For many people, midlife is a time of evaluation, assessment, and reflection in terms of the work they do and want to do in the future (Moen, 2009). Among the work issues that some people face in midlife are recognizing limitations in career progress, deciding whether to change jobs or careers, deciding whether to rebalance family and work, and planning for retirement (Sterns & Huyck, 2001).

Couples increasingly have both spouses in the workforce who are expecting to retire. Historically retirement has been a male transition, but today far more couples are planning two retirements—his and hers (Moen, 2009; Moen, Kelly, & Magennis, 2008).

developmental connection

Work

Work defines people in fundamental ways, influencing their financial standing, housing, the way they spend their time, where they live, their friendships, and their health. Chapter 13, p. 442

What characterizes work in middle adulthood?

The recent economic downturn and recession in the United States has forced some middle-aged individuals into premature retirement because of job loss and fear of not being able to reenter the work force. Such premature retirement also may result in accumulating insufficient financial resources to cover an increasingly long retirement period (Lusardi, Mitchell, & Curto, 2012; Szinovacz, 2011; Wang, 2012).

CAREER CHALLENGES AND CHANGES

Middle-aged workers face several important challenges in the twenty-first century (Blossfeld, 2009). These include the globalization of work, rapid developments in information technologies, downsizing of organizations, early retirement, and concerns about pensions and health care.

Globalization has replaced what was once a primarily White male workforce with employees of different ethnic and national backgrounds. To improve profits, many companies are restructuring, downsizing, and outsourcing jobs. One of the outcomes of these changes is to offer incentives to middle-aged employees to retire early—in their fifties, or in some cases even forties, rather than their sixties.

The decline in defined-benefit pensions and increased uncertainty about the fate of health insurance are decreasing the sense of personal control among middle-aged workers. As a consequence, many are delaying retirement.

Some midlife career changes are self-motivated; others are the consequence of losing one's job (Moen, 2009). Some individuals in middle age decide that they don't want to spend the rest of their lives doing the same kind of work they have been doing (Hoyer & Roodin, 2009). One aspect of middle adulthood involves adjusting idealistic hopes to realistic possibilities in light of how much time individuals have before they retire and how fast they are reaching their occupational goals (Levinson, 1978). If individuals perceive that they are behind schedule, if their goals are unrealistic, they don't like the work they are doing, or their job has become too stressful, they could become motivated to change jobs.

A final point to make about career development in middle adulthood is that cognitive factors earlier in development are linked to occupational attainment in middle age. In one study, task persistence at 13 years of age was related to occupational success in middle age (Andersson & Bergman, 2011).

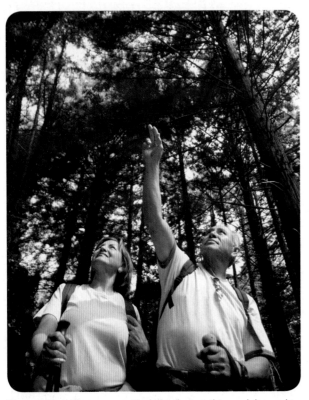

Sigmund Freud once commented that the two things adults need to do well to adapt to society's demands are to work and to love. To his list we add "to play." In our fast-paced society, it is all too easy to get caught up in the frenzied, hectic pace of our achievement-oriented work world and ignore leisure and play. Imagine your life as a middle-aged adult. *What would be the ideal mix of work and leisure? What leisure activities do you want to enjoy as a middle-aged adult?*

leisure The pleasant times after work when individuals are free to pursue activities and interests of their own choosing.

religion An organized set of beliefs, practices, rituals, and symbols that increases an individual's connection to a sacred or transcendent other (God, higher power, or higher truth).

religiousness The degree to which an individual is affiliated with an organized religion, participates in prescribed rituals and practices, feels a sense of connection with its beliefs, and is involved in a community of believers.

LEISURE

As adults, not only must we learn how to work well, but we also need to learn how to relax and enjoy leisure (Gibson, 2009). **Leisure** refers to the pleasant times after work when individuals are free to pursue activities and interests of their own choosing—hobbies, sports, or reading, for example. In one analysis of research on what U.S. adults regret the most, not engaging in more leisure was one of the top six regrets (Roese & Summerville, 2005).

Leisure can be an especially important aspect of middle adulthood (Parkes, 2006). By middle adulthood, more money is available to many individuals, and there may be more free time and paid vacations. In short, midlife changes may produce expanded opportunities for leisure.

In one study, 12,338 men 35 to 57 years of age were assessed each year for five years regarding whether or not they took vacations (Gump & Matthews, 2000). Then the researchers examined the medical and death records over nine years for men who lived for at least a year after the last vacation survey. Compared with those who never took vacations, men who went on annual vacations were 21 percent less likely to die over the nine years and 32 percent less likely to die of coronary heart disease.

Adults at midlife need to begin preparing psychologically for retirement. Constructive and fulfilling leisure activities in middle adulthood are an important part of this preparation (Danigelis, 2007). If an adult develops leisure activities that can be continued into retirement, the transition from work to retirement can be less stressful.

Review *Connect* Reflect

LG4 Characterize career development, work, and leisure in middle adulthood.

Review
- What are some issues that workers face in midlife?
- What career challenges and changes might people experience in middle adulthood?
- What characterizes leisure in middle age?

Connect
- In this section you learned about the leisure time of adults in middle age. What did you learn about cultural differences and leisure time in adolescence in Chapter 12?

Reflect *Your Own Personal Journey of Life*
- What do you want your work life and leisure to be like in middle age? If you are middle-aged, what is your work life and leisure like? If you are an older adult, what were they like in middle age?

5 Religion, Spirituality, and Meaning in Life

LG5 Explain the roles of religion, spirituality, and meaning in life during middle adulthood.

| Religion, Spirituality, and Adult Lives | Religion, Spirituality, and Health | Meaning in Life |

What roles do religion and spirituality play in our development as adults? Is the meaning of life an important theme for many middle-aged adults?

RELIGION, SPIRITUALITY, AND ADULT LIVES

Can religion be distinguished from spirituality? Recent analysis by Pamela King and her colleagues (2011) provides the following distinctions:

- **Religion** is an organized set of beliefs, practices, rituals, and symbols that increases an individual's connection to a sacred or transcendent other (God, higher power, or ultimate truth).
- **Religiousness** refers to the degree of affiliation with an organized religion, participation in its prescribed rituals and practices, connection with its beliefs, and involvement in a community of believers.
- **Spirituality** involves experiencing something beyond oneself in a transcendent manner and living in a way that benefits others and society.

What roles do religion and spirituality play in the lives of middle-aged adults?

In the MacArthur Study of Midlife Development, more than 70 percent of U.S. middle-aged adults said they are religious and consider spirituality a major part of their lives (Brim, 1999).

In thinking about religion, spirituality, and adult development, it is important to consider the role of individual differences. Religion and spirituality are powerful influences for some

spirituality Experiencing something beyond oneself in a transcendent manner and living in a way that benefits others and society.

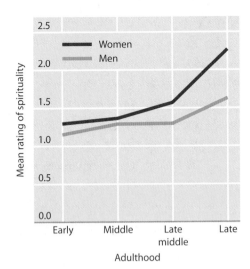

FIGURE **15.6**

LEVEL OF SPIRITUALITY IN FOUR ADULT AGE PERIODS. In a longitudinal study, the spirituality of individuals in four different adult age periods—early (thirties), middle (forties), late middle (mid-fifties/early sixties), and late (late sixties/early seventies) adulthood—was assessed (Wink & Dillon, 2002). Based on responses to open-ended questions in interviews, the spirituality of the individuals was coded on a 5-point scale with 5 being the highest level of spirituality and 1 the lowest.

- - - - - - - - - - - ➤

developmental **connection**

Religion

Religion and spirituality play important roles in the lives of many older adults. Chapter 18, p. 590

When more time stretches behind than stretches before one, some assessments, however reluctantly and incompletely, begin to be made.

—JAMES BALDWIN

American Novelist, 20th Century

meaning-making coping Involves drawing on beliefs, values, and goals to change the meaning of a stressful situation, especially in times of chronic stress such as when a loved one dies.

adults but hold little or no significance for others (McCullough & others, 2005). Further, the influence of religion and spirituality in people's lives may change as they develop (Sapp, 2010). In John Clausen's (1993) longitudinal investigation, some individuals who had been strongly religious in their early adult years became less so in middle age, while others became more religious in middle age. In a longitudinal study of individuals from their early thirties through their late sixties/early seventies, a significant increase in spirituality occurred between late middle (mid-fifties/early sixties) and late adulthood (Wink & Dillon, 2002) (see Figure 15.6).

Women have consistently shown a stronger interest in religion and spirituality than men have. In the longitudinal study just described, the spirituality of women increased more than men in the second half of life (Wink & Dillon, 2002).

RELIGION, SPIRITUALITY, AND HEALTH

How might religion influence physical health? Some cults and religious sects encourage behaviors that are damaging to health, such as ignoring sound medical advice (Williams & Sternthal, 2007). For individuals in the religious mainstream, researchers increasingly are finding that spirituality/religion is positively linked to health (McCullough & Willoughby, 2009). Researchers have found that religious commitment helps to moderate blood pressure and hypertension, and that religious attendance is linked to a reduction in hypertension (Gillum & Ingram, 2007). And in a recent analysis of a number of studies, adults with a higher level of spirituality/religion had an 18 percent reduction in mortality (Lucchetti, Lucchetti, & Koenig, 2011). In this analysis, a high level of spirituality/religion had a stronger link to mortality than 60 percent of 25 other health interventions (such as eating fruits and vegetables and taking statin drugs for cardiovascular disease). In *Connecting Development to Life,* we explore links between religion, spirituality, and coping.

In sum, various dimensions of religion and coping can help some individuals cope more effectively with their lives (Olson & others, 2012; Park, 2010, 2012a; Thune-Boyle & others, 2012). Religious counselors often advise people about mental health and coping. To read about the work of one religious counselor, see *Connecting with Careers.*

MEANING IN LIFE

Austrian psychiatrist Viktor Frankl's mother, father, brother, and wife died in the concentration camps and gas chambers in Auschwitz, Poland. Frankl survived the concentration camp and went on to write about meaning in life. In his book *Man's Search for Meaning,* Frankl (1984) emphasized each person's uniqueness and the finiteness of life. He argued that examining the finiteness of our existence and the certainty of death adds meaning to life. If life were not finite, said Frankl, we could spend our life doing just about whatever we pleased because time would continue forever.

Frankl said that the three most distinct human qualities are spirituality, freedom, and responsibility. Spirituality, in his view, does not have a religious underpinning. Rather, it refers to a human being's uniqueness of spirit, philosophy, and mind. Frankl proposed that people need to ask themselves such questions as why they exist, what they want from life, and what the meaning of their life might be.

It is in middle adulthood that individuals begin to be faced with death more often, especially the deaths of parents and other older relatives. Also faced with less time in their life, many individuals in middle age begin to ask and evaluate the questions that Frankl proposed (Cohen, 2009). And, as indicated in *Connecting Development to Life,* meaning-making coping is especially helpful in times of chronic stress and loss.

Having a sense of meaning in life can lead to clearer guidelines for living one's life and enhanced motivation to take care of oneself and reach goals. A higher level of meaning in life also is linked to a higher level of psychological well-being and physical health (Park, 2012b).

Roy Baumeister and Kathleen Vohs (2002, pp. 610–611) argue that the quest for a meaningful life can be understood in terms of four main needs for meaning that guide how people try to make sense of their lives:

- *Need for purpose.* "Present events draw meaning from their connection with future events." Purposes can be divided into (1) goals and (2) fulfillments. Life can be oriented toward a future anticipated state, such as living happily ever after or being in love.

Religion, Spirituality, and Coping

What is the relation between religion, spirituality, and the ability to cope with stress? In a study of 850 medically ill patients admitted to an acute-care hospital, religious coping was related to low depression (Koenig & others, 1992). Religious coping is often beneficial during times of high stress (Koenig, 2001). For example, in one study individuals were divided into those who were experiencing high stress and those with low stress (Manton, 1989). In the high-stress group, spiritual support was significantly related to low depression and high self-esteem. No such links were found in the low-stress group. One study revealed that when religion was an important aspect of people's lives, they frequently prayed, had positive religious core beliefs, worried less, were less anxious, and had a lower level of depressive symptoms (Rosmarin, Krumrei, & Andersson, 2009).

A recent interest in linking religion and coping focuses on **meaning-making coping**, which involves drawing on beliefs, values, and goals to change the meaning of a stressful situ-

How is religion linked to the ability to cope with stress?

ation, especially in times of chronic stress such as when a loved one dies. In Crystal Park's (2005, 2007, 2010, 2012a) view, religious individuals experience more disruption of their beliefs, values, and goals immediately after the death of a loved one than individuals who are not religious. Eventually, though, individuals who are religious often show better adjustment to the loss. Initially, religion is linked with more depressed feelings about a loved one's death. Over time, however, as religious individuals search for meaning in their loss, the depressed feelings lessen. Thus, religion can serve as a meaning system through which bereaved individuals are able to reframe their loss and even find avenues of personal growth.

If religion is linked to the ability to cope with stress better and if stress is linked to disease (as indicated earlier in the chapter), what then can be concluded about a possible indirect link between religion and disease?

Gabriel Dy-Liacco, Pastoral Counselor

Gabriel Dy-Liacco is a pastoral counselor at the Pastoral Counseling and Consultation Centers of Greater Washington, DC. He obtained his Ph.D. in pastoral counseling from Loyola College in Maryland and also has experience as a psychotherapist in mental health settings such as a substance-abuse program, military family center, psychiatric clinic, and community mental health center. As a pastoral counselor, he works with adolescents and adults in the aspects of their lives that they show the most concern about—psychological, spiritual, or the interface of both. Having lived in Peru, Japan, and the Philippines, he brings considerable multicultural experience to the counseling setting. Dr. Dy-Liacco also is a professor in the Graduate School of Psychology and Counseling at Regent University in the Washington, DC, area.

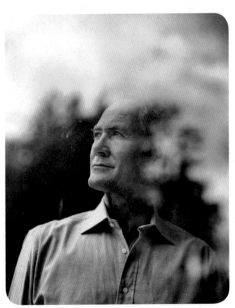

What characterizes the search for meaning in life?

- *Need for values.* This "can lend a sense of goodness or positive characterization of life and justify certain courses of action. Values enable people to decide whether certain acts are right or wrong." Frankl's (1984) view of meaning in life emphasized value as the main form of meaning that people need.
- *Need for a sense of efficacy.* This involves the "belief that one can make a difference. A life that had purposes and values but no efficacy would be tragic. The person might know what is desirable but could not do anything with that knowledge." With a sense of efficacy, people believe that they can control their environment, which has positive physical and mental health benefits (Bandura, 2009).
- *Need for self-worth.* Most individuals want to be "good, worthy persons. Self-worth can be pursued individually."

Researchers are increasingly studying the factors involved in a person's exploration of meaning in life and whether developing a sense of meaning in life is linked to positive developmental outcomes. Research indicates that many individuals state that religion played an important role in increasing their exploration of meaning in life (Krause, 2008, 2009). Studies also suggest that individuals who have found a sense of meaning in life are more physically healthy, happier, and experience less depression than their counterparts who report that they have not discovered meaning in life (Debats, 1990; Krause, 2004, 2009; Parquart, 2002).

Review Connect Reflect

LG5 Explain the roles of religion, spirituality, and meaning in life during middle adulthood.

Review

- What are some characteristics of religion and spirituality in middle-aged individuals?
- How are religion and spirituality linked to physical and mental health?
- What role does meaning in life play in middle adulthood?

Connect

- In this section, you read about religion and spirituality and middle adulthood. In Chapter 12, what did you learn about the role of religion in adolescents' lives?

Reflect *Your Own Personal Journey of Life*

- How important is meaning in life to you at this point in your development? What do you think the most important aspects of meaning in life are?

topical **connections**

In Chapter 17, you will read about biological views on why people age and what people can do to possibly slow down the aging process. You also will learn about the factors that influence life expectancy and what the lives of centenarians—people who live to be 100 or older—are like. The many physical changes that occur in late adulthood, including those involving the brain, also will be described in Chapter 17. In Chapter 18, you will learn about numerous cognitive changes in older adults, as well as work and retirement, mental health, and religion in their lives.

looking forward

Physical and Cognitive Development in Middle Adulthood

1 The Nature of Middle Adulthood

LG1 Explain how midlife is changing, and define middle adulthood.

- Changing Midlife

- Defining Middle Adulthood

- As more people live to an older age, what we think of as middle age seems to be occurring later. A major reason developmentalists are beginning to study middle age is the dramatic increase in the number of individuals entering this period of the life span.

- Middle age involves extensive individual variation. With this variation in mind, we will consider middle adulthood to be entered at about 40 to 45 years of age and exited at approximately 60 to 65 years of age. Middle adulthood is the age period in which gains and losses as well as biological and sociocultural factors balance each other. Some experts conclude that sociocultural factors influence development in midlife more than biological factors do.

2 Physical Development

LG2 Discuss physical changes in middle adulthood.

- Physical Changes

- Health, Disease, Stress, and Control

- Mortality Rates

- Sexuality

- The physical changes of midlife are usually gradual. Genetic and lifestyle factors play important roles in whether chronic diseases will appear and when. Among the physical changes of middle adulthood are changes in physical appearance (wrinkles, age spots); height (decrease) and weight (increase); strength, joints, and bones; vision and hearing; cardiovascular system; lungs; and sleep.

- In middle age, the frequency of accidents declines and individuals are less susceptible to colds and allergies. Chronic disorders rarely appear in early adulthood, increase in middle adulthood, and become more common in late adulthood. Arthritis is the leading chronic disorder in middle age, followed by hypertension. Men have more fatal chronic disorders, women more nonfatal ones in middle age. Immune system functioning declines with age. Emotional stress likely is an important factor contributing to cardiovascular disease. People who live in a chronically stressed condition are likelier to smoke, overeat, and not exercise. All of these stress-related behaviors are linked with cardiovascular disease. Culture and ethnicity play important roles in health and disease. Having a sense of control peaks in middle adulthood and is linked to many aspects of health and disease.

- In middle adulthood, chronic diseases are the main causes of death. Until recently, cardiovascular disease was the leading cause of death in middle age, but now cancer is the leading cause of death in this age group.

- Climacteric is the midlife transition in which fertility declines. The vast majority of women do not have serious physical or psychological problems related to menopause, which usually takes place in the late forties or early fifties, but menopause is an important marker because it signals the end of childbearing capability. Hormone replacement therapy (HRT) augments the declining levels of reproductive hormone production by the ovaries. HRT consists of various forms of estrogen, usually combined with progestin. Recent evidence of risks associated with HRT suggests that its long-term use should be seriously evaluated. Men do not experience an inability to father children in middle age, although their testosterone levels decline. A male menopause, like the dramatic decline in estrogen in women, does not occur. Sexual behavior occurs less frequently in middle adulthood than in early adulthood. Nonetheless, a majority of middle-aged adults show a moderate or strong interest in sex.

3 Cognitive Development

 LG3 Identify cognitive changes in middle adulthood.

Intelligence

- Horn argued that crystallized intelligence (accumulated information and verbal skills) continues to increase in middle adulthood, whereas fluid intelligence (ability to reason abstractly) begins to decline. Schaie and Willis found that longitudinal assessments of intellectual abilities are less likely than cross-sectional assessments to find declines in middle adulthood and are more likely to find improvements. The highest level of four intellectual abilities (vocabulary, verbal memory, inductive reasoning, and spatial orientation) occurred in middle age. Recent analysis shows considerable individual variation in intellectual abilities across middle adulthood and indicates that variations in some abilities are more predictive of cognitive impairment in late adulthood than others. Salthouse argues that decline in a number of cognitive functions begins in early adulthood and continues through the fifties. Declines have recently been identified in some aspects of neurobiological functioning that may be linked to age-related changes in cognitive functioning.

Information Processing

- Speed of information processing, often assessed through reaction time, continues to decline in middle adulthood. Although Schaie found that verbal memory increased in middle age, some researchers have found that memory declines in middle age. Working memory declines in late middle age. Memory is more likely to decline in middle age when individuals don't use effective strategies. Expertise involves having an extensive, highly organized knowledge and an understanding of a particular domain. Expertise often increases in middle adulthood. Practical problem solving remains stable in early and middle adulthood but declines in late adulthood.

4 Careers, Work, and Leisure

LG4 Characterize career development, work, and leisure in middle adulthood.

Work in Midlife

- For many people, midlife is a time of reflection, assessment, and evaluation of their current work and what they plan to do in the future. One important issue is whether individuals will continue to do the type of work they currently do or change jobs or careers.

Career Challenges and Changes

- Today's middle-aged workers face challenges such as the globalization of work, rapid developments in information technologies, downsizing of organizations, pressure to take early retirement, and concerns about pensions and health care. Midlife job or career changes can be self-motivated or forced on individuals.

Leisure

- We not only need to learn to work well, but we also need to learn to enjoy leisure. Midlife may be an especially important time for leisure because of the physical changes that occur and because of a desire to prepare for an active retirement.

5 Religion, Spirituality, and Meaning in Life

 LG5 Explain the roles of religion, spirituality, and meaning in life during middle adulthood.

Religion, Spirituality, and Adult Lives

- Religion and spirituality are important dimensions of many Americans' lives. Women show a stronger interest in religion and spirituality than men do. It is important to consider individual differences in religious and spiritual interest.

Religion, Spirituality, and Health

- In some cases, religion and spirituality can be negatively linked to physical health, as when cults or religious sects discourage individuals from obtaining medical care. In mainstream religions, researchers are increasingly finding that religion is positively related to health. Religion and spirituality can enhance coping for some individuals.

Meaning in Life

- Frankl argues that examining the finiteness of our existence leads to exploration of meaning in life. Faced with the death of older relatives and less time to live themselves, many middle-aged individuals increasingly examine life's meaning. Baumeister and Vohs argue that a quest for a meaningful life involves fulfilling four main needs: purpose, values, efficacy, and self-worth.

key terms

middle adulthood 485
metabolic syndrome 488
chronic disorders 490
climacteric 491

menopause 491
erectile dysfunction (ED) 493
crystallized intelligence 495
fluid intelligence 495

leisure 500
religion 500
religiousness 500
spirituality 501

meaning-making
coping 502

key people

Gilbert Brim 485
David Almeida 490
Margie Lachman 491
John Horn 495

K. Warner Schaie 495
Sherry Willis 496
Timothy Salthouse 497
Denise Park 498

Nancy Denney 498
Pamela King 501
John Clausen 502
Crystal Park 503

Viktor Frankl 502
Roy Baumeister 502
Kathleen Vohs 502

Chapter *15* | PHYSICAL AND COGNITIVE DEVELOPMENT IN MIDDLE ADULTHOOD

Connecting with

Learning Objectives	Application Activities	Activity Type	Page Reference
Discuss physical changes in middle adulthood.	Middle Adulthood Perspectives on Body Image	Milestones: Transitions	pp. 486–489
Discuss sexuality in middle adulthood.	Middle Adulthood Perspectives on Sexuality	Milestones: Transitions	pp. 491–494
Explain information processing in middle adulthood.	Middle Adulthood Perspectives on Thinking and Memory	Milestones: Transitions	pp. 497–499
	Working Memory	Interactive exercise	

SOCIOEMOTIONAL DEVELOPMENT IN MIDDLE ADULTHOOD

chapter **outline**

Forty-five-year-old Sarah feels tired, depressed, and angry when she looks back on the way her life has gone. She became pregnant when she was 17 and married Ben, the baby's father. They stayed together for three years after their son was born, and then Ben left her for another woman. Sarah went to work as a salesclerk to make ends meet. Eight years later, she married Alan, who had two children from a previous marriage. Sarah stopped working for several years to care for the children. Then, like Ben, Alan started seeing someone else. Sarah found out about it from a friend. Nevertheless, Sarah stayed with Alan for another year. Finally, he was gone so much that she could not take it anymore and decided to divorce him. Sarah went back to work again as a salesclerk; she has been in the same position for 16 years now. During those 16 years, she dated a number of men, but the relationships never seemed to work out. Her son never finished high school and has drug problems. Her father died last year, and Sarah is trying to help her mother financially, although she can barely pay her own bills. Sarah looks in the mirror and does not like what she sees. She sees her past as a shambles, and her future does not look rosy, either.

Forty-five-year-old Wanda feels energetic, happy, and satisfied. As a young woman, she graduated from college and worked for three years as a high school math teacher. She married Andy, who had just finished law school. One year later, they had their first child, Josh. Wanda stayed home with Josh for two years, and then returned to her job as a math teacher. Even during her pregnancy, Wanda stayed active and exercised regularly, playing tennis almost every day. After her pregnancy, she kept up her exercise habits. Wanda and Andy had another child, Wendy. Now, as they move into their middle-age years, their children are both off at college, and Wanda and Andy are enjoying spending more time with each other. Last weekend, they visited Josh at his college, and the weekend before they visited Wendy at hers. Wanda continued working as a high school math teacher until six years ago. She had developed computer skills as part of her job and had taken some computer courses at a nearby college.

topical **connections**

Emerging adulthood, which occurs from approximately 18 to 25 years of age, is a transitional period between adolescence and early adulthood, during which time individuals intensely explore their identity and experience instability in different contexts. A secure attachment style benefits young adults. Love and possibly marriage become central aspects of many young adults' socioemotional development. Searching for a balance between the need for independence and freedom and the need for intimacy and commitment characterizes the lives of many young adults. Many young adults not only are marrying later or not at all but are having children later than in past decades. Many young adults cohabit with a romantic partner.

*looking **back***

She resigned her math teaching job and took a job with a computer company, where she has already worked her way into management. Wanda looks in the mirror and likes what she sees. She sees her past as enjoyable, although not without hills and valleys, and she looks toward the future with enthusiasm.

preview

As with Sarah and Wanda, there are individual variations in the way people experience middle age. To begin the chapter, we will examine personality theories and development in middle age, including ideas about individual variation. Then we will turn our attention to how much individuals change or stay the same as they go through the adult years. Finally we will explore a number of aspects of close relationships during middle adulthood.

1 Personality Theories and Adult Development

LG1 Describe personality theories and socioemotional development in middle adulthood.

- Stages of Adulthood
- The Life-Events Approach
- Stress and Personal Control in Midlife
- Context of Midlife Development

What is the best way to conceptualize middle age? Is it a stage or a crisis? How extensively is middle age influenced by life events? Do middle-aged adults experience stress and personal control differently from adults at other life stages? Is personality linked with contexts such as the point in history when individuals go through midlife, their culture, and their gender?

> The generations of living things pass in a short time, and like runners, hand on the torch of life.
>
> —LUCRETIUS
> *Roman Poet, 1st Century B.C.*

STAGES OF ADULTHOOD

Adult stage theories have been plentiful, and they have contributed to the view that midlife brings a crisis in development. Two prominent theories that define stages of adult development are Erik Erikson's life-span view and Daniel Levinson's seasons of a man's life.

Erikson's Stage of Generativity Versus Stagnation Erikson (1968) proposed that middle-aged adults face a significant issue—generativity versus stagnation, which is the name Erikson gave to the seventh stage in his life-span theory. Generativity encompasses adults' desire to leave legacies of themselves to the next generation (Busch & Hofer, 2012). Through these legacies adults achieve a kind of immortality. By contrast, stagnation (sometimes called "self-absorption") develops when individuals sense that they have done nothing for the next generation.

Middle-aged adults can develop generativity in a number of ways (Kotre, 1984). Through biological generativity, adults have offspring. Through parental generativity, adults nurture and guide children. Through work generativity, adults develop skills that are passed down to others. And through cultural generativity, adults create, renovate, or conserve some aspect of culture that ultimately survives.

Adults promote and guide the next generation by parenting, teaching, leading, and doing things that benefit the community. One of the participants in a study of aging said: "From twenty to thirty I learned how to get along with my wife. From thirty to forty I learned how to be a success at my job, and at forty to fifty I worried less about myself and more about the children" (Vaillant, 2002, p. 114). Generative adults commit themselves to the continuation

developmental **connection**

Personality

Erikson's early adulthood stage is intimacy versus isolation and his late adulthood stage is integrity versus despair. Chapter 14, p. 457; Chapter 19, p. 596

and improvement of society as a whole through their connection to the next generation. Generative adults develop a positive legacy of the self and then offer it as a gift to the next generation.

Does research support Erikson's theory that generativity is an important dimension of middle age? Yes, it does (Newton & Stewart, 2012). In George Vaillant's (2002) longitudinal studies of aging, generativity (defined in this study as "taking care of the next generation") in middle age was more strongly related than intimacy to whether individuals would have an enduring and happy marriage at 75 to 80 years of age.

Other research also supports Erikson's (1968) view on the importance of generativity in middle adulthood. In one study, Carol Ryff (1984) examined the views of women and men at different ages and found that middle-aged adults especially were concerned about generativity. In a longitudinal study of Smith College women, the desire for generativity increased as the participants aged from their thirties to their fifties (Stewart, Ostrove, & Helson, 2001) (see Figure 16.1). And in a recent study, generativity was strongly linked to middle-aged adults' positive social engagement in contexts such as family life and community activities (Cox & others, 2010).

FIGURE 16.1

CHANGES IN GENERATIVITY FROM THE THIRTIES THROUGH THE FIFTIES. Generativity increased in Smith College women as they aged from their thirties through their fifties (Stewart, Ostrove, & Helson, 2001). The women rated themselves on a 3-point scale indicating the extent to which they thought the statements about generativity were descriptive of their lives. Higher scores reflect greater generativity.

Levinson's Seasons of a Man's Life In *The Seasons of a Man's Life* (1978), clinical psychologist Daniel Levinson reported the results of extensive interviews with 40 middle-aged men. The interviews were conducted with hourly workers, business executives, academic biologists, and novelists. Levinson bolstered his conclusions with information from the biographies of famous men and the development of memorable characters in literature. Although Levinson's major interest focused on midlife change, he described a number of stages and transitions during the period from 17 to 65 years of age, as shown in Figure 16.2. Levinson emphasizes that developmental tasks must be mastered at each stage.

At the end of one's teens, according to Levinson, a transition from dependence to independence should occur. This transition is marked by the formation of a dream—an image of the kind of life the youth wants to have, especially in terms of a career and marriage. Levinson sees the twenties as a novice phase of adult development. It is a time of reasonably free experimentation and of testing the dream in the real world. In early adulthood, the two major tasks to be mastered are exploring the possibilities for adult living and developing a stable life structure.

From about the ages of 28 to 33, a man goes through a transition period in which he must face the more serious question of determining his goals. During the thirties, he usually focuses on family and career development. In the later years of this period, he enters a phase of Becoming One's Own Man (or BOOM, as Levinson calls it). By age 40, he has reached a stable point in his career, has outgrown his earlier, more tenuous attempts at learning to become an adult, and now must look forward to the kind of life he will lead as a middle-aged adult.

According to Levinson, the transition to middle adulthood lasts about five years (ages 40 to 45) and requires the adult male to come to grips with four major conflicts that have existed in his life since adolescence: (1) being young versus being old, (2) being destructive versus being constructive, (3) being masculine versus being feminine, and (4) being attached to others versus being separated from them. Seventy to 80 percent of the men Levinson interviewed found the midlife transition tumultuous and psychologically painful, as many aspects of their lives came into question. According to Levinson, the success of the midlife

Late adult transition: Age 60 to 65

Era of late adulthood: 60 to ?

Middle adult transition: Age 40 to 45

Culminating life structure for middle adulthood: 55 to 60

Age 50 transition: 50 to 55

Entry life structure for middle adulthood: 45 to 50

Early adult transition: Age 17 to 22

Culminating life structure for early adulthood: 33 to 40

Age 30 transition: 28 to 33

Entry life structure for early adulthood: 22 to 28

FIGURE 16.2

LEVINSON'S PERIODS OF ADULT DEVELOPMENT. According to Daniel Levinson, adulthood for men has three main stages that are surrounded by transition periods. Specific tasks and challenges are associated with each stage.

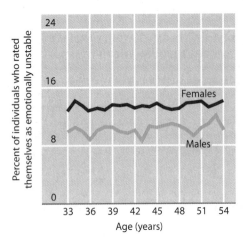

FIGURE **16.3**

EMOTIONAL INSTABILITY AND AGE. In one longitudinal study, the emotional instability of individuals was assessed from age 33 to age 54 (McCrae & Costa, 1990). No significant increase in emotional instability occurred during the middle-aged years.

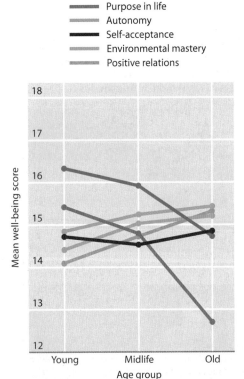

FIGURE **16.4**

AGE AND WELL-BEING. In one study, six dimensions of well-being (self-acceptance, positive relations, personal growth, purpose in life, environmental mastery, and autonomy) were assessed in three different age groups of individuals (young adults, middle-aged adults, and older adults) (Keyes & Ryff, 1998). An increase or little change in most of the dimensions of well-being occurred during middle adulthood.

transition rests on how effectively the individual reduces the polarities and accepts each of them as an integral part of his being.

Because Levinson interviewed middle-aged men, we can consider the data about middle adulthood more valid than the data about early adulthood. When individuals are asked to remember information about earlier parts of their lives, they may distort and forget things. The original Levinson data included no women, although Levinson (1996) reported that his stages, transitions, and the crisis of middle age hold for women as well as men. Levinson's work included no statistical analysis. However, the quality and quantity of the Levinson biographies make them outstanding examples of the clinical tradition.

How Pervasive Are Midlife Crises? Levinson (1978) views midlife as a crisis, arguing that the middle-aged adult is suspended between the past and the future, trying to cope with this gap that threatens life's continuity. George Vaillant (1977) has a different view. Vaillant's study—called the "Grant Study"—involved Harvard University men in their early thirties and in their late forties who initially had been interviewed as undergraduates. He concludes that just as adolescence is a time for detecting parental flaws and discovering the truth about childhood, the forties are a decade of reassessing and recording the truth about the adolescent and adulthood years. However, whereas Levinson sees midlife as a crisis, Vaillant maintains that only a minority of adults experience a midlife crisis:

> Just as pop psychologists have reveled in the not-so-common high drama of adolescent turmoil, also the popular press, sensing good copy, had made all too much of the mid-life crisis. The term *mid-life crisis* brings to mind some variation of the renegade minister who leaves behind four children and the congregation that loved him in order to drive off in a magenta Porsche with a 25-year-old striptease artiste. As with adolescent turmoil, mid-life crises are much rarer in community samples. (pp. 222–223)

Thus, for most people midlife is not a crisis (Pudrovska, 2009). As we saw in Chapter 15, many cognitive skills, such as vocabulary, verbal memory, and inductive reasoning, peak in midlife, and many individuals reach the height of their career success in midlife. Further, reports of general well-being and life satisfaction tend to be high during middle adulthood (Martin, Grunendahl, & Martin, 2001).

A number of research studies have documented that midlife is not characterized by pervasive crises:

- One study found that 26 percent of middle-aged U.S. adults said they had experienced a midlife crisis, but most attributed the crisis to negative life events rather than aging (Wethington, Kessler, & Pixley, 2004).
- A longitudinal study of more than 2,000 individuals found few midlife crises (McCrae & Costa, 1990; Siegler & Costa, 1999). In this study, the emotional instability of individuals did not significantly increase during their middle-aged years (see Figure 16.3).
- A study of individuals described as young (average age 19), middle-aged (average age 46), and older (average age 73) adults found that their ability to master their environment, autonomy, and personal relations improved during middle age (Keyes & Ryff, 1998) (see Figure 16.4).

Adult development experts are virtually unanimous in their belief that midlife crises have been exaggerated (Brim, Ryff, & Kessler, 2004; Lachman, 2004; Pudrovska, 2009; Wethington, Kessler, & Pixley, 2004). In sum:

- The stage theories place too much emphasis on crises in development, especially midlife crises.
- There often is considerable individual variation in the way people experience the stages, a topic that we will turn to next.

Individual Variations Stage theories focus on the universals of adult personality development as they try to pin down stages that all individuals go through in their adult lives. These theories do not adequately address individual variations in adult development. One extensive study of a random sample of 500 men at midlife, for example, found extensive individual variation among men (Farrell & Rosenberg, 1981). In the individual variations view, middle-aged adults interpret, shape, alter, and give meaning to their lives.

Some individuals may experience a midlife crisis in some contexts of their lives but not others (Lachman, 2004). For example, turmoil and stress may characterize a person's life at work even while things are going smoothly at home.

Researchers have found that in one-third of the cases in which individuals have reported going through a midlife crisis, the "crisis is triggered by life events such as a job loss, financial problems, or illness" (Lachman, 2004, p. 315). Let's now explore the role of life events in midlife development.

THE LIFE-EVENTS APPROACH

Age-related stages represent one major way to examine adult personality development. A second major way to conceptualize adult personality development is to focus on life events (Luhmann & others, 2012; Schwarzer & Luszezynska, 2013). In the early version of the life-events approach, life events were viewed as taxing circumstances for individuals, forcing them to change their personality (Holmes & Rahe, 1967). Events such as the death of a spouse, divorce, marriage, and so on were believed to involve varying degrees of stress, and therefore likely to influence the individual's development.

Today's life-events approach is more sophisticated. In the **contemporary life-events approach,** how life events influence the individual's development depends not only on the life event itself but also on mediating factors (such as physical health and family supports), the individual's adaptation to the life event (such as appraisal of the threat and coping strategies), the life-stage context, and the sociohistorical context (see Figure 16.5). For example, if individuals are in poor health and have little family support, life events are likely to be more stressful. And a divorce may be more stressful after many years of marriage when adults are in their fifties than when they have been married only several years and are in their twenties, a finding indicating that the life-stage context of an event makes a difference. The sociohistorical context also makes a difference. For example, adults may be able to cope more effectively with divorce today than in the 1950s because divorce has become more commonplace and accepted in today's society. Whatever the context or mediating variables, however, one individual may perceive a life event as highly stressful, whereas another individual may perceive the same event as a challenge.

Although the life-events approach offers valuable insights for understanding adult development, it has its drawbacks. One drawback is that the life-events approach places too much emphasis on change. It does not adequately recognize the stability that, at least to some degree, characterizes adult development.

Another drawback is that it may not be life's major events that are the primary sources of stress, but our daily experiences (Almeida & others, 2011). Enduring a boring but tense job or living in poverty does not show up on scales of major life events. Yet the everyday pounding from these conditions can add up to a highly stressful life and eventually illness. Greater insight into the source of life's stresses might come from focusing more on daily hassles and daily uplifts (McIntosh, Gillanders, & Rodgers, 2010). Researchers have found that young and middle-aged adults experience a greater daily frequency of stressors than older individuals (Almeida & Horn, 2004). In a recent study, healthy older adult women 63 to 93 years of age reported their daily experiences over the course of one week (Charles & others, 2010). In this study, the older the women were, the fewer stressors and less frequent negative affect they reported.

One study found that the most frequent daily hassles of college students were wasting time, concerns about meeting high standards, and being lonely (Kanner & others, 1981).

> Mid-life crises are greatly exaggerated in America.
>
> —**George Vaillant**
> *Contemporary Psychologist, Harvard University*

developmental **connection**

Stress

Adolescence has been characterized too negatively, dating from Hall's storm and stress view of adolescents. Chapter 11, p. 356

FIGURE 16.5

A CONTEMPORARY LIFE-EVENTS FRAMEWORK FOR INTERPRETING ADULT DEVELOPMENTAL CHANGE. According to the contemporary life-events approach, the influence of a life event depends on the event itself, on mediating variables, on the life-stage and sociohistorical context, and on the individual's appraisal of the event and coping strategies.

contemporary life-events approach Approach emphasizing that how a life event influences the individual's development depends not only on the life event, but also on mediating factors, the individual's adaptation to the life event, the life-stage context, and the sociohistorical context.

Daily Hassles	Percentage of Times Checked
Concerns about weight	52.4
Health of family member	48.1
Rising prices of common goods	43.7
Home maintenance	42.8
Too many things to do	38.6
Misplacing or losing things	38.1
Yardwork/outside home maintenance	38.1
Property, investment, or taxes	37.6
Crime	37.1
Physical appearance	35.9

Daily Uplifts	
Relating well with your spouse or lover	76.3
Relating well with friends	74.4
Completing a task	73.3
Feeling healthy	72.7
Getting enough sleep	69.7
Eating out	68.4
Meeting your responsibilities	68.1
Visiting, phoning, or writing someone	67.7
Spending time with family	66.7
Home (inside) pleasing to you	65.5

FIGURE **16.6**

THE TEN MOST FREQUENT DAILY HASSLES AND UPLIFTS OF MIDDLE-AGED ADULTS OVER A NINE-MONTH PERIOD.
How do these hassles compare with your own?

How do women and men differ in the way they experience and respond to stressors?

Among the most frequent uplifts of the college students were entertainment, getting along well with friends, and completing a task. In this same study, the most frequent daily hassles of middle-aged adults were concerns about weight and the health of a family member, while their most frequent daily uplifts involved relating well with a spouse or lover, or a friend (see Figure 16.6). And the middle-aged adults were more likely than the college students to report that their daily hassles involved economic concerns (rising prices and taxes, for example).

The manner in which different stressors affect health varies—life events often produce prolonged arousal whereas daily stressors are linked to spikes in arousal (Piazza & others, 2010). Consider caring for a spouse who has Alzheimer disease. In this case, a life event (spouse diagnosed with an incurable disease) produces chronic stress for the caregiver, which also is linked to the daily stressors involved in caring for the individual.

Critics of the daily hassles approach argue that some of the same problems involved with life-events scales occur when daily hassles are assessed. For example, knowing about an adult's daily hassles tells us nothing about physical changes, about how the individual copes with hassles, or about how the individual perceives hassles.

STRESS AND PERSONAL CONTROL IN MIDLIFE

As we have seen, there is conclusive evidence that midlife is not a time when a majority of adults experience a tumultuous crisis, but when they do experience a midlife crisis it is often linked to stressful life events. Do middle-aged adults experience stress differently from young adults and older adults?

Stress, Personal Control, and Age   One study using daily diaries over a one-week period found that both young and middle-aged adults had more days that were stressful and that were characterized by multiple stresses than older adults (Almeida & Horn, 2004). In this study, although young adults experienced daily stressors more frequently than middle-aged adults, middle-aged adults experienced more "overload" stressors that involved juggling too many activities at once. Another study also revealed that middle-aged and older adults showed a smaller increase in psychological distress to interpersonal stressors than did younger adults, and middle-aged adults were less physically reactive to work stressors than were younger adults (Neupert, Almeida, & Charles, 2007).

To what extent do middle-aged adults perceive that they can control what happens to them? As you read in Chapter 15, researchers have found that on average a sense of personal control peaks in midlife and then declines (Lachman, 2006). In one study, approximately 80 percent of the young adults (25 to 39 years of age), 71 percent of the middle-aged adults (40 to 59 years of age), and 62 percent of the older adults (60 to 75 years of age) reported that they were often in control of their lives (Lachman & Firth, 2004). However, some aspects of personal control increase with age while others decrease (Lachman, Neupert, & Agrigoroaei, 2011). For example, middle-aged adults feel they have a greater sense of control over their finances, work, and marriage than younger adults but less control over their sex life and their children (Lachman & Firth, 2004).

Stress and Gender   Women and men differ in the way they experience and respond to stressors (Almeida & others, 2011). Women are more vulnerable to social stressors such as those involving romance, family, and work. For example, women experience higher levels of stress when things go wrong in romantic and marital relationships. Women also are more likely than men to become depressed when they encounter stressful life events such as divorce or the death of a friend. A recent study of more than 2,800 adults 50 years and older in Taiwan also found that women were more susceptible to depressive symptoms when they felt constant stress from finances, increasing stress from jobs, and fluctuating stress in family relationships (Lin & others, 2011).

When men face stress, they are more likely to respond in a **fight-or-flight** manner—become aggressive, socially withdraw, or drink alcohol. By contrast, according to

Shelley Taylor and her colleagues (2011a, b, c; Taylor & others, 2000), when women experience stress, they are more likely to engage in a **tend-and-befriend** pattern, seeking social alliances with others, especially friends. Taylor argues that when women experience stress an influx of the hormone *oxytocin*, which is linked to nurturing in animals, is released.

CONTEXTS OF MIDLIFE DEVELOPMENT

Both Sarah and Wanda, whose stories appeared at the beginning of this chapter, are working mothers. In almost every other way, however, their lives could scarcely be more different. Why? Part of the answer might lie in the different contexts of their lives. The contemporary life-events approach (like Bronfenbrenner's theory, discussed in Chapter 1) highlights the importance of the complex setting of our lives—of everything from our income and family supports to our sociohistorical circumstances. Let's examine how three aspects of the contexts of life influence development during middle adulthood: historical contexts (cohort effects), gender, and culture.

Historical Contexts (Cohort Effects)   Some developmentalists conclude that changing historical times and different social expectations influence how different cohorts—groups of individuals born in the same year or time period—move through the life span (Schaie, 2010, 2012). Bernice Neugarten (1986) argues that our values, attitudes, expectations, and behaviors are influenced by the period in which we live. For example, individuals born during the difficult times of the Great Depression may have a different outlook on life from those born during the optimistic 1950s, says Neugarten.

Neugarten (1986) holds that the social environment of a particular age group can alter its **social clock**—the timetable on which individuals are expected to accomplish life's tasks, such as getting married, having children, or establishing themselves in a career. Social clocks provide guides for our lives; individuals whose lives are not synchronized with these social clocks find life to be more stressful than those who are on schedule, says Neugarten. For example, the fact that Sarah's pregnancy occurred when she was a teenager probably increased the stressfulness of that pregnancy. Neugarten argues that today there is much less agreement than in the past on the right age or sequence for the occurrence of major life events such as having children or retiring. Indeed, one study found that between the late 1950s and the late 1970s, there was a dramatic decline in adults' beliefs that there is a "best age" for major life events and achievements (Passuth, Maines, & Neugarten, 1984) (see Figure 16.7).

Gender Contexts   Critics say that the stage theories of adult development have a male bias. For example, the central focus of stage theories is on career choice and work achievement, which historically have dominated men's life choices and life chances more than women's. The stage theories do not adequately address women's concerns about relationships, interdependence, and caring (Gilligan, 1982). The adult stage theories have also placed little importance on childbearing and child rearing. Women's family roles are complex and often have a higher salience in their lives than in men's lives. The role demands that women experience in balancing career and family are usually not experienced as intensely by men.

Should midlife and the years beyond be feared by women as a time of declining youth and opportunity? Or is middle adulthood a new prime of life, a time for renewal, for shedding preoccupations with a youthful appearance and body, and for seeking new challenges, valuing maturity, and enjoying change?

In one study, the early fifties were indeed a new prime of life for many women (Mitchell & Helson, 1990). In this sample of 700 women aged 26 to 80, women in their early fifties most often described their lives as "first-rate." Conditions that distinguished the lives of women in their early fifties from those of women in other age periods included more "empty nests," better health, higher income, and more concern for parents. Women in their early fifties showed confidence, involvement, security, and breadth of personality.

In sum, the view that midlife is a negative age period for women is stereotypical, as so many perceptions of age periods are. Midlife is a diversified, heterogeneous period for women, just as it is for men.

developmental **connection**

Research Methods

Cohort effects have also been described as normative, history-graded influences. Chapter 1, p. 34

Critics say the stage theories of adult development reflect a male bias by emphasizing career choice and achievement, and that they do not adequately address women's concerns about relationships, interdependence, and caring. The stage theories assume a normative sequence of development, but as women's roles have become more varied and complex, determining what is normative is difficult. *What kinds of changes have taken place in middle-aged women's lives in recent years?*

fight-or-flight The view that when men experience stress, they are more likely to engage in a fight-or-flight pattern, as reflected in being aggressive, withdrawing from social contact, or drinking alcohol.

tend-and-befriend Taylor's view that when women experience stress, they are likely to engage in a tend-and-befriend pattern, seeking social alliances with others, especially female friends.

social clock The timetable according to which individuals are expected to accomplish life's tasks, such as getting married, having children, or establishing themselves in a career.

Activity/event	Appropriate age range	Percent who agree (late '50s study)		Percent who agree (late '70s study)	
		Men	Women	Men	Women
Best age for a man to marry	20–25	80	90	42	42
Best age for a woman to marry	19–24	85	90	44	36
When most people should become grandparents	45–50	84	79	64	57
Best age for most people to finish school and go to work	20–22	86	82	36	38
When most men should be settled on a career	24–26	74	64	24	26
When most men hold their top jobs	45–50	71	58	38	31
When most people should be ready to retire	60–65	83	86	66	41
When a man has the most responsibilities	35–50	79	75	49	50
When a man accomplishes most	40–50	82	71	46	41
The prime of life for a man	35–50	86	80	59	66
When a woman has the most responsibilities	25–40	93	91	59	53
When a woman accomplishes the most	30–45	94	92	57	48

FIGURE **16.7**

INDIVIDUALS' CONCEPTIONS OF THE BEST AGE FOR MAJOR LIFE EVENTS AND ACHIEVEMENTS: LATE 1950S AND LATE 1970S. *What do you think is the best age to experience each of these major life events and accomplishments?*

Cultural Contexts   In many cultures, especially nonindustrialized cultures, the concept of middle age is not very clear, or in some cases is absent. It is common in nonindustrialized societies to describe individuals as young or old but not as middle-aged (Grambs, 1989). Some cultures have no words for "adolescent," "young adult," or "middle-aged adult."

Consider the Gusii culture, located south of the equator in the African country of Kenya. The Gusii divide the life course differently for females and males (LeVine, 1979): females: (1) infant, (2) uncircumcised girl, (3) circumcised girl, (4) married woman, and (5) female elder; males: (1) infant, (2) uncircumcised boy, (3) circumcised boy warrior, and (4) male elder. Thus, movement from one status to the next is due primarily to life events, not age, in the Gusii culture.

Although the Gusii do not have a clearly labeled midlife transition, some of the Gusii adults do reassess their lives around the age of 40. At this time, these Gusii adults examine their current status and the limited time they have remaining in their lives. Their physical strength is decreasing, and they know they cannot farm their land forever, so they seek spiritual powers by becoming ritual practitioners or healers. As in the American culture, however, a midlife crisis in the Gusii culture is the exception rather than the rule.

What is middle age like for women in other cultures? It depends on the modernity of the culture and the culture's view of gender roles. Some anthropologists conclude that when women become middle-aged in nonindustrialized societies they may experience certain advantages (Brown, 1985). First, they are often freed from cumbersome restrictions that were placed on them when they were younger. For example, in middle age they enjoy greater geographical mobility. Child care has ceased or can be delegated, and domestic chores are reduced. They may venture forth from the village for commercial opportunities, visits to relatives living at a distance, and religious events. Second, with middle age a woman has the right to exercise authority over specified younger kin. Middle-aged women can extract labor from younger family members. The work of middle-aged women tends to be administrative, delegating tasks

Gusii dancers perform on habitat day in Nairobi, Kenya. Movement from one status to another in the Gusii culture is due primarily to life events, not age. The Gusii do not have a clearly labeled midlife transition.

and making assignments to younger women. Middle-aged women also make important decisions for certain members of the younger generation: what a grandchild is to be named, who is ready to be initiated, and who is eligible to marry whom. A third major change brought on by middle age in nonindustrialized societies is eligibility for special statuses and the possibility that these provide recognition beyond the household. These statuses include the vocations of midwife, curer, holy woman, and matchmaker.

Review *Connect* Reflect

 LG1 Describe personality theories and socioemotional development in middle adulthood.

Review

- What are some theories of adult stages of development?
- What is the life-events approach?
- How do middle-aged adults experience stress and personal control differently from young and older adults?
- How do contexts influence midlife development?

Connect

- In this section, you read that some researchers criticize the stage theories of

adult development as having a male bias. What did you learn about gender bias in research in Chapter 1?

Reflect *Your Own Personal Journey of Life*

- Which approach makes more sense—adult stage or life events—in explaining your own development as you go through adulthood? Or do you think both approaches should be considered in understanding your adult development? Explain your answer.

2 Stability and Change

LG2 Discuss stability and change in development during middle adulthood, as reflected in longitudinal studies.

Longitudinal Studies

Conclusions

Sarah's adult life, described in the chapter opening, has followed a painful path. Were her sorrows inevitable as a result of how she learned to cope with problems earlier in life? Is it possible for her, in middle age, to change her coping strategies or how she relates to other people?

LONGITUDINAL STUDIES

We will examine four longitudinal studies to help us understand the extent to which there is stability or change in adult development: Costa and McCrae's Baltimore Study, the Berkeley Longitudinal Studies, Helson's Mills College Study, and Vaillant's studies.

Costa and McCrae's Baltimore Study A major study of adult personality development continues to be conducted by Paul Costa and Robert McCrae (1998; McCrae & Costa, 2003, 2006). They focus on what are called the **big five factors of personality,** which are openness to experience, conscientiousness, extraversion, agreeableness, and neuroticism (emotional stability); they are described in Figure 16.8. (Notice that if you create an acronym from these factor names, you will get the word OCEAN.) A number of research studies point toward these factors as important dimensions of personality (Hill & others, 2012; Lucas & Donnellan, 2011; Roberts, Donnellan, & Hill, 2013).

Using their five-factor personality test, Costa and McCrae (1995, 2000) studied approximately 1,000 college-educated men and women ages 20 to 96, assessing the same individuals over many years. Data collection began in the 1950s to the mid-1960s and is ongoing. Costa and McCrae concluded that considerable stability occurs in the five personality factors—emotional stability, extraversion, openness, agreeableness, and conscientiousness. However, more recent research indicates greater developmental changes in the five personality factors in adulthood (Lucas & Donnellan, 2011; Soto & others, 2011). For example, a recent study found that

developmental **connection**

Life-Span Perspective

The extent to which development is characterized by stability and/or change is one of the key issues in the study of life-span development. Chapter 1, p. 7

big five factors of personality Emotional stability (neuroticism), extraversion, openness to experience, agreeableness, and conscientiousness.

Openness	**C**onscientiousness	**E**xtraversion	**A**greeableness	**N**euroticism (emotional stability)
• Imaginative or practical • Interested in variety or routine • Independent or conforming	• Organized or disorganized • Careful or careless • Disciplined or impulsive	• Sociable or retiring • Fun-loving or somber • Affectionate or reserved	• Softhearted or ruthless • Trusting or suspicious • Helpful or uncooperative	• Calm or anxious • Secure or insecure • Self-satisfied or self-pitying

FIGURE 16.8

THE BIG FIVE FACTORS OF PERSONALITY.
Each of the broad supertraits encompasses more narrow traits and characteristics. Use the acronym OCEAN to remember the Big Five personality factors: openness, conscientiousness, extraversion, agreeableness, neuroticism.

developmental **connection**

Personality

The big five factors are linked to how old people will live to be. Chapter 19, p. 603

Based on their study of middle-aged women, Ravenna Helson and her colleagues described the women as experiencing a midlife consciousness rather than a midlife crisis. *What were some other findings in the Mills College study?*

emotional stability, extraversion, openness, and agreeableness were lower in early adulthood, peaked between 40 and 60 years of age, and decreased in late adulthood, while conscientiousness showed a continuous increase from early adulthood to late adulthood (Specht, Egloff, & Schukle, 2011). In this study, personality traits changed the most in early adulthood and late adulthood, but most research studies indicate that the greatest change occurs in early adulthood (Lucas & Donnellan, 2011; Roberts, Donnellan, & Hill, 2013; Roberts, Walton, & Viechtbauer, 2006).

Further evidence for the importance of the big five factors indicates that they are related to such important aspects of a person's life as health, intelligence, achievement and work, and relationships (McCrae, Gaines, & Wellington, 2013). The following research reflects these links:

- Across a 10-year period, four of the five big five factors (the exception being openness) predicted health outcomes involving physical health, blood pressure, and number of days limited at work or home due to physical health factors (Turiano & others, 2012). Individuals high on neuroticism report more health complaints (Carver & Connor-Smith, 2010).
- One study revealed that openness was related to superior cognitive functioning and IQ across the life span (Sharp & others, 2010).
- A study found that conscientiousness was related to college students' grade point averages (Noftle & Robins, 2007). A meta-analysis revealed that openness was linked to pursuing entrepreneurial goals such as starting a new business, and to success in those pursuits (Zhao, Seibert, & Lumpkin, 2010).
- Individuals high on agreeableness were more likely to have satisfying romantic relationships (Donnellan, Larsen-Rife, & Conger, 2005).

The big five factors also are related to changing historical circumstances. In a longitudinal study of women in their twenties to their seventies, the big five factors were linked to cultural influences, such as changes in the traditional feminine role, the women's movement, and graduate education in careers (George, Helson, & John, 2011).

Berkeley Longitudinal Studies   In the Berkeley Longitudinal Studies, more than 500 children and their parents were initially studied in the late 1920s and early 1930s. The book *Present and Past in Middle Life* (Eichorn & others, 1981) profiles these individuals as they became middle-aged. The results from early adolescence through a portion of midlife did not support either extreme in the debate over whether personality is characterized by stability or change. Some characteristics were more stable than others, however. The most stable characteristics were the degree to which individuals were intellectually oriented, self-confident, and open to new experiences. The characteristics that changed the most included the extent to which the individuals were nurturant or hostile and whether or not they had good self-control.

John Clausen (1993), one of the researchers in the Berkeley Longitudinal Studies, stresses that too much attention has been given to discontinuities for all members of the human species, as exemplified in the adult stage theories. He points out that some people experience recurrent crises and change a great deal over the life course, whereas others have more stable, continuous lives and change far less.

Helson's Mills College Study   Another longitudinal investigation of adult personality development was conducted by Ravenna Helson and her colleagues (George, Helson, & John, 2011; Helson, 1997; Helson & Wink, 1992; Stewart, Ostrove, & Helson, 2001). They initially studied 132 women who were seniors at Mills College in California in the late 1950s and then studied them again when they were in their thirties, forties, and fifties. Helson and her colleagues distinguished three main groups among the Mills women: family-oriented, career-oriented (whether or not they also wanted families), and those who followed neither path (women without children who pursued only low-level work).

During their early forties, many of the women shared the concerns that stage theorists such as Levinson found in men: concern for young and old, introspectiveness, interest in roots, and awareness of limitations and death. However, the researchers in the Mills College Study concluded that rather than being in a midlife crisis, the women were experiencing *midlife consciousness*. The researchers also indicated that commitment to the tasks of early adulthood—whether to a career or family (or both)—helped women learn to control their impulses, develop interpersonal skills, become independent, and work hard to achieve goals. Women who did not commit themselves to one of these lifestyle patterns faced fewer challenges and did not develop as fully as the other women (Rosenfeld & Stark, 1987).

In the Mills College Study, some women moved toward becoming "pillars of society" in their early forties to early fifties. Menopause, caring for aging parents, and an empty nest were not associated with an increase in responsibility and self-control (Helson & Wink, 1992). And as you read earlier, in a recent study that assessed the Mills college women from their twenties to their seventies, the big five factors were linked to changing historical circumstances in the women's lives (George, Helson, & John, 2011).

George Vaillant's Studies Longitudinal studies by George Vaillant help us explore a question that differs somewhat from the topics examined by the studies described so far: Does personality at middle age predict what a person's life will be like in late adulthood? Vaillant (2002) has conducted three longitudinal studies of adult development and aging: (1) a sample of 268 socially advantaged Harvard graduates born about 1920 (called the Grant Study); (2) a sample of 456 socially disadvantaged inner-city men born about 1930; and (3) a sample of 90 middle-SES, intellectually gifted women born about 1910. These individuals have been assessed numerous times (in most cases, every two years), beginning in the 1920s to 1940s and continuing today for those still living. The main assessments involve extensive interviews with the participants, their parents, and teachers.

Vaillant categorized 75- to 80-year-olds as "happy-well," "sad-sick," or "dead." He used data collected from these individuals when they were 50 years of age to predict which categories they were likely to end up in at 75 to 80 years of age. Alcohol abuse and smoking at age 50 were the best predictors of which individuals would be dead at 75 to 80 years of age. Other factors at age 50 that were linked with being in the "happy-well" category at 75 to 80 years of age included getting regular exercise, avoiding being overweight, being well-educated, having a stable marriage, being future-oriented, being thankful and forgiving, empathizing with others, being active with other people, and having good coping skills.

Wealth and income at age 50 were not linked with being in the "happy-well" category at 75 to 80 years of age. Generativity in middle age (defined as "taking care of the next generation") was more strongly related than intimacy to whether individuals would have an enduring and happy marriage at 75 to 80 years of age (Vaillant, 2002).

The results for one of Vaillant's studies, the Grant Study of Harvard men, are shown in Figure 16.9. Note that when individuals at 50 years of age were not heavy smokers, did not abuse alcohol, had a stable marriage, exercised, maintained a normal weight, and had good coping skills, they were more likely to be alive and happy at 75 to 80 years of age.

CONCLUSIONS

What can be concluded about stability and change in personality development during the adult years? According to a research review by leading researchers Brent Roberts and Daniel Mroczek (2008), there is increasing evidence that personality traits continue to change during the adult years, even into late

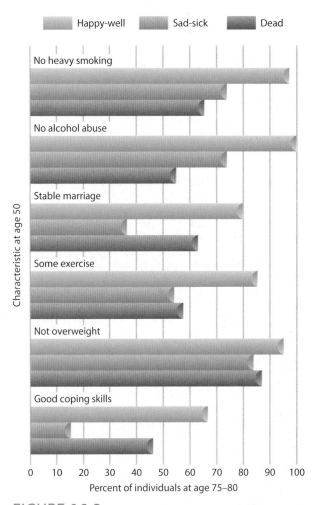

FIGURE 16.9

LINKS BETWEEN CHARACTERISTICS AT AGE 50 AND HEALTH AND HAPPINESS AT AGE 75 TO 80. In a longitudinal study, the characteristics shown above at age 50 were related to whether individuals were happy-well, sad-sick, or dead at age 75 to 80 (Vaillant, 2002).

adulthood. However, in a meta-analysis of 92 longitudinal studies, the greatest change in personality traits occurred in early adulthood—from about 20 to 40 years of age (Roberts, Walton, & Viechbauer, 2006).

Thus, people show more stability in their personality when they reach midlife than they did when they were younger adults (Roberts, Donnellan, & Hill, 2013). These findings support what is called a cumulative personality model of personality development, which states that with time and age people become more adept at interacting with their environment in ways that promote increased stability in personality (Caspi & Roberts, 2001).

This does not mean that change is absent throughout middle and late adulthood. Ample evidence shows that social contexts, new experiences, and sociohistorical changes can affect personality development, but the changes in middle and late adulthood are usually not as great as those in early adulthood (Mroczek, Spiro, & Griffin, 2006).

In general, changes in personality traits across adulthood also occur in a positive direction. Over time, "people become more confident, warm, responsible, and calm" (Roberts & Mroczek, 2008, p. 33). Such positive changes equate with becoming more socially mature.

In sum, recent research contradicts the old view that stability in personality begins to set in at about 30 years of age (McAdams & Olson, 2010; Roberts & Mroczek, 2008; Roberts, Wood, & Caspi, 2008; Roberts & others, 2009). Although there are some consistent developmental changes in the personality traits of large numbers of people, at the individual level people can show unique patterns of personality traits—and these patterns often reflect life experiences related to themes of their particular developmental period (Roberts & Mroczek, 2008). For example, researchers have found that individuals who are in a stable marriage and a solid career track become more socially dominant, conscientious, and emotionally stable as they go through early adulthood (Roberts & Wood, 2006). And for some of these individuals there is greater change in their personality traits than for other individuals (McAdams & Olson, 2010; Roberts & Mroczek, 2008; Roberts & others, 2009; Roberts, Donnellan, & Hill, 2013).

At age 55, actor Jack Nicholson said, "I feel exactly the same as I've always felt: a slightly reined-in voracious beast." Nicholson felt his personality had not changed much. Some others might think they have changed more. *How much does personality change and how does it stay the same through adulthood?*

Review *Connect* Reflect

LG2 Discuss stability and change in development during middle adulthood, as reflected in longitudinal studies.

Review
- Identify four longitudinal studies and describe their results.
- What conclusions can be reached about stability and change in development during middle adulthood?

Connect
- This section discussed four different longitudinal studies. What are the pros and cons of using a longitudinal study to collect data (as discussed in Chapter 1)?

Reflect *Your Own Personal Journey of Life*
- How much stability and change have characterized your life so far? How much stability and change do you predict will characterize your future development as an adult? Explain.

3 Close Relationships

LG3 Identify some important aspects of close relationships in middle adulthood.

Love and Marriage at Midlife | The Empty Nest and Its Refilling | Sibling Relationships and Friendships | Grandparenting | Intergenerational Relationships

There is a consensus among middle-aged Americans that a major component of well-being involves positive relationships with others, especially parents, spouse, and offspring (Blieszner & Roberto, 2012; Markus & others, 2004). To begin our examination of midlife relationships, let's explore love and marriage in middle-aged adults.

LOVE AND MARRIAGE AT MIDLIFE

Remember from Chapter 14 that two major forms of love are romantic love and affectionate love. The fires of romantic love are strong in early adulthood. Affectionate, or companionate, love increases during middle adulthood. That is, physical attraction, romance, and passion are more important in new relationships, especially in early adulthood. Security, loyalty, and mutual emotional interest become more important as relationships mature, especially in middle adulthood.

One study revealed that marital satisfaction increased in middle age (Gorchoff, John, & Helson, 2008). Some of the marriages that were difficult and rocky during early adulthood improved during middle adulthood. Although the partners may have lived through a great deal of turmoil, they eventually discovered a deep and solid foundation on which to anchor their relationship. In middle adulthood, the partners may have fewer financial worries, less housework and chores, and more time with each other. Middle-aged partners are more likely to view their marriage as positive if they engage in mutual activities.

What characterizes marriage in middle adulthood?

Most individuals in midlife who are married voice considerable satisfaction with being married. In a large-scale study of individuals in middle adulthood, 72 percent of those who were married said their marriage was either "excellent" or "very good" (Brim, 1999). Possibly by middle age, many of the worst marriages already have dissolved. However, a recent study revealed that married and partnered middle-aged adults were more likely to view their relationships with ambivalence or indifference than their late adulthood counterparts (Windsor & Butterworth, 2010).

Divorce in middle adulthood may be more positive in some ways, more negative in others, than divorce in early adulthood. On one hand, for mature individuals, the perils of divorce can be fewer and less intense than for younger individuals. They have more resources, and they can simplify their lives by disposing of possessions, such as a large home, which they no longer need. Their children are adults and may be able to cope with their parents' divorce more effectively. The partners may have gained a better understanding of themselves and may be searching for changes that could include ending a poor marriage. One study found that women who initiated a divorce in midlife were characterized more by self-focused growth and optimism than were women whose husbands initiated the divorce (Sakraida, 2005).

On the other hand, the emotional and time commitment to marriage that has existed for so many years may not be lightly given up. Many midlife individuals perceive a divorce as a failure in what could have been the best years of their lives. The divorcer might see the situation as an escape from an untenable relationship, but the divorced partner usually sees it as betrayal, the ending of a relationship that had been built up over many years and that involved a great deal of commitment and trust. Also, divorce may lower the economic standing of some middle-aged and older women who have a limited number of options (Mitchell, 2007). These women may lack the necessary education, skills, and employment experience to maintain a standard of living that is as high as when they were married. In sum, divorce in midlife may have positive outcomes for some individuals and negative outcomes for others (Pudrovska, 2009).

A survey by AARP (2004) of 1,148 40- to 79-year-olds who were divorced at least once in their forties, fifties, or sixties found that staying married because of their children was by far the main reason many people took so long to become divorced. Despite the worry and stress involved in going through a divorce, three in four of the divorcees said they had made the right decision to dissolve their marriage and reported a positive outlook on life. Sixty-six percent of the divorced women said they had initiated the divorce, compared with only 41 percent of the divorced men. The divorced women were much more afraid of having financial problems (44 percent) than were the divorced men (11 percent). Following are the main reasons the middle-aged and older adult women cited for their divorce: (1) verbal, physical, or emotional abuse (23 percent); (2) alcohol or drug abuse (18 percent); and (3) cheating (17 percent). The main reasons the middle-aged and older men cited for their divorce were (1) no

What are some ways that divorce might be more positive or more negative in middle adulthood than in early adulthood?

obvious problems, just fell out of love (17 percent); (2) cheating (14 percent); and (3) different values, lifestyles (14 percent).

THE EMPTY NEST AND ITS REFILLING

An important event in a family is the launching of a child into adult life. Parents undergo adjustments as a result of the child's absence. Students usually think that their parents suffer from their absence. In fact, parents who live vicariously through their children might experience the **empty nest syndrome,** which includes a decline in marital satisfaction after children leave the home. For most parents, however, marital satisfaction does not decline after children have left home but rather increases during the years after child rearing (Fingerman & Baker, 2006). With their children gone, marital partners have time to pursue career interests and more time for each other. A recent study revealed that the transition to an empty nest increased marital satisfaction and this increase was linked to an increase in the quality of time—but not the quantity of time—spent with partners (Gorschoff, John, & Helson, 2008).

In today's uncertain economic climate, the refilling of the empty nest is becoming a common occurrence as adult children return home after several years of college, after graduating from college, or to save money after taking a full-time job (Merrill, 2009). Young adults also may move in with their parents after an unsuccessful career or a divorce. And some individuals don't leave home at all until their middle to late twenties because they cannot financially support themselves. Numerous labels have been applied to these young adults who return to their parents' homes to live, including "boomerang kids," and "B2B" (or Back-to-Bedroom) (Furman, 2005).

The middle generation has always provided support for the younger generation, even after the nest is bare. Through loans and monetary gifts for education, and through emotional support, the middle generation has helped the younger generation. Adult children appreciate the financial and emotional support their parents provide them at a time when they often feel considerable stress about their career, work, and lifestyle. And parents feel good that they can provide this support. A recent study of 40- to 60-year-old parents revealed that they provided financial, practical, and emotional support on average every few weeks to each of their children over 18 years of age (Fingerman & others, 2009).

However, as with most family living arrangements, there are both pluses and minuses when adult children return home. A common complaint voiced by both adult children and their parents is a loss of privacy. The adult children complain that their parents restrict their independence, cramp their sex lives, reduce their music listening, and treat them as children rather than adults. Parents often complain that their quiet home has become noisy, that they stay up late worrying when their adult children will come home, that meals are difficult to plan because of conflicting schedules, that their relationship as a married couple has been invaded, and that they have to shoulder too much responsibility for their adult children. In sum, when adult children return home to live, a disequilibrium in family life is created, which requires considerable adaptation on the part of parents and their adult children. To read about strategies that young adults and their parents can use to get along better, see *Connecting Development to Life*.

empty nest syndrome A decrease in marital satisfaction after children leave home, because parents derive considerable satisfaction from their children.

Doonesbury

BY GARRY TRUDEAU

Strategies for Parents and Their Young Adult Children

When adult children ask to return home to live, parents and their adult children should agree beforehand on the conditions and expectations. For example, they might discuss and agree on whether young adults will pay rent, wash their own clothes, cook their own meals, do any household chores, pay their phone bills, come and go as they please, be sexually active or drink alcohol at home, and so on. If these conditions aren't negotiated at the beginning, conflict often results because the expectations of parents and young adult children will likely be violated.

Parents need to treat young adult children more like adults than children and let go of much of their parenting role. Parents should interact with young adult children not as dependent children who need to be closely monitored and protected but rather as adults who are capable of responsible, mature behavior. Adult children have the right to choose how much they sleep and eat, how they dress, whom they choose as friends and lovers, what career they pursue, and how they spend their money. However, if the young adult children act in ways that interfere with their parents' lifestyles, parents need to say so. The discussion should focus not on the young adult children's choices but on how their activities are unacceptable while living together in the same home.

Some parents don't let go of their young adult children when they should. They engage in "permaparenting," which can impede not only their adult children's movement toward independence and responsibility but also their own postparenting lives. "Helicopter parents" is another label used for parents who hover too closely in their effort to ensure that

What are some strategies that can help parents and their young adult children get along better?

their children succeed in college and adult life (Paul, 2003). Although well intentioned, this intrusiveness by parents can slow the process by which their children become responsible adults.

When they move back home, young adult children need to think about how they will need to change their behavior to make the living arrangement work. Elina Furman (2005) provides some good recommendations in *Boomerang Nation: How to Survive Living with Your Parents . . . the Second Time Around.* She recommends that when young adult children move back home they expect to make adjustments. And as recommended earlier, she urges young adults to sit down with their parents and negotiate the ground rules for living at home before they actually move back. Furman also recommends that young adults set a deadline for how long they will live at home and then stay focused on their goals (whether they want to save enough money to pay off their debts, save enough to start a business or buy their own home, finish graduate school, and so on). Too often young adults spend the money they save by moving home on luxuries such as spending binges, nights on the town, expensive clothes, and unnecessary travel, further delaying their ability to move out of their parents' home.

Children who leave college and return to live at home with their parents are on the cusp of young adulthood, a time called emerging adulthood (as described in Chapter 12). What characterizes individuals' identity development during this time?

SIBLING RELATIONSHIPS AND FRIENDSHIPS

Sibling relationships persist over the entire life span for most adults (Whiteman, McHale, & Soli, 2011). Eighty-five percent of today's adults have at least one living sibling. Sibling relationships in adulthood may be extremely close, apathetic, or highly rivalrous (Bedford, 2009). The majority of sibling relationships in adulthood are close (Cicirelli, 2009). Those siblings who are psychologically close to each other in adulthood tended to be that way in childhood. It is rare for sibling closeness to develop for the first time in adulthood (Dunn, 1984, 2007). One study revealed that adult siblings often provide practical and emotional support to each other (Voorpostel & Blieszner, 2008). Another study revealed that men who had poor sibling relationships in childhood were more likely to develop depression by age 50 than men who had more positive sibling relationships as children (Waldinger, Vaillant, & Orav, 2007).

developmental **connection**

Family and Peers

Many siblings have mixed feelings about each other. Chapter 8, p. 261

Friendships are as important in middle adulthood as they were in early adulthood (Blieszner & Roberto, 2012). It takes time to develop intimate friendships, so friendships that have endured over the adult years are often deeper than those that are newly formed in middle adulthood.

GRANDPARENTING

The increase in longevity is influencing the nature of grandparenting (Monserud, 2011). In 1900 only 4 percent of 10-year-old children had four living grandparents but in 2000 that figure had risen to more than 40 percent. And in 1990 only about 20 percent of children at 30 years of age had living grandparents, a figure that is projected to increase to 80 percent in 2020 (Hagestad & Uhlenberg, 2007). Further increases in longevity are likely to support this trend in the future, although the current trend in delaying childbearing is likely to undermine it (Szinovacz, 2009).

Grandparents play important roles in the lives of many grandchildren (Lumby, 2010; Newton & Stewart, 2012). Many adults become grandparents for the first time during middle age. Researchers have consistently found that grandmothers have more contact with grandchildren than do grandfathers (Watson, Randolph, & Lyons, 2005). Perhaps women tend to define their role as grandmothers as part of their responsibility for maintaining ties between family members across generations. Men may have fewer expectations about the grandfather role and see it as more voluntary.

Grandparent Roles and Styles   What is the meaning of the grandparent role? Three prominent meanings are attached to being a grandparent (Neugarten & Weinstein, 1964). For some older adults, being a grandparent is a source of biological reward and continuity. For others, being a grandparent is a source of emotional self-fulfillment, generating feelings of companionship and satisfaction that may have been missing in earlier adult-child relationships. And for yet others, being a grandparent is a remote role. A recent study revealed that grandparenting can provide a sense of purpose and a feeling of being valued during middle and late adulthood when generative needs are strong (Thiele & Whelan, 2008).

The grandparent role may have different functions in different families, in different ethnic groups and cultures, and in different situations (Watson, Randolph, & Lyons, 2005). For example, in one study of White, African American, and Mexican American grandparents and grandchildren, the Mexican American grandparents saw their grandchildren most frequently, provided the most support for the grandchildren and their parents, and had the most satisfying relationships with their grandchildren (Bengtson, 1985). And in a study of three generations of families in Chicago, grandmothers had closer relationships with their children and grandchildren and gave more personal advice than grandfathers did (Hagestad, 1985).

The diversity of grandparenting also was apparent in an early investigation of how grandparents interacted with their grandchildren (Neugarten & Weinstein, 1964). Three styles were dominant—formal, fun-seeking, and distant. In the formal style, the grandparent performed what was considered to be a proper and prescribed role. These grandparents showed a strong interest in their grandchildren but were careful not to give child-rearing advice. In the fun-seeking style, the grandparent was informal and playful. Grandchildren were a source of leisure activity; mutual satisfaction was emphasized. A substantial portion of grandparents were distant figures. In the distant-figure style, the grandparent was benevolent but interaction was infrequent. Grandparents who were over the age of 65 were more likely to display a formal style of interaction; those under 65 were more likely to display a fun-seeking style. Because the grandparent role links three generations—grandparents, parents, and grandchildren—the grandparent role is often mediated by parents at least until grandchildren become adults (Szinovacz, 2009).

The Changing Profile of Grandparents   In 2009, 7.8 million children lived with at least one grandparent, a 64 percent increase since 1981 when 4.7 million children were living with at least one grandparent (U.S. Census Bureau, 2011). Divorce, adolescent pregnancies, and drug use by parents are the main reasons that grandparents are thrust back into the "parenting" role they thought they had shed.

What are some grandparents' roles and styles?

One study revealed that grandparent involvement was linked with better adjustment in single-parent and stepparent families than in two-parent biological families (Attar-Schwartz & others, 2009).

Less than 20 percent of grandparents whose grandchildren move in with them are 65 years old or older. Almost half of the grandchildren who move in with grandparents are raised by a single grandmother. These families are mainly African American (53 percent). When both grandparents are raising grandchildren, the families are overwhelmingly non-Latino White.

A majority of the grandparents living with their children contributed to the family income and provided child care while parents worked. Only about 10 percent of the grandparents who move in with their children and grandchildren are in poverty. Almost half of the grandparents who move in with their children are immigrants. Partly because women live longer than men, more grandmothers than grandfathers live with their children. About 70 percent of the grandparents who move in with their children are grandmothers.

Grandparents who are full-time caregivers for grandchildren are at elevated risk for health problems, depression, and stress (Silverstein, 2009). Caring for grandchildren is linked with these problems in part because full-time grandparent caregivers are often characterized by low-income, minority status, and by not being married (Minkler & Fuller-Thompson, 2005). Grandparents who are part-time caregivers are less likely to have the negative health portrait that full-time grandparent caregivers have. In a recent study of part-time grandparent caregivers, few negative effects on grandparents were found (Hughes & others, 2007).

In some cases, divorce may increase children's contact with grandparents, as when grandparents assume a stronger caregiving role; in others, a custodial parent may try to restrict grandparents' time with children. One recent study revealed that when children's relationships with their father deteriorated after a divorce, their relationships with their paternal grandparents also were distant, negative, or nonexistent (Ahrons, 2007).

As divorce and remarriage have become more common, a special concern of grandparents is visitation privileges with their grandchildren (Kivnik & Sinclair, 2007). In the last two decades, more states have passed laws giving grandparents the right to petition a court for visitation privileges with their grandchildren, even if a parent objects. Whether such forced visitation rights for grandparents are in the child's best interest is still being debated.

What characterizes recent changes in the profile of grandparents?

INTERGENERATIONAL RELATIONSHIPS

Family is important to most people. When 21,000 adults aged 40 to 79 in 21 countries were asked, "When you think of who you are, you think mainly of _____," 63 percent said "family," 9 percent said "religion," and 8 percent said "work" (HSBC Insurance, 2007). In this study, in all 21 countries, middle-aged and older adults expressed a strong feeling of responsibility between generations in their family, with the strongest intergenerational ties indicated in Saudi Arabia, India, and Turkey. More than 80 percent of the middle-aged and older adults reported that adults have a duty to care for their parents (and parents-in-law) in time of need later in life.

Adults in midlife play important roles in the lives of the young and the old (Birditt & Wardjiman, 2012; Fingerman & Birditt, 2011). Middle-aged adults share their experience and transmit values to the younger generation. They may be launching children and experiencing the empty nest, adjusting to having grown children return home, or becoming grandparents. They also may be giving or receiving financial assistance, caring for a widowed or sick parent, or adapting to being the oldest generation after both parents have died.

Middle-aged and older adults around the world show a strong sense of family responsibility. A recent study of middle-aged and older adults in 21 countries revealed the strongest intergenerational ties in Saudi Arabia.

Middle-aged adults have been described as the "sandwich," "squeezed," or "overload" generation because of the responsibilities they have for their adolescent and young adult children as well as their aging parents (Etaugh & Bridges, 2010; Pudrovska, 2009). However, an alternative view is that in the United States, a "sandwich" generation, in which the middle

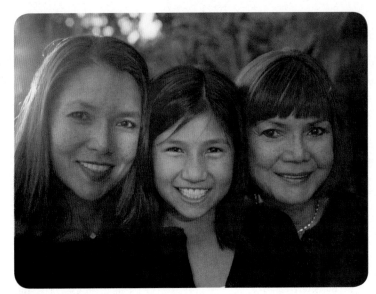

What is the nature of intergenerational relationships?

generation cares for both grown children and aging parents simultaneously, occurs less often than a "pivot" generation, in which the middle generation alternates attention between the demands of grown children and aging parents (Birditt & Wardjiman, 2012; Fingerman & Birditt, 2011).

Many middle-aged adults experience considerable stress when their parents become very ill and die. One survey found that when adults enter midlife, 41 percent have both parents alive, but that 77 percent leave midlife with no parents alive (Bumpass & Aquilino, 1994). By middle age, more than 40 percent of adult children (most of them daughters) provide care for aging parents or parents-in-law (Bliezner & Roberto, 2012; National Alliance for Caregiving, 2009). However, two recent studies revealed that middle-aged parents are more likely to provide support to their grown children than to their parents (Fingerman & others, 2011a, 2012). When middle-aged adults have a parent with a disability, their support for that parent increases (Fingerman & others, 2011b). This support might involve locating a nursing home and monitoring its quality, procuring medical services, arranging public service assistance, and handling finances. In some cases, adult children provide direct assistance with daily living, including such activities as eating, bathing, and dressing. Even less severely impaired older adults may need help with shopping, housework, transportation, home maintenance, and bill paying.

Some researchers have found that relationships between aging parents and their children are usually characterized by ambivalence (Birditt, Fingerman, & Zarit, 2010; Birditt & Wardjiman, 2012; Fingerman & Birditt, 2011; Fingerman & others, 2011a). Perceptions include love, reciprocal help, and shared values on the positive side and isolation, family conflicts and problems, abuse, neglect, and caregiver stress on the negative side. A recent study, though, revealed that affection and support, reflecting solidarity, was more prevalent than ambivalence in intergenerational relationships (Hogerbrugge & Komter, 2012).

With each new generation, personality characteristics, attitudes, and values are replicated or changed. As older family members die, their biological, intellectual, emotional, and personal legacies are carried on in the next generation. Their children become the oldest generation and their grandchildren the second generation. As adult children become middle-aged, they often develop more positive perceptions of their parents (Field, 1999). Both similarity and dissimilarity across generations are found. For example, similarity between parents and an adult child is most noticeable in religion and politics, least in gender roles, lifestyle, and work orientation.

The following studies provide further evidence of the importance of intergenerational relationships in development:

- The motivation of adult children to provide social support to their older parents was linked with earlier family experiences (Silverstein & others, 2002). Children who spent more time in shared activities with their parents and received more financial support from them earlier in their lives provided more support to their parents as they became older.
- Children of divorced parents were disproportionately likely to end their own marriage than were children from intact, never divorced families, although the transmission of divorce across generations has declined in recent years (Wolfinger, 2011).
- Adult children of divorced parents who were classified as securely attached were less likely to divorce in the early years of their marriage than their insecurely attached counterparts (Crowell, Treboux, & Brockmeyer, 2009).
- Parents who smoked early and often, and who persisted in becoming regular smokers, were more likely to have adolescents who became smokers (Chassin & others, 2008).

Gender differences also characterize intergenerational relationships (Etaugh & Bridges, 2010). Women have an especially important role in maintaining family relationships across generations. Women's relationships across generations are typically closer than other family bonds (Merrill, 2009). In one study, mothers and their daughters had much closer relationships during their adult years than mothers and sons, fathers and daughters, and

How Do Mothers' and Daughters' Descriptions of Enjoyable Visits Differ at Different Points in Adult Development?

Karen Fingerman (2000) studied 48 pairs of older adult mothers (mean age, 76 years) and their middle-aged daughters (mean age, 46 years), and 44 pairs of middle-aged mothers (mean age, 47 years) and their young adult daughters (mean age, 21 years). Interviewers asked participants (p. 98):

> Think about the last time you had a particularly enjoyable visit with your daughter/mother. By visit, I mean a time when you got together, went to the other's house (or your daughter came home from college), or talked on the phone. Tell a little about what went on. Please provide as much information as you can about the visit, what happened, and why it was particularly enjoyable.

Transcriptions of descriptions of the visits were coded, and the results for the coded categories were summarized as follows (Fingerman, 2000, pp. 100–102):

- *Investment and connection.* Mothers in both age groups were more invested in their relationships with their daughters than their daughters were with them.
- *Family.* Older mothers and daughters were more likely than younger pairs to describe the larger kin network, such as the daughter's children, siblings, father, husband, or the family in general. By contrast, younger pairs "were more likely to stick to their own relationship and to discuss situations in which the two of them had enjoyed a special event."
- *Nurturance.* "Young adult daughters and older adult mothers were more likely to report pleasure from having the other party help them in some way than were middle-aged women."
- *Interacting.* Younger mothers tended to focus on activities in which they enjoyed their daughters' emergence as young adults. "Younger daughters derived pleasure from having their mothers around as sounding boards, whereas older daughters" enjoyed the link to the past that their mothers represented.
- *Negative comments.* Mothers and daughters in the older pairs "were more likely to say something negative than were younger mothers and daughters," although these comments were still infrequent.

In sum, mothers' and daughters' perceptions of their visits reflected a combination of individual developmental needs. Although the focus of mothers' and daughters' relationships may change, in general mothers were more invested in relationships with their daughters than the reverse throughout adulthood.

---

fathers and sons (Rossi, 1989). Also in this study, married men were more involved with their wives' kin than with their own. Also, a recent study revealed that mothers' intergenerational ties were more influential for grandparent-grandchild relationships than fathers' (Monserud, 2008). To further explore intergenerational relationships, see the *Connecting Through Research* interlude.

When adults immigrate to another country, intergenerational stress may increase. In the last several decades, increasing numbers of Mexicans have immigrated to the United States, and their numbers are expected to increase. The pattern of immigration usually involves separation from the extended family (Parra-Cardona & others, 2006). It may also involve separation of immediate family members, with the husband coming first and then later bringing his wife and children. Those initially isolated, especially the wife, experience considerable stress due to relocation and the absence of family and friends. Within several years, a social network is usually established in the ethnic neighborhood.

As soon as some stability in their lives is achieved, Mexican families may sponsor the immigration of extended family members, such as a maternal or paternal sister or mother who provides child care and enables the mother to go to work. In some cases, the older generation remains behind and joins their grown children in old age. The accessibility of Mexico facilitates visits to and from the village for vacations or at a time of crisis, such as when an adolescent runs away from home.

The discrepancies between acculturation levels can give rise to conflicting expectations within the Mexican American family (Sarkisian, Gerena, & Gerstel, 2006; Simpkins, Vest, & Price, 2011). The immigrant parents' model of child rearing may be out of phase with the dominant culture's model, which may cause reverberations through the family's generations, as discussed in earlier chapters. For

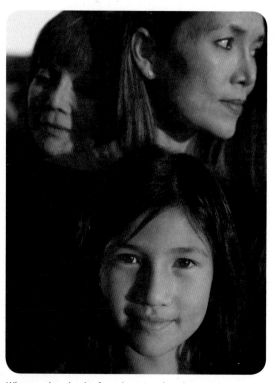

What are three levels of acculturation that characterize many Mexican American families?

Lillian Troll, Professor of Psychology and Life-Span Development and Researcher on Families and Aging Women

Lillian Troll has been a leading figure in the field of adult development and aging. She graduated from the University of Chicago with a joint major in psychology and premedicine. During World War II, she dropped out of graduate school to work in Washington, where she helped develop an array of Army screening and achievement tests. After the war she became a suburban housewife and mother, following her husband's career moves from city to city. For a decade, the closest Troll came to a career in life-span development was founding a nursery school in New Jersey.

Many years later, after her divorce, Troll returned to the University of Chicago and in 1967 completed a Ph.D. in life-span development. She then began teaching and conducting research on generations in the family and women's development, first at Wayne State University in Detroit and then as a 60-year-old grandmother at Rutgers University Psychology Department. In 1986 she retired and moved to California, where she continued doing research at the University of California at San Francisco, collaborating with Colleen Johnson on a longitudinal study of the "oldest-old" (people over 85).

Lillian Troll (*left*) with participants in a study of aging women.

For more information about what professors and researchers do, see page 44 in the Careers in Life-Span Development appendix.

example, parents and grandparents may be especially resistant to the demands for autonomy and dating made by adolescent daughters (Wilkinson-Lee & others, 2006). And in recent years an increasing number of female youth have left their Mexican American homes to further their education, an event that is often stressful for families with strong ties to Mexican values.

Lillian Troll has conducted research on intergenerational relations and women's development in midlife. To read about her work, see the *Connecting with Careers* profile.

Review *Connect* Reflect

LG3 Identify some important aspects of close relationships in middle adulthood.

Review

- How can love and marriage at midlife be characterized?
- What is the empty nest? How has it been refilling?
- What are sibling relationships and friendships like in middle adulthood?
- What is the nature of grandparenting?
- What are relationships across generations like?

Connect

- In this section, you read about divorce in middle adulthood. In Chapter 14, what did you learn was one of the most common characteristics of divorced adults?

Reflect *Your Own Personal Journey of Life*

- What was or is the nature of your relationship with your grandparents? What are intergenerational relationships like in your family?

Erikson's eighth and final stage of development—integrity versus despair—occurs in late adulthood. In this stage, individuals engage in a life review. Being active is linked with life satisfaction in late adulthood. Older adults become more selective about their social networks and choose to spend more time with emotionally rewarding relationships and less time with peripheral relationships. Older adults also experience more positive emotions and fewer negative emotions than younger adults. The personality traits of conscientiousness and agreeableness also increase in late adulthood. Because of losses (declines in physical or cognitive skills, for example), older adults often have to use accommodative strategies to reach their goals.

looking *forward* ---→

reach your **learning goals**

Socioemotional Development in Middle Adulthood

1 Personality Theories and Adult Development

LG1 Describe personality theories and socioemotional development in middle adulthood.

Stages of Adulthood

- Erikson says that the seventh stage of the human life span, generativity versus stagnation, occurs in middle adulthood. Four types of generativity are biological, parental, work, and cultural. In Levinson's theory, developmental tasks must be mastered at different points in development, and changes in middle age focus on four conflicts: being young versus being old, being destructive versus being constructive, being masculine versus being feminine, and being attached to others versus being separated from them. Levinson asserted that a majority of Americans, especially men, experience a midlife crisis. Research, however, indicates that midlife crises are not pervasive. There is considerable individual variation in development during the middle adulthood years.

The Life-Events Approach

- According to the early version of the life-events approach, life events produce taxing circumstances that create stress. In the contemporary version of the life-events approach, how life events influence the individual's development depends not only on the life event but also on mediating factors, adaptation to the event, the life-stage context, and the sociohistorical context.

Stress and Personal Control in Midlife

- Researchers have found that young and middle-aged adults experience more stressful days and more multiple stressors than do older adults. On average, a sense of personal control decreases as adults become older—however, some aspects of personal control increase. Women and men differ in the way they experience and respond to stressors. Women are more likely to respond to stress in a tend-and-befriend manner, men in a flight-or-flight manner.

Contexts of Midlife Development

- Neugarten argues that the social environment of a particular cohort can alter its social clock—the timetable according to which individuals are expected to accomplish life's tasks. Critics say that the adult stage theories are male biased because they place too much emphasis on achievement and careers and do not adequately address women's concerns about relationships. Midlife is a heterogeneous period for women, as it is for men. For some women, midlife is the prime of their lives. Many cultures do not have a clear concept of middle age. In many nonindustrialized societies, a woman's status improves in middle age.

2 Stability and Change

 Discuss stability and change in development during middle adulthood, as reflected in longitudinal studies.

Longitudinal Studies

- In Costa and McCrae's Baltimore Study, the big five personality factors—openness to experience, conscientiousness, extraversion, agreeableness, and neuroticism—showed considerable stability. However, researchers recently have found that the greatest change in personality occurs in early adulthood, with positive aspects of the factors peaking in middle age. The big five factors are linked to important aspects of a person's life, such as health and work. In the Berkeley Longitudinal Studies, extremes in the stability-change argument were not supported. The most stable characteristics were intellectual orientation, self-confidence, and openness to new experiences. The characteristics that changed the most were nurturance, hostility, and self-control. Helson's Mills College Study of women distinguished family-oriented and career-oriented women, and those who followed neither path. In their early forties, women experienced many of the concerns that Levinson described for men. However, rather than a midlife crisis, women experienced midlife consciousness. George Vaillant's research revealed links between a number of characteristics at age 50 and health and well-being at 75 to 80 years of age.

Conclusions

- The cumulative personality model states that with time and age personality becomes more stable. Changes in personality traits occur more in early adulthood than middle and late adulthood, but a number of aspects of personality do continue to change after early adulthood. Change in personality traits across adulthood occurs in a positive direction, reflecting social maturity. At the individual level, changes in personality are often linked to life experiences related to a particular developmental period. Some people change more than others.

3 Close Relationships

 Identify some important aspects of close relationships in middle adulthood.

Love and Marriage at Midlife

- Affectionate love increases in midlife, especially in marriages that have endured many years. A majority of middle-aged adults who are married say that their marriage is very good or excellent. Researchers recently have found that the perils of divorce in midlife can be fewer and less intense than those for divorcing young adults.

The Empty Nest and Its Refilling

- Rather than decreasing marital satisfaction as once thought, the empty nest increases it for most parents. Following an unsuccessful career or a divorce, an increasing number of young adults are returning home to live with their parents. Some young adults do not leave home until their middle to late twenties because they are unable to financially support themselves.

Sibling Relationships and Friendships

- Sibling relationships continue throughout life. Some are close; others are distant. Friendships continue to be important in middle age.

Grandparenting

- There are different grandparent roles and styles. Grandmothers spend more time with grandchildren than grandfathers, and the grandmother role involves greater expectations for maintaining ties across generations than the grandfather role. The profile of grandparents is changing because of such factors as divorce and remarriage. An increasing number of U.S. grandchildren live with their grandparents.

Intergenerational Relationships

- Family members usually maintain contact across generations. Mothers and daughters have the closest relationships. The middle-aged generation, which has been called the "sandwich" or "squeezed" generation, plays an important role in linking generations.

key terms

contemporary life-events approach 513

fight-or-flight 515
tend-and-befriend 515

social clock 515
big five factors of personality 517

empty nest syndrome 522

key people

Chapter 16 | SOCIOEMOTIONAL DEVELOPMENT IN MIDDLE ADULTHOOD

Connecting with

Learning Objectives	Application Activities	Activity Type	Page Reference
Describe contexts of midlife development.	Middle Adulthood Perspectives on Emotion	Milestones: Transitions	pp. 515–517
Discuss stability and change in development during middle adulthood, including longitudinal studies.	Trait Theory of Personality	Interactive exercise	pp. 517–520
Discuss love and marriage at midlife.	Falling in Love in Middle Adulthood	Video	pp. 521–522
Explain grandparenting.	On Becoming a Grandmother	Video	pp. 524–525
	Being a Grandfather	Video	
	Being a Grandmother	Video	

To be seventy years young is sometimes far more cheerful and hopeful than to be forty years old.

—OLIVER WENDELL HOLMES, SR.
American Physician, 19th Century

Late Adulthood

The rhythm and meaning of human development eventually wend their way to late adulthood, when each of us stands alone at the heart of the earth and suddenly it is evening. We shed the leaves of youth and are stripped by the winds of time down to the truth. We learn that life is lived forward but understood backward. We trace the connection between the end and the beginning of life and try to figure out what this whole show is about before it is out. Ultimately, we come to know that we are what survives of us. Section 9 contains three chapters: "Physical Development in Late Adulthood (Chapter 17), "Cognitive Development in Late Adulthood" (Chapter 18), and "Socioemotional Development in Late Adulthood" (Chapter 19).

chapter 17

PHYSICAL DEVELOPMENT IN LATE ADULTHOOD

chapter **outline**

1 Longevity

Learning Goal 1 Characterize longevity and discuss the biological theories of aging.

Life Expectancy and Life Span
The Young-Old and the Oldest-Old
Biological Theories of Aging

2 The Course of Physical Development in Late Adulthood

Learning Goal 2 Describe how a person's brain and body change in late adulthood.

The Aging Brain
Sleep
The Immune System
Physical Appearance and Movement
Sensory Development
The Circulatory System and Lungs
Sexuality

3 Health

Learning Goal 3 Identify health problems in older adults and describe how they can be treated.

Health Problems
Substance Use and Abuse
Exercise, Nutrition, and Weight
Health Treatment

Jonathan Swift said, "No wise man ever wished to be younger." Without a doubt, a 70-year-old body does not work as well as it once did. It is also true that an individual's fear of aging is often greater than need be. As more individuals live to a ripe *and* active old age, our image of aging is changing. While on average a 75-year-old's joints should be stiffening, people can practice not to be average. For example, a 75-year-old man might *choose* to train for and run a marathon; an 80-year-old woman whose capacity for work is undiminished might *choose* to make and sell children's toys.

Consider 85-year-old Sadie Halperin, who has been working out for 11 months at a rehabilitation center for the aged in Boston. She lifts weights and rides a stationary bike. She says that before she started working out, almost everything she did—shopping, cooking, walking—was a major struggle. Sadie says she always felt wobbly and held on to a wall when she walked. Now she walks down the center of the hallways and reports that she feels wonderful. Initially she could lift only 15 pounds with both legs; now she lifts 30 pounds. At first she could bench-press only 20 pounds; now she bench-presses 50 pounds. Sadie's exercise routine has increased her muscle strength and is helping her to battle osteoporosis by slowing calcium loss from her bones and reducing the risk of deadly fractures (Ubell, 1992).

Eighty-five-year-old Sadie Halperin engaging in her exercise routine.

topical **connections**

As more individuals are living healthier lives and medical discoveries are slowing down the aging process, middle age appears to be starting later and lasting longer. Increasingly, early middle age (40–54) is distinguished from late middle age (55–65). However, middle age is a time of declining physical skills—such as loss of height, impaired vision and hearing, and reduced cardiovascular functioning. Sleep also becomes more problematic. Sexual changes occur as women enter menopause, many middle-aged men begin to experience erectile dysfunction, and couples engage less frequently in sexual intercourse.

looking back

preview

The story of Sadie Halperin's physical development and well-being raises some truly fascinating questions about life-span development, which we will explore in this chapter. They include: Why do we age, and what, if anything, can we do to slow down the process? How long can we live? What chance do we have of living to be 100? How does the body change in old age? Can certain eating habits and exercise help us live longer? How can we enhance older adults' quality of life?

1 Longevity

LG1 Characterize longevity and discuss the biological theories of aging.

- Life Expectancy and Life Span
- The Young-Old and the Oldest-Old
- Biological Theories of Aging

In his eighties, Nobel-winning chemist Linus Pauling argued that vitamin C slows the aging process. Aging researcher Roy Walford fasted two days a week because he believed calorie restriction slows the aging process. What do we really know about longevity?

LIFE EXPECTANCY AND LIFE SPAN

We are no longer a youthful society. The proportion of individuals at different ages has become increasingly similar. Since the beginning of recorded history, **life span,** the maximum number of years an individual can live, has remained at approximately 120 to 125 years of age. But since 1900, improvements in medicine, nutrition, exercise, and lifestyle have increased our life expectancy an average of 30 additional years. Keep in mind that it is not just improvements in the health and well-being of adults that has contributed to increased longevity but also the substantial reduction in infant deaths in recent decades.

Recall from Chapter 1 that **life expectancy** is the number of years that the average person born in a particular year will probably live. The average life expectancy of individuals born today in the United States is 78.3 years (U.S. Census Bureau, 2011). Sixty-five-year-olds in the United States today can expect to live an average of 18.6 more years (19.9 for females, 17.2 for males) (U.S. Census Bureau, 2011). Older adults who are 100 years of age can only expect to live an average of 2.3 years longer (U.S. Census Bureau, 2011).

> Each of us stands alone at the heart of the earth, pierced through by a ray of sunshine: And suddenly it is evening.
>
> —Salvatore Quasimodo
> *Italian Poet, 20th Century*

Life Expectancy How does the United States fare in life expectancy, compared with other countries around the world? We do considerably better than some and somewhat worse than others. In 2011, Monaco had the highest estimated life expectancy at birth (90 years), followed by Macau (a region of China near Hong Kong), Japan, and Singapore (84 years) (Central Intelligence Agency, 2012). Of 221 countries, the United States ranked fiftieth at 78 years. The lowest estimated life expectancy in 2011 occurred in the African countries of Chad, Guinea-Bissau, South Africa, and Swaziland (49 years). Differences in life expectancies across countries are due to such factors as health conditions and medical care throughout the life span.

Life expectancy also differs for various ethnic groups within the United States and for men and women (Centers for Disease Control and Prevention, 2012a). For example, the life expectancy of African Americans (74) in the United States is five years lower than the life expectancy for non-Latino Whites (79)

life span The maximum number of years an individual can live. The life span of human beings is about 120 to 125 years of age.

life expectancy The number of years that will probably be lived by the average person born in a particular year.

(Centers for Disease Control and Prevention, 2012a). Non-Latino White women have a life expectancy of 81, followed by African American women (77), non-Latino White men (76 years), and African American men (70 years) (National Center for Health Statistics, 2010).

In 2010 the overall life expectancy for women was 80.8 years of age, and for men it was 75.7 years of age (Centers for Disease Control and Prevention, 2012a). Beginning in the mid-thirties, women outnumber men; this gap widens during the remainder of the adult years. By the time adults are 75 years of age, more than 61 percent of the population is female; for those 85 and over, the figure is almost 70 percent female. Why can women expect to live longer than men? Social factors such as health attitudes, habits, lifestyles, and occupation are probably important (Saint Onge, 2009). Men are more likely than women to die from most of the leading causes of death in the United States, including cancer of the respiratory system, motor vehicle accidents, cirrhosis of the liver, emphysema, and coronary heart disease (Robine, 2011). These causes of death are associated with lifestyle. For example, the sex difference in deaths due to lung cancer and emphysema occurs because men are heavier smokers than women.

The sex difference in longevity also is influenced by biological factors (Soerensen, 2012). In virtually all species, females outlive males. Women have more resistance to infections and degenerative diseases (Pan & Chang, 2012). For example, the female's estrogen production helps to protect her from arteriosclerosis (hardening of the arteries). And the additional X chromosome that women carry in comparison with men may be associated with the production of more antibodies to fight off disease. The sex difference in mortality is still present but less pronounced in late adulthood than earlier in adulthood and is especially linked to the higher level of cardiovascular disease in men than women (Yang & Kozloski, 2011).

What about your own life expectancy? What is the likelihood that you will live to be 100? To evaluate this possibility, see Figure 17.1 on page 538.

Centenarians In industrialized countries, the number of centenarians (individuals 100 years and older) is increasing at a rate of approximately 7 percent each year (Perls, 2007). In the United States, there were only 15,000 centenarians in 1980, a number that rose to 72,000 in 2010 and is projected to reach 600,000 by 2050 (U.S. Census Bureau, 2011). The United States has the most centenarians, followed by Japan, China, and England/Wales (Hall, 2008). It is estimated that there are 75 to 100 supercentenarians (individuals 110 years or older) in the United States and about 300 to 450 worldwide (Perls, 2007).

Many people expect that "the older you get, the sicker you get." However, researchers are finding that this is not true for some centenarians (Davinelli, Willcox, & Scapagnini, 2012; Li & others, 2011). One study of 93 centenarians revealed that despite some physical limitations, they had a low rate of age-associated diseases and most had good mental health (Selim & others, 2005). And a recent study of centenarians from 100 to 119 years of age found that

developmental **connection**

Life Expectancy

In the twentieth century alone, life expectancy in the United States increased 30 years. Chapter 1, p. 8

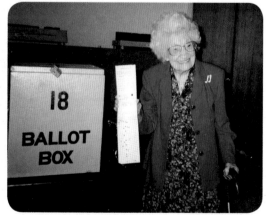

Three participants in the New England Centenarian Study: (*Left*) Adelaide Kruger, age 101, watering her flowers; (*middle*) Waldo McBurney, age 104, active beekeeper, gardener, and runner who has earned five gold medals and set international records in track and field events in his age group; (*right*) Daphne Brann, age 110, voting in an election.

Life Expectancy

Decide how each item applies to you and add or subtract the appropriate number of years from your basic life expectancy.

1. Family history
____ Add five years if two or more of your grandparents lived to 80 or beyond.
____ Subtract four years if any parent, grandparent, sister, or brother died of a heart attack or stroke before 50.
____ Subtract two years if anyone died from these diseases before 60.
____ Subtract three years for each case of diabetes, thyroid disorder, breast cancer, cancer of the digestive system, asthma, or chronic bronchitis among parents or grandparents.

2. Marital status
____ If you are married, add four years.
____ If you are over 25 and not married, subtract one year for every unmarried decade.

3. Economic status
____ Add two years if your family income is over $60,000 per year.
____ Subtract three years if you have been poor for the greater part of your life.

4. Physique
____ Subtract one year for every 10 pounds you are overweight.
____ For each inch your girth measurement exceeds your chest measurement deduct two years.
____ Add three years if you are over 40 and not overweight.

5. Exercise
____ Add three years if you exercise regularly and moderately (jogging three times a week).
____ Add five years if you exercise regularly and vigorously (long-distance running three times a week).
____ Subtract three years if your job is sedentary.
____ Add three years if your job is active.

6. Alcohol
____ Add two years if you are a light drinker (one to three drinks a day).
____ Subtract five to ten years if you are a heavy drinker (more than four drinks per day).
____ Subtract one year if you are a teetotaler.

7. Smoking
____ Subtract eight years if you smoke two or more packs of cigarettes per day.
____ Subtract two years if you smoke one to two packs per day.
____ Subtract two years if you smoke less than one pack.
____ Subtract two years if you regularly smoke a pipe or cigars.

8. Disposition
____ Add two years if you are a reasoned, practical person.
____ Subtract two years if you are aggressive, intense, and competitive.
____ Add one to five years if you are basically happy and content with life.
____ Subtract one to five years if you are often unhappy, worried, and often feel guilty.

9. Education
____ Subtract two years if you have less than a high school education.
____ Add one year if you attended four years of school beyond high school.
____ Add three years if you attended five or more years beyond high school.

10. Environment
____ Add four years if you have lived most of your life in a rural environment.
____ Subtract two years if you have lived most of your life in an urban environment.

11. Sleep
____ Subtract five years if you sleep more than nine hours a day.

12. Temperature
____ Add two years if your home's thermostat is set at no more than 68° F.

13. Health care
____ Add three years if you have regular medical checkups and regular dental care.
____ Subtract two years if you are frequently ill.

____ **Your Life Expectancy Total**

FIGURE 17.1

CAN YOU LIVE TO BE 100? This test gives you a rough guide for predicting your longevity. The basic life expectancy for men is age 75, and for women it is 81. Write down your basic life expectancy. If you are in your fifties or sixties, you should add ten years to the basic figure because you have already proved yourself to be a durable individual. If you are over age 60 and active, you can even add another two years.

developmental **connection**

Nature and Nurture

The nature-nurture issue is a key aspect of understanding development throughout the human life span. Chapter 1, p. 19; Chapter 2, p. 71

the older the age group (110 to 119—referred to as *supercentenarians*—compared with 100 to 104, for example), the later the onset of diseases such as cancer and cardiovascular disease, as well as functional decline (Andersen & others, 2012). The research just described was conducted as part of the ongoing New England Centenarian Study. In this study, the majority of the centenarians have had difficult lives, dealing with challenges such as surviving the Holocaust and living in extreme poverty as an immigrant to the United States (Perls, Lauerman, & Silver, 1999). One factor that has contributed to their survival is their ability to cope effectively with stress.

What chance do you have of living to be 100? Genes play an important role in surviving to an extreme old age (Balistreri & others, 2012). As we saw in Chapter 2, "Biological Beginnings," the search for longevity genes has recently intensified (Conneely & others, 2012; Soerensen, 2012; Tabara & others, 2012). But there are additional factors at work such as family history, health (weight, diet, smoking, and exercise), education, personality, and lifestyle. Remember from Chapter 2 that in the epigenetic approach, there is increasing interest in determining gene x environment (G x E) interactions that influence development (Davinelli, Willcox, & Scapagnini, 2012; Eaton & others, 2012).

To further examine the factors that are involved in living to a very old age, let's journey to the island of Okinawa in the East China Sea where individuals live longer than anywhere else in the world. In Okinawa, there are 34.7 centenarians for every 100,000 inhabitants, the highest ratio in the world. In comparison, the United States has about 10 centenarians for every 100,000 residents. The life expectancy in Okinawa is 81.2 years (86 for women, 78 for men), also the highest in the world.

What is responsible for such longevity in Okinawa? Some possible explanations include the following (Willcox, Willcox, & Suzuki, 2002; Willcox & others, 2007, 2008):

- *Diet.* Okinawans eat very healthy food, heavy on grains, fish, and vegetables, light on meat, eggs, and dairy products. The risk of dying from cancer is far lower among Okinawans than among Japanese and Americans (see Figure 17.2). About 100,000 Okinawans moved to Brazil and quickly adopted the eating regimen of their new home, one heavy on red meat. The result: The life expectancy of the Brazilian Okinawans is now 17 years lower than Okinawa's 81 years!

- *Low-stress lifestyle.* The easygoing lifestyle in Okinawa more closely resembles that of a laid-back South Sea island than that of the high-stress world on the Japanese mainland.

- *Caring community.* Okinawans look out for each other and do not isolate or ignore their older adults. If older adults need help, they don't hesitate to ask a neighbor. Such support and caring is likely responsible for Okinawa having the lowest suicide rate among older women in East Asia, an area noted for its high suicide rate among older women.

- *Activity.* Many older adults in Okinawa are physically vigorous, engaging in activities such as taking walks and working in their gardens. Many older Okinawans also continue working at their jobs.

- *Spirituality.* Many older adults in Okinawa find a sense of purpose in spiritual practice. Prayer is commonplace and believed to ease the mind of stress and problems.

Teru Kingjo, 88, who continues to work as a weaver on Okinawa Island, Japan. She, like many Okinawans, believes that having a sense of purpose helps people to live longer.

To me old age is always fifteen years older than I am.

—**Bernard Baruch**
American Statesman, 20th Century

THE YOUNG-OLD AND THE OLDEST-OLD

Do you want to live to be 100, or 90? As we discussed in Chapter 1, these ages are part of late adulthood, which begins in the sixties and extends to approximately 120 to 125 years of age. This is the longest span of any period of human development—50 to 60 years. Increasingly, a distinction is being made between the *young-old* (65 to 84 years of age) and *oldest-old* (85 years and older). An increased interest in successful aging is producing a portrayal of the oldest-old that is more optimistic than past stereotypes (Andersen & others, 2012; Li & others, 2011). Interventions such as cataract surgery and a variety of rehabilitation strategies are improving the functioning of the oldest-old. And there is cause for optimism in the development of new regimens of prevention and intervention, such as engaging in regular exercise (Buchman & others, 2012; Katzel & Steinbrenner, 2012).

Many experts on aging prefer to talk about such categories as the young-old and oldest-old in terms of *function* rather than age. Remember from Chapter 1 that we described age not only in terms of chronological age but also in terms of biological age, psychological age, and social age. Thus, in terms of *functional age*—the person's actual ability to function—an 85-year-old might well be more biologically and psychologically fit than a 65-year-old.

Still, there are some significant differences between adults in their sixties or seventies and adults who are 85 and older. As we discussed in Chapter 1, Paul Baltes and his colleagues (Baltes, 2003; Scheibe, Freund, & Baltes, 2007) argue that the oldest-old (85 and over) face a number of problems, including sizable losses in cognitive potential and ability to learn; an increase in chronic stress; a substantial prevalence of physical and mental disabilities; high levels of frailty;

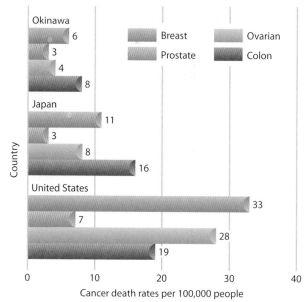

FIGURE **17.2**

RISKS OF DYING FROM CANCER IN OKINAWA, JAPAN, AND THE UNITED STATES. The risk of dying from different forms of cancer is lower in Okinawa than in the United States and Japan (Willcox, Willcox, & Suzuki, 2002). Okinawans eat lots of tofu and soy products, which are rich in flavonoids (substances that are believed to lower the risk of breast and prostate cancer). They also consume large amounts of fish, especially tuna, mackerel, and salmon, which reduce the risk of breast cancer.

(a)

(b)

(*a*) Frenchwoman Jeanne Louise Calment, who died at the age of 122. Greater ages have been claimed, but scientists say the maximum human life span is about 120 to 125 years. (*b*) Heredity is an important component of how long we will live. For example, in Figure 17.1, you were able to add five years to your life expectancy if two or more of your grandparents lived to 80 or beyond. And if you were born a female, you start out with a basic life expectancy that is six years more than if you were born a male. The three sisters shown here, all in their eighties, are celebrating the youngest sister's (*center*) eightieth birthday.

increased loneliness; and the difficulty of dying at older ages with dignity. He contrasts the problems of the oldest-old with the increase in successful aging of adults in their sixties and seventies. Compared with the oldest-old, the young-old have a substantial potential for physical and cognitive fitness, higher levels of emotional well-being, and more effective strategies for mastering the gains and losses of old age.

The oldest-old today are mostly female, and the majority of these women are widowed and live alone if they are not institutionalized. The majority also are hospitalized at some time in the last years of life, and the majority die alone in a hospital or institution. Their needs, capacities, and resources are often different from those of older adults in their sixties and seventies (Scheibe, Freund, & Baltes, 2007).

Despite the negative portrait of the oldest-old by Baltes and his colleagues, they are a heterogeneous, diversified group. In the New England Centenarian Study, 15 percent of the individuals 100 years and older were living independently at home, 35 percent with family members or in assisted living, and 50 percent in nursing homes (Perls, 2007).

A significant number of the oldest-old have cognitive impairments, but many do not (Andersen & others, 2012). Almost one-fourth of the oldest-old are institutionalized, and many report some limitation of activity or difficulties in caring for themselves. However, more than three-fourths are not institutionalized. The majority of older adults aged 80 and over continue to live in the community. More than one-third of older adults 80 and over who live in the community report that their health is excellent or good; 40 percent say that they have no activity limitations (Suzman & others, 1992). Less than 50 percent of U.S. 85- to 89-year-olds have a disability (Siegler, Bosworth, & Poon, 2003), and a substantial subgroup of the oldest-old are robust and active. The oldest-old who have aged successfully have often been unnoticed and unstudied.

BIOLOGICAL THEORIES OF AGING

Even if we stay remarkably healthy, we begin to age at some point. In fact, some life-span experts argue that biological aging begins at birth (Schaie, 2000). What are the biological explanations of aging? Intriguing explanations of why we age are provided by five biological theories: evolutionary theory, cellular clock theory, free-radical theory, mitochondrial theory, and hormonal stress theory.

Evolutionary Theory

Recall from Chapter 2 the view that the benefits conferred by evolutionary selection decrease with age (Baltes, 2003). In the **evolutionary theory of aging,** natural selection has not eliminated many harmful conditions and nonadaptive characteristics in older adults (Le Couteur & Simpson, 2011; Wensink & others, 2012). Why? Because natural selection is linked to reproductive fitness, which is present only in the earlier part of adulthood. For example, consider Alzheimer disease, an irreversible brain disorder that does not appear until late middle adulthood or late adulthood. In evolutionary theory, if Alzheimer disease occurred earlier in development, it might have been eliminated many centuries ago.

Cellular Clock Theory

Cellular clock theory is Leonard Hayflick's (1977) theory that cells can divide a maximum of about 75 to 80 times, and that as we age our cells become less capable of dividing. Hayflick found that cells extracted from adults in their fifties to seventies divided fewer than 75 to 80 times. Based on the ways cells divide, Hayflick places the upper limit of the human life-span potential at about 120 to 125 years of age.

In the last decade, scientists have tried to fill in a gap in cellular clock theory (Niajou & others, 2012; Phillips, 2012). Hayflick did not know why cells die. The answer may lie at the tips of chromosomes, at telomeres, which are DNA sequences that cap chromosomes (Kim & others, 2012; Uringa & others, 2012).

Each time a cell divides, the telomeres become shorter and shorter (see Figure 17.3). After about 70 or 80 replications, the telomeres are dramatically reduced, and the cell no longer can reproduce. One study revealed that healthy centenarians had longer telomeres than unhealthy centenarians (Terry & others, 2008). And a recent study even found that telomere length was linked to social relationships (Uchino & others, 2012). In this study of middle-aged and older adults, women (but not men) with shorter telomeres had more ambivalent relationships with friend, parents, and acquaintances.

Injecting the enzyme telomerase into human cells grown in the laboratory has been found to substantially extend the life of the cells beyond the approximately 70 to 80 normal cell divisions (Aubert & Lansdorp, 2008; Harrison, 2012). However, telomerase is present in approximately 85 to 90 percent of cancerous cells and thus may not produce healthy life extension of cells (Fakhoury, Nimmo, & Autexier, 2007). To capitalize on the high presence of telomerase in cancerous cells, researchers currently are investigating telomerase-related gene therapies that inhibit telomerase and lead to the death of cancerous cells while keeping healthy cells alive (Bernardes de Jesus & others, 2012; Londono-Vallejo & Wellinger, 2012). A recent focus of these gene therapies is on stem cells and their renewal (Hoffmeyer & others, 2012). Telomeres and telomerase are increasingly thought to be key components of the stem cell regeneration process, providing a possible avenue to restrain cancer and delay aging (Piper & others, 2012; Shay, Reddel, & Wright, 2012).

Free-Radical Theory

A second microbiological theory of aging is **free-radical theory,** which states that people age because when cells metabolize energy, the by-products include unstable oxygen molecules known as *free radicals*. The free radicals ricochet around the cells, damaging DNA and other cellular structures (Bachschmid & others, 2012). The damage can lead to a range of disorders, including cancer and arthritis (Manivannan & others, 2012). Overeating is linked with an increase in free radicals, and researchers recently have found that calorie restriction—a diet restricted in calories although adequate in proteins, vitamins, and minerals—reduces the oxidative damage created by free radicals (Cerqueira & others, 2012; Kowaltowski, 2011). In addition to diet, researchers also are exploring the role that exercise might play in reducing oxidative damage in cells (Muthusamy & others, 2012).

Mitochondrial Theory

There is increasing interest in the role that *mitochondria*—tiny bodies within cells that supply essential energy for function, growth, and repair—might play in aging (Lee & Wei, 2012) (see Figure 17.4). **Mitochondrial theory** states that aging is due

FIGURE **17.3**
TELOMERES AND AGING. The photograph shows actual telomeres lighting up the tips of chromosomes.

evolutionary theory of aging This theory states that natural selection has not eliminated many harmful conditions and nonadaptive characteristics in older adults; thus, the benefits conferred by evolution decline with age because natural selection is linked to reproductive fitness.

cellular clock theory Leonard Hayflick's theory that the maximum number of times that human cells can divide is about 75 to 80. As we age, our cells have less capability to divide.

free-radical theory A microbiological theory of aging that states that people age because inside their cells normal metabolism produces unstable oxygen molecules known as free radicals. These molecules ricochet around inside cells, damaging DNA and other cellular structures.

mitochondrial theory The theory that aging is caused by the decay of mitochondria, tiny cellular bodies that supply energy for function, growth, and repair.

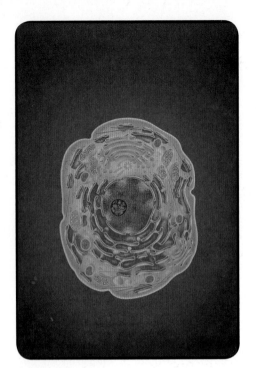

FIGURE **17.4**

MITOCHONDRIA. This color-coded illustration of a typical cell shows mitochondria in green. The illustration also includes the nucleus (pink) with its DNA (brown). *What are ways that changes in mitochondria might be involved in aging?*

hormonal stress theory The theory that aging in the body's hormonal system can lower resistance to stress and increase the likelihood of disease.

to the decay of mitochondria. It appears that this decay is primarily caused by oxidative damage and loss of critical micronutrients supplied by the cell (Eckert, Lipka, & Muller, 2012).

How does this damage and loss of nutrients occur? Among the by-products of mitochondrial energy production are the free radicals we just described. According to the mitochondrial theory, the damage caused by free radicals initiates a self-perpetuating cycle in which oxidative damage impairs mitochondrial function, which results in the generation of even greater amounts of free radicals. The result is that over time the affected mitochondria become so inefficient that they cannot generate enough energy to meet cellular needs (Schulz & others, 2012).

Defects in mitochondria are linked with cardiovascular disease, neurodegenerative diseases such as Alzheimer disease, Parkinson disease, and decline in liver functioning (Eckmann & others, 2012; Moslehi, DePinho, & Sahin, 2012). Mitochondria likely play important roles in neuronal plasticity (de Oliveira, Ferreira Lima, & El-Bacha, 2012). However, it is not known whether the defects in mitochondria cause aging or are merely accompaniments of the aging process (Brand, 2011).

Hormonal Stress Theory Cellular clock, free-radical, and mitochondrial theories attempt to explain aging at the cellular level. In contrast, **hormonal stress theory** argues that aging in the body's hormonal system can lower resistance to stress and increase the likelihood of disease (Finch & Seeman, 1999).

When faced with external challenges, such as stressful situations, the human body adapts by altering internal physiological processes (Almeida & others, 2011). This process of adaptation and adjustment is referred to as *allostasis*. Allostasis is adaptive in the short term; however, continuous accommodation of physiological systems in response to stressors may result in *allostatic load*, a wearing down of body systems due to constant activity (Tomiyama & others, 2012).

Normally, when people experience stressors, the body responds by releasing certain hormones. As people age, the hormones stimulated by stress remain at elevated levels longer than they did when people were younger (Finch, 2011). These prolonged, elevated levels of stress-related hormones are associated with increased risks for many diseases, including cardiovascular disease, cancer, diabetes, and hypertension (Steptoe & Kivimaki, 2012).

Recently, a variation of hormonal stress theory has emphasized the role of a decline in immune system functioning with aging (Cavanagh, Weyand, & Goronzy, 2012; Solana & others, 2012). Aging contributes to immune system deficits that give rise to infectious diseases in older adults (Stowell, Robles, & Kane, 2013). The extended duration of stress and diminished restorative processes in older adults may accelerate the effects of aging on immunity.

Which of these biological theories best explains aging? That question has not yet been answered. It might turn out that more than one—or perhaps all—of these biological processes contribute to aging (Miller, 2009).

Review *Connect* Reflect

LG1 Characterize longevity and discuss the biological theories of aging.

Review

- What is the difference between life span and life expectancy? What characterizes centenarians? What sex differences exist in longevity?
- How can the differences between the young-old and oldest-old be summarized?
- What are the five main biological theories of aging?

Connect

- Go back to Figure 17.1 and see if you can link any of the items listed with research or theories you read about in this section or in earlier chapters (for example, item 2 states "If you are married, add four years," and in Chapter 14 we read that "Individuals who are happily married live longer, healthier lives than either divorced individuals or those who are unhappily married").

Reflect *Your Own Personal Journey of Life*

- To what age do you think you will live? Why? To what age would you like to live?

2 The Course of Physical Development in Late Adulthood

LG2 Describe how a person's brain and body change in late adulthood.

The Aging Brain	Sleep	The Immune System	Physical Appearance and Movement	Sensory Development	The Circulatory System and Lungs	Sexuality

The physical decline that accompanies aging usually occurs slowly, and sometimes lost function can even be restored. We'll examine the main physical changes behind the losses of late adulthood and describe ways that older adults can age successfully.

THE AGING BRAIN

How does the brain change during late adulthood? Does it retain plasticity?

The Shrinking, Slowing Brain   On average, the brain loses 5 to 10 percent of its weight between the ages of 20 and 90. Brain volume also decreases (Fjell & Walhovd, 2010). A recent study found a decrease in total brain volume and volume in key brain structures such as the frontal lobes and hippocampus from 22 to 88 years of age (Sherwood & others, 2011). Another study found that the volume of the brain was 15 percent less in older adults than younger adults (Shan & others, 2005). A recent analysis concluded that in healthy aging the decrease in brain volume is due mainly to shrinkage of neurons, lower numbers of synapses, and reduced length of axons but only to a minor extent attributable to neuron loss (Fjell & Walhovd, 2010).

Some areas of the brain shrink more than others (Raz & others, 2010). The prefrontal cortex is one area that shrinks with aging, and recent research has linked this shrinkage with a decrease in cognitive functioning and slower motor behavior in older adults (Rosano & others, 2012; Sakatini, Tanida, & Katsuyama, 2010).

A general slowing of function in the brain and spinal cord begins in middle adulthood and accelerates in late adulthood (Rosano & others, 2012). Both physical coordination and intellectual performance are affected. For example, after age 70 many adults no longer show a knee jerk reflex, and by age 90 most reflexes are much slower (Spence, 1989). The slowing of the brain can impair the performance of older adults on intelligence tests and various cognitive tasks, especially those that are timed (Lu & others, 2011). For example, a neuroimaging study revealed that older adults were more likely to be characterized by slower processing in the prefrontal cortex during retrieval of information on a cognitive task than were younger adults (Rypma, Eldreth, & Rebbechi, 2007).

Aging has also been linked to a reduction in synaptic functioning and the production of some neurotransmitters, including acetylcholine, dopamine, and gamma-aminobutyric acid (GABA) (Juraska & Lowry, 2012; Marcello & others, 2012). Reductions in acetylcholine have been linked to small declines in memory functioning and to the severe memory loss associated with Alzheimer disease, which will be further discussed in Chapter 18 (Newman & others, 2012). Normal age-related reductions in dopamine may cause problems in planning and carrying out motor activities (Balarajah & Cavanna, 2012). Severe reductions in the production of dopamine have been linked with age-related diseases characterized by a loss of motor control, such as Parkinson disease (Sutachan & others, 2012). GABA helps to control the preciseness of the signal sent from one neuron to another, decreasing "noise," and its production decreases with aging (Garrido & others, 2011).

The Adapting Brain   The story of the aging brain is far from being limited to loss and decline in functioning. The aging brain has remarkable adaptive capabilities (Nyberg & Backman, 2011; Vance & others, 2012). Even in late adulthood, the brain loses only a portion of its ability to function, and the activities older adults engage in can influence the brain's development (Ando, 2012; Kraft, 2012). For example, in one fMRI study, higher levels of aerobic fitness

developmental **connection**

Brain Development

Substantial growth in the prefrontal cortex occurs throughout infancy, childhood, and adolescence. Chapter 4, p. 112; Chapter 7, p. 211; Chapter 9, p. 282; Chapter 11, p. 361

FIGURE **17.5**

GENERATING NEW NERVE CELLS IN ADULT MICE. Researchers have found that exercise (running) and an enriched environment (a larger cage and many toys) can cause brain cells to divide and form new brain cells (Kempermann, van Praag, & Gage, 2000). Cells were labeled with a chemical marker that becomes integrated into the DNA of dividing cells (red). Four weeks later, they were also labeled to mark neurons (nerve cells). As shown here, both the running mice and the mice in an enriched environment had many cells that were still dividing (red) and others that had differentiated into new nerve cells (orange).

Exercise   Enriched Environment

developmental **connection**

Brain Development

At the peak of neurogenesis in prenatal development, it is estimated that as many as 200,000 neurons are being generated every minute. Chapter 3, p. 82

were linked with greater volume in the hippocampus, which translates into better memory (Erickson & others, 2009).

Can adults, even aging adults, generate new neurons? Researchers have found that **neurogenesis,** the generation of new neurons, does occur in lower mammalian species, such as mice. Also, research indicates that exercise and an enriched, complex environment can generate new brain cells in rats and mice, and that stress reduces their survival rate (Mustroph & others, 2012; Salmaso & others, 2012) (see Figure 17.5). And a recent study revealed that coping with stress stimulated hippocampal neurogenesis in adult monkeys (Lyons & others, 2010). Researchers also have discovered that if rats are cognitively challenged to learn something, new brain cells survive longer (Shors, 2009).

It also is now accepted that neurogenesis can occur in human adults (Goritz & Frisen, 2012). However, researchers have documented neurogenesis in only two brain regions: the hippocampus, which is involved in memory, and the olfactory bulb, which is involved in smell (Ming & Song, 2011; Xu & others, 2012). It also is not known what functions these new brain cells perform, and at this point researchers have documented that they last for only several weeks (Nelson, 2006). Researchers currently are studying factors that might inhibit or promote neurogenesis, including various drugs, stress, and exercise (Gil-Mohapel & others, 2010). They also are examining how the grafting of neural stem cells to various regions of the brain, such as the hippocampus, might increase neurogenesis (Decimo & others, 2012). Interest also is being directed to the possible role neurogenesis might play in neurogenerative diseases, such as Alzheimer disease, Parkinson disease, and Huntington disease (Walton & others, 2012).

Dendritic growth can occur in human adults, possibly even in older adults (Eliasieh, Liets, & Chalupa, 2007). Recall from Chapter 4, "Physical Development in Infancy," that dendrites are the receiving portion of the neuron. One study compared the brains of adults at various ages (Coleman, 1986). From the forties through the seventies, the growth of dendrites increased. However, among people in their nineties dendritic growth no longer occurred. This dendritic growth might compensate for the possible loss of neurons through the seventies but not in the nineties. Lack of dendritic growth in older adults could be due to a lack of environmental stimulation and activity. Further research is needed to clarify what changes characterize dendrites during aging.

Stanley Rapaport (1994), chief of the neurosciences laboratory at the National Institute on Aging, demonstrated another way in which the aging brain can adapt. He compared the brains of younger and older people engaged in the same tasks. The older brains had rewired themselves to compensate for losses. If one neuron was not up to the job, neighboring neurons helped to pick up the slack. Rapaport concluded that as brains age, they can shift responsibility for a given task from one region to another.

Changes in lateralization may provide one type of adaptation in aging adults (Zhu, Zacks, & Slade, 2010). Recall that lateralization is the specialization of function in one hemisphere of the brain or the other. Using neuroimaging techniques, researchers found that brain activity in the prefrontal cortex is lateralized less in older adults than in younger adults when they are engaging in cognitive tasks (Angel & others, 2011; Cabeza, 2002; Manenti & others, 2011;

developmental **connection**

Language

Speech and grammar are strongly lateralized, depending on activity in the left hemisphere. Chapter 4, p. 112

neurogenesis The generation of new neurons.

Rossi & others, 2005). For example, Figure 17.6 shows that when younger adults are given the task of recognizing words they have previously seen, they process the information primarily in the right hemisphere; older adults are more likely to use both hemispheres (Madden & others, 1999). The decrease in lateralization in older adults likely plays a compensatory role in the aging brain. That is, using both hemispheres may improve the cognitive functioning of older adults.

FIGURE **17.6**

THE DECREASE IN BRAIN LATERALIZATION IN OLDER ADULTS. Younger adults primarily used the right prefrontal region of the brain (*top left photo*) during a recall memory task, whereas older adults used both the left and right prefrontal regions (*bottom two photos*).

Of course, there are individual differences in how the brain changes in older adults (Nyberg & others, 2012). Consider highly successful businessman 80-year-old T. Boone Pickens, who continues to lead a highly active lifestyle, regularly exercising and engaging in cognitively complex work. Pickens recently underwent an fMRI in cognitive neuroscientist Denise Park's laboratory, during which he was presented with various cognitive tasks. Instead of both hemispheres being active, his left hemisphere was dominant, just as is the case for most younger adults (Helman, 2008). Indeed, as the cognitive tasks became more complex, Pickens was more likely to use the left hemisphere of his brain (see Figure 17.7). Further indication of variation in the link between brain lateralization and cognitive processing was found in a recent study (Manenti, Cotelli, & Miniussi, 2010). Older adults who performed better on memory tasks showed less asymmetry in the prefrontal cortex than their counterparts who performed more poorly on the tasks.

Does staying intellectually challenged affect one's quality of life and longevity? To read further about aging and the brain, see *Connecting Through Research*.

Left Hemisphere   **Right Hemisphere**

SLEEP

Approximately 50 percent of older adults complain of having difficulty sleeping (Neikrug & Ancoli-Israel, 2010). Poor sleep can result in earlier death and is linked to a lower level of cognitive functioning (Naismith, Lewis, & Rogers, 2011). For example, researchers found that spending more time in sleep benefitted older adults' memory (Aly & Moscovitch, 2010). And a recent research review indicated that improving older adults' sleep through behavioral and pharmaceutical treatments may enhance their cognitive skills (Pace-Schott & Spencer, 2011).

Many of the sleep problems of older adults are associated with health problems (Rothman & Mattson, 2012). Strategies to help older adults sleep better at night include avoiding caffeine, avoiding over-the-counter sleep remedies, staying physically active during the day, staying mentally active, and limiting naps (Morin, Savard, & Ouellet, 2013). A recent study revealed that regular exercise improves the sleep profile of older adults (Lira & others, 2011).

THE IMMUNE SYSTEM

Decline in the functioning of the body's immune system with aging is well documented (Cavanaugh, Weyand, & Goronzy, 2012; Stowell, Robles, & Kane, 2013). As indicated earlier in our discussion of hormonal stress theory, the extended duration of stress and diminished restorative processes in older adults may accelerate the effects of aging on immunity (Solana & others, 2012). Also, malnutrition involving low levels of protein is linked to a decrease in T cells that destroy infected cells and hence to deterioration in the immune system (Hughes & others, 2009). Exercise can improve immune system functioning (Spielmann & others, 2011). Because of the decline in the functioning of the immune system that accompanies aging, vaccination against influenza is especially important in older adults (Parodi & others, 2011).

PHYSICAL APPEARANCE AND MOVEMENT

In late adulthood, the changes in physical appearance that began occurring during middle age (as discussed in Chapter 15) become more pronounced. Wrinkles and age spots are the most noticeable changes.

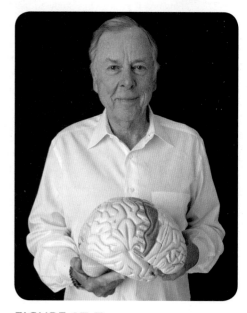

FIGURE **17.7**

INDIVIDUAL DIFFERENCES IN HEMISPHERIC SPECIALIZATION IN OLDER ADULTS. On tough questions—such as "Are 'zombies' and 'unicorns' living or nonliving?"—the red patches indicate that 80-year-old T. Boone Pickens (above, holding a model of the brain) was relying mainly on the left hemisphere of his brain to make a decision. Most older adults show a stronger bilateral activation, using both hemispheres more equally than Pickens, whose lateralization was more characteristic of younger adults.

connecting through research

Does Staying Intellectually Challenged Affect One's Quality of Life and Longevity?

The Nun Study, directed by David Snowdon, is an intriguing ongoing investigation of aging in 678 nuns, many of whom live in a convent in Mankato, Minnesota (Snowdon, 2003; Tyas & others, 2007). Each of the 678 nuns agreed to participate in annual assessments of their cognitive and physical functioning. They also agreed to donate their brains for scientific research when they die, and they are the largest group of brain donors in the world. Examination of the nuns' donated brains, as well as others', has led neuroscientists to believe that the brain has a remarkable capacity to change and grow, even in old age. The Sisters of Notre Dame in Mankato lead intellectually challenging lives, and brain researchers believe this contributes to their quality of life as older adults and possibly to their longevity.

Findings from the Nun Study so far include the following:

(a) **(b)**

(a) Sister Marcella Zachman (*left*) finally stopped teaching at age 97. Now, at 99, she helps ailing nuns exercise their brains by quizzing them on vocabulary or playing a card game called Skip-Bo, at which she deliberately loses. Sister Mary Esther Boor (*right*), also 99 years of age, is a former teacher who stays alert by doing puzzles and volunteering to work the front desk. (b) A technician holds the brain of a deceased Mankato nun. The nuns donate their brains for research that explores the effects of stimulation on brain growth.

- Idea density, a measure of linguistic ability assessed early in the adult years (age 22), was linked with higher brain weight, fewer incidences of mild cognitive impairment, and fewer characteristics of Alzheimer disease in 75- to 95-year-old nuns (Riley & others, 2005).
- Positive emotions early in adulthood were linked to longevity (Danner, Snowdon, & Friesen, 2001). Handwritten autobiographies from 180 nuns, composed when they were 22 years of age, were scored for emotional content. The nuns whose early writings had higher scores for positive emotional content were more likely to still be alive at 75 to 95 years of age than their counterparts whose early writings were characterized by negative emotional content.
- Sisters who had taught for most of their lives showed more moderate declines in intellectual skills than those who had spent most of their

lives in service-based tasks, which supports the notion that stimulating the brain with intellectual activity keeps neurons healthy and alive (Snowdon, 2002).

This and other research provides hope that scientists will discover ways to tap into the brain's capacity to adapt in order to prevent and treat brain diseases (Mortimer, 2012). For example, scientists might learn more effective ways to improve older adults' cognitive functioning, reduce Alzheimer disease, and help older adults recover from strokes (Bornstein & Poon, 2012; Farias & others, 2012; Wang & others, 2012). Even when areas of the brain are permanently damaged by stroke, new message routes can be created to get around the blockage or to resume the function of that area, indicating that the brain does adapt.

developmental **connection**

Biological Processes

On average, men lose 1 to 2 inches in height from 30 to 70 years of age and women can lose an much as 2 inches in height from age 25 to 75. Chapter 15, p. 486

We also become shorter as we get older. As we saw in Chapter 15, both men and women become shorter in late adulthood because of bone loss in their vertebrae (Hoyer & Roodin, 2009).

Our weight usually drops after we reach 60 years of age. This likely occurs because we lose muscle, which also gives our bodies a "sagging" look (Evans, 2010). Figure 17.8 shows the declining percentage of muscle and bone from age 25 to age 75, and the corresponding increase in the percentage of fat.

Older adults move more slowly than young adults, and this slowing occurs for movements with a wide range of difficulty (Davis & others, 2013) (see Figure 17.9). Adequate mobility is an important aspect of maintaining an independent and active lifestyle in late adulthood

(Clark & others, 2011). Recent research indicates that obesity contributes to mobility limitation in older adults (Vincent, Raiser, & Vincent, 2012). The good news is that regular walking decreases the onset of physical disability and reduces functional limitations in older adults (Mullen & others, 2012; Newman & others, 2006). Also, a recent study found that a combined program of physical activity and weight loss was linked to preserving mobility in older, obese adults in poor cardiovascular health (Rejeski & others, 2011).

SENSORY DEVELOPMENT

Seeing, hearing, and other aspects of sensory functioning are linked with our ability to perform everyday activities (Hochberg & others, 2012; Schneider & others, 2011). This link was documented in a study of more than 500 adults, 70 to 102 years of age, in which sensory acuity, especially visual capacity, was related to whether and how well older adults bathed and groomed themselves, completed household chores, engaged in intellectual activities, and watched TV (Marsiske, Klumb, & Baltes, 1997). How do vision, hearing, taste, smell, touch, and pain change in late adulthood?

Vision   With aging, visual acuity, color vision, and depth perception decline. Several diseases of the eye also may emerge in aging adults.

Visual Acuity   In late adulthood, the decline in vision that began for most adults in early or middle adulthood becomes more pronounced (Casco & others, 2011; Polat & others, 2012). Visual processing speed declines in older adults (Owsley, 2011). Night driving is especially difficult, to some extent because of diminishing sensitivity to contrasts and reduced tolerance for glare (Naumann, Dellinger, & Kresnow, 2011; van Rijn & others, 2011). Dark adaptation is slower—that is, older individuals take longer to recover their vision when going from a well-lighted room to semidarkness. The area of the visual field becomes smaller, a change suggesting that the intensity of a stimulus in the peripheral area of the visual field needs to be increased if the stimulus is to be seen. Events taking place away from the center of the visual field might not be detected (West & others, 2010).

This visual decline often can be traced to a reduction in the quality or intensity of light reaching the retina (Nag & Wadhwa, 2012). At 60 years of age, the retina receives only about one-third as much light as it did at 20 years of age (Scialfa & Kline, 2007). In extreme old age, these changes might be accompanied by degenerative changes in the retina, causing severe difficulty in seeing. Large-print books and magnifiers might be needed in such cases.

An extensive study of visual changes in adults found that the age of older adults was a significant factor in how extensively their visual functioning differed from that of younger adults (Brabyn & others, 2001). Beyond 75, and more so beyond age 85, older adults showed significantly worse performance on a number of visual tasks when compared with young adults and older adults in their sixties and early seventies. The greatest decline in visual perception beyond 75, and especially beyond 85, involved glare. The older adults, especially those 85 and older, fared much worse in being able to see clearly when glare was present, and they took much longer to recover from glare than younger adults did (see Figure 17.10). For example, whereas young adults recover vision following glare in less than 10 seconds, 50 percent of 90-year-olds have not recovered vision after 1.5 minutes.

Recent research has shown that sensory decline in older adults is linked to a decline in cognitive functioning. One study of individuals in their 70s revealed that visual decline was related to slower speed of processing information, which in turn was associated with greater cognitive decline (Clay & others, 2009). And a recent study found that hearing loss was associated with a reduction in cognitive functioning in older adults (Lin, 2011).

Color Vision   Color vision also may decline with age in older adults as a result of the yellowing of the lens of the eye (Scialfa & Kline, 2007). This decline is most likely to occur in the green-blue-violet part of the color spectrum. As a result, older adults may have trouble accurately matching closely related colors such as navy socks and black socks.

Percentage of total weight

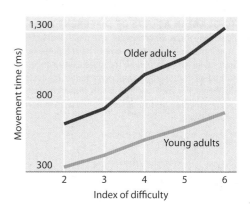

FIGURE 17.8

CHANGES IN BODY COMPOSITION OF BONE, MUSCLE, AND FAT FROM 25 TO 75 YEARS OF AGE. Notice the decrease in bone and muscle and the increase in fat from 25 to 75 years of age.

FIGURE 17.9

MOVEMENT AND AGING. Older adults take longer to move than young adults, and this change occurs across a range of movement difficulty (Ketcham & Stelmach, 2001).

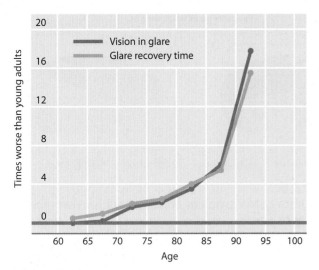

FIGURE **17.10**

RATES OF DECLINE IN VISUAL FUNCTIONING RELATED TO GLARE IN ADULTS OF DIFFERENT AGES. Older adults, especially those 85 and older, fare much worse than younger adults in being able to see clearly when glare is present, and their recovery from glare is much slower. These data were collected from a random sample of community-dwelling older adults living in Marin County, California. For each age, the graph shows the factor by which the group's median performance was worse than normative values for young adults.

developmental **connection**

Perception

The visual cliff was used to determine if infants have depth perception. Chapter 4, p. 135

FIGURE **17.11**

MACULAR DEGENERATION. This simulation of the effect of macular degeneration shows how individuals with this eye disease can see their peripheral field of vision but can't clearly see what is in their central visual field.

Depth Perception   As with many areas of perception, depth perception changes little after infancy until adults become older. Depth perception typically declines in late adulthood, which can make it difficult for the older adult to determine how close or far away or how high or low something is (Bian & Anderson, 2008). A decline in depth perception can make steps or street curbs difficult to manage.

Diseases of the Eye   Three diseases that can impair the vision of older adults are cataracts, glaucoma, and macular degeneration:

- **Cataracts** involve a thickening of the lens of the eye that causes vision to become cloudy, opaque, and distorted (Choi & others, 2012). By age 70, approximately 30 percent of individuals experience a partial loss of vision due to cataracts. Initially, cataracts can be treated by glasses; if they worsen, the cloudy lens should be removed and replaced with an artificial one (Chung & others, 2009). Diabetes is a risk factor for the development of cataracts (Olafsdottir, Andersson, & Stefansson, 2012).

- **Glaucoma** involves damage to the optic nerve because of the pressure created by a buildup of fluid in the eye (Kokotas & others, 2012). Approximately 1 percent of individuals in their seventies and 10 percent of those in their nineties have glaucoma, which can be treated with eye drops. If left untreated, glaucoma can ultimately destroy a person's vision.

- **Macular degeneration** involves deterioration of the macula of the retina, which corresponds to the focal center of the visual field. Individuals with macular degeneration may have relatively normal peripheral vision but be unable to see clearly what is right in front of them (Taylor, 2012) (see Figure 17.11). This condition affects 1 in 25 individuals from 66 to 74 years of age and 1 in 6 of those 75 years old and older. One study revealed that cigarette smoking contributes to macular degeneration (Schmidt & others, 2006). If the disease is detected early, it can be treated with laser surgery (Sorensen & Kemp, 2010). However, macular degeneration is difficult to treat and thus is a leading cause of blindness in older adults (Cacho & others, 2010). A recent study found that macular degeneration was linked to increased risk of falls in adults 77 years and older (Wood & others, 2011).

Hearing   For hearing as for vision, the age of older adults is important in determining the degree of decline (Pacala & Yeuh, 2012) (see Figure 17.12). The decline in vision and hearing is much greater in individuals 75 years and older than in individuals 65 to 74 years of age (Charness & Bosman, 1992).

Hearing impairment usually does not become much of an impediment until late adulthood (Li-Korotky, 2012). Only 19 percent of individuals from 45 to 54 years of age experience some type of hearing problem (Harris, 1975). By contrast, a recent national survey revealed that 63 percent of adults 70 years and older had a hearing loss defined as an inability to hear sounds at frequencies higher than 25 dB with their better ear (Lin & others, 2011). In this study, hearing aids were used by 40 percent of those with moderate hearing loss. Fifteen percent of the population over the age of 65 is estimated to be legally deaf, usually due to degeneration of the *cochlea*, the primary neural receptor for hearing in the inner ear (Adams, 2009).

Older adults often don't recognize that they have a hearing problem, deny that they have one, or accept it as a part of growing old (Pacala & Yeuh, 2012). Older women are more likely to seek treatment for their hearing problem than older men (Fowler & Leigh-Paffenroth, 2007). A recent study found that the severity of age-related hearing loss was linked to impaired activities in daily living (Gopinath & others, 2012).

Two devices can be used to minimize the problems linked to hearing loss in older adults: (1) hearing aids that amplify sound to reduce middle ear–based conductive hearing loss, and (2) cochlear implants that restore some hearing following neurosensory hearing loss (Kidd & Bao, 2012). Currently, researchers are exploring the use of stem cells as an alternative to cochlear implants (Parker, 2011).

Perceptual System	65 to 74 years	75 years and older
Vision	There is a loss of acuity even with corrective lenses. Less transmission of light occurs through the retina (half as much as in young adults). Greater susceptibility to glare occurs. Color discrimination ability decreases.	There is a significant loss of visual acuity and color discrimination, and a decrease in the size of the perceived visual field. In late old age, people are at significant risk for visual dysfunction from cataracts and glaucoma.
Hearing	There is a significant loss of hearing at high frequencies and some loss at middle frequencies. These losses can be helped by a hearing aid. There is greater susceptibility to masking of what is heard by noise.	There is a significant loss at high and middle frequencies. A hearing aid is more likely to be needed than in young-old age.

FIGURE **17.12**
VISION AND HEARING DECLINE IN LATE ADULTHOOD

Smell and Taste   Most older adults lose some of their sense of smell or taste, or both (Murphy, 2009). These losses often begin around 60 years of age (Hawkes, 2006). A majority of individuals age 80 and older experience a significant reduction in smell (Lafreniere & Mann, 2009). Researchers have found that older adults show a greater decline in their sense of smell than in their taste (Schiffman, 2007). Smell and taste decline less in healthy older adults than in their less healthy counterparts.

Reductions in the ability to smell and taste can reduce enjoyment of food and life satisfaction (Rolls & Drewnowski, 2007). Also, a declining sense of smell can reduce the ability to detect smoke from a fire. If elderly individuals need to be encouraged to eat more, compounds that stimulate the olfactory nerve are sometimes added to food. However, many older adults compensate for their diminished taste and smell by eating sweeter, spicier, and saltier foods, which can lead to eating more low-nutrient, highly seasoned "junk food" (Hoyer & Roodin, 2009). Further, one study of people aged 19 to 39, 40 to 59, and 60 and older revealed that although adults' ability to detect a smell declined as they got older, the perceived pleasantness of a smell increased in the older group (Markovic & others, 2007).

Touch and Pain   Changes in touch and pain sensitivity are also associated with aging (Pho & others, 2012). One study found that with aging individuals could detect touch less in the lower extremities (ankles, knees, and so on) than in the upper extremities (wrists, shoulders, and so on) (Corso, 1977). For most older adults, a decline in touch sensitivity is not problematic (Hoyer & Roodin, 2009). And one study revealed that older adults who are blind retain a high level of touch sensitivity, which likely is linked to their use of active touch in their daily lives (Legge & others, 2008).

Older adults are less sensitive to pain and suffer from it less than younger adults do (Harkins, Price, & Martinelli, 1986). Although decreased sensitivity to pain can help older adults cope with disease and injury, it can also mask injuries and illnesses that need to be treated.

Researchers have found that most older adults show reductions in their senses of smell and taste. However, a recent study revealed that the perceived pleasantness of a smell increased in older adults (Markovic & others, 2007).

THE CIRCULATORY SYSTEM AND LUNGS

Cardiovascular disorders increase in late adulthood (Emery, Anderson, & Goodwin, 2013; Veronica & Esther, 2012). In one analysis, 57 percent of 80-year-old men and 60 percent of 81-year-old women had hypertension, and 32 percent of the men and 31 percent of the women had experienced a stroke (Aronow, 2007).

Today, most experts on aging recommend that consistent blood pressures above 120/80 should be treated to reduce the risk of heart attack, stroke, or kidney disease (Krakoff, 2008). A rise in blood pressure with age can be linked to illness, obesity, stiffening of blood vessels, stress, or lack of exercise (Shizukuda, Plummer, & Harrelson, 2010). The longer any of these factors persist, the higher the individual's blood pressure gets. A recent national analysis found that resistant hypertension (hypertension that cannot be controlled with at least four

cataracts A thickening of the lens of the eye that causes vision to become cloudy, opaque, and distorted.

glaucoma Damage to the optic nerve because of the pressure created by a buildup of fluid in the eye.

macular degeneration A disease that involves deterioration of the macula of the retina, which corresponds to the focal center of the visual field.

developmental **connection**

Sexuality

Older adults may express their sexuality differently than younger adults, especially enjoying touching and caressing in their sexual relationship when sexual intercourse becomes difficult. Chapter 19, p. 609

What are some characteristics of sexuality in older adults? How does sexuality change as older adults go through the late adulthood period?

antihypertensive agents) is increasing in the United States, likely because of increases in obesity and the number of older adults (Roberie & Elliott, 2012). Resistant hypertension is more common in the elderly.

Various drugs, a healthy diet, and exercise can reduce the risk of cardiovascular disease in many older adults (Guirado & others, 2012). One recent study revealed that diminished exercise capacity and lack of walking were the best predictors of earlier death in older adults with heart problems (Reibis & others, 2010).

Lung capacity drops 40 percent between the ages of 20 and 80, even when disease is not present (Fozard, 1992). Lungs lose elasticity, the chest shrinks, and the diaphragm weakens (Marek & others, 2011). The good news, though, is that older adults can improve lung functioning with diaphragm-strengthening exercises. Severe impairments in lung functioning and death can result from smoking (Wilhelmsen & others, 2011).

SEXUALITY

In the absence of two circumstances—disease and the belief that old people are or should be asexual—sexuality can be lifelong (Benbow & Beeston, 2012; Marshall, 2012). Aging, however, does induce some changes in human sexual performance, more so in males than in females (Gray & Garcia, 2012; Taylor & Gosney, 2011).

Orgasm becomes less frequent in males with age, occurring in every second to third attempt rather than every time. More direct stimulation usually is needed to produce an erection. From 65 to 80 years of age, approximately one out of four men have serious problems getting and/or keeping erections, and after 80 years of age the percentage rises to one out of two men (Butler & Lewis, 2002). However, with recent advances in erectile dysfunction medications, such as Viagra, an increasing number of older adults, especially the young-old, are able to have an erection (Lowe & Costabile, 2012; Rubio-Aurioles & others, 2012).

An interview study of more than 3,000 adults 57 to 85 years of age revealed that many older adults are sexually active as long as they are healthy (Lindau & others, 2007). Sexual activity did decline through the later years of life: 73 percent of people 57 to 64 years old, 53 percent of people 65 to 74 years old, and 26 percent of adults 75 to 85 years old reported that they were sexually active. Even in the sexually active oldest group (75 to 85), more than 50 percent said they still have sex at least two to three times a month. Fifty-eight percent of sexually active 65- to 74-year-olds and 31 percent of 75- to 85-year-olds said they engage in oral sex. As with middle-aged and younger adults, older adults who did not have a partner were far less likely to be sexually active than those who had a partner. For older adults with a partner who reported not having sex, the main reason was poor health, especially the male partner's physical health.

A recent large-scale study of individuals from 57 to 85 years of age revealed that sexual activity, a good-quality sexual life, and interest in sex were positively related to health in middle and late adulthood (Lindau & Gavrilova, 2010). Also in this study, these aspects of sexuality were higher for aging males than aging women, and this gap widened with age. Further, sexually active life expectancy was longer for men than women, but men lost more years of sexually active life due to poor health than women did.

As indicated in Figure 17.13, sexual activity with a partner declined from the last part of middle adulthood through late adulthood, with a lower rate of sexual activity with a partner for women than men. Indeed, a challenge for a sexually interested older woman is not having a partner. At 70 years of age, approximately 70 percent of women don't have a partner compared with only about 35 percent of men. Many older women's husbands have died, and many older men are in relationships with younger women.

Various therapies for older adults who report sexual difficulties have been effective (Bain, 2010). In one study, sex education—which consisted largely of simply giving sexual information—led to increased sexual interest, knowledge, and activity in older adults (White & Catania, 1981). Even when intercourse is impaired by infirmity, other relationship needs persist, among them closeness, sensuality, and being valued as a man or a woman. We discuss these needs in Chapter 19.

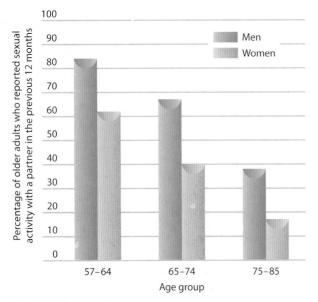

FIGURE **17.13**

SEXUAL ACTIVITY IN OLDER ADULTS WITH A PARTNER

Review *Connect* Reflect

LG2 Describe how a person's brain and body change in late adulthood.

Review

- How much plasticity and adaptability does the aging brain have?
- What characterizes older adults' sleep?
- How does the immune system change with aging?
- What changes in physical appearance and movement characterize late adulthood?
- How do vision, hearing, smell and taste, touch, and sensitivity to pain change in older adults?
- How does the circulatory system change in older adults? How do the lungs change in older adults?
- What is the nature of sexuality in late adulthood?

Connect

- Many of the declines in the functioning of individuals in late adulthood start occurring in middle adulthood. Which declines in functioning occur mainly in late adulthood?

Reflect *Your Own Personal Journey of Life*

- If you could interview the Mankato nuns, what questions would you want to ask them to help you improve your understanding of successful aging?

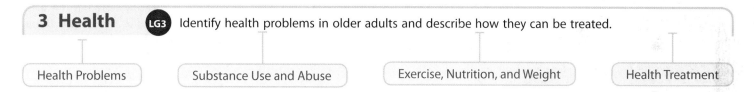

3 Health   **LG3** Identify health problems in older adults and describe how they can be treated.

| Health Problems | Substance Use and Abuse | Exercise, Nutrition, and Weight | Health Treatment |

How healthy are older adults? What types of health problems do they have, and what can be done to maintain or improve their health and ability to function in everyday life?

HEALTH PROBLEMS

As we age, we become more susceptible to disease or illness. The majority of adults who are still alive at 80 years of age or older are likely to have some type of impairment. Chronic diseases (those with a slow onset and a long duration) are rare in early adulthood, increase in middle adulthood, and become more common in late adulthood (Tinetti & others, 2011). As indicated in Figure 17.14, 84 percent of U.S. adults 65 years of age and older have one or more chronic conditions, and 62 percent have two or more chronic conditions (Partnership for Solutions, 2002).

As shown in Figure 17.15, arthritis is the most common chronic disorder in late adulthood, followed by hypertension. Older women have a higher incidence of arthritis and hypertension and are more likely to have visual problems, but are less likely to have hearing problems, than older men are.

Although adults over the age of 65 often have a physical impairment, many of them can still carry on their everyday activities or work. Chronic conditions associated with the greatest limitations on work are heart conditions (52 percent), diabetes (34 percent), asthma (27 percent), and arthritis (27 percent). Conflict in relationships has been linked with greater decline in older adults with diabetes or hypertension (Seeman & Chen, 2002). Low income is also strongly related to health problems in late adulthood (Ferraro, 2006). Approximately three times as many poor as non-poor older adults report that their activities are limited by chronic disorders.

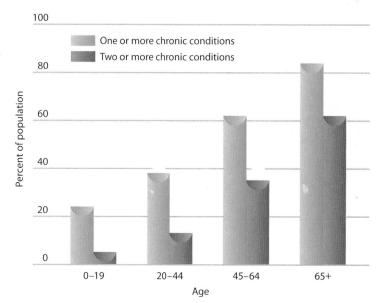

FIGURE 17.14

PERCENT OF U.S. POPULATION WITH CHRONIC CONDITIONS ACROSS AGE GROUPS

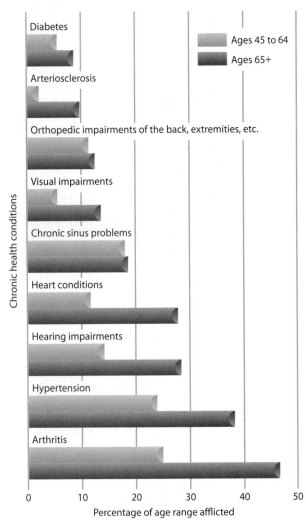

FIGURE **17.15**
THE MOST PREVALENT CHRONIC CONDITIONS IN MIDDLE AND LATE ADULTHOOD

How many of us older persons have really been prepared for the second half of life, for old age, and eternity?

—Carl Jung
Swiss Psychoanalyst, 20th Century

arthritis Inflammation of the joints that is accompanied by pain, stiffness, and movement problems; this disease is especially common in older adults.

osteoporosis A chronic condition that involves an extensive loss of bone tissue and is the main reason many older adults walk with a marked stoop. Women are especially vulnerable to osteoporosis.

Recent studies document links between low socioeconomic status and health problems (Aittomaki & others, 2012; Friedman & Herd, 2010). One study revealed that frailty increased for low-income older adults, regardless of their ethnicity (Szanton & others, 2010).

Causes of Death in Older Adults Nearly 60 percent of U.S. adults 65 to 74 years old die of cancer or cardiovascular disease (Murphy, Xu, & Kochanek, 2012). As we saw in Chapter 15, cancer recently replaced cardiovascular disease as the leading cause of death in U.S. middle-aged adults. The same realignment of causes of death has also occurred in 65- to 74-year-olds, with cancer now the leading cause of death in this age group (National Center for Health Statistics, 2010). The decline in cardiovascular disease in middle-aged and older adults is due to improved drugs, a decrease in smoking, better diet, and an increase in exercise. However, in the age groups 75 to 84 and 85 and over, cardiovascular disease still is the leading cause of death (National Center for Health Statistics, 2010). As individuals age through the late adult years, the older they are the more likely they are to die of cardiovascular disease rather than cancer (National Center for Health Statistics, 2010).

Ethnicity is linked with the death rates of older adults (National Center for Health Statistics, 2010). Among ethnic groups in the United States, African Americans have high death rates for stroke, heart disease, lung cancer, and female breast cancer. Asian Americans and Latinos have low death rates for these diseases. In the last decade, death rates for most diseases in African Americans, Latinos, and Asian Americans have decreased. However, death rates for most diseases still remain high for African Americans (U.S. Census Bureau, 2011).

Arthritis **Arthritis** is an inflammation of the joints accompanied by pain, stiffness, and movement problems. Arthritis is especially common in older adults (Davis & others, 2013). This disorder can affect hips, knees, ankles, fingers, and vertebrae. Individuals with arthritis often experience pain and stiffness, as well as problems in moving about and performing routine daily activities. There is no known cure for arthritis. However, the symptoms of arthritis can be reduced by drugs such as aspirin, range-of-motion exercises for the afflicted joints, weight reduction, and in extreme cases, replacement of the crippled joint with a prosthesis (Xu & others, 2010). Recent studies also document the benefits of exercise in older adults with arthritis (Baruth & Wilcox, 2011; Semanik, Chang, & Dunlop, 2012). For example, a high-intensity, 16-week strength-training program significantly increased the strength and reduced the pain of arthritis patients (Flint-Wagner & others, 2009).

Osteoporosis Normal aging brings some loss of bone tissue, but in some instances loss of bone tissue can become severe. **Osteoporosis** involves an extensive loss of bone tissue. Osteoporosis is the main reason many older adults walk with a marked stoop. Women are especially vulnerable to osteoporosis, which is the leading cause of broken bones in women (Davis & others, 2013; Ragucci & Shrader, 2011). Approximately 80 percent of osteoporosis cases in the United States occur in females, 20 percent in males. Almost two-thirds of all women over the age of 60 are affected by osteoporosis. It is more common in non-Latina White, thin, and small-framed women.

Osteoporosis is related to deficiencies in calcium, vitamin D, estrogen, and lack of exercise (Howe & others, 2011; Roghani & others, 2012). To prevent osteoporosis, young and middle-aged women should eat foods rich in calcium (such as dairy products, broccoli, turnip greens, and kale), exercise regularly, and avoid smoking (Bonjour & others, 2012; Forsyth, Quon, & Konkle, 2011). Drugs such as Fosamax can be used to reduce the risk of osteoporosis. Aging women should also get bone density checks.

Accidents Unintended accidents are the ninth leading cause of death among older adults (U.S. Census Bureau, 2011). Injuries resulting from a fall at home or a traffic accident in which an older adult is a driver or an older pedestrian is hit by a vehicle are common (Verghese & others, 2010). Falls are the leading cause of injury deaths among adults who are 65 years and older. Each year, approximately 200,000 adults over the age of 65 (most of them women) fracture a hip in a fall. Half of these older adults die within 12 months, frequently from pneumonia. Because healing and recuperation are slower in older adults, an accident that is only a temporary setback for a younger person may result in long-term hospital or home care for an older adult (Duque, Demontiero, & Troen, 2009). One study revealed that participation in an exercise class once a week for three years reduced the fall risk and the number of falling incidents in older adults who were at high risk for falling (Yokoya, Demura, & Sato, 2009). In another study, Tai Chi, a form of balance training, improved the coordination of older adults in challenging conditions (Wong & others, 2001).

SUBSTANCE USE AND ABUSE

In many cases, older adults are taking multiple medications, which can increase the risks associated with consuming alcohol or other drugs. For example, when combined with tranquilizers or sedatives, alcohol use can impair breathing, produce excessive sedation, and be fatal.

How extensive is substance abuse in older adults? A national survey found that in 2010 the percentage of individuals who engaged in binge drinking (defined as four or more drinks for women and five or more drinks for men on one occasion in the past 30 days) declined considerably in the middle and late adulthood years (Centers for Disease Control and Prevention, 2012b) (see Figure 17.16). However, the frequency of binge drinking in the past 30 days was highest among older adults (5.5 episodes).

Despite the decline in the percentage of individuals who engage in binge drinking in late adulthood, the Substance Abuse and Mental Health Services Administration (2003) has identified substance abuse among older adults as the "invisible epidemic" in the United States. The belief is that substance abuse often goes undetected in older adults, and there is concern about older adults who abuse not only illicit drugs but prescription drugs as well (Wu & Blazer, 2011). Too often, screening questionnaires are not appropriate for older adults, and the consequences of alcohol abuse—such as depression, inadequate nutrition, congestive heart failure, and frequent falls—may erroneously be attributed to other medical or psychological conditions (Hoyer & Roodin, 2009). Because of the dramatic increase in the number of older adults anticipated over the twenty-first century, substance abuse is likely to characterize an increasing number of older adults (Atkinson, Ryan, & Turner, 2001).

Late-onset alcoholism is the label used to describe the onset of alcoholism after the age of 65. Late-onset alcoholism is often related to loneliness, loss of a spouse, or a disabling condition.

Researchers have found a protective effect of moderate alcohol use in older adults (Giacosa & others, 2012; Holahan & others, 2012). One study revealed better physical and mental health, and increased longevity in older adults who drank moderately compared with those who drank heavily or did not drink at all (Rozzini, Ranhoff, & Trabucchi, 2007). Benefits of moderate drinking include better physical and mental performance, greater openness to social contacts, and ability to assert mastery over one's life.

Researchers have especially found that moderate drinking of red wine is linked to better health and increased longevity (Fernandez & Fraga, 2011). Explanations of the benefits of red wine center on its role in lowering stress and reducing the risk of coronary heart disease (Stockley, 2012; Wu & Hsieh, 2011). Evidence is increasing that a chemical in the skin of red wine grapes—resveratrol—plays a key role in red wine's health benefits (Das, Mukherjee, & Ray, 2011; Tome-Carneiro & others, 2012). One study found that red wine, but not white, killed several lines of cancer cells (Wallenborg & others, 2009). Scientists are exploring how resveratrol, as well as calorie restriction, increases SIRT1, an enzyme that is involved in DNA repair and aging (Baur & others, 2012).

Osteoporosis

What characterizes osteoporosis? What factors contribute to osteoporosis?

Age Group	Percent	Drinks Per Occasion	Frequency
18–24	28	9	4.2
25–34	28	8	4.2
35–44	19	8	4.1
45–64	13	7	4.7
65 & over	4	5	5.5

FIGURE **17.16**

BINGE DRINKING THROUGH THE LIFE SPAN. *Note:* Percent refers to percent of individuals in a particular age group who engaged in binge drinking on an occasion in the past 30 days (4 or more drinks for women, 5 or more for men). Drinks per occasion reflects the intensity of the binge drinking. Frequency indicates the number of occasions in which binge drinking occurred in the past 30 days.
Source: After data presented by the Centers for Disease Control and Prevention, 2012b, Table 1.

What might explain the finding that drinking red wine in moderation is linked to better health and increased longevity?

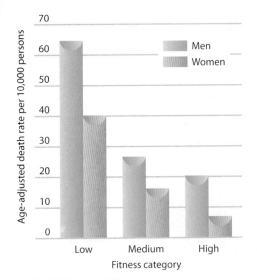

FIGURE **17.17**

PHYSICAL FITNESS AND MORTALITY. In this study of middle-aged and older adults, being moderately fit or highly fit meant that individuals were less likely to die over a period of eight years than their less fit (sedentary) counterparts (Blair & others, 1989).

FIGURE **17.18**

THE JOGGING HOG EXPERIMENT. Jogging hogs reveal the dramatic effects of exercise on health. In one investigation, a group of hogs was trained to run approximately 100 miles per week (Bloor & White, 1983). Then the researchers narrowed the arteries that supplied blood to the hogs' hearts. The hearts of the jogging hogs developed extensive alternate pathways for blood supply, and 42 percent of the threatened heart tissue was salvaged, compared with only 17 percent in a control group of nonjogging hogs.

EXERCISE, NUTRITION, AND WEIGHT

Can exercise slow the aging process? Can eating a nutritious but calorie-reduced diet increase longevity? Let's examine how exercise, nutrition, and weight control might influence how healthily we age.

Exercise Although we may be in the evening of our lives in late adulthood, we are not meant to live out our remaining years passively. Everything we know about older adults suggests that the more active they are, the healthier and happier they are likely to be (Freund, Nikitin, & Riediger, 2013; Siegler & others, 2013a, b).

In one study, exercise literally made the difference between life and death for middle-aged and older adults. More than 10,000 men and women were divided into categories of low fitness, medium fitness, and high fitness (Blair & others, 1989). Then they were studied over a period of eight years. As shown in Figure 17.17, sedentary participants (low fitness) were more than twice as likely to die during the eight-year time span of the study than those who were moderately fit and more than three times as likely to die as those who were highly fit. The positive effects of being physically fit occurred for both men and women in this study. Further, a recent study revealed that 60-year-old and older adults who were in the lowest fifth in terms of physical fitness as determined by a treadmill test were four times more likely to die over a 12-year period than their counterparts who were in the top fifth of physical fitness (Sui & others, 2007). Also in this study, older adults who were physically fit but overweight had a lower mortality risk over the 12 years than their normal-weight counterparts who were low in fitness (Sui & others, 2007). A longitudinal study found that men who exercised regularly at 72 years of age had a 30 percent higher probability of still being alive at 90 years of age than their sedentary counterparts (Yates & others, 2008). And a recent study of more than 11,000 women found that low cardiorespiratory fitness was a significant predictor of death (Farrell & others, 2010).

Gerontologists increasingly recommend strength training in addition to aerobic activity and stretching for older adults (Geirsdottir & others, 2012; Semanik, Chang, & Dunlop, 2012). The average person's lean body mass declines with age—about 6.6 pounds of lean muscle are lost each decade during the adult years. The rate of loss accelerates after age 45. Resistance exercises can preserve and possibly increase muscle mass in older adults (Forbes, Little, & Candow, 2012).

Exercise is an excellent way to maintain health (Siegler & others, 2013a, b). The current recommended level of aerobic activity for adults 60 years of age and older is 30 minutes of moderately intense activity, such as brisk walking or riding a stationary bicycle, five or more days a week, and strength training on two or more days a week (Der Ananian & Prohaska, 2007). Flexibility and balance exercises also are recommended.

Researchers continue to document the positive effects of exercise in older adults. Exercise helps people to live independent lives with dignity in late adulthood (Katzel & Steinbrenner, 2012). At 80, 90, and even 100 years of age, exercise can help prevent older adults from falling down or even being institutionalized. Being physically fit means being able to do the things you want to do, whether you are young or old. More about research on exercise's positive benefits for health is shown in Figure 17.18.

Researchers who study exercise and aging have made the following discoveries:

- *Exercise is linked to increased longevity.* A recent study of older adults found that total daily physical activity was linked to increased longevity across a four-year period (Buchman & others, 2012). In a longitudinal study of Chinese women, those who exercised regularly were less likely to die over approximately a six-year period (Matthews & others, 2007). And in one analysis, energy expenditure by older adults during exercise that burns up at least 1,000 calories a week was estimated to increase life expectancy by about 30 percent, while burning up 2,000 calories a week in exercise was estimated to increase life expectancy by about 50 percent (Lee & Skerrett, 2001).

- *Exercise is related to prevention of common chronic diseases.* Exercise can reduce the risk of developing cardiovascular disease, type 2 diabetes, osteoporosis, stroke, and breast cancer (Chae & others, 2012; Kirshner, 2012).

- *Exercise is associated with improvement in the treatment of many diseases.* When exercise is used as part of the treatment, individuals with these diseases show improvement in symptoms: arthritis, pulmonary disease, congestive heart failure, coronary artery disease, hypertension, type 2 diabetes, obesity, and Alzheimer disease (Ohta & others, 2012; Vincent, Raiser, & Vincent, 2012).

- *Exercise improves older adults' cellular functioning.* Researchers increasingly are finding that exercise improves cellular functioning in older adults (Gielen & others, 2011). For example, researchers recently have found that aerobic exercise is linked to greater telomere length in older adults (Du & others, 2012; Kim & others, 2012). And a recent study revealed that exercise buffered the effects of chronic stress on telomere length in post-menopausal women (Puterman & others, 2010).

- *Exercise improves immune system functioning in older adults* (Simpson & others, 2012). One study revealed that following exercise, a number of components of immune system functioning in older adult women improved (Sakamoto & others, 2009).

- *Exercise can optimize body composition and reduce the decline in motor skills as aging occurs.* Exercise can increase muscle mass and bone mass, as well as decrease bone fragility (Perry & Downey, 2012). One study found that participation in exercise activities was linked to a delay in the onset and progression of frailty (Peterson & others, 2009).

- *Exercise reduces the likelihood that older adults will develop mental health problems and can be effective in the treatment of mental health problems.* For example, exercise reduces the likelihood that older adults will develop depression and can be effective in treating depression in older adults (Lavie & Milani, 2011; Villaverde Gutierrez & others, 2012).

- *Exercise is linked to improved brain and cognitive functioning in older adults.* Older adults who exercise show better brain functioning and process information more effectively than older adults who don't exercise (Mortimer & others, 2012; Prakash & others, 2011). For example, a recent study of older adults revealed that exercise increased the size of the hippocampus and improved memory (Erickson & others, 2011). Another recent study of older adults found that engaging in exercise decreased the negative effects of stress on hippocampal volume and memory (Head, Singh, & Bugg, 2012).

Despite the extensive documentation of exercise's power to improve older adults' health and quality of life, a national survey revealed that older adults have increased their exercise levels only slightly in recent years (Centers for Disease Control and Prevention, 2008) (see Figure 17.19). Possible explanations of older adults' failure to substantially increase their exercise focus on such factors as chronic illnesses, life crises (such as a spouse's death) that disrupt exercise schedules, embarrassment at being around others who are in better shape (especially if they haven't exercised much earlier in life), and the "why bother?" factor (not believing that exercise will improve their lives much) (Painter, 2008). But as we have seen, it is never too late to begin exercising, and older adults can significantly benefit from regular exercise (Guirado & others, 2012). We will further discuss the influence of exercise on older adults' cognitive functioning in Chapter 18.

Nutrition and Weight

Three aspects of nutrition are especially important in older adults: (1) Getting adequate nutrition, (2) avoiding overweight and obesity, and (3) the role of calorie restriction in improving health and extending life.

Healthy Nutrition Eating a healthy, balanced diet and taking appropriate vitamins are important in helping older adults maintain their health. One change in eating behavior in older adults is a decrease in snacking between meals, which contributes to harmful weight loss, especially in women. Among the strategies for increasing weight gain in these women are the use of taste enhancers and calorie supplements between meals.

Overweight and Obesity A recent national survey found that 28 percent of U.S. adults 60 years of age and older were obese in 2011 (Centers for Disease Control and Prevention,

Johnny Kelley, loosening up before one of the many Boston Marathons he ran as an older adult. In 1981, Kelley ran his fiftieth Boston Marathon. In 2000, he was named "Runner of the Century" by *Runner's World* magazine. At 70 years of age, Kelley was still running approximately 50 miles a week. At that point in his life, Kelley said, "I'm afraid to stop running. I feel so good. I want to stay alive." Kelley went on to live 27 more years and died at age 97 in 2004.

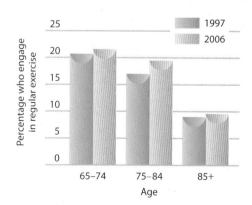

FIGURE **17.19**

REGULAR EXERCISE BY U.S. OLDER ADULTS: 1997 TO 2006

developmental **connection**

Health

Being physically fit and cognitively fit are key aspects of successful aging. Chapter 19, p. 615

2012a). Obesity is linked to the acceleration of diseases in many older adults. However, some recent studies have reported that overweight adults live longer than normal-weight adults or that being overweight is not a risk factor for earlier death, especially in older adults (Berraho & others, 2010; Chang & others, 2012; Flicker & others, 2010). A magazine article even mentioned that chubby might be the new healthy (Kolata, 2007). It's not clear why a few extra pounds that place someone in the overweight category might be linked to longevity. Possibly for some older adults, such as those recovering from surgery or those who develop pneumonia, the pounds may be protective.

Some researchers argue that studies revealing a link between being overweight and living longer is likely due to inclusion of participants who have preexisting diseases (sometimes labeled "reverse causality") or sarcopenia (loss of lean body mass) (Greenberg, 2006).

Despite the several studies that have not found a link between being overweight and living longer, the majority of studies have revealed that being overweight is a risk factor for an earlier death (de Hollander & others, 2012a; Katzmarzyk & others, 2012; Preston & Stokes, 2011). For example, a recent study of 70- to 75-year-olds revealed that a higher body mass index (BMI) was associated with all-cause mortality risk, with the greatest risk occurring for death due to cardiovascular disease (de Hollander & others, 2012b). Also, a recent national study of biomarkers (inflammation, metabolic function, and cardiovascular function) of 20- to 80-year-olds' health found that being overweight consistently was associated with the worst health risk profiles (Zajacova, Dowd, & Burgard, 2011).

In addition to the current controversy about whether being overweight is a risk factor for early death in older adults, another controversy involves what is the best measure of overweight or obesity in predicting longevity (de Hollander & others, 2012b). This debate has mainly focused on whether BMI or waist circumference (WC) is the best predictor. A recent study found that both an elevated BMI and a higher WC were linked to earlier death, with WC being a better predictor (Staiano & others, 2012).

Researchers also consistently find that when individuals are overweight and fit, they have a much better health profile and greater longevity than those who are overweight and not fit (Matheson, King, & Everett, 2012; O'Donovan & others, 2011). Some leading researchers now conclude that inactivity and low cardiorespiratory fitness are greater threats to health and longevity than being overweight (McAuley & Blair, 2011).

Calorie Restriction Seventeenth-century English philosopher and essayist Francis Bacon was the first author to recommend scientific evaluation of diet and longevity. He advocated a frugal diet. Does a restricted intake of food increase longevity? Could it possibly even extend the human life span?

Scientists have accumulated considerable evidence that caloric restriction (CR) in laboratory animals (in most cases rats) can increase the animals' life span (Minor & others, 2010; Roth & Polotsky, 2012). Animals who are fed diets restricted in calories, although adequate in protein, vitamins, and minerals, live as much as 40 percent longer than animals given unlimited access to food (Jolly, 2005). And chronic problems such as cardiovascular, kidney, and liver diseases appear at a later age (Han & others, 2012; Kemnitz, 2011). CR also delays biochemical alterations such as the age-related rise in cholesterol and triglycerides observed in both humans and animals (Fontana, 2009). And recent research indicates that CR may provide neuroprotection for an aging central nervous system (Willette & others, 2012) (see Figure 17.20). For example, a recent study revealed that following CR for three months, the verbal memory of older adults improved (Witte & others, 2009).

Why does CR increase the life span of animals? Some scientists argue that CR might lower the level of free radicals and reduce oxidative stress in cells (Bloomer & others, 2011). Others argue that calorie restriction might trigger a state of emergency called "survival mode" in which the body eliminates all unnecessary functions to focus only on staying alive. This survival mode likely is the result of evolution in which calorie restriction allowed animals to survive periods of famine, and thus the genes remain in the genomes of animal and human species today (Chen & Guarente, 2007).

Whether similar very low-calorie diets can stretch the human life span is not known (Blagosklonny, 2010; Stein & others, 2012). In some instances, the animals in these studies ate

What characterizes the current controversy about longevity and being overweight?

40 percent less than normal. In humans, a typical level of calorie restriction involves a 30 percent decrease, which translates to about 1,120 calories a day for the average woman and 1,540 for the average man.

Do underweight women and men live longer? One study revealed that women who were 20 pounds or more underweight lived longer even after controlling for smoking, hypertension, alcohol intake, and other factors (Wandell, Carlsson, & Theobald, 2009). In this study, underweight men did not live longer when various factors were controlled.

The Controversy Over Vitamins and Aging For years, most experts on aging and health argued that a balanced diet was all that was needed for successful aging; vitamin supplements were not recommended. However, recent research suggests the possibility that some vitamin supplements—mainly a group called "antioxidants," which includes vitamin C, vitamin E, and beta-carotene—help to slow the aging process and improve the health of older adults.

The theory is that antioxidants counteract the cell damage caused by free radicals, which are produced both by the body's own metabolism and by environmental factors such as smoking, pollution, and bad chemicals in the diet (Gandhi & Abramov, 2012). When free radicals cause damage (oxidation) in one cell, a chain reaction of damage follows. Antioxidants are theorized to act much like a fire extinguisher, helping to neutralize free-radical activity and reduce oxidative stress (Da Costa, Badawi, & El-Sohemy, 2012).

What have research studies found about the role of antioxidants in health? Recent research reviews have not supported the belief that antioxidant vitamin supplements can reduce the incidence of cancer and cardiovascular disease (Chen & others, 2012; Dolara, Bigagli, & Collins, 2012). However, a recent meta-analysis of seven studies concluded that dietary intakes (not vitamin supplements) of vitamin E, C, and beta-carotene were linked to a reduced risk of Alzheimer disease (Li, Shen, & Ji, 2012).

There still are many uncertainties about the role of antioxidant vitamins in health. For example, it is unclear which vitamins should be taken, how large a dose should be taken, what the restraints are, and so on. Critics also argue that the key experimental studies documenting the effectiveness of the vitamins in slowing the aging process have not been conducted. The studies in this area thus far have been so-called population studies that are correlational rather than experimental in nature. Other factors—such as exercise, better health practices, and good nutritional habits—might be responsible for the positive findings about vitamins and aging rather than vitamins per se. Also, the free-radical theory is a theory and not a fact, and is only one of a number of theories about why we age.

FIGURE **17.20**

CALORIE RESTRICTION IN MONKEYS. Shown here are two male monkeys at the Wisconsin Primate Research Center. Both are 24 years old. The monkey in the top photograph was raised on a calorie-restricted diet, while the monkey in the bottom photograph was raised on a normal diet. Notice that the monkey on the calorie-restricted diet looks younger; he also has lower glucose and insulin levels. The monkey raised on a normal diet has higher triglycerides and more oxidative damage to his cells.

HEALTH TREATMENT

The increase in the aging population is predicted to dramatically escalate health care costs over the foreseeable future. As older adults live longer, disease management programs will need to be expanded to handle the chronic disorders of older adults. The increasing demand for health services among the expanding population of older adults is likely to bring shortages of many types of health care professionals, including geriatric nurses, doctors, and health care aides (Bardach & Rowles, 2012).

What is the quality of health treatment that older adults in the United States receive? A study of older adults with health problems revealed that they receive the recommended medical care they need only half the time (Wenger & others, 2003). The researchers examined the medical records of 372 frail older adults who had been treated by two managed-care

connecting with careers

Sarah Kagan, Geriatric Nurse

Sarah Kagan is a professor of nursing at the University of Pennsylvania School of Nursing. She provides nursing consultation to patients, their families, nurses, and physicians regarding the complex needs of older adults related to their hospitalization. She also consults on research and the management of patients who have head and neck cancers. Kagan teaches in the undergraduate nursing program, where she directs a course on "Nursing Care in the Older Adult." In 2003, she was awarded a MacArthur Fellowship for her work in the field of nursing.

In Kagan's own words:

> I'm lucky to be doing what I love—caring for older adults and families—and learning from them so that I can share this knowledge and develop or investigate better ways of caring. My special interests in the care of older adults who have cancer allow me the intimate privilege of being with patients at the best and worst times of their lives. That intimacy acts as a beacon—it reminds me of the value I and nursing as a profession contribute to society and the rewards offered in return (Kagan, 2008, p. 1).

Sarah Kagan with a patient.

For more information about what geriatric nurses do, see page 46 in the Careers in Life-Span Development appendix.

organizations over the course of one year. Then they documented the medical care each patient received and judged it using standard indicators of quality. For example, many older adults with an unsteady gait didn't get the help they need, such as physical therapy to improve their walking ability. Clearly, the quality of health treatment provided to older adults needs to be significantly improved.

Geriatric nurses can be especially helpful in treating the health care problems of older adults. To read about the work of one geriatric nurse, see *Connecting with Careers*.

The development of alternative home and community-based care has decreased the percentage of older adults who live in nursing homes (Katz & others, 2009). Still, as older adults age, their probability of being in a nursing home increases (see Figure 17.21). The quality of nursing homes and other extended-care facilities for older adults varies enormously and is a source of continuing concern (Wagner, McDonald, & Castle, 2012; Shah & others, 2012). More than one-third of these facilities are seriously deficient. They fail federally mandated inspections because they do not meet the minimum standards for physicians, pharmacists, and various rehabilitation specialists (occupational and physical therapists). Further concerns focus on the patient's right to privacy, access to medical information, safety, and lifestyle freedom within the individual's range of mental and physical capabilities.

Because of the inadequate quality of many nursing homes and the escalating costs for nursing home care, many specialists in the health problems of the aged stress that home health care, elder-care centers, and preventive medicine clinics are good alternatives (Berenson & others, 2012; Katz & others, 2009). They are potentially less expensive than hospitals and nursing homes. They also are less

FIGURE **17.21**

PERCENTAGE OF U.S. OLDER ADULTS OF DIFFERENT AGES IN NURSING HOMES

Health Care Providers and Older Adults

The attitudes of both the health care provider and the older adult are important aspects of the older adult's health care (Miller, 2010). Unfortunately, health care providers too often share society's stereotypes and negative attitudes toward older adults (Eymard & Douglas, 2012). In a health care setting, these attitudes can take the form of avoidance, dislike, and begrudged tolerance rather than positive, hopeful treatment. Health care personnel are more likely to be interested in treating younger persons, who more often have acute problems with a higher prognosis for successful recovery. They often are less motivated to treat older persons, who are more likely to have chronic problems with a lower prognosis for successful recovery.

Not only are physicians less responsive to older patients, but older patients often take a less active role in medical encounters with health care personnel than do younger patients. Older adults should be encouraged to take a more active role in their own health care.

Mathilde Spett (*right*), who is 91 years old, injured herself in a fall but recently graduated from a walker to a cane and learned how to stay on a better diet with the help of home-care aide Marilyn Ferguson (*left*). The demand for home-care aides is predicted to increase dramatically in the next several decades because of the likely doubling of the 65-year-and-older population and older adults' preference for remaining out of nursing homes (Moos, 2007). Not only is it important to significantly increase the number of health care professionals available to treat older adults, but it is also very important that they not harbor negative stereotypes of older adults and that they show very positive attitudes toward them.

likely to engender the feelings of depersonalization and dependency that occur so often in residents of institutions. Currently, there is an increased demand for, but shortage of, home-care workers because of the increase in population of older adults and their preference to stay out of nursing homes (Moos, 2007).

In a classic study, Judith Rodin and Ellen Langer (1977) found that an important factor related to health, and even survival, in a nursing home is the patient's feelings of control and self-determination. A group of elderly nursing home residents were encouraged to make more day-to-day choices and thus feel they had more responsibility for control over their lives. They began to decide such matters as what they ate, when their visitors could come, what movies they saw, and who could come to their rooms. A similar group in the same nursing home was told by the administrator how caring the nursing home was and how much the staff wanted to help, but these residents were given no opportunity to take more control over their lives. Eighteen months later, the residents given responsibility and control were more alert and active, and said they were happier, than the residents who were only encouraged to feel that the staff would try to satisfy their needs. And the "responsible" or "self-control" group had significantly better improvement in their health than did the "dependent" group. Even more important was the finding that after 18 months only half as many nursing home residents in the "responsibility" group had died as in the "dependent" group (see Figure 17.22). Perceived control over one's environment, then, can literally be a matter of life or death.

Rodin's research shows that simply giving nursing home residents options for control can change their behavior and improve their health. To read further about health care providers and older adults, see *Connecting Development to Life*.

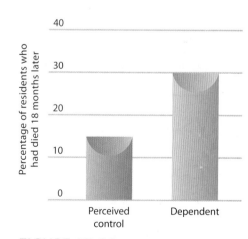

FIGURE **17.22**

PERCEIVED CONTROL AND MORTALITY. In the study by Rodin and Langer (1977), nursing home residents who were encouraged to feel more in control of their lives were more likely to be alive 18 months later than those who were treated as being more dependent on the nursing home staff.

Review

- What are some common health problems in older adults? What are the main causes of death in older adults?
- What characterizes substance abuse in late adulthood?
- How do exercise, nutrition, and weight influence development in late adulthood?
- What are some options and issues in the health treatment of older adults?

Connect

- In this section, we learned that older adults fare better when they are given more responsibility and control in various aspects of their lives. At what other age stages is giving individuals more responsibility and control particularly important for their development? In what way(s)?

Reflect *Your Own Personal Journey of Life*

- What changes in your lifestyle now might help you age more successfully when you become an older adult?

---

topical **connections** ----------

Eventually, the human life span ends with death. Compared with younger adults and children, most older adults are closer to death and more likely to know that they will die gradually over a period of time rather than suddenly. Physical impairments—such as cardiovascular disease and cancer—are the most likely reasons older adults will die. Actual death is sometimes difficult to determine and involves which portions of the brain are no longer functioning. Care for the dying often involves providing comfort and managing pain.

looking forward ---→

---

reach your **learning goals**

Physical Development in Late Adulthood

1 Longevity

LG1 Characterize longevity and discuss the biological theories of aging.

Life Expectancy and Life Span

- Life expectancy refers to the number of years that will probably be lived by an average person born in a particular year. Life span is the maximum number of years an individual can live. Life expectancy has dramatically increased; life span has not. An increasing number of individuals live to be 100 or older. Genetics, health, and coping well with stress can contribute to becoming a centenarian. On the average, females live about six years longer than males do. The sex difference is likely due to biological and social factors.

The Young-Old and the Oldest-Old

- In terms of chronological age, the young-old have been described as being 65 to 84 years of age and the oldest-old as 85 years and older. Many experts on aging prefer to describe the young-old, old-old, and oldest-old in terms of functional age rather than chronological age. This view accounts for the fact that some 85-year-olds are more biologically and psychologically fit than some 65-year-olds. However, those 85 and older face significant problems, whereas those in their sixties and seventies are experiencing an increase in successful aging.

Biological Theories of Aging

- Five biological theories are evolutionary theory, cellular clock theory, free-radical theory, mitochondrial theory, and hormonal stress theory. The evolutionary theory of aging proposes that natural selection has not eliminated many harmful conditions and nonadaptive characteristics in older adults; thus, the benefits conferred by evolution decline with age because natural selection is linked to reproductive fitness. Hayflick proposed the cellular clock theory, which states that cells can divide a maximum of about 75 to 80 times, and that as we age, our cells become less capable of dividing. Telomeres are likely to be involved in explaining why cells lose their capacity to divide. According to free-radical theory, people age because unstable oxygen molecules called free radicals are produced in the cells and damage cellular structures. According to mitochondrial theory, aging is due to the decay of mitochondria, which are tiny cellular bodies that supply energy for function, growth, and repair. According to hormonal stress theory, aging in the body's hormonal system can lower resilience to stress and increase the likelihood of disease.

2 The Course of Physical Development in Late Adulthood

 LG2 Describe how a person's brain and body change in late adulthood.

The Aging Brain

- The brain loses weight and volume with age, and there is a general slowing of function in the central nervous system that begins in middle adulthood and increases in late adulthood. However, researchers have recently found that older adults can generate new neurons, and at least through the seventies, new dendrites. The aging brain retains considerable plasticity and adaptiveness. For example, it may compensate for losses in some regions of the brain by shifting responsibilities to other regions. A decrease in lateralization may reflect this kind of compensation, or it may reflect an age-related decline in the specialization of function.

Sleep

- Approximately 50 percent of older adults complain of having difficulty sleeping. Poor sleep can result in earlier death and lower cognitive functioning. Many sleep problems among older adults are linked to health conditions.

The Immune System

- Declines in immune system functioning with aging are well documented. Exercise can improve immune system functioning.

Physical Appearance and Movement

- The most obvious signs of aging are wrinkled skin and age spots on the skin. People get shorter as they age, and their weight often decreases after age 60 because of loss of muscle. The movement of older adults slows across a wide range of movement tasks.

Sensory Development

- Declines in visual acuity, color vision, and depth perception usually occur with age, especially after age 75. The yellowing of the eye's lens with age reduces color differentiation. The ability to see the periphery of a visual field also declines in older adults. Significant declines in visual functioning related to glare characterize adults 75 years and older and are even prevalent among those 85 and older. Three diseases that can impair the vision of older adults are cataracts, glaucoma, and macular degeneration. Hearing decline can begin in middle age but usually does not become much of an impediment until late adulthood. Hearing aids (for conductive hearing loss) and cochlear implants (for neurosensory hearing loss) can diminish hearing problems for many older adults. Smell and taste can decline, although the decline is minimal in healthy older adults. Changes in touch sensitivity are associated with aging, although this does not present a problem for most older adults. Sensitivity to pain decreases in late adulthood.

The Circulatory System and Lungs

- Cardiovascular disorders increase in late adulthood. Consistent high blood pressure should be treated to reduce the risk of stroke, heart attack, and kidney disease. Lung capacity does drop with age, but older adults can improve lung functioning with diaphragm-strengthening exercises.

Sexuality

- Aging in late adulthood does include some changes in sexual performance, more for males than females. Nonetheless, there are no known age limits to sexual activity.

3 Health

LG3 Identify health problems in older adults and describe how they can be treated.

Health Problems

- As we age, our probability of disease or illness increases. Chronic disorders are rare in early adulthood, increase in middle adulthood, and become more common in late adulthood. The most common chronic disorder in late adulthood is arthritis. Nearly three-fourths of older adults die of cancer, heart disease, or stroke. Osteoporosis is the main reason many older adults walk with a stoop; women are especially vulnerable. Accidents are usually more debilitating to older than to younger adults.

Substance Use and Abuse

- The percentage of older adults who engage in binge drinking declines compared with earlier in adulthood, but moderate drinking of red wine can bring health benefits. Abuse of illicit and prescription drugs is a growing problem in the United States, although it is more difficult to detect in older adults than in younger adults.

Exercise, Nutrition, and Weight

- The physical benefits of exercise have clearly been demonstrated in older adults. Aerobic exercise and weight lifting are both recommended if the adults are physically capable of them. It is important for older adults to eat healthy foods and take appropriate vitamins. Current controversy involves whether overweight adults live longer than normal-weight adults. Being overweight is linked to health problems, and being obese predicts earlier death. Caloric restriction (CR) in animals can increase the animals' life span, but whether this works with humans is not known. In humans, there has been recent controversy about whether being overweight is associated with an increased mortality rate in older adults. Most nutritional experts recommend a well-balanced, low-fat diet for older adults but do not recommend an extremely low-calorie diet. Controversy surrounds the question of whether vitamin supplements—especially the antioxidants vitamin C, vitamin E, and beta-carotene—can slow the aging process and improve older adults' health. Recent research reviews concluded that taking antioxidant vitamin supplements does not reduce this risk of cancer and cardiovascular disease.

Health Treatment

- Although only 3 percent of adults over 65 reside in nursing homes, 23 percent of adults 85 and over do. The quality of nursing homes varies enormously. Alternatives to nursing homes are being proposed. Simply giving nursing home residents options for control can change their behavior and improve their health. The attitudes of both the health care provider and the older adult patient are important aspects of the older adult's health care. Too often health care personnel share society's negative view of older adults.

key terms

life span 536
life expectancy 536
evolutionary theory of
   aging 541

cellular clock theory 541
free-radical theory 541
mitochondrial
   theory 541

hormonal stress theory 542
neurogenesis 544
cataracts 549
glaucoma 549

macular degeneration 549
arthritis 552
osteoporosis 552

key people

Leonard Hayflick 541   Stanley Rapaport 544   Judith Rodin 559   Ellen Langer 559

Chapter 17 | PHYSICAL DEVELOPMENT IN LATE ADULTHOOD

Connecting with

Learning Objectives	Application Activities	Activity Type	Page Reference
Define aging including young-old, old-old, and oldest-old.	What Is Old Age?	Video	pp. 539–540
Describe the biological theories of aging.	Biological Theories of Aging	Click & drag activity	pp. 540–542
Describe physical appearance and movement in late adulthood.	Late Adulthood Perspectives on Body Image	Milestones: Transitions	pp. 545–547
Discuss sexuality in late adulthood.	Late Adulthood Perspectives on Sexuality	Milestones: Transitions	pp. 550–551
	Sex in Later Adulthood	Video	

chapter 18

COGNITIVE DEVELOPMENT IN LATE ADULTHOOD

chapter **outline**

1 Cognitive Functioning in Older Adults

Learning Goal 1 Describe the cognitive functioning of older adults.

Multidimensionality and Multidirectionality
Education, Work, and Health
Use It or Lose It
Training Cognitive Skills
Cognitive Neuroscience and Aging

2 Language Development

Learning Goal 2 Characterize changes in language in older adults.

3 Work and Retirement

Learning Goal 3 Discuss aging and adaptation to work and retirement.

Work
Retirement in the United States and in Other Countries
Adjustment to Retirement

4 Mental Health

Learning Goal 4 Describe mental health problems in older adults.

Depression
Dementia, Alzheimer Disease, and Other Afflictions
Fear of Victimization, Crime, and Elder Maltreatment

5 Religion and Spirituality

Learning Goal 5 Explain the role of religion and spirituality in the lives of older adults.

In 2010, 90-year-old Helen Small completed her master's degree at the University of Texas at Dallas (UT-Dallas). The topic of her master's degree research project was romantic relationships in late adulthood. Helen said that she only interviewed one individual who was older than she was at the time—a 92-year-old man.

I (your author, John Santrock) first met Helen when she took my undergraduate course in life-span development in 2006. After the first test, Helen stopped showing up and I wondered what had happened to her. It turns out that she had broken her shoulder when she tripped over a curb while hurrying to class. The next semester, she took my class again and did a great job in it, even though the first several months she had to take notes with her left hand (she's right-handed) because of her lingering shoulder problem.

Helen grew up in the Great Depression and first went to college in 1938 at the University of Akron, where she only attended for one year. She got married and her marriage lasted 62 years. After her husband's death, Helen went back to college in 2002, first at Brookhaven Community College and then at UT-Dallas. When I interviewed her recently, she told me that she had promised her mother that she would finish college. Her most important advice for college students, "Finish college and be persistent. When you make a commitment, always see it through. Don't quit. Go after what you want in life."

Helen not only is cognitively fit, she also is physically fit. She works out three times a week for about an hour each time—aerobically on a treadmill for about 30 minutes and then on six different weight machines.

What struck me most about Helen when she took my undergraduate course in life-span development was how appreciative she was of the opportunity to learn and how tenaciously she pursued studying and doing well in the course. Helen was quite popular with the younger students in the course and she was a terrific role model for them.

Helen Small with the author of your text, John Santrock, in his undergraduate course on life-span development at the University of Texas at Dallas in spring 2012. Helen now returns each semester to talk with students in the class about cognitive aging. This past semester, I had to reschedule the date of the topic because Helen had other work commitments the day it was originally scheduled.

topical connections

Most individuals reach the peak of their cognitive functioning in middle adulthood. However, some cognitive processes increase while others decline in middle age. For example, vocabulary peaks and speed of processing decreases in middle age. Expertise also typically increases during this adult age period. For many people, midlife is a time when individuals reflect and evaluate their current work and what they plan to do in the future. Many middle-aged adults increasingly examine life's meaning.

◄ *looking back*

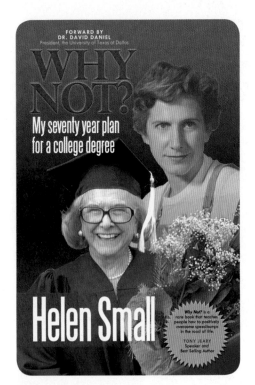

Helen Small published her first book, *Why Not? My Seventy Year Plan for a College Degree,* in 2011 at the age of 91.

After her graduation, I asked her what she planned to do the next few years and she responded, "I've got to figure out what I'm going to do with the rest of my life." Helen now comes each semester to my course in life-span development when we are discussing cognitive aging. She wows the class and has been an inspiration to all who come in contact with her.

What has Helen done the last several years to stay cognitively fit? She has worked as a public ambassador for Dr. Denise Park's Center for Vital Longevity at UT-Dallas and wrote her first book: *Why Not? My Seventy Year Plan for a College Degree* (Small, 2011). It's a wonderful, motivating invitation to live your life fully and reach your potential no matter what your age.

preview

Helen Small leads a very active cognitive life as an older adult. Just how well older adults can and do function cognitively is an important question we will explore in this chapter. We also will examine the important topics of language development, work and retirement, mental health, and religion.

1 Cognitive Functioning in Older Adults

LG1 Describe the cognitive functioning of older adults.

Multidimensionality and Multidirectionality	Education, Work, and Health	Use It or Lose It	Training Cognitive Skills	Cognitive Neuroscience and Aging

At age 76, Anna Mary Robertson Moses, better known as Grandma Moses, took up painting and became internationally famous, staging 15 one-woman shows throughout Europe. At age 89, Arthur Rubinstein gave one of his best performances at New York's Carnegie Hall. When Pablo Casals was 95, a reporter asked him, "Mr. Casals, you are the greatest cellist who ever lived. Why do you still practice six hours a day?" Mr. Casals replied, "Because I feel like I am making progress" (Canfield & Hansen, 1995).

Grandma Moses, known in her time as the "grand old lady of American art," took up painting at the age of 76 and continued to paint past her 100th birthday.

MULTIDIMENSIONALITY AND MULTIDIRECTIONALITY

In thinking about the nature of cognitive change in adulthood, it is important to consider that cognition is a multidimensional concept (Dixon & others, 2013). It is also important to consider that, although some dimensions of cognition might decline as we age, others might remain stable or even improve.

Cognitive Mechanics and Cognitive Pragmatics Paul Baltes (2003; Baltes, Lindenberger, & Staudinger, 2006) clarified the distinction between those aspects of the aging mind that show decline and those that remain stable or even improve:

- **Cognitive mechanics** are the "hardware" of the mind and reflect the neurophysiological architecture of the brain developed through evolution. Cognitive mechanics consist of these components: speed and accuracy of the processes involved in sensory input,

FIGURE **18.1**

THEORIZED AGE CHANGES IN COGNITIVE MECHANICS AND COGNITIVE PRAGMATICS. Baltes argues that cognitive mechanics decline during aging, whereas cognitive pragmatics do not decline for many people until they become very old. Cognitive mechanics have a biological/genetic foundation; cognitive pragmatics have an experiential/cultural foundation. The broken lines from 75 to 100 years of age indicate possible individual variations in cognitive pragmatics.

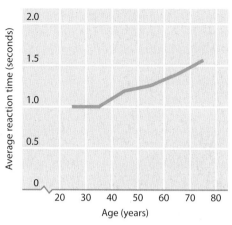

FIGURE **18.2**

THE RELATION OF AGE TO REACTION TIME. In one study, the average reaction time began to slow in the forties, and this decline accelerated in the sixties and seventies (Salthouse, 1994). The task used to assess reaction time required individuals to match numbers with symbols on a computer screen.

developmental **connection**

Intelligence

Fluid intelligence is the ability to reason abstractly; crystallized intelligence is an individual's accumulated information and verbal skills. Chapter 15, p. 495

attention, visual and motor memory, discrimination, comparison, and categorization. Because of the strong influence of biology, heredity, and health on cognitive mechanics, their decline with aging is likely. Some researchers conclude that the decline in cognitive mechanics may begin as soon as early midlife (Salthouse, 2012a, b).

- **Cognitive pragmatics** are the culture-based "software programs" of the mind. Cognitive pragmatics include reading and writing skills, language comprehension, educational qualifications, professional skills, and also the type of knowledge about the self and life skills that help us to master or cope with life. Because of the strong influence of culture on cognitive pragmatics, their improvement into old age is possible. Thus, although cognitive mechanics may decline in old age, cognitive pragmatics may actually improve, at least until individuals become very old (see Figure 18.1).

The distinction between cognitive mechanics and cognitive pragmatics is similar to the one between fluid (mechanics) and crystallized (pragmatics) intelligence that was described in Chapter 15. Indeed, the similarity is so strong that some experts now use these terms to describe cognitive aging patterns: *fluid mechanics* and *crystallized pragmatics* (Lovden & Lindenberger, 2007).

What factors are most likely to contribute to the decline in fluid mechanics in late adulthood? Among the most likely candidates are declines in processing speed, working memory capacity, and suppressing irrelevant information (inhibition) (Lovden & Lindenberger, 2007).

Now that we have examined the distinction between fluid mechanics and crystallized pragmatics, let's explore some of the more specific cognitive processes that reflect these two general domains, beginning with speed of processing.

Speed of Processing It is now well accepted that the speed of processing information declines in late adulthood (Salthouse, 2012a, b). Figure 18.2 illustrates this decline through the results of a study of slowing reaction times in adults.

Although speed of processing information slows down in late adulthood, there is considerable individual variation in this ability. Accumulated knowledge may compensate to some degree for slower processing speed in older adults.

The decline in processing speed in older adults is likely due to a decline in functioning of the brain and central nervous system (Finch, 2009, 2011). Health and exercise may influence the extent to which processing speed declines. For example, one study found that following six months of aerobic exercise older adults showed improvement on reaction time tasks (Kramer & others, 1999).

Attention Changes in attention are important aspects of cognitive aging. Researchers have found that older adults are less able to ignore distracting information than younger adults, and this distractibility becomes more pronounced as attentional demands increase (Mund, Bell, & Buchner, 2010). Recent research indicates that the greater distractibility of older adults

cognitive mechanics The "hardware" of the mind, reflecting the neurophysiological architecture of the brain. Cognitive mechanics involve the speed and accuracy of the processes involving sensory input, visual and motor memory, discrimination, comparison, and categorization.

cognitive pragmatics The culture-based "software programs" of the mind. Cognitive pragmatics include reading and writing skills, language comprehension, educational qualifications, professional skills, and also the type of knowledge about the self and life skills that help us to master or cope with life.

What are some developmental changes in attention in late adulthood?

developmental **connection**

Attention

Young children make progress in many aspects of attention, including sustained attention and executive attention. Chapter 7, p. 224

selective attention Focusing on a specific aspect of experience that is relevant while ignoring others that are irrelevant.

divided attention Concentrating on more than one activity at the same time.

sustained attention Focused and extended engagement with an object, task, event, or other aspect of the environment.

executive attention Aspects of thinking that include planning actions, allocating attention to goals, detecting and compensating for errors, monitoring progress on tasks, and dealing with novel or difficult circumstances.

is associated with less effective functioning in neural networks running through the frontal and parietal lobes of the brain, which are involved in cognitive control (Campbell & others, 2012).

In Chapter 7, "Physical and Cognitive Development in Early Childhood," you read about two types of attention—sustained and executive. Here we will discuss those two types of attention in older adults plus two other types of attention: selective and divided attention:

- **Selective attention** is focusing on a specific aspect of experience that is relevant while ignoring others that are irrelevant. An example of selective attention is the ability to focus on one voice among many in a crowded room or a noisy restaurant. Another is making a decision about which stimuli to attend to when making a left turn at an intersection. Generally, older adults are less adept at selective attention than younger adults are (Caban-Holt & others, 2012). However, on simple tasks involving a search for a feature, such as determining whether a target item is present on a computer screen, age differences are minimal when individuals are given sufficient practice.

- **Divided attention** involves concentrating on more than one activity at the same time. When the two competing tasks are reasonably easy, age differences among adults are minimal or nonexistent. However, the more difficult the competing tasks are, the less effectively older adults divide attention than younger adults (Bucur & Madden, 2007). In one study, the ability to engage in a conversation while simultaneously driving a simulator through highway traffic (in an experimental laboratory) was examined in 17- to 25-year-olds, 26- to 49-year-olds, and 50- to 80-year-olds (McKnight & McKnight, 1993). A nondistraction control condition also was included. Overall, the participants performed more poorly in the divided attention condition than in the nondistraction control condition. Also, the older adults (50 to 80 years old) performed worse in the divided attention condition than the younger two groups but not in the control condition. Thus, placing more demands on the attention of the older adults led them to perform more poorly on the driving task.

- **Sustained attention** is focused and extended engagement with an object, task, event, or some other aspect of the environment. Sometimes sustained attention is referred to as *vigilance*. On tests of simple vigilance and sustained attention, older adults usually perform as well as younger adults. For example, a recent study revealed that sustained attention increased in early adulthood but remained unchanged thereafter through 77 years of age (Carriere & others, 2010). However, on complex vigilance tasks, older adults' performance usually drops (Bucur & Madden, 2007). And a recent study of older adults found that the greater the variability in their sustained attention (vigilance), the more likely they were to experience falls (O'Halloran & others, 2012).

- **Executive attention** involves action planning, allocating attention to goals, error detection and compensation, monitoring progress on tasks, and dealing with novel or difficult circumstances. A recent study found that older adults had deficiencies in executive attention (Mahoney & others, 2010). In this study, a lower level of executive attention in older adults was linked to low blood pressure, which likely is related to reduced blood flow to the brain's frontal lobes.

Memory   Let's examine a research study that addresses how we remember as we age. Non-Latino adults of various ages in the United States were studied to determine how much Spanish they remembered from classes they had taken in high school or college (Bahrick, 1984). The individuals chosen for the study had used Spanish very little since they initially learned it in high school or college. Not surprisingly, the young adults who had taken Spanish within the last three years remembered Spanish best. After that, the deterioration in memory was gradual (see Figure 18.3). For example, older adults who had studied Spanish 50 years earlier remembered about 80 percent of what young adults did who had studied it in the last three years! The most important factor in the adults' memory of Spanish was not how long ago they studied it but how well they had initially learned it—those who got an A in Spanish 50 years earlier remembered more Spanish than adults who got a C when taking Spanish only one year earlier.

Memory does change during aging, but not all memory changes with age in the same way (Brehmer, Westerberg, & Backman, 2012; Dixon & others, 2012; El Haj & Allain, 2012; Small & others, 2012b). The main dimensions of memory and aging that have been studied include episodic memory, semantic memory, cognitive resources (such as working memory and perceptual speed), source memory, prospective memory, and noncognitive influences such as health, education, and socioeconomic factors.

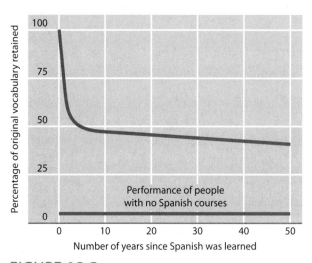

FIGURE 18.3

MEMORY FOR SPANISH AS A FUNCTION OF AGE SINCE SPANISH WAS LEARNED. An initial steep drop over about a three-year period in remembering the vocabulary learned in Spanish classes occurred. However, there was little dropoff in memory for Spanish vocabulary from three years after taking Spanish classes to 50 years after taking them. Even 50 years after taking Spanish classes, individuals still remembered almost 50 percent of the vocabulary.

Episodic Memory   **Episodic memory** is the retention of information about the where and when of life's happenings. For example, what was the color of the walls in your bedroom when you were a child, what was your first date like, what were you doing when you heard that airplanes had struck the World Trade Center, and what did you eat for breakfast this morning?

Younger adults have better episodic memory than older adults have (Talamini & Gorree, 2012). A study of 18- to 94-year-olds revealed that increased age was linked to increased difficulty in retrieving episodic information, facts, and events (Siedlecki, 2007). Also, older adults think that they can remember older events better than more recent events, typically reporting that they can remember what happened to them years ago but can't remember what they did yesterday. However, researchers consistently have found that, contrary to such self-reports, in older adults the older the memory, the less accurate it is. This has been documented in studies of memory for high school classmates, foreign language learned in school over the life span, names of grade school teachers, and autobiographical facts kept in diaries (Smith, 1996).

Semantic Memory   **Semantic memory** is a person's knowledge about the world. It includes a person's fields of expertise, such as knowledge of chess for a skilled chess player; general academic knowledge of the sort learned in school, such as knowledge of geometry; and "everyday knowledge" about the meanings of words, famous individuals, important places, and common things, such as what day is Valentine's Day. Semantic memory appears to be independent of an individual's personal identity with the past. For example, you can access a fact—such as "Lima is the capital of Peru"—and not have the foggiest idea of when and where you learned it.

Does semantic memory decline with age? Among the tasks that researchers often use to assess semantic memory are those involving vocabulary, general knowledge, and word identification (Mardh, Nagga, & Samuelsson, 2012; Miotto & others, 2012). Older adults do often take longer to retrieve semantic information, but usually they can ultimately retrieve it. However, the ability to retrieve very specific information (such as names) usually declines in older adults (Luo & Craik, 2008). For the most part, episodic memory declines more than semantic memory in older adults (Nyberg & Backman, 2011; Small & others, 2012b).

Although many aspects of semantic memory are reasonably well preserved in late adulthood, a common memory problem for older adults is the *tip-of-the-tongue (TOT) phenomenon*,

episodic memory The retention of information about the where and when of life's happenings.

semantic memory A person's knowledge about the world—including one's fields of expertise, general academic knowledge of the sort learned in school, and "everyday knowledge."

in which individuals can't quite retrieve familiar information but have the feeling that they should be able to retrieve it (Bucur & Madden, 2007). Researchers have found that older adults are more likely to be experience TOT states than younger adults (Bucur & Madden, 2007). A recent study of older adults found that the most commonly reported errors in memory they reported having in the last 24 hours were those involving tip-of-the-tongue (Ossher, Flegal, & Lustig, 2012).

Cognitive Resources: Working Memory and Perceptual Speed   One view of memory suggests that a limited number of cognitive resources can be devoted to any cognitive task. Two important cognitive resource mechanisms are working memory and perceptual speed (Baddeley, 2012; Salthouse, 2012a). Recall from Chapters 9 and 15 that *working memory* is closely linked to short-term memory but places more emphasis on memory as a place for mental work. Working memory is like a mental "workbench" that allows children and adults to manipulate and assemble information when making decisions, solving problems, and comprehending written and spoken language (Baddeley, 2007, 2010, 2012). Researchers have found declines in working memory during the late adulthood years (Nyberg & others, 2012). A recent study revealed that working memory continued to decline from 65 to 89 years of age (Elliott & others, 2011). Another recent study found that multitasking especially produced a disruption in older adults' working memory, likely because of an interruption in retrieving information (Clapp & others, 2011). Explanation of the decline in working memory in older adults often focuses on their less efficient inhibition in preventing irrelevant information from entering working memory and their increased distractibility (Lustig & Hasher, 2009).

Perceptual speed is a cognitive resource that involves the ability to perform simple perceptual-motor tasks such as deciding whether pairs of two-digit or two-letter strings are the same or different or determining the time required to step on the brakes when the car directly ahead stops. Perceptual speed shows considerable decline in late adulthood and is strongly linked with declines in working memory (Dirk, 2012; Eckert, 2011; Salthouse, 2012a).

Explicit and Implicit Memory   Researchers also have found that aging is linked with a decline in explicit memory (Kim & Giovanello, 2011). **Explicit memory** is memory of facts and experiences that individuals consciously know and can state. Explicit memory also is sometimes called declarative memory. Examples of explicit memory include being at a grocery store and remembering what you wanted to buy, being able to name the capital of Illinois, or recounting the events of a movie you have seen. **Implicit memory** is memory without conscious recollection; it involves skills and routine procedures that are automatically performed. Examples of implicit memory include driving a car, swinging a golf club, or typing on a computer keyboard without having to consciously think about how to perform these tasks.

Implicit memory is less likely to be adversely affected by aging than explicit memory (Norman, Holmin, & Bartholomew, 2011; Nyberg & others, 2012). Thus, older adults are more likely to forget what items they wanted to buy at a grocery store (unless they write them down on a list and take it with them) than they are to forget how to drive a car. Their perceptual speed might be slower in driving the car, but they remember how to do it.

Source Memory   **Source memory** is the ability to remember where one learned something. Failures of source memory increase with age in the adult years and they can create awkward situations, as when an older adult forgets who told a joke and retells it to the source (El Haj & Allain, 2012; Ruiz-Gallego-Largo, Simon, & Suengas, 2012).

Lynn Hasher (2003, p. 1301) argues that age differences are substantial in many studies of memory, such as resource memory, when individuals are asked "for a piece of information that just doesn't matter much. But if you ask for information that is important, old people do every bit as well as young adults . . . young people have mental resources to burn. As people get older, they get more selective in how they use their resources."

Prospective Memory   **Prospective memory** involves remembering to do something in the future, such as remembering to take your medicine or remembering to do an errand. Although some researchers have found a decline in prospective memory with age (Kelly & others, 2012), a number of studies show that whether there is a decline depends on such factors as the nature of the task, what is being assessed, and the context of the assessment (Einstein & McDaniel,

This older woman has forgotten where she put the keys to her car. *What type of memory is involved in this situation?*

explicit memory Memory of facts and experiences that individuals consciously know and can state.

implicit memory Memory without conscious recollection; involves skills and routine procedures that are automatically performed.

source memory The ability to remember where one learned something.

prospective memory Remembering to do something in the future.

some of the decline in intellectual performance found for older adults is likely due to health-related factors rather than to age per se (Morra & others, 2012).

K. Warner Schaie (1994) concluded that although some diseases—such as hypertension and diabetes—are linked to cognitive drop-offs, they do not directly cause mental decline. Rather, the lifestyles of the individuals with the diseases might be the culprits. For example, poor eating habits, inactivity, and stress are related to both physical and mental decline (Annweiler & others, 2012; Kraft, 2012). For example, a recent study found that older adults who had a high level of trans fat in their blood plasma showed lower cognitive functioning (Bowman & others, 2012). And researchers have found age-related cognitive decline in adults with mood disorders such as depression (van den Kommer & others, 2012).

A number of research studies have found that lifestyle and exercise are linked to improved cognitive functioning in older adults (Small & others, 2012a). Here are the results of three of these studies:

- Community-dwelling women 65 years of age and older did not have cognitive impairment or physical limitations when they were initially assessed (Yaffe & others, 2001). Six to eight years later, the women with higher physical activity when they were initially assessed were less likely to experience cognitive decline.

- One hundred twenty-four individuals 60 to 75 years of age whose primary activity was sitting around the house were tested for their level of aerobic endurance and their level of cognitive functioning (Kramer & others, 1999). Cognitive functioning was assessed by tasks on working memory, planning, and scheduling. Half the group was randomly assigned to engage in yoga-type stretching activities and the other half was randomly assigned to start walking three times a week. After six months, the walkers averaged a mile in 16 minutes, a minute faster than at the beginning, and the stretchers had become more flexible. When their cognitive functioning was retested after six months, the walkers scored up to 25 percent higher on the cognitive tests than the stretchers did.

- A higher level of cardiorespiratory fitness in older adults was linked to better performance on a cognitive task through recruitment of neural circuits in the prefrontal and parietal regions of the brain (Prakash & others, 2011).

Other research has found that aerobic exercise is related to improved memory and reasoning (Head, Singh, & Bugg, 2012; Miller & others, 2012). Walking or any other aerobic exercise appears to get blood and oxygen pumping to the brain, which can help people think more clearly (Jak, 2011).

Recent studies have documented that the mental health of older adults can also influence their cognitive functioning (van den Kommer & others, 2012). In one study, depressive symptoms predicted cognitive decline in older adults (Kohler & others, 2010).

A final aspect of health that is important to consider in cognitive functioning in older adults is *terminal decline*. This concept emphasizes that changes in cognitive functioning may be linked more to distance from death or cognition-related pathology than to distance from birth (Wilson & others, 2012). A recent study revealed that although the trajectory of pre-death cognitive change was characterized by a steeper decline than typical age-related change, the decline was still best described as slow and steady (MacDonald, Hultsch, & Dixon, 2011).

USE IT OR LOSE IT

Changes in cognitive activity patterns might result in disuse and consequent atrophy of cognitive skills (Hindin & Zelinski, 2012; Marioni & others, 2012; Small & others, 2012a). This concept is captured in the concept of "use it or lose it." The mental activities that likely benefit the maintenance of cognitive skills in older adults are activities such as reading books, doing crossword puzzles, and going to lectures and concerts. "Use it or lose it" also is a significant component of the engagement model of cognitive optimization that emphasizes how intellectual and social engagement can buffer age-related declines in intellectual development (Park & Bischof, 2011; Park & Reuter-Lorenz, 2009; Stine-Morrow & Basak,

developmental **connection**

Health

Exercise is linked to increased longevity and the prevention of common chronic diseases. Chapter 17, p. 555

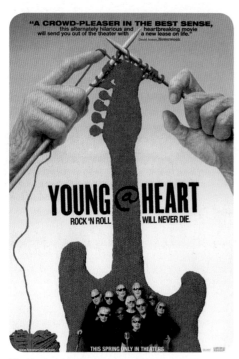

The Young@Heart chorus—whose average age is 80. Young@Heart became a hit documentary in 2008. The documentary displays the singing talents, energy, and optimism of a remarkable group of older adults, who clearly are on the "use it" side of "use it or lose it."

2011). The following studies support the "use it or lose it" concept and the engagement model of cognitive optimization:

- In the Victoria Longitudinal Study, when middle-aged and older adults participated in intellectually engaging activities it served to buffer them against cognitive decline (Hultsch & others, 1999). Further analyses of the participants in this study revealed that engagement in cognitively complex activities was linked to faster and more consistent processing speed (Bielak & others, 2007). And in the most recent analysis of these older adults over a 12-year period, those who reduced their cognitive lifestyle activities (such as using a computer, playing bridge) subsequently showed decline in cognitive functioning in verbal speed, episodic memory, and semantic memory (Small & others, 2012a). The decline in cognitive functioning was linked to subsequent lower engagement in social activities.

- In a longitudinal study of 801 Catholic priests 65 years and older, those who regularly read books, did crossword puzzles, or otherwise exercised their minds were 47 percent less likely to develop Alzheimer disease than the priests who rarely engaged in these activities (Wilson & others, 2002).

- Reading daily was linked to increased longevity for men in their seventies (Jacobs & others, 2008).

- At the beginning of a longitudinal study, 75- to 85-year-olds indicated how often they participated in six activities—reading, writing, doing crossword puzzles, playing card or board games, having group discussions, and playing music—on a daily basis (Hall & others, 2009). Across the five years of the study, the point at which memory loss accelerated was assessed and it was found that for each additional activity the older adult engaged in, the onset of rapid memory loss was delayed by .18 years. For older adults who participated in 11 activities per week compared with their counterparts who engaged in only 4 activities per week, the point at which accelerated memory decline occurred was delayed by 1.29 years.

TRAINING COGNITIVE SKILLS

If older adults are losing cognitive skills, can they be retrained? An increasing number of research studies indicate that this is possible to some degree (Boron, Willis, & Schaie, 2007; Kramer & Morrow, 2012; Lovden & others, 2012; Stine-Morrow & Basak, 2011; Szelag & Skolimowska, 2012; Valdes, O'Connor, & Edwards, 2012). Two key conclusions can be derived from research in this area: (1) training can improve the cognitive skills of many older adults, but (2) there is some loss in plasticity in late adulthood, especially in those who are 85 years and older (Baltes, Lindenberger, & Staudinger, 2006). Let's now examine the results of several cognitive training studies involving older adults.

In an extensive study by Sherry Willis and her colleagues (2006), older adults were randomly assigned to one of four groups: training in (1) reasoning, (2) memory, (3) speed of processing, or (4) a control group that received no training. Each type of training showed an immediate effect in its domain—reasoning training improved reasoning, memory training improved memory, and speed of processing training improved speed of processing. However, the training effects did not transfer across cognitive domains, such that speed of processing training did not benefit the older adults' memory or reasoning, for example. The older adults who were given reasoning training did have less difficulty in the activities of daily living than a control group who did not receive this training. The activities of daily living that were assessed included how independently the older adults were able to prepare meals, do housework, do finances, go shopping, and engage in health maintenance. Each intervention maintained its effects on the specific targeted ability across the five years of the study. However, neither memory nor speed of processing training benefited the older adults' activities of daily living.

Another study had older adults participate in a 20-week activity called Senior Odyssey, a team-based program involving creative problem solving that is derived from the Odyssey of the Mind program for children and emerging adults (Stine-Morrow & others, 2007). In a field experiment, compared with a control group who did not experience Senior Odyssey, the Senior

Odyssey participants showed improved processing speed, somewhat improved creative thinking, and increased mindfulness. *Mindfulness* involves generating new ideas, being open to new information, and being aware of multiple perspectives (Langer, 2000, 2007).

Another study trained older adults to increase their processing speed (Ball, Edwards, & Ross, 2007). As a result of the training, older adults increased their processing speed, and the gain was maintained for two years. The benefits of the processing speed training translated into improvements in everyday activities, such as safer driving performance. And in a recent study, older adults who participated in an 8-week memory training program improved their source memory and the training was linked to a thickening of certain areas of the cerebral cortex (Engvig & others, 2010).

As we discussed earlier in the chapter, researchers are also finding that improving the physical fitness of older adults can improve their cognitive functioning (Head, Singh, & Bugg, 2012; Hindin & Zelinski, 2012; Jak, 2011). A research review revealed that aerobic fitness training improved planning, scheduling, working memory, resistance to distraction, and processing involving multiple tasks in older adults (Colcombe & Kramer, 2003).

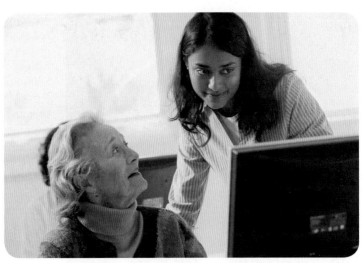

To what extent can training improve cognitive functioning of older adults?

The Stanford Center for Longevity (2011) recently reported information based on a consensus of leading scientists in the field of aging. One of their concerns is the misinformation given to the public touting products to improve the functioning of the mind for which there is no scientific evidence. Nutritional supplements, games, and software products have all been advertised as "magic bullets" to slow the decline of mental functioning and improve the mental ability of older adults. Some of the claims are reasonable but not scientifically tested, while others are unrealistic and implausible. A recent research review of dietary supplements and cognitive aging did indicate that ginkgo biloba was linked with improvements in some aspects of attention in older adults and that omega-3 polyunsaturated fatty acids was related to reduced risk of age-related cognitive decline (Gorby, Brownawell, & Falk, 2010). In this research review, there was no evidence of cognitive improvements in aging adults who took supplements containing ginseng and glucose. Overall, research has not provided consistent plausible evidence that dietary supplements can accomplish major cognitive goals in aging adults over the long term. However, some software-based cognitive training games have been found to improve older adults' cognitive functioning (Hertzog & others, 2009; Lange & others, 2010). Nonetheless, the training games may improve cognitive skills in a laboratory setting but not generalize to gains in the real world.

In sum, the cognitive vitality of older adults can be improved to some extent through cognitive and fitness training (Gross & Rebok, 2011; Kramer & Morrow, 2012). However, benefits have not been observed in all studies (Salthouse, 2012a). Also, there is a difference between short-term improvement and long-term changes from cognitive training in older adults. If older adults' goal is to improve their ability to remember peoples' names at a forthcoming community meeting, research indicates there are good chances that this can be accomplished. However, if the goal is to reduce the rate of memory decline over a decade or two in older adults, no intervention has yet been able to document this result (Stanford Center for Longevity, 2011). Further research is needed to determine more precisely which cognitive improvements occur in older adults (Buitenweg, Murre, & Ridderinkhof, 2012; Luszcz, 2011; Salthouse, 2012a).

COGNITIVE NEUROSCIENCE AND AGING

On several occasions in this chapter and in Chapter 17, we have discussed that certain regions of the brain are involved in links between aging and cognitive functioning. In this section, we further explore the substantial increase in interest in the brain's role in aging and cognitive functioning. The field of *cognitive neuroscience* has emerged as the major discipline that studies links between brain activity and cognitive functioning (Fletcher & Rapp, 2013; Nyberg & others, 2012). This field especially relies on brain imaging techniques, such as fMRI, PET, and DTI (diffusion tensor imaging) to reveal the areas of the brain that

developmental **connection**

Brain Development

The activities older adults engage in can influence the brain's development. Chapter 17, p. 544

FIGURE 18.5

THE PREFRONTAL CORTEX. Advances in neuroimaging are allowing researchers to make significant progress in connecting changes in the brain with cognitive development. Shown here is an fMRI of the brain's prefrontal cortex. *What links have been found between the prefrontal cortex, aging, and cognitive development?*

are activated when individuals engage in certain cognitive activities (Carmichael & Lockhart, 2012; DeCarli & others, 2012; Pacheco & others, 2012). For example, as an older adult is asked to encode and then retrieve verbal materials or images of scenes, the older adult's brain activity will be monitored by an fMRI brain scan.

Changes in the brain can influence cognitive functioning, and changes in cognitive functioning can influence the brain. For example, aging of the brain's prefrontal cortex may produce a decline in working memory (Takeuchi & others, 2012). And when older adults do not regularly use their working memory (recall the section on "Use It or Lose It"), neural connections in the prefrontal lobe may atrophy. Further, cognitive interventions that activate older adults' working memory may increase these neural connections.

Although in its infancy as a field, the cognitive neuroscience of aging is beginning to uncover some important links between aging, the brain, and cognitive functioning (Tanev & others, 2012). These include:

- Neural circuits in specific regions of the brain's prefrontal cortex decline, and this decline is linked to poorer performance by older adults on complex reasoning tasks, working memory, and episodic memory tasks (Grady & others, 2006) (see Figure 18.5).

- Recall from Chapter 17 that older adults are more likely than younger adults to use both hemispheres of the brain to compensate for aging declines in attention, memory, and language (Dennis & Cabeza, 2008; Davis & others, 2012). Two recent neuroimaging studies revealed that older adults showed better memory performance when both hemispheres of the brain were active in processing information (Angel & others, 2011; Manenti, Cotelli, & Miniussi, 2011).

- Functioning of the hippocampus declines to a lesser degree than the functioning of the frontal lobes in older adults. In K. Warner Schaie's (2012) recent research, individuals whose memory and executive functioning declined in middle age had more hippocampal atrophy in late adulthood, but those whose memory and executive functioning improved in middle age did not show a decline in hippocampal functioning in late adulthood.

- Patterns of neural decline with aging are larger for retrieval than encoding (Gutchess & others, 2005).

- Compared with younger adults, older adults often show greater activity in the frontal and parietal lobes of the brain on simple tasks but as attentional demands increase, older adults display less effective functioning in the frontal and parietal lobes of the brain that involve cognitive control (Campbell & others, 2012).

- Younger adults have better connectivity between brain regions than older adults do (Goh, 2011; Waring, Addis, & Kensinger, 2012). For example, a recent study revealed that younger adults had more connections between brain activations in frontal, occipital, and hippocampal regions than older adults during a difficult encoding task (Leshikar & others, 2010).

- An increasing number of cognitive and fitness training studies include brain-imaging techniques such as fMRI to assess the results of such training on brain function (Erickson & others, 2010; Head, Singh, & Bugg, 2012). In one study, older adults who walked one hour a day three days a week for six months showed increased volume in the frontal and temporal lobes of the brain (Colcombe & others, 2006).

Denise Park and Patricia Reuter-Lorenz (2009) proposed a neurocognitive scaffolding view of connections between the aging brain and cognition. In this view, increased activation in the prefrontal cortex with aging reflects an adaptive brain that is compensating for declining neural structures and function and declines in various aspects of cognition, including working memory and long-term memory. Scaffolding involves the use of complementary neural circuits to protect cognitive functioning in an aging brain. Among the factors that can strengthen brain scaffolding are cognitive engagement and exercise.

Review *Connect* Reflect

LG1 Describe the cognitive functioning of older adults.

Review

- How is cognition multidimensional and multidirectional in older adults? What changes in cognitive processes take place in aging adults?
- How do education, work, and health affect cognition in aging adults?
- What is the concept of "use it or lose it"?
- To what extent can older adults' cognitive skills be retrained?
- What characterizes the cognitive neuroscience of aging?

Connect

- The term *scaffolding* was used in this section to describe the use of complementary neural circuits to protect cognitive functioning in an aging brain. How has the term *scaffolding* been used elsewhere in the text?

Reflect *Your Own Personal Journey of Life*

- Can you think of older adults who have made significant contributions in late adulthood other than those we mentioned in the chapter? Spend some time reading about these individuals and evaluate how their intellectual interests contributed to their life satisfaction as older adults. What did you learn from their lives that might benefit your cognitive development and life satisfaction as an older adult?

---

2 Language Development

LG2 Characterize changes in language in older adults.

Most research on language development has focused on infancy and childhood. It is generally thought that for most of adulthood individuals maintain their language skills (Thornton & Light, 2006). The vocabulary of individuals often continues to increase throughout most of the adult years, at least until late adulthood (Schaie, 2012; Singh-Manoux & others, 2012). Many older adults maintain or improve their word knowledge and word meaning (Burke & Shafto, 2004).

In late adulthood, however, some decrements in language may appear (Obler, 2009). Among the most common language-related complaints reported by older adults are difficulty in retrieving words to use in conversation and problems understanding spoken language in certain contexts (Clark-Cotton, Williams, & Goral, 2007). This often involves the *tip-of-the-tongue phenomenon*, in which individuals are confident that they can remember something but just can't quite seem to retrieve it from memory, which we discussed earlier in the section on memory and aging (Ossher, Flegal, & Lustig, 2012). Older adults also report that in less than ideal listening conditions they can have difficulty in understanding speech. This difficulty is most likely to occur when speech is rapid, competing stimuli are present (a noisy room, for example), and when they can't see their conversation partner (in a telephone conversation, for example). The difficulty in understanding speech may be due to hearing loss (Benichov & others, 2012). In general, though, most language skills decline little among older adults if they are healthy (Clark-Cotton & others, 2007).

Some aspects of the phonological skills of older adults are different from those of younger adults (Clark-Cotton & others, 2007; Singh-Manoux & others, 2012). Older adults' speech is typically lower in volume, slower, less precisely articulated, and less fluent (more pauses, fillers, repetition, and corrections). Despite these age differences, most older adults' speech skills are adequate for everyday communication.

Researchers have found conflicting information about changes in *discourse* (extended verbal expression in speech or writing) with aging. "Some (researchers) have reported increased elaborateness, while others have reported less varied and less complex syntax" (Obler, 2009, p. 459). One aspect of discourse where age differences have been found involves retelling a story or giving instructions for completing a task. When engaging in this type of discourse, older adults are more likely than younger adults to omit key elements, creating discourse that is less fluent and more difficult to follow (Clark-Cotton & others, 2007). A

What are some differences in the ways older and younger adults communicate?

recent study found that when retelling a story, older adults were more likely than younger adults to compress discourse and less likely to improve the cohesiveness of their narratives (Saling, Laroo, & Saling, 2012).

Nonlanguage factors may be responsible for some of the decline in language skills that do occur in older adults (Obler, 2009). Slower information-processing speed and a decline in working memory, especially in being able to keep information in mind while processing, likely contribute to lowered language efficiency in older adults (Salthouse, 2012a; Stine-Morrow, 2007).

Language does change among individuals with Alzheimer disease, which we will discuss later in the chapter (Obler, 2009). Word-finding/generating difficulties are one of the earliest symptoms of Alzheimer disease (Haugrud, Crossley, & Vrbancic, 2011). Individuals with Alzheimer disease especially have difficulty on tests of semantic verbal fluency, in which they have to say as many words as possible in a category (fruits or animals, for example) in a given time, typically one minute (Pakhomov, Hemmy, & Lim, 2012). Most individuals with the disease do retain much of their ability to produce well-formed sentences until the late stages of the disease. Nonetheless, they do make more grammatical errors than older adults without the disease (Huang, Meyer, & Federmeier, 2012; Kail, Lemaire, & Lecacheur, 2012).

Review Connect Reflect

LG2 Characterize changes in language in older adults.

Review

- What are the main changes in language development in older adults?

Connect

- In this section, we learned that some aspects of the phonological skills of older adults are different from those of younger adults. By what age are children typically capable of producing all the vowel sounds and most of the consonant sounds of their language (discussed in Chapter 7)?

Reflect *Your Own Personal Journey of Life*

- What might you be able to do as an older adult to preserve or even enhance your language skills?

3 Work and Retirement

LG3 Discuss aging and adaptation to work and retirement.

Work

Retirement in the United States and Other Countries

Adjustment to Retirement

What percentage of older adults continue to work? How productive are they? Who adjusts best to retirement? What is the changing pattern of retirement in the United States and around the world? Let's look at the answers to these and other questions.

WORK

The percentage of older U.S. adult men who are still working or returning to work has been increasing since the early 1990s. As more women have entered the workforce, the percentage of older adult women still working also has increased. Figure 18.6 shows the increase in the percentage of men and women 65 to 69 years old who were still working or looking for work from 1998 to 2008 (U.S. Bureau of Labor Statistics, 2008).

Since the mid-1990s, a significant shift has occurred in the percentage of older adults working part-time or full-time (U.S. Bureau of Labor Statistics, 2008). As shown in Figure 18.7, after 1995, of the adults 65 and older in the workforce, those engaging in full-time work rose substantially and those working part-time decreased considerably. This significant rise in full-time employment likely reflects the increasing number of older adults who realize that they may not have adequate money to fund their retirement (Rix, 2011). Older adults are increasingly

developmental **connection**

Work

In the United States, approximately 80 percent of individuals 40 to 59 years of age are employed. Chapter 15, p. 499

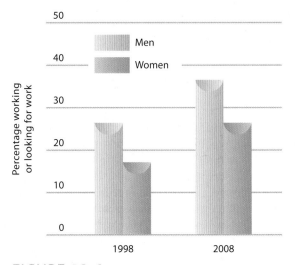

FIGURE **18.6**

PERCENTAGE OF 65- TO 69-YEAR-OLD U.S. MEN AND WOMEN WORKING OR LOOKING FOR WORK IN 1998 AND 2008

Ninety-two-year-old Russell "Bob" Harrell (right) puts in 12-hour days at Sieco Consulting Engineers in Columbus, Indiana. A highway and bridge engineer, he designs and plans roads. James Rice (age 48), a vice president of client services at Sieco, says that Bob wants to learn something new every day and that he has learned many life lessons from being around him. Harrell says he is not planning to retire. *What are some variations in work and retirement in older adults?*

seeking some type of bridge employment that permits a gradual rather than a sudden movement out of the work context (Bowen, Noack, & Staudinger, 2011).

Cognitive ability is one of the best predictors of job performance in older adults. And older workers have lower rates of absenteeism, fewer accidents, and higher job satisfaction than their younger counterparts (Warr, 2004). Thus, the older worker can be of considerable value to a company, above and beyond the older worker's cognitive competence. Changes in federal law now allow individuals over the age of 65 to continue working (Shore & Goldberg, 2005). Also, remember from our discussion earlier in this chapter that substantively complex work is linked with a higher level of intellectual functioning (Schooler, 2007). In sum, a cognitively stimulating work context promotes successful aging (Bowen, Noack, & Staudinger, 2011).

In sum, age affects many aspects of work. Nonetheless, many studies of work and aging—such as evaluation of hiring and performance—have yielded inconsistent results. Important contextual factors—such as age composition of departments or applicant pools, occupations, and jobs—all affect decisions about older workers. It also is important to recognize that ageist stereotypes of workers and of tasks can limit older workers' career opportunities and can encourage early retirement or other forms of downsizing that adversely affect older workers (Finkelstein & Farrell, 2007).

> The night hath not yet come: We are not quite cut off from labor by the failing of light; some work remains for us to do and dare.
>
> —HENRY WADSWORTH LONGFELLOW
> *American Poet, 19th Century*

FIGURE **18.7**

PERCENTAGE OF U.S. ADULTS 65 YEARS AND OLDER IN THE LABOR FORCE WHO ARE WORKING FULL-TIME OR PART-TIME

Continue working as long as possible

Retire when I am old enough to receive my pension

Retire when I am eligible for early retirement

Retire when my employer forces me to

Retire when my friends/colleagues do

Reasons

Percentage

FIGURE 18.8

RESPONSES GIVEN BY PEOPLE WHO WERE ASKED WHEN THEY EXPECTED TO RETIRE FROM WORK

In the study of work and retirement in 21 countries, what were some variations across countries regarding the extent to which retirees missed work and money?

RETIREMENT IN THE UNITED STATES AND IN OTHER COUNTRIES

At what age do most people retire in the United States? Do many people return to the workforce at some point after they have retired? What is retirement like in other countries?

Retirement in the United States   The option to retire is a late-twentieth-century phenomenon in the United States (Higo & Williamson, 2009). It exists largely because of the 1935 implementation of the Social Security system, which gives benefits to older workers when they retire. On average, today's workers will spend 10 to 15 percent of their lives in retirement. A survey revealed that as baby boomers move into their sixties, they expect to retire later than either their parents or their grandparents (Frey, 2007). In 2011, in the United States, the average age of retirement was 64 for men and 62 for women (Munnell, 2011).

In the past, when most people reached an accepted retirement age, such as some point in their sixties, retirement meant a one-way exit from full-time work to full-time leisure. Leading expert Phyllis Moen (2007) described how today, when people reach their sixties, the life path they follow is less clear:

- some individuals don't retire, continuing in their career jobs
- some retire from their career work and then take up a new and different job
- some retire from career jobs but do volunteer work
- some retire from a post-retirement job and go on to yet another job
- some move in and out of the workforce, so they never really have a "career" job from which they retire
- some individuals who are in poor health move to a disability status and eventually into retirement
- some who are laid off define it as "retirement."

Approximately 7 million retired Americans return to work after they have retired (Putnam Investments, 2006). When retired adults return to the labor force, it occurs on average four years after retirement (Hardy, 2006). In many instances, the jobs pay much less than their pre-retirement jobs. In one study of older adults who returned to work, approximately two-thirds said they were happy they had done so, while about one-third indicated they were forced to go back to work to meet financial needs (Putnam Investments, 2006).

Just as the life path after individuals reach retirement age may vary, so do the reasons for working. For example, some older adults who reach retirement age work for financial reasons, others to stay busy, and yet others to "give back" (Moen, 2007).

Work and Retirement in Other Countries   What characterizes work and retirement in other countries? A large-scale study of 21,000 individuals aged 40 to 79 in 21 countries examined patterns of work and retirement (HSBC Insurance, 2007). On average, 33 percent of individuals in their sixties and 11 percent in their seventies were still in some kind of paid employment. In this study, 19 percent of those in their seventies in the United States were still working. As indicated in Figure 18.8, a substantial percentage of individuals expect to continue working as long as possible before retiring (HSBC Insurance, 2007).

In the study of work and retirement in 21 countries, Japanese retirees missed the work slightly more than they expected and the money considerably less than they expected (HSBC Insurance, 2007). U.S. retirees missed both the work and the money slightly less than they expected. German retirees were the least likely to miss the work, Turkish and Chinese retirees the most likely to miss it. Regarding the money, Japanese and Chinese retirees were the least likely to miss it, Turkish retirees the most likely to miss it.

Early retirement policies were introduced by many companies in the 1970s and 1980s with the intent of making room for younger workers (Coe & others, 2012). However, the recent survey indicated that an increasing number of adults are beginning to reject the early retirement option as they hear about people who retired and then regretted it. In the 21-country study, on average only 12 percent of individuals in their forties and fifties expected to take early retirement while 16 percent in their sixties and seventies had taken early retirement. Only in Germany, South Korea, and Hong Kong did a higher percentage of individuals expect to take earlier retirement than in the past.

ADJUSTMENT TO RETIREMENT

Retirement is a process, not an event (Wang, 2012). Much of the research on retirement has been cross-sectional rather than longitudinal and has focused on men rather than women. One study found that men had higher morale when they had retired within the last two years compared with men who had been retired for longer periods of time (Kim & Moen, 2002). Another study revealed that retired married and remarried women reported being more satisfied with their lives and in better health than retired women who were widowed, separated, divorced, or had never been married (Price & Joo, 2005). Yet another study indicated that women spend less time planning for retirement than men do (Jacobs-Lawson, Hershey, & Neukam, 2005). And a recent study revealed that higher levels of financial assets and job satisfaction were more strongly linked to men's higher psychological well-being in retirement, while preretirement social contacts were more strongly related to women's psychological well-being in retirement (Kubicek & others, 2010).

What are some keys to adjusting effectively in retirement?

Older adults who adjust best to retirement are healthy, have adequate income, are active, are better educated, have an extended social network including both friends and family, and usually were satisfied with their lives before they retired (Jokela & others, 2010). Older adults with inadequate income and poor health, and who must adjust to other stress that occurs at the same time as retirement, such as the death of a spouse, have the most difficult time adjusting to retirement (Reichstadt & others, 2007). A study also found that individuals who had difficulty in adjusting to retirement had a strong attachment to work, including full-time jobs and a long work history, lack of control over the transition to retirement, and low self-efficacy (van Solinge & Henkens, 2005).

The U.S. retirement system is in transition (Butrica, Smith, & Iams, 2012; Kramer, 2012). Following are the results of a 2007 survey on retirement (Helman, VanDerhei, & Copeland, 2007): Half of the workers were not confident about their pension benefits; many workers count on benefits that won't be there when they retire; workers often don't heed advice about retirement even when they are provided the advice; workers overestimate long-term care coverage; most workers' savings are modest; and many workers know little about the Social Security income they will receive when they retire.

The recent economic downturn, high unemployment rate, and potential changes in Social Security and health insurance coverage for retired individuals in the United States has made having enough money for retirement an even greater concern (Bosworth, 2012). A 2012 survey indicated that confidence in having enough money to live comfortably in retirement dropped to 14 percent (Helman, Copeland, & VanDerhei, 2012). In this survey, the percent of workers who reported that they expect to retire after the age of 65 grew to 37 percent (compared to 11 percent in 1991). With regard to retirement income, the two main worries of individuals as they approach retirement are: (1) drawing retirement income from savings, and (2) paying for health care expenses (Yakoboski, 2011).

Flexibility is also a key factor in whether individuals adjust well to retirement (Wang, 2012). When people retire, they no longer have the structured environment they had when they were working, so they need to be flexible and discover and pursue their own interests. Cultivating interests and friends unrelated to work improves adaptation to retirement.

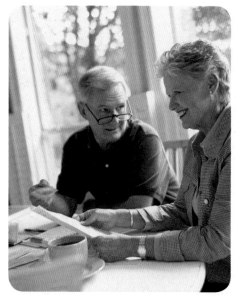

In addition to financial planning, what are some other aspects of retirement planning that need to be carried out?

Planning and then successfully carrying out the plan are important aspects of adjusting well in retirement (Adams & Rau, 2011). A special concern in retirement planning involves women, who are likely to live longer than men, more likely to live alone, and have lower retirement income (less likely to remarry and more likely to be widowed) (Moen, 2007; Prickett & Angel, 2011; Silver, 2010).

Individuals who view retirement planning only in terms of finances don't adapt as well to retirement as those who have a more balanced retirement plan (Birren, 1996). It is important not only to plan financially for retirement but also to consider other aspects of your life (Shultz & Wang, 2011). In addition to financial planning, individuals need to ask questions about retirement such as these: What am I going to do with my leisure time? What am I going to do to stay active? What am I going to do socially? What am I going to do to keep my mind active?

Review *Connect* Reflect

 LG3 Discuss aging and adaptation to work and retirement.

Review

- What characterizes the work of older adults?
- Compare retirement in the United States with retirement in other countries.
- How can individuals adjust effectively to retirement?

Connect

- In Chapter 12, you learned that U.S. adolescents spend much more time in unstructured leisure activities than East Asian adolescents do. How might establishing challenging lifelong leisure activities as an adolescent benefit an individual at retirement age?

Reflect *Your Own Personal Journey of Life*

- At what age would you like to retire? Or would you prefer to continue working as an older adult as long as you are healthy?

4 Mental Health   **LG4** Describe mental health problems in older adults.

Depression

Dementia, Alzheimer Disease, and Other Afflictions

Fear of Victimization, Crime, and Elder Maltreatment

Although a substantial portion of the population can now look forward to a longer life, that life may unfortunately be hampered by a mental disorder in old age (Knight & Kellough, 2013). This prospect is both troubling to the individual and costly to society. Mental disorders make individuals increasingly dependent on the help and care of others. The cost of caring for older adults with mental health disorders is estimated to be more than $40 billion per year in the United States. More important than the loss in dollars, though, is the loss of human potential and the suffering involved for individuals and their families. Although mental disorders in older adults are a major concern, it is important to understand that older adults do not have a higher incidence of mental disorders than younger adults do (Busse & Blazer, 1996).

DEPRESSION

Major depression is a mood disorder in which the individual is deeply unhappy, demoralized, self-derogatory, and bored. The person does not feel well, loses stamina easily, has a poor appetite, and is listless and unmotivated. Major depression has been called the "common cold" of mental disorders. However, a recent review concluded that depression is less common among older adults than younger adults (Fiske, Wetherell, & Gatz, 2009). More than half of the cases of depression in older adults represent the first time these individuals have developed depression in their life (Fiske, Wetherell, & Gatz, 2009).

One study found that the lower frequency of depressive symptoms in older adults compared with middle-aged adults was linked to fewer economic hardships, fewer negative social interchanges, and increased religiosity (Schieman, van Gundy, & Taylor, 2004). Other research indicates that older adults who engage in regular exercise, especially aerobic exercise, are less likely to be depressed, whereas those who are in poor health and experiencing pain are more likely to be depressed (Cimpean & Drake, 2011; Tinetti & others, 2011). Depressive symptoms increase among the oldest-old (85 years and older), and this increase is associated with a higher percentage of women in the group, more physical disability, greater cognitive impairment, and lower socioeconomic status (Hybels & Blazer, 2004).

major depression A mood disorder in which the individual is deeply unhappy, demoralized, self-derogatory, and bored. The person does not feel well, loses stamina easily, has poor appetite, and is listless and unmotivated. Major depression is so widespread that it has been called the "common cold" of mental disorders.

dementia A global term for any neurological disorder in which the primary symptoms involve a deterioration of mental functioning.

Alzheimer disease A progressive, irreversible brain disorder characterized by a gradual deterioration of memory, reasoning, language, and eventually, physical function.

In the childhood, adolescent, and early adulthood years, females show higher rates of depression than males do (Nolen-Hoeksema, 2011). Does this gender difference hold for middle-aged and older adults? A longitudinal study found more depression in women than men at 50 and 60 years of age, but not at 80 years of age (Barefoot & others, 2001). Men showed increases in depressive symptoms from 60 to 80, but women did not. In this cohort, men may have undergone more profound role shifts after 60 years of age because they were more likely than women to have retired from active involvement in the work world. Thus, the absence of a gender difference in depression in older adults may be cohort-specific and may not hold as women who have entered the workforce in greater numbers are assessed in late adulthood.

Among the most common predictors of depression in older adults are earlier depressive symptoms, poor health, disability, loss events such as the death of a spouse, and low social support (Bland, 2012; Ng & others, 2010). Insomnia is often overlooked as a risk factor for depression in older adults (Fiske, Wetherell, & Gatz, 2009). Curtailment of daily activities is a common pathway to late-life depression (Fiske, Wetherell, & Gatz, 2009). Often accompanying this curtailment of activity is an increase in self-critical thinking that exacerbates depression. A recent meta-analysis found that the following living arrangements were linked to risk for depression in older adults: living alone, in a nursing home, or in an institutionalized setting (Xiu-Ying & others, 2012).

Depression is a treatable condition, not only in young adults but in older adults as well (Kohen & others, 2011; Piazza & Charles, 2012). Unfortunately, as many as 80 percent of older adults with depressive symptoms receive no treatment at all. Combinations of medications and psychotherapy produce significant improvement in almost four out of five older adults with depression (Koenig & Blazer, 1996). Also, engagement in valued activities and religious/spiritual involvement can reduce depressive symptoms (Fiske, Wetherell, & Gatz, 2009). Life review/reminiscence therapy, which we will discuss further in Chapter 19, is underutilized in the treatment of depression in older adults (Fiske, Wetherell, & Gatz, 2009).

Major depression can result not only in sadness but also in suicidal tendencies (Bergman-Levy & others, 2011). Nearly 25 percent of individuals who commit suicide in the United States are 65 years of age or older (Church, Siegel, & Fowler, 1988). The older adult most likely to commit suicide is a male who lives alone, has lost his spouse, and is experiencing failing health (Ruckenhauser, Yazdani, & Ravaglia, 2007).

What characterizes depression in older adults?

developmental **connection**

Gender

One reason that females have higher rates of depression is that they ruminate more in their depressed mood and amplify it more than males do. Chapter 12, p. 408

DEMENTIA, ALZHEIMER DISEASE, AND OTHER AFFLICTIONS

Among the most debilitating of mental disorders in older adults are the dementias (Clare & others, 2011). In recent years, extensive attention has been focused on the most common dementia, Alzheimer disease.

Dementia   **Dementia** is a global term for any neurological disorder in which the primary symptoms involve a deterioration of mental functioning. Individuals with dementia often lose the ability to care for themselves and can become unable to recognize familiar surroundings and people—including family members (Clare, 2011). It is estimated that 23 percent of women and 17 percent of men 85 years and older are at risk for developing dementia (Alzheimer's Association, 2012). However, these estimates may be high because of the Alzheimer's Association's lobbying efforts to increase funding for research and treatment facilities. Dementia is a broad category, and it is important that every effort is made to determine the specific cause of deteriorating mental functioning (Taney & others, 2012).

Alzheimer Disease   One form of dementia is **Alzheimer disease**—a progressive, irreversible brain disorder that is characterized by a gradual deterioration of memory, reasoning, language, and eventually, physical function. In 2012, an estimated 5.4 million adults in the United States had Alzheimer disease, and it is projected that 10 million baby boomers will develop Alzheimer disease in their lifetime (Alzheimer's Association, 2012). Figure 18.9 shows the estimated

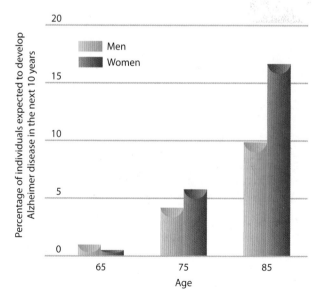

FIGURE 18.9

ESTIMATED RISKS FOR DEVELOPING ALZHEIMER DISEASE AT DIFFERENT AGES FOR WOMEN AND MEN.
Source: Alzheimer's Association (2010).

FIGURE **18.10**

TWO BRAINS: NORMAL AGING AND ALZHEIMER DISEASE. The photograph on the top shows a slice of a normal aging brain and the photograph on the bottom shows a slice of a brain ravaged by Alzheimer disease. Notice the deterioration and shrinking in the Alzheimer disease brain.

risks for developing Alzheimer disease at different ages for women and men (Alzheimer's Association, 2010). Women are more likely than men to develop Alzheimer disease because they live longer than men and their longer life expectancy increases the number of years during which they can develop it. It is estimated that Alzheimer disease triples the health care costs of Americans 65 years of age and older (Alzheimer's Association, 2012). Because of the increasing prevalence of Alzheimer disease, researchers have stepped up their efforts to discover the causes of the disease and find more effective ways to treat it (Gamba & others, 2012; Genin & others, 2012).

Causes   Alzheimer disease involves a deficiency in the important brain messenger chemical acetylcholine, which plays an important role in memory (Hunter & others, 2012). Also, as Alzheimer disease progresses, the brain shrinks and deteriorates (see Figure 18.10). This deterioration is characterized by the formation of *amyloid plaques* (dense deposits of protein that accumulate in the blood vessels) and *neurofibrillary tangles* (twisted fibers that build up in neurons) (Luan, Rosales, & Lee, 2012; Hickman & Khoury, 2012).

There is increasing interest in the role that oxidative stress might play in Alzheimer disease (Ferreiro & others, 2012; Gonfloni & others, 2012). Oxidative stress occurs when the body's antioxidant defenses don't cope with free radical attacks and oxidation in the body. Recall from Chapter 17 that free radical theory is a major theory of aging.

Although scientists are not certain what causes Alzheimer disease, age is an important risk factor and genes also are likely to play an important role (Park, Lee, & Han, 2012). The number of individuals with Alzheimer disease doubles every five years after the age of 65. A gene called *apolipoprotein E* (*ApoE*) is linked to increasing presence of plaques and tangles in the brain (Schellenberg & Montine, 2012). Special attention has focused on an allele (an alternative form of a gene) labeled ApoE4, an allele that is a strong risk factor for Alzheimer disease (Caselli, 2012; Ward & others, 2012). In K. Warner Schaie's (2012) recent research, individuals who had the ApoE4 allele showed more cognitive decline beginning in middle age. A recent study found that the ApoE4 gene created a cascade of molecular signaling that causes blood vessels to become more porous, allowing toxic substances to leak into the brain and damage neurons (Bell & others, 2012).

Despite links between the presence of the ApoE4 gene and Alzheimer disease, less than 50 percent of the individuals who are carriers of the ApoE4 gene develop dementia in old age. Advances as a result of the Human Genome Project have recently resulted in identification of other genes that are risk factors for Alzheimer disease, although they are not as strongly linked to the disease as the ApoE4 gene (Schellenberg & Montine, 2012).

Although individuals with a family history of Alzheimer disease are at greater risk, the disease is complex and likely caused by a number of factors, including lifestyles (Lopez, Becker, & Kuller, 2012). Researchers are finding that healthy lifestyle factors may lower the risk of Alzheimer disease or delay the onset of the disease. For example, older adults with Alzheimer disease are more likely to have cardiovascular disease than are individuals who do not have Alzheimer disease (Obisesan & others, 2012). Recently, more cardiac risk factors have been implicated in Alzheimer disease—obesity, smoking, atherosclerosis, high cholesterol, and lipids (Businaro & others, 2012). One of the best strategies for intervening in the lives of people who are at risk for Alzheimer disease is to improve their cardiac functioning through diet, drugs, and exercise (Geda & others, 2010; Gelber, Launer, & White, 2012; Wagner & others, 2012). One study of older adults found that those who exercised three or more times a week were less likely to develop Alzheimer disease over a six-year period than those who exercised less (Larson & others, 2006).

Early Detection and Drug Treatment   *Mild cognitive impairment* (*MCI*) represents a transitional state between the cognitive changes of normal aging and very early Alzheimer disease and other dementias. MCI is increasingly recognized as a risk factor for Alzheimer disease. Estimates indicate that as many as 10 to 20 percent of individuals 65 years of age and older have MCI (Alzheimer's Association, 2012). Many individuals with MCI do not go on to develop Alzheimer disease, but MCI is a risk factor for Alzheimer disease.

Distinguishing between individuals who merely have age-associated declines in memory and those with MCI is difficult, as is predicting which individuals with MCI will subsequently develop Alzheimer disease (Palmqvist & others, 2012; Macdonald & others, 2012). A recent research review concluded that fMRI measurement of neuron loss in the medial temporal lobe is a predictor of memory loss and eventually dementia (Vellas & Aisen, 2010). Further, a recent study revealed that amyloid beta—a protein fragment that forms plaques in the brain—was present in the spinal fluid of approximately 75 percent of the individuals with mild cognitive impairment (De Meyer & others, 2010). Every one of the older adults with mild cognitive impairment who had the amyloid beta in their spinal fluid developed Alzheimer disease within five years.

Drug Treatment of Alzheimer Disease   Several drugs called cholinerase inhibitors have been approved by the U.S. Food and Drug Administration to treat Alzheimer disease. They are designed to improve memory and other cognitive functions by increasing levels of acetylcholine in the brain (Gil-Bea & others, 2012). Keep in mind, though, that the drugs used to treat Alzheimer disease only slow the downward progression of the disease; they do not address its cause (Alves & others, 2012). Also, no drugs have yet been approved by the Federal Drug Administration for the treatment of MCI (Alzheimer's Association, 2010).

Caring for Individuals with Alzheimer Disease   A special concern is caring for Alzheimer patients (Bursch & Butcher, 2012; Clare, 2011). Health-care professionals emphasize that the family can be an important support system for the Alzheimer patient, but this support can have costs for the family, who can become emotionally and physically drained by the extensive care required for a person with Alzheimer disease (Carling-Jenkins & others, 2012). A recent study compared family members' perception of caring for someone with Alzheimer disease, cancer, or schizophrenia (Papastavrou & others, 2012). In this study, the highest perceived burden was reported for Alzheimer disease.

Former president Ronald Reagan was diagnosed with Alzheimer disease at age 83.

   Respite care (services that provide temporary relief for those who are caring for individuals with disabilities, illnesses, or the elderly) has been developed to help people who have to meet the day-to-day needs of Alzheimer patients. This type of care provides an important break from the burden of providing chronic care (de la Cuesta-Benjumea, 2011).

   There are many career opportunities for working with individuals who have Alzheimer disease. To read about the work of a director of an Alzheimer association, see *Connecting with Careers.*

Parkinson Disease   Another type of dementia is **Parkinson disease,** a chronic, progressive disease characterized by muscle tremors, slowing of movement, and partial facial paralysis. Parkinson disease is triggered by degeneration of dopamine-producing neurons in the brain (Feve, 2012; Nishikawa & others, 2012). Dopamine is a neurotransmitter that is necessary for normal brain functioning. Why these neurons degenerate is not known.

   The main treatment for Parkinson disease involves administering drugs that enhance the effect of dopamine (dopamine agonists) in the disease's earlier stages and later administering the drug L-dopa, which is converted by the brain into dopamine (Reese & others, 2012). However, it is difficult to determine the correct level of dosage of L-dopa and it loses efficacy over time (Nomoto & others, 2009).

   Another treatment for advanced Parkinson disease is deep brain stimulation (DBS), which involves implantation of electrodes within the brain (Tsang & others, 2012). The electrodes are then stimulated by a pacemaker-like device. Recent studies indicated that deep brain stimulation may provide benefits for individuals with Parkinson disease (Weaver & others, 2012). Other recent studies indicate that certain types of dance, such as the tango, can improve the movement skills of individuals with Parkinson disease (Hackney & Earhart, 2010a, b; Ransmayr, 2011). Stem cell transplantation and gene therapy also offer hope for treating the disease (Pardal & Lopez-Barneo, 2012; Politis & Lindvall, 2012).

Muhammad Ali, one of the world's leading sports figures, has Parkinson disease.

FEAR OF VICTIMIZATION, CRIME, AND ELDER MALTREATMENT

Some of the physical decline and limitations that characterize development in late adulthood contribute to a sense of vulnerability and fear among older adults. For some older adults, fear

Parkinson disease A chronic, progressive disease characterized by muscle tremors, slowing of movement, and partial facial paralysis.

Jan Weaver, Director of the Alzheimer's Association of Dallas

Dr. Weaver joined the Alzheimer's Association, Greater Dallas Chapter, as director of services and education in 1999. Prior to that time, she served as associate director of education for the Texas Institute for Research and Education on Aging and director of the National Academy for Teaching and Learning About Aging at the University of North Texas. As a gerontologist, Weaver plans and develops services and educational programs that address patterns of human development related to aging. Among the services that Weaver supervises at the Alzheimer's Association are a resource center and helpline, a family assistance program, a care program, support groups, referral and information, educational conferences, and community seminars.

Weaver recognizes that people of all ages should have an informed and balanced view of older adults that helps them perceive aging as a process of growth and fulfillment rather than a process of decline and dependency. Weaver earned her Ph.D. in sociology, with an emphasis in gerontology, from the University of Texas in 1996.

Jan Weaver giving a lecture on Alzheimer disease.

of crime may become a deterrent to travel, attendance at social events, and the pursuit of an active lifestyle. Almost one-fourth of older adults say they have a basic fear of being the victim of a crime. However, in reality, possibly because of the precautions they take, older adults are less likely than younger adults to be the victim of a crime. However, the crimes committed against older adults are likely to be serious offenses such as armed robbery. Older adults are also victims of nonviolent crimes such as fraud, vandalism, purse snatching, and harassment (Navarro & others, 2012). Estimates of the incidence of crimes against older adults may be low because older adults may not report crimes, fearing retribution from criminals or believing the criminal justice system cannot help them.

How often does elder abuse occur? A research review indicated that 6 percent of older adults reported experiencing significant abuse in the last month (Cooper, Selwood, & Livingston, 2008). In this study, 16 percent of home-care staff admitted to significant psychological abuse of older adults. Elder maltreatment may be perpetuated by anyone, but it is primarily carried out by family members (Dakin & Pearlmutter, 2009). As with child maltreatment, elder maltreatment can involve neglect, psychological abuse, or physical abuse (Mysyuk, Westendorp, & Lindenberg, 2012). Older adults are most often abused by their spouses. A special concern is the burden older women carry in facing possible physical violence. In the research review described above, 5.6 percent of older adult couples said they had experienced physical violence in their relationship in the last month.

Older adults also can experience institutional abuse, which involves mistreatment of older adults living in facilities such as nursing homes, hospitals, or long-term care centers (Natan, Lowenstein, & Eisikovits, 2011). Institutional abuse of older adults include the staff engaging in rough handling, hitting, or slapping patients, inappropriate treatment, and psychological abuse, such as social isolation and threats.

Maltreated older adults, as well as older adults who are depressed, have a dementia, or have another mental disorder, may need mental health treatment (Cisler & others, 2012). To read about this topic, see *Connecting Development to Life.*

Meeting the Mental Health Needs of Older Adults

Older adults receive disproportionately fewer mental health services than young or middle-aged adults (Moak, 2011). One estimate is that only 2.7 percent of all clinical services provided by psychologists go to older adults, although individuals aged 65 and over make up more than 11 percent of the population. Psychotherapy can be expensive. Although reduced fees and sometimes no fee can be arranged in public hospitals for older adults from low-income backgrounds, many older adults who need psychotherapy do not get it (Knight & others, 2006). It has been said that psychotherapists like to work with young, attractive, verbal, intelligent, and successful clients (called YAVISes) rather than those who are quiet, ugly, old, institutionalized, and different (called QUOIDs). Psychotherapists have been accused of failing to see older adults because they perceive that older adults have a poor prognosis for therapy success; they do not feel they have adequate training to treat older adults, who may have special problems requiring special treatment; and they may have stereotypes that label older adults as low-status and unworthy recipients of treatment (Virnig & others, 2004).

How can we better meet the mental health needs of older adults? First, mental health professionals must be encouraged to include greater numbers of older adults in their client lists, and older adults must be convinced that they can benefit from therapy (Baskin & others, 2011; Knight & Kellough, 2013). Second, we must make mental health care affordable. For example, Medicare continues to fall short of providing many mental health services for older adults, especially those in need of long-term care (Knight & Lee, 2007).

Margaret Gatz (*right*) has been a crusader for better mental health treatment of older adults. She believes that mental health professionals need to be encouraged to include greater numbers of older adults in their client lists and that we need to better educate the elderly about how they can benefit from therapy. *What are some common mechanisms of change that can be used to improve the mental health of older adults?*

Earlier in this chapter, we discussed stereotypes and ageism with regard to older adults in the workforce. How are those concepts related to what you just read in this interlude?

Review *Connect* Reflect

 LG4 Describe mental health problems in older adults.

Review

- What is the nature of depression in older adults?
- What are dementia, Alzheimer disease, and Parkinson disease like in older adults?
- How extensive is fear of victimization, crime, and maltreatment in older adults?

Connect

- We also discussed depression in adolescence in Chapter 12. What are some differences in how depression is characterized in adolescence as opposed to late adulthood?

Reflect *Your Own Personal Journey of Life*

- Have any older adults in your family background experienced mental health problems as adults? If so, what were these mental health problems? If they have experienced mental health problems, what were the likely causes of the problems?

5 Religion and Spirituality

LG5 Explain the role of religion and spirituality in the lives of older adults.

In Chapter 15, we discussed religion, spirituality, and meaning in life with a special focus on middle age, including links between religion/spirituality and health. Here we will continue our exploration of religion and spirituality by considering their importance in the lives of many older adults.

In many societies around the world, older adults are the spiritual leaders in their churches and communities. For example, in the Catholic Church more popes have been elected in their eighties than in any other 10-year period of the human life span.

The religious patterns of older adults have increasingly been studied (Krause, 2012; Sun & others, 2012; Vahia & others, 2011a, b). One study revealed that religious attendance at least weekly compared with never was linked to a lower risk of mortality (Gillum & others, 2008). Another study revealed that African American and Caribbean Black older adults reported higher levels of religious participation, religious coping, and spirituality than non-Latino White older adults (Taylor, Chatters, & Jackson, 2007). And in a recent study, older adults who reported having a higher level of spirituality had more resilience in the face of stressful and difficult circumstances (Vahia & others, 2011a).

Individuals over 65 years of age are more likely than younger people to say that religious faith is the most significant influence in their lives, that they try to put religious faith into practice, and that they attend religious services (Gallup & Bezilla, 1992). A recent study of more than 500 African Americans 55 to 105 years of age revealed that they had a strong identification with religious institutions and high levels of attendance and participation in religious activities (Williams, Keigher, & Williams, 2012). And a Pew poll found that belief in God was higher in older adults than in any other age period (Pew Forum on Religion and Public Life, 2008).

Is religion related to a sense of well-being and life satisfaction in old age? In one study, older adults' self-esteem was highest when they had a strong religious commitment and lowest when they had little religious commitment (Krause, 1995). In another study, older adults who derived a sense of meaning in life from religion had higher levels of life satisfaction, self-esteem, and optimism (Krause, 2003).

Religion and spirituality can meet some important psychological needs in older adults, helping them to face impending death, to find and maintain a sense of meaningfulness in life, and to accept the inevitable losses of old age (Koenig, 2004). Socially, the religious community can serve many functions for older adults, such as social activities, social support, and the opportunity to assume teaching and leadership roles (Krause, 2012; Moxey & others, 2011).

During late adulthood, many individuals increasingly engage in prayer. *How might this be linked with longevity?*

developmental **connection**

Religion and Spirituality

Meaning-making coping involves drawing on beliefs, values, and goals to change the meaning of a stressful situation, especially in times of chronic stress, such as when a loved one dies. Chapter 15, p. 503

Review *Connect* Reflect

 LG5 Explain the role of religion and spirituality in the lives of older adults.

Review

- What are some characteristics of religion and spirituality in older adults?

Connect

- We just learned that prayer and meditation may reduce stress and dampen the body's production of stress

hormones. Why is this especially important in the aging process?

Reflect *Your Own Personal Journey of Life*

- Do you think you will become more or less religious as an older adult than you are now? Explain.

topical connections

In Chapter 19, you will read about a number of theories that seek to explain older adults' socioemotional development, including Erikson's final stage (integrity versus despair). Older adults become more selective than middle-aged adults about the people they want to spend time with. There is considerable diversity in older adults' lifestyles, and an increasing number of older adults cohabit. Social support is especially important in older adults' lives and is linked to their physical and mental health. An important aspect of late adulthood is not dwelling too extensively on the negative aspects of aging but rather determining the key dimensions of successful aging.

looking *forward* --- ⟶

reach your **learning goals**

Cognitive Development in Late Adulthood

1 Cognitive Functioning in Older Adults

 LG1 Describe the cognitive functioning of older adults.

Multidimensionality and Multidirectionality

- Cognitive mechanics (the neurophysiological architecture, including the brain) are more likely to decline in older adults than are cognitive pragmatics (the culture-based software of the mind). Speed of processing declines in older adults. Older adults' attention declines more on complex than simple tasks. Regarding memory, in late adulthood, episodic memory declines more than semantic memory; working memory declines; explicit memory declines more than implicit memory; and noncognitive factors such as health, education, and socioeconomic status are linked with memory in older adults.

  Components of executive functioning—such as cognitive control and working memory—decline in late adulthood. Decision making is reasonably well preserved in older adults. Wisdom is expert knowledge about the practical aspects of life that permits excellent judgment about important matters. Baltes and his colleagues have found that high levels of wisdom are rare, the time frame of late adolescence and early adulthood is the main window for wisdom to emerge, factors other than age are critical for wisdom to develop, and personality-related factors are better predictors of wisdom than cognitive factors such as intelligence. Sternberg argues that wisdom involves both academic and practical aspects of intelligence.

Education, Work, and Health

- Successive generations of Americans have been better educated. Education is positively correlated with scores on intelligence tests. Older adults may return to college for a number of reasons. Successive generations have had work experiences that include a stronger emphasis on cognitively oriented labor. The increased emphasis on information processing in jobs likely enhances an individual's intellectual abilities. Poor health is related to decreased performance on intelligence tests by older adults. Exercise is linked to higher cognitive functioning in older adults.

Use It or Lose It

- Researchers are finding that older adults who engage in cognitive activities, especially challenging ones, have higher cognitive functioning than those who don't use their cognitive skills.

Training Cognitive Skills

- Two main conclusions can be derived from research on training cognitive skills in older adults: (1) training can improve the cognitive skills of many older adults, and (2) there is some loss in plasticity in late adulthood.

| Cognitive Neuroscience and Aging | • There has been considerable recent interest in the cognitive neuroscience of aging that focuses on links among aging, the brain, and cognitive functioning. This field especially relies on fMRI and PET scans to assess brain functioning while individuals are engaging in cognitive tasks. One of the most consistent findings in this field is a decline in the functioning of specific regions in the prefrontal cortex in older adults and links between this decline and poorer performance on tasks involving complex reasoning, working memory, and episodic memory. |

2 Language Development

LG2 Characterize changes in language in older adults.

- For many individuals, knowledge of words and word meanings continues unchanged or may even improve in late adulthood. However, some decline in language skills may occur in retrieving words for use in conversation, understanding speech, phonological skills, and some aspects of discourse. These changes in language skills in older adults likely occur as a consequence of declines in hearing or memory, or in the speed of processing information, or as a result of disease.

3 Work and Retirement

LG3 Discuss aging and adaptation to work and retirement.

Work

- Today, the percentage of men over 65 who continue to work full-time is less than at the beginning of the twentieth century. An important change in older adults' work patterns is the increase in part-time work. Some individuals continue a life of strong work productivity throughout late adulthood.

Retirement in the United States and in Other Countries

- A retirement option for older workers is a late-twentieth-century phenomenon in the United States. Americans are more likely to continue working in their seventies than are workers in other countries.

Adjustment to Retirement

- The pathways individuals follow when they reach retirement age today are less clear than in the past. Those who adjust best to retirement are individuals who are healthy, have adequate income, are active, are better educated, have an extended social network of friends and family, and are satisfied with their lives before they retire.

4 Mental Health

LG4 Describe mental health problems in older adults.

Depression

- Depression has been called the "common cold" of mental disorders. However, a majority of older adults with depressive symptoms never receive mental health treatment.

Dementia, Alzheimer Disease, and Other Afflictions

- Dementia is a global term for any neurological disorder in which the primary symptoms involve a deterioration of mental functioning. Alzheimer disease is by far the most common dementia. This progressive, irreversible disorder is characterized by gradual deterioration of memory, reasoning, language, and eventually physical functioning. Special efforts are being made to discover the causes of Alzheimer disease and effective treatments for it. The increase in amyloid plaques and neurofibrillary tangles in Alzheimer patients may hold important keys to improving our understanding of the disease. Alzheimer disease is characterized by a deficiency in acetylcholine that affects memory. Also, in Alzheimer disease the brain shrinks and deteriorates as plaques and tangles form. Important concerns are the financial implications of caring for Alzheimer patients and the burdens placed on caregivers. In addition to Alzheimer disease, another type of dementia is Parkinson disease.

Fear of Victimization, Crime, and Elder Maltreatment

- Some of the physical decline and limitations that characterize development in late adulthood contribute to a sense of vulnerability and fear among older adults. Almost one-fourth of older adults say they have a basic fear of being the victim of a crime. Older women are more likely than older men to be victimized or abused.

5 Religion and Spirituality

 Explain the role of religion and spirituality in the lives of older adults.

- Many older adults are spiritual leaders in their church and community. Religious interest increases in old age and is related to a sense of well-being in the elderly.

key terms

key people

Chapter 18 | COGNITIVE DEVELOPMENT IN LATE ADULTHOOD

Connecting with Mc Graw Hill connect®

Learning Objectives	Application Activities	Activity Type	Page Reference
Discuss cognitive functioning in older adults.	Late Adulthood Perspectives on Thinking and Memory	Milestones: Transitions	pp. 565–573
Discuss cognitive neuroscience and aging.	Types of Memory	Click & drag activity	pp. 577–578
Describe retirement in the Unites States and other countries.	Retirement	Video	pp. 582–583
Describe planning and adjustment to retirement.	Moving to a Retirement Home	Video	pp. 583–584

SOCIOEMOTIONAL DEVELOPMENT IN LATE ADULTHOOD

chapter **outline**

1 Theories of Socioemotional Development

Learning Goal 1 Discuss four theories of socioemotional development and aging.

Erikson's Theory
Activity Theory
Socioemotional Selectivity Theory
Selective Optimization with Compensation Theory

2 Personality, the Self, and Society

Learning Goal 2 Describe links between personality and mortality, and identify changes in the self and society in late adulthood.

Personality
The Self and Society
Older Adults in Society

3 Families and Social Relationships

Learning Goal 3 Characterize the families and social relationships of aging adults.

Lifestyle Diversity
Older Adult Parents and Their Adult Children
Great-Grandparenting
Friendship
Social Support and Social Integration
Altruism and Volunteerism

4 Ethnicity, Gender, and Culture

Learning Goal 4 Summarize how ethnicity, gender, and culture are linked with aging.

Ethnicity
Gender
Culture

5 Successful Aging

Learning Goal 5 Explain how to age successfully.

Bob Cousy was a star player on Boston Celtics teams that won numerous National Basketball Association championships. In recognition of his athletic accomplishments, Cousy was honored by ESPN as one of the top 100 athletes of the twentieth century. After he retired from basketball, he became a college basketball coach and then into his seventies was a broadcaster of Boston Celtics basketball games. Now in his eighties, Cousy has retired from broadcasting but continues to play golf and tennis on a regular basis. He has a number of positive social relationships, including a marriage of more than 50 years, children and grandchildren, and many friends.

As is the case with many famous people, Cousy's awards reveal little about his personal life and contributions. Two examples illustrate his humanitarian efforts to help others (McClellan, 2004). First, when Cousy played for the Boston Celtics, his African American teammate, Chuck Cooper, was refused a room on a road trip because of his race. Cousy expressed anger to his coach about the situation and then accompanied an appreciative Cooper on a train back to Boston. Second, "Today the Bob Cousy Humanitarian Fund honors individuals who have given their lives to using the game of basketball as a medium to help others" (p. 4). The Humanitarian Fund reflects Cousy's motivation to care for others, be appreciative and give something back, and make the world less self-centered.

Bob Cousy as a Boston Celtics star when he was a young adult (*left*) and as an older adult (*right*). *What are some changes he has made in his life as an older adult?*

-topical **connections** -

Middle adulthood is a time when individuals become more conscious of the young-old polarity in life and the shrinking amount of time left in their lives. And it is a time when individuals seek to transmit something meaningful to the next generation. The concept of midlife crisis has been exaggerated; when people do experience this crisis, it often is linked to negative life events. Stability of personality peaks in middle adulthood, and marital satisfaction often increases at this time. Many middle-aged adults become grandparents and the middle-aged generation plays a key role in intergenerational relationships, with middle-aged women especially connecting generations.

◄ - - - *looking back* -

preview

Bob Cousy's life as an older adult reflects some of the themes of socioemotional development in older adults that we will discuss in this chapter. These include the important role that being active plays in life satisfaction, the need to adapt to changing skills, and the ways in which close relationships with friends and family contribute to an emotionally fulfilling life.

1 Theories of Socioemotional Development

LG1 Discuss four theories of socioemotional development and aging.

Erikson's Theory · Activity Theory · Socioemotional Selectivity Theory · Selective Optimization with Compensation Theory

We will explore four main theories that focus on socioemotional development in late adulthood: Erikson's theory, activity theory, socioemotional selectivity theory, and selective optimization with compensation theory.

ERIKSON'S THEORY

We initially discussed Erik Erikson's (1968) eight stages of the human life span in Chapter 1, and as we explored different periods of development in this book, we examined the stages in more detail. Here we will discuss his final stage.

Integrity Versus Despair   **Integrity versus despair** is Erikson's eighth and final stage of development, which individuals experience during late adulthood. This stage involves reflecting on the past and either piecing together a positive review or concluding that one's life has not been well spent. Through many different routes, the older adult may have developed a positive outlook in each of the preceding periods. If so, retrospective glances and reminiscences will reveal a picture of a life well spent, and the older adult will be satisfied (integrity). But if the older adult resolved one or more of the earlier stages in a negative way (being socially isolated in early adulthood or stagnating in middle adulthood, for example), retrospective glances about the total worth of his or her life might be negative (despair). Figure 19.1 portrays how positive resolutions of Erikson's eight stages can culminate in wisdom and integrity for older adults.

Life Review   Life review is prominent in Erikson's final stage of integrity versus despair. Life review involves looking back at one's life experiences, evaluating them, interpreting them, and often reinterpreting them (George, 2010; Wu & others, 2012). A leading expert on aging, Robert Butler, provided this perspective on life review: ". . . there are chances for pain, anger, guilt, and grief, but there are also opportunities for resolution and celebration, for affirmation and hope, for reconciliation and personal growth" (Butler, 2007, p. 72).

Butler (2007) states that the life review is set in motion by looking forward to death. Sometimes the life review proceeds quietly; at other times it is intense, requiring considerable work to achieve some sense of personality integration. The life review may be observed initially in stray and insignificant thoughts about oneself and one's life history. These thoughts may continue to emerge in brief intermittent spurts or become essentially continuous. One 76-year-old man commented, "My life is in the back of my mind. It can't be any other way. Thoughts of the past play on me. Sometimes I play with them, encouraging and savoring them; at other times I dismiss them."

Life reviews can include sociocultural dimensions, such as culture, ethnicity, and gender. Life reviews also can include interpersonal, relationship dimensions, including sharing and intimacy with family members or a friend (Randall, 2012). And life reviews can include personal dimensions, which might involve the creation and discovery of meaning and coherence.

developmental **connection**

Erikson's Theory

Erikson's other two adult stages are intimacy versus isolation (early adulthood) and generativity versus stagnation (middle adulthood). Chapter 14, p. 457; Chapter 16, p. 510

integrity versus despair Erikson's eighth and final stage of development, which individuals experience during late adulthood. This involves reflecting on the past and either piecing together a positive review or concluding that one's life has not been well spent.

Conflict and Resolution	Culmination in Old Age
Old age Integrity vs. despair: wisdom	Existential identity; a sense of integrity strong enough to withstand physical disintegration.
Middle adulthood Generativity vs. stagnation: care	Caring for others, and empathy and concern.
Early adulthood Intimacy vs. isolation: love	Sense of complexity of relationships; value of tenderness and loving freely.
Adolescence Identity vs. confusion: fidelity	Sense of complexity of life; merger of sensory, logical, and aesthetic perception.
School age Industry vs. inferiority: competence	Humility; acceptance of the course of one's life and unfulfilled hopes.
Early childhood Initiative vs. guilt: purpose	Humor; empathy; resilience.
Toddlerhood Autonomy vs. shame: will	Acceptance of the cycle of life, from integration to disintegration.
Infancy Basic trust vs. mistrust: hope	Appreciation of interdependence and relatedness.

FIGURE **19.1**

ERIKSON'S VIEW OF HOW POSITIVE RESOLUTION OF THE EIGHT STAGES OF THE HUMAN LIFE SPAN CAN CULMINATE IN WISDOM AND INTEGRITY IN OLD AGE. In Erikson's view, each stage of life is associated with a particular psychosocial conflict and a particular resolution. In this chart, Erikson describes how the issue from each of the earlier stages can mature into the many facets of integrity and wisdom in old age. At left, Erikson is shown with his wife Joan, an artist.

These personal dimensions might unfold in such a way that the pieces do or don't make sense to the older adult. In the final analysis, each person's life review is to some degree unique.

As the past marches in review, the older adult surveys it, observes it, and reflects on it. Reconsideration of previous experiences and their meaning occurs, often with revision or expanded understanding taking place. This reorganization of the past may provide a more valid picture for the individual, bringing new and significant meaning to one's life. It may also help prepare the individual for death and in the process reduce fear (O'Rourke, Cappeliez, & Claxton, 2011). A recent study revealed that one particular life-review course, "Looking for Meaning," reduced the depressive symptoms of middle-aged and older adults (Pot & others, 2010).

One aspect of life review involves identifying and reflecting on not only the positive aspects of one's life but also on regrets as part of developing mature levels of wisdom and self-understanding (Choi & Jun, 2009). The hope is that by examining not only the positive aspects of one's life, but also what one has regretted doing, a more accurate vision of the complexity of one's life and possibly increased life satisfaction will be attained (King & Hicks, 2007).

Following is a sampling of recent studies on regrets in older adults:

- For low-income older adults, regrets about education, careers, and marriage were common, but the intensity of regrets was greater for finance/money, family conflict and children's problems, loss and grief, and health (Choi & Jun, 2009). Common sources of pride involved children and parenting, careers, volunteering/informal caregiving, having a long/strong marriage, and personal growth.

- Making downward social comparisons, such as "I'm better off than most people," was linked to a reduction in the intensity of regrets in older adults (Bauer, Wrosch, & Jobin, 2008).

- Following the death of a loved one, resolving regrets was related to lower depression and improved well-being (Torges, Stewart, & Nolen-Hoeksema, 2008). In this study, older adults were more likely to resolve their regrets than were younger adults.

Although thinking about regrets can be helpful as part of a life review, recent research indicates that it is important for older adults to not dwell on regrets, especially since opportunities to

What characterizes a life review in late adulthood?

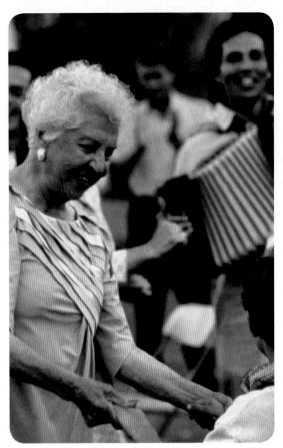

Should adults stay active or become more disengaged as they become older? Explain.

undo regrettable actions decline with age (Suri & Gross, 2012). One study revealed that an important factor among older adults who showed a higher level of emotion regulation and successful aging was reduced responsiveness to regrets (Brassen & others, 2012).

When working with older clients, some clinicians use *reminiscence therapy*, which involves discussing past activities and experiences with another individual or group (Cotelli, Manenti, & Zanetti, 2012; Fujiwara & others, 2012). The therapy may include the use of photographs, familiar items, and video/audio recordings. Researchers have found that reminiscence therapy improves the mood of older adults, including those with dementia (Subramaniam & Woods, 2012). A recent meta-analysis of 128 studies found that through reminiscence therapy clients attained a higher sense of integrity (based on Erikson's concept of integrity versus despair) (Pinquart & Forstemeier, 2012). Smaller effects occurred for purpose in life, preparing for death, mastery, positive well-being, social integration, and cognitive performance. The largest improvements were made for depressive symptoms in depressed individuals and persons with chronic physical disease.

ACTIVITY THEORY

Activity theory states that the more active and involved older adults are, the more likely they are to be satisfied with their lives. Researchers have found strong support for activity theory, beginning in the 1960s and continuing into the twenty-first century (Neugarten, Havighurst, & Tobin, 1968; Riebe & others, 2005). These researchers have found that when older adults are active, energetic, and productive, they age more successfully and are happier than if they disengage from society. A recent study found that older adults were happiest when they combined effortful social, physical, cognitive, and household activities with restful activities (Oerlemans, Bakker, & Veenhoven, 2011).

Activity theory suggests that many individuals will achieve greater life satisfaction if they continue their middle-adulthood roles into late adulthood. If these roles are stripped from them (as in early retirement), it is important for them to find substitute roles that keep them active and involved.

SOCIOEMOTIONAL SELECTIVITY THEORY

Socioemotional selectivity theory states that older adults become more selective about their social networks. Because they place a high value on emotional satisfaction, older adults spend more time with familiar individuals with whom they have had rewarding relationships. Developed by Laura Carstensen (1998, 2006, 2008, 2009; Carstensen & others, 2011), this theory states that older adults deliberately withdraw from social contact with individuals peripheral to their lives while maintaining or increasing contact with close friends and family members with whom they have had enjoyable relationships. This selective narrowing of social interaction maximizes positive emotional experiences and minimizes emotional risks as individuals become older.

Socioemotional selectivity theory challenges the stereotype that the majority of older adults are in emotional despair because of their social isolation (Carstensen & Fried, 2012). Rather, older adults consciously choose to decrease the total number of their social contacts in favor of spending increasing time in

Laura Carstensen (*right*), in a caring relationship with an older woman. Her theory of socioemotional selectivity is gaining recognition as an important perspective on aging.

activity theory The theory that the more active and involved older adults are, the more likely they are to be satisfied with their lives.

socioemotional selectivity theory The theory that older adults become more selective about their social networks. Because they place a high value on emotional satisfaction, older adults often spend more time with familiar individuals with whom they have had rewarding relationships.

emotionally rewarding moments with friends and family. That is, they systematically hone their social networks so that available social partners satisfy their emotional needs.

Is there research evidence to support life-span differences in the composition of social networks? Researchers have found that older adults have far smaller social networks than younger adults (Charles & Carstensen, 2010; Wrzus & others, 2012). In one study of individuals 69 to 104 years of age, the oldest participants had fewer peripheral social contacts than the relatively younger participants but about the same number of close emotional relationships (Lang & Carstensen, 1994).

Socioemotional selectivity theory also focuses on the types of goals that individuals are motivated to achieve (Biggs, Carstensen, & Hogan, 2012; Carstensen & others, 2011). It states that two important classes of goals are (1) knowledge-related and (2) emotional. This theory emphasizes that the trajectory of motivation for knowledge-related goals starts relatively high in the early years of life, peaking in adolescence and early adulthood, and then declines during middle and late adulthood (see Figure 19.2). The emotion trajectory is high during infancy and early childhood, declines from middle childhood through early adulthood, and increases in middle and late adulthood.

A recent study revealed that younger adults performed better in decision making about health care choices when they had an information focus (focus on specific attributes, report details about options, then make a choice), whereas older adults did better on these decision making tasks when they had an emotion focus (focus on emotional reactions to options, report feelings about the options, and then make a choice) (Mikels & others, 2010).

One of the main reasons given for these changing trajectories in knowledge-related and emotion-related goals involves the perception of time (Carstensen, 2006; Carstensen & others, 2011). When time is perceived as open-ended, as it is when individuals are younger, people are more strongly motivated to pursue information, even at the cost of emotional satisfaction. But as older adults perceive that they have less time left in their lives, they are motivated to spend more time pursuing emotional satisfaction (Kaszniak & Menchola, 2012). Are older adults more emotionally satisfied than younger adults? To read further about how emotion changes across the life span, see the *Connecting Through Research* interlude.

In general, compared with younger adults, the feelings of older adults mellow. Emotional life is on a more even keel, with fewer highs and lows. It may be that although older adults have less extreme joy, they have more contentment, especially when they are connected in positive ways with friends and family. Compared with younger adults, older adults react less to negative circumstances, are better at ignoring irrelevant negative information, and remember more positive than negative information (Mather, 2012).

A recent study revealed that positive emotion increased and negative emotion (except for sadness) decreased from 50 years of age through the mid-eighties (Stone & others, 2010). In this study, a pronounced decline in anger occurred from the early twenties and sadness was essentially unchanged from the early twenties through the mid-eighties. Another recent study found that aging was linked to more positive overall well-being and greater emotional stability (Carstensen & others, 2011). In this study, adults who experienced more positive than negative emotions were more likely to remain alive over a 13-year period. Other research also indicates that happier people live longer (Frey, 2011). Thus, the emotional life of older adults is more positive than stereotypes suggest (Lynchard & Radvansky, 2012; Carstensen & Fried, 2012; Yeung, Wong, & Lok, 2011).

How might the brain be involved in the changes that take place in older adults' emotion? Although links between the aging brain and emotion have only just begun to be studied, recent research suggests some possible connections (Samanez-Larkin & Carstensen, 2011). Reduced negative emotion in older adults may be associated with decreased physiological arousal of emotion with aging in the amygdala and autonomic nervous system (Kaszniak & Menchola, 2012). More effective emotion regulation may be related to this reduction in subcortical activation and also to increased activation in the prefrontal cortex (Samanez-Larkin & Carstensen, 2011).

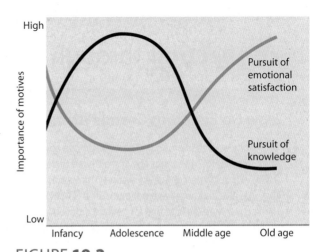

FIGURE **19.2**

IDEALIZED MODEL OF SOCIOEMOTIONAL SELECTIVITY THROUGH THE LIFE SPAN. In Carstensen's theory of socioemotional selectivity, the motivation to reach knowledge-related and emotion-related goals changes across the life span.

How Do Emotions Change Across Adulthood?

One study examined emotional changes across adulthood in 2,727 persons from 25 to 74 years of age in the United States (Mroczek & Kolarz, 1998). Participants completed a survey that assessed the frequency of their positive and negative emotions over a 30-day time frame. Two six-item scales were created: one for positive emotion, the other for negative emotion. Participants rated each of the following items on a scale ranging from 1 = none of the time to 5 = all of the time:

Positive Affect	Negative Affect
1. Cheerful	1. So sad nothing could cheer you up
2. In good spirits	2. Nervous
3. Extremely happy	3. Restless or fidgety
4. Calm or peaceful	4. Hopeless
5. Satisfied	5. That everything was an effort
6. Full of life	6. Worthless

Thus, scores could range from 6 to 30 for positive affect and for negative affect.

Overall, older adults reported experiencing more positive emotion and less negative emotion than younger adults, and the increase in positive emotion with age in adults occurred at an accelerating rate

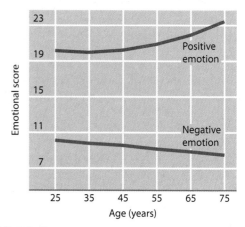

FIGURE **19.3**

CHANGES IN POSITIVE AND NEGATIVE EMOTION ACROSS THE ADULT YEARS. Positive and negative scores had a possible range of 6 to 30 with higher scores reflecting positive emotion and lower scores negative emotion. Positive emotion increased in middle adulthood and late adulthood while negative emotion declined.

(see Figure 19.3). In sum, researchers have found that the emotional life of older adults is more positive than was once believed (Carstensen & others, 2011).

SELECTIVE OPTIMIZATION WITH COMPENSATION THEORY

Selective optimization with compensation theory states that successful aging depends on three main factors: selection, optimization, and compensation (SOC). The theory describes how people can produce new resources and allocate them effectively to the tasks they want to master (Freund, Nikitin, & Riediger, 2013; Riediger, Li, & Lindenberger, 2006; Staudinger & Jacobs, 2010). *Selection* is based on the concept that older adults have a reduced capacity and loss of functioning, which require a reduction in performance in most life domains. *Optimization* suggests that it is possible to maintain performance in some areas through continued practice and the use of new technologies. *Compensation* becomes relevant when life tasks require a level of capacity beyond the current level of the older adult's performance potential. Older adults especially need to compensate in circumstances involving high mental or physical demands, such as when thinking about and memorizing new material in a very short period of time, reacting quickly when driving a car, or running fast. When older adults develop an illness, the need for compensation is obvious.

Selective optimization with compensation theory was proposed by Paul Baltes and his colleagues (Baltes, 2003; Baltes, Lindenberger, & Staudinger, 2006). They describe the life of the late Arthur Rubinstein to illustrate their theory. When he was interviewed at 80 years of age, Rubinstein said that three factors were responsible for his ability to maintain his status as an admired concert pianist into old age. First, he mastered the weakness of old age by reducing the scope of his performances and playing fewer pieces (which reflects selection). Second,

developmental **connection**

Life-Span Perspective

Baltes proposed eight main characteristics of the life-span perspective, one of which is that development involves growth, maintenance, and regulation of loss. Chapter 1, p. 9

selective optimization with compensation theory The theory that successful aging is related to three main factors: selection, optimization, and compensation.

Strategies for Effectively Engaging in Selective Optimization with Compensation

What are some good strategies that aging adults can engage in to attain selective optimization with compensation? According to Paul Baltes and his colleagues (Baltes, Lindenberger, & Staudinger, 2006; Freund & Baltes, 2002), these strategies are likely to be effective:

Selection Strategies

- Focus on the most important goal at a particular time.
- Think about what you want in life and commit yourself to one or two major goals.
- To reach a particular goal, you may need to abandon other goals.

Optimization Strategies

- Keep working on what you have planned until you are successful.
- Persevere and keep trying until you reach your goal.

- When you want to achieve something, you may need to be patient until the right moment arrives.

Compensation Strategies

- When things don't go the way they used to, search for other ways to achieve what you want.
- If things don't go well for you, be willing to let others help you.
- When things don't go as well as in the past, keep trying other ways until you can achieve results that are similar to what you accomplished earlier in your life.

How might you revise these guidelines to include the use of new technologies?

he spent more time at practice than earlier in his life (which reflects optimization). Third, he used special strategies, such as slowing down before fast segments, thus creating the image of faster playing (which reflects compensation).

The process of selective optimization with compensation is likely to be effective whenever people pursue successful outcomes (Hutchinson & Nimrod, 2012; Freund, Nikitin, & Riediger, 2013; Staudinger & Jacobs, 2010). What makes SOC attractive to aging researchers is that it makes explicit how individuals can manage and adapt to losses. By using SOC, they can continue to live satisfying lives, although in a more restricted manner. Loss is a common dimension of old age, although there are wide variations in the nature of the losses involved. Because of these individual variations, the specific form of selection, optimization, and compensation will likely vary, depending on the person's life history, pattern of interests, values, health, skills, and resources. To read about some strategies for effectively engaging in selective optimization with compensation, see *Connecting Development to Life*.

In Baltes' view (2003; Baltes, Lindenberger, & Staudinger, 2006), the selection of domains and life priorities is an important aspect of development. Life goals and priorities likely vary across the life course for most people. For many individuals, it is not just the sheer attainment of goals, but rather the attainment of *meaningful* goals, that makes life satisfying.

A cross-sectional study by Ursula Staudinger (1996) assessed the personal life investments of 25- to 105-year-olds (see Figure 19.4). From 25 to 34 years of age, participants said that they personally invested more time in work, friends, family, and independence, in that order. From 35 to 54 and 55 to 65 years of age, family became more important than friends to them in terms of their personal investment. Little changed in the rank ordering of persons 70 to 84 years old, but for participants 85 to 105 years old, health became the most important personal investment. Thinking about life showed up for the first time on the most important list for those who were 85 to 105 years old.

One point to note about the study just described is the demarcation of late adulthood into the subcategories of 70 to 84 and 85 to 105 years of age. This fits with our comments on a number of occasions in this book that researchers increasingly recognize the importance of comparing older adults of different ages rather than studying them as one age group.

25 to 34 Years	35 to 54 Years	55 to 65 Years	70 to 84 Years	85 to105 Years
Work	Family	Family	Family	Health
Friends	Work	Health	Health	Family
Family	Friends	Friends	Cognitive fitness	Thinking about life
Independence	Cognitive fitness	Cognitive fitness	Friends	Cognitive fitness

FIGURE 19.4

DEGREE OF PERSONAL LIFE INVESTMENT AT DIFFERENT POINTS IN LIFE. Shown here are the top four domains of personal life investment at different points in life. The highest degree of investment is listed at the top (for example, work was the highest personal investment from 25 to 34 years of age, family from 35 to 84, and health from 85 to 105).

Review Connect Reflect

LG1 Discuss four theories of socioemotional development and aging.

Review

- What is Erikson's theory of late adulthood?
- What is activity theory?
- What is socioemotional selectivity theory?
- What is selective optimization with compensation theory?

Connect

- How does the life reflection of older adults differ from the life reflection of individuals in middle adulthood when approaching retirement age?

Reflect *Your Own Personal Journey of Life*

- Which of the four theories best describes the lives of older adults you know? Explain.

2 Personality, the Self, and Society

LG2 Describe links between personality and mortality, and identify changes in the self and society in late adulthood.

Personality · The Self and Society · Older Adults in Society

Do some personality traits change in late adulthood? Is personality linked to mortality in older adults? Do self-perceptions and self-control change in late adulthood? How are older adults perceived and treated by society? We will explore these and other topics in the next few pages.

PERSONALITY

We described the Big Five factors of personality in Chapter 16, "Socioemotional Development in Middle Adulthood." Researchers have found that several of the Big Five factors of personality continue to change in late adulthood (Roberts, Donnellan, & Hill, 2013). For example, in one study conscientiousness continued to increase in late adulthood (Roberts, Walton, & Bogg, 2005) and in another study older adults were more conscientious and agreeable than middle-aged and younger adults (Allemand, Zimprich, & Hendriks, 2008).

Might certain personality traits be related to how long older adults live? Researchers have found that some personality traits are associated with the mortality of older adults (Roberts, Donnellan, & Hill, 2013). A longitudinal study of more than 1,200 individuals across seven decades revealed that a higher score on the Big Five personality factor of conscientiousness predicted a lower risk of earlier death from childhood through late adulthood (Martin, Friedman, & Schwartz, 2007). Another study found that two of the Big Five factors were linked to older adults' mortality in one study, with low conscientiousness and high neuroticism predicting earlier death (Wilson & others, 2004). In a five-year longitudinal study, higher levels of conscientiousness, extraversion, and openness were related to a lower risk of earlier death (Iwasa & others, 2008). And in a recent study, a higher level of conscientiousness predicted greater longevity in older adults (Hill & others, 2011).

Following are the results of three other studies of the Big Five factors in older adults:

- The transition into late adulthood was characterized by increases in these aspects of conscientiousness: impulse control, reliability, and conventionality (Jackson & others, 2009).

- A higher level of neuroticism was linked to older adults' medication non-adherence across a six-year time frame (Jerant & others, 2011).

- Elevated neuroticism, lower conscientiousness, and lower openness were related to an increased risk of older adults' developing Alzheimer disease across a period of six years (Duberstein & others, 2011).

Affect and outlook on life are also linked to mortality in older adults (Carstensen & others, 2011). Older adults characterized by negative affect don't live as long as those who display more positive affect, and optimistic older adults who have a positive outlook on life live longer than their counterparts who are more pessimistic and have a negative outlook on life (Mosing & others, 2012).

THE SELF AND SOCIETY

Our exploration of the self focuses on changes in self-esteem, possible selves, self-acceptance, and self-control. In Chapter 12, we described how self-esteem drops in adolescence, especially for girls. How does self-esteem change during the adult years?

Self-Esteem In the cross-sectional study of self-esteem described in Chapter 12, a very large, diverse sample of more than 300,000 individuals from 9 to 90 years of age were assessed (Robins & others, 2002). About two-thirds of the participants were from the United States. The individuals were asked to respond to the item "I have high self-esteem" on the following five-point scale:

1	2	3	4	5
Strongly Disagree				Strongly Agree

Self-esteem increased in the twenties, leveled off in the thirties and forties, rose considerably in the fifties and sixties, and then dropped significantly in the seventies and eighties (see Figure 19.5). Throughout most of the adult years, the self-esteem of males was higher than the self-esteem of females. However, in the seventies and eighties, the self-esteem of males and females converged.

Why might self-esteem decline in older adults? Explanations include deteriorating physical health and negative societal attitudes toward older adults, although these factors were not examined in the large-scale study just described. Researchers have found that in late adulthood, being widowed, institutionalized, or physically impaired, having a low religious commitment, and experiencing a decline in health are linked to low self-esteem (Giarrusso & Bengtson, 2007).

developmental **connection**

Personality

The Big Five factors of personality are openness, conscientiousness, extraversion, agreeableness, and neuroticism. Chapter 16, p. 517

FIGURE **19.5**

SELF-ESTEEM ACROSS THE LIFE SPAN. One cross-sectional study found that self-esteem was high in childhood, dropped in adolescence, increased through early and middle adulthood, then dropped in the seventies and eighties (Robins & others, 2002). More than 300,000 individuals were asked the extent to which they have high self-esteem on a five-point scale, with 5 being "Strongly Agree" and 1 being "Strongly Disagree."

I am the family face;
Flesh perishes,
I live on,
Projecting trait and trace
Through time to times anon,
And leaping from place to
place
Over oblivion.

—**Thomas Hardy**
English Novelist and Poet, 19th Century

Is self-esteem more stable at some points in the life span than at others? A meta-analysis revealed that self-esteem was the least stable in early childhood (Trzesniewski, Donnellan, & Robins, 2003). One reason for this may be that young children don't completely understand the questions they are asked about their self-esteem but rather provide responses based on their current mood. The stability of self-esteem increased in late adolescence and early adulthood. By late adolescence, individuals are experiencing less dramatic physical changes (compared with pubertal change, for example) and are able to better engage in self-control, which likely contributed to the increased stability of self-esteem. The stability of self-esteem decreased in late adulthood, a time during which dramatic life changes and shifting social circumstances (such as the death of a loved one and deteriorating health) may occur.

Although older adults may derive self-esteem from earlier successes in some domains, such as work and family, some aspects of their lives require continued support for self-esteem (Smith, 2009). For example, older adults' self-esteem benefits when they are told they are nice and accepted by others. A recent study revealed that older adults had higher self-esteem when they had a youthful identity and more positive personal experiences (Westerhof, Whitbourne, & Freeman, 2012). And another recent study also found that older adults with higher self-esteem were more likely to be characterized by successful aging factors (Cha, Seo, & Sok, 2012).

Possible Selves   **Possible selves** are what individuals might become, what they would like to become, and what they are afraid of becoming (Bolkan & Hooker, 2012; Kornadt & Rothermund, 2012; Markus & Nurius, 1987). Acceptance of ideal and future selves decreases and acceptance of past selves increases in older adults (Ryff, 1991).

One study of older adults (mean age of 81) revealed that hope-related activities had more positive effect and a higher probability of survival over a 10-year period (Hoppmann & others, 2007). Also in this study, hoped-for selves were linked to more likely participation in these domains. Another study of older adults 70 to 100-plus years found that over time 72 percent of the older adults added new domains of hope and 53 percent added new fears (Smith & Freund, 2002). In this study, hopes and fears about health were reported more often than ones related to family and social relationships. Also, when some individuals are middle-aged adults, their possible selves center on attaining hoped-for selves, such as acquiring material possessions, but as older adults they become more concerned with maintaining what they have acquired and preventing or avoiding health problems and dependency (Smith, 2009).

Self-Control   Although older adults are aware of age-related losses, most still effectively maintain a sense of self-control (Lewis, Todd, & Xu, 2011). A survey across a range of 21 developed and developing countries revealed that a majority of adults in their sixties and seventies reported being in control of their lives (HSBC Insurance, 2007). In developed countries such as Denmark, the United States, and Great Britain, adults in their sixties and seventies said

possible selves What individuals might become, what they would like to become, and what they are afraid of becoming.

they had more control over their lives than did their counterparts in their forties and fifties. Older adults in Denmark reported the highest perceptions of control.

It is important, however, to consider not only general perceptions of control but also how people self-regulate their behavior in specific areas of their lives (Bertrand, Graham, & Lachman, 2013; Bolkan & Hooker, 2012). One study examined individuals from 13 to 90 years of age. For the oldest group (60 to 90 years of age), control was lowest in the physical domain; for the youngest group (13 to 18 years of age), it was lowest in the social domain (Bradley & Webb, 1976). Other researchers have found a decline in perceived control of cognitive functioning in older adults (Bertrand & Lachman, 2003).

OLDER ADULTS IN SOCIETY

Does society negatively stereotype older adults? What are some social policy issues in an aging society?

Stereotyping Older Adults   Social participation by older adults is often discouraged by **ageism,** which is prejudice against others because of their age, especially prejudice against older adults (Bolkan & Hooker, 2012; Kornadt & Rothermund, 2012). Older adults are often perceived as incapable of thinking clearly, learning new things, enjoying sex, contributing to the community, or holding responsible jobs. Many older adults face painful discrimination and might be too polite and timid to attack it. Because of their age, older adults might not be hired for new jobs or might be eased out of old ones; they might be shunned socially; and they might be edged out of their family life.

The personal consequences of negative stereotyping about aging can be serious (Kalache & Blewitt, 2012; Kornadt & Rothermund, 2012). A physician (60 years old himself) told an 80-year-old: "Well, of course, you are tired. You just need to slow down. Don't try to do so much. After all, you are very old." Many older adults accept this type of advice even though it is rooted in age stereotyping rather than medical records.

Ageism is widespread (Hummert, 2011; Milner, Van Norman, & Milner, 2012). One study found that men were more likely to negatively stereotype older adults than were women (Rupp, Vodanovich, & Crede, 2005). Research indicates that the most frequent form is disrespect for older adults, followed by assumptions about ailments or frailty caused by age (Palmore, 2004). However, the increased number of adults living to an older age has led to active efforts to improve society's image of older adults, obtain better living conditions for older adults, and gain political clout.

Policy Issues in an Aging Society   The aging society and older persons' status in this society raise policy issues about the well-being of older adults (Fisher & others, 2013; Greenlund & others, 2012). These include the status of the economy, the provision of health care, supports for families who care for older adults, and generational inequity, each of which we consider in turn.

Status of the Economy   An important issue involving the economy and aging is the concern that our economy cannot bear the burden of so many older persons, who by reason of their age alone are usually consumers rather than producers. However, not all persons 65 and over are nonworkers, and not all persons 18 to 64 are workers. Thus, it is incorrect to simply describe older adults as consumers and younger adults as producers. However, the recent economic crisis has placed considerable burdens on many older adults, who have seen their nongovernment retirement funds drop precipitously (Strand, 2010). Especially bothersome is the low rate of savings of U.S. adults, which further exacerbated the financial problems of older adults in the recent economic downturn (Gould & Hertel-Fernandez, 2010). As indicated in Chapter 18, recent surveys indicate that Americans' confidence in their ability to retire comfortably has reached all-time lows in recent years (Helman, Copeland, & VanDerhei, 2012).

Health Care   An aging society also brings with it various problems involving health care (Hellander & Bhargavan, 2012; Siegler & others, 2013a, b). Escalating health care costs are currently the focus of considerable concern (Alzheimer's Association, 2012; Fried, Hogan, & Rowe, 2012). One factor that contributes to the surge in health costs is the increasing number

A study in 21 countries revealed that older adults in Denmark reported the highest perceptions of control over their lives (HSBC Insurance, 2007).

ageism Prejudice against others because of their age, especially prejudice against older adults.

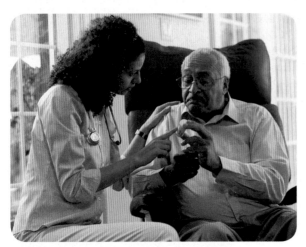

What are some concerns about health care for older adults?

of older adults. Older adults have more illnesses than younger adults, despite the fact that many older adults report their health as good. Older adults see doctors more often, are hospitalized more often, and have longer hospital stays. Approximately one-third of the total health bill of the United States is for the care of adults 65 and over, who comprise only 12 percent of the population. The health care needs of older adults are reflected in Medicare and Medicaid (Hansen, 2012). Of interest is the fact that until the Affordable Care Act was recently enacted, the United States was the only developed country that did not have a national health care system. Older adults themselves still pay about one-third of their total health care costs. Thus, older adults as well as younger adults are adversely affected by rising medical costs (McDonough, 2012).

A special concern is that while many of the health problems of older adults are chronic rather than acute, the medical system is still based on a "cure" rather than a "care" model. Chronic illness is long-term, often lifelong, and requires long-term, if not life-term, management (Harris, Pan, & Mukhtar, 2010). Chronic illness often follows a pattern of an acute period that may require hospitalization, followed by a longer period of remission, and then repetitions of this pattern. The patient's home, rather than the hospital, often becomes the location for managing the patient's chronic illness. In a home-based system, a new type of cooperative relationship between doctors, nurses, patients, family members, and other service providers needs to be developed (Kamp, Wellman, & Russell, 2010). Health care personnel need to be trained and be available to provide home services (Irish, 2011).

Eldercare   **Eldercare** is the physical and emotional caretaking of older members of the family, whether that care involves day-to-day physical assistance or responsibility for arranging and overseeing such care. An important issue involving eldercare is how it can best be provided (Beverly & others, 2010; Zacher, Jimmieson & Winter, 2012). With so many women in the labor market, who will replace them as caregivers? An added problem is that many caregivers are in their sixties, and many of them are ill themselves. They may find it especially stressful to be responsible for the care of relatives who are in their eighties or nineties.

Generational Inequity   Yet another policy issue involving aging is **generational inequity,** the view that our aging society is being unfair to its younger members because older adults pile up advantages by receiving an inequitably large allocation of resources. Some authors have argued that generational inequity produces intergenerational conflict and divisiveness in the society at large (Longman, 1987). The generational equity issue raises questions about whether the young should be required to pay for the old (Auerbach & Lee, 2011; Daniels, 2012; Williamson, 2011).

Income   Many older adults are understandably concerned about their income (Ehnes, 2012; Laboul, 2012). Of special concern are older adults who are poor (Reno & Veghte, 2011). Researchers have found that poverty in late adulthood is linked to an increase in physical and mental health problems (Herd, Robert, & House, 2011). Poverty also is linked to lower levels of physical and cognitive fitness in older adults (Johnson & others, 2011). And one study revealed that low SES increased the risk of earlier death in older adults (Krueger & Chang, 2008).

Census data suggest that the overall number of older people living in poverty has declined since the 1960s, but in 2010, 9 percent of older adults in the United States still were living in poverty (Administration on Aging, 2011). In 2010, U.S. women 65 years and older (11 percent) were much more likely to live in poverty than their male counterparts (7 percent) (U.S. Census Bureau, 2010). Nineteen percent of single, divorced, or widowed women 65 years and older lived in poverty. There is a special concern about poverty among older women and considerable discussion about the role of Social Security in providing a broad economic safety net for them (Jokinen-Gordon, 2012; Soneji & King, 2012).

Poverty rates among ethnic minorities are two to three times higher than the rate for non-Latino Whites. Combining gender and ethnicity, 41 percent of older Latinas and 31 percent of African American women lived in poverty in 2010 (U.S. Census Bureau, 2011). Also, the oldest-old are the age subgroup of older adults most likely to be living in poverty.

eldercare Physical and emotional caretaking for older members of the family, whether by giving day-to-day physical assistance or by being responsible for overseeing such care.

generational inequity The view that our aging society is being unfair to its younger members because older adults pile up advantages by receiving inequitably large allocations of resources.

Living Arrangements   One stereotype of older adults is that they are often residents in institutions—hospitals, mental hospitals, nursing homes, and so on. However, nearly 95 percent of older adults live in the community. Almost two-thirds of older adults live with family members—their spouse, a child, or a sibling, for example—and almost one-third live alone. The older people become, the greater are their odds for living alone. Half of older women 75 years and older live alone. The majority of older adults living alone are widowed, encompassing three times as many women as men (U.S. Census Bureau, 2010). Older adults who live alone often report being more lonely than their counterparts who live with someone (Kirkevold & others, 2012). However, as with younger adults, living alone as an older adult does not mean being lonely. Older adults who can sustain themselves while living alone often have good health and few disabilities, and they may have regular social exchanges with relatives, friends, and neighbors.

Technology   The Internet plays an increasingly important role in providing access to information and communication for adults as well as youth (Bers & Kazakoff, 2013). How well are older adults keeping up with changes in technology? Older adults are less likely to have a computer in their home and less likely to use the Internet than younger adults, but older adults are the fastest-growing segment of Internet users (Czaja & others, 2006). A 2003 survey indicated that 32 percent of U.S. adults who are 65 and older (about 11 million) and 61 percent of 50- to 64-year-olds are online (Harris Interactive, 2003). Older adults log more time on the Internet (an average of 8.3 hours per week), visit more Web sites, and spend more money on the Internet than their younger adult counterparts. They are especially interested in learning to use e-mail and going online for health information (Westlake & others, 2007). Increasing numbers of older adults use e-mail to communicate with relatives. As with children and younger adults, cautions about verifying the accuracy of information—especially on topics involving health care—on the Internet should always be kept in mind (Miller & Bell, 2012).

Links between older adults' use of technology and their cognitive development also are being studied. A recent study found that frequent computer use was linked to higher performance on cognitive tasks in older adults (Tun & Lachman, 2010). And researchers are examining the role that video games could play in maintaining or improving older adults' cognitive skills (McDougall & House, 2012). For example, a research study found that a lengthy 40-hour video game training program improved older adults' attention and memory (Smith & others, 2009). And a recent study revealed that a brain training game that elderly adults played about 15 minutes a day for 4 weeks improved their executive functioning and speed of processing information (Nouchi & others, 2012).

Are older adults keeping up with changes in technology?

Review *Connect* Reflect

 Describe links between personality and mortality, and identify changes in the self and society in late adulthood.

Review

- How are personality traits related to mortality in older adults?
- How does self-esteem change in late adulthood? What characterizes possible selves, self-acceptance, and self-control in older adults?
- How are older adults perceived and treated by society?

Connect

- We learned in this section that poverty is linked to lower levels of physical and cognitive fitness in older adults. What did we learn about poverty and young children in earlier chapters?

Reflect *Your Own Personal Journey of Life*

- What do you envision your life will be like as an older adult?

3 Families and Social Relationships

LG3 Characterize the families and social relationships of aging adults.

| Lifestyle Diversity | Older Adult Parents and Their Adult Children | Great-Grandparenting | Friendship | Social Support and Social Integration | Altruism and Volunteerism |

Are the close relationships of older adults different from those of younger adults? What are the lifestyles of older adults like? What characterizes the relationships of older adult parents and their adult children? Is the role of great-grandparents different from the role of grandparents? What do friendships and social networks contribute to the lives of older adults? What types of social support do older adults need and want? How might older adults' altruism and volunteerism contribute to positive outcomes?

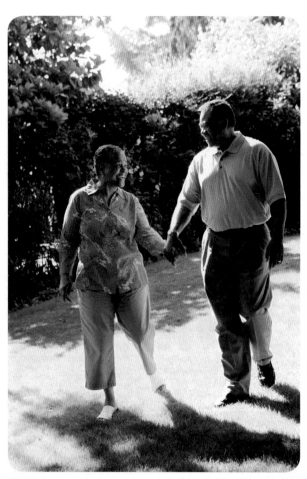

What are some adaptations that many married older adults need to make?

developmental **connection**

Marriage

The benefits of a happy marriage involve less physical and emotional stress, which puts less wear and tear on the body. Chapter 14, p. 464

LIFESTYLE DIVERSITY

The lifestyles of older adults are changing. Formerly, the later years of life were likely to consist of marriage for men and widowhood for women. With demographic shifts toward marital dissolution characterized by divorce, one-third of adults can now expect to marry, divorce, and remarry during their lifetime. Let's now explore some of the diverse lifestyles of older adults, beginning with those who are married or partnered.

Married Older Adults   In 2010, 57 percent of U.S. adults over 65 years of age were married (U.S. Census Bureau, 2011). In 2010, 27 percent of U.S. adults over 65 years of age were widowed (U.S. Census Bureau, 2011). There were more than four times as many widows as widowers.

The time from retirement until death is sometimes referred to as the "final stage in the marriage process." The portrait of marriage in the lives of older adults is a positive one for many couples (Piazza & Charles, 2012; Strout & Howard, 2012). Individuals who are in a marriage or a partnership in late adulthood are usually happier, are less distressed, and live longer than those who are single (Peek, 2009). A recent study of octogenarians revealed that marital satisfaction helped to protect their happiness from daily fluctuations in perceived health (Waldinger & Schulz, 2010). Also, a longitudinal study of adults 75 years of age and older revealed that individuals who were married were less likely to die during a seven-year time span (Rasulo, Christensen, & Tomassini, 2005).

Retirement alters a couple's lifestyle, requiring adaptation (Price & Nesteruk, 2010). The greatest changes occur in the traditional family structure in which the husband works and the wife is a homemaker. The husband may not know what to do with his time, and his wife may feel uneasy having him around the house so much of the day. In traditional families, both partners may need to move toward more expressive roles. The husband must adjust from being the provider outside of the home to being a helper around the house; the wife must change from being the only homemaker to being a partner who shares and delegates household duties. Marital happiness as an older adult is also affected by each partner's ability to deal with personal challenges, including aging, illness, and eventual death.

In late adulthood, married individuals are more likely to find themselves having to care for a sick partner with a limiting health condition (Blieszner & Roberto, 2012). The stress of caring for a spouse who has a chronic disease can place demands on intimacy.

Divorced and Remarried Older Adults   In 2010, 11 percent of women and 9 percent of men 65 years and older in the United States were divorced or separated (U.S. Census Bureau, 2011). Many of these individuals were divorced or separated before they entered late adulthood. The majority of divorced older adults are women, due to their greater longevity. Men are more likely to remarry, thus removing themselves from the pool of divorced older adults (Peek, 2009). Divorce is far less common among older adults than younger adults, likely reflecting cohort effects rather than age effects since divorce was somewhat rare when current cohorts of older adults were young (Peek, 2009).

There are social, financial, and physical consequences of divorce for older adults (Butrica & Smith, 2012; Piazza & Charles, 2012). Divorce can weaken kinship ties when it occurs in later life, especially in the case of older men. Divorced older women are less likely to have adequate financial resources than married older women, and older adults who are divorced have more health problems than those who are not (Bennett, 2006).

Rising divorce rates, increased longevity, and better health have led to an increase in remarriage by older adults (Ganong & Coleman, 2006). What happens when an older adult wants to remarry or does remarry? Researchers have found that some older adults perceive negative social pressure about their decision to remarry (McKain, 1972). These negative sanctions range from raised eyebrows to rejection by adult children (Ganong & Coleman, 2006). However, the majority of adult children support the decision of their older adult parents to remarry. Researchers have found that remarried parents and stepparents provide less support to adult stepchildren than parents in first marriages (White, 1994).

Cohabiting Older Adults

An increasing number of older adults cohabit (Noel-Miller, 2011). In 1960, hardly any older adults cohabited (Chevan, 1996). In 2010, 3 percent of older adults were cohabiting (Mykyta & Macartney, 2012). It is expected that the number of cohabiting older adults will increase even further as the large cohort of baby boomers become 65 years of age and older and bring their historically more nontraditional values about love, sex, and relationships to late adulthood. In many cases, the cohabiting is more for companionship than for love. In other cases, such as when one partner faces the potential for expensive care, a couple may decide to maintain their assets separately and thus not marry. One study found that older adults who cohabited had a more positive, stable relationship than younger adults who cohabited, although older adults were less likely to have plans to marry their partner (King & Scott, 2005).

Does cohabiting affect an individual's health? A study of more than 8,000 51- to 61-year-old adults revealed that the health of couples who cohabited did not differ from the health of married couples (Waite, 2005). However, another study of individuals 50 years of age and older found that those who cohabited were more depressed than their married counterparts (Brown, Bulanda, & Lee, 2005). And a recent study indicated that cohabiting older adults were less likely to receive partner care than married older adults (Noel-Miller, 2011).

Romance and Sex in Older Adults' Relationships

Few of us imagine older couples taking an interest in sex or romantic relationships. We might think of them as being interested in a game of bridge or a conversation on the porch, but not much else. In fact, a number of older adults date. The increased health and longevity of older adults have resulted in a much larger pool of active older adults. And the increased divorce rate has added more older adults to the adult dating pool.

Regarding their sexuality, older adults may express their sexuality differently from younger adults, especially when engaging in sexual intercourse becomes difficult. Older adults especially enjoy touching and caressing as part of their sexual relationship. When older adults are healthy, they still may engage in sexual activities (Benbow & Beeston, 2012; Marshall, 2012). For example, a recent U.S. study found that among 75- to 85-year-olds, 40 percent of women and 78 percent of men reported having a stable sexual partner (Waite & others, 2009). The gender differential is likely due to women's higher likelihood of being widowed, age difference in spouses, and women's probability of living longer than men do. With the increased use of drugs to treat erectile dysfunction, older adults can be expected to increase their sexual activity (Lowe & Costabile, 2012; Rubio-Aurioles & others, 2012). However, companionship often becomes more important than sexual activity in older adults. Older couples often emphasize intimacy over sexual prowess.

developmental **connection**

Sexuality

Middle-aged men want sex more, think about it more, and masturbate more than middle-aged women. Chapter 15, p. 493

What are some ways that older adults retain their sexuality?

OLDER ADULT PARENTS AND THEIR ADULT CHILDREN

Parent-child relationships in later life differ from those earlier in the life span (Birditt & Wardjiman, 2012; Fingerman & Birditt, 2011; Fingerman & others, 2011a, b). They are influenced by a lengthy joint history and extensive shared experiences and memories.

Approximately 80 percent of older adults have living children, many of whom are middle-aged. About 10 percent of older adults have children who are 65 years or older. Adult children are an important part of the aging parent's social network. Researchers have found that older adults with children have more contacts with relatives than those without children (Johnson & Troll, 1992).

Increasingly, diversity characterizes the lifestyles of older adult parents and their adult children. Divorce, remarriage, cohabitation, and nonmarital childbearing are more common in the history of older adults today than in the past.

Gender plays an important role in relationships involving older adult parents and their children (Ward-Griffin & others, 2007). Adult daughters are more likely than adult sons to be involved in the lives of their aging parents. For example, adult daughters are three times more likely than are adult sons to give parents assistance with daily living activities (Dwyer & Coward, 1991).

As discussed in Chapter 16, "Socioemotional Development in Middle Adulthood," middle-aged adults are more likely to provide support if their parents have a disability (Fingerman & others, 2011b; Birditt & Wardjiman, 2012). A valuable service that adult children can perform is to coordinate and monitor services for an aging parent who becomes disabled (Jones & others, 2011). Even less severely impaired older adults may need help with shopping, housework, transportation, home maintenance, and bill paying.

As discussed in Chapter 16, some researchers have found that relationships between aging parents and their children are usually characterized by ambivalence (Fingerman & Birditt, 2011; Birditt & Wardjiman, 2012). Perceptions include love, reciprocal help, and shared values on the positive side and isolation, family conflicts and problems, abuse, neglect, and caregiver stress on the negative side. A study of adult children's relationships with their older adult parents revealed that ambivalence was likely to be present when relationships involved in-laws, those in poor health, and adult children with poor parental relationships in early life (Wilson, Shuey, & Elder, 2003). A recent study, though, revealed that affection and support, reflecting solidarity, were more prevalent than ambivalence in intergenerational relationships (Hogerbrugge & Komter, 2012).

GREAT-GRANDPARENTING

Because of increased longevity, more grandparents today than in the past are also great-grandparents. At the turn of the twentieth century, the three-generation family was common, but now the four-generation family is common. One contribution of great-grandparents is to transmit family history by telling their children, grandchildren, and great-grandchildren where the family came from, what their members achieved, what they endured, and how their lives changed over the years (Harris, 2002).

There has been little research on great-grandparenting. One study examined the relationship between young adults and their grandparents and great-grandparents (Roberto & Skoglund, 1996). The young adults interacted with, and participated in more activities with, their grandparents than great-grandparents. They also perceived their grandparents as having a more defined role and being more influential in their lives than great-grandparents.

FRIENDSHIP

In early adulthood, friendship networks expand as new social connections are made away from home. In late adulthood, new friendships are less likely to be forged, although some adults do seek out new friendships, especially following the death of a spouse (Zettel-Watson & Rook, 2009).

Aging expert Laura Carstensen (1998) concluded that people choose close friends over new friends as they grow older. And as long as they have several close people in their network,

At the beginning of the twentieth century, the three-generation family was common, but now the four-generation family is common as well. Thus, an increasing number of grandparents are also great-grandparents. The four-generation family shown here is the Jordans—author John Santrock's mother-in-law, daughter, granddaughter, and wife.

developmental **connection**

Family and Peers

It takes time to develop intimate friendships, so friendships that have endured over the adult years are often deeper than those that have just been formed in middle adulthood. Chapter 16, p. 524

they seem content, says Carstensen. Supporting Carstensen's view, in one study older adults said they experienced less intense positive emotions with new friends and more intense positive emotions with established friends (Charles & Piazza, 2007) (see Figure 19.6).

In one study of 128 married older adults, women were more depressed than men if they did not have a best friend, and women who did have a friend reported lower levels of depression (Antonucci, Lansford, & Akiyama, 2001). Similarly, women who did not have a best friend were less satisfied with life than women who did have a best friend.

The following studies document the importance of friendship in older adults:

- In late adulthood, friendships were more important than family relationships in predicting mental health (Fiori, Antonucci, & Cortina, 2006). For example, older adults whose social contacts were mainly restricted to their family members were more likely to have depressive symptoms. Friends likely provide emotional intimacy and companionship, as well as integration into the community (Antonucci, Akiyama, & Sherman, 2007).

- Older adults who had close ties with friends were less likely to die across a seven-year age span (Rasulo, Christensen, & Tomassini, 2005). The findings were stronger for women than men.

SOCIAL SUPPORT AND SOCIAL INTEGRATION

Social support and social integration play important roles in the physical and mental health of older adults (Antonucci, Birditt, & Ajrouch, 2013).

Social Support In the **convoy model of social relations,** individuals go through life embedded in a personal network of individuals to whom they give and from whom they receive social support (Antonucci, Birditt, & Ajrouch, 2013). For older adults, social support is related to their physical and mental health (Cheng, Lee, & Chow, 2010). It is linked with a reduction in symptoms of disease, with the ability to meet one's own health care needs, and reduced mortality (Rook & others, 2007). A higher level of social support also is related to a lower probability of an older adult being institutionalized and depressed (Herd & others, 2011; Richardson & others, 2011). Further, a recent study revealed that older adults who experienced a higher level of social support showed later cognitive decline than their counterparts with a lower level of social support (Dickinson & others, 2011).

Social support for older adults can be provided by different adults (Antonucci, Birditt, & Ajrouch, 2013). Older adults who are married are less likely to need formal social supports,

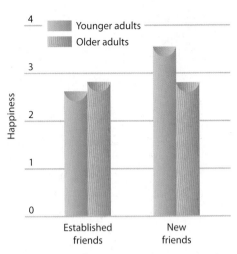

FIGURE 19.6

HAPPINESS OF YOUNGER ADULTS AND OLDER ADULTS WITH NEW AND ESTABLISHED FRIENDS. *Note:* The happiness scale ranged from 0 to 6, with participants rating how intensely they experienced happiness (0 = not at all, 6 = extremely intense). Older adults' mean age was 71; younger adults' mean age was 23.

What are some characteristics of older adults' friendships?

convoy model of social relations Model in which individuals go through life embedded in a personal network of individuals to whom they give and from whom they receive support.

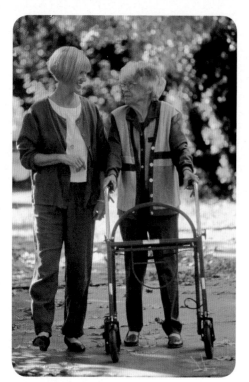

What role does social support play in the health of older adults?

such as home nursing care, adult day care, and home-delivered meals, than are nonmarried older adults. Families play important roles in social support for older adults, but friends also can provide invaluable resources for social support (Blieszner & Roberto, 2012). Also, social support for older adults may vary across cultures. For example, in the United States, the focal support person for an older adult is most likely to be a daughter, whereas in Japan it is most likely to be a daughter-in-law.

Social Integration   Social integration also plays an important role in the lives of many older adults (Antonucci, Birditt, & Ajrouch, 2013; Fingerman, Brown, & Blieszner, 2011; Hawkley & Cacioppo, 2013). Remember from our earlier discussion of socioemotional selectivity theory that many older adults choose to have fewer peripheral social contacts and more emotionally positive contacts with friends and family (Carstensen & others, 2011). Thus, a decrease in the overall social activity of many older adults may reflect their greater interest in spending more time in the small circle of friends and families where they are less likely to have negative emotional experiences. Researchers have found that older adults tend to report being less lonely than younger adults and less lonely than would be expected based on their circumstances (Schnittker, 2007). Their reports of feeling less lonely than younger adults likely reflect their more selective social networks and greater acceptance of solitude in their lives (Antonucci, Birditt, & Ajrouch, 2013).

Researchers have found that a low level of social integration is linked with coronary heart disease in older adults (Shankar & others, 2011). Also, in one study, being part of a social network was related to longevity, especially for men (House, Landis, & Umberson, 1988). Being lonely and socially isolated is a significant health risk factor in older adults (Smith, 2012; Ye & others, 2012). For example, one study found that loneliness predicted increased blood pressure four years later in middle-aged and older adults (Hawkley & others, 2010). Also, another study revealed that social isolation in late adulthood was linked to a greater risk of being inactive, smoking, and engaging in other health-risk behaviors (Shankar & others, 2011). And three recent longitudinal studies found that feelings of loneliness were linked to an earlier death (Holwerda & others, 2012; Luo & others, 2012; Perissinotto, Stijacic Cenzer, & Covinsky, 2012).

ALTRUISM AND VOLUNTEERISM

A common perception is that older adults need to be given help rather than give help themselves. However, a 12-year longitudinal study revealed that older adults who had persistently low or declining feelings of usefulness to others had an increased risk of earlier death (Gruenewald & others, 2009). Further, researchers have found that when older adults engage in altruistic behavior and volunteering they benefit from these activities (Pilkington & others, 2012). Volunteering peaks in middle adulthood and then shows a slight downturn in late adulthood (Corporation for National and Community Service, 2006). However, older adults are more likely than any other age group to volunteer more than 100 hours annually (Burr, 2009). Almost 50 percent of the volunteering efforts of older adults are for services provided by religious organizations (Burr, 2009).

One study followed 423 older adult couples for five years (Brown & others, 2003). At the beginning of the study, the couples were asked about the extent to which they had given or received emotional or practical help in the past year. Five years later, those who said they had helped others were half as likely to have died. One possible reason for this finding is that helping others may reduce the output of stress hormones, which improves cardiovascular health and strengthens the immune system. A recent study revealed that older adults who volunteered for other-oriented reasons had a decreased mortality risk but those who volunteered for self-oriented reasons had a mortality risk similar to nonvolunteers (Konrath & others, 2012). Researchers also have found that the more older adults engage in volunteering, the healthier they are and the happier they are (Dulin & others, 2012; Krause & others, 1999). Among the reasons for the positive outcomes of volunteering are its provision of constructive activities and productive roles, social integration, and enhanced meaningfulness (Tan & others, 2007).

Ninety-eight-year-old volunteer Iva Broadus plays cards with 10-year-old DeAngela Williams in Dallas, Texas. Iva recently was recognized as the oldest volunteer in the Big Sister program in the United States. Iva says that card-playing helps to keep her memory and thinking skills sharp and can help DeAngela's as well.

developmental **connection**

Community and Culture

Service learning is linked with numerous positive outcomes in youth. Chapter 11, p. 381

4 Ethnicity, Gender, and Culture

LG4 Summarize how ethnicity, gender, and culture are linked with aging.

Ethnicity · · · Gender · · · Culture

How is ethnicity linked to aging? Do gender roles change in late adulthood? What are the social aspects of aging in different cultures?

ETHNICITY

Of special concern are ethnic minority older adults, especially African Americans and Latinos, who are overrepresented in poverty statistics (Jackson, Govia, & Sellers, 2011). Consider Harry, a 72-year-old African American who lives in a run-down hotel in Los Angeles. He suffers from arthritis and uses a walker. He has not been able to work for years, and government payments are barely enough to meet his needs.

Comparative information about African Americans, Latinos, and Whites indicates a possible double jeopardy for elderly ethnic minority individuals. They face problems related to both ageism and racism (Hatzfeld, Laveist, & Gaston-Johansson, 2012). Both the wealth and the health of ethnic minority older adults decrease more rapidly than for elderly non-Latino Whites (Yee & Chiriboga, 2007). Older ethnic minority individuals are more likely to become ill but less likely to receive treatment (Shenson & others, 2012). They also are more likely to have a history of less education, higher levels of unemployment, worse housing conditions, and shorter life expectancies than their non-Latino White counterparts (Gee, Walsemann, & Brondolo, 2012). And many ethnic minority workers never enjoy the Social Security and Medicare benefits to which their earnings contribute, because they die before reaching the age of eligibility for benefits (Jackson, Govia, & Sellers, 2011).

Despite the stress and discrimination older ethnic minority individuals face, many of these older adults have developed coping mechanisms that allow them to survive in the dominant non-Latino White world. Extension of family networks helps older minority-group individuals cope with the bare essentials of living and gives them a sense of being loved (Karasik & Hamon, 2007). Churches in African American and Latino communities provide avenues for meaningful social participation, feelings of power, and a sense of internal satisfaction (Hill & others, 2006). And residential concentrations of ethnic minority groups give their older members a sense of belonging. Thus, it always is important to consider individual variations

A special concern is the stress faced by older African American women, many of whom view religion as a source of strength to help them cope. *What are some other characteristics of being female, a member of an ethnic minority, and old?*

Norma Thomas, Social Work Professor and Administrator

Dr. Norma Thomas has worked for more than three decades in the field of aging. She obtained her undergraduate degree in social work from Pennsylvania State University and her doctoral degree in social work from the University of Pennsylvania. Thomas' activities are varied. Earlier in her career, as a social work practitioner, she provided services to older adults of color in an effort to improve their lives. She currently is a professor and academic administrator at Widener University in Chester, Pennsylvania, a fellow of the Institute of Aging at the University of Pennsylvania, and the chief executive officer and cofounder of the Center on Ethnic and Minority Aging (CEMA). CEMA was formed to provide research, consultation, training, and services to benefit aging individuals of color, their families, and their communities. Thomas has created numerous community service events that benefit older adults of color, especially African Americans and Latinos. She has also been a consultant to various national, regional, and state agencies in her effort to improve the lives of aging adults of color.

Norma Thomas

For more information about what professors and social workers do, see pages 44 and 45 in the Careers in Life-Span Development appendix.

in the lives of aging minorities. To read about one individual who is providing help for aging minorities, see *Connecting with Careers*.

GENDER

Do our gender roles change when we become older adults? Some developmentalists conclude that femininity decreases in women and that masculinity decreases in men when they reach late adulthood (Gutmann, 1975). The evidence suggests that older men do become more feminine—nurturant, sensitive, and so on—but it appears that older women do not necessarily become more masculine—assertive, dominant, and so on (Turner, 1982). Keep in mind that cohort effects are especially important to consider in areas such as gender roles. As sociohistorical changes take place and are assessed more frequently in life-span investigations, what were once perceived to be age effects may turn out to be cohort effects (Schaie, 2012).

A possible double jeopardy also faces many women—the burden of both ageism and sexism (Meyer & Parker, 2011). Not only is it important to be concerned about older women's double jeopardy of ageism and sexism, but special attention also needs to be devoted to female ethnic minority older adults (Jackson, Govia, & Sellers, 2011). They face what could be described as triple jeopardy—ageism, sexism, and racism (Hinze, Lin, & Andersson, 2012). Older women in ethnic minority groups have faced considerable stress in their lives. In the face of this stress, they have shown remarkable adaptability, resilience, responsibility, and coping skills.

CULTURE

What promotes a good old age in most cultures? One analysis indicated that three factors are important in living the "good life" as an older adult: health, security, and kinship/support (Fry, 2007).

Another important question is: What factors are associated with whether older adults are accorded a position of high status in a culture? In one view, seven factors are most likely to predict high status for older adults in a culture (Sangree, 1989):

- Older persons have valuable knowledge.
- Older persons control key family/community resources.
- Older persons are permitted to engage in useful and valued functions as long as possible.
- There is role continuity throughout the life span.
- Age-related role changes involve greater responsibility, authority, and advisory capacity.
- The extended family is a common family arrangement in the culture, and the older person is integrated into the extended family.
- In general, respect for older adults is greater in collectivistic cultures (such as China and Japan) than in individualistic cultures (such as the United States). However, some researchers are finding that this collectivistic/individualistic difference in respect for older adults is not as strong as it used to be, and that in some cases older adults in individualistic cultures receive considerable respect (Antonucci, Vandewater, & Lansford, 2000).

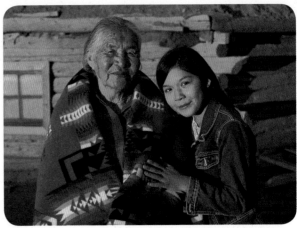

Cultures vary in the prestige they give to older adults. In the Navajo culture, older adults are especially treated with respect because of their wisdom and extensive life experiences. *What are some other factors that are linked with respect for older adults in a culture?*

Review *Connect* Reflect

 LG4 Summarize how ethnicity, gender, and culture are linked with aging.

Review

- How does ethnicity modify the experience of aging?
- Do gender roles change in late adulthood? Explain.
- How is aging experienced in different cultures?

Connect

- In this section, you read that ethnic minorities face additional challenges in aging. What did you learn about ethnicity and life expectancy in Chapter 17?

Reflect *Your Own Personal Journey of Life*

- How would you describe the experiences of the older adults in your family background that were influenced by their ethnicity, gender, and culture?

5 Successful Aging

 LG5 Explain how to age successfully.

For too long, the positive dimensions of late adulthood were ignored (Biggs, Carstensen, & Hogan, 2012). Throughout this book, we have called attention to the positive aspects of aging. There are many robust, healthy older adults (Depp, Vahia, & Jeste, 2012). With a proper diet, an active lifestyle, mental stimulation and flexibility, positive coping skills, good social relationships and support, and the absence of disease, many abilities can be maintained or in some cases even improved as we get older (Antonucci, Birditt, & Ajrouch, 2013). Even when individuals develop a disease, improvements in medicine mean that increasing numbers of older adults can continue to lead active, constructive lives (Siegler & others, 2013a, b).

Being active is especially important to successful aging (Katzel & Steinbrenner, 2012). Older adults who exercise regularly, attend meetings, participate in church activities, and go on trips are more satisfied with their lives than their counterparts who disengage from society (Buchman & others, 2012). Older adults who engage in challenging cognitive activities are more likely to retain their cognitive skills for a longer period of time (Dixon & others, 2013). Older adults who are emotionally selective, optimize their choices, and compensate effectively for losses increase their chances of aging successfully (Baltes & Smith, 2008; Carstensen & others, 2011; Freund, Nikitin, & Riediger, 2013).

developmental **connection**

Health

Regular exercise is linked to increased longevity and prevention of many chronic diseases. Chapter 17, p. 555

Eighty-two-year-old Warren Buffett, one of the world's richest individuals, continues to have a very active, successful life. He recently donated more than $30 billion to several foundations, with the bulk of the money given to the Bill and Melinda Gates Foundation, which plans to use it to reduce poverty, improve education, and solve health problems.

Successful aging also involves perceived control over the environment (Graham & Lachman, 2012). In Chapter 17, we described how perceived control over the environment had a positive effect on nursing home residents' health and longevity. In recent years, the term *self-efficacy* has often been used to describe perceived control over the environment and the ability to produce positive outcomes (Bandura, 2010, 2012). Researchers have found that many older adults are quite effective in maintaining a sense of control and have a positive view of themselves (Dunbar, Leventhal, & Leventhal, 2007). For example, a study of centenarians found that many were very happy and that self-efficacy and an optimistic attitude were linked to their happiness (Jopp & Rott, 2006). And a recent study revealed that maximizing psychological resources (self-efficacy and optimism) was linked to a higher level quality of life in the future for older adults (Bowling & Lliffe, 2011). Examining the positive aspects of aging is an important trend in life-span development that is likely to benefit future generations of older adults (Depp, Vahai, & Jeste, 2012; Freund, Nikitin, & Riediger, 2013). And a very important agenda is to continue to improve our understanding of how people can live longer, healthier, more productive and satisfying lives (Beard & others, 2012).

Review Connect Reflect

 Explain how to age successfully.

Review

- What factors are linked with aging successfully?

Connect

- In this section, you read that self-efficacy and an optimistic attitude are linked to the happiness of centenarians. In Chapter 17, what factors did you learn play an important role in surviving to an extreme old age?

Reflect *Your Own Personal Journey of Life*

- How might your ability to age successfully as an older adult be related to what you are doing in your life now?

topical **connections**

In death, dying, and grieving, dying individuals and those close to them experience intense emotions. The dying individual doesn't go through a set sequence of stages, but at various points may show denial, anger, or acceptance. It is important for family and friends to communicate effectively with a dying person. In coping with the death of another person, grief may be experienced as emotional numbness, separation anxiety, despair, sadness, or loneliness. In some cases, grief may last for years. Among the most difficult losses are the death of a child or a spouse. Social support benefits widows and widowers.

looking forward

Socioemotional Development in Late Adulthood

---

1 Theories of Socioemotional Development

LG1 Discuss four theories of socioemotional development and aging.

- Erikson's Theory

- Activity Theory

- Socioemotional Selectivity Theory

- Selective Optimization with Compensation Theory

- Erikson's eighth and final stage of development, which individuals experience in late adulthood, involves reflecting on the past and either integrating it positively or concluding that one's life has not been well spent. Life review is an important theme in Erikson's stage of integrity versus despair.

- Activity theory states that the more active and involved older adults are, the more likely they are to be satisfied with their lives. This theory has been strongly supported by research.

- Socioemotional selectivity theory states that older adults become more selective about their social networks. Because they place a high value on emotional satisfaction, they are motivated to spend more time with familiar individuals with whom they have had rewarding relationships. Knowledge-related and emotion-related goals change across the life span, with emotion-related goals being more important when individuals get older.

- Selective optimization with compensation theory states that successful aging is linked with three main factors: (1) selection, (2) optimization, and (3) compensation. These are especially likely to be relevant when loss occurs.

---

2 Personality, the Self, and Society

LG2 Describe links between personality and mortality, and identify changes in the self and society in late adulthood.

- Personality

- The Self and Society

- Older Adults in Society

- The personality traits of conscientiousness and agreeableness increase in late adulthood. Lower levels of conscientiousness, extraversion, and openness to experience, a higher level of neuroticism, negative affect, pessimism, and a negative outlook on life are related to earlier death in late adulthood.

- In one large-scale study, self-esteem increased through most of adulthood but declined in the seventies and eighties. Further research is needed to verify these developmental changes in self-esteem. The stability of self-esteem declines in older adults. Possible selves are what individuals might become, what they would like to become, and what they are afraid of becoming. Possible selves change during late adulthood and are linked to engagement in various activities and longevity. Changes in types of self-acceptance occur through the adult years as acceptance of ideal and future selves decreases with age and acceptance of past selves increases. Most older adults effectively maintain a sense of self-control, although self-regulation may vary by domain. For example, older adults often show less self-regulation in the physical domain than younger adults.

- Ageism is prejudice against others because of their age. Too many negative stereotypes of older adults continue to exist. Social policy issues in an aging society include the status of the economy and the viability of the Social Security system, the provision of health care, eldercare, and generational inequity. Of special concern are older adults who are in poverty. Poverty rates are especially high among older women who live alone and ethnic minority older adults. Most older adults live in the community, not in institutions. Almost two-thirds of older adults live with family members. Older adults are less likely to have a computer in their home and less likely to use the Internet than younger adults, but they are the fastest-growing age segment of Internet users.

3 Families and Social Relationships

 Characterize the families and social relationships of aging adults.

Lifestyle Diversity

- Older adult men are more likely to be married than older adult women. Retirement alters a couple's lifestyle and requires adaptation. Married older adults are often happier than single older adults. There are social, financial, and physical consequences of divorce for older adults. More divorced older adults, increased longevity, and better health have led to an increase in remarriage by older adults. Some older adults perceive negative pressure about their decision to remarry, although the majority of adult children support the decision of their older adult parents to remarry. An increasing number of older adults cohabit. Older adults especially enjoy touching and caressing as part of their sexual relationship.

Older Adult Parents and Their Adult Children

- Approximately 80 percent of older adults have living children, many of whom are middle-aged. Increasingly, diversity characterizes the relationships of older parents and their adult children. Adult daughters are more likely than adult sons to be involved in the lives of aging parents. An important task that adult children can perform is to coordinate and monitor services for an aging parent who becomes disabled. Ambivalence can characterize the relationships of adult children with their aging parents.

Great-Grandparenting

- Because of increased longevity, more grandparents today are also great-grandparents. One contribution of great-grandparents is knowledge of family history. One research study found that young adults have a more involved relationship with grandparents than with great-grandparents.

Friendship

- There is more continuity than change in friendship for older adults.

Social Support and Social Integration

- Social support is linked with improved physical and mental health in older adults. Older adults who participate in more organizations live longer than their counterparts who have low participation rates. Older adults often have fewer peripheral social ties but a strong motivation to spend time in relationships with close friends and family members that are emotionally rewarding.

Altruism and Volunteerism

- Altruism is linked to having a longer life. Volunteering is associated with higher life satisfaction, less depression and anxiety, better physical health, and more positive emotions.

4 Ethnicity, Gender, and Culture

 Summarize how ethnicity, gender, and culture are linked with aging.

Ethnicity

- Aging minorities cope with the double burden of ageism and racism. Nonetheless, there is considerable variation in the lives of aging minorities.

Gender

- There is stronger evidence that men become more feminine (nurturant, sensitive) as older adults than there is that women become more masculine (assertive). Older women face a double jeopardy of ageism and sexism.

Culture

- Historically, respect for older adults in China and Japan was high, but today their status is more variable. Factors that predict high status for the elderly across cultures range from their valuable knowledge to integration into the extended family.

5 Successful Aging

 Explain how to age successfully.

- Increasingly, the positive aspects of older adulthood are being studied. Factors that are linked with successful aging include an active lifestyle, positive coping skills, good social relationships and support, and the absence of disease.

key terms

integrity versus despair 596
activity theory 598
socioemotional selectivity
  theory 598

selective optimization
  with compensation
  theory 600
possible selves 604

ageism 605
eldercare 606
generational
  inequity 606

convoy model of social
  relations 611

key people

Erik Erikson 596
Robert Butler 596

Laura Carstensen 598
Paul Baltes 600

Ursula Staudinger 601

Chapter 19 | SOCIOEMOTIONAL DEVELOPMENT IN LATE ADULTHOOD

Connecting with

Learning Objectives	Application Activities	Activity Type	Page Reference
Discuss Erikson's theory of socioemotional development and aging.	Late Adulthood Perspectives on Emotion	Milestones: Transitions	pp. 596–600
Identify changes in the self and society in late adulthood.	When I Was Young	Video	pp. 603–605
Discuss older adults in society including ageism, policy issues, income, living arrangements, and technology.	What Is Old?	Video	pp. 605–607
	A Day in the Life of a Nursing Home Resident	Video	
	Nursing Home Environment	Video	

Years following years steal something every day;
At last they steal us from ourselves away.

—ALEXANDER POPE
English Poet, 18th Century

Endings

Our life ultimately ends—when we approach life's grave sustained and soothed with unfaltering trust or rave at the close of day; when at last years steal us from ourselves; and when we are linked to our children's children's children by an invisible cable that runs from age to age. This final section contains one chapter: "Death, Dying, and Grieving" (Chapter 20).

DEATH, DYING, AND GRIEVING

chapter **outline**

1 The Death System and Cultural Contexts

Learning Goal 1 Describe the death system and its cultural and historical contexts.

The Death System and Its Cultural Variations

Changing Historical Circumstances

2 Defining Death and Life/Death Issues

Learning Goal 2 Evaluate issues in determining death and decisions regarding death.

Issues in Determining Death

Decisions Regarding Life, Death, and Health Care

3 A Developmental Perspective on Death

Learning Goal 3 Discuss death and attitudes about it at different points in development.

Causes of Death

Attitudes Toward Death at Different Points in the Life Span

4 Facing One's Own Death

Learning Goal 4 Explain the psychological aspects involved in facing one's own death and the contexts in which people die.

Kübler-Ross' Stages of Dying

Perceived Control and Denial

The Contexts in Which People Die

5 Coping with the Death of Someone Else

Learning Goal 5 Identify ways to cope with the death of another person.

Communicating with a Dying Person

Grieving

Making Sense of the World

Losing a Life Partner

Forms of Mourning

Paige Farley-Hackel and her best friend Ruth McCourt teamed up to take McCourt's 4-year-old daughter, Juliana, to Disneyland. They were originally booked on the same flight from Boston to Los Angeles, but McCourt decided to use her frequent flyer miles and go on a different airplane. Both their flights exploded 17 minutes apart after terrorists hijacked them, then rammed them into the twin towers of the World Trade Center in New York City on 9/11/2001.

Forty-five-year-old Ruth McCourt was a homemaker from New London, Connecticut, who had met Farley-Hackel at a day spa she used to own in Boston. McCourt gave up the business when she married, but the friendship between the two women lasted. They often traveled together and shared their passion for reading, cooking, and learning.

Forty-six-year-old Farley-Hackel was a writer, motivational speaker, and spiritual counselor who lived in Newton, Massachusetts. She was looking forward to the airing of the first few episodes of her new radio program, "Spiritually Speaking," and wanted to eventually be on *The Oprah Winfrey Show*, said her husband, Allan Hackel. Following 9/11, Oprah provided a memorial tribute to Farley-Hackel, McCourt, and Juliana.

-topical **connections**

In the United States, the leading cause of death in infancy is sudden infant death syndrome (SIDS). In early childhood, motor vehicle accidents are the leading cause of death, followed by cancer and cardiovascular disease. Injuries are the leading cause of death during middle and late childhood, and the most common cause of severe injury and death in this period is motor vehicle accidents, either as a pedestrian or as a passenger. The three leading causes of death in adolescence are accidents, homicide, and suicide. Emerging adults have more than twice the mortality rate of adolescents. For many years, heart disease was the leading cause of death in middle adulthood, followed by cancer; however, in 2005 more individuals 45 to 64 years of age in the United States died of cancer, followed by cardiovascular disease. Men have higher mortality rates than women for all of the leading causes of death. Nearly 60 percent of 65- to 74-year-old U.S. adults die of cancer or cardiovascular disease, with cancer now the leading cause of death. However, in the age groups of 75 to 84 and 85 and over, cardiovascular disease is the leading cause of death.

◄ - - - *looking back* -

preview

In this final chapter of the book, we will explore many aspects of death and dying. Among the questions that we will ask are: What characterizes the death system and its cultural and historical contexts? How can death be defined? What are some links between development and death? How do people face their own death? How do individuals cope with the death of someone they love?

---

1 The Death System and Cultural Contexts

LG1 Describe the death system and its cultural and historical contexts.

The Death System and Its Cultural Variations

Changing Historical Circumstances

Today in the United States, deaths of older adults account for approximately two-thirds of the 2 million deaths that occur each year. Thus, what we know about death, dying, and grieving mainly is based on information about older adults. Youthful death is far less common. What has changed historically in the United States is when, where, and how people die. And how we deal with death is part of our culture. Every culture has a death system, and variations in this death system occur across cultures.

THE DEATH SYSTEM AND ITS CULTURAL VARIATIONS

Robert Kastenbaum (2009, 2012) emphasizes that the *death system* in any culture comprises the following components:

- *People.* Because death is inevitable, everyone is involved with death at some point, either their own death or the death of others. Some individuals have a more systematic role with death, such as those who work in the funeral industry and the clergy, as well as people who work in life-threatening contexts such as firemen and policemen.
- *Places or contexts.* These include hospitals, funeral homes, cemeteries, hospices, battlefields, and memorials (such as the Vietnam Veterans Memorial wall in Washington, DC).
- *Times.* Death involves times or occasions, such as Memorial Day in the United States and the Day of the Dead in Mexico, which are times to honor those who have died. Also, anniversaries of disasters such as D-Day in World War II, 9/11/2001, and Hurricane Katrina in 2005, as well as the 2004 tsunami in Southeast Asia that took approximately 100,000 lives, are times when those who died are remembered in special ways such as ceremonies.
- *Objects.* Many objects in a culture are associated with death, including caskets, various black objects such as clothes, armbands, and hearses.
- *Symbols.* Symbols such as a skull and crossbones, as well as last rites in the Catholic religion and various religious ceremonies, are connected to death.

What are some cultural variations in the death system? To live a full life and die with glory was the prevailing goal of the ancient Greeks. Individuals are more conscious of death in times of war, famine, and plague. Whereas Americans are conditioned from early in life to live as though they were immortal, in much of the world this fiction cannot be maintained. Death crowds the streets of Calcutta in daily overdisplay, as it does in the impoverished villages of Africa's Sahel. By

These children's parents died when they were swept away by the tsunami in Indonesia in 2004. The death system includes events such as the 2004 tsunami. *What are some other components of the death system?*

contrast, in the United States it is not uncommon to reach adulthood without having seen someone die.

Most societies throughout history have had philosophical or religious beliefs about death, and most societies have a ritual that deals with death (Bruce, 2007). Death may be seen as a punishment for one's sins, an act of atonement, or a judgment from a just God. For some, death means loneliness; for others, death is a quest for happiness. For still others, death represents redemption, a relief from the trials and tribulations of the earthly world. Some embrace death and welcome it; others abhor and fear it. For those who welcome it, death may be seen as the fitting end to a fulfilled life. From this perspective, how we depart from Earth is influenced by how we have lived.

In most societies, death is not viewed as the end of existence—after the biological body has died, the spiritual body is believed to live on. This religious perspective is favored by most Americans as well (Gowan, 2003). Cultural variations in attitudes toward death include belief in reincarnation, which is an important aspect of the Hindu and Buddhist religions (Dillon, 2003). In the Gond culture of India, death is believed to be caused by magic and demons. The members of the Gond culture react angrily to death. In the Tanala culture of Madagascar, death is believed to be caused by natural forces. The members of the Tanala culture show a much more peaceful reaction to death than members of the Gond culture. Figure 20.1 shows a ritual associated with death in South Korea.

In many ways, we in the United States are death avoiders and death deniers (Norouzieh, 2005). This denial can take many forms, including our persistent search for a fountain of youth through diet, surgery, and other means, as well as the tendency of the funeral industry to gloss over death and fashion lifelike qualities in the dead.

A body lies in the flooded streets of New Orleans in the aftermath of Hurricane Katrina.

developmental **connection**

Life Expectancy

The upper boundary of the human life span is 122 years of age (based on the oldest age documented). Chapter 1, p. 8

CHANGING HISTORICAL CIRCUMSTANCES

One historical change involves the age group in which death most often occurs. Two hundred years ago, almost one of every two children died before the age of 10, and one parent died before children grew up. Today, death occurs most often among older adults (Carr, 2009). Life expectancy has increased from 47 years for a person born in 1900 to 78 years for someone born today (U.S. Census Bureau, 2011). In 1900, most people died at home, cared for by their family. As our population has aged and become more mobile, greater numbers of older adults die apart from their families (Carr, 2009). In the United States today, more than 80 percent of all deaths occur in institutions or hospitals. The care of a dying older person has shifted away from the family and minimized our exposure to death and its painful surroundings (Gold, 2011).

FIGURE **20.1**

A RITUAL ASSOCIATED WITH DEATH. Family memorial day at the national cemetery in Seoul, South Korea.

Review Connect Reflect

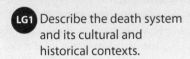

LG1 Describe the death system and its cultural and historical contexts.

Review

· What characterizes the death system in a culture? What are some cultural variations in the death system?
· What are some changing sociohistorical circumstances regarding death?

Connect

· You just read about how changes in life expectancy over time have affected our

experience of death. In earlier chapters, what did you learn about life expectancy and the age span that encompasses older adulthood?

Reflect *Your Own Personal Journey of Life*

· How extensively have death and dying been discussed in your family? Explain.

Issues in Determining Death

Decisions Regarding Life, Death, and Health Care

Is there one point in the process of dying that is the point at which death takes place, or is there more of a gradual transition between life and death? What are some decisions individuals can make about life, death, and health care?

ISSUES IN DETERMINING DEATH

Twenty-five years ago, determining whether someone was dead was simpler than it is today. The end of certain biological functions, such as breathing and blood pressure, and the rigidity of the body (rigor mortis) were considered to be clear signs of death. In recent decades, defining death has become more complex (Goswami & others, 2012; Jeret, 2011).

Brain death is a neurological definition of death, which states that a person is brain dead when all electrical activity of the brain has ceased for a specified period of time. A flat EEG (electroencephalogram) reading for a specified period of time is one criterion of brain death. The higher portions of the brain often die sooner than the lower portions. Because the brain's lower portions monitor heartbeat and respiration, individuals whose higher brain areas have died may continue to breathe and have a heartbeat (Binderman, Krakauer, & Solomon, 2012). The definition of brain death currently followed by most physicians includes the death of both the higher cortical functions and the lower brain stem functions (Sung & Greer, 2011).

Some medical experts argue that the criteria for death should include only higher cortical functioning. If the cortical death definition were adopted, then physicians could declare that a person is dead when there is no cortical functioning in that person, even though the lower brain stem is functioning. Supporters of the cortical death policy argue that the functions we associate with being human, such as intelligence and personality, are located in the higher cortical part of the brain. They believe that when these functions are lost, the "human being" is no longer alive.

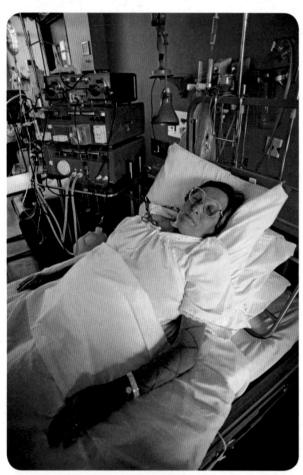

What are some issues in determining death?

DECISIONS REGARDING LIFE, DEATH, AND HEALTH CARE

In cases of catastrophic illness or accidents, patients might not be able to respond adequately to participate in decisions about their medical care. To prepare for this situation, some individuals make choices earlier.

Advanced Care Planning *Advance care planning* refers to the process of patients thinking about and communicating their preferences about end-of-life care (Carr, 2012; Tinetti, 2012). For many patients in a coma, it is not clear what their wishes regarding termination of treatment might be if they still were conscious. Recognizing that some terminally ill patients might prefer to die rather than linger in a painful or vegetative state, the organization "Choice in Dying" created the *living will*, a legal document that reflects the patient's advance care planning.

Physicians' concerns over malpractice suits and the efforts of people who support the living will concept have produced natural death legislation. Laws in all 50 states now accept an *advance directive*, such as a living will. An advance directive states such preferences as whether life-sustaining procedures should or should not be used to prolong the life of an individual when death is imminent (Dunlay & others, 2012). An advance directive must be signed while the individual still is able to think clearly (Spoelhof & Elliott, 2012). A study of

brain death A neurological definition of death. A person is brain dead when all electrical activity of the brain has ceased for a specified period of time. A flat EEG recording is one criterion of brain death.

end-of-life planning revealed that only 15 percent of patients 18 years of age and older had a living will (Clements, 2009). Almost 90 percent of the patients reported that it was important to discuss health care wishes with their family, but only 60 percent of them had done so.

Recently, Physican Orders for Life-Sustaining Treatment (POLST), a document that is more specific than previous advanced directives, was created (Bomba & others, 2012; Hammes & others, 2012). POLST translates treatment preferences into medical orders such as those involving cardiopulmonary resuscitation, extent of treatment, and artificial nutrition via a tube (Fromme & others, 2012). POLST involves the health care professional and the patient or surrogate conferring to determine and state the wishes of the patient. POLST is currently available or being considered in 34 states.

Euthanasia   Euthanasia ("easy death") is the act of painlessly ending the lives of individuals who are suffering from an incurable disease or severe disability (Augestad & others, 2012; Kouwenhoven & others, 2012). Sometimes euthanasia is called "mercy killing." Distinctions are made between two types of euthanasia: passive and active.

- **Passive euthanasia** occurs when a person is allowed to die by withholding available treatment, such as withdrawing a life-sustaining device. For example, this might involve turning off a respirator or a heart-lung machine.
- **Active euthanasia** occurs when death is deliberately induced, as when a lethal dose of a drug is injected.

Terri Schiavo (*right*) shown with her mother in an undated photo. *What issues did the Terri Schiavo case raise?*

Technological advances in life-support devices raise the issue of quality of life (Blanker & others, 2012). Nowhere was this more apparent than in the highly publicized case of Terri Schiavo, who suffered severe brain damage related to cardiac arrest and a lack of oxygen to the brain. She went into a coma and spent 15 years in a vegetative state. Across the 15 years, the question of whether passive euthanasia should be implemented or whether she should be kept in the vegetative state with the hope that her condition might change for the better was debated between family members and eventually at a number of levels in the judicial system. At one point toward the end of her life in the early spring of 2005, a court ordered that her feeding tube be removed. However, subsequent appeals led to its reinsertion twice. The feeding tube was removed a third and final time on March 18, 2005, and she died 13 days later.

Should individuals like Terri Schiavo be kept alive in a vegetative state? The trend is toward acceptance of passive euthanasia in the case of terminally ill patients (Seay, 2011). However, a study revealed that family members were reluctant to have their relatives disconnected from a ventilator but rather wanted an escalation of treatment for them (Sviri & others, 2009). In this study, most of the individuals said that in similar circumstances they would not want to be chronically ventilated or resuscitated.

The inflammatory argument that once equated this practice with suicide rarely is heard today. However, experts do not yet entirely agree on the precise boundaries or the exact mechanisms by which treatment decisions should be implemented (Seay, 2011). Can a comatose patient's life-support systems be disconnected when the patient has left no written instructions to that effect? Does the family of a comatose patient have the right to overrule the attending physician's decision to continue life-support systems? These questions have no simple or universally agreed-upon answers (Chambers & others, 2012; McLachlan, 2011). The most widely publicized cases of active euthanasia involve "assisted suicide." Jack Kevorkian, a Michigan physician, assisted a number of terminally ill patients in ending their lives. After a series of trials, Kevorkian was convicted of second-degree murder and given a 10- to 15-year sentence. He was released from prison at age 79 for good behavior in June 2007 and promised not to participate in any further assisted suicides. Kevorkian died recently at the age of 83.

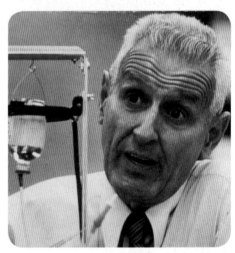

Dr. Jack Kevorkian assisted a number of people in Michigan to end their lives through active euthanasia. *Where do you stand on the use of active euthanasia?*

euthanasia The act of painlessly ending the lives of persons who are suffering from incurable diseases or severe disabilities; sometimes called "mercy killing."

passive euthanasia The withholding of available treatments, such as life-sustaining devices, in order to allow a person to die.

active euthanasia Death induced deliberately, as by injecting a lethal dose of a drug.

Active euthanasia is a crime in most countries and in all states in the United States except Oregon and Washington. In 1994, the state of Oregon passed the Death With Dignity Act, which allows active euthanasia. Through 2001, 91 individuals were known to have died by active euthanasia in Oregon. In January 2006, the U.S. Supreme Court upheld Oregon's active euthanasia law. Active euthanasia is legal in the Netherlands, Belgium, Luxembourg, and Uruguay (Smets & others, 2010).

A Dutch study of almost 7,000 dying persons revealed that only 7 percent requested passive or active euthanasia, and of those who requested it, approximately one-third of the requests were granted (Onwuteaka-Philipsen & others, 2010). A recent Belgian study found that approximately 50 percent of the requests for euthanasia were granted (Van Wesemael & others, 2011). And another study found that in the Netherlands approximately 75 percent of the requests for euthanasia came from cancer patients and the main reason for the requests was pain (van Alphen, Donker, & Marquet, 2010).

Needed: Better Care for Dying Individuals   Death in America is often lonely, prolonged, and painful. Dying individuals often get too little or too much care. Scientific advances sometimes have made dying harder by delaying the inevitable. And even though painkillers are available, too many people experience severe pain during the last days and months of life (Kreuter & Herth, 2011). Many health care professionals have not been trained to provide adequate end-of-life care or to understand its importance. One study revealed that in many cases doctors don't give dying patients adequate information about how long they are likely to live or how various treatments will affect their lives (Harrington & Smith, 2008). For example, in this study of patients with advanced cancer, only 37 percent of doctors told patients how long they were likely to live.

Care providers are increasingly interested in helping individuals experience a "good death" (Cheng & others, 2012). One view is that a good death involves physical comfort, support from loved ones, acceptance, and appropriate medical care. For some individuals, a good death involves accepting one's impending death and not feeling like a burden to others (Carr, 2009).

There are few fail-safe measures for avoiding pain at the end of life. Still, you can follow these suggestions (Cowley & Hager, 1995):

- Make a living will, and be sure there is someone who will draw your doctor's attention to it.
- Give someone the power of attorney, and make sure this person knows your wishes regarding medical care.
- Give your doctors specific instructions—from "Do not resuscitate" to "Do everything possible"—for specific circumstances.
- If you want to die at home, talk it over with your family and doctor.
- Check to see whether your insurance plan covers home care and hospice care.

Hospice is a program committed to making the end of life as free from pain, anxiety, and depression as possible (Fauci & others, 2012). Whereas a hospital's goals are to cure illness and prolong life, hospice care emphasizes **palliative care,** which involves reducing pain and suffering and helping individuals die with dignity (Bull & others, 2012). Health care professionals work together to treat the dying person's symptoms, make the individual as comfortable as possible, show interest in the person and the person's family, and help them cope with death (De Lima & others, 2012; Junger & others, 2012).

The hospice movement began toward the end of the 1960s in London, when a new kind of medical institution, St. Christopher's Hospice, opened. Little effort is made to prolong life at St. Christopher's—there are no heart-lung machines and there is no intensive care unit, for example. A primary goal is to bring pain under control and to help dying patients face death in a psychologically healthy way (Campbell & Cox, 2012). The hospice also makes every effort to include the dying individual's family; it is believed that this strategy benefits not only the dying individual but family members as well, probably diminishing their guilt after the death (Kastenbaum, 2012).

The hospice movement has grown rapidly in the United States. More than 1,500 community groups are involved nationally in establishing hospice programs. Hospices are more likely to serve people with terminal cancer than those with other life-threatening conditions (Kastenbaum, 2012). Hospice advocates underscore that it is possible to control pain for almost any dying individual and to create an environment for the patient that is superior to that found in most hospitals (Hayslip, 1996). For hospice services to be covered by Medicare, a patient must be deemed by a physician to have six months or fewer to live. Also, some hospice

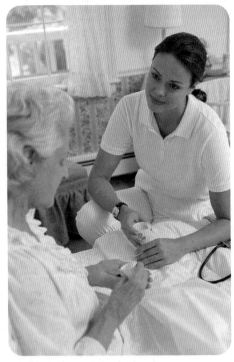

What characterizes hospice care?

hospice A program committed to making the end of life as free from pain, anxiety, and depression as possible. The goals of hospice contrast with those of a hospital, which are to cure disease and prolong life.

palliative care The type of care emphasized in a hospice, which involves reducing pain and suffering and helping individuals die with dignity.

connecting with careers

Kathy McLaughlin, Home Hospice Nurse

Kathy McLaughlin is a home hospice nurse in Alexandria, Virginia. She provides care for individuals with terminal cancer, Alzheimer disease, and other diseases. There currently is a shortage of home hospice nurses in the United States.

McLaughlin says that she has seen too many people dying in pain, away from home, hooked up to needless machines. In her work as a home hospice nurse, she comments, "I know I'm making a difference. I just feel privileged to get the chance to meet this person who is not going to be around much longer. I want to enjoy the moment with this person. And I want them to enjoy the moment. They have great stories. They are better than novels." (McLaughlin, 2003, p. 1)

Kathy McLaughlin checks the vital signs of Kathryn Francis, 86, who is in an advanced stage of Alzheimer disease.

providers require that the patient have a family caregiver in the home (or nearby) before agreeing to provide services for the patient.

Approximately 90 percent of hospice care is provided in patients' homes (Hayslip & Hansson, 2007). In some cases, home-based care is provided by community-based health care professionals or volunteers; in other cases, home-based care is provided by home health care agencies or the Visiting Nurse Associations. There is a rapidly growing need for competent home health aides in hospice and palliative care (Brown, 2012; Marrelli, 2012). Also, some hospice care is provided in free-standing, full-service hospice facilities and in hospice units in hospitals. To read about the work of a home hospice nurse, see *Connecting with Careers*.

Review *Connect* Reflect

 LG2 Evaluate issues in determining death and decisions regarding death.

Review

- What are some issues regarding the determination of death?
- What are some decisions to be made regarding life, death, and health care?

Connect

- In this section, you learned that one of the things that hospices try to provide dying

patients is adequate pain management. What did you learn about older adults in Chapter 17 that might help them deal with pain better than younger adults?

Reflect *Your Own Personal Journey of Life*

- Have you signed an advance directive (living will)? Why or why not?

---

3 A Developmental Perspective on Death

 LG3 Discuss death and attitudes about it at different points in development.

Causes of Death   Attitudes Toward Death at Different Points in the Life Span

Do the causes of death vary across the human life span? Do we have different expectations about death as we develop through the life span? What are our attitudes toward death at different points in our development?

developmental connection

Conditions, Diseases, and Disorders

Nearly 3,000 deaths of infants a year in the U.S. are attributed to SIDS. Chapter 4, p. 116

CAUSES OF DEATH

Death can occur at any point in the human life span. Death can occur during prenatal development through miscarriages or stillborn births. Death can also occur during the birth process or in the first few days after birth, which usually happens because of a birth defect or because infants have not developed adequately to sustain life outside the uterus. In Chapter 4, "Physical Development in Infancy," we described *sudden infant death syndrome (SIDS)*, in which infants stop breathing, usually during the night, and die without apparent cause (Moon & Fu, 2012). SIDS currently is the leading cause of infant death in the United States, with the risk highest at 2 to 4 months of age (NICHD, 2011).

In childhood, death occurs most often because of accidents or illness. Accidental death in childhood can be the consequence of events such as an automobile accident, drowning, poisoning, fire, or a fall from a high place. Major illnesses that cause death in children are heart disease, cancer, and birth defects.

Compared with childhood, death in adolescence is more likely to occur because of motor vehicle accidents, suicide, and homicide. Many motor vehicle accidents that cause death in adolescence are alcohol-related. We will examine suicide in greater depth shortly.

Older adults are more likely to die from chronic ailments such as heart disease and cancer, whereas younger adults are more likely to die from accidents. Older adults' diseases often incapacitate before they kill, which produces a course of dying that slowly leads to death. Of course, many young and middle-aged adults also die of heart disease, cancer, and other diseases.

ATTITUDES TOWARD DEATH AT DIFFERENT POINTS IN THE LIFE SPAN

The ages of children and adults influence the way they experience and think about death (Torbic, 2011). A mature, adult-like conception of death includes an understanding that death is final and irreversible, that death represents the end of life, and that all living things die. Most researchers have found that as children grow, they develop a more mature approach to death (Hayslip & Hansson, 2003).

Childhood   Young children do not perceive time the way adults do. Even brief separations may be experienced as total losses. For most infants, the reappearance of the caregiver provides a continuity of existence and a reduction of anxiety. We know very little about the infant's actual experiences with bereavement, although the loss of a parent, especially if the caregiver is not replaced, can negatively affect the infant's health.

Even children 3 to 5 years of age have little or no idea of what death means. They may confuse death with sleep or ask in a puzzled way, "Why doesn't it move?" Preschool-aged children rarely get upset by the sight of a dead animal or by being told that a person has died. They believe that the dead can be brought back to life spontaneously by magic or by giving them food or medical treatment. Young children often believe that only people who want to die, or who are bad or careless, actually die. They also may blame themselves for the death of someone they know well, illogically reasoning that the event may have happened because they disobeyed the person who died.

Sometime in the middle and late childhood years, more realistic perceptions of death develop. In a review of research on children's conception of death, it was concluded that children probably do not view death as universal and irreversible until about 9 years of age (Cuddy-Casey & Orvaschel, 1997). Most children under 7 do not see death as likely. If they do, they tend to perceive it as reversible.

The death of a parent is especially difficult for children (Crawford, 2011). When a child's parent dies, the child's school performance and peer relationships often worsen. For some children, as well as adults, a parent's death can be devastating and result in a hypersensitivity about death, including a fear of losing others close to the individual. In some cases, loss of a sibling can result in similar

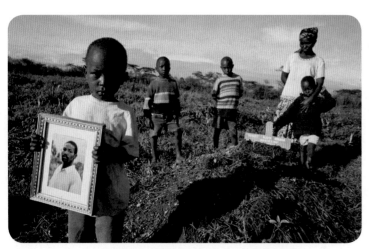

Three- to nine-year-old children with their mother visiting their father's grave in Kenya. *What are some developmental changes in children's conceptions of death?*

negative outcomes (Sood & others, 2006). However, a number of factors, such as the quality of the relationship and type of the death (whether due to an accident, long-standing illness, suicide, or murder, for example), can influence the individual's development following the death of a person close to the individual.

Most psychologists emphasize that honesty is the best strategy in discussing death with children. Treating the concept as unmentionable is thought to be an inappropriate strategy, yet most of us have grown up in a society in which death is rarely discussed.

In addition to honesty, the best response to a child's query about death might depend on the child's maturity level. For example, a preschool child requires a less elaborate explanation than an older child. Death can be explained to preschool children in simple physical and biological terms. Actually, what young children need more than elaborate explanations of death is reassurance that they are loved and will not be abandoned. Regardless of children's age, adults should be sensitive and sympathetic, encouraging them to express their own feelings and ideas.

It is not unusual for terminally ill children to distance themselves from their parents as they approach the final phase of their illness. The distancing may be due to the depression that many dying patients experience, or it may be a child's way of protecting parents from the overwhelming grief they will experience at the death. Most dying children know they have a terminal illness. Their developmental level, social support, and coping skills influence how well they cope with knowing they will die.

Adolescence Deaths of friends, siblings, parents, or grandparents bring death to the forefront of adolescents' lives. Deaths of peers who commit suicide "may be especially difficult for adolescents who feel . . . guilty for having failed to prevent the suicide or feel that they should have died, or . . . feel they are being rejected by their friends who hold them responsible for the death" (Hayslip & Hansson, 2003, p. 441).

Adolescents develop more abstract conceptions of death than children do. For example, adolescents describe death in terms of darkness, light, transition, or nothingness (Wenestam & Wass, 1987). They also develop religious and philosophical views about the nature of death and whether there is life after death.

Recall from Chapter 11 adolescents' concepts of egocentrism and personal fable—that is, adolescents' preoccupation with themselves and their belief that they are invincible and unique. Thus, it is not unusual for some adolescents to think that they are somehow immune to death and that death is something that happens to other people but not to them. However, as we indicated in Chapter 11, an increasing number of research studies suggest that rather than perceiving themselves to be invulnerable, adolescents tend to portray themselves as vulnerable to experiencing a premature death (Fischhoff & others, 2010; Reyna & Rivers, 2008).

Adulthood There is no evidence that a special orientation toward death develops in early adulthood. An increase in consciousness about death accompanies individuals' awareness that they are aging, which usually intensifies in middle adulthood. In our discussion of middle adulthood, we indicated that midlife is a time when adults begin to think more about how much time is left in their lives. Researchers have found that middle-aged adults actually fear death more than do young adults or older adults (Kalish & Reynolds, 1976). Older adults, though, think about death more and talk about it more in conversation with others than do middle-aged and young adults. They also have more direct experience with death as their friends and relatives become ill and die (Hayslip & Hansson, 2003). Older adults are forced to examine the meanings of life and death more frequently than are younger adults.

Younger adults who are dying often feel cheated more than do older adults who are dying (Kalish, 1987). Younger adults are more likely to feel they have not had the opportunity to do what they want to do with their lives. Younger adults perceive they are losing what they might achieve, while older adults perceive they are losing what they already have.

In old age, one's own death may take on an appropriateness it lacked in earlier years. Some of the increased thinking and conversing about death, and an

> We keep on thinking and rethinking death after we have passed through childhood's hour.
>
> **—Robert Kastenbaum**
> *Professor Emeritus in Gerontology and Communications*

What are children's and adolescents' attitudes about death?

How might older adults' attitudes about death differ from those of younger adults?

increased sense of integrity developed through a positive life review, may help older adults accept death. Older adults are less likely to have unfinished business than are younger adults. They usually do not have children who need to be guided to maturity, their spouses are more likely to be dead, and they are less likely to have work-related projects that require completion. Lacking such anticipations, death may be less emotionally painful to them. Even among older adults, however, attitudes toward death vary (Whitbourne & Meeks, 2011).

Review Connect Reflect

 LG3 Discuss death and attitudes about it at different points in development.

Review

- What are some developmental changes in the cause of death?
- What are some attitudes about death at different points in development?

Connect

- In this section, you learned that children 3 to 5 years of age often believe that the dead can be brought back to life spontaneously by magic or by giving them food or medical treatment. During which of Piaget's stages of development is a child's cognitive world dominated by egocentrism and magical beliefs?

Reflect *Your Own Personal Journey of Life*

- What is your current attitude about death? Has it changed since you were an adolescent? If so, how?

---

4 Facing One's Own Death

LG4 Explain the psychological aspects involved in facing one's own death and the contexts in which people die.

| Kübler-Ross' Stages of Dying | Perceived Control and Denial | The Contexts in Which People Die |

Sustained and soothed by an unfaltering trust,
approach thy grave,
Like one who wraps the drapery of his couch
About him, and lies down to pleasant dreams.

—WILLIAM CULLEN BRYANT
American Poet, 19th Century

denial and isolation Kübler-Ross' first stage of dying, in which the dying person denies that she or he is really going to die.

anger Kübler-Ross' second stage of dying, in which the dying person's denial gives way to anger, resentment, rage, and envy.

bargaining Kübler-Ross' third stage of dying, in which the dying person develops the hope that death can somehow be postponed.

depression Kübler-Ross' fourth stage of dying, in which the dying person comes to accept the certainty of her or his death. A period of depression or preparatory grief may appear.

Knowledge of death's inevitability permits us to establish priorities and structure our time accordingly. As we age, these priorities and structurings change in recognition of diminishing future time. Values concerning the most important uses of time also change. For example, when asked how they would spend their six remaining months of life, younger adults described such activities as traveling and accomplishing things they previously had not done; older adults described more inner-focused activities—contemplation and meditation, for example (Kalish & Reynolds, 1976).

Most dying individuals want an opportunity to make some decisions regarding their own life and death (Kastenbaum, 2012). Some individuals want to complete unfinished business; they want time to resolve problems and conflicts and to put their affairs in order.

One study examined the concerns of 36 dying individuals from 38 to 92 years of age with a mean age of 68 (Terry & others, 2006). The three areas of concern that consistently appeared were (1) privacy and autonomy, mainly in regard to their families; (2) inadequate information about physical changes and medication as they approached death; (3) the motivation to shorten their life, which was indicated by all patients.

KÜBLER-ROSS' STAGES OF DYING

Might there be a sequence of stages we go through as we face death? Elisabeth Kübler-Ross (1969) divided the behavior and thinking of dying persons into five stages: denial and isolation, anger, bargaining, depression, and acceptance.

Denial and isolation is Kübler-Ross' first stage of dying, in which the person denies that death is really going to take place. The person may say, "No, it can't be me. It's not possible." This is a common reaction to terminal illness. However, denial is usually only a temporary defense. It is eventually replaced with increased awareness when the person is confronted with such matters as financial considerations, unfinished business, and worry about surviving family members.

Anger is Kübler-Ross' second stage of dying, in which the dying person recognizes that denial can no longer be maintained. Denial often gives way to anger, resentment, rage, and envy. The dying person's question is, "Why me?" At this point, the person becomes increasingly difficult to care for as anger may become displaced and projected onto physicians, nurses, family members, and even God. The realization of loss is great, and those who symbolize life, energy, and competent functioning are especially salient targets of the dying person's resentment and jealousy.

Bargaining is Kübler-Ross' third stage of dying, in which the person develops the hope that death can somehow be postponed or delayed. Some persons enter into a bargaining or negotiation—often with God—as they try to delay their death. Psychologically, the person is saying, "Yes, me, but . . ." In exchange for a few more days, weeks, or months of life, the person promises to lead a reformed life dedicated to God or to the service of others.

Depression is Kübler-Ross' fourth stage of dying, in which the dying person comes to accept the certainty of death. At this point, a period of depression or preparatory grief may appear. The dying person may become silent, refuse visitors, and spend much of the time crying or grieving. This behavior is normal and is an effort to disconnect the self from love objects. Attempts to cheer up the dying person at this stage should be discouraged, says Kübler-Ross, because the dying person has a need to contemplate impending death.

Acceptance is Kübler-Ross' fifth stage of dying, in which the person develops a sense of peace, an acceptance of his or her fate, and in many cases, a desire to be left alone. In this stage, feelings and physical pain may be virtually absent. Kübler-Ross describes this fifth stage as the end of the dying struggle, the final resting stage before death. A summary of Kübler-Ross' dying stages is presented in Figure 20.2.

What is the current evaluation of Kübler-Ross' approach? According to Robert Kastenbaum (2009, 2012), there are some problems with Kübler-Ross' approach:

- The existence of the five-stage sequence has not been demonstrated by either Kübler-Ross or independent research.
- The stage interpretation neglected the patients' situations, including relationship support, specific effects of illness, family obligations, and institutional climate in which they were interviewed.

However, Kübler-Ross' pioneering efforts were important in calling attention to those who are attempting to cope with life-threatening illnesses. She did much to encourage attention to the quality of life for dying persons and their families.

Because of the criticisms of Kübler-Ross' stages, some psychologists prefer to describe them not as stages but as potential reactions to dying. At any one moment, a number of emotions may wax and wane. Hope, disbelief, bewilderment, anger, and acceptance may come and go as individuals try to make sense of what is happening to them.

In facing their own death, some individuals struggle until the end, desperately trying to hang on to their lives. Acceptance of death never comes for them. Some psychologists believe that the harder individuals fight to avoid the inevitable death they face and the more they deny it, the more difficulty they will have in dying peacefully and in a dignified way; other psychologists argue that not confronting death until the end may be adaptive for some individuals (Lifton, 1977).

The extent to which people have found meaning and purpose in their lives is linked with how they approach death (Carr, 2009; Park, 2012). One study revealed that individuals with a chronic, life-threatening illness—congestive heart failure—were trying to understand meaning in life (Park & others, 2008). In another study, individuals with less than three months to live who had found purpose and meaning in their lives felt the least despair in the final weeks, whereas dying individuals who saw no reason for living were the most distressed and wanted to hasten death (McClain, Rosenfeld, & Breitbart, 2003). In this and other studies, spirituality helped to buffer dying individuals from severe depression (Smith, McCullough, & Poll, 2003).

Do individuals become more spiritual as they get closer to death? A study of more than 100 patients with advanced congestive heart failure who were studied at two times six months apart found that as the patients perceived they were closer to death, they became more spiritual (Park, 2009).

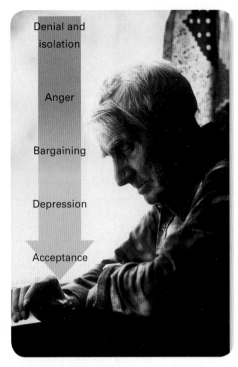

FIGURE 20.2

KÜBLER-ROSS' STAGES OF DYING. According to Elisabeth Kübler-Ross, we go through five stages of dying: denial and isolation, anger, bargaining, depression, and acceptance. *Does everyone go through these stages, and do we go through them in the same order? Explain.*

Man is the only animal that finds his own existence a problem he has to solve and from which he cannot escape. In the same sense man is the only animal who knows he must die.

—ERICH FROMM
American Psychotherapist, 20th Century

developmental **connection**

Religion

Religion can fulfill some important psychological needs in older adults, helping them face impending death and accept the inevitable losses in old age. Chapter 18, p. 590

acceptance Kübler-Ross' fifth stage of dying, in which the dying person develops a sense of peace, an acceptance of her or his fate, and, in many cases, a desire to be left alone.

What are some positive and negative aspects of dying at home compared with dying in a hospital?

PERCEIVED CONTROL AND DENIAL

Perceived control may work as an adaptive strategy for some older adults who face death. When individuals are led to believe they can influence and control events—such as prolonging their lives—they may become more alert and cheerful. Remember from Chapter 17 that giving nursing home residents options for control improved their attitudes and increased their longevity (Rodin & Langer, 1977).

Denial also may be a fruitful way for some individuals to approach death. It can be adaptive or maladaptive. Denial can be used to avoid the destructive impact of shock by delaying the necessity of dealing with one's death. Denial can insulate the individual from having to cope with intense feelings of anger and hurt; however, if denial keeps us from having a life-saving operation, it clearly is maladaptive. Denial is neither good nor bad; its adaptive qualities need to be evaluated on an individual basis.

THE CONTEXTS IN WHICH PEOPLE DIE

For dying individuals, the context in which they die is important (Hooyman & Kiyak, 2011). More than 50 percent of Americans die in hospitals, and nearly 20 percent die in nursing homes. Some people spend their final days in isolation and fear (Clay, 1997). An increasing number of people choose to die in the humane atmosphere of a hospice.

Hospitals offer several important advantages to the dying individual; for example, professional staff members are readily available, and the medical technology present may prolong life. But a hospital may not be the best place for many people to die (Pantilat & Isaac, 2008). Most individuals say they would rather die at home (Jackson & others, 2010; Kalish & Reynolds, 1976). Many feel, however, that they will be a burden at home, that there is limited space there, and that dying at home may alter relationships. Individuals who are facing death also worry about the competency and availability of emergency medical treatment if they remain at home.

Review *Connect* Reflect

 Explain the psychological aspects involved in facing one's own death and the contexts in which people die.

Review

*   What are Kübler-Ross' five stages of dying? What conclusions can be reached about them?
*   What roles do perceived control and denial play in facing one's own death?
*   What are the contexts in which people die?

Connect

*   In this section, you learned that the extent to which people have found meaning and

purpose in their lives is linked with how they approach death. In Chapter 15, what did Roy Baumeister and Kathleen Vohs say are the four main needs for meaning that guide how people try to make sense of their lives?

Reflect *Your Own Personal Journey of Life*

*   How do you think you will psychologically handle facing your own death?

5 Coping with the Death of Someone Else

 Identify ways to cope with the death of another person.

| Communicating with a Dying Person | Grieving | Making Sense of the World | Losing a Life Partner | Forms of Mourning |

Loss can come in many forms in our lives—divorce, a pet's death, loss of a job—but no loss is greater than that which comes through the death of someone we love and care for—a parent, sibling, spouse, relative, or friend. In the ratings of life's stresses that require the most adjustment, death of a spouse is given the highest number. How should we communicate with a dying individual? How do we cope with the death of someone we love?

COMMUNICATING WITH A DYING PERSON

Most psychologists argue that it is best for dying individuals to know that they are dying and that significant others know they are dying so they can interact and communicate with each other on the basis of this mutual knowledge (Banja, 2005). What are some of the advantages of this open awareness for the dying individual? First, dying individuals can close their lives in accord with their own ideas about proper dying. Second, they may be able to complete some plans and projects, can make arrangements for survivors, and can participate in decisions about a funeral and burial. Third, dying individuals have the opportunity to reminisce and to converse with others who have been important in their life. And fourth, individuals who know they are dying have more understanding of what is happening within their bodies and what the medical staff is doing for them (Kalish, 1981).

In addition to keeping communication open, some experts reason that conversation should not focus on mental pathology or preparation for death but should focus on strengths of the individual and preparation for the remainder of life. Since external accomplishments are not possible, communication should be directed toward internal growth. Keep in mind also that important support for a dying individual may come not only from mental health professionals but also from nurses, physicians, a spouse, or intimate friends. In *Connecting Development to Life*, you can read further about effective communication strategies with a dying person.

GRIEVING

Our exploration of grief focuses on dimensions of grieving, the dual-process model of coping with bereavement, and cultural diversity in healthy grieving.

Dimensions of Grieving **Grief** is the emotional numbness, disbelief, separation anxiety, despair, sadness, and loneliness that accompany the loss of someone we love. Grief is not a simple emotional state but rather a complex, evolving process with multiple dimensions (Wakefield, 2012). In this view, pining for the lost person is one important dimension. Pining or yearning reflects an intermittent, recurrent wish or need to recover the lost person. One study revealed that the death of a loved one is most frequently followed by yearning and acceptance, with most of the negative feelings associated with the death diminishing by six months after the death (Maciejewski & others, 2007). In this study, yearning was more common than depression following a loved one's death. Another important dimension of grief is separation anxiety, which not only includes pining and preoccupation with thoughts of the deceased person but also focuses on places and things associated with the deceased, as well as crying or sighing. Grief may also involve despair and sadness, which include a sense of hopelessness and defeat, depressive symptoms, apathy, loss of meaning for activities that used to involve the person who is gone, and growing desolation (Shear & Skritskaya, 2012).

These feelings occur repeatedly shortly after a loss (Shear, 2012a, b). As time passes, pining and protest over the loss tend to diminish, although episodes of depression and apathy may remain or increase. The sense of separation anxiety and loss may continue to the end of one's life, but most of us emerge from grief's tears, turning our attention once again to productive tasks and regaining a more positive view of life. One study of recently widowed men and women revealed that in the course of their bereavement experiencing humor, laughter, and happiness was strongly related to more favorable bereavement adjustment (lower levels of grief and depression) (Lund & others, 2008–2009).

The grieving process is more like a roller-coaster ride than an orderly progression of stages with clear-cut time frames (Lund, 2007). The ups and downs of grief often involve rapidly changing emotions, meeting the challenges of learning new skills, detecting personal weaknesses and limitations, creating new patterns of behavior, and forming new friendships and relationships (Feldon, 2003). For most individuals, grief becomes more manageable over time,

> Everyone can master grief but he who has it.
>
> **—William Shakespeare**
> *English Playwright, 17th Century*

grief The emotional numbness, disbelief, separation anxiety, despair, sadness, and loneliness that accompany the loss of someone we love.

Effective Strategies for Communicating with a Dying Person

Effective strategies for communicating with a dying person include the following suggestions:

- Establish your presence, be at the same eye level; don't be afraid to touch the dying person—dying individuals are often starved for human touch.
- Eliminate distraction—for example, ask if it is okay to turn off the TV. Realize that excessive small talk can be a distraction.
- Dying individuals who are very frail often have little energy. If the dying person you are visiting is very frail, you may not want to visit for very long.
- Don't insist that the dying person feel acceptance about death if the dying person wants to deny the reality of the situation; on the other hand, don't insist on denial if the dying individual indicates acceptance.
- Allow the dying person to express guilt or anger; encourage the expression of feelings.
- Don't be afraid to ask the person what the expected outcome for the illness is. Discuss alternatives and unfinished business.
- Sometimes dying individuals don't have access to other people. Ask the dying person if there is anyone he or she would like to see that you can contact.
- Encourage the dying individual to reminisce, especially if you have memories in common.

What are some good strategies for communicating with a dying person?

- Talk with the individual when she or he wishes to talk. If this is impossible, make an appointment and keep it.
- Express your regard for the dying individual. Don't be afraid to express love, and don't be afraid to say good-bye.

---

with fewer abrupt highs and lows. But many grieving spouses report that even though time has brought some healing, they have never gotten over their loss. They have just learned to live with it.

Cognitive factors are involved in the severity of grief after a loved one has died. One study focused on adults who had suffered the loss of a first-degree relative (parent, child, or sibling) (Boelen, van den Bout, & van den Hout, 2003). The more negative beliefs and self-blame the adults had, the more severe were their symptoms of traumatic grief, depression, and anxiety.

Long-term grief is sometimes masked and can predispose individuals to become depressed and even suicidal (Miller, 2012). Good family communication can help reduce the incidence of depression and suicidal thoughts. An estimated 80 to 90 percent of survivors experience normal or uncomplicated grief reactions that include sadness and even disbelief or considerable anguish. By six months after their loss, they accept it as a reality, are more optimistic about the future, and function competently in their everyday lives.

However, six months after their loss, approximately 10 to 20 percent of survivors have difficulty moving on with their life, feel numb or detached, believe their life is empty without the deceased, and feel that the future has no meaning. This type of grief that involves enduring despair that is still unresolved over an extended period of time has been labeled complicated grief or **prolonged grief disorder** by Holly Prigerson and her colleagues (2011). Complicated or prolonged grief usually has negative consequences for physical and mental health (Greer & others, 2011; Wetherell, 2012). A person who loses someone he or she was emotionally dependent on is often at greatest risk for developing prolonged grief (Rodriquez Villar & others, 2012). Complicated grief or prolonged grief disorder is now being considered

prolonged grief disorder Grief that involves enduring despair and remains unresolved over an extended period of time.

for possible inclusion in DSM-V, the psychiatric classification system of mental health disorders (Bryant, 2012; Pies, 2012; Shear, 2012a, b).

Recently, there has been a substantial increase in research on complicated or prolonged grief (Shear, 2012a, b). The following studies provide further information about this topic:

- Prolonged grief was more likely to occur when individuals had lost their spouse, lost a loved one unexpectedly, or spent time with the deceased every day in the last week of the person's life (Fujisawa & others, 2010).
- Adults with depression were more likely to also have complicated grief (Sung & others, 2011).
- Complicated grief was more likely to be present in older adults when the grief was in response to the death of a child or a spouse (Newsom & others, 2011).

Another type of grief is *disenfranchised grief,* which describes an individual's grief over a deceased person that is a socially ambiguous loss that can't be openly mourned or supported (Spidell & others, 2011). Examples of disenfranchised grief include a relationship that isn't socially recognized such as an ex-spouse, a hidden loss such as an abortion, and circumstances of the death that are stigmatized such as death because of AIDS. Disenfranchised grief may intensify an individual's grief because the feelings cannot be publicly acknowledged. This type of grief may be hidden or repressed for many years, only to be reawakened by later deaths.

What are some different types of grief?

Dual-Process Model of Coping with Bereavement
The **dual-process model** of coping with bereavement has two main dimensions: (1) loss-oriented stressors, and (2) restoration-oriented stressors (Stroebe & Schut, 2010; Stroebe, Schut, & Boerner, 2010). Loss-oriented stressors focus on the deceased individual and can include grief work and both positive and negative reappraisals of the loss. A positive reappraisal of the loss might include acknowledging that death brought relief at the end of suffering, whereas a negative reappraisal might involve yearning for the loved one and ruminating about the death. Restoration-oriented stressors involve the secondary stressors that emerge as indirect outcomes of bereavement. They can include a changing identity (such as from "wife" to "widow") and mastering skills (such as dealing with finances). Restoration rebuilds "shattered assumptions about the world and one's own place in it."

In the dual-process model, effective coping with bereavement often involves an oscillation between coping with loss and coping with restoration (Bennett, 2009; Shear, 2010). Earlier models often emphasized a sequence of coping with loss through such strategies as grief work as an initial phase, followed by restoration efforts. However, in the dual-process model, coping with loss and engaging in restoration can be carried out concurrently (Richardson, 2007). According to this model, the person coping with death might be involved in grief group therapy while settling the affairs of the loved one. Oscillation might occur in the short term during a particular day as well as across weeks, months, and even years. Although loss and restoration coping can occur concurrently, over time there often is an initial emphasis on coping with loss followed by greater emphasis on restoration (Milberg & others, 2008).

Coping and Type of Death
The impact of death on surviving individuals is strongly influenced by the circumstances under which the death occurs (Gold, 2011; Kristensen, Weisaeth, & Heir, 2012). Deaths that are sudden, untimely, violent, or traumatic are likely to have more intense and prolonged effects on surviving individuals and make the coping process more difficult for them (Maercker & Laior, 2012). Such deaths often are accompanied by posttraumatic stress disorder (PTSD) symptoms, such as intrusive thoughts, flashbacks, nightmares, sleep disturbance, problems in concentrating, and others (Nakajima & others, 2012). Death of a child can be especially devastating and extremely difficult for parents to cope with (Caeymaex & others, 2012; Lang & others, 2011).

Cultural Diversity in Healthy Grieving
Some approaches to grieving emphasize the importance of breaking bonds with the deceased and returning to autonomous lifestyles. People who persist in holding on to the deceased are believed to be in need of therapy.

dual-process model A model of coping with bereavement that emphasizes oscillation between two dimensions: (1) loss-oriented stressors, and (2) restoration-oriented stressors.

How might grieving vary across individuals and cultures?

These restaurant workers, who lost their jobs on 9/11/01, have made a bittersweet return by establishing a New York restaurant they call their own. Colors, named for the many nationalities and ethnic groups among its owners, is believed to be the city's first cooperative restaurant. World-famous restaurant Windows on the World was destroyed and 73 workers killed when the Twin Towers were destroyed by terrorists. The former Windows survivors at the new venture planned to split 60 percent of the profits between themselves and to donate the rest to a fund to open other cooperative restaurants.

developmental **connection**

Stress

Meaning-making coping involves drawing on beliefs, values, and goals to change the meaning of a stressful situation, especially in times of chronic stress such as when a loved one dies. Chapter 15, p. 503

However, some doubt has been cast on whether this recommendation is always the best therapeutic advice (Reisman, 2001).

Analyses of non-Western cultures suggest that beliefs about continuing bonds with the deceased vary extensively. Maintenance of ties with the deceased is accepted and sustained in the religious rituals of Japan. Among the Hopi of Arizona, the deceased are forgotten as quickly as possible and life is carried on as usual. Their funeral ritual concludes with a break-off between mortals and spirits. The diversity of grieving is nowhere more clear than in two Muslim societies—one in Egypt, the other in Bali. In Egypt, the bereaved are encouraged to dwell at length on their grief, surrounded by others who relate similarly tragic accounts and express their own sorrow. By contrast, in Bali, the bereaved are encouraged to laugh and be joyful.

Consider also the responses of parents whose sons died in two Israeli wars, 13 and 4 years earlier (Rubin & Malkinson, 2001; Schuchter & Zisook, 1993). Even many years after the death of their sons, the Israeli parents showed a strong involvement with them. They idealized the lost sons in ways that were not present in the descriptions by a control group of parents of sons who had recently left home.

In sum, people grieve in a variety of ways (Shear, 2012a, b). The diverse grieving patterns are culturally embedded practices. Thus, there is no one right, ideal way to grieve. There are many different ways to feel about a deceased person and no set series of stages that the bereaved must pass through to become well adjusted. The stoic widower may need to cry out over his loss at times. The weeping widow may need to put her husband's wishes aside as she becomes the financial manager of her estate. What is needed is an understanding that healthy coping with the death of a loved one involves growth, flexibility, and appropriateness within a cultural context.

MAKING SENSE OF THE WORLD

Not only do many individuals who face death search for meaning in life, so do many bereaved individuals (Carr, 2009; Park, 2010, 2012). One beneficial aspect of grieving is that it can stimulate people to try to make sense of their world (Kalish, 1981). A common occurrence is to go over again and again all of the events that led up to the death. In the days and weeks after the death, the closest family members share experiences with each other, sometimes reminiscing over family experiences. In one study, women who became widowed in midlife were challenged by the crisis of their husband's death to examine meaningful directions for their lives (Danforth & Glass, 2001). Another study found that mourners who expressed positive themes of hope showed better adjustment than those who focused on negative themes of pain and suffering (Gamino & Sewell, 2004). And one study revealed that finding meaning in the death of a spouse was linked to a lower level of anger during bereavement (Kim, 2009).

When a death is caused by an accident or a disaster, the effort to make sense of it is pursued more vigorously. As added pieces of news come trickling in, they are integrated into the puzzle. The bereaved want to put the death into a perspective that they can understand—divine intervention, a curse from a neighboring tribe, a logical sequence of cause and effect, or whatever it may be. A study of more than 1,000 college students found that making sense was an important factor in their grieving of a violent loss by accident, homicide, or suicide (Currier, Holland, & Neimeyer, 2006).

LOSING A LIFE PARTNER

In 2009 in the United States, 13 percent of men and 41 percent of women age 65 and older were widowed (U.S. Census Bureau, 2011). Those left behind after the death of an intimate

What Are Some Connections Between Marital Status and Length of Widowhood and Health in Women?

One three-year longitudinal study of more than 130,000 women aged 50 to 79 years in the United States as part of the Women's Health Initiative examined the relation of widowhood to physical and mental health, health behaviors, and health outcomes (Wilcox & others, 2003). Women were categorized as (1) remaining married, (2) transitioning from married to widowed, (3) remaining widowed, and (4) transitioning from widowed to married. Widows were further subdivided into the recently widowed (widowed for less than one year) and longer-term widowed (widowed for more than one year).

The measures used to assess the older women's health were:

- *Physical health.* Blood pressure was assessed after five minutes of quiet rest using the average of two readings with 30 seconds between the readings. Hypertension was defined as more than 140/90. Body mass index (BMI) was calculated and used to determine whether a woman was obese. A health survey assessed physical function and health status.
- *Mental health.* Depressive symptoms were assessed using a six-item depression scale, with participants rating the frequency of their depressed thoughts during the past week. The participants' self-report of antidepressant medicine use was also obtained. Information about social functioning and mental health was based on participants' responses on the Social Functioning Scale (Ware, Kosinski, & Dewey, 2000).

- *Health behaviors.* Dietary behaviors were assessed with a modified version of the National Cancer Institute—Health Habits and History Questionnaire. Participants also were asked if they smoked tobacco, and if so, how much. To assess physical activity, participants were asked how often they walked outside the home each week and the extent to which they engaged in strenuous or moderate exercise. To assess health care use, they were asked whether they had visited their doctor in the past year.
- *Health outcomes.* Cardiovascular disease and cancer occurrences were assessed annually and any overnight hospitalizations were noted.

At the beginning of the three-year study, married women reported better physical and mental health, and better health in general, than widowed women. Women who remained married over the three-year period of the study showed stability in mental health, recent widows experienced marked impairments in mental health, and longer-term widows showed stability or slight improvements in mental health. Both groups of widows (recent and longer-term) reported more unintentional weight loss across the three years.

The findings underscore the resilience of older women and their capacity to reestablish connections but also point to the need for services that strengthen social support for those who have difficulty making the transition from marriage to widowhood.

partner often suffer profound grief and may endure financial loss, loneliness, increased physical illness, and psychological disorders, including depression (Holm & Severinsson, 2012). A recent study of widowed individuals 75 years and older found that loss of a spouse increases the likelihood of psychiatric visits and an earlier death (Moller & others, 2011).

Surviving spouses seek to cope with the loss of their spouse in various ways (Hahn & others, 2011; Park, 2012). In one study, widowed individuals were more likely to intensify their religious and spiritual beliefs following the death of a spouse, and this increase was linked with a lower level of grief (Brown & others, 2004). Another study revealed that finding meaning in the death of a spouse was linked to a lower level of anger during bereavement (Kim, 2009).

Many widows are lonely and benefit considerably from social support (Ben-Zur, 2012; Utz, Caserta, & Lund, 2012). The poorer and less educated they are, the lonelier they tend to be. The bereaved are also at increased risk for many health problems (Mechakra-Tahiri & others, 2010). How might you expect widowhood to affect a woman's physical and mental health, for instance? The *Connecting Through Research* interlude above examines how researchers have investigated the links between bereavement and health.

Optimal adjustment after a death depends on several factors. Women do better than men largely because in our society women are responsible for the emotional life of a couple, whereas men usually manage the finances and material goods (Fry, 2001). Thus, women have better networks of friends, closer relationships with relatives, and experience in taking care

A widow with the urn containing the remains of her husband, who was killed while working in Iraq. *What are some factors that are related to the adjustment of a widow after the death of her husband?*

developmental **connection**

Community and Culture

For older adults, social support is linked with a reduction in the symptoms of disease and mortality. Chapter 19, p. 611

of themselves psychologically (Antonucci, Birditt, & Ajrouch, 2013; Taylor, 2011a, b, c). Older widows do better than younger widows, perhaps because the death of a partner is more expected for older women. For their part, widowers usually have more money than widows do, and they are much more likely to remarry. However, a recent study of older adults revealed that widowhood was linked to a higher risk of depression in men than in women (Mechakra-Tahiri & others, 2010).

For both widows and widowers, social support helps them adjust to the death of a spouse (Antonucci, Birditt, & Ajrouch, 2013). The Widow-to-Widow program, begun in the 1960s, provides support for newly widowed women. Volunteer widows reach out to other widows, introducing them to others who may have similar problems, leading group discussions, and organizing social activities. The program has been adopted by the American Association of Retired Persons and disseminated throughout the United States as the Widowed Persons Service. The model has since been adopted by numerous community organizations to provide support for those going through a difficult transition. Other widow support groups also are often beneficial in reducing bereaved spouses' depression (Maruyama & Atencio, 2008).

Researchers have found that religiosity and coping skills are related to well-being following the loss of a spouse in late adulthood (Leighton, 2008). Further, one study revealed that compared with continually married counterparts, adults aged 50 and older who experienced the death of a spouse reported a higher participation in volunteer work several years after the death (Li, 2007). The volunteer work helped to protect the spouses from depressive symptoms, and an increase in volunteer hours enhanced their self-efficacy. Another study also found that when older adults helped others following the death of a spouse, they experienced an accelerated decline in depressive symptoms (Brown & others, 2008).

FORMS OF MOURNING

One decision facing the bereaved is what to do with the body. In the United States, in 2007, 66 percent of corpses were disposed of by burial, 34 percent by cremation—a significant increase from a cremation rate of 15 percent in 1985 (Cremation Association of North America, 2012). Projections indicate that by 2015, 44 percent of corpses will be cremated (Cremation Association of North America, 2012). Cremation is more popular in the Pacific region of the United States, less popular in the South. Cremation also is more popular in Canada than in the United States and most popular of all in Japan and many other Asian countries.

The funeral is an important aspect of mourning in many cultures. In one study, bereaved individuals who were personally religious derived more psychological benefits from a funeral,

developmental **connection**

Religion

Religious participation is positively linked to health and longevity. Chapter 15, p. 502

(*Left*) A widow leading a funeral procession in the United States. (*Right*) A crowd gathered at a cremation ceremony in Bali, Indonesia, balancing decorative containers on their heads.

participated more actively in the rituals, and adjusted more positively to the loss (Hayslip, Edmondson, & Guarnaccia, 1999). In the United States, the trend is away from public funerals and displaying the dead body in an open casket and toward private funerals followed by a memorial ceremony (Callahan, 2009).

The funeral industry has been the source of controversy in recent years. Funeral directors and their supporters argue that the funeral provides a form of closure to the relationship with the deceased, especially when there is an open casket. Their critics claim that funeral directors are just trying to make money and that embalming is grotesque. One way to avoid being exploited during bereavement is to purchase funeral arrangements in advance. However, in one survey only 24 percent of individuals 60 and over had made any funeral arrangements (Kalish & Reynolds, 1976).

In some cultures, a ceremonial meal is held after a death; in others, a black armband is worn for one year following a death. Cultures vary in how they practice mourning. Two of those cultures are the Amish and traditional Judaism (Worthington, 1989).

The Amish are a conservative group with approximately 80,000 members in the United States, Ontario, and several small settlements in South and Central America. The Amish live in a family-oriented society in which family and community support are essential for survival. Today, they live at the same unhurried pace as that of their ancestors, using horses instead of cars and facing death with the same steadfast faith as their forebears. At the time of death, close neighbors assume the responsibility of notifying others of the death. The Amish community handles virtually all aspects of the funeral.

The funeral service is held in a barn in the warmer months and in a house during colder months. Calm acceptance of death, influenced by a deep religious faith, is an integral part of the Amish culture. Following the funeral, a high level of support is given to the bereaved family for at least a year. Visits to the family, special scrapbooks and handmade items for the family, new work projects started for the widow, and quilting days that combine fellowship and productivity are among the supports given to the bereaved family. A profound example of the Amish culture's religious faith and acceptance of death occurred after Charles Roberts shot and killed five Amish schoolgirls and then apparently took his own life in October 2006 in Bart Township, Pennsylvania. Soon after the murders and suicide, members of the Amish community visited his widow and offered their support and forgiveness.

The family and community also have specific and important roles in mourning in traditional Judaism. The program of mourning is divided into graduated time periods, each with its appropriate practices. The observance of these practices is required of the spouse and the immediate blood relatives of the deceased. The first period is aninut, the period between death and burial. The next two periods make up avelut, or mourning proper. The first of these is shivah, a period of seven days, which commences with the burial. It is followed by sheloshim, the 30-day period following the burial, including shivah. At the end of sheloshim, the mourning process is considered over for all but one's parents. For parents, mourning continues for 11 months, although observances are minimal.

The seven-day period of the shivah is especially important in traditional Judaism. The mourners, sitting together as a group through an extended period, have an opportunity to project their feelings to the group as a whole. Visits from others during shivah may help the mourner deal with feelings of guilt. After shivah, the mourner is encouraged to resume normal social interaction. In fact, it is customary for the mourners to walk together a short distance as a symbol of their return to society. In its entirety, the elaborate mourning system of traditional Judaism is designed to promote personal growth and to reintegrate the individual into the community.

(*Top*) A funeral procession of horse-drawn buggies on their way to the burial of five young Amish girls who were murdered in October 2006. A remarkable aspect of their mourning involved the outpouring of support and forgiveness they gave to the widow of the murderer. (*Bottom*) Meeting in a Jewish graveyard.

Review

- What are some strategies for communicating with a dying person?
- What is the nature of grieving?
- How is making sense of the world a beneficial outcome of grieving?
- What are some characteristics and outcomes of losing a life partner?
- What are some forms of mourning? What is the nature of the funeral?

Connect

- In this section, we learned that one advantage of knowing you are dying is

that you have the opportunity to reminisce. Which of Erikson's stages of development involves reflecting on the past and either piecing together a positive review or concluding that one's life has not been well spent?

Reflect *Your Own Personal Journey of Life*

- What are considered appropriate forms of mourning in the culture in which you live?

---

topical **connections**

We have arrived at the end of this book. I hope this book and course have been a window to the life span of the human species and a window to your own personal journey in life.

Our study of the human life span has been long and complex. You have read about many physical, cognitive, and socioemotional changes that take place from conception through death. This is a good time to reflect on what you have learned. Which theories, studies, and ideas were especially interesting to you? What did you learn about your own development?

I wish you all the best in the remaining years of your journey through the human life span.

looking forward ---►

---

reach your **learning goals**

Death, Dying, and Grieving

1 The Death System and Cultural Contexts

LG1 Describe the death system and its cultural and historical contexts.

The Death System and Its Cultural Variations

- In Kastenbaum's view, every culture has a death system that involves these components: people, places, times, and objects and symbols. Most cultures do not view death as the end of existence—spiritual life is thought to continue. Most societies throughout history have had philosophical or religious beliefs about death, and most societies have rituals that deal with death. The United States has been described as more of a death-denying and death-avoiding culture than most cultures.

| Changing Historical Circumstances | | • When, where, and why people die have changed historically. Today, death occurs most often among older adults. More than 80 percent of all deaths in the United States now occur in a hospital or other institution; our exposure to death in the family has been minimized. |

2 Defining Death and Life/Death Issues

 LG2 Evaluate issues in determining death and decisions regarding death.

Issues in Determining Death

• Twenty-five years ago, determining whether someone was dead was simpler than it is today. Brain death is a neurological definition of death, which states that a person is brain dead when all electrical activity of the brain has ceased for a specified period of time. Medical experts debate whether this should mean the higher and lower brain functions or just the higher cortical functions. Currently, most physicians define brain death as the death of both the higher cortical functions and the lower brain stem functions.

Decisions Regarding Life, Death, and Health Care

• Decisions regarding life, death, and health care can involve whether to create a living will, to consider the possibility of euthanasia, and to arrange for hospice care. Living wills and advance directives are increasingly used. Euthanasia ("mercy killing") is the act of painlessly ending the life of a person who is suffering from an incurable disease or disability. Distinctions are made between active and passive euthanasia. Hospice care emphasizes reducing pain and suffering rather than prolonging life.

3 A Developmental Perspective on Death

 LG3 Discuss death and attitudes about it at different points in development.

Causes of Death

• Although death is more likely to occur in late adulthood, death can come at any point in development. In children and younger adults, death is more likely to occur because of accidents or illness; in older adults, death is more likely to occur because of chronic diseases such as heart disease or cancer.

Attitudes Toward Death at Different Points in the Life Span

• Infants do not have a concept of death. Preschool children also have little concept of death. Preschool children sometimes blame themselves for a person's death. In the elementary school years, children develop a more realistic orientation toward death. Most psychologists argue that honesty is the best strategy for helping children cope with death. Death may be glossed over in adolescence. Adolescents have more abstract, philosophical views of death than children do. Recent research indicates that rather than perceiving themselves as invulnerable, many adolescents believe they are likely to experience an early death. There is no evidence that a special orientation toward death emerges in early adulthood. Middle adulthood is a time when adults show a heightened consciousness about death and death anxiety. Older adults often show less death anxiety than middle-aged adults, but older adults experience and converse about death more. Attitudes about death may vary considerably among adults of any age.

4 Facing One's Own Death

 LG4 Explain the psychological aspects involved in facing one's own death and the contexts in which people die.

Kubler-Ross' Stages of Dying

• Kübler-Ross proposed five stages of dying: denial and isolation, anger, bargaining, depression, and acceptance. Not all individuals go through the same sequence.

Perceived Control and Denial

• Perceived control and denial may work together as an adaptive orientation for the dying individual. Denial can be adaptive or maladaptive, depending on the circumstances.

The Contexts in Which People Die

• The fact that most deaths in the United States occur in hospitals has advantages and disadvantages. Most individuals say they would rather die at home, but they worry that they will be a burden and they worry about the lack of medical care.

5 Coping with the Death of Someone Else

 LG5 Identify ways to cope with the death of another person.

Communicating with a Dying Person

• Most psychologists recommend an open communication system with the dying. Communication should not dwell on mental pathology or preparation for death but should emphasize the dying person's strengths.

Grieving	
	• Grief is the emotional numbness, disbelief, separation anxiety, despair, sadness, and loneliness that accompany the loss of someone we love. Grief is multidimensional and in some cases may last for years. Prolonged grief involves enduring despair and is still unresolved after an extended period of time. In the dual-process model of coping with bereavement, oscillation occurs between two dimensions: (1) loss-oriented stressors, and (2) restoration-oriented stressors. Grief and coping vary with the type of death. There are cultural variations in grieving.
Making Sense of the World	• The grieving process may stimulate individuals to strive to make sense out of their world. When a death is caused by an accident or disaster, the effort to make sense of it is pursued more vigorously.
Losing a Life Partner	• The death of an intimate partner often leads to profound grief. The bereaved are at risk for many health problems, although there are variations in the distress experienced by a surviving spouse. Social support benefits widows and widowers.
Forms of Mourning	• Forms of mourning vary across cultures. Approximately two-thirds of corpses are disposed of by burial, one-third by cremation. An important aspect of mourning in many cultures is the funeral. In recent years, the funeral industry has been the focus of controversy. In some cultures, a ceremonial meal is held after death.

key terms

brain death 626
euthanasia 627
passive euthanasia 627
active euthanasia 627

hospice 628
palliative care 628
denial and isolation 632
anger 632

bargaining 632
depression 632
acceptance 633
grief 635

prolonged grief disorder 636
dual-process model 637

key people

Robert Kastenbaum 624

Elisabeth Kübler-Ross 632

Holly Prigerson 636

Chapter 20 | DEATH, DYING, AND GRIEVING

Connecting with McGraw Hill **connect**®

Learning Objectives	Application Activities	Activity Type	Page Reference
Evaluate decisions regarding life, death, and health care.	On Dying at Age 72	Video	pp. 626–629
Discuss attitudes about death at different points in the life span.	Life-span Perspectives on Death and Dying Fear of Dying at Age 72	Milestones: Transitions Video	pp. 630–632

glossary

A

acceptance   Kübler-Ross' fifth stage of dying, in which the dying person develops a sense of peace, an acceptance of her or his fate, and, in many cases, a desire to be left alone.

accommodation   Piagetian concept of adjusting schemes to fit new information and experiences.

active euthanasia   Death induced deliberately, as by injecting a lethal dose of a drug.

active (niche-picking) genotype-environment correlations   Correlations that exist when children seek out environments they find compatible and stimulating.

activity theory   The theory that the more active and involved older adults are, the more likely they are to be satisfied with their lives.

addiction   A pattern of behavior characterized by an overwhelming involvement with using a drug and securing its supply.

adolescent egocentrism   The heightened self-consciousness of adolescents.

adoption study   A study in which investigators seek to discover whether, in behavior and psychological characteristics, adopted children are more like their adoptive parents, who provided a home environment, or more like their biological parents, who contributed their heredity. Another form of the adoption study is to compare adoptive and biological siblings.

aerobic exercise   Sustained exercise (such as jogging, swimming, or cycling) that stimulates heart and lung activity.

affectionate love   In this type of love, also called companionate love, an individual desires to have the other person near and has a deep, caring affection for the other person.

affordances   Opportunities for interaction offered by objects that fit within our capabilities to perform functional activities.

afterbirth   The third stage of birth, when the placenta, umbilical cord, and other membranes are detached and expelled.

ageism   Prejudice against others because of their age, especially prejudice against older adults.

Alzheimer disease   A progressive, irreversible brain disorder characterized by a gradual deterioration of memory, reasoning, language, and eventually physical function.

amnion   The life-support system that is a bag or envelope that contains a clear fluid in which the developing embryo floats.

amygdala   The region of the brain that is the seat of emotions.

androgyny   The presence of positive masculine and feminine characteristics in the same individual.

anger   Kübler-Ross' second stage of dying, in which the dying person's denial gives way to anger, resentment, rage, and envy.

anger cry   A variation of the basic cry, with more excess air forced through the vocal cords.

animism   The belief that inanimate objects have life-like qualities and are capable of action.

anorexia nervosa   An eating disorder that involves the relentless pursuit of thinness through starvation.

A-not-B error   Error that occurs when infants make the mistake of selecting the familiar hiding place (A) rather than the new hiding place (B) as they progress into substage 4 in Piaget's sensorimotor stage; also called $A\bar{B}$ error.

anxious attachment style   An attachment style that describes adults who demand closeness, are less trusting, and are more emotional, jealous, and possessive.

Apgar Scale   A widely used method to assess the health of newborns at one and five minutes after birth. The Apgar Scale evaluates an infant's heart rate, respiratory effort, muscle tone, body color, and reflex irritability.

aphasia   A loss or impairment of language ability caused by brain damage.

arthritis   Inflammation of the joints that is accompanied by pain, stiffness, and movement problems; especially common in older adults.

Asperger syndrome   A relatively mild autism spectrum disorder in which the child has relatively good verbal language, milder nonverbal language problems, and a restricted range of interests and relationships.

assimilation   Piagetian concept of using existing schemes to deal with new information or experiences.

attachment   A close emotional bond between two people.

attention   The focusing of mental resources on select information.

attention deficit hyperactivity disorder (ADHD)   A disability in which children consistently show one or more of the following characteristics: (1) inattention, (2) hyperactivity, and (3) impulsivity.

authoritarian parenting   A restrictive, punitive style in which parents exhort the child to follow their directions and to respect their work and effort. The authoritarian parent places firm limits and controls on the child and allows little verbal exchange. Authoritarian parenting is associated with children's social incompetence.

authoritative parenting   A parenting style in which parents encourage their children to be independent but still place limits and controls on their actions. Extensive verbal give-and-take is allowed, and parents are warm and nurturant toward the child. Authoritative parenting is associated with children's social competence.

autism spectrum disorders (ASD)   Also called pervasive developmental disorders, they range from the severe disorder labeled autistic disorder to the milder disorder called Asperger syndrome. Children with these disorders are characterized by problems in social interaction, verbal and nonverbal communication, and repetitive behaviors.

autistic disorder   A severe autism spectrum disorder that has its onset in the first three years of life and includes deficiencies in social relationships, abnormalities in communication, and restricted, repetitive, and stereotyped patterns of behavior.

autonomous morality   In Piaget's theory, displayed by older children (about 10 years of age and older). The child becomes aware that rules and laws are created by people and that in judging an action one should consider the actor's intentions as well as the consequences.

average children   Children who receive an average number of both positive and negative nominations from peers.

avoidant attachment style   An attachment style that describes adults who are hesitant about getting involved in romantic relationships and once in a relationship tend to distance themselves from their partner.

B

bargaining   Kübler-Ross' third stage of dying, in which the dying person develops the hope that death can somehow be postponed.

basic cry   A rhythmic pattern usually consisting of a cry, a briefer silence, a shorter inspiratory whistle that is higher pitched than the main cry, and then a brief rest before the next cry.

Bayley Scales of Infant Development   Scales developed by Nancy Bayley that are widely used in the assessment of infant development. The current version has three components: a mental scale, a motor scale, and an infant behavior profile.

behavior genetics   The field that seeks to discover the influence of heredity and environment on individual differences in human traits and development.

Big Five factors of personality Emotional stability (neuroticism), extraversion, openness to experience, agreeableness, and conscientiousness.

biological processes Changes in an individual's physical nature.

blastocyst The inner layer of cells that develops during the germinal period. These cells later develop into the embryo.

bonding The formation of a close connection, especially a physical bond, between parents and their newborn in the period shortly after birth.

brain death A neurological definition of death. A person is brain dead when all electrical activity of the brain has ceased for a specified period of time. A flat EEG recording is one criterion of brain death.

brainstorming A technique in which individuals are encouraged to come up with creative ideas in a group, play off each other's ideas, and say practically whatever comes to mind.

Brazelton Neonatal Behavioral Assessment Scale (NBAS) A measure that is used in the first month of life to assess the newborn's neurological development, reflexes, and reactions to people and objects.

breech position The baby's position in the uterus that causes the buttocks to be the first part to emerge from the vagina.

Broca's area An area in the brain's left frontal lobe that is involved in speech production.

Bronfenbrenner's ecological theory Bronfenbrenner's environmental systems theory that focuses on five environmental systems: microsystem, mesosystem, exosystem, macrosystem, and chronosystem.

bulimia nervosa An eating disorder in which the individual consistently follows a binge-and-purge pattern.

C

care perspective The moral perspective of Carol Gilligan, which views people in terms of their connectedness with others and emphasizes interpersonal communication, relationships with others, and concern for others.

case study An in-depth look at a single individual.

cataracts A thickening of the lens of the eye that causes vision to become cloudy, opaque, and distorted.

cellular clock theory Leonard Hayflick's theory that the maximum number of times that human cells can divide is about 75 to 80. As we age, our cells have less capability to divide.

centration The focusing of attention on one characteristic to the exclusion of all others.

cephalocaudal pattern The sequence in which the earliest growth always occurs at the top—the head—with physical growth in size, weight, and feature differentiation gradually working from top to bottom.

cesarean delivery The baby is removed from the mother's uterus through an incision made in her abdomen.

child-centered kindergarten Education that involves the whole child by considering both the child's physical, cognitive, and socioemotional development and the child's needs, interests, and learning styles.

child-directed speech Language spoken in a higher pitch than normal with simple words and sentences.

chromosomes Threadlike structures that come in 23 pairs, one member of each pair coming from each parent. Chromosomes contain the genetic substance DNA.

chronic disorders Disorders that are characterized by slow onset and long duration. They are rare in early adulthood, they increase during middle adulthood, and they become common in late adulthood.

climacteric The midlife transition in which fertility declines.

clique A small group that ranges from 2 to about 12 individuals, averaging about 5 to 6 individuals, and can form because adolescents engage in similar activities.

cognitive mechanics The "hardware" of the mind, reflecting the neurophysiological architecture of the brain. Cognitive mechanics involve the speed and accuracy of the processes involving sensory input, visual and motor memory, discrimination, comparison, and categorization.

cognitive pragmatics The culture-based "software programs" of the mind. Cognitive pragmatics include reading and writing skills, language comprehension, educational qualifications, professional skills, and also the type of knowledge about the self and life skills that help us to master or cope with life.

cognitive processes Changes in an individual's thought, intelligence, and language.

cohort effects Effects due to a person's time of birth, era, or generation but not to actual age.

commitment Marcia's term for the part of identity development in which adolescents show a personal investment in identity.

conscience An internal regulation of standards of right and wrong that involves an integration of moral thought, feeling, and behavior.

consensual validation An explanation of why individuals are attracted to people who are similar to them. Our own attitudes and behavior are supported and validated when someone else's attitudes and behavior are similar to our own.

conservation In Piaget's theory, awareness that altering an object's or a substance's appearance does not change its basic properties.

constructive play Play that combines sensorimotor and repetitive activity with symbolic representation of ideas. Constructive play occurs when children engage in self-regulated creation or construction of a product or a solution.

constructivist approach A learner-centered approach that emphasizes the importance of individuals actively constructing their knowledge and understanding with guidance from the teacher.

contemporary life-events approach Approach emphasizing that how a life event influences the individual's development depends not only on the life event, but also on mediating factors, the individual's adaptation to the life event, the life-stage context, and the sociohistorical context.

continuity-discontinuity issue Focuses on the extent to which development involves gradual, cumulative change (continuity) or distinct stages (discontinuity).

controversial children Children who are frequently nominated both as a best friend and as being disliked.

conventional reasoning The second, or intermediate, level in Kohlberg's theory of moral development. At this level, individuals abide by certain standards but they are the standards of others such as parents or the laws of society.

convergent thinking Thinking that produces one correct answer and is characteristic of the kind of thinking tested by standardized intelligence tests.

convoy model of social relations Model in which individuals go through life embedded in a personal network of individuals to whom they give and from whom they receive support.

coordination of secondary circular reactions Piaget's fourth sensorimotor substage, which develops between 8 and 12 months of age. Actions become more outwardly directed, and infants coordinate schemes and act with intentionality.

core knowledge approach States that infants are born with domain-specific innate knowledge systems.

corpus callosum The location where fibers connect the brain's left and right hemispheres.

correlation coefficient A number based on statistical analysis that is used to describe the degree of association between two variables.

correlational research The goal is to describe the strength of the relationship between two or more events or characteristics.

creative thinking The ability to think in novel and unusual ways and to come up with unique solutions to problems.

crisis Marcia's term for a period of identity development during which the adolescent is exploring alternatives.

critical thinking Thinking reflectively and productively, as well as evaluating the evidence.

cross-cultural studies Comparison of one culture with one or more other cultures. These provide information about the degree to which development is similar, or universal, across cultures, and the degree to which it is culture-specific.

cross-sectional approach   A research strategy in which individuals of different ages are compared at one time.

crowd   A crowd is a larger group structure than a clique and is usually formed based on reputation; members may or may not spend much time together.

crystallized intelligence   Accumulated information and verbal skills, which increase in middle adulthood, according to Horn.

cultural-familial retardation   Retardation that is characterized by no evidence of organic brain damage, but the individual's IQ is generally between 50 and 70.

culture   The behavior patterns, beliefs, and all other products of a group that are passed on from generation to generation.

culture-fair tests   Tests of intelligence that are designed to be free of cultural bias.

D

date or acquaintance rape   Coercive sexual activity directed at someone with whom the perpetrator is at least casually acquainted.

deferred imitation   Imitation that occurs after a delay of hours or days.

dementia   A global term for any neurological disorder in which the primary symptoms involve a deterioration of mental functioning.

denial and isolation   Kübler-Ross' first stage of dying, in which the dying person denies that she or he is really going to die.

depression   Kübler-Ross' fourth stage of dying, in which the dying person comes to accept the certainty of her or his death. A period of depression or preparatory grief may appear.

descriptive research   Has the purpose of observing and recording behavior.

development   The pattern of change that begins at conception and continues through the life span. Most development involves growth, although it also includes decline brought on by aging and dying.

developmental quotient (DQ)   An overall score that combines subscores in motor, language, adaptive, and personal-social domains in the Gesell assessment of infants.

developmentally appropriate practice Education that focuses on the typical developmental patterns of children (age-appropriateness) and the uniqueness of each child (individual-appropriateness).

difficult child   A child who tends to react negatively and cry frequently, engages in irregular daily routines, and is slow to accept change.

direct instruction approach   A structured, teacher-centered approach that is characterized by teacher direction and control, mastery of academic skills, high expectations for students' progress, maximum time spent on learning tasks, and efforts to keep negative effect to a minimum.

dishabituation   Recovery of a habituated response after a change in stimulation.

divergent thinking   Thinking that produces many answers to the same question and is characteristic of creativity.

divided attention   Concentrating on more than one activity at the same time.

DNA   A complex molecule that contains genetic information.

doula   A caregiver who provides continuous physical, emotional, and educational support for the mother before, during, and after childbirth.

Down syndrome   A chromosomally transmitted form of mental retardation, caused by the presence of an extra copy of chromosome 21.

dual-process model   States that decision making is influenced by two systems—one analytical and one experiential, which compete with each other; in this model, it is the experiential system—monitoring and managing actual experiences—that benefits adolescent decision making. (Chapter 7)

dual-process model   A model of coping with bereavement that emphasizes oscillation between two dimensions: (1) loss-oriented stressors, and (2) restoration-oriented stressors. (Chapter 20)

dynamic systems theory   The perspective on motor development that seeks to explain how motor behaviors are assembled for perceiving and acting.

dyscalculia   Also known as developmental arithmetic disorder; a learning disability that involves difficulty in math computation.

dysgraphia   A learning disability that involves difficulty in handwriting.

dyslexia   A category of learning disabilities involving a severe impairment in the ability to read and spell.

E

easy child   A child who is generally in a positive mood, quickly establishes regular routines in infancy, and adapts easily to new experiences.

eclectic theoretical orientation   An orientation that does not follow any one theoretical approach, but rather selects from each theory whatever is considered the best in it.

ecological view   The view that perception functions to bring organisms in contact with the environment and to increase adaptation.

egocentrism   The inability to distinguish between one's own perspective and someone else's (salient feature of the first substage of preoperational thought).

eldercare   Physical and emotional caretaking for older members of the family, whether by giving day-to-day physical assistance or by being responsible for overseeing such care.

embryonic period   The period of prenatal development that occurs two to eight weeks after conception. During the embryonic period, the rate of cell differentiation intensifies, support systems for the cells form, and organs appear.

emerging adulthood   The transition from adolescence to adulthood (approximately 18 to 25 years of age) that involves experimentation and exploration.

emotion   Feeling, or affect, that occurs when a person is in a state or interaction that is important to him or her. Emotion is characterized by behavior that reflects (expresses) the pleasantness or unpleasantness of the state a person is in or the transactions being experienced.

emotional and behavioral disorders   Serious, persistent problems that involve relationships, aggression, depression, fears associated with personal or school matters, as well as other inappropriate socioemotional characteristics.

empty nest syndrome   A decrease in marital satisfaction after children leave home, because parents derive considerable satisfaction from their children.

epigenetic view   Emphasizes that development is the result of an ongoing, bidirectional interchange between heredity and environment.

episodic memory   The retention of information about the where and when of life's happenings.

equilibration   A mechanism that Piaget proposed to explain how children shift from one stage of thought to the next.

erectile dysfunction   The inability to adequately achieve and maintain an erection that results in satisfactory sexual performance.

Erikson's theory   Includes eight stages of human development. Each stage consists of a unique developmental task that confronts individuals with a crisis that must be resolved.

ethnic gloss   Using an ethnic label such as African American or Latino in a superficial way that portrays an ethnic group as being more homogeneous than it really is.

ethnic identity   An enduring, basic aspect of the self that includes a sense of membership in an ethnic group and the attitudes and feelings related to that membership.

ethnicity   A characteristic based on cultural heritage, nationality characteristics, race, religion, and language.

ethology   Stresses that behavior is strongly influenced by biology, is tied to evolution, and is characterized by critical or sensitive periods.

euthanasia   The act of painlessly ending the lives of persons who are suffering from incurable diseases or severe disabilities; sometimes called "mercy killing."

evocative genotype-environment correlations Correlations that exist when the child's genotype elicits certain types of physical and social environments.

evolutionary psychology Emphasizes the importance of adaptation, reproduction, and "survival of the fittest" in shaping behavior.

evolutionary theory of aging This theory states that natural selection has not eliminated many harmful conditions and nonadaptive characteristics in older adults; thus, the benefits conferred by evolutionary theory decline with age because natural selection is linked to reproductive fitness.

executive attention Involves action planning, allocating attention to goals, error detection and compensation, monitoring progress on tasks, and dealing with novel or difficult circumstances.

experiment A carefully regulated procedure in which one or more of the factors believed to influence the behavior being studied are manipulated while all other factors are held constant.

explicit memory Memory of facts and experiences that individuals consciously know and can state.

F

fertilization A stage in reproduction whereby an egg and a sperm fuse to create a single cell, called a zygote.

fetal alcohol spectrum disorders (FASD) A cluster of abnormalities that appears in the offspring of mothers who drink alcohol heavily during pregnancy.

fetal period Lasting about seven months, the prenatal period between two months after conception and birth in typical pregnancies.

fine motor skills Motor skills that involve more finely tuned movements, such as finger dexterity.

first habits and primary circular reactions Piaget's second sensorimotor substage, which develops between 1 and 4 months of age. In this substage, the infant coordinates sensation and two types of schemes: habits and primary circular reactions.

fluid intelligence The ability to reason abstractly, which begins to decline from middle adulthood on, according to Horn.

fragile X syndrome A genetic disorder involving an abnormality in the X chromosome, which becomes constricted and often breaks.

free-radical theory A microbiological theory of aging that states that people age because inside their cells normal metabolism produces unstable oxygen molecules known as free radicals. These molecules ricochet around inside cells, damaging DNA and other cellular structures.

fuzzy trace theory States that memory is best understood by considering two types of memory representations: (1) verbatim memory trace, and (2) gist. In this theory, older children's better memory is attributed to the fuzzy traces created by extracting the gist of information.

G

games Activities engaged in for pleasure that include rules and often competition with one or more individuals.

gender The characteristics of people as males or females.

gender identity The sense of being male or female, which most children acquire by the time they are 3 years old.

gender role A set of expectations that prescribes how females or males should think, act, and feel.

gender schema theory The theory that gender-typing emerges as children develop gender schemas of their culture's gender-appropriate and gender-inappropriate behavior.

gender stereotypes Broad categories that reflect our impressions and beliefs about females and males.

gender typing Acquisition of a traditional masculine or feminine role.

gene × environment (G × E) interaction The interaction of a specific measured variation in the DNA and a specific measured aspect of the environment.

generational inequity The view that our aging society is being unfair to its younger members because older adults pile up advantages by receiving inequitably large allocations of resources.

genes Units of hereditary information composed of DNA. Genes direct cells to reproduce themselves and manufacture the proteins that maintain life.

genotype A person's genetic heritage; the actual genetic material.

germinal period The period of prenatal development that takes place in the first two weeks after conception. It includes the creation of the zygote, continued cell division, and the attachment of the zygote to the uterine wall.

gifted Having above-average intelligence (an IQ of 130 or higher) and/or superior talent for something.

glaucoma Damage to the optic nerve because of the pressure created by a buildup of fluid in the eye.

goodness of fit Refers to the match between a child's temperament and the environmental demands with which the child must cope.

grasping reflex A neonatal reflex that occurs when something touches the infant's palms. The infant responds by grasping tightly.

grief The emotional numbness, disbelief, separation anxiety, despair, sadness, and loneliness that accompany the loss of someone we love.

gross motor skills Motor skills that involve large-muscle activities, such as walking.

H

habituation Decreased responsiveness to a stimulus after repeated presentations of the stimulus.

heteronomous morality Kohlberg's first stage of preconventional reasoning in which moral thinking is tied to punishment.

heteronomous morality The first stage of moral development in Piaget's theory, occurring from approximately 4 to 7 years of age. Justice and rules are conceived of as unchangeable properties of the world, removed from the control of people.

hormonal stress theory The theory that aging in the body's hormonal system can lower resistance to stress and increase the likelihood of disease.

hormones Powerful chemical substances secreted by the endocrine glands and carried through the body by the bloodstream.

hospice A program committed to making the end of life as free from pain, anxiety, and depression as possible. The goals of hospice contrast with those of a hospital, which are to cure disease and prolong life.

hypotheses Specific assumptions and predictions that can be tested to determine their accuracy.

hypothetical-deductive reasoning Piaget's formal operational concept that adolescents have the cognitive ability to develop hypotheses, or best guesses, about ways to solve problems, such as an algebraic equation.

I

identity achievement Marcia's term for the status of individuals who have undergone a crisis and have made a commitment.

identity diffusion Marcia's term for the status of individuals who have not yet experienced a crisis (explored meaningful alternatives) or made any commitments.

identity foreclosure Marcia's term for the status of individuals who have made a commitment but have not experienced a crisis.

identity moratorium Marcia's term for the status of individuals who are in the midst of a crisis, but their commitments are either absent or vaguely defined.

imaginary audience Involves adolescents' belief that others are as interested in them as they themselves are, as well as attention-getting behavior motivated by a desire to be noticed, visible, and "on stage."

immanent justice The concept that if a rule is broken punishment will be meted out immediately.

implicit memory Memory without conscious recollection; involves skills and routine procedures that are automatically performed.

inclusion Educating a child with special education needs full-time in the regular classroom.

individual differences The stable, consistent ways in which people are different from each other.

individualism, instrumental purpose, and exchange Kohlberg's second stage of preconventional reasoning. At this stage, individuals pursue their own interests but also let others do the same.

individualized education plan (IEP) A written statement that spells out a program specifically tailored to a child with a disability.

indulgent parenting A style of parenting in which parents are highly involved with their children but place few demands or controls on them. Indulgent parenting is associated with children's social incompetence, especially a lack of self-control.

infinite generativity The ability to produce an endless number of meaningful sentences using a finite set of words and rules.

information-processing theory Emphasizes that individuals manipulate information, monitor it, and strategize about it. Central to this theory are the processes of memory and thinking.

insecure avoidant babies Babies that show insecurity by avoiding the caregiver.

insecure disorganized babies Babies that show insecurity by being disorganized and disoriented.

insecure resistant babies Babies that often cling to the caregiver, then resist the caregiver by fighting against the closeness, perhaps by kicking or pushing away.

integrity versus despair Erikson's eighth and final stage of development, which individuals experience in late adulthood. This involves reflecting on the past and either piecing together a positive review or concluding that one's life has not been well spent.

intelligence Problem-solving skills and the ability to learn from and adapt to the experiences of everyday life.

intelligence quotient (IQ) A person's mental age divided by chronological age, multiplied by 100.

intermodal perception The ability to relate and integrate information from two or more sensory modalities, such as vision and hearing.

internalization of schemes Piaget's sixth and final sensorimotor substage, which develops between 18 and 24 months of age. In this substage, the infant develops the ability to use primitive symbols.

intimacy in friendships Self-disclosure and the sharing of private thoughts.

intuitive thought substage Piaget's second substage of preoperational thought, in which children begin to use primitive reasoning and want to know the answers to all sorts of questions (between 4 and 7 years of age).

J

joint attention Process that occurs when individuals focus on the same object and an ability to track another's behavior is present, one individual directs another's attention, and reciprocal interaction is present.

justice perspective A moral perspective that focuses on the rights of the individual; individuals independently make moral decisions.

juvenile delinquent An adolescent who breaks the law or engages in behavior that is considered illegal.

K

kangaroo care Treatment for preterm infants that involves skin-to-skin contact.

Klinefelter syndrome A chromosomal disorder in which males have an extra X chromosome, making them XXY instead of XY.

kwashiorkor A condition caused by severe protein deficiency in which the child's abdomen and feet become swollen with water; usually appears between 1 to 3 years of age.

L

laboratory A controlled setting in which many of the complex factors of the "real world" are removed.

language A form of communication, whether spoken, written, or signed, that is based on a system of symbols. Language consists of the words used by a community and the rules for varying and combining them.

language acquisition device (LAD) Chomsky's term that describes a biological endowment enabling the child to detect the features and rules of language, including phonology, syntax, and semantics.

lateralization Specialization of function in one hemisphere of the cerebral cortex or the other.

learning disability Describes a child who has difficulty in learning that involves understanding or using spoken or written language, and the difficulty can appear in listening, thinking, reading, writing, and spelling. A learning disability also may involve difficulty in doing mathematics. To be classified as a learning disability, the learning problem is not primarily the result of visual, hearing, or motor disabilities; mental retardation; emotional disorders; or due to environmental, cultural, or economic disadvantage.

least restrictive environment (LRE) A setting that is as similar as possible to the one in which children who do not have a disability are educated.

leisure The pleasant times after work when individuals are free to pursue activities and interests of their own choosing.

life expectancy The number of years that will probably be lived by the average person born in a particular year.

life span The upper boundary of life, the maximum number of years an individual can live. The maximum life span of human beings is about 120 to 125 years of age.

life-span perspective The perspective that development is lifelong, multidimensional, multidirectional, plastic, multidisciplinary, and contextual; involves growth, maintenance, and regulation; and is constructed through biological, sociocultural, and individual factors working together.

longitudinal approach A research strategy in which the same individuals are studied over a period of time, usually several years or more.

long-term memory A relatively permanent type of memory that holds huge amounts of information for a long period of time.

low birth weight infants An infant that weighs less than 5½ pounds at birth.

M

macular degeneration A disease that involves deterioration of the macula of the retina, which corresponds to the focal center of the visual field.

major depression A mood disorder in which the individual is deeply unhappy, demoralized, self-derogatory, and bored. The person does not feel well, loses stamina easily, has poor appetite, and is listless and unmotivated. Major depression is so widespread that it has been called the "common cold" of mental disorders.

marasmus A wasting away of body tissues in the infant's first year, caused by severe protein-calorie deficiency.

matching hypothesis States that although we prefer a more attractive person in the abstract, in the real world we end up choosing someone who is close to our own level.

meaning-making coping Involves drawing on beliefs, values, and goals to change the meaning of a stressful situation, especially in times of chronic stress as when a loved one dies.

meiosis A specialized form of cell division that occurs to form eggs and sperm (or gametes).

memory A central feature of cognitive development, pertaining to all situations in which an individual retains information over time.

menarche A girl's first menstruation.

menopause Cessation of a woman's menstrual periods, usually in the late forties or fifties.

mental age (MA) Binet's measure of an individual's level of mental development, compared with that of others.

mental retardation A condition of limited mental ability in which an individual has a low IQ, usually below 70 on a traditional test of intelligence, and has difficulty adapting to everyday life.

metacognition   Cognition about cognition, or knowing about knowing.

metalinguistic awareness   Refers to knowledge about language, such as knowing what a preposition is or the ability to discuss the sounds of a language.

middle adulthood   The developmental period that begins at approximately 40 to 45 years of age and extends to about 60 to 65 years of age.

mindfulness   Being alert, mentally present, and cognitively flexible while going through life's everyday activities and tasks.

mindset   The cognitive view, either fixed or growth, that individuals develop for themselves.

mitochondrial theory   The theory that aging is caused by the decay of mitochondria, tiny cellular bodies that supply energy for function, growth, and repair.

mitosis   Cellular reproduction in which the cell's nucleus duplicates itself with two new cells being formed, each containing the same DNA as the parent cell, arranged in the same 23 pairs of chromosomes.

Montessori approach   An educational philosophy in which children are given considerable freedom and spontaneity in choosing activities and are allowed to move from one activity to another as they desire.

moral development   Development that involves thoughts, feelings, and behaviors regarding rules and conventions about what people should do in their interactions with other people.

Moro reflex   A neonatal startle response that occurs in reaction to a sudden, intense noise or movement. When startled, the newborn arches its back, throws its head back, and flings out its arms and legs. Then the newborn rapidly closes its arms and legs to the center of the body.

morphology   Units of meaning involved in word formation.

multi-infarct dementia   Sporadic and progressive loss of intellectual functioning caused by repeated temporary obstruction of blood flow in cerebral arteries.

mutual interpersonal expectations, relationships, and interpersonal conformity   Kohlberg's third stage of moral development. At this stage, individuals value trust, caring, and loyalty to others as a basis of moral judgments.

myelination   The process by which the nerve cells are covered and insulated with a layer of fat cells, which increases the speed at which information travels through the nervous system.

N

narcissism   A self-centered and self-concerned approach toward others.

natural childbirth   This method attempts to reduce the mother's pain by decreasing her fear through education about childbirth and relaxation techniques during delivery.

naturalistic observation   Observing behavior in real-world settings.

nature-nurture issue   Refers to the debate about whether development is primarily influenced by nature or nurture. Nature refers to an organism's biological inheritance, nurture to its environmental experiences. The "nature proponents" claim biological inheritance is the most important influence on development; the "nurture proponents" claim that environmental experiences are the most important.

neglected children   Children who are infrequently nominated as a best friend but are not disliked by their peers.

neglectful parenting   A style of parenting in which the parent is very uninvolved in the child's life; it is associated with children's social incompetence, especially a lack of self-control.

Neonatal Intensive Care Unit Neurobehavioral Scale (NNNS)   An "offspring" of the NBAS, the NNNS provides an assessment of the newborn's behavior, neurological and stress responses, and regulatory capacities.

neo-Piagetians   Developmentalists who argue that Piaget got some things right but that his theory needs considerable revision. They have elaborated on Piaget's theory, giving more emphasis to information processing, strategies, and precise cognitive steps.

neurogenesis   The generation of new neurons.

neurons   Nerve cells, which handle information processing at the cellular level in the brain.

nonnormative life events   Unusual occurrences that have a major impact on an individual's life.

nonshared environmental experiences   The child's own unique experiences, both within the family and outside the family, that are not shared by another sibling. Thus, experiences occurring within the family can be part of the "nonshared environment."

normal distribution   A symmetrical distribution with most scores falling in the middle of the possible range of scores and a few scores appearing toward the extremes of the range.

normative age-graded influences   These are influences that are similar for individuals in a particular age group.

normative history-graded influences   Influences that are common to people of a particular generation because of historical circumstances.

O

object permanence   The Piagetian term for understanding that objects and events continue to exist, even when they cannot directly be seen, heard, or touched.

operations   In Piaget's theory, these are reversible mental actions that allow children to do mentally what they formerly did physically.

organic retardation   Mental retardation that is caused by a genetic disorder or brain damage.

organization   Piaget's concept of grouping isolated behaviors and thoughts into a higher-order, more smoothly functioning cognitive system.

organogenesis   Organ formation that takes place during the first two months of prenatal development.

osteoporosis   A chronic condition that involves an extensive loss of bone tissue and is the main reason many older adults walk with a marked stoop. Women are especially vulnerable to osteoporosis.

P

pain cry   A sudden appearance of a long, initial loud cry without preliminary moaning, followed by breath holding.

palliative care   Care emphasized in a hospice, which involves reducing pain and suffering and helping individuals die with dignity.

Parkinson disease   A chronic, progressive disease characterized by muscle tremors, slowing of movement, and partial facial paralysis.

passive euthanasia   The withholding of available treatments, such as life-sustaining devices, allowing the person to die.

passive genotype-environment correlations   Correlations that exist when the natural parents, who are genetically related to the child, provide a rearing environment for the child.

perception   The interpretation of what is sensed.

personal fable   The part of adolescent egocentrism that involves an adolescent's sense of uniqueness and invincibility (or invulnerability).

perspective taking   The ability to assume other people's perspectives and understand their thoughts and feelings.

phenotype   The way an individual's genotype is expressed in observed and measurable characteristics.

phenylketonuria (PKU)   A genetic disorder in which an individual cannot properly metabolize an amino acid. PKU is now easily detected but, if left untreated, results in mental retardation and hyperactivity.

phonics approach   The idea that reading instruction should teach the basic rules for translating written symbols into sounds.

phonology   The sound system of the language, including the sounds that are used and how they may be combined.

Piaget's theory   States that children actively construct their understanding of the world and go through four stages of cognitive development.

placenta   A life-support system that consists of a disk-shaped group of tissues in which small blood vessels from the mother and offspring intertwine.

popular children Children who are frequently nominated as a best friend and are rarely disliked by their peers.

possible selves What individuals might become, what they would like to become, and what they are afraid of becoming.

postconventional reasoning The highest level in Kohlberg's theory of moral development. At this level, the individual recognizes alternative moral courses, explores the options, and then decides on a personal moral code.

postformal thought A form of thought that is qualitatively different from Piaget's formal operational thought. It involves understanding that the correct answer to a problem can require reflective thinking, that the correct answer can vary from one situation to another, and that the search for truth is often an ongoing, never-ending process. It also involves the belief that solutions to problems need to be realistic and that emotion and subjective factors can influence thinking.

postpartum depression Characteristic of women who have such strong feelings of sadness, anxiety, or despair that they have trouble coping with daily tasks in the postpartum period.

postpartum period The period after childbirth when the mother adjusts, both physically and psychologically, to the process of childbirth. This period lasts for about six weeks or until her body has completed its adjustment and returned to a near prepregnant state.

practice play Play that involves repetition of behavior when new skills are being learned or when physical or mental mastery and coordination of skills are required for games or sports.

pragmatics The appropriate use of language in different contexts.

precocious puberty The very early onset and rapid progression of puberty.

preconventional reasoning The lowest level in Kohlberg's theory of moral development. The individual's moral reasoning is controlled primarily by external rewards and punishment.

preoperational stage Piaget's second stage, lasting from about 2 to 7 years of age, during which children begin to represent the world with words, images, and drawings, and symbolic thought goes beyond simple connections of sensory information and physical action; stable concepts are formed, mental reasoning emerges, egocentrism is present, and magical beliefs are constructed.

prepared childbirth Developed by French obstetrician Ferdinand Lamaze, this childbirth strategy is similar to natural childbirth but includes a special breathing technique to control pushing in the final stages of labor and a more detailed anatomy and physiology course.

pretense/symbolic play Play in which the child transforms the physical environment into a symbol.

preterm infants Those born before the completion of 37 weeks of gestation (the time between fertilization and birth).

primary circular reaction A scheme based on the attempt to reproduce an event that initially occurred by chance.

primary emotions Emotions that are present in humans and other animals and emerge early in life; examples are joy, anger, sadness, fear, and disgust.

Project Head Start A government-funded program that is designed to provide children from low-income families with the opportunity to acquire the skills and experiences important for school success.

prolonged grief Grief that involves enduring despair and is still unresolved over an extended period of time.

prospective memory Remembering to do something in the future.

proximodistal pattern The sequence in which growth starts at the center of the body and moves toward the extremities.

psychoanalytic theories Describe development as primarily unconscious and heavily colored by emotion. Behavior is merely a surface characteristic, and the symbolic workings of the mind have to be analyzed to understand behavior. Early experiences with parents are emphasized.

psychoanalytic theory of gender A theory deriving from Freud's view that the preschool child develops a sexual attraction to the opposite-sex parent, by approximately 5 or 6 years of age renounces this attraction because of anxious feelings, and subsequently identifies with the same-sex parent, unconsciously adopting the same-sex parent's characteristics.

puberty A period of rapid physical maturation, occurring primarily in early adolescence, that involves hormonal and bodily changes.

R

rape Forcible sexual intercourse with a person who does not consent to it.

rapport talk The language of conversation; it is a way of establishing connections and negotiating relationships.

reciprocal socialization Socialization that is bidirectional; children socialize parents, just as parents socialize children.

reflexes Built-in reactions to stimuli that govern the newborn's movements, which are automatic and beyond the newborn's control.

reflexive smile A smile that does not occur in response to external stimuli. It happens during the month after birth, usually during sleep.

rejected children Children who are infrequently nominated as a best friend and are actively disliked by their peers.

report talk Talk that is designed to give information and includes public speaking.

rite of passage A ceremony or ritual that marks an individual's transition from one status to another. Most rites of passage focus on the transition to adult status.

romantic love Also called passionate love, or eros, romantic love has strong sexual and infatuation components and often predominates in the early period of a love relationship.

rooting reflex A newborn's built-in reaction that occurs when the infant's cheek is stroked or the side of the mouth is touched. In response, the infant turns his or her head toward the side that was touched, in an apparent effort to find something to suck.

S

scaffolding Parents time interactions so that infants experience turn-taking with the parents.

schemes In Piaget's theory, actions or mental representations that organize knowledge.

scientific method An approach that can be used to obtain accurate information. It includes these steps: (1) conceptualize the problem, (2) collect data, (3) draw conclusions, and (4) revise research conclusions and theory.

secondary circular reactions Piaget's third sensorimotor substage, which develops between 4 and 8 months of age. In this substage, the infant becomes more object-oriented, moving beyond preoccupation with the self.

secure attachment style An attachment style that describes adults who have positive views of relationships, find it easy to get close to others, and are not overly concerned or stressed out about their romantic relationships.

securely attached babies Babies that use the caregiver as a secure base from which to explore the environment.

selective attention Focusing on a specific aspect of experience that is relevant while ignoring others that are irrelevant.

selective optimization with compensation theory The theory that successful aging is related to three main factors: selection, optimization, and compensation.

self-concept Domain-specific evaluations of the self.

self-conscious emotions Emotions that require self-awareness, especially consciousness and a sense of "me"; examples include jealousy, empathy, and embarrassment.

self-efficacy The belief that one can master a situation and produce favorable outcomes.

self-esteem The global evaluative dimension of the self. Self-esteem is also referred to as self-worth or self-image.

self-understanding The child's cognitive representation of self, the substance and content of the child's self-conceptions.

semantic memory A person's knowledge about the world—including a person's fields of expertise, general academic knowledge of the sort learned in school, and "everyday knowledge."

semantics   The meaning of words and sentences.

sensation   The product of the interaction between information and the sensory receptors—the eyes, ears, tongue, nostrils, and skin.

sensorimotor play   Behavior engaged in by infants to derive pleasure from exercising their existing sensorimotor schemas.

sensorimotor stage   The first of Piaget's stages, which lasts from birth to about 2 years of age; infants construct an understanding of the world by coordinating sensory experiences with motoric actions.

separation protest   An infant's distressed crying when the caregiver leaves.

seriation   The concrete operation that involves ordering stimuli along a quantitative dimension (such as length).

service learning   A form of education that promotes social responsibility and service to the community.

sexually transmitted infections (STIs)   Infections that are contracted primarily through sexual contact, including oral-genital and anal-genital contact.

shape constancy   The recognition that an object's shape remains the same even though its orientation to us changes.

shared environmental experiences   Siblings' common environmental experiences, such as their parents' personalities and intellectual orientation, the family's socioeconomic status, and the neighborhood in which they live.

short-term memory   The memory component in which individuals retain information for up to 30 seconds, assuming there is no rehearsal of the information.

sickle-cell anemia   A genetic disorder that affects the red blood cells and occurs most often in people of African descent.

simple reflexes   Piaget's first sensorimotor substage, which corresponds to the first month after birth. In this substage, sensation and action are coordinated primarily through reflexive behaviors.

size constancy   The recognition that an object remains the same even though the retinal image of the object changes as you move toward or away from the object.

slow-to-warm-up child   A child who has a low activity level, is somewhat negative, and displays a low intensity of mood.

small for date infants   Also called small for gestational age infants, these infants' birth weights are below normal when the length of pregnancy is considered. Small for date infants may be preterm or full term.

social clock   The timetable according to which individuals are expected to accomplish life's tasks,

such as getting married, having children, or establishing themselves in a career.

social cognitive theory   The view of psychologists who emphasize behavior, environment, and cognition as the key factors in development.

social cognitive theory of gender   A theory that emphasizes that children's gender development occurs through the observation and imitation of gender behavior and through the rewards and punishments children experience for gender-appropriate and gender-inappropriate behavior.

social constructivist approach   An approach that emphasizes the social contexts of learning and that knowledge is mutually built and constructed. Vygotsky's theory reflects this approach.

social contract or utility and individual rights   The fifth Kohlberg stage. At this stage, individuals reason that values, rights, and principles undergird or transcend the law.

social conventional reasoning   Thoughts about social consensus and convention, in contrast to moral reasoning, which stresses ethical issues.

social play   Play that involves social interactions with peers.

social policy   A national government's course of action designed to promote the welfare of its citizens.

social referencing   "Reading" emotional cues in others to help determine how to act in a particular situation.

social role theory   A theory that gender differences result from the contrasting roles of men and women.

social smile   A smile in response to an external stimulus, which early in development is typically a face.

social systems morality   The fourth stage in Kohlberg's theory of moral development. Moral judgments are based on understanding the social order, law, justice, and duty.

socioeconomic status (SES)   Refers to the grouping of people with similar occupational, educational, and economic characteristics.

socioemotional processes   Changes in an individual's relationships with other people, emotions, and personality.

socioemotional selectivity theory   The theory that older adults become more selective about their social networks. Because they place a high value on emotional satisfaction, older adults often spend more time with familiar individuals with whom they have had rewarding relationships.

source memory   The ability to remember where one learned something.

stability-change issue   Involves the degree to which we become older renditions of our early experience (stability) or whether we develop into someone different from who we were at an earlier point in development (change).

standardized test   A test with uniform procedures for administration and scoring. Many

standardized tests allow a person's performance to be compared with the performance of other individuals.

Strange Situation   An observational measure of infant attachment that requires the infant to move through a series of introductions, separations, and reunions with the caregiver and an adult stranger in a prescribed order.

stranger anxiety   An infant's fear and wariness of strangers; it tends to appear in the second half of the first year of life.

strategies   Deliberate mental activities to improve the processing of information.

sucking reflex   A newborn's built-in reaction to automatically suck an object placed in its mouth. The sucking reflex enables the infant to get nourishment before he or she has associated a nipple with food and also serves as a self-soothing or self-regulating mechanism.

sudden infant death syndrome (SIDS)   A condition that occurs when an infant stops breathing, usually during the night, and suddenly dies without an apparent cause.

sustained attention   Focused and extended engagement with an object, task, event, or other aspect of the environment.

symbolic function substage   Piaget's first substage of preoperational thought, in which the child gains the ability to mentally represent an object that is not present (between about 2 and 4 years of age).

syntax   The ways words are combined to form acceptable phrases and sentences.

T

telegraphic speech   The use of short and precise words without grammatical markers such as articles, auxiliary verbs, and other connectives.

temperament   Involves individual differences in behavioral styles, emotions, and characteristic ways of responding.

teratogen   From the Greek word *tera*, meaning "monster." Any agent that causes a birth defect. The field of study that investigates the causes of birth defects is called teratology.

tertiary circular reactions, novelty, and curiosity   Piaget's fifth sensorimotor substage, which develops between 12 and 18 months of age. In this substage, infants become intrigued by the many properties of objects and by the many things that they can make happen to objects.

theory   An interrelated, coherent set of ideas that helps to explain and make predictions.

theory of mind   The awareness of one's own mental processes and the mental processes of others.

top-dog phenomenon   The circumstance of moving from the top position in elementary school to the lowest position in middle or junior high school.

transitivity The ability to logically combine relations to understand certain conclusions.

triarchic theory of intelligence Sternberg's theory that intelligence consists of analytical intelligence, creative intelligence, and practical intelligence.

trophoblast The outer layer of cells that develops in the germinal period. These cells provide nutrition and support for the embryo.

Turner syndrome A chromosome disorder in females in which either an X chromosome is missing, making the person XO instead of XX, or the second X chromosome is partially deleted.

twin study A study in which the behavioral similarity of identical twins is compared with the behavioral similarity of fraternal twins.

U

umbilical cord A life-support system containing two arteries and one vein that connects the baby to the placenta.

universal ethical principles The sixth and highest stage in Kohlberg's theory of moral development. Individuals develop a moral standard based on universal human rights.

V

visual preference method A method used to determine whether infants can distinguish one stimulus from another by measuring the length of time they attend to different stimuli.

Vygotsky's theory A sociocultural cognitive theory that emphasizes how culture and social interaction guide cognitive development.

W

Wernicke's area An area in the brain's left hemisphere that is involved in language comprehension.

whole-language approach An approach to reading instruction based on the idea that instruction should parallel children's natural language learning. Reading materials should be whole and meaningful.

wisdom Expert knowledge about the practical aspects of life that permits excellent judgment about important matters.

working memory The mental "workbench," where individuals manipulate and assemble information when decision making, problem solving, and comprehending language.

X

XYY syndrome A chromosomal disorder in which males have an extra Y chromosome.

Z

zone of proximal development (ZPD) Vygotsky's term for tasks too difficult for children to master alone but that can be mastered with the assistance of adults or more-skilled children.

zygote A single cell formed through fertilization.

references

A

AARP. (2004). *The divorce experience: A study of divorce at midlife and beyond.* Washington, DC: AARP.

Abbasi, M., & others. (2010). The effect of hypnosis on pain relief during labor and childbirth in Iranian pregnant women. *International Journal of Clinical and Experimental Hypnosis, 57,* 174–183.

Abbate-Daga, G., Gramaglia, C., Amianto, F., Marzola, E., & Fassino, S. (2010). Attachment insecurity, personality, and body dissatisfaction in eating disorders. *Journal of Nervous and Mental Disease, 198,* 520–524.

Abbott, B. D., & Barber, B. L. (2010). Embodied image: Gender differences in functional and aesthetic body image among Australian adolescents. *Body Image, 7,* 22–31.

Abbott, L. C., & Winzer-Serhan, U. H. (2012). Smoking during pregnancy: Lessons learned from epidemiological studies and experimental studies using animals. *Critical Reviews in Toxicology, 42,* 279–303.

ABC News. (2005, December 12). Larry Page and Sergey Brin. Retrieved September 16, 2007, from http://abcnews.go.com?Entertainment/12/8/05

Abrams, L. (2009). Exploring the generality of retest effects: Commentary on "When does age-related cognitive decline begin?" *Neurobiology of Aging, 30,* 525–527.

Accornero, V. H., Anthony, J. C., Morrow, C. E., Xue, L., & Bandstra, E. S. (2006). Prenatal cocaine exposure: An examination of childhood externalizing and internalizing behavior problems at age 7 years. *Epidemiology, Psychiatry, and Society, 15,* 20–29.

Achieve, Inc. (2005). *An action agenda for improving America's high schools.* Washington, DC: Author.

Ackerman, J. P., Riggins, T., & Black, M. M. (2010). A review of the effects of prenatal cocaine exposure among school-aged children. *Pediatrics, 125,* 554–565.

Adams, G. A., & Rau, B. L. (2011). Putting off tomorrow to do what you want today: Planning for retirement. *American Psychologist, 66,* 180–192.

Adams, J. C. (2009). Immunocytochemical traits of type IV fibrocytes and their possible relation to cochlear function and pathology. *Journal of the Association for Research in Otolaryngology, 10,* 369–382.

Adams, K. F., & others. (2006). Overweight, obesity, and mortality in a large prospective cohort of persons 50 to 71 years old. *New England Journal of Medicine, 355,* 763–768.

Adamson, L., & Frick, J. (2003). The still face: A history of a shared experimental paradigm. *Infancy, 4,* 451–473.

Adkins, D. E., Daw, J. K., McClay, J. L., & van den Oord, E. J. (2012). The influence of five monoamine genes on trajectories of depressive symptoms across adolescence and young adulthood. *Development and Psychopathology, 24,* 267–285.

Administration for Children and Families. (2008). *Statistical Fact Sheet Fiscal Year 2008.* Washington, DC: Author.

Administration on Aging. (2011). *A profile of older Americans: 2011.* Washington, DC: U.S. Department of Health and Human Services.

Adolph, K. E. (1997). Learning in the development of infant locomotion. *Monographs of the Society for Research in Child Development, 62* (3, Serial No. 251).

Adolph, K. E., & Berger, S. E. (2005). Physical and motor development. In M. H. Bornstein & M. E. Lamb (Eds.), *Developmental psychology* (5th ed.). Mahwah, NJ: Erlbaum.

Adolph, K. E., & Berger, S. E. (2013, in press). Development of the motor system. In H. Pashler, T. Crane, M. Kinsbourne, F. Ferreira, & R. Zemel (Eds.), *The encyclopedia of the mind.* Thousand Oaks, CA: Sage.

Adolph, K. E., Karasik, L. B., & Tamis-LeMonda, C. S. (2010). Moving between cultures: Cross-cultural research on motor development. In M. Bornstein & L. R. Cote (Ed.), *Handbook of cross-cultural developmental science: Vol. 1. Domains of development across cultures.* Clifton, NJ : Psychology Press.

Adoph, K. E., & Kretch, K. S. (2012, in press). Infants on the edge: Beyond the visual cliff. In A. Slater & P. Quinn (Eds.), *Developmental psychology: Revisiting the classic studies.* New York: Oxford University Press.

Adolph, K. E., & Robinson, S. R. R. (2013, in press). The road to walking: What learning to walk tells us about development. In P. Zelazo (Ed.) *Oxford handbook of developmental psychology.* New York: Oxford University Press.

Adolph, K. E., Vereijken, B., & Shrout, P. E. (2003). What changes in infant walking and why? *Child Development, 74,* 475–497.

Adolph, K. E., & others. (2012, in press). How do you learn to walk? Thousands of steps and dozens of falls per day. *Psychological Science.*

Agency for Healthcare Research and Quality. (2007). *Evidence report/Technology assessment Number 153: Breastfeeding and maternal and infant health outcomes in developed countries.* Rockville, MD: U.S. Department of Health and Human Services.

Agras, W. S., & others. (2004). Report of the National Institutes of Health workshop on overcoming barriers to treatment research in anorexia nervosa. *International Journal of Eating Disorders, 35,* 509–521.

Agras, W. S., Hammer, L. D., McNicholas, F., & Karemer, H. C. (2004). Risk factors for childhood overweight: A prospective study from birth to 9.5 years. *Journal of Pediatrics, 145,* 20–25.

Ahluwalia, I. B., Tessaro, I., Grumer-Strawn, L. M., MacGowan, C., & Benton-Davis, S. (2000). Georgia's breastfeeding promotion program for low-income women. *Pediatrics, 105,* E-85–E-87.

Ahmed, S., & others. (2011). Community kangaroo mother care: Implementation and potential for neonatal survival and health in very low-income settings. *Journal of Perinatology, 31,* 361–367.

Ahrens, C. E., & Aldana, E. (2012). The ties that bind: Understanding the impact of sexual assault disclosure on survivors' relationships with friends, family, and partners. *Journal of Trauma & Dissociation, 13,* 226–243.

Ahrons, C. (2004). *We're still family.* New York: HarperCollins.

Ahrons, C. (2007). Family ties after divorce: Long term implications for children. *Family Process, 46,* 53–65.

Ailshire, J. A., & Burgard, S. A. (2012). Family relationships and troubled sleep among U.S. adults: Examining the influences of contact frequency and relationship quality. *Journal of Health and Social Behavior, 53,* 248–262.

Ainsworth, M. D. S. (1979). Infant-mother attachment. *American Psychologist, 34,* 932–937.

Aishworiya, R., & others. (2012). Sleep behavior in a sample of preschool children in Singapore. *Annals of the Academy of Medicine, Singapore, 41,* 99–106.

Aittomaki, A., & others. (2012, in press). Household economic resources, labor-market advantage and health problems—A study on causal relationships using prospective register data. *Social Science and Medicine.*

Ajayi, G. O. (2011). Ultrasound-guided amniocentesis in singleton pregnancies: A review of the first 1,000 cases. *Clinical and Experimental Obstetrics and Gynecology, 38,* 405–407.

Akbari, A., & others. (2011). Parity and breastfeeding are preventive measures against breast cancer in Iranian women. *Breast Cancer, 18,* 51–55.

Akhavan, S., & Lundgren, I. (2012). Midwives' experiences of doula support for immigrant women in Sweden—A qualitative study. *Midwifery, 28,* 80–85.

Akhtar, N., & Herold, K. (2008). Pragmatic development. In M. M. Haith & J. B. Benson (Eds.), *Encyclopedia of infant and early childhood development.* Oxford, UK: Elsevier.

Alberga, A. S., & others. (2012a). Healthy eating, aerobic and resistance training in youth (HEARTY): Study rationale, design, and methods. *Contemporary Clinical Trials, 33,* 839–847.

Alberga, A. S., & others. (2012b, in press). Overweight and obese teenagers: Why is adolescence a critical period? *Pediatric Obesity.*

Albert, D., & Steinberg, L. (2011a). Judgment and decision making in adolescence. *Journal of Research on Adolescence, 21,* 211–224.

Albert, D., & Steinberg, L. (2011b). Peer influences on adolescent risk behavior. In M. Bardo, D. Fishbein, & R. Milich (Eds.), *Inhibitory control and drug abuse prevention: From research to translation.* New York: Springer.

Alberts, E., Elkind, D., & Ginsberg, S. (2007). The personal fable and risk taking in early adolescence. *Journal of Youth and Adolescence, 36,* 71–76.

Albright, J. A., Stevens, S. A., & Beussman, D. J. (2012). Detecting ketamine in beverage residues: Application in date rape detection. *Drug Testing and Analysis, 4,* 337–341.

Aleksandrova-Howell, M., Abramson, C. I., & Craig, D. P. (2012). Coverage of Russian psychological contributions in American psychology textbooks. *International Journal of Psychology, 47,* 76–87.

Alexander, N., & others. (2012, in press). Interaction of serotonin transporter-linked polymorphic region and environmental adversity: Increased amygdala-hypothalamus connectivity as a potential mechanism linking neural and endocrine hyperreactivity. *Biological Psychiatry.*

Ali, M. M., & Dwyer, D. S. (2011). Estimating peer effects in sexual behavior among adolescents. *Journal of Adolescence, 34,* 183–190.

Allaire, J. C. (2012). Everyday cognition. In S. K. Whitbourne & M. Sliwinski (Eds.), *Wiley-Blackwell handbook of adult development and aging.* New York: Wiley.

Allemand, M., Zimprich, D., & Hendriks, A. A. J. (2008). Age differences in five personality domains across the life span. *Developmental Psychology, 44,* 758–770.

Allen, J. P., & Miga, E. M. (2010). Attachment in adolescence: A move to the level of emotion regulation. *Journal of Social and Personal Relationships, 27,* 226–234.

Allen, J. P., Philliber, S., Herring, S., & Kuperminc, G. P. (1997). Preventing teen pregnancy and academic failure: Experimental evaluation of a developmentally-based approach. *Child Development, 68,* 729–742.

Allen, J. P. & others. (2009, April). *Portrait of the secure teen as an adult.* Paper presented at the meeting of the Society for Research in Child Development, Denver.

Allen, K., & Diamond, L. M. (2012, in press). Same-sex relationships. In M. Fine & F. Fincham (Eds.), *Family theories.* New York: Routledge.

Allen, M., Svetaz, M. V., Hardeman, R., & Resnick, M. D. (2008, February). *What research tells us about parenting practices and their relationship to youth sexual behavior.* Campaign to Prevent Teen and Unplanned Pregnancy. Retrieved December 2, 2008, from http://www.TheNationalCampaign.org

Allen, T. D. (2013). The work-family role interface: A synthesis of the research from industrial and organizational psychology. In I. B. Weiner & others (Eds.), *Handbook of psychology* (2nd ed., Vol. 12). New York: Wiley.

Allor, J., & Al Otaiba, S. A. (2013). In B. G. Cook & M. G. Tankersley (Eds.), *Research-based practices in special education.* Upper Saddle River, NJ: Pearson.

Almeida Montes, L. G., & others. (2012, in press). Brain cortical thickness in ADHD: Age, sex, and clinical correlations. *Journal of Attention Disorders.*

Almeida, D. M., & Horn, M. C. (2004). Is daily life more stressful during middle adulthood? In C. D. Ryff & R. C. Kessler (Eds.), *A portrait of midlife in the United States.* Chicago: University of Chicago Press.

Almeida, D. M., Piazza, J. R., Stawski, R. S., & Klein, L. C. (2011). The speedometer of life: Stress, health, and aging. In K. W. Schaie & S. L. Willis (Eds.), *Handbook of the psychology of aging* (7th ed.). New York: Elsevier.

Alsaker, F. D., & Valanover, S. (2012). The Bernese program against victimization in kindergarten and elementary school. *New Directions in Youth Development, 133,* 15–28.

Alvarez, O., & others. (2012, in press). Effect of hydroxyurea on renal function parameters: Results from the multi-center placebo controlled Baby Hug clinical trial for infants with sickle cell anemia. *Pediatric Blood and Cancer.*

Alves, L., Correia, A. S., Miguel, R., Alegria, P., & Bugalho, P. (2012, in press). Alzheimer's disease: A clinical practice-oriented review. *Frontiers in Neurology.*

Aly, M., & Moscovitch, M. (2010). The effects of sleep on episodic memory in older and younger adults. *Memory, 18,* 327–334.

Alzheimer's Association. (2010). 2010 Alzheimer's disease facts and figures. *Alzheimer's Disease & Dementia, 6,* 158–194.

Alzheimer's Association. (2012). 2012 Alzheimer's disease facts and figures. *Alzheimer's Disease and Dementia, 8,* 131–168.

Amabile, T. M. (1993). Commentary. In D. Goleman, P. Kaufman, & M. Ray. *The creative spirit.* New York: Plume.

Amato, P. R. (2007). Transformative processes in marriage: Some thoughts from a sociologist. *Journal of Marriage and the Family, 69,* 305–309.

Amato, P. R. (2010). Research on divorce: Continuing trends and new developments. *Journal of Marriage and the Family, 72,* 650–666.

Amato, P. R., & Booth, A. (1996). A prospective study of divorce and parent-child relationships. *Journal of Marriage and the Family, 58,* 356–365.

Amato, P. R., & Dorius, C. (2010). Fathers, children, and divorce. In M. E. Lamb (Ed.), *The role of the father in child development* (5th ed.). New York: Wiley.

Ambrose, D., Sternberg, R. J., & Sriraman, B. (2012). Considering the effects of dogmatism on giftedness and talent development. In D. Ambrose, R. J. Sternberg, & B. Sriraman (Eds.), *Confronting dogmatism in gifted education.* New York: Taylor & Francis.

Ament, B. H., & others. (2012, in press). Resources as a protective factor for negative outcomes of frailty in elderly people. *Gerontology.*

American Academy of Pediatrics & Reiff, M. I. (2011). *ADHD: What every parent needs to know* (2nd ed.). Washington, DC: Author.

American Academy of Pediatrics Section on Breastfeeding. (2012). Breastfeeding and the use of human milk. *Pediatrics, 129,* e827–e841.

American Academy of Pediatrics Task Force on Infant Positioning and SIDS. (2000). Changing concepts of sudden infant death syndrome. *Pediatrics, 105,* 650–656.

American Association of University Women. (2006). *Drawing the line: Sexual harassment on campus.* Washington, DC: American Association of University Women.

American Cancer Society. (2012). *Information and resources for cancer.* Retrieved June 24, 2012, from http:www.cancer.org

American College Health Association. (2008). American College Health Association National College Health Assessment, spring 2007. *Journal of American College Health, 56,* 469–479.

American Pregnancy Association. (2012). *Mercury levels in fish.* Retrieved April 12, 2011, from www.americanpregnancy.org/pregnancyhealth/fishmercury.htm

American Psychological Association. (2003). *Psychology: Scientific problem solvers.* Washington, DC: Author.

American Psychological Association. (2007). *Stress in America.* Washington, DC: American Psychological Association.

Amsel, E., & Smetana, J. G. (Eds.). (2011). *Adolescent vulnerabilities and opportunities: Constructivist and developmental perspectives.* New York: Cambridge University Press.

Amso, D., & Johnson, S. P. (2010). Building object knowledge from perceptual input. In B. Hood & L. Santos (Eds.), *The origins of object knowledge.* New York: Oxford University Press.

Amstadter, A. B., McCauley, J. L., Ruggiero, K. J., Resnick, H. S., & Kilpatrick, D. G. (2011). Self-rated health in relation to rape and mental health disorders in a national sample of women. *American Journal of Orthopsychiatry, 81,* 202–210.

Amsterdam, B. K. (1968). *Mirror behavior in children under two years of age.* Unpublished doctoral dissertation. University of North Carolina, Chapel Hill.

Anderman, E. M. (2012). Adolescence. In K. L. Harris, S. Graham, & T. Urdan (Eds.), *APA educational psychology handbook.* Washington, DC: American Psychological Association.

Andersen, S. L., Sebastiani, P., Dworkis, D. A., Feldman, L., & Perls, T. T. (2012). Health span approximates life span among many supercentenarians: Compression of morbidity at the approximate limit of life span. *Journals of Gerontology A: Biological Sciences and Medical Sciences, 67A,* 395–405.

Anderson, E., Greene, S. M., Hetherington, E. M., & Clingempeel, W. G. (1999). The dynamics of parental remarriage. In E. M. Hetherington (Ed.), *Coping with divorce, single parenting, and remarriage.* Mahwah, NJ: Erlbaum.

Anderson, E. R., & Greene, S. M. (2011). "My child and I are a package deal": Balancing adult and child concerns in repartnering after divorce. *Journal of Family Psychology, 25,* 741–750.

Anderson, P. J., & others. (2011). Attention problems in a representative sample of extremely preterm/extremely low birth weight children. *Developmental Neuropsychology, 36,* 57–73.

Anderson, S. A., & Sabatelli, R. M. (2011). *Family interaction* (5th ed.). Upper Saddle River, NJ: Pearson.

Anderson, S. E., Gooze, R. A., Lemeshow, S., & Whitaker, R. C. (2012). Quality of early maternal-child relationship and risk of adolescent obesity. *Pediatrics, 129,* 132–140.

Andersson, H., & Bergman, L. R. (2011). The role of task persistence in young adolescence for successful educational and occupational attainment in middle adulthood. *Developmental Psychology, 47,* 950–960.

Andersson, U. (2010). The contribution of working memory capacity to foreign language comprehension in children. *Memory, 18,* 458–472.

Ando, S. (2012). Neuronal dysfunction with aging and its amelioration. *Proceedings of the Japanese Academy. Series B, Physical and Biological Sciences, 88,* 266–282.

Ang, M., Evans, J. R., & Mehta, J. S. (2012, in press). Manual small incision cataract surgery (MSICS) with posterior chamber intraocular lens versus extracapsular cataract extraction (ECCE) with posterior chamber intraocular lens for age-related cataract. *Cochrane Database of Systematic Reviews*, 18, 4: CD008811.

Angel, L., Fay, S., Bouazzaoui, B., & Isingrini, M. (2011). Two hemispheres for better memory in old age: Role of executive functioning. *Journal of Cognitive Neuroscience*, 23, 3767–3777.

Angelone, D. J., Mitchell, D., & Lucente, L. (2012, in press). Predicting perceptions of date rape: An examination of perpetrator motivation, relationship length, and gender role beliefs. *Journal of Interpersonal Violence*.

Annweiler, C., Montero-Odasso, M., Bartha, R., & Beauchet, O. (2012). Nutrient biomarker patterns, cognitive function, and MRI measures of brain aging. *Neurology*, 78, 1281.

Anspaugh, D., & Ezell, G. (2013). *Teaching today's health* (10th ed.). Upper Saddle River, NJ: Pearson.

Antonopoulos, C., & others. (2011). Maternal smoking during pregnancy and childhood lymphoma: A meta-analysis. *International Journal of Cancer*, 129, 2694–2703.

Antonucci, R., & others. (2012, in press). Use of non-steroidal anti-inflammatory drugs in pregnancy: Impact on the fetus and newborn. *Current Drug Metabolism*.

Antonucci, T. C., Akiyama, H., & Sherman, A. M. (2007). Social networks, support, and integration. In J. E. Birren (Ed.), *Encyclopedia of gerontology* (2nd ed.). San Diego: Academic Press.

Antonucci, T. C., Birditt, K. S., & Ajrouch, K. (2011). Agency and control striving across the life span. In K. L. Fingerman, C. A. Berg, J. Smith, & T. C. Antonucci (Eds.), *Handbook of life-span development*. New York: Springer.

Antonucci, T. C., Birditt, K. S., & Ajrouch, K. (2013, in press). Social relationships and aging. In I. B. Weiner & others (Eds.), *Handbook of psychology* (2nd ed., Vol. 6). New York: Wiley.

Antonucci, T. C., Lansford, J. E., & Akiyama, H. (2001). The impact of positive and negative aspects of marital relationships and friendships on the well-being of older adults. In J. P. Reinhardt (Ed.), *Negative and positive support*. Mahwah, NJ: Erlbaum.

Antonucci, T. C., Vandewater, E. A., & Lansford, J. E. (2000). Adulthood and aging: Social processes and development. In A. Kazdin (Ed.), *Encyclopedia of psychology*. Washington, DC, and New York: American Psychological Association and Oxford University Press.

Apperly, I. A. (2012, in press). EPS prize lecture. "What is theory of mind?": Concepts, cognitive processes, and individual differences. *Quarterly Journal of Experimental Psychology*.

Arabi, M., Frongillo, E. A., Avula, R., & Mangasaryan, N. (2012). Infant and young child feeding in developing countries. *Child Development*, 83, 32–45.

Arbib, M. A. (2012). *How the brain got language*. New York: Oxford University Press.

Archontaki, D., Lewis, G. J., & Bates, T. C. (2012, in press). Genetic influences on psychological well-being: A nationally representative twin study. *Journal of Personality*.

Ardelt, M. (2011). Wisdom, age, and well-being (2011). In K. W. Schaie & S. L. Willis (Eds.), *Handbook of the psychology of aging* (7th ed.). New York: Elsevier.

Arfe, B., Dockrell, J., & Berninger, V. (Eds.) (2013). *Writing development and instruction in children with hearing, speech, and language disorders*. New York: Oxford University Press.

Ariceli, G., Castro, J., Cesena, J., & Toro, J. (2005). Anorexia nervosa in male adolescents: Body image, eating attitudes, and psychological traits. *Journal of Adolescent Health*, 36, 221–226.

Arnett, J. J. (2004). *Emerging adulthood*. New York: Oxford University Press.

Arnett, J. J. (2006). Emerging adulthood: Understanding the new way of coming of age. In J. J. Arnett & J. L. Tanner (Eds.), *Emerging adults in America*. Washington, DC: American Psychological Association.

Arnett, J. J. (2007). Socialization in emerging adulthood. In J. E. Grusec & P. D. Hastings (Eds.), *Handbook of socialization*. New York: Guilford.

Arnett, J. J. (2010). Oh, grow up! Generational grumbling and the new life stage of emerging adulthood—Commentary on Trzesniewski & Donnellan (2010), *Perspectives on Psychological Science*, 5, 89–92.

Arnett, J. J. (Ed.). (2012). *Adolescent psychology around the world*. New York: Psychology Press.

Arnold, A. (2012, April). *Reframing sexual differentiation in the brain*. Paper presented at the Gender Development Research conference, San Francisco.

Aron, A., Aron, E. N., & Coups, E. (2013). *Statistics for psychology* (6th ed.). Upper Saddle River, NJ: Pearson.

Aronow, W. S. (2007). Cardiovascular system. In J. E. Birren (Ed.), *Encyclopedia of gerontology* (2nd ed.). San Diego: Academic Press.

Aronson, E. (1986, August). *Teaching students things they think they already know about: The case of prejudice and desegregation*. Paper presented at the meeting of the American Psychological Association, Washington, DC.

Arseth, A., Kroger, J., Martinussen, M., & Marcia, J. E. (2009). Meta-analytic studies of identity status and the relational issues of attachment and intimacy. *Identity*, 9, 1–32.

Arterberry, M. E. (2008). Perceptual development. In M. E. Haith & J. B. Benson (Eds.), *Encyclopedia of infant and early childhood development*. Oxford, UK: Elsevier.

Asendorph, J. B., Denissen, J. J. A., & van Aken, M. A. G. (2008). Inhibited and aggressive preschool children at 23 years of age: Personality and social transitions into adulthood. *Developmental Psychology*, 44, 997–1011.

Aslan, A., Zellner, M., & Bauml, K. H. (2010). Working memory capacity predicts listwise directed forgetting in adults and children. *Memory*, 18, 442–450.

Aslin, R. N. (2012). Infant eyes: A window on cognitive development. *Infancy*, 17, 126–140.

Aslin, R. N., Jusczyk, P. W., & Pisoni, D. B. (1998). Speech and auditory processing during infancy: Constraints on and precursors to language. In W. Damon (Ed.), *Handbook of child psychology* (5th ed., Vol. 2). New York: Wiley.

Aslin, R. N., & Lathrop, A. L. (2008). Visual perception. In M. M. Haith & J. B. Benson (Eds.), *Encyclopedia of infant and early childhood development*. Oxford, UK: Elsevier.

Assadi, F. (2012, in press). The growing epidemic of hypertension among children and adolescents: A challenging road ahead. *Pediatric Cardiology*.

Astell-Burt, T., Maynard, M. J., Lenguerrand, E., & Harding, S. (2012). Racism, ethnic density, and psychological well-being through adolescence: Evidence from Determinants of Adolescent Social Well-Being and Health longitudinal study. *Ethnicity and Health*, 17, 71–87.

Astington, J. W., & Hughes, C. (2013). Theory of mind: Self-reflection and social understanding. In P. D. Zelazo (Ed.), *Oxford handbook of developmental psychology*. New York: Oxford University Press.

Athanasiadis, A. P., & others. (2011). Correlation of 2nd trimester amniotic fluid amino acid profile with gestational age and estimated fetal weight. *Journal of Maternal-Fetal and Neonatal Medicine*, 24, 1033–1038.

Atkinson, J., & Braddick, O. (2013). Visual development. In P. D. Zelazo (Ed.), *Oxford handbook of developmental psychology*. New York: Oxford University Press.

Atkinson, R. M., Ryan, S. C., & Turner, J. A. (2001). Variation among aging alcoholic patients in treatment. *American Journal of Geriatric Psychiatry*, 9, 275–282.

Attar-Schwartz, S., Tan, J. P., Buchanan, A., Flouri, E., & Griggs, J. (2009). Grandparenting and adolescent development in two-parent biological, lone-parent, and step-families. *Journal of Family Psychology*, 23, 67–75.

Aubert, G., & Lansdorp, P. M. (2008). Telomeres and aging. *Physiological Review*, 88, 557–579.

Aud, S., & others. (2011). *The condition of education 2011*. Washington, DC: U.S. Department of Education.

Auerbach, A. J., & Lee, R. (2011). Welfare and generational equity in sustainable unfunded pension systems. *Journal of Public Economics*, 95, 16–27.

Augestad, L. A., Rand-Hendriksen, K., Staverm, K., & Kristiansen, I. S. (2012, in press). Time trade-off and attitudes toward euthanasia: Implications of using 'death' as an anchor in health state valuation. *Quality of Life Research*.

Avent, N. D. (2012). Refining noninvasive prenatal diagnosis with single-molecule next generation sequencing. *Clinical Chemistry*, 58, 657–658.

Avis, N. E., & others. (2009). Longitudinal changes in sexual functioning as women transition through menopause: Results from the Study of Women's Health Across the Nation. *Menopause*, 16, 442–452.

Ayoub, C., Vallotton, C. D., & Mastergeorge, A. M. (2011). Developmental pathways to integrated social skills: The role of parenting and early intervention. *Child Development*, 82, 583–600.

B

Babbar, S., Parks-Savage, A. C., & Chauhan, S. P. (2012, in press). Yoga during pregnancy. *American Journal of Perinatology*.

Baber, R. (2011). Breast cancer in postmenopausal women after hormone therapy. *JAMA*, 305, 466.

Bachman, J. G., O'Malley, P. M., Schulenberg, J., Johnston, L. D., Bryant, A. L., & Merline, A. C. (2002). *The decline of substance abuse in young adulthood.* Mahwah, NJ: Erlbaum.

Bachman, J. G., O'Malley, P. M., Schulenberg, J. E., Johnston, L. D., Freedman-Doan, P., & Messersmith, E. E. (2008). *The education-drug use connection.* Clifton, NJ: Psychology Press.

Bachrach, R. L., Merrill, J. E., Bytschkow, K. M., & Read, J. P. (2012, in press). Development and initial validation of a measure of motives for pregaming in college students. *Addictive Behaviors.*

Bachschmid, M. M., & others. (2012, in press). Vascular aging: Chronic oxidative stress and impairment of redox signaling—Consequences for vascular homeostatis and disease. *Annals of Medicine.*

Backhans, M. C., & Hemmingsson, T. (2012). Unemployment and mental health—Who is (not) affected? *European Journal of Public Health, 22,* 429–433.

Baddeley, A. (2007). *Working memory, thought, and action.* New York: Oxford University Press.

Baddeley, A. (2012). Working memory. *Annual Review of Psychology* (Vol. 63). Palo Alto, CA: Annual Reviews.

Baddeley, A. D. (1990). *Human memory: Theory and practice.* Boston: Allyn & Bacon.

Baddeley, A. D. (2001). *Is working memory still working?* Paper presented at the meeting of the American Psychological Association, San Francisco.

Baddeley, A. D. (2007). *Working memory, thought, and action.* New York: Oxford University Press.

Baddeley, A. D. (2010). Working memory. *Current Biology, 20,* 136–140.

Baddeley, A. D. (2012a). Prefatory. *Annual Review of Psychology* (Vol. 63). Palo Alto, CA: Annual Reviews.

Baddeley, A. D. (2012b). Working memory: Theories, models, and controversies. *Annual Review of Psychology* (Vol. 63). Palo Alto, CA: Annual Reviews.

Baer, J., & Kaufman, J. C. (2013, in press). *Being creative inside and outside the classroom.* The Netherlands: Sense Publishers.

Bagnato, S. J., & Macy, M. (2012). The authentic alternative for assessment in early childhood intervention. In T. Kehle (Ed.), *Oxford handbook of psychological assessment.* New York: Oxford University Press.

Bahrick, H. P. (1984). Semantic memory content in permastore: Fifty years of memory for Spanish learned in school. *Journal of Experimental Psychology: General. 113,* 1–35.

Bahrick, L. E. (2010). Intermodal perception and selective attention to intersensory redundancy: Implications for social development and autism. In J. G. Bremner & T. D. Wachs (Eds.), *Wiley-Blackwell handbook of infant development* (2nd ed.). New York: Wiley.

Bahrick, L. E., & Hollich, G. (2008). Intermodal perception. In M. M. Haith & J. B. Benson (Eds.), *Encyclopedia of infant and early childhood development.* Oxford, UK: Elsevier.

Baillargeon, R. (1995). The object concept revisited: New directions in the investigation of infants' physical knowledge. In C. E. Granrud (Ed.), *Visual perception and cognition in infancy.* Hillsdale, NJ: Erlbaum.

Baillargeon, R. (2004). The acquisition of physical knowledge in infancy: A summary in eight lessons. In U. Goswami (Ed.), *Blackwell handbook of childhood cognitive development.* Malden, MA: Blackwell.

Baillargeon, R. (2008). Innate ideas revisited: For a principle of persistence in infants' physical reasoning. *Perspectives on Psychological Science, 3,* 2–13.

Baillargeon, R., & Carey, S. (2012, in press). Core cognition and beyond: The acquisition of physical and numerical knowledge. In S. Pauen & M. Bornstein (Eds.), *Early childhood development and later outcome.* New York: Cambridge University Press.

Baillargeon, R., & DeVos, J. (1991). Object permanence in young children: Further evidence. *Child Development, 62,* 1227–1246.

Baillargeon, R., Li, J., Gertner, Y., & Wu, D. (2011). How do infants reason about physical events? In U. Goswami (Ed.), *Wiley-Blackwell handbook of childhood cognitive development* (2nd ed.). New York: Wiley.

Baillargeon, R., & others. (2012, in press). Object individuation and physical reasoning in infancy: An integrative account. *Language, Learning, and Development.*

Baimel, C., Borgland, S. L., & Corrigall, W. (2012). Cocaine and nicotine research illustrates a range of hypocretin mechanisms in addiction. *Vitamins and Hormones, 89,* 291–313.

Bain, J. (2010). Testosterone and the aging male: To treat or not to treat? *Maturitas, 66,* 16–22.

Bakeman, R., & Brown, J. V. (1980). Early interaction: Consequences for social and mental development at three years. *Child Development, 51,* 437–447.

Bakeman, R., & Quera, V. (2012). Behavioral observation. In H. Cooper (Ed.), *APA handbook of research methods in psychology.* Washington, DC: American Psychological Association.

Baker, J. H., Thorton, L. M., Lichtenstein, P., & Bulik, C. M. (2012, in press). Pubertal development predicts eating behaviors in adolescents. *International Journal of Eating Disorders.*

Baker, J. K., Fenning, R. M., & Crnic, K. A. (2011). Emotion socialization by mothers and fathers: Coherence among behaviors and associations with parent attitudes and children's competence. *Social Development, 20,* 412–430.

Bakermans-Kranenburg, M. J., & van IJzendoorn, M. H. (2011). Differential susceptibility to rearing environment depending on dopamine-related genes: New evidence and a meta-analysis. *Development and Psychopathology, 23,* 39–52.

Balaji, P., Dhillon, P., & Russell, I. F. (2009). Low-dose epidural top up for emergency cesarean delivery: A randomized comparison of levobpivacaine versus lidocaine/epinephrine/fentanyl. *International Journal of Obstetric Anesthesia, 18,* 335–341.

Balarajah, S., & Cavanna, A. E. (2012, in press). The pathophysiology of impulse control disorders in Parkinson disease. *Behavioral Neurology.*

Baldwin, S. A., Christian, S., Berkeljon, A., & Shadish, W. R. (2012). The effects of family therapies for adolescent delinquency and substance abuse: A meta-analysis. *Journal of Marital and Family Therapy, 38,* 281–304.

Balistreri, C. R., & others. (2012, in press). Genetics of longevity. Data from the studies of Sicilian centenarians. *Immunity and Aging.*

Ball, K., Edwards, J. D., & Ross, L. A. (2007). The impact of speed of process training on cognitive and everyday functions. *Journals of Gerontology B: Psychological Sciences and Social Sciences, 62,* P19–P31.

Ballard, S. (2011). Blood tests for investigating maternal well-being. 4. When nausea and vomiting in pregnancy becomes pathological: Hyperemesis gravidarum. *Practicing Midwife, 14,* 37–41.

Balsa, A. I., Giuliano, L. M., & French, M. T. (2011). The effects of alcohol use on academic achievement in high school. *Economics of Education Review, 30,* 1–15.

Balsam, K., & Hughes, T. (2013, in press). Sexual orientation, victimization, and hate crimes. In C. J. Patterson & A. R. D'Augelli (Eds.), *Handbook of psychology and sexual orientation.* New York: Oxford University Press.

Balsano, Theokas, C., & Bobek, D. L. (2009). A shared commitment to youth: The integration of theory, research, and policy. In R. M. Lerner & L. Steinberg (Eds.), *Handbook of adolescent psychology* (3rd ed.). New York: Wiley.

Baltes, P. B. (1987). Theoretical propositions of life-span developmental psychology: On the dynamics between growth and decline. *Developmental Psychology, 23,* 611–626.

Baltes, P. B. (2003). On the incomplete architecture of human ontogeny: Selection, optimization, and compensation as foundation of developmental theory. In U. M. Staudinger & U. Lindenberger (Eds.), *Understanding human development.* Boston: Kluwer.

Baltes, P. B. (2006). *Facing our limits. The very old and the future of aging.* Unpublished manuscript, Max Planck Institute, Berlin.

Baltes, P. B., & Kunzmann, U. (2007). Wisdom and aging: The road toward excellence in mind and character. In D. C. Park & N. Schwarz (Eds.), *Cognitive aging: A primer* (2nd ed.). Philadelphia: Psychology Press.

Baltes, P. B., Lindenberger, U., & Staudinger, U. (2006). Life span theory in developmental psychology. In. W. Damon & R. Lerner (Eds.), *Handbook of child psychology* (6th ed.), New York: Wiley.

Baltes, P. B., Reuter-Lorenz, P., & Rösler, F. (Eds.). (2006). *Lifespan development and the brain.* New York: Cambridge University Press.

Baltes, P. B., & Smith, J. (2003). New frontiers in the future of aging: From successful aging of the young old to the dilemmas of the fourth age. *Gerontology, 49,* 123–135.

Baltes, P. B., & Smith, J. (2008). The fascination of wisdom: Its nature, ontogeny, and function. *Perspectives in Psychological Sciences, 3,* 56–64.

Bandura, A. (1986). *Social foundations of thought and action: A social cognitive theory.* Englewood Cliffs, NJ: Prentice Hall.

Bandura, A. (1998, August). *Swimming against the mainstream: Accentuating the positive aspects of humanity.* Paper presented at the meeting of the American Psychological Association, San Francisco.

Bandura, A. (2001). Social cognitive theory. *Annual Review of Psychology.* Palo Alto, CA: Annual Reviews.

Bandura, A. (2004, May). *Toward a psychology of human agency.* Paper presented at the meeting of the American Psychological Society, Chicago.

Bandura, A. (2008). Reconstrual of free will from the agentic perspective of social cognitive theory. In J. Baer, J. C. Kaufman, & R. F. Baumeister (Eds.), *Are we free? Psychology and free will.* Oxford, UK: Oxford University Press.

Bandura, A. (2009). Social policy impact of social cognitive theory. In M. Mark, S. Donaldson, & B. Campbell (Eds.), *Social psychology and program/ policy evaluation.* New York: Guilford.

Bandura, A. (2010a). Self-efficacy. In D. Matsumoto (Ed.), *Cambridge dictionary of psychology.* New York: Cambridge University Press.

Bandura, A. (2010b). Vicarious learning. In D. Matsumoto (Ed.), *Cambridge dictionary of psychology.* New York: Cambridge University Press.

Bandura, A. (2012). Social cognitive theory. *Annual Review of Clinical Psychology* (Vol. 8). Palo Alto, CA: Annual Reviews.

Banerjee, S. (2011). Hearing aids in the real world: Use of multimemory and multivolume controls. *Journal of the American Academy of Audiology, 22,* 359–374.

Bangdiwala, S. I., & others. (2010). NIH consensus development conference draft statement on vaginal birth after cesarean: new insights. *NIH Consensus Statements and Scientific Statements, 27,* 3.

Banja, J. (2005). Talking to the dying. *Case Manager, 16,* 37–39.

Bank, L., Burraston, B., & Snyder, J. (2004). Sibling conflict and ineffective parenting as predictors of adolescent boys' antisocial behavior and peer difficulties: Additive and interactive effects. *Journal of Research on Adolescence. 14,* 99–125.

Barakat, R., & others. (2011). Exercise during pregnancy improves maternal health perception: A randomized controlled trial. *American Journal of Obstetrics and Gynecology, 204,* e1–e7.

Bardach, S. H., & Rowles, G. D. (2012, in press). Geriatric education in the health professions: Are we making progress? *Gerontologist.*

Barefoot, J. C., Mortensen, E. L., Helms, J., Avlund, K., & Schroll, M. (2001). A longitudinal study of gender differences in depressive symptoms from age 50 to 80. *Psychology and Aging, 16,* 342–345.

Bargh, J. A., & McKenna, K. Y. A. (2004). The Internet and social life. *Annual Review of Psychology* (Vol. 55). Palo Alto, CA: Annual Reviews.

Barker, R., & Wright, H. F. (1951). *One boy's day.* New York: Harper & Row.

Barnett, J. E., & Frances, A. L. (2012). Using higher-order thinking questions to foster critical thinking: A classroom study. *Educational Psychology, 32,* 201–211.

Barnett, W. S., & others. (2006). Educational effectiveness of the Tools of the Mind curriculum: A randomized trial. New Brunswick, NJ: National Institute of Early Education Research, Rutgers University.

Baron, C. (2012). Using the gradient of human cortical bone properties to determine age-related bone changes via ultrasonic guided waves. *Ultrasound in Medicine and Biology, 38,* 972–981.

Baron, I. S., Erickson, K., Ahronovich, M. D., Baker, R., & Litman, F. R. (2011). Neuropsychological and behavioral outcomes of extremely low birth weight at age three. *Developmental Neuropsychology, 36,* 5–21.

Baron, N. S. (1992). *Growing up with language.* Reading, MA: Addison-Wesley.

Baron-Cohen, S. (2008). Autism, hypersystemizing, and truth. *Quarterly Journal of Experimental Psychology, 61,* 64–75.

Baron-Cohen, S. (2011). The empathizing-systematizing (E-S) theory of autism: A cognitive developmental account. In U. Goswami (Ed.), *Wiley-Blackwell handbook of childhood cognitive development* (2nd ed.). New York: Wiley.

Baron-Cohen, S., Golan, O., Chapman, E., & Granader, Y. (2007). Transported to a world of emotion. *The Psychologist, 20,* 76–77.

Barrett, D. E., Radke-Yarrow, M., & Klein, R. E. (1982). Chronic malnutrition and child behavior: Effects of calorie supplementation on social and emotional functioning at school age. *Developmental Psychology, 18,* 541–556.

Barrett, T. M., Traupman, E., & Needham, A. (2008). Infants' visual anticipation of object structure in grasp planning. *Infant Behavior and Development, 31,* 1–9.

Bartel, M. A., Weinstein, J. R., & Schaffer, D. V. (2012, in press). Directed evolution of novel adeno-associated viruses for therapeutic gene delivery. *Gene Therapy.*

Barth, T. (2012). Relationships and sexuality of imprisoned men in the German penal system—a survey of inmates in a Berlin prison. *International Journal of Law and Psychiatry, 35,* 153–158.

Bartsch, K., & Wellman, H. M. (1995). *Children talk about the mind.* New York: Oxford University Press.

Baruth, M., & Wilcox, S. (2011). Effectiveness of two evidence-based programs in participants with arthritis: Findings from the Active For Life Initiative. *Arthritis Care & Research, 63,* 1038–1047.

Basaran, A., Basaran, M., & Topatan, B. (2011). Chorionic villus sampling and the risk of preeclampsia: A systematic review and meta-analysis. *Archives of Gynecology and Obstetrics, 283,* 1175–1181.

Baskin, F., & others. (2011). Coalitions on mental health and aging: Lessons learned for policy and practice. *Journal of Aging and Social Policy, 23,* 323–332.

Bassett, C. L. (2012). Wisdom and its development: Learning to become wise(r). In C. Hoare (Ed.), *Oxford handbook of reciprocal adult development and learning.* New York: Oxford University Press.

Bassett, H. H., Denham, S. A., Mincic, M. M., & Graling, K. (2012, in press). The structure of preschoolers' relationship knowledge: Model equivalence and validity using an SEM approach. *Early Education and Development.*

Bates, E. (1990). Language about me and you: Pronomial reference and the emerging concept of self. In D. Cicchetti & M. Beeghly (Eds.), *The self in transition: Infancy to childhood.* Chicago: University of Chicago Press.

Bates, J. E. (2012a). Behavioral regulation as a product of temperament and environment. In S. L. Olson & A. J. Sameroff (Eds.), *Biopsychosocial regulatory processes in the development of childhood behavioral problems.* New York: Cambridge University Press.

Bates, J. E. (2012b). Temperament as a tool in promoting early childhood development. In S. L. Odom, E. P. Pungello, & N. Gardner-Neblett (Eds.), *Infants, toddlers, and families in poverty.* New York: Guilford University Press.

Bateson, D. J., Weisberg, E., McCaffery, K. J., & Luscombe, G. M. (2012). When online becomes Online: Attitudes to safer sex practices in older and younger women using an Australian internet dating service. *Sexual Health, 9,* 152–159.

Bauer, I., Wrosch, C., & Jobin, J. (2008). I'm better off than most people: The role of social comparisons for coping with regret in young adulthood and old age. *Psychology and Aging, 23,* 800–811.

Bauer, P. J. (2009a). Learning and memory: Like a horse and carriage. In A. Woodward & A. Needham (Eds.), *Learning and the infant mind.* New York: Oxford University Press.

Bauer, P. J. (2009b). Neurodevelopmental changes in infancy and beyond: Implications for learning and memory. In O. A. Barbarin & B. H. Wasik (Eds.), *Handbook of child development and early education.* New York: Guilford.

Bauer, P. J. (2013). Memory. In P. D. Zelazo (Ed.), *Oxford handbook of developmental psychology.* New York: Oxford University Press.

Bauer, P. J., & Fivush, R. (Eds.) (2013, in press). *Wiley-Blackwell handbook of children's memory.* New York: Oxford University Press.

Bauer, P. J., Larkina, M., & Deocampo, J. (2011). Early memory development. In U. Goswami (Ed.), *Wiley-Blackwell handbook of childhood cognitive development* (2nd ed.). New York: Wiley.

Bauer, P. J., Wenner, J. A., Dropik, P. I., & Wewerka, S. S. (2000). Parameters of remembering and forgetting in the transition from infancy to early childhood. *Monographs of the Society for Research in Child Development, 65* (4, Serial No. 263).

Bauer, R. M., & Dunn, C. B. (2013, in press). Research methods in neuropsychology. In I. B. Weiner & others (Eds.), *Handbook of psychology* (2nd ed., Vol. 2). New York: Wiley.

Bauland, C. G., & others. (2012). Similar risk for hemangiomas after amniocentesis and transabdominal chorionic villus sampling. *Journal of Obstetrics and Gynecology Research, 38,* 371–375.

Bauman, K. E., Ennett, S. T., Foshee, V. A., Pemberton, M., King, T. S., & Koch, G. G. (2002). Influence of a family program on adolescent smoking and drinking prevalence. *Prevention Science, 3,* 35–42.

Baumeister, R.F. (2013, in press). Self-esteem. In E. Anderson (Ed.), *Psychology of classroom learning: An encyclopedia.* Detroit: Macmillan.

Baumeister, R. F., Campbell, J. D., Krueger, J. I., & Vohs, K. D. (2003). Does high self-esteem cause better performance, interpersonal success, happiness, or healthier lifestyles? *Psychological Science in the Public Interest, 4*(1), 1–44.

Baumeister, R. F., & Vohs, K. D. (2002). The pursuit of meaningfulness in life. In C. R. Snyder & S. J. Lopez (Eds.), *Handbook of positive psychology.* New York: Oxford University Press.

Baumrind, D. (1971). Current patterns of parental authority. *Developmental Psychology Monographs, 4* (1, Pt. 2).

Baumrind, D. (1999, November). Unpublished review of J. W. Santrock's *Child development* (9th ed.). New York: McGraw-Hill.

Baumrind, D., Larzelere, R. E., & Cowan, P. A. (2002). Ordinary physical punishment: Is it harmful? Comment on Gershoff. *Psychological Bulletin, 128,* 590–595.

Baumrind, D., Larzelere, R. E., & Owens, E. B. (2010). Effects of preschool parents' power assertive patterns and practices on adolescent development. *Parenting, 10,* 157–201.

Baur, J. A., & others. (2012). Are sirtuins viable targets for improving healthspan and lifespan? Nature Reviews. *Drug Discovery, 11,* 443–461.

Bauserman, R. (2002). Child adjustment in joint-custody versus sole-custody arrangements: A meta-analytical review. *Journal of Family Psychology, 16,* 91–102.

Bayley, N. (1969). *Manual for the Bayley Scales of Infant Development.* New York: Psychological Corporation.

Bayley, N. (2006). *Bayley Scales of Infant and Toddler Development* (3rd ed.). San Antonio: Harcourt Assessment.

Beall, S. A., & Decherny, A. (2012). History and challenges surrounding ovarian stimulation in the treatment of infertility. *Fertility and Sterility, 97,* 795–801.

Beard, J. R., & others. (2012). Introduction. *Global population aging: Peril or promise?* Geneva, SWIT: World Economic Forum.

Bearman, S. K., Presnall, K., Martinez, E., & Stice, E. (2006). The skinny on body dissatisfaction: A longitudinal study of adolescent girls and boys. *Journal of Youth and Adolescence, 35,* 217–229.

Beauchamp, G., & Mennella, J. A. (2009). Early flavor learning and its impact on later feeding behavior. *Journal of Pediatric Gastroenterology and Nutrition, 48* (Suppl 1), S25–S30.

Beaulieu, D. A., & Bugental, D. B. (2007). An evolutionary approach to socialization. In J. E. Grusec & P. D. Hastings (Eds.). *Handbook of socialization.* New York: Guilford.

Beaver, K. M., Vaughn, M. G., Wright, J. P., & Delisi, M. (2012). An interaction between perceived stress and 5HTTLPR genotype in the prediction of stable depressive symptomatology. *American Journal of Orthopsychiatry, 82,* 260–266.

Bechtold, A. G., Bushnell, E. W., & Salapatek, P. (1979, April). Infants' visual localization of visual and auditory targets. Paper presented at the meeting of the Society for Research in Child Development, San Francisco.

Beck, C. T. (2006). Postpartum depression: It isn't just the blues. *American Journal of Nursing, 106,* 40–50.

Beck, D. M., Schaefer, C., Pang, K., & Carlson, S. M. (2011). Executive functioning in preschool children: Test-retest reliability. *Journal of Cognition and Development, 12,* 169–193.

Bedford, R., & others. (2012, in press). Precursors to social and communication difficulties in infants at risk for autism: Gaze following and attentional engagement. *Journal of Autism and Developmental Disorders.*

Bedford, V. H. (2009). Sibling relationships: Adulthood. In D. Carr (Ed.), *Encyclopedia of the life course and human development.* Boston: Gale Cengage.

Bednar, R. L., Wells, M. G., & Peterson, S. R. (1995). *Self-esteem* (2nd ed.). Washington, DC: American Psychological Association.

Beebe, D. W. (2011). Cognitive, behavioral, and functional consequences of inadequate sleep in children and adolescents. *Pediatric Clinics of North America, 58,* 649–665.

Beech, A. R., Ward, T., & Fisher, D. (2006). The identification of sexual and violent motivations in men who assault women: Implications for treatment. *Journal of Interpersonal Violence, 21,* 1635–1653.

Beeghly, M., Martin, B., Rose-Jacobs, R., Cahral, H., Heeren, T., Augustyn, M., & others. (2006). Prenatal cocaine exposure and children's language functioning at 6 and 9.5 years: Moderating effects of child age, birthweight, and gender. *Journal of Pediatric Psychology, 31,* 98–115.

Beets, M. W., & Foley, J. T. (2008). Association of father involvement and neighborhood quality with kindergarteners' physical activity: A multilevel structural equation model. *American Journal of Health Promotion, 22*(3), 195–203.

Behrens, H. (2012). Grammatical categories. In E. L. Bavin (Ed.), *Cambridge handbook of child language.* New York: Cambridge University Press.

Beins, B. C. (2013). *Research methods* (3rd ed.). Upper Saddle River, NJ: Pearson.

Bekman, S., & Aksu-Koc, A. (Eds.) (2012). *Perspectives on human development, family, and culture.* New York: Cambridge University Press.

Belk, C., & Maier, V. B. (2013). *Biology* (4th ed.). Upper Saddle River, NJ: Pearson.

Bell, J. T., & Saffery, R. (2012). The value of twins in epigenetic epidemiology. *International Journal of Epidemiology, 4,* 140–150.

Bell, M. A. (2012). A psychobiological perspective on working memory performance at 8 months of age. *Child Development, 83,* 251–265.

Bell, M. A., & Calkins, S. D. (2012). Attentional control and emotion regulation in early development. In M. I. Posner (Ed.), *Cognitive neuroscience of attention* (2nd ed.). New York: Guilford.

Bell, M. A., & Cuevas, K. (2012, in press). Psychobiology of executive function in early development. In J. A. Griffin, L. S. Freund, & P. McCardle (Eds.), *Executive functioning in preschool age children.* Washington, DC: American Psychological Association.

Bell, M. A., & Diaz, A. (2012, in press). EEG/ERP measures of emotion-cognition integration during development. In T. A. Dennis, K. A. Buss, & P. D. Hastings (Eds.), Physiological measures of emotion from a developmental perspective: State of the science. *Monographs of the Society for Research in Child Development.*

Bell, R. D., & others. (2012, in press). Apolipoprotein E controls cerebrovascular integrity via cyclophillin. *Nature.*

Bell, S. M., & Ainsworth, M. D. S. (1972). Infant crying and maternal responsiveness. *Child Development, 43,* 1171–1190.

Belsky, J. (1981). Early human experience: A family perspective. *Developmental Psychology, 17,* 3–23.

Belsky, J., & others. (2007). Are there long-term effects of early child care? *Child Development, 78,* 681–701.

Bem, S. I. (1977). On the utility of alternative procedures for assessing psychological androgyny. *Journal of Consulting and Clinical Psychology, 45,* 196–205.

Benbow, S. M., & Beeston, D. (2012). Sexuality, aging, and dementia. *International Psychogeriatrics, 24,* 1026–1033.

Bendersky, M., & Sullivan, M. W. (2007). Basic methods in infant research. In A. Slater & M. Lewis (Eds.), *Introduction to infant development* (2nd ed.). New York: Oxford University Press.

Benenson, J. F., Apostolaris, N. H., & Parnass, J. (1997). Age and sex differences in dyadic and group interaction. *Developmental Psychology, 33,* 538–543.

Bengtson, V. L. (1985). Diversity and symbolism in grandparental roles. In V. L. Bengtson & J. Robertson (Eds.). *Grandparenthood.* Newbury Park, CA: Sage.

Bengtsson, H., & Arvidsson, A. (2011). The impact of developing social perspective-taking skills on emotionality in middle and late childhood. *Social Development, 20,* 353–375.

Benichov, J., Cox, L. C., Tun, P. A., & Wingfield, A. (2012). Word recognition within a linguistic context: Effects of age, hearing acuity, verbal ability, and cognitive function. *Ear and Hearing, 33,* 250–256.

Bennett, J. S., Boyle, P. A., James, B. D., & Bennett, D. A. (2012, in press). Correlates of health and financial literacy in older adults without dementia. *BMC Geriatrics.*

Bennett, K. M. (2006). Does marital status and marital status change predict physical health in older adults? *Psychological Medicine, 36,* 1313–1320.

Bennett, K. M. (2009). Widowhood. In D. Carr (Ed.), *Encyclopedia of the life course and human development.* Boston: Gale Cengage.

Bennett, S. A., Bagot, C. N., & Arya, R. (2012, in press). Pregnancy loss and thrombophilia: The elusive link. *British Journal of Hematology.*

Benoit, D., Coolbear, J., & Crawford, A. (2008). Abuse, neglect, and maltreatment of infants. In M. M. Haith & J. B. Benson (Eds.), *Encyclopedia of infant and early childhood development.* Oxford, UK: Elsevier.

Benokraitis, N. (2012). *Marriage and families* (7th ed.). Upper Saddle River, NJ: Pearson.

Benowitz-Fredericks, C. A., Garcia, K., Massey, M., Vassagar, B., & Borzekowski, D. L. (2012). Body image, eating disorders, and the relationship to adolescent media use. *Pediatric Clinics of North America, 59,* 693–704.

Benson, P. L. (2010). *Parent, teacher, mentor, friend: How every adult can change kids' lives.* Minneapolis: Search Institute Press.

Benson, P. L., Mannes, M., Pittman, K., & Ferber, T. (2004). Youth development, developmental assets, and public policy. In R. Lerner & L. Steinberg (Eds.),

Handbook of adolescent psychology (2nd ed.). New York: Wiley.

Benson, P. L., Roehlkepartain, E. C., & Scales, P. C. (2012, in press). Spirituality and positive youth development. In L. Miller (Ed.), *Oxford handbook of spirituality and consciousness.* New York: Oxford University Press.

Benson, P. L., & Scales, P. C. (2009). The definition and preliminary measurement of thriving in adolescence. *Journal of Positive Psychology, 4,* 85–104.

Benson, P. L., & Scales, P. C. (2011). Thriving and sparks: Development and emergence of new core concepts in positive youth development. In R. J. R. Levesque (Ed.), *Encyclopedia of adolescence.* Berlin: Springer.

Bentley, M. E., Wasser, H. M., & Creed-Kanashiro, H. M. (2011). Responsive feeding and child undernutrition in low- and middle-income countries. *Journal of Nutrition, 141,* 502–507.

Ben-Zur, H. (2012). Loneliness, optimism, and well-being among married, divorced, and widowed individuals. *Journal of Psychology, 146,* 23–36.

Berenbaum, S. A., & Beltz, A. M. (2011). Sexual differentiation of human behavior: Effects of prenatal and pubertal organization hormones. *Frontiers in Neuroscience, 32,* 183–200.

Berenson, J., Doty, M. M., Abram, M. K., & Shih, A. (2012). Achieving better quality of care for low-income populations: The roles of health insurance and the medical home in reducing health inequities. *Issues Brief, 11,* 1–18.

Bergen, D. (1988). Stages of play development. In D. Bergen (Ed.), *Play as a medium for learning and development.* Portsmouth, NH: Heinemann.

Bergman Levy, T., Barak, Y., Sigler, M., & Aizenberg, D. (2011). Suicide attempts and burden of physical illness among depressed elderly patients. *Archives of Gerontology and Geriatrics, 52,* 115–117.

Berk, L. E. (1994). Why children talk to themselves. *Scientific American, 271*(5), 78–83.

Berk, L. E., & Spuhl, S. T. (1995). Maternal interaction, private speech, and task performance in preschool children. *Early Childhood Research Quarterly, 10,* 145–169.

Berko, J. (1958). The child's learning of English morphology. *Word, 14,* 150–177.

Berko Gleason, J. (2009). The development of language: An overview. In J. Berko Gleason & N. B. Rather (Eds.), *The development of language* (7th ed.). Boston: Allyn & Bacon.

Berkowitz, M. W. (2012). Moral and character education. In K. R. Harris, S. Graham, & T. Urdan (Eds.), *APA educational psychology handbook.* Washington, DC: American Psychological Association.

Berlin, L. J. (2012). Leveraging attachment research to re-vision infant/toddler care for poor families. In S. L. Odom, E. P. Pungello, & N. Gardner-Neblett (Eds.), *Infants, toddlers, and families in poverty.* New York: Guilford.

Berlin, L. J. & others. (2009). Correlates and consequences of spanking and verbal punishment for low-income White, African-American, and Mexican American toddlers. *Child Development, 80,* 1403–1420.

Berlyne, D. E. (1960). *Conflict, arousal, and curiosity.* New York: McGraw-Hill.

Bernard, K., & Dozier, M. (2008). Adoption and foster placement. In M. M. Haith & J. B. Benson (Eds.), *Encyclopedia of infant and early childhood development.* Oxford, UK: Elsevier.

Bernard, K., & others. (2012). Enhancing attachment organization among maltreated children: Results from a randomized clinical trial. *Child Development, 83,* 623–636.

Bernardes de Jesus, B., & others. (2012, in press). Telomerase gene therapy in adult and old mice delays aging and increases longevity without increasing cancer. *EMBO Molecular Medicine.*

Berndt, T. J., & Perry, T. B. (1990). Distinctive features and effects of early adolescent friendships. In R. Montemayor (Ed.), *Advances in adolescent research.* Greenwich, CT: JAI Press.

Berninger, V., & Dunn, M. (2012). Brain and behavioral response to intervention for specific reading, writing, and math disabilities: What works for whom? In B. Wong & D. Butler (Eds.), *Learning about LD* (4th ed.). New York: Elsevier.

Berninger, V. W., & O'Malley, M. M. (2011). Evidence-based diagnosis and treatment for specific learning disabilities involving impairments in written and/or oral language. *Journal of Learning Disabilities, 44,* 167–183.

Berookhim, B. M., & Bar-Charma, N. (2011). Medical implications of erectile dysfunction. *Medical Clinics of North America, 95,* 213–221.

Berraho, M., & others. (2010). Body mass index, disability, and 13-year mortality in older French adults. *Journal of Aging and Health, 22,* 68–83.

Berry, D., Deater-Deckard, K., McCartney, K., Wang, Z., & Petrill, S.A. (2012, in press). Gene-environment interaction between DRD4 7-repeat VNTR and early maternal sensitivity predicts inattention trajectories across middle childhood. *Development and Psychopathology.*

Bers, M. U., & Kazakoff, E. R. (2013, in press). Developmental technologies: Technology and human development. In I. B. Weiner & others (Eds.), *Handbook of aging* (2nd ed., Vol. 6). New York: Wiley.

Berscheid, E. (1988). Some comments on love's anatomy: Or, whatever happened to old-fashioned lust? In R. J. Sternberg (Ed.), *Anatomy of love.* New Haven, CT: Yale University Press.

Berscheid, E. (2010). Love in the fourth dimension. *Annual Review of Psychology* (Vol. 61). Palo Alto, CA: Annual Reviews.

Bertenthal, B. I. (2008). Perception and action. In M. M. Haith & J. B. Benson (Eds.), *Encyclopedia of infant and early childhood development.* Oxford, UK: Elsevier.

Bertenthal, B. I., Longo, M. R., & Kenny, S. (2007). Phenomenal permanence and the development of predictive tracking in infancy. *Child Development, 78,* 350–363.

Bertrand, R., Graham, E. K., & Lachman, M. E. (2013). Personality development in adulthood and old age. In I. B. Weiner & others (Eds.), *Handbook of psychology* (2nd ed., Vol. 6). New York: Wiley.

Best, J. R. (2010). Effects of physical activity on children's executive function: Contributions of experimental research on aerobic exercise. *Developmental Review, 30,* 331–351.

Beverly, C., Burger, S. G., Maas, M. L., & Specht, J. K. (2010). Aging issues: Nursing imperatives for healthcare reform. *Nursing Administration Quarterly, 34,* 95–109.

Beyene, Y. (1986). Cultural significance and physiological manifestations of menopause: A biocultural analysis. *Culture, Medicine and Psychiatry, 10,* 47–71.

Beyerlein, A., & others. (2011). Is low birth weight in the causal pathway of the association between maternal smoking in pregnancy and higher BMI in the offspring? *European Journal of Epidemiology, 26,* 413–420.

Beyers, E., & Seiffge-Krenke, I. (2010). Does identity precede intimacy? Testing Erikson's theory on romantic development in emerging adults of the 21st century. *Journal of Adolescent Research, 25,* 387–415.

Bhutta, Z. A., & Reddy, K. S. (2012). Achieving equality in global health: So near and yet so far. *Journal of the American Medical Association, 307,* 2035–2036.

Bialystok, E. (1997). Effects of bilingualism and biliteracy on children's emerging concepts of print. *Developmental Psychology, 33,* 429–440.

Bialystok, E. (2001). *Bilingualism in development: Language, literacy, and cognition.* New York: Cambridge University Press.

Bialystok, E. (2007). Acquisition of literacy in preschool children. A framework for research. *Language Learning, 57,* 45–77.

Bialystok, E. (2011). *Becoming bilingual: Emergence of cognitive outcomes of bilingualism in immersion education.* Paper presented at the meeting of the Society for Research in Child Development, Montreal.

Bialystok, E., & Craik, F. I. M. (2010). Cognitive and linguistic processing in the bilingual mind. *Current Directions in Psychological Science, 19,* 19–23.

Bian, Z., & Anderson, G. J. (2008). Aging and the perceptual organization of 3-D scenes. *Psychology and Aging, 23,* 342–352.

Biehle, S. N., & Mickelson, K. D. (2012). First-time parents' expectations about the division of childcare and play. *Journal of Family Psychology, 26,* 36–45.

Bielak, A. A. M., Hughes, T. F., Small, B. J., & Dixon, R. A. (2007). It's never too late to engage in lifestyle activities: Significant concurrent but not change relationships between lifestyle activities and cognitive speed. *Journals of Gerontology: Psychological Sciences and Social Sciences, 62B,* P331–P339.

Bierman, K. L., & Powers, C. J. (2009). Social skills training to improve peer relations. In K. H. Rubin, W. M. Bukowski, & B. Laursen (Eds.), *Handbook of peer interactions, relationships, and groups.* New York: Guilford.

Bierman, K. L., & others. (2008). Executive functions and school readiness intervention: Impact, moderation, and mediation in the Head Start-REDI Program. *Development and Psychopathology, 20,* 821–843.

Bigelow, A. E., & Power, M. (2012). The effect of mother-infant and skin-to-skin contact on infants' response to the Still Face Task from newborn to three months of age. *Infant Behavior and Development, 35*, 240–251.

Bigelow, A. E., & others. (2010). Maternal sensitivity throughout infancy: Continuity and relation to attachment security. *Infant Behavior and Development, 33*, 50–60.

Biggs, S., Carstensen, L. L., & Hogan, P. (2012). Social capital, lifelong learning, and social innovation. *Global population aging: Peril or promise?* Geneva, SWIT: World Economic Forum.

Bihagi, S. W., & others. (2012, in press). Do epigenetic pathways initiate late onset Alzheimer disease (LOAD)? Towards a new paradigm. *Current Alzheimer Research.*

Bill and Melinda Gates Foundation. (2008). *Report gives voice to dropouts.* Retrieved July 5, 2008, from http://www.gatesfoundation.org/UnitedStates/Education/TransformingHighSchools/Related

Bill and Melinda Gates Foundation. (2011). *College-ready education.* Retrieved August 21, 2011, from www.gatesfoundation.org/college-ready-education/Pages/default.aspx

Binderman, C. D., Krakauer, E. L., & Solomon, M. Z. (2012). Time to revise the approach to cardiopulmonary resuscitation status. *JAMA, 307*, 917–918.

Birditt, K. S., Fingerman, K. L., & Zarit, S. (2010). Adult children's problems and successes: Implications for intergenerational ambivalence. *Journals of Gerontology B: Psychological Sciences and Social Sciences, 65B*, 145–153.

Birditt, K. S., & Wardjiman, E. (2012a). Intergenerational relationships and aging. In S. K. Whitbourne & M. J. Sliwinski (Eds.), *Wiley-Blackwell handbook of adult development and aging.* New York: Wiley.

Birditt, K. S., & Wardjiman, E. (2012b). Partners and friends in adulthood. In S. K. Whitbourne & M. Sliwinski (Eds.), *Wiley-Blackwell handbook of adult development and aging.* New York: Wiley.

Birman, B. F., & others. (2007). *State and local implementation of the "No Child Left Behind act." Volume II—Teacher Quality under "NCLB": Interim report.* Jessup, MD: U.S. Department of Education.

Birren, J. E. (Ed.). (1996). *Encyclopedia of gerontology.* San Diego: Academic Press.

Bisceglia, R., & others. (2012). Arginine vasopressin 1a receptor gene and maternal behavior: Evidence of association and moderation. *Genes, Brain, and Behavior, 11*, 262–268.

Bishop, D. V., & others. (2011). Autism, language, and communication in children with sex chromosome trisomies. *Archives of Disease in Childhood, 96*, 954–959.

Bisiacchi, P. S., Tarantino, V., & Ciccola, A. (2008). Aging and prospective memory: The role of working memory and monitoring processes. *Aging: Clinical and Experimental Research, 20*, 569–577.

Bjorklund, D. F. (2007). *Why youth is not wasted on the young.* Malden, MA: Blackwell.

Bjorklund, D. F. (2012). *Children's thinking* (8th ed.). Boston: Cengage.

Bjorklund, D. F. (2013). Cognitive development: An overview. In P. D. Zelazo (Ed.), *Oxford handbook of developmental psychology.* New York: Oxford University Press.

Bjorklund, D. F., & Pellegrini, A. D. (2002). *The origins of human nature.* New York: Oxford University Press.

Black, M. M., & Hurley, K. M. (2007). Helping children develop healthy eating habits. In Tremblay, R. E., Barr, R. G., Peters, R., & Boivin, M. (Eds.), *Encyclopedia on early childhood development* (rev. ed.). Retrieved March 11, 2008, from www.child-encyclopedia.com/documents/Black-HurleyANGxp_rev-Eating.pdf

Black, M. M., & Lozoff, B. (2008). Nutrition and diet. In M. M. Haith & J. B. Benson (Eds.), *Encyclopedia of infant and early childhood development.* Oxford, UK: Elsevier.

Blackwell, L. S., & Dweck, C. S. (2008). *The motivational impact of a computer-based program that teaches how the brain changes with learning.* Unpublished manuscript, Department of Psychology, Stanford University, Palo Alto, CA.

Blackwell, L. S., Trzesniewski, K. H., & Dweck, C. S. (2007). Implicit theories of intelligence predict achievement across an adolescent transition: A longitudinal study and an intervention. *Child Development, 78*, 246–263.

Blaga, O. M., Shaddy, D. J., Anderson, C. J., Kannass, K. N., Little, T. D., & Colombo, J. (2009). Structure and continuity of intellectual development in early childhood. *Intelligence, 37*, 106–113.

Blagosklonny, M. V. (2010). Calorie restriction: Decelerating mTOR-driven aging from cells to organisms (including humans). *Cell Cycle, 9*, 683–688.

Blair, C., & Raver, C. C. (2012, in press). Child development in the context of poverty: Experiential canalization of brain and behavior. *American Psychologist.*

Blair, C., & Razza, R. P. (2007). Relating effortful control, executive functioning, and false belief understanding to emerging math and literacy ability in kindergarten. *Child Development, 78*, 647–663.

Blair, M., & Somerville, S. C. (2009). The importance of differentiation in young children's acquisition of expertise. *Cognition, 112*, 259–280.

Blair, S. N., Kohl, H. W., Paffenbarger, R. S., Clark, D. G., Cooper, K. H., & Gibbons, L. W. (1989). Physical fitness and all-cause mortality: A prospective study of healthy men and women. *Journal of the American Medical Association, 262*, 2395–2401.

Blakemore, J. E. O., Berenbaum, S. A., & Liben, L. S. (2009). *Gender development.* Clifton, NJ: Psychology Press.

Blakemore, S.-J. (2012). Development of the social brain in adolescence. *Journal of the Royal Society of Medicine, 105*, 111–116.

Blakemore, S. J., Dahl, R. E., Frith, U., & Pine, D. S. (2011, in press). Developmental cognitive neuroscience. *Developmental Cognitive Neuroscience, 1*(1), 3–6.

Blakey, J. (2011). Normal births or spontaneous vertex delivery? *Practicing Midwife, 14*, 12–13.

Bland, P. (2012). Tackling anxiety and depression in older people in primary care. *Practitioner, 256*, 17–20.

Blandthorn, J., Forster, D. A., & Love, V. (2011). Neonatal and maternal outcomes following maternal use of buprenophine or methadone during pregnancy: Findings of a retrospective audit. *Women and Birth, 24*, 32–39.

Blanker, M. H., & others. (2012, in press). Pressure during decision making of continuous sedation in end-of-life situations in Dutch general practice. *BMC Family Practice.*

Blieszner, R. (2009). Friendship, adulthood. In D. Carr (Ed.), *Encyclopedia of the life course and human development.* Boston: Gale Cengage.

Blieszner, R., & Roberto, K. A. (2012a). Intergenerational relationships and aging. In S. K. Whitbourne & M. Sliwinski (Eds.), *Wiley-Blackwell handbook of adult development and aging.* New York: Wiley.

Blieszner, R., & Roberto, K.A. (2012b). Partner and friend relationships in adulthood. In S. K. Whitbourne & M. Sliwinski (Eds.), *Wiley-Blackwell handbook of adult development and aging.* New York: Wiley.

Block, J. (1993). Studying personality the long way. In D. Funder, R. D. Parke, C. Tomlinson-Keasey, & K. Widaman (Ed.), *Studying lives through time.* Washington, DC: American Psychological Association.

Bloom, B. (1985). *Developing talent in young people.* New York. Ballantine.

Bloom, L., Lifter, K., & Broughton, J. (1985). The convergence of early cognition and language in the second year of life. Problems in conceptualization and measurement. In M. Barren (Ed.), *Single word speech.* London: Wiley.

Bloom, P., & German, T. P. (2000). Two reasons to abandon the false belief task as a test of theory of mind. *Cognition, 77*, B25–B31.

Bloomer, R. J., Kabir, M. M., Trepanowski, J. F., Canale, R. E., & Farney, T. M. (2011). A 21 day Daniel Fast improves selected biomarkers of antioxidant status and oxidative stress in men and women. *Nutrition and Metabolism, 8*, 17.

Bloor, C., & White, F. (1983). *Unpublished manuscript.* La Jolla, CA: University of California at San Diego.

Blossfeld, H-P. (2009). Globalization. In D. Carr (Ed.), *Encyclopedia of the life course and human development.* Boston: Gale Cengage.

Bodrova, E., & Leong, D. J. (2007). *Tools of the mind* (2nd ed.). Geneva, Switzerland: International Bureau of Education. UNESCO.

Bodrova, E., Leong, D. J., & Akhutina, T. V. (2011). When everything new is well-forgotten old: Vygotsky/Luria insights in the development of executive functions. In *New Directions for Child and Adolescent Development, 133*, 11–28.

Boelen, P. A., van den Bout, J., & van den Hout, M. A. (2003). The role of cognitive variables in psychological functioning after the death of a first degree relative. *Behavior Research and Therapy, 41*, 1123–1136.

Bohlin, G., Eninger, L., Brocki, K. C., & Thorell, L. B. (2012). Disorganized attachment and inhibitory capacity: Predicting externalizing problem behaviors. *Journal of Abnormal Child Psychology, 40,* 449–458.

Bohlin, G., & Hagekull, B. (2009). Socio-emotional development: From infancy to young adulthood. *Scandinavian Journal of Psychology, 50,* 592–601.

Bolkan, C., & Hooker, K. (2012). Self-regulation and social cognition in adulthood: The gyroscope. In S. K. Whitbourne & M. J. Sliwinski (Eds.), *Wiley-Blackwell handbook of adult development and aging.* New York: Wiley.

Bomba, P. A., Kemp, M., & Black, J. S. (2012). POLST: An improvement over traditional advance directives. *Cleveland Clinic Journal of Medicine, 79,* 457–464.

Bonjour, J. P., Benoit, V., Rousseau, B., & Souberbielle, J. C. (2012). Consumption of vitamin D- and calcium-fortified soft white cheese lowers the biochemical marker of bone reabsorption TRAP 5b in postmenopausal women at moderate risk of osteoporosis fracture. *Journal of Nutrition, 142,* 698–703.

Booth, A. (2006). Object function and categorization in infancy: Two mechanisms of facilitation. *Infancy, 10,* 145–169.

Booth, M. (2002). Arab adolescents facing the future: Enduring ideals and pressures to change. In B. B. Brown, R. W. Larson & T. S. Saraswath (Eds.), *The world's youth.* New York: Cambridge University Press.

Booth-LaForce, C., & Kerns, K. A. (2009). Child-parent attachment relationships, peer relationships, and peer-group functioning. In K. H. Rubin, W. M. Bukowski, & B. Laursen (Eds.), *Handbook of peer interactions, relationships, and groups.* New York: Guilford.

Bor, W., McGee, T. R., & Fagan, A. A. (2004). Early risk factors for adolescent antisocial behavior: An Australian longitudinal study. *Australian and New Zealand Journal of Psychiatry, 38,* 365–372.

Borella, E., Ghisletta, P., & de Ribaupierre, A. (2011). Age differences in text processing: The role of working memory, inhibition, and processing speed. *Journals of Gerontology B: Psychological Sciences and Social Sciences, 66B,* 311–320.

Borella, E., Ludwig, C., Dirck, J., & de Ribaupierre, A. (2011). The influence of time of testing on interference, working memory, processing speed, and vocabulary: Age differences in adulthood. *Experimental Aging Research, 37,* 76–107.

Bornstein, M. H. (1975). Qualities of color vision in infancy. *Journal of Experimental Child Psychology, 19,* 401–409.

Bornstein, M. H., Arterberry, M. E., & Mash, C. (2011). Perceptual development. In M. H. Bornstein & M. E. Lamb (Eds.), *Developmental psychology: An advanced textbook* (6th ed.). New York: Psychology Press.

Bornstein, M. H., & Colombo, J. (2012, in press). Infant cognitive functioning and mental development. In S. Pauen & M. Bornstein (Eds.), *Early childhood development and later outcome.* New York: Cambridge University Press.

Bornstein, M. H., Jager, J., & Steinberg, L. (2013, in press). Adolescents, parents/friends/peers: A relationship model. In I. Weiner & others (Eds.), *Handbook of psychology* (2nd ed., Vol. 6). New York: Wiley.

Bornstein, N., & Poon, W. S. (2012). Accelerated recovery from acute brain injuries: Clinical efficacy of neurotrophic treatment in stroke and traumatic brain injuries. *Drugs Today.*

Boron, J. B., Willis, S. L., & Schaie, K. W. (2007). Cognitive training gain as a predictor of mental status. *Journals of Gerontology: Psychological Sciences and Social Sciences, 62B,* P45–P52.

Borup, L., & others. (2009). Acupuncture as pain relief during delivery: A randomized controlled trial. *Birth, 36,* 5–12.

Bosl, W., Tierney, A., Tager-Flusberg, H., & Nelson, C. (2011). EEG complexity as a biomarker for autism spectrum disorder risk. *BMC Medicine, 9,* 60.

Bosworth, B. (2012, February). *Economic consequences of the great recession: Evidence from the Panel Study of Income Dynamics.* Chestnut Hill, MA: Center for Retirement Research at Boston College.

Botwinick, J. (1978). *Aging and behavior* (2nd ed.). New York: Springer.

Bouchard, T. J., Lykken, D. T., McGue, M., Segal, N. L., & Tellegen, A. (1990). Source of human psychological differences. The Minnesota Study of Twins Reared Apart. *Science, 250,* 223–228.

Boucher, J. (2012a, in press). Putting theory of mind in its place: Psychological explanations of the socio-emotional-communicative impairments in autism spectrum disorder. *Autism.*

Boucher, J. (2012b). Research review: Structural language in autistic spectrum disorder—characteristics and causes. *Journal of Child Psychology and Psychiatry, 53,* 219–233.

Boucher, J., Mayes, A., & Bigham, S. (2012). Memory in autism spectrum disorder. *Psychological Bulletin, 138,* 458–496.

Boutot, E. A., & Myles, B. S. (2011). *Autism spectrum disorders.* Upper Saddle River, NJ: Merrill.

Bowen, C. E., Noack, M. G., & Staudinger, U. M. (2011). Aging in the work context. In K. W. Schaie & S. L. Willis (Eds.), *Handbook of the psychology of aging* (7th ed.). New York: Elsevier.

Bower, T. G. R. (1966). Slant perception and shape constancy in infants. *Science, 151,* 832–834.

Bowlby, J. (1969). *Attachment and loss* (Vol. 1). London: Hogarth.

Bowlby, J. (1989). *Secure and insecure attachment.* New York: Basic Books.

Bowling, A., & Iliffe, S. (2011). Psychological approach to successful aging predicts future quality of life in older adults. *Health Quality and Life Outcomes, 9,* 13.

Bowman, G. L., & others. (2012). Nutrient biomarker patterns, cognitive function, and MRI measures of brain aging. *Neurology, 78,* 241–249.

Bowman, N. A. (2010). The development of psychological well-being in first-year college students. *Journal of College Student Development, 51,* 180–200.

Boyer, K., & Diamond, A. (1992). Development of memory for temporal order in infants and young children. In A. Diamond (Ed.), *Development and neural bases of higher cognitive function.* New York: Academy of Sciences.

Boyle, J., & Cropley, M. (2004). Children's sleep: Problems and solutions. *Journal of Family Health Care, 14,* 61–63.

Boyle, P. A., Yu, L., Buchman, A. S., & Bennett, D. A. (2012, in press). Risk aversion is associated with decision making among community-based older persons. *Frontiers in Psychology.*

Brabyn, J. A., Schneck, M. E., Haegerstrom-Portnoy, G., & Lott, L. (2001). The Smith-Keuttewell Institute (SKI). Longitudinal study of vision function and its impact among the elderly. An overview. *Ophthalmology and Vision Science, 78,* 2464–2469.

Bradley, R. E., & Webb, R. (1976). Age-related differences in locus of control orientation in three behavior domains. *Human Development, 19,* 49–55.

Brainerd, C. J., & Reyna, V. E. (1993). Domains of fuzzy-trace theory. In M. L. Howe & R. Pasnak (Eds.), *Emerging themes in cognitive development.* New York: Springer.

Bralic, I., & others. (2012). Association of early menarche age and overweight/obesity. *Journal of Pediatric Endocrinology and Metabolism, 25,* 57–62.

Brand, M. (2011). Mitochondrial functioning and aging. In E. Masoro & S. Austad (Eds.), *Handbook of the biology of aging* (7th ed.). New York: Elsevier.

Brand, M., & Markowitsch, H. J. (2010). Mechanisms contributing to decision-making difficulties in late adulthood: Theoretical approaches, speculations, and empirical evidence. *Gerontology, 56,* 319–324.

Bransford, J., & others. (2006). Learning theories in education. In P. A. Alexander & P. H. Winne (Eds.), *Handbook of educational psychology* (2nd ed.). Mahwah, NJ: Erlbaum.

Brassard, A., & others. (2012). Romantic attachment insecurity predicts sexual dissatisfaction in couples seeking marital therapy. *Journal of Sexual and Marital Therapy, 38,* 245–262.

Brassen, S., & others. (2012). Don't look back in anger! Responsiveness to missed chances in successful and unsuccessful aging. *Science, 336,* 612–614.

Brazelton, T. B. (2004). Preface: The Neonatal Intensive Care Unit Network Neurobehavioral Scale. *Pediatrics, 113* (Suppl.), S632–S633.

Brechwald, W. A., & Prinstein, M. J. (2011). Beyond homophily: A decade of advances in understanding peer influence processes. *Journal of Research on Adolescence, 21,* 166–179.

Brecklin, L. R., & Ullman, S. E. (2010). The roles of victim and offender substance use in sexual assault outcomes. *Journal of Interpersonal Violence, 25,* 1503–1522.

Bredekamp, S. (2011). *Effective practices in early childhood education.* Upper Saddle River, NJ: Merrill.

Brehmer, Y., Westerberg, H., & Backman, L. (2012, in press). Working-memory training in younger and older adults: Training gains, transfer, and maintenance. *Frontiers in Human Neuroscience.*

Bremner, J. G., Slater, A. M., Johnson, S. P., Mason, U. C., & Spring, J. (2012, in press). The effects of auditory information on 4-month-old infants' perception of trajectory continuity. *Child Development.*

Brendgen, M., Lamarche, V., Wanner, B., & Vitaro, F. (2010). Links between friendship relations and early adolescents' trajectories of depressed mood. *Developmental Psychology, 46,* 491–501.

Brent, R. L. (2009). Saving lives and changing family histories: Appropriate counseling of pregnant women and men and women of reproductive age concerning the risk of diagnostic radiation exposure during and before pregnancy. *American Journal of Obstetrics and Gynecology, 200,* 4–24.

Brent, R. L. (2011). The pulmonologist's role in caring for pregnant women with regard to reproductive risks of diagnostic radiological studies or radiation therapy. *Clinics in Chest Medicine.*

Brent, R. L., Christian, M. S., & Diener, R. M. (2011). Evaluation of the reproductive and developmental risks of caffeine. *Birth Defects Research B: Developmental and Reproductive Toxicology, 92,* 152–187.

Breslau, J., & others. (2011). A multinational study of mental disorders, marriage, and divorce. *Acta Psychiatrica Scandinavica, 124,* 474–486.

Bretherton, I. (2012). Afterword. In K. H. Brisch, *Treating attachment disorders* (2nd ed.). New York: Guilford.

Bretherton, I., Stolberg, U., & Kreye, M. (1981). Engaging strangers in proximal interaction: Infants' social initiative. *Developmental Psychology, 17,* 746–755.

Bril, B. (1999). Dires sur l'enfant selon les cultures. Etat des lieux et perspectives. In B. Brill, P. R. Dasen, C. Sabatier, & B. Krewer (Eds.), *Propos sur l'enfant et l'adolescent. Quels enfants pour quelles cultures?* Paris: L'Harmattan.

Brim, G. (1992, December 7). Commentary, *Newsweek,* p. 52.

Brim, G., Ryff, C. D., & Kessler, R. (Eds.). (2004). *How healthy we are: A national study of well-being in midlife.* Chicago: University of Chicago Press.

Brim, O. (1999). *The MacArthur Foundation study of midlife development.* Vero Beach, FL: MacArthur Foundation.

Brion, M., & others. (2012, in press). Sarcomeric gene mutations in sudden infant death syndrome (SIDS). *Forensic Science International.*

Brisch, K. H. (2012). *Treating attachment disorders* (2nd ed.). New York: Guilford.

Britto, P. R., & Ulkuer, N. (2012). Child development in developing countries: Child rights and policy implications. *Child Development, 83,* 92–103.

Britton, J. R., Britton, H. L., & Gronwaldt, V. (2006). Breastfeeding, sensitivity, and attachment. *Pediatrics, 118,* e1436–e1443.

Broadbelt, K. G., & others. (2012, in press). Brainstem deficiency of the 14-3-3 regulator of serotonin synthesis: A proteomics analysis in the sudden infant death syndrome. *Molecular and Cellular Proteomics.*

Brocardo, P. S., Gil-Mohapel, J., & Christie, B. R. (2011). The role of oxidative stress in fetal alcohol spectrum disorders. *Brain Research Reviews, 67,* 209–225.

Broderick, R. (2003, July/August). A surgeon's saga. *Minnesota: The magazine of the University of Minnesota Alumni Association,* 26–31.

Brodsky, J. L., Viner-Brown, S., & Handler, A. S. (2009). Changes in maternal cigarette smoking among pregnant WIC participants in Rhode Island. *Maternal and Child Health Journal, 13*(6), 822–831.

Brody, G. H., Kogan, S. M., & Chen, Y. F. (2012). Perceived discrimination and longitudinal increases in adolescent substance use: Gender differences and mediational pathways. *American Journal of Public Health, 102,* 1006–1011.

Brody, N. (2000). Intelligence. In A. Kazdin (Ed.), *Encyclopedia of psychology.* Washington, DC, & New York: American Psychological Association and Oxford University Press.

Brody, N. (2007). Does education influence intelligence? In P. C. Kyllonen, R. D. Roberts, & L. Stankov (Eds.), *Extending intelligence.* Mahwah, NJ: Erlbaum.

Brody, R. M., & Costa, R. M. (2009). Satisfaction (sexual, life, relationship, and mental health) is associated directly with penile-vaginal intercourse, but inversely related to other sexual behavior frequencies. *Journal of Sexual Medicine, 6,* 1947–1954.

Brody, S. (2010). The relative health benefits of different sexual activities. *Journal of Sexual Medicine, 7,* 1336–1361.

Brodzinsky, D. M., & Pinderhughes, E. (2002). Parenting and child development in adoptive families. In M. H. Bornstein (Ed.), *Handbook of parenting* (Vol. 1). Mahwah, NJ: Erlbaum.

Broekhuizen, L. N., & others. (2011). Physical activity, metabolic syndrome, and coronary risk: The EPIC-Norfolk prospective population study. *European Journal of Cardiovascular Prevention and Rehabilitation, 18,* 209–217.

Bronfenbrenner, U. (1986). Ecology of the family as a context for human development: Research perspectives. *Developmental Psychology, 22,* 723–742.

Bronfenbrenner, U. (2004). *Making human beings human.* Thousand Oaks, CA: Sage.

Bronfenbrenner, U., & Morris, P. (1998). The ecology of developmental processes. In W. Damon (Ed.), *Handbook of child psychology* (5th ed., Vol. 1). New York: Wiley.

Bronfenbrenner, U., & Morris, P. A. (2006). The ecology of human development. In W. Damon & R. Lerner (Eds.), *Handbook of child psychology* (6th ed.). New York: Wiley.

Bronstein, P. (2006). The family environment: Where gender role socialization begins. In J. Worell & C. D. Goodheart (Eds.), *Handbook of girls' and women's psychological health.* New York: Oxford University Press.

Brook, J. S., Brook, D. W., Gordon, A. S., Whiteman, M., & Cohen, P. (1990). The psychological etiology of adolescent drug use: A family interactional approach. *Genetic Psychology Monographs, 116*(2).

Brooker, R. J. (2012). *Genetics* (4th ed.). New York: McGraw-Hill.

Brooks, J. G., & Brooks, M. G. (2001). *The case for constructivist classrooms* (2nd ed.). Upper Saddle River, NJ: Erlbaum.

Brooks-Gunn, J. (2003). Do you believe in magic?: What we can expect from early childhood programs. *Social Policy Report, Society for Research in Child Development, XVII* (No. 1), 1–13.

Brooks-Gunn, J., Han, W-J., & Waldfogel, J. (2010). First-year maternal employment and child development in the first seven years. *Monographs of the Society for Research in Child Development, 75*(2), 1–147.

Brooks-Gunn, J., & Warren, M. P. (1989). The psychological significance of secondary sexual characteristics in 9- to 11-year-old girls. *Child Development 59,* 161–169.

Brotman, L. M., & others. (2012). Early childhood family intervention and long-term obesity prevention among high-risk minority youth. *Pediatrics, 129,* e621–e628.

Brown, A., & Lee, M. (2011). Maternal child-feeding style during the weaning period: Association with weight and maternal eating style. *Eating Behavior, 12,* 108–111.

Brown, B. B. (2011). Popularity in peer group perspective: The role of status in adolescent peer systems. In A. H. N. Cillessen, D. Schwartz, & L. Mayeux (Eds.), *Popularity in the peer system.* New York: Guilford.

Brown, B. B., & Bakken, J. P. (2011). Parenting and peer relationships: Invigorating research on family-peer linkages in adolescence. *Journal of Research on Adolescence, 21,* 153–165.

Brown, B. B., Bakken, J. P., Ameringer, S. W., & Mahon, S. D. (2008). A comprehensive conceptualization of the peer influence process in adolescence. In M. J. Prinstein & K. A. Dodge (Eds.), *Understanding peer influence in children and adolescents.* New York: Guilford.

Brown, B. B., & Larson, J. (2009). Peer relationships in adolescence. In R. M. Lerner & L. Steinberg (Eds.), *Handbook of adolescent development* (3rd ed.). New York: Wiley.

Brown, B. B., & Larson, R. W. (2002). The kaleidoscope of adolescence: Experiences of the world's youth at the beginning of the 21st century. In B. B. Brown, R. W. Larson, & T. S. Saraswathi (Eds.), *The world's youth.* New York: Cambridge University Press.

Brown, D. (2013, in press). Morphological typology. In J. J. Song (Ed.), *Oxford handbook of linguistic typology.* New York: Oxford University Press.

Brown, D., Chumakina, M., & Corbett, G. G. (2013). *Canonical morphology and syntax.* New York: Oxford University Press.

Brown, J. D., & Bobkowski, P. S. (2011). Older and newer media: Patterns of use and effects on adolescents' health and well-being. *Journal of Research on Adolescence, 21,* 95–113.

Brown, J. K. (1985). Introduction. In J. K. Brown & V. Kerns (Eds.), *In her prime: A new view of middle-aged women.* South Hadley, MA: Bergin & Garvey.

Brown, L. (2012). Creative forces for retention of home health aides in hospitals and palliative care. *Home Healthcare Nurse, 30,* 420–429.

Brown, L. D., Feinberg, M., & Kan, M. L. (2012). Predicting engagement in a transition to parenthood program for couples. *Evaluation and Program Planning, 35,* 1–8.

Brown, L. M., Hansen, C. T., Huberty, A. F., & Castonquay, T. W. (2011). Traits of the metabolic syndrome after corpulent obesity in LAN, SHR, and DSS rats: Behavioral and metabolic interactions with adrenalectomy. *Physiology and Behavior, 103,* 98–103.

Brown, L. S. (1989). New voices, new visions: Toward a lesbian/gay paradigm for psychology. *Psychology of Women Quarterly, 13,* 445–458.

Brown, M. J., & Henriquez, E. (2011). Support for gay and lesbian rights: Development of a new scale. *Journal of Homosexuality, 58,* 462–475.

Brown, R. (1958). *Words and things.* Glencoe, IL: Free Press.

Brown, R. (1973). *A first language: The early stages.* Cambridge, MA: Harvard University Press.

Brown, S. L., Bulanda, J. R., & Lee, G. R. (2005). The significance of nonmarital cohabitation: Marital status and mental health benefits among middle-aged and older adults. *Journals of Gerontology B: Psychological Sciences and Social Sciences, 60,* S21–S29.

Brown, S. L., Nesse, R. M., House, J. S., & Utz, R. L. (2004). Religion and emotional compensation: Results from a prospective study of widowhood. *Personality and Social Psychology Bulletin, 30,* 1165–1174.

Brown, S. L., Nesse, R. M., Vinokur, A. D., & Smith, D. M. (2003). Providing social support may be more beneficial than receiving it: Results from a prospective study of mortality. *Psychological Science, 14,* 320–327.

Brown, W. H., Pfeiffer, K. A., McIver, K. L., Dowda, M., Addy, C. L., & Pate, R. R. (2009). Social and environmental factors associated with preschoolers' nonsedentary physical activity. *Child Development, 80,* 45–58.

Brownell, C. A., Ramani, G. B., & Zerwas, S. (2006). Becoming a social partner with peers: Cooperation and social understanding in one- and two-year-olds. *Child Development, 77,* 803–821.

Brownell, C. A., Svetlova, M., Anderson, R., Nichols, S. R., & Drummond, J. (2012, in press). Socialization of early prosocial behavior: Parents' talk about emotions is associated with sharing and helping in toddlers. *Infancy.*

Bruce, A. (2007). Time(lessness): Buddhist perspectives and end-of-life. *Nursing Philosophy, 8,* 151–157.

Bruchmiller, K., Margraf, J., & Schneider, S. (2012). Is ADHD diagnosed in accord with diagnostic criteria? Overdiagnosis and influence of client gender on diagnosis. *Journal of Consulting and Clinical Psychology, 80,* 128–138.

Bruck, M., & Ceci, S. J. (1999). The suggestibility of children's memory. *Annual Review of Psychology, 50,* 419–439.

Bruck, M., & Ceci, S. J. (2012). Forensic developmental psychology in the courtroom. In D. Faust & M. Ziskin (Eds.), *Coping with psychiatric and psychological testimony.* New York: Cambridge University Press.

Brumariu, L. E., & Kerns, K. A. (2010). Parent-child attachment and internalizing symptomatology in childhood and adolescence: A review of empirical findings and future direction. *Development and Psychopathology, 22,* 177–203.

Brumariu, L. E., Kerns, K. A., & Seibert, A. C. (2012, in press). Mother-child attachment, emotion regulation, and anxiety symptoms in middle childhood. *Personal Relationships.*

Brun, C., & Brock-Utne, J. G. (2012). Paralyzed by beauty. *Journal of Clinical Anesthesia, 24,* 77–78.

Brune, M., & others. (2012). The crisis of psychiatry—insights and prospects from evolutionary theory. *World Psychiatry, 11,* 55–57.

Brunton, P. J., & Russell, J. A. (2011). Neuroendocrine control of maternal stress responses and fetal programming by stress in pregnancy. *Progress in Neuro-Pharamacology and Biological Psychiatry, 23,* 1079–1090.

Bryant, D. P., & others. (2013). Instructional practices for improving student outcomes in solving arithmetic combinations. In B. G. Cook & M. G. Tankersley (Eds.), *Research-based practices in special education.* Upper Saddle River, NJ: Pearson.

Bryant, J. A. (Ed.). (2007). *The children's television community.* Mahwah, NJ: Erlbaum.

Bryant, J. B. (2012). Pragmatic development. In E. L. Bavin (Ed.), *Cambridge handbook of child language.* New York: Cambridge University Press.

Bryant, R. A. (2012). Grief as a psychiatric disorder. *British Journal of Psychiatry, 201,* 9–10.

Brynes, J. P. (2012). How neuroscience contributes to our understanding of learning and development in typically developing and special needs students. In K. R. Harris, S. Graham, & T. Urdan (Eds.), *APA educational psychology handbook.* Washington, DC: American Psychological Association.

Bryom, S., & Symon, A. (2011). Developing the midwife's role in public health. *Practicing Midwife, 14,* 16–17.

Buchanan, S. L., & others. (2012). Trends in morbidity associated with oxytocin use in labor in nulliparas at term. *Australian and New Zealand Journal of Obstetrics and Gynecology, 52,* 173–178.

Buchman, A. S., Yu, L., Boyle, P. A., Shah, R. C., & Bennett, D. A. (2012). Total daily physical activity and longevity in old age. *Archives of Internal Medicine, 172,* 444–446.

Buckner, J. C., Mezzacappa, E., & Beardslee, M. R. (2009). Self-regulation and its relations to adaptive functioning in low income youths. *American Journal of Orthopsychiatry, 79,* 19–30.

Bucur, B., & Madden, D. J. (2007). Information processing/cognition. In J. E. Birren (Ed.), *Encyclopedia of gerontology* (2nd ed.). San Diego: Academic Press.

Bucur, B., & Madden, D. J. (2010). Effects of adult age and blood pressure on executive function and speed of processing. *Experimental Aging Research, 36,* 153–168.

Bugental, D., & Grusec, J. (2006). Socialization processes. In W. Damon & R. Lerner (Eds.), *Handbook of child psychology* (6th ed.). New York: Wiley.

Buhl, H. M., & Lanz, M. (2007). Emerging adulthood in Europe: Common traits and variability across five European countries. *Journal of Adolescent Research, 22,* 439–443.

Buhler, E., Bachmann, C., Govert, H., Heinzel-Gutenbrunner, M., & Kamp-Becker, I. (2011). Differential diagnosis of autism spectrum disorder and attention deficit hyperactivity disorder by means of inhibitory control and 'theory of mind.' *Journal of Autism and Developmental Disorders, 41*(12), 1718–1726.

Buhrmester, D. (1998). Need fulfillment, interpersonal competence, and the developmental contexts of early adolescent friendship. In W. M. Bukowski & A. F. Newcomb (Eds.), *The company they keep: Friendship in childhood and adolescence.* New York: Cambridge University Press.

Buitenweg, J. I., Murre, J. M., & Ridderinkhof, K. R. (2012, in press). Brain training in progress: A review of trainability in seniors. *Frontiers in Human Neuroscience.*

Bukowski, R., & others. (2008, January). *Folic acid and preterm birth.* Paper presented at the meeting of the Society for Maternal-Fetal Medicine, Dallas.

Bukowski, W. M., Buhrmester, D., & Underwood, M. K. (2011). Peer relations as a developmental context. In M. K. Underwood & L. M. Rosen (Eds.), *Social development.* New York: Guilford.

Bukowski, W., Ittel, A., & Juang, L. (2012, April). *Gender, culture, and positive and negative experiences with peers.* Paper presented at the Gender Development Research Conference, San Francisco.

Bulik, C. M., Berkman, N. D., Brownley, K. A., Sedway, J. A., & Lhor, K. N. (2007). Anorexia nervosa treatment: A systematic review of randomized controlled trials. *International Journal of Eating Disorders, 40,* 310–320.

Bull, J. H., & others. (2012, in press). Demonstration of a sustainable community-based model of care across the palliative continuum. *Journal of Pain and Symptom Management.*

Bullock, C. M., & Beckson, M. (2011). Male victims of sexual assault: Phenomenology, psychology, and physiology. *Journal of American Academy of Psychiatry and the Law, 39,* 197–205.

Bumpass, L., & Aquilino, W. (1994). *A social map of midlife: Family and work over the middle life course.* Center for Demography and Ecology, University of Wisconsin, Madison, WI.

Bumpus, M. F., Crouter, A. C., & McHale, S. M. (2001). Parental autonomy granting during adolescence: Gender differences in context. *Developmental Psychology, 37,* 163–173.

Bundick, M. J. (2011). The benefits of reflecting on and discussing purpose in life in emerging adulthood. *New Directions in Youth Development, 2011,* 89–103.

Burack, J. A., Enns, J. T., & Fox, N. A. (Eds.) (2013, in press). *Cognitive science, development, and technology.* New York: Oxford University Press.

Burgess-Champoux, T. L., Larson, N., Neumark-Sztainer, D., Hannan, P. J., & Story, M. (2009). Are family meal patterns associated with overall diet quality during the transition from early to middle adolescence? *Journal of Nutrition Education and Behavior, 41,* 79–86.

Burke, D. M., & Shafto, M. A. (2004). Aging and language production. *Current Directions in Psychological Science, 13,* 21–24.

Burke, J. D. (2011). The relationship between conduct disorder and oppositional defiant disorder and their continuity with antisocial behaviors. In D. Shaffer, E. Leibenluft, & L. A. Rohde (Eds.), *Externalizing disorders of childhood: Refining the research agenda for DSM-V.* Arlington, VA: American Psychiatric Association.

Burnham, D., & Mattock, K. (2010). Auditory development. In J. G. Bremner & T. D. Wachs (Eds.), *Wiley-Blackwell handbook of infant development* (2nd ed.). New York: Wiley.

Burns, C., Dunn, A., Brady, M., Starr, N., & Blosser, C. (2013). *Pediatric primary care* (5th ed.). New York: Elsevier.

Burr, J. (2009). Volunteering, later life. In D. Carr (Ed.), *Encyclopedia of the life course and human development*. Boston: Gale Cengage.

Bursch, H. C., & Butcher, H. K. (2012). Caregivers' deepest feelings in living with Alzheimer's disease: A ricoeurian interpretation of family caregivers' journals. *Research in Gerontological Nursing.*

Burstyn, I., Kuhle, S., Allen, A. C., & Veugelers, P. (2012). The role of maternal smoking in effect of fetal growth restriction on poor scholastic achievement in elementary school. *International Journal of Environmental Research and Public Health, 9*, 408–420.

Burt, K. B., & Paysnick, A. A. (2012). Resilience in the transition to adulthood. *Development and Psychopathology, 24*, 493–505.

Busch, H., & Hofer, J. (2012). Self-regulation and milestones of adult development: Intimacy and generativity. *Developmental Psychology, 48*, 282–293.

Bushel, P. R., & others. (2012). Population differences in transcript-regulator expression quantitative trait loci. *PLoS One, 7*(3), e34286.

Bushnell, I. W. R. (2003). Newborn face recognition. In O. Pascalis & A. Slater (Eds.), *The development of face processing in infancy and early childhood*. New York: NOVA Science.

Businaro, R., Ippoliti, F., Ricci, S., Canitano, N., & Fuso, A. (2012, in press). Alzheimer's disease promotion by obesity: Induced mechanisms-molecular links and perspectives. *Current Gerontology and Geriatric Research.*

Buss, D. M. (1995). Psychological sex differences: Origins through sexual selection. *American Psychologist, 50*, 164–168.

Buss, D. M. (2004). *Evolutionary psychology* (2nd ed.). Boston: Allyn & Bacon.

Buss, D. M. (2008). *Evolutionary psychology* (3rd ed.). Boston: Allyn & Bacon.

Buss, D. M. (2012). *Evolutionary psychology* (4th ed.). Boston: Allyn & Bacon.

Buss, D. M., & Barnes, M. (1986). Preferences in human mate selection. *Journal of Personality and Social Psychology, 50*, 559–570.

Buss, D. M., & others. (1990). International preferences in selecting mates: A study of 37 cultures. *Journal of Cross-Cultural Psychology, 21*, 5–47.

Buss, K. A. (2011). Which fearful toddlers should we worry about? Context, fear regulation, and anxiety risk. *Developmental Psychology, 47*, 804–819.

Busse, E. W., & Blazer, D. G. (1996). *The American Psychiatric Press textbook of geriatric psychiatry* (2nd ed.). Washington, DC: American Psychiatric Press.

Bussey, K., & Bandura, A. (1999). Social cognitive theory of gender development and differentiation. *Psychological Review, 106*, 676–713.

Butler, R. N. (2007). Life review. In J. E. Birren (Ed.), *Encyclopedia of gerontology* (2nd ed.). San Diego: Academic Press.

Butler, R. N., & Lewis, M. (2002). *The new love and sex after 60.* New York: Ballantine.

Butrica, B. A., & Smith, K. E. (2012). The retirement prospects of divorced women. *Social Security Bulletin, 72*, 11–22.

Butrica, B. A., Smith, K. E., & Iams, H. M. (2012). This is not your parents' retirement: Comparing retirement income across generations. *Social Security Bulletin, 72*, 37–58.

Butterworth, G. (2004). Joint visual attention in infancy. In G. Bremner & A. Slater (Eds.), *Theories of infant development*. Malden, MA: Blackwell.

Buzwell, S., & Rosenthal, D. (1996). Constructing a sexual self: Adolescents sexual self-perceptions and sexual risk-taking. *Journal of Research on Adolescence, 6*, 489–513.

Byrd-Bredbenner, C., Moe, G., Beshgetoor, D., & Berning, J. (2013). *Wardlaw's perspectives in nutrition* (9th ed.). New York: McGraw-Hill.

C

Caban-Holt, A., & others. (2012, in press). Age-expanded normative data for the Ruff 2&7 Selective Attention Test: Evaluating cognition in older males. *Clinical Neuropsychology.*

Cabeza, R. (2002). Hemispheric asymmetry reduction in older adults: The HAROLD model. *Psychology and Aging, 17*, 85–100.

Cabrera, N. J., Hofferth, S. L., & Chae, S. (2011). Patterns and predictors of father-infant engagement across race/ethnic groups. *Early Childhood Research Quarterly, 26*, 365–375.

Cacho, I., Dickinson, C. M., Smith, H. J., & Harper, P. A. (2010). Clinical impairment measures and reading performance in a large age-related macular degeneration group. *Optometry and Vision Science, 87*(5), 344–349.

Caddy, S. C., & others. (2011). Pregnancy and neonatal outcomes of women with reactive syphilis serology in Alberta, 2002–2006. *Journal of Obstetrics and Gynecology Canada, 33*, 453–459.

Caeymaex, L., & others. (2012, in press). Perceived role in end-of-life decision making in the NICU affects long-term parental grief response. *Archives of Disease in Childhood. Fetal and Neonatal Edition.*

Cahill, K., Stead, L. F., & Lancaster, T. (2012). Nicotine receptor partial agonists for smoking cessation. *Cochrane Database of Systematic Reviews, 18*(4), CD006103.

Caldwell, S. (2013). *Statistics unplugged* (4th ed.). Boston: Cengage.

Calkins, S. D. (2012). Regulatory competence and early disruptive behavior problems: Role of physiological regulation. In S. L. Olson & A. J. Sameroff (Eds.), *Biopsychosocial regulatory processes in the development of childhood behavioral problems*. New York: Cambridge University Press.

Callaghan, T. (2013). Symbols and symbolic thought. In P. D. Zelazo (Ed.), *Oxford handbook of developmental psychology*. New York: Oxford University Press.

Callahan, D. (2009). Death, mourning, and medical practice. *Perspectives in Biological Medicine, 52*, 103–115.

Cameron, J. M., Heidelberg, N., Simmons, L., Lyle, S. B., Kathakali, M-V., & Correia, C. (2010). Drinking game participation among undergraduate students attending National Alcohol Screening Day. *Journal of American College Health, 58*, 499–506.

Campbell, C. S., & Cox, J. C. (2012). Hospice-assisted death? A study of Oregon hospices on death with dignity. *American Journal of Hospice and Palliative Care, 29*, 227–235.

Campbell, F. A., Pungello, E. P., Miller-Johnson, S., Burchinal, M., & Ramey, C. T. (2001). The development of cognitive and academic abilities: Growth curves from an early childhood educational experiment. *Developmental Psychology, 37*, 231–243.

Campbell, I. G., Grimm, K. J., de Bie, E., & Feinberg, I. (2012). Sex, puberty, and the timing of sleep EEG measured in adolescent brain maturation. *Proceedings of the National Academy of Sciences U.S.A., 109*, 5740–5743.

Campbell, K. L., Grady, C. L., Ng, C., & Hasher, L. (2012, in press). Age differences in the frontoparietal cognitive control network: Implications for distractibility. *Neuropsychologia.*

Campbell, L., Campbell, B., & Dickinson, D. (2004). *Teaching and learning through multiple intelligences* (3rd ed.). Boston: Allyn & Bacon.

Campos, J. J. (2005). Unpublished review of J. W. Santrock's *Life-span development* (10th ed.). New York: McGraw-Hill.

Campos, J. J., Langer, A., & Krowitz, A. (1970). Cardiac responses on the visual cliff in prelocomotor human infants. *Science, 170*, 196–197.

Canfield, J., & Hansen, M. V. (1995). *A second helping of chicken soup for the soul.* Deerfield Beach, FL: Health Communications.

Canfield, R. L., & Haith, M. M. (1991). Young infants' visual expeciations for symmetric and asymmetric stimulus sequences. *Developmental Psychology, 27*, 198–208.

Carl, J. D. (2012). *Short introduction to the U.S. Census*. Upper Saddle River, NJ: Pearson.

Carling-Jenkins, R., Torr, J., Iacono, T., & Bigby, C. (2012). Experiences of supporting people with Down syndrome and Alzheimer's disease in aged care and family environments. *Journal of Intellectual and Developmental Disability, 37*, 54–60.

Carlisle, J., Kenney, C., & Vereb, A. (2013). Vocabulary instruction for students with or at risk for learning disabilities: Promising approaches for learning words from text. In B. G. Cook & M. G. Tankersley (Eds.), *Research-based practices in special education*. Upper Saddle River, NJ: Pearson.

Carlson, S. M. (2010). Development of conscious control and imagination. In R. F. Baumeister, A. R. Mele, & K. D. Vohs (Eds.), *Free will and consciousness: How might they work?* New York: Oxford University Press.

Carlson, S. M. (2011). Introduction to the special issue: Executive function. *Journal of Experimental Child Psychology, 108*, 411–413.

Carlson, S. M., Davis, A. C., & Leach, J. G. (2005). Executive function and symbolic representation in preschool children. *Psychological Science, 16*, 609–616.

Carlson, S. M., & White, R. (2011). *Unpublished research.* Minneapolis: Institute of Child Development, University of Minnesota.

Carlson, S. M., & White, R. (2013, in press). Executive function and imagination. In M. Taylor (Ed.), *Handbook of imagination*. New York: Oxford University Press.

Carlson, S. M., Zelazo, P. D., & Faja, S. (2013). Executive function. In P. D. Zelazo (Ed.), *Oxford handbook of developmental psychology*. New York: Oxford University Press.

Carmichael, O., & Lockhart, S. (2012). The role of diffusion tensor imaging in the study of cognitive aging. *Current Topics in Behavioral Neuroscience, 11,* 289–320.

Carnethon, M. R., Gidding, S. S., Nehgme, R., Sidney, S., Jacobs, D. R., & Liu, K. (2003). Cardiorespiratory fitness in young adulthood and the development of cardiovascular disease risk factors. *Journal of the American Medical Association, 290,* 3092–3100.

Carpendale, J. I., & Chandler, M. J. (1996). On the distinction between false belief understanding and subscribing to an interpretive theory of mind. *Child Development, 67,* 1686–1706.

Carpenter, J., Nagell, K., & Tomasello, M. (1998). Social cognition, joint attention, and communicative competence from 9 to 15 months of age. *Monographs of the Society for Research in Child Development, 70* (1, Serial No. 279).

Carpenter, M. (2011). Social cognition and social motivations in infancy. In U. Goswami (Ed.), *Wiley-Blackwell handbook of childhood cognitive development* (2nd ed.). New York: Wiley.

Carr, D. (2009). Death and dying. In D. Carr (Ed.), *Encyclopedia of the life course and human development.* Boston: Gale Cengage.

Carr, D. (2012, in press). "I don't want to die like that . . .": The impact of significant others' death quality on advance care planning. *Gerontologist.*

Carr, R., & Peebles, R. (2012). Developmental considerations of media exposure risk for eating disorders. In J. Lock (Ed.), *Oxford handbook of child and adolescent eating disorders: Developmental perspectives.* New York: Oxford University Press.

Carriere, J. S., Cheyne, J. A., Solman, G. J., & Smilek, D. (2010). Age trends for failures in sustained attention. *Psychology and Aging, 25*(3), 569–574.

Carroll, D., & others. (2011). Low cognitive ability in early adulthood is associated with reduced lung function in middle age: The Vietnam Experience Study. *Thorax, 66,* 884–888.

Carroll, D. J., & others. (2012, in press). How do alternative ways of responding influence 3- and 4-year-olds' performance on tests of executive function and theory of mind? *Journal of Experimental Child Psychology.*

Carroll, J. L. (2013). *Sexuality now* (4th ed.). Boston: Cengage.

Carskadon, M. A. (2004). Sleep difficulties in young people. *Archives of Pediatric and Adolescent Medicine, 158,* 597–598.

Carskadon, M. A. (2005). Sleep and circadian rhythms in children and adolescents: Relevance for athletic performance of young people. *Clinical Sports Medicine, 24,* 319–328.

Carskadon, M. A. (2011a). Sleep in adolescents: The perfect storm. *Pediatric Clinics of North America, 58,* 637–647.

Carskadon, M. A. (2011b). Sleep's effects on cognition and learning in adolescence. *Progress in Brain Research, 190,* 137–143.

Carstensen, L. L. (1998). A life-span approach to social motivation. In J. Heckhausen & C. Dweck (Eds.), *Motivation and self-regulation across the life span.* New York: Cambridge University Press.

Carstensen, L. L. (2006). The influence of a sense of time on human development. *Science, 312,* 1913–1915.

Carstensen, L. L. (2008, May). *Long life in the 21st century.* Paper presented at the meeting of the Association of Psychological Science, Chicago.

Carstensen, L. L. (2009). *A long bright future.* New York: Random House.

Carstensen, L. L., & Fried, L. P. (2012). The meaning of old age. *Global population aging: Peril or promise?* Geneva, SWIT: World Economic Forum.

Carstensen, L. L., & others. (2011). Emotional experience improves with age: Evidence based on over 10 years of experience sampling. *Psychology & Aging, 26,* 21–33.

Carta, J. J., Greenwood, C., Baggett, K., Buzhardt, J., & Walker, D. (2012). Research-based approaches for individualizing caregiving and educational interventions for infants and toddlers in poverty. In S. L. Odom, E. P. Pungello, & N. Gardner-Neblett (Eds.), *Infants, toddlers, and families in poverty.* New York: Guilford.

Cartwright, K. B., Galupo, M. P., Tyree, S. D., & Jennings, J. G. (2009). Reliability and validity of the Complex Postformal Thought Questionnaire: Assessing adults' cognitive development. *Journal of Adult Development, 16,* 183–189.

Cartwright, R., Agargun, M. Y., Kirkby, J., & Friedman, J. K. (2006). Relation of dreams to waking concerns. *Psychiatry Research, 141,* 261–270.

Carver, C. S., & Connor-Smith, J. (2010). Personality and coping. *Annual Review of Psychology* (Vol. 61). Palo Alto, CA: Annual Reviews.

Carver, K., Joyner, K., & Udry, J. R. (2003). National estimates of romantic relationships. *Annual Review of Psychology* (Vol. 54). Palo Alto, CA: Annual Reviews.

Carver, L. J., & Bauer, P. J. (2001). The dawning of the past: The emergence of long-term explicit memory in infancy. *Journal of Experimental Psychology: General, 130,* 726–745.

Casco, C., Robol, V., Barollo, M., & Cansino, S. (2011). Effects of aging on visual contour integration and segmentation. *Investigative Ophthalmology and Vision Science, 52,* 3955–3961.

Case, R., & Mueller, M. R. (2001). Differentiation, integration, and covariance mapping as fundamental processes in cognitive and neurological growth. In J. L. McClelland & R. S. Slegler (Eds.), *Mechanisms of cognitive development.* Mahwah, NJ: Erlbaum.

Caselli, R. J. (2012, in press). Phenotypic differences between apolipoprotein E genetic subgroups: Research and clinical implications. *Alzheimer's Research and Therapy.*

Casey, B. J., Jones, R. M., & Somerville, L. H. (2011). Braking and accelerating of the adolescent brain. *Journal of Research on Adolescence, 21,* 21–33.

Caspers, K. M., Paradiso, S., Yucuis, R., Troutman, B., Arndt, S., & Philibert, R. (2009). Association between the serotonin transporter promoter polymorphism (5-HTTLPR) and adult unresolved attachment. *Developmental Psychology, 45,* 64–76.

Caspi, A., & Roberts, B. W. (2001). Personality development across the life course; The argument for change and continuity. *Psychological Inquiry, 12,* 49–66.

Caspi, A., & others. (2003). Influence of life stress on depression: Moderation by a polymorphism in the 5-HTT gene. *Science, 301,* 386–389.

Cassidy, J., & others. (2011). Enhancing infant attachment security: An examination of treatment efficacy and differential susceptibility. *Development and Psychopathology, 23,* 131–148.

Castle, J., & others. (2010). Parents' evaluation of adoption success: A follow-up study of intercountry and domestic adoptions. *American Journal of Orthopsychiatry, 79,* 522–531.

Catalano, R. F., & others. (2012). Worldwide application of prevention science in adolescent health. *Lancet, 379,* 1653–1664.

Catenacci, V. A., & others. (2008). Physical activity patterns in the National Weight Control Registry. *Obesity, 16,* 153–161.

Cavanagh, S. E. (2009). Puberty. In D. Carr (Ed.), *Encyclopedia of the life course and human development.* Boston: Gale Cengage.

Cavanaugh, M. M., Weyand, C. M., & Goronzky, J. J. (2012, in press). Chronic inflammation and aging: DNA damage tips the balance. *Current Opinion in Immunology.*

Caviola, S., Mammarella, I. C., Comoldi, C., & Lucangeli, D. (2012). The involvement of working memory in children's exact and approximate mental addition. *Journal of Experimental Child Psychology, 112,* 141–160.

Ceci, S. J., & Gilstrap, L. L. (2000). Determinants of intelligence: Schooling and intelligence. In A. Kazdin (Ed.), *Encyclopedia of Psychology.* Washington, DC, & New York: American Psychological Association and Oxford University Press.

Ceci, S. J., & Klemfuss, J. Z. (2010). Children's suggestibility: Knowns and unknowns. *The Advocate: Division 37 of APA, 33,* 3–7.

Center for Science in the Public Interest. (2008). *Obesity on the kids' menu at top chains.* Retrieved October 24, 2008, from www.cspinet.org/nes/200808041.html

Center for Survey Research at the University of Connecticut. (2000). *Hours on the job.* Storrs: University of Connecticut, Center for Survey Research.

Centers for Disease Control and Prevention. (2007). *Autism and developmental disabilities monitoring (ADDM) network.* Atlanta: Author.

Centers for Disease Control and Prevention. (2008). *National Health Interview Study.* Atlanta: Author.

Centers for Disease Control and Prevention. (2010). Prevalence of overweight, infants and children less than two years of age: United States, 2003–2004. Retrieved April 22, 2012, from www.cdc.gov/nchs/data/hestat/overweight/overweight_child_u...

Centers for Disease Control and Prevention. (2011). *Breastfeeding report card 2011, United States: Outcome indicators.* Retrieved from www.cdc.gov/breastfeeding/data/reportcard2.htm

Centers for Disease Control and Prevention. (2012). *Birth data.* Atlanta: Author.

Centers for Disease Control and Prevention. (2012). *Body mass index for children and teens.* Atlanta: Centers for Disease Control and Prevention.

Centers for Disease Control and Prevention. (2012). *By the numbers full year 2011: Health measures from the National Health Interview Study, January–December 2011.* Atlanta: Author.

Centers for Disease Control and Prevention. (2012). CDC estimates 1 in 88 children in the United States has been identified as having an autism spectrum disorder. *CDC Division of News & Electronic Media, 404,* 639–3286.

Centers for Disease Control and Prevention. (2012). *Fast facts: Tobacco.* Retrieved June 8, 2012, from www.cdc.gov/tobacco/data_statistics/fact_sheets/fast_facts/

Centers for Disease Control and Prevention. (2012). Prepregnancy contraceptive use among teens with unintended pregnancies resulting in live births—Pregnancy Risk Assessment Monitoring System (PRAMS), 2004–2008. *MMWR Morbidity and Morality Weekly Report, 61*(2), 25–29.

Centers for Disease Control and Prevention. (2012). *Sexually transmitted disease surveillance.* Atlanta, GA: U.S. Department of Health and Human Services.

Centers for Disease Control and Prevention. (2012, January 13). Vital signs: Binge drinking prevalence, frequency, and intensity among adults—United States, 2010. *Morbidity and Mortality Weekly Report (MMWR), 61*(1), 14–19.

Central Intelligence Agency. (2012). *The world factbook: Life expectancy at birth.* Washington, DC: CIA.

Cernin, P. A., Lysack, C., & Lichtenberg, P. A. (2011). A comparison of self-rated and objectively measured successful aging constructs in an urban sample of African American older adults. *Clinical Gerontologist, 34,* 89–102.

Cerqueira, F. M., Cunha, F. M., Laurindo, F. R., & Kowaltowski, A. J. (2012). Calorie restriction increases cerebral mitochondrial respiratory capacity in a NO mediated mechanism: Impact on neuronal survival. *Free Radical and Biological Medicine, 52,* 1236–1241.

Cha, N. H., Seo, E .J., & Sok, S. R. (2012, in press). Factors influencing the successful aging of older Korean adults. *Gerontological Nursing.*

Chae, J. S., & others. (2012, in press). Supervised exercise program, BMI, and risk of type 2 diabetes in subjects with normal or impaired fasting glucose. *Diabetes Care.*

Chahrour, M. H., & others. (2012). Whole-exome sequencing and homozygosity analysis implicate depolarization-regulated neuronal genes in autism. *PLoS One, 8*(4), e1002635.

Chambers, J. A., & Swanson, V. (2012). Stories of weight management: Factors associated with successful and unsuccessful weight maintenance. *British Journal of Health Psychology, 17,* 223–243.

Chambers, K., & others. (2012, in press). Age-based disparities in end-of-life decisions in Belgium: A population-based death certificate survey. *BMC Public Health.*

Chandra, A., Mosher, W. D., Copen, C., & Sionean, C. (2011, March 3). Sexual behavior, sexual attraction, and sexual identity in the United States: Data from the 2006–2008 National Survey of Family Growth. *National Health Statistics Reports, 36,* 1–28.

Chang, S. H., Beason, T. S., Hunleth, J. M., & Colditz, G. A. (2012). A systematic review of body fat distribution and mortality in older people. *Maturitas, 72,* 175–191.

Chang, Y. K., Liu, S., Yu, H. H., & Lee, Y. H. (2012). Effect of acute exercise on executive function in children with attention deficit hyperactivity disorder. *Archives of Clinical Neuropsychology, 27,* 225–237.

Chang, Z., Lichtenstein, P., & Larsson, H. (2012). The effects of childhood ADHD symptoms on early-onset substance use: A Swedish twin study. *Journal of Abnormal Child Psychology, 40,* 425–435.

Chantler, P. D., & Lakatta, E. G. (2012, in press). Arterial-ventricular coupling with aging and disease. *Frontiers in Physiology.*

Chao, R. K. (2001). Extending research on the consequences of parenting style for Chinese Americans and European Americans. *Child Development, 72,* 1832–1843.

Chao, R. K. (2005, April). *The importance of* Guan *in describing control of immigrant Chinese.* Paper presented at the meeting of the Society for Research in Child Development, Atlanta.

Chao, R. K. (2007, March). *Research with Asian Americans: Looking back and moving forward.* Paper presented at the meeting of the Society for Research in Child Development, Boston.

Chao, R. K., & Otsuki-Clutter, M. (2011). Racial and ethnic differences: Sociocultural and contextual explanations. *Journal of Research on Adolescence, 21,* 47–60.

Chao, R. K., & Tseng, V. (2002). Parenting of Asians. In M. H. Bornstein (Ed.), *Handbook of parenting* (2nd ed., Vol. 4). Mahwah, NJ: Erlbaum.

Chaplin, J. E., & others. (2012, in press). Improvements in behavior and self-esteem following growth hormone treatment in short prepubertal children. *Hormone Research in Pediatrics.*

Chaplin, T. M., & others. (2012). Parent-adolescent conflict interactions and adolescent alcohol use. *Addictive Behaviors, 37,* 605–612.

Charles, S. T., & Carstensen, L. L. (2010). *Social and emotional aging.* In S. Fiske & S. Taylor (Eds.), *Annual Review of Psychology* (Vol. 61). Palo Alto, CA: Annual Reviews.

Charles, S. T., & Luong, G. (2011). Emotional experience across the life span. In K. L. Fingerman, C. A. Berg, J. Smith, & T. C. Antonucci (Eds.), *Handbook of life-span development.* New York: Springer.

Charles, S. T., Luong, G., Almeida, D. M., Ryff, C., Sturm, M., & Love, G. (2010). Fewer ups and downs: Daily stressors mediate age differences in negative affect. *Journals of Gerontology B: Psychological Sciences and Social Sciences, 65B,* 279–286.

Charles, S. T., & Piazza, J. R. (2007). Memories of social interactions: Age differences in emotion intensity. *Psychology and Aging, 22,* 300–309.

Charlet, J., Schnekenburger, M., Brown, K. W., & Diederich, M. (2012). DNA demethylation increases sensitivity of neuroblastoma cells to chemotherapeutic drugs. *Biochemical Pharmacology, 83,* 858–865.

Charness, N., & Bosman, E. A. (1992). Human factors and aging. In F. I. M. Craik & T. A. Salthouse (Eds.), *The handbook of aging and cognition.* Hillsdale, NJ: Erlbaum.

Charness, N., & Krampe, R. T. (2008). Expertise and knowledge. In D. F. Alwin & S. M. Hofer (Eds.), *Handbook on cognitive aging.* Thousand Oaks, CA: Sage.

Chassin, L., Presson, C., Sco, D. C., Sherman, S. J., Macy, J., Wirth, R. J., & others. (2008). Multiple trajectories of cigarette smoking and the intergenerational transmission of smoking: A multigenerational, longitudinal study of a midwestern community sample. *Health Psychology, 27,* 819–828.

Chen, A. F., & others. (2012). Free radical biology of the cardiology system. *Clinical Science, 123,* 73–91.

Chen, C., & Stevenson, H. W. (1989). Homework: A cross-cultural comparison. *Child Development, 60,* 551–561.

Chen, D., & Guarente, L. (2007). SIR2: A potential target for calorie restriction mimetics. *Trends in Molecular Medicine, 13,* 64–71.

Chen, J. J., & Brooks-Gunn, J. (2012). Neighborhoods, schools, and achievement. In K. R. Harris, S. Graham, & T. Urdan (Eds.), *APA handbook of educational psychology.* Washington, DC: American Psychological Association.

Chen, K. C., Wang, T. Y., & Chen, C. H. (2012). Associations between HIV and human pathways revealed by protein-protein interactions and correlated gene expression profiles. *PLoS One, 7*(3), e3420.

Chen, P., & Jacobson, K. C. (2012). Developmental trajectories of substance use from early adolescence to young adulthood: Gender and racial/ethnic differences. *Journal of Adolescent Health, 50,* 154–163.

Chen, X., Chung, J., Lechcier-Kimel, R., & French, D. (2011). Culture and social development. In P. K. Smith & C. H. Hart (Eds.), *Wiley-Blackwell handbook of childhood social development* (2nd ed.). New York: Wiley.

Chen, X., Hastings, P. D., Rubin, K. H., Chen, H., Cen, G., & Stewart, S. L. (1998). Childrearing attitudes and behavioral inhibition in Chinese and Canadian toddlers: A cross-cultural study. *Developmental Psychology, 34,* 677–686.

Cheng, D., Kettinger, L., Uduhiri, K., & Hurt, L. (2011). Alcohol consumption during pregnancy: Prevalence and provider assessment. *Obstetrics and Gynecology, 117*(2, Pt. 2), 212–217.

Cheng, S., Koch, W. H., & Wu, L. (2012, in press). Co-development of a companion diagnostic for targeted cancer therapy. *New Biotechnology.*

Cheng, S. H., & others. (2012, in press). A study on the sleep quality of incoming university students. *Psychiatry Research.*

Cheng, S. T., Lee, C. K., & Chow, P. K. (2010, in press). Social support and psychological well-being of nursing home residents in Hong Kong. *International Geriatrics.*

Cheng, S. Y., & others. (2012, in press). Factors affecting the improvement of quality of dying of terminally ill patients with cancer through palliative care: A 10-year experience. *Journal of Palliative Medicine.*

Cheng, Y., Lou, C., Gao, E., Emerson, M. R., & Zabin, L. S. (2012). The relationship between contact and unmarried adolescents' and young adults' traditional beliefs in three East Asian cities: A cross-cultural analysis. *Journal of Adolescent Health, 50*(Suppl. 3), S4–S11.

Cheong, K.C., & others. (2012, in press). Optimal BMI cut-off values for predicting diabetes, hypertension, and hypercholesterolaemia in a multi-ethnic population. *Public Health Nutrition.*

Cherlin, A. J. (2009). *The marriage-go-round*. New York: Random House.

Cherlin, A. J., & Furstenberg, F. F. (1994). Stepfamilies in the United States: A reconsideration. In J. Blake & J. Hagen (Eds.), *Annual review of sociology*. Palo Alto, CA: Annual Reviews.

Chess, S., & Thomas, A. (1977). Temperamental individuality from childhood to adolescence. *Journal of Child Psychiatry, 16,* 218–226.

Chess, S., & Thomas, A. (1987). *Origins and evolution of behavior disorders*. Cambridge, MA: Harvard University Press.

Cheung, C., & Pomerantz, E. M. (2012, in press). Why does parental involvement in children's learning enhance children's achievement? The role of parent-oriented motivation. *Journal of Educational Psychology.*

Chevan, A. (1996). As cheaply as one: Cohabitation in the older population. *Journal of Marriage and the Family, 58*(August), 656–667.

Chi, M. T. (1978). Knowledge structures and memory development. In R. S. Siegler (Ed.), *Children's thinking: What develops?* Hillsdale, NJ: Erlbaum.

Chick, C. F., & Reyna, V. F. (2012). A fuzzy trace theory of adolescent risk taking: Beyond self-control and sensation seeking. In V. F. Reyna & others (Eds.), *The adolescent brain*. Washington, DC: American Psychological Association.

Chiu, R. W., & Lo, Y. M. (2012). Noninvasive prenatal diagnosis empowered by high-throughput sequencing. *Prenatal Diagnosis, 32,* 401–406.

Chlebowski, R. T., & others. (2011). Estrogen plus progestin and breast cancer in postmenopausal women. *JAMA, 304,* 1684–1692.

Choi, D., Suramethakul, P., Lindstrom, R. L., & Singh, K. (2012). Glaucoma surgery with and without cataract surgery: Revolution or evolution? *Journal of Cataract and Refractory Surgery, 38,* 1121–1122.

Choi, H., & Marks, N. F. (2011). Socioeconomic status, marital status continuity and change, and mortality. *Journal of Aging and Health, 23,* 714–742.

Choi, N. G., & Jun, J. (2009). Life regrets and pride among low-income older adults: Relationships with depressive symptoms, current life stressors, and coping resources. *Aging and Mental Health, 13,* 213–225.

Choi, N. G., & Landeros, C. (2011). Wisdom from life's challenges: Qualitative interviews with low- and moderate-income older adults who were nominated as being wise. *Journal of Gerontological Social Work, 54,* 592–614.

Chomsky, N. (1957). *Syntactic structures*. The Hague: Mouton.

Choudhry, Z., & others. (2012, in press). LPHN3 and attention deficit/hyperactivity disorder: Interaction with maternal stress during pregnancy. *Journal of Child Psychology and Psychiatry.*

Choy, S. C., & Oo, P. S. (2012). Reflective thinking and teaching practices: A precursor for incorporating critical thinking into the classroom? *International Journal of Instruction, 5,* 167–182.

Christensen, L. (2012). Types of designs using random assignment. In H. Cooper (Ed.), *APA handbook of research methods in psychology*. Washington, DC: American Psychological Association.

Chung, J. K., Park, S. H., Lee, W. J., & Lee, S. J. (2009). Bilateral cataract surgery: A controlled clinical trial. *Japan Journal of Ophthalmology, 53,* 107–113.

Church, D. K., Siegel, M. A., & Fowler, C. D. (1988). *Growing old in America*. Wylie, TX: Information Aids.

Cicchetti, D. (2011). Pathways to resilient functioning in maltreated children: From single to multilevel investigations. In D. Cicchetti & G. I. Roisman (Eds.), *The origins and organization of adaptation and maladaptation: Minnesota Symposia on Child Psychology* (Vol. 36). New York: Wiley.

Cicchetti, D. (2013, in press). Developmental psychopathology. In P. Zelazo (Ed.), *Oxford handbook of developmental psychology*. New York: Oxford University Press.

Cicchetti, D., & Rogosch, F. A. (2012, in press). Neuroendocrine regulation and emotional adaptation in the context of child maltreatment. In T. Dennis, P. Hastings, & K. Buss (Eds.), *Physiological measures of emotion from a developmental perspective: State of the Science. SRCD Monographs in Child Development*. New York: Wiley.

Cicchetti, D., & Toth, S. L. (2006). Developmental psychopathology and preventive intervention. In W. Damon & R. Lerner (Eds.). *Handbook of child psychology* (6th ed.). New York: Wiley.

Cicchetti, D., Toth, S. L., Nilsen, W. J., & Manley, J. T. (2012, in press). What do we know and why does it matter? The dissemination of evidence-based interventions for child maltreatment. In H. R. Schaeffer & K. Durkin (Eds.), *Blackwell handbook of developmental psychology in action*. New York: Blackwell.

Cicchetti, D., Toth, S. L., & Rogosch, F. A. (2005). *A prevention program for child maltreatment*. Unpublished manuscript. University of Rochester, Rochester, NY.

Cichy, K. E., Stawski, R. S., & Almeida, D. M. (2012, in press). Racial difference in exposure and reactivity to daily stressors. *Journal of Marriage and the Family.*

Cicirelli, V. (2009). Sibling relationships, later life. In D. Carr (Ed.), *Encyclopedia of the life course and human development*. Boston: Gale Cengage.

Cignini, P., & others. (2010). The role of ultrasonography in the diagnosis of fetal isolated complete agenesis of the corpus callosum: A long-term prospective study. *Journal of Maternal-Fetal and Neonatal Medicine, 23,* 1504–1509.

Cillessen, A. H. N., & Bellmore, A. D. (2011). Social skills and social competence in interactions with peers. In P. K. Smith & C. H. Hart (Eds.), *Wiley-Blackwell handbook of childhood social development* (2nd ed.). New York: Wiley.

Cillessen, A. H. N., Schwartz, D., & Mayeux, L. (Eds.). (2011). *Popularity in the peer system*. New York: Guilford.

Cillessen, A. H. N., & van den Berg, Y. H. M. (2012). Popularity and school adjustment. In A. M. Ryan & G. W. Ladd (Eds.), *Peer relationships and adjustment at school*. Charlotte, NC: Information Age Publishing.

Cimpean, D., & Drake, R. E. (2011). Treating co-morbid chronic medical conditions and anxiety/depression. *Epidemiology and Psychiatric Science, 20,* 141–150.

Cisler, J. M., Begle, A. M., Amstadter, A. B., & Acierno, R. (2012). Mistreatment and self-reported emotional symptoms: Results from the National Elder Mistreatment Study. *Journal of Elder Abuse and Neglect, 24,* 216–230.

Citkovitz, C., Schnyer, R. N., & Hoskins, I. A. (2011). Acupuncture during labor: Data are more promising than a recent review suggests. *British Journal of Obstetrics and Gynecology, 118,* 101.

Claes, H. I., & others. (2010). Understanding the effects of sildenafil treatment on erection maintenance and erection hardness. *Journal of Sexual Medicine, 7*(6), 2184–2191.

Clapp, W. C., Rubens, M. T., Sabharwal, J., & Gazzaley, A. (2011). Deficit switching between functional brain networks underlies the impact of multitasking on working memory in older adults. *Proceedings of the National Academy of Sciences U.S.A., 108,* 7212–7217.

Clare, L., & others. (2011). Longitudinal trajectories of awareness in early-stage dementia. *Alzheimer Disease and Associated Disorders, 26,* 140–147.

Clark, B. (2008). *Growing up gifted* (7th ed.). Upper Saddle River, NJ: Prentice Hall.

Clark, D. J., Patten, C., Reid, K. F., Carabello, R. J., Phillips, E. M., & Fielding, R. A. (2011). Muscle performance and physical function are associated with voluntary rate of neuromuscular activation in older adults. *Journals of Gerontology A: Biological Sciences and Medical Sciences, 66A,* 115–121.

Clark, E. V. (1993). *The lexicon in acquisition*. New York: Cambridge University Press.

Clark, E. V. (2009). What shapes children's language? Child-directed speech and the process of acquisition. In V. C. M. Gathercole (Ed.), *Routes to Language: Essays in honor of Melissa Bowerman*. New York: Psychology Press.

Clark, E. V. (2012). Lexical meaning. In E. L. Bavin (Ed.), *Cambridge handbook of child language*. New York: Cambridge University Press.

Clark-Cotton, M. R., Williams, R. K., & Goral. M. (2007). Language and communication in aging. In J. E. Birren (Ed.), *Encyclopedia of gerontology* (2nd ed.). San Diego: Academic Press.

Clarke-Stewart, A. K., & Miner, J. L. (2008). Child and day care, effects of. In M. M. Haith & J. B. Benson (Eds.), *Encyclopedia of infant and early childhood development*. Oxford, UK: Elsevier.

Class, Q. A., Lichtenstein, P., Langstrom, N., & D'Onofrio, B. M. (2011). Timing of prenatal maternal exposure to severe life events and adverse pregnancy outcomes: A population study of 2.6 million pregnancies. *Psychosomatic Medicine, 73,* 234–241.

Clausen, J. A. (1993). *American lives*. New York: Free Press.

Clay, O. J., & others. (2009). Visual function and cognitive speed of processing mediate age-related decline in memory span and fluid intelligence. *Journal of Aging and Health, 21,* 547–566.

Clay, R. (2001, February). Fulfilling an unmet need. *Monitor on Psychology,* 2.

Clay, R. A. (1997, April). Helping dying patients let go of life in peace. *APA Monitor,* p. 42.

Clearfield, M. W., Diedrich, F. J., Smith, L. B., & Thelen, E. (2006). Young infants reach correctly in A-not-B tasks: On the development of stability and perseveration. *Infant Behavior and Development, 29,* 435–444.

Clements, J. M. (2009). Patient perceptions on the use of advanced directives and life prolonging technology. *American Journal of Hospice and Palliative Care, 26,* 270–276.

Cleveland, M. J., Feinberg, M. E., Osgood, D. W., & Moody, J. (2012). Do peers' parents matter? A new link between positive parenting and adolescent substance use. *Journal of Studies on Alcohol and Drugs, 73,* 423–433.

Clifton, R. K., Morrongiello, B. A., Kulig, J. W., & Dowd, J. M. (1981). Developmental changes in auditory localization in infancy. In R. N. Aslin, J. R. Alberts, & M. R. Petersen (Eds.), *Development of perception* (Vol. 1). Orlando, FL: Academic Press.

Clifton, R. K., Muir, D. W., Ashmead, D. H., & Clarkson, M. G. (1993). Is visually guided reaching in early infancy a myth? *Child Development, 64,* 1099–1110.

Clouchoux, C., & Limperopoulos, C. (2012). Novel applications of MRI for the fetal brain. *Pediatric Radiology, 42*(Suppl. 1), S24–S32.

Cluett, E. R., & Burns, E. (2009). Immersion in water in labour and birth. *Cochrane Database of Systematic Reviews,* CD000111.

Coe, N. B., von Gaudecker, H. M., Lindeboom, M., & Maurer, J. (2012). The effect of retirement on cognitive functioning. *Health Economics, 21,* 913–927.

Cogmed. (2013). *Cogmed: Working memory is the engine of learning.* Upper Saddle River, NJ: Pearson.

Cohen, D. (2012). *How the child's mind develops* (2nd ed.). New York: Psychology Press.

Cohen, F., Kemeny, M. E., Zegans, L. S., Johnson, P., Kearney, K. A., & Stites, D. P. (2007). Immune function declines with unemployment and recovers after stressor termination. *Psychosomatic Medicine, 69,* 225–234.

Cohen, G. D. (2009). Creativity, later life. In D. Carr (Ed.), *Encyclopedia of the life course and human development.* Boston: Gale Cengage.

Cohen, G. L., & Prinstein, M. J. (2006). Peer contagion of aggression and health-risk behavior among adolescent males: An experimental investigation of effects on public conduct and private attitudes. *Child Development, 77,* 967–983.

Cohen, K. M., & Savin-Williams, R. C. (2013, in press). Coming out to self and others: Unfolding of developmental milestones. In P. Levounis, J. Drescher, & M. Barber (Eds.), *Working with lesbian, gay, bisexual, and transgender people: Basic principles and case studies.* Arlington, VA: American Psychiatric Publishing.

Cohen, L. B. (2002, April). *Can infants really add and subtract?* Paper presented at the meeting of the International Conference on Infant Studies, Toronto.

Cohen, P. (2012). *In our prime: The invention of middle age.* New York: Scribner.

Cohen, P., Kasen, S., Chen, H., Hartmark, C., & Gordon, K. (2003). Variations in patterns of developmental transitions in the emerging adulthood period. *Developmental Psychology, 39,* 657–669.

Coie, J. (2004). The impact of negative social experiences on the development of antisocial behavior. In J. B. Kupersmidt & K. A. Dodge (Eds.), *Children's peer relations: From development to intervention.* Washington, DC: American Psychological Association.

Colby, A., Koblberg, L., Gibbs, J., & Lieberman, M. (1983). A longitudinal study of moral judgment. *Monographs of the Society for Research in Child Development* (Serial No. 201).

Colcombe, S., & Kramer, A. F. (2003). Fitness effects on the cognitive function of older adults: A meta-analytic study. *Psychological Science, 14,* 125–130.

Colcombe, S. J., & others. (2006). Aerobic exercise training increases brain volume in aging humans. *Journals of Gerontology: Medical Sciences, 61A,* 1166–1170.

Cole, M., & Packer, M. (2011). Culture in development. In M. H. Bornstein & M. E. Lamb (Eds.), *Cognitive development.* New York: Psychology Press.

Cole, P. M., Dennis, T. A., Smith-Simon, K. E., & Cohen, L. H. (2009). Preschoolers' emotion regulation strategy understanding: Relations with maternal socialization and child behavior. *Social Development, 18*(2), 324–352.

Cole, P. M., & Hall, S. E. (2012). Emotion dysregulation as a risk factor for psychopathology. In T. Beauchaine & S. Hinshaw (Eds.), *Developmental Psychopathology.* New York: Wiley.

Cole, P. M., & Tan, P. Z. (2007). Emotion socialization from a cultural perspective. In J. E. Grusec & P. D. Hastings (Eds.), *Handbook of socialization.* New York: Guilford.

Coleman, M., Ganong, L., & Fine, M. (2004). Communication in stepfamilies. In A. L. Vangelisti (Ed.), *Handbook of family communication.* Mahwah, NJ: Erlbaum.

Coleman, P. D. (1986, August). *Regulation of dendritic extent: Human aging brain and Alzheimer's disease.* Paper presented at the meeting of the American Psychological Association, Washington, DC.

Coleman-Phox, M. P. H., Odouli, R., & Li, D. K. (2008). Use of a fan during sleep and the risk of sudden infant death syndrome. *Archives of Pediatric and Adolescent Medicine, 162,* 963–968.

Collaku, A., & others. (2004). A genome-wide linkage scan for dietary energy and nutrient intakes. *American Journal of Clinical Nutrition, 79,* 881–886.

Collins, C. E., & others. (2011). Parent diet modification, child activity, or both in obese children: An RCT. *Pediatrics, 127,* 619–627.

Collins, J. S., Atkinson, K. K., Dean, J. H., Best, R. G., & Stevenson, R. E. (2011). Long term maintenance of neural tube defects prevention in a high prevalence state. *Journal of Pediatrics. Alcoholism, Clinical and Experimental Research, 159,* 143–149.

Collins, W. A., & van Dulmen, M. (2006). The significance of middle childhood peer competence for work and relationships in early childhood. In A. C. Huston & M. N. Ripke (Eds.), *Developmental contexts in middle childhood.* New York: Cambridge University Press.

Collins, W. A., Welsh, D. P., & Furman, W. (2009). Adolescent romantic relationships. *Annual Review of Psychology* (Vol. 60). Palo Alto, CA: Annual Reviews.

Colombo, J., Kapa, L., & Curtendale, L. (2011). Varieties of attention in infancy. In L. Oakes, C. Cashon, M. Casasola, & D. Rakison (Eds.), *Infant perception and cognition.* New York: Oxford University Press.

Colonnesi, C., Stams, G. J., Koster, I., & Noom, M. J. (2010). The relation between pointing and language development: A meta-analysis. *Developmental Review, 30,* 352–366.

Colrain, I. M., & Baker, F. C. (2011). Changes in sleep as a function of adolescent development. *Neuropsychology Review, 21,* 5–21.

Comer, J. (1988). Educating poor minority children. *Scientific American, 259,* 42–48.

Comer, J. (2004). *Leave no child behind.* New Haven, CT: Yale University Press.

Comer, J. (2006). Child development: The under-weighted aspect of intelligence. In P. C. Kyllonen, R. D. Roberts, & L. Stankov (Eds.), *Extending intelligence.* Mahwah, NJ: Erlbaum.

Comer, J. (2010). Comer School Development Program. In J. Meece & J. Eccles (Eds.), *Handbook of research on schools, schooling, and human development.* New York: Routledge.

Committee on Injury, Violence, and Poison Prevention. (2011). Child passenger safety. *Pediatrics, 127,* e1050–e1066.

Common Sense Media. (2011). *Zero to eight: Children's media use in America.* Retrieved June 21, 2012, from www.commonsensemedia.org/research

Commoner, B. (2002). Unravelling the DNA myth: The spurious foundation of genetic engineering. *Harper's Magazine, 304,* 39–47.

Commons, M. L., & Bresette, L. M. (2006). Illuminating major creative scientific innovators with postformal stages. In C. Hoare (Ed.), *Handbook of adult development and learning.* New York: Oxford University Press.

Conde-Aguedelo, A., Belizan, J. M., & Diaz-Rossello, J. (2011). Kangaroo care to reduce morbidity and mortality in low birthweight infants. *Cochrane Database of Systematic Reviews, 16*(3) CD002771.

Conduct Problems Prevention Research Group. (2011). The effects of Fast Track preventive intervention on the development of conduct disorder across childhood. *Child Development, 82,* 331–345.

Conduct Problems Prevention Research Group. (2010). The difficulty of maintaining positive intervention effects: A look at disruptive behavior, deviant peer relations, and social skills during the middle school years. *Journal of Early Adolescence, 30*(4), 593–624.

Cong, X., Ludington-Hoe, S. M., & Walsh, S. (2011). Randomized crossover trial of kangaroo care to reduce biobehavioral pain responses in preterm infants: A pilot study. *Biological Research for Nursing, 13,* 204–216.

Cong, Z., Feng, D., Liu, Y., & Esperat, M. C. (2012). Sedentary behaviors among Hispanic children: Influences of parental support in a school intervention program. *American Journal of Health Promotion, 26,* 270–280.

Conger, R. D., & Chao, W. (1996). Adolescent depressed mood. In R. L. Simons (Ed.), *Understanding differences between divorced and intact families: Stress, interaction, and child outcome.* Thousand Oaks, CA: Sage.

Conger, R. D., & others. (2012). Resilience and vulnerability of Mexican origin youth and their families: A test of a culturally-informed model of family economic stress. In P. K. Kerig, M. S. Schulz, & S. T. Hauser (Eds.), *Adolescence and beyond*. New York: Oxford University Press.

Conneely, K. N., & others. (2012). Human longevity and common variations in the LMNA gene: A meta-analysis. *Aging Cell, 11*, 475–481.

Connell, A. M., Dishion, T. J., & Klostermann, S. (2012, in press). Family check-up effects on adolescent arrest trajectories: Variation by developmental subtype. *Journal of Research on Adolescence.*

Connolly, J. A., & McIsaac, C. (2009). Romantic relationships in adolescence. In R. M. Lerner & L. Steinberg (Eds.), *Handbook of adolescent psychology* (3rd ed.), New York: Wiley.

Conry-Murray, C., Kim, J. M., & Turiel, E. (2012, April). *U.S. and Korean children's judgments of gender norm violations.* Paper presented at the Gender Development Research conference, San Francisco.

Conway, A., & Stifter, C. A. (2012, in press). Longitudinal antecedents of executive function in preschoolers. *Child Development.*

Cook, E. C., Buehler, C., & Blair, B. L. (2012, in press). Adolescent emotional reactivity across relationship contexts. *Developmental Psychology.*

Cook, M., & Birch, R. (1984). Infant perception of the shapes of tilted plane forms. *Infant Behavior and Development, 7*, 389–402.

Cookston, J., & McHale, S. (2012, April). *Family gender dynamics: Parent-child, marital, and sibling relationships.* Paper presented at the Gender Development Research conference, San Francisco.

Cooper, C. (2012). *Intelligence and abilities* (2nd ed.). New York: Psychology Press.

Cooper, C., Selwood, A., & Livingston, G. (2008). The prevalence of elder abuse and neglect: A systematic review. *Age and Aging, 37*, 151–160.

Cooper, C. R. (2011). *Bridging multiple worlds.* New York: Oxford University Press.

Cooper, H. (Ed.) (2012). *APA handbook of research methods in psychology.* Washington, DC: American Psychological Association.

Cooper, J. N., & others. (2012, in press). Effects of an intensive weight loss intervention consisting of caloric restriction with or without physical activity on common carotid artery remodeling in seriously obese adults. *Metabolism.*

Coovadia, H. M., & others. (2012). Efficacy and safety of extended nevirapine regimen in infant children of breastfeeding mothers with HIV-1 infection for prevention of postnatal HIV-1 transmission (HPTN 046): A randomized, double-blind, placebo-controlled trial. *Lancet, 379*, 221–228.

Copen, C. E., Daniels, K., Vespa, J., & Mosher, W. D. (2012). First marriages in the United States: Data from the 2006–2010 National Survey of Family Growth. *National Health Statistics Reports, 49*, 1–22.

Coplan, R. J., & Arbeau, K. A. (2009). Peer interactions and play in early childhood. In K. H. Rubin, W. M. Bukowski, & B. Laursen (Eds.), *Handbook of peer interactions, relationships, and groups.* New York: Guilford.

Cordier, S. (2008). Evidence for a role of paternal exposure in developmental toxicity. *Basic and Clinical Pharmacology and Toxicology, 102*, 176–181.

Cornew, L., & others. (2012, in press). Atypical social referencing in infant siblings of children with autism spectrum disorders. *Journal of Autism and Developmental Disorders.*

Corporation for National and Community Service. (2006). *Volunteer growth in America.* Washington, DC: Author.

Corrada, M. M., Berlau, D. J., & Kawas, C. H. (2012, in press). A population-based clinicopathological study in the oldest-old: The 901 study. *Current Alzheimer Research.*

Corsica, J. A., & Perri, M. G. (2013). Obesity. In I. B. Weiner & others (Eds.), *Handbook of psychology* (2nd ed., Vol. 9). New York: Wiley.

Corso, J. F. (1977). Auditory perception and communication. In J. E. Birren & K. W. Schaie (Eds.), *Handbook of the psychology of aging.* (2nd ed.). New York: Van Nostrand Reinhold.

Cortes, E., Basra, R., & Kelleher, C. J. (2011). Waterbirth and pelvic floor injury: A retrospective study and postal survey using ICIQ modular long form questionnaires. *European Journal of Obstetrics, Gynecology, and Reproductive Biology, 155*, 27–30.

Cosmides, L. (2013). Evolutionary psychology. *Annual Review of Psychology* (Vol. 6). Palo Alto, CA: Annual Reviews.

Costa, P. T., & McCrae, R. R. (1995). Solid ground on the wetlands of personality: A reply to Black. *Psychological Bulletin, 117*, 216–220.

Costa, P. T., & McCrae, R. R. (1998). Personality assessment. In H. S. Friedman (Ed.), *Encyclopedia of mental health* (Vol. 3). San Diego: Academic Press.

Costa, P. T., & McCrae, R. R. (2000). Contemporary personality psychology. In C. E. Coffey and J. L. Cummings (Eds.). *Textbook of geriatric neuropsychiatry.* Washington, DC: American Psychiatric Press.

Costa, R., & Figueiredo, B. (2011). Infants' psychophysiological profile and temperament at 3 and 12 months. *Infant Behavior and Development, 34*, 270–279.

Costley, K. C. (2012). An overview of the life, central concepts, including classroom applications for Lev Vygotsky. *ERIC*, ED529565.

Cote, J., & Bynner, J. M. (2008). Changes in the transition to adulthood in the UK and Canada: The role of structure and aging in emerging adulthood. *Journal of Youth Studies, 11*, 251–258.

Cotelli, M., Manenti, R., & Zanetti, O. (2012). Reminiscence therapy in dementia: A review. *Maturitas, 72*, 203–205.

Council of Economic Advisors. (2000). *Teens and their parents in the 21st century: An examination of trends in teen behavior and the role of parent involvement.* Washington, DC: Author.

Courage, M. L., & Richards, J. E. (2008). Attention. In M. M. Haith & J. B. Benson (Eds.), *Encyclopedia of infant and early childhood development.* Oxford, UK: Elsevier.

Couraud, S., Zalcman, G., Milleron, B., Morin, F., & Souquet, P. J. (2012, in press). Lung cancer in never smokers—A review. *European Journal of Cancer.*

Cousineau, T. M., Goldstein, M., & Franco, D. L. (2005). A collaborative approach to nutrition education for college students. *Journal of American College Health, 53*, 79–84.

Cowan, C. P., & Cowan, P. A. (2000). *When partners become parents.* Mahwah, NJ: Erlbaum.

Cowan, P., Cowan, C., Ablow, J., Johnson, V. K., & Measelle, J. (2005). *The family context of parenting in children's adaptation to elementary school.* Mahwah, NJ: Erlbaum.

Cowley, G., & Hager, M. (1995, December 4). Terminal care: Too painful, too prolonged. *Newsweek,* pp. 74–75.

Cox, K. S., Wilt, J., Olson, B., & McAdams, D. P. (2010). Generativity, the Big Five, and psychosocial adaptation in midlife adults. *Journal of Personality, 78*, 1185–1208.

Coxon, J. P., Van Impe, A., Wenderoth, N., & Swinnen, S. P. (2012). Aging and inhibitory control of action: Cortio-subthalamic connection strength predicts stopping performance. *Journal of Neuroscience, 32*, 8401–8412.

Coyne, S. M., Nelson, D. A., & Underwood, M. K. (2011). Aggression in children. In P. K. Smith & C. H. Hart (Eds.), *Wiley-Blackwell handbook of childhood social development* (2nd ed.). New York: Wiley.

Crain, S. (2012). Sentence scope. In E. L. Bavin (Ed.), *Cambridge handbook of child language.* New York: Cambridge University Press.

Crain, S., & Zhou, P. (2012, in press). Semantics and pragmatics: Acquisition of logical connectives and focus. In C. T. J. Huang & R. Sybesma (Eds.), *Encyclopedia of Chinese language and linguistics.* The Netherlands: Brill.

Crawford, D. (2011). Understanding a child's grief takes care and compassion. *Nursing Children and Young People, 23*, 6–7.

Crawford, D., & others. (2010). The longitudinal influence of home and neighborhood environments on children's body mass index and physical activity over 5 years: The CLAN study. *International Journal of Obesity, 34*, 1177–1187.

Cremation Association of North America. (2012). *Statistics about cremation trends.* Retrieved July 12, 2012, from www.cremationassociation/org/Media/Cremation Statistics/tabid/95/Default.aspx

Crijns, H. J., & others. (2012, in press). Prescriptive contraceptive use among isotretinoin users in the Netherlands in comparison with non-users: A drug utilization study. *Pharmacoepidemiology and Drug Safety.*

Crockenberg, S. B. (1986). Are temperamental differences in babies associated with predictable differences in caregiving? In J. V. Lerner & R. M. Lerner (Eds.), *Temperament and social interaction during infancy and childhood.* San Francisco: Jossey-Bass.

Crone, E. A., & others. (2009). Neurocognitive development of relational reasoning. *Developmental Science, 12*, 55–66.

Cronk, C. E., & others. (2011). Effects of a culturally tailored intervention on changes in body mass index and health-related quality of life of Latino children and their parents. *American Journal of Health Promotion, 25*, e1–e11.

Crooks, R. L., & Baur, K. (2011). *Our sexuality* (11th ed.). Boston: Cengage.

Crosnoe, R. (2011). *Fitting in, standing out*. New York: Cambridge University Press.

Crosnoe, R., Wu, N., & Bonazzo, C. (2012). Child health and early education. In V. Maholmes & R. B. King (Eds.), *Oxford handbook of poverty and child development*. New York: Oxford University Press.

Cross, T. P., Matthews, B., Tommyr, L., Scott, D., & Quimet, C. (2012, in press). Child welfare policy and practice on children's exposure to domestic violence. *Child Abuse and Neglect*.

Crouter, A. C. (2006). Mothers and fathers at work. In A. Clarke-Stewart & J. Dunn (Eds.), *Families count*. New York: Cambridge University Press.

Crouter, A. C., & McHale, S. (2005). The long arm of the job revisited: Parenting in dual-earner families. In T. Luster & L. Okasagi (Eds.), *Parenting*. Mahwah, NJ: Erlbaum.

Crowell, J. A., Treboux, D., & Brockmeyer, S. (2009). Parental divorce and adult children's attachment representations and marital status. *Attachment and Human Development, 11*, 87–101.

Crowley, K., Callahan, M. A., Tenenbaum, H. R., & Allen, E. (2001). Parents explain more to boys than to girls during shared scientific thinking. *Psychological Science, 12*, 258–261.

Crowley, S. J., & Carskadon, M. A. (2010). Modifications to weekend recovery sleep delay circadian phase in older adolescents. *Chronobiology International, 27*, 1469–1492.

Cruz, J. E., Emery, R. E., & Turkheimer, E. (2012, in press). Peer network drinking predicts increasing alcohol use from adolescence to early adulthood after controlling for genetic and shared environmental selection. *Developmental Psychology*.

Csikszentmihalyi, M. (1995). *Creativity*. New York: HarperCollins.

Csikszentmihalyi, M. (2000). Creativity: An overview. In A. Kazdin (Ed.), *Encyclopedia of psychology*. Washington, DC, & New York: American Psychological Association and Oxford University Press.

Cubbin, C., Brindis, C. D., Jain, S., Santelli, J., & Braveman, P. (2010). Neighborhood poverty, aspirations and expectations, and initiation of sex. *Journal of Adolescent Health, 47*, 399–406.

Cubillo, A., Halari, R., Smith, A., Taylor, E., & Rubia, K. (2012). A review of fronto-spatial brain abnormalities in children and adults with Attention Deficit Hyperactivity Disorder (ADHD) and new evidence for dysfunction in adults with ADHD during motivation and attention. *Cortex, 48*, 194–215.

Cuddy-Casey, M., & Orvaschel, H. (1997). Children's understanding of death in relation to child suicidality and homicidality. *Death Studies, 17*, 33–45.

Cuevas, K., Swingler, M. M., Bell, M. A., Marcovitch, S., & Calkins, S. D. (2012). Measures of frontal lobe functioning and the emergence of inhibitory control process at 10 months of age. *Developmental Cognitive Neuroscience, 2*, 235–243.

Cummings, E. M., & Davies, P. T. (2010). *Marital conflict and children: An emotional security perspective*. New York: Guilford.

Cummings, E. M., El-Sheikh, M., & Kouros, C. D. (2009). Children and violence: The role of children's regulation in the marital aggression-child adjustment link. *Clinical Child and Family Psychology Review, 12*(1), 3–15.

Cummings, E. M., Braungart-Rieker, J. M., & Du Rocher-Schudlich, T. (2013, in press). Emotion and personality development. In I. B. Weiner & others (Eds.), *Handbook of psychology* (2nd ed., Vol. 6). New York: Wiley.

Cummings, E. M., Papp, L. M., & Kouros, C. D. (2012, in press). Regulatory processes in children's coping with exposure to marital conflict. In S. L. Olson & A. J. Sameroff (Eds.), *Biopsychosocial regulatory processes in the development of childhood behavioral problems*. New York: Cambridge University Press.

Cummings, E. M., & Schatz, J. N. (2012). Family conflict, emotional security, and child development: Translating research findings into a prevention program for community families. *Clinical Child and Family Psychology Review, 15*, 14–27.

Cunningham, M. (2009). Housework. In D. Carr (Ed.), *Encyclopedia of the life course and human development*. Boston: Gale Cengage.

Cunningham, P. M. (2013). *Phonics they use: Words for reading and writing* (6th ed.). Boston: Allyn & Bacon.

Curran, K., DuCette, J., Eisenstein, J., & Hyman, I. A. (2001, August). *Statistical analysis of the cross-cultural data: The third year*. Paper presented at the meeting of the American Psychological Association, San Francisco, CA.

Currie, C., & others. (2012). Is obesity at individual and national level associated with lower age at menarche? Evidence from 34 countries in the Health Behavior in School-aged Children study. *Journal of Adolescent Health, 50*, 621–626.

Currie, K. D., McKelvie, R. S, & MacDonald, M. J. (2012, in press). Flow-mediated dilation is acutely improved following high-density interval exercise. *Medicine and Science in Sports and Exercise*.

Currier, J. M., Holland, J. M., & Neimeyer, R. A. (2006). Sense-making, grief, and the experience of violent loss: Toward a mediational model. *Death Studies, 30*, 403–428.

Cvencek, D., Meltzoff, A. N., & Greenwald, A. G. (2011). Math-gender stereotypes in elementary school children. *Child Development, 82*, 766–779.

Czaja, S. J., & others. (2006). Factors predicting the use of technology: Findings from the Center for Research and Education on Aging and Technology (CREATE). *Psychology and Aging, 21*, 333–352.

D

D'Angelo, D. V., & others. (2011). Birth outcomes of intended pregnancies among women who used assisted reproductive technology, ovulation stimulation, or no treatment. *Fertility and Sterility, 96*, 314–320.

D'Augelli, A. R. (1991). Gay men in college: Identity processes and adaptations. *Journal of College Student Development, 32*, 140–146.

Da Costa, L. A., Badawi, A., & El-Sohemy, A. (2012). Nutrigenetics and modulation of oxidative stress. *Annals of Nutrition and Metabolism* (Suppl. 3), S27–S36.

da Fonseca, E. B., Bittar, R. E., Damiao, R., & Zugiab, M. (2009). Prematurity prevention: The role of progesterone. *Current Opinion in Obstetrics and Gynecology, 21*, 142–147.

Dafnis, I., & others. (2012, in press). An apolipoprotein E4 fragment affects matrix metalloproteinase 9, tissue inhibitor of metalloproteinase 1 and cytokine levels in brain cell lines. *Neuroscience*.

Dahl, R. E. (2004). Adolescent brain development: A period of vulnerability and opportunity. *Annals of the New York Academy of Sciences, 1021*, 1–22.

Dahlen, H. G., Jackson, M., & Stevens, J. (2011). Homebirth, freebirth, and doulas: Casualty and consequences of a broken maternity system. *Women and Birth, 24*, 47–50.

Dakin, E., & Pearlmutter, S. (2009). Older women's perceptions of elder maltreatment and ethical dilemmas in adult protective services: A cross-cultural, exploratory study. *Journal of Elder Abuse and Neglect, 21*, 15–57.

Daley, A. J., Macarthur, C., & Winter, H. (2007). The role of exercise in treating postpartum depression: A review of the literature. *Journal of Midwifery & Women's Health, 52*, 56–62.

Dalley, J. W., & Roiser, J. P. (2012, in press). Dopamine, serotonin, and impulsivity. *Neuroscience*.

Damon, W. (1988). *The moral child*. New York: Free Press.

Damon, W. (2008). The path to purpose. New York: Free Press.

Danforth, M. M., & Glass, J. C. (2001). Listen to my words, give meaning to my sorrow: A study in cognitive constructs in middle-aged bereaved widows. *Death Studies, 25*, 513–548.

Daniels, H. (2011). Vygotsky and psychology. In U. Goswami (Ed.), *Wiley-Blackwell handbook of childhood cognitive development* (2nd ed.). New York: Wiley.

Daniels, N. (2012). Aging and intergenerational equity. *Global population aging: Peril or promise?* Geneva, SWIT: World Economic Forum.

Danigelis, N. L. (2007). Leisure. In J. E. Birren (Ed.), *Encyclopedia of gerontology* (2nd ed.). San Diego: Academic Press.

Danner, D., Snowdon, D., & Friesen, W. (2001). Positive emotions in early life and longevity: Findings from the Nun Study. *Journal of Personality and Social Psychology, 80*(5), 804–813.

Darcy, E. (2012). Gender issues in child and adolescent eating disorders. In J. Lock (Ed.), *Oxford handbook of child and adolescent eating disorders: Developmental perspectives*. New York: Oxford University Press.

Darwin, C. (1859). *On the origin of species*. London: John Murray.

Das, D. K., Mukherjee, S., & Ray, D. (2011). Erratum to: Resveratrol and red wine, healthy heart and longevity. *Heart Failure Review, 16*, 425–435.

Dastani, Z., & others. (2012). Novel loci for adiponectin levels and their influence on type 2 diabetes and metabolic traits: A multi-ethnic meta-analysis of 45,891 individuals. *PLoS One, 8*(3), e1002607.

Dattilo, A. M., & others. (2012, in press). Need for early interventions in the prevention of pediatric overweight: A review and upcoming directions. *Journal of Obesity*.

Davalos, D. B., Yadon, C. A., & Tregellas, H. C. (2012). Untreated maternal depression and the potential risks to offspring: A review. *Archives of Women's Mental Health, 15*, 1–14.

Davidov, M., & Grusec, J. E. (2006). Untangling the links of parental responsiveness to distress and warmth to child outcomes. *Child Development, 77,* 44–58.

Davidson, J. (2000). Giftedness. In A. Kazdin (Ed.), *Encyclopedia of psychology.* Washington, DC, & New York: American Psychological Association and Oxford University Press.

Davidson, M. R., Davidson, M., London, M. L., & Ladewig, P. W. (2012). *Olds' maternal-newborn nursing and women's health across the lifespan: International edition.* (9th ed.). Upper Saddle River, NJ: Pearson.

Davidson, W. S., Jimenez, T. R., Onifade, E., & Hankins, S. S. (2010). Student experiences of the adolescent diversion project: A community-based exemplar in the pedagogy of service-learning. *American Journal of Community Psychology, 46,* 442–458.

Davies, G., & others. (2011). Genome-wide association studies establish that human intelligence is highly heritable and polygenic. *Molecular Psychiatry, 16,* 996–1005.

Davies, J., & Brember, I. (1999). Reading and mathematics attainments and self-esteem in years 2 and 6—an eight-year cross-sectional study. *Educational Studies, 25,* 145–157.

Davies, M., Gilston, J., & Rogers, P. (2012, in press). Examining the relationship between male rape myth acceptance, female rape myth acceptance, victim blame, homophobia, gender roles, and ambivalent sexism. *Journal of Interpersonal Violence.*

Davinelli, S., Willcox, D. C., & Scapagnini, G. (2012, in press). Extending healthy aging: Nutrient sensitive pathway and centenarian population. *Immunity and Aging.*

Davis, A. E., Hyatt, G., & Arrasmith, D. (1998, February). "I Have a Dream" program. *Class One Evaluation Report,* Portland, OR: Northwest Regional Education Laboratory.

Davis, B. E., Moon, R. Y., Sachs, M. C., & Ottolini, M. C. (1998). Effects of sleep position on infant motor development. *Pediatrics, 102,* 1135–1140.

Davis, C. F., Lazariu, V., & Sekhobo, J. P. (2010). Smoking cessation in the WIC program. *Maternal and Child Health Journal 14*(3), 474–477.

Davis, C. L., & Cooper, S. (2011). Fitness, fatness, cognition, behavior, and academic achievement in overweight children: Do cross-sectional associations correspond to exercise trial outcomes? *Preventive Medicine, 52* (Suppl. 1), S65–S69.

Davis, C. L., & others. (2007). Effects of aerobic exercise on overweight children's cognitive functioning: A randomized controlled trial. *Research Quarterly for Exercise and Sport, 78,* 510–519.

Davis, C. L., & others. (2011). Exercise improves executive functioning and alters neural activation in overweight children. *Health Psychology, 30,* 91–98.

Davis, L., & Keyser, J. (1997). *Becoming the parent you want to be: A sourcebook of strategies for the first five years.* New York: Broadway.

Davis, M. C., Burke, H. M., Zautra, A. J., & Stark, S. (2013, in press). Arthritis and musculoskeletal conditions. In I. B. Weiner & others (Eds.), *Handbook of psychology* (2nd ed., Vol. 9). New York: Wiley.

Davis, S. W., Kragel, J. E., Madden, D. J., & Cabesa, R. (2012). The architecture of cross-hemispheric communication in the aging brain: Linking behavior to functional and structural connectivity. *Cerebral Cortex, 22,* 232–242.

Day, N. L., Goldschmidt, L., & Thomas, C. A. (2006). Prenatal marijuana exposure contributes to the prediction of marijuana use at age 14. *Addiction, 101,* 1313–1322.

Day, R. H., & McKenzie, B. E. (1973). Perceptual shape constancy in early infancy. *Perception, 2,* 315–320.

De Decker, E., & others. (2012). Influencing factors of screen time in preschool children: An exploration of parents' perceptions through focus groups in six European countries. *Obesity Reviews, 13* (Suppl. 1), S75–S84.

De Giovanni, N., & Marchetti, D. (2012). Cocaine and its metabolites in the placenta: A systematic review of the literature. *Reproductive Toxicology, 33,* 1–14.

de Haan, M., & Gunnar, M. R. (Eds.) (2009). *Handbook of developmental social neuroscience.* New York: Guilford.

de Haan, M., & Matheson, A. (2009). The development and neural bases of processing emotion in faces and voices. In M. De Haan & M. R. Gunnar (Eds.), *Handbook of developmental social neuroscience.* New York: Guilford.

de Hevia, M. D., & Spelke, E. S. (2010). Number-space mapping in human infants. *Psychological Science, 21,* 653–660.

de Hollander, E. L., & others. (2012, in press). The association between waist circumference and risk of mortality considering body mass index in 65- to 74-year-olds: A meta-analysis of 29 cohorts involving more than 58,000 elderly persons. *International Journal of Epidemiology.*

de Hollander, E. L., & others. (2012). The impact of body mass index on old age on cause-specific mortality. *Journal of Nutrition, Health, and Aging, 16,* 100–116.

de la Cuesta-Benjumea, C. (2011). Strategies for the relief of burden in advanced dementia care-giving. *Journal of Advanced Nursing, 67,* 1790–1799.

de la Sierra, A., & Barrios, V. (2012, in press). Blood pressure control with angiotensin receptor blocker-based three-drug combinations: Key trials. *Advances in Therapy.*

de Leo, D., & Heller, T. (2008). Social modeling in the transmission of suicidality. *Crisis, 29,* 11–19.

De Lima, L., & others. (2012). International Association for Hospice and Palliative Care (IAHPC) list of essential practices in palliative care. *Journal of Pain and Palliative Care Pharmacotherapy, 26,* 118–126.

De Meyer, G., & others. (2010). Diagnosis-independent Alzheimer disease biomarker signature in cognitively normal people. *Archives in Neurology, 67,* 949–956.

de Oliveira, D. M., Ferreira Lima, R. M., & El-Bache, R. S. (2012). Brain rust: Recent discoveries on the role of oxidative stress in neurodegenerative diseases. *Nutritional Neuroscience, 15,* 94–102.

De Rose, L. M., Shiyko, M. P., Foster, H., & Brooks-Gunn, J. (2011). Associations between menarcheal timing and behavioral developmental trajectories for girls from age 6 to age 15. *Journal of Youth and Adolescence, 40,* 1329–1342.

de Villars, J., & de Villiers, P. (2013). Syntax acquisition. In P. D. Zelazo (Ed.), *Oxford handbook of developmental psychology.* New York: Oxford University Press.

de Wit, L., & others. (2010). Depression and obesity: A meta-analysis of community-based studies. *Psychiatry Research, 178,* 230–235.

Deary, I. J. (2012). Intelligence. *Annual Review of Intelligence* (Vol. 63). Palo Alto, CA: Annual Reviews.

Deater-Deckard, K., & Dodge, K. (1997). Externalizing behavior problems and discipline revisited: Non-linear effects and variation by culture, context and gender. *Psychological Inquiry, 8,* 161–175.

Debats, D. L. (1990). The Life Regard Index: Reliability and validity. *Psychological Reports, 67,* 27–34.

Decarli, C., & others. (2012, in press). Session II: Mechanisms of age-related cognitive change and targets for intervention: Neural circuits, networks, and plasticity. *Journals of Gerontology A: Biological Sciences and Medical Sciences.*

DeCasper, A. J., & Spence, M. J. (1986). Prenatal maternal speech influences newborns' perception of speech sounds. *Infant Behavior and Development, 9,* 133–150.

Decimo, I., Bifari, F., Krampera, M., & Fumagalli, G. (2012). Neural stem cell niches in health and diseases. *Current Pharmaceutical Design, 18,* 1755–1783.

Deeg, D. J. H. (2005). The development of physical and mental health from late midlife to early old age. In S. L. Willis & M. Martin (Eds.), *Middle adulthood.* Thousand Oaks, CA: Sage.

DeGenova, M. K., Rice, F. P., Stinnett, N., & Stinnett, N. L. (2011). *Intimate relationships, marriages, and families* (8th ed.). New York: McGraw-Hill.

DeJong, W., DeRicco, B., & Schneider, S. K. (2010). Pregaming: An exploratory study of strategic drinking by college students in Pennsylvania. *Journal of American College Health, 58,* 307–316.

Del Giudice, M. (2011). Sex differences in romantic attachment: A meta-analysis. *Personality and Social Psychology Bulletin, 37,* 193–214.

Del Tredici, K., & Braak, H. (2008). Neurofibrillary changes of the Alzheimer type in very elderly individuals: Neither inevitable nor benign. Commentary on no disease in the brain of a 115-year-old woman. *Neurobiology of Aging, 29,* 1133–1136.

Delgado. J., & others. (2012, in press). Differences in blood pressure control in a large population-based sample of older African Americans and non-Hispanic Whites. *Journals of Gerontology A: Biological Sciences and Medical Sciences.*

DeLoache, J. S. (2011). Early development of the understanding and use of symbolic artifacts. In U. Goswami (Ed.), *Wiley-Blackwell handbook of childhood cognitive development* (2nd ed.). New York: Wiley.

DeLoache, J. S., Simcock, G., & Macari, S. (2007). Planes, trains, and automobiles—and tea sets: Extremely intense interests in very young children. *Developmental Psychology, 43,* 1579–1586.

Demerouti, E. (2012). The spillover and crossover of resources among partners: The role of work-self and family-self facilitation. *Journal of Occupational Health Psychology, 17,* 184–195.

Dempster, F. N. (1981). Memory span: Sources of individual and developmental differences. *Psychological Bulletin, 80*, 63–100.

Dencker, M., & others. (2012, in press). Body fat, abdominal fat, and body fat distribution related to cardiovascular risk factors in prepubertal children. *Acta Pediatrica.*

Denham, S., & others. (2011). Emotions and social development in childhood. In P. K. Smith & C. H. Hart (Eds.), *Wiley-Blackwell handbook of childhood social development* (2nd ed.). New York: Wiley.

Denham, S., & others. (2012, in press). Preschoolers' emotion knowledge: Self-regulatory foundations and predictors of school success. *Cognition and Emotion.*

Denham, S., Warren, H., von Salisch, M., Benga, O., Chin, J-C., & Geangu, E. (2011). Emotions and social development in childhood. In P. K. Smith & C. H. Hart (Eds.), *Wiley-Blackwell handbook of childhood social development* (2nd ed.). New York: Wiley.

Denham, S. A., Bassett, H. H., & Wyatt, T. (2007). The socialization of emotional competence. In J. E. Grusec & P. D. Hastings (Eds.), *Handbook of socialization.* New York: Guilford.

Denmark, F. L., Russo, N. F., Frieze, I. H., & Eschuzur, J. (1988). Guidelines for avoiding sexism in psychological research: A report of the ad hoc committee on nonsexist research. *American Psychologist. 43*, 582–585.

Denney, N. W. (1986, August). *Practical problem solving.* Paper presented at the meeting of the American Psychological Association, Washington, DC.

Denney, N. W. (1990). Adult age differences in traditional and practical problem solving. *Advances in Psychology, 72*, 329–349.

Dennis, N. A., & Cabeza, R. (2008). Neuroimaging of healthy cognitive aging. In F. I. M. Craik & T. A. Salthouse (Eds.). *Handbook of aging and cognition* (3rd ed.). Mahwah, NJ: Erlbaum.

Deodati, A., & Cianfarani, S. (2011). Impact of growth hormone therapy on adult height of children idiopathic short stature: Systematic reiew. *British Medical Journal, 342*, c7157.

DePaulo, B. (2006). *Singled out.* New York: St. Martin's Press.

DePaulo, B. (2011). Living single: Lightening up those dark, dopey myths. In W. R. Cupach & B. H. Spitzberg (Eds.), *The dark side of close relationships.* New York: Routledge.

Depp, C. A., Vahia, I. V., & Jeste, D. V. (2012). Successful aging. In S. K. Whitbourne & M. J. Sliwinski (Ed.), *Wiley-Blackwell handbook of adult development and aging.* New York: Wiley.

Der Ananian, C., & Prohaska, T. R. (2007). Exercise and physical activity. In J. E. Birren (Ed.), *Encyclopedia of gerontology* (2nd ed.). San Diego: Academic Press.

DeRose, L., & Brooks-Gunn, J. (2008). Pubertal development in early adolescence: Implications for affective processes. In N. B. Allen & L. Sheeber (Eds.), *Adolescent emotional development and the emergence of depressive disorders.* New York: Cambridge University Press.

Derry, P. S., & Derry, P. N. (2012). Menstruation, perimenopause, and chaos theory. *Perspectives in Biology and Medicine, 1*, 26–42.

Devaney, S. A., Palomaki, G. E., Scott, J. A., & Bianchi, D. W. (2011). Noninvasive fetal sex determination using cell-free fetal DNA: A systematic review and meta-analysis. *Journal of the American Medical Association, 306*, 627–636.

DeWall, C. N., & others. (2011). So far away from one's partner, yet so close to romantic alternatives: Avoidant attachment, interest in alternatives, and infidelity. *Journal of Personality and Social Psychology, 101*, 1302–1316.

Di Ciommo, V., Forcella, E., & Cotugno, G. (2012). Living with phenylketonuria from the point of view of children, adolescents, and young adults: A qualitative study. *Journal of Developmental and Behavioral Pediatrics, 33*, 229–235.

Diamond, A. (1985). Development of the ability to use recall to guide action, as indicated by infants' performance on AB. *Child Development, 56*, 868–883.

Diamond, A. (2010). Commentary in E. Galinsky, *Mind in the making.* New York: Harper.

Diamond, A. (2013). Executive functioning. *Annual Review of Psychology* (Vol. 64). Palo Alto, CA: Annual Reviews.

Diamond, A., Barnett, W. S., Thomas, J., & Munro, S. (2007). Preschool program improves cognitive control. *Science, 318*, 1387–1388.

Diamond, A., Casey, B. J., & Munakata, Y. (2011). *Developmental cognitive neuroscience.* New York: Oxford University Press.

Diamond, A., & Lee, K. (2011). Interventions shown to aid executive function development in children 4 to 12 years old. *Science, 333*, 959–964.

Diamond, L. M. (2013, in press). Concepts of female sexual orientation. In C. Patterson & A. R. D'Augelli (Eds.), *The psychology of sexual orientation.* New York: Cambridge University Press.

Diamond, L. M., & Savin-Williams, R. C. (2011). Same-sex activity in adolescence: Multiple meanings and implications. In R. F. Fassinger & S. L. Morrow (Eds.), *Sex in the margins.* Washington, DC: American Psychological Association.

Diaz-Rico, L. T. (2012). *Course for teaching English Language Learners* (2nd ed.). Boston: Allyn & Bacon.

Dickinson, W. J., & others. (2011). Change in stress and social support as predictors of cognitive decline in older adults with and without depression. *International Journal of Geriatric Psychiatry, 26*, 1267–1274.

Diego, M. A., Field, T., & Hernandez-Reif, M. (2008). Temperature increases in preterm infants during massage therapy. *Infant Behavior and Development, 31*, 149–152.

Diener, E. (2012). *Subjective well-being.* Retrieved April 5, 2012, from http://internal.psychology.illinois.edu/~ediener/SWLS.html

Diener, E., Emmons, R. A., Larson, R. J., & Griffin, S. (1985). The Satisfaction with Life Scale. *Journal of Personality Assessment, 49*, 71–75.

Dietz, P. M., & others. (2010). Infant morbidity and mortality attributable to prenatal smoking in the U.S. *American Journal of Preventive Medicine, 39*, 45–62.

Dillon, J. (2003). Reincarnation: The technology of death. In C. D. Bryant (Ed.), *Handbook of death and dying.* Thousand Oaks, CA: Sage.

Dilworth-Anderson, P., Pierre, G., & Hilliard, T. S. (2012). Social justice, health disparities, and culture in the care of the elderly. *Journal of Law, Medicine, and Ethics, 40*, 26–32.

Dindia, K. (2005). Men are from North Dakota, women are from South Dakota. In K. Dindia & D. J. Canary (Eds.), *Sex differences and similarities in communication.* Mahwah, NJ: Erlbaum.

Dirk, J. (2012). Processing speed. In S. K. Whitbourne & M. Sliwinski (Eds.), *Wiley-Blackwell handbook of adulthood and aging.* New York: Wiley.

Dirk, J., & Schmiedek, F. (2012). Processing speed. In S. K. Whitbourne & M. Sliwinski (Eds.), *Wiley-Blackwell handbook of adult development and aging.* New York: Wiley.

Dishion, T. J., & Piehler, T. F. (2009). Deviant by design: Peer contagion in development, interventions, and schools. In K. H. Rubin, W. M. Bukowski, & B. Laursen (Eds.), *Handbook of peer interactions, relationships, and groups.* New York: Guilford.

Diwadkar, V. A., & others. (2012, in press). Differences in cortico-striatal-cerebellar activation during working memory in syndromal and nonsyndromal children with prenatal exposure to alcohol. *Human Brain Mapping.*

Dixon, R. A., McFall, G. P., Whitehead, B. P., & Dolcos, S. (2013, in press). Cognitive development and aging. In I. B. Weiner & others (Eds.), *Handbook of psychology* (2nd ed., Vol. 6). New York: Wiley.

Dixon, R. A., Small, B. J., MacDonald, S. W. S., & McArdle, J. J. (2012). Yes, memory declines with age—but when, how, and why? In M. Naveh Benjamin & N. Ohta (Eds.), *Memory and aging.* New York: Psychology Press.

Dixon, S. V., Graber, J. A., & Brooks-Gunn, J. (2008). The roles of respect for parental authority and parenting practices in parent-child conflict among African American, Latino, and European American families. *Journal of Family Psychology, 22*, 1–10.

Dodge, E. (2012). Family evolution and process during the child and adolescent years in eating disorders. In J. Lock (Ed.)., *Oxford handbook of child and adolescent eating disorders: Developmental perspectives.* New York: Oxford University Press.

Dodge, K. A. (1983). Behavioral antecedents of peer social status. *Child Development, 54*, 1386–1399.

Dodge, K. A. (2011a). Context matters in child and family policy. *Child Development, 82*, 433–442.

Dodge, K. A. (2011b). Social information processing models of aggressive behavior. In M. Mikulincer & P. R. Shaver (Eds.), *Understanding and reducing aggression, violence, and their consequences.* Washington, DC: American Psychological Association.

Dodge, K. A., & McCourt, S. N. (2010). Translating models of antisocial behavioral development into efficacious intervention policy to prevent adolescent violence. *Developmental Psychobiology, 52*, 277–285.

Doherty, M. (2008). *Theory of mind.* Philadelphia: Psychology Press.

Dolara, P., Bigagli, E., & Collins, A. (2012, in press). Antioxidant vitamins and mineral supplementation, life span expansion, and cancer incidence: A critical commentary. *European Journal of Nutrition.*

Domsch, H., Lohaus, A., & Thomas, H. (2009). Prediction of childhood cognitive abilities from a set of early indicators of information processing capabilities. *Infant Behavior and Development, 32,* 91–102.

Donatelle, R. J. (2013). *Health* (10th ed.). Upper Saddle River, NJ: Pearson.

Dondi, M., Simion, F., & Caltran, G. (1999). Can newborns discriminate between their own cry and the cry of another newborn infant? *Developmental Psychology, 35*(2), 418–426.

Donnellan, M. B., Larson-Rife, D., & Conger, R. D. (2005). Personality, family history, and competence in early adult romantic relationships. *Journal of Personality and Social Psychology, 88,* 562–576.

Donnerstein, E. (2012). Internet bullying. *Pediatric Clinics of North America, 59,* 623–633.

Doria, E., Buonocore, D., Focarelli, A., & Marzatico, F. (2012, in press). Relationship between human aging muscle and oxidative system pathway. *Oxidative Medicine and Cellular Longevity.*

Dorn, L. H., & Biro, F. M. (2011). Puberty and its measurement: A decade in review. *Journal of Research on Adolescence, 21,* 180–195.

Dorresteijn, J. A., Visseren, F. L., & Spiering, W. (2012). Mechanisms linking obesity to hypertension. *Obesity Reviews, 13,* 17–26.

Doss, B. D., Rhoades, G. K., Stanley, S. M., Markman, H. J., & Johnson, C. A. (2009). Differential use of premarital education in first and second marriages. *Journal of Family Psychology, 23,* 268–273.

Doty, R. L., & Shah, M. (2008). Taste and smell. In M. M. Haith & J. B. Benson (Eds.), *Encyclopedia of infant and early childhood development.* Oxford, UK: Elsevier.

Dougall, A. L., & Baum, A. (2012). Health and illness. In A. Baum, T. A. Revenson, & J. Singer (Eds.), *Handbook of health psychology* (2nd ed.). New York: Psychology Press.

Dougall, A. L., Biglan, C. W., Swanson, J. N., & Baum, A. (2013, in press). Stress, coping, and immune function. In I. B. Weiner & others (Eds.), *Handbook of psychology* (2nd ed., Vol. 3). New York: Wiley.

Dow, B. J., & Wood, J. (Eds.) (2006). *The Sage handbook of gender and communication.* Thousand Oaks, CA: Sage.

Dow, R. S., & Baer, G. T. (2013). *Self-paced phonics* (5th ed.). Boston: Allyn & Bacon.

Dowdy, S., & others. (2012, in press). Empower U: Effectiveness of an adolescent outreach and prevention program with sixth-grade boys and girls: A pilot study. *Journal of Pediatric Nursing.*

Dozier, M., Stovall-McClough, K. C., & Albus, K. E. (2009). Attachment and psychopathology in adulthood. In J. Cassidy & P. R. Shaver (Eds.), *Handbook of attachment* (2nd ed.). New York: Guilford.

Draghi-Lorenz, R. (2007, July). *Self-conscious emotions in young infants and the direct perception of self and others in interaction.* Paper presented at the meeting of the International Society for Research on Emotions, Sunshine Coast, Australia.

Draghi-Lorenz, R., Reddy, V., & Costall, A. (2001). Rethinking the development of "nonbasic" emotions: A critical review of existing theories. *Developmental Review, 21,* 263–304.

Drey, M., & others. (2012, in press). C-terminal agrin fragment as a marker for sarcopenia caused by degeneration of the neuromuscular junction. *Experimental Gerontology.*

Dryfoos, J. G. (1990). *Adolescents at risk: Prevalence or prevention.* New York: Oxford University Press.

Dryfoos, J. G., & Barkin, C. (2006). *Growing up in America today.* New York: Oxford University Press.

Du, M., & others. (2012). Physical activity, sedentary behavior, and leukocyte telomere length in women. *American Journal of Epidemiology, 175,* 414–422.

Dubern, B., & Clement, K. (2012, in press). Leptin and leptin receptor-related monogenic obesity. *Biochemie.*

Duberstein, P. R., & others. (2011). Personality and risk for Alzheimer's disease in adults 72 years of age and older: A 6-year follow-up. *Psychology and Aging, 26,* 351–362.

Dubois, L., & others. (2012). Genetic and environmental contributions to weight, height, and BMI from birth to 19 years of age: An international study of over 12,000 twin pairs. *PLoS One, 7*(2), E30153.

Duck, S. (2011). *Rethinking relationships.* Thousand Oaks, CA: Sage.

Dufour-Rainfray, D., & others. (2011). Fetal exposure to teratogens: Evidence of genes involved in autism. *Neuroscience and Biobehavioral Reviews, 35,* 1254–1265.

Duke, J., & others. (2011). A study of burn hospitalizations for children younger than 5 years of age: 1983–2008. *Pediatrics, 27,* e971–e977.

Dulin, P. L., Gavala, J., Stephens, C., Kostick M., & McDonald, J. (2012, in press). *Volunteering predicts happiness among Maori and non-Maori in the New Zealand Health, Work, and Retirement Study.*

Dulloo, A. G., Jacquet, J., & Montani, J. P. (2012, in press). How dieting makes some fatter: From a perspective of human body composition autoregulation. *Proceedings of the Nutrition Society.*

Dunbar, L., Leventhal, H., & Leventhal, E. A. (2007). Self-regulation, health, and behavior. In J. E. Birren (Ed.), *Encyclopedia of gerontology* (2nd ed.). San Diego: Academic Press.

Duncan, A. F., & others. (2011). Elevated systolic blood pressure in preterm very-low-birthweight infants at 3 years of life. *Pediatric Nephrology, 26,* 1115–1121.

Duncan, G. J. (2012). Give us this day our daily breadth. *Child Development, 83,* 6–15.

Duncan, G. J., Ziol-Guest, K. M., & Kalil, A. (2010). Early-childhood poverty and adult attainment, behavior, and health. *Child Development, 81,* 306–325.

Duncan, G., Magnuson, K., Kalil, A., & Ziol-Guest, K. (2013, in press). *Social indicators research.*

Duncombe, M. E., Havighurst, S. S., Holland, K. A., & Frankling, E. J. (2012, in press). The contribution of parenting practice and parent emotion factors in children at risk for disruptive behavior disorders. *Child Psychiatry and Human Development.*

Dunkel Schetter, C. (2011). Psychological science in the study of pregnancy and birth. *Annual Review of Psychology* (Vol. 62). Palo Alto, CA: Annual Reviews.

Dunlay, S. M., Swetz, K. M., Mueller, P. S., & Roger, V. L. (2012). Advance directives in community patients with heart failure. *Circulation, Cardiovascular Quality and Outcomes, 5,* 283–289.

Dunn, J. (1984). Sibling studies and the developmental impact of critical incidents. In P. B. Baltes & O. G. Brim (Eds.), *Life-span development and behavior* (Vol. 6). Orlando, FL: Academic Press.

Dunn, J. (2007). Siblings and socialization. In J. E. Grusec & P. D. Hastings (Eds.), *Handbook of socialization.* New York: Guilford.

Dunn, J., & Kendrick, C. (1982). *Siblings.* Cambridge, MA: Harvard University Press.

Dunsmore, J. C., Booker, J. A., & Ollendick, T. H. (2012, in press). Parental emotion coaching and child emotion regulation as protective factors for children with oppositional defiant disorder. *Social Development.*

Dupre, M. E., & Meadows, S. O. (2007). Disaggregating the effects of marital trajectories on health. *Journal of Family Issues, 28,* 623–652.

Duque, G., Demontiero, O., & Troen, B. R. (2009). Prevention and treatment of senile osteoporosis and hip fractures. *Minerva Medica, 100,* 79–94.

Durbin, D. R. (2011). Technical report—child passenger safety. *Pediatrics, 127,* e1050–e1066.

Duriez, B., Luyckx, K., Soenens, B., & Berzonsky, M. (2012). A process-content approach to adolescent identity formation: Examining longitudinal associations between identity styles and goal pursuits. *Journal of Personality, 80,* 135–161.

Durrant, J. E. (2008). Physical punishment, culture, and rights: Current issues for professionals. *Journal of Developmental and Behavioral Pediatrics, 29,* 55–66.

Durrant, R., & Ellis, B. (2013, in press). Evolutionary psychology. In M. Gallagher, R. J. Nelson, & I. B. Weiner & others (Eds.), *Handbook of psychology* (2nd ed., Vol. 3). New York: Wiley.

Durston, S., & others. (2006). A shift from diffuse to focal cortical activity with development. *Developmental Science, 9,* 1–8.

Dvornyk, V., & Waqar-ul-Haq, H. (2012). Genetics of age at menarche: A systematic review. *Human Reproduction Update, 18,* 198–210.

Dweck, C. S. (2006). *Mindset.* New York: Random House.

Dweck, C. S. (2013, in press). Social development. In P. Zelazo (Ed.), *Oxford handbook of developmental psychology.* New York: Oxford University Press.

Dweck, C. S., & Master, A. (2009). Self-theories and motivation: Students' beliefs about intelligence. In K. R. Wentzel & A. Wigfield (Eds.), *Handbook of motivation at school.* New York: Routledge.

Dworkin, S. L., & Santelli, J. (2007). Do abstinence-plus interventions reduce sexual risk behavior among youth? *PLoS Medicine, 4,* 1437–1439.

Dwyer, J. W., & Coward, R. T. (1991). A multivariate comparison of the involvement of adult sons versus daughters in the care of impaired parents. *Journal of Gerontology B: Psychological Sciences and Social Sciences, 46,* S259–S269.

Dykes, M. J., & Cassidy, J. (2011). Attachment and the processing of social information across the life span: Theory and evidence. *Psychological Bulletin, 137,* 19–46.

E

Eagly, A. H. (2001). Social role theory of sex differences and similarities. In J. Worrell (Ed.), *Encyclopedia of women and gender*. San Diego: Academic Press.

Eagly, A. H. (2010). Gender roles. In J. Levine & M. Hogg (Eds.), *Encyclopedia of group process and intergroup relations*. Thousand Oaks, CA: Sage.

Eagly, A. H. (2012, in press). Women as leaders: Paths through the labryrinth. In M. C. Bligh & R. Riggio (Eds.), *When near is far and far is near: Exploring distance in leader-follower relationships*. New York: Wiley.

Eagly, A. H., & Crowley, M. (1986). Gender and helping: A meta-analytic review of the social psychological literature. *Psychological Bulletin, 108,* 233–256.

Eagly, A. H., & Steffen, V. J. (1986). Gender and aggressive behavior: A meta-analytic review of the social psychological literature. *Psychological Bulletin, 100,* 309–330.

Eagly, A. H., & Wood, W. (2012, in press). Social role theory. In P. Lange, A. Kruglanski, & E. T. Higgins (Eds.), *Handbook of theories in social psychology*. Thousand Oaks, CA: Sage.

Early Growth Genetics (EGG) Consortium & others. (2012, in press). A genome-wide association meta-analysis identifies new childhood obesity loci. *Nature: Genetics.*

Easterbrooks, M. A., Bartlett, J. D., Beeghly, M., & Thompson, R. A. (2013). Social and emotional development in infancy. In I. B. Weiner & others (Eds.), *Handbook of psychology* (2nd ed., Vol. 6). New York: Wiley.

Eastwick, P. W., & Finkel, E. J. (2008). Sex differences in mate preferences revisited: Do people know what they initially desire in a romantic partner? *Journal of Personality and Social Psychology, 94,* 245–264.

Eaton, D. K., & others. (2010, June 4). Youth risk behavior surveillance—United States, 2009. *MMWR Surveillance Summaries, 59*(5), 1–142.

Eaton, N. R., & others. (2012). Genes, environment, personality, and successful aging: Toward a comprehensive developmental model in later life. *Journals of Gerontology A: Biological Sciences and Medical Sciences, 67,* 480–488.

Ebstein, R. P., Knafo, A., Mankuta, D., Chew, S. H., & Lai, P. S. (2012). The contributions of oxytocin and vasopressin pathway genes to human behavior. *Hormones and Behavior, 61,* 359–379.

Eccles, J. S. (2007). Families, schools, and developing achievement-related motivations and engagement. In J. E. Grusec & P. D. Hastings (Eds.), *Handbook of socialization*. New York: Guilford.

Eccles, J. S., & Roeser, R. W. (2013). Schools as developmental contexts in adolescence. In I. B. Weiner & others (Eds.), *Handbook of psychology* (2nd ed., Vol. 6). New York: Wiley.

Echevarria, J. J., Vogt, M. J., & Short, D. J. (2013). *Making content comprehensible for English learners: The SIOP Model* (4th ed.). Boston: Allyn & Bacon.

Eckenrode, J., & others. (2010). Long-term effects of prenatal and infancy nurse home visitation on the life course of youths: 19-year follow-up of a randomized trial. *Archives of Pediatric and Adolescent Medicine, 164,* 9–15.

Eckerman, C., & Whitehead, H. (1999). How toddler peers generate coordinated action: A cross-cultural exploration. *Early Education & Development, 10,* 241–266.

Eckert, G. P., Lipka, U., & Muller, W. E. (2012, in press). Omega-3 fatty acids in neurogenerative diseases: Focus on mitochondria. *Prostaglandins, Leukotrienes, and Essential Fatty Acids.*

Eckert, M. A. (2011). Slowing down: Age-related neurobiological predictors of processing speed. *Frontiers in Neuroscience, 5,* 25.

Eckmann, J., & others. (2012, in press). MITOCHONDRIA: Mitochondrial membranes in aging and neurodegeneration. *International Journal of Biochemistry and Cell Biology.*

Educational Testing Service. (1992, February). *Cross-national comparisons of 9- to 13-year-olds' science and math achievement.* Princeton, NJ: Educational Testing Service.

Edwardson, C. L., & Gorely, T. (2010). Activity-related parenting practices and children's objectively measured physical activity. *Pediatric Exercise Science, 22,* 105–113.

Egan, S. K., & Perry, D. G. (2001). Gender identity: A multidimensional analysis with implications for psychosocial adjustment. *Developmental Psychology, 37,* 451–463.

Egli, T., Bland, M. W., Melton, B. F., & Czech, D. R. (2011). Influence of age, sex, and race on college students' exercise motivation of physical activity. *Journal of American College Health, 59,* 399–406.

Ehnes, J. (2012). Aging and financial (in)security. *Global population aging: Peril or promise?* Geneva, SWIT: World Economic Forum.

Eibach, R. P. & Mock, S. E. (2011). Idealizing parenthood to rationalize parental investments. *Psychological Science, 22,* 203–208.

Eichorn, D. H., Clausen, J. A., Haan, N., Honzik, M. P., & Mussen, P. H. (Eds.). (1981). *Present and past in middle life*. New York: Academic Press.

Eiferman, R. R. (1971). Social play in childhood. In R. Herron & B. Sutton-Smith (Eds.), *Child's play*. New York: Wiley.

Einstein, G. O., & McDaniel, M. A. (2005). Prospective memory. *Current Directions in Psychological Science, 14,* 286–290.

Eisenberg, M. E., Bernat, D. H., Bearinger, L. H., & Resnick, M. D. (2008). Support for comprehensive sexuality education: Perspectives from parents of school-aged youth. *Journal of Adolescent Research, 42,* 352–359.

Eisenberg, N., & Morris, A. S. (2004). Moral cognitions and social responding in adolescence. In R. L. Lerner & L. Steinberg (Eds.), *Handbook of adolescent psychology* (2nd ed.). New York: Wiley.

Eisenberg, N., Morris, A. S., McDaniel, B., & Spinrad, T. L. (2009). Moral cognitions and prosocial responding in adolescence. In R. M. Lerner & L. Steinberg (Eds.), *Handbook of adolescent psychology* (3rd ed.). New York: Wiley.

Eisenberg, N., Spinrad, T. R., & Eggum, N. D. (2010). Emotion-focused self-regulation and its relation to children's maladjustment. *Annual Review of Clinical Psychology* (Vol. 6). Palo Alto, CA: Annual Reviews.

Eisenberg, N., Spinrad, T. L., & Morris, A. S. (2013). Prosocial development. In P. D. Zelazo (Ed.), *Oxford handbook of developmental psychology*. New York: Oxford University Press.

El Haj, M., & Allain, P. (2012). Relationship between source monitoring in episodic memory and executive function in normal aging. *Geriatrie et Psychologie Neuropsychiatrie du Viellissement, 10,* 197–205.

Elbourne, P. (2012). *Meaning.* New York: Oxford University Press.

El-Dib, M., Massaro, A. N., Glass, P., & Aly, H. (2012). Neurobehavioral assessment as a predictor of neurodevelopmental outcome in preterm infants. *Journal of Perinatology, 32,* 299–303.

Eliasieh, K., Liets, L. C., & Chalupa, L. M. (2007). Cellular reorganization in the human retina during normal aging. *Investigative Ophthalmology and Visual Science, 48,* 2824–2830.

Elkind, D. (1970, April 5). Erik Erikson's eight ages of man. *New York Times Magazine.*

Elkind, D. (1976). *Child development and education: A Piagetian perspective*. New York: Oxford University Press.

Elliott, E. M., & others. (2011). Working memory in the oldest-old: Evidence from output serial position curves. *Memory and Cognition, 10,* 20–27.

Elliott, S. N., Kurz, A., & Neergaard, L. (2012). Large-scale assessment for educational accountability. In K. R. Harris, S. Graham, & T. Urdan (Eds.), *APA educational psychology handbook*. Washington, DC: American Psychological Association.

Elsabbagh, M., & others. (2012). Global prevalence of autism and other pervasive developmental disorders. *Autism Research, 5,* 160–179.

Else, L. J., Taylor, S., Back, D. J., & Khoo, S. H. (2011). Pharmacokinetics of antiretroviral drugs in anatomical sanctuary sites: The fetal compartment (placenta and amniotic fluid). *Antiviral Therapy, 16,* 1139–1147.

El-Sheikh, M., Keiley, M., Erath, S. A., & Dyer, W. J. (2012, in press). Marital conflict and growth in children's internalizing behavior: The role of autonomic nervous system activity. *Developmental Psychology.*

Emery, C. F., Anderson, D. R., & Goodwin, C. L. (2013, in press). Coronary heart disease and hypertension. In I. B. Weiner & others (Eds.), *Handbook of psychology* (2nd ed., Vol. 9). New York: Wiley.

Emes, R. D., & Grant, S. G. N. (2013). Evolution of synapse complexity and diversity. *Annual Review of Neuroscience,* Vol. 35. Palo Alto, CA: Annual Reviews.

Engvig, A., & others. (2010). Effects of memory training on cortical thickness in the elderly. *Neuroimage, 52,* 1667–1676.

Ensembl Human. (2010). *Explore the Homo sapiens genome.* Retrieved March 17, 2010, from www.ensembl.org/Homo_sapiens/index.html

Ensor, R., Spencer, D., & Hughes, C. (2011). You feel sad? Emotional understanding mediates effects of verbal ability and mother-child mutuality on prosocial behaviors: Findings from 2 to 4 years. *Social Development, 20,* 93–100.

Epstein, D., & Barnette, W. S. (2012). Early education in the United States: Programs and access. In R. C. Pianta (Ed.), *Handbook of early childhood education*. New York: Guilford.

Epstein, M., & Ward, L. M. (2008). "Always use protection": Communication boys receive about sex education from parents, peers, and the media. *Journal of Youth and Adolescence, 37*, 113–126.

Erickson, K. I., & others. (2009). Aerobic fitness is associated with hippocampal volume in elderly humans. *Hippocampus, 19*, 1030–1039.

Erickson, K. I., & others. (2010). Physical activity predicts gray matter volume in late adulthood: The Cardiovascular Health Study. *Neurology, 145*, 1415–1422.

Erickson, K. I., & others. (2011). Exercise training increases the size of the hippocampus and improves memory. *Proceedings of the National Academy of Sciences U.S.A., 108*, 3017–3022.

Ericson, N. (2001, June). *Addressing the problem of juvenile bullying*. Washington, DC: Office of Juvenile Justice and Delinquency Prevention, Office of Justice Programs, U.S. Department of Justice.

Ericsson, K. A., Krampe, R., & Tesch-Romer, C. (1993). The role of deliberate practice in the acquisition of expert performance. *Psychological Review, 100*, 363–406.

Erikson, E. H. (1950). *Childhood and society*. New York: W. W. Norton.

Erikson, E. H. (1968). *Identity: Youth and crisis*. New York: W. W. Norton.

Eriksson, U. J. (2009). Congenital malformations in diabetic pregnancy. *Seminars in Fetal and Neonatal Medicine. 14*, 85–93.

Erixon-Lindroth, N., Farde, L., Robins Whalin, T. B., Sovago, J., Halldin, C., & Backman, L. (2005). The role of the striatal dopamine transporter in cognitive aging. *Psychiatry Research: Neuroimaging, 138*, 1–12.

Escobar-Chaves, S. L., & Anderson, C. A. (2008). Media and risky behavior. *Future of Children, 18*, 147–180.

ESHRE Capri Workshop Group. (2011). Perimenopausal risk factors and future health. *Human Reproduction Update, 17*, 706–717.

Estigarribia, B., Martin, G. E., & Roberts, J. E. (2012, in press). Cognitive, environmental, and linguistic predictors of syntax in fragile X syndrome and Down syndrome. *Journal of Speech, Language, and Hearing Research*.

Etaugh, C., & Bridges, J. S. (2010). *Women's lives* (2nd ed.). Boston: Allyn & Bacon.

Evans, G. W., Chen, E., Miller, G., & Seeman, T. (2012). How poverty gets under the skin: A life-course perspective. In V. Maholmes & R. B. King (Eds.), *Oxford handbook of poverty and child development*. New York: Oxford University Press.

Evans, G. W., & English, G. W. (2002). The environment of poverty. *Child Development, 73*, 1238–1248.

Evans, G. W., & Kim, P. (2007). Childhood poverty and health: Cumulative risk exposure and stress dysregulation. *Psychological Science, 18*, 953–957.

Evans, W. J. (2010). Skeletal muscle loss: Cachexia, sarcopenia, and inactivity. *American Journal of Clinical Nutrition, 91*, S1123–S1127.

Eymard, A. S., & Douglas, D. H. (2012). Ageism among health care providers and interventions to improve their attitudes toward older adults: An integrative review. *Journal of Gerontological Nursing, 38*, 26–35.

F

Fabbri, R., & others. (2012, in press). Cryopreservation of ovarian tissue for pediatric patients. *Obstetrics and Gynecology International*.

Fabiano, G. A., Pelham, W. E., Coles, E. K., Gnagy, E. M., Chronis-Tuscano, A., & O'Connor, B. C. (2009). A meta-analysis of behavioral treatments for attention deficit/hyperactivity disorder. *Clinical Psychology Review, 29*, 129–140.

Fabricius, W. V., Braver, S. L., Diaz, P., & Schenck, C. (2010). Custody and parenting time: Links to family relationships and well-being after divorce. In M. E. Lamb (Ed.), *The role of the father in child development* (5th ed.). New York: Wiley.

Fagan, J. F. (1992). Intelligence. A theoretical viewpoint. *Current Directions in Psychological Science, 1*, 82–86.

Fagan, J. F., Holland, C. R., & Wheeler, K. (2007). The prediction, from infancy, of adult IQ and achievement. *Intelligence, 35*, 225–231.

Fagot, B. I., Rogers, C. S., & Leinbach, M. D. (2000). Theories of gender socialization. In T. Eckes & H. M. Trautner (Eds.), *The developmental social psychology of gender*. Mahwah, NJ: Erlbaum.

Fahey, T. D., Insel, P. M., & Roth, W. T. (2013). *Fit and well* (10th ed.). New York: McGraw-Hill.

Faith, M. S., & others. (2012). Evaluating parents and adult caregivers as "agents of change" for treating obese children: Evidence for parent behavior change strategies and research gaps: A scientific statement from the American Heart Association. *Circulation, 125*, 1186–1207.

Fakhoury, J., Nimmo, G. A., & Autexier, C. (2007). Harnessing telomerase in cancer therapeutics. *Anti-Cancer Agents in Medicinal Chemistry, 7*, 475–483.

Falbo, T., & Poston, D. L. (1993). The academic, personality, and physical outcomes of only children in China. *Child Development, 64*, 18–35.

Falck-Yttere, T., & others. (2012, in press). Gaze performance in children with autism spectrum disorder when observing communicative actions. *Journal of Autism and Developmental Disorders*.

Fall, A. M., & Roberts, G. (2012, in press). High school dropouts: Interactions between social context, self perceptions, school engagement, and student dropout. *Journal of Adolescence*.

Fancy, S. P. J., & others. (2012). Myelin regeneration: A recapitulation of development? *Annual Review of Neuroscience* (Vol. 34). Palo Alto, CA: Annual Reviews.

Fantz, R. L. (1963). *Pattern vision in newborn infants*. Science, 140, 286–297.

Farias, S. T., & others. (2012, in press). Idea density measured in late life predicts subsequent cognitive trajectories: Implications for the measurement of cognitive reserve. *Journal of Gerontology B: Psychological Sciences and Social Sciences*.

Faroogi, A., Hagglof, B., Sedin, G., & Serenius, F. (2011). Impact at 11 years of major neonatal morbidities in children born extremely preterm. *Pediatrics, 127*, e1247–e1257.

Farrell, M. P., & Rosenberg, S. D. (1981). *Men at mid-life*. Boston: Auburn House.

Farrell, S. W., Fitzgerald, S. J., McAuley, P., & Barlow, C. E. (2010). Cardiorespiratory fitness, adiposity, and all-cause mortality in women. *Medicine and Science in Sports and Exercise, 42*(11), 2006–2012.

Farrow, C. V. (2012). Do parental feeding practices moderate the relationships between impulsivity and eating in children? *Eating Behavior, 13*, 150–153.

Fasig, L. (2000). Toddlers' understanding of ownership: Implications for self-concept development. *Social Development, 9*, 370–382.

Fatusi, A. O., & Hindin, M. J. (2010). Adolescents and youths in developing countries: Health and development issues in context. *Journal of Adolescence, 33*, 499–508.

Fauci. J., & others. (2012, in press). The utilization of palliative care in gynecologic oncology patients near the end of life. *Gynecologic Oncology*.

Fava, N. M., & Bay-Cheng, L. Y. (2012, in press). Young women's adolescent experiences of oral sex: Relation of age of initiation to sexual motivation, sexual coercion, and psychological functioning. *Journal of Adolescence*.

Feeney, S., Moravcik, E., & Nolte, S. (2013). *Who am I in the lives of children?* (9th ed.). Upper Saddle River, NJ: Pearson.

Feil, R., & Fraga, M. F. (2012). Epigenetics and the environment: Emerging patterns and implications. *Nature Reviews: Genetics, 1*, 97–109.

Feinglass, J., & others. (2012). Association of functional status with changes in physical activity: Insights from a behavioral intervention for participants with arthritis. *Archives of Physical Medicine and Rehabilitation, 93*, 172–175.

Feinstein, E. E., Richter, L., & Foster, S. E. (2012). Addressing the critical health problem of adolescent substance use through health care, research, and public policy. *Journal of Adolescent Health, 50*, 431–436.

Feldman, D. H. (2013, in press). Cognitive development in childhood: A contemporary perspective. In I. B. Weiner & others (Eds.), *Handbook of psychology* (Vol. 6). New York: Wiley.

Feldman, R. (2007). Parent-infant synchrony. *Current Directions in Psychological Science, 16*, 340–345.

Feldman, R. (2012). Oxytocin and social affiliation in humans. *Hormones and Behavior, 61*, 380–391.

Feldman, S. S., & Elliott, G. R. (1990). Progress and promise of research on normal adolescent development. In S. S. Feldman & G. Elliott (Eds.), *At the threshold: The developing adolescent*. Cambridge, MA: Harvard University Press.

Feldman, S. S., Turner, R., & Araujo, K. (1999). Interpersonal context as an influence on sexual timetables of youths: Gender and ethnic effects. *Journal of Research on Adolescence, 9*, 25–52.

Feldon, J. M. (2003). Grief as a transformative experience: Weaving through different lifeworlds after a loved one has committed suicide. *International Journal of Mental Health Nursing, 12*, 74–85.

Ferguson, D. M., Harwood, L. J., & Shannon, F. T. (1987). Breastfeeding and subsequent social adjustment in 6- to 8-year-old children. *Journal of Child Psychology and Psychiatry, 28*, 378–386.

Fernandez, A. F., & Fraga, M. F. (2011). The effects of dietary polyphenol resveratrol on human healthy aging and lifespan. *Epigenetics, 6,* 870–874.

Fernandez-Martinez, F. J. & others. (2012). Noninvasive fetal sex determination in maternal plasma: A prospective feasibility study. *Genetics in Medicine, 14,* 101–106.

Ferrari, M., & Weststrate, N. (Eds.) (2013, in press). *Personal wisdom.* New York: Springer.

Ferraro, K. F. (2006). Health and aging. In R. H. Binstock & L. K. George (Eds.). *Handbook of aging and the social sciences* (6th ed.). San Diego: Academic Press.

Ferreiro, E., & others. (2012, in press). Mitochondrial- and endoplasmic reticulum-associated oxidative stress in Alzheimer's disease: From pathogenesis to biomarkers. *International Journal of Cell Biology.*

Ferrie, J. E., & others. (2011). Change in sleep duration and cognitive function: Findings from the Whitehall II Study. *Sleep, 34,* 565–573.

Feve, A. P. (2012). Current status of tyrosine hydroxylase in management of Parkinson's disease. *CNS and Neurological Disorders Drug Targets, 11,* 450–455.

Field, D. (1999). A cross-cultural perspective on continuity and change in social relations in old age: Introduction to a special issue. *International Journal of Aging and Human Development, 48,* 257–262.

Field, R. D., England, D. E., Andrews, C. Z., Martin, C. L., & Zosuls, K. M. (2012, April). *"I understand girls but not boys": Assessing gender-based relationship efficacy.* Paper presented at the Gender Development Research conference, San Francisco.

Field, T. M. (2001). Massage therapy facilitates weight gain in preterm infants. *Current Directions in Psychological Science, 10,* 51–55.

Field, T. M. (2007). *The amazing infant.* Malden, MA: Blackwell.

Field, T. M. (2010a). Postpartum depression effects on early interactions, parenting, and safety practices: A review. *Infant Behavior and Development, 33,* 1–6.

Field, T. M. (2010b). Pregnancy and labor massage. *European Review of Obstetrics and Gynecology, 5,* 177–181.

Field, T. M., Diego, M., & Hernandez-Reif, M. (2008). *International Journal of Neuroscience, 118,* 277–289.

Field, T. M., Diego, M., & Hernandez-Reif, M. (2011). Preterm infant massage therapy research: A review. *Infant Behavior and Development, 34,* 383–389.

Field, T. M., Diego, M., Hernandez-Reif, M., Medina, L., Delgado, J., & Hernandez, A. (2012). Yoga and massage therapy reduce prenatal depression and prematurity. *Journal of Bodywork and Movement Therapies, 16,* 204–209.

Field, T. M., Figueiredo, B., Hernandez-Reif, M., Diego, M., Deeds, O., & Ascencio, A. (2008). Massage therapy reduces pain in pregnant women, alleviates prenatal depression in both parents and improves their relationships. *Journal of Bodywork and Movement Therapies, 12,* 146–150.

Field, T. M., Grizzle, N., Scafidi, F., & Schanberg, S. (1996). Massage and relaxation therapies' effects on depressed adolescent mothers. *Adolescence, 31,* 903–911.

Field, T. M., Henteleff, T., & others. (1998). Children with asthma have improved pulmonary functions after message therapy. *Journal of Pediatrics, 132,* 854–858.

Field, T., & Hernandez-Reif, M. (2008). Touch and pain. In M. M. Haith & J. B. Benson (Eds.), *Encyclopedia of infant and early childhood development.* Oxford, UK: Elsevier.

Field, T. M., Hernandez-Reif, M., Diego, M., Feijo, L., Vera, Y., & Gil, K. (2004). Massage therapy by parents improves early growth and development. *Infant Behavior & Development, 27,* 435–442.

Field, T. M., Hernandez-Reif, M., Feijo, L., & Freedman, J. (2006). Prenatal, perinatal, and neonatal stimulation. *Infant Behavior & Development, 29,* 24–31.

Field, T. M., Hernandez-Reif, M., & Freedman, J. (2004, Fall). Stimulation programs for preterm infants. *SRCD Social Policy Reports, 28*(1), 1–20.

Field, T. M., Hernandez-Reif, M., Taylor, S., Quintino, O., & Burman, I. (1997). Labor pain is reduced by massage therapy. *Journal of Psychosomatic Obstetrics and Gynecology, 18,* 286–291.

Field, T. M., Lasko, D., & others. (1997). Brief report: Autistic children's attentiveness and responsivity improve after touch therapy. *Journal of Autism and Developmental Disorders, 27,* 333–338.

Field, T. M., Quintino, O., Hernandez-Reif, M., & Koslosky, G. (1998). Adolescents with attention deficit hyperactivity disorder benefit from massage therapy. *Adolescence, 33,* 103–108.

Finch, C. E. (2009). The neurobiology of middle-age has arrived. *Neurobiology of Aging, 30,* 503–520.

Finch, C. E. (2011). Inflammation and aging. In E. Masoro & S. Austad (Eds.), *Handbook of the biology of aging* (7th ed.). New York: Elsevier.

Finch, C. E., & Seeman, T. E. (1999). Stress theories of aging. In V. L. Bengtson & K. W. Schaie (Eds.), *Handbook of theories of aging.* New York: Springer.

Fincham, F. D., Stanley, S. M., & Beach, S. R. H. (2007). Transformative processes in marriage: An analysis of emerging trends. *Journal of Marriage and the Family, 69,* 275–292.

Finger, B., Hans, S. L., Bernstein, V. J., & Cox, S. M. (2009). Parent relationship quality and infant-mother attachment. *Attachment and Human Development, 11,* 285–306.

Fingerhut, A. W., & Peplau, L. A. (2013). Same-sex romantic relationships. In C. J. Patterson & A. R. D'Augelli (Eds.), *Handbook of psychology and sexual orientation.* New York: Oxford University Press.

Fingerman, K. L. (2000). Age and generational differences in mothers' and daughters' descriptions of enjoyable visits. *Journals of Gerontology B: Psychological Sciences and Social Sciences, 55,* P95–P106.

Fingerman, K. L., & Baker, B. (2006). Socioemotional aspects of aging. In J. Wilmouth & K. Ferraro (Eds.), *Perspectives in Gerontology* (3rd ed.). New York: Springer.

Fingerman, K. L., & Birditt, K. S. (2011). Relationships between adults and their aging parents. In K. W. Schaie & S. L. Willis (Eds.), *Handbook of the psychology of aging* (7th ed.). New York: Elsevier.

Fingerman, K. L., Brown, B. B., & Blieszner, R. (2011). Informal ties across the lifespan: Peers, consequential strangers, and people we encounter in daily life. In K. L. Fingerman, C. A. Berg, J. Smith, & T. C. Antonucci (Eds.), *Handbook of life-span development.* New York: Springer.

Fingerman, K. L., Chan, W., Pitzer, L. M., Birditt, K. S., Franks, M. M., & Zarit, S. (2011a). Who gets what and why: Help middle-aged adults provide to parents and grown children. *Journal, of Gerontology B: Psychological Sciences and Social Sciences, 66,* 87–98.

Fingerman, K. L., Cheng, Y. P., Tighe, L., Birditt, K. S., & Zarit, S. (2011b, in press). Parent-child relationships in young adulthood. In A. Booth & others (Eds.), *Early adulthood in a family context.* New York: Springer.

Fingerman, K. L., Miller, L., Birditt, K., & Zarit, S. (2009). Giving to the good and needy: Parental support of grown children. *Journal of Marriage and the Family, 71,* 1220–1233.

Fingerman, K. L., Pillemer, K. A., Silverstein, M., & Suitor, J. J. (2012). The Baby Boomers' intergenerational relationships. *Gerontologist, 52,* 199–209.

Finkelstein, E. A., & others. (2012). Obesity and severe obesity forecasts through 2030. *American Journal of Preventive Medicine, 42,* 563–570.

Finkelstein, L. M., & Farrell, S. K. (2007). An expanded view of age bias in the workplace. In K. S. Shultz & G. A. Adams (Eds.), *Aging and work in the 21st century.* Mahwah, NJ: Erlbaum.

Fiori, K. L., Antonucci, T. C., & Cortina, K. S. (2006). Social network typologies and mental health among older adults. *Journals of Gerontology B: Psychological Sciences and Social Sciences, 61,* P25–P32.

Fischhoff, B., Bruine de Bruin, W., Parker, A. M., Millstein, S. G., & Halpern-Felsher, B. L. (2010). Adolescents' perceived risk of dying. *Journal of Adolescent Health, 46,* 265–269.

Fisher, B. S., Cullen, F. T., Turner, M. G. (2000). *The sexual victimization of college women.* Washington, DC: National Institute of Justice.

Fisher, C. B., Busch-Rossnagel, N. A., Jopp, D. S., & Brown, J. L. (2013, in press). Applied developmental psychology across the life span. In I. B. Weiner & others (Eds.), *Handbook of psychology* (2nd ed., Vol. 6). New York: Wiley.

Fisher, H. L. & others. (2012, in press). Bullying victimization and risk of self-harm in early adolescence: Longitudinal cohort study. *British Medical Journal.*

Fisher, P. A. (2005, April). *Translational research on underlying mechanisms of risk among foster children: Implications for prevention science.* Paper presented at the meeting of the Society for Research in Child Development, Washington, DC.

Fiske, A., Wetherell, J. L., & Gatz, M. (2009). Depression in older adults. *Annual Review of Clinical Psychology* (Vol. 5). Palo Alto, CA: Annual Reviews.

Fitzpatrick, K. K. (2012). Developmental considerations when treating anorexia nervosa in adolescents and young adults. In J. Lock (Ed.)., *Oxford handbook of child and adolescent eating disorders: Developmental perspectives.* New York: Oxford University Press.

Fivush, R. (1993). Developmental perspectives on autobiographical recall. In G. S. Goodman, & B. Bottoms (Eds.). *Child victims and child witnesses: Understanding and improving testimony.* New York: Guilford.

Fivush, R. (2011). The development of autobiographical memory. *Annual Review of Psychology* (Vol. 62). Palo Alto, CA: Annual Reviews.

Fjell, A. M., & Walhovd, K. B. (2010). Structural brain changes in aging: Courses, causes, and consequences. *Reviews in the Neurosciences, 21,* 187–222.

Flavell, J. H. (2004). Theory-of-mind development: Retrospect and prospect. *Merrill-Palmer Quarterly, 50,* 274–290.

Flavell, J. H., Friedrichs, A., & Hoyt, J. (1970). Developmental changes in memorization processes. *Cognitive Psychology, 1,* 324–340.

Flavell, J. H., Green, F. L., & Flavell, E. R. (1993). Children's understanding of the stream of consciousness. *Child Development, 64,* 95–120.

Flavell, J. H., Green, F. L., & Flavell, E. R. (1998). The mind has a mind of its own: Developing knowledge about mental uncontrollability. *Cognitive Development, 13,* 127–138.

Flavell, J. H., & Miller, P. H. (1998). Social cognition. In W. Damon (Ed.), *Handbook of child psychology* (5th ed.). New York: Wiley.

Flavell, J., Mumme, D., Green, F., and Flavell, E. (1992). Young children's understanding of different types of beliefs. *Child Development, 63,* 960–977.

Fletcher, B. R., & Rapp, P. R. (2013, in press). Normal neurocognitive aging. In I. B. Weiner & others (Eds.), *Handbook of psychology* (2nd ed.). New York: Wiley.

Flicker, L., & others. (2010). Body mass index and survival in men and women 70 to 75. *Journal of the American Geriatric Society, 58,* 234–241.

Flint, M. S., Baum, A., Chambers, W. H., & Jenkins, F. J. (2007). Induction of DNA damage, alteration of DNA repair, and transcriptional activation by stress hormones. *Psychoneuroendocrinology, 32,* 470–479.

Flint-Wagner, H. G., & others. (2009). Assessment of a sixteen-week training program on strength, pain, and function in rheumatoid arthritis patients. *Journal of Clinical Rheumatology, 15,* 165–171.

Flom, R., & Pick, A. D. (2003). Verbal encouragement and joint attention in 18-month-old infants. *Infant Behavior and Development, 26,* 121–134.

Florsheim, P., Moore, D., & Edgington, C. (2003). Romantic relationships among pregant and parenting adolescents. In P. Florsheim (Ed.), *Adolescent romantic relations and sexual behavior.* Mahwah, NJ: Erlbaum.

Flynn, J. R. (1999). Searching for justice: The discovery of IQ gains over time. *American Psychologist, 54,* 5–20.

Flynn, J. R. (2007). The history of the American mind in the 20th century: A scenario to explain IQ gains over time and a case for the relevance of g. In P. C. Kyllonen, R. D. Roberts, & L. Stankov (Eds.), *Extending intelligence.* Mahwah, NJ: Erlbaum.

Flynn, J. R. (2011). Secular changes in intelligence. In R. J. Sternberg & S. B. Kaufman (Eds.), *Cambridge handbook of intelligence.* New York: Cambridge University Press.

Flynn, J. R. (2012). *Are we getting smarter?* New York: Cambridge University Press.

Fogel, A. (2010). *Infant development.* New York: Sloan.

Fontana, L. (2009). The scientific basis of caloric restriction leading to longer life. *Current Opinion in Gastroenterology, 25,* 144–150.

Fontenot, H. B. (2007). Transition and adaptation to adoptive motherhood. *Journal of Obstetrics, Gynecologic, and Neonatal Nursing, 36,* 175–182.

Forbes, S. C., Little, J. P., & Candow, D. G. (2012, in press). Exercise and nutritional interventions for improving aging and muscle health. *Endocrine.*

Ford, R. M., Driscoll, T., Shum, D., & Macaulay, C. E. (2012). Executive and theory-of-mind contributions to event-based prospective memory in children: Exploring the self-projection hypothesis. *Journal of Experimental Child Psychology, 111,* 468–489.

Forget-Dubois, N., Dionne, G., Lemelin, J-P., Perusse, D., Tremblay, R. E., & Boivan, M. (2009). Early child language mediates the relation between home environment and school readiness. *Child Development, 80,* 736–749.

Forsyth, A. L., Quon, D. V., & Konkle, B. A. (2011, in press). Role of exercise and physical activity on haemophilc arthropathy, fall prevention, and osteoporosis. *Haemophilia.*

Fosco, G. M., Frank, J. L., & Dishion, T. J. (2012). Understanding the influence of deviant peers on problem behavior: Coercion and contagion in peer, family, and school environments. In S. R. Jimerson & others (Eds.), *Handbook of school violence and school safety.* New York: Routledge.

Fosco, G. M., Stomrmshak, E. A., Dishion, T. J., & Winter, C. E. (2012). Family relationships and parental monitoring during middle school as predictors of early adolescent problem behavior. *Journal of Clinical Child and Adolescent Psychology, 41,* 202–213.

Fowler, C. G., & Leigh-Paffenroth, E. D. (2007). Hearing. In J. E. Birren (Ed.), *Encyclopedia of gerontology* (2nd ed.). San Diego: Academic Press.

Fox, B. J. (2012). *Word identification strategies* (5th ed.). Boston: Allyn & Bacon.

Fox, M. K., Pac, S., Devancy, B., & Jankowski, L. (2004). Feeding infants and toddlers study: What foods are infants and toddlers eating? *American Dietetic Association Journal, 104* (Suppl.), S22–S30.

Fox, M. K., & others. (2010). Food consumption patterns of young preschoolers: Are they starting off on the right path? *Journal of the American Dietetic Association, 110* (Suppl. 12), S52–S59.

Fozard, J. L. (1992, December 6). Commentary in "We can age successfully." *Parade Magazine,* pp. 14–15.

Franchak, J. M., Kretch, K. S., Soska, K. C., & Adolph, K. E. (2011). Head-mounted eye-tracking: A new method to describe the visual ecology of infants. *Child Development, 82,* 1738–1750.

Francis, J., Fraser, G., & Marcia, J. E. (1989). *Cognitive and experimental factors in moratorium-achievement (MAMA) cycles.* Unpublished manuscript, Department of Psychology, Simon Fraser University, Burnaby, British Columbia.

Franco, P., Kato, I., Richardson, H. L., Yang, J. S., Montemitro, E., & Horne, R. S. (2010). Arousal from sleep mechanisms in infants. *Sleep Medicine, 11,* 603–614.

Frank, M. C., Vul, E., & Johnson, S. P. (2009). Development of infants' attention to faces during the first year. *Cognition, 110,* 160–170.

Frankl, V. (1984). *Man's search for meaning.* New York: Basic Books.

Franklin, A., Bevis, L., Ling, Y., & Hulbert, A. (2010). Biological components of color preference in infancy. *Developmental Science, 13,* 346–354.

Franks, B. A. (2011). Moving targets: A developmental framework for understanding children's changes following disasters. *Journal of Applied Developmental Psychology, 32,* 58–69.

Franz, C. E. (1996). The implications of preschool tempo and motoric activity level for personality decades later. Reported in A. Caspi, Personality development across the life course, in W. Damon (Ed.), *Handbook of child psychology* (Vol. 3) New York: Wiley.

Frederikse, M., Lu, A., Aylward, E., Barta, P., Sharma, T., & Pearlson, G. (2000). Sex differences in inferior lobule volume in schizophrenia. *American Journal of Psychiatry, 157,* 422–427.

Fredricks, J. A., & Eccles, J. S. (2010). Breadth of extracurricular participation and adolescent adjustment among African-American and European-American youth. *Journal of Research on Adolescence, 20,* 307–333.

Freeman, R. (2011). Reggio Emilia, Vygotsky, and family childcare: Four American providers describe their pedagogical practice. *Child Care in Practice, 17,* 227–246.

Freiheit, E. A., & others. (2012). A dynamic view of depressive symptoms and neurocognitive change among patients with coronary artery disease. *Archives of General Psychiatry, 69,* 244–255.

Freitag, C. M., Asherson, P., & Hebebrand, J. (2012). Behavioral genetics of childhood disorders. *Current Topics in Behavioral Neuroscience, 12,* 395–428.

Freud, S. (1917). *A general introduction to psychoanalysis.* New York: Washington Square Press.

Freund, A. M., & Baltes, P. B. (2002). Life-management strategies of selection, optimization, and compensation: Measurement by self-report and construct validity. *Journal of Personality and Social Psychology, 82,* 642–662.

Freund, A. M., Nikitin, J., & Riediger, M. (2013, in press). Successful aging. In I. B. Weiner & others (Eds.), *Handbook of psychology* (2nd ed., Vol. 6). New York: Wiley.

Frey, B. S. (2011). Happy people live longer. *Science, 331,* 542–543.

Frey, W. H. (2007). *Mapping the growth of older America: Seniors and boomers in the early 21st century.* Washington, DC: The Brookings Institution.

Freyer-Adam, J., Gaertner, B., Tobschall, S., & John, U. (2011). Health risk factors and self-rated health among job-seekers. *BMC Public Health, 11,* 659.

Fried, A. L. (2012). Ethnics in psychological research: Guidelines and regulations. In H. Cooper (Ed.), *APA handbook of research methods in psychology.* Washington, DC: American Psychological Association.

Fried, L. P., Hogan, P., & Rowe, J. (2012). Design and operation of health systems in wealthy nations. *Global population aging: Peril or promise?* Geneva, SWIT: World Economic Forum.

Friedman, D., Nessler, D., Johnson, R., Ritter, W., & Bersick, M. (2008). Age-related changes in executive function: An event-related potential (ERP) investigation of task-switching. *Aging, Neuropsychology, and Cognition, 15,* 95–128.

Friedman, E. M., & Herd, P. (2010). Income, education, and inflammation: Differential associations in a national probability sample (the MIDUS study). *Psychosomatic Medicine, 72*(3), 290–300.

Friedman, S. L., Melhuish, E., & Hill, C. (2010). Childcare research at the dawn of a new millennium: An update. In G. Bremner & T. Wachs (Eds.), *Wiley-Blackwell handbook of infant development* (2nd ed.). Oxford, UK: Wiley-Blackwell.

Friend, M. (2011). *Special education* (3rd ed.). Upper Saddle River, NJ: Merrill.

Friese, R. S., & others. (2012, in press). Integrated computational and experimental analysis of the neuroendocrine transcriptome in genetic hypertension identifies novel control points for the cardio-metabolic syndrome. *Circulation: Cardiovascular Genetics.*

Frieske, D. A., & Park, D. C. (1999). Memory for news in young and old adults. *Psychology and aging, 14*, 90–98.

Frisen, A., & Holmqvist, K. (2010). What characterizes early adolescents with a positive body image? A qualitative investigation of Swedish boys and girls. *Body Image, 7*, 205–212.

Frodl, T., & O'Keane, V. (2012, in press). How does the brain deal with cumulative stress? A review with focus on developmental stress, HPA axis function, and hippocampal structure in humans. *Neurobiology of Disease.*

Fromme, E. K., & others. (2012). POLST registry do-not-resuscitate orders and other patient treatment preferences. *JAMA, 307*, 34–35.

Frost, D. M. (2011). Stigma and intimacy in same-sex relationships: A narrative approach. *Journal of Family Psychology, 25*, 1–10.

Frost, J. E., Wortham, S. C., & Reifel, S. C. (2012). *Play and child development* (4th ed.). Upper Saddle River, NJ: Pearson.

Fry, C. L. (2007). Comparative and cross-cultural studies. In J. E. Birren (Ed.), *Encyclopedia of gerontology* (2nd ed.). San Diego: Academic Press.

Fry, P. S. (2001). The unique contribution of key existential factors to the prediction of psychological well-being of older adults following spousal loss. *The Gerontologist, 41*, 69–81.

Fujisawa, D., & others. (2010). Prevalence and determinants of complicated grief in general population. *Journal of Affective Disorders, 127*, 352–358.

Fujiwara, E., & others. (2012). Usefulness of reminiscence therapy for community mental health. *Psychiatry and Clinical Neuroscience, 66*, 74–79.

Fung, C. K. H., & Cheng, D. P. W. (2012). Consensus or disconsensus? Stakeholders' views on the role of play in learning. *Early years: An International Journal of Research and Development, 32*, 17–33.

Fung, L. K., Quintin, E. M., Haas, B. W., & Reiss, A. L. (2012). Conceptualizing neurodevelopmental disorders through a mechanistic understanding of fragile X syndrome and Williams syndrome. *Current Opinion in Neurology, 25*, 112–124.

Furman, E. (2005). *Boomerang nation.* New York: Fireside.

Furman, W., Low, S., & Ho, M. J. (2009). Romantic experience and psychosocial adjustment in middle adolescence. *Journal of Clinical Child and Adolescent Psychology, 38*, 75–90.

Furstenberg, F. F. (2007). The future of marriage. In A. S. Skolnick & J. H. Skolnick (Eds.), *Family in transition* (14th ed.). Boston: Allyn & Bacon.

Furth, H. G., & Wachs, H. (1975). *Thinking goes to school.* New York: Oxford University Press.

G

Gabbe, S., & others. (Eds.). (2012). *Obstetrics* (6th ed.). New York: Elsevier.

Gadi, R., Amanullah, A., & Figueredo, V. M. (2012, in press). HDL-C: Does it matter? An update on novel HDL-directed pharmaco-therapeutic strategies. *International Journal of Cardiology.*

Gahagan, S. (2012). Development of eating behavior: Biology and context. *Journal of Developmental and Behavioral Pediatrics*, 261–271.

Gaias, L. M., & others. (2012). Cross-cultural temperamental differences in infants, children, and adults in the United States of America and Finland. *Scandinavian Journal of Psychology, 53*, 119–128.

Gaiha, R., Kulkarni, V. S., Pandey, M. K., & Imai, K. S. (2012). On hunger and mortality in India. *Journal of Asian and African Studies, 47*, 3–17.

Gaither, S. E., Pauker, K., & Johnson, S. P. (2012, in press). Biracial and monoracial infant own-race face perception: An eye tracking study. *Developmental Science.*

Galambos, N. L., Howard, A. L., & Maggs, J. L. (2011). Rise and fall of sleep quality with student experiences across the first year of the university. *Journal of Research on Adolescence, 21*, 342–349.

Galbally, M., Lewis, A. J., IJzendoorn, M., & Permezel, M. (2011). The role of oxytocin in mother-infant relations: A systematic review of human studies. *Harvard Review of Psychiatry, 19*, 1–14.

Galinsky, E. (2010). *Mind in the making.* New York: Harper Collins.

Galinsky, E., & David, J. (1988). *The preschool years: Family strategies that work—from experts and parents.* New York: Times Books.

Galland, B. C., Taylor, B. J., Edler, D. E., & Herbison, P. (2012). Normal sleep patterns in infants and children: A systematic review of observational studies. *Sleep Medicine Review, 16*, 213–222.

Galler, J. R., & others. (2012). Infant malnutrition is associated with persisting attention deficits in middle childhood. *Journal of Nutrition, 142*, 788–794.

Galloway, J. C., & Thelen, E. (2004). Feet first: Object exploration in young infants. *Infant Behavior & Development, 27*, 107–112.

Gallup, G. W., & Bezilla, R. (1992). *The religious life of young Americans.* Princeton, NJ: Gallup Institute.

Galupo, M. P., Cartwright, K. B., & Savage, L. S. (2010). Cross-category friendships and postformal thought among college students. *Journal of Adult Development, 17*, 208–214.

Gamba, P., & others. (2012). The link between arterial cholesterol metabolism and Alzheimer's disease. *Annals of the New York Academy of Sciences, 1259*, 54–64.

Gamble, T. K., & Gamble, M. (2008). *Communication works* (9th ed.) New York: McGraw-Hill.

Gamino, L. A., & Sewell, K. W. (2004). Meaning constructs as predictors of bereavement adjustment: A report from the Scott & White grief study. *Death Studies, 28*, 397–421.

Gandhi, S., & Abramov, A. Y. (2012, in press). Mechanism of oxidative stress in neurodegeneration. *Oxidative Medicine and Cellular Longevity.*

Ganong, L., & Coleman, M. (2006). Obligations to stepparents acquired in later life: Relationship quality and acuity of needs. *Journals of Gerontology B: Psychological Sciences and Social Sciences, 61*, S80–S88.

Ganong, L., Coleman, M., & Hans, J. (2006). Divorce as prelude to stepfamily living and the consequences of re-divorce. In M. A. Fine & J. H. Harvey (Eds.), *Handbook of divorce and relationship dissolution.* Mahwah, NJ: Erlbaum.

Gao, Z. (2012, in press). Urban Latino school children's physical activity correlates and daily physical activity participation: A social cognitive approach. *Psychology, Health, and Medicine.*

Garber, J., & Cole, D. A. (2010). Intergenerational transmission of depression: A launch and grow model of change across adolescence. *Development and Psychopathology, 22*, 819–830.

Gardner, H. (1983). *Frames of mind.* New York: Basic Books.

Gardner, H. (1993). *Multiple intelligences.* New York: Basic Books.

Gardner, H. (2002). The pursuit of excellence through education. In M. Ferrari (Ed.), *Learning from extraordinary minds.* Mahwah, NJ: Erlbaum.

Gardner, M., Martin, A., & Brooks-Gunn, J. (2012). Exploring the link between caregiver affect and adolescent sexual behavior: Does neighborhood disadvantage matter? *Journal of Research on Adolescence, 22*, 135–149.

Garofalo, R. (2010). Cytokines in human milk. *Journal of Pediatrics, 156* (Suppl. 2), S36–S40.

Garrido, P., De Blas, M., Gine, E., Santos, A., & Mora, F. (2011). Aging impairs the control of prefrontal cortex on the release of corticosterone in response to stress and on memory consolidation. *Neurobiology of Aging, 33*(4), 827.

Garrison, M. M., Liekweg, K., & Christakis, D. A. (2011). Media use and child sleep: The impact of content, timing, and environment. *Pediatrics, 128*(1), 128–135.

Garvey, C. (2000). *Play* (Enlarged ed.). Cambridge, MA: Harvard University Press.

Gasser, L., & Keller, M. (2009). Are the competent morally good? Perspective taking and moral motivation of children involved in bullying. *Social Development, 18*, 798–816.

Gates, W. (1998, July 20). Charity begins when I'm ready (interview). *Fortune magazine.*

Gathwala, G., Singh, B., & Singh, J. (2010). Effect of kangaroo care on physical growth, breastfeeding, and its acceptability. *Tropical Doctor, 40*, 199–202.

Gauthier, B., & Shi, R. (2011). A connectionist study on the role of pitch in infant-directed speech. *Journal of the Acoustical Society of America, 130*, 380–386.

Gauvain, M. (2008). Vygotsky's sociocultural theory. In M. M. Haith & J. B. Benson (Eds.), *Encyclopedia of* *infant and early childhood development.* Oxford, UK: Elsevier.

Gauvain, M. (2011). Applying the cultural approach to cognitive development. *Journal of Cognition and Development, 12,* 121–133.

Gauvain, M. (2013). Sociocultural contexts of development. In P. D. Zelazo (Ed.), *Oxford handbook of developmental psychology.* New York: Oxford University Press.

Gauvain, M., & Parke, R. D. (2010). Socialization. In M. H. Bornstein (Ed.), *Handbook of cultural developmental science.* New York: Psychology Press.

Geaghan, S. M. (2012). Fetal laboratory medicine: On the frontier of maternal-fetal medicine. *Clinical Chemistry, 58,* 337–352.

Geda, Y. E., & others. (2010). Physical exercise, aging, and mild cognitive impairment: A population-based study. *Archives of Neurology, 67,* 80–86.

Gee, C. C., Walsemann, K. M., & Brondolo, E. (2012). A life course perspective on how racism may be related to health inequities. *American Journal of Public Health, 102,* 967–974.

Gee, C. L., & Heyman, G. D. (2007). Children's evaluations of other people's self-descriptions. *Social Development, 16,* 800–818.

Geirsdottir, O. G., & others. (2012). Physical function predicts improvement in quality of life in elderly Icelanders after 12 weeks of resistance exercise. *Journal of Nutrition, Health, and Aging, 16,* 62–66.

Geisinger, K. F. (2012). Norm- and criterion-referenced testing. In H. Cooper (Ed.), *APA handbook of research methods in psychology.* Washington, DC: American Psychological Association.

Gelber, R. P., Launer, L. J., & White, L. R. (2012, in press). The Honolulu-Asia Aging Study: Epidemiologic and neuropathogenic research on cognitive impairment. *Current Alzheimer Research.*

Gelman, R. (1969). Conservation acquisition: A problem of learning to attend to relevant attributes. *Journal of Experimental Child Psychology, 7,* 67–87.

Gelman, S. A. (2009). Learning from others: Children's construction of concepts. *Annual Review of Psychology, 60,* 115–140.

Gelman, S. A. (2013). Concepts in development. In P. Zelazo (Ed.), *Oxford handbook of developmental psychology.* New York: Oxford University Press.

Gelman, S. A., & Kalish, C. W. (2006). Conceptual development. In W. Damon & R. Lerner (Eds.), *Handbook of child psychology* (6th ed.). New York: Wiley.

Geng, X., & others. (2012, in press). Quantitative tract-based white matter development from birth to age 2 years. *Neuroimage.*

Genin, E., & others. (2012). APOE and Alzheimer disease: A major gene with semi-dominant inheritance. *Molecular Psychiatry, 16,* 903–907.

Gennetian, L. A., & Miller, C. (2002). Children and welfare reform: A view from an experimental welfare reform program in Minnesota. *Child Development, 73,* 601–620.

Gentile, D. A. (2011). The multiple dimensions of video game effects. *Child Development Perspectives, 5,* 75–81.

Georgakilas, A. G. (2011). From chemistry of DNA damage to repair and biological significance. Comprehending the future. *Mutation Research, 711,* 1–2.

George, L. G., Helson, R., & John, O. P. (2011). The "CEO" of women's work lives: How Big Five Conscientiousness, Extraversion, and Openness predict 50 years of work experiences in a changing sociocultural context. *Journal of Personality and Social Psychology, 101*(4), 812–830.

George, L. K. (2010). Still happy after all these years: Research frontiers on subjective well-being in later life. *Journals of Gerontology B: Psychological Sciences and Social Sciences, 65B,* 331–339.

Gershoff, E. T. (2002). Corporal punishment by parents and associated child behaviors and experiences: A meta-analysis and theoretical review. *Psychological Bulletin, 128,* 539–579.

Gershoff, E. T., Lansford, J. E., Sexton, H. R., Davis-Kean, P., & Sameroff, A. (2012). Longitudinal links between spanking and children's externalizing behaviors in a national sample of White, Black, Hispanic, and Asian American families. *Child Development, 83,* 838–843.

Gershoff, E. T., & others. (2010). Parent discipline practices in an international sample: Associations with child behaviors and moderation by perceived normativeness. *Child Development, 81,* 487–502.

Gerstorff, D., & Ram, N. (2012). Late-life: A venue for studying the mechanisms by which contextual factors influence individual development. In S. K. Whitbourne & M. Sliwinski (Eds.), *Wiley-Blackwell handbook of adult development and aging.* New York: Wiley.

Gertner, Y., & Fisher, C. (2012, in press). Predicted errors in children's early sentence comprehension. *Cognition.*

Gesell, A. (1934). *An atlas of infant behavior.* New Haven, CT: Yale University Press.

Gesell, A. L. (1934). *Infancy and human growth.* New York: Macmillan.

Gewirtz, J. (1977). Maternal responding and the conditioning of infant crying: Directions of influence within the attachment-acquisition process. In B. C. Etzel, J. M. LeBlanc, & D. M. Baer (Eds.), *New developments in behavioral research.* Hillsdale, NJ: Erlbaum.

Ghetti, S., & Alexander, K. W. (2004). "If it happened, I would remember it": Strategic use of event memorability in the rejection of false autobiographical events. *Child Development, 75,* 542–561.

Ghetti, S., & Bauer, P. J. (Eds.). (2012). *Origins and development of recollection.* New York: Oxford University Press.

Ghosh, S., Feingold, E., Chakaborty, S., & Dey, S. K. (2010). Telomere length is associated with types of chromosome 21 nondisjunction: A new insight into the maternal age effect on Down syndrome birth. *Human Genetics, 127,* 403–409.

Giacosa, A., & others. (2012). Alcohol and wine in relation to cancer and other diseases. *European Journal of Cancer Prevention, 21,* 103–108.

Giarrusso, R., & Bengtson, V. L. (2007). Self-esteem. In J. E. Birren (Ed.), *Encyclopedia of gerontology* (2nd ed.). San Diego: Academic Press.

Gibbons, L., & others. (2012, in press). Inequities in the use of cesarean section deliveries in the world. *American Journal of Obstetrics and Gynecology, 206.*

Gibbs, J. C. (2010). *Moral development and reality* (2nd ed.). Boston: Allyn & Bacon.

Gibbs, J. C., Basinger, K. S., Grime, R. L., & Snarey, J. R. (2007). Moral judgment development across cultures: Revisiting Kohlberg's universality claims. *Developmental Review, 27,* 443–500.

Gibson, E. J. (1969). *Principles of perceptual learning and development.* New York: Appleton-Century-Crofts.

Gibson, E. J. (1989). Exploratory behavior in the development of perceiving, acting, and the acquiring of knowledge. *Annual Review of Psychology* (Vol. 39). Palo Alto, CA: Annual Reviews.

Gibson, E. J. (2001). *Perceiving the affordances.* Mahwah, NJ: Erlbaum.

Gibson, E. J., Riccio, G., Schmuckler, M. A., Stoffregen, T. A., Rosenberg, D., & Taormina, J. (1987). Detection of the traversability of surfaces by crawling and walking infants. *Journal of Experimental Psychology: Human Perception and Performance, 13,* 533–544.

Gibson, E. J., & Walk, R. D. (1960). The "visual cliff." *Scientific American, 202,* 64–71.

Gibson, E. L., & others. (2012). A narrative review of psychological and educational strategies applied to young children's eating behaviors aimed at reducing obesity risk. *Obesity Reviews, 13*(Suppl. 1), S85–S95.

Gibson, H. J. (2009). Leisure and travel, adulthood. In D. Carr (Ed.), *Encyclopedia of the life course and human development.* Boston: Gale Cengage.

Gibson, J. J. (1966). *The senses considered as perceptual systems.* Boston: Houghton Mifflin.

Gibson, J. J. (1979). *The ecological approach to visual perception.* Boston: Houghton Mifflin.

Giedd, J. N., & others. (2012). Automatic magnetic resonance imaging of the developing child and adolescent brain. In V. F. Reyna & others (Eds.), *The adolescent brain.* Washington, DC: American Psychological Association.

Gielen, S., Sandri, M., Erbs, S., & Adams, V. (2011). Exercise-induced modulation of endothelial nitric oxide production. *Current Pharmaceutical Biotechnology, 12*(9), 1375.

Gil-Bea, F. J., & others. (2012, in press). Cholinergic deactivation exacerbates amyloid pathology and induces hippocampal atrophy in Tg2576 mice. *Neurobiology of Disease.*

Gilliam, M., & others. (2011). Developmental trajectories of the corpus callosum in attention-deficit/hyperactivity disorder. *Biological Psychiatry, 69,* 839–846.

Gillig, P. M., & Sanders, R. D. (2011). Higher cortical functions: Attention and vigilance. *Innovations in Clinical Neuroscience, 8,* 43–46.

Gilligan, C. (1982). *In a different voice.* Cambridge, MA: Harvard University Press.

Gilligan, C. (1992, May). *Joining the resistance: Girls' development in adolescence.* Paper presented at the symposium on development and vulnerability in close relationships, Montreal, Quebec.

Gilligan, C. (1996). The centrality of relationships in psychological development: A puzzle, some evidence, and a theory. In G. G. Noam & K. W. Fischer (Eds.), *Development and vulnerability in close relationships.* Hillsdale, NJ: Erlbaum.

Gillum, R. F., & Ingram, D. D. (2007). Frequency of attendance at religious services, hypertension, and blood pressure: The third National Health and Nutrition Examination Survey. *Psychosomatic Medicine, 68,* 382–385.

Gillum, R. F., King, D. E., Obisesan, T. O., & Koenig, H. G. (2008). Frequency of attendance at religious services and mortality in a U.S. National cohort. *Annals of Epidemiology, 18,* 124–129.

Gil-Mohapel, J., Simpson, J. M., Titerness, A. K., & Christie, B. R. (2010). Characterization of the neurogenesis quiet zone in the rodent brain: Effects of age and exercise. *European Journal of Neuroscience, 31,* 797–807.

Gilmore, A. K., Granato, H. F., & Lewis, M. A. (2012, in press). The use of drinking and condom-related protective strategies in association with condom use and sex-related alcohol use. *Journal of Sex Research.*

Giorgis, C., & Glazer, J. (2013). *Literature for young children: Supporting emergent literacy, ages 0–8* (7th ed.). Upper Saddle River, NJ: Pearson.

Giovannini, M., Verduci, E., Salvatici, E., Paci, S., & Riva, E. (2012, in press). Phenylketonuria: Nutritional advances and challenges. *Nutrition and Metabolism.*

Girls, Inc. (1991). *Truth, trusting, and technology: New research oil preventing adolescent pregnancy.* Indianapolis: Author.

Glei, D. A. (1999). Measuring contraceptive use patterns among teenage and adult women. *Family Planning Perspectives, 31,* 73–80.

Glick, J. E., & Clark, R. (2012). Cognitive development and family resources among children in immigrant families. In V. Maholmes & R. B. King (Eds.), *Oxford handbook of poverty and child development.* New York: Wiley.

Gluck, M. E., Venti, C. A., Lindsay, R. S., Knowler, W. C., Salbe, A. D., & Krakoff, J. (2009). Maternal influence, not diabetic intrauterine environment, predicts children's energy intake. *Obesity, 17*(4), 772–777.

Goble, P. M., Martin, C. L., Hanish, L. D., & Fabes, R. A. (2012, April). *Defining preschool gender-typed activities.* Paper presented at the Gender Development Research conference, San Francisco.

Goga, A. E., & others. (2012, in press). Infant feeding practices at routine PMTCT site, South Africa: Results of a prospective observational study amongst HIV exposed and unexposed infants—birth to 9 months. *International Breastfeeding Journal.*

Gogtay, N., & Thompson, P. M. (2010). Mapping gray matter development: Implications for typical development and vulnerability to psychopathology. *Brain and Cognition, 72,* 6–15.

Goh, J. O. (2011). Functional dedifferentiation and altered connectivity in older adults: Neural accounts of cognitive aging. *Aging and Disease, 2,* 30–48.

Gold, D. (2011). Death and dying. In R. H. Binstock & L. K. George (Eds.), *Handbook of aging and the social sciences* (7th ed.). New York: Elsevier.

Goldberg, M. E., Gee, A., Ipata, A., Bisley, J., & Gottlieb, J. (2012). In G. R. Mangun, *Neuroscience of attention: Attentional control and selection.* New York: Oxford University Press.

Goldberg, W. A., & Lucas-Thompson, R. (2008). Maternal and paternal employment, effects of. In M. M. Haith & J. B. Benson (Eds.), *Encyclopedia of infant and early childhood development.* Oxford, UK: Elsevier.

Goldenberg, R. L., & Culhane, J. F. (2007). Low birth weight in the United States. *American Journal of Clinical Nutrition, 85*(Suppl.), S584–S590.

Goldfield, G. S. (2012). Making access to TV contingent on physical activity: Effects on liking and relative reinforcing value of TV and physical activity in overweight and obese children. *Journal of Behavioral Medicine, 35,* 1–7.

Goldin-Meadow, S. (2012, in press). What modern-day gesture can tell us about language evolution. In K. Gibson & M. Tallerman (Eds.), *Oxford handbook of language evolution.* New York: Oxford University Press.

Goldin-Meadow, S., & Alibali, M. W. A. (2013, in press). Gesture's role in learning and development. In P. Zelazo (Ed.), *Oxford University handbook of developmental psychology.* New York: Oxford University Press.

Goldschmidt, L., Richardson, G. A., Willford, J., & Day, N. L. (2008). Prenatal marijuana exposure and intelligence test performance at age 6. *Journal of the American Academy of Child and Adolescent Psychiatry, 47,* 254–263.

Goldstein, M. H., King, A. P., & West, M. J. (2003). Social interaction shapes babbling: Testing parallels between birdsong and speech. *Proceedings of the National Academy of Sciences, 100*(13), 8030–8035.

Goldston, D. B., Molock, S. D., Whitbeck, L. B., Murakami, J. L., Zayas, L. H., & Hall, G. C. (2008). Cultural considerations in adolescent suicide prevention and psychosocial treatment. *American Psychologist, 63,* 14–31.

Golley, R. K., & others. (2012, in press). An index measuring adherence to complementary feeding guidelines has convergent validity as a measure of infant diet quality. *Journal of Nutrition.*

Gollnick, D. M., & Chinn, P. C. (2013). *Multicultural education in a pluralistic society* (9th ed.). Boston: Allyn & Bacon.

Golombok, S. (2011a). Children in new family forms. In R. Gross (Ed.), *Psychology* (6th ed.). London: Hodder Educaiton.

Golombok, S. (2011b). Why I study lesbian families. In S. Ellis & others (Eds.), *LGBTQ psychologies.* New York: Cambridge University Press.

Golombok, S., MacCallum, F., & Goodman, E. (2001). The "test-tube" generation: Parent-child relationships and the psychological well-being of in vitro fertilization children at adolescence. *Child Development, 72,* 599–608.

Golombok, S., Rust, J., Zervoulis, K., & Croudace, T., Golding, J., & Hines, M. (2008). Developmental trajectories of sex-typed behavior in boys and girls: A longitudinal general population study of children aged 2.5–8 years. *Child Development, 79,* 1583–1593.

Golombok, S., & Tasker, F. (2010). Gay fathers. In M. E. Lamb (Ed.), *The role of the father in child development* (5th ed.). New York: Wiley.

Gomes, R. S., & others. (2011). Primary versus secondary hypertension in children followed up at an outpatient tertiary unit. *Pediatric Nephrology, 26,* 441–447.

Gompel, A., & Santen, R. J. (2012). Hormone therapy and breast cancer risk 10 years after the WHI. *Climacteric, 15,* 241–249.

Goncu, A., & Gauvain, M. (2011). Sociocultural approaches to educational psychology: Theory, research, and application. In K. R. Harris, S. Graham, & T. Urdan (Eds.), *APA educational psychology handbook.* Washington, DC: American Psychological Association.

Gonfloni, S., & others. (2012). Oxidative stress, DNA damage, and c-Abl signaling: At the crossroad in neurodegenerative diseases? *International Journal of Cell Biology.*

Gonsalves, S. (2011). Connecting curriculum with community. *Education Digest, 76*(6), 56–59.

Gonzales, M., Jones, D. J., Kincaid, C. Y., & Cuellar, J. (2012). Neighborhood context and adjustment in African American youths from single mother homes: The intervening role of hopelessness. *Cultural Diversity and Ethnic Minority Psychology, 18,* 109–117.

Gonzales, V., Yawkey, T. D., & Minaya-Rowe, L. (2006). *English-as-a-second language (ESL) teaching and learning.* Boston: Allyn & Bacon.

Gonzalez, A., Atkinson, L., & Fleming, A. S. (2009). Attachment and the comparative psychobiology of mothering. In M. de Haan & M. R. Gunnar (Eds.), *Developmental social neuroscience.* New York: Guilford.

Good, M., & Willoughby, T. (2008). Adolescence as a sensitive period for spiritual development. *Child Development Perspectives, 2,* 32–37.

Goodenough, J., & McGuire, B. A. (2012). *Biology of humans* (4th ed.). Upper Saddle River, NJ: Pearson.

Goodman, E., Evans, W. D., & DiPietro, L. (2012). Preliminary evidence for school-based physical activity policy needs in Washington, D.C. *Journal of Physical Activity and Health, 9,* 124–128.

Goodnough, L. T., & others. (2011). How we treat: Transfusion medicine support of obstetric services. *Transfusion, 204,* e1–e12.

Goodvin, R., Meyer, S., Thompson, R. A., & Hayes, R. (2008). Self-understanding in early childhood: Associations with child attachment security and maternal negative affect. *Attachment and Human Development, 10,* 433–450.

Gopinath, B., & others. (2012). Severity of age-related hearing loss is associated with impaired activities of daily living. *Age and Aging, 41,* 195–200.

Gopnik, A. (2010). Commentary in E. Galinsky (2010), *Mind in the making.* New York: Harper Collins.

Gorby, H. E., Brownawell, A. M., & Falk, M. C. (2010). Do specific dietary constituents and supplements affect mental energy? Review of the evidence. *Nutrition Reviews, 68,* 697–718.

Gorchoff, S. M., John, O. P., & Helson, R. (2008). Contextualizing change in marital satisfaction during middle age: An 18-year longitudinal study. *Psychological Science, 19,* 1194–1200.

Gordh, A. H., Brkic, S., & Soderpalm, B. (2011). Stress and consumption of alcohol in humans with a

Type 1 family history alcoholism in an experimental laboratory setting. *Pharmacology, Biochemistry, and Behavior, 99*, 696–703.

Goritz, C., & Frisen, J. (2012). Neural stem cells and neurogenesis in the adult. *Cell: Stem Cell, 10*, 657–659.

Gorrese, A., & Ruggieri, R. (2012). Peer attachment: A meta-analytic review of gender and age differences and associations with parent attachment. *Journal of Youth and Adolescence, 41*, 650–672.

Gosden, R. G. (2007). Menopause. In J. E. Birren (Ed.), *Encyclopedia of gerontology* (2nd ed.). San Diego: Academic Press.

Gosselin, J. (2010). Individual and family factors related to psychosocial adjustment in stepmother families with adolescents. *Journal of Divorce and Remarriage, 51*, 108–123.

Goswami, S., & others. (2012, in press). Determination of brain death by apnea test adapted to extracorporeal cardiopulmonary resuscitation. *Journal of Cardiothoracic and Vascular Anesthesia.*

Gottlieb, G. (2007). Probabalistic epigenesis. *Developmental Science, 10*, 1–11.

Gottlieb, G., Wahlsten, D., & Lickliter, R. (2006). The significance of biology for human development: A developmental psychobiological systems view. In W. Damon & R. Lerner (Eds.), *Handbook of child psychology* (6th ed.). New York: Wiley.

Gottman, J. M. (1994). *What predicts divorce?* Mahwah, NJ: Erlbaum.

Gottman, J. M. (2002) *The relationship cure.* New York: Three Rivers Press.

Gottman, J. M. (2006, April 29). Secrets of long term love. *New Scientist, 2549*, 40.

Gottman, J. M. (2011). *The science of trust.* New York: Norton.

Gottman, J. M. (2012a). *Bringing home baby.* Retrieved April 27, 2012, from www.bbhonline.org/

Gottman, J. M. (2012b). *Research on parenting.* Retrieved May 8, 2012, from www.gottman.com/ parenting/research

Gottman, J. M., & Parker, J. G. (Eds.). (1987). *Conversations of friends.* New York: Cambridge University Press.

Gottman, J. M., Shapiro, A. F., Parthemer, J. (2004). Bringing baby home: A preventative intervention program for expectant couples. *International Journal of Childbirth Education, 19*, 28–30.

Gottman, J. M., & Silver, N. (1999). *The seven principles for making marriages work.* New York: Crown.

Gouin, K., & others. (2011). Effects of cocaine use during pregnancy on low birthweight and preterm birth: Systematic and metanalyses. *American Journal of Obstetrics and Gynecology, 204*(4), 1.e1–1.e12.

Gould, E., & Hertel-Fernandez, A. (2010). Early retiree and near-elderly health insurance in a recession. *Journal of Aging and Social Policy, 22*, 172–187.

Gould, S. J. (1981). *The mismeasure of man.* New York: W. W. Norton.

Gouldner, H., & Strong, M. M. (1987). *Speaking of friendship.* New York: Greenwood Press.

Gove, W. R., Style, C. B., & Hughes, M. (1990). The effect of marriage on the well-being of adults. *Journal of Marriage and the Family, 11*, 4–35.

Gowan, D. E. (2003). Christian beliefs concerning death and life after death. In C. D. Bryant (Ed.), *Handbook of death and dying.* Thousand Oaks, CA: Sage.

Graber, J. A., Brooks-Gunn, J., & Warren, M. P. (2006). Pubertal effects on adjustment in girls: Moving from demonstrating effects to identifying pathways. *Journal of Youth and Adolescence, 35*, 391–401.

Graber, J. A., & Sontag, L. M. (2009). Internalizing problems during adolescence. In R. M. Lerner & L. Steinberg (Eds.), *Handbook of adolescent psychology* (3rd ed.). New York: Wiley.

Graber, K. C., & Woods, A. M. (2013). *Physical education and activity for elementary classroom teachers.* New York: McGraw-Hill.

Gradisar, M., Gardner, G., & Dohnt, H. (2011). Recent worldwide sleep patterns and problems during adolescence: A review and meta-analysis of age, region, and sleep. *Sleep Medicine, 12*, 110–118.

Grady, C. L., Springer, M. V., Hongwanishkul, D., McIntosh, A. R., & Winocur, G. (2006). Age-related changes in brain activity across the adult lifespan. *Journal of Cognitive Neuroscience, 18*, 227–241.

Grafenhain, M., Behne, T., Carpenter, M., & Tomasello, M. (2009). Young children's understanding of joint commitments. *Developmental Psychology, 45*, 1430–1443.

Graham, E. K., & Lachman, M. E. (2012). Personality and aging: Cognitive perspectives and processes. In S. K. Whitbourne & M. J. Sliwinski (Eds.), *Wiley-Blackwell handbook of adult development and aging.* New York: Wiley.

Graham, G. M., Holt-Hale, S., & Parker, M. A. (2013). *Children moving* (9th ed.). New York: McGraw-Hill.

Graham, S. (2005, February 16). Commentary in *USA TODAY,* p. 20.

Grambs, J. D. (1989). *Women over forty* (rev. ed.). New York: Springer.

Grant, J. (1993). *The state of the world's children.* New York: UNICEF and Oxford University Press.

Grant, N., Wardle, J., & Steptoe, A. (2009). The relationship between life satisfaction and health behavior: A cross-cultural analysis of young adults. *International Journal of Behavioral Medicine, 16*, 259–268.

Graven, S. (2006). Sleep and brain development. *Clinical Perinatology, 33*, 693–706.

Gravetter, R. J., & Forzano, L. B. (2012). *Research methods for the behavioral sciences* (4th ed.). Boston: Cengage.

Gray, P. B., & Garcia, J. R. (2012, in press). *Aging and human sexual behavior: Biocultural perspectives—a mini-review.*

Graziano, A. M., & Raulin, M. L. (2013). *Research methods* (8th ed.). Upper Saddle River, NJ: Pearson.

Gredler, M. E. (2012). Understanding Vygotsky for the classroom: Is it too late? *Educational Psychology Review, 24*, 113–131.

Green, J., Muir, H., & Maher, M. (2011). Child pedestrian casualties and deprivation. *Accidents: Analysis and Prevention, 43*, 714–723.

Green, M. J., Espie, C A., Hunt, K., & Benzeval, M. (2012). The longitudinal course of insomnia symptoms: Inequalities by sex and occupational class among two different age cohorts followed for 20 years in the west of Scotland. *Sleep, 35*, 815–823.

Greenberg, J. A. (2006). Correcting biases in estimates of mortality attributable to obesity. *Obesity, 14*, 2071–2079.

Greenhaus, J. H. (2013). Career dynamics. In I. B. Weiner & others (Eds.), *Handbook of psychology* (2nd ed., Vol. 12). New York: Wiley.

Greenlund, K. J., & others. (2012, in press). Public health options for improving cardiovascular health among older Americans. *American Journal of Public Health.*

Greer, F. R., Sicherer, S. H., Burks, A. W., & The Committee on Nutrition and Section on Allergy and Immunology. (2008). Effects of early nutritional interventions on the development of atopic disease in infants and children: The role of maternal dietary restriction, breast feeding, timing of introduction of complementary foods, and hydrolyzed formulas. *Pediatrics, 121*, 183–191.

Greer, J. A., & others. (2011). Anxiety disorders in long-term survivors of adult cancers. *Psychosomatics, 52*, 417–423.

Gregorson, M., Kaufman, J. C., & Snyder, H. (Eds.) (2013, in press). *Teaching creatively and teaching creativity.* New York: Springer.

Greif, M. L., & Needham, A. (2012). The development of tool use early in life. In T. McCormack, C. Hoerl, & S. Butterfill (Eds.), *Tool use and causal cognition.* New York: Oxford University Press.

Griffiths, J. D., Marslen-Wilson, W. D., Stamatakis, E. A., & Tyler, L. K. (2012, in press). Functional organization of the neural language system: Dorsal and ventral pathways are critical for syntax. *Cerebral Cortex.*

Grigorenko, E. (2000). Heritability and intelligence. In R. J. Sternberg (Ed.). *Handbook of intelligence.* New York: Cambridge U. Press.

Grigorenko, E. L., & Takanishi, R. (Eds.). (2012). *Immigration, diversity, and education.* New York: Routledge.

Groh, A. M., & others. (2012). The significance of insecure and disorganized attachment for children's internalizing symptoms: A meta-analytic study. *Child Development, 83*, 591–610.

Gross, A., & Rebok, G. W. (2011). Memory training and strategy use in older adults: Results from the ACTIVE Study. *Psychology and Aging, 26*, 503–517.

Gross, J. J., Fredrickson, B. L., & Levenson, R. W. (1994). The psychophysiology of crying. *Psychophysiology, 31*, 460–468.

Gross, L. S. (2013). *Electronic media* (11th ed.). New York: McGraw-Hill.

Gross, R. S., & others. (2011). Maternal controlling feeding styles during early infancy. *Clinical Pediatrics, 50*(12), 1125–1133.

Gross, R. S., & others. (2012, in press). Food insecurity and obesogenic maternal infant feeding Styles and practices in low-income families. *Pediatrics.*

Grossman, I., Na, J., Varnum, M. E., Park, D. C., Kitayama, S., & Nisbett, R. E. (2010). Reasoning about social conflicts improves into old age. *Proceedings of the National Academy of Sciences U.S.A., 107*, 7246–7250.

Grossmann, K., Grossmann, K. E., Spangler, G., Suess, G., & Unzner, L. (1985). Maternal sensitivity and newborns' orientation responses as related to quality of attachment in northern Germany. In L. Bretherton & E. Waters (Eds.), Growing points of attachment theory and research. *Monographs of the Society for Research in Child Development, 50*(1–2, Serial No. 209).

Grotevant, H. D., & von Korff, L. (2011). Adoptive identity. In S. Schwartz, K. Luyckx, & V. L. Vignoies (Eds.), *Handbook of identity theory and research.* New York: Springer.

Gruber, K. J. (2012). A comparative assessment of early adult life status of graduates of the North Carolina adolescent parenting program. *Journal of Child and Adolescent Psychiatric Nursing, 25*, 75–83.

Gruenewald, T. L., Karlamangia, A. S., Greendale, G. A., Singer, B. H., & Seeman, T. E. (2009). Increased mortality risk in older adults with persistently low or declining feelings of usefulness to others. *Journal of Aging and Health, 21*, 398–425.

Grusec, J. E. (2011a). Human development: Development in the family. *Annual Review of Psychology* (Vol. 62). Palo Alto, CA: Annual Reviews.

Grusec, J. E. (2011b). Socialization processes in the family: Social and emotional development. *Annual Review of Psychology* (Vol. 62). Palo Alto, CA: Annual Reviews.

Grusec, J. E., Chaparro, M. P., Johnston, M., & Sherman, A. (2013). Social development and social relationships in middle childhood. In I. B. Weiner & others (Eds.), *Handbook of psychology* (2nd ed., Vol. 6). New York: Wiley.

Grusec, J. E., & Davidov, M. (2010). Integrating different perspectives on socialization theory and research: A domain-specific approach. *Child Development, 81*, 687–709.

Grusec, J. E., & Sherman, A. (2011). Prosocial behavior. In M. K. Underwood & L. H. Rosen (Eds.), *Social development.* New York: Guilford.

Guerrero, L. K., Andersen, P. A., & Afifi, W. A. (2011). *Close encounters: Communication in relationships* (3rd ed.). Thousand Oaks, CA: Sage.

Guilford, J. P. (1967). *The structure of intellect.* New York: McGraw-Hill.

Guirado, G. N., & others. (2012). Combined exercise training in asymptomatic elderly with controlled hypertension: Effects of functional capacity and cardiac diastolic function. *Medical Science Monitor, 28*, CR461–CR465.

Gump, B., & Matthews, K. (2000, March). *Annual vacations, health, and death.* Paper presented at the meeting of the American Psychosomatic Society, Savannah, GA.

Gunderson, E. A., Ramirez, G., Beilock, S. L., & Levine, S. C. (2012). The role of parents and teachers in the development of gender-related attitudes. *Sex Roles, 66*, 153–166.

Gunnar, M. R., Malone, S., & Fisch, R. O. (1987). The psychobiology of stress and coping in the human neonate: Studies of the adrenocortical activity in response to stress in the first week of life. In T. Field, P. McCabe, & N. Scheiderman (Eds.). *Stress and coping.* Hillsdale, NJ: Erlbaum.

Gunnar, M., & Quevado, K. (2007). The neurobiology of stress and development. *Annual Review of Psychology* (Vol. 58). Palo Alto, CA: Annual Reviews.

Gunnar, M. R., Fisher, P. A., & The Early Experience, Stress, and Prevention Network. (2006). Bringing basis research on early experience and stress neurobiology to bear on preventive interventions for neglected and maltreated children. *Development and Psychopathology, 18*, 651–677.

Gunning, T. G. (2013). *Creating literacy instruction for all children in grades Pre-K to 4* (2nd ed.). Boston: Allyn & Bacon.

Gupta, A., Thornton, J. W., & Huston, A. C. (2008). Working families should not be poor—the New Hope Program. In D. R. Crane & T. B. Heaton (Eds.), *Handbook of families and poverty.* Thousand Oaks, CA: Sage.

Gur, R. C., & others. (1995). Sex differences in regional cerebral glucose metabolism during a resting state. *Science, 267*, 528–531.

Gurwitch, R. H., Silovksy, J. F., Schultz, S., Kees, M., & Burlingame, S. (2001). *Reactions and guidelines for children following trauma/disaster.* Norman, OK: Department of Pediatrics, University of Oklahoma Health Sciences Center.

Gustafsson, J-E. (2007). Schooling and intelligence. Effects of track of study on level and profile of cognitive abilities. In P. C. Kyllonen, R. D. Roberts, & L. Stankov (Eds.), *Extending intelligence.* Mahwah, NJ: Erlbaum.

Gustafsson, P. E., Persson, M., & Hammarstrom, A. (2011). Life course origins of the metabolic syndrome in middle-aged women and men: The role of socioeconomic status and metabolic risk in adolescence and early adulthood. *Annals of Epidemiology, 21*, 103–110.

Gutchess, A. H., & others. (2005). Aging and the neural correlates of successful picture encoding: Frontal activations compensate for decreased medial-temporal activity. *Journal of Cognitive Neuroscience, 17*, 84–96.

Gutmann, D. L. (1975). Parenthood: A key to the comparative study of the life cycle. In N. Datan & L. Ginsberg (Eds.), *Life-span developmental psychology: Normative life crises.* New York: Academic Press.

Guttmannova, K., & others. (2012). Examining explanatory mechanisms of the effects of early alcohol use on young adult alcohol competence. *Journal of Studies of Alcohol and Drugs, 73*, 379–390.

H

Hackney, M. E., & Earhart, G. M. (2010a). Effects of dance on balance and gait in severe Parkinson disease: A case study. *Disability and Rehabilitation, 32*, 679–684.

Hackney, M. E., & Earhart, G. M. (2010b). Effects of dance on gait and balance in Parkinson's disease: A comparison of partnered and nonpartnered dance movement. *Neurorehabilitation and Neural Repair, 24*, 384–392.

Hagen, J. W., & Lamb-Parker, F. G. (2008). Head Start. In M. M. Haith & J. B. Benson (Eds.), *Encyclopedia of infant and early childhood development.* Oxford, UK: Elsevier.

Hagestad, G. O. (1985). Continuity and connectedness. In V. L. Bengston & J. Robertson (Eds.). *Grandparenthood.* Newbury Park, CA: Sage.

Hagestad, G. O., & Uhlenberg, P. (2007). The impact of demographic changes on relations between age groups and generations: A comparative perspective. In K. W. Schaie & P. Uhlenberg (Eds.), *Demographic changes and the well-being of older persons.* New York: Springer.

Hagman, J. O., & Frank, G. K. W. (2012). Developmental concerns in psychopharmacological treatment of children and adolescents with eating disorders. In J. Lock (Ed.), *Oxford handbook of child and adolescent eating disorders: Developmental perspectives.* New York: Oxford University Press.

Hahn, D. B., Payne, W. A., & Lucas, E. B. (2013). *Focus on health* (11th ed.). New York: McGraw-Hill.

Hahn, E. A., Cichy, K. E., Almeida, D. M., & Haley, W. E. (2011). Time use and well-being in older widows: Adaptation and resilience. *Journal of Women and Aging, 23*, 149–159.

Haith, M. M., Hazen, C., & Goodman, G. S. (1988). Expectation and anticipation of dynamic visual events by 3.5-month-old babies. *Child Development, 59*, 467–479.

Hakuta, K. (2001, April). *Key policy milestones and directions in the education of English language learners.* Paper prepared for the Rockefeller Symposium on Educational Equity, Washington, DC.

Hakuta, K. (2005, April). *Bilingualism at the intersection of research and public policy.* Paper presented at the meeting of the Society for Research in Child Development, Atlanta.

Hakuta, K., Butler, Y. G., & Witt, D. (2000). *How long does it take English learners to attain proficiency?* Berkeley, CA: The University of California Linguistic Minority Research Institute Policy Report 2000–1.

Halford, W. K., Markman, H. J., & Stanley, S. (2008). Strengthening couples' relationships with education: Social policy and public health perspectives. *Journal of Family Psychology, 22*, 497–505.

Hall, C. B., Lipton, R. B., Sliwinski, M., Katz, M. J., Derby, C. A., & Verghese, J. (2009). Cognitive activities delay onset of memory decline in persons who develop dementia. *Neurology, 73*, 356–361.

Hall, G. S. (1904). *Adolescence* (Vols. 1 & 2). Englewood Cliffs, NJ: Prentice Hall.

Hall, L. J. (2013). *Autism spectrum disorders* (2nd ed.). Upper Saddle River, NJ: Pearson.

Hall, W. J. (2008). Centenarians: Metaphor becomes reality. *Archives of Internal Medicine, 168*, 262–263.

Hallahan, D. P., Kaufmann, J. M., & Pullen, P. C. (2012). *Exceptional learners* (12th ed.). Boston: Allyn & Bacon.

Halonen, J., & Santrock, J. W. (2013). *Your guide to college success* (7th ed.). Boston: Cengage.

Halpern, D. F. (2012). *Sex differences in cognitive abilities* (2nd ed.). New York: Psychology Press.

Halpern, D. F., Benbow, C. P., Geary, D. C., Gur, R. C., Hyde, J. S., & Gernsbacher, M. A. (2007). The science of sex differences in science and mathematics. *Psychological Science in the Public Interest, 8*, 1–51.

Hammen, C. (2009). Adolescent depression: Stressful interpersonal contexts and risk for recurrence. *Current Directions in Psychological Science, 18*, 200–204.

Hammes, B. J., & others. (2012). THE POLST program: A retrospective review of the demographics of use and outcomes in one community where advance directives are prevalent. *Journal of Palliative Medicine, 15*, 77–85.

Hampstead, B. M., & others. (2012a, in press). Mnemonic strategy training improves memory for object location associations in both healthy elderly and patients with amnestic mild cognitive impairment: A randomized, single-blind study. *Neuropsychology.*

Hampstead, B. M., & others. (2012b, in press). Mnemonic strategy training partially restores hippocampal activity in patients with mild cognitive impairment. *Hippocampus.*

Han, W-J. (2009). Maternal employment. In D. Carr (Ed.). *Encyclopedia of the life course and human development.* Boston: Gale Cengage.

Han, X., & others. (2012, in press). Influence of long-term caloric restriction on myocardial and cardiomycte contractile function and autophagy in mice. *Journal of Nutritional Biochemistry.*

Handrinos, J., Cooper, P., Pauletti, R., & Perry, D. G. (2012, April). *Influences on girls' aggression toward gender-atypical boys.* Paper presented at the Gender Development Research conference, San Francisco.

Hanish, L. D., & Guerra, N. G. (2004). Aggressive victims, passive victims, and bullies: Developmental continuity or developmental change? *Merrill-Palmer Quarterly, 50,* 17–38.

Hansard, K. (2012). Compassion and empathy—a doula's best friends. *Midwifery Today and International Midwife, 31,* 69.

Hansell, N. K., & others. (2012). Genetic co-morbidity between neuroticism, anxiety/depression, and somatic distress in a sample of adolescent and young adult twins. *Psychological Medicine, 42,* 1249–1260.

Hansen, M. (2012). Confronting costs: Medicaid spending is at the top of many legislative lists. *State Legislatures, 38,* 30–32.

Hansen, M. L., Gunn, P. W., & Kaelber, D. C. (2007). Underdiagnosis of hypertension in children and adolescents. *Journal of the American Medical Association, 298,* 874–879.

Harakeh, Z., & others. (2012, in press). Individual and environmental predictors of health risk behaviors among Dutch adolescents: The HBSC study. *Public Health.*

Harden, K. P., & Mendle, J. (2011). Adolescent sexual activity and the development of delinquent behavior: The role of relationship context. *Journal of Youth and Adolescence, 40,* 825–838.

Hardy, M. (2006). Older workers. In R. H. Binstock & L. K. George (Eds.), *Handbook of aging and the social sciences* (6th ed.). San Diego: Academic Press.

Hardy, S. A., Walker, L. J., Rackham, D. D., & Olsen, J. A. (2012, in press). Religiosity and adolescent empathy and aggression: The mediating role of moral identity. *Psychology of Religion and Spirituality.*

Harkins, S. W., Price, D. D., & Martinelli, M. (1986). Effects of age on pain perception. *Journal of Gerontology, 41,* 58–63.

Harkness, S., & Super, E. M. (1995). Culture and parenting. In M. H. Bornstein (Ed.), *Handbook of parenting* (Vol. 3). Hillsdale, NJ: Erlbaum.

Harlow, H. F. (1958). The nature of love. *American Psychologist, 13,* 673–685.

Harrington, S. E., & Smith, T. J. (2008). The role of chemotherapy at the end of life: "When is enough, enough?" *Journal of the American Medical Association, 299,* 2667–2678.

Harris Interactive. (2003, February 5). *Harris Poll #8: Adults on the Internet.* Rochester, NY: Author.

Harris, C. D., Pan, L., & Mukhtar, Q. (2010). Changes in receiving preventive care services among U.S. adults with diabetes, 1997–2007. *Preventing Chronic Disease, 7*(3), A56.

Harris, G. (2002). *Grandparenting: How to meet its responsibilities.* Los Angeles: The Americas Group.

Harris, J., Golinkoff, R. M., & Hirsh-Pasek, K. (2011). Lessons from the crib for the classroom: How children really learn vocabulary. In S. B. Neuman & D. K. Dickinson (Eds.), *Handbook of early literacy research.* New York: Guilford.

Harris, J. J., & Attwell, D. (2012). The energetics of CNS white matter. *Journal of Neuroscience, 32,* 356–371.

Harris, J. R. (1998). *The nurture assumption: Why children turn out the way they do: Parents matter less than you think and peers matter more.* New York: Free Press.

Harris, J. R. (2009). *The nurture assumption* (Rev. ed.). New York: The Free Press.

Harris, K. M., Gorden-Larsen, P., Chantala, K., & Udry, J. R. (2006). Longitudinal trends in race/ethnic disparities in leading health indicators from adolescence to young adulthood. *Archives of Pediatrics and Adolescent Medicine, 160,* 74–81.

Harris, K. R., Graham, S., Brindle, M., & Sandmel, K. (2010). Metacognition and children's writing. In D. Hacker, J. Dunlosky, & A. Graesser (Eds.), *Handbook of metacognition in education.* Mahwah, NJ: Erlbaum.

Harris, K. R., Graham, S., & Urdan, T. (Eds.) (2012). *APA educational psychology handbook.* Washington, DC: American Psychological Association.

Harris, L. (1975). *The myth and reality of aging in America.* Washington, DC: National Council on Aging.

Harris, M. F. (2012, in press). Access to preventive care by immigrant populations. *BMC Medicine.*

Harris, P. L. (2000). *The work of the imagination.* New York: Oxford University Press.

Harris, P. L. (2006). Social cognition. In W. Damon & R. Lerner (Eds.), *Handbook of child psychology* (6th ed.). New York: Wiley.

Harrison, C. (2012). Aging: Telomerase gene therapy increases longevity. *Nature Reviews/Drug Discovery, 11,* 518.

Harrison-Hale, A. O., McLoyd, V. C., & Smedley, B. (2004). Racial and ethnic status: Risk and protective processes among African-American families. In K. L. Maton, C. J. Schellenbach, B. J. Leadbetter, & A. L. Solarz (Eds.), *Investing in children, families, and communities.* Washington, DC: American Psychological Association.

Hart, B., & Risley, T. R. (1995). *Meaningful differences in the everyday experience of young Americans.* Baltimore: Paul H. Brookes.

Hart, C. H., Yang, C., Charlesworth, R., & Burts, D. C. (2003, April). *Early childhood teachers' curriculum beliefs, classroom practices, and children's outcomes: What are the connections?* Paper presented at the biennial meeting of the Society for Research in Child Development, Tampa, FL.

Hart, C. N., Cairns, A., & Jelalian, E. (2011). Sleep and obesity in children and adolescents. *Pediatric Clinics of North America, 58,* 15–33.

Hart, D., & Karmel, M. P. (1996). Self-awareness and self-knowledge in humans, great apes, and monkeys. In A. Russori, K. Bard, & S. Parker (Eds.), *Reaching into thought.* New York: Cambridge University Press.

Hart, D., Matsuba, M. K., & Atkins, R. (2008). The moral and civic effects of learning to serve. In L. Nucci & D. Narvaez (Eds.), *Handbook of moral and character education.* Clinton, NJ: Psychology Press.

Hart, S., & Carrington, H. (2002). Jealousy in 6-month-old infants: *Infancy, 3,* 395–402.

Harter, S. (2006). The self. In W. Damon & R. Lerner (Eds.), *Handbook of child psychology* (6th ed.). New York: Wiley.

Harter, S. (2012). *The construction of the self* (2nd ed.). New York: Wiley.

Hartley, A. (2006). Changing role of the speed of processing construct in the cognitive psychology of human aging. In J. E. Birren & K. W. Schaie (Eds.), *Handbook of the psychology of aging* (6th ed.). San Diego: Academic Press.

Hartshorne, H., & May, M. S. (1928–1930). *Moral studies in the nature of character.* New York: Macmillan.

Hartup, W. W. (1983). The peer system. In P. H. Mussen (Ed.), *Handbook of child psychology* (4th ed., Vol. 4). New York: Wiley.

Hartup, W. W. (1996). The company they keep: Friendships and their developmental significance. *Child Development, 67,* 1–13.

Hartup, W. W. (2009). Critical issues and theoretical viewpoints. In K. H. Rubin, W. M. Bukowski, & B. Laursen (Eds.), *Handbook of peer interactions, relationships, and groups.* New York: Guilford.

Hartup, W. W. (2009). Critical issues and theoretical viewpoints. In K. H. Rubin, W. M. Bukowski, & B. Laursen (Eds.), *Handbook of peer interactions, relationships, and groups.* New York: Guilford.

Hasher, L. (2003, February 28). Commentary in "The wisdom of the wizened." *Science, 299,* 1300–1302.

Hasher, L., Chung, C., May, C. P., & Foong, N. (2001). Age, time of testing, and proactive interference. *Canadian Journal of Experimental Psychology, 56,* 200–207.

Hastings, P. D., Utendale, W. T., & Sullivan, C. (2007). The socialization of prosocial development. In J. E. Grusec & P. D. Hastings (Eds.), *Handbook of socialization.* New York: Guilford.

Hattery, A. J., & Smith, E. (2007). *African American families.* Thousand Oaks, CA: Sage.

Hatzfeld, J. J., Laveist, T. A., & Gaston-Johansson, F. G. (2012, in press). Racial/ethnic disparities in the prevalence of selected chronic diseases among U.S. Air Force members, 2008. *Preventing Chronic Disease.*

Hauck, F. R., Signore, C., Fein, S. B., & Raju, T. N. (2008). Infant sleeping arrangements and practices during the first year of life. *Pediatrics, 122* (Suppl. 2), S113–S120.

Hauck, F. R., & others. (2011). Breastfeeding and reduced risk of sudden infant death syndrome : A meta-analysis. *Pediatrics, 128,* 103–110.

Haugrud, N., Crossley, M., & Vrbancic, M. (2011). Clustering and switching strategies during verbal fluency performance differentiate Alzheimer's disease and healthy aging. *Journal of the International Alzheimer's Society, 17,* 1153–1157.

Hawkes, C. (2006). Olfaction in neurogenerative disorder. *Advances in Otorhinollaryngology, 63,* 133–151.

Hawkins, J. A., & Berndt, T. J. (1985, April). *Adjustment following the transition to junior high school.* Paper presented at the biennial meeting of the Society for Research in Child Development, Toronto.

Hawkley, L. C., & Cacioppo, J. T. (2013, in press). Social connection and relationships in successful aging. In J. M. Rippe (Ed.), *Encyclopedia of lifestyle medicine and health.* Thousand Oaks, CA: Sage.

Hawkley, L. C., Thisted, R. A., Masi, C. M., & Cacioppo, J. T. (2010). Loneliness predicts increased blood pressure: 5-year cross-lagged analyses in middle-aged and older adults. *Psychology and Aging, 25,* 132–141.

Haydon, A., & Halpern, G. T. (2010). Older romantic partners and depressive symptoms during adolescence. *Journal of Youth and Adolescence, 39,* 1240–1251.

Haydon, A. A., Herring, A. H., Prinstein, M. J., & Halpern, C. T. (2012). Beyond age at first sex: Patterns of emerging sexual behavior in adolescence and young adulthood. *Journal of Adolescent Health, 50,* 456–463.

Hayes, J. R., & Berninger, V. (2013, in press). Cognitive processes in writing: A framework. In B. Arte, J. Dockrell, & V. Berninger (Eds.), *Writing development and instruction in children with hearing, speech, and language disorders.* New York: Oxford University Press.

Hayflick, L. (1977). The cellular basis for biological aging. In C. E. Finch & L. Hayflick (Eds.), *Handbook of the biology of aging.* New York: Van Nostrand.

Hayslip, B. (1996). Hospice. In J. E. Birren (Ed.), *Encyclopedia of gerontology* (Vol. 1). San Diego: Academic Press.

Hayslip, B., Edmondson, R., & Guarnaccia, C. (1999, November). *Religiousness, perceptions of funerals, and bereavement adjustment in adulthood.* Paper presented at the meeting of the Gerontological Society of America, San Francisco.

Hayslip, B., & Hansson, R. (2003). Death awareness and adjustment across the life span. In C. D. Bryant (Ed.), *Handbook of death and dying.* Thousand Oaks, CA: Sage.

Hayslip, B., & Hansson, R. O. (2007). Hospice. In J. E. Birren (Ed.), *Encyclopedia of gerontology* (2nd ed.). San Diego: Academic Press.

Hazan, C., & Shaver, P. R. (1987). Romantic love conceptualized as an attachment process. *Journal of Personality and Social Psychology, 52,* 522–524.

Head, D., Singh, T., & Bugg, J. M. (2012). The moderating role of exercise on stress-related effects on the hippocampus and memory in late adulthood. *Neuropsychology, 26,* 133–143.

Healey, M. K., & Hasher, L. (2009). Limitations to the deficit attenuation hypothesis: Aging and decision making. *Journal of Consumer Psychology, 19,* 17–22.

Heard, E., & others. (2011). Mediating effects of social support on the relationship between perceived stress, depression, and hypertension in African Americans. *Journal of the American Medical Association, 103,* 116–122.

Hebl, M. R., & Avery, D. R. (2013). Diversity in organizations. In I. B. Weiner & others (Eds.), *Handbook of psychology* (2nd ed., Vol.12). New York: Wiley.

Hegaard, H. K., Hedegaard, M., Damm, P., Ottesen, B., Petersson, K., & Henriksen, T. B. (2008). Leisure time physical activity is associated with a reduced risk of preterm delivery. *American Journal of Obstetrics and Gynecology, 198,* e1–e5.

Heiman, G. W. (2013). *Basic statistics for the behavioral sciences* (7th ed.). Boston: Cengage.

Heimann, M., Strid, K., Smith, L., Tjus, T., Ulvund, S. E., & Melzoff, A. N. (2006). Exploring the relation between memory, gestural communication, and the emergence of language in infancy: A longitudinal study. *Infant and Child Development, 15,* 233–249.

Helgeson, V. S. (2012). *Psychology of gender* (4th ed.). Upper Saddle River, NJ: Pearson.

Hellander, I., & Bhargavan, R. (2012). Report from the United States: The U.S. health crisis deepens amid rising inequality—a review of data, fall 2011. *International Journal of Health Services, 42,* 161–175.

Helman, C. (2008). Inside T. Boone Pickens' brain. *Forbes.* Retrieved June 15, 2008, from http://www.forbes.com/billionaires/forbes/2008/0630/076.html

Helman, R., Copeland, C., & Van Derhei, J. (2012). The 2012 Retirement Confidence Survey: Job insecurity, debt weigh on retirement confidence, savings. *EBRI Issue Brief, 369,* 5–32.

Helman, R., VanDerhei, J., & Copeland, C. (2007). The retirement system in transition: The 2007 Retirement Confidence Survey. *Employment Benefit Research Institute Issue Brief, 304*(1), 4–24.

Helmuth, L. (2003). The wisdom of the wizened. *Science, 299,* 1300–1302.

Helson, R. (1997, August). *Personality change: When is it adult development?* Paper presented at the meeting of the American Psychological Association, Chicago.

Helson, R., & Wink, P. (1992). Personality change in women from the early 40s to early 50s. *Psychology and Aging, 7,* 46–55.

Helwig, C. C., & Turiel, E. (2011). Children's social and moral reasoning. In P. K. Smith & C. H. Hart (Eds.), *Wiley-Blackwell handbook of childhood social development* (2nd ed.). New York: Wiley.

Henderson, V. W. (2011). Gonadal hormones and cognitive aging: A midlife perspective. *Women's Health, 7,* 81–93.

Henggeler, S. W., & Sheidow, L. J. (2012). Empirically supported family-based treatments for conduct disorder and delinquency in adolescents. *Journal of Marital and Family Therapy, 38,* 30–58.

Hennessey, B. A. (2011). Intrinsic motivation and creativity: Have we come full circle? In R. A. Beghetto & J. C. Kaufman (Eds.), *Nurturing creativity in the classroom.* New York: Cambridge University Press.

Henninger, D. E., Madden, D. J., & Huettel, S. A. (2010). Processing speed and memory mediate age-related differences in decision making. *Psychology and Aging, 25,* 262–270.

Henninger, M. L. (2013). *Teaching young children* (5th ed.). Upper Saddle River, NJ: Pearson.

Henretta, J. C. (2010). Lifetime marital history and mortality after age 50. *Journal of Aging and Health, 22*(8), 1198–1212.

Henriksen, T. B., & others. (2004). Alcohol consumption at the time of conception and spontaneous abortion. *American Journal of Epidemiology, 160,* 661–667.

Herd, P., Robert, S. A., & House, J. S. (2011). Health disparities among older adults: Life course influences and policy solutions. In R. H. Binstock & L. K. George (Eds.), *Handbook of aging and the social sciences* (7th ed.). New York: Elsevier.

Herek, G. M. (2009). Hate crimes and stigma-related experiences among sexual minority adults in the United States: Prevalence estimates from a national probability sample. *Journal of Interpersonal Violence, 24,* 54–74.

Herman-Giddens, M. E. (2007). The decline in the age of menarche in the United States: Should we be concerned? *Journal of Adolescent Health, 40,* 201–203.

Hern, B., & Chard, D. (2013). Strategies for improving students' reading fluency. In B. G. Cook & M. G. Tankersley (Eds.), *Research-based practices in special education.* Upper Saddle River, NJ: Pearson.

Hernandez-Reif, M., Diego, M., & Field, T. (2007). Preterm infants show reduced stress behaviors and activity after 5 days of massage therapy. *Infant Behavior and Development, 30,* 557–561.

Hertzog, C., Kramer, A. F., Wilson, R. S., & Lindenberger, U. (2009). Enrichment effects on adult cognitive development. *Psychological Perspectives in the Public Interest, 9,* 1–65.

Hetherington, E. M. (1993). An overview of the Virginia Longitudinal Study of Divorce and Remarriage with a focus on early adolescence. *Journal of Family Psychology, 7,* 39–56.

Hetherington, E. M. (2000). Divorce. In A. Kazdin (Ed.), *Encyclopedia of psychology.* Washington, DC, & New York: American Psychological Association and Oxford University Press.

Hetherington, E. M. (2006). The influence of conflict, marital problem solving, and parenting on children's adjustment in nondivorced, divorced, and remarried families. In A. Clarke-Stewart & J. Dunn (Eds.), *Families count.* New York: Oxford University Press.

Hetherington, E. M., & Kelly, J. (2002). *For better or for worse: Divorce reconsidered.* New York: Norton.

Hetherington, E. M., & Stanley-Hagan, M. (2002). Parenting in divorced and remarried families. In M. H. Bornstein (Ed.), *Handbook of parenting* (2nd ed., Vol. 3). Mahwah, NJ: Erlbaum.

Hetzner, N. M. P., & Brooks-Gunn, J. (2012). Employment in low-income families. In V. Maholmes & R. B. King (Eds.), *Oxford handbook of poverty and children's development.* New York: Oxford University Press.

Hewlett, B. S. (1991). *Intimate fathers: The nature and context of Aka Pygmy.* Ann Arbor, MI: University of Michigan Press.

Hewlett, B. S. (2000). Culture, history, and sex: Anthropological perspectives on father involvement. *Marriage and Family Review, 29,* 324–340.

Hewlett, B. S., & MacFarlan, S. J. (2010). Fathers' roles in hunter-gatherer and other small-scale cultures. In M. E. Lamb (Ed.) *The role of the father in child development* (5th ed.). New York: Wiley.

Heyman, G. D., & Legare, C. H. (2005). Children's evaluation of sources of information about traits. *Developmental Psychology, 41,* 636–647.

Hickman, S. E., & el Khoury, J. (2012, in press). The neuroimmune system in Alzheimer's disease: The glass is half full. *Journal of Alzheimer's Disease.*

Higginbotham, B., Davis, P., Smith, L., Dansie, L., Skogrand, L., & Reck, K. (2012). Stepfathers and stepfamily education. *Journal of Divorce & Remmarriage, 53,* 76–90.

High/Scope Resource. (2005, Spring). The High/Scope Perry Preschool Study and the man who began it. *High/Scope Resource 9.* Ypsilanti, MI: High/Scope Press.

Highfield, R. (2008, April 30). *Harvard's baby brain research lab.* Retrieved January 24, 2009, from www.telegraph.co.uk/scienceandtechnology/science/sciencenews/3341166/Harvards-baby-brain-research-lab.html

Highhouse, S., & Schmitt, N. (2013). A snapshot in time: Industrial-organizational psychology today. In I. B. Weiner & others (Eds.), *Handbook of psychology* (2nd ed., Vol. 12). New York: Wiley.

Higo, M., & Williamson, J. B. (2009). Retirement. In D. Carr (Ed.), *Encyclopedia of the life course and human development.* Boston: Gale Cengage.

Hildebrant, T., Bacow, T., Markella, M., & Loeb, K. L. (2012, in press). Anxiety in anorexia nervosa and its management using family-based treatment. *European Eating Disorders Review.*

Hill, C. R., & Stafford, E. P. (1980). Parental care of children: Time diary estimate of quantity, predictability, and variety. *Journal of Human Resources, 15,* 219–239.

Hill, P. L., Turiano, N. A., Mroczek, D. K., & Roberts, B. W. (2012, in press). Examining concurrent and longitudinal relations between personality traits and social well-being in adulthood. *Social Psychological and Personality Science.*

Hill, P. L., & others. (2011). Conscientiousness and longevity: An examination of possible Mediators. *Health Psychology, 30,* 536–541.

Hill, T. D., Burdette, A. M., Angel, J. L., & Angel, R. J. (2006). Religious attendance and cognitive functioning among older Mexican Americans. *Journals of Gerontology B: Psychological Sciences and Social Sciences, 61,* P3–P9.

Hillemeier, M. M., Morgan, P. L., Farkas, G., & Maczuga, S. A. (2012, in press). Quality disparities in child care for at-risk children: Comparing Head Start and non-Head Start settings. *Maternal and Child Health Journal.*

Hilliard, L., & Liben, L. (2012, April). *No boys in ballet: Response to gender bias in mother-child conversations.* Paper presented at the Gender Development Research conference, San Francisco.

Hillier, A., & others. (2012, in press). The impact of WIC food package changes on access to healthful food in two low-income neighborhoods. *Journal of Nutrition Education and Behavior.*

Himes, C. L. (2009). Age structure. In D. Carr (Ed.), *Encyclopedia of the life course and human development.* Boston: Gale Cengage.

Hindin, S. B., & Zelinski, E. M. (2012). Extended practice and aerobic exercise interventions benefit untrained cognitive outcomes in older adults: A meta-analysis. *Journal of the American Geriatric Association, 60,* 136–141.

Hindman, A. H., Skibbek, L. E., Miller, A., & Zimmerman, M. (2010). Ecological contexts and early learning: Contributions of child, family, and classroom factors during Head Start to literacy and mathematics growth through first grade. *Early Childhood Research Quarterly, 25,* 235–250.

Hines, M. (2011). Gender development and the human brain. *Annual Review of Neuroscience, 34,* Palo Alto, CA: Annual Reviews.

Hines, M. (2013). Sex and sex differences. In P. D. Zelazo (Ed.), *Oxford handbook of developmental psychology.* New York: Oxford University Press.

Hinkle, J. S., Tuckman, B. W., & Sampson, J. P. (1993). The psychology, physiology, and the creativity of middle school aerobic exercisers. *Elementary School Guidance & Counseling, 28,* 133–145.

Hinze, S. W., Lin, J., & Andersson, T. E. (2012). Can we capture the intersections? Older Black women, education, and health. *Women's Health Issues, 22,* e91–e98.

Hirotani, M., Stets, T., Striano, T., & Friederici, A. D. (2009). Joint attention helps infants learn new words: Event-related potential evidence. *Neuroreport, 20,* 600–605.

Hirsch, B. J., & Rapkin, B. D. (1987). The transition to junior high school: A longitudinal study of self-esteem, psychological symptomatology, school life, and social support. *Child Development, 58,* 1235–1243.

Hirsh-Pasek, K., & Golinkoff, R. M. (2012a, in press). Early language and literacy: Six principles. In S. Gilford (Ed.), *Head Start teacher's guide.* New York: Teacher's College Press.

Hirsh-Pasek, K., & Golinkoff, R. M. (2012b, in press). How babies talk: Six principles of early language development: In S. Odom, E. Pungello, & N. Gardner-Neblett (Eds.), *Re-visioning the beginning: Implications of developmental and health science for infant/toddler care and poverty.* New York: Guilford Press.

Hirsh-Pasek, K., & Golinkoff, R. M. (2013, in press). Early language and literacy: Six principles. In S. Gilford (Ed.), *Head Start Teacher's Guide.* New York: Teacher's College Press.

Hirsh-Pasek, K., Golinkoff, R. M., Singer, D., & Berk, L. (2009). *A mandate for playful learning in preschool: Presenting the evidence.* New York: Oxford University Press.

Ho, J., Yeh, M., McCabe, K., & Lau, A. (2012). Perceptions of the acceptability of parent training among Chinese immigrant parents: Contributions of cultural factors and clinical need. *Behavior Therapy, 43,* 436–449.

Hochberg, C., & others. (2012). Association of vision loss in glaucoma and age-related macular degeneration with IADL disability. *Investigative Ophthalmology and Visual Science, 53,* 3201–3206.

Hock, R. R. (2012). *Human sexuality* (3rd ed.). Upper Saddle River, NJ: Pearson.

Hodis, H. N., Collins, P., Mack, W. J., & Schierbeck, L. L. (2012). The timing hypothesis for coronary heart disease prevention with hormone therapy: Past, present, and future in perspective. *Climacteric, 15,* 217–228.

Hoefnagels, M. (2013). *Biology essentials.* New York: McGraw-Hill.

Hoelter, L. (2009). Divorce and separation. In D. Carr (Ed.), *Encyclopedia of the life course and human development.* Boston: Gale Cengage.

Hoeve, M., & others. (2012, in press). A meta-analysis of attachment to parents and delinquency. *Journal of Abnormal Child and Adolescent Psychology.*

Hofer, A., & others. (2007). Sex differences in brain activation patterns during processing of positively and negatively balanced emotional stimuli. *Psychological Medicine, 37,* 109–119.

Hofer, S. M., Rast, P., & Piccinin, A. M. (2012). Methodological issues in research on adult development and aging. In S. K. Whitbourne & M. J. Sliwinski (Eds.), *Wiley-Blackwell handbook of adult development and aging.* New York: Wiley.

Hoff, E. (2012, in press). Interpreting the early language trajectories of children from low-SES and language minority homes: Implications for closing achievement gaps. *Developmental Psychology.*

Hoff, E., Laursen, B., & Tardif, T. (2002). Socioeconomic status and parenting. In M. H. Bornstein (Ed.), *Handbook of parenting* (2nd ed.). Mahwah, NJ: Erlbaum.

Hofferth, S. L., & Reid, L. (2002). Early childbearing and children's achievement behavior over time. *Perspectives on Sexual and Reproductive Health, 34,* 41–49.

Hoffman, E., & Ewen, D. (2007). Supporting families, nurturing young children. *CLASP Policy Brief No. 9,* 1–11.

Hoffmeyer, K., & others. (2012). Wnt/B-catenin signaling regulates telomerase in stem cells and cancer cells. *Science, 336,* 1549–1554.

Hogan, M. J. (2012). Prosocial effects of media. *Pediatric Clinics of North America, 59,* 635–645.

Hogan, M. J., Kelly, C. A. M., Verrier, D., Newell, J., Hasher, L., & Robertson, I. H. (2009). Optimal time-of-day and consolidation of learning in younger and older adults. *Experimental Aging Research, 28,* 107–128.

Hogerbrugge, M. J., & Komter, A. E. (2012). Solidarity and ambivalence: Comparing two perspectives on intergenerational relations using longitudinal panel data. *Journals of Gerontology B: Psychological Sciences and Social Sciences, 67,* 372–383.

Holahan, C. J., & others. (2012). Wine consumption and 20-year mortality among late-life moderate drinkers. *Journal of Studies in Alcohol and Drugs, 73,* 80–88.

Holden, G. W., Vittrup, B., & Rosen, L. H. (2011). Families, parenting, and discipline. In M. K. Underwood & L. H. Rosen (Eds.), *Social development.* New York: Guilford.

Holland, A. S., & Roisman, G. I. (2010). Adult attachment security and young adults' dating relationships over time: Self-reported, observational, and physiological evidence. *Developmental Psychology, 46,* 552–557.

Hollister, M. (2011). Employment stability in the U.S. labor market: Rhetoric versus reality. *Annual Review of Sociology* (Vol. 37). Palo Alto, CA: Annual Reviews.

Holloway, D. (2010). Clinical update on hormone replacement therapy. *British Journal of Nursing, 19,* 496, 498–504.

Holloway, I. W., & others. (2012, in press). Effects of sexual expectancies on early sexualized behavior among urban minority youth. *Journal of the Society for Social Work and Research.*

Holm, A. L., & Severinsson, E. (2012). Systematic review of emotional state and self-management of widows. *Nursing and Health Sciences, 14,* 109–120.

Holman, A., & Sillars, A. (2012). Talk about "hooking up": The influence of college student social networks on nonrelationship sex. *Health Communication, 27,* 205–217.

Holmes, L. B. (2011). Human teratogens: Update 2010. *Birth Defects Research Part A: Clinical and Molecular Teratology, 91,* 1–7.

Holmes, L. B., & Westgate, M. N. (2011). Inclusion and exclusion criteria for malformations in newborn infants exposed to potential teratogens. *Birth Defects Research Part A: Clinical and Molecular Teratology, 91,* 807–812.

Holmes, R. M., Little, K. C., & Welsh, D. (2009). Dating and romantic relationships, adulthood. In D. Carr (Ed.), *Encyclopedia of the life course and human development.* Boston: Gale Cengage.

Holmes, T. H., & Rahe, R. H. (1967). The social readjustment rating scale. *Journal of Psychosomatic Research. 11,* 213–218.

Holsen, I., Carlson Jones, D., & Skogbrott Birkeland, M. (2012). Body image satisfaction among Norwegian adolescents and young adults: A longitudinal study of the influence of interpersonal relationships and BMI. *Body Image, 9,* 201–208.

Holtz, P., & Appel, M. (2011). Internet use and video gaming predict problem behavior in early adolescence. *Journal of Adolescence, 17,* 37–44.

Holwerda, T. J., & others. (2012). Increased risk of mortality associated with social isolation in older men: Only when feeling lonely? Results from the Amsterdam Study of the Elderly (AMSTEL). *Psychological Medicine, 42,* 843–853.

Hooper, S. R., & others. (2008). Executive functions in young males with fragile X syndrome in comparison to mental age-matched controls: baseline findings from a longitudinal study. *Neuropsychology, 22,* 36–47.

Hooyman, N. R., & Kiyak, H. A. (2011). *Social gerontology* (9th ed.). Upper Saddle River, NJ: Pearson.

Hopkins, B. (1991). Facilitating early motor development: An intracultural study of West Indian mothers and their infants living in Britain. In J. K. Nugent, B. M. Lester, & T. B. Brazelton (Eds.), *The cultural context of infancy:* Vol. 2. *Multicultural and interdisciplinary approaches to parent-infant relations.* Westport, CT: Ablex.

Hopkins, B., & Westra, T. (1990). Motor development, maternal expectations, and the role of handling. *Infant Behavior and Development, 13,* 117–122.

Hoppmann, C. A., Gerstorf, D., Smith, J., & Klumb, P. L. (2007). Linking possible selves and behavior: Do domain-specific hopes and fears translate into daily activities in very old age? *Journals of Gerontology B: Psychological Sciences and Social Sciences, 62,* P104–P111.

Horn, J. L., & Donaldson, G. (1980). Cognitive development II: Adulthood development of human abilities. In O. G. Brim & J. Kagan (Eds.), *Constancy and change in human development.* Cambridge, MA: Harvard University Press.

Horne, R. S., Franco, P., Adamson, T. M., Groswasser, J., & Kahn, A. (2002). Effects of body position on sleep and arousal characteristics in infants. *Early Human Development, 69,* 25–33.

Hornor, G. (2012). Medical evaluation for child physical abuse: What the PNP needs to know. *Journal of Pediatric Health Care, 26,* 163–170.

Horowitz, E. K. (2013). *Becoming a second language teacher* (2nd ed.). Boston: Allyn & Bacon.

Hospital for Sick Children, Dipchard, A., Friedman, J., Gupta, S., Bismilla, Z., & Lam, C. (2010). *The Hospital for Sick Children's handbook of pediatrics* (11th ed.). London: Elsevier.

Houde, O., & others. (2011). Functional magnetic resonance imaging study of Piaget's conservation-of-number task in preschool and school-age children: A neo-Piagetian approach. *Journal of Experimental Child Psychology, 110*(3), 332–346.

House, J. S., Landis, K. R., & Umberson, D. (1988). Social relationships and health. *Science, 241,* 540–545.

Houston, D., Golinkoff, R., Ma, W., & Hirsh-Pasek, I. (2012, in press). Word learning in infant- and adult-directed speech. *Language Learning and Development.*

Howe, G. W., Homberger, A. P., Weihs, K., Moreno, F., & Neiderhiser, J. M. (2012). Higher-order structure in the trajectories of depression and anxiety following sudden involuntary unemployment. *Journal of Abnormal Psychology, 121,* 325–338.

Howe, N., Ross, H. S., & Recchia, H. (2011). Sibling relations in early and middle childhood. In P. K. Smith & C. H. Hart (Eds.), *Wiley-Blackwell handbook of childhood social development* (2nd ed.). New York: Wiley.

Howe, T. E., & others. (2011, July 6). Exercise for preventing and treating osteoporosis in postmenopausal women. *Cochrane Database of Systematic Reviews, 7,* CD00033.

Howell, A., & Evans, G. D. (2011). Hormone replacement therapy and cancer. *Recent Results in Cancer Research, 188,* 115–124.

Howerton, C. L., & Bale, T. L. (2012, in press). Prenatal programming: At the intersection of maternal stress and immune activation. *Hormones and Behavior.*

Howes, C. (2009). Friendship in early childhood. In K. H. Rubin, W. M. Bukowski, & B. Laursen (Eds.), *Handbook of peer interactions, relationships, and groups.* New York: Guilford.

Hoyer, W. J., & Roodin, P. A. (2009). *Adult development and aging* (6th ed.). New York: McGraw-Hill.

Hoyert, D. L., Mathews, T. J., Meancker, F., Strobino, D. M., & Guyer, B. (2006). Annual summary of vital statistics: 2004. *Pediatrics, 117,* 168–183.

Hoyt, M. A., & Stanton, A. (2012). Adjustment to chronic illness. In A. Baum, T. A. Revenson, & J. Singer (Eds.), *Handbook of health psychology* (2nd ed.). New York: Psychology Press.

HSBC Insurance. (2007). *The future of retirement: The new old age global report.* London: HSBC.

Hsu, J. L. & others. (2008). Gender differences and age-related white matter changes of the human brain: A diffusion tensor imaging study. *NeuroImage, 39,* 566–577.

Huang, H. W., Meyer, A. M., & Federmeier, K. D. (2012). A "concrete view" of aging: Event related potentials reveal age-related changes in basic integrated processes in language. *Neuropsychologia, 50,* 26–35.

Huang, J-H., DeJong, W., Towvim, L. G., & Schneider, S. K. (2009). Sociodemographic and psychobehavioral characteristics of U.S. college students who abstain from alcohol. *Journal of American College Health, 57,* 395–410.

Huang, P. M., Smock, P. J., Manning, W. D., & Bergstrom-Lynch, C. A. (2011). He says, she says: Gender and cohabitation. *Journal of Family Issues, 32,* 876–905.

Huberman, H. S., & Mendelsohn, A. L. (2012). Preventive interventions: Parenting and the home environment. In V. Maholmes & R. B. King (Eds.), *Oxford handbook of poverty and child development.* New York: Oxford University Press.

Hudley, C., & Irving, M. (2012). Ethnic and racial identity in childhood and adolescence. In K. R. Harris, S. Graham, & T. Urdan (Eds.), *APA handbook of educational psychology.* Washington, DC: American Psychological Association.

Huebner, A. M., & Garrod, A. C. (1993). Moral reasoning among Tibetan monks: A study of Buddhist adolescents and young adults in Nepal. *Journal of Cross-Cultural Psychology, 24,* 167–185.

Huesmann, L. R., Dubow, E. F., Eron, L. D., & Boxer, P. (2006). Middle childhood family-contextual and personal factors as predictors of adult outcomes. In A. G. Huston & M. N. Ripke (Eds.), *Developmental contexts in middle childhood: Bridges to adolescence and adulthood.* New York: Cambridge University Press.

Huesmann, L. R., Moise-Titus, J., Podolski, C., & Eron, L. D. (2003). Longitudinal relations between children's exposure to TV violence and their aggressive and violent behavior in young adulthood, 1977–1992. *Developmental Psychology, 39,* 201–221.

Hughes, D., Hagelskamp, C., Way, N., & Foust, M. D. (2009). The role of mothers' and adolescents' perceptions of ethnic-racial socialization in shaping ethnic-racial identity among early adolescent boys and girls. *Journal of Youth and Adolescence, 38,* 605–626.

Hughes, D., Way, N., & Rivas-Drake, D. (2011). Stability and change in private and public ethnic regard among African American, Puerto Rican, Dominican, and Chinese American early adolescents. *Journal of Research on Adolescence, 21,* 861–870.

Hughes, J. F., & Rozen, S. (2012). Genomics and genetics of human and primate Y chromosomes. *Annual Review of Genomics and Human Genetics* (Vol. 13). Palo Alto, CA: Annual Reviews.

Hughes, M. E., Waite, L. J., LaPierre, T. A., & Luo, Y. (2007). All in the family: The impact of caring for grandchildren on grandparents' health. *Journals of Gerontology B: Psychological Sciences and Social Sciences, 62,* S108–S119.

Hughes, S. M., Amadi, B., Mwiya, M., Nkamba, H., Tomkins, A., & Goldblatt, D. (2009). Dendritic cell anergy results from endotoxemia in severe malnutrition. *Journal of Immunology, 183,* 2818–2826.

Huh, S. Y., Rifas-Shiman, S. L., Taveras, E. M., Oken, E., & Gillman, M. W. (2011). Timing of solid food introduction and risk of obesity in preschool children. *Pediatrics, 3,* e544–e551.

Hultsch, D. F., Hertzog, C., Small, B. J., & Dixon, R. A. (1999). Use it or lose it: Engaged lifestyle as a buffer of cognitive decline in aging? *Psychology and Aging, 14,* 245–263.

Hummert, M. L. (2011). Age stereotypes and aging. In K. W. Schaie & S. L. Willis (Eds.), *Handbook of the psychology of aging* (7th ed.). New York: Elsevier.

Hunt, K. J., & others. (2011). Diabetes is more lethal in Mexicans and Mexican Americans compared to non-Hispanic Whites. *Annals of Epidemiology, 21*, 899–906.

Hunter, J. M., & others. (2012). Morphological and pathological evolution of the brain microcirculation in aging and Alzheimer's disease. *PLoS One, 7*(5), e36893.

Hurt, H., Brodsky, N. L., Roth, H., Malmud, F., & Giannetta, J. M. (2005). School performance of children with gestational cocaine exposure. *Neurotoxicology and Teratology, 27*, 203–211.

Hustedt, J. T., Friedman, A. H., & Barnett, W. S. (2012). Investments in early education: Resources at the federal and state levels. In R. C. Pianta (Ed.), *Handbook of early childhood education.* New York: Guilford.

Huston, A. C. (2012). How welfare and employment policies influence children's development. In V. Malholmes & R. King (Eds.), *Oxford handbook of poverty and child development.* New York: Oxford University Press.

Huston, A. C., Epps, S. R., Shim, M. S., Duncan, G. J., Crobsy, D. A., & Ripke, M. N. (2006). Effects of a poverty intervention program last from middle childhood to adolescence. In A. C. Huston & M. N. Ripke (Eds.), *Developmental contexts of middle childhood: Bridges to adolescence and adulthood.* New York: Cambridge University Press.

Huston, A. C., & Ripke, N. N. (2006). Experiences in middle and late childhood and children's development. In A. C. Huston & M. N. Ripke (Eds.), *Developmental contexts in middle childhood.* New York: Cambridge University Press.

Hutchinson, S. L., & Nimrod, G. (2012). Leisure as a resource for successful aging by older adults with chronic health conditions. *International Journal of Aging and Human Development, 74*, 41–65.

Huttenlocher, J., Haight, W., Bruk, A., Seltzer, M., & Lyons, T. (1991). Early vocabulary growth: Relation to language input and gender. *Developmental Psychology, 27*, 236–248.

Huttenlocher, P. R., & Dabholkar, A. S. (1997). Regional differences in synaptogenesis in human cerebral cortex. *Journal of Comparative Neurology, 37*(2), 167–178.

Hwang, S. H., Hwang, J. H., Moon, J. S., & Lee, D. H. (2012). Environmental tobacco smoke and children's health. *Korean Journal of Pediatrics, 55*, 35–41.

Hybels, C. F., & Blazer, D. G. (2004). Epidemiology of the late-life mental disorders. *Clinical Geriatric Medicine, 19*, 663–696.

Hyde, D. C., & Spelke, E. S. (2012, in press). Spatio-temporal dynamics of numerical processing: An ERP source localization study. *Human Brain Mapping.*

Hyde, J. S. (2005). The gender similarities hypothesis. *America Psychologist, 60*, 581–592.

Hyde, J. S. (2007). *Half the human experience* (6th ed.). Boston: Houghton Mifflin.

Hyde, J. S., & DeLamater, J. D. (2011). *Understanding human sexuality* (11th ed.). New York: McGraw-Hill.

Hyde, J. S., & Else-Quest, N. (2013). *Half the human experience* (8th ed.). Boston: Cengage.

Hyde, J. S., Lindberg, S. M., Linn, M. C., Ellis, A. B., & Williams, C. C. (2008). Gender similarities characterize math performance. *Science, 321*, 494–495.

Hymel, S., Closson, L. M., Caravita, C. S., & Vaillancourt, T. (2011). Social status among peers: From sociometric attraction to peer acceptance to perceived popularity. In P. K. Smith & C. H. Hart (Eds.), *Wiley-Blackwell handbook of childhood social development* (2nd ed.). New York: Wiley.

Hyoun, S. C., Obican, S. G., & Scialli, A. R. (2012). Teratogen update: Methotrexate. *Birth Defects Research A: Clinical and Molecular Teratology, 94*, 187–204.

Hyson, M. C., Copple, C., & Jones, J. (2006). Early childhood development and education. In W. Damon & R. Lerner (Eds.), *Handbook of child psychology* (6th ed.). New York: Wiley.

I

Ibrahim, R., & Eviatar, Z. (2012, in press). The contribution of two hemispheres to lexical decision in different languages. *Behavioral and Brain Functions.*

Ickovics, J. R., & others. (2011). Effects of group prenatal care on psychosocial risk in pregnancy: Results from a randomized controlled trial. *Psychology and Health, 26*, 235–250.

"I Have a Dream" Foundation. (2012). *About us.* Retrieved June 3, 2012, from www.ihad.org

Ige, F., & Shelton, D. (2004). Reducing the risk of sudden infant death syndrome (SIDS) in African-American communities. *Journal of Pediatrics, Nursing, 19*, 290–292.

Impett, E. A., Schoolder, D., Tolman, L., Sorsoli, L., & Henson, J. M. (2008). Girls' relationship authenticity and self-esteem across adolescence, *Developmental Psychology, 44*, 722–733.

Insel, P. M., & Roth, W. T. (2012). *Connect core concepts in health* (12th ed.). New York: McGraw-Hill.

International Montessori Council. (2006). Larry Page and Sergey Brin, founders of Google.com, credit their Montessori education for much of their success on prime-time television. Retrieved June 24, 2006, from http://www.Montessori.org/enews/Barbara_walters.html

Iovannone, R. (2013). Teaching students with autism spectrum disorders. In B. G. Cook & M. G. Tankerslee (Ed.), *Research based practices in special education.* Upper Saddle River, NJ: Pearson.

Ip, S., Chung, M., Raman, G., Trikaliinos, T. A., & Lau, J. (2009). A summary of the Agency for Healthcare Research and Quality's evidence report on breastfeeding in developed countries. *Breastfeeding Medicine, 4*(Suppl. 1), S17–S30.

Iqbal, M., & others. (2012). Placental drug transporters and their role in fetal protection. *Placenta, 33*, 137–142.

Irish, C. (2011). Home health care: Helping to prevent and treat diabetes. *Caring, 30*, 28–32.

Iruka, I. U., Laforett, D. R., & Odom, E. C. (2012, in press). Examining the validity of the family investment and stress models and relationships to children's school readiness across five cultural groups. *Journal of Family Psychology.*

Isaacs, B. (2012). *Understanding the Montessori approach: Early years education practice.* New York: Routledge.

Ishaque, S., & others. (2011). Effectiveness of interventions to screen and manage infections during pregnancy on reducing stillbirths: A review. *BMC Public Health, 11*(Suppl. 3), S3.

Issel, L. M., & others. (2011). A review of prenatal home-visiting effectiveness for improving birth outcomes. *Journal of Obstetrics, Gynecologic, and Neonatal Nursing, 40*, 157–165.

Iwasa, H., Masul, Y., Gondo, Y., Inagaki, H., Kawaal, C., & Suzuki, T. (2008). Personality and all-cause mortality among older adults dwelling in a Japanese community: A five-year population-based prospective cohort study. *American Journal of Geriatric Psychiatry, 16*, 399–405.

Izard, C. E. (2009). Emotion theory and research: Highlights, unanswered questions, and emerging issues. *Annual Review of Psychology* (Vol. 60). Palo Alto, CA: Annual Reviews.

Izard, V., Dehaene-Lambertz, G., & Dehaene, S. (2008). Distinct cerebral pathways for object identity and number in human infants. *PLOS Biology, 6*, e11.

Izard, V., Pica, P., Dehaene, S., Hinchey, D., & Spelke, E. S. (2011). Geometry as a universal mental construction. In E. Brannon & S. Dehaene (Eds.), *Space, time, and number in the brain.* New York: Oxford University Press.

J

Jackson, A., Purkis, J., Burnham, E., Hundt, G. L., & Blaxter, L. (2010). Views of relatives, careers, and staff on end-of-life care pathways. *Emergency Nurse, 17*, 22–26.

Jackson, C. A., Henderson, M., Frank, J. W., & Haw, S. J. (2012). An overview of prevention of multiple risk behavior in adolescence and young adulthood. *Journal of Public Health, 34* (Suppl. 1), S131–S140.

Jackson, J. J., & others. (2009). Not all conscientiousness scales change alike: A multimethod, multisample study of age differences in the facets of conscientiousness. *Journal of Personality and Social Psychology, 96*, 446–459.

Jackson, J. S., Govia, I. O., & Sellers, S. L. (2011). Racial and ethnic influences over the life course. In R. H. Binstock & L. K. George (Eds.), *Handbook of aging and the social sciences* (7th ed.). New York: Elsevier.

Jackson, L. A., & others. (2012). The digital divide. In J. R. Levesque (Ed.), *Encyclopedia of adolescence.* New York: Springer.

Jacobs, J. M., Hammerman-Rozenberg, R., Cohen, A., & Stressman, J. (2008). Reading daily predicts reduced mortality among men from a cohort of community dwelling 70-year-olds. *Journals of Gerontology B: Psychological Sciences and Social Sciences, 63*, S73–S80.

Jacobs-Lawson, J. M., Hershey, D. A., & Neukam, K. A. (2005). Gender differences in factors that influence time spent planning for retirement. *Journal of Women and Aging, 16*, 55–69.

Jaeggi, S. M., Berman, M. G., & Jonides, J. (2009). Training attentional processes. *Trends in Cognitive Science, 37*, 644–654.

Jaffee, S., & Hyde, J. S. (2000). Gender differences in moral orientation: A meta-analysis. *Psychological Bulletin, 126,* 703–726.

Jak, A. J. (2011). The impact of physical and mental activity on cognitive aging. *Current Topics in Behavioral Neurosciences, 10,* 273–291.

James, J., Ellis, B. J., Scholmer, G. L., & Garber, J. (2012). Sex-specific pathways to early puberty, sexual debut, and sexual risk taking: Tests of an integrated evolutionary-developmental model. *Developmental Psychology, 48,* 687–702.

James, W. (1890/1950). *The principles of psychology.* New York: Dover.

Jan, J. E., & others. (2010). Long-term sleep disturbances in children: A cause of neuronal loss. *European Journal of Pediatric Neurology, 14,* 380–390.

Jansen, J., de Weerth, C., & Riksen-Walraven, J. M. (2008). Breastfeeding and the mother-infant relationship—A review. *Developmental Review, 28,* 503–521.

Janssen, I., & others. (2005). Comparison of overweight and obesity prevalence in school-aged youth from 34 countries and their relationships with physical activity and dietary patterns. *Obesity Reviews, 6,* 123–132.

Jardri, R., & others. (2012). Assessing fetal response to maternal speech using a noninvasive functional brain imaging technique. *International Journal of Developmental Neuroscience, 30,* 159–161.

Javaroni, V., & Neves, M. F. (2012, in press). Erectile dysfunction and hypertension: Impact on cardiovascular risk and treatment. *International Journal of Hypertension.*

Jazaieri, H., Goldin, P. R., Werner, K., Ziv, M., & Gross, J. J. (2012, in press). A randomized trial of MBSR versus aerobic exercise for social anxiety disorder. *Journal of Clinical Psychology.*

Jefferson, A. L., & others. (2011). A life course model of cognitive activities, socioeconomic status, education, reading ability, and cognition. *Journal of the American Geriatric Society, 59,* 1403–1411.

Jenkins, J. M., & Astington, J. W. (1996). Cognitive factors and family structure associated with theory of mind development in young children. *Developmental Psychology, 32,* 70–78.

Jennings, J. R., & Egizio, V. (2012). How psychophysiology contributes to health psychology. In A. Baum, T. R. Revenson, & J. Singer (Eds.), *Handbook of health psychology* (2nd ed.). New York: Psychology Press.

Jerant, A., Chapman, B., Duberstein, P., Robbins, J., & Franks, P. (2011). Personality and medication non-adherence among older adults enrolled in a six-year trial. *British Journal of Health Psychology, 16,* 151–159.

Jeret, J. S. (2011). Evidence-based guidelines update: Determining brain death in adults: Report of the Quality Standards Subcommittee of the American Academy of Neurology. *Neurology, 76,* 307–308.

Jex, S. M., Swanson, N., & Grubb, P. (2013). Healthy workplaces. In I. B. Weiner & others (Eds.), *Handbook of psychology* (2nd ed., Vol. 12). New York: Wiley.

Ji, B. T., & others. (1997). Paternal cigarette smoking and the risk of childhood cancer among offspring of nonsmoking mothers. *Journal of the National Cancer Institute, 89,* 238–244.

Jia, R., & Schoppe-Sullivan, S. J. (2011). Relations between coparenting and father involvement in families with preschool-age children. *Developmental Psychology, 47,* 106–118.

Jiao, S., Ji, G., & Jing, Q. (1996). Cognitive development of Chinese urban only children and children with siblings. *Child Development, 67,* 387–395.

Jin, M. K., Jacobvitz, D., Hagen, N., & Jung, S. H. (2012). Maternal sensitivity and infant attachment security in Korea: Cross-cultural validation of the Strange Situation. *Attachment and Human Development, 14,* 33–44.

Jinyao, Y., & others. (2012, in press). Insecure attachment as a predictor of depressive and anxious symptomatology. *Depression and Anxiety.*

Jitendra, A., & Montague, M. (2013). Strategies for improving student outcomes in mathematical reasoning. In B. G. Cook & M. G. Tankersley (Eds.), *Research-based practices in special education.* Upper Saddle River, NJ: Pearson.

Joel, S., MacDonald, G., & Shimotomai, A. (2011). Conflicting pressures on romantic relationship commitment for anxiously attached individuals. *Journal of Personality, 79,* 51–73.

Joffe, H., & others. (2011). Increased estradiol and improved sleep, but not hot flashes, predict enhanced mood during the menopausal transition. *Journal of Clinical Endocrinology and Metabolism, 90,* E1044–E1054.

Johansson, B., & Berg, A. I. (2012). Effects of remaining time for psychological well-being and cognition. In S. K. Whitbourne & M. Sliwinksi (Eds.), *Wiley-Blackwell handbook of adult development and aging.* New York: Wiley.

Johns Hopkins University. (2006, February 17). Undergraduate honored for launching health program in India. Baltimore: Johns Hopkins University News Releases.

Johnson, A. D., & Brooks-Gunn, J. (2012). Child care and early education for low-income families: Choices and consequences. In V. Maholmes & R. B. King (Eds.), *Oxford handbook of poverty and child development.* New York: Oxford University Press.

Johnson, C. L., & Troll, L. E. (1992). Family functioning in late late life. *Journals of Gerontology, 47,* S66–S72.

Johnson, J. S., & Newport, E. L. (1991). Critical period effects on universal properties of language: The status of subjacency in the acquisition of a second language. *Cognition, 39,* 215–258.

Johnson, L., Giordano, P. C., Manning, W. D., & Longmore, M. A. (2011, in press). Parent-child relations and offending during young adulthood. *Journal of Youth and Adolescence.*

Johnson, M. (2008, April 30). Commentary in R. Highfield *Harvard's baby brain research lab.* Retrieved January 24, 2008, from www.telegraph.co.uk/scienceandtechnology/science/sciencenews/3341166/Harvards-baby-brain-research-lab.html

Johnson, M. D. (2012). *Human biology* (6th ed.). Upper Saddle River, NJ: Pearson.

Johnson, M. H., & de Haan, M. (2012). *Developmental cognitive neuroscience* (3rd ed.). New York: Wiley-Blackwell.

Johnson, M. H., Grossmann, T., and Cohen-Kadosh, K. (2009). Mapping functional brain development: Building a social brain through Interactive Specialization. *Developmental Psychology, 45,* 151–159.

Johnson, S. P. (2004). Development of perceptual completion in infancy. *Psychological Science, 15,* 769–775.

Johnson, S. P. (2009). Developmental origins of object perception. In A. Woodward & A. Needham (Eds.), *Learning and the infant mind.* New York: Oxford University Press.

Johnson, S. P. (2010). Perceptual completion in infancy. In S. P. Johnson (Ed.), *Neoconstructivism: The new science of cognitive development.* New York: Oxford University Press.

Johnson, S. P. (2011). A constructivist view of object perception in infancy. In L. M. Oakes & others (Eds.), *Infant perception and cognition.* New York: Oxford University Press.

Johnson, S. P. (2012, in press). Development of the visual system. In P. Rakic & J. Rubenstein (Eds.), *Developmental neuroscience—Basic and clinical mechanisms.* New York: Oxford University Press.

Johnson, S. P. (2013, in press). Object perception. In P. D. Zelazo (Ed.), *Handbook of developmental psychology.* New York: Oxford University Press.

Johnson, S. P., Bremner, J. G., Slater, A., & Mason, U. (2000). The role of good form in young infants' perception of partly occluded objects. *Journal of Experimental Child Psychology, 76,* 1–25.

Johnson, W., Corley, J., Starr, J. M., & Deary, I. J. (2011). Psychological and physical health at age 70 in the Lothian Birth Cohort 1936: Links with early life IQ, SES, and current cognitive function and neighborhood environment. *Health Psychology, 30,* 1–11.

John-Steiner, V. (2007). Vygotsky on thinking and speaking. In H. Daniels, J. Wertsch, & M. Cole (Eds.), *The Cambridge companion to Vygotsky.* New York: Cambridge University Press.

Johnston, L. D., O'Malley, P. M., Bachman, J. G., & Schulenberg, J. E. (2008a). *Monitoring the Future national survey results on drug use, 1975–2007 (Vol. 1, Secondary school students)* (NIH Publication No. 08-6418A). Bethesda, MD: National Institute on Drug Abuse.

Johnston, L. D., O'Malley, P. M., Bachman, J. G., & Schulenberg, J. E. (2008b). *Monitoring the Future national survey results on drug use, 1975–2007 (Vol. 2: College students and adults ages 19–45).* Washington, DC: National Institute of Drug Abuse.

Johnston, L. D., O'Malley, P. M., Bachman, J. G., & Schulenberg, J. E. (2011). *Monitoring the Future national survey results on drug use, 1975–2010 (Vol. 2: College students and adults ages 19–50).* Bethesda, MD: National Institute on Drug Abuse.

Johnston, L. D., O'Malley, P. M., Bachman, J. G., & Schulenberg, J. E. (2012). *Monitoring the Future national survey results on adolescent drug use: Overview of key findings, 2011.* Institute for Social Research, University of Michigan, Ann Arbor.

Jokela, M., & others. (2010). From midlife to early old age: Health trajectories associated with retirement. *Epidemiology, 21,* 284–290.

Jokinen-Gordon, H. (2012). Still penalized? Parity, age at first birth, and women's income in later life. *Journal of Women and Aging, 24,* 227–241.

Jolivette, K. & others. (2013). Strategies to prevent problem behavior. In B. G. Cook & M. G. Tankersley (Eds.), *Research-based practices in special education.* Upper Saddle River, NJ: Pearson.

Jolly, C. A. (2005). Diet manipulation and prevention of aging, cancer, and autoimmune disease. *Current Opinions in Clinical Nutrition and Metabolic Care, 8,* 382–387.

Jones, D., & others. (2010). The impact of the Fast Track prevention trial on health services utilization by youth at risk for conduct problems. *Pediatrics, 125,* 130–136.

Jones, L., & others. (2012). Pain management for women in labor: An overview of systematic reviews. *Cochrane Database of Systematic Reviews, 14*(3), CD009234.

Jones, M. C. (1965). Psychological correlates of somatic development. *Child Development, 36,* 899–911.

Jones, M. D., & Galliher, R. V. (2007). Ethnic identity and psychosocial functioning in Navajo adolescents. *Journal of Research on Adolescence, 17,* 683–696.

Jones, N. A. (2012). Delayed reactive cries demonstrate emotional and physiological dysregulation in newborns of depressed mothers. *Biological Psychology, 89,* 374–381.

Jones, P. S., & others. (2011). Development of a caregiver empowerment model to promote positive outcomes. *Journal of Family Nursing, 17,* 11–28.

Jonson-Reid, M., Kohl, P. L., & Drake, B. (2012). Child and adolescent outcomes of chronic child maltreatment. *Pediatrics, 129,* 839–845.

Jopp, D., & Rott, C. (2006). Adaptation in very old age: Exploring the role of resources and attitudes for centenarians' happiness. *Psychology and Aging, 21,* 266–280.

Jose, A., O'Leary, K. D., & Moyer, A. (2010). Does premarital cohabitation predict subsequent marital stability and marital quality? A meta-analysis. *Journal of Marriage and the Family, 72,* 105–116.

Joseph, J. (2006). *The missing gene.* New York: Algora.

Jozkowski, K. N., & Sanders, N. A. (2012). Health and sexual outcomes of women who have experienced forced or coercive sex. *Women's Health, 52,* 108–118.

Judd, F. K., Hickey, M., & Bryant, C. (2012). Depression and midlife: Are we overpathologizing the menopause? *Journal of Affective Disorders, 136,* 199–211.

Juffer, F., & van IJzendoorn, M. H. (2007). Adoptees do not lack self-esteem: A meta-analysis of studies on self-esteem of transracial, international, and domestic adoptees. *Psychological Bulletin, 133,* 1067–1083.

Jung, C. (1933). *Modern man in search of a soul.* New York: Harcourt Brace.

Junger, S., & others. (2012, in press). Consensus building in palliative care: A Europe-wide delphi study on common understandings and conceptual differences. *Journal of Pain and Symptom Management.*

Juraska, J. M., & Lowry, N. C. (2012). Neuroanatomical changes associated with cognitive aging. *Current Topics in Behavioral Neuroscience, 10,* 137–162.

Just, M. A., Keller, T. A., Malave, V. L., Kana, R. K., & Varma, S. (2012). Autism as a neural systems disorder: A theory of frontal-posterior underconnectivity. *Neuroscience and Biobehavioral Reviews, 36,* 1292–1313.

K

Kagan, J. (1987). Perspectives on infancy. In J. D. Osofsky (Ed.), *Handbook on infant development* (2nd ed.). New York: Wiley.

Kagan, J. (2002). Behavioral inhibition as a temperamental category. In R. J. Davidson, K. R. Scherer, & H. H. Goldsmith (Eds.), *Handbook of affective sciences.* New York: Oxford University Press.

Kagan, J. (2008). Fear and wariness. In M. M. Haith & J. B. Benson (Eds.), *Encyclopedia of infant and early childhood development.* Oxford, UK: Elsevier.

Kagan, J. (2010). Emotions and temperament. In M. H. Burnstein (Ed.), *Handbook of cultural developmental science.* New York: Psychology Press.

Kagan, J. (2013). Temperamental contributions to inhibited and uninhibited profiles. In P. D. Zelazo (Ed.), *Oxford handbook of developmental psychology.* New York: Oxford University Press.

Kagan, J. J., Kearsley, R. B., & Zelazo, P. R. (1978). *Infancy: Its place in human development.* Cambridge, MA: Harvard University Press.

Kagan, S. H. (2008). Faculty profile, University of Pennsylvania School of Nursing. Retrieved January 5, 2008, from www.nursing.upenn.edu/faculty/profile.asp

Kahn, J. A., & others. (2008). Patterns and determinants of physical activity in U.S. adolescents. *Journal of Adolescent Health, 42,* 369–377.

Kail, M., Lemaire, P., & Lecacheur, M. (2012). Online grammaticality judgments in Fench young and older adults. *Experimental Aging Research, 38,* 186–207.

Kail, R. V. (2007). Longitudinal evidence that increases in processing speed and working memory enhance children's reasoning. *Psychological Science, 18,* 312–313.

Kalache, A., & Blewitt, R. (2012). Human rights in older age. *Global population aging: Peril or promise?* Geneva, SWIT: World Economic Forum.

Kalder, M., Knoblauch, K., Hrgovic, I., & Munstedt, K. (2011). Use of complementary and alternative medicine during pregnancy and delivery. *Archives of Gynecology and Obstetrics, 283*(3), 475–482.

Kalish, R. A. (1981). *Death, grief, and caring relationships,* Monterey, CA: Brooks/Cole.

Kalish, R. A. (1987). Death. In G. L. Maddox (Ed.), *Encyclopedia of aging.* New York: Springer.

Kalish, R. A., & Reynolds, D. K. (1976). *An overview of death and ethnicity.* Farmingdale, NY: Baywood.

Kamp, B. J., Wellman, N. S., & Russell, C. (2010). Position of the American Dietetic Association, American Society for Nutrition, and Society for Nutrition Education: Food and nutrition programs for community-residing older adults. *Journal of Nutrition Education and Behavior, 42,* 72–82.

Kanner, A. D., Coyne, J. C., Schaefer, C., & Lazarus, R. S. (1981). Comparison of two modes of stress measurement: Daily hassles and uplifts versus major life events. *Journal of Behavioral Medicine, 4,* 1–39.

Kapornai, K., & Vetro, A. (2008). Depression in children. *Current Opinion in Psychiatry, 21,* 1–7.

Kar, B. R., Rao, S. L., & Chandramouli, B. A. (2008). Cognitive development in children with chronic energy malnutrition. *Behavioral and Brain Functions, 4,* 31.

Karasik, R. J., & Hamon, R. R. (2007). Cultural diversity and aging families. In B. S. Trask & R. R. Hamon (Eds.), *Cultural diversity and families.* Thousand Oaks, CA: Sage.

Karg, K., & Sen, S. (2012, in press). Gene x environment interaction models in psychiatry. *Current Topics in Behavioral Neuroscience.*

Karniol, R., Grosz, E., & Schorr, I. (2003). Caring, gender-role orientation, and volunteering. *Sex Roles, 49,* 11–19.

Karoly, L. A., & Bigelow, J. H. (2005). *The economics of investing in universal preschool education in California.* Santa Monica, CA: RAND Corporation.

Karreman, A., van Tuijl, C., van Aken, M. A., & Dekovic, M. (2008). Parenting, coparenting, and effortful control in preschoolers. *Journal of Family Psychology, 22,* 30–40.

Kastenbaum, R. J. (2009). *Death, society, and human experience* (10th ed.). Boston: Allyn & Bacon.

Kastenbaum, R. J. (2012). *Death, society, and human experience* (11th ed.). Boston: Allyn & Bacon.

Kaszniak, A.W., & Menchola, M. (2012). Behavioral neuroscience of emotion in aging. *Current Topics in Behavioral Neuroscience, 10,* 51–56.

Kato, T. (2005). The relationship between coping with stress due to romantic break-ups and mental health. *Japanese Journal of Social Psychology, 20,* 171–180.

Katz, E. S., Mitchell, R. B., & D'Ambrosio, C. M. (2012). Obstructive sleep apnea in infants. *American Journal of Respiratory and Critical Care Medicine, 185,* 805–816.

Katz, L. (1999). Curriculum disputes in early childhood education. *ERIC Clearinghouse on Elementary and Early Childhood Education,* Document EDO-PS-99-13.

Katz, P. R., Karuza, J., Intrator, O., & Mor, V. (2009). Nursing home physician specialists: A response to the workforce crisis in long-term care. *Annals of Internal Medicine, 150,* 411–413.

Katzel, L. I., & Steinbrenner, G. M. (2012). Physical exercise and health. In S. K. Whitbourne & M. J. Sliwinski (Eds.), *Wiley-Blackwell handbook of adult development and aging.* New York: Wiley.

Katzmarzyk, P. T., & others. (2012). Body mass index and risk of cardiovascular disease, cancer, and all-cause mortality. *Canadian Journal of Public Health, 103,* 147–151.

Kauffman, J. M., McGee, K., & Brigham, M. (2004). Enabling or disabling? Observations on changes in special education. *Phi Delta Kappan, 85,* 613–620.

Kaufman, J. C., & Sternberg, R. J. (2013, in press). The creative mind. In C. Jones, M. Lorenzen, & R. F. Proctor (Eds.), *Handbook of psychology: Experimental psychology* (Vol. 4). New York: Wiley.

Kaur, A., & Phadke, S. R. (2012, in press). Analysis of short stature cases referred for genetic evaluation. *Indian Journal of Pediatrics.*

Kavsek, M. (2004). Predicting IQ from infant visual habituation and dishabituation: A meta-analysis. *Journal of Applied Developmental Psychology, 25,* 369–393.

Kawabata, Y., Tseng, W. L., Murray-Close, D., & Crick, N. R. (2012, in press). Developmental trajectories of Chinese children's relational and physical aggression: Associations with social-psychological adjustment problems. *Journal of Abnormal Child Psychology.*

Keating, D. P. (1990). Adolescent thinking. In S. S. Feldman & G. R. Elliott (Eds.), *At the threshold: The developing adolescent.* Cambridge, MA: Harvard University Press.

Keating, D. P. (2004). Cognitive and brain development. In R. Lerner & L. Steinberg (Ed.), *Handbook of Adolescent Psychology.* New York: Wiley.

Keating, D. P. (2009). Developmental science and giftedness: An integrated life-span framework. In F. D. Horowitz, R. F. Subotnik, & D. J. Matthews (Eds.), *The development of giftedness and talent across the life span.* Washington, DC: American Psychological Association.

Keen, R. (2005). Unpublished review of J. W. Santrock's *Topical approach to life-span development* (3rd ed.). New York: McGraw-Hill.

Keen, R. (2011). The development of problem solving in young children: A critical cognitive skill. *Annual Review of Psychology* (Vol. 62). Palo Alto, CA: Annual Reviews.

Keijsers, L., & Laird, R. D. (2010). Introduction to special issue: Careful conversations: Adolescents managing their parents' access to information. *Journal of Adolescence, 33,* 255–259.

Keiley-Moore, J. (2009). Chronic illness, adulthood and later life. In D. Carr (Ed.), *Encyclopedia of the life course and human development.* Boston: Gale Cengage.

Keller, A., Ford, L., & Meacham, J. (1978). Dimensions of self concept in preschool children. *Developmental Psychology, 14,* 485–489.

Keller, H., Kartner, J., Borke, J., Yvosi, R., & Kleis, A. (2005). Parenting styles and the development of the categorical self: A longitudinal study on mirror self-recognition in Cameroonian Nso and German families. *International Journal of Behavioral Development, 29,* 496–504.

Kellman, P. J., & Arterberry, M. E. (2006). Infant visual perception. In W. Damon & R. Lerner (Eds.), *Handbook of child psychology* (6th ed.). New York: Wiley.

Kellman, P. J., & Banks, M. S. (1998). Infant visual perception. In W. Damon (Eds.), *Handbook of child psychology* (5th ed., Vol. 2). New York: Wiley.

Kelly, A. J., Hertzog, C., Hayes, M. G., & Smith, A. D. (2012, in press). The effects of age and focality on delay-execute prospective memory. *Neuropsychology, Development, and Cognition B. Aging, Neuropsychology, and Cognition.*

Kelly, D. J., & others. (2005). Three-month-olds, but not newborns, prefer own-race faces. *Developmental Science, 8,* F31–F36.

Kelly, D. J., & others. (2007). Cross-race preferences for same-race faces extend beyond the African versus Caucasian contrast in 3-month-old infants. *Infancy, 11,* 87–95.

Kelly, J. P., Borchert, J., & Teller, D. Y. (1997). The development of chromatic and achromatic sensitivity in infancy as tested with the sweep VEP. *Vision Research, 37,* 2057–2072.

Kemnitz, J. W. (2011). Calorie restriction and aging in nonhuman primates. *ILAR Journal, 52,* 66–77.

Kempermann, G., van Praag, H., & Gage, F. H. (2000). Activity-dependent regulation of neuronal plasticity and self repair. *Progress in Brain Research 127,* 35–48.

Kendler, K. S., & others. (2012, in press). Genetic and familial environmental influences on the risk for drug abuse: A national Swedish adoption study. *Archives of General Psychiatry.*

Kendrick, K., Jutengren, G., & Stattin, H. (2012, in press). The protective role of supportive friends against bullying perpetration and victimization. *Journal of Adolescence.*

Kennell, J. H. (2006). Randomized controlled trial of skin-to-skin contact from birth versus conventional incubator for physiological stabilization in 1200g to 2199g newborns. *Acta Paediatica (Swedent), 95,* 15–16.

Kennell, J. H., & McGrath, S. K. (1999). Commentary: Practical and humanistic lessons from the third world for perinatal caregivers everywhere. *Birth, 26,* 9–10.

Kenney, J. (2012). *Loosening the grip: A handbook of alcohol information* (10th ed.). New York: McGraw-Hill.

Kern, L., Hilt-Panehon, A., & Mukherjee, A. D. (2013). Strategies for addressing internalizing behavior problems. In B. G. Cook & M. G. Tankersley (Eds.), *Research-based practices in special education.* Upper Saddle River, NJ: Pearson.

Kerns, K. A., & Seibert, A. C. (2012, in press). Finding your way through the thicket: Promising approaches to assessing attachment in middle childhood. In E. Waters & B. Vaughn (Eds.), *Measuring attachment.* New York: Guilford.

Kerns, K. A., Siener, S., & Brumariu, L. E. (2011). Mother-child relationships, family context, and child characteristics as predictors of anxiety symptoms in middle childhood. *Development and Psychopathology, 23,* 593–604.

Ketcham, C. J., & Stelmach, G. E. (2001). Age-related declines in motor control. In J. E. Birren & K. W. Schale (Eds.), *Handbook of the psychology of aging* (5th ed.). San Diego: Academic Press.

Keyes, C. L. M., & Ryff, C. D. (1998). Generativity in adult lives: Social structure contours and quality of life consequences. In D. P. McAdams & E. de St. Aubin (Eds.). *Generativity and adult development: How and why we care for the next generation.* Washington, DC: American Psychological Association.

Khan, M. R., Berger, A. T., Wells, B. E., & Cleland, C. M. (2012). Longitudinal associations between adolescent alcohol use and adult sexual risk behavior and sexually transmitted infection in the United States: Assessment of differences by race. *American Journal of Public Health, 102,* 867–876.

Khandekar, A. A., Augustyn, M., Sanders, L., & Zuckerman, B. (2011). Improving early literacy promotion: A quality-improvement project for Reach Out and Read. *Pediatrics, 127,* e1067–e1072.

Khashan, A. S., Baker, P. N., & Kenny, L. C. (2010). Preterm birth and reduced birthweight in first and second teenage pregnancies: A register-based cohort study. *BMC Pregnancy and Childbirth, 10,* 36.

Khurana, A., & others. (2012, in press). Early adolescent sexual debut: The mediating role of working memory ability, sensation seeking, and impulsivity. *Developmental Psychology.*

Kidd, A. R., & Bao, J. (2012, in press). Recent advances in the study of age-related hearing loss: A mini-review. *Gerontology.*

Kidd, E. (2012). Implicit statistical learning is directly associated with the acquisition of syntax. *Developmental Psychology, 48,* 171–184.

Kielsmeier, J. (2011). The time is now. *Prevention Researcher, 18,* 3–7.

Kilic, S., & others. (2012, in press). Environmental tobacco smoke exposure during intrauterine period promotes granulosa cell apoptosis: A prospective, randomized study. *Journal Maternal-Fetal and Neonatal Medicine.*

Kim, H., & Johnson, S. P. (2010). Infant perception. In B. Goldstein (Ed.), *Encyclopedia of perception.* Thousand Oaks, CA: Sage.

Kim, J., & others. (2006). Trends in overweight from 1980 through 2001 among preschool-aged children enrolled in a health maintenance organization. *Obesity, 14,* 1107–1112.

Kim, J. E., & Moen, P. (2002). Retirement transitions, gender, and psychological well-being: A life-course, ecological model. *Journals of Gerontology B: Psychological Sciences and Social Sciences, 57B,* P212–P222.

Kim, J. H., Ko, J. H., Lee, D. C., Lim, I., & Bang, H. (2012, in press). Habitual physical exercise has beneficial effects on telomere length in postmenopausal women. *Menopause.*

Kim, K. H. (2010, May). Unpublished data. School of Education, College of William & Mary, Williamsburg, VA.

Kim, S. H. (2009). The influence of finding meaning and worldview of accepting death on anger among bereaved older spouses. *Aging and Mental Health, 13,* 38–45.

Kim, S., & others. (2012). Telomere maintenance genes SIRT1 and XRCC6 impact age-related decline in telomere length but only SIRT1 is associated with human longevity. *Biogerontology, 13,* 119–131.

Kim, S. Y., & Giovanello, K. S. (2011). The effects of attention on age-related relational memory deficits: Evidence from a novel attentional manipulation. *Psychology and Aging, 26,* 678–688.

Kimble, M., Neacsiu, A. D., Flack, W. F., & Horner, J. (2008). Risk of unwanted sex for college women: Evidence for a red zone. *Journal of American College Health, 57,* 331–338.

King, L. A. (2013). *Experience psychology* (2nd ed.). New York: McGraw-Hill.

King, L. A., & Hicks, J. A. (2007). Whatever happened to "What might have been?" Regrets, happiness, and maturity. *American Psychologist, 62,* 625–636.

King, P. E., Carr, A., & Boiter, C. (2011). Spirituality, religiosity, and youth thriving. In R. M. Lerner, J. V. Lerner, & J. B. Benson (Eds.), *Advances in child development and behavior: Positive youth development.* New York: Elsevier.

King, P. E., Ramos, J. S., & Clardy, C. E. (2013, in press). Searching for the sacred: Religious and spiritual development among adolescents. In K. I.

Pargament, J. Exline, & J. Jones (Eds.), *APA handbook of psychology, religion, and spirituality.* Washington, DC: American Psychological Association.

King, P. E., & Roeser, R.W. (2009). Religion and spirituality in adolescent development. In R. M. Lerner & L. Steinberg (Eds.), *Handbook of adolescent psychology* (3rd ed.). New York: Wiley.

King, V., & Scott, M. E. (2005). A comparison of cohabiting relationships among older and younger adults. *Journal of Marriage and the Family, 67,* 271–285.

Kingsmore, S. F., & others. (2012, in press). Next-generation community genetics for low- and middle-income countries. *Genomic Medicine.*

Kini, S., Morrell, D., Thong, K. J., Kopakaki, A., Hillier, S., & Irvine, D. S. (2010). Lack of impact of semen quality on fertilization in assisted conception. *Scottish Medicine, 55,* 20–23.

Kinney, J. (2012). *Loosening the grip: A handbook of alcohol information* (10th ed.). New York: McGraw-Hill.

Kins, E., & Beyers, W. (2010). Failure to launch, failure to achieve criteria for adulthood? *Journal of Adolescent Research, 25,* 743–777.

Kirk, R. E. (2013, in press). Experimental design. In I. B. Weiner & others (Eds.), *Handbook of psychology* (2nd ed., Vol. 2). New York: Wiley.

Kirkevold, M., Moyle, W., Wilkinson, C., Meyer, J., & Haughe, S. (2012, in press). Facing the challenge of adapting to life 'alone' in old age: The influence of losses. *Journal of Advanced Nursing.*

Kirkham, N. Z., Wagner, J. B., Swan, K. A., & Johnson, S. P. (2012). Sound support: Intermodal information facilitates infants' perception of an occluded trajectory. *Infant Behavior and Development, 35,* 174–178.

Kirkorian, H. L., Anderson, D. R., & Keen, R. (2012). Age differences in online processing of video: An eye movement study. *Child Development, 83,* 497–507.

Kirshner, H. S. (2012, in press). Antiplatelet and anticoagulation strategies in the prevention and treatment of ischemic stroke. *Current Pharmaceutical Design.*

Kisilevsky, B. S., & others. (2003). Effects of experience on fetal voice recognition. *Psychological Science, 14,* 220–224.

Kisilevsky, B. S., & others. (2009). Fetal sensitivity to properties of maternal speech and language. *Infant Behavior and Development, 32,* 59–71.

Kistner, J. A., David-Ferdon, C. F., Repper, K. K., & Joiner, T. E. (2006). Bias and accuracy of children's perceptions of peer acceptance: Prospective associations with depressive symptoms. *Journal of Abnormal Child Psychology, 34,* 349–361.

Kitayama, S., & Uskul, A. K. (2011). Culture, mind, and the brain: Current evidence and future directions. *Annual Review of Psychology* (Vol. 62). Palo Alto, CA: Annual Reviews.

Kitsantas, P., & Gaffney, K. F. (2010). Racial/ethnic disparities in infant mortality. *Journal of Perinatal Medicine, 38,* 87–94.

Kitts, R. L., & Goldman, S. J. (2012). Education and depression. *Child and Adolescent Psychiatry Clinics of North America, 21,* 421–426.

Kitzinger, S. (2011). Human rights and midwifery. *Birth, 38,* 86–87.

Kivnik, H. Q., & Sinclair, H. M. (2007). Grandparenthood. In J. E. Birren (Ed.), *Encyclopedia of gerontology* (2nd ed.). San Diego: Academic Press.

Klaczynski, P. (2001). The influence of analytic and heuristic processing on adolescent reasoning and decision making. *Child Development, 72,* 844–861.

Klaus, M., & Kennell, H. H. (1976). *Maternal-infant bonding.* St. Louis: Mosby.

Kliegman, R., Stanton, B., St. Geme, J., Schor, N., & Behrman, R. (2012). *Nelson textbook of pediatrics* (19th ed.). New York: Elsevier.

Klima, C., Norr, K., Conderheld, S., & Handler, A. (2009). Introduction of Centering Pregnancy in a public health clinic. *Journal of Midwifery and Women's Health, 54,* 27–34.

Klimstra, T. A., Hale, W. W., Raaijmakers, Q. A. W., Branje, S. J. T., & Meeus, W. H. H. (2010). Identity formation in adolescence: Change or stability? *Journal of Youth and Adolescence, 39,* 150–162.

Klinenberg, E. (2012). *Going solo: The extraordinary rise and surprising appeal of living alone.* New York: Penguin.

Klomek, A. B., Marrocco, F., Kleinman, M., Schonfeld, I. S., & Gould, M. S. (2008). Peer victimization, depression, and suicidality in adolescents. *Suicide and Life Threatening Behavior, 38,* 166–180.

Knight, B. B., & Kellough, J. (2013, in press). Psychotherapy with older adults within a family context. In I. B. Weiner & others (Eds.), *Handbook of psychology* (2nd ed., Vol. 8). New York: Wiley.

Knight, B. G., Kaski, B., Shurgot, G. R., & Dave, J. (2006). Improving the mental health of older adults. In J. E. Birren & K. W. Schaie (Eds.), *Handbook of the psychology of aging* (6th ed.). San Diego: Academic Press.

Knight, B. G., & Lee, L. (2007). Mental health. In J. E. Birren (Ed.), *Encyclopedia of gerontology* (2nd ed.). San Diego: Academic Press.

Knopik, V. S. (2009). Maternal smoking during pregnancy and child outcomes: Real or spurious effect? *Developmental Neuropsychology, 34,* 1–36.

Knox, M. (2010). On hitting children: A review of corporal punishment in the United States. *Journal of Pediatric Health Care, 24,* 103–107.

Kochanek, K. D., & others. (2011). Deaths: Preliminary data 2009. *National Vital Statistics Reports, 59*(4), 1–51.

Kochanska, G., & Aksan, N. (2007). Conscience in childhood: Past, present, and future. *Merrill-Palmer Quarterly, 50,* 299–310.

Kochanska, G., Barry, R. A., Jimenez, N. B., Hollatz, A. L., & Woodard, J. (2009). Guilt and effortful control: Two mechanisms that prevent disruptive developmental trajectories. *Journal of Personality and Social Psychology, 97,* 322–333.

Kochanska, G., & Kim, S. (2012a, in press). Early attachment organization with both parents and future behavior problems: From infancy to middle childhood. *Child Development.*

Kochanska, G., & Kim, S. (2012b, in press). Toward a new understanding of the legacy of early attachments for future antisocial trajectories: Evidence from two longitudinal studies. *Development and Psychopathology.*

Kochanska, G., Koenig, J. L., Barry, R. A., Kim, S., & Yoon, J. E. (2010). Children's conscience during toddler and preschool years, moral self, and a competent, adaptive developmental trajectory. *Developmental psychology, 46,* 1320–1322.

Koenig, H. G. (2001). Religion and medicine II: Religion, mental health, and related behaviors. *International Journal of Psychiatry, 31,* 97–109.

Koenig, H. G. (2004). Religion, spirituality, and medicine: Research findings and implications for clinical practice. *Southern Medical Journal, 97,* 1194–2000.

Koenig, H. G., & Blazer, D. G. (1996). Depression. In J. E. Birren (Ed.), *Encyclopedia of gerontology* (Vol. 1). San Diego: Academic Press.

Koenig, H. G., & others. (1992). Religious coping and depression in elderly hospitalized medically ill men. *American Journal of Psychiatry, 149,* 1693–1700.

Koenig, L. B., McGue, M., & Iacono, W. G. (2008). Stability and change in religiousness during emerging adulthood. *Developmental Psychology, 44,* 523–543.

Kohen, D. E., Leventhal, T., Dahinten, V. S., & McIntosh, C. N. (2008). Neighborhood disadvantage: Pathways of effects for young children. *Child Development, 79,* 156–169.

Kohen, R., & others. (2011). Response to psychosocial treatment in poststroke depression is associated with serotonin transporter polymorphisms. *Stroke, 42,* 2068–2070.

Kohlberg, L. (1958). The development of modes of moral thinking and choice in the years 10 to 16. Unpublished doctoral dissertation, University of Chicago.

Kohlberg, L. (1969). Stage and sequence: The cognitive-developmental approach to socialization. In D. A. Goslin (Ed.), *Handbook of socialization theory and research.* Chicago: Rand McNally.

Kohlberg, L. (1986). A current statement of some theoretical issues. In S. Modgil & C. Modgil (Eds.), *Lawrence Kohlberg.* Philadelphia: Falmer.

Kohler, M., & others. (2012, in press). Effect of cardiovascular and metabolic disease on cognitive test performance and cognitive change in older adults. *Journal of the American Geriatric Society.*

Kohler, S., & others. (2010). Depressive symptoms and cognitive decline in community-dwelling older adults. *Journal of the American Geriatrics Society, 55,* 873–879.

Kok, R., & others. (2012, in press). Attachment insecurity predicts child active resistance to parental requests in a compliance task. *Child Care Health and Development.*

Kokkevi, A., & others. (2012, in press). Multiple substance use and self-reported suicide attempts by adolescents in 16 countries. *European Child and Adolescent Psychiatry.*

Kokotas, H., & others. (2012). Biomarkers in primary open angle glaucoma. *Clinical Chemistry and Laboratory Medicine, 29,* 1–13.

Kolata, G. (2007, Nov. 11). Chubby gets a second look. *New York Times,* p. D4.

Kolialexi, A. (2012). Early non-invasive detection of fetal Y chromosome sequences in maternal plasma using multiplex PCR. *European Journal of Obstetrics, Gynecology, and Reproductive Medicine, 161,* 34–37.

Kolotkin, R. L., Zunker, C., & Ostbye, T. (2012, in press). Sexual functioning and obesity: A review. *Obesity*.

Konrath, S., Fuhrel-Forbis, A., Lou, A., & Brown, S. (2012). Motives for volunteering are associated with mortality risk in older adults. *Health Psychology, 31*, 87–96.

Koo, Y. J., & others. (2012). Pregnancy outcomes according to increasing maternal age. *Taiwan Journal of Obstetrics and Gynecology, 51*, 60–65.

Kopp, F., & Lindenberger, U. (2011). Effects of joint attention on long-term memory in 9-month-old infants: An event-related potentials study. *Developmental Science, 14*, 660–672.

Korat, O. (2009). The effect of maternal teaching talk on children's emergent literacy as a function of type of activity and maternal education level. *Journal of Applied Developmental Psychology, 30*, 34–42.

Koren, G., & Nordeng, H. (2012, in press). Antidepressant use during pregnancy: The benefit-risk ratio. *American Journal of Obstetrics and Gynecology*.

Kornadt, A. E., & Rothermund, K. (2012). Internalization of age stereotypes into the self-concept via future self-views: A general model and domain-specific differences. *Psychology and Aging, 27*, 164–172.

Koropeckyj-Cox, T. (2009). Singlehood. In D. Carr (Ed.), *Encyclopedia of the life course and human development*, Boston: Gale Cengage.

Koss, K. J. & others. (2011). Understanding children's emotional processes and behavioral strategies in the context of marital conflict. *Journal of Experimental Child Psychology, 109*, 336–352.

Koss, K. J., & others. (2012, in press). Patterns of children's adrenocortical reactivity to interparental conflict and associations with child adjustment: A growth mixture modeling approach. *Developmental Psychology*.

Kostovic, I., Judas, M., & Sedmak, G. (2011). Developmental history of the subplate zone, subplate neurons, and interstitial white matter neurons: Relevance for schizophrenia. *International Journal of Developmental Neuroscience*.

Kotovsky, L., & Baillargeon, R. (1994). Calibration-based reasoning about collision events in 11-month-old infants. *Cognition, 51*, 107–129.

Kotre, J. (1984). *Outliving the self: Generativity and the interpretation of lives*. Baltimore: Johns Hopkins University Press.

Kottak, C. P. (2009). *Cultural anthropology* (13th ed.). New York: McGraw-Hill.

Kottak, C. P., & Kozaitis, K. A. (2012). *On being different* (4th ed.). New York: McGraw-Hill.

Kotter-Gruhn, D., & Smith, J. (2011). When time is running out: Changes in positive future perception and their relationships to changes in well-being in old age. *Psychology and Aging, 26*, 381–387.

Kouwenhoven, P. S., & others. (2012, in press). Opinions of health care professionals and the public after eight years of euthanasia legislation in the Netherlands: A mixed method approach. *Palliative Medicine*.

Kowalski, R. M., Limber, S. P., & Agatston, P. W. (2012). *Cyberbullying* (2nd ed.). New York: Wiley.

Kowaltowski, A. J. (2011). Caloric restriction and redox state: Does this diet increase or decrease oxidant production? *Redox Report, 16*, 237–241.

Kozol, J. (2005). *The shame of the nation*. New York: Crown.

Kraft, E. (2012). Cognitive function, physical activity, and aging: Possible biological links and implications for multimodal interventions. *Neuropsychology, Development, and Cognition. Section B, Aging, Neuropsychology, Cognition, 19*, 248–263.

Kraft, J. M., & others. (2012, in press). Sex education and adolescent sexual behavior: Do community characteristics matter? *Contraception*.

Krakoff, L. R. (2008). Older patients need better guidelines for optimal treatment of high blood pressure: One size fits few. *Hypertension, 51*, 817–818.

Krakowiak, P., & others. (2012, in press). Maternal metabolic conditions and risk for autism and other neurodevelopmental disorders. *Pediatrics*.

Kramer, A. F., & Morrow, D. (2012, in press). Cognitive training and expertise. In D. Park & N. Schwartz (Eds.), *Cognitive aging: A primer* (2nd ed.). New York: Psychology Press.

Kramer, A. F., & others. (1999, July). Aging, fitness, and neurocognitive function. *Nature, 400*, 418–419.

Kramer, J. R., & others. (2008). Multiple-domain predictors of problematic alcohol use in young adulthood. *Journal of Studies in Alcohol and Drugs, 69*, 649–659.

Kramer, L. (2006, July 10). Commentary in "How your siblings make you who you are" by J. Kluger, *Time*, pp. 46–55.

Kramer, L., & Perozynski, L. (1999). Parental beliefs about managing sibling conflict. *Developmental Psychology, 35*, 489–499.

Kramer, L., & Radey, C. (1997). Improving sibling relationships among young children: A social skills training model. *Family Relations, 46*, 237–246.

Kramer, W. E. (2012). Large employers see scenarios under which they could move workers and retirees to exchanges. *Health Affairs, 31*, 299–305.

Krause, N. (1995). Religiosity and self-esteem among older adults. *Journal of Gerontology B: Psychological Science, 50*, P236–P246.

Krause, N. (2003). Religious meaning and subjective well-being in late life. *Journals of Gerontology B: Psychological Sciences and Social Sciences, 58*, S160–S170.

Krause, N. (2004). Stressors in highly valued roles, meaning in life, and the physical health status of older adults. *Journal of Gerontology: Social Sciences, 59*, S287–S297.

Krause, N. (2008). The social foundations of religious meaning in life. *Research on Aging, 30*(4), 395–427.

Krause, N. (2009). Deriving a sense of meaning in late life. In V. L. Bengtson, D. Gans, N. M. Putney, & M. Silverstein (Eds.), *Handbook of theories of aging*. New York: Springer.

Krause, N. (2012). Valuing the life experience of old adults and change in depressive symptoms: Exploring an overlooked benefit of involvement in religion. *Journal of Aging Health, 24*, 227–247.

Krause, N., Ingersoll-Dayton, B., Liang, J., & Sugisawa, H. (1999). Religion social-behavior and health among the Japanese elderly. *Journal of Health and Social Behavior, 40*, 405–421.

Kreuter, M., & Herth, F. J. (2011). Supportive and palliative care of advanced nonmalignant lung disease. *Respiration, 82*, 307–316.

Kreutzer, M., Leonard, C., & Flavell, J. H. (1975). An interview study of children's knowledge about memory. *Monographs of the Society for Research in Child Development, 40*(1. Serial No. 159).

Kriemler, S., & others. (2011). Effect of school-based interventions on activity and fitness in children and adolescents: A review of reviews and systematic update. *British Journal of Sports Medicine, 45*, 923–930.

Kring, A. M. (2000). Gender and anger. In A. H. Fischer (Ed.), *Gender and emotion: Social psychological perspectives*. New York: Cambridge University Press.

Kristensen, P., Weisaeth, L., & Heir, T. (2012). Bereavement and mental health after sudden and violent losses: A review. *Psychiatry, 75*, 76–97.

Kristjuhan, U., & Taidre, E. (2010). Postponed aging in university teachers. *Rejuvenation Research, 13*, 356–358.

Kroger, J. (2012). The status of identity developments in identity research. In P. K. Kerig, M. S. Schulz, & S. T. Hauser (Eds.), *Adolescence and beyond*. New York: Oxford University Press.

Kroger, J., Martinussen, M., & Marcia, J. E. (2010). Identity change during adolescence and young adulthood: A meta-analysis. *Journal of Adolescence, 33*, 683–698.

Kronenberg, G., & others. (2010). Impact of actin filament stabilization on adult hippocampal and olfactory bulb neurogenesis. *Journal of Neuroscience, 30*, 3419–3431.

Krueger, J. I., Vohs, K. D., & Baumeister, R. F. (2008). Is the allure of self-esteem a mirage after all? *American Psychologist, 63*, 64.

Krueger, P. M., & Chang, V. W. (2008). Being poor and coping with stress: Health behaviors and the risk of death. *American Journal of Public Health, 98*, 889–896.

Kruger, J., Blanck, H. M., & Gillespie, C. (2006). Dietary and physical activity behaviors among adults successful at weight loss management. *International Journal of Behavioral Nutrition and Physical Activity, 3*, 17.

Kubarych, T. S., & others. (2012, in press). A multivariate twin study of hippocampal volume, self-esteem and well-being in middle-aged men. *Genes, Brain, and Behavior*.

Kubicek, B., Korunka, C., Hoonakker, P., & Raymo, J. M. (2010). Work and family characteristics as predictors of early retirement in men and women. *Research on Aging, 32*, 467–498.

Kübler-Ross, E. (1969). *On death and dying*. New York: Macmillan.

Kuebli, J. (1994, March). Young children's understanding of everyday emotions. *Young Children*, 36–48.

Kuhl, P. K. (1993). Infant speech perception: A window on psycholinguistic development. *International Journal of Psycholinguistics, 9*, 33–56.

Kuhl, P. K. (2000). A new view of language acquisition. *Proceedings of the National Academy of Science, 97*(22), 11850–11857.

Kuhl, P. K. (2007). Is speech learning "gated" by the social brain? *Developmental Science, 10*, 110–120.

Kuhl, P. K. (2009). Linking infant speech perception to language acquisition: Phonetic learning predicts language growth. In J. Colombo, P. McCardle, & L. Freund (Eds.), *Infant pathways to language*. New York: Psychology Press.

Kuhl, P. K. (2011). Social mechanisms in early language acquisition: Understanding integrated brain systems and supporting language. In J. Decety & J. Cacioppo (Eds.), *Handbook of social neuroscience*. New York: Oxford University Press.

Kuhl, P. K. (2012, in press). Language learning and the developing brain: Cross-cultural studies unravel the effects of biology and culture. *Journal of the Acoustical Society of America*.

Kuhl, P. K., & Damasio, A. (2012). Language. In E. R. Kandel & others (Eds.), *Principles of neural science* (5th ed.). New York: McGraw-Hill.

Kuhn, D. (1998). Afterword to Volume 2: Cognition, perception, and language. In W. Damon (Ed.), *Handbook of child psychology* (5th ed., Vol. 2). New York: Wiley.

Kuhn, D. (2009). Adolescent thinking. In R. M. Lerner & L. Steinberg (Eds.), *Handbook of adolescent psychology* (3rd ed.). New York: Wiley.

Kuhn, D. (2011). What is scientific thinking and how does it develop? In U. Goswami (Ed.), *Wiley-Blackwell handbook of childhood cognitive development* (2nd ed.). New York: Wiley.

Kuhn, D., Cheney, R., & Weinstock, M. (2000). The development of epistemological understanding. *Cognitive Development, 15*, 309–328.

Kulkofsky, S., & Klemfuss, J. Z. (2008). What the stories children tell can tell about their memory: Narrative skill and young children's suggestibility. *Developmental Psychology, 44*, 1442–1456.

Kuo, L. J., & Anderson, R. C. (2012). Effects of early bilingualism on learning phonological regularities in a new language. *Journal of Experimental Child Psychology, 111*, 455–467.

Kuo, S. Y., & others. (2012, in press). Trajectories of depressive symptoms and fatigue among postpartum women. *Journal of Obstetric, Gynecologic, and Neonatal Nursing*.

Kupersmidt, J. B., & Coie, J. D. (1990). Preadolescent peer status, aggression, and school adjustment as predictors of externalizing problems in adolescence. *Child Development, 61*, 1350–1363.

Kurdek, L. A. (2006). Differences between partners from heterosexual, gay, and lesbian cohabiting couples. *Journal of Marriage and the Family, 68*, 509–528.

Kurdek, L. A. (2007). The allocation of household labor between partners in gay and lesbian couples. *Journal of Family Issues, 28*, 132–148.

Kwan, M. Y., Cairney, J., Faulkner, G. E., & Pullenayegum, E. E. (2012). Physical activity and other health-risk behaviors during the transition into early adulthood: A longitudinal cohort study. *American Journal of Preventive Medicine, 42*, 14–20.

L

La Rooy, D. J., Malloy, L. C., & Lamb, M. E. (2012). The development of memory in childhood. In M. E. Lamb, D. J. La Rooy, L. C. Malloy, & C. Katz (Eds.), *Children's testimony*. New York: Wiley.

Laboul, A. (2012). Financial education and older adults. *Global population aging: Peril or promise?* Geneva, SWIT: World Economic Forum.

Labouvie-Vief, G. (1986, August). *Modes of knowing and life-span cognition*. Paper presented at the meeting of the American Psychological Association, Washington, DC.

Labouvie-Vief, G. (2009). Cognition and equilibrium regulation in development and aging. In V. Bengtson & others (Eds.), *Handbook of theories of aging*. New York: Springer.

Labouvie-Vief, G., Gruhn, D., & Studer, J. (2010). Dynamic integration of emotion and cognition: Equilibrium regulation in development and aging. In M. E. Lamb, A. Freund, & R. M. Lerner (Eds.), *Handbook of life-span development* (Vol. 2). New York: Wiley.

LaBrie, J. W., Hummer, J., Kenney, S., Lac, A., & Pedersen, E. (2011). Identifying factors that increase the likelihood for alcohol-induced blackouts in the prepartying context. *Substance Use and Misuse, 46*, 992–1002.

Lacelle, C., Hebert, M., Lavoie, F., Vitaro, F., & Tremblay, R. E. (2012). Sexual health in women reporting a history of child sexual abuse. *Child Abuse and Neglect, 36*, 247–259.

Lachausse, R. G. (2012). My student body: Effects of an internet-based prevention program to decrease obesity among college students. *Journal of American College Health, 60*, 324–330.

Lachman, M. E. (2004). Development in midlife. *Annual Review of Psychology* (Vol. 55). Palo Alto, CA: Annual Reviews.

Lachman, M. E. (2006). Perceived control over aging-related declines. *Current Directions in Psychological Science, 15*, 282–286.

Lachman, M. E., Agrigoroaei, S., Murphy, C., & Tun, P. A. (2010). Frequent cognitive activity compensates for education differences in episodic memory. *American Journal of Geriatric Psychiatry, 18*, 4–10.

Lachman, M. E., & Firth, K. M. P. (2004). The adaptive value of feeling in control during midlife. In O. G. Brim, C. D. Ruff, & R. C. Kessler (Eds.), *How healthy are we?* Chicago: University of Chicago Press.

Lachman, M. E., Maier, H., & Budner, R. (2000). *A portrait of midlife*. Unpublished manuscript, Brandeis University, Waltham, MA.

Lachman, M. E., Neupert, S., & Agrigoraei, S. (2011). The relevance of control beliefs for health and aging. In K. W. Schaie & S. L. Willis (Eds.), *Handbook of the psychology of aging* (7th ed.). New York: Elsevier.

Lachman, M. E., Rosnick, C., & Rocke, C. (2009). The rise and fall of control beliefs predict exercise behavior during and after an exercise intervention. *Journal of Aging and Physical Activity, 16*, 1–16.

Ladd, G., Buhs, E., & Troop, W. (2004). School adjustment and social skills training. In P. K. Smith & C. H. Hart (Eds.), *Blackwell handbook of childhood social development*. Malden, MA: Blackwell.

Ladd, G. W., Kochenderfer-Ladd, Visconti, J., & Ettekal, I. (2012). Classroom peer relations and children's social and scholastic development. In A. M. Ryan & G. W. Ladd (Eds.), *Peer relationships and adjustment at school*. Charlotte, NC: Information Age Publishing.

LaFrance, M., Hecht, M. A., & Paluck, E. L. (2003). The contingent smile: A meta-analysis of sex differences in smiling. *Psychological Bulletin, 129*, 305–334.

Lafreniere, D., & Mann, N. (2009). Anosmia: Loss of smell in the elderly. *Otolaryngologic Clinics of North America, 42*, 123–131.

Lahey, B. B., Van Hulle, C. A., D'Onofrio, B. M., Rodgers, J. L., & Waldman, I. D. (2008). Is parental knowledge of their adolescent offspring's whereabouts and peer associations spuriously associated with offspring delinquency? *Journal of Abnormal Child Psychology, 36*, 807–823.

Laible, D., & Thompson, R. A. (2007). Early socialization: A relationship perspective. In J. E. Grusec & P. D. Hastings (Eds.), *Handbook of socialization*. New York: Guilford.

Laird, R. D., & Marrero, M. D. (2010). Information management and behavior problems: Is concealing misbehavior necessarily a sign of trouble? *Journal of Adolescence, 33*, 297–308.

Lamb, M. E. (1994). Infant care practices and the application of knowledge. In C. B. Fisher & R. M. Lerner (Eds.), *Applied developmental psychology*. New York: McGraw-Hill.

Lamb, M. E. (2000). The history of research on father involvement: An overview. *Marriage and Family Review, 29*, 23–42.

Lamb, M. E. (2010). How do fathers influence children's development? In M. E. Lamb (Ed.), *The role of the father in child development* (5th ed.). New York: Wiley.

Lamb, M. E. (2012, in press). Non-parental care and emotional development. In S. Pauen & M. Bornstein (Eds.), *Early childhood development and later outcomes*. New York: Cambridge University Press.

Lamb, M. E., Bornstein, M. H., & Teti, D. M. (2002). *Development in infancy* (4th ed.). Mahwah, NJ: Erlbaum.

Lamb, M. E., & Malloy, L. C. (2013, in press). Child development and the law. In I. B. Weiner & others (Eds.), *Handbook of psychology* (2nd ed., Vol. 6). New York: Wiley.

Lambertini, L., & others. (2012, in press). Imprinted gene expression in fetal growth and development. *Placenta*.

Lampard, A. M., Byrne, S. M., McLean, N., & Fursland, A. (2012). The Eating Disorder Inventory-2 perfectionism scale: Factor structrure and associations with dietary restraint and weight and shape concern in eating disorders. *Eating Behaviors, 13*, 49–53.

Lamy, C. (2012). Poverty is a knot, preschool is an untangler. In R. C. Pianta (Ed.), *Handbook of early childhood education*. New York: Guilford.

Landau, B., Smith, L., & Jones, S. (1998). Object perception and object naming in early development. *Trends in Cognitive Science, 2*, 19–24.

Lane, H. (1976). *The wild boy of Aveyron*. Cambridge, MA: Harvard University Press.

Lane, K. L., & others. (2013). Strategies for decreasing aggressive, coercive behavior: A call for preventive efforts. In B. G. Cook & M. G. Tankersley (Eds.),

Research-based practices in special education. Upper Saddle River, NJ: Pearson.

Lang, A., & others. (2011). Perinatal loss and parental grief: The challenge of ambiguity and disenfranchised grief. *Omega, 63,* 183–196.

Lang, F. R., & Carstensen, L. L. (1994). Close emotional relationships in late life: Further support for proactive aging in the social domain. *Psychology and Aging, 9,* 315–324.

Lange, B. S., & others. (2010). The potential of virtual reality and gaming to assist successful aging with disability. *Physical Medicine and Rehabilitation Clinics of North America, 21,* 339–356.

Langer, E. (2005). *On becoming an artist.* New York: Ballantine.

Langer, E. J. (2000). Mindful learning. *Current Directions in Psychological Science, 9,* 220–223.

Langer, E. J. (2007, August). *Counterclockwise: Mindfulness and aging.* Paper presented at the meeting of the American Psychological Association, San Francisco.

Langstrom, N., Rahman, Q., Carlstrom, E., & Lichtenstein, P. (2010). Genetic and environmental effects on same-sex sexual behaviour: A population study of twins in Sweden. *Archives of Sexual Behavior, 39,* 75–80.

Lansford, J. E. (2012a). Divorce. In R. J. R. Levesque (Ed.), *Encyclopedia of adolescence.* New York: Springer.

Lansford, J. E. (2012b, in press). Single- and two-parent families. In J. Hattie & E. Anderman (Eds.), *International handbook of student achievement.* New York: Routledge.

Lansford, J. E., & Deater-Deckard, K. (2012, in press). Childrearing discipline and violence in developing countries. *Child Development.*

Lansford, J. E., Wager, L. B., Bates, J. E., Pettit, G. S., & Dodge, K. A. (2012, in press). Forms of spanking and children's externalizing problems. *Family Relations.*

Lansford, J. E., Yu, T., Erath, S. A., Pettit, G. S., Bates, J. E., & Dodge, K. A. (2010). Developmental precursors of number of sexual partners from ages 16 to 22. *Journal of Research on Adolescence, 20,* 651–677.

Lansford, J. E., & others. (2005). Cultural normativeness as a moderator of the link between physical discipline and children's adjustment: A comparison of China, India, Italy, Kenya, Philippines, and Thailand. *Child Development, 76,* 1234–1246.

Lansford, J. E., & others. (2011). Reciprocal relations between parents' physical discipline and children's externalizing behavior during middle childhood and adolescence. *Development and Psychopathology, 23,* 225–238.

Laopaiboon, M., & others. (2009). Music during caesarean section under regional anaesthesia for improving maternal and infant outcomes. *Cochrane Database of Systematic Reviews,* CD006914.

Larson, F. B., & others. (2006). Exercise is associated with reduced risk for incident dementia among persons 65 years of age and older. *Annals of Internal Medicine, 144,* 73–81.

Larson, R. W. (2001). How U.S. children and adolescents spend their time: What it does (and doesn't) tell us about their development. *Current Directions in Psychological Science, 10,* 160–164.

Larson, R. W., & Angus, R. (2011). Adolescents' development of skills for agency in youth programs: Learning to think strategically. *Child Development, 82,* 277–294.

Larson, R. W., & Dawes, N. P. (2013, in press). Cultivating intrinsic motivation in American youth programs. In M. Csikszentmihalyi (Ed.), *Education and youth development in cross-cultural psychology: Contributions from positive psychology.* New York: Springer.

Larson, R. W., Rickman, A., Gibbons, C., & Walker, K. (2009). Practitioner expertise: Creating quality within the daily tumble of events in youth settings. *New Directions in Youth Development, 121,* 71–88.

Larson, R. W., & Verma, S. (1999). How children and adolescents spend time across the world: Work, play, and developmental opportunities. *Psychological Bulletin, 125,* 701–736.

Larson, R. W., & Walker, K. C. (2010). Dilemmas of practice: Challenges to program quality encountered by youth program leaders. *American Journal of Community Psychology, 45,* 338–349.

Larson, R. W., & Wilson, S. (2004). Adolescence across place and time; Globalization and the changing pathways to adulthood. In R. Lerner & L. Steinberg (Eds.), *Handbook of Adolescent Psychology.* New York: Wiley.

Larson, R. W., Wilson, S., & Rickman, A. (2009). Globalization, societal change, and adolescence across the world. In R. M. Lerner & L. Steinberg (Eds.), *Handbook of adolescent psychology* (3rd ed.). New York: Wiley.

Larzelere, R. E., & Kuhn, B. R. (2005). Comparing child outcomes of physical punishment and alternative disciplinary tactics: A meta-analysis. *Clinical Child and Family Psychology Review, 8,* 1–37.

Laslett, A. M., Room, R., Dietze, P., & Ferris, J. (2012, in press). Alcohol's involvement in recurrent child abuse and neglect cases. *Addiction.*

Laubjerg, M., & Petersson, B. (2011). Juvenile delinquency and psychiatric contact among adoptees compared to non-adoptees in Denmark: A nationwide register-based comparative study. *Nordic Journal of Psychiatry, 65,* 365–372.

Lauer, R. H., & Lauer, J. C. (2012). *Marriage and the family* (8th ed.). New York: McGraw-Hill.

Laumann, E. O., Glasser, D. B., Neves, R. C., & Moreira, E. D. (2009). A population-based survey of sexual activity, sexual problems, and associated help-seeking behavior patterns in mature adults in the United States of America. *International Journal of Impotence Research, 21,* 171–178.

Laurent, H. K., Ablow, J. C., & Measelle, J. (2012). Taking stress response out of the box: Stability, discontinuity, and temperament effects on HPA and SNS across social stressors in mother-infant dyads. *Developmental Psychology, 48,* 35–45.

Laursen, B., & Pursell, G. (2009). Conflict in peer relationships. In K. H. Rubin, W. M. Bukowski, & B. Laursen (Eds.), *Handbook of peer interactions, relationships, and groups.* New York: Guilford.

Laus, M. F., Vales, L. D., Costa, T. M., & Almeida, S. S. (2011). Early postnatal protein-calorie malnutrition and cognition: A review of human and animal studies. *International Journal of Environmental Research and Public Health, 8,* 590–612.

Lavie, C. J., & Milani, R.V. (2011). Depression, autonomic function, and cardiorespiratory fitness: comment on Hughes et al. (2010), *Perceptual and Motor Skills, 112,* 319–321.

Lavner, J. A., & Bradbury, T. N. (2012). Why do even satisfied newlyweds eventually go on to divorce? *Journal of Family Psychology, 26,* 1–10.

Lavoie-Tremblay, M., Leclerc, E., Marchionni, C., & Drevniok, U. (2010). The needs and expectations of generation Y nurses in the workplace. *Journal for Nurses in Staff Development, 26,* 2–8.

Lawrence, R. A. (2012). Breastfeeding—a public health issue, not just a matter of choice. *Breastfeeding Medicine, 7,* 67–68.

Le Couteur, D. G., & Simpson, S. J. (2011). Adaptive senectitude: The prolongevity effects on aging. *Journals of Gerontology A: Biological Sciences and Medical Sciences, 66A,* 179–182.

Leaper, C. (2013). Gender development during childhood. In P. D. Zelazo (Ed.), *Oxford handbook of developmental psychology.* New York: Oxford University Press.

Leaper, C., & Bigler, R. S. (2011). Gender. In M. H. Underwood & L. H. Rosen (Eds.), *Social development.* New York: Guilford.

Leaper, C., & Smith, T. E. (2004). A meta-analytic review of gender variations in children's language use: Talkativeness, affiliative speech, and assertive speech. *Developmental Psychology, 40,* 993–1027.

Leatherdale, S. T. (2010). Factors associated with communication-based sedentary behaviors among youth: Are talking on the phone, texting, and instant messaging new sedentary behaviors to be concerned about? *Journal of Adolescent Health, 47,* 315–318.

Lebel, C., & others. (2012). Diffusion tensor imaging of white matter tract evolution over the lifespan. *Neuroimage, 60,* 340–352.

Ledesma, K. (2012). A place to call home. *Adoptive Families.* Retrieved August 8, 2012, from www.adoptivefamilies.com/articles.php?aid=2129

Lee, H. C., & Wei, Y. H. (2012). Mitochondria and aging. *Advances in Experimental Medicine and Biology, 942,* 311–327.

Lee, I. M., & Skerrett, P. J. (2001). Physical activity and all-cause mortality: What is the dose-response relation? *Medical Science and Sports Exercise, 33* (6 Suppl.), S459–S471.

Lee, K., Cameron, C. A., Doucette, J., & Talwar, V. (2002). Phantoms and fabrications: Young children's detection of implausible lies. *Child Development, 73,* 1688–1702.

Lee, K., Quinn, P. C., Pascalis, O., & Slater, A. (2013). Development of face processing ability in childhood. In P. D. Zelazo (Ed.), *Oxford handbook of developmental psychology.* New York: Oxford University Press.

Lee, K. Y., & others. (2011). Effects of combined radiofrequency radiation exposure on the cell cycle and its regulatory proteins. *Bioelectromagnetics, 32,* 169–178.

Lee, L. A., Sbarra, D. A., Mason, A. E., & Law, R. W. (2011). Attachment anxiety, verbal immediacy, and blood pressure: Results from a laboratory-analog study following marital separation. *Personal Relationships, 18,* 285–301.

Lee, Y. S., Turkeltaub, P., Granger, R., & Raizada, R. D. (2012). Categorical speech processing in Broca's area: An fMRI study using multivariate pattern-based analysis. *Journal of Neuroscience, 32,* 3942–3948.

Leedy, P. D., & Ormrod, J. E. (2013). *Practical research* (10th ed.). Upper Saddle River, NJ: Pearson.

Leerkes, E. M. (2011). Maternal sensitivity during distressing tasks: A unique predictor of attachment security. *Infant Behavior and Development, 34,* 443–446.

Leerkes, E. M., Parade, S. H., & Gudmundson, J. A. (2011, in press). Mothers' emotional reactions to crying pose risk for subsequent attachment insecurity. *Journal of Family Psychology, 25,* 635–643.

Lefkowitz, E. S., & Gillen, M. M. (2006). "Sex is just a normal part of life": Sexuality in emerging adulthood. In J. J. Arnett & J. L. Tanner (Eds.), *Emerging adults in America.* Washington, DC: American Psychological Association.

Legear, M., & others. (2012, in press). A window of opportunity? Motor skills and perceptions of competence of children in kindergarten. *International Journal of Behavioral Nutrition and Physical Activity.*

Legerstee, M. (1997). Contingency effects of people and objects on subsequent cognitive functioning in 3-month-old infants. *Social Development, 6,* 307–321.

Legge, G. E., Madison, C., Vaughn, B. N., Cheong, A. M., & Miller, J. C. (2008). Retention of high tactile acuity throughout the lifespan in blindness. *Perception and Psychophysics, 70,* 1471–1488.

Lehman, E. B., & others. (2010.) Long-term stability of young children's eyewitness accuracy, suggestibility, and resistance to misinformation. *Journal of Applied Developmental Psychology, 31,* 145–154.

Lehman, H. C. (1960). The age decrement in outstanding scientific creativity. *American Psychologist, 15,* 128–134.

Lehr, C. A., Hanson, A., Sinclair, M. F., & Christensen, S. I. (2003). Moving beyond dropout prevention towards school completion. *School Psychology Review, 32,* 342–364.

Leighton, S. (2008). Bereavement therapy with adolescents: Facilitating a process of spiritual growth. *Journal of Child and Adolescent Psychiatric Nursing, 21,* 24–34.

Lempers, J. D., Flavell, E. R., & Flavell, J. H. (1977). The development in very young children of tacit knowledge concerning visual perception. *Genetic Psychology Monographs, 95,* 3–53.

Lemstra, M. E., Nielsen, G., Rogers, M. R., Thompson, A. T., & Moraros, J. S. (2012). Risk indicators and outcomes associated with bullying in youth aged 9-15 years. *Canadian Journal of Public Health, 103,* 9–13.

Lenhart, A., Purcell, K., Smith, A., & Zickuhr, K. (2010, February 3). *Social media and young adults.* Washington, DC: Pew Research Center.

Lennon, E. M., Gardner, J. M., Karmel, B. Z., & Flory, M. J. (2008). Bayley Scales of Infant Development. In M. M. Haith & J. B. Benson (Eds.), *Encyclopedia of infant and early childhood development.* Oxford, UK: Elsevier.

Lenoir, C. P., Mallet, E., & Calenda, E. (2000). Siblings of sudden infant death syndrome and near miss in about 30 families: Is there a genetic link? *Medical Hypotheses, 54,* 408–411.

Lenroot, R. K., & Giedd, J. N. (2006). Brain development in children and adolescents: Insights from anatomical magnetic resonance imaging. *Neuroscience and Biobehavioral Reviews, 30,* 718–729.

Leonardi-Bee, J. A., Smyth, A. R., Britton, J., & Coleman, T. (2008). Environmental tobacco smoke on fetal health: Systematic review and analysis. *Archives of Disease in Childhood: Fetal and Neonatal Edition, 93,* F351–F361.

Leppanen, J. M., Moulson, M., Vogel-Farley, V. K., & Nelson, C. A. (2007). An ERP study of emotional face processing in the adult and infant brain. *Child Development, 78,* 232–245.

Lerner, H. G. (1989). *The dance of intimacy.* New York: Harper & Row.

Lerner, J. V., & others. (2013, in press). Positive youth development: Processes, philosophies, and programs. In I. B. Weiner & others (Eds.), *Handbook of psychology* (2nd ed., Vol. 6). New York: Wiley.

Lerner, J. W., & Johns, B. (2012). *Learning disabilities and related mild disabilities* (12th ed.). Boston: Cengage.

Lerner, R. M., Boyd, M., & Du, D. (2008). Adolescent development. In I. B. Weiner & C. B. Craighead (Eds.). *Encyclopedia of psychology* (4th ed). Hoboken, NJ: Wiley.

Lerner, R. M., Easterbrooks, M. A., & Mistry, J. (2013, in press). Developmental science across the life span: An introduction. In I. B. Weiner & others (Eds.), *Handbook of psychology* (2nd ed., Vol. 6). New York: Wiley.

Lerner, R. M., Roeser, R. W., & Phelps, E. (Eds.). (2009). *Positive youth development and spirituality: From theory to research.* West Conshohocken, PA: Templeton Foundation Press.

Lerner-Geva, L., Boyko, V., Blumstein, T., & Benyamini, Y. (2010). The impact of education, cultural background, and lifestyle on symptoms of the menopausal transition: The Women's Health at Midlife Study. *Journal of Women's Health, 19,* 975–985.

Leshikar, E. D., Gutchess, A. H., Hebrank, A. C., Sutton, B. P., & Park, D. C. (2010). The impact of increased relational encoding demands in frontal and hippocampal function in older adults. *Cortex, 46,* 507–521.

Lesley, C. (2005). *Burning fence: A Western memoir of fatherhood.* New York: St. Martin's Press.

Lessow-Hurley, J. (2013). *Foundations of dual language instruction.* (6th ed.). Boston: Allyn & Bacon.

Lester, B. M., & others. (2002). The maternal lifestyle study: Effects of substance exposure during pregnancy on neurodevelopmental outcome in 1-month-old infants. *Pediatrics, 110,* 1182–1192.

Lester, B. M., & others. (2011). Infant neurobehavioral development. *Seminars in Perinatology, 35,* 8–19.

Letourneau, N., & others. (2012). Support intervention needs and preferences for fathers affected by postpartum depression. *Journal of Perinatal and Neonatal Nursing, 26,* 69–80.

Levant, R. F. (2002). Men and masculinity. In J. Worell (Ed.), *Encyclopedia of women and gender.* San Diego: Academic Press.

Levelt, W. J. M. (1989). *Speaking: From intention to articulation.* Cambridge, MA: MIT Press.

Leventhal, T., & Brooks-Gunn, J. (2011). Changes in neighborhood poverty from 1990 to 2000 and youth's problem behaviors. *Developmental Psychology, 47,* 1680–1696.

LeVine, S. (1979). *Mothers and wives: Gusii women of East Africa.* Chicago: University of Chicago Press.

Levine, T. P., & others. (2008). Effects of prenatal cocaine exposure on special education in school-aged children. *Pediatrics, 122,* e83–e91.

Levinson, D. J. (1978). *The seasons of a man's life.* New York: Knopf.

Levinson, D. J. (1996). *Seasons of a woman's life.* New York: Alfred Knopf.

Levinson, P. (2013). *New new media* (2nd ed.). Upper Saddle River, NJ: Pearson.

Lewallen, L. P. (2012, in press). Breastfeeding is important for cognitive development in term and preterm infants. *Evidence Based Nursing.*

Lewis, A. C. (2007). Looking beyond NCLB. *Phi Delta Kappan, 88,* 483–484.

Lewis, C., Hill, M., Skirton, H., & Chitty, L. S. (2012, in press). Non-invasive prenatal diagnosis for fetal sex determination: Benefits and disadvantages from the service users' perspective. *European Journal of Genetics.*

Lewis, M. (2005). Selfhood. In B. Hopkins (Ed.), *The Cambridge encyclopedia of child development.* Cambridge, UK: Cambridge University Press.

Lewis, M. (2007). Early emotional development. In A. Slater & M. Lewis (Eds.), *Introduction to infant development.* Malden, MA: Blackwell.

Lewis, M. (2008). The emergence of human emotions. In M. Lewis, J. M. Haviland Jones, & L. Feldman Barrett (Eds.), *Handbook of emotions* (3rd ed.). New York: Guilford.

Lewis, M. (2010). The emergence of consciousness and its role in human development. In W. F. Overton & R. M. Lerner (Eds.), *Handbook of life-span development* (2nd ed.). New York: Wiley.

Lewis, M., & Brooks-Gunn, J. (1979). *Social cognition and the acquisition of the self.* New York. Plenum.

Lewis, M., Feiring, C., & Rosenthal, S. (2000). Attachment over time. *Child Development, 71,* 707–720.

Lewis, M. D. (2013). The development of emotional regulation: Integrating normal and individual differences through developmental neuroscience. In P. D. Zelazo (Ed.), *Oxford handbook of developmental psychology.* New York: Oxford University Press.

Lewis, M. D., Todd, R., & Xu, X. (2011). The development of emotion regulation: A neuropsychological perspective. In R. M. Lerner, W. F. Overton, A. M. Freund, & M. E. Lamb (Eds.), *Handbook of life-span development.* New York: Wiley.

Lewis, R. (2012). *Human genetics* (10th ed.). New York: McGraw-Hill.

Lewis, R. J., Kholodkov, T., & Derlega, V. J. (2012). Still stressful after all these years: A review of lesbians' and bisexual women's minority stress. *Journal of Lesbian Studies, 16,* 30–44.

Lhila, A., & Long, S. (2011). What is driving the black-white difference in low birthweight in the U.S.? *Health Economics, 21,* 301–315.

Li, B. J., Jiang, Y. J., Yuan, F., & Ye, H. X. (2010). Exchange transfusion of least incompatible blood for severe hemolytic disease of the newborn due to anti-Rh17. *Transfusion Medicine, 20,* 66–69.

Li, C., Goran, M. I., Kaur, H., Nollen, N., & Ahluwalia, J. S. (2007). Developmental trajectories of overweight during childhood: Role of early life factors. *Obesity, 15,* 760–761.

Li, D., Zhao, H., & Gelenter, J. (2012, in press). Further clarification of the contribution of the ADH1C gene to vulnerability of alcoholism and selected liver diseases. *Human Genetics.*

Li, F. J., Shen, L., & Ji, H. F. (2012, in press). Dietary intakes of vitamin E, vitamin C, and b-carotene, and risk of Alzheimer's disease: A meta-analysis. *Journal of Alzheimer's Disease.*

Li, J., Olsen, J., Vestergaard, M., & Obel, C. (2011). Low Apgar scores and risk of childhood attention deficit hyperactivity disorder. *Journal of Pediatrics, 158,* 775–779.

Li, J. M., Chen, Y. R., Li, X. T., & Xu, W. C. (2011). Screening of Herpes simplex virus 2 infection among pregnant women in southern China. *Journal of Dermatology, 38,* 120–124.

Li, T., & Chan, D. K-S. (2012). How anxious and avoidant attachment affect romantic relationship quality differently: A meta-analytic review, *42,* 406–419.

Li, Y. (2007). Recovering from spousal bereavement in later life: Does volunteer participation play a role? *Journals of Gerontology: Psychological Sciences and Social Sciences, 62B,* S257–S266.

Li, Y., Zou, X., Lv, J., Yang, L., Li, H., & Wang, W. (2011). Trace elements in the fingernails of healthy Chinese centenarians. *Biological Trace Element Research, 409,* 1385–1390.

Li, Z., & Heber, D. (2012). Sarcopenic obesity in the elderly and strategies for weight management. *Nutrition Reviews, 70,* 57–64.

Liben, L. S. (1995). Psychology meets geography: Exploring the gender gap on the national geography bee. *Psychological Science Agenda, 8,* 8–9.

Libertus, K., & Needham, A. (2010). Teach to reach: The effects of active versus passive reading experiences on action and perception. *Vision Research, 50,* 2750–2757.

Lie, E., & Newcombe, N. (1999). Elementary school children's explicit and implicit memory for faces of preschool classmates. *Developmental Psychology, 35,* 102–112.

Lieven, E. (2008). Language development: overview. In M. M. Haith & J. B. Benson (Eds.), *Encyclopedia of infant and early childhood development.* Oxford, UK: Elsevier.

Lieven, E., & Stoll, S. (2010). Language. In M. Borstein (Ed.), *Handbook of cultural developmental science.* New York: Psychology Press.

Lifton, R. J. (1977). The sense of immortality: On death and the continuity of life. In H. Feifel (Ed.), *New meanings of death.* New York: McGraw-Hill.

Li-Korotky, H. S. (2012). Age-related hearing loss: Quality of care for quality of life. *Gerontologist, 52,* 265–271.

Lillard, A. (2006). Pretend play in toddlers. In C. A. Brownell & C. B. Kopp (Eds.), *Socioemotional development in the toddler year.* New York: Oxford University Press.

Lin, F. R. (2011). Hearing loss and cognition among older adults in the United States, *Journals of Gerontology A: Biological Sciences and Medical Sciences, 66,* 1131–1136.

Lin, F. R., Thorpe, R., Gordon-Salant, S., & Ferrucci, L. (2011). Hearing loss prevalence and risk factors among older adults in the United States. *Journals of Gerontology A: Biological Sciences and Medical Sciences.* doi: 10.1093/gerona/glr002

Lin, H. W., Hsu, H. C., & Chang, M. C. (2011). Gender differences in the association between stress trajectories and depressive symptoms among middle aged and older adults in Taiwan. *Journal of Women and Aging, 23,* 233–245.

Lindau, S. T., & Gavrilova, N. (2010). Sex, health, and years of sexually active life gained due to good health: Evidence from two U.S. population based cross sectional surveys of aging. *British Medical Journal, 340,* c810.

Lindau, S. T., Schumm, L. P., Laumann, E. O., Levinson, W., O'Muircheartaigh, C. A., & Waite, L. J. (2007). A study of sexuality and health among older adults in the United States. *New England Journal of Medicine, 357,* 162–174.

Lindberg, S. M., Hyde, J. S., Petersen, J. L., & Lin, M. C. (2010). New trends in gender and mathematics performance: A meta-analysis. *Psychological Bulletin, 136,* 1123–1135.

Lindblad, F., & Hjern, A. (2010). ADHD after fetal exposure to maternal smoking. *Nicotine and Tobacco Research, 12,* 408–415.

Lindqvist, K., & Dalal, K. (2012). The impact of child safety promotion on different social strata in a WHO safe community. *Journal of Injury and Violence Research, 4,* 20–25.

Lindstrom, M. (2010). Social capital, economic conditions, marital status, and daily smoking: A population-based study. *Public Health, 124,* 71–77.

Lippman, L. A., & Keith, J. D. (2006). The demographics of spirituality among youth: International perspectives. In E. Roehlkepartain, P. E. King, L. Wagener, & P. L. Benson (Eds.), *The handbook of spirituality in childhood and adolescence.* Thousand Oaks, CA: Sage.

Lipton, J., & Spelke, E. (2004). Discrimination of large and small numerosities by human infants. *Infancy, 5,* 271–290.

Lira, F. S., & others. (2011). Exercise training improves sleep pattern and metabolic profile in elderly people in a time-dependent manner. *Lipids in Health and Disease, 10,* 1–6.

Liu, J., & others. (2010, in press). Neonatal neurobehavior predicts medical and behavioral outcome. *Pediatrics, 125,* e90–e98.

Liu, S., Quinn, P. C., Wheeler, A., Xiao, N., Ge, L., & Lee, K. (2011). Similarity and difference in the processing of same- and other-race faces as revealed by eye-tracking in 4- to 9-month-old infants. *Journal of Experimental Child Psychology, 108,* 180–189.

Liu, Y. H., Chang, M. Y., & Chen, C. H. (2010). Effects of music therapy on labor pain and anxiety in Taiwanese first-time mothers. *Journal of Clinical Nursing, 19,* 1065–1072.

Lively, W., & Bromley, D. (1973). *Person perception in childhood and adolescence.* New York: Wiley.

Lleo, A., Moroni, L., Caliari, L., & Invernizzi, P. (2012). Autoimmunity and Turner's syndrome. *Autoimmunity Reviews, 11,* A538–A543.

Lock, J. (2012a). Developmental translational research: Adolescence, brain circuitry, cognitive processes, and eating disorders. In J. Lock (Ed.), *Oxford handbook of child and adolescent eating disorders.* New York: Oxford University Press.

Lock, J. (2012b) (Ed.). *Oxford handbook of child and adolescent eating disorders.* New York: Oxford University Press.

Lock, M. (1998). Menopause: Lessons from anthropology. *Psychosomatic Medicine, 60,* 410–419.

Loeber, R., & Burke, J. D. (2011). Developmental pathways in juvenile externalizing and internalizing problems. *Journal of Research on Adolescence, 21,* 34–46.

Logan, A. G. (2011). Hypertension in aging patients. *Expert Review of Cardiovascular Therapy, 9,* 113–120.

Logsdon, M. C., Wisner, K., & Hanusa, B. H. (2009). Does maternal role functioning improve with antidepressant treatment in women with postpartum depression? *Journal of Women's Health, 18,* 85–90.

Londono-Vallejo, J. A., & Wellinger, R. J. (2012, in press). Telomeres and telomerase dance to the rhythm of the cell cycle. *Trends in Biochemical Science.*

Longman, P. (1987). *Born to pay: The new politics of aging in America.* Boston: Houghton Mifflin.

Loos, R. J. (2012). Genetic determinants of common obesity and their values in prediction. *Best Practices & Research: Clinical Endocrinology and Metabolism, 26,* 211–226.

Lopez, A. B., Huynh, V. W., & Fuligni, A. J. (2011, in press). A longitudinal study of religious identity and participation during adolescence. *Child Development.*

Lopez, O. L., Becker, J. T., & Kuller, L. H. (2012, in press). Patterns of compensation and vulnerability in normal subjects at risk for Alzheimer's disease. *Journal of Alzheimer's Disease.*

Loponen, M., Hublin, C., Kalimo, R., Manttari, M., & Tenkanen, L. (2010). Joint effect of self-reported sleep problems and three components of the metabolic syndrome on risk of coronary heart disease. *Journal of Psychosomatic Research, 68,* 149–158.

Lorenz, K. Z. (1965). *Evolution and the modification of behavior.* Chicago: University of Chicago Press.

Lovden, M., Brehmer, Y., Li, S. C., & Lindenberger, U. (2012, in press). Training-induced compensation versus magnification of individual differences in memory performance. *Frontiers in Human Neuroscience.*

Lovden, M., & Lindenberger, U. (2007). Intelligence. In J. E. Birren (Ed.), *Encyclopedia of gerontology* (2nd ed.). San Diego: Academic Press.

Low, J., & Simpson, S. (2012, in press). Effects of labeling on preschoolers' explicit false belief performance: Outcomes of cognitive flexibility or inhibitory control? *Child Development.*

Lowdermilk, D. L., & Perry (2012). *Maternity and women's health care* (10th ed.). New York: Elsevier.

Lowe, G., & Costabile, R. A. (2012, in press). 10-year analysis of adverse event reports to the Food and Drug Administration for phosphodiesterase type-5 inhibitors. *Journal of Sexual Medicine.*

Lowe, J. R., & others. (2012). Association of maternal interaction with emotional regulation in 4- and 9-month old infants during the Still Face Paradigm. *Infant Behavior and Development, 35,* 295–302.

Loyens, S. M. M., Kirschner, P. A., & Paas, F. (2012). Problem-based learning. In K. R. Harris, S. Graham, & T. Urdan (Eds.), *APA handbook of educational psychology.* Washington, DC: American Psychological Association.

Lu, C. J., Yu, J. J., & Deng, J. W. (2012). Disease-syndrome combination clinical study of psoriasis: Present status, advantages, and prospects. *China Journal of Integrative Medicine, 18,* 166–171.

Lu, P. H., & others. (2011). Age-related slowing in cognitive processing speed is associated with myelin integrity in a very healthy elderly sample. *Journal of Clinical and Experimental Neuropsychology, 33,* 1059–1068.

Luan, K., Rosales, J. L., & Lee, K. Y. (2012, in press). Viewpoint: Crosstalks between neurofibrillary tangles and amyloid plaque formation. *Aging Research and Review.*

Lucas, R. E., Clark, A. E., Yannis, G., & Diener, E. (2004). Unemployment alters the setpoint for life satisfaction. *Psychological Science, 15,* 8–13.

Lucas, R. E., & Donnellan, M. B. (2011). Personality development across the life span: Longitudinal analyses with a national sample in Germany. *Journal of Personality and Social Psychology, 10,* 847–861.

Lucchetti, G., Lucchetti, A. L., & Koenig, H. G. (2011). Impact of spirituality/religiosity on mortality: Comparison with other health interventions. *Explore, 7,* 234–238.

Lucovnik, M., & others. (2011). Progestin treatment for the prevention of preterm births. *Acta Obstetrica et Gynecologica Scandinavica, 90,* 1057–1069.

Luders, E., & others. (2004). Gender differences in cortical complexity. *Nature Neuroscience, 1,* 799–800.

Ludington-Hoe, S. M., Lewis, T., Morgan, K., Cong, X., Anderson, L., & Reese, S. (2006). Breast and infant temperatures with twins during kangaroo care. *Journal of Obstetric, Gynecologic, and Neonatal Nursing, 35,* 223–231.

Luhmann, M., Hofmann, W., Eid, M., & Lucas, R. E. (2012). Subjective well-being and adaptation to life events: A meta-analysis. *Journal of Personality and Social Psychology 102,* 592–615.

Lumby, J. (2010). Grandparents and grandchildren: A grand connection. *International Journal of Evidence Based Healthcare, 8,* 28–31.

Lumeng, J. C., & others. (2012). Observed assertive and intrusive maternal feeding behaviors increase child adiposity. *American Journal of Clinical Nutrition, 95,* 640–647.

Lund, B., & others. (2011). Risk factors for treatment related mortality in childhood acute lymphoblastic leukemia. *Pediatric Blood Cancer, 56,* 551–559.

Lund, D. A. (2007). Bereavement and loss. In J. E. Birren (Ed.), *Encyclopedia of gerontology* (2nd ed.). San Diego: Academic Press.

Lund, D. A., Utz, R., Caserta, M. S., & De Vries, B. (2008–2009). Humor, laughter, and happiness in the lives of recently bereaved spouses. *Omega, 58,* 87–105.

Lund, H. G., Reider, B. D., Whiting, A. B., & Prichard, J. R. (2010). Sleep patterns and predictors of disturbed sleep in a large population of college students. *Journal of Adolescent Health, 46,* 124–132.

Lundin, A., Backhans, M., & Hemmingsson, T. (2012). Unemployment and hospitalization owing to alcohol-related diagnosis among middle-aged men in Sweden. *Alcoholism: Clinical and Experimental Research, 36,* 663–669.

Luo, L., & Craik, F. I. M. (2008). Aging and memory: A cognitive approach. *Canadian Journal of Psychology, 53,* 346–353.

Luo, Y., & Baillargeon, R. (2010). Toward a mentalistic account of early psychological reasoning. *Current Directions in Psychological Science, 19,* 301–307.

Luo, Y., Hawkley, L. C., Waite, L. J., & Cacioppo, J. T. (2012). Loneliness, health, and mortality in old age: A national longitudinal study. *Social Science and Medicine, 74,* 907–914.

Luria, A., & Herzog, E. (1985, April). *Gender segregation across and within settings.* Paper presented at the biennial meeting of the Society for Research in Child Development, Toronto.

Lusardi, A., Mitchell, O. S., & Curto, V. (2012). *Financial sophistication in the older population.* Retrieved June 12, 2012, from www.pensionresearchcouncil.org/publications/document.php?fi . . .

Lusis, A. J. (2012). Genetics of atherosclerosis. *Trends in Genetics 28*(6), 267–275.

Lustig, C., & Hasher, L. (2009). Interference. In R. Schulz, L. Noelker, K. Rockwood, & R. Sprott (Eds.), *Encyclopedia of Aging* (4th ed.). New York: Springer Publishing.

Luszcz, M. (2011). Executive functioning and cognitive aging. In K. W. Schaie & S. L. Willis (Eds.), *Handbook of the psychology of aging* (7th ed.). New York: Elsevier.

Lyberg, A., Viken, B., Haruna, M., & Severinsson, E. (2012). Diversity and challenges in the management of maternal care for migrant women. *Journal of Nursing Management, 20,* 287–295.

Lykken, D. (2001). *Happiness: What studies on twins show us about nature, nurture, and the happiness set point.* New York: Golden Books.

Lynchard, N. A., & Radvansky, G. A. (2012, in press). Age-related perspectives and emotion processing. *Psychology and Aging.*

Lyndaker, C., & Hulton, L. (2004). The influence of age on symptoms of perimenopause. *Journal of Obstetric, Gynecological, and Neonatal Nursing, 33,* 340–347.

Lyon, T. D., & Flavell, J. H. (1993). Young children's understanding of forgetting over time. *Child Development, 64,* 789–800.

Lyons, D. M., & others. (2010). Stress coping stimulates hippocampal neurogenesis in adult monkeys. *Proceedings of the National Academy of Sciences U.S.A., 107,* 14823–14827.

Lytle, L. A. (2012, in press). Dealing with the childhood obesity epidemic: A public health approach. *Abdominal Imaging.*

M

Maalouf, F. T., & Brent, D. A. (2012). Child and adolescent depression intervention overview: What works for whom and how well? *Child and Adolescent Psychiatry Clinics of North America, 21,* 299–312.

Maccoby, E. E. (1998). *The two sexes: Growing up apart, coming together.* Cambridge, MA: Harvard University Press.

Maccoby, E. E. (2002). Gender and group processes. *Current Directions in Psychological Science, 11,* 54–58.

Maccoby, E. E., & Martin, J. A. (1983). Socialization in the context of the family: Parent-child interaction. In P. H. Mussen (Ed.), *Handbook of child psychology* (4th ed., Vol. 4). New York: Wiley.

Macdonald, K. E., & others. (2012, in press). The value of hippocampal and temporal horn volume and rates of change in predicting future conversion to Alzheimer's disease. *Alzheimer Disease and Associated Disorders.*

MacDonald, S. W., DeCarlo, C. A., & Dixon, R. A. (2011). Linking biological and cognitive aging: Toward improving characterizations of developmental time. *Journals of Gerontology B: Psychological Sciences and Social Sciences, 66B*(Suppl. 1), i59–i70.

MacDonald, S. W., Hultsch, D. F., & Dixon, R. A. (2011). Aging and the shape of cognitive change before death: Terminal decline or terminal drop? *Journals of Gerontology B: Psychological Sciences and Social Sciences, 66B,* 292–301.

Macdorman, M. F., Declercq, E., & Menacker, F. (2011). Trends and characteristics of home births in the United States by race and ethnicity, 1990–2006. *Birth, 38,* 17–23.

MacEvoy, J. P., & Asher, S. R. (2012). When friends disappoint: Boys' and girls' responses to transgressions of friendship expectations. *Child Development, 83,* 104–119.

MacFarlane, J. A. (1975). Olfaction in the development of social preferences in the human neonate. In *Parent-infant interaction.* Ciba Foundation Symposium No. 33. Amsterdam: Elsevier.

MacGeorge, E. L. (2003). Gender differences in attributions and emotions in helping contexts. *Sex Roles, 48,* 175–182.

Maciejewski, P. K., Zhang, B., Block, S. D., & Prigerson, H. G. (2007). An empirical examination of the stage theory of grief. *Journal of the American Medical Association, 297,* 716–723.

Madden, D. J., & others. (1999). Aging and recognition memory: Changes in regional cerebral blood flow associated with components of reaction time distributions. *Journal of Cognitive Neuroscience, II,* 511–520.

Mader, S. S. (2012). *Connect biology* (3rd ed.). New York: McGraw-Hill.

Mader, S. S. (2013). *Biology* (11th ed.). New York: McGraw-Hill.

Mader, S. S., & Windelspecht, M. (2013). *Biology* (11th ed.). New York: McGraw-Hill.

Madill, A. (2012). Interviews and interviewing techniques. In H. Cooper (Ed.), *APA handbook of research methods in psychology.* Washington, DC: American Psychological Association.

Maercker, A., & Lalor, J. (2012). Diagnostic and clinical considerations in prolonged grief disorder. *Dialogues in Clinical Neuroscience, 14,* 167–176.

Magarey, A. M., & others. (2011). A parent-led family-focused treatment program for overweight children aged 5 to 9 years: The PEACH RCT. *Pediatrics, 127,* 214–222.

Mahn, H., & John-Steiner, V. (2013, in press). Vygotsky and sociocultural approaches to teaching and learning. In I. B. Weiner & others (Eds.), *Handbook of psychology* (2nd ed., Vol. 7). New York: Wiley.

Maholmes, V., & King, R. B. (Eds.) (2012). *Oxford handbook of poverty and child development*. New York: Oxford University Press.

Mahoney, J. R., Verghese, J., Goldin, Y., Lipton, R., & Holtzer, R. (2010). Altering orienting and executive attention in older adults. *Journal of the International Neuropsychological Society, 16*(5), 877–889.

Major Depressive Disorder Working Group of the Psychiatric GWAS Consortium. (2012, in press). A mega-analysis of genome-wide association studies for major depressive disorder. *Molecular Psychiatry.*

Malamitsi-Puchner, A., & Boutsikikou, T. (2006). Adolescent pregnancy and perinatal outcome. *Pediatric Endocrinology Review, 3*(Suppl 1), S170–S171.

Malizia, B. A., Hacker, M. R., & Penzias, A. S. (2009). Cumulative live-birth rates after in vitro fertilization. *New England Journal of Medicine, 360,* 236–243.

Mallin, B. M., & Richards, J. E. (2012, in press). Peripheral stimulus location by infants of moving stimuli on complex backgrounds. *Infancy.*

Malloy, L. C., La Rooy, D. J., Lamb, M. A., & Katz, C. (2012). Developmentally sensitive interviewing for legal purposes. In M. E. Lamb, D. J. La Rooy, L. C. Malloy, & C. Katz (Eds.), *Children's testimony* (2nd ed.). New York: Wiley.

Mandara, J. (2006). The impact of family functioning on African American males' academic achievement: A review and clarification of the empirical literature. *Teachers College Record, 108,* 206–233.

Mandler, J. M. (2004). *The foundations of the mind: Origins of conceptual thought.* New York: Oxford University Press.

Mandler, J. M. (2009). Conceptual categorization. In D. H. Rakison & L. M. Oakes (Eds.), *Early category and concept development.* New York: Oxford University Press.

Mandler, J. M., & DeLoach, J. (2012, in press). The beginnings of conceptual development. In S. Pauen & M. Bornstein (Eds.), *Early child development and later outcome.* New York: Cambridge University Press.

Mandler, J. M., & McDonough, L. (1993). Concept formation in infancy. *Cognitive Development, 8,* 291–318.

Manenti, R., Cotelli, M., & Miniussi, C. (2011). Successful physiological aging and episodic memory: A brain stimulation study. *Behavioral Brain Research, 216,* 153–158.

Mangione, R., & others. (2011). Neurodevelopmental outcome following prenatal diagnosis of an isolated anomaly of the corpus callosum. *Ultrasound in Obstetrics and Gyencology, 37,* 290–295.

Manivannan, S., Scheckhuber, C. Q., Veenhuis, M., & van der Klei, I. J. (2012, in press). The impact of peroxisomes on cellular aging and death. *Frontiers in Oncology.*

Mann, T., Tomiyama, A. J., Westling, E., Lew, A-M., Samuels, B., & Chatman, J. (2007). Medicare's search for effective obesity treatments. *American Psychologist, 62,* 220–233.

Manning, W. D., & Cohen, J. (2012, in press). Premarital cohabitation and marital dissolution: An examination of recent marriages. *Journal of Marriage and the Family.*

Manongdo, J. A., & Garcia, J. I. R. (2011). Maternal parenting and mental health of Mexican American youth: A bidirectional and prospective approach. *Developmental Psychology, 25,* 261–270.

Manton, K. I. (1989). The stress buffering role of spiritual support: Cross-sectional and prospective investigations. *Journal for the Scientific Study of Religion, 28,* 310–323.

Marceau, K., Dorn, L. D., & Susman, E. J. (2012, in press). Stress and puberty-related hormone reactivity, negative emotionality, and parent-adolescent relationships. *Psychoneuroimmunology.*

Marceau, K., Neiderhiser, J. M., Lichtenstein, P., & Reis, D. (2012, in press). Genetic and environmental influences on the association between pubertal maturation and internalizing symptoms. *Journal of Youth and Adolescence.*

Marcell, J. J. (2003). Sarcopenia: Causes, consequences, and preventions. *Journals of Gerontology A: Biological Sciences and Medical Sciences,* M911–M916.

Marcello, E., Epis, R., Saraceno, C., & Di Luca, M. (2012). Synaptic dysfunction in Alzheimer's disease. *Advances in Experimental Medicine and Biology, 970,* 573–601.

Marcia, J. E. (1980). Ego identity development. In J. Adelson (Ed.), *Handbook of adolescent psychology:* New York: Wiley.

Marcia, J. E. (1994). The empirical study of ego identity. In H. A. Bosma, T. L. G. Graafsma, H. D. Grotevant, & D. J. De Levita (Eds.), *Identity and development.* Newbury Park, CA: Sage.

Marcia, J. E. (2002). Identity and psychosocial development in adulthood. *Identity: An International Journal of Theory and Research, 2,* 7–28.

Marcotte, T. D., Bekman, N. M., Meyer, R. A., & Brown, S. A. (2012, in press). High-risk driving behaviors among binge drinkers. *American Journal of Drug and Alcohol Abuse.*

Mardh, S., Nagga, K., & Samuelsson, S. (2012, in press). A longitudinal study of semantic memory impairment in patients with Alzheimer's disease. *Cortex.*

Marek, W., & others. (2011). Lung function in our aging population. *European Journal of Medical Research, 16,* 108–114.

Margrett, J. A., & Deshpande-Kamat, N. (2009). Cognitive functioning and decline. In D. Carr (Ed.), *Encyclopedia of the life course and human development.* Boston: Gale Cengage.

Marie, C., & Trainor, L. J. (2012, in press). Development of simultaneous pitch encoding: Infants show a high voice superiority effect. *Cerebral Cortex.*

Marinkovic, K., & others. (2012). Right hemisphere has the last laugh: Neural dynamics of joke appreciation. *Cognitive, Affective, and Behavioral Neuroscience, 11,* 113–130.

Marioni, R. E., & others. (2012). Active cognitive lifestyle associates with cognitive recovery and a reduced risk of cognitive decline. *Journal of Alzheimer's Disease, 28,* 223–230.

Mariscal, S., & Gallego, C. (2012). The relationship between early lexical and grammatical development in Spanish: Evidence in children with different linguistic levels. *Spanish Journal of Psychology, 15,* 112–123.

Markham, C. M., & others. (2010). Connectedness as a predictor of sexual and reproductive health outcomes for youth. *Journal of Adolescent Health, 46* (Suppl. 3), S23–S41.

Markovic, K., & others. (2007). Good news for elderly persons: Olfactory pleasure increases at later stages of the life span. *Journals of Gerontology: Biological Sciences and Medical Sciences, 62A,* 1287–1293.

Marks, D. F. (2013, in press). Health psychology: Overview. In I. B. Weiner & others (Eds.), *Handbook of psychology* (2nd ed., Vol. 9). New York: Wiley.

Markus, H., & Nurius, P. (1987). Possible selves: The interface between motivation and self-concept. In K. M. Yardley & T. M. Honess (Eds.), *Self and identity.* New York: Wiley.

Markus, H. R., Ryff, C. D., Curhan, K., & Palmersheim, K. (2004). In their own words: Well-being among high school and college-educated adults. In G. Brim, C. D. Ryff, & R. Kessler (Eds.), *How healthy we are: A national study of well-being in midlife.* Chicago: University of Chicago Press.

Marquie, J. C., & others. (2010). Higher mental stimulation at work is associated with improved cognitive functioning in both young and older workers. *Ergonomics, 53,* 1287–1301.

Marrelli, T. (2012). Home health and hospice aides and integrating evidence-based information into practice, operations, and management: Two themes that will continue as the revised world view of our healthcare system evolves. *Home Healthcare Nurse, 30,* 381–383.

Marret, S., & others. (2010). Prenatal low-dose aspirin and neurobehavioral outcomes of children born very preterm. *Pediatrics, 125,* e29–e34.

Marsh, H., Ellis, L., & Craven, R. (2002). How do preschool children feel about them selves? Unraveling measurement and multidimensional self-concept structure. *Developmental Psychology, 38,* 376–393.

Marsh, H. W., Martin, A. J., & Xu, M. (2012). Self-concept: Synergy of theory, mind, and application. In K. R. Harris, S. Graham, & T. Urdan (Eds.), *APA educational psychology handbook.* Washington, DC: American Psychological Association.

Marshall, B. L. (2012). Medicalization and the refashioning of age-related limits on sexuality. *Journal of Sexual Research, 49,* 337–343.

Marsiske, M., Klumb, P. L., & Baltes, M. M. (1997). Everyday activity patterns and sensory functioning in old age. *Psychology and Aging, 12,* 444–457.

Marti, C. N., Stice, E., & Springer, D. W. (2010). Substance use and abuse trajectories across adolescence: A latent trajectory analysis of a community-recruited sample of girls. *Journal of Adolescence, 33,* 449–461.

Martin, C., & Evaldsson, A-C. (2012). Affordances for participation: Children's appropriation of rules in a Reggio Emilia school. *Mind, Culture, and Activity, 19,* 51–74.

Martin, C. L., & Ruble, D. N. (2010). Patterns of gender development. *Annual Review of Psychology* (Vol. 61). Palo Alto, CA: Annual Reviews.

Martin, J. A., Hamilton, B. E., Menacker, F., Sutton, P. D., & Matthews, T. J. (2005, November 15). Preliminary births for 2004: Infant and maternal health. *Health E-Stats*. Atlanta: National Center for Health Statistics.

Martin, L. R., Friedman, H. S., & Schwartz, J. E. (2007). Personality and mortality risk across the life span: The importance of conscientiousness as a biopsychosocial attribute. *Health Psychology, 26*, 428–436.

Martin, M., Grunendahl, M., & Martin, P. (2001). Age differences in stress, social resources, and well-being in middle and older age. *Journals of Gerontology: Psychological Sciences and Social Sciences. 56B*, P214–P222.

Maruyama, N. C., & Atencio, C. V. (2008). Evaluating a bereavement support group. *Palliative Support and Care, 6*, 43–49.

Marzo, L., Gousset, K., & Zurzolo, C. (2012, in press). Multifaceted roles of tunneling nanotubes in intercellular communication. *Frontiers in Physiology*.

Mascalo, M. F., & Fischer, K. W. (2010). The dynamic development of thinking, feeling, and acting over the life span. In W. F. Overton & R. M. Lerner (Eds.), *Handbook of life-span development* (Vol. 1). New York: Wiley.

Mason, L., Harris, K. L., & Graham, S. (2013). Strategies for improving student outcomes in written expression. In B. G. Cook & M. G. Tankersley (Eds.), *Research-based practices in special education*. Upper Saddle River, NJ: Pearson.

Masselli, G., & others. (2011). MR imaging in the evaluation of placental abruption: Correlation with sonographic findings. *Radiology*.

Masten, A. S. (2006). Developmental psychopathology: Pathways to the future. *International Journal of Behavioral Development, 31*, 46–53.

Masten, A. S. (2009). Ordinary Magic: Lessons from research on resilience in human development. *Education Canada, 49*(3), 28–32.

Masten, A. S. (2011). Resilience in children threatened by extreme adversity: Frameworks for research, practice, and translational synergy. *Development and Psychopathology, 23*, 141–153.

Masten, A. S. (2013, in press). Risk and resilience in development. In P. D. Zelazo (Ed.), *Oxford handbook of developmental psychology*. New York: Oxford University Press.

Masten, A. S., Burt, K., & Coatsworth, J. D. (2006). Competence and psychopathology in development. In D. Cicchetti & D. Cohen (Eds.), *Developmental psychopathology (Vol. 3): Risk, disorder, and psychopathology* (2nd ed.). New York: Wiley.

Masten, A. S., Liebkind, K., & Hernandez, D. J. (2012, in press). *Realizing the potential of immigrant youth*. New York: Cambridge University Press.

Masten, A. S., & Narayan, A. J. (2012). Child development in the context of disaster, war, and psychopathology: The legacy of Norman Garmezy. *Annual Review of Psychology* (Vol. 63). Palo Alto, CA: Annual Reviews.

Masten, A. S., Obradovic, J., & Burt, K. B. (2006). Resilience in emerging adulthood: Developmental perspectives on continuity and transformation. In J. J. Arnett & J. L. Tanner (Eds.), *Emerging adults in America*. Washington, DC: American Psychological Association.

Masten, A. S., & Tellegen, A. (2012). Resilience in developmental psychology: Contributions of the Project Competence Longitudinal Study. *Development and Psychopathology, 24*, 345–361.

Masters, C. (2008, January 17). We just clicked. *Time magazine*, pp. 84–89.

Match.com. (2011). The Match.com Single in America Study. Retrieved February 7 from http://blog.match.com/singles-study

Match.com. (2012). *Singles in America 2012*. Retrieved June 10, 2012, from http://blog.match.com/singles-in-america/

Mather, M. (2012, in press). The emotion paradox in the human brain. *Annals of the New York Academy of Sciences*.

Matheson, E. M., King, D. E., & Everett, C. J. (2012). Healthy lifestyle habits and mortality in overweight and obese individuals. *Journal of the American Board of Family Medicine, 25*, 9–15.

Matlin, M. W. (2012). *The psychology of women* (7th ed.). Boston: Cengage.

Matlin, S. L., Molock, S. D., & Tebes, J. K. (2011). Suicidality and depression among African American adolescents: The role of family and peer support and community connectedness. *American Journal of Orthopsychiatry, 81*, 108–117.

Matos, A. P., Ferreira, J. A., & Haase, R. F. (2012). Television and aggression: A test of a mediated model with a sample of Portuguese students. *Journal of Social Psychology, 152*, 75–91.

Matsuda, H., Yoshida, M., Wakamatsu, H., & Furuya, K. (2011). Fetal intraperitoneal injection of immunoglobulin diminishes alloimmune hemolysis. *Journal of Perinatology, 31*, 289–292.

Matsumoto, D., & Juang, L. (2012). *Culture and psychology* (5th ed.). Boston: Cengage.

Matthews, C. E., & others. (2007). Influence of exercise, walking, cycling, and overall nonexercise physical activity on mortality in Chinese women. *American Journal of Epidemiology, 165*, 1343–1350.

Matthews, N. L., & others. (2012). Does theory of mind performance differ in children with early-onset and regressive autism? *Developmental Science, 15*, 25–34.

Mattson, S., & Smith, J. E. (2011). *Core curriculum for maternal-newborn nursing* (4th ed.). New York: Elsevier.

Maxson, S. (2013, in press). Behavioral genetics. In I. B. Weiner & others (Eds.), *Handbook of psychology* (2nd ed., Vol. 3). New York: Wiley.

Mayer, K. D., & Zhang, L. (2009). Short-and long-term effects of cocaine abuse during pregnancy on heart development. *Therapeutic Advances in Cardiovascular Disease, 3*, 7–16.

Mayer, R. E. (2012). Information processing. In K. R. Harris, S. Graham, & T. Urdan (Eds.), *APA educational psychology handbook*. Washington, DC: American Psychological Association.

Mayo Clinic. (2012). *Pregnancy and fish: What's safe to eat?* Retrieved April 12, 2012, from www.mayoclinic.com/health/pregnancy-and-fish/PR00158

Mazzuco, T. L., & others. (2012, in press). Genetic aspects of adrenocortical tumors. *Clinical Endocrinology*.

Mbugua Gitau, G., Liversedge, H., Goffey, D., Hawton, A., Liversedge, N., & Taylor, M. (2009). The influence of maternal age on the outcomes of pregnancy complicated by bleeding at less than 12 weeks. *Acta Obstetricia et Gynecologica Scandinavica, 88*, 116–118.

McAdams, D. P., & Olson, B. D. (2010). Personality development: Continuity and change over the life course. *Annual Review of Psychology* (Vol. 61). Palo Alto, CA: Annual Reviews.

McAuley, P. A., & Blair, S. N. (2011). Obesity paradoxes. *Journal of Sports Sciences, 29*, 773–782.

McBride-Chang, C. (2004). *Children's literacy development*. New York: Oxford University Press.

McCabe, D. P., & Loaiza, V. M. (2012). Working memory. In S. K. Whitbourne & M. Sliwinski (Eds.), *Wiley-Blackwell handbook of adult development and aging*. New York: Wiley.

McCardle, P., Miller, B., Lee, J. R., & Tzeng, O. J. (2011). *Dyslexia across languages*. Baltimore: Brookes.

McCartney, K. (2003, July 16). Interview with Kathleen McCartney in A. Bucuvalas, "Child care and behavior." *HGSE News*, pp. 1–4. Cambridge, MA: Harvard Graduate School of Education.

McCartney, K., Dearing, E., Taylor, B. A., & Bub, K. L. (2007). Quality child care supports the achievement of low-income children: Direct and indirect pathways through caregiving and the home environment. *Journal of Applied Developmental Psychology, 28*, 411–426.

McClain, C. S., Rosenfeld, B., & Breitbart, W. S. (2003, March). The influence of spirituality on end-of-life despair in cancer patients close to death. Paper presented at the meeting of American Psychosomatic Society, Phoenix.

McClellan, M. D. (2004, February 9). Captain Fantastic: The interview. *Celtic Nation*, pp. 1–9.

McClelland, K., Bowles, J., & Koopman, P. (2012). Male sex determination: Insights into molecular mechanisms. *Asian Journal of Andrology, 14*, 164–171.

McCombs, B. L. (2013, in press). Educational psychology and educational transformation. In I. B. Weiner & others (Eds.), *Handbook of psychology* (2nd ed., Vol. 7). New York: Wiley.

McCormack, L. A., & others. (2011). Weight-related teasing in a racially diverse sample of sixth-grade children. *Journal of the American Dietetic Association, 111*, 431–436.

McCormack, T., Hoerl, C., & Butterfill, C. (2012). *Tool use and causal cognition*. New York: Oxford University Press.

McCormick, C. B., Dimmitt, C., & Sullivan, F. R. (2013, in press). Metacognition, learning, and instruction. In I. B. Weiner & others (Eds.), *Handbook of psychology* (2nd ed., Vol. 7). New York: Wiley.

McCoy, D. C., & Raver, C. C. (2012, in press). Caregiver emotional expressiveness, child emotion regulation, and child behavior problems among Head Start families. *Social Development*.

McCrae, R. R., & Costa, P. T. (1990). *Personality in adulthood*. New York: Guilford.

McCrae, R. R., & Costa, P. T. (2006). Cross-cultural perspectives on adult personality trait development. In D. K. Mroczek & T. D. Little (Eds.). *Handbook of personality development*. Mahwah, NJ: Erlbaum.

McCrae, R. R., Gaines, J. F., & Wellington, M. A. (2013, in press). The five-factor model in fact and fiction. In I. B. Weiner & others (Eds.), *Handbook of psychology* (2nd ed., Vol. 5). New York: Wiley.

McCullough, M. E., Enders, C. K., Brion, S. L., & Jain, A. R. (2005). The varieties of religious development in adulthood: A longitudinal investigation of religion and rational choice. *Journal of Personality and Social Psychology, 89*, 78–89.

McCullough, M. E., & Willoughby, B. L. (2009). Religion, self-regulation, and self-control: Associations, explanations, and implications. *Psychological Bulletin, 135*, 69–93.

McCutcheon, V. V., & others. (2012, in press). Environmental influences predominate in remission from alcohol use disorder in young adult twins. *Psychological Medicine.*

McDermott, B. M., & Cobham, V. E. (2012, in press). Family functioning in the aftermath of a disaster. *BMC Psychiatry.*

McDonald, S., & others. (2009). Preterm birth and low birth weight among in vitro fertilization singletons: A systematic review and meta-analyses. *European Journal of Obstetrics, Gynecology, and Reproductive Biology, 146*, 138–148.

McDonald, S. D., & others. (2010). Preterm birth and low birth weight among in vitro fertilization twins: A systematic review and meta-analyses. *European Journal of Obstetrics, Gynecology, and Reproductive Biology, 148*, 105–113.

McDonough, J. E. (2012, in press). The road ahead for the Affordable Care Act. *New England Journal of Medicine.*

McDougall, S., & House, B. (2012). Brain training in older adults: Evidence of transfer to memory span performance and pseudo-Matthew effects. *Neuropsychology, Development, and Cognition B. Aging, Neuroscience, and Cognition, 19*, 195–221.

McElhaney, K. B., & Allen, J. P. (2012). Sociocultural perspectives on adolescent autonomy. In P. K. Kreig, M. S. Schulz, & S. T. Hauser (Eds.), *Adolescence and beyond.* New York: Oxford University Press.

McElwain, N. L., & Booth-LaForce, C. (2006). Maternal sensitivity to infant distress and nondistress as predictors of infant-mother attachment security. *Journal of Family Psychology, 2*, 247–255.

McGarry, J., Kim, H., Sheng, X., Egger, M., & Baksh, L. (2009). Postpartum depression and help seeking behavior. *Journal of Midwifery and Women's Health, 54*, 50–56.

McGee, L. M., & Richgels, D. J. (2012). *Literacy's beginnings* (6th ed.). Boston: Allyn & Bacon.

McGettigan, C., & others. (2012). An application of univariate and multivariate approaches to fMRI to quantifying the hemispheric lateralization of acoustic and linguistic processes. *Journal of Cognitive Neuroscience, 24*, 636–652.

McGillivray, G., & others. (2012). Genetic counseling and ethical issues with chromosome microarray analysis in prenatal testing. *Prenatal Diagnosis, 2*, 389–395.

McHale, J., & Sullivan, M. (2008). Family systems. In M. Hersen & A. Gross (Eds.), *Handbook of Clinical Psychology* (Vol. 2). New York: Wiley.

McIntosh, C. G., Tonkin, S. L., & Gunn, A. J. (2010). What is the mechanism of sudden infant deaths associated with co-sleeping? *New Zealand Medical Journal, 122*, 69–75.

McIntosh, E., Gillanders, D., & Rodgers, S. (2010). Rumination, goal linking, daily hassles, and life events in major depression. *Clinical Psychology and Psychotherapy, 17*, 33–43.

McKain, W. C. (1972). A new look at older marriages. *The Family Coordinator, 21*, 61–69.

McKinney, E., & Murray, S. (2013). *Maternal-child nursing* (4th ed.). New York: Elsevier.

McKnight, A. J., & McKnight, A. S. (1993). The effect of cellular phone use upon driver attention. *Accident Analysis and Prevention, 25*, 259–265.

McKnight, J. R., & others. (2011). Obesity in pregnancy: Problems and potential solutions. *Frontiers in Bioscience, 3*, 442–552.

McLachlan, H. (2011). Moral duties and euthanasia: Why to kill us is not necessarily the same as to let us die. *Journal of Medical Ethics, 37*, 766–767.

McLaughlin, K. (2003, December 30). Commentary in K. Painter, "Nurse dispenses dignity for dying." *USA Today*, Section D, pp. 1–2.

McLaughlin, K. A., Fox, N. A., Zeanah, C. H., & Nelson, C. A. (2011). Adverse rearing environments and neural development in children: The development of frontal electroencephalogram asymmetry. *Biological Psychiatry, 70*, 1008–1015.

McLeskey, J. M., Rosenberg, M. S., & Westling, D. L. (2013). *Inclusion* (2nd ed.). Upper Saddle River, NJ: Pearson.

McLoyd, V. C., Kaplan, R., Purtell, K. M., & Huston, A. C. (2011). Assessing the effects of a work-based antipoverty program for parents on youths' future orientation and employment experiences. *Child Development, 82*, 113–132.

McMahon, E. M., Reulbach, U., Keeley, H., Perry, I. J., & Arensman, E. (2012). Reprint of: Bullying victimization, self-harm, and associated factors in Irish boys. *Social Science and Medicine, 74*, 490–497.

McNamara, F., & Sullivan, C. E. (2000). Obstructive sleep apnea in infants. *Journal of Pediatrics, 136*, 318–323.

McNeil, D. A., & others. (2012, in press). Getting more than they realized they needed: A qualitative study of women's experience of group prenatal care. *BMC Pregnancy and Childbirth.*

McNeill, K. L., & Krajcik, J. S. (2012). *Supporting grade 5-8 students in constructing explanations in science.* Boston: Allyn & Bacon.

McNulty, J. K., Karney, B. R., & Neff, L.A. (2008). Beyond initial attraction: physical attractiveness in newlywed marriage. *Journal of Family Psychology, 22*, 135–143.

McRae, K., & others. (2012). The development of emotion regulation: An fMRI study of cognitive reappraisal in children, adolescents, and adults. *Social Cognitive and Affective Neuroscience, 7*, 11–22.

McWilliams, L. A., & Bailey, S. J. (2010). Association between adult attachment rating and health conditions: Evidence from the National Comorbidity Survey replication. *Health Psychology, 29*, 446–453.

Meade, C. S., Kershaw, T. S., & Ickovics, J. R. (2008). The intergenerational cycle of teenage motherhood: An ecological approach. *Health Psychology, 27*, 419–429.

Meaney, M. J. (2010). Epigenetics and the biological definition of gene x environment interactions. *Child Development, 81*, 41–79.

Mechakra-Tahiri, S. D., Zunzunegui, M. V., Preville, M., & Dube, M. (2010). Gender, social relationships and depressive disorders in adults aged 65 and over in Quebec. *Chronic Diseases in Canada, 30*, 56–65.

Meerlo, P., Sgoifo, A., & Suchecki, D. (2008). Restricted and disrupted sleep: Effects on autonomic function, neuroendocrine stress systems, and stress responsivity. *Sleep Medicine Review.*

Mehari, A., & others. (2012). Mortality in adults with sickle-cell disease and pulmonary hypertension. *Journal of the American Medical Association, 307*, 1254–1256.

Mehl, M. R., Vazire, S., Ramirez-Esparza, N., Slatcher, R. B., & Pennebaker, J. W. (2007). Are women really more talkative than men? *Science, 317*, 82.

Meltzi, G., & Ely, R. (2009). Language development in the school years. In J. B. Gleason & N. Ratner (Eds.), *The development of language* (7th ed.). Boston: Allyn & Bacon.

Meltzoff, A. N. (1988). Infant imitation and memory: Nine-month-old infants in immediate and deferred tests. *Child Development, 59*, 217–225.

Meltzoff, A. N. (2004). Imitation as a mechanism of social cognition: Origins of empathy, theory of mind, and the representation of action. In U. Goswami (Ed.), *Blackwell handbook of childhood cognitive development.* Malden, MA: Blackwell.

Meltzoff, A. N. (2005). Imitation. In B. Hopkins (Ed.), *Cambridge encyclopedia of child development.* Cambridge: Cambridge University Press.

Meltzoff, A. N. (2007). Infants' causal learning. In A. Gopnik & L. Schulz (Eds.), *Causal learning.* New York: Oxford University Press.

Meltzoff, A. N. (2008). Unpublished review of J. W. Santrock's *Life-span development* (12th ed.). New York: McGraw-Hill.

Meltzoff, A. N. (2011). Social cognition and the origins of imitation, empathy, and theory of mind. In U. Goswami (Ed.), *Wiley-Blackwell handbook of childhood cognitive development* (2nd ed.). New York: Wiley.

Meltzoff, A. N., & Brooks, R. (2006). Eyes wide shut: The importance of eyes in infant gaze following and understanding of other minds. In R. Flom, K. Lee, & D. Muir (Eds.), *Gaze following: Its development and significance.* Mahwah, NJ: Erlbaum.

Meltzoff, A. N., & Moore, M. K. (1998). Object representation, identity, and the paradox of early permanence: Steps toward a new framework. *Infant Behavior and Development, 21*, 201–235.

Meltzoff, A. N., & Moore, M. K. (1999). A new foundation for cognitive development in infancy: The birth of the representational infant. In E. K. Skolnick, K. Nelson, S. A. Gelman, & P. H. Miller (Eds.), *Conceptual development*, Mahwah. NJ: Erlbaum.

Meltzoff, A. N., & Williamson, R. A. (2010). The importance of imitation for theories of social-cognitive development. In J. G. Bremner & T. D. Wachs (Eds.), *Wiley-Blackwell handbook of infant development* (2nd ed.). New York: Wiley.

Meltzoff, A. N., & Williamson, R. A. (2013). Imitation: Social, cognitive, and theoretical Perspectives. In P. D. Zelazo (Ed.), *Oxford handbook of developmental psychology.* New York: Oxford University Press.

Melzi, G., Schick, A. R., & Kennedy, J. L. (2011). Narrative elaboration and participation: Two dimensions of maternal elicitation style. *Child Development, 82,* 1282–1296.

Memari, A., Ziaee, V., Mirfaxeli, F., & Kordi, R. (2012). Investigation of autism comorbidities and associations in a school-based community sample. *Journal of Child and Adolescent Psychiatric Nursing, 25,* 84–90.

Mendez, M. A., & others. (2012, in press). The brain GABA-benzodiazepine receptor alpha-5 subtype in autism spectrum disorder: A pilot [(11)C] Ro15-4513 positron emission tomography study. *Neuropharmacology.*

Menendez, S., Hidalgo, M.V., Jiminez, L., & Moreno, M. C. (2011). Father involvement and marital relationship during transition to parenthood: Differences between dual and single earners. *Spanish Journal of Psychology, 14,* 639–647.

Menn, L., & Stoel-Gammon, C. (2009). Phonological development: Learning sounds and sound patterns. In J. Berko Gleason (Ed.), *The development of language* (7th ed.). Boston: Allyn & Bacon.

Mennella, J. A. (2009). Taste and smell. In R. A. Shweder & others (Eds.), *The child: An encyclopedic companion.* Chicago: University of Chicago Press.

Menon, R., & others. (2011). Cigarette smoking induces oxidative stress and atopsis in normal fetal membranes. *Placenta, 32,* 317–322.

Menyuk, P., Liebergott, J., & Schultz, M. (1995). *Early language development in full-term and premature infants.* Hillsdale, NJ: Erlbaum.

Mepham, S. O., Bland, R. M., & Newell, M. L. (2011). Prevention of mother-to-child transmission of HIV in resource-rich and -poor settings. *BJOG, 118,* 202–218.

Meredith, N. V. (1978). Research between 1960 and 1970 on the standing height of young children in different parts of the world. In H. W. Reece & L. P. Lipsitt (Eds.), *Advances in child development and behavior* (Vol. 12). New York: Academic Press.

Merewood, A., & others. (2007). Breastfeeding duration rates and factors affecting continued breastfeeding among infants born at an inner-city U.S. baby-friendly hospital. *Journal of Human Lactation, 23,* 157–164.

Merrill, D. A., & others. (2012). Self-reported memory impairment and brain PET of amyloid and tau in middle-aged and older adults without dementia. *International Psychogeriatrics, 24,* 1076–1084.

Merrill, D. M. (2009). Parent-child relationships: Later-life. In D. Carr (Ed.), *Encyclopedia of the life course and human development.* Boston: Gale Cengage.

Mesman, J., van Ijzendoorn, M. H., & Bakermans-Kranenburg, M. J. (2009). The many facets of the still-face paradigm: A review and meta analysis. *Developmental Review, 29,* 120–162.

Messiah, S. E., Miller, T. L., Lipshultz, S. E., & Bandstra, E. S. (2011). Potential latent effects of prenatal cocaine exposure on growth and the risk of cardiovascular and metabolic disease in childhood. *Progress in Pediatric Cardiology, 31,* 59–65.

Meyer, M. H., & Parker, W. M. (2011). Gender, aging, and social policy. In R. H. Binstock & L. K. George (Eds.), *Handbook of aging and the social sciences* (7th ed.). New York: Elsevier.

Meyer, S. L., Weible, C. M., & Woeber, K. (2010). Perceptions and practice of waterbirth: A survey of Georgia midwives. *Journal of Midwifery and Women's Health, 55,* 55–59.

Meyers, J. (2010, April 1). Suicides open eyes to bullying. *Dallas Morning News,* pp. 1A–2A.

Michael, R. T., Gagnon, J. H., Laumann, E. O., & Kolata, G. (1994). *Sex in America.* Boston: Little, Brown.

Mikels, J. A., & others. (2010). Following your heart or your head: Focusing on emotions versus information differentially influences the decisions of younger and older adults. *Journal of Experimental Psychology: Applied, 17,* 87–95.

Mikulincer, M., & Shaver, P. R. (2007). *Attachment in adulthood.* New York: Guilford.

Mikulincer, M., & Shaver, P. R. (2012). Attachment theory expanded: A behavioral systems approach to personality. In K. Deaux & M. Snyder (Eds.), *Oxford handbook of personality and social psychology.* New York: Oxford University Press.

Mikulincer, M., Shaver, P. R., Bar-on, N., & ein-Dor, T. (2010). The pushes and pulls of close relationships: Attachment insecurities and relational ambivalence. *Journal of Personality and Social Psychology, 98,* 450–468.

Milberg, A., Olsson, E. C., Jakobsson, M., Olsson, M., & Friedrichsen, M. (2008). Family members' perceived needs for bereavement follow-up. *Journal of Pain and Symptom Management, 35,* 58–69.

Milburn, N. G., & others. (2012). A family intervention to reduce sexual risk behavior, substance use, and delinquency among newly homeless youth. *Journal of Adolescent Health, 50,* 358–364.

Miller, B. C., Benson, B., & Galbraith, K. A. (2001). Family relationships and adolescent pregnancy risk: A research synthesis. *Developmental Review, 21,* 1–38.

Miller, C. F., Lurye, L. E., Zusuls, K. M., & Ruble, D. N. (2009). Accessibility of gender stereotype domains: Developmental and gender differences in children. *Sex Roles, 60,* 870–881.

Miller, D. I., Taler, V., Davidson, P. S., & Messier, C. (2012). Measuring the impact of exercise on cognitive aging: Methodological issues. *Neurobiology of Aging, 33,* e29–e43.

Miller, G. T., & Spoolman, S. (2012). *Living in the environment* (17th ed.). Boston: Cengage.

Miller, J. (2007). Cultural psychology of moral development. In S. Kitayama & D. Cohen (Eds.), *Handbook of cultural psychology.* New York: Guilford.

Miller, J. B. (1986). *Toward a new psychology of women* (2nd ed.). Boston: Beacon Press.

Miller, J. G., & Kinsbourne, M. (2012). Culture and neuroscience in developmental psychology: Contributions and challenges. *Child Development Perspectives, 6,* 35–41.

Miller, K. G. (2010). Long-term care: Facility quality and safety, Issue brief. *Policy Tracking Service, 4,* 1–42.

Miller, L. M., & Bell, R. A. (2012). Online health information seeking: The influence of age, information trustworthiness, and search challenges. *Journal of Aging and Health, 24,* 525–541.

Miller, M., Ho, J., & Hinshaw, S. P. (2012). Executive functions in girls with ADHD followed prospectively into young adulthood. *Neuropsychology, 26,* 278–287.

Miller, M. D. (2012). Complicated grief in late life. *Dialogues in Clinical Neuroscience 14,* 195–202.

Miller, P. H. (2011). Piaget's theory: Post, present, and future. In U. Goswami (Ed.), *Wiley-Blackwell handbook of childhood cognitive development* (2nd ed.). New York: Wiley.

Miller, R. (2012). *Intimate relationships* (6th ed.). New York: McGraw-Hill.

Miller, R. A. (2009). Cell stress and aging: New emphasis on multiplex resistance mechanisms. *Journals of Gerontology A: Biological Sciences and Medical Sciences, 64,* 179–182.

Miller, S., Malone, P., Dodge, K. A., & Conduct Problems Prevention Research Group. (2011). Developmental trajectories of boys' and girls' delinquency: Sex differences and links to later adolescent outcomes. *Journal of Abnormal Child Psychology, 38,* 1021–1033.

Miller, S. A. (2012). *Theory of mind: Beyond the preschool years.* New York: Psychology Press.

Miller-Perrin, C. L., Perrin, R. D., & Kocur, J. L. (2009). Parental, physical, and psychological aggression: Psychological symptoms in young adults. *Child Abuse and Neglect, 33,* 1–11.

Mills, B., Reyna, V., & Estrada, S. (2008). Explaining contradictory relations between risk perception and risk taking. *Psychological Science, 19,* 429–433.

Mills, C. M., Danovitch, J. H., Grant, M. G., & Elashi, F. B. (2012). Little pitchers with their big ears: Preschoolers solve problems by listening to others ask questions. *Child Development, 83,* 568–580.

Mills, C. M., Elashi, F. B., & Archacki, M. A. (2011, March). *Evaluating sources of information and misinformation: Developmental and individual differences in the elementary school years.* Paper presented at the biennial meeting of the Society for Research in Child Development, Montreal.

Mills, D., & Mills, C. (2000). *Hungarian kindergarten curriculum translation.* London: Mills Production.

Mills-Koonce, W. R., Propper, C. B., & Barnett, M. (2012). Poor infant soothability and later insecure-ambivalent attachment: Developmental change in phenotypic markers of risk or two measures of the same construct? *Infant Behavior and Development, 35,* 215–235.

Milne, E., & others. (2012). Parental prenatal smoking and risk of childhood acute lymphoblastic leukemia. *American Journal of Epidemiology, 175,* 43–53.

Milner, C., Van Norman, K., & Milner, J. (2012). The media's portrayal of aging. *Global population aging: Peril or promise?* Geneva, SWIT: World Economic Forum.

Miltenberger, R. G. (2012). *Behavior modification* (5th ed.). Boston: Cengage.

Minde, K., & Zelkowitz, P. (2008). Premature babies. In M. M. Haith & J. B. Benson (Eds.), *Encyclopedia of infancy and early childhood development.* Oxford, UK: Elsevier.

Mindell, J. A., Sadeh, A., Kohyama, J., & How, T. H. (2010). Parental behaviors and sleep outcomes in infants and toddlers: A cross-cultural comparison. *Sleep Medicine, 11,* 393–399.

Mindell, J. A., Sadeh, A., Wiegand, B., How, T. H., & Goh, D. Y. (2010). Cross-cultural differences in infant and toddler sleep. *Sleep Medicine, 11,* 274–280.

Ming, G. L., & Song, H. (2011). Adult neurogenesis in the mammalian brain: Significant answers and significant questions. *Neuron, 70,* 687–702.

Ming, L., & others. (2012, in press). Synchronization between embryo development and endometrium is a contributing factor for rescue ICSI outcome. *Reproductive Biomedicine Online.*

Minguez-Milio, J. A., & others. (2011). Perinatal outcome and long-term follow-up of extremely low birth weight infants depending on the mode of delivery. *Journal of Maternal-Fetal and Neonatal Medicine, 24,* 1235–1238.

Minkler, M., & Fuller-Thompson, E. (2005). African American grandparents raising grandchildren: A national study using the Census 2000 American Community Survey. *Journals of Gerontology B: Psychological Sciences and Social Sciences, 60,* S82–S92.

Minnes, S., & others. (2010). The effects of prenatal cocaine exposure on problem behavior in children 4-10 years. *Neurotoxicology and Teratology, 32,* 443–451.

Minnesota Family Investment Program. (2009). *Longitudinal study of early MFIP recipients.* Retrieved January 12, 2009, from http://www.dhs.state.mn.us/main/idcplg?IdcService5GET_DYNAMIC_CONVERSION&...

Minor, R. K., Allarad, J. S., Younts, C. M., Ward, T. M., & de Cabo, R. (2010). Dietary interventions to extend life span and health span based on calorie restriction. *Journals of Gerontology A: Biological Sciences and Medical Sciences, 65,* 695–703.

Miotto, E. C., & others. (2012, in press). Semantic strategy training increases memory performance and brain activity in patients with prefrontal cortex lesions. *Clinical Neurology and Neurosurgery.*

Mirman, J. H., Albert, D., Jacobsohn, L. S., & Winston, F. K. (2012). Factors associated with adolescents' propensity to drive with multiple passengers and to engage in risky driving behaviors. *Journal of Adolescent Health, 50,* 634–640.

Mischel, W. (2004). Toward an integrative science of the person. *Annual Review of Psychology* (Vol. 55). Palo Alto, CA: Annual Reviews.

Mischel, W., & others. (2011). 'Willpower' over the life span: Decomposing self-regulation. *Social Cognitive and Affective Neuroscience, 6,* 252–256.

Mishra, G. D., Cooper, R., Tom, S. E., & Kuh, D. (2009). Early life circumstances and their impact on menarche and menopause. *Women's Health, 5,* 175–190.

Mistry, J., Contreras, M., & Dutta, R. (2013, in press). Culture and child development. In I. B. Weiner & others (Eds.), *Handbook of psychology* (2nd ed., Vol. 6). New York: Wiley.

Mitchell, B. A. (2007). Marriage and divorce. In J. E. Birren (Ed.), *Encyclopedia of gerontology* (2nd ed.). San Diego: Academic Press.

Mitchell, E. A., Stewart, A. W., Crampton, P., & Salmond, C. (2000). Deprivation and sudden infant death syndrome. *Social Science and Medicine, 51,* 147–150.

Mitchell, V., & Helson, R. (1990). Women's prime of life: Is it the 50s? *Psychology of Women Quarterly, 14,* 451–470.

Miura, M., & others. (2011). Clinical application of fetal sex determination using cell-free fetal DNA in pregnant carriers of X-linked genetic disorders. *Journal of Human Genetics, 56,* 296–299.

Miyake, K., Chen, S., & Campos, J. (1985). Infants' temperament, mothers' mode of interaction and attachment in Japan: An interim report. In I. Bretherton & F. Waters (Eds.), Growing points of attachment theory and research, *Monographs of the Society for Research in Child Development, 50* (1–2, Serial No. 109), 276–297.

Mize, K. D., & Jones, N. A. (2012). Infant physiological and behavioral responses to loss of maternal attention to a social-rival. *International Journal of Psychophysiology, 83,* 16–23.

MMWR. (2006, June 9). Youth risk behavior surveillance—United States 2005 (Vol. 255). Atlanta: Centers for Disease Control and Prevention.

Moak, G. S. (2011). Treatment of late-life mental disorders in primary care: We can do a better job. *Journal of Aging and Social Policy, 23,* 274–285.

Moen, P. (2007). Unpublished review of J. W. Santrock's *Life-span development* (12th ed.). New York: McGraw-Hill.

Moen, P. (2009a). Careers. In D. Carr (Ed.), *Encyclopedia of the life course and human development.* Boston: Gale Cengage.

Moen, P. (2009b). Dual-career couples. In D. Carr (Ed.), *Encyclopedia of the life course and human development.* Boston: Gale Cengage.

Moen, P., Kelly, E., and Magennis, R. (2008). Gender strategies: Social and institutional convoys, mystiques, and cycles of control. In M. C. Smith & T. G. Reio (Eds.), *Handbook of research on adult development and learning.* Mahwah: Erlbaum.

Mok, A., & Morris, M. W. (2012). Managing two cultural identities: The malleability of bicultural identity integration as a function of induced global or local processing. *Personality and Social Psychology Bulletin, 38,* 233–246.

Molina, R. C., Roca, C. G., Zamorano, J. S., & Araya, E. G. (2010). Family planning and adolescent pregnancy. *Best Practices and Research: Clinical Obstetrics and Gynecology, 24,* 209–222.

Moller, J., Bjorkeenstam, E., Ljung, R., & Yngwe, M. A. (2011). Widowhood and the risk of psychiatric care, psychotropic medication, and all-cause mortality: A cohort of 658,022 elderly people in Sweden. *Aging and Mental Health, 15,* 259–266.

Monahan, C. J., & others. (2012). Health-related quality of life among heavy-drinking college students. *American Journal of Health Behavior, 36,* 289–299.

Monk, C., Fitelson, E. M., & Werner, E. (2011). Mood disorders and their pharmacological treatment during pregnancy: Is the future child affected? *Pediatric Research, 69,* 3R–10R.

Monserud, M. A. (2008). Intergenerational relationships and affectual solidarity between grandparents and young adults. *Journal of Marriage and the Family, 70,* 182–195.

Monserud, M. A. (2011). Changes in grandchildren's adult role statuses and their relationships to grandparents. *Journal of Family Issues, 32,* 425–451.

Montagna, P., & Chokroverty, S. (2011). *Sleep disorders.* New York: Elsevier.

Monti, J. M., Hillman, C. H., & Cohen, N. J. (2012, in press). Aerobic fitness enhances relational memory in preadolescent children: The FITKids randomized control trial. *Hippocampus.*

Montirosso, R., & others. (2012, in press). Level of NICU quality and developmental care and neurobehavioral performance in very preterm infants. *Pediatrics.*

Montoya Arizabaleta, A. V., & others. (2010). Aerobic exercise during pregnancy improves health-related quality of life: A randomized trial. *Journal of Physiotherapy, 56,* 253–258.

Moon, R. Y., & Fu, L. (2012). Sudden infant death syndrome: An update. *Pediatrics in Review, 33,* 314–320.

Moon, R. Y., & others. (2012). Pacifier use and SIDS: Evidence for a consistently reduced risk. *Maternal and Child Health Journal, 16,* 609–614.

Moore, D. (2001). *The dependent gene.* New York: W. H. Freeman.

Moore, D. (2013). Behavioral genetics, genetics, and epigenetics. In P. D. Zelazo (Ed.), *Oxford handbook of developmental psychology.* New York: Oxford University Press.

Moore, K. A., Murphey, D., & Bandy, T. (2012, in press). Positive child well-being: An index based on data for individual children. *Maternal and Child Health Journal.*

Moore, M. (2012). Behavioral sleep problems in children and adolescents. *Journal of Clinical Psychology in Medical Settings, 19,* 77–83.

Moos, B. (2007, July 4). Who'll care for aging boomers? Dallas Morning News, A1–A2.

Morales-Campos, D. Y., Markham, C., Peskin, M. F., & Fernandez, M. E. (2012). Sexual initiation, parent practices, and acculturation in Hispanic seventh graders. *Journal of School Health, 82,* 75–81.

Moran, S., & Gardner, H. (2006). Extraordinary achievements. In W. Damon & R. Lerner (Eds.), *Handbook of child psychology* (6th ed.). New York: Wiley.

Moran, S., & Gardner, H. (2007). Hill, skill, and will: Executive function from a multiple intelligences perspective. In L. Meltzer (ed.), *Executive function in education.* New York: Guilford.

Morasch, K. C., & Bell, M. A. (2012). Self-regulation of negative affect at 5 and 10 months. *Developmental Psychobiology, 54,* 215–221.

Morasch, K. C., Raj, V. R., & Bell, M. A. (2013, in press). The development of cognitive control from infancy through childhood. In D. Reisberg (Ed.), *Oxford handbook of cognitive psychology.* New York: Oxford University Press.

Moravcik, E., Nolte, S., & Feeney, S. (2012). *Meaningful curriculum for young children.* Upper Saddle River, NJ: Pearson.

Moreau, C., Beltzer, N., Bozon, M., Bajos, N., & the CSF Group. (2011). Sexual-risk taking following relationship break-ups. *European Journal of Contraception and Reproductive Health Care, 16,* 95–99.

Morgante, J. C., Zolfaghari, R., & Johnson, S. P. (2012). A critical test of temporal and spatial accuracy of the Tobii T60XL eye tracker. *Infancy, 17,* 9–32.

Morin, C. M., Savard, J., & Ouellet, M-C. (2013, in press). Nature and treatment of insomnia. In I. B. Weiner & others (Eds.), *Handbook of psychology* (2nd ed., Vol. 9). New York: Wiley.

Morra, L., Zade, D., McGlinchey, R. E., & Milberg, W. P. (2012, in press). Normal aging and cognition: The unacknowledged contribution of cerebrovascular risk factors. *Neuropsychology, Development, and Cognition B. Aging, Neuropsychology, and Cognition.*

Morra, S., Gobbo, C., Marini, Z., & Sheese, R. (2008). *Cognitive development: Neo-Piagetian perspectives.* Mahwah, NJ: Erlbaum.

Morris, A., Cui, L., & Steinberg, L. (2013, in press). Arrested development: The effects of incarceration on the development of psychosocial immaturity. *Development and Psychopathology.*

Morris, B. J., & others. (2012, in press). A 'snip' in time: What is the best age to circumcise? *BMC Pediatrics.*

Morrison, G. S. (2012). *Early childhood education today* (12th ed.). Upper Saddle River, NJ: Pearson.

Morrison, J. H., & Baxter, M. G. (2012). The aging cortical synapse: Hallmarks and implications for cognitive decline. *Nature Reviews: Neuroscience, 13,* 240–250.

Morrissey, T. W. (2009). Multiple child-care arrangements and young children's behavioral outcomes. *Child Development, 80,* 59–76.

Morrow, C. E., & others. (2006). Learning disabilities and intellectual functioning in school-aged children with prenatal cocaine exposure. *Developmental Neuropsychology, 30,* 905–931.

Morrow, L. (2012). *Literacy development in the early years* (7th ed.). Boston: Allyn & Bacon.

Mortensen, O., Torsheim, T., Melkevik, O., & Thuen, F. (2012). Adding a baby to the equation. Married and cohabiting women's relationship satisfaction in the transition to parenthood. *Family Process, 51,* 122–139.

Mortimer, J. A. (2012, in press). The Nun Study: Risk factors for pathology and clinical-pathologic correlations. *Current Alzheimer Research.*

Mortimer, J. A., & others. (2012). Changes in brain volume and cognition in a randomized trial of exercise and social interaction in a community-based sample of non-demented Chinese elders. *Journal of Alzheimer's Disease, 30,* 757–766.

Moshman, D. (2011). *Adolescent rationality and development: Cognition, morality, and identity* (3rd ed.). New York: Psychology Press.

Mosing, M. A., & others. (2012). Genetic influences on life span and its relationship to personality: A 16-year follow-up study of a sample of aging twins. *Psychosomatic Medicine, 74,* 16–22.

Moslehi, J., DePinho, R. A., & Sahin, E. (2012). Telomeres and mitochondria in the aging heart. *Circulation Research, 110,* 1226–1237.

Motowidlo, S. J., & Kell, H. J. (2013). Job performance. In I. B. Weiner & others (Eds.), *Handbook of psychology* (2nd ed., Vol. 12). New York: Wiley.

Moxey, A., McEvoy, M., Bowe, S., & Attia, J. (2011). Spirituality, religion, social support, and health among older Australian adults. *Australasian Journal of Aging, 30,* 82–88.

Mroczek, D. K., & Kolarz, C. M. (1998). The effect of age on positive and negative affect: A developmental perspective on happiness. *Journal of Personality and Social Psychology, 75,* 1333–1349.

Mroczek, D. K., Spiro, A., & Griffin, P. W. (2006). Personality and aging. In J. E. Birren & K. W. Schale (Eds.). *Handbook of the psychology of aging* (6th ed.). San Diego: Academic Press.

Mullen, S. P., & others. (2012). Physical activity and functional limitations in older adults: The influence of self-efficacy and functional performance. *Journals of Gerontology B: Psychological Sciences and Social Sciences, 67,* 354–361.

Muller, U., & others. (2012). Knowing minds, controlling actions: The developmental relations between theory of mind and executive function from 2 to 4 years of age. *Journal of Experimental Child Psychology, 111,* 331–348.

Muluye, D., Woldeyohannes, D., Gizchew, M., & Tiruneh, M. (2012, in press). Infant feeding practice and associated factors of HIV positive mothers attending prevention of mother to child transmission and antiretroviral therapy clinics in Gondar Town health institutions, Northwest Ethiopia. *BMC Public Health.*

Mund, I., Bell, R., & Buchner, A. (2010). Age differences in reading with distraction: Sensory or inhibitory deficits. *Psychology and Aging, 25,* 886–897.

Mundy, P., Block, J., Delgado, C., Pomares, Y., Van Hecke, A. V., & Parlade, M. V. (2007). Individual differences and the development of joint attention in infancy. *Child Development, 78,* 938–954.

Munnell, A. H. (2011). *What is the average retirement age?* (Issue Brief No.11-11). Chestnut Hill, MA: Center for Retirement Research, Boston College.

Murphy, C. (2009). The chemical senses and nutrition in older adults. *Journal of Nutrition for the Elderly, 27,* 247–265.

Murphy, M. M., & Mazzocco, M. M. (2008). Mathematics learning disabilities in girls with fragile X or Turner syndrome during late elementary school. *Journal of Learning Disabilities, 41,* 29–46.

Murphy, S. L., Xu, J., Kochanek, K. D. (2012, January 12). Deaths: Preliminary data for 2010. Table 7. *National Vital Statistics Reports, 60*(4), 54–58.

Murphy-Hoefer, R., Alder, S., & Higbee, C. (2004). Perceptions about cigarette smoking and risks among college students. *Nicotine and Tobacco Research, 6*(Suppl. 3), S371–S374.

Murray, A. (2011). Montessori elementary philosophy reflects current motivation theories. *Montessori Life, 23,* 22–33.

Musick, K., & Bumpass, L. (2012). Re-examining the case for marriage: Union formation and changes in well-being. *Journal of Marriage and the Family, 74,* 1–18.

Mussen, P. H., Honzik, M., & Eichorn, D. (1982). Early adult antecedents of life satisfaction at age 70. *Journal of Gerontology, 37,* 316–322.

Mustroph, M. L., & others. (2012, in press). Aerobic exercise is a key variable in an enriched environment that increases hippocampal neurogenesis and water maze learning in male C57BL/6J mice. *Neuroscience.*

Muthusamy, V. R., & others. (2012). Acute exercise stress activates Nrf2/ARE signaling and promotes antioxidant mechanisms in myocardium. *Free Radical Biology and Medicine, 52,* 366–372.

Myers, D. G. (2010). *Psychology* (9th ed.). New York: Worth.

Myerson, J., Rank, M. R., Raines, F. Q., & Schnitzler, M. A. (1998). Race and general cognitive ability: The myth of diminishing returns in education. *Psychology Science, 9,* 139–142.

Mykyta, L., & Macartney, S. (2012, June). Sharing a household. Composition and economic well-being: 2007–2010. *Current Population Report,* P60-242. Washington, DC: U.S. Department of Commerce.

Mysyuk, Y., Westendorp, R. G., & Lindenberg, J. (2012, in press). Added value of elder abuse definitions: A review. *Journal of Elder Abuse and Neglect.*

N

Nabhan, Z. M., & Hannon, T. S. (2012). Cardiovascular risk factors for American children: What can be learned from current trends? *Journal of Adolescent Health, 50,* 107–109.

Nader, K. (2001). Treatment methods for childhood trauma. In J. P. Wilson, M. J. Friedman, & J. Lindy (Eds.), *Treating psychological trauma and PTSD.* New York: Guilford Press.

Nader, P., & others. (2006). Identifying risk for obesity in early childhood. *Pediatrics, 118,* e594–e601.

Nader, P. R., Bradley, R. H., Houts, R. M., McRitchie, S. L., & O'Brian, M. (2008). Moderate-to-vigorous physical activity from 9 to 15 years. *Journal of the American Medical Association, 300,* 295–305.

NAEYC (National Association for the Education of Young Children). (2009). Developmentally appropriate practice in early childhood programs serving children from birth through age 8. Washington, DC: Author.

Nag, T. C., & Wadhwa, S. (2012). Ultrastructure of the human retina in aging and various pathological states. *Micron, 43,* 759–781.

Nagasawa, M., Okabe, S., Mogi, K., & Kikusui, T. (2012, in press). Oxytocin and mutual communication in mother-infant bonding. *Frontiers in Human Neuroscience.*

Nagata, D. K., Kohn-Wood, L., & Suzuki, L. A. (Eds.) (2012). *Qualitative strategies for ethnocultural research.* Washington, DC: American Psychological Association.

Nagel, B. J., & others. (2011). Altered white matter microstructure in children with attention-deficit/hyperactivity disorder. *Journal of the American Academy of Child and Adolescent Psychiatry, 50,* 283–292.

Naismith, S. L., Lewis, S. J., & Rogers, N. L. (2011). Sleep-wake changes and cognition in neurogenerative diseases. *Progress in Brain Research, 190,* 21–52.

Najar, B., Hamadani, J. D., Ahmed, T., Tofail, F., Rahman, A., Huda, S. N., & others. (2008). Effects of psychosocial stimulation on growth and development of severely malnourished children in a nutrition unit in Bangladesh. *European Journal of Clinical Nutrition, 63*(6), 725–731.

Najman, J. M., Hayatbakhsh, M. R., Heron, M. A., Bor, W., O'Callaghan, M. J., & Williams, G. M. (2009). The impact of episodic and chronic poverty on child cognitive development. *Journal of Pediatrics, 154,* 284–289.

Najman, J. M., & others. (2010). Timing and chronicity of family poverty and development of unhealthy behaviors in children: A longitudinal study. *Journal of Adolescent Health, 46,* 538–544.

Nakajima, S., Masaya, I., Akemi, S., & Takako, K. (2012). Complicated grief in those bereaved by violent death: The effects of post-traumatic stress disorder on complicated grief. *Dialogues in Clinical Neuroscience, 14*, 210–214.

Nanni, V., Uher, R., & Danese, A. (2012). Childhood maltreatment predicts unfavorable course of illness and treatment outcome in depression: A meta-analysis. *American Journal of Psychiatry, 169*, 141–151.

Nansel, T. R., Overpeck, M., Pilla, R., Ruan, W., Simons-Morton, B., & Scheidt, P. (2001). Bullying behaviors among U.S. youth. *Journal of the American Medical Association, 285*, 2094–2100.

Naoi, N., & others. (2012). Cerebral responses to infant-directed speech and the effect of talker familiarity. *Neuroimage, 59*, 1733–1744.

Narváez, D. (2010). Moral complexity: The fatal attraction of truthiness and the importance of mature moral functioning. *Perspectives on Psychological Science, 5*(2), 163–181.

Narváez, D., & Hill, P. L. (2010). The relation of multicultural experiences to moral judgment and mindsets. *Journal of Diversity in Higher Education, 3*, 43–55.

Narvaez, D., Panskepp, J., Schore, A., & Gleason, T. (2012, in press). *Evolution, early experience, and human development.* New York: Oxford University Press.

Nash-Ditzel, S. (2010). Metacognitive reading strategies can improve comprehension. *Journal of College Reading and Learning, 40*, 45–63.

Natalizia, A., Casale, M., Guglielmelli, E., Rinaldi, V., Vressi, F., & Savinelli, F. (2010). An overview of hearing impairment in older adults: Perspectives for rehabilitation with hearing aids. *European Review for Medical and Pharmaceutical Sciences, 14*, 223–229.

Natan, M. B., Lowenstein, A., & Eisikovits, Z. (2011). Psycho-social factors affecting elders' maltreatment in long-term care facilities. *International Nursing Review, 57*, 113–120.

National Alliance for Caregiving. (2009). *Caregiving in the United States 2009.* Retrieved June 29, 2012, from www.caregiving.org/pdf/research/Caregiving

National Assessment of Educational Progress. (2005). *The nation's report card: 2005.* Washington, DC: National Center for Education Statistics.

National Assessment of Educational Progress. (2007). *The nation's report card: 2007.* Washington, DC: U.S. Department of Education.

National Association for Sport and Physical Education. (2002). *Active start: A statement of physical activity guidelines for children birth to five years.* Reston, VA: National Association for Sport and Physical Education Publications.

National Autism Association. (2011). *All about autism.* Retrieved July 30, 2011, from http://www.nationalautismassociation.org/definitions.php

National Cancer Institute. (2012). *Childhood cancer.* Rockville, MD: Author.

National Center for Education Statistics. (2002). *Work during college.* Washington, DC: U.S. Office of Education.

National Center for Education Statistics. (2007). *The condition of education 2007.* Washington, DC: U.S. Department of Education.

National Center for Education Statistics. (2009). *Comparative indicators of education in the United States and other G-8 countries: 2009.* Washington, DC: U.S. Department of Education.

National Center for Education Statistics. (2010). *The condition of education 2010.* Washington, DC: U.S. Department of Education.

National Center for Education Statistics. (2011). *The condition of education 2011.* Washington, DC: U.S. Department of Education.

National Center for Health Statistics. (2000). *Health United States 2000, with adolescent health chartbook.* Bethesda, MD: U.S. Department of Health and Human Services.

National Center for Health Statistics. (2002). *Sexual behavior and selected health measures: Men and women 15–44 years of age, United States, 2002,* PHS 2003-1250. Atlanta: Centers for Disease Control and Prevention.

National Center for Health Statistics. (2004). *Health United States.* Atlanta: Centers for Disease Control and Prevention.

National Center for Health Statistics. (2008). *Death by age and selected causes: 2005.* Table 114. *National Vital Statistics Report: Final data for 2005, 56*(10).

National Center for Health Statistics. (2009, January 7). *Public Release Statement: Preterm births rise 36 percent since early 1980s.* Atlanta: Centers for Disease Control and Prevention.

National Center for Health Statistics. (2010). Deaths, percentage of total deaths, and death rates for 10 leading causes of death in selected age groups, by race and sex: United States, 2006. *National Vital Statistics Reports, 58*(14), 25.

National Center for Health Statistics. (2011, March). Adult obesity prevalence in the United States and Canada. *NCHS Data Brief, No. 56.*

National Center for Health Statistics. (2011). *Births.* Atlanta: Centers for Disease Control and Prevention.

National Center for Health Statistics. (2011). *Sexually transmitted diseases.* Atlanta: Centers for Disease Control and Prevention.

National Center for Health Statistics. (2012). *Death rates.* Atlanta: Centers for Disease Control and Prevention.

National Center for Health Statistics. (2012). *Sexually transmitted diseases.* Atlanta: Centers for Disease Control and Prevention.

National Center for Vital Statistics. (2010). Births, marriages, divorces, deaths: Provisional data for November 2009. *National Vital Statistics Reports, 58*(23), 1–5.

National Center on Shaken Baby Syndrome. (2012). *Shaken baby syndrome.* Retrieved April, 20, 2011, from www.dontshake.org/

National Clearinghouse on Child Abuse and Neglect. (2004). *What is child abuse and neglect?* Washington, DC: U.S. Department of Health and Human Services.

National Council on Aging. (2000, March). *Myths and realities survey results.* Washington, DC: Author.

National Human Genome Research Institute. (2012). *Genome-wide association studies.* Retrieved April 11, 2012, from www.genome.gov/20019523

National Institute of Mental Health. (2012). *Autism spectrum disorders (pervasive developmental disorders).* Retrieved May 11, 2012, from www.nimh.nih.gov/Publicat/autism.clm

National Institutes of Health. (2004). *Women's Health Initiative Hormone Therapy Study.* Bethesda, MD: National Institutes of Health.

National Institutes of Health. (2008). Clinical trial.gov. Retrieved April 22, 2008.

National Marriage Project. (2011). *Unmarried cohabitation.* Retrieved June 9, 2012, from www.stateofouruniions.org/2011/social_indicators.php

National Sleep Foundation. (2006). *Sleep in America poll 2006.* Washington, DC: Author.

National Sleep Foundation. (2007). *Sleep in America poll 2007.* Washington, DC: Author.

National Sleep Foundation. (2012). *Children's sleep habits.* Retrieved April 30, 2012, from www.sleepfoundation.org

National Vital Statistics Report. (2004, March 7). *Deaths: Leading causes for 2002.* Atlanta: Centers for Disease Control and Prevention.

Naumann, R. B., Dellinger, A. M., & Kresnow, M. J. (2011). Driving self-restriction in high-risk conditions: How do older drivers compare to others? *Journal of Safety Research, 42*, 67–71.

Navab, A., Gillespie-Lynch, K., Johnson, S. P., Sigman, M., & Hutman, T. (2012, in press). Eye tracking as a measure of responsiveness to joint attention in infants at risk for autism. *Infancy.*

Navarro, A. E., Gassoumis, Z. D., & Wilber, K. H. (2012, in press). Holding abusers accountable: An elder abuse forensic center increases criminal prosecution of financial exploitation. *Gerontologist.*

Needham, A. (2009). Learning in infants' object perception, object-directed action, and tool use. In A. Needham & A. Woodward (Eds.), *Learning and the infant mind.* New York: Oxford University Press.

Needham, A., Barrett, T., & Peterman, K. (2002). A pick-me-up for infants' exploratory skills: Early simulated experiences reaching for objects using 'sticky mittens' enhances young infants' object exploration skills. *Infant Behavior and Development, 25*, 279–295.

Negriff, S., Susman, E. J., & Trickett, P. K. (2011). The development pathway from pubertal timing to delinquency and sexual activity from early to late adolescence. *Journal of Youth and Adolescence, 40*, 1343–1356.

Neikrug, A. B., & Ancoli-Israel, S. (2010). Sleep disorders in the older adult: A mini-review. *Gerontology, 56*, 181–189.

Nelson, A. M. (2012, in press). A comprehensive review of the evidence and current recommendations related to pacifier use. *Journal of Pediatric Nursing.*

Nelson, C. A. (2003). Neural development and lifelong plasticity. In R. M. Lerner, F. Jacobs, & D. Wertlieb (Eds.), *Handbook of applied developmental science* (Vol. 1). Thousand Oaks, CA: Sage.

Nelson, C. A. (2006). Unpublished review of J. W. Santrock's *Topical approach to life-span development* (4th ed.) New York: McGraw-Hill.

Nelson, C. A. (2007). A developmental cognitive neuroscience approach to the study of atypical development: A model system involving infants of diabetic mothers. In D. Coch, G. Dawson, & K. W. Fischer (Eds.), *Human behavior, learning, and the developing brain*. New York: Guilford.

Nelson, C. A. (2012). Brain development and behavior. In A. M. Rudolph, C. Rudolph, L. First, G. Lister, & A. A. Gersohon (Eds.), *Rudolph's pediatrics* (22nd ed.). New York: McGraw-Hill.

Nelson, C. A. (2013, in press). Neural development and lifelong plasticity. In D. P. Keating (Ed.), *Nature and nurture in early childhood development*. New York: Cambridge University Press.

Nelson, C. A., Thomas, K. M., & de Haan, M. (2006). Neural bases of cognitive development. In W. Damon & R. Lerner (Eds.), *Handbook of child psychology* (6th ed.). New York: Wiley.

Nelson, J. A., Leerkes, E. M., O'Brien, M., Calkins, S. D., & Maracovitch, S. (2012). African American and European American mothers' beliefs about negative emotions and emotion socialization practices. *Parenting, 12,* 22–41.

Nelson, J. L., Palonsky, S. B., & McCarthy, M. R. (2013). *Critical issues in education* (8th ed.). New York: McGraw-Hill.

Nelson, K. (1999). Levels and modes of representation: Issues for the theory of conceptual change and development. In E. K. Skolnick, K. Nelson, S. A. Gelman, & P. H. Miller (Eds.), *Conceptual development*. Mahwah, NJ: Erlbaum.

Nelson, L. J., Padilla-Walker, L. M., Carroll, J. S., Madsen, S. D., Barry, C. M., & Badger, S. (2007). "If you want me to treat you like an adult, start acting like one!" Comparing the criteria that emerging adults and their parents have for adulthood. *Journal of Family Psychology, 21,* 665–674.

Neugarten, B. L. (1986). The aging society. In A. Pifer & L. Bronte (Eds.). *Our aging society: Paradox and promise*. New York: W. W. Norton.

Neugarten, B. L. (1988, August). *Policy issues for an aging society*. Paper presented at the meeting of the American Psychological Association, Atlanta.

Neugarten, B. L., Havighurst, R. J., & Tobin, S. S. (1968). Personality and patterns of aging. In B. L. Neugarten (Ed.), *Middle age and aging*. Chicago: University of Chicago Press.

Neugarten, B. L., & Weinstein, K. K. (1964). The changing American grandparent. *Journal of Marriage and the Family, 26,* 199–204.

Neupert, S. D., Almeida, D. M., & Charles, S. T. (2007). Age differences in reactivity to daily stressors: The role of personal control. *Journals of Gerontology B: Psychological Sciences and Social Sciences, 62B,* P316–P225.

Nevarez, M. D., & others. (2010). Associations of early life risk factors with infant sleep duration. *Academic Pediatrics, 10,* 187–193.

Neville, H. J. (2006). Different profiles of plasticity within human cognition. In Y. Munakata & M. H. Johnson (Eds.). *Attention and Performance XXI: Processes of change in brain and cognitive development.* Oxford, UK: Oxford University Press.

Newcombe, N. (2008). The development of implicit and explicit memory. In N. Cowan & M. Courage (Eds.), *The development of memory in childhood*. Philadelphia: Psychology Press.

Newell, K., Scully, D. M., McDonald, P. V., & Ballargeon, R. (1989). Task constraints and infant grip configurations. *Developmental Psychobiology, 22,* 817–832.

Newman, A. B., & others. (2006). Association of long-distance corridor walk performance with mortality, cardiovascular disease, mobility limitation, and disability. *Journal of the American Medical Association, 295,* 2018–2026.

Newman, E. L., & others. (2012, in press). Cholinergic modulation of cognitive processing: Insights drawn from computational models. *Frontiers in Behavioral Neuroscience.*

Newman, M. L., Groom, C. J., Handelman, L. D., & Pennebaker, J. W. (2008). *Discourse Perspectives, 45,* 211–236.

Newsom, R. S., Boelen, P. A., Hofman, A., & Tiemeier, H. (2011). The prevalence and characteristics of complicated grief in older adults. *Journal of Affective Disorders, 132,* 231–238.

Newton, N. J., & Stewart, A. J. (2012). Personality development in adulthood. In S. K. Whitbourne & M. Sliwinski (Eds.), *Wiley-Blackwell handbook of adult development and aging*. New York: Wiley.

Nezu, A. M., Raggio, G., Evans, A. N., & Zezu, C. M. (2013, in press). Diabetes mellitus. In I. B Weiner & others (Eds.), *Handbook of psychology* (2nd ed., Vol. 9). New York: Wiley.

Ng, T. P., Feng, L., Niti, M., & Yap, K. B. (2010). Low blood pressure and depressive symptoms among Chinese older subjects: A population-based study. *American Journal of Medicine, 123,* 342–349.

Nguyen, T. V., & others. (2012, in press). Testosterone-related cortical maturation across childhood and adolescence. *Cerebral Cortex.*

Niajou, O. T., & others. (2012, in press). Shorter telomeres are associated with obesity and weight gain in the elderly. *International Journal of Obesity.*

NICHD. (2011). *SIDS facts.* Retrieved September 17, 2011, from http://www.nichd.nih/gov/sids

NICHD Early Child Care Research Network. (2000). Factors associated with fathers' caregiving activities and sensitivity with young children. *Developmental Psychology, 14,* 200–219.

NICHD Early Child Care Research Network. (2001). Nonmaternal care and family factors in early development: An overview of the NICHD study of Early Child Care. *Journal of Applied Developmental Psychology, 22,* 457–492.

NICHD Early Child Care Research Network. (2002). Structure → Process → Outcome: Direct and indirect effects of child care quality on young children's development. *Psychological Science, 13,* 199–206.

NICHD Early Child Care Research Network. (2003). Does amount of time spent in child care predict socioemotional adjustment during the transition to kindergarten? *Child Development, 74,* 976–1005.

NICHD Early Child Care Research Network. (2004). Type of child care and children's development at 54 months. *Early Childhood Research Quarterly, 19,* 203–230.

NICHD Early Child Care Research Network. (2005a). *Child care and development*. New York: Guilford.

NICHD Early Child Care Research Network. (2005b). Duration and developmental timing of poverty and children's cognitive and social development from birth through third grade. *Child Development, 76,* 795–810.

NICHD Early Child Care Research Network. (2005c). Predicting individual differences in attention, memory, and planning in first graders from experiences at home, child care, and school. *Developmental Psychology, 41,* 99–114.

NICHD Early Child Care Research Network. (2006). Infant-mother attachment classification: Risk and protection in relation to changing maternal caregiving quality. *Developmental Psychology, 42,* 38–58.

NICHD Early Child Care Research Network. (2009). Family-peer linkages: The mediational role of attentional processes. *Social Development, 18*(4), 875–895.

Nielsen, M. B., & Einarsen, S. (2012). Prospective relationships between workplace sexual harassment and psychological distress. *Occupational Medicine, 62,* 226–228.

Nieto, S., & Bode, P. (2012). *Affirming diversity* (6th ed.). Boston: Allyn & Bacon.

Nigro, G., & others. (2011). Role of the infections in recurrent spontaneous abortion. *Journal of Maternal-Fetal and Neonatal Medicine, 24,* 983–989.

Nisbett, R. E. (2003). *The geography of thought.* New York: Free Press.

Nisbett, R. E., & others. (2012, in press). Intelligence: New findings and theoretical developments. *American Psychologist.*

Nishikawa, N., & others. (2012, in press). Coadministration of Doperidone increases plasma Levodopa concentration in patients with Parkinson disease. *Clinical Neuropharmacology.*

Nixon, S. A., Rubincam, C., Casale, M., & Flicker, S. (2011). Is 80% a passing grade? Meanings attached to condom use in an abstinence-plus HIV prevention programme in South Africa. *AIDS Care, 23,* 213–220.

Noddings, N. (2007). *When school reform goes wrong.* New York: Teachers College Press.

Nodine, P. M., & Hastings-Tolsma, M. (2012). Maternal obesity: Improving pregnancy outcomes. *MCN American Journal of Maternal Child Nursing, 37,* 110–115.

Noel-Miller, C. M. (2011). Partner caregiving in older cohabiting couples. *Journals of Gerontology B: Psychological Sciences and Social Sciences, 66B,* 341–353.

Noftle, E. E., & Robins, R. W. (2007). Personality predictors of academic outcomes: Big Five correlates of GPA and SAT scores. *Journal of Personality and Social Psychology, 93,* 116–130.

Nolen-Hoeksema, S. (2011). *Abnormal psychology* (5th ed.). New York: McGraw-Hill.

Nolen-Hoeksema, S. (2012). Emotion regulation and psychopathology: The role of gender. *Annual Review of Clinical Psychology* (Vol. 8). Palo Alto, CA: Annual Review.

Nomoto, M., & others. (2009). Inter- and intra-individual variation in L-dopa pharmacokinetics in the treatment of Parkinson's disease. *Parkinsonism and Related Disorders, 15*(Suppl. 1), S21–S24.

Norman, J. F., Holmin, J. S., & Bartholomew, A. N. (2011). Visual memories for perceived length are well preserved in older adults. *Vision Research, 51,* 2057–2062.

Norouzieh, K. (2005). Case management of the dying child. *Case Manager, 16,* 54–57.

Norton, P. J., & Grellner, K. W. (2011). A retrospective study on infant bed-sharing in a clinical population. *Maternal and Child Health Journal, 15,* 507–513.

Nottelmann, E. D., & others. (1987). Gonadal and adrenal hormone correlates of adjustment in early adolescence. In R. M. Lerner & T. T. Foch (Eds.), *Biological-psychological interactions in early adolescence.* Hillsdale, NJ: Erlbaum.

Nouchi, R., & others. (2012). Brain training game improves executive functions and processing speed in the elderly: A randomized controlled trial. *PLoS One, 7(1),* e29676.

Noymer, A., & Lee, R. (2012, in press). Immigrant health around the world: Evidence from the World Values Survey. *Journal of Immigrant and Minority Health.*

Nucci, L. (2006). Education for moral development. In M. Killen & J. Smetana (Eds.), *Handbook of moral development.* Mahwah, NJ: Erlbaum.

Nunez, Y. O., & Mayfield, R. D. (2012, in press). Understanding alcoholism through microRNA signatures in brains of human alcoholics. *Frontiers in Genetics.*

Nurmsoo, E., Einav, S., & Hood, B. M. (2012). Best friends: Children use mutual gaze to identify friendship in others. *Developmental Science, 15,* 417–425.

Nyberg, L., & Backman, L. (2011a). Influences of biological and self-initiated factors on brain and cognition in adulthood and aging. In P. B. Baltes, P. A. Reuter-Lorenz, & F. Rosler (Eds.), *Lifespan development and the brain.* New York: Cambridge University Press.

Nyberg, L., & Backman, L. (2011b). Memory changes and the aging brain: A multimodal imaging approach. In K. W. Schaie & S. L. Willis (Eds.), *Handbook of the psychology of aging* (7th ed.). New York: Elsevier.

Nyberg, L., Lovden, M., Rilund, K., Lindenberger, U., & Backman, L. (2012). Memory aging and brain maintenance. *Current Trends in Cognitive Science, 16,* 292–305.

Nyberg, L., & others. (2012). Memory aging and brain maintenance. *Trends in Cognitive Science, 16,* 292–305.

Nylund, K., Bellmore, A., Nishina, A., & Graham, S. (2007). Subtypes, severity, and structural stability of peer victimization: What does latent class analysis say? *Child Development, 78,* 1706–1722.

O

O'Brien, M., & Moss, P. (2010). Fathers, work, and family policies in Europe. In M. E. Lamb (Ed.), *The father's role in child development* (5th ed.). New York: Wiley.

O'Callaghan, F. V., & others. (2010). The link between sleep problems in infancy and early childhood and attention problems at 5 and 14 years: Evidence from a birth cohort study. *Early Human Development, 86,* 419–424.

O'Callahan, M., & others. (2013, in press). Coronary heart disease and hypertension. In I. B. Weiner & others (Eds.), *Handbook of psychology* (2nd ed., Vol. 9). New York: Wiley.

O'Connor, D. B., & others. (2011). The relationships between sex hormones and sexual function in middle-aged and older European men. *Journal of Clinical Endocrinology and Metabolism, 96,* E1577–E1587.

O'Connor, E., & McCartney, K. (2007). Attachment and cognitive skills: An investigation of mediating mechanisms. *Journal of Applied Developmental Psychology, 28,* 458–476.

O'Donnell, A. M. (2012). Constructivism. In K. R. Harris, S. Graham, & T. Urdan (Eds.), *APA educational psychology handbook.* Washington, DC: American Psychological Association.

O'Donnell, E., Kirwan, L. D., & Goodman, J. M. (2009). Aerobic exercise training in healthy postmenopausal women: Effects of hormone therapy. *Menopause, 16,* 770–776.

O'Donovan, G., Kearney, E., Sherwood, R., & Hillsdon, M. (2011). Fatness, fitness, and cardiometabolic risk factors in middle-aged white men. *Metabolism, 61(2),* 213–220.

O'Halloran, A. M., & others. (2012, in press). Falls and fall efficacy: The role of sustained attention in older adults. *BMC Geriatrics.*

O'Hara, R. E., Gibbons, F. X., Weng, C. Y., Gerrard, M., & Simons, R. L. (2012). Perceived racial discrimination as a barrier to college enrollment for African Americans. *Personality and Social Psychology Bulletin, 38,* 77–89.

O'Rourke, N., Cappeliez, P., & Claxton, A. (2011). Functions of reminiscence and the psychological well-being of young-old and older adults over time. *Aging and Mental Health, 15,* 272–281.

Oakes, L. M. (2012). Advances in eye-tracking in infancy research. *Infancy, 17,* 1–8.

Oakes, L. M., Kannass, K. N., & Shaddy, D. J. (2002). Developmental changes in endogenous control of attention: The role of target familiarity on infants' distraction latency. *Child Development, 73,* 1644–1655.

Oates, J., & Abraham, S. (2010). *Llewellyn-Jones fundamentals of obstetrics and gynecology* (9th ed.). New York: Elsevier.

Obermann, M. L. (2011). Moral disengagement in self-reported and peer-nominated school bullying. *Aggressive Behavior, 37,* 133–144.

Obisesan, T. O., & others. (2012, in press). Neuroprotection and neurodegeneration in Alzhiemer's disease: Role of cardiovascular disease factors, implications for dementia rates, and prevention with aerobic exercise in African Americans. *International Journal of Alzheimer's Disease.*

Obler, L. K. (2009). Development in the older years. In Berko Gleason (Ed.), *The development of language* (7th ed.). Boston: Allyn & Bacon.

Occupational Outlook Handbook. (2012). Washington, DC: U.S. Department of Labor, Bureau of Labor Statistics.

Ochs, E., & Schieffelin, B. (2008). Language socialization and language acquisition. In P. A. Duff & N. H. Hornberger (Eds.), *Encyclopedia of language and education.* New York: Springer.

OECD. (2010a). *Obesity and the economics of prevention—Fit not fat.* Paris: OECD.

OECD. (2010b). *Strong performers and successful reformers in education: Lessons from PISA for the United States.* Paris, France: OECD.

Oerlemans, W. G., Bakker, A. B., & Veenhoven, R. (2011). Finding the key to happy aging: A day reconstruction of happiness. *Journals of Gerontology B: Psychological Sciences and Social Sciences, 66B,* 665–674.

Offer, D., Ostrov E., Howard, K. I., & Atkinson, R. (1988). *The teenage world: Adolescents' self-image in ten countries.* New York: Plenum.

Ogden, C. L., Carroll, M. D., Kit, B. K., & Flegal, K. M. (2012, January). Prevalence of obesity in the United States, 2009–2010. *NCHS Data Brief,* No. 82, pp. 1–9. Hyattsville, MD: National Center for Health Statistics.

Ogden, L. G., & others. (2012, in press). Cluster analysis of the National Weight Control Registry to identify distinct subgroups maintaining successful weight loss. *Obesity.*

Ohta, M., Tajiri, Y., Yamato, H., & Ikeda, M. (2012, in press). Effects of exercise therapy alone and in combination with a calcium channel blocker or an angiotensin receptor blocker in hypertensive patients. *Clinical and Experimental Hypertension.*

Okosun, I. S., Seale, J. P., Boltri, J. M., & Davis-Smith, M. (2012). Trends and clustering cardiometabolic risk factors in American adolescents from 1999 to 2008. *Journal of Adolescent Health, 50,* 132–139.

Olafsdottir, E., Andersson, D. K., & Stefansson, E. (2012). The prevalence of cataract in a population of with and without type 2 diabetes mellitus. *Acta Ophthalmologica, 90,* 334–340.

Olds, D. L., & others. (2004). Effects of home visits by paraprofessionals and nurses: Age four follow-up of a randomized trial. *Pediatrics, 114,* 1560–1568.

Olds, D. L., & others. (2007). Effects of nurse home visiting on maternal and child functioning: Age 9 follow-up of a randomized trial. *Pediatrics, 120,* e832–e845.

Olmstead, S. B., Pasley, K., & Fincham, F. D. (2012, in press). Hooking up and penetrative hookups: Correlates that differentiate college men. *Archives of Sexual Behavior.*

Olson, B. H., Haider, S. J., Vangjel, L., Bolton, T. A., & Gold, J. G. (2010a). A quasi-experimental evaluation of a breastfeeding support program for low income women in Michigan. *Maternal and Child Health Journal, 14(1),* 86–93.

Olson, B. H., Horodynski, M. A., Brophy-Herb, H., & lwanski, K. C. (2010b). Health professionals' perspectives on the infant feeding practices of low income mothers. *Maternal and Child Health Journal, 14(1),* 75–85.

Olson, D. H., DeFrain, J., & Skogrand, L. (2011). *Marriages and families* (7th ed.). New York: McGraw-Hill.

Olson, M. M., Trevino, D. B., Geske, J. A., & Vanderpool, H. (2012). Religious coping and mental health outcomes: An exploratory study of socioeconomically disadvantaged patients. *Explore, 8,* 172–176.

Olweus, D. (2003). Prevalence estimation of school bullying with the Olweus bully/victim questionnaire. *Aggressive Behavior, 29(3),* 239–269.

Onwudiwe, N. C., Stuart, B., Zuckerman, I. H., & Sorkin, J. D. (2011). Obesity and Medicare expenditure: Accounting for age-related height loss. *Obesity, 19,* 204–211.

Onwuteaka-Philipsen, B. D., Rurup, M. L., Pasman, H. R., & van der Heide, A. (2010). The last phase of life: Who requests and who receives euthanasia or physician-assisted suicide. *Medical Care, 48,* 596–603.

Opfer, J. E., & Gelman, S. A. (2011). Development of the animate-inanimate distinction. In U. Goswami (Ed.), *Wiley-Blackwell handbook of childhood cognitive development* (2nd ed.). New York: Wiley.

Ophir, E., Nass, C., & Wagner, A. D. (2009). Cognitive control in media multitaskers. *Proceedings of the National Academy of Sciences USA, 106,* 15583–15587.

Orbach, Y., Lamb, D., La Rooy, D., & Pipe, M-E. (2012). A case study of witness consistency and memory recovery across multiple investigative interviews. *Applied Cognitive Psychology, 26,* 118–129.

Ornstein, P., Coffman, J. L., & Grammer, J. K. (2007, April). *Teachers' memory-relevant conversations and children's memory performance.* Paper presented at the biennial meeting of the Society for Research in Child Development, Boston.

Ornstein, P. A., Coffman, J. L., & Grammer, J. K. (2009). Learning to remember. In O. A. Barbarin & B. H. Wasik (Eds.), *Handbook of child development and early education.* New York: Guilford.

Ornstein, P. A., Coffman, J. L., Grammer, J. K., San Souci, P. P., & McCall, L. E. (2010). Linking the classroom context and the development of children's memory skills. In J. Meece & J. Eccles (Eds.), *Handbook of research on schools, schooling, and human development.* New York: Routledge.

Orsi, C. M., Hale, D. E., & Lynch, J. L. (2011). Pediatric obesity epidemiology. *Current Opinion in Endocrinology, Diabetes, and Obesity, 18,* 14–22.

Ortega, M. I., & others. (2012). Migration, agribusiness, and nutritional status of children under five in Northwest Mexico. *International Journal of Environmental Research and Public Health, 9,* 33–43.

Ortigosa Gomez, S., & others. (2011). Use of illicit drugs over gestation and their neonatal impact. Comparison between periods 1982–1988 and 2002–2008. *Medicina Clinica, 136,* 423–430.

Ossher, L., Flegal, K. E., & Lustig, C. (2012, in press). Everyday memory errors in older adults. *Neuropsychology, Development, and Cognition, B. Aging, Neuroscience, and Cognition.*

Ostchega, Y., Carroll, M., Prineas, R. J., McDowell, M. A., Louis, T., & Tilert, T. (2009). Trends of elevated blood pressure among children and adolescents: data from the National Health and Nutrition Examination Survey 1988–2006. *American Journal of Hypertension, 22,* 59–67.

Otsuka, Y., & others. (2012). Perception of mooney faces by young infants: The role of local feature visibility, contrast polarity, and motion. *Journal of Experimental Child Psychology, 111,* 164–179.

Owen, J. J., Rhoades, G. K., Stanley, S. M., & Markman, H. J. (2011). The role of leaders' working alliance in premarital education. *Journal of Family Psychology, 25,* 49–57.

Owens, J., & Mindell, J. (2011). *Sleep in children and adolescents.* New York: Elsevier.

Owens, J. A., Belon, K., & Moss, P. (2010). Impact of delaying school start time on adolescent sleep, mood, and behavior. *Archives of Pediatric and Adolescent Medicine, 164,* 608–614.

Owsley, C. (2011). Aging and vision. *Vision Research, 51,* 1610–1622.

P

Paas, F., van Merrienboer, J. G., & van Gog, T. A. J. M. (2012). Designing instruction for the contemporary learning landscape. In K. R. Harris, S. Graham, & T. Urdan (Eds.), *APA educational psychology handbook.* Washington, DC: American Psychological Association.

Pacala, J. T., & Yeuh, B. (2012). Hearing defects in the older patient: "I didn't notice anything." *JAMA, 307,* 1185–1194.

Pace-Schott, E. F., & Spencer, R. M. (2011). Age-related changes in the cognitive function of sleep. *Progress in Brain Research, 191,* 75–89.

Pacheco, J., Beevers, C. G., McGeary, J. E., & Schnyer, D. M. (2012, in press). Memory monitoring performance and PFC activity are associated with 5-HTTLPR genotype in older adults. *Neuropsychologia.*

Padilla-Walker, L. M., & Coyne, S. M. (2011). "Turn that thing off!" Parent and adolescent predictors of proactive media monitoring. *Journal of Youth and Adolescence, 34,* 705–715.

Painter, A., Williams, A. D., & Burd, L. (2012a). Fetal alcohol spectrum disorders—implications for child neurology, part 1: Prenatal exposure and dosimetry. *Journal of Child Neurology, 27,* 258–263.

Painter, A., Williams, A. D., & Burd, L. (2012b). Fetal alcohol spectrum disorders—implications for child neurology, part 2: Diagnosis and management. *Journal of Child Neurology, 27,* 355–362.

Painter, K. (2008, June 16). Older, wiser, but less active. *USA Today,* p. 4D.

Pakhomov, S. V., Hemmy, L. S., & Lim, K. O. (2012, in press). Automated indices related to cognitive function and rate of cognitive decline. *Neuropsychologia.*

Palmore, E. B. (2004). Research note: Ageism in Canada and the United States. *Journal of Cross Cultural Gerontology, 19,* 41–46.

Palmqvist, S., & others. (2012). Comparison of brief cognitive tests and CSF biomarkers in predicting Alzheimer disease in mild cognitive impairment: Six-year follow-up study. *PLoS One, 7*(6), e38639.

Palu, A. K., West, B. J., & Jensen, J. (2011). Noni-based nutritional supplementation and exercise interventions influence body composition. *North American Journal of Medical Sciences, 3,* 552–556.

Pan, B. A., Rowe, M. L., Singer, J. D., & Snow, C. E. (2005). Maternal correlates of growth in toddler vocabulary production in low-income families. *Child Development, 76,* 763–782.

Pan, B.A., & Uccelli, P. (2009). Semantic development. In J. Berko Gleason & N. B. Rather (Eds.) (2009). *The development of language* (7th ed.). Boston: Allyn & Bacon.

Pan, Z., & Chang, C. (2012). Gender and the regulation of longevity: Implications for autoimmunity. *Autoimmunity Reviews, 11,* A393–A403.

Panigraphy, A., & others. (2012). Neuroimaging biomarkers of preterm brain injury: Toward developing the preterm connectome. *Pediatric Radiology, 42*(Suppl. 1), S33–S61.

Panter-Brick, C., Lende, D., & Kohrt, B. (2012). Children in global adversity: Physical health, mental health, behavioral health, and symbolic health. In V. Maholmes & R. B. King (Eds.), *Oxford handbook of poverty and child development.* New York: Oxford University Press.

Pantilat, S. Z., & Isaac, M. (2008). End-of-life care for the hospitalized patient. *Medical Clinics of North America, 92,* 349–370.

Papastavrou, E., Charlalambous, A., Tsangari, H., & Karayiannis, G. (2012). The burdensome and depressive experience of caring: What cancer, schizophrenia, and Alzheimer's disease caregivers have in common. *Cancer Nursing, 35,* 187–194.

Pardal, R., & Lopez-Barneo, J. (2012). Neural stem cells and transplantation studies in Parkinson's disease. *Advances in Experimental Medicine and Biology, 741,* 206–216.

Parens, E., & Johnston, J. (2009). Facts, values, and attention-deficit hyperactivity disorder (ADHD): An update on the controversies. *Child and Adolescent Psychiatry and Mental Health, 3,* 1.

Paris, S., Yeung, A., Wong, H. M., & Luo, S. W. (2012). Global perspectives on education during middle childhood. In K. R. Harris, S. Graham, & T. Urdan (Eds.), *APA educational psychology handbook.* Washington, DC: American Psychological Association.

Parish-Morris, J., Golinkoff, R. M., & Hirsh-Pasek, K. (2013). From coo to code: A brief story of language development. In P. D. Zelazo (Ed.), *Oxford handbook of developmental psychology.* New York: Oxford University Press.

Parish, S. L., Rose, R. A., Dababnah, S., Yoo, J., & Cassiman, S. A. (2012). State-level income inequality and family burden of U.S. families raising children with special health care needs. *Social Science and Medicine, 74,* 399–407.

Park, B., Lee, W., & Han, K. (2012). Modeling the interactions of Alzheimer-related genes from the whole brain microarray data and diffusion tensor images of human brain. *BMC Informatics, 13*(Suppl. 7), S10.

Park, C. J., Yelland, G. W., Taffe, J. R., & Gray, K. M. (2012). Morphological and syntactic skills in language samples of pre-school aged children with autism: Atypical development? *International Journal of Speech and Language Pathology, 14,* 95–108.

Park, C. L. (2005). Religion as a meaning-making system. *Psychology of Religion Newsletter, 30*(2), 1–9.

Park, C. L. (2007). Religiousness/spirituality and health: A meaning systems perspective. *Journal of Behavioral Medicine, 30,* 319–328.

Park, C. L. (2009). Meaning making in cancer survivorship. In P. T. P. Wong & P. S. Fry (Eds.), *The human quest for meaning* (2nd ed.). New York: Psychology Press.

Park, C. L. (2010). Making sense out of the meaning literature: An integrative review of meaning making and its effect on adjustment to stressful life events. *Psychological Bulletin, 136,* 257–301.

Park, C. L. (2012a, in press). Meaning making in cancer survivorship. In P. T. P. Wong (Ed.), *Handbook of meaning* (2nd ed.). Thousand Oaks, CA: Sage.

Park, C. L. (2012b). Meaning, spirituality, and growth: Protective and resilience factors in health and illness. In A. S. Baum, T. A. Revenson,

& J. E. Singer (Eds.), *Handbook of health psychology* (2nd ed.). New York: Sage.

Park, C. L., Malone, M. R., Suresh, D. P., Bliss, D., & Rosen, R. I. (2008). Coping, meaning in life, and the quality of life in congestive heart failure patients. *Quality of Life Research, 17,* 21–26.

Park, D. (2001). Commentary in R. Restak, *The secret life of the brain.* Washington, DC: Joseph Henry Press.

Park, D. C., & Bischof, G. N. (2011). Neuroplasticity, aging, and cognitive function. In K. W. Schaie & S. L. Willis (Eds.), *Handbook of the psychology of aging* (7th ed.). New York: Elsevier.

Park, D. C., & Reuter-Lorenz, P. (2009). The adaptive brain: Aging and neurocognitive scaffolding. *Annual Review of Psychology* (Vol. 60). Palo Alto, CA: Annual Reviews.

Park, M. J., Paul Mulye, T., Adams, S. H., Brindis, C. D., & Irwin, C. E. (2006). The health status of young adults in the United States. *Journal of Adolescent Health, 39,* 305–317.

Parkay, F. W. (2013). *Becoming a teacher* (9th ed.). Upper Saddle River, NJ: Pearson.

Parke, R. D., & Buriel, R. (2006). Socialization in the family. Ethnic and ecological perspectives. In W. Damon & R. Lerner (Eds.). *Handbook of child psychology* (6th ed.). New York: Wiley.

Parke, R. D., & Clarke-Stewart, A. K. (2011). *Social development.* New York: Wiley.

Parke, R. D., Coltrane, S., & Schofield, T. (2011). The bicultural advantage. In J. Marsh, R. Mendoza-Denton, & J. A. Smith (Eds.), *Are we born racist?* Boston: Beacon Press.

Parker, M. A. (2011). Biotechnology in the treatment of sensorineural hearing loss: Foundations and future of hair cell regeneration. *Journal of Speech, Language, and Hearing Research, 54,* 1709–1731.

Parkes, K. R. (2006). Physical activity and self-rated health: Interactive effects of activity in work and leisure domains. *British Journal of Health Psychology, 11,* 533–550.

Parkinson, P. (2010). Changing policies regarding separated fathers in Australia. In M. E. Lamb (Ed.), *The role of the father in child development* (5th ed.). New York: Wiley.

Parodi, V., de Florentiis, D., Martini, M., & Ansaldi, F. (2011). Inactivated influenza vaccines: Recent progress and implications for the elderly. *Drugs and Aging, 28,* 93–106.

Parquart, M. (2002). Creating and maintaining purpose in life in old age: A meta-analysis. *Aging International, 27,* 90–114.

Parra Cardona, J. R., & others. (2012). Culturally adapting an evidence-based parenting intervention for Latino immigrants: The need to integrate fidelity and cultural relevance. *Family Process, 51,* 56–72.

Parra-Cardona, J. R., Bulock, L. A., Imig, D. R., Villarruel, F. A., & Gold, S. J. (2006). "Trabajanco duro todos los dias": Learning from the life experiences of Mexican-origin migrant families. *Family Relations, 55,* 361–375.

Parrett, A. L., & others. (2011). Adiposity and aerobic fitness are associated with metabolic disease risk in children. *Applied Physiology, Nutrition, and Metabolism, 36,* 72–79.

Parsons, C. E., & others. (2010). The functional neuroanatomy of the evolving parent-infant relationship. *Progress in Neurobiology, 91,* 220–241.

Partnership for Solutions. (2002). *Multiple chronic conditions: Complications in care and treatment.* Baltimore: Johns Hopkins University.

Pasley, K., & Moorefield, B. S. (2004). Stepfamilies. In M. Coleman & L. Ganong (Eds.), *Handbook of contemporary families.* Thousand Oaks, CA: Sage.

Pasquali, T., & Krueger, R. (2012). Topography-guided laser refractory surgery. *Current Opinion in Ophthalmology, 23,* 264–268.

Pasquini, E. S., Corriveau, K. H., Koenig, M., & Harris, P. L. (2007). Preschoolers monitor the relative accuracy of informants. *Developmental Psychology, 43,* 1216–1226.

Passini, S. (2012). The delinquency-drug relationship: The influence of social reputation and moral disengagement. *Addictive Behaviors, 37,* 577–579.

Passuth, P. M., Maines, D. R., & Neugarten, B. L. (1984). *Age norms and age constraints twenty years later.* Paper presented at the annual meeting of the Midwest Sociological Society, Chicago.

Patel, R., & others. (2011). European guidelines for the management of genital herpes, 2010. *International Journal of STD and AIDS, 22,* 1–10.

Patrick, M. E., & Schulenberg, J. E. (2010). Alcohol use and heavy episodic drinking prevalence among national samples of American eighth- and tenth-grade students. *Journal of Studies on Alcohol and Drugs, 71,* 41–45.

Pattanapisalsak, C. (2011). Obstetric outcomes of teenage primigravida in Su-Ngai Kolok Hospital, Narathiwat, Thailand. *Journal of the Medical Association of Thailand, 94,* 139–146.

Patterson, C. J. (2012, in press). Sexual minority youth with sexual minority parents. In A. Ben-Arieh & others (Eds.), *Handbook of child research.* Thousand Oaks, CA: Sage.

Patterson, C. J., & D'Augelli, A. R. (Eds.) (2013, in press) *The psychology of sexual orientation.* New York: Cambridge University Press.

Patterson, C. J., & Farr, R. H. (2012, in press). Children of lesbian and gay parents: Reflections on the research-policy interface. In H. R. Schaffer & K. Durkin (Eds.), *Blackwell handbook of developmental psychology in action.* New York: Blackwell.

Patton, G. C., & others. (2011). Overweight and obesity between adolescence and early adulthood: A 10-year prospective study. *Journal of Adolescent Health, 45,* 275–280.

Paul, P. (2003, Sept/Oct). The PermaParent trap. *Psychology Today, 36*(5), 40–53.

Pauletti, R. E., Menon, M., Menon, M., Tobin, D. D., & Perry, D. G. (2012). Narcissism and adjustment in preadolescence. *Child Development, 83,* 831–837.

Paulhus, D. L. (2008). Birth order. In M. M. Haith & J. B. Benson (Eds.), *Encyclopedia of infant and early childhood development.* Oxford, UK: Elsevier.

Paus, T., & others. (2007). Morphological properties of the action-observation cortical network in adolescents with low and high resistance to peer influence. *Social Neuroscience 3*(3), 303–316.

Payer, L. (1991). The menopause in various cultures. In H. Burger & M. Boulet (Eds.), *A portrait of the menopause.* Park Ridge, NJ: Parthenon.

Pea, R., & others. (2012). Media use, face-to-face communication, media multitasking, and social well-being among 8- to 12-year-old girls. *Developmental Psychology, 48,* 327–336.

Pedersen, W., & Mastekaasa, A. (2011). Conduct disorder symptoms and subsequent pregnancy, childbirth, and abortion: A population-based longitudinal study of adolescents. *Journal of Adolescence, 34,* 1025–1033.

Pedroso, F. S. (2008). Reflexes. In M. H. Haith & J. B. Benson (Eds.), *Encyclopedia of infant and early childhood development.* Oxford, UK: Elsevier.

Peek, M. K. (2009). Marriage in later life. In D. Carr (Ed.), *Encyclopedia of the life course and human development.* Boston: Gale Cengage.

Peets, K., Hodges, E. V. E., & Salmivalli, C. (2011). Actualization of social cognitions into aggressive behavior toward disliked targets. *Social Development, 20,* 233–250.

Pelaez, M., Virues-Ortega, J., & Gewirtz, J. L. (2012). Acquisition of social referencing via discrimination training in infants. *Journal of Applied Behavior Analysis, 45,* 23–36.

Pellegrini, A. D. (2013). Play. In P. D. Zelazo (Ed.), *Oxford handbook of developmental psychology.* New York: Oxford University Press.

Pellegrini, A. (2013). Play. In P. D. Zelazo (Ed.), *Oxford handbook of developmental psychology.* New York: Oxford University Press.

Pellicano, E. (2010). Individual differences in executive function and central coherence predict developmental changes in theory of mind in autism. *Developmental Psychology, 46,* 530–544.

Pelton, S. L., & Leibovitz, E. (2009). Recent advances in otitis media. *Pediatric Infectious Disease Journal, 28*(Suppl. 10), S133–S137.

Peltz, C. B., Gratton, G., & Fabiani, M. (2011). Age-related changes in electrophysiological and neuropsychological indices of working memory, attention control, and cognitive flexibility. *Frontiers in Psychology, 2,* 190.

Peltzer-Karpf, A. (2012). The dynamic matching of neural and cognitive growth cycles. *Nonlinear Dynamics, Psychology, and Life Sciences, 16,* 61–78.

Penela, E. C., & others. (2012, in press). Maternal caregiving moderates the relation between temperamental fear and social behavior with peers. *Infancy.*

Pennell, A., Salo-Coombs, V., Hering, A., Spielman, F., & Fecho, K. (2011). Anesthesia and analgesia-related preferences and outcomes of women who have birth plans. *Journal of Midwifery and Women's Health, 56,* 376–381.

Pereira-Lancha, L. L., Campos-Ferraz, P. L., & Junior, L. A. H. (2012). Obesity: Considerations about etiology, metabolism, and the use of experimental models. *Diabetes, Metabolic Syndrome, and Obesity, 5,* 75–87.

Perissinotto, C. M., Stijacic Cenzer, I., & Covinsky, K. E. (2012, in press). Loneliness in older persons: A predictor of functional decline and death loneliness in older persons. *Archives of Internal Medicine.*

Perls, T., Lauerman, J. F., & Silver, M. H. (1999). *Living to 100.* New York: Basic Books.

Perls, T. T. (2007). Centenarians. In J. E. Birren (Ed.), *Encyclopedia of Gerontology* (2nd ed.). San Diego: Academic Press.

Perry, D. (2012, April). *The intrapsychics of gender.* Paper presented at the Gender Development Research conference, San Francisco.

Perry, N. B., Nelson, J. A., Leerkes, E. M., O'Brien, M., Calkins, S. D., & Maracovitch, S. (2012, in press). The relation between maternal emotional support and child physiological regulation across the preschool years. *Developmental Psychobiology.*

Perry, S. B., & Downey, P. A. (2012). Fracture risk and prevention: A multidimensional approach. *Physical Therapy, 92,* 164–178.

Persky, H. R., Dane, M. C., & Jin, Y. (2003). *The nation's report card writing: 2002.* Washington, DC: U.S. Department of Education.

Persson, K. E., Fridlund, B., Kvist, L. J., & Dykes, A.K. (2011). Mothers' sense of security in the first postnatal week: Interview study. *Journal of Advanced Nursing, 67,* 105–116.

Pesce, C., Crova, C., Cereatti, L., Casella, R., & Bellucci, M. (2009). Physical activity and mental performance in preadolescents: Effects of acute exercise on free-recall memory. *Mental Health and Physical Activity, 2*(1), 16–22.

Peskin, H. (1967). Pubertal onset and ego functioning. *Journal of Abnormal Psychology, 72,* 1–15.

Pessia, E., & others. (2012). Mammalian X chromosome inactivation evolved as a dosage-compensation mechanism for dosage-sensitive genes on the X chromosome. *Proceedings of the National Academy of Sciences USA, 109,* 5346–5351.

Peters, K. F., & Petrill, S. A. (2011). Comparison of background, needs, and expectations for genetic counseling of adults with experience with Down syndrome, Marfan syndrome, and neurofibromatosis. *American Journal of Medical Genetics A, 155,* 684–696.

Petersen, I. T., & others. (2012, in press). Interaction between serotonin transporter polymorphism (5-HTTLPR) and stressful life events in adolescents' trajectories of anxious/depressed symptoms. *Developmental Psychology.*

Petersen, J. L., & Hyde, J. S. (2010). A meta-analytic review of research on gender differences in sexuality, 1973–2007. *Psychological Bulletin, 136,* 21–38.

Peterson, C. C. (2005). Mind and body: Concepts of human cognition, physiology and false belief in children with autism or typical development. *Journal of Autism and Developmental Disorders, 35,* 487–497.

Peterson, C. C., Garnett, M., Kelly, A., & Attwood, T. (2009). Everyday social and conversation applications of theory-of-mind understanding by children with autism spectrum disorders or typical development. *European Child and Adolescent Psychiatry, 18,* 105–115.

Peterson, C. C., Wellman, H. M., & Slaughter, V. (2012). The mind behind the message: Advancing theory-of-mind scales for typically developing children, and those with deafness, autism, or Asperger syndrome. *Child Development, 83,* 469–485.

Petrick-Steward, E. (2012). *Beginning writers in the zone of proximal development.* New York: Psychology Press.

Pew Forum on Religion and Public Life. (2008). *U.S. religious landscape study.* Washington, DC: Pew Research Center.

Pew Research Center. (2010). *The decline of marriage and rise of new families.* Washington, DC: Author.

Pew Research Center. (2010). *Millennials: Confident, connected, open to change.* Washington, DC: Pew Research Center.

Pew Research Center. (2011, December). *Barely half of U.S. adults are married—a record low.* Washington, DC: Pew Research Center.

Pfeifer, J. H., & Blakemore, S. J. (2012). Adolescent social cognitive and affective neuroscience: Past, present, and future. *Social Cognitive and Affective Neuroscience, 7,* 1–10.

Pfeifer, M., Goldsmith, H. H., Davidson, R. J., & Rickman, M. (2002). Continuity and change in inhibited and uninhibited children. *Child Development, 73,* 1474–1485.

Philip, R. C., & others. (2012). A systematic review and meta-analysis of the fMRI investigation of autism spectrum disorders. *Neuroscience and Biobehavioral Reviews, 36,* 901–942.

Philips, S., & others. (2012, in press). Whole genome amplification of DNA for genotyping pharmacogenetics candidate genes. *Frontiers in Pharmacology.*

Phillips, D. A., & Lowenstein, A. (2011, in press). Early care, education, and child development. *Annual review of psychology* (Vol. 62). Palo Alto, CA: Annual Reviews.

Phillips, M. I. (2012, in press). Gene, stem cell, and future therapies for orphan diseases. *Clinical Pharmacology and Therapeutics.*

Phinney, J. S. (2008). Bridging identities and disciplines: Advances and challenges in understanding multiple identities. In M. Azmitia, M. Syed, & K. Radmacher (Eds.), *The intersections of personal and social identities. New Directions for Child and Adolescent Development, 120,* 97–109.

Phinney, J. S., & Baldelomar, O. A. (2011). Identity development in multiple developmental contexts. In L. Jensen (Ed.), *Bridging cultural and developmental approaches to psychology.* New York: Oxford University Press.

Phinney, J. S., & Ong, A. D. (2007). Ethnic identity in immigrant families. In J. E. Lansford, K. Deater-Deckard, & M. H. Bornstein (Eds.), *Immigrant families in contemporary society.* New York: Guilford.

Pho, A. T., & others. (2012, in press). Nursing strategies for promoting and maintaining function among community-living older adults: The CAPABLE intervention. *Geriatric Nursing.*

Piaget, J. (1932). *The moral judgment of the child.* New York: Harcourt Brace Jovanovich.

Piaget, J. (1952). *The origins of intelligence in children.* (M. Cook, Trans.). New York: International Universities Press.

Piaget, J. (1954). *The construction of reality in the child.* New York: Basic Books.

Piaget, J. (1962). *Play, dreams, and imitation.* New York: W.W. Norton.

Piaget, J., & Inhelder, B. (1969). *The child's conception of space* (F. J. Langdon & J. L. Lunger, Trans.). New York: W. W. Norton.

Piasta, S. B., Justice, L. M., McGinty, A. S., & Kaderavek, J. N. (2012, in press). Increasing young children's contact with print during shared reading: Longitudinal effects on literacy achievement. *Child Development.*

Piazza, J. R., Almeida, D. M., Dmitrieva, N. O., & Klein, L. C. (2010). Frontiers in the use of biomarkers of health in research on stress and aging. *Journals of Gerontology B: Psychological Sciences and Social Sciences, 65B,* 513–525.

Piazza, J. R., & Charles, S. T. (2012). Affective disorders and age: The view through a developmental lens. In S. K. Whitbourne & M. J. Sliwinski (Eds.), *Wiley-Blackwell handbook of adult development and aging.* New York: Wiley.

Pidsley, R., Dempster, E., Troakes, C., Al-Sarraj, S., & Mill, J. (2012). Epigenetic and genetic variation at the IGF2/H19 imprinting control region on 11p15.5 is associated with cerebellum weight. *Epigenetics, 7,* 155–163.

Piehler, T. F., Veronneau, M. H., & Dishion, T. J. (2012, in press). Substance use progression from adolescence to early adulthood: Effortful control in the context of friendship influence and early-onset use. *Journal of Abnormal Child Psychology.*

Pienaar, A. E., & others. (2012). Change over three years in adolescents' physical activity levels and patterns after a physical activity intervention: Play study. *Journal of Sports Medicine and Physical Fitness, 52,* 300–310.

Pieperhoff, P., & others. (2008). Deformation field morphometry reveals age-related structural differences between the brains of adults up to 51 years. *Journal of Neuroscience, 28,* 828–842.

Pies, R. (2012). Bereavement, complicated grief, and the rationale for diagnosis in psychiatry. *Dialogues in Clinical Neuroscience, 14,* 111–113.

Pietilainen, K. H., Saarni, S. E., Kaprio, J., & Rissanen, A. (2012). Does dieting make you fat? A twin study. *International Journal of Obesity, 36,* 456–464.

Piko, B. F., & Balazs, M. A. (2012). Authoritative parenting style and adolescent smoking and drinking. *Addictive Behaviors, 37,* 353–356.

Pilkington, P. D., Windsor, T. D., & Crisp, D. A. (2012). Volunteering and subjective well-being in midlife and older adults: The role of supportive social networks. *Journals of Gerontology B: Psychological Sciences and Social Sciences, 67,* 249–260.

Pines, A., Sturdee, D. W., & Maclennan, A. H. (2012). Quality of life and the role of menopausal hormone therapy. *Climacteric, 15,* 213–216.

Ping, H., & Hagopian, W. (2006). Environmental factors in the development of type 1 diabetes. *Reviews in Endocrine and Metabolic Disorders, 7,* 149–162.

Pinquart, M., & Frostmeier, S. (2012). Effects of reminiscence interventions on psychosocial outcomes: A meta-analysis. *Aging and Mental Health, 16,* 541–558.

Pinsker, J. E. (2012, in press). Turner syndrome: Updating the paradigm of clinical care. *Journal of Clinical and Endocrinology and Metabolism.*

Piper, B. J., & others. (2011). Abnormalities in parentally rated executive function in methamphetamine/polysubstance exposed children. *Pharmacology, Biochemistry, and Behavior, 98,* 432–439.

Piper, S. L., & others. (2012, in press). Inducible immortality in hTERT-human mesenchymal stem cells. *Journal of Orthopedic Research*.

Pistrang, N., & Barker, C. (2012). Varieties of qualitative research: A pragmatic approach to selecting methods. In H. Cooper (Ed.), *APA handbook of research methods in psychology*. Washington, DC: American Psychological Association.

Pitkänen, T., Lyyra, A. L., & Pulkkinen L. (2005). Age of onset of drinking and the use of alcohol in adulthood: A follow-up study from age 8–42 for females and males. *Addiction, 100*, 652–661.

Pizza, V., & others. (2011). Neuromm-aging and neurogenerative diseases: An overview. *CNS & Neurological Disorders Drug Targets, 10*, 621–634.

Pleck, J. H. (1995). The gender-role strain paradigm. In R. E. Levant & W. S. Pollack (Eds.), *A new psychology of men*. New York: Basic Books.

Plener, P. L., Singer, H., & Goldbeck, L. (2011). Traumatic events and suicidality in a German adolescent community sample. *Journal of Traumatic Stress, 24*, 121–124.

Plomin, R. (1999). Genetics and general cognitive ability. *Nature, 402*(Suppl.), C25–C29.

Plomin, R. (2004). Genetics and developmental psychology. *Merrill-Palmer Quarterly, 50*, 341–352.

Plomin, R. (2012, in press). Child development and molecular genetics: 14 years later. *Child Development*.

Plomin, R., & Daniels, D. (2011). Why are children in the same family so different from one another? *International Journal of Epidemiology, 3*, 563–582.

Plomin, R., DeFries, J. C., McClearn, G. E., & McGuffin, P. (2009). *Behavioral genetics* (5th ed.). New York: W. H. Freeman.

Plucker, J. (2010, July 19). Commentary in P. Bronson & A. Merryman, The creativity crisis. *Newsweek*, pp. 45–46.

Polat, U., & others. (2012, in press). Training the brain to overcome the effect of aging on the human eye. *Science Reports*.

Politis, M., & Lindvall, O. (2012, in press). Clinical application of stem cell therapy in Parkinson's disease. *BMC Medicine*.

Pollack, W. (1999). *Real boys*. New York: Owl Books.

Pollak, S., & others. (2010). Neurodevelopmental effects of early deprivation in postinstitutionalized children, *81, Child Development*, 224–236.

Polo-Kantola, P. (2011). Sleep problems in midlife and beyond. *Maturitas, 68*, 224–232.

Pomerantz, E. M., Cheung, C. S., & Qin, L. (2012). Relatedness between children and parents: Implications for motivation. In R. Ryan (Ed.), *Oxford handbook of motivation*. New York: Oxford University Press.

Pomerantz, E. M., Kim, E. M., & Cheung, C. S. (2012). Parents' involvement in children's learning. In K. R. Harris & others (Eds.), *APA educational psychology handbook*. Washington, DC: American Psychological Association.

Poorthuis, A. M., & others. (2012, in press). Prosocial tendencies predict friendship quality, but not for popular children. *Journal of Experimental Child Psychology*.

Popenoe, D. (2009). *The state of our unions 2008. Updates of social indicators: Tables and charts*. Piscataway, NJ: The National Marriage Project.

Posada, G., & Kaloustian, G. (2010). Parent-infant interaction. In J. G. Bremner & T. D. Wachs (Eds.), *Wiley-Blackwell handbook of infant development* (2nd ed.). New York: Wiley.

Posner, M. I. (Ed.) (2011). *Cognitive neuroscience of attention* (2nd ed.). New York: Guilford.

Posner, M. I., & Rothbart, M. K. (2007). *Educating the human brain*. Washington, DC: American Psychological Association.

Postert, C., Dannlowski, U., Muller, J. M., & Konrad, C. (2012). Beyond the blues: Cross-cultural phenomenology of depressed mood. *Psychopathology, 45*, 185–192.

Pot, A. M., & others. (2010). The impact of life review on depression in older adults: A randomized controlled trial. *International Psychogeriatrics, 22*, 572–581.

Potochnick, S., Perreira, K. M., & Fuligni, A. (2012). Fitting in: The roles of social acceptance and discrimination in shaping the daily psychological well-being of Latino youth. *Social Science Quarterly, 93*, 173–190.

Poulin, F., Kiesner, J., Pedersen, S., & Dishion, T. J. (2011). A short-term longitudinal analysis of friendship selection on early adolescent substance use. *Journal of Adolescence, 34*, 249–256.

Poulin, F., & Pedersen, S. (2007). Developmental changes in gender composition of friendship networks in adolescent girls and boys. *Developmental Psychology, 43*, 1484–1496.

Powell, S. D. (2012). *Your introduction to education* (2nd ed.). Upper Saddle River, NJ: Pearson.

Power, T. G. (2011). Social play. In P. K. Smith & C. H. Hart (Eds.), *Wiley-Blackwell handbook of childhood social development* (2nd ed.). New York: Wiley.

Powers, C. J., & Bierman, K. L. (2012, in press). The multifaceted impact of peer relations on aggressive-disruptive behavior in early elementary school. *Developmental Psychology*.

Prabhakar, H. (2007). Hopkins interactive guest blog: The public health experience at Johns Hopkins. Retrieved January 31, 2008, from http://hopkins.typepad.com/guest/2007/03/the_public_heal.html

Prakash, R. S., & others. (2011). Cardiorespiratory fitness and attentional control in the aging brain. *Frontiers in Human Neuroscience, 4*(229), 1–12.

Prameela, K. K. (2011). Breastfeeding—anti-viral potential and relevance to the influenza virus pandemic. *Medical Journal of Malaysia, 66*, 166–169.

Pratt, C., & Bryant, P. E. (1990). Young children understand that looking leads to knowing (so long as they are looking in a single barrel). *Child Development, 61*, 973–982.

Preer, G., Sorrentino, D., & Newton, A.W. (2012). Child abuse pediatrics: Prevention, evaluation, and treatment. *Current Opinion in Pediatrics, 24*, 266–273.

Pressley, M. (2003). Psychology of literacy and literacy instruction. In I. B. Weiner (Ed.), *Handbook of psychology*. New York: Wiley.

Pressley, M. (2007). An interview with Michael Pressley by Terri Flowerday and Michael Shaughnessy. *Educational Psychology Review, 19*, 1–12.

Pressley, M., Dolezal, S. E., Raphael, L. M., Welsh, L. M., Bogner, K., & Roehrig, A. D. (2003). *Motivating primary-grades teachers*. New York: Guilford.

Pressley, M., Mohan, L., Fingeret, L., Reffitt, K., & Raphael-Bogaert, L. R. (2007). Writing instruction in engaging and effective elementary settings. In S. Graham. C. A. MacArthur, & J. Fitzgerald (Eds.), *Best practices in writing instruction*. New York: Guilford.

Pressley, M., Raphael, L., Gallagher, D., & DiBella, J. (2004). Providence-St. Mel School: How a school that works for African-American students works. *Journal of Educational Psychology, 96*, 216–235.

Preston, S. H., & Stokes, A. (2011). Contribution of obesity to international differences in life expectancy. *American Journal of Public Health, 101*, 2137–2143.

Price, C. A., & Joo, E. (2005). Exploring the relationship between marital status and women's retirement satisfaction. *International Journal of Aging and Human Development, 61*, 37–55.

Price, C. A., & Nesteruk, O. (2010). Creating retirement paths: Examples from the lives of women. *Journal of Women and Aging, 22*, 136–149.

Prickett, K. C., & Angel, J. L. (2011). The new health care law: How will women near retirement fare? *Women's Health Issues, 21*, 331–337.

Prigerson, H. G., & others. (2011). Prolonged grief disorder: Psychometric validation of criteria for proposed for DSM-V and ICD-11. *PLOS Medicine, 6*(8), e1000121.

Prinstein, M. J. (2007). Moderators of peer contagion: A longitudinal examination of depression socialization between adolescents and their best friends. *Journal of Clinical Child and Adolescent Psychology, 36*, 159–170.

Prinstein, M. J., & Dodge, K. A. (2008). Current issues in peer influence. In M. J. Prinstein & K. A. Dodge (Eds.), *Understanding peer influence in children and adolescents*. New York: Guilford.

Prior, J. C., & Hitchcock, C. L. (2011). The endocrinology of perimenopause: Need for a paradigm shift. *Frontiers in Bioscience, 3*, 474–486.

Pruden, S., Goksun, T., Roseberry, S., Hirsh-Pasek, K., & Golinkoff, R. M. (2012, in press). Infant categorization of path relations during dynamic events. *Child Development*.

Pryor, J. H., DeAngelo, L., Blake, L. P. (2011). *The American freshman: National norms for fall 2011*. Los Angeles: Higher Education Research Institute, UCLA.

Pudrovska, T. (2009). Midlife crises and transitions. In D. Carr (Ed.), *Encyclopedia of the life course and human development*. Boston: Gale Cengage.

Pufal, M. A., & others. (2012, in press). Prevalence of overweight children of obese patients: A dietary overview. *Obesity Surgery*.

Puma, M., & others. (2010). *Head Start impact study. Final report*. Washington, DC: Administration for Children & Families.

Putallaz, M., Grimes, C. L., Foster, K. J., Kupersmidt, J. B., Clie, J. D., & Dearing, K. (2007). Overt and relational aggression and victimization: Multiple perspectives within the school setting. *Journal of School Psychology. 45*, 523–547.

Puterman, E., & others. (2010). The power of exercise: Buffering the effects of chronic stress on telomere length. *PLoS One, 5*(5), e10837.

Putnam Investments. (2006). *Survey of the working retired.* Franklin, MA: Putnam Investments.

Puzzanchera, C., & Sickmund, M. (2008, July). *Juvenile court statistics 2005.* Pittsburgh: National Center for Juvenile Justice.

Q

Qiu, M-G., & others. (2011). Changes of brain structure and function in ADHD children. *Brain Topography, 24*(3-4), 243–252.

R

Rachner, T. D., Khosia, S., & Hofbauer, L. C. (2011). Osteoporosis: Now and the future. *Lancet, 377,* 1276–1287.

Ragucci, K. R., & Shrader, S. P. (2011). Osteoporosis treatment: An evidence-based approach. *Journal of Gerontological Nursing, 37,* 17–22.

Raikes, H. A., & Thompson, R. A. (2009). Attachment security and parenting quality predict children's problem-solving, attributions, and loneliness with peers. *Attachment and Human Development, 10,* 319–344.

Raikes, H., & others. (2006). Mother-child bookreading in low-income families: Correlates and outcomes during the first three years of life. *Child Development, 77,* 924–953.

Raj, T., & others. (2012). Alzheimer disease susceptibility loci: Evidence for a protein network under natural selection. *American Journal of Human Genetics, 90,* 720–726.

Rajaraman, P., & others. (2011). Early life exposure to diagnostic radiation and ultrasound scans and risk of childhood cancer: Case-control study. *British Medical Journal, 342,* d472.

Rakison, D. H., & Lawson, C. A. (2013). Categorization. In P. D. Zelazo (Ed.), *Oxford handbook of developmental psychology.* New York: Oxford University Press.

Rakoczy, H. (2012). Do infants have a theory of mind? *British Journal of Developmental Psychology, 30,* 59–74.

Ram, K. T., & others. (2008). Duration of lactation is associated with lower prevalence of the metabolic syndrome in midlife—SWAN, the study of women's health across the nation. *American Journal of Obstetrics and Gynecology, 198,* e1–e6.

Ramchandani, P. G., & others. (2011). Paternal depression: An examination of its links with father, child, and family functioning in the postnatal period. *Depression and Anxiety, 28,* 471–477.

Ramey, C. T., & Campbell, F. A. (1984). Preventive education for high-risk children: Cognitive consequences of the Carolina Abecedarian Project. *American Journal of Mental Deficiency, 88,* 515–532.

Ramey, C. T., & Ramey, S. L. (1998). Early prevention and early experience. *American Psychologist, 53,* 109–120.

Ramey, C. T., Ramey, S. L., & Lanzi, R. G. (2001). Intelligence and experience. In R. J. Sternberg & E. I. Grigorenko (Eds.), *Environment effects on cognitive development.* Mahwah, NJ: Erlbaum.

Ramey, S. L. (2005). Human developmental science serving children and families: Contributions of the NICHD study of early child care. In NICHD Early Child Care Research Network (Eds.), *Child care and development.* New York: Guilford.

Ramus, F., & Ahissar, M. (2012, in press). Developmental dyslexia: The difficulties of interpreting poor performance, and the importance of normal performance. *Cognitive Neuropsychology.*

Randall, W. L. (2012, in press). The importance of being ironic: Narrative openness and personal resilience in later life. *Gerontologist.*

Ransdell, H. L., Oller, D. K., Buder, E. H., Ethington, C. A., & Chorna, L. (2012, in press). Identification of prelinguistic phonological categories. *Journal of Speech, Language, and Hearing Research.*

Ransmayr, G. (2011). Physical, occupational, speech, and swallowing therapies and exercise in Parkinson's disease. *Journal of Neural Transmission, 118,* 773–781.

Rapaport, S. (1994, November 28). Interview. *U.S. News & World Report,* p. 94.

Rasmussen, S. A. (2012). Human teratogens update 2011: Can we ensure safety during pregnancy? *Birth Defects Research A: Clinical and Molecular Teratology, 94,* 123–128.

Rasulo, D., Christensen, K., & Tomassini, C. (2005). The influence of social relations on mortality in later life: A study on elderly Danish twins. *Gerontologist, 45,* 601–608.

Rathunde, K., & Csikszentmihalyi, M. (2006). The developing person: An experiential perspective. In W. Damon & R. Lerner (Eds.), *Handbook of child psychology* (6th ed.). New York: Wiley.

Raudsepp, L., & Neissaar, I. (2012, in press). Brief report: Relationships between physical activity and depressive symptoms in adolescent girls. *Journal of Adolescence.*

Raver, C. C., & others. (2011). CSRP's impact on low-income preschoolers preacademic skills: Self-regulation as a mediating mechanism. *Child Development, 82,* 362–378.

Raver, C. C., & others. (2012, in press). Testing models of children's self-regulation within educational contexts: Implications for measurement. *Advances in Child Development and Behavior.*

Raz, N., Ghisletta, P., Rodrique, K. M., Kennedy, K. M., & Lindenberger, U. (2010). Trajectories of brain imaging in middle-aged and older adults: Regional and individual differences. *Neuroimage, 51*(2), 501–511.

Read, J. P., Merrill, J. E., & Bytschkow, K. (2010). Before the party starts: Risk factors and reasons for "pregaming" in college students. *Journal of American College Health, 58,* 461–472.

Realini, J. P., Buzi, R. S., Smith, P. B., & Martinez, M. (2010). Evaluation of "big decisions": An abstinence-plus sexuality. *Journal of Sex and Marital Therapy, 36,* 313–326.

Reef, S. E., & others. (2011). Progress toward control of rubella and prevention of congenital rubella syndrome—worldwide, 2009. *Journal of Infectious Diseases, 204*(Suppl. 1), S24–S27.

Reese, J. P., & others. (2012). Pharmacoeconomic considerations in treating patients with advanced Parkinson's disease. *Expert Opinion in Pharmacotherapy, 13,* 939–958.

Reeve, C. L., & Charles, J. E. (2008). Survey of opinions on the primacy of g and social consequences of ability testing: A comparison of expert and non-expert views. *Intelligence, 36,* 681–688.

Regalado, M., Sareen, H., Inkelas, M., Wissow, L. S., & Halfon, N. (2004). Parents' discipline of young children: Results from the National Survey of Early Childhood Health. *Pediatrics, 113,* 1952–1958.

Regev, R. H., & others. (2003). Excess mortality and morbidity among small-for-gestational-age premature infants: A population based study. *Journal of Pediatrics, 143,* 186–191.

Reibis, R. K., Treszi, A., Wegscheider, K., Ehrlich, B., Dissmann, R., & Voller, H. (2010). Exercise capacity is the most powerful predictor of 2-year mortality in patients with left ventricular systolic dysfunction. *Herz, 35,* 104–110.

Reich, S. M., & Vandell, D. L. (2011). The interplay between parents and peers as socializing influences on children's development. In P. K. Smith & C. H. Hart (Eds.), *Wiley-Blackwell handbook of childhood social development* (2nd ed.). New York: Wiley.

Reichstadt, J., Depp, C. A., Palinkas, L. A., Folsom, D. P., & Jeste, D. V. (2007). Building blocks of successful aging: A focus group study of older adults' perceived contributors to successful aging. *American Journal of Geriatric Psychiatry, 15,* 194–201.

Reid, P. T., & Zalk, S. R. (2001). Academic environments: Gender and ethnicity in U.S. higher education. In J. Worell (Ed.), *Encyclopedia of women and gender.* San Diego: Academic Press.

Reijmerink, N. E., & others. (2011). Toll-like receptors and microbial exposure: Gene-gene and gene-environment interaction in the development of atopy. *European Respiratory Journal, 128,* 948–955.

Reindollar, R. H., & Goldman, M. B. (2012). Gonadotropin therapy: A 20th century relic. *Fertility and Sterility, 97,* 813–818.

Reinhold, S. (2010). Reassessing the link between marital cohabitation and marital instability. *Demography, 47,* 719–733.

Reisman, A. S. (2001). Death of a spouse: Basic assumptions and continuation of bonds. *Death Studies, 25,* 445–460.

Rejeski, W. J., & others. (2011). Translating weight loss and physical activity into the community to preserve mobility in older, obese adults in poor cardiovascular health. *Archives of Internal Medicine, 171*(10), 880–886.

Ren, Q., Zhang, Z., & Zhao, J. (2012, in press). Effect of information transfer of synaptic pruning driven by spike-timing-dependent plasticity. *Physical Review. E., Statistical, Nonlinear, and Soft Matter Physics.*

Rendall, M. S., Weden, M. M., Faveault, M. M., & Waldron, H. (2011). The protective effect of marriage for survival: A review and update. *Demography, 48,* 481–506.

Rende, R. (2012, in press). Behavioral resilience in the post-genomic era: Emerging models linking genes with environment. *Frontiers in Human Neuroscience.*

Reno, V. P., & Veghte, B. (2011). Economic status of the aged in the United States. In R. H. Binstock & L. K. George (Eds.), *Handbook of aging and the social sciences* (7th ed.). New York: Elsevier.

Repacholi, B. M., & Gopnik, A. (1997). Early reasoning about desires: Evidence from 14- and 18-month-olds. *Developmental Psychology, 33*, 12–21.

Repetti, R., Flook, L., & Sperling, J. (2011). Family influences in development across the life span. In K. L. Fingerman, C. A. Berg, J. Smith, & T. C. Antonucci (Eds.), *Handbook of life-span development.* New York: Springer.

Reproductive Endocrinology and Infertility Committee & others. (2012). Advanced reproductive age and fertility. *Journal of Obstetrics and Gynecology Canada.*

Resick, P. A., & others. (2012). Long-term consequences of cognitive-behavioral treatments for posttraumatic stress disorder among female rape survivors. *Journal of Consulting and Clinical Psychology, 80*, 201–210.

Reutzel, D. R., & Cooter, R. B. (2012). *Teaching children to read* (6th ed.). Boston: Allyn & Bacon.

Reutzel, D. R., & Cooter, R. B. (2013). *Essentials of teaching children to read* (3rd ed.). Boston: Allyn & Bacon.

Reyna, V. F. (2004). How people make decisions that involve risk: A dual-process approach. *Current Directions in Psychological Science, 13*, 60–66.

Reyna, V. F., Chapman, S. B., Dougherty, M. R., & Confrey, J. (Eds.) (2012). *The adolescent brain.* Washington, DC: American Psychological Association.

Reyna, V. F., & Farley, F. (2006). Risk and rationality on adolescent decision-making: Implications for theory, practice, and public policy. *Psychological Science in the Public Interest, 7*, 1–44.

Reyna, V. F., & Rivers, S. E. (2008). Current theories of risk and rational decision making. *Developmental Review, 28*, 1–11.

Reynolds, F. (2010). The effects of maternal labour analgesia on the fetus. *Best Practices & Research. Clinical Obstetrics & Gynaecology, 24*, 289–302.

Rhemtulla, M., & Tucker-Drob, E. M. (2012, in press). Gene-by-socioeconomic status interaction on school readiness. *Behavior Genetics.*

Rhoades, G. K., Kamp Dusch, C. M., Atkins, D. C., Stanley, S. M., & Markman, H. J. (2011). Breaking up is hard to do: The impact of unmarried relationship dissolution on mental health and life satisfaction. *Journal of Family Psychology 25*, 366–374.

Rhoades, G. K., Stanley, S. M., & Markman, H. J. (2009). The pre-engagement cohabitation effect: A replication and extension of previous findings. *Journal of Family Psychology, 23*, 107–111.

Rhoades, G. K., Stanley, S. M., & Markman, H. J. (2012). The impact of transition to cohabitation on relationship functioning: Cross-sectional and longitudinal findings. *Journal of Family Psychology, 26*, 348–358.

Richards, J. E. (2009). Attention to the brain in infancy. In S. Johnson (Ed.), *Neuroconstructivism: The new science of cognitive development.* New York: Oxford University Press.

Richards, J. E. (2010). Infant attention, arousal, and the brain. In L. Oakes, C. Cashon, M. Casasola, & D. Rakison (Eds.), *Infant perception and cognition.* New York: Oxford University Press.

Richards, J. E., Reynolds, G. D., & Courage, M. I. (2010). The neural bases of infant attention. *Current Directions in Psychological Science, 19*, 41–46.

Richardson, C. R., Faulkner, G., McDevitt, J., Skrinar, G. S., Hutchinson, D. S., & Piette, J. D. (2005). Integrating physical activity into mental health services for persons with serious mental illness. *Psychiatric Services, 56*, 324–331.

Richardson, G. A., Goldschmidt, L., Leech, S., & Williford, J. (2011). Prenatal cocaine exposure: Effects on mother- and teacher-rated behavior problems and growth in school-aged children. *Neurotoxicology and Teratology, 33*, 69–77.

Richardson, G. A., Goldschmidt, L., & Willford, J. (2008). The effects of prenatal cocaine use on infant development. *Neurotoxicology and Teratology, 30*, 96–106.

Richardson, T. M., & others. (2011, in press). Depression and its correlates among older adults accessing social services. *Journal of Nursing Care Quality.*

Richardson, V. E. (2007). A dual process model of grief counseling: Findings from the Changing Lives of Older Couples (CLOC) study. *Journal of Gerontological Social Work, 48*, 311–329.

Richmond, J., & Nelson, C. A. (2009). Relational memory during infancy: Evidence from eye tracking. *Developmental Science, 12*, 549–556.

Rideout, V., Foehr, U. G., & Roberts, D. P. (2010). *Generation M: Media in the lives of 8- to 18-year-olds.* Menlo Park, CA: Kaiser Family Foundation.

Rider, O. J., & others. (2010). The effect of obesity and weight loss on aortic pulse wave velocity as assessed by magnetic resonance imaging. *Obesity, 18*, 2311–2316.

Riebe, D., & others. (2005). Physical activity, physical function, and stages of change in older adults. *American Journal of Health Behavior, 29*, 70–80.

Riediger, M., Li, S-C., & Lindenberger, U. (2006). Selection, optimization, and compensation as developmental mechanisms of adaptive resource allocation: Review and preview. In J. E. Birren & K. W. Schaie (Eds.), *Handbook of the psychology of aging* (6th ed.). San Diego: Academic Press.

Riesch, S. K., & others. (2012, in press). Modifiable family factors among treatment-seeking families of children with high body mass index: Report of a pilot study. *Journal of Pediatric Health Care.*

Riggins, T. (2012, in press). Building blocks of recollection. In S. Ghetti & P. J. Bauer (Eds.), *Origins and development of recollection.* New York: Oxford University Press.

Riley, K. P., Snowdon, D. A., Derosiers, M. F., & Markesbery, W. R. (2005). Early life linguistic ability, late life cognitive function, and neuropathology: Findings from the Nun Study. *Neurobiology of Aging, 26*, 341–347.

Riley, M., & Bluhm, B. (2012). High blood pressure in children and adolescents. *American Family Physician, 85*, 693–700.

Rimsza, M. E., & Kirk, G. M. (2005). Common medical problems of the college student. *Pediatric Clinics of North America, 52*, 9–24.

Rix, S. (2011). Employment and aging. In R. H. Binstock & L. K. George (Eds.), *Handbook of aging and the social sciences* (7th ed.). New York: Elsevier.

Rizzo, M. S. (1999, May 8). Genetic counseling combines science with a human touch. *Kansas City Star*, p. 3.

Robbers, S., & others. (2012, in press). Childhood problem behavior and parental divorce: Evidence for gene-environment interaction. *Social Psychiatry and Psychiatric Epidemiology.*

Roberie, D. R., & Elliott, W. J. (2012). What is the prevalence of resistant hypertension in the United States? *Current Opinion in Cardiology, 27*, 386–391.

Roberto, K. A., & Skoglund, R. R. (1996). Interactions with grandparents and great grandparents: A comparison of activities, influences, and relationships. *International Journal of Aging and Human Development, 43*, 107–117.

Roberts, B. W., Donnellan, M. B., & Hill, P. L. (2013, in press). Personality trait development in adulthood: Findings and implications. In I. B. Weiner & others (Eds.), *Handbook of psychology* (2nd ed., Vol. 5). New York: Wiley.

Roberts, B. W., Edmonds, G., & Grijalva, E. (2010). It is developmental me, not generation me: Developmental changes are more important than generational changes in narcissism—Commentary on Trzesniewski & Donnellan (2010), *Perspectives on Psychological Science*, pp. 97–102.

Roberts, B. W., Jackson, J. J., Fayard, J. V., Edmonds, G., & Meints, J. (2009). Conscientiousness. In M. Leary & R. Hoyle (Eds.). *Handbook of individual differences in social behavior.* New York: Guilford.

Roberts, B. W., & Mroczek, D. (2008). Personality trait change in adulthood. *Current Directions in Psychological Science, 17*, 31–35.

Roberts, B. W., Walton, K. E., & Bogg, T. (2005). Conscientiousness and health across the life course. *Review of General Psychology, 9*, 156–168.

Roberts, B. W., Walton, K. E., & Viechtbauer, W. (2006). Patterns of mean-level change in personality traits across the life course. A meta-analysis of longitudinal studies. *Psychological Bulletin, 132*, 1–25.

Roberts, B. W., & Wood, D. (2006). Personality development in the context of the Neo-Socioanalytic Model of personality. In D. Mroczek & T. Little (Eds.), *Handbook of personality development.* Mahwah, NJ: Erlbaum.

Roberts, B. W., Wood, D., & Caspi, A. (2008). Personality development. In O. P. John, R. W. Robins, & L. A. Pervin (Eds.), *Handbook of personality* (3rd ed.). New York: Guilford.

Roberts, D. F., & Foehr, U. G. (2008). Trends in media use. *Future of Children, 18*(1), 11–37.

Roberts, M. E., & others. (2012). From racial discrimination to risky sex: Prospective relations involving peers and parents. *Developmental Psychology, 48*, 89–102.

Robine, J. M. (2011). The weaker sex. *Aging: Clinical and Experimental Research, 23*, 80–83.

Robins, R. W., Trzesniewski, K. H., Tracey, J. L., Potter, J., & Gosling, S. D. (2002). Age differences in self-esteem from age 9 to 90. *Psychology and Aging, 17*, 423–434.

Robinson-Riegler, B., & Robinson-Riegler, G. L. (2012). *Cognitive psychology* (3rd ed.). Upper Saddle River, NJ: Pearson.

Robledo-Colonia, A. F., & others. (2012). Aerobic exercise training during pregnancy reduces symptoms in nulliparous women: A randomized trial. *Journal of Physiotherapy, 58,* 9–15.

Rochat, P. (2013). Self-conceptualizing in development. In P. D. Zelazo (Ed.), *Oxford handbook of developmental psychology.* New York: Oxford University Press.

Rochlen, A. B., McKelley, R. A., Suizzo, M-A., & Scaringi, V. (2008). Predictors of relationship satisfaction, psychological well-being, and life-satisfaction among stay-at-home fathers. *Psychology of Men and Masculinity, 9,* 17–28.

Rode, S. S., Chang, P., Fisch, R. O., & Sroufe, L. A. (1981). Attachment patterns of infants separated at birth. *Developmental Psychology, 17,* 188–191.

Rodin, J., & Langer, E. J. (1977). Long-term effects of a control-relevant intervention with the institutionalized aged. *Journal of Personality and Social Psychology, 35,* 397–402.

Rodkin, P. C., & Ryan, A. M. (2012). Child and adolescent peer relationships in educational context. In K. R. Harris, S. Graham, & T. Urdan (Eds.), *APA handbook of educational psychology.* Washington, DC: American Psychological Association.

Rodrigo, M. J., Almeida, A., Spiel, C., & Koops, W. (2012). Introduction: Evidence-based parent education programs to promote positive parenting. *European Journal of Developmental Psychology, 9,* 2–10.

Rodriguez, E. T., & others. (2009). The formative role of home literacy experiences across the first three years of life in children from low-income families. *Journal of Applied Developmental Psychology, 30*(6), 677–694.

Rodriquez Villar, S., & others. (2012). Prolonged grief disorder in the next of kin of adult patients who die during or after admission to intensive care. *Chest, 141,* 1635–1636.

Roeber, B. J., Tober, C. L., Bolt, D. M., & Pollak, S. D. (2012). Gross motor development in children from orphanage settings. *Developmental Medicine and Child Neurology, 54,* 527–531.

Roelfs, D. J., Shor, E., Davidson, K. W., & Schwartz, J. E. (2011). Losing life and livelihood: A systematic review and meta-analysis of unemployment and all-cause mortality. *Social Science & Medicine, 72,* 840–854.

Roese, N. J., & Summerville, A. (2005). What we regret most . . . and why. *Personality and Social Psychology Bulletin, 31,* 1273–1285.

Rogers, L. O., Zosuals, K. M., Halilm, M. L., Ruble, D., Hughes, D., & Fuligni, A. (2012). Meaning making in middle childhood: An exploration of the meaning of ethnic identity. *Cultural Diversity and Ethnic Minority Psychology, 18,* 99–108.

Roghani, T., & others. (2012, in press). Effects of short-term aerobic exercise with and without external loading on bone metabolism and balance in postmenopausal women with osteoporosis. *Rheumatology International.*

Rogoff, B. (2003). *The cultural nature of human development.* New York: Oxford University Press.

Roisman, G. I., & Groh, A. M. (2011). Attachment theory and research in developmental psychology: An overview and appreciative critique. In M. K. Underwood & L. H. Rosen (Eds.), *Social development.* New York: Wiley.

Rojas, A., Khoo, A., Tejedo, J. R., Bedoya, F. J., Soria, B., & Martin, F. (2010). Islet cell development. *Advances in Experimental Medicine and Biology, 654,* 59–75.

Roland, E., & Midthassel, U. V. (2012). *The Zero Program. New Directions in Youth Development, 133,* 29–39.

Roll, J., Koglin, U., & Petermann, F. (2012, in press). Emotion regulation and childhood aggression: Longitudinal associations. *Child Psychiatry and Human Development.*

Rolland, Y., & others. (2011). Treatment strategies for sarcopenia and frailty. *Medical Clinics of North America, 95,* 427–438.

Rolls, B. J., & Drewnowski, A. (2007). Diet and nutrition. In J. E. Birren (ed.), *Encyclopedia of gerontology* (2nd ed.). San Diego: Academic Press.

Romans, S., Cohen, M., & Forte, T. (2011). Rates of depression and anxiety in urban and rural Canada. *Social Psychiatry and Psychiatric Epidemiology, 46,* 567–575.

Ronald, A., & Hoekstra, R. A. (2011). Autism spectrum disorders and autistic traits: A decade of new twin studies. *American Journal of Medical Genetics B: Neuropsychiatric Genetics, 156,* 255–274.

Ronninger, M., & others. (2012). Interaction analysis between HLA-DRB1 shared epitope alleles and MHC class II transactivator CIITA gene with regard to risk of rheumatoid arthritis. *PLoS One, 7*(3), e32861.

Rook, K. S., Mavandadi, S., Sorkin, D. H., & Zettel, L. A. (2007). Optimizing social relationships as a resource for health and well-being in later life. In C. M. Aldwin, C. L. Park, & A. Spiro (Eds.), *Handbook of health psychology and aging.* New York: Guilford.

Rosano, C., & others. (2012). Slower gait, slower information processing, and smaller prefrontal area in older adults. *Age and Aging, 41,* 58–64.

Rose, A. J., Carlson, W., & Waller, E. M. (2007). Prospective associations of co-rumination with friendship and emotional adjustment: Considering the socioemotional trade-offs of co-rumination. *Developmental Psychology, 43,* 1019–1031.

Rose, A. J., & others. (2012). How girls and boys expect disclosure about problems will make them feel: Implications for friendship. *Child Development, 83,* 844–863.

Rose, S. A. (1990). Cross-modal transfer in human infants: What is being transferred? *Annals of the New York Academy of Sciences, 608,* 38–47.

Rosenblith, J. F. (1992). *In the beginning* (2nd ed.). Newbury Park, CA: Sage.

Rosenfeld, A., & Stark, E. (1987, May). The prime of our lives. *Psychology Today,* pp. 62–72.

Rosengard, C. (2009). Confronting the intendedness of adolescent rapid repeat pregnancy. *Journal of Adolescent Health, 44,* 5–6.

Rosenstein, D., & Oster, H. (1988). Differential facial responses to four basic tastes in newborns. *Child Development, 59,* 1555–1568.

Rosmarin, D. H., Krumrei, E. J., & Andersson, G. (2009). Religion as a predictor of psychological distress in two religious communities. *Cognitive Behavior Therapy, 38,* 54–64.

Rosnow, R. L., & Rosenthal, R. (2013). *Beginning psychological research* (7th ed.). Boston: Cengage.

Ross, J. L., & others. (2012). Behavioral and social phenotypes in boys with 47, XYY syndrome or 47, XXY Klinefelter syndrome. *Pediatrics, 129,* 769–778.

Rossi, A. S. (1989). A life-course approach to gender, aging, and intergenerational relations. In K. W. Schaie & C. Schooler (Eds.), *Social structure and aging.* Hillsdale, NJ: Erlbaum.

Rossi, S., Minlussi, C., Pasqualetti, P., Babilioni, C., Rossini, P. M., & Cappa, S. F. (2005). Age-related functional changes of prefrontal cortex in long-term memory: A repetitive transcranial magnetic stimulation study. *Journal of Neuroscience, 24,* 7939–7944.

Rote, W. M., & others. (2012). Associations between observed mother-adolescent interactions and adolescent information management. *Journal of Research on Adolescence, 22,* 206–214.

Rotermann, M. (2007). Marital breakdown and subsequent depression. *Health Reports, 18,* 33–44.

Roth, J., Brooks-Gunn, J., Murray, L., & Foster, W. (1998). Promoting healthy adolescents: Synthesis of youth development program evaluations. *Journal of Research on Adolescence, 8,* 423–459.

Roth, L. W., & Polotsky, A. J. (2012). Can we live longer by eating less? A review of caloric restriction and longevity. *Maturitas, 71,* 315–319.

Rothbart, M. K. (2004). Temperament and the pursuit of an integrated developmental psychology. *Merrill-Palmer Quarterly, 50,* 492–505.

Rothbart, M. K. (2007). Temperament, development, and personality. *Current Directions in Psychological Science, 16,* 207–212.

Rothbart, M. K. (2011). *Becoming who we are.* New York: Guilford Press.

Rothbart, M. K., & Bates, J. E. (2006). Temperament. In W. Damon & R. Lerner (Eds.), *Handbook of child psychology* (6th ed.). New York: Wiley.

Rothbart, M. K., & Gartstein, M. A. (2008). Temperament. In M. M. Haith & J. B. Benson (Eds.), *Encyclopedia of infant and early childhood development.* Oxford, UK: Elsevier.

Rothbaum, F., Poll, M., Azuma, H., Miyake, K., & Welsz, J. (2000). The development of close relationships in Japan and the United States: Paths of symbiotic harmony and generative tension. *Child Development, 71,* 1121–1142.

Rothman, S. M., & Mattson, M. P. (2012, in press). Sleep disturbances in Alzheimer's and Parkinson's diseases. *Neuromolecular Medicine.*

Rousssotte, F. F. (2011). Abnormal brain activation during working memory in children with prenatal exposure to drugs of abuse: The effects of methamphetamine, alcohol, and polydrug exposure. *NeuroImage, 54,* 3067–3075.

Rovee-Collier, C. (1987). Learning and memory in children. In J. D. Osofsky (Ed.), *Handbook of infant development* (2nd ed.). New York: Wiley.

Rovee-Collier, C. (2004). Infant learning and memory. In U. Goswami (Ed.). *Blackwell handbook of childhood cognitive development.* Malden, MA: Blackwell.

Rovee-Collier, C. (2008). The development of infant memory. In N. Cowan & M. Courage (Eds.), *The development of memory in infancy and childhood* (2nd ed.). Philadelphia: Psychology Press.

Rovee-Collier, C., & Barr, R. (2010). Infant learning and memory. In U. J. G. Bremner & T. D. Wachs (Ed.),

Wiley-Blackwell handbook of infant development (2nd ed.). New York: Wiley.

Rowe, M., & Goldin-Meadow, S. A. (2009). Differences in early gesture explain SES disparities in child vocabulary size at school entry. *Science, 323*, 951–953.

Rowley, S. R., Kurtz-Costas, B., & Cooper, S. M. (2011). The role of schooling in ethnic minority achievement and attainment. In J. Meece & J. Eccles (Eds.), *Handbook of research on schools, schooling, and human development*. Clifton, NJ: Psychology Press.

Royer-Pokora, B. (2012, in press). Genetics of pediatric renal tumors. *Pediatric Nephrology*.

Roza, S. J., & others. (2010). Maternal folic acid supplement use in early pregnancy and child behavioural problems: The Generation R study. *British Journal of Nutrition, 103*, 445–452.

Rozzini, R., Ranhoff, A., & Trabucchi, M. (2007). Alcoholic beverage and long-term mortality in elderly people living at home. *Journals of Gerontology: Biological Sciences and Medical Sciences, 62A*, M1313–M1314.

Rubin, K. H., Bowker, J. C., McDonald, K. L., & Menzer, M. (2013). Peer relationships in childhood. In P. D. Zelazo (Ed.), *Oxford handbook of developmental psychology*. New York: Oxford University Press.

Rubin, K. H., Bowker, J. C., McDonald, K.L., & Menzer, M. (2013). Peer relationships in childhood. In P. D. Zelazo (Ed.), *Oxford handbook of developmental psychology*. New York: Oxford University Press.

Rubin, K. H., Bukowski, W., & Parker, J. G. (1998). Peer interactions, relationships, and groups. In N. Eisenberg (Ed.), *Handbook of child psychology* (5th ed., Vol. 3). New York: Wiley.

Rubin, K. H., Bukowski, W., & Parker, J. G. (2006). Peer interactions, relationships, and groups. In W. Damon & R. Lerner (Eds.), *Handbook of child psychology* (6th ed.). New York: Wiley.

Rubin, K. H., Coplan, R. J., Bowker, J. C., & Menzer, M. (2011). Social withdrawal and shyness. In P. K. Smith & C. H. Hart (Eds.), *Wiley-Blackwell handbook of childhood social development* (2nd ed.). New York: Wiley.

Rubin, S., & Malkinson, R. (2001). Parental response to child loss across the life-cycle. Clinical and research perspectives. In M. Stroebe, R. Hansson, W. Stroebe & H. Schut (Eds), *Handbook of bereavement research: Consequences, coping and care*. Washington, DC: American Psychological Association.

Rubio-Aurioles, E., & others. (2012, in press). A randomized open-label trial with a cross-over comparison of sexual self-confidence and other treatment outcomes following tadalafil once a day vs. tadalafil or sildenafil on-demand in men with erectile dysfunction. *Journal of Sexual Medicine*.

Ruble, D. (1983). The development of social comparison processes and their role in achievement-related self-socialization. In E. Higgins, D. Ruble, & W. Hartup (Eds.), *Social cognitive development: A social-cultural perspective*. New York: Cambridge University Press.

Ruchat, S. M., & others. (2012, in press). Nutrition and exercise reduce excessive weight gain in normal-weight pregnant women. *Medicine and Science in Sports and Exercise*.

Ruckenhauser, G., Yazdani, F., & Ravaglia, G. (2007). Suicide in old age: Illness or autonomous

decision of the will? *Archives of Gerontology and Geriatrics, 44*(Suppl. 6), S355–S358.

Rudang, R., Mellstrom, D., Clark, E., Ohlsson, C., & Lorentzon, M. (2012). Advancing maternal age is associated with lower bone mineral density in young adult male offspring. *Osteoporosis International, 23*, 475–482.

Rueda, M. R., Posner, M. I., & Rothbart, M. K. (2005). The development of executive attention: Contributions to the emergence of self-regulation. *Developmental Neuropsychology, 28*, 573–594.

Ruff, H. A., & Capozzoli, M. C. (2003). Development of attention and distractibility in the first 4 years of life. *Developmental Psychology, 39*, 877–890.

Ruffman, T., Slade, L., & Crowe, E. (2002). The relation between children's and mothers' mental state language and theory-of-mind understanding. *Child Development, 73*, 734–751.

Ruiter, M., & others. (2012, June 11). Short sleep predicts stroke symptoms in persons of normal weight. Paper presented at the annual meeting of the Associated Professional Sleep Societies (APSS), Boston.

Ruiz-Gallego-Largo, T., Simon, T., & Suengas, A. G. (2012). Age differences in source monitoring and referent discrimination. *Spanish Journal of Psychology, 15*, 20–28.

Rumberger, R. W. (1983). Dropping out of high school: The influence of race, sex, and family background. *American Educational Research Journal, 20*, 194–220.

Runco, M., & Spritzker, S. (Eds.) (2011). *Encyclopedia of creativity* (2nd ed.). New York: Elsevier.

Runquist, J. (2007). Persevering through postpartum fatigue. *Journal of Obstetric, Gynecologic, and Neonatal Nursing, 36*, 28–37.

Rupp, D. E., Vodanovich, S. J., & Crede, M. (2005). The multidimensional nature of ageism: Construct validity and group differences. *Journal of Social Psychology, 145*, 335–362.

Russell, M., & Airasian, P. W. (2012). *Classroom assessment* (7th ed.). New York: McGraw-Hill.

Russell, S. T., Crockett, L. J., & Chao, R. K. (2010). *Asian American parenting and parent-adolescent relationships*. New York: Springer.

Rutter, M. (2013, in press). Biological and experiential influences on psychological development. In D. P. Keating (Ed.), *Nature and nurture in early childhood development*. New York: Cambridge University Press.

Ryan, A. M. (2011). Peer relationships and academic adjustment during early adolescence. *Journal of Early Adolescence, 31*, 5–12.

Ryan, A. M., & Ladd, G. W. (Eds.). (2012, in press). *Peer relationships and adjustment at school*. Charlotte: Information Age Publishing.

Ryan, R. M., Fauth, R. C., & Brooks-Gunn, J. (2006). Childhood poverty: Implications for school readiness and early childhood education. In B. Spodek & O. N. Saracho (Eds.), *Handbook of research on the education of young children*. Mahwah, NJ: Erlbaum.

Ryff, C. D. (1984). Personality development from the inside: The subjective experience of change in adulthood and aging. In P. B. Baltes & O. G. Brim (Eds.), *Life-span development and behavior*. New York: Academic Press.

Ryff, C. D. (1991). Possible selves in adulthood and old age: A tale of shifting horizons. *Psychology and Aging, 6*, 286–295.

Rypma, B., Eldreth, D. A., & Rebbechi, D. (2007). Age-related differences in activation-performance relations in delayed-response tasks: A multiple component analyses. *Cortex, 43*, 65–76.

S

Saarni, C. (1999). *The development of emotional competence*. New York: Guilford.

Saarni, C., Campos, J., Camras, L. A., & Witherington, D. (2006). Emotional development. In W. Damon & R. Lerner (Eds.), *Handbook of child psychology* (6th ed.). New York: Wiley.

Sabbagh, M. A., Xu, F., Carlson, S. M., Moses, L. J., & Lee, K. (2006). The development of executive functioning and theory of mind: A comparison of Chinese and U. S. preschoolers. *Psychological Science, 17*, 74–81.

Sadeh, A. (2008). Sleep. In M. M. Haith & J. B. Benson (Eds.), *Encyclopedia of infant and early childhood development*. Oxford, UK: Elsevier.

Sadker, D. M., & Zittleman, K. (2012). *Teachers, schools, and society* (3rd ed.). New York: McGraw-Hill.

Sagiv, S. K., Epstein, J. N., Bellinger, D. C., & Korrick, S. A. (2012, in press). Pre- and postnatal risk factors for ADHD in a nonclinical pediatric population. *Journal of Attention Disorders*.

Saifer, S. (2007, August 29). *Tools of the Mind—A Vygotskian-inspired early childhood curriculum*. Paper presented at the 17th Annual Conference of the European Early Childhood Education Research Association, Prague.

Saint Onge, J. M. (2009). Mortality. In D. Carr (Ed.), *Encyclopedia of the life course and human development*. Boston: Gale Cengage.

Sakamoto, Y., & others. (2009). Effect of exercise, aging, and functional capacity on acute secretory immunoglobulin A response in elderly people over 75 years of age. *Geriatrics and Gerontology International, 9*, 81–88.

Sakatini, K., Tanida, M., & Katsuyama, M. (2010). Effects of aging on activity in the prefrontal cortex and autonomic nervous system during mental stress task. *Advances in Experimental Medicine and Biology, 662*, 473–478.

Sakraida, T. J. (2005). Divorce transition differences of midlife women. *Issues in Mental Health Nursing, 26*, 225–249.

Sakuma, I. (2012, in press). What type of statin and what level of low-density lipoprotein cholesterol should be appropriate for secondary prevention for Japanese patients with coronary artery disease? *Circulation Journal*.

Salat, D. H., & others. (2004). Thinning of the cerebral cortex in aging. *Cerebral Cortex, 14*, 721–730.

Sales, J. M., Brown, J. L., Vissman, A. T., & Diclemente, R. J. (2012). The association between alcohol use and sexual risk behaviors among African American women across three developmental periods: A review. *Current Drug Abuse Reviews, 5*, 117–128.

Saling, L. L., Laroo, N., & Saling, M. M. (2012). When more is less: Failure to compress discourse with re-telling in normal aging. *Acta Psychologica, 139*, 220–224.

Salloum, A., & Overstreet, S. (2012). Grief and trauma intervention for children after disaster:

Exploring coping skills versus trauma narration. *Behavior Research and Therapy, 50,* 169–179.

Salmaso, N., & others. (2012). Environmental enrichment increases the GFAP+ stem cell pool and reverses hypoxia-induced cognitive deficits in juvenile mice. *Journal of Neuroscience, 32,* 8930–8939.

Salmivalli, C., Garandeau, C. F., & Veenstra, R. (2012). KiVa Anti-Bullying Program: Implications for school adjustment. In A. M. Ryan & G. W. Ladd (Eds.), *Peer relationships and adjustment at school.* Charlotte, NC: Information Age Publishing.

Salmivalli, C., & Peets, K. (2009). Bullies, victims, and bully-victim relationships in middle childhood and adolescence. In K. H. Rubin, W. M. Bukowski, & B. Laursen (Eds.), *Handbook of peer interactions, relationships, and groups.* New York: Guilford.

Salmivalli, C., Peets, K., & Hodges, E. V. E. (2011). Bullying. In P. K. Smith & C. H. Hart (Eds.), *Wiley-Blackwell handbook of childhood social development* (2nd ed.). New York: Wiley.

Salthouse, T. A. (1994). The nature of influence of speed on adult age differences in cognition. *Developmental Psychology, 30,* 240–259.

Salthouse, T. A. (2009). When does age-related cognitive decline begin? *Neurobiology of Aging, 30,* 507–514.

Salthouse, T. A. (2010). The paradox of cognitive change. *Journal of Clinical and Experimental Neuropsychology, 32*(6), 622–629.

Salthouse, T. A. (2012a). Consequences of age-related cognitive declines. *Annual Review of Psychology* (Vol. 63). Palo Alto, CA: Annual Reviews.

Salthouse, T. A. (2012b, in press). Within-cohort age differences in cognitive functioning. *Psychological Science.*

Salthouse, T. A. (2013, in press). Executive functioning. In D. C. Park & N. Schwartz (Eds.), *Cognitive aging* (2nd ed.). New York: Psychology Press.

Salthouse, T. A., & Skovronek, E. (1992). Within-context assessment of working memory. *Journal of Gerontology, 47,* P110–P117.

Salvatore, J. E., Kuo, S. I., Steele, R. D., Simpson, J. A., & Collins, W. A. (2011). Recovering from conflict in romantic relationships: A developmental perspective. *Psychological Science, 22,* 376–383.

Samanez-Larkin, G. R., & Carstensen, L. L. (2011). Socioemotional functioning and the aging brain. In J. Decety & J. T. Cacioppo (Eds.), *Handbook of social neuroscience.* New York: Oxford University Press.

Sameroff, A. J. (2009). The transactional model. In A. J. Sameroff (Ed.), *The transactional model of development: How children and contexts shape each other.* Washington, DC: American Psychological Association.

Sameroff, A. J. (2012, in press). Conceptual issues in studying the development of self-regulation. In S. L. Olson & A. J. Sameroff (Eds.), *Biopsychosocial regulatory processes in the development of childhood behavioral problems.* New York: Cambridge University Press.

Sanders, E. (2008). Medial art and play therapy with accident survivors. In C. A. Malchiodi (Ed.), *Creative interventions with traumatized children.* New York: Guilford.

Sangree, W. H. (1989). Age and power: Life-course trajectories and age structuring of power relations in East and West Africa. In D. I. Kertzer & K. W. Schaie (Eds.), *Age structuring in comparative perspective.* Hillsdale, NJ: Erlbaum.

Sankupellay, M., & others. (2011). Characteristics of sleep EEG power spectra in healthy infants in the first two years of life. *Clinical Neurophysiology, 122,* 236–243.

Sanson, A., & Rothbart, M. K. (1995). Child temperament and parenting. In M. H. Bornstein (Ed.), *Handbook of parenting* (Vol. 4). Hillsdale, NJ: Erlbaum.

Santrock, J. W., Sitterle, K. A., & Warshak, R. A. (1988). Parent-child relationships in stepfather families. In P. Bronstein & C. P. Cowan (Eds.), *Fatherhood today: Men's changing roles in the family.* New York: Wiley.

Sapp, S. (2010). What have religion and spirituality to do with aging? Three approaches. *Gerontologist, 50,* 271–275.

Sarkisian, N., Gerena, M., & Gerstel, N. (2006). Extended family ties among Mexicans, Puerto Ricans, and Whites: Superintegration or disintegration? *Family Relations, 55,* 330–334.

Saroglou, V. (2013, in press). Religion, spirituality, and altruism. In K. I. Pargament, J. Exline, & J. Jones (Eds.), *Handbook of psychology, religion, and spirituality.* Washington, DC: American Psychological Association.

Sasson, N. J., & Elison, J. T. (2012, in press). Eye tracking in young children with autism. *Journal of Visualized Experiments.*

Saunders, N. R., Liddelow, S. A., & Dziegielewska, K. M. (2012, in press). Barrier mechanisms in the developing brain. *Frontiers in pharmacology.*

Savendahl, L., & others. (2012). Gender influences short-term growth hormone treatment response in children. *Hormone Research in Pediatrics, 77,* 188–194.

Savin-Williams, R. C. (2011). Identity development in sexual-minority youth. In S. Schwartz, K. Luyckx, & V. Vignoles (Eds.), *Handbook of identity theory and research.* New York: Springer.

Savin-Williams, R. C. (2013, in press). The new sexual-minority teenager. In J. S. Kaufman & D. A. Powell (Eds.), *Sexual identities.* Thousand Oaks, CA: Sage.

Sayer, L. C. (2006). Economic aspects of divorce and relationship dissolution. In M. A. Fine & J. H. Harvey (Eds.), *Handbook of divorce and relationship dissolution.* Mahwah, NJ: Erlbaum.

Sbarra, D. A. (2012, in press). Marital dissolution and physical health outcomes: A review of mechanisms. *The science of the couple. The Ontario Symposium* (Vol. 12). New York: Psychology Press.

Scales, P. C., Benson, P. L., & Roehlkepartain, E. C. (2011). Adolescent thriving: The role of sparks, relationships, and empowerment. *Journal of Youth and Adolescence, 40,* 263–277.

Scarr, S. (1993). Biological and cultural diversity: The legacy of Darwin for development. *Child Development, 64,* 1333–1353.

Schachter, A. D., & Kohane, I. S. (2011). Drug target-gene signatures that predict teratogenicity are enrichers for developmentally related genes. *Reproductive Toxicology, 45,* 984–990.

Schaffer, H. R. (1996). *Social development.* Cambridge, MA: Blackwell.

Schaffer, M. A., Goodhue, A., Stennes, K., & Lanigan, C. (2012). Evaluation of a public health nurse visiting program for pregnant and parenting teens. *Public Health Nursing, 29,* 218–231.

Schaie, K. W. (1994). The life course of adult intellectual abilities. *American Psychologist, 49,* 304–313.

Schaie, K. W. (1996). *Intellectual development in adulthood: The Seattle Longitudinal Study.* New York: Cambridge University Press.

Schaie, K. W. (2000). Unpublished review of J. W. Santrock's *Life-span development* (8th ed). New York: McGraw-Hill.

Schaie, K. W. (2005). *Developmental influences on adult intelligence: The Seattle Longitudinal Study.* New York: Oxford University Press.

Schaie, K. W. (2007). Generational differences: Age-period cohort. In J. E. Birren (Ed.), *Encyclopedia of gerontology* (2nd ed.). San Diego: Academic Press.

Schaie, K. W. (2008). Historical processes and patterns of cognitive aging. In S. M. Hofer & D. F. Alwin (Eds.), *Handbook on cognitive aging: Interdisciplinary perspectives.* Thousand Oaks, CA: Sage.

Schaie, K. W. (2009). When does age-related cognitive decline begin? Salthouse again reifies the "cross-sectional fallacy." *Neurobiology of Aging, 30,* 528–529.

Schaie, K. W. (2010). Adult intellectual abilities. *Corsini encyclopedia of psychology.* New York: Wiley.

Schaie, K. W. (2011). Historical influences on aging and behavior. In K.W. Schaie & S. L. Willis (Eds.), *Handbook of the psychology of aging* (7th ed.). New York: Elsevier.

Schaie, K. W. (2012). *Developmental influences on adult intelligence: The Seattle Longitudinal Study* (2nd ed.). New York: Oxford University Press.

Schaie, K. W., & Zanjani, F. (2012). The interface of adult learning and intelligence. In C. Hoare (Ed.), *Oxford handbook of reciprocal adult development and learning.* New York: Oxford University Press.

Schattschneider, C., Fletcher, J. M., Francis, D. J., Carlson, C. D., & Foorman, B. R. (2004). Kindergarten prediction of reading skills: A longitudinal comparative analysis. *Journal of Educational Psychology, 96,* 265–282.

Scheeren, A. M., Koot, H. M., & Begeer, S. (2012, in press). Social interaction style of children and adolescents with high-functioning autism spectrum disorder. *Journal of Autism and Developmental Disorders.*

Scheibe, S., Freund, A. M., & Baltes, P. B. (2007). Toward a psychology of life-longings: The optimal (utopian) life. *Developmental Psychology, 43,* 778–795.

Scheier, M. F., Carver, C. S., & Armstrong, G. H. (2012). Behavioral self-regulation, health, and illness. In A. Baum, T. A. Revenson, & J. Singer (Eds.), *Handbook of health psychology* (2nd ed.). New York: Psychology Press.

Schellenberg, G. D., & Montine, T. J. (2012, in press). The genetics and neuropathology of Alzheimer's disease. *Acta Neuropathologica.*

Scher, A., & Harel, J. (2008). Separation and stranger anxiety. In M. M. Haith & J. B. Benson (Eds.), *Encyclopedia of infant and early childhood development.* Oxford, UK: Elsevier.

Schieffelin, B. (2005). *The give and take of everyday life*. Tucson, AZ: Fenestra.

Schieman, S., van Gundy, K., & Taylor, J. (2004). The relationship between age and depressive symptoms: A test of competing explanatory and suppression influences. *Journal of Aging Health*, 14, 260–285.

Schiff, W. J. (2013). *Nutrition for healthy living* (3rd ed.). New York: McGraw–Hill.

Schiffman, S. S. (2007). Smell and taste. In J. E. Birren (Ed.), *Encyclopedia of gerontology* (2nd ed.). San Diego: Academic Press.

Schilling, E. A., Aseltine, R. H., Glanovsky, J. L., James, A., & Jacobs, D. (2009). Adolescent alcohol use, suicidal ideation, and suicide attempts. *Journal of Adolescent Health*, 44, 335–341.

Schlee, W., Leirer, V., Kolassa, I. T., Weisz, N., & Elbert, T. (2012). Age-related changes in neural functional connectivity and its behavioral relevance. *BMC Neuroscience*, 13, 16.

Schlegel, A. (2009). Cross-cultural issues in the study of adolescent development. In R. M. Lerner & L. Steinberg (Eds.), *Handbook of adolescent psychology* (3rd ed.). New York: Wiley.

Schlegel, M. (2000). All work and play. *Monitor on Psychology*, 31(11), 50–51.

Schlomer, G. L., & Belsky, J. (2012, in press). Maternal age, investment, parent-child conflict: A mediational test of terminal investment hypothesis. *Journal of Family Psychology*.

Schmidt, M. E., & others. (2012, in press). Systematic review of effective strategies for reducing screen time among young children. *Obesity*.

Schmidt, S., & others. (2006). Cigarette smoking strongly modifies the association of LOC387715 and age related macular degeneration. *American Journal of Human Genetics*, 78, 852–864.

Schneider, J. M., & others. (2011). Dual sensory impairment in older age. *Journal of Aging and Health*, 23, 1309–1324.

Schneider, W. (2011). Memory development in childhood. In U. Goswami (Ed.), *Wiley-Blackwell handbook of childhood cognitive development* (2nd ed.). New York: Wiley-Blackwell.

Schnittker, J. (2007). Look (closely) at all the lonely people: Age and social psychology of social support. *Journal of Aging and Health*, 19, 659–682.

Schoeneberger, J. (2012). Longitudinal attendance patterns: Developing high school dropouts. *Clearinghouse*, 85, 7–14.

Schoenemann, P. T. (2012). Evolution of brain and language. *Progress in Brain Research*, 195, 443–459.

Schoffstall, C. L., & Cohen, R. (2012, in press). Cyber aggression: The relation of online offenders and offline social competence. *Social Development*.

Schooler, C. (2007). Use it—and keep it, longer, probably: A reply to Salthouse (2006). *Perspectives on Psychological Science*, 2, 24–29.

Schooler, C., Mulatu, S., & Oates, G. (1999). The continuing effects of substantively complex work on the intellectual functioning of older workers. *Psychology and Aging*, 14, 483–506.

Schoon, I., Jones, E., Cheng, H., & Maughan, B. (2012, in press). Family hardship, family instability, and cognitive development. *Journal of Epidemiology and Community Health*.

Schuchter, S., & Zisook, S. (1993). The course of normal grief. In M. Stroebe, W. Stroebe, & R. O. Hanson (Eds.), *Handbook of bereavement*. New York: Cambridge University Press.

Schueller-Weidekamm, C., & Kautzky-Willer, A. (2012, in press). Challenges of work-life balance for women physicians/mothers working in leadership positions. *Gender Medicine*.

Schulenberg, J., O'Malley, P. M., Bachman, J. G., & Johnson, L. D. (2000). "Spread your wings and fly": The course of health and well-being during the transition to young adulthood. In L. J. Crockett & R. K. Silbereisen (Eds.), *Negotiating adolescence in times of social change*. New York: Cambridge University Press.

Schulenberg, J. E., & Zarrett, N. R. (2006). Mental health during emerging adulthood: Continuity and discontinuity in courses, causes, and functions. In J. J. Arnett & J. L. Tanner (Eds.), *Emerging adults in America*. Washington, DC: American Psychological Association.

Schulz, E., Wenzel, P., Munzel, T., & Daiber, A. (2012, in press). Mitochondrial redox signaling: Interaction of mitochondrial reactive oxygen species with other sources of oxidative stress. *Antioxidants and Redox Signaling*.

Schunk, D. H. (2012). *Learning theories: An educational perspective* (5th ed.). Upper Saddle River, NJ: Prentice Hall.

Schwalbe, C. S., Gearing, R. E., MacKenzie, M. J., Brewer, K. B., & Ibrahim, R. (2012). A meta-analysis of experimental studies of diversion programs for juvenile defenders. *Clinical Psychology Review*, 32, 26–33.

Schwartz, D., Kelly, B. M., Duong, M., & Badaly, D. (2010). Contextual perspective on intervention and prevention efforts for bully/victim problems. In E. M. Vernberg & B. K. Biggs (Eds.), *Preventing and treating bullying and victimization*. New York: Oxford University Press.

Schwartz, M. A., & Scott, B. M. (2012). *Marriages and families, census update* (6th ed.). Upper Saddle River, NJ: Pearson.

Schwartz, S. J., Donnellan, M. B., Ravert, R. D., Luyckx, K., & Zamboanga, B. L. (2013, in press). Identity development, personality, and well-being in adolescence and emerging adulthood: Theory, research, and recent advances. In I. B. Weiner & others (Eds.), *Handbook of psychology* (2nd ed., Vol. 6). New York: Wiley.

Schwartz, S. J., & others. (2011). Examining the light and dark sides of emerging adults' identity status differences in positive and negative psychosocial functioning. *Journal of Youth and Adolescence*, 40, 839–859.

Schwarz, B., Stutz, M., & Ledermann, T. (2012, in press). Perceived interparental conflict and early adolescents' friendships: The role of attachment security and emotion regulation. *Journal of Youth and Adolescence*.

Schwarzer, R., & Luszczynska, A. (2013, in press). Stressful life events. In I. B. Weiner & others (Eds.), *Handbook of psychology* (2nd ed., Vol. 9). New York: Wiley.

Schweinhart, L. J., Montie, J., Xiang, Z., Barnett, W. S., Belfield, C. R., & Nores, M. (2005). *Lifetime effects: The High/Scope Perry Preschool Study through age 40*. Ypsilanti, MI: High/Scope Press.

Scialfa, C. T., & Kline, D. W. (2007). Vision. In J. E. Birren (ed.), *Encyclopedia of gerontology* (2nd ed.). San Diego: Academic Press.

Sciberras, E., & Ukoumunne, O. C., & Efron, D. (2011). Predictors of parent-reported attention-deficit/hyperactivity disorder in children aged 6–7 years: A national longitudinal study. *Journal of Abnormal Child Psychology*, 39, 1025–1034.

Science Daily. (2008, January 15). Human gene count tumbles again, p. 1.

Sclar, D. A., & others. (2012, in press). Attention deficit/hyperactivity disorder among children and adolescents in the United States: Trends in diagnosis and use of pharmacotherapy by gender. *Clinical Pediatrics*.

Scott, J. A., Ng, S. Y., & Cobiac, L. (2012, in press). The relationship between breastfeeding and weight status in a national sample of Australian children and adolescents. *BMC Public Health*.

Scourfield, J., Van den Bree, M., Martin, N., & McGuffin, P. (2004). Conduct problems in children and adolescents: A twin study. *Archives of General Psychiatry*, 61, 489–496.

Scullin, M. K., Bugg, J. M., & McDaniel, M. A. (2012). Whoops, I did it again: Commission errors in prospective memory. *Psychology of Aging*, 27, 46–53.

Search Institute. (2010). *Teen voice*. Minneapolis: Search Institute.

Seaton, E. K., Neblett, E. W., Upton, R. D., Hammond, W. P., & Sellers, R. M. (2011). The moderating capacity of racial identity between perceived discrimination and psychological well-being over time in African American youth. *Child Development*, 82, 1850–1867.

Seay, G. (2011). Euthanasia and common sense: A reply to Garcia. *Journal of Medical Philosophy*, 36, 321–327.

Seccombe, K. (2012). *Exploring marriages and families*. Upper Saddle River, NJ: Pearson.

Seefeldt, C., Galper, A., & Jones, I. (2012). *Active experiences for active children* (3rd ed.). Upper Saddle River, NJ: Pearson.

Seeman, T. E., & Chen, X. (2002). Risk and protective factors for physical functioning in older adults with and without chronic conditions: MacArthur Studies of Successful Aging. *PB: Social Sciences*, 57B, S135–S144.

Seiter, L. N., & Nelson, L. J. (2011). An examination of emerging adulthood in college students and nonstudents in India. *Journal of Adolescent Research*, 26, 506–536.

Sekhobo, J. P., Edmunds, L. S., Reynolds, D. K., Dalenius, K., & Sharma, A. (2010). Trends in the prevalence of obesity and overweight among children enrolled in the New York State WIC program, 2002–2007. *Public Health Reports*, 125, 218–224.

Selim, A. J., & others. (2005). Comprehensive health status assessment of centenarians: Results from the 1999 Large Health Survey of Veteran Enrollees. *Journals of Gerontology A: Biological Sciences and Medical Sciences*, 60, 515–519.

Sellers, R. M., Copeland-Linder, N., Martin, P. P., & Lewis, R. L. (2006). Racial identity matters: The relationship between racial discrimination and psychological functioning in African American adolescents. *Journal of Research on Adolescence, 16*, 187–216.

Selman, R. L. (1980). *The growth of interpersonal understanding.* New York: Academic Press.

Semanik, P. A., Chang, R. W., & Dunlop, D. D. (2012). Aerobic activity in prevention and symptom control of osteoarthritis. *PM & R, 4*(5, Suppl.), S37–S44.

Sen, B. (2010). The relationship between frequency of family dinner and adolescent problem behaviors after adjusting for other characteristics. *Journal of Adolescence, 33*, 187–196.

Senter, L., Sackoff, J., Landi, K., & Boyd, L. (2010). Studying sudden and unexpected deaths in a time of changing death certification and investigation practices: Evaluating sleep-related risk factors for infant death in New York City. *Maternal and Child Health, 15*(2), 242–248.

Serra, M. J., & Metcalfe, J. (2010). Effective implementation of metacognition. In D. J. Hacker, J. Dunlosky, & A. C. Graesser (Eds.), *Handbook of metacognition and education.* New York: Psychology Press.

Sethna, V., Murray, L., & Ramchandani, P. G. (2012, in press). Depressed fathers' speech to their 3-month-old infants: A study of cognitive and mentalizing features in paternal speech. *Psychological Medicine.*

Setterson, R. A. (2009). Neugarten, Bernice. In D. Carr (Ed.), *Encyclopedia of the life course and human development.* Boston: Gale Cengage.

Setterson, R. A., & Trauten, M. E. (2009). The new terrain of old age: hallmarks, freedoms, and risks. In V. L. Bengtson, D. Gans, N. M. Putney, & M. Silverstein (Eds.), *Handbook of theories of aging.* New York: Springer.

Sgandurra, G., & others. (2012). Longitudinal study of unimanual actions and grasping forces during infancy. *Infant Behavior and Development, 35*, 205–214.

Shah, R., & others. (2012, in press). Prenatal methamphetamine exposure and short-term maternal and infant medical outcomes. *American Journal of Perinatology.*

Shah, S. M., Carey, I. M., Harris, T., Dewilde, S., & Cook, D. G. (2012). Quality of prescribing in care homes and the community in England and Wales. *British Journal of General Practice, 62*, 329–336.

Shamah, T., & Villalpando, S. (2006). The role of enriched foods in infant and child nutrition. *British Journal of Nutrition, 96*(Suppl. 1), S73–S77.

Shan, Z. Y., Liu, J. Z., Sahgal, V., Wang, B., & Yue, G. H. (2005). Selective atrophy of left hemisphere and frontal lobe of the brain in older men. *Journals of Gerontology A: Biological Sciences and Medical Sciences, 60*, A165–A174.

Shankar, A., McMunn, A., Banks, J., & Steptoe, A. (2011). Loneliness, social isolation, and behavioral and biological health indicators in older adults. *Health Psychology, 30*, 377–385.

Shankaran, S., & others. (2010). Prenatal cocaine exposure and BMI and blood pressure at 9 years of age. *Journal of Hypertension, 28*, 1166–1175.

Shankaran, S., & others. (2011). Risk for obesity in adolescence starts in early childhood. *Journal of Perinatology, 31*, 711–716.

Shapiro, A. F., and Gottman, J. M. (2005). Effects on marriage of a psycho-education intervention with couples undergoing the transition to parenthood, evaluation at 1 year post-intervention. *Journal of Family Communication, 5*, 1–24.

Shapiro, C. J., Prinz, R. J., & Sanders, M. R. (2012). Facilitators and barriers to implementation of an evidence-based parenting intervention to prevent child maltreatment: The Triple P-Positive Parenting Program. *Child Maltreatment, 17*, 86–95.

Sharp, E. S., Reynolds, C. A., Pedersen, N. L., & Gatz, M. (2010). Cognitive engagement and cognitive aging: Is openness protective? *Psychology and Aging, 25*, 60–73.

Shatz, M., & Gelman, R. (1973). The development of communication skills: Modifications in the speech of young children as a function of the listener. *Monographs of the Society for Research in Child Development, 38* (Serial No. 152).

Shaw, P., & others. (2007). Attention-deficit/hyperactivity disorder is characterized by a delay in cortical maturation. *Proceedings of the National Academy of Sciences, 104*(49), 19649–19654.

Shay, J. W., Reddel, R. R., & Wright, W. E. (2012). Cancer and telomeres—An ALTernative to telomerase. *Science, 336*, 1388–1390.

Shaywitz, B. A., Lyon, G. R., & Shaywitz, S. E. (2006). The role of functional magnetic resonance imaging in understanding reading and dyslexia. *Developmental Neuropsychology, 30*, 613–632.

Shaywitz, S. E., Gruen, J. R., & Shaywitz, B. A. (2007). Management of dyslexia, its rationale and underlying neurobiology. *Pediatric Clinics of North America, 54*, 609–623.

Shear, M. K. (2010). Exploring the role of experiential avoidance from the perspective of attachment theory and the dual process model. *Omega, 61*, 357–369.

Shear, M. K. (2012a). Getting straight about grief. *Depression and Anxiety, 29*, 461–464.

Shear, M. K. (2012b). Grief and mourning gone awry: Pathway and course of complicated grief. *Dialogues in Clinical Neuroscience, 14*, 119–128.

Shear, M. K., & Skritskaya, N. A. (2012). Bereavement and anxiety. *Current Psychiatry Reports, 14*, 169–175.

Shehata, F., & others. (2011). Placenta/birthweight ratio and perinatal outcome: A retrospective cohort analysis. *BJOG, 118*, 741–747.

Shek, D. T. (2012, in press). Spirituality as a positive youth development construct: A conceptual review. *Scientific World Journal.*

Shen, L. H., Liao, M. H., & Tseng, Y. C. (2012, in press). Recent advances in imaging of dopaminergic neurons for evaluation of neuropsychiatric disorders. *Journal of Biomedicine and Biotechnology.*

Shenson, D., & others. (2012, in press). Developing an integrated strategy to reduce ethnic and racial disparities in the delivery of clinical preventive services for older Americans. *American Journal of Public Health.*

Sherwood, C. C., & others. (2011). Aging of the cerebral cortex differs between humans and chimpanzees. *Proceedings of the National Academy of Sciences U.S.A., 108*, 13029–13034.

Shi, Y., de Groh, M., & Morrison, H. (2012, in press). Increasing blood pressure and its associated factors in Canadian children and adolescents from Canadian Health Measures Survey. *BMC Public Health, 29.*

Shin, S. H., Hong, H. G., & Hazen, A. L. (2010). Childhood sexual abuse and adolescence substance use: A latent class analysis. *Drug and Alcohol Dependence, 109*, 226–235.

Shipley, B. A., Der, G., Taylor, M. D., & Deary, I. J. (2007). Association between mortality and cognitive change over 7 years in a large representative sample of UK residents. *Psychosomatic Medicine, 69*, 640–650.

Shirom, A., Toker, S., Alkaly, Y., Jacobson, O., & Balicer, R. (2011). Work-based predictors of mortality: A 20-year follow-up of healthy employees. *Health Psychology, 30*, 268–275.

Shizukuda, Y., Plummer, S. L., & Harrelson, A. (2010). Customized exercise echocardiography: Beyond detection of coronary artery disease. *Echocardiography, 27*, 186–194.

Shor, E., Roelfs, D. J., Bugyi, P., & Schwartz, J. E. (2012). Meta-analysis of marital dissolution and mortality: Reevaluating the intersection of gender and age. *Social Science and Medicine, 75*, 46–59.

Shore, L. M., & Goldberg, C. B. (2005). Age discrimination in the work place. In R. L. Dipobye & A. Colella (Eds.), *Discrimination at work.* Mahwah, NJ: Erlbaum.

Shors, T. J. (2009). Saving new brain cells. *Scientific American, 300*, 46–52.

Shuai, L., Chan, R. C., & Wang, Y. (2011). Executive function profile of Chinese boys with attention-deficit hyperactivity disorder: Different subtypes and comorbidity. *Archives of Clinical Neuropsychology, 26*, 120–132.

Shuaib, A. A., Frass, K. A., Al-Harazi, A. H., & Ghanem, N. S. (2011). Pregnancy outcomes of mothers aged 17 years of less. *Saudi Medical Journal, 32*, 166–170.

Shukla, D. K., Keehn, B., Smylie, D. M., & Muller, R. A. (2011). Microstructural abnormalities of short-distance white matter tracts in autism spectrum disorders. *Neuropsychologia, 49*, 1378–1382.

Shulman, S., Davila, J., & Shachar-Shapira, L. (2011). Assessing romantic competence among older adolescents. *Journal of Adolescence, 34*, 397–406.

Shultz, K. S., & Wang, M. (2011). Psychological perspectives on the changing nature of retirement. *American Psychologist, 66*, 170–179.

Siedlecki, K. L. (2007). Investigating the structure and age invariance of episodic memory across the adult life span. *Psychology and Aging, 22*, 251–268.

Siegler, I. C., Bosworth, H. B., Davey, A., & Elias, M. F. (2013a, in press). Disease, health, and aging in the first decade of the 21st century. In I. B. Weiner & others (Eds.), *Handbook of psychology* (Vol. 6). New York: Wiley.

Siegler, I. C., Bosworth, H. B., & Poon, L. W. (2003). Disease, health, and aging. In I. B. Welner (Eds.), *Handbook of psychology* (Vol. 6), New York: Wiley.

Siegler, I. C., & Costa, P. T. (1999, August). *Personality change and continuity in midlife: UNC Alumni Heart Study.* Paper presented at the meeting of the American Psychological Association, Boston.

Siegler, I. C., Elias, M. F., Brummett, B. H., & Bosworth, H. B. (2013b, in press). Adult development and aging. In I. B. Weiner & others (Eds.), Handbook of psychology (Vol. 9). New York: Wiley.

Siegler, R. S. (2006). Microgenetic analysis of learning. In W. Damon & R. Lerner (Eds.). *Handbook of child psychology* (6th ed.). New York: Wiley.

Siegler, R. S. (2007). Cognitive variability. *Developmental Science, 10,* 104–109.

Siegler, R. S. (2012). From theory to application and back: Following in the giant footsteps of David Klahr. In S. M. Carver & J. Shrager (Eds.), *The journey from child to scientist: Integrating cognitive development and the education sciences.* Thousand Oaks, CA: Sage.

Siegler, R. S. (2013, in press). How do people become experts? In J. Staszewski (Ed.), *Expertise and skill acquisition: The impact of William C. Chase.* New York: Taylor & Francis.

Siegler, R. S., & Mu, Y. (2008). Chinese children excel on novel mathematics problems even before elementary school. *Psychological Science, 19,* 759–763.

Siener, S., & Kerns, K. A. (2012). Emotion regulation and depressive symptoms in preadolescence. *Child Psychiatry and Human Development, 43,* 414–430.

Sievert, L. L., & Obermeyer, C. M. (2012). Symptom clusters at midlife: A four-country comparison of checklist and qualitative responses. *Menopause, 19,* 133–144.

Sigal, A., Sandler, I., Wolchik, S., & Braver, S. (2011). Do parent education programs promote healthy post-divorce parenting? Critical directions and distinctions and a review of the evidence. *Family Court Review, 49,* 120–129.

Silva, C. (2005, October 31). When the dynamo talks, city listens. *Boston Globe,* pp. B1, B4.

Silver, M. P. (2010). Women's retirement and self-assessed well-being: An analysis of three measures of well-being among recent and long-term retirees relative to homemakers. *Women and Health, 50,* 1–19.

Silverstein, M. (2009). Caregiving. In D. Carr (Ed.), *Encyclopedia of the life course and human development.* Boston: Gale Cengage.

Silverstein, M., Conroy, S. J., Wang, H., Giarrusso, R., & Bengtson, V. L. (2002). Reciprocity in parent-child relation over the adult life course. *Journals of Gerontology B: Psychological Sciences and Social Sciences, 57B,* S3–S13.

Simkin, P., & Bolding, A. (2004). Update on nonpharmacological approaches to relieve labor pain and prevent suffering. *Journal of Midwifery and Women's Health, 49,* 489–504.

Simmons, D. (2011). Diabetes and obesity in pregnancy. *Best Practice and Research, Clinical Obstetrics and Gynecology, 25,* 25–36.

Simmons, R. G., & Blyth, D. A. (1987). *Moving into adolescence.* Hawthorne, NY: Aldine.

Simon, E. J., Dickey, J. L., & Reece, J. B. (2013). *Campbell essential biology* (5th ed.). Upper Saddle River, NJ: Pearson.

Simon, G. E., & others. (2011). Obesity, depression, and health service costs among middle-aged women. *Journal of General Internal Medicine, 26,* 1284–1290.

Simon, R. W., & Barrett, A. E. (2010). Nonmarital romantic relationships and mental health in early adulthood: Does the association differ for women and men? *Journal of Health and Social Behavior, 51,* 168–182.

Simonetti, G. D., & others. (2011). Determinants of blood pressure in preschool children: The role of parental smoking. *Circulation, 123,* 292–298.

Simonton, D. K. (1996). Creativity. In J. E. Birren (Ed.), *Encyclopedia of aging.* San Diego: Academic Press.

Simpkins, S. D., Delgado, M. Y., Price, C. D., Quach, A., & Starbuck, E. (2012, in press). Socioeconomic status, ethnicity, culture, and immigration: Examining the potential mechanisms underlying Mexican-origin adolescents' organized activity participation. *Developmental Psychology.*

Simpkins, S. D., Fredricks, J. A., Davis-Kean, P. E., & Eccles, J. S. (2006). Healthy mind, healthy habits: The influence of activity involvement in middle childhood. In A. C. Huston & M. N. Ripke (Eds.), *Developmental contexts in middle childhood.* New York: Cambridge University Press.

Simpkins, S. D., Vest, A. E., & Price, C. D. (2011). Intergenerational continuity and discontinuity in Mexican-origin youths' participation in organized activities: Insights from mixed-methods. *Journal of Family Psychology, 25,* 814–824.

Simpson, R. J., & others. (2012). Exercise and the aging immune system. *Aging Research and Reviews, 1,* 404–420.

Singer, D., Golinkoff, R. M., & Hirsh-Pasek, K. (Eds.). (2006). *Play = learning: How play motivates and enhances children's cognitive and social-emotional growth.* New York: Oxford University Press.

Singer, T. (2012, in press). The past, present, and future of social neuroscience: A European perspective. *Neuroimage.*

Singh-Manoux, A., & others. (2012). Timing and onset of cognitive decline: Results from Whitehall II prospective cohort study. *BMJ, 344,* d7622.

Sinha, J. W., Cnaan, R. A., & Gelles, R. J. (2006). Adolescent risk behaviors and religion: Findings from a national study. *Journal of Adolescence, 30,* 231–249.

Sinnott, J. D. (2003). Postformal thought and adult development: Living in balance. In J. Demick & C. Andreoletti (Eds.), *Handbook of adult development.* New York: Kluwer.

Sinnott, J. D., & Johnson, L. (1997). Brief report: Complex formal thought in skilled research administrators. *Journal of Adult Development, 4,* 45–53.

Sirsch, U., Dreher, E., Mayr, E., & Willinger, U. (2009). What does it take to be an adult in Australia? Views of adulthood in Australian adolescents, emerging adults and adults. *Journal of Adolescent Research, 24,* 275–292.

Sisson, S. B., Broyles, S. T., Baker, B. L., & Katzmarzyk, P. T. (2010). Screen time, physical activity, and overweight in U.S. youth: National Survey of Children's Health 2003. *Journal of Adolescent Health, 47,* 309–311.

Skinner, B. F. (1938). *The behavior of organisms: An experimental analysis.* New York: Appleton-Century-Crofts.

Skinner, B. F. (1957). *Verbal behavior.* New York: Appleton-Century-Crofts.

Slatcher, R. B., & Trentacosta, C. J. (2012, in press). Influences of parent and child negative emotionality on young children's everyday behaviors. *Emotion.*

Slater, A. (2012). Imitation in infancy: Revisiting Meltzoff & Moore's study. In A. M. Slater & P. C. Quinn (Eds.), *Developmental psychology: Revisiting the classic studies.* Thousand Oaks, CA: Sage.

Slater, A. M., Bremner, J. G., Johnson, S. P., & Hayes, R. (2011). The role of perceptual processes in infant addition/subtraction events. In L. M. Oakes, C. H. Cashon, M. Casasola, & D. H. Rakison (Eds.), *Early perceptual and cognitive development.* New York: Oxford University Press.

Slater, A., Field, T., & Hernandez-Reif, M. (2007). The development of the senses. In A. Slater & M. Lewis (Eds.), *Introduction to infant development* (2nd ed.). New York: Oxford University Press.

Slater, A. M., Morison, V., & Somers, M. (1988). Orientation discrimination and cortical function in the human newborn. *Perception, 17,* 597–602.

Slavin, R. E. (2012). Classroom applications of cooperative learning. In K. R. Harris, S. Graham, & T. Urdan (Eds.), *APA educational psychology handbook.* Washington, DC: American Psychological Association.

Sleet, D. A., & Mercy, J. A. (2003). Promotion of safety, security, and well-being. In M. H. Bornstein, L. Davidson, C. L. M. Keyes, & K. A. Moore (Eds.), *Well-being.* Mahwah, NJ: Erlbaum.

Sliwinski, M. J. (2011). Approaches to modeling intraindividual and interindividual facets of change for developmental research. In K. L. Fingerman, C. A. Berg, J. Smith, & T. C. Antonucci (Eds.), *Handbook of life-span development.* New York: Springer.

Slobin, D. (1972, July). Children and language: They learn the same way all around the world. *Psychology Today,* 71–76.

Slomko, H., Heo., H. J., & Einstein, F. H. (2012). Minireview: Epigenetics of obesity and diabetes in humans. *Endrocrinology, 15,* 1025–1030.

Slutske, W. S., Moffitt, T. E., Poulton, R., & Caspi, A. (2012). Undercontrolled temperament at age 3 predicts disordered gambling at age 32: A longitudinal study of a complete birth cohort. *Psychological Science, 23,* 510–516.

Small, B. J., Dixon, R. A., McArdle, J. J., & Grimm, K. J. (2012a). Do changes in lifestyle engagement moderate cognitive decline in normal aging? Evidence from the Victoria Longitudinal Study. *Neuropsychology, 26,* 144–155.

Small, B. J., Rawson, K. S., Eisel, S., & McEvoy, C. L. (2012b). Memory and aging. In S. K. Whitbourne & M. Sliwinski (Eds.), *Wiley-Blackwell handbook of adulthood and aging.* New York: Wiley.

Small, H. (2011). *Why not? My seventy year plan for a college degree.* Franklin, TN: Carpenter's Son Publishing.

Smetana, J. G. (2010). The role of trust in adolescent-parent relationships: To trust is to tell you. In K. Rotenberg (Ed.), *Trust and trustworthiness during childhood and adolescence.* New York: Cambridge University Press.

Smetana, J. G. (2011a). *Adolescents, families, and social development: How adolescents construct their worlds.* New York: Wiley-Blackwell.

Smetana, J. G. (2011b). Adolescents' social reasoning and relationships with parents: Conflicts and coordinations within and across domains. In E. Amsel & J. Smetana, J. (Eds.), *Adolescent vulnerabilities and opportunities: Constructivist and developmental perspectives.* New York: Cambridge University Press.

Smets, T., & others. (2010). Euthanasia in patients dying at home in Belgium: Interview study on adherence to legal standards. *British Journal of General Practice, 60*, e163–e170.

Smink, F. R., van Hoeken, D., & Hoek, H. W. (2012, in press). Epidemiology of eating disorders: Incidence, prevalence, and mortality rates. *Current Psychiatry Reports.*

Smith, A. D. (1996). Memory. In J. E. Birren (Ed.), *Encyclopedia of gerontology* (Vol. 2). San Diego: Academic Press.

Smith, C., & Denton, M. (2005). *Soul searching: The religious and spiritual lives of American teenagers.* New York: Oxford University Press.

Smith, C. A., Levett, K. M., Collins, C. T., & Jones, L. (2012). Massage, reflexology, and other manual methods for pain management. *Cochrane Database of Systematic Reviews, 15*(2), CD009290.

Smith, G. E., & others. (2009). A cognitive training program based on principles of brain plasticity: Results from the improvement in memory with plasticity-based adaptive cognitive training (IMPACT) study. *Journal of the American Geriatrics Society, 57*, 594–603.

Smith, J. (2009). Self. In D. Carr (Ed.), *Encyclopedia of the life course and human development.* Boston: Gale Cengage.

Smith, J. M. (2012). Toward a better understanding of loneliness in community-dwelling older adults. *Journal of Psychology, 146*, 293–311.

Smith, J., & Freund, A. M. (2002). The dynamics of possible selves in old age. *Journals of Gerontology B: Psychological Sciences and Social Sciences, 57*, P492–P500.

Smith, L. E., & Howard, K. S. (2008). Continuity of paternal social support and depressive symptoms among new mothers. *Journal of Family Psychology, 22*, 763–773.

Smith, P. H., Hornish, G. G., Leonard, K. E., & Cornelius, J. R. (2012, in press). Women ending marriage to a problem drinking partner decrease their own risk for problem drinking. *Addiction.*

Smith, R. A., & Davis, S. F. (2013). *Psychologist as detective* (6th ed.). Upper Saddle River, NJ: Pearson.

Smith, R. L., Rose, A. J., & Schwartz-Mette, R. A. (2010). Relational and overt aggression in childhood and adolescence: Clarifying mean-level gender differences and associations with peer acceptance. *Social Development, 19*, 243–269.

Smith, T. B., McCullough, M. E., & Poll, J. (2003). Religiousness and depression. Evidence for a main effect and the moderating influence of stressful life events. *Psychological Bulletin, 129*, 614–636.

Smith, T. E. C., Polloway, E. A., Patton, J. R., & Dowdy, C. A. (2012). *Teaching students with special needs in inclusive settings* (6th ed.). Upper Saddle River, NJ: Pearson.

Smoreda, Z., & Licoppe, C. (2000). Gender-specific use of the domestic telephone. *Social Psychology Quarterly, 63*, 238–252.

Snarey, J. (1987, June). A question of morality. *Psychology Today*, pp. 6–8.

Snel, M., & others. (2012). Effects of adding exercise to a 16-week very low-calorie diet in obese, insulin-dependent type 2 diabetes mellitus patients. *Journal of Clinical Endocrinology and Metabolism.*

Snow, C. E., & Kang, J. Y. (2006). Becoming bilingual, biliterate, and bicultural. In W. Damon & R. Lerner (Eds.), *Handbook of child psychology* (6th ed.). New York: Wiley.

Snowdon, D. A. (2002). *Aging with grace: What the Nun Study teaches us about leading longer, healthier, and more meaningful lives.* New York: Bantam.

Snowdon, D. A. (2003). Healthy aging and dementia: Findings from the Nun Study. *Annals of Internal Medicine, 139*, 450–454.

Snyder, J. A., Scherer, H. L., & Fisher, B. S. (2012). Social organization and social ties: Their effects on sexual harassment victimization in the workplace. *Work, 42*, 137–150.

Snyder, K. A., & Torrence, C. M. (2008). Habituation and novelty. In M. M. Haith & J. B. Benson (Eds.), *Encyclopedia of infant and early childhood development.* Oxford, UK: Elsevier.

Soares, N. S., & Patel, D. R. (2012). Office screening and early identification of children with autism. *Pediatric Clinics of North America, 59*, 89–102.

Soenens, B., & Beyers, W. (2012). The cross-cultural significance of control and autonomy in parent-adolescent relationships. *Journal of Adolescence, 35*, 243–248.

Soerensen, M. (2012). Genetic variation and human longevity. *Danish Medical Journal, 59*, B4454.

Soerensen, M., & others. (2012, in press). Human longevity and variation in GH/IGF-1/insulin signaling, DNA damage signaling and repair and pro/antioxidant pathway genes: Cross sectional and longitudinal studies. *Experimental Gerontology.*

Sokol, B. W., Snjezana, H., & Muller, U. (2010). Social understanding and self-regulation: From perspective-taking to theory-of-mind. In B. Sokol, U. Muller, J. Carpendale, A. Young, & G. Iarocci (Eds.), *Self- and social-regulation.* New York: Oxford University Press.

Solana, R., & others. (2012, in press). Innate immunosenescence: Effect of aging on cells and receptors of the innate immune system in humans. *Seminars in Immunology.*

Solanans-Barkca, M., & others. (2012, in press). Apolipoprotein E gene mutations in subjects with hyperlipidemia and a clinical diagnosis of familial combined hyperlipidemia. *Atherosclerosis.*

Solheim, K. N., & others. (2011). The effect of cesarean delivery rates on the future incidence of placenta previa, placenta accrete, and maternal mortality. *Journal of Maternal-Fetal and Neonatal Medicine, 24*, 1341–1346.

Solmeyer, A. R., McHale, S. M., Killoren, S. E., & Updegraff, K. A. (2011). Coparenting around siblings' differential treatment in Mexican-origin families. *Developmental Psychology, 25*, 251–260.

Soneji, S., & King, G. (2012, in press). Statistical security for social security. *Demography.*

Song, A. V., & Halpern-Felsher, B. L. (2010). Predictive relationship between adolescent oral and vaginal sex: Results from a prospective, longitudinal study. *Archives of Pediatric and Adolescent Medicine, 165*, 243–249.

Song, J. J. (Ed.) (2013, in press). *Oxford handbook of linguistic typology.* New York: Oxford University Press.

Sonnentag, S., & Frese, M. (2013). Stress in organizations. In I. B. Weiner & others (Eds.), *Handbook of psychology* (2nd ed., Vol. 12). New York: Wiley.

Sonuga-Berke, E. J. S. (2013). Attention deficit/hyperactivity disorder. In P. D. Zelazo (Ed.), *Oxford handbook of developmental psychology.* New York: Oxford University Press.

Sood, A. B., Razdan, A., Weller, E. B., & Weller, R. A. (2006). Children's reactions to parental and sibling death. *Current Psychiatry Reports, 8*, 115–120.

Sophian, C. (1985). Perseveration and infants' search: A comparison of two- and three-location tasks. *Developmental Psychology, 21*, 187–194.

Sorensen, K., & others. (2012). Recent secular trends in pubertal timing: Implications for evaluation and diagnosis of precocious puberty. *Hormone Research in Pediatrics, 77*, 137–145.

Sorensen, T. L., & Kemp, H. (2010). Ranibizumab treatment in patients with neovascular age-related macular degeneration and very low vision. *Acta Ophthalmologica, 89*(1), e97.

Soter, A. O. (2013). *Grammar, usage, and punctuation.* Boston: Allyn & Bacon.

Soto, C. J., John, O. P., Gosling, S. D., & Potter, J. (2011). Age differences in personality traits from 10 to 65: Big Five domains and facets in a large cross-sectional sample. *Journal of Personality and Social Psychology, 100*, 333–348.

South, M., & Isaacs, D. (2013). *Practical pediatrics.* New York: Elsevier.

Sowell, E. R., Thompson, P. M., Leonard, C. M., Welcome, S. E., Kan, E., & Toga, A. W. (2004). Longitudinal mapping of cortical thickness and brain growth in children. *Journal of Neuroscience, 24*, 8223–8231.

Spangler, G., Johann, M., Ronai, Z., & Zimmermann, P. (2009). Genetic and environmental influence on attachment disorganization. *Journal of Child Psychology and Psychiatry, 50*, 952–961.

Specht, J., Egloff, B., & Schukle, S. C. (2011). Stability and change of personality across the life course: The impact of age and major life events on mean-level and rank-order stability of the Big Five. *Journal of Personality and Social Psychology, 101*(4), 862–882.

Spelke, E. S. (1979). Perceiving bimodally specified events in infancy. *Developmental Psychology, 5*, 626–636.

Spelke, E. S. (1991). Physical knowledge in infancy: Reflections on Piaget's theory. In S. Carey & R. Gelman (Eds.), *The epigenesis of mind: Essays on biology and cognition.* Hillsdale, NJ: Erlbaum.

Spelke, E. S. (2000). Core knowledge. *American Psychologist, 55*, 1233–1243.

Spelke, E. S. (2003). Developing knowledge of space: Core systems and new combinations. In S. M. Kosslyn & A. Galaburda (Eds.), *Languages of the brain.* Cambridge, MA: Harvard University Press.

Spelke, E. S. (2011). Natural number and natural geometry. In E. Brannon & S. Dehaene (Eds.), *Space, time, and number in the brain.* New York: Oxford University Press.

Spelke, E. S., Breinlinger, K., Macomber, J., & Jacobson, K. (1992). Origins of knowledge. *Psychological Review, 99,* 605–632.

Spelke, E. S., & Hespos, S. J. (2001). Continuity competence, and the object concept. In E. Dupoux (Ed.), *Language, brain, and behavior.* Cambridge, MA: Bradford/MIT Press.

Spelke, E. S., & Kinzler, K. D. (2007). Core knowledge. *Developmental Science 10,* 89–96.

Spelke, E. S., & Kinzler, K. D. (2009). Innateness, learning and rationality. *Cognitive Development Perspectives, 3,* 96–98.

Spelke, E. S., & Lee, S. A. (2012, in press). Core systems of geometry in animal minds. *Philosophical Transactions of the Royal Society, B.*

Spelke, E. S., & Owsley, C. J. (1979). Intermodal exploration and knowledge in infancy. *Infant Behavior and Development, 2,* 13–28.

Spence, A. P. (1989). *Biology of human aging.* Englewood Cliffs, NJ: Prentice Hall.

Spence, J. T., & Helmreich, R. (1978). *Masculinity and femininity: Their psychological dimensions.* Austin: University of Texas Press.

Sperling, R. A., Richmond, A. S., Ramsay, C. M., & Klapp, M. (2012). The measurement and predictive ability of metacognition in middle school learners. *Journal of Educational Research, 105,* 1–7.

Spidell, S., & others. (2011). Grief in healthcare chaplains: An investigation of disenfranchised grief. *Journal of Health Care Chaplaincy, 17,* 75–86.

Spieker, S. J., & others. (2012). Relational aggression in middle childhood: Predictors and adolescent outcomes. *Social Development, 21,* 354–375.

Spielmann, G., & others. (2011). Aerobic fitness is associated with lower proportions of senescent blood T cells in man. *Brain, Behavior, and Immunity, 25,* 1521–1529.

Spilman, S. K., Neppl, T. K., Donnellan, M. B., Schofield, T. J., & Conger, R. D. (2012, in press). Incorporating religiosity into a developmental model of positive family functioning across generations. *Developmental Psychology.*

Spoelhof, G. D., & Elliott, B. (2012). Implementing advance directives in office practice. *American Family Physician, 85,* 461–466.

Spohn, C., & Tellis, K. (2012). The criminal justice system's response to sexual violence. *Violence Against Women, 18,* 169–192.

Spring, J. (2013). *Deculturalization and the struggle for equality* (7th ed.). New York: McGraw-Hill.

Spruijt, E., & Duindam, V. (2010). Joint physical custody in the Netherlands and the well-being of children. *Journal of Divorce and Remarriage, 51,* 65–82.

Squires, J., Pribble, L., Chen, C-I., & Pomes, M. (2013, in press). Early childhood education: Improving outcomes for young children and families. In I. B. Weiner & others (Eds.), *Handbook of psychology* (2nd ed., Vol. 7). New York: Wiley.

Sroufe, L. A., Coffino, B., & Carlson, E. A. (2010). Conceptualizing the role of early experience: Lessons from the Minnesota longitudinal study. *Developmental Review, 30,* 36–51.

Sroufe, L. A., Egeland, B., Carlson, E., & Collins, W. A. (2005). The place of early attachment in developmental context. In K. E. Grossman, K. Krossman, & E. Waters (Eds.), *The power of longitudinal attachment research: From infancy and childhood to adulthood.* New York: Guilford.

Sroufe, L. A., Waters, E., & Matas, L. (1974). Contextual determinants of infant affectional response. In M. Lewis & L. Rosenblum (Eds.), *Origins of fear.* New York: Wiley.

Stager, L. (2009–2010). Supporting women during labor and birth. *Midwifery Today with International Midwife, 23,* 12–15.

Staiano, A. E., & others. (2012, in press). Body mass index versus waist circumference as predictors of mortality in Canadian adults. *International Journal of Obesity.*

Stanford Center for Longevity. (2011). *Experts consensus on brain health.* Retrieved April 30, 2011, from http://longevity.stanford.edu/my mind/cognitiveagingstatement

Stanford University Medical Center. (2012). *Growth hormone deficiency.* Palo Alto, CA: Author.

Stanley, S. M., Amato, P. R., Johnson, C. A., & Markman, H. J. (2006). Premarital education, marital quality, and marital stability: Findings from a large, household survey. *Journal of Family Psychology, 20,* 117–126.

Stanovich, K. E., West, R. F., & Toplak, M. E. (2012). Judgment and decision making in adolescence: Separating intelligence from rationality. In V. F. Reyna (Ed.), *The adolescent brain.* Washington, DC: American Psychological Association.

Starr, C., Taggart, R., Evers, C., & Starr, L. (2013). *Evolution of life* (13th ed.). Boston: Cengage.

Starr, L. R., & others. (2012, in press). Love hurts (in more ways than one): Specificity of psychological symptoms as predictors and consequences of romantic activity among early adolescent girls. *Journal of Clinical Psychology.*

Staszewski, J. (Ed.) (2013, in press). *Expertise and skill acquisition: The impact of William C. Chase.* New York: Taylor & Francis.

Staudinger, U. M. (1996). Psychologische Produktivität und Selbstentfaltung im Alter. In M. M. Baltes & L. Montada (Eds.), *Produktives Leben im Alter.* Frankfurt: Campus.

Staudinger, U. M., & Dorner, J. (2007). Wisdom. In J. E. Birren (Ed.), *Encyclopedia of gerontology* (2nd ed.). San Diego: Academic Press.

Staudinger, U. M., & Gluck, J. (2011). Psychological wisdom research. *Annual Review of Psychology* (Vol. 62). Palo Alto, CA: Annual Reviews.

Staudinger, U. M., & Jacobs, C. B. (2010). Life-span perspectives on positive personality development in adulthood and old age. In R. M. Lerner, W. F. Overton, A. M. Freund, & M. E. Lamb (Eds.), *Handbook of life-span development.* New York: Wiley.

Steel, A. J., & Sutcliffe, A. (2010). Long-term health implications for children conceived by IVF/ ICSI. *Human Fertility, 12,* 21–27.

Steele, J., Waters, E., Crowell, J., & Treboux, D. (1998, June). *Self-report measures of attachment: Secure bonds to other attachment measures and attachment theory.* Paper presented at the meeting of the International Society for the Study of Personal Relationships, Saratoga Springs, NY.

Stein, P. K., & others. (2012, in press). Caloric restriction may reverse age-related autonomic decline in humans. *Aging Cell.*

Steinberg, L. (2011). Adolescent risk-taking: A social neuroscience perspective. In E. Amsel & J. Smetana (Eds.), *Adolescent vulnerabilities and opportunities.* New York: Cambridge University Press.

Steinberg, L. (2012, Spring). Should the science of adolescent brain development inform social policy? *Issues in Science and Technology,* 67–78.

Steinberg, L. (2013, in press). How should the science of adolescent brain development inform legal policy? In J. Bhabha (Ed.), *Coming of age: A new framework for adolescent rights.* Philadelphia: University of Pennsylvania Press.

Steinberg, L., & Collins, W. A. (2011). Psychosocial development and behavior. In M. Fisher & others (Eds.), *Textbook of adolescent health care.* Elk Grove Village, IL: American Academy of Pediatrics.

Steinberg, L. D., & Silk, J. S. (2002). Parenting adolescents. In M. Bornstein (Ed.), *Handbook of parenting* (2nd ed., Vol. I). Mahwah, NJ: Erlbaum.

Steiner, J. E. (1979). Human facial expressions in response to taste and smell stimulation. In H. Reese & L. Lipsitt (Eds.), *Advances in child development and behavior, 13,* 257–295.

Steming, C. (2008). Centering Pregnancy: Group prenatal care. *Creative Nursing, 14,* 182–183.

Steptoe, A., & Kivimaki, M. (2012). Stress and cardiovascular disease. *Nature Reviews. Cardiology, 9,* 360–370.

Stergiakouli, E., & others. (2012). Investigating the contribution of common genetic variants to the risk and pathogenesis of ADHD. *American Journal of Psychiatry, 169,* 186–194.

Stern, D. N. (2010). A new look at parent-infant interaction: Infant arousal dynamics. In B. M. Lester & J. D. Sparrow (Eds.), *Nurturing children and families: Building on the legacy of T. Berry Brazelton.* New York: Wiley.

Stern, D. N., Beebe, B., Jaffe, J., & Bennett, S. L. (1977). The infant's stimulus world during social interaction: A study of caregiver behaviors with particular reference to repetition and timing. In H. R. Schaffer (Ed.), *Studies in mother-infant interaction.* London: Academic Press.

Stern, S. J., Matok, I., Kapur, B., & Koren, G. (2011). A comparison of folic acid pharmacokinetics in obese and nonobese women of childbearing age. *Therapeutic Drug Monitoring, 33,* 336–340.

Sternberg, K., & Sternberg, R. J. (2013, in press). Love. In H. Pashler (Ed.), *Encyclopedia of the mind.* Thousand Oaks, CA: Sage.

Sternberg, R. J. (1986). *Intelligence applied.* San Diego. Harcourt Brace Jovanovich.

Sternberg, R. J. (1988). *The triangle of love.* New York: Basic Books.

Sternberg, R. J. (2004). Individual differences in cognitive development. In U. Goswami (Ed.), *Blackwell handbook of childhood cognitive development*. Malden, MA: Blackwell.

Sternberg, R. J. (2010). Human intelligence. In V. S. Ramachandran (Ed.), *Encyclopedia of human behavior*. New York: Elsevier.

Sternberg, R. J. (2012). The assessment of creativity: An investment-based approach. *Creativity Research Journal, 24*, 3–12.

Sternberg, R. J. (2012, in press). Building wisdom and character. In S. J. Lynn & others (Eds.), *Psychological science and well-being*. Thousand Oaks, CA: Sage.

Sternberg, R. J. (2012). Human intelligence. In V. S. Ramachandran (Ed.), *Encyclopedia of human behavior* (2nd ed.). New York: Elsevier.

Sternberg, R. J. (2012). Intelligence. In I. Weiner & D. Freedheim (Eds.), *Handbook of psychology* (2nd Ed.). New York: Wiley.

Sternberg, R. J. (2012). Intelligence in its cultural context. In M. Gelfand, C-Y Chiu, & Y-Y Hong (Eds.), *Advances in cultures and psychology* (Vol. 2). New York: Oxford University Press.

Sternberg, R. J. (2013). Contemporary theories of intelligence. In I. B. Weiner & others (Eds.), *Handbook of psychology* (2nd ed., Vol. 7). New York: Wiley.

Sternberg, R. J. (2013, in press). Personal wisdom in the balance. In M. Ferrari & N. Westrate (Eds.), *Personal wisdom*. New York: Springer.

Sternberg, R. J. (2013, in press). Teaching for wisdom. In I. Boniwell (Ed.), *Oxford handbook of happiness*. New York: Oxford University Press.

Sternberg, R. J. (2013). The triarchic theory of successful intelligence. In D. P. Flanagan & P. L. Harrison (Eds.), *Contemporary intellectual assessment* (3rd ed.). New York: Guilford.

Sternberg, R. J., & Sternberg, K. (2012). *Cognitive psychology* (7th ed.). Boston: Cengage.

Sterns, H., & Huyck, M. H. (2001). The role of work in midlife. In M. Lachman (Ed.), *Handbook of midlife development*. New York: Wiley.

Steur, F. B., Applefield, J. M., & Smith, R. (1971). Televised aggression and interpersonal aggression of preschool children. *Journal of Experimental Child Psychology, 11*, 442–447.

Stevenson, H. W. (1995). Mathematics achievements of American students: First in the world by the year 2000: In C. A. Nelson (Ed.), *Basic and applied perspectives on learning, cognition, and development*. Minneapolis: University of Minnesota Press.

Stevenson, H. W. (2000). Middle childhood: Education and schooling. In A. Kazdin (Ed.), *Encyclopedia of psychology*. Washington, DC, & New York: American Psychological Association and Oxford University Press.

Stevenson, H. W., Hofer, B. K., & Randel, B. (1999). *Middle childhood: Education and schooling*. Unpublished manuscript, Dept. of Psychology, University of Michigan, Ann Arbor.

Stevenson, H. W., Lee, S., Chen, C., Stigler, J. W., Hsu, C., & Kitamure, S. (1990). Contexts of achievement. *Monograph of the Society for Research in Child Development, 55* (Serial No. 221).

Stevenson, H. W., Lee, S., & Stigler, J. W. (1986). Mathematics achievement of Chinese, Japanese, and American children. *Science, 231*, 693–699.

Stevenson, H. W., & Newman, R. S. (1986). Long-term prediction of achievement and attitudes in mathematics and reading. *Child Development, 57*, 646–659.

Stevenson, H. W., & Zusho, A. (2002). Adolescence in China and Japan: Adapting to a changing environment. In B. B. Brown, R. W. Larson, & T. S. Saraswathi (Eds.), *The world's youth*. New York: Cambridge University Press.

Stewart, A. D., & others. (2012). Body image, shape, and volumetric assessments using 3D whole body laser scanning and 2D digital photography in females with a diagnosed eating disorder: Preliminary novel findings. *British Journal of Psychology, 103*, 183–202.

Stewart, A. J., Ostrove, J. M., & Helson, R. (2001). Middle aging in women: Patterns of personality change from the 30s to the 50s. *Journal of Adult Development, 8*, 23–37.

Stidham-Hall, K., Moreau, C., & Trussell, J. (2012). Patterns and correlates of parental and formal sexual and reproductive health communication for adolescent women in the United States, 2002–2008. *Journal of Adolescent Health, 50*, 410–413.

Stiggins, R. (2008). *Introduction to student involved assessment for learning* (5th ed.). Upper Saddle River, NJ: Prentice Hall.

Stiles-Shields, C., Hoste, R. R., Doyle, P. M., & Le Grange, D. (2012). A review of family-based treatment for adolescents with eating disorders. *Reviews on Recent Clinical Trials, 7*, 133–140.

Stine-Morrow, E. A. L. (2007). The Dumbledore hypothesis of cognitive aging. *Current Directions in Psychological Science, 16*, 295–299.

Stine-Morrow, E. A. L., & Basak, C. (2011). Cognitive interventions. In K. W. Schaie & S. L. Willis (Eds.), *Handbook of the psychology of aging* (7th ed.). New York: Elsevier.

Stine-Morrow, E. A. L., Parisi, J. M., Morrow, d. G., Greene, J., & Park, D. C. (2007). An engagement model of cognitive optimization through adulthood. *Journals of Gerontology B: Psychological Sciences and Social Sciences, 62*, P62–P69.

Stipek, D. (2005, February 16). Commentary in *USA TODAY*, p. 10.

Stochholm, K., & others. (2012). Criminality in men with Klinefelter's syndrome and XYY syndrome: A cohort study. *BMJ Open, 2*, e000650.

Stockley, C. S. (2012). Is it merely a myth that alcoholic beverages such as red wine can be cardioprotective? *Journal of the Science of Food and Agriculture, 92*, 1815–1821.

Stokes, C. E., & Raley, R. K. (2009). Cohabitation. In D. Carr (Ed.), *Encyclopedia of the life course and human development*. Boston: Gale Cengage.

Stoll, C., Dott, B., Alembik, Y., & Roth, M. P. (2011). Associated malformations among infants with neural tube defects. *American Journal of Medical Genetics A, 155*(3), 565–568.

Stone, A. A., Schwartz, J. E., Broderick, J. E., & Deaton, A. (2010). A snapshot of the age distribution of psychological well-being in the United States. *Proceedings of the National Academy of Sciences USA, 107*, 9985–9990.

Stone, H. F., Zhu, Z., Thach, T. Q., & Ruegg, C. L. (2011). Characterization of diffusion and duration of action of a new botulinum toxin type A formulation. *Toxicon, 58*, 159–167.

Stones, M., & Stones, L. (2007). Sexuality, sensuality, and intimacy. In J. E. Birren (Ed.), *Encyclopedia of gerontology* (2nd ed.). San Diego: Academic Press.

Stosic, L., & others. (2012). Household environmental tobacco smoke and respiratory diseases among children in Nis (Serbia). *Central European Journal of Public Health, 20*, 29–32.

Stowell, J. R., Robles, T., & Kane, H. S. (2013, in press). Psychoneuroimmunology: Mechanisms, individual differences, and interventions. In I. B. Weiner & others (Eds.), *Handbook of psychology* (2nd ed., Vol. 9). New York: Wiley.

Strand, A. (2010). Low levels of retirement resources in the near-elderly time period and future participation in means-tested programs. *Social Security Bulletin, 70*, 1–21.

Strasburger, V. C., Jordan, A. B., & Donnerstein, E. (2012). Children, adolescents, and the media: Health effects. *Pediatric Clinics of North America, 59*, 533–587.

Strathearn, L., Iyenger, U., Fonagy, P., Kim, S. (2012). Maternal oxytocin response during mother-infant interaction: Associations with adult temperament. *Hormones and Behavior, 61*, 429–435.

Strauss, M. A., Sugarman, D. B., & Giles-Sims, J. (1997). Spanking by parents and subsequent anti-social behavior in children. *Archives of Pediatrics and Adolescent Medicine, 151*, 761–767.

Streri, A. (1987) Tactile discrimination of shape and intermodal transfer in two- to three-month-old infants. *British Journal of Developmental Psychology, 5*, 213–220.

Streuling, I., & others. (2011). Physical activity and gestational weight gain: A meta-analysis of intervention trials. *BJOG, 118*, 278–284.

Striegel-Moore, R. H., & Bulik, C. M. (2007). Risk factors for eating disorders. *American Psychologist, 62*, 181–198.

Stroebe, M., & Schut, H. (2010). The dual process model of coping with bereavement: A decade on. *Omega, 61*, 273–289.

Stroebe, M., Schut, H., & Boerner, K. (2010). Continuing bonds in adaptation to bereavement: Toward theoretical integration. *Clinical Psychology Review, 30*, 259–268.

Strohmeier, D., & Noam, G. G. (2012). Bullying in schools: What is the problem and how can educators solve it? *New Directions in Youth Development, 133*, 7–13.

Stroobant, N., Buijs, D., & Vingerhoets, G. (2009). Variation in brain lateralization during various language tasks: A functional transcranial Doppler study. *Behavioral Brain Research, 199*, 190–196.

Strout, K. A., & Howard, E. (2012, in press). The six dimensions of wellness and cognition in aging adults. *Journal of Holistic Nursing*.

Stuart, S. (2012). Interpersonal psychotherapy for postpartum depression. *Clinical Psychology and psychotherapy, 19*, 134–140.

Stuebe, A. M., & Schwartz, E. G. (2010). The risks and benefits of infant feeding practices for women and their children. *Journal of Perinatology, 30*, 155–162.

Sturm, J., & others. (2012, in press). Physical exercise through mountain hiking in high-risk suicide patients: A randomized crossover trial. *Acta Psychiatrica Scandinavica*.

Sturman, M. C. (2003). Searching for the inverted U-shaped relationship between time and performance: Meta-analyses of the experience/performance, tenure/performance, and age-performance relationships. *Journal of Management, 29*, 609–640.

Su, M. W., & others. (2012). Gene-gene and gene-environmental interactions of childhood asthma: A multifactor dimension reduction approach. *PLoS One, 7*(2), e30694.

Subramaniam, P., & Woods, B. (2012). The impact of individual reminiscence therapy for people with dementia: Systematic review. *Expert Review of Neurotherapeutics, 12*, 545–555.

Substance Abuse and Mental Health Services Administration. (2003). *Aging and substance abuse*. Washington, DC: U.S. Department of Health and Human Services.

Sugita, Y. (2004). Experience in early infancy is indispensable for color perception. *Current Biology, 14*, 1267–1271.

Sui, X., & others. (2007). Cardiorespiratory fitness and adiposity as mortality predictors in older adults. *Journal of the American Medical Association, 298*, 2507–2516.

Sullivan, H. S. (1953). *The interpersonal theory of psychiatry*. New York: W.W. Norton.

Sullivan, K., & Sullivan, A. (1980). Adolescent-parent separation. *Developmental Psychology, 16*, 93–99.

Sum, A. M. (2012). *Trends in the levels and distribution of the annual incomes of young families, 1973 to 2010: Deteriorating real incomes amidst steep inequality*. Washington, DC: Children's Defense Fund.

Summerbell, C. D., & others. (2012). Evidence-based recommendations for the development of obesity prevention programs targeted at preschool children. *Obesity Reviews, 13*(Suppl. 1), S129–S132.

Sun, F., & others. (2012). Predicting the trajectories of depressive symptoms among southern community-dwelling older adults: The role of religiosity. *Aging and Mental Health, 16*, 189–198.

Sun, S. S., & others. (2008). Childhood obesity predicts adult metabolic syndrome: The Fels Longitudinal Study. *Journal of Pediatrics, 152*, 191–200.

Sun, Y., Tao, F., Hao, J., & Wan, Y. (2010). The mediating effects of stress and coping on depression among adolescents in China. *Journal of Child and Adolescent Psychiatric Nursing, 23*, 173–180.

Sund, A. M., Larsson, B., & Wichstrom, L. (2011). Role of physical and sedentary activities in the development of depressive symptoms in early adolescence. *Social Psychiatry and Psychiatric Epidemiology, 46*, 431–441.

Sung, G., & Greer, D. (2011). The case for simplifying brain death criteria. *Neurology, 76*, 113–114.

Sung, S. C., & others. (2011). Complicated grief among individuals with major depression: Prevalence, comorbidity, and associated features. *Journal of Affective Disorders, 134*, 453–458.

Supekar, K., & Menon, V. (2012). Developmental maturation of dynamic causal control signals in higher-order cognition: A neurocognitive network model. *PLoS Computational Biology, 8*(2), e1002374.

Super, C., & Harkness, S. (1997). The cultural structuring of child development. In J. W. Berry, Y. H. Poortinga, & J. Pandey (Eds.), *Handbook of cross-cultural psychology: Theory and method* (Vol. 2). Boston: Allyn & Bacon.

Suri, G., & Gross, J. J. (2012, in press). Emotion regulation and successful aging. *Trends in Cognitive Science*.

Susman, E. J., & Dorn, L. D. (2013, in press). Puberty: Its role in development. In I. B. Weiner & others (Eds.), *Handbook of psychology* (2nd ed., Vol. 6). New York: Wiley.

Sutachan, J. J., & others. (2012). Cellular and molecular mechanisms of antioxidants in Parkinson's disease. *Nutritional Neuroscience, 15*, 120–126.

Sutcliffe, K., & others. (2012, in press). Comparing midwife-led and doctor-led maternity care: A systematic review of reviews. *Journal of Advanced Nursing*.

Sutherland, K. E., Altenhofen, S., & Biringen, Z. (2012). Emotional availability during mother-child interactions in divorcing and intact married families. *Journal of Divorce and Remarriage, 53*, 126–141.

Suzman, R. M., Harris, T., Hadley, E. C., Kovar, M. G., & Weindruch, R. (1992). The robust oldest old: Optimistic perspectives for increasing healthy life expectancy. In R. M. Suzman, D. P. Willis, & K. G. Manton (Eds.), *The oldest old*. New York: Oxford University Press.

Sviri, S., & others. (2009). Contraindications in end-of-life decisions for self and other, expressed by relatives of chronically ventilated persons. *Journal of Critical Care, 24*, 293–301.

Swaiman, K., Ashwal, S., Ferriero, D., & Schor, N. (2012). *Swaiman's pediatric neurology*. New York: Elsevier.

Swamy, G. K., Ostbye, T., & Skjaerven, R. (2008). Association of preterm birth with long-term survival, reproduction, and next-generation preterm birth. *Journal of the American Medical Association, 299*, 1429–1436.

Swan, G., & others. (2013, in press). Tobacco dependence. In I. B. Weiner & others (Eds.), *Handbook of psychology* (2nd ed.). New York: Wiley.

Swanson, D. P., Edwards, M. C., & Spencer, M. B. (Eds.). (2010). *Adolescence: Development during a global era*. Burlington, MA: Academic Press.

Sweeney, M. M. (2009). Remarriage. In D. Carr (Ed.), *Encyclopedia of the life course and human development*. Boston: Gale Cengage.

Sweeney, M. M. (2010). Remarriage and stepfamilies: Strategic sites for family scholarship in the 21st century. *Journal of Marriage and the Family, 72*, 667–684.

Sweet, S., Moen, P., & Meiksins, P. (2007). Dual earners in double jeopardy: Preparing for job loss in the new risk economy. In B. A. Rubin (Ed.), *Research in the sociology of work*. New York: Elsevier.

Swing, E. L., Gentile, D. A., Anderson, C. A., & Walsh, D. A. (2010). Television and video game exposure and the development of attention problems. *Pediatrics, 126*, 214–221.

Syed, M. (2010). Developing an integrated self: Academic and ethnic identities among ethnically-diverse college students. *Developmental Psychology, 46*, 1590–1604.

Syed, M. (2013, in press). Assessment of ethnic identity and acculturation. In K. Geisinger (Ed.), *APA handbook of testing and assessment in psychology*. Washington, DC: American Psychological Association.

Sykes, C. J. (1995). *Dumbing down our kids: Why America's children feel good about themselves but can't read, write, or add*. New York: St. Martin's Press.

Symon, B., & Bammann, M. (2012). Feeding in the first year of life—emerging benefits of introducing complementary solids from 4 months. *Australian Family Physician, 41*, 226–229.

Szanton, S. L., Seplaki, C. L., Thorpe, R. J., Allen, J. K., & Fried, L. P. (2010). Socioeconomic status is associated with frailty: The Women's Health and Aging Studies. *Journal of Epidemiology and Community Health, 64*, 63–67.

Szelag, E., & Skolimowska, J. (2012, in press). Cognitive function in elderly can be ameliorated by training temporal information processing. *Restorative Neurology and Neuroscience*.

Szinovacz, M. E. (2009). Grandparenthood. In D. Carr (Ed.), *Encyclopedia of the life course and human development*. Boston: Gale Cengage.

Szinovacz, M.E. (2011). Introduction: The aging workforce: Challenges for societies, employers, and older workers. *Journal of Aging and Social Policy, 23*, 95–100.

Szwedo, D. E., Mikami, A. Y., & Allen, J. P. (2011). Qualities of peer relations on social networking websites: Predictions from negative mother-teen interactions. *Journal of Research on Adolescence, 21*, 595–607.

Szymanski, L. M., & Satin, A. J. (2012). Exercise during pregnancy: Fetal responses to current public health guidelines. *Obstetrics and Gynecology, 119*, 603–610.

T

Tabara, Y., Kohara, K., & Miki, T. (2012). Hunting for genes for hypertension: The Millennium Genome Project for Hypertension. *Hypertension Research, 35*(6), 567–573.

Taige, N. M., & others. (2007). Antenatal maternal stress and long-term effects on child neurodevelopment: How and why? *Journal of Child Psychology and Psychiatry, 48*, 245–261.

Takeuchi, H., & others. (2012). Neural correlates of the differences between working memory speed and simple sensorimotor speed: an fMRI study. *PLoS One, 7*(1), e30579.

Talamini, L. M., & Gorree, E. (2012). Aging memories: Differential decay of episodic memory components. *Learning and Memory, 19*, 239–246.

Talaulikar, V. S., & Arulkumaran, S. (2011). Folic acid in obstetric practice: A review. *Obstetrical and Gynecological Survey, 66*, 240–247.

Taler, S. J. (2009). Hypertension in women. *Current Hypertension Reports, 11*, 23–28.

Tallerman, M. (2013). *Understanding syntax*. New York: Oxford University Press.

Tamashiro, K. L. (2011). Chronic stress, metabolism, and metabolic syndrome. *Stress, 14*, 468–474.

Tamis-LeMonda, C. S., & Song, L. (2013, in press). Parent-infant communicative interactions in cultural context. In R. M. Lerner (Ed.), *Handbook of psychology* (Vol. 6). New York: Wiley.

Tan, E. J., Xue, Q. L., Li, T., Carlson, M. C., & Fried, L. P. (2007). Volunteering: A physical activity intervention for older adults—The Experience Corps program in Baltimore. *Journal of Urban Health, 83,* 954–969.

Tan, L. J., & others. (2012). Molecular genetic studies of gene identification for sarcopenia. *Human Genetics, 131,* 1–31.

Tandon, S. D., & others. (2011). Preventing perinatal depression in low-income home visiting clients: A randomized controlled trial. *Journal of Consulting and Clinical Psychology, 79,* 707–712.

Tanev, K., Sablosky, M., Vento, J., & O'Hanlon, D. (2012). Structural and functional neuroimaging methods in the diagnosis of dementias: A retrospective chart and brain imaging review. *Neurocase, 18,* 224–234.

Tang, Y., & Posner, M. I. (2009). Attention training and attention state training. *Trends in Cognitive Science, 13,* 222–227.

Tannen, D. (1990). *You just don't understand: Women and men in conversation.* New York: Ballantine.

Tarokh, L., & Carskadon, M. A. (2010). Developmental changes in the human sleep EEG during early adolescence. *Sleep, 33,* 801–809.

Tashiro, T., & Frazier, P. (2003). "I'll never be in a relationship like that again": *Personal Relationships, 10,* 113–128.

Task Force on Sudden Infant Death Syndrome & Moon, R. Y. (2011). SIDS and other sleep-related infant deaths: Expansion of recommendations for a safe infant sleeping environment. *Pediatrics, 128,* 1030–1039.

Tasker, F. L., and Golombok, S. (1997). *Growing up in a lesbian family: Effects on child development.* New York: Guilford.

Taylor, A. (2012, in press). Introduction to the issue regarding research on age-related macular degeneration. *Molecular Aspects of Medicine.*

Taylor, A., & Gosney, M. A. (2011). Sexuality in older age: Essential considerations for healthcare professionals. *Age and Aging, 40,* 538–543.

Taylor, C. A., Manganello, J. A., Lee, S. J., & Rice, J. C. (2010). Mothers' spanking of 3-year-old children and subsequent risk of children's aggressive behavior. *Pediatrics, 125,* e1057–e1065.

Taylor, L. M., & Fratto, J. M. (2012). *Transforming learning through 21st century skills.* Boston: Allyn & Bacon.

Taylor, M., Bates, G., & Webster, J. D. (2011). Comparing the properties of two measures of wisdom: Predicting forgiveness and psychological well-being with the Self-Assessed Wisdom Scale (SAWS) and the Three-Dimensional Wisdom Scale (3D-WS). *Experimental Aging Research, 37,* 129–141.

Taylor, R. D., & Lopez, E. I. (2005). Family management practice, school achievement, and problem behavior in African American adolescents: Mediating processes. *Applied Developmental Psychology, 26,* 39–49.

Taylor, R. J., Chatters, L. M., & Jackson, J. S. (2007). Religious and spiritual involvement among older African Americans, Caribbean Blacks, and non-Hispanic Whites: Findings from the National Survey of American Life. *Journals of Gerontology: Psychological and Social Sciences (Vol. 62b),* S238–S250.

Taylor, S. E. (2011a). Affiliation and stress. In S. S. Folkman (Ed.), *Oxford handbook of stress, health, and coping.* New York: Oxford University Press.

Taylor, S. E. (2011b). *Health psychology* (8th ed.). New York: McGraw-Hill.

Taylor, S. E. (2011c). Tend and befriend theory. In A. M. van Lange, A.W. Kruglanski, & E. T. Higgins (Eds.), *Handbook of theories of social psychology.* Thousand Oaks, CA: Sage.

Taylor, S. E., & others. (2000). Biobehavioral responses to stress in females: Tend-and-befriend, not fight-or-flight. *Psychological Review, 107,* 411–429.

Taylor, Z. E., Widaman, K. F., Robins, R. W., Jochem, R., Early, D. R., & Conger, R. D. (2012). Dispositional optimism: A psychological resource for Mexican-origin families experiencing economic stress. *Journal of Family Psychology, 26,* 133–139.

te Velde, S. J., & others. (2012). Energy balance-related behaviors associated with overweight and obesity in preschool children: A systematic review of prospective studies. *Obesity Reviews, 13* (Suppl. 1), S56–S74.

Teery-McElrath, Y. M., O'Malley, P. M., & Johnston, L. D. (2011). Exercise and substance use among American youth, 1991–2009. *American Journal of Preventive Medicine, 40,* 530–540.

Telkemeyer, S., & others. (2011). Acoustic processing of temporally modulated sounds in infants: Evidence from a combined near-infrared spectroscopy and EEG study. *Frontiers in Psychology, 2,* 62.

Temple, C. A., Nathan, R., & Temple, C. (2013). *Beginnings of writing* (4th ed.). Boston: Allyn & Bacon.

Terman, L. (1925). *Genetic studies of genius. Vol. 1: Mental and physical traits of a thousand gifted children.* Stanford, CA: Stanford University Press.

Terry, D. F., Nolan, V. G., Andersen, S. L., Perls, T. T., & Cawthon, R. (2008). Association of longer telomeres with better health in centenarians. *Journals of Gerontology A: Biological Sciences and Medical Sciences, 63,* 809–812.

Terry, W., Olson, L. G., Wilss, L., & Boulton-Lewis, G. (2006). Experience of dying: Concerns of dying patients and of carers. *Internal Medicine Journal, 36,* 338–346.

Teti, D. M., Kim, B. R., Mayer, G., & Countermine, M. (2010). Maternal availability at bedtime predicts infant sleep quality. *Journal of Family Psychology, 24,* 307–315.

Thapar, A., Collishaw, S., Pine, D. S., & Thapar, A. K. (2012). Depression in adolescence. *Lancet, 379,* 1056–1067.

Tharp, R. G. (1994). Intergroup differences among Native Americans in socialization and child cognition: An erthogenetic analysis. In P. M. Greenfield & R. Cocking (Eds.), *Cross-cultural roots of minority child development.* Mahwah, NJ: Erlbaum.

The, N. S., & others. (2010). Association of adolescent obesity with risk of severe obesity in adulthood. *Journal of the American Medical Association, 304,* 2042–2047.

Thelen, E. (2000). Perception and motor development. In A. Kazdin (Ed.), *Encyclopedia of psychology.* Washington, DC, & New York: American Psychological Association and Oxford University Press.

Thelen, E., Corbetta, D., Kamm, K., Spencer, J. P., Schneider, K., & Zernicke, R. F. (1993). The transition to reaching: Mapping intention and intrinsic dynamics. *Child Development, 64,* 1058–1098.

Thelen, E., & Smith, L. B. (1998). Dynamic systems theory. In W. Damon & R. Lerner (Eds.), *Handbook of child psychology* (5th ed., Vol. 1). New York: Wiley.

Thelen, E., & Smith, L. B. (2006). Dynamic development of action and thought. In W. Damon & R. Lerner (Eds.), *Handbook of child psychology* (6th ed.). New York: Wiley.

Therrell, B. L., & others. (2010). Newborn Screening System Performance Evaluation Assessment (PEAS). *Seminars in Perinatology, 34,* 105–120.

Thiele, D. M., & Whelan, T. A. (2008). The relationship between grandparent satisfaction, meaning, and generativity. *International Journal of Aging and Human Development, 66,* 21–48.

Thio, A. (2010). *Deviant behavior* (10th ed.). Boston: Allyn & Bacon.

Thomas, A., & Chess, S. (1991). Temperament in adolescence and its functional significance. In R. M. Lerner, A. C. Petersen, & J. Brooks-Gunn (Eds.), *Encyclopedia of adolescence* (Vol. 2). New York: Garland.

Thomas, M. S. C., & Johnson, M. H. (2008). New advances in understanding sensitive periods in brain development. *Current Directions in Psychological Science, 17,* 1–5.

Thomason, M. E., & Thompson, P. M. (2011). Diffusion imaging, white matter, and psychopathology. *Annual Review of Clinical Psychology* (Vol. 7). Palo Alto, CA: Annual Reviews.

Thompson, J., & Manore, M. (2013). *Nutrition for life* (3rd ed.). Upper Saddle River, NJ: Pearson.

Thompson, M. P., Kuruwita, C., & Foster, E. M. (2009). Transitions in suicide risk in a nationally representative sample of adolescents. *Journal of Adolescent Health, 44,* 458–463.

Thompson, R. A. (2006). The development of the person. In W. Damon & R. Lerner (Eds.), *Handbook of child psychology* (6th ed.). New York: Wiley.

Thompson, R. A. (2009). Early foundations: Conscience and the development of moral character. In D. Narvaez & D. Lapsley (Eds.), *Moral self, identity and character: Prospects for a new field of study.* New York: Cambridge University Press.

Thompson, R. A. (2010). Feeling and understanding: Through the prism of relationships. In S. D. Calkins & M. A. Bell (Eds.), *Child development at the intersection of emotion and cognition.* Washington, DC: American Psychological Association.

Thompson, R. A. (2011). The emotionate child. In D. Cicchetti & G. I. Roissman (Eds.), *The origins and organization of adaptation and maladaptation. Minnesota Symposium on Child Psychology* (Vol. 36). New York: Wiley.

Thompson, R. A. (2012, in press). Whither the preoperational child? Toward a life-span moral development theory. *Child Development.*

Thompson, R. A. (2013a, in press). Attachment and its development: Precis and prospect. In P. Zelazo (Ed.), *Oxford handbook of developmental psychology.* New York: Oxford University Press.

Thompson, R. A. (2013b, in press). Interpersonal relations. In A. Ben-Arieh, I. Frones, F. Cases, & J. Korbin (Eds.), *Handbook of child well-being.* New York: Springer.

Thompson, R. A. (2013c, in press). Relationships, regulation, and development. In R. M. Lerner (Ed.), *Handbook of child psychology* (7th ed.). New York: Wiley.

Thompson, R. A. (2013d, in press). Socialization of emotion regulation in the family. In J. Gross (Ed.), *Handbook of emotion regulation* (2nd ed.). New York: Guilford.

Thompson, R. A., Meyer, S. C., & McGinley, M. (2006). Understanding values in relationships: The development of conscience. In M. Killen & J. Smetana (Eds.), *Handbook of moral development.* Mahwah, NJ: Erlbaum.

Thompson, R. A., Meyer, S., Virmani, E., Waters, S., Raikes, H. A., & Jochem, R. (2009, April). *Parent-child relationships, conversation, and developing emotion regulation.* Paper presented at the meeting of the Society for Research in Child Development, Denver.

Thompson, R. A., & Murachver, T. (2001). Predicting gender from electronic discourse. *British Journal of Social Psychology, 40,* 193–208.

Thompson, R. A., & Virmani, E. A. (2010). Self and personality. In M. H. Bornstein (Ed.), *Handbook of cultural developmental science.* New York: Psychology Press.

Thompson, R. A., Winer, A. C., & Goodvin, R. (2011). The individual child: Temperament, emotion, self, and personality. In M. Bornstein & M. E. Lamb (Eds.), *Developmental science: An advanced textbook* (6th ed.). New York: Psychology Press.

Thornton, R., & Light, L. C. (2006). Aging and language. In J. E. Birren & K. W. Schaie (Eds.), *Handbook of the psychology of aging* (6th ed.). San Diego: Academic Press.

Thorton, A., & Camburn, D. (1989). Religious participation and sexual behavior and attitudes. *Journal of Marriage and the Family, 49,* 117–128.

Thune-Boyle, I. C., & others. (2012, in press). Religious/spiritual coping resources and their relationship with adjustment in patients newly diagnosed with breast cancer in the U.K. *Psychooncology.*

Tikotzky, L., Sadeh, A., & Glickman-Gavrieli, T. (2010). Infant sleep and paternal involvement in infant caregiving during the first 6 months of life. *Journal of Pediatric Psychology, 36*(1), 36–46.

Tikotzky, L., & Shaashua, L. (2012). Infant sleep and early parental sleep-related cognitions predict sleep in pre-school children. *Sleep Medicine, 13,* 185–192.

Timmermans, S., & others. (2011). Individual accumulation of heterogeneous risks explains inequalities within deprived neighborhoods. *European Journal of Epidemiology.*

Tincoff, R., & Jusczyk, P. W. (2012, in press). Six-month-olds comprehend words that refer to parts of the body. *Infancy.*

Tinetti, M. E. (2012). The retreat from advanced care planning. *JAMA, 307,* 915–916.

Tinetti, M. E., & others. (2011a). Contribution of multiple chronic conditions to universal health outcomes. *Journal of the American Geriatric Society, 59,* 1686–1691.

Tinetti, M. E., & others. (2011b). Effect of chronic disease-related symptoms and impairments on universal outcomes in older adults. *Journal of the American Geriatric Society, 59,* 1618–1627.

To, W. W. (2012). Prenatal diagnosis and assessment of facial clefts: Where are we now? *Hong Kong Medical Journal, 18,* 146–152.

Tobler, A. L., & Komro, K. A. (2010). Trajectories of parental monitoring and communication and effects on drug use among urban young adolescents. *Journal of Adolescent Health, 46,* 560–568.

Tolani, N., & Brooks-Gunn, J. (2008). Family support, international trends. In M. M. Haith & J. B. Benson (Eds.), *Encyclopedia of infant and early childhood development.* Oxford, UK: Elsevier.

Tolman, D. L., & McClelland, S. I. (2011). Normative sexuality development in adolescence: A decade in review, 2000–2009. *Journal of Research on Adolescence, 21,* 242–255.

Tolou-Shams, M., Hadley, W., Conrad, S. M., & Brown, L. K. (2012). The role of family affect in juvenile drug court offenders' substance use and HIV risk. *Journal of Child and Family Studies, 21,* 449–456.

Toma, C., & others. (2012, in press). Neurotransmitter systems and neurotrophic factors in autism: Association study of 37 genes suggests involvement of DDC. *World Journal of Biology.*

Tomasello, M. (2003). *Constructing a language: A usage-based theory of language acquisition.* Cambridge, MA: Harvard University Press.

Tomasello, M. (2006). Acquiring linguistic constructions. In W. Damon & R. Lerner (Eds.), *Handbook of child psychology* (6th ed.). New York: Wiley.

Tomasello, M. (2011). Language development. In U. Goswami (Ed.), *Wiley-Blackwell handbook of childhood cognitive development* (2nd ed.). New York: Wiley.

Tomasello, M., & Hamann, K. (2012). Collaboration in young children. *Quarterly Journal of Experimental Psychology, 65,* 1–12.

Tomasi, D., & Volkow, N. D. (2012). Abnormal functional connectivity in children with attention-deficit/hyperactivity disorder. *Biological Psychiatry, 71,* 443–450.

Tome-Carneiro, J., & others. (2012, in press). One-year consumption of a grape nutraceutical containing resveratrol improves the inflammatory and fibrinolytic status of patients in primary prevention of cardiovascular disease. *American Journal of Cardiology.*

Tomiyama, A. J., & others. (2012). Does cellular aging relate to patterns of allostasis? An examination of basal and stress reactive HPA axis activity and telomere length. *Physiology and Behavior, 106,* 40–45.

Tompkins, G. E. (2013). *Language arts* (8th ed.). Boston: Allyn & Bacon.

Torbic, H. (2011). Children and grief: But what about the children?: A guide for home care and hospice clinicians. *Home Healthcare Nurse, 29,* 67–77.

Torges, C. M., Stewart, A. J., & Nolen-Hoeksema, S. (2008). Regret resolution, aging, and adapting to loss. *Psychology and Aging, 23,* 169–180.

Tortora, G. J., Funke, B. R., & Case, C. L. (2013). *Microbiology* (11th ed.). Upper Saddle River, NJ: Pearson.

Toure, K., & others. (2012, in press). Positioning women's and children's health in African union policy-making: A policy analysis. *Global Health.*

Tran, S., & Simpson, J. A. (2012, in press). Attachment, commitment, and relationship maintenance: When partners really matter. *The science of the couple. The Ontario Symposium* (Vol. 12). New York: Psychology Press.

Trasande, L., & Elbel, B. (2012). The economic burden placed on healthcare systems by childhood obesity. *Expert Review of Pharmacoeconomics and Outcomes Research, 12,* 39–45.

Trautner, H. M., Ruble, D. N., Cyphers, L., Kirsten, B., Behrendt, R., & Hartmann, P. (2005). Rigidity and flexibility of gender stereotypes in children: Developmental or differential? *Infant and Child Development, 14,* 365–381.

Trehub, S. E., Schneider, B. A., Thorpe, L. A., & Judge, P. (1991). Observational measures of auditory sensitivity in early infancy. *Developmental Psychology, 27,* 40–49.

Tremblay, M. S., & others. (2012). Canadian sedentary behavior guidelines for the early years (0–4 years). *Applied Physiology, Nutrition, and Metabolism, 37,* 370–380.

Triche, E. W., & Hossain, N. (2007). Environmental factors implicated in the causation of adverse pregnancy outcome. *Seminars in Perinatology, 31,* 240–242.

Trickett, P. K., & Negriff, S. (2011). Child maltreatment and social relationships. In M. H. Underwood & L. H. Rosen (Eds.), *Social development.* New York: Guilford.

Trickett, P. K., Negriff, S., Ji, J., & Peckins, M. (2011). Child maltreatment and adolescent development. *Journal of Research on Adolescence, 21,* 3–20.

Trimble, J. E. (1988. August). *The enculturation of contemporary psychology.* Paper presented at the meeting of the American Psychological Association, New Orleans.

Trommsdorff, G. (2012). A social change and human development perspective on the value of children. In S. Bekman & A. Aksu-Koc (Eds.), *Perspectives on human development, families, and culture.* New York: Cambridge University Press.

Tronick, E. (2010). Infants and mothers: Self- and mutual regulation and meaning making. In B. M. Lester & J. D. Sparrow (Eds.), *Nurturing children and families: Building on the legacy of T. Berry Brazelton.* New York: Wiley.

Trost, S. G., Fees, B., & Dzewaltowski, D. (2008). Feasibility and efficacy of "move and learn" physical activity curriculum in preschool children. *Journal of Physical Activity and Health, 5,* 88–103.

Trzesniewski, K. H., & Donnellan, M. B. (2010). Rethinking "generation me": A study of cohort effects from 1976–2006. *Perspectives on Psychological Science, 5,* 58–75.

Trzesniewski, K. H., Donnellan, M. B., Caspi, A., Moffitt, T. E., Robins, R. W., & Poultin, R. (2006). Adolescent low self-esteem is a risk factor for adult poor health, criminal behavior, and limited economic prospects. *Developmental Psychology, 42*, 381–390.

Trzesniewski, K. H., Donnellan, M. B., & Robins, R. W. (2003). Stability of self-esteem across the life span. *Journal of Personality and Social Psychology, 84*, 205–220.

Trzesniewski, K. H., Donnellan, M. B., & Robins, R. W. (2008a). Do today's young people really think they are so extraordinary? An examination of secular trends in narcissism and self-enhancement. *Psychological Science, 19*, 181–188.

Trzesniewski, K. H., Donnellan, M. B., & Robins, R. W. (2008b). Is "Generation Me" really more narcissistic than previous generations? *Journal of Personality, 76*, 903–918.

Tsai, S. Y., & Thomas, K. A. (2012, in press). Sleep disturbances and depressive symptoms in healthy postpartum women: A pilot study. *Research in Nursing and Health.*

Tsang, E. W., & others. (2012). Subthalamic deep brain stimulation at individualized frequencies of Parkinson disease. *Neurology, 78*, 1930–1938.

Tschann, J. M., Flores, E., de Groat, C. L., Deardorff, J., & Wibbelsman, C. J. (2010). Condom negotiation strategies and actual condom use among Latino youth. *Journal of Adolescent Health, 47*, 254–262.

Tucker, J. S., & others. (2012). Resisting smoking when a best friend smokes: Do intrapersonal and contextual factors matter? *Journal of Research on Adolescence, 22*, 113–122.

Tucker-Drob, E. M., & Harden, K. P. (2012). Early childhood cognitive development and parental cognitive stimulation: Evidence for reciprocal gene-environment transactions. *Developmental Science, 15*, 250–259.

Tull, M. T., Weiss, N. H., Adams, C. E., & Gratz, K. L. (2012, in press). The contribution of emotion regulation difficulties to risky sexual behavior within a sample of patients in residential substance abuse treatment. *Addictive Behaviors.*

Tun, P. A., & Lachman, M. E. (2010). The association between computer use and cognition across adulthood: Use it so you won't lose it? *Psychology and Aging, 25*(3), 560–568.

Turiano, N. A., Pitzer, L., Armour, C., Karlamangia, A., Ryff, C. D., & Mroczek, D. K. (2012). Personality trait level and change as predictors of health outcomes: Findings of a national study of Americans (MIDUS). *Journals of Gerontology B: Psychological Sciences and Social Sciences, 67*, 4–12.

Turkeltaub, P. E., Gareau, L., Flowers, D. L., Zeffiro, T. A., & Eden, G. F. (2003). Development of neural mechanisms for reading. *Nature Neuroscience, 6*, 767–773.

Turnbull, A., Rutherford-Turnbull, H., Wehmeyer, M. L., & Shogren, K. A. (2013). *Exceptional lives* (7th ed.). Upper Saddle River, NJ: Pearson.

Turner, B. F. (1982). Sex-related differences in aging. In B. B. Wolman (Ed.). *Handbook of developmental psychology.* Englewood Cliffs, NJ: Prentice Hall.

Turner, G. R., & Spreng, R. N. (2012, in press). Executive functions and neurocognitive aging: Dissociable patterns of brain activity. *Neurobiology of Aging.*

Turner, H. A., & others. (2012). Family context, victimization, and child trauma symptoms: Variations in safe, stable, and nurturing relationships during early and middle childhood. *American Journal of Orthopsychiatry, 82*, 209–219.

Twardosz, S., & Bell, M. A. (2012). Introduction to special issue on neuroscience perspectives on early education and development. *Early Education and Development, 23*, 1–3.

Twenge, J. M., Konrath, S., Foster, J. D., Campbell, W. K., & Bushman, B. J. (2008a). Egos inflating over time: A cross-temporal meta-analysis of the Narcissistic Personality Inventory, *Journal of Personality, 76*, 875–902.

Twenge, J. M., Konrath, S., Foster, J. D., Campbell, W. K., & Bushman, B. J. (2008b). Further evidence of an increase in narcissism among college students. *Journal of Personality, 76*, 919–928.

Tyas, S. L., & others. (2007). Transitions to mild cognitive impairments, dementia, and death: Findings from the Nun Study. *American Journal of Epidemiology, 165*, 1231–1238.

Tyrka, A. R., & others. (2012, in press). Neuroendocrine predictors of emotional and behavioral adjustment in boys: Longitudinal follow-up of a community sample. *Psychoneuroimmunology.*

U

Ubell, C. (1992, December 6). We can age successfully. *Parade*, pp. 14–15.

Uchino, B. N., & others. (2012, in press). Social relationships and health: Is feeling positive, negative, or both (ambivalent) about your social ties related to telomeres? *Health Psychology.*

Uher, R., & Rutter, M. (2012). Classification of feeding and eating disorders: Review of evidence and proposals for ICD-11. *World Psychiatry, 11*, 80–92.

Umana-Taylor, A. J., Updegraff, K. A., & Gonzales-Bracken, M. A. (2011). Mexican-origin adolescent mothers' stressors and psychological functioning: Examining ethnic identity affirmation and familism as moderators. *Journal of Youth and Adolescence, 40*, 140–157.

Umana-Taylor, A. J., Wong, J. J., Gonzalez, N. A., & Dumka, L. E. (2012, in press). Ethnic identity and gender as moderators of the association between discrimination and academic adjustment among Mexican-origin adolescents. *Journal of Adolescence.*

UNAIDS. (2011). *AIDS at 30: Nations at a crossroads.* Geneva, SWIT: United Nations.

Underwood, M. (2004). Sticks and stones and social exclusion: Aggression among boys and girls. In P. K. Smith & C. H. Hart (Eds.), *Blackwell handbook of childhood social development.* Malden, MA: Blackwell.

Underwood, M. K. (2011). Aggression. In M. K. Underwood & L. H. Rosen (Eds.), *Social development.* New York: Wiley.

Underwood, M. K., & others. (2012). The BlackBerry project: Capturing the content of adolescents' text messaging. *Developmental Psychology, 48*, 295–302.

UNICEF. (2004). *The state of the world's children 2004.* Geneva, SWIT: UNICEF.

UNICEF. (2007). *The state of the world's children 2007.* Geneva, SWIT: UNICEF

UNICEF. (2011). *The state of the world's children 2011.* Geneva, SWIT: UNICEF.

UNICEF. (2012). *The state of the world's children 2012.* Geneva, SWIT: UNICEF.

UNICEF. (2013). *The state of the world's children 2013.* Geneva, SWIT: UNICEF.

United Nations. (2002). *Improving the quality of life of girls.* New York: United Nations.

Updegraff, K. A., Kim, J-Y., Killoren, S. E., & Thayer, S. M. (2010). Mexican American parents' involvement in adolescents' peer relationships: Exploring the role of culture and adolescents' peer experiences. *Journal of Research on Adolescence, 20*, 65–87.

Urdan, T. (2012). Factors affecting the motivation and achievement of immigrant students. In K. R. Harris, S. Graham, & T. Urdan (Eds.), *APA handbook of educational psychology.* Washington, DC: American Psychological Association.

Uringa, E. J., & others. (2012, in press). RTEL1 contributes to DNA replication, repair, and telomere maintenance. *Molecular Biology of the Cell.*

U.S. Bureau of Labor Statistics. (2008). *Employment of older workers.* Washington, DC: U. S. Department of Labor.

U.S. Census Bureau. (2010, May). *Facts for features: Older Americans month: May 2010.* Washington, DC: U.S. Census Bureau.

U.S. Census Bureau. (2010). *People.* Washington, DC: U.S. Department of Labor.

U.S. Census Bureau. (2011). *Births, deaths, marriages, divorces: Life expectancy.* Table 102. Author: U.S. Department of Labor.

U.S. Census Bureau. (2011). Census Bureau reports 64 percent increase in the number of children living with a grandparent over the last two decades. Retrieved September 2, 2011, from www.census.gov/prod/2011pubs/p.70-126.pdf

U.S. Census Bureau. (2011, September). Income, poverty, and health insurance coverage in the United States: 2010. *Current Population Survey, Annual Social and Economic Supplement*, P60-239.

U.S. Census Bureau. (2011). *People.* Washington, DC: U.S. Department of Labor.

U.S. Census Bureau. (2011, May 8). *Mother's day: May 8, 2011.* Retrieved August 28, 2011, from www.census/gov/newsroom/releases/archives/facts_for_features_special_editions/cb

U.S. Census Bureau. (2012). *People: Poverty.* Washington, DC: U.S. Department of Labor.

U.S. Department of Energy. (2001). *The human genome project.* Washington, DC: U.S. Department of Energy.

U.S. Department of Health and Human Services. (2010). *Child maltreatment 2009.* Washington, DC: Author.

U.S. Department of Health and Human Services. (2012). Retrieved April 12, 2012, from www.cdc.gov/ncbddd/folicacid/

Utz, R. L., Caserta, M., & Lund, D. (2012). Grief, depressive symptoms, and physical health among recently bereaved spouses. *Gerontologist, 52*, 460–471.

V

Vacca, J. A., Vacca, R. T., Gove, M. K., Burkey, L. C., Lenhart, L. A., & McKeon, C. A. (2012). *Reading and learning to read* (8th ed.). Boston: Allyn & Bacon.

Vahia, I. V., & others. (2011a). Correlates of spirituality in older women. *Aging and Mental Health, 15*(1), 97–102.

Vahia, I. V., & others. (2011b). Psychological protective factors across the lifespan: Implications for psychiatry. *Psychiatric Clinics of North America, 34*, 231–248.

Vaillant, G. E. (1977). *Adaptation of life.* Boston: Little, Brown.

Vaillant, G. E. (1992). Is there a natural history of addiction? In C. P. O'Brien & J. H. Jaffe (Eds.), *Addictive states.* Cambridge, MA: Harvard University Press.

Vaillant, G. E. (2002). *Aging well.* Boston: Little, Brown.

Vaish, A., Carpenter, M., & Tomasello, M. (2010). Young children selectively avoid helping people with harmful intentions. *Child Development, 81*, 1661–1669.

Valdes, E. G., O'Connor, M. L., & Edwards, J. D. (2012, in press). The effects of cognitive speed of processing training among older adults with psychometrically-defined mild cognitive impairment. *Current Alzheimer Research.*

Valenzuela, C. F., Morton, R. A., Diaz, M. R., & Topper, L. (2012, in press). Does moderate drinking harm the fetal brain? Insights from animal models. *Trends in Neuroscience.*

Valkenburg, P. M., & Peter, J. (2011). Online communication among adolescents: An integrated model of its attraction, opportunities, and risks. *Journal of Adolescent Health, 48*, 121–127.

van Alphen, J. E., Donker, G. A., & Marquet, R. L. (2010). Requests for euthanasia in general practice before and after implementation of the Dutch Euthanasia Act. *British Journal of General Practice, 60*, 263–267.

van den Boom, D. C. (1989). Neonatal irritability and the development of attachment. In G. A. Kohnstamm, J. E. Bates, & M. K. Rothbart (Eds.), *Temperament in childhood.* New York: Wiley.

van den Dries, L., Juffer, F., van IJzendoorn, M. H., & Bakersman-Kranenburg, M. J. (2010). Infants' physical and cognitive development after international adoption from foster care or institutions in China. *Journal of Developmental and Behavioral Pediatrics, 31*, 144–150.

van den Hoodakker, B. J., & others. (2012). Dopamine transporter gene moderates response to behavioral parent training in children with ADHD: A pilot study. *Developmental Psychology, 48*, 567–574.

van den Kommer, T. N., & others. (2012, in press). Depression and cognition: How do they interrelate in old age? *American Journal of Geriatric Psychiatry.*

Van der Haegen, L., Cai, Q., Seurinck, R., & Brysbaert, M. (2011). Further fMRI validation of the visual half field technique as an indicator of language laterality: A large-group analysis. *Neuropsychologia, 49*, 2879–2888.

van Dijk, M., Hunnius, S., & van Geert, P. (2012). The dynamics of feeding during the introduction to solid food. *Infant Behavior and Development, 35*, 226–239.

van Harmelen, A. L., & others. (2010). Child abuse and negative explicit and automatic self-associations: The cognitive scars of emotional maltreatment. *Behavior Research and Therapy, 48*, 486–494.

Van Hecke, V., & others. (2012). Infant responding to joint attention, executive processes, and self-regulation in preschool children. *Infant Development and Behavior, 35*, 303–311.

van IJzendoorn, M. H., & Kroonenberg, P. M. (1988). Cross-cultural patterns of attachment: A meta-analysis of the Strange Situation. *Child Development, 59*, 147–156.

Van Norstrand, D. W., & others. (2012). Connexin43 mutation causes heterogeneous gap junction loss and sudden infant death. *Circulation, 125*, 474–481.

van Rijn, L. J., & others. (2011). Prevalence of impairment of visual function in European drivers. *Acta Ophthalmologica, 89*, 124–131.

Van Ryzin, M. J., Carlson, E. A., & Sroufe, L. A. (2011). Attachment discontinuity in a high-risk sample. *Attachment and Human Development, 13*, 381–401.

Van Ryzin, M. J., & Dishion, T. J. (2012, in press). The impact of a family-centered intervention on the ecology of adolescent antisocial behavior: Modeling developmental sequelae and trajectories during adolescence. *Development and Psychopathology.*

Van Ryzin, M. J., Johnson, A. B., Leve, L. D., & Kim, H. K. (2011). The number of sexual partners and health-risking sexual behavior: Prediction from high school entry to high school exit. *Archives of Sexual Behavior, 40*, 939–949.

Van Solinge, H., & Henkens, K. (2005). Couples' adjustment to retirement: A multiactor panel study. *Journals of Gerontology B: Psychological Sciences and Social Sciences, 60*, S11–S20.

Van Wesemael, Y., & others. (2011). Process and outcomes of euthanasia requests under the Belgian Act on Euthanasia: A nationwide survey. *Journal of Pain and Symptom Management, 42*, 721–733.

Vance, D. E., & others. (2012). Neuroplasticity and successful cognitive aging: A brief overview for nursing. *Journal of Neuroscience Nursing, 44*, 218–227.

Vandell, D. L., & others. (2010). Do effects of early childcare extend to age 15 years? From the NICHD Study of Early Child Care and Youth Development. *Child Development, 81*, 737–756.

Vanhalst, J., Luyckx, K., Raes, F., & Goossens, L. (2012). Loneliness and depression symptoms: The mediating and moderating role of uncontrollable ruminative thoughts. *Journal of Psychology, 146*, 259–276.

VanKim, N. A., & Laska, M. N. (2012, in press). Socioeconomic disparities in emerging adult weight and weight behaviors. *American Journal of Health Behavior.*

Vasquez, M. J., & Berg, O. R. (2012). The Baby-Friendly journey in a U.S. public hospital. *Journal of Perinatal and Neonatal Nursing, 26*, 37–46.

Vaughan, C. A., & Halpern, C. T. (2010). Gender differences in depressive symptoms during adolescence: The contributions of weight-related concerns and behaviors. *Journal of Research on Adolescence, 20*, 389–419.

Vaughn, S. R., & Bos, C. S. (2012). *Strategies for teaching children with learning and behavior problems* (8th ed.). Upper Saddle River, NJ: Pearson.

Vazsonyi, A. T., & Huang, L. (2010). Where self-control comes from: On the development of self-control and its relationship to deviance over time. *Developmental Psychology, 46*, 245–257.

Veerman, J. L., & others. (2012, in press). Television viewing time and reduce life expectancy: A life table analysis. *British Journal of Sports Medicine.*

Velez, C. E., Wolchik, S. A., Tein, J. Y., & Sandler, I. (2011). Protecting children from the consequences of divorce: A longitudinal study of the effects of parenting on children's coping responses. *Child Development, 82*, 244–257.

Vellas, B., & Aisen, P. S. (2010). Editorial: Early Alzheimer's trials: New developments. *Journal of Nutrition, Health, and Aging, 14*, 293.

Venners, S. A., & others. (2004). Paternal smoking and pregnancy loss: A prospective study using a biomarker of pregnancy. *American Journal of Epidemiology, 159*, 993–1001.

Ventura, S. J., & Hamilton, B.E. (2011, February). U.S. teenage birth rate resumes decline. *NCHS Data Brief, 58*, 1–3.

Verdejo-Garcia, A., Clark, L., & Dunn, B. D. (2012, in press). The role of interoception in addiction: A critical review. *Neuroscience and Biobehavioral Reviews.*

Verghese, J., Ambrose, A. F., Lipton, R. B., & Wang, C. (2010). Neurological gait abnormalities and risk of falls in older adults. *Journal of Neurology, 257*, 392–398.

Veronica, G., & Esther, R. R. (2012). Aging, metabolic syndrome, and the heart. *Aging and Disease, 3*, 269–279.

Vesco, K. K., & others. (2012, in press). Healthy Moms, a randomized trial to promote and evaluate weight maintenance among obese pregnant women: Study design and rationale. *Contemporary Clinical Trials.*

Viachantoni, A. (2012, in press). Financial inequality and gender in older people. *Maturitas.*

Villanueva, C. M., & Buriel, R. (2010). Speaking on behalf of others: A qualitative study of the perceptions and feelings of adolescent Latina language brokers. *Journal of Social Issues, 66*, 197–210.

Villaverde Gutierrez, C., & others. (2012). Influence of exercise on mood in postmenopausal women. *Journal of Clinical Nursing, 21*, 923–928.

Villegas, R., & others. (2008). Duration of breast-feeding and the incidence of type 2 diabetes mellitus in the Shanghai Women's Health Study. *Diabetologia., 51*, 258–266.

Vincent, H. K., Raiser, S. N., & Vincent, K. R. (2012). The aging musculoskeletal system and obesity-related considerations with exercise. *Aging Research and Reviews, 11*, 361–373.

Vinik, J., Almas, A., & Grusec, J. (2011). Mothers' knowledge of what distresses and comforts their children predicts children's coping, empathy, and prosocial behavior. *Parenting: Science and Practice, 11*, 56–71.

Virnig, B., Huang, Z., Lurie, N., Musgrave, D., McBean, A. M., & Dowd, B. (2004). Does Medicare managed care provide equal treatment for mental illness across race? *Archives of General Psychiatry, 61*, 201–205.

Visher, E., & Visher, J. (1989). Parenting coalitions after remarriage: Dynamics and therapeutic guidelines. *Family Relations, 38*, 65–70.

Vitaro, F., Boivin, M., & Bukowski, W. M. (2009). The role of friendship in child and adolescent psychological development. In K. H. Rubin, W. M. Bukowski, & B. Laursen (Eds.), *Handbook of peer interaction, relationships, and groups*. New York: Guilford.

Vittrup, B., Holden, G. W., & Buck, M. (2006). Attitudes predict the use of physical punishment: A prospective study of the emergence of disciplinary practices. *Pediatrics, 117*, 2055–2064.

Vladutiu, C. J., Evenson, K. R., & Marshall, S. W. (2010). Physical activity and injuries during pregnancy. *Journal of Physical Activity and Health, 7*, 761–769.

Volbrecht, M. M., & Goldsmith, H. H. (2010). Early temperamental and family predictors of shyness and anxiety. *Developmental Psychology, 46*, 1192–1205.

Von Korff, L., & Grotevant, H. D. (2011). Contact in adoption and adoptive family identity formation: The mediating role of family conversation. *Journal of Family Psychology, 25*, 393–401.

Von Polier, G. G., Vioet, T. D., & Herpertz-Dahlmann, B. (2012). ADHD and delinquency—A developmental perspective. *Behavioral Sciences and the Law, 30*, 121–139.

Vong, K-I. (2012). Play—A multimodal manifestation in kindergarten education in China. *Early Years: An International Journal of Research and Development, 32*(1), 35–48.

Voorpostel, M., & Blieszner, R. (2008). Intergenerational solidarity and support between adult siblings. *Journal of Marriage and the Family, 70*, 157–167.

Votruba-Drzal, E., Coley, R. L., & Chase-Lansdale, P. L. (2004). Child care and low-income children's development: Direct and moderated effects. *Child Development, 75*, 296–312.

Vrangalova, Z., & Savin-Williams, R. C. (2013). Mostly heterosexual and mostly gay/lesbian: New sexual orientation identities and the sexual orientation continuum. *Archives of Sexual Behavior.*

Vreeman, R. C., & Carroll, A. E. (2007). A systematic review of school-based interventions to prevent bullying. *Archives of Pediatric and Adolescent Medicine, 161*, 78–88.

Vukelich, C., Christie, J. F., & Enz, B. J. (2012). *Helping children learn language and literacy* (3rd ed.). Boston: Allyn & Bacon.

Vurpillot, E. (1968). The development of scanning strategies and their relation to visual differentiation. *Journal of Experimental Child Psychology, 6*, 632–650.

Vygotsky, L. S. (1962). *Thought and language*. Cambridge, MA: MIT Press.

W

Waasdorp, T. E., Bradshaw, C. P., & Leaf, P. J. (2012). The impact of schoolwide positive behavioral interventions and supports on bullying and peer rejection: A randomized controlled effectiveness trial. *Archives of Pediatric and Adolescent Medicine, 166*, 149–156.

Waber, D. P. (2010). *Rethinking learning disabilities*. New York: Guilford University Press.

Wachs, T. D. (1994). Fit, context and the transition between temperament and personality. In C. Halverson, G. Kohnstamm, & R. Martin (Eds.), *The developing structure of personality from infancy to adulthood*. Hillsdale, NJ: Erlbaum.

Wachs, T. D. (2000). *Necessary but not sufficient*. Washington, DC: American Psychological Association.

Wachs, T. D., & Bates, J. E. (2010). Temperament. In J. G. Bremner & T. D. Wachs (Eds.), *Wiley-Blackwell handbook of infant development* (2nd ed.). New York: Wiley

Waddell, L. (2012). The power of vitamins. *Journal of Family Health Care, 22*, 16–20, 22–25.

Wagner, G., & others. (2012). Antihypertensive treatment and risk of dementia: A retrospective database study. *International Journal of Clinical Pharmacology and Therapy, 50*, 195–201.

Wagner, L., & Hoff, E. (2013, in press). Language development. In I. B. Weiner & others (Eds.), *Handbook of psychology* (2nd ed.). New York: Wiley.

Wagner, L. M., McDonald, S. M., & Castle, N. G. (2012). Relationship between nursing home safety culture and joint commission accreditation. *Joint Commission on Accreditation of Healthcare Organizations, 38*, 207–215.

Waite, L. J. (2005, June). *The case for marriage*. Paper presented at the Ninth Annual Smart Marriages conference, Dallas.

Waite, L. J. (2009). Marriage. In D. Carr (Ed.), *Encyclopedia of the life course and human development*. Boston: Gale Cengage.

Waite, L. J., Das, A., & Laumann, E. O. (2009). Sexual activity, later life. In D. Carr (Ed.), *Encyclopedia of the life course and human development*. Boston: Gale Cengage.

Waite, L. J., Laumann, E. O., Das, A., & Schumm, L. P. (2009). Sexuality: Measures of partnerships, practices, attitudes, and problems in the National Social Life, Health, and Aging Project. *Journals of Gerontology B: Psychological Sciences and Social Sciences, 64B* (Suppl. 1), S56–S66.

Wakefield, J. D. (2012). Should prolonged grief be reclassified as a mental disorder in DSM-5?: Reconsidering the empirical and conceptual arguments for complicated grief disorder. *Journal of Nervous and Mental Disease, 200*, 499–511.

Wakeling, E. L. (2011). Silver-Russell syndrome. *Archives of Disease in Childhood, 96*, 1156–1161.

Walden, T. (1991). Infant social referencing. In J. Garber & K. Dodge (Eds.), *The development of emotional regulation and dysregulation*. New York: Cambridge University Press.

Waldfogel, J. (2012). Work-family policies and child well-being in low-income families. In V. Maholmes & R. B. King (Eds.), *Oxford handbook of poverty and child development*. New York: Oxford University Press.

Waldinger, R. J., & Schulz, M. C. (2010). What's love got to do with it? Social functioning, perceived health, and daily happiness in married octogenarians. *Psychology and Aging, 25*, 422–431.

Waldinger, R. J., Vaillant, G. E., & Orav, E. J. (2007). Childhood sibling relationships as a predictor of

major depression in adulthood: A 30-year prospective study. *American Journal of Psychiatry, 164*, 949–954.

Walker, L. (1982). The sequentiality of Kohlberg's stages of moral development. *Child Development, 53*, 1130–1136.

Walker, L. J. (2002). In W. Damon (Ed.), *Bringing in a new era of character education*. Stanford, CA: Hoover Press.

Walker, L. J. (2004). Progress and prospects in the psychology of moral development. *Merrill-Palmer Quarterly, 50*, 546–557.

Walker, L. J., & Frimer, J. A. (2008). Being good for goodness' sake: Transcendence in the lives of moral heroes. In F. Oser & W. Veugelers (Eds.), *Getting involved: Global citizenship development and sources of moral values*. Rotterdam, The Netherlands: Sense Publishers.

Walker, L. J., & Frimer, J. A. (2009). "The song remains the same": Rebuttal to Sherblom's re-envisioning of the legacy of the care challenge. *Journal of Moral Education, 38*, 53–68.

Walker, L. J., & Frimer, J. A. (2011). The science of moral development. In M. K. Underwood & L. Rosen (Eds.), *Social development*. New York: Guilford.

Walker, S. (2006). Unpublished review of J. W. Santrock's *Topical approach to life-span development* (3rd ed.). New York: McGraw-Hill.

Wallenborg, K., & others. (2009). Red wine triggers cell death and thiroredoxin reductase inhibition: Effects beyond resveratrol and SIRT 1. *Experimental Cell Research, 315*, 1360–1371.

Waller, E. M., & Rose, A. J. (2010). Adjustment trade-offs of co-rumination in mother-adolescent relationships. *Journal of Adolescence, 33*, 487–497.

Wallerstein, J. S. (2008). Divorce. In M. M. Haith & J. B. Benson (Eds.), *Encyclopedia of infant and early childhood development*. Oxford, UK: Elsevier.

Wallin, K., & others. (2012, in press). Midlife rheumatoid arthritis increases the risk of cognitive impairment two decades later: A population-based study. *Journal of Alzheimer's Disease.*

Walsh, R. (2011). Lifestyle and mental health. *American Psychologist, 66*(7), 579–592.

Walton, N. M., & others. (2012). Adult neurogenesis transiently generates oxidative stress. *PLoS One, 7*(4), e35264.

Wan, G. W. Y., & Leung, P. W. L. (2010). Factors accounting for youth suicide attempt in Hong Kong: A model building. *Journal of Adolescence, 33*, 575–582.

Wandell, P. E., Carlsson, A. C., & Theobold, H. (2009). The association between BMI value and long-term mortality. *International Journal of Obesity, 33*, 577–582.

Wang, H., & others. (2012). Blood folate is associated with asymptomatic or partially symptomatic Alzheimer's disease in the Nun Study. *Journal of Alzheimer's Disease, 28*, 637–645.

Wang, J., Nansel, T. R., & Iannotti, R. J. (2011). Cyber and traditional bullying: Differential association with depression. *Journal of Adolescent Health, 48*(4), 415–417.

Wang, M. (2012). Retirement: An adult development perspective. In S. K. Whitbourne & M. J. Sliwinski (Eds.), *Wiley-Blackwell handbook of adult development and aging*. New York: Wiley.

Wang, M., Kviz, F. J., & Miller, A. M. (2012, in press). The mediating role of parent-child bonding to prevent adolescent alcohol abuse among Asian American families. *Journal of Immigrant and Minority Health*.

Wang, N., & others. (2012). Effects of television viewing on body fatness among Chinese children and adolescents. *Chinese Medical Journal, 125*, 1500–1503.

Wang, R., Li, J., Fang, H., Tian, M., & Liu, J. (2012). Individual differences in holistic processing predict face recognition ability. *Psychological Science, 23*, 169–177.

Wang, Z., Deater-Deckard, K., Petrill, S. A., & Thompson, L. (2012, in press). Externalizing problems, attention regulation, and household chaos: A longitudinal behavioral genetic study. *Development and Psychopathology*.

Ward, A., & others. (2012). Prevalence of apolipoprotein E4 genotype and homozygotes (APOEe4/4) among patients diagnosed with Alzheimer's disease: A systematic review and meta-analysis. *Neuroepidemiology*.

Ward, L. M., Epstein, M., Caruthers, A., & Merriwether, A. (2011). Men's media use, sexual cognitions, and sexual risk behavior: Testing a meditational model. *Developmental Psychology, 47*, 592–602.

Ward-Griffin, C., Oudshoorn, A., Clark, K., & Bol, N. (2007). Mother-adult daughter relationships within dementia care: A critical analysis. *Journal of Family Nursing, 13*, 13–32.

Wardlaw, G. M., & Smith, A. M. (2012). *Contemporary nutrition* (2nd ed.). New York: McGraw-Hill.

Ware, J. E., Kosinski, M., Dewey, J. E. (2000). *How to score Version 2 of the SF-36 Health Survey*. Boston: QualityMetric.

Waring, J. D., Addis, D. R., & Kensinger, E. A. (2012, in press). Effects of aging on neural connectivity underlying selective memory for emotional scenes. *Neurobiology of Aging*.

Warr, P. (2004). Work, well-being, and mental health. In J. Baring, E. K. Kelloway, & M. R. Frone (Eds.), *Handbook of work stress*. Thousand Oaks, CA: Sage.

Warshak, R. A. (2007, January). Personal communication. Department of Psychology, University of Texas at Dallas, Richardson.

Watamura, S. E., Phillips, D. A., Morrissey, D. A., McCartney, T. W., & Bub, K. (2011). Double jeopardy: Poorer social-emotional outcomes for children in the NICHD SECCYD who experience home and child-care environments that convey risk. *Child Development, 82*, 48–65.

Waterman, A. S. (1985). Identity in the context of adolescent psychology. In A. S. Waterman (Ed.), *Identity in adolescence: Processes and contents*. San Francisco: Jossey-Bass.

Waterman, A. S. (1999). Identity, the identity statuses, and identity status development: A contemporary statement. *Developmental Review, 19*, 591–621.

Watson, D. (2012). Objective tests as instruments of psychological theory and research. In H. Cooper (Ed.), *APA handbook of research methods in psychology*. Washington, DC: American Psychological Association.

Watson, J. A., Randolph, S. M., & Lyons, J. L. (2005). African-American grandmothers as health educators in the family. *International Journal of Aging and Human Development, 60*, 343–356.

Watson, J. B. (1928). *Psychological care of infant and child*. New York: W. W. Norton.

Watts, C., & Zimmerman, C. (2002). Violence against women: Global scope and magnitude. *Lancet, 359*, 1232–1237.

Waugh, C. K., & Gronlund, N. E. (2013). *Assessment of student achievement* (10th ed.). Upper Saddle River, NJ: Pearson.

Waxman, S., & Goswami, U. (2012). Acquiring language: Learning the spoken and written word. In S. Pauen & M. Bornstein (Eds.), *Early child development and later outcome*. New York: Cambridge University Press.

Way, N., & Silverman, L. R. (2012). The quality of friendships across adolescence: Patterns across context, culture, and age. In P. K. Kerig, M. S. Schulz, & S. T. Hauser (Eds.), *Adolescence and beyond*. New York: Oxford University Press.

Wayne, A. (2011). Commentary in interview: Childhood cancers in transition. Retrieved April 12, 2011, from http://home.ccr.cancer.gov/connections/2010/Vol4_No2/clinic2.asp

Weaver, F. M., & others. (2012). Randomized trial of deep brain stimulation for Parkinson disease: Thirty-six-month outcomes. *Neurology, 79*, 55–65.

Webb, L. D., Metha, A., & Jordan, K. F. (2013). *Foundations of American education* (7th ed.). Upper Saddle River, NJ: Pearson.

Webb, M. B. (2012). Children and families in poverty: Federal perspectives on applied research and evaluation. In V. Maholmes & R. B. King (Eds.), *Oxford handbook on poverty and child development*. New York: Oxford University Press.

Webster, N. S., & Worrell, F. C. (2008). Academically talented students' attitudes toward service in the community. *Gifted Child Quarterly, 52*, 170–179.

Wechsler, H., Lee, J. E., Kuo, M., Selbring, M., Nelson, T. F., & Lee, H. (2002). Trends in college binge drinking during a period of increased prevention efforts: Findings from 4 Harvard School of Public Health college alcohol study surveys: 1993–2001. *Journal of American College Health, 50*, 203–217.

Wehby, G. L., & others. (2011). The impact of maternal smoking during pregnancy on early child neurodevelopment. *Journal of Human Capital, 5*, 207–254.

Weikert, D. P. (1993). Long-term positive effects in the Perry Preschool Head Start Program. Unpublished data, High Scope Foundation, Ypsilanti, MI.

Weiner, C. P., & Buhimschi, C. (2009). *Drugs for pregnant and lactating women* (2nd ed.). London: Elsevier.

Weinraub, M., & others. (2012, in press). Patterns of developmental change in infants' nighttime sleep awakenings from 6 to 36 months of age. *Developmental Psychology*.

Weiss, L. A., & others. (2008). Association between microdeletion and microduplication at 16p11.2 and autism. *New England Journal of Medicine, 358*. 667–675.

Welch, K. J. (2011). *THINK human sexuality*. Upper Saddle River, NJ: Pearson.

Welch, K. J. (2012). *Family life now census update* (2nd ed.). Upper Saddle River, NJ: Pearson.

Wellman, H. M. (2011). Developing a theory of mind. In U. Goswami (Ed.), *Wiley-Blackwell handbook of childhood cognitive development* (2nd ed.). New York: Wiley.

Wellman, H. M., Cross, D., & Watson, J. (2001). Meta-analysis of theory-of-mind development: The truth about false belief. *Child Development, 72*, 655–684.

Wellman, H. M., & Woolley, J. D. (1990). From simple desires to ordinary beliefs: The early development of everyday psychology. *Cognition, 35*, 245–275.

Wells, E. M., & others. (2011). Body burdens of mercury, lead, selenium, and copper among Baltimore newborns. *Environmental Research, 111*, 411–417.

Welsh, J. A., Nix, R. L., Blair, C., Bierman, K. L., & Nelson, K. E. (2010). The development of cognitive skills and gains in academic school readiness for children from low-income families. *Journal of Educational Psychology, 102*, 43–53.

Wenestam, C. G., & Wass, H. (1987). Swedish and U.S. children's thinking about death: A qualitative study and cross-cultural comparison. *Death Studies, 11*, 99–121.

Wenger, N. K., & others. (2003). The quality of medical care provided to vulnerable community-dwelling older patients. *Annals of Internal Medicine, 139*, 740–747.

Wensink, M. J., van Heemst, D., Rozing, M. P., & Westendorp, R. G. (2012). The maintenance gap: A new theoretical perspective on the evolutionary theory of aging. *Biogerontology, 13*, 197–201.

Wentzel, K. R. (1997). Student motivation in middle school: The role of perceived pedagogical caring. *Journal of Educational Psychology, 89*, 411–419.

Wentzel, K. R. (2013). School adjustment. In I. B. Weiner & others (Eds.), *Handbook of psychology* (2nd ed., Vol. 7). New York: Wiley.

Wentzel, K. R., & Asher, S. R. (1995). The academic lives of neglected, rejected, popular and controversial children. *Child Development. 66*, 754–763.

Wentzel, K. R., Barry, C. M., & Caldwell, K. A. (2004). Friendships in middle schools: Influences on motivation and school adjustment. *Journal of Educational Psychology, 96*, 195–203.

Wentzel, K. R., Donlan, A., & Morrison, D. (2012). Peer relationships and social motivational processes. In A. M. Ryan & G. W. Ladd (Eds.), *Peer relationships and adjustment at school*. Charlotte, NC: Information Age Publishing.

West, S. K., & others. (2010). Older drivers and failure to stop at red lights. *Journals of Gerontology A: Biological Sciences and Medical Sciences, 65A*, 179–183.

Westerhof, G. J. (2009). Age identity. In D. Carr (Ed.), *Encyclopedia of the life course and human development*. Boston: Gale Cengage.

Westerhof, G. J., Whitbourne, S. K., & Freeman, G. P. (2012). The aging self in a cultural context: The relation of conceptions of aging to identity processes and self-esteem in the United States and the Netherlands. *Journals of Gerontology B: Psychological Sciences and Social Sciences, 67*, 52–60.

Westerman, G., Thomas, M. S. C., & Karmiloff-Smith, A. (2011). Neuroconstructivism. In U. Goswami (Ed.),

Wiley-Blackwell handbook of childhood cognitive development (2nd ed.). New York: Wiley.

Westlake, C., Evangelista, L. S., Stromberg, A., Ter-Galstanyan, A., Vazirani, S., & Dracup, K. (2007). Evaluation of a web-based education and counseling pilot for older heart failure patients. *Progress in Cardiovascular Nursing, 22,* 20–26.

Wetherell, J. L. (2012). Complicated grief therapy as a new treatment approach. *Dialogues in Clinical Neuroscience, 14,* 159–166.

Wethington, E., Kessler, R. C., & Pixley, J. E. (2004). Turning points in adulthood. In O. G. Brim, C. D. Ryff, & R. C. Kessler (Eds.), *How healthy are we?* Chicago: University of Chicago Press.

Whaley, L. (2013, in press). Syntactic typology. In J. J. Song (Ed.), *Oxford handbook of linguistic typology.* New York: Oxford University Press.

Whaley, S. E., Jiang, L., Gomez, J., & Jenks, E. (2011). Literacy promotion for families participating in the Women, Infants, and Children program. *Pediatrics, 127,* 454–461.

Whaley, S. E., Ritchie, L. D., Spector, P., & Gomez, J. (2012, in press). Revised WIC food package improves diets of WIC families. *Journal of Nutrition and Education Behavior.*

Wheeden, A., Scafidi, F. A., Field, T., Ironson, G., Valdeon, C., & Bandstra, E. (1993). Massage effects on cocaine-exposed preterm neonates. *Journal of Developmental and Behavioral Pediatrics, 14,* 318–322.

Wheeler, A., & others. (2011). Caucasian infants scan own- and other-race faces differently. *PLoS One, 6,* e18621.

Whitbourne, S. K., & Meeks, S. (2011). Psychopathology, bereavement, and aging. In K. W. Schaie & S. L. Willis (Eds.), *Handbook of the psychology of aging* (7th ed.). New York: Elsevier.

Whitbourne, S. K., & Sliwinski, M. (Eds.). (2012). *Wiley-Blackwell handbook of adulthood and aging.* New York: Wiley.

White, B. A., & Kistner, J. A. (2011). Biased self-perceptions, peer rejection, and aggression in children. *Journal of Abnormal Child Psychology, 39,* 645–656.

White, C. B., & Catania, J. (1981). Psychoeducational intervention for sexuality with the aged, family members of the aged, and people who work with the aged. *International Journal of Aging and Human Development, 13,* 71–77.

White, J. W. (2001). Aggression and gender. In J. Worell (Ed.), *Encyclopedia of gender and women.* San Diego: Academic Press.

White, L. (1994). Stepfamilies over the life course: Social support. In A. Booth and J. Dunne (Eds.), *Stepfamilies: Who benefits and who does not.* Hillsdale, NJ: Erlbaum.

Whitehead, B. D., & Popenoe, D. (2003). *The state of our Unions.* Piscataway, NJ: The National Marriage Project, Rutgers University.

Whiteman, S. D., McHale, S. M., & Soli, A. (2011). Theoretical perspectives on sibling relationships. *Journal of Family Theory and Review, 3,* 124–139.

Whitfield, K. E., Thorpe, R., & Szanton, S. (2011). Health disparities, social class, and aging. In K.W. Schaie & S. L. Willis (Eds.), *Handbook of the psychology of aging* (7th ed.). New York: Elsevier.

WIC New York. (2011). *The new look of the women, infants, and children (WIC) program.* Retrieved July 30, 2009, from www.health.state.ny.us/prevention/nutrition/wic/the_new_look_of_wic.htm

Wickelgren, I. (1999). Nurture helps to mold able minds. *Science, 283,* 1832–1834.

Widman, L., & McNulty, J. K. (2010). Sexual narcissism and the perpetration of sexual aggression. *Archives of Sexual Behavior, 39,* 939–946.

Widom, C. S., Czaja, S. J., Bentley, T., & Johnson, M. S. (2012, in press). A prospective investigation of physical health outcomes in abused and neglected children: New findings from a 30-year follow-up. *American Journal of Public Health.*

Widom, C. S., & Nikulina, V. (2012). Long-term consequences of child neglect in low-income families. In V. Maholmes & R. B. King (Eds.), *Oxford handbook of poverty and child development.* New York: Oxford University Press.

Wiesel, A., & others. (2011). Maternal occupational exposure to ionizing radiation and birth defects. *Radiation and Environmental Biophysics, 50,* 325–328.

Wilcox, J. (2009–2010). The easiest birth yet. *Midwifery Today with International Midwife, 23,* 63–64.

Wilcox, S., Evenson, K. R., Aragaki, A., Wassertheil-Smoller, S., Mouton, C. P., & Loevinger, B. L. (2003). The effects of widowhood on physical and mental health, health behaviors, and health outcomes: The women's health initiative. *Health Psychology, 22,* 513–522.

Wilcox, S., Sharpe, P. A., Parra-Medina, D., Granner, M., & Hutto, B. (2011). A randomized trial of a diet and exercise intervention for overweight and obese women from economically disadvantaged neighborhoods: Sisters Taking Action for Real Success (STARS). *Contemporary Clinical Trials, 32*(6), 931–945.

Wilhelmsen, L., & others. (2011). Factors associated with reaching 90 years of age: A study of men born in 1913 in Gothenberg, Sweden. *Journal of Internal Medicine, 269,* 441–451.

Wilkinson-Lee, A. M., Russell, S. T., Lee, F. C. H., & the Latina/o Teen Pregnancy Prevention Workgroup. (2006). Practitioners' perspectives on cultural sensitivity in Latina pregnancy prevention. *Family Relations, 55,* 376–389.

Willcox, B. J., Willcox, M. D., & Suzuki, M. (2002). *The Okinawa Program.* New York: Crown.

Willcox, D. C., Willcox, B. J., He, Q., Wang, N. C., & Suzuki, M. (2008). They really are that old: A validation study of centenarian prevalence in Okinawa. *Journals of Gerontology A: Biological Sciences and Medical Sciences, 63,* 338–349.

Willcox, D. C., Willcox, B. J., Sokolovsky, J., & Sakihara, S. (2007). The cultural context of "successful aging" among older women weavers in a Northern Okinawan village: The role of productive activity. *Journal of Cross Cultural Gerontology, 22,* 137–165.

Willett, W. (2013, in press). The current evidence on healthy eating. *Annual Review of Nutrition* (Vol. 34). Palo Alto, CA: Annual Reviews.

Willette, A. A., & others. (2012). Calorie restriction reduces the influence of glucoregulatory dysfunction on regional brain volume in aged rhesus monkeys. *Diabetes, 61,* 1036–1042.

Williams, B. K., Sawyer, S. C., & Wahlstrom, C. M. (2012). *Marriages, families, and intimate relationships* (2nd ed.). Upper Saddle River, NJ: Pearson.

Williams, D. L., & Schwartz, M. W. (2011). Neuroanatomy of body weight control: Lessons from leptin. *Journal of Clinical Investigation, 121,* 2152–2155.

Williams, D. R., & Sternthal, M. J. (2007). Spirituality, religion, and health: Evidence and research directions. *Medical Journal of Australia, 186* (Suppl.), S47–S50.

Williams, G. L., Keigher, S., & Williams, A. V. (2012). Spiritual well-being among older African Americans in a midwestern city. *Journal of Religion and Health, 51*(2), 355–370.

Williams, N. M., & others. (2012). Genome-wide analysis of copy number variants in attention deficit hyperactivity disorder: The role of rare variants and duplications at 15q13.3. *American Journal of Psychiatry, 169,* 195–204.

Williamson, J. B. (2011). The future of retirement security. In R. H. Binstock & L. K. George (Eds.), *Handbook of aging and the social sciences* (7th ed.). New York: Elsevier.

Willis, S. L., & Martin, M. (2005). Preface. In S. C. Willis & M. Martin (Eds.), *Middle adulthood.* Thousand Oaks, CA: Sage.

Willis, S. L., & Schaie, K. W. (2005). Cognitive trajectory in midlife and cognitive functioning in old age. In S. K. Wills & M. Martin (Eds.), *Middle adulthood.* Thousand Oaks, CA: Sage.

Willis, S. L., & Schaie, K. W. (2006). A co-constructionist view of the third age: The case of cognition. *Annual Review of Gerontology and Geriatrics, 26,* 131–152.

Willis, S. L., & others. (2006). Long-term effects of cognitive training on everyday functional outcomes in older adults. *Journal of the American Medical Association, 296,* 2805–2814.

Willis, T. A., Potrata, B., Hunt, C., & Rudolf, M. C. (2012, in press). Training community practitioners to work more effectively with parents to prevent childhood obesity: The impact of HENRY upon children centers and their staff. *Journal of Human Nutrition and Dietetics.*

Willoughby, K. A., Desrocher, M., Levine, B., & Rovet, J. F. (2012, in press). Episodic and semantic autobiographical memory and everyday memory during late childhood and early adolescence. *Frontiers in Psychology.*

Willoughby, V., Heger, A., Rogers, C., & Sathyavagiswaran, L. (2012). Sexual assault documentation program. *American Journal of Forensic Medicine and Pathology, 33,* 22–25.

Wilson, A. E., Shuey, K. M., & Elder, G. H. (2003). Ambivalence in relationships of adult children to aging parents and in-laws. *Journal of Marriage and the Family, 65,* 1055–1072.

Wilson, B. J. (2008). Media and children's aggression, fear, and altruism. *Future of Children, 18*(1), 87–118.

Wilson, D., & Hockenberry, M. (2012). *Wong's clinical manual of pediatric nursing* (7th ed.). New York: Elsevier.

Wilson, G. T., & Zandberg, L. J. (2012). Cognitive-behavioral guided self-help for eating disorders: Effectiveness and scalability. *Clinical Psychology Review, 32,* 343–357.

Wilson, K. R., Havighurst, S. S., & Harley, A. E. (2012). Tuning in to kids: An effectiveness trial of a parenting program targeting emotion socialization of preschoolers. *Journal of Family Psychology, 26,* 56–65.

Wilson, R. S., Mendes de Leon, C. F., Bienas, J. L., Evans, D. A., & Bennett, D. A. (2004). Personality and mortality in old age. *Journals of Gerontology B: Psychological Sciences and Social Sciences, 59,* P110–P116.

Wilson, R. S., & others. (2002). Participation in cognitively stimulating activities and risk of incident Alzheimer disease. *Journal of the American Medical Association, 287,* 742–748.

Wilson, R. S., & others. (2012). Terminal dedifferentiation of cognitive abilities. *Neurology, 78,* 1116–1122.

Windle, M. (2012). Longitudinal data analysis. In H. Cooper (Ed.), *APA handbook of research methods in psychology.* Washington, DC: American Psychological Association.

Windsler, A., & others. (2012, in press). Child, family, and childcare predictors of delayed school entry and kindergarten retention among linguistically and ethnically diverse children. *Developmental Psychology.*

Windsor, T. D., & Butterworth, P. (2010). Supportive, aversive, ambivalent, and indifferent partner evaluations in midlife and young-old adulthood. *Journals of Gerontology B: Psychological Sciences and Social Sciences, 65B,* 287–295.

Wing, R., Tate, D. F., Gorin, A. A., Raynor, H. A., Fava, J. L., & Machan, J. (2007). "STOP Regain": Are there negative effects of daily weighing? *Journal of Consulting and Clinical Psychology, 75,* 652–656.

Wink, P., & Dillon, M. (2002). Spiritual development across the adult life course. Findings from a longitudinal study. *Journal of Adult Development, 9,* 79–94.

Winner, E. (1996). *Gifted children: Myths and realitics.* New York: Basic Books.

Winner, E. (2006). Development in the arts. In W. Damon & R. Lerner (Eds.), *Handbook of child psychology* (6th ed.). New York: Wiley.

Winner, E. (2009). Toward broadening our understanding of giftedness: The spatial domain. In F. D. Horowitz, R. F. Subotnik, & D. J. Matthews (Eds.), *The development of giftedness and talent across the life span.* Washington, DC: American Psychological Association.

Winner, F. (1986, August.). Where pelicans kiss seals. *Psychology Today,* pp. 24–35.

Winsler, A., Carlton, M. P., & Barry, M. J. (2000). Age-related changes in preschool children's systematic use of private speech in a natural setting. *Journal of Child Language, 27,* 665–687.

Winsper, C., Lereya, T., Zanarini, M., & Wolke, D. (2012). Involvement in bullying and suicide-related behavior at 11 years: A prospective birth cohort study. *Journal of the Academy of Child and Adolescent Psychiatry, 51,* 271–282.

Wise, P. M. (2006). Aging of the female reproductive system. In E. J. Masoro & S. N. Austad (Eds.), *Handbook of the biology of aging* (6th ed.). San Diego: Academic Press.

Wit, J.M., Kiess, W., & Mullis, P. (2011). Genetic evaluation of short stature. *Best Practices and Research. Clinical Endocrinology and Metabolism, 25,* 1–17.

Witherington, D. C., Campos, J. J., Harriger, J. A., Bryan, C., & Margett, T. E. (2010). Emotion and its development in infancy. In J. G. Bremner & T. D. Wachs (Eds.), *Wiley-Blackwell handbook of infant development* (2nd ed.). New York: Wiley.

Witkin, H. A., & others. (1976). Criminality in XYY and XXY men. *Science, 193,* 547–555.

Witte, A. V., Fobker, M., Gellner, R., Knecht, S., & Fioel, A. (2009). Caloric restriction improves memory in elderly humans. *Proceedings of the National Academy of Sciences U.S.A., 106,* 1255–1260.

Witte, R. (2012). *Classroom assessment for teachers.* New York: McGraw-Hill.

Wittig, S. L., & Spatz, D. L. (2008). Induced lactation: Gaining a better understanding. *MCN, The Journal of Maternal Child Nursing, 33,* 76–81.

Wittmeier, K. D., Mollard, R. C., & Kriellaars, D. J. (2008). Physical activity intensity and risk of overweight and adiposity in children. *Obesity, 16,* 415–420.

Wojtowicz, A., & others. (2011). Aspirin resistance may be associated with adverse pregnancy outcomes. *Neuroendocrinology Letters, 32,* 334–339.

Wolfinger, N. H. (2011). More evidence for trends in the intergenerational transmission of divorce: A completed cohort approach using data from the general social survey. *Demography, 48,* 581–592.

Wolitzky-Taylor, K. B., & others. (2011). Reporting rape in a national sample of college women. *American Journal of College Health, 59,* 582–587.

Wolke, D., Schreier, A., Zanarini, M. C., & Winsper, C. (2012, in press). Bullied by peers in childhood and borderline personality symptoms at 11 years of age: A prospective study. *Journal of Child Psychology and Psychiatry.*

Wong Briggs, T. W. (2004, October 14). USA Today's 2004 all-USA team. *USA Today,* p. 6D.

Wong Briggs, T. W. (2007, October 18). All-USA teacher team. *USA Today,* p. 6D.

Wong, A. M., Lin, Y. C., Chou, S. W., Tang, F. T., & Wong, P. Y. (2001). Coordination exercise and postural stability in elderly people: Effect of Tai Chi Chuan. *Archives of Physical Medicine & Rehabilitation, 82,* 608–612.

Wong, C. G., & Stevens, M. C. (2012). The effects of stimulant medication on working memory functional connectivity in attention-deficit/hyperactivity disorder. *Biological Psychiatry, 71,* 458–466.

Wong, M. M., & Brower, K. J. (2012, in press). The prospective relationship between sleep problems and suicidal behavior in the National Longitudinal Study of Adolescent Health.

Wong, M. M., Brower, K. J., & Zucker, R. A. (2010). Childhood sleep problems, early onset of substance use, and behavioral problems in adolescence. *Alcoholism: Clinical and Experimental Research, 34,* 1033–1044.

Wong, S. S., Sugimoto-Matsuda, J. J., Chang, J. Y., & Hishinuma, E. S. (2012). Ethnic differences in risk factors for suicide among American high school students, 2009: The vulnerability of multiracial and Pacific Islander adolescents. *Archives of Suicide Research, 16,* 159–173.

Wood, A., & others. (2011). Retinal and choroidal thickness in early age-related macular degeneration. *American Journal of Ophthalmology, 152,* 1030–1038.

Woodward, A. L., & Markman, E. M. (1998). Early word learning. In D. Kuhn & R. S. Siegler (Eds.), *Handbook of child psychology* (5th ed., Vol. 2). New York: Wiley.

Woolett, L. A. (2011). Review: Transport of maternal cholesterol to the fetal circulation. *Placenta, 32*(Suppl. 2), S18–S21.

Woolgar, M., & Tranah, T. (2010). Cognitive vulnerability to depression in young people in secure accommodation: The influence of ethnicity and current suicidal ideation. *Journal of Adolescence, 33,* 653–651.

World Health Organization. (2000, February 2). *Adolescent health behavior in 28 countries.* Geneva, SWIT: World Health Organization.

Worthington, E. L. (1989). Religious faith across the life span: Implications for counseling and research. *Counseling Psychologist, 17,* 555–612.

Wright, J. (2006, March 16). Boomers in the bedroom: Sexual attitudes and behaviours in the boomer generation. Ipsos Reid survey. Retrieved February 28, 2009, from http://www.ipsos-na-com.

Wright, R. H., Mindel, C. H., Tran, T. V., & Habenstein, R. W. (2012). *Ethnic families in America* (5th ed.). Upper Saddle River, NJ: Pearson.

Wrzus, C., Hanel, M., Wagner, J., & Neyer, F. J. (2012, in press). Social network changes and life events across the life span: A meta-analysis. *Psychological Bulletin.*

Wu, J. M., & Hsieh, T. C. (2011). Resveratrol: A cardioprotective substance. *Annals of the New York Academy of Sciences, 1215,* 16–21.

Wu, L. F., Chuo, L. J., & Wu, S. T. (2012). The effect of group instrumental reminiscence therapy in older single veterans who live in a veterans home in Taiwan. *International Journal of Geriatric Psychiatry, 27,* 107–108.

Wu, L. T., & Blazer, D. G. (2011). Illicit and nonmedical drug use among older adults: A review. *Journal of Aging and Health, 23,* 481–504.

Wu, T., Gao, X., Chen, M., & van Dam, R. M. (2009). Long-term effectiveness of diet-plus-exercise interventions vs. diet-only interventions for weight loss: A meta-analysis. *Obesity Review, 10,* 313–323.

Wu, W. S., Liu, Z., & Ho, S. C. (2010). Metabolic syndrome and all-cause mortality: A meta-analysis of prospective cohort studies. *European Journal of Epidemiology, 25,* 375–384.

Wu, Z. C., Yu, J. T., Li, Y., & Tan, L. (2012). Clusterin in Alzheimer's disease. *Advances in Clinical Chemistry, 56,* 155–173.

Wuest, D. A., & Fisette, J. L. (2012). *Foundations of physical education, exercise science, and sports* (17th ed.). New York: McGraw-Hill.

Wynn, K. (1992). Addition and subtraction by human infants. *Nature, 358,* 749–570.

X

Xiao, Y., & others. (2012, in press). Systematic identification of functional modules related to heart failure with different etiologies. *Gene.*

Xie, Q., & Young, M. E. (1999). Integrated child development in rural China. *Education: The World Bank.* Washington, DC: The World Bank.

Xiu-Ying, H., & others. (2012). Living arrangements and risk for late life depression: A meta-analysis of published literature. *International Journal of Psychiatry in Medicine, 43,* 19–34.

Xu, F., Spelke, E., & Goddard, S. (2005). Number sense in human infants. *Developmental Science, 8,* 88–101.

Xu, H., & others. (2012, in press). The function of BMP4 during neurogenesis in the adult hippocampus in Alzheimer's disease. *Aging Research and Reviews.*

Xu, Z. Z., & others. (2010). Resolvins RvE1 and RvD1 attenuate inflammatory pain via central and peripheral actions. *Nature Medicine, 16,* 592–597.

Xue, F., Holzman, C., Rahbar, M. H., Trosko, K., & Fischer, L. (2007). Maternal fish consumption, mercury levels, and risk of preterm delivery. *Environmental Health Perspectives, 115,* 42–47.

Y

Yaffe, K., Barnes, D., Nevitt, M., Lui, L., & Covinsky, K. (2001). A prospective study of physical activity and cognitive decline in elderly women. *Archives of Internal Medicine, 161,* 1703–1708.

Yakoboski, P. J. (2011). Worries and plans as individuals approach retirement. *Benefits Quarterly, 27,* 34–37.

Yang, X. P., & Reckelhoff, J. F. (2011). Estrogen, hormonal replacement therapy, and cardiovascular disease. *Current Opinion in Nephrology and Hypertension, 20,* 133–138.

Yang, Y. (2008). Social inequalities in happiness in the United States, 1972–2004: An age-period-cohort analysis. *American Sociological Review, 73,* 204–226.

Yang, Y., & Kozloski, M. (2011). Sex differences in age trajectories of physiological dysregulation: Inflammation, metabolic syndrome, and allostatic load. *Journals of Gerontology A: Biological Sciences and Medical Sciences, 66A,* 493–500.

Yarber, W., Sayad, B., & Strong, B. (2013). *Human sexuality* (8th ed.). New York: McGraw-Hill.

Yashion, R., & Cummings, M. (2012). *Human genetics and society* (2nd ed.). Boston: Cengage.

Yassin, A. A., Akhras, F., El-Sakka, A. I., & Saad, F. (2011). Cardiovascular diseases and erectile dysfunction: The two faces of the coin on androgen deficiency. *Andrologia, 43,* 1–8.

Yates, D. (2012, in press). Neurogenetics: Unraveling the genetics of autism. *Nature Reviews: Neuroscience.*

Yates, L. B., Djuousse, L., Kurth, T., Buring, J. E., & Gaziano, J. M. (2008). Exceptional longevity in men: Modifiable factors associated with survival and function to age 90 years. *Archives of Internal Medicine, 168,* 284–290.

Ye, L., Hawkley, L. C., Waite, L., & Cacioppo, J. T. (2012, in press). Loneliness, health, and mortality in old age: A national longitudinal study. *Social Science and Medicine.*

Yee, B. W. K., & Chiriboga, D. A. (2007). Issues of diversity in health psychology and aging. In C. M. Aldwin, C. L. Park, & A. Spiro (Eds.), *Handbook of health psychology and aging.* New York: Guilford.

Yeung, D. Y., Wong, C. K., & Lok, D. P. (2011). Emotion regulation mediates age differences in emotions. *Aging and Mental Health, 15,* 414–418.

Yi, O., & others. (2012). Association between environmental tobacco smoke exposure of children and parental socioeconomic status: A cross-sectional study in Korea. *Nicotine and Tobacco Research, 14,* 607–615.

Yi, S., & others. (2010). Role of risk and protective factors in risky sexual behavior among high school students in Cambodia. *BMC Public Health, 10,* 477.

Yiallourou, S. R., Sands, S. A., Walker, A. M., & Horne, R. S. (2011). Baroreflex sensitivity during sleep in infants: Impact of sleeping position and sleep state. *Sleep, 34,* 725–732.

Yin, R. K. (2012). Case study methods. In H. Cooper (Ed.), *APA handbook of research methods in psychology.* Washington, DC: American Psychological Association.

Yokoya, T., Demura, S., & Sato, S. (2009). Three-year follow-up of the fall risk and physical function characteristics of the elderly participating in a community exercise class. *Journal of Physiological Anthropology, 28,* 55–62.

Yolton, K., & others. (2010). Associations between secondhand smoke and exposure and sleep patterns in children. *Pediatrics, 125,* e261–e268.

Yoon, C., Cole, C. A., & Lee, M. P. (2009). Consumer decision making and aging: Current knowledge and future directions. *Journal of Consumer Psychology, 19,* 2–16.

Yoon, C., May, C. P., Goldstein, D., & Hasher, L. (2010). Aging, circadian arousal patterns and cognition. In D. Park and N. Schwarz (Eds.), *Cognitive aging: A primer* (2nd ed.). Psychology Press.

Yoshikawa, H. (2011). *Immigrants raising citizens: Undocumented parents and their young children.* New York: Russell Sage.

Young, K. T. (1990). American conceptions of infant development from 1955 to 1984: What the experts are telling parents. *Child Development, 61,* 17–28.

Youniss, J., McLellan, J. A., & Yates, M. (1999). Religion, community service, and identity in American youth. *Journal of Adolescence, 22,* 243–253.

Youth Risk Behavior Survey. (2011). *Trends in the prevalence of suicide-related behaviors National YRB: 1991–2011.* Retrieved June 6, 2012, from www.cdc.gov/yrbss

Yu, C. Y., & others. (2012, in press). Prenatal predictors for father-infant attachment after childbirth. *Journal of Clinical Nursing.*

Yudof, M. G., Levin, B., Moran, R., & Ryan, J. M. (2012). *Educational policy and the law* (5th ed.). Boston: Cengage.

Z

Zacher, H., Jimmieson, N. L., & Winter, G. (2012). Eldercare demands, mental health, and work performance: The moderating role of satisfaction with eldercare tasks. *Journal of Occupational Health Psychology.*

Zaff, J. F., Hart, D., Flanagan, C., Youniss, J., & Levin, P. (2010). Developing civic engagement within a civic context. In M. E. Lamb, A. M. Freund, & R. M. Lerner (Eds.), *Handbook of life-span development* (Vol. 2). New York: Wiley.

Zajacova, A., Dowd, J. B., & Burgard, S. A. (2011). Overweight adults may have the lowest mortality—Do they have the best health? *American Journal of Epidemiology, 173,* 430–437.

Zannas, A. S., & others. (2012, in press). Stressful life events, perceived stress, and 12-month course of geriatric depression: Direct effects and moderation by the 5-HTTLPR and COMT Val158Met polymorphisms. *Stress.*

Zayas, L., Gulbas, L. E., Fedoravicius, N., & Cabassa, L. J. (2010). Patterns of distress, precipitating events, and reflections on suicide attempts by young Latinas. *Social Science & Medicine, 70*(11), 1773–1779.

Zeiders, K. H., Roosa, M. W., & Tein, J. Y. (2011). Family structure and family processes in Mexican-American families. *Family Process, 50,* 77–91.

Zeifman, D., & Hazan, C. (2008). Pair bonds as attachments: Reevaluating the evidence. In J. Cassidy & P. R. Shaver (Eds.), *Handbook of attachment* (2nd ed.). New York: Guilford.

Zeisel, S. H. (2011). The supply of choline is important for fetal progenitor cells. *Seminars in Cell and Developmental Biology, 22,* 624–628.

Zekry, D., & others. (2012). Telomere length, comorbidity, functional, nutritional, and cognitive status as predictors of 5 years post hospital discharge survival in the oldest old. *Journal of Nutrition, Health, and Aging, 16,* 225–230.

Zelazo, P. D., & Muller, U. (2011). Executive function in typical and atypical children. In U. Goswami (Ed.), *Wiley-Blackwell handbook of childhood cognitive development* (2nd ed.). New York: Wiley.

Zembal-Saul, C. L., McNeill, K., & Hershberger, K. (2013). *What's your evidence: Engaging K-5 children in constructing explanations in science.* Boston: Allyn & Bacon.

Zentner, M., & Shiner, R. L. (Eds.) (2012). Fifty years of progress in temperament research: A synthesis of major themes, findings, challenges, and a look forward. In M. Zentner & R. Shiner (Eds.), *Handbook of temperament.* New York: Guilford.

Zeskind, P. S., Klein, L., & Marshall, T. R. (1992). Adults' perceptions of experimental modifications of durations and expiratory sounds in infant crying. *Developmental Psychology, 28,* 1153–1162.

Zettel-Watson, L., & Rook, K. S. (2009). Friendship, later life. In D. Carr (Ed.). *Encyclopedia of the life course and human development.* Boston: Gale Cengage.

Zhai, F., Raver, C. C., & Jones, S. (2012, in press). Quality of subsequent schools and impacts of early interventions: Evidence from a randomized controlled trial in Head Start settings. *Children and Youth Services Review.*

Zhang, L., Zhang, X. H., Liang, M. Y., & Ren, M. H. (2010). Prenatal cytogenetic diagnosis study of 2782 cases of high-risk pregnant women. *China Medicine (English), 123,* 423–430.

Zhao, H., Seibert, S. E., & Lumpkin, G. T. (2010). The relationship of personality to entrepreneurial intentions and performance: A meta-analytic review. *Journal of Management, 36,* 381–404.

Zhou, P., Su, Y. E., Crain, S., Gao, L., & Zhan, L. (2012, in press). Children's use of phonological information in ambiguity resolution: A view from Mandarin Chinese. *Journal of Child Language.*

Zhu, D. C., Zacks, R. T., & Slade, J. M. (2010). Brain activation during interference resolution in young and older adults: An fMRI study. *Neuroimage, 50,* 810–817.

Zielinksi, A. E., Rochette, L. M., & Smith, G. A. (2012). Stair-related injuries to young children treated in U.S. emergency departments, 1999–2008. *Pediatrics, 129,* 721–729.

Zielinski, D. S. (2009). Child maltreatment and adult socioeconomic well-being. *Child Abuse and Neglect, 33,* 666–678.

Ziemer, C. J., Plumert, J. M., & Pick, A. D. (2012, in press). To grasp or not to grasp: Infants' actions toward objects and pictures. *Infancy.*

Zigler, E. F., Gilliam, W. S., & Barnett, W. S. (Eds.) (2011). *The pre-K debates: Controversies and Issues.* Baltimore: Brookes.

Zigler, E. F., Gilliam, W. S., & Jones, S. M. (2006). *A vision for universal preschool education.* New York: Cambridge University Press.

Zigler, E. F., & Styfco, S. J. (1994). Head Start: Criticisms in a constructive context. *American Psychologist, 49,* 127–132.

Zigler, E. F., & Styfco, S. J. (2010). *The hidden history of Head Start.* New York: Oxford University Press.

Zimmerman, F. I., Ortiz, S. E., Christakis, D. A., & Elkun, D. (2012). The value of social-cognitive theory to reducing preschool TV viewing: A pilot randomized trial. *Preventive Medicine, 54,* 212–218.

Ziol-Guest, K. M. (2009). Child custody and support. In D. Carr (Ed.), *Encyclopedia of the life course and and human development.* Boston: Gale Cengage.

Zotter, H., & Pichler, G. (2012, in press). Breast feeding is associated with decreased risk of sudden infant death syndrome. *Evidence Based Medicine.*

Zozuls, K., Martin, C., England, D., Andrews, N., & Borders, A. (2012, April). *"I don't want to talk to them because I don't know how to": The role of relationship efficacy in children's gender-related intergroup processes.* Paper presented at the Gender Development Research conference, San Francisco.

Zuckerman, M. (2012). Models of adult temperament. In M. Zentner & R. L. Shiner (Eds.), *Handbook of temperament.* New York: Guilford.

Zugazaga Cortazar, A., & Martin Martinez, C. (2012, in press). Usefulness of magnetic resonance imaging in the prenatal study of malformations of the face and neck. *Radiologia.*

credits

Chapter 1

Opener: © Geri Lavrov/Flickr/Getty Images RF; p.4: © Barros & Barros/The Image Bank/Getty Images; p.5 (Kaczynski adult): © Seanna O'Sullivan; p.5 (Kaczynski teen): © WBBM-TV/AFP/Getty Images; p.5 (Walker adult): © AP Wide World Photos; p.5 (Walker child): Courtesy of Alice Walker; 1.1 (tortoise): © Digital Vision/PunchStock RF; 1.1 (mouse): © Redmond Durrell/Alamy RF; p.7: Margaret M. and Paul B. Baltes Foundation; 1.2: © istockphoto.com/leezsnow; p.8: © Walter Hodges/Corbis; p.9 (top): FEMA Photo/Andrea Booher; p.9 (bottom): © Comstock Images/Jupiter Images/Alamy RF; p.10 (top): Courtesy of Luis Vargas; p.10 (bottom): National Association for the Education of Young Children, Robert Maust/Photo Agora; p.11 (top left): © Nancy Agostini; p.11 (top right): © Andy Nelson/The Christian Science Monitor via Getty Images; p.11 (bottom): Naser Siddique/UNICEF Bangladesh; p.12: Courtesy of Children's Defense Fund; p.14: © Dennis Brack Ltd./Black Star Photo; 1.8 (left to right): © Brand X Pictures/PunchStock RF; Courtesy of John Santrock; © Laurence Mouton/PhotoAlto/PictureQuest RF; © Digital Vision RF; © Getty Images/SW Productions RF; © Blue Moon Stock/Alamy Images RF; © Corbis RF; © Ronnie Kaufman/Blend Images LLC RF; p.18: © Jetta Productions/Blend Images/Getty Images; p.19 (top left): © Jay Syverson/Corbis; p.19 (top right): © Owaki-Kulla/Corbis; p.19 (bottom): © Rubberball/PictureQuest RF; p.22 (top): © Bettmann/Corbis; p.22 (bottom): © Sarah Putman; p.23: © Yves de Braine/Black Star/Stock Photo; 1.13 (left to right): © Stockbyte/Getty Images RF; © BananaStock/PunchStock RF; © image100/Corbis RF; © RF/Corbis; p.24: A.R. Lauria/Dr. Michael Cole, Laboratory of Human Cognition, University of California, San Diego; p.25 (top): © Creatas Images/Jupiter Images RF; p.25 (bottom): © AP Wide World Photos; p.26: © Linda A. Cicero/Stanford News Service; p.27: © Time & Life Pictures/Getty Images; p.28: Courtesy of Urie Bronfenbrenner; p.30: © Philadelphia Inquirer/MCT/Landov Images; p.31: © Bettmann/Corbis; 1.18: Dr. Susan Tapert, University of California at San Diego; 1.19: © Digital Vision/PunchStock RF; p.35 (top left): George Grantham Bain Collection, Library of Congress, Reproduction Number #LC-USZ62-63966; p.35 (top right): © Jamie Grill/Blend Images/Corbis RF; p.35 (bottom): © Inti St. Clair/Digital Vision/Getty Images RF; p.36: © The McGraw-Hill Companies, Inc./Mark Dierker, photographer; p.38: Courtesy of Dr. Pam Reid, University of Saint Joseph; p.39 (top left): © Anthony Cassidy/Stone/Getty Images; p.39 (top right): © Punchstock/Digital Vision RF.

Chapter 2

Opener: © Petit Format/Nestle/PhotoResearchers; p.50: © China Tourism Press/The Image Bank/Getty Images; p.51: © Enrico Ferorelli Enterprises; p.52: © Frans Lemmens/Corbis; 2.1: © Alan and Sandy Carey/Photodisc/Getty Images RF; p.54: © David Wilkie; p.56: © Rick Rickman; 2.4: © Science Source/Photo Researchers; 2.5: © Custom Medical Stock Photo; p.59: © Joel Gordon Photography; p.60: From R. Simensen and R. Curtis Rogers, "Fragile X Syndrome" in *American Family Physician*, 39(5): 186, May 1989 © American Academy of Family Physicians; p.61: © Andrew Eccles/August Images; p.62: Courtesy of Holly Ishamel; p.63: © Jacques Pavlousky/Sygma/Corbis; 2.8: © Larry Berman; p.65: © Science Source/Photo Researchers; p.66: © AP Wide World Photos; p.67: © Randy Santos; p.68: © Myrleen Pearson/PhotoEdit; p.70: © Cuomo/Corbis.

Chapter 3

Opener: © Lennart Nilsson/Scanpix Sweden AB; p.77: Courtesy of John Santrock; 3.3 (top): © Last Refuge, LTD., PhotoTakeUSA.com; 3.3 (middle): © Neil Bromhall/Photo Researchers, Inc.; 3.3 (bottom): © Brand X Pictures/PunchStock RF; p.82: © AP Wide World Photos; 3.4: © Lennart Nilsson/Scanpix Sweden AB; p.84: Courtesy of Ann Streissguth; p.85 (top): © Anthony West/Corbis; p.85 (bottom): © John Chiasson; p.86: © R.I.A. Novosti/Gamma/H.P.P./Eyedea; p.87: © Betty Press/Woodfin Camp & Associates; p.88 (top): © Barbara Penoyar/Getty Images RF; p.88 (bottom): © Rafal Strzechowski/age fotostock; p.89 (top): © Ryan Pyle/Ryan Pyle/Corbis; p.89 (bottom): © Tracy Frankel/The Image Bank/Getty Images; p.90: © Mark Randall/Sun Sentinel. All Rights Reserved; p.91: © Jonathan Nourok/Corbis; p.92 (top): © Viviane Moos/Corbis; p.92 (bottom): © RF/Corbis; p.93 (top): Courtesy of Linda Pugh; p.93 (bottom): © Barros & Barros/Stockbyte/Getty Images RF; p.94: Dr. Holly Beckwith; p.95: © Stephen Marks/The Image Bank/Getty Images; p.96: © AP Wide World Photos; p.97: © iStockphoto.com/casenbina; p.98: Courtesy of Dr. Tiffany Field; p.100: Courtesy of Diane Sanford, Photograph: © Tony Schanuel; p.101: © Howard Grey/Getty Images RF.

Chapter 4

Opener: © Jose Luis Pelaez, Inc./Getty Images RF; p.108: © Image Source/Getty Images RF; p.109 (top): © Wendy Stone/Corbis; p.109 (bottom): © Dave Bartruff/Corbis; p.111: © Benjamin Benschneider/The Seattle Times; 4.3: © A. Glauberman/Photo Researchers; 4.4: © ER Productions/Getty Images RF; 4.8: Courtesy of Dr. Harry T. Chugani, Children's Hospital of Michigan; 4.9a: © David Grugin Productions, Inc. Reprinted by permission; 4.9b: Image courtesy of Dana Boatman, Ph.D., Department of Neurology, John Hopkins University, reprinted with permission from *The Secret Life of the Brain*, Joseph Henry Press; p.117 (top): © Marla Teljeiro/Cultura/Getty Images RF; p.117 (bottom): © The McGraw-Hill Companies, Inc./Mark Steinmetz, photographer; p.119: © Blend Images/Getty Images; p.120: © Bob Daemmrich/The Image Works; p.121 (top): © USDA Food and Nutrition Service, Supplemental Nutrition Assistance Program; p.121 (bottom): Courtesy Brazelton Touchpoints Center; p.122: Courtesy of Esther Thelen; p.123: © Harry Bartlett/Taxi/Getty Images; 4.13 (moro): © Petit Format/Photo Researchers; 4.13 (grasping): © Stockbyte/PunchStock RF; 124: © Fabio Cardoza/zefa/Corbis; 4.14: © Dr. Karen Adolph, New York University; 4.15 (left to right): © Barbara Penoyar/Getty Images RF; © Digital Vision/Getty Images RF; © Image Source/Getty Images RF; Titus/Getty Images RF; © Digital Vision RF; © BananaStock/Getty Images RF; © Corbis/PictureQuest RF; © BrandX/Punchstock RF; p.126 (bottom left): © Michael Greenlar/The Image Works; p.126 (bottom right): © Frank Baily Studios; p.127: © Newstockimages/SuperStock RF; 4.16: Courtesy Amy Needham, Duke University; p.129: © Trish Gant/Dorling Kindersley/Getty Images; 4.17: © David Linton; 4.19: Image courtesy of Dr. Karen E. Adolph; 4.20: © Kevin Peterson/Getty Images/Simulation by Vischeck RF; 4.22: © Mark Richards/PhotoEdit; 4.23a: ©McGraw-Hill Companies, Inc./Jill Braaten, photographer; 4.23b: Dr. Melanie Spence, University of Texas; 4.24: © Jean Guichard/Corbis; 4.25: Rosenstein, D & Oster, H (1988) Differential facial responses to four basic tastes in newborns. *Child Development*, 59, p.1561; p.137 (top): © Dorling Kindersley/Getty Images; p.137 (bottom): © altrendo images/Getty Images; p.138: © Anthony Cain/Flickr/Getty Images RF.

Chapter 5

Opener: © Marcus Mok/Asia Images/Corbis; p.145 (top): © Laura Dwight/Corbis; p.145 (bottom): © Plush Studios/Brand X Pictures/JupiterImages RF; p.147: © Johnny Valley/Cultura/Getty Images RF; 5.2: © Doug Goodman/Photo Researchers; p.150: © Joe McNally; p.152: © baobao ou/Flickr/Getty Images RF; 5.5: Courtesy of Dr. Carolyn Rovee-Collier; 5.6: Photos from Meltzoff, A.N., & Brooks, R. (2007). *Intersubjectivity before language: Three windows on preverbal sharing*. In S. Braten (Ed.), *On being moved: From mirror neurons to empathy* (pp. 149–174). Philadelphia, PA: John Benjamins; p.154 (top): © Myrleen Pearson/PhotoEdit; p.154 (bottom): © Tom Stewart/Corbis; 5.9: © Andrew Meltzoff; 5.10: From Jean Mandler, University of California, San Diego. Reprinted by permission of Oxford University Press, Inc.; p.157: Courtesy of John Santrock; p.159 (top): Courtesy of John Santrock; p.159 (bottom): Bayley Scales of Infant and Toddler Development-Third Edition (Bayley-III). Copyright © 2006 by NCS Pearson, Inc. Reproduced with permission. All rights reserved; p.161: © Vanessa Davies/Dorling Kindersley/Getty Images; 5.13: © 2003 University of Washington, Institute for Learning and Brain Sciences (I-LABS); p.163: © Don Hammon/Design Pics/Corbis RF; p.164 (top): © Niki Mareschal/Photographer's Choice/Getty Images; p.164 (bottom): © Yang Liu/Corbis; p.165 (top): © ABPL Image Library/Animals Animals/Earth Scenes; p.165 (bottom): © Digital Vision/PunchStock RF; 5.17: © Michael Goldstein, Cornell University; p.168: © Elyse Lewin/Brand X Pictures/Getty Images RF; p.169: © John Carter/Photo Researchers.

Chapter 6

Opener: © Vanessa Gavalya/Stockbyte/Getty Images RF; p.176: © Rick Gomez/Corbis; p.177: © Jose Luis Pelaez Inc./Getty Images RF; 6.1 (joy): © BananaStock/PictureQuest RF; 6.1 (sadness): © The McGraw-Hill Companies, Inc./Jill Braaten, photographer; 6.1 (fear): © David Sacks/Getty Images; 6.1 (surprise): © Getty Images RF; 6.2: Photo by Kenny Braun and courtesy of Dr. Sybil L. Hart, Texas Tech University; p.179: © Andy Cox/Stone/Getty Images; p.180: © Photodisc Collection/Getty Images RF; p.181: © Girl Ray/Getty Images; p.182–183: © Tom Merton/Getty Images RF; p.184: © MIXA/Getty Images RF; 6.4: © Digital Vision/Getty Images RF; p.186: © iStockphoto.com/Derek Latta; p.187: © Britt Erlanson/Getty Images; 6.5: Courtesy of Celia A. Brownell, University of Pittsburgh; p.188: © Dan Lepp/ETSA/Corbis; p.189: © Martin Rogers/Stock Boston; p.190: © Camille Tokerud/Getty Images RF; p.191 (top): © George Doyle/Stockbyte/Getty Images RF; p.191 (bottom left): © iStockphoto.com/Yuko Hirao; p.191 (bottom right): © iStockphoto.com/Andrew Rich; p.192: © Penny Tweedie/Stone/Getty Images; 6.9: © Photodisc/Getty Images RF; p.194: © Corbis RF; p.195 (top): © BrandXPictures/Getty Images RF; p.195 (middle): © BrandX/Punchstock RF; p.195 (bottom): © Jessie Jean/Taxi/Getty Images; p.196: Courtesy of Dr. Barry Hewlett; p.197 (top): Polka Dot Images/PhotoLibrary RF; p.197 (bottom): © Lawrence Schwartzwald; p.198: Courtesy of Wanda Mitchell; p.199: © Reena Rose Sibayan/The Jersey Journal /Landov Images.

Chapter 7

Opener: © Ariel Skelley/Corbis; p.208: © Ariel Skelley/Blend Images/Getty Images RF; p.209: From *'Open Window'* © 1994 Municipality of Reggio Emilia Infant-Toddler Centers and Preschools Published by Reggio Children; p.210: © DK Stock/Robert Glen; 7.1: © Photo Researchers; p.212 (top): © C Squared Studios/Getty Images RF; p.212 (bottom): © Medioimages/Photodisc/Getty Images RF; p.213 (top): © BrandX/Punchstock RF; p.213 (bottom): © Lilian Perez/Corbis; p.214: © RubberBall Productions/Getty Images RF; p.215: © AP Wide World Photos; 7.6: © Paul Fusco/Magnum Photos; 7.8: © Elizabeth Crews/The Image Works; p.221 (top): © James Wertsch/Washington University, St.Louis; p.221 (bottom): © BananaStock/PunchStock RF; 7.9: Images courtesy of E. Bodrova and D.J. Leong, from *Tools of the Mind*, 2007; 7.10a: A.R. Lauria/Dr. Michael Cole, Laboratory of Human Cognition, University of California, San Diego; 7.10b: © Bettmann/Corbis; p.224: © BananaStock/PunchStock RF; p.225: © 2012 www.polychromemedia/jameskamp; 7.13: Photo by Dawn Villella, Courtesy of Stephanie Carlson; p.227: Courtesy of Helen Hadani; p.229 (top): © Robin Nelson/PhotoEdit; p.229 (bottom): © Joe Baker, Images.com/Corbis; p.232 (top): © Hill Street Studios/Blend Images/agefotostock RF; p.232 (bottom): © JGI/Jamie Grill/Blend Images/Getty Images RF; p.234 (top): © iStockphoto.com/fatihhoca; p.234 (bottom): © James Leynse/Corbis Images; p.235: © BananaStock/PunchStock RF; p.237 (top): Courtesy of Yolanda Garcia; p.237 (bottom): © Ronnie Kaufman/The Stock Market/Corbis.

Chapter 8

Opener: © Fotosearch/PhotoLibrary RF; p.246 (top): © Roger Allyn Lee/SuperStock; p.246 (bottom): © RF/Corbis; p.247: © James Woodson/Digital Vision/Getty Images RF; p.248 (top): © LWA-Dann Tardif/Corbis; p.248 (bottom): © Catherine Ledner/Stone/Getty Images; p.250: © Tom Grill/Corbis RF; p.251: © Tanya Constantine/Blend Images/Getty Images RF;

Chapter 20

Opener: © Hans Neleman/Getty Images; p.622: © Fuse/Getty Images RF; p.624: © Lynsey Addario/VII; p.625: © Robert Galbrait/Reuters/Corbis; 20.1: © Patrick Ward/Stock Boston, Inc.; p.626: © Dario Mitidieri/Getty Images; p.627 (top): © Handout Courtesy of the Schiavo Family/Corbis Images; p.627 (bottom): © The Detroit News Archives/Craig Porter; p.628: © Comstock Images/PictureQuest RF; p.629: Photo courtesy of the family of Mary Monteiro; p.630: © Per-Anders Pettersson/Getty Images; p.631 (top): Photo by Molly Hayden, U.S. Army Garrison-Hawaii Public Affairs; p.631 (bottom): © Corbis RF; 20.2: © Eastcott Momatinck/The Image Works; p.635: © Photodisc/Getty Images RF; p.636: © Stockbroker/PhotoLibrary RF; p.637: © Digital Vision RF; p.638 (top): © Tao Ming/XinHua/Xinhua Press/Corbis; p.638 (bottom): © Thomas Hinton/Splash News/Newscom; p.639: © Matt Moyer/Getty Images; p.640 (left): © Russell Underwood/Corbis; p.640 (right): © Paul Almasy/Corbis; p.641 (top): © Reprinted with permission of The Baltimore Sun Media Group. All Rights Reserved/Photo by Sun Photographer Glenn Fawcett; p.641 (bottom): © Robert Mulder/Godong/Corbis.

TEXT AND LINE ART CREDITS

Chapter 1

TA 1.3, p 5a: Peanuts: © United Feature Syndicate, Inc. TA 1.3, p 5a: From "Percentage of Children 7 to 18 Years of Age Around the World Who Have Never Been to School of Any Kind," 2004, *The State of the World's Children*, Geneva, Switzerland: UNICEF, Fig. 5, p. 27. TA 1.14, p 24a: © Robert Weber/The New Yorker Collection/www.cartoonbank.com Fig 1.15, p 47a: From "Bronfenbrenner's Ecological Theory of Development," in C.B. Kopp & J.B. Krakow, 1982, *Child Development in the Social Context*, p. 648. Addison-Wesley Longman, Inc. Reprinted by permission of Pearson Education, Inc. Fig. 1.19, p 57a: From Santrock *Children*, 9/e, Figure 2.12. Copyright © 2007 The McGraw-Hill Companies. Reproduced by permission of The McGraw-Hill Companies.

Chapter 2

Fig. 2.2, p 8a: *Annual Review of Psychology*, Vol. 50 by Baltes, Staudinger, and Lindenberger. Copyright 1999 by Annual Reviews, Inc. Reproduced with permission of Annual Reviews, Inc. in the format Textbook via Copyright Clearance Center. For e-book citation use: "Other Book" instead of "Textbook." Fig. 2.3, p 11a: From Santrock, *Psychology*, 7/e. Copyright © 2003 The McGraw-Hill Companies. Reproduced by permission of The McGraw-Hill Companies. Fig. 2.11, p 37a: From Santrock, *Children*, 9/e Figure 3.10. Copyright © 2007 The McGraw-Hill Companies. Reproduced by permission of The McGraw-Hill Companies. TA 2.7, p 12b: CALVIN AND HOBBES © Watterson. Dist. by UNIVERSAL UCLICK. Reprinted with permission. All rights reserved. Ch. 2, p 151–152: From *Handbook of Parenting Vol. 1: Children and Parenting* by D. Brodzinsky and E. Pinderhughes. Copyright 2002 by Taylor & Francis Group LLC – Books. Reproduced with permission of Taylor & Francis Group LLC – Books in the format Textbook via Copyright Clearance Center. For e-book citation use: "Other Book" instead of "Textbook." Ch. 2, p 154–155: From *Handbook of Parenting Vol. 1: Children and Parenting* by D. Brodzinsky and E. Pinderhughes. Copyright 2002 by Taylor & Francis Group LLC – Books. Reproduced with permission of Taylor & Francis Group LLC – Books in the format Textbook via Copyright Clearance Center. For e-book citation use: "Other Book" instead of "Textbook."

Chapter 3

Fig. 3.3, p 8a: From Santrock *Children*, 9/e, Figure 4.3. Copyright © 2007 The McGraw-Hill Companies. Reproduced by permission of The McGraw-Hill Companies. Fig. 3.5, p 12a: Adapted from K.L. Moore and T.V.N. Persaud from *Before We Are Born*, p. 130. © 1993, with permission from Elsevier. Ch. 3, p 35a: From Virginia A. Apgar, 1975, "A Proposal for a New Method of Evaluation of a Newborn Infant," in *Anesthesia and Analgesia*, Vol. 32, pp. 260–267. Reprinted by permission of Lippincott Williams & Wilkins. Fig. 3.7, p 38a: From Santrock, *Children*, 10/e. Copyright © 2008 The McGraw-Hill Companies. Reproduced by permission of The McGraw-Hill Companies. Fig. 3.11: From Santrock, *Child Development*, 10/e,

Figure 4.11. Copyright © 2004 The McGraw-Hill Companies. Reproduced by permission of The McGraw-Hill Companies.

Chapter 4

Fig. 4.1, p 6a: From Santrock, *Children*, 9/e, Figure 6.1. Copyright © 2007 The McGraw-Hill Companies. Reproduced by permission of The McGraw-Hill Companies. Fig. 4.5, p10a: From Santrock, *Child Development*, 10/e, Figure 5.2. Copyright © 2004 The McGraw-Hill Companies. Reproduced by permission of The McGraw-Hill Companies. Fig. 4.7, p 12a: From Santrock, *Child Development*, 11/e, Figure 5.11. Copyright © 2007 The McGraw-Hill Companies. Reproduced by permission of The McGraw-Hill Companies. Fig. 4.10, p 17a: From Santrock, *Child Development*, 11/e, Figure 5.23. Copyright © 2007 The McGraw-Hill Companies. Reproduced by permission of The McGraw-Hill Companies. Fig. 4.11, p 22a: From J. Kim (2006). *Obesity*, 14, 1107–1112. Reprinted by permission from Macmillan Publishers, Ltd. Fig. 4.12, p 23a: From Santrock, *Child Development*, 10/e, Figure 5.11. Copyright © 2004 The McGraw-Hill Companies. Reproduced by permission of The McGraw-Hill Companies. Fig. 4.15, p 37a: Reprinted from *Journal of Pediatrics*, Vol. 71, W.K. Frankenburg and J.B. Dobbs, "The Denver Development Screening Test" pp. 181–191. Copyright © 1967 with permission from Elsevier. Fig. 4.17A, p 46a: Adapted from "The Origin of Form Perception" by R.L. Frantz. Copyright © 1961 by Scientific American, Inc. Fig. 4.18 a and b, p 47a: From A. Slater, V. Morison, & M. Somers, 1988, "Orientation Discrimination and Cortical Functions in the Human Newborn," *Perception*, Vol. 17, pp. 597–602, Fig. 1 and Table 1. Reprinted by permission of Pion, Ltd. London. Fig. 4.20, p 50a: From Santrock, *Child Development*, 10/e, Figure 5.18. Copyright © 2004 The McGraw-Hill Companies. Reproduced by permission of The McGraw-Hill Companies. Fig. 4.21, p 53a: From B.I Bertenthal, M.R. Longo, and S. Kenny, "Phenomenal Permanence and the Development of Predictive Tracking in Infancy," 2007. *Child Development*, 78, p. 354. Reprinted by permission of John Wiley and Sons, Ltd.

Chapter 5

Fig. 5.3, p 14a: From R. Baillargeon & J. DeVoe, "Using the Violation of Expectations Method to Study Object Permanence in Infants," 1991, "Object Permanence in Young Children: Further Evidence," *Child Development*, 62, pp. 1227–1246. Reprinted by permission of John Wiley and Sons, Ltd. Fig. 5.4, p 19a: From K. Wynn (1992). *Nature*, 358, Fig. 1, p. 749. Reprinted by permission from Macmillan Publishers, Ltd. Fig. 5.7, p 28a: From *Learning and the Infant Mind* by Bauer, Table 1, p. 12. © by Amanda Woodward and Amy Needham. By permission of Oxford University Press, Inc. Fig. 5.11, p 32b: From DeLoache, Simcock, and Mecari, "Planes, Trains and Automobiles," *Developmental Psychology* 43:1579–1586. Copyright © 2007 by the American Psychological Association. Fig. 5.12, p 42a: From "The Rule Systems of Language," from S.L. Haight, *Language Overview*. Reprinted by permission. Fig. 5.14, p 45a: From Santrock, *A Topical Approach to Life Span Development*, 4/e, Figure 9.3. Copyright © 2008 The McGraw-Hill Companies. Reproduced by permission of The McGraw-Hill Companies. Fig. 5.15, p 47a: From Santrock, *Children*, 9/e, Figure 7.11. Copyright © 2007 The McGraw-Hill Companies. Reproduced by permission of The McGraw-Hill Companies. Fig. 5.16, p 48a: From Santrock, *A Topical Approach to Life-Span Development*, 4/e, Figure 10.2. Copyright © 2008 The McGraw-Hill Companies. Reproduced by permission of The McGraw-Hill Companies. Fig. 5.18, p 51a: From Hart & Risley (1995), *Meaningful Differences in the Everyday Experiences of Young American Children*, Baltimore: Paul H. Brookes Publishing Co. Reprinted by permission of Paul H. Brookes Publishing Co. TA 5.13, p 40a: FRANK & ERNEST: © Thaves/Dist. by United Feature Syndicate, Inc. Ch. 5, p 2–3: From J. Piaget, *The Origins of Intelligence*, pp. 27, 159, 225, 273, 339. Reprinted with permission by International Universities Press, Inc. and Taylor & Francis Books UK.

Chapter 6

Fig. 6.4, p 21a: From Santrock, *Life-Span Development*, 4/e. Copyright © 1999 The McGraw-Hill Companies. Reproduced by permission of The McGraw-Hill Companies. Fig. 6.7, p 32a: From van Ijzendoorn & Kroonenberg, 1988, "Cross Cultural Patterns of Attachment," *Child Development*, 59, 147–156. Adapted by permission of Blackwell Publishing. Fig. 6.8, p 37a: From Jay Belsky, "Early Human Experiences: A Family Perspective," in *Developmental Psychology*, Vol. 17,

pp. 3–23. Copyright © 1981 by the American Psychological Association. TA 6.8, p 16a: © Barbara Smaller/The New Yorker Collection/www.cartoonbank.com Fig 6.9, p 41a: Reproduced with permission from *Pediatrics*, Vol. 117, Pages 2055–2064, Copyright 2006 by the AAP.

Chapter 7

Fig. 7.4, p 19a: From Santrock, *Psychology*, 7/e. Copyright © 2003 The McGraw-Hill Companies. Reproduced by permission of The McGraw-Hill Companies. Fig. 7.5, p 20a: "The Symbolic Drawings of Young Children," reprinted courtesy of D. Wolf and J. Nove. Reprinted by permission of Dennie Palmer Wolf, Annenberg Institute, Brown University. Fig. 7.9 a and b, p 22a: Elena Bodrova, Deborah J. Leong. Fig. 7.11, p 32a: From Santrock, *Children*, 7/e. Copyright © 2003 The McGraw-Hill Companies. Reproduced by permission of The McGraw-Hill Companies. Fig. 7.15, p 41a: From U. Frith, 1989. *Autism: Explaining the Enigma*, p. 83. Reproduced with permission of Blackwell Publishing, Ltd. Fig. 7.17, p 47a: From Jean Berko, 1958, "The Child's Learning of English Morphology," in *Word*, Vol. 14, p. 154. Reprinted courtesy of Jean Berko Gleason. TA 7.10, p 20b: © Lee Lorenz/The New Yorker Collection/www.cartoonbank.com Ch. 7, p 510–511: From Bruck and Ceci, "The Suggestibility of Children's Memory" in *Annual Review of Psychology*, 50, pp. 429–430. Used with permission by M. Bruck.

Chapter 8

Fig. 8.1, p 22b: From Santrock, *Child Development*, 10/e, Figure 13.3. Copyright © 2004 The McGraw-Hill Companies. Reproduced by permission of The McGraw-Hill Companies. TA 8.12, p 21a: © Edward Koren/The New Yorker Collection/www.cartoonbank.com TA 8.14, p 25a: CALVIN AND HOBBES © Watterson. Dist. by UNIVERSAL UCLICK. Reprinted with permission. All rights reserved. TA 8.31, p 59a: © Martha F. Campbell/www.CartoonStock.com Ch. 8, p. 546–547: 3 pages of text From BURNING FENCE: A WESTERN MEMOUR OF FATHERHOOD Copyright © 2005 by Craig Lesley and reprinted by permission of St. Martin's Press, LLC.

Chapter 9

Fig. 9.1, p 6a: From Santrock, *Children*, 9/e, Figure 9.3. Copyright © 2007 The McGraw-Hill Companies. Reproduced by permission of The McGraw-Hill Companies. Fig. 9.5, p 19b: From Shaw et al. (2007). "Attention Deficit/Hyperactivity Disorder is Characterized by a Delay in Cortical Maturation," *Proceedings of the National Academy of Sciences*, Vol. 104, p. 19650, Fig. 2. Copyright © 2007 National Academy of Sciences, U.S.A. Used with permission. Fig. 9.10, p 32b: From *Children's Thinking: What Develops?* By M.T.H. Chi in F.S. Seigler. Copyright 1978 by Taylor & Francis Group LLC – Books. Reproduced with permission of Taylor & Francis Group LLC – Books in the format Textbook via Copyright Clearance Center. For e-book citation: use "Other Book" instead of "Textbook." Fig. 9.12, p 45a: Wechsler Intelligence Scale for Children, Fourth Edition (WISC-IV). Copyright © 2003 by NCS Pearson, Inc. Reproduced with permission. All rights reserved. "Weschsler Intelligence Scale for Children", "WISC" and "Raven's Progressive Matrices" are trademarks, in the US and/or other countries, of Pearson Education, Inc. or its affiliates(s). Fig. 9.14, p 51a: From "The Rise in IQ Scores from 1932 to 1997" from "The Increase in IQ Scores from 1932 to 1997," by Ulric Neisser. Reprinted by permission. Fig. 9.15, p 55a: *Raven's Progressive Matrices*. Copyright © 1998 by NCS Pearson, Inc. Reproduced with permission. All rights reserved. "Weschsler Intelligence Scale for Children", "WISC" and "Raven's Progressive Matrices" are trademarks, in the US and/or other countries, of Pearson Education, Inc. or its affiliates(s). TA 9.14, p 35b: © Sam Gross/The New Yorker Collection/www.cartoonbank.com TA 9.13, p 37a: ScienceCartoonsPlus.com TA 9.21, p 46a: © Donald Reilly/The New Yorker Collection/www.cartoonbank.com TA 9.23, p 55b: ScienceCartoonsPlus.com TA 9.28, p 64a: Peanuts: © United Feature Syndicate, Inc. TA 9.29, *BERKO GLEASON, JEAN, THE DEVELOPMENT OF LANGUAGE, 3rd*, © 1993. Printed and Electronically reproduced by permission of Pearson Education, Inc., Upper Saddle River, New Jersey.

Chapter 10

Fig. 10.2, p 14a: From Colby et al. "A Longitudinal Study of Moral Judgment," *Monographs of the Society for Research in Child Development*, Serial No. 201. Reprinted with permission of Blackwell Publishing. **Fig. 10.3, p 22b:** From Santrock, *A Topical Approach to Life-Span Development,* 3/e, Figure 12.4. Copyright © 2007 The McGraw-Hill Companies. Reproduced by permission of The McGraw-Hill Companies. **Fig. 10.4, p 24a:** Reproduced by special permission of the Publisher, Mind Garden, Inc., www.mindgarden.com from the Bem Sex Role Inventory by Sandra Bem. Copyright 1978, 1981 by consulting Psychologists Press, Inc. Further reproduction is prohibited without the Publisher's written consent. **Fig. 10.5, p 33b:** From Nansel et al., 2001, "Bullying Behaviors Among U.S. Youth," *Journal of the American Medical Association,* Vol. 285, pp. 2094–2100. **Fig. 10.6, p 45b:** From Stevenson et al., 1986, Figure 6, "Mathematics Achievement of Chinese, Japanese, and American Children," *Science* Vol. 231, pp. 693–699. Reprinted with permission from AAAS. **TA 10.14, p 22a:** © Joel Pett. Author rights reserved.

Chapter 11

Fig. 11.1, p 10a: From J.M. Tanner et al., "Standards from birth to Maturity for Height, Weight, Height Velocity: British Children in 1965" in *Archives of Diseases in Childhood* 41, 1966. With permission from BMJ Publishing Group. **Fig. 11.2, p 12a:** From A.F. Roache, "Secular Trends in Stature, Weight and Maturation," *Monographs of the Society for Research in Child Development,* n. 179. © Blackwell Publishing, Ltd. Used with permission. **Fig. 11.3, p 14a:** From R.B. Simmons, D.A. Blyth, and K.L. McKinney, "The Social and Psychological Effects of Puberty on White Females." In J. Brooks-Gunn & A.C. Petersen (eds.). *Girls at Puberty: Biological and Psychological Perspectives,* pp. 229–272, 1983. With the kind permission of Springer Science and Business Media. **Fig. 11.4, p 16a:** From Santrock, *Essentials of Life-Span Development,* 1/e. Copyright © 2008 The McGraw-Hill Companies. Reproduced by permission of The McGraw-Hill Companies. **Fig. 11.6, p 23a:** From Facts at a Glance: A fact sheet reporting national, state-level, and city-level trends in teen childbearing: Publication #2008-29 by Child Trends. Copyright 2008 by Child Trends Incorporated. Reproduced with permission of Child Trends Incorporated in the format Textbook via Copyright Clearance Center. For e-book citation: Use "Other Book" instead of "Textbook." **Fig. 11.10, p 37a:** From "Young Adolescents' Reports of Alcohol Use in the Family Matters Program," from K.E. Bauman, S.T. Ennett, et al., 2002, "Influence of a Family Program on Adolescent Smoking and Drinking Prevalence," *Prevention Science* 3, 2002, pp. 35–42. With kind permission of Springer Science and Business Media. **Fig. 11.8, p 32a:** From Santrock, *Adolescence,* 12/e, Figure 2.13. © 2008 The McGraw-Hill Companies. Reproduced by permission of The McGraw-Hill Companies. **Fig. 11.9, p 34a:** From Santrock, *Children,* 10/e, Figure 15.3. Copyright © 2004 The McGraw-Hill Companies. Reproduced by permission of The McGraw-Hill Companies. **TA 11.6, p 9a:** ZITS © ZITS PARTNERSHIP, KING FEATURES SYNDICATE **TA 11.22, p 42a:** © Edward Koren/The New Yorker Collection/www.cartoonbank.com

Chapter 12

Fig. 12.5, p 23a: From Santrock, *Child Development,* 11/e, Figure 16.4. Copyright © 2007 The McGraw-Hill Companies. Reproduced by permission of The McGraw-Hill Companies. **Fig. 12.8, p 48a:** From D.B. Goldston et al., "Cultural Considerations in Adolescent Suicide Prevention and Psychosocial Treatment" *American Psychologist,* 63, 14–31. Copyright © 2008 American Psychological Association.

Chapter 13

Fig. 13.1, p 9a: From The American College Health Association National College Health Assessment Spring 2007 Reference Group Date Report (abridged). *Journal of American College Health,* 56, Table 17, p. 478. Used with permission by American College Health Association. **Fig. 13.2, p 12a:** Reprinted from *Journal of Adolescent Health,* Vol. 39, M. Jane Park, et al., "The Health Status of Young Adults in the United States," pp. 305–317. Copyright © 2006, with permission from Elsevier. **Fig. 13.3, p 14b:** From Santrock, *Topical LifeSpan Development,* 6/e, Figure 4.12. Copyright © The McGraw-Hill Companies. Reproduced by permission of The McGraw-Hill Companies. **Fig. 13.4, p 17a:** From J. Kruger, H.M. Blanck, and C. Gillespie (2006). "Dietary and Physical Activity Behaviors Among Adults Successful at Weight Loss Management" *International Journal of Behavioral Nutrition and Physical Activity,* 3, 17. **Fig. 13.6, p 25a:** From *Sex in America* by John Gagnon. Copyright © 1994 by CSG Enterprises, Inc., Edward O. Laumann, Robert T. Michael, and Gina Kolata. By permission of Little, Brown & Company and Brockman, Inc. **Fig. 13.7, p 29a:** From Santrock, *Children,* 9/e, Figure 15.8. Copyright © 2007 The McGraw-Hill Companies. Used by permission of The McGraw-Hill Companies. **TA 13.8, p 14a:** www.CartoonStock.com **Fig. 13.9, p 39a:** From Santrock, *Adolescence,* 14/e, Figure 3.5. Copyright © The McGraw-Hill Companies. Reproduced by permission of The McGraw-Hill Companies. **TA 13.12, p 21a:** © Michael Shaw/The New Yorker Collection/www.cartoonbank.com **TA 13.19, p 45a:** © Joseph Farris/The New Yorker Collection/www.cartoonbank.com

Chapter 14

Fig. 14.1, p 7a: From *Developing Structure of Temperament and Personality from Infancy to Adulthood* by T.D. Wachs in C. Halverson, et al. Copyright 1994 by Taylor & Francis Group LLC – Books. Reproduced with permission by Taylor & Francis Group LLC – Books in the format Textbook via Copyright Clearance Center. For e-book citation: Use "Other Book" instead of "Textbook." **Fig. 14.3, p 23a:** From "Examples of Positive Changes in the Aftermath of a Romantic Breakup" by T. Tashiro & P. Frazier, 2003, "I'll Never Be in a Relationship Like That Again: Personal Growth Following Romantic Relationship Breakups," *Personal Relationships,* 10, after Table 1, p. 120. Reprinted by permission of John Wiley and Sons, Ltd. **Fig. 14.5, p 29a:** From Popenoe, David and Barbara DaFoe Whitehead. *The State of Our Unions: The Social Health of Marriage in America, 2005,* copyright 2005 by The National Projects at Rutgers University. **Fig. 14.8, p 40a:** Random House credit TBD **TA 14.5, p 13a:** DILBERT: © Scott Adams/Dist. By United Feature Syndicate, Inc. **TA 14.6, p 14a:** © Fran Orford, www.francartoons.com **TA 14.19, p 47a:** Copyright © Don Orehek – Reprinted by permission. **TA 14.20, p 49a:** (C) Barbara Smaller/The New Yorker Collection/www.cartoonbank.com **Ch. 14, p 895–896:** Excerpt from pp. 44–5 from *The Dance of Intimacy* by Harriet Goldhor Lerner. Copyright © 1989 by Harriet Goldhor Lerner. Reprinted by permission of HarperCollins Publishers. **Ch. 14, p 937–938:** From *For Better Or For Worse: Divorce Reconsidered* by E. Mavis Hetherington & John Kelly. Copyright © 2002 by E. Mavis Hetherington and John Kelly. Used by permission of W.W. Norton & Company, Inc.

Chapter 15

Fig. 15.1, p 13a: Adapted from *Newsweek,* "Health for Life," Special Section, Fall/Winter 2001. Copyright © Newsweek, Inc. All rights reserved. Used by permission and protected by the Copyright Laws of the United States. The printing, copying, redistribution, or retransmission of the Material without express written permission is prohibited. **Fig. 15.2, p 17a:** Adapted from *Newsweek,* "Health for Life," Special Section, Fall/Winter 2001. Copyright © Newsweek, Inc. All rights reserved. Used by permission and protected by the Copyright Laws of the United States. The printing, copying, redistribution, or retransmission of the Material without express written permission is prohibited. **Fig. 15.4, p 26a:** From *Sex in America* by Robert T. Michael, John H. Gagnon, Edward O. Laumann and Gina Kolata. Copyright © 1994 by CSG Enterprises, Inc. Edward O. Laumann, Robert T. Michael and Gina Kolata. By permission of Little, Brown and Company and Brockman, Inc. **Fig. 15.6, p 31a:** From *Developmental Influences on Adult Intelligence: The Seattle Longitudinal Study* by K.W. Schaie, Figure 5.7a, p. 127. By permission of Oxford University Press, Inc. **Fig. 15.7, p 31b:** From Santrock, *Life-Span Development,* 8/e. © The McGraw-Hill Companies. Reproduced by permission of The McGraw-Hill Companies. **TA 15.14, p 40a:** HAGAR © 1987 KING FEATURES SYNDICATE **Ch. 15, p 955–956:** From Jim Croce, "Time in a Bottle." Copyright © 1972, 1985 Denjac Music, Co. Reprinted with permission.

Chapter 16

Fig. 16.1, p 6a: From "Changes in Generativity and Identity Certainty from the 30s through the 50s," from Stewart, Osgrove and Helson, 2002, "Middle Aging in Women: Patterns of Personality Change from the 30s to the 50s," Fig. 3, *Journal of Adult Development,* Vol. 8, pp. 23–37. With kind permission of Springer Science and Business Media. **Fig. 16.2:** From "Items Used to Assess Generativity and Identity Certainty," from Steward, Osgrove & Helson, 2002, "Middle Aging in Women: Patterns of Personality Change from the 30s to the 50s, "Table II, *Journal of Adult Development,* Vol. 8, pp. 23–37. With kind permission of Springer Science and Business Media. **Fig. 16.3, p 10a:** From Santrock, *A Topical Approach to Life-Span Development,* 3/e, Figure 11.12. Copyright © 2007 The McGraw-Hill Companies. Reproduced by permission of The McGraw-Hill Companies. **Fig 16.4, p 10b:** From Nansel et al., 2001. "Bullying Behaviors Among U.S. Youth," *Journal of the American Medical Association,* Vol. 285, pp. 2094–2100. **Fig. 16.7, p 17a:** From "Individuals' Conceptions of the Right Age for Major Life Events and Achievements: Late 1950s and Late 1970s," from D.F. Hultsch and J.K. Plemons, "Life Events and Life Span Development" in *Life Span Development and Behavior,* Vol. 2, by P.B. Baltes and O.G Brun (eds.). **Fig. 16.8, p 21a:** From Santrock, *Psychology,* 7/3, Figure 12.11. Copyright © 2003 The McGraw-Hill Companies. Reproduced by permission of The McGraw-Hill Companies. **TA 16.8, p 31a:** DOONESBURY © 1991 G.B. Trudeau. Reprinted with permission of UNIVERSAL UCLICK. All rights reserved.

Chapter 17

Fig. 17.1, p 7a: From *The Psychology of Death, Dying and Bereavement,* by Richard Schultz. Copyright © 1978 The McGraw-Hill Companies. Reproduced by permission of The McGraw-Hill Companies. **Fig. 17.2, p 9a:** From *The Okinawa Diet Plan* by Bradley J. Willcox, M.D. and D. Craig Willcox, Ph.D., Makoto Suzuki, M.D. with Leah Feldon. Copyright © 2004 by Bradley J. Willcox and D. Craig Willcox. Used by permission of Clarkson Potter/Publishers, an imprint of the Crown Publishing Group, a division of Random House, Inc. **Fig. 17.8, p 25a:** Adapted from *Newsweek,* "Health for Life," Special Section, Fall/Winter 2001. Copyright © Newsweek, Inc. All rights reserved. Used by permission and protected by the Copyright Laws of the United States. The printing, copying, redistribution, or retransmission of the Material without express written permission is prohibited. **Fig. 17.14, p 36a:** From Partnerships for Solutions (2002). Baltimore: Johns Hopkins University. Used with permission by Dr. Gerard Anderson. **Fig. 17.16, p 40:** From "Age and the Consumption of Five or More Drinks on at Least One Day in the United States," from National Center for Health Statistics, 2002. **Fig. 17.21, p 53a:** From Santrock, *A Topical Approach to Life-Span Development,* 4/e. Copyright © 2008 The McGraw-Hill Companies. Reproduced by permission of The McGraw-Hill Companies.

Chapter 18

Fig. 18.1, p 5a: From S.C. Li et al., 2004, *Psychological Science,* 15, p. 158. Reprinted by permission of Sage Publications. **Fig. 18.6, p 35a:** From Santrock, *Topical LifeSpan Development,* 6/e, Figure 16.11. Copyright © The McGraw-Hill Companies. Reproduced by permission of The McGraw-Hill Companies. **Fig. 18.7, p 35b:** From Santrock, *Topical LifeSpan Development,* 6/e, Figure 16.12. Copyright © The McGraw-Hill Companies. Reproduced by permission of The McGraw-Hill Companies. **Fig. 18.8, p 38a:** From HSBC's The Future of Retirement Survey 2007. Reproduced with permission. **Fig. 18.9, p 45a:** Reprinted from *Alzheimer's & Dementia,* Vol. 5. Alzheimer's Association. Copyright © 2009 with permission from Elsevier. **TA 18.5, p 7a:** GARFIELD © 2001 Paws, Inc. Reprinted with permission of UNIVERSAL UCLICK. All rights reserved.

Chapter 19

Fig. 19.2, p 9a: From L. Carstensen, et al., "The Social Context of Emotion" in the *Annual Review of Gerontology and Geriatrics* by Schaie/Lawton, 1997, Vol. 17, p. 331. Copyright © 1997 by Springer Publishing Company. Adapted by permission of Springer Publishing Company, LLC, New York, NY 10036. **Fig. 19.3, p 11a:** From "Changes in Positive and Negative Emotion Across the Adult Years," from D. Mroczek and C.M. Kolarz, "The Effect of Age in Positive and Negative Affect" in *Journal of Personality and Social Psychology,* Vol. 75, pp. 1333–1349. Copyright © 1998 by the American Psychological Association. Reprinted by permission.

name index

Barkin, C., 410
Barlow, C. E., 554
Barnard, C., 422
Barnes, D., 575
Barnes, M., 457
Barnett, J. E., 295
Barnett, W. S., 222, 235, 237, 238, 270
Barnette, W. S., 237
Barollo, M., 547
Baron, C., 487
Baron, I. S., 97
Bar-on, N., 453, 454
Baron, N. S., 169
Baron-Cohen, S., 229, 290
Barr, R., 153
Barrett, A. E., 460
Barrett, D. E., 120
Barrett, T., 127
Barrett, T. M., 127
Barrios, V., 488
Barry, C. M., 339, 423
Barry, M. J., 220
Barry, R. A., 251
Barta, P., 329
Bartel, M. A., 59
Barth, T., 436
Bartha, R., 575
Bartholomew, A. N., 570, 571
Bartlett, J. D., 177, 178, 180, 183, 245, 395, 452, 453
Bartsch, K., 227
Baruch, B., 539
Baruth, M., 552
Basak, C., 575–576
Basaran, A., 64
Basaran, M., 64
Basinger, K. S., 325, 326
Baskin, F., 589
Basra, R., 94
Bassett, C. L., 8, 10, 18
Bassett, H. H., 247, 321
Bates, E., 186
Bates, G., 573
Bates, J. E., 181–184, 201, 257, 258, 363
Bates, T. C., 68
Bates, T. E., 452
Bateson, D. J., 456
Bauer, C. R., 85
Bauer, I., 597
Bauer, P., 295
Bauer, P. J., 155, 224, 225
Bauland, C. G., 64
Baum, A., 56, 490
Bauman, K. E., 372
Baumeister, R. F., 319, 320, 388, 502, 506
Bauml, K. H., 294
Baumrind, D., 70, 255, 256, 258
Baur, J. A., 553
Baur, K., 433
Bauserman, R., 264
Baxter, M. G., 31
Bay-Cheng, L. Y., 363
Bayley, N., 158, 159–160, 172
Beach, S. R. H., 468
Beall, S. A., 65
Beard, J. R., 616
Beardslee, M. R., 321
Bearinger, L. H., 366
Bearman, S. K., 360
Beauchamp, G., 136
Beauchet, O., 575
Beaulieu, D. A., 249
Beaver, K. M., 408
Bechtold, A. G., 136
Beck, C. T., 100
Beck, D. M., 226
Becker, J. T., 586
Beckson, M., 436
Bedford, R., 132, 188
Bedford, V. H., 523
Bednar, R. L., 320
Bedoya, F. J., 80
Beebe, B., 195
Beebe, D. W., 368
Beech, A. R., 436

Beecher, H. W., 470
Beeghly, M., 85, 177, 178, 180, 183, 245, 395, 452, 453
Beeston, D., 550, 609
Beets, M. W., 214
Begeer, S., 229
Begle, A. M., 588
Behne, T., 247
Behrendt, R., 329
Behrens, H., 307
Behrman, R., 282
Beilock, S. L., 330
Beins, B. C., 29
Bekman, N. M., 369, 370
Bekman, S., 265
Belfield, C. R., 237
Belizan, J. M., 97
Belk, C., 55
Bell, J. T., 68
Bell, K., 355
Bell, M. A., 15, 112, 114, 152, 177, 180, 223
Bell, R., 567
Bell, R. A., 607
Bell, R. D., 586
Bell, S. M., 180
Bellinger, D. C., 85
Bellmore, A., 268, 337
Bellucci, M., 283
Belon, K., 369
Belsky, J., 53, 194, 199, 202
Beltz, A. M., 433
Beltzer, N., 460
Bem, S. I., 331
Benbow, C. P., 329
Benbow, S. M., 550, 609
Bendersky, M., 130, 131
Benenson, J. F., 254
Benga, O., 321
Bengtson, V. L., 524, 526, 603
Bengtsson, H., 319
Benichov, J., 579
Bennett, D. A., 539, 554, 573, 603, 615
Bennett, K. M., 609, 637
Bennett, S. A., 83
Bennett, S. L., 195
Benoit, D., 259
Benoit, V., 552
Benokraitis, N., 461
Benowitz-Fredericks, C. A., 360, 372
Benson, B., 363
Benson, P. L., 357
Bentley, M. E., 120
Bentley, T., 260
Benton-Davis, S., 119
Benyamini, Y., 492
Benzeval, M., 489
Ben-Zur, H., 471, 639
Berenbaum, S. A., 251, 254, 326, 329, 331, 433
Berensen, J., 491
Berenson, J., 558
Berg, A. I., 13
Berg, O. R., 118
Bergen, D., 269, 271
Berger, A. T., 430
Berger, S. E., 122, 124, 125, 137, 188
Bergman, L. R., 500
Bergstrom-Lynch, C. A., 462
Berk, L., 271
Berk, L. E., 220
Berkeljon, A., 407
Berkman, N. D., 372
Berko, J., 230–231
Berko, J., 240
Berko Gleason, J., 161, 168–169, 230, 308
Berkowitz, M. W., 325
Berlau, D. J., 17
Berlin, L. J., 197, 198, 257, 333
Berlyne, D. E., 269
Berman, M. G., 224
Bernard, K., 66, 67, 192
Bernardes de Jesus, B., 541
Bernat, D. H., 366
Berndt, T. J., 339, 378
Berning, J., 117

Berninger, V., 287, 288
Berninger, V. W., 341
Bernstein, V. J., 192
Berookhim, B. M., 493
Berraho, M., 556
Berry, D., 71
Bers, M. U., 607
Berscheid, E., 457, 459
Bersick, M., 571
Bertenthal, B. I., 134
Bertenthal, B. L., 134
Bertrand, R., 486, 605
Berzonsky, M., 389
Beshgetoor, D., 117
Best, J. R., 283
Best, R. G., 82, 88
Beussman, D. J., 436
Beverly, 606
Bevis, L., 133
Beyene, Y., 492
Beyerlein, A., 85
Beyers, E., 457–458
Beyers, W., 357, 423
Bezilla, R., 590
Bhargavan, R., 605
Bhutta, Z. A., 491
Bialystok, E., 39, 310
Bian, Z., 548
Bianchi, D. W., 64
Biehle, S. N., 194
Bielak, A. A. M., 576
Bienas, J. L., 603
Bierman, K. L., 294, 336, 339
Bifari, F., 544
Bigagli, E., 557
Bigby, C., 587
Bigelow, A. E., 187, 192, 195
Bigelow, J. H., 238
Biggs, S., 599, 615
Bigham, S., 229
Biglan, C. W., 490
Bigler, R. S., 253, 329, 331
Bihagi, S. W., 71
Binderman, C. D., 626
Binet, A., 299
Birch, R., 133
Birditt, K., 522
Birditt, K. S., 13, 525, 526, 610–612, 615, 640
Biringen, Z., 263, 264
Birman, B. F., 341
Biro, F. M., 31, 358, 359
Birren, J. E., 583
Bisceglia, R., 193
Bischof, G. N., 8, 15, 575
Bishop, D. V., 60
Bisiacchi, P. S., 571
Bisley, J., 153
Bittar, R. E., 96
Bjorkeenstam, E., 639
Bjorklund, D. F., 53, 376
Black, J. S., 627
Black, M. M., 85, 117, 213
Blackwell, L. S., 346
Blaga, O. M., 159
Blagosklonny, M. V., 556
Blair, B. L., 397
Blair, C., 248, 294, 299
Blair, M., 294
Blair, S. N., 554, 556
Blake, L. P., 392, 424
Blake, W., 179, 269
Blakemore, J. E. O., 251, 254, 326, 329, 331
Blakemore, S. J., 15, 114, 181, 193, 361
Blakey, J., 93
Blanck, H. M., 428
Bland, M. W., 429
Bland, P., 585
Bland, R. M., 110
Blandthorn, J., 86
Blankenship, L., 365
Blanker, M. H., 627
Blaxter, L., 634
Blazer, D. G., 503, 553, 584, 585
Blewitt, R., 605

Blieszner, R., 20, 458, 520, 523, 524, 526, 608, 612
Bliss, D., 633
Block, J., 167, 453
Block, S. D., 635
Bloom, B., 306
Bloom, L., 164
Bloom, P., 228
Bloomer, R. J., 556
Bloor, C., 554
Blosser, C., 111, 210, 211, 282
Blossfeld, H-P., 500
Blue, J. H., 359
Bluhm, B., 213
Blumstein, T., 492
Blyth, D. A., 360
Bobby, P., 119
Bobkowski, P. S., 271
Bode, P., 10, 266, 303, 343
Bodrova, E., 222, 299
Boelen, P. A., 636, 637
Boerner, K., 637
Bogg, T., 602–603
Bogner, K., 298
Bohlin, G., 181, 192, 453
Boiter, C., 501
Boivan, M., 232
Boivin, M., 339
Bol, N., 610
Bolding, A., 94
Bolkan, C., 604, 605
Bolton, T. A., 121
Boltri, J. M., 367
Bomba, P. A., 627
Bonazzo, C., 20
Bonde, J. P., 85
Bonjour, J. P., 552
Booker, J. A., 248
Boor, M. E., 546
Booth, A., 156, 264
Booth, M., 401
Booth-LaForce, C., 180, 268
Bor, W., 342, 407
Borchert, J., 133
Borders, A., 253
Borgland, S. L., 431
Bornstein, M. H., 133, 137, 145, 152, 395, 397
Bornstein, N., 546
Boron, J. B., 576
Borup, L., 94
Borzekowski, D. L., 360, 372
Bos, C. S., 287
Bosl, W., 229
Bosman, E. A., 548
Bosworth, B., 583
Bosworth, H. B., 540, 554, 605, 615
Botkin, D., 259
Botwinick, J., 18
Bouazzaoui, B., 544–555, 578
Bouchard, T. J., 51, 52
Boucher, J., 229
Boulton-Lewis, G., 632
Boutot, E. A., 290
Boutskikou, T., 365
Bowe, S., 590
Bowen, C. E., 581
Bower, T. G. R., 133
Bowker, J. C., 268, 337
Bowlby, J., 26, 179, 180, 189, 190, 192, 202, 203
Bowles, J., 58
Bowman, G. L., 575
Bowman, N. A., 424
Boxer, P., 335
Boyd, L., 116, 117
Boyd, M., 361
Boyer, K., 155
Boyko, V., 492
Boyle, J., 212
Boyle, P. A., 539, 554, 573, 615
Bozon, M., 460
Braak, H., 497
Brabyn, J. A., 547
Bradbury, T. N., 462
Bradley, R. E., 605

Bradley, R. H., 368
Bradshaw, C. P., 338
Brady, M., 111, 210, 211, 282
Brainerd, C. J., 295
Bralic, I., 360
Brand, M., 542, 573
Branje, S. J. T., 391
Brann, D., 537
Bransford, J., 341
Brassard, A., 455
Brassen, S., 568
Braungart-Rieker, J. M., 247
Braveman, P., 363
Braver, S., 263, 264
Braver, S. L., 264
Brazelton, T. B., 95, 98, 103, 120, 121
Brechwald, W. A., 339
Brecklin, L. R., 436
Bredekamp, S., 235
Brehmer, Y., 569, 576
Breinlinger, K., 150
Breitbart, W. S., 633
Brember, I., 319
Bremner, J. G., 133–134, 136, 137
Brendgen, M., 408
Brent, D. A., 408–409
Brent, R. L., 83, 86
Bresette, L. M., 440
Breslau, J., 465
Bretherton, I., 180, 191, 333
Brewer, K. B., 407
Bridges, J. S., 525
Bril, B., 125
Brim, G., 485, 512
Brim, O., 494, 501, 521
Brin, S., 234
Brindis, C. D., 363, 409, 426
Brion, M., 117
Brion, S. L., 502
Brisch, K. H., 191, 395
Britto, P. R., 12
Britton, H. L., 119
Britton, J., 85
Britton, J. R., 119
Brkic, S., 430
Broadbent, K. G., 117
Broadus, I., 612
Brocardo, P. S., 84
Brocki, K. C., 192
Brockmeyer, S., 526
Brock-Utne, J. G., 486
Brockwell, S., 494
Broderick, J. E., 18, 599
Broderick, R., 423
Brodsky, J. L., 121
Brodsky, N. L., 85
Brody, G. H., 391
Brody, N., 301, 303
Brody, R. M., 433
Brody, S., 433
Brodzinsky, D. M., 65–67
Broekhuizen, L. N., 488
Bromley, D., 318
Brondolo, E., 613
Bronfenbrenner, U., 27, 28, 41, 43, 215, 265,
    331, 515
Bronstein, P., 253
Brook, D. W., 396
Brook, J. S., 396
Brooker, R. J., 58
Brooks, J. G., 296
Brooks, M. G., 296
Brooks, R., 154
Brooks-Gunn, J., 13, 168, 185, 197, 236, 257, 262,
    303, 342, 357, 359, 360, 363, 366, 403, 407
Brophy-Herb, H., 121
Brotman, L. M., 285
Broughton, J., 164
Brower, K. J., 212, 369
Brown, A., 118
Brown, B. B., 266, 268, 398–399, 401, 612, 640
Brown, C. A., 134
Brown, D., 161
Brown, J. D., 271
Brown, J. K., 516

Brown, J. L., 363, 605
Brown, J. V., 101
Brown, K. W., 83
Brown, L., 629
Brown, L. D., 194
Brown, L. K., 407
Brown, L. M., 427
Brown, L. S., 434
Brown, M. J., 466
Brown, R., 166, 168
Brown, S., 612
Brown, S. A., 369, 370
Brown, S. L., 609, 612, 639
Brown, W. H., 214
Brownawell, A. M., 577
Brownell, C. A., 178, 188
Brownley, K. A., 372
Broyles, S. T., 368
Bruce, A., 625
Bruchmiller, K., 288
Bruck, M., 225, 226
Bruine de Bruin, W., 631
Bruk, A., 167
Brumariu, L. E., 333–334
Brummett, B. H., 554, 605, 615
Brun, C., 486
Brune, M., 53
Brunton, P. J., 88
Bryan, C., 177, 179
Bryant, A. L., 429, 430
Bryant, C., 492
Bryant, D. P., 287
Bryant, J. A., 272
Bryant, P. E., 227
Bryant, W. C., 632
Brynes, J. P., 361, 374, 375
Bryom, S., 91
Brysbaert, M., 112
Bub, K., 200
Bub, K. L., 198
Buchanan, A., 525
Buchanan, S. L., 92
Buchman, A. S., 539, 554, 573, 615
Buchner, A., 567
Buck, M., 195, 196
Buckner, J. C., 321
Buckner, R. K., 497
Bucur, B., 568, 570, 574
Buder, E. H., 163
Budner, R., 484
Buehler, C., 397
Buffett, W., 616
Bugalho, P., 587
Bugental, D., 253
Bugental, D. B., 249
Bugg, J. M., 555, 570–571, 575, 577, 578
Bugyi, P., 464
Buhimschi, C., 92
Buhl, H. M., 422–423
Buhler, E., 289
Buhrmester, D., 268, 397
Buhs, E., 336
Buijus, D., 112
Buitenweg, J. I., 577
Bukowski, R., 88
Bukowski, W., 253, 268, 335, 336, 339
Bulanda, J. R., 609
Bulik, C. M., 360–361, 372
Bull, J. H., 628
Bullock, C. M., 436
Bulock, L. A., 527
Bumpass, L., 461, 526
Bumpus, M. F., 395
Bundick, M. J., 443
Buonocore, D., 487
Burack, J. A., 152
Burchinal, M., 199, 304
Burd, L., 84
Burdette, A. M., 613
Burgard, S. A., 485
Burgard, S.A., 556
Burger, S. G., 606
Burgess-Champoux, T. L., 367
Buriel, R., 38, 39, 403
Buring, J. E., 554

Burke, D. M., 579
Burke, H. M., 546, 552
Burke, J. D., 406
Burkey, L. C., 30, 309
Burks, A. W., 118
Burlingame, S., 322
Burman, I., 98
Burnham, D., 135
Burnham, E., 634
Burns, C., 111, 210, 211, 282
Burns, E., 94
Burr, J., 612
Burraston, B., 407
Bursch, H. C., 587
Burstyn, I., 85
Burt, K., 13
Burt, K. B., 423
Burton, R., 53
Burts, D. C., 235
Busch, H., 510
Busch-Rossnagel, N. A., 605
Bushel, P. R., 59
Bushman, B. J., 389
Bushnell, E. W., 136
Bushnell, I. W. R., 132
Businaro, R., 586
Buss, D. M., 20, 21, 53, 252, 457, 463
Buss, K. A., 181
Busse, E. W., 584
Bussey, K., 253
Butcher, H. K., 587
Butler, R., 596
Butler, R. N., 596
Butler, R. N., 550
Butler, Y. G., 310
Butrica, B. A., 583, 609
Butterfill, C., 127
Butterworth, G., 154
Butterworth, P., 521
Buzhardt, J., 198
Buzi, R. S., 366
Buzwell, S., 362
Bynner, J. M., 423
Byrd-Bredbenner, C., 117
Byrne, S. M., 373
Bytschkow, K., 430
Bytschkow, K. M., 430

Caban-Holt, A., 568
Cabassa, L. J., 409
Cabesa, R., 578
Cabeza, R., 544–545, 578
Cabrera, N. J., 196
Caccioppo, J. T., 612
Cacho, I., 548
Cacioppo, J. T., 612
Caddy, S. C., 87
Caeymaex, L., 637
Cahill, K., 85
Cahral, H., 85
Cai, Q., 112
Cain, V. S., 494
Cairney, J., 368
Cairns, A., 212
Caldwell, K. A., 339
Caldwell, S., 32
Calenda, E., 117
Caliari, L., 60
Calkins, S. D., 15, 112, 152, 177, 180, 248
Callahan, D., 641
Callahan, M. A., 30
Calment, J. L., 540
Caltran, G., 179
Camburn, D., 362
Cameron, C. A., 246
Cameron, J. M., 430
Campbell, B., 301
Campbell, C. S., 628
Campbell, F. A., 304
Campbell, I. G., 113, 568
Campbell, J. D., 319, 320
Campbell, L., 301
Campbell, W. K., 389
Campos, J., 178, 190, 322
Campos, J. J., 134, 177–179

Campos-Ferraz, P. L., 285
Camras, L. A., 178, 322
Canale, R. E., 556
Candow, D. G., 554
Canfield, J., 566
Canfield, R. L., 150
Canitano, N., 586
Cansino, S., 547
Capozzoli, M. C., 153
Cappa, S. F., 544–555
Cappeliez, P., 597
Carabello, R. J., 546–547
Caravita, C. S., 335, 336
Carey, S., 148–150, 374
Carl, J. D., 470
Carling-Jenkins, R., 587
Carlisle, J., 287
Carlson, C. D., 232
Carlson, E., 191
Carlson, E. A., 191–192, 453
Carlson, M. C., 612
Carlson, S. M., 226, 229, 248, 298
Carlson, W., 408
Carlsson, A. C., 557
Carlstrom, E., 433
Carlton, M. P., 220
Carmichael, O., 578
Carnethon, M. R., 489
Carpendale, J. I., 228
Carpenter, J., 154
Carpenter, M., 154, 167, 247, 250
Carr, A., 501
Carr, D., 625, 626, 628, 633, 638
Carr, R., 372
Carriere, J. S., 568
Carrington, H., 178
Carroll, A. E., 338
Carroll, D., 489
Carroll, D. J., 229
Carroll, J. L., 366
Carroll, J. S., 423
Carroll, L., 389
Carroll, M., 285
Carroll, M. D., 367
Carskadon, M. A., 369
Carstensen, L. L., 15, 18, 19, 598–600, 603,
    610–612, 615
Carta, J. J., 198
Cartwright, K. B., 439, 440
Cartwright, R., 116
Caruthers, A., 362
Carver, C. S., 491, 518
Carver, K., 400
Carver, L. J., 155
Casale, M., 366, 487
Casals, P., 566
Casco, C., 547
Case, C. L., 55
Case, R., 293
Casella, R., 283
Caselli, R. J., 586
Caserta, M., 639
Caserta, M. S., 635
Casey, B. J., 211, 376
Cash, J. E., 387, 388
Caspers, K. M., 71, 455
Caspi, A., 71, 388, 453, 520
Cassidy, J., 20, 395
Cassiman, S. A., 13
Castle, J., 66
Castle, N. G., 558
Castonquay, T. W., 427
Castro, J., 371
Catalano, R. F., 367, 370
Catania, J., 550
Catenacci, V. A., 428
Cavanagh, S. E., 361
Cavanaugh, M. M., 490, 542, 545
Cavanna, A. E., 543
Caviola, S., 294
Cawthon, R., 541
Ceci, S. J., 225, 226, 302
Cen, G., 183
Cereatti, L., 283
Cernin, P. A., 574

Dzewaltowski, D., 214
Dziegielewska, K. M., 79

Eagly, A., 252
Eagly, A. H., 252, 330, 331
Earhart, G. M., 587
Early, D. R., 265
Easterbrooks, M. A., 177, 178, 180, 183, 245, 395, 452, 453
Eastwick, P. W., 457
Eaton, D. K., 362, 363, 368, 369, 409
Eaton, N. R., 72, 538
eaver, J., 588
Ebel, B., 285
Ebstein, R. P., 193
Eccles, J. S., 333, 357, 378–379, 381
Echevarria, J. J., 310
Eckenrode, J., 90
Eckerman, C., 187–188
Eckert, G. P., 542
Eckert, M. A., 570
Eckmann, J., 542
Edelman, M. W., 12
Eden, G. F., 283
Edgington, C., 400
Edison, T., 440
Edler, D. E., 115
Edmonds, G., 389, 520
Edmondson, R., 640–641
Edmunds, L. S., 121
Edwards, J. D., 576, 577
Edwards, M. C., 355
Edwardson, C. L., 283
Efron, D., 288
Egan, S. K., 251
Egeland, B., 191
Egger, M., 100
Eggers, D., 421, 422
Eggum, N. D., 331
Egizio, V., 490
Egli, T., 429
Egloff, B., 517–518
Ehnes, J., 606
Ehrlich, B., 550
Eibach, R. P., 470
Eichorn, D., 426
Eichorn, D. H., 518
Eid, M., 513
Eiferman, R. R., 271
Einarsen, S., 437
Einav, S., 339
Einstein, A., 29
Einstein, F. H., 71
Einstein, G. O., 570–571
Eisel, S., 498, 569
Eisenberg, M. E., 366
Eisenberg, N., 327, 331
Eisenstein, J., 257
Eisikovits, Z., 588
Elashi, F. B., 246, 319
Elasy, T., 119
El-Bache, R. S., 542
Elbel, B., 213
Elbert, T., 497
Elbourne, P., 162
Elder, G. H., 610
El-Dib, M., 95
Eldreth, D. A., 543
El Haj, M., 569, 570
Elias, M. F., 554, 605, 615
Eliasieh, K., 544
Elison, J. T., 132
Elkind, D., 218, 321, 375, 383
Elkun, D., 271
Elliott, B., 626
Elliott, E. M., 570
Elliott, G. R., 356
Elliott, S. N., 341
Elliott, W. J., 488, 550
Ellis, A. B., 330
Ellis, B. J., 359
Ellis, L., 246
Elsabbagh, M., 229
El-Sakka, A. I., 492
Else, L. J., 79

Else-Quest, N., 253, 265, 330, 474
El-Sheikh, M., 263
El-Sohemy, A., 557
Ely, R., 308
Emerson, M. R., 400
Emerson, R. W., 161, 375
Emery, C. F., 488, 490, 549
Emery, R. E., 371
Emes, R. D., 113
Emmons, R. A., 18
Enders, C. K., 502
England, D., 253
English, G. W., 12
Engvig, A., 577
Eninger, L., 192
Ennett, S. T., 372
Enns, J. T., 152
Ensor, R., 247
Enz, B. J., 168, 233
Epis, R., 543
Epps, S. R., 342
Epstein, D., 237
Epstein, J. N., 85
Epstein, M., 362
Erath, S. A., 263, 363
Erbs, S., 555
Erickson, K., 97
Erickson, K. I., 543–544, 555, 578
Ericson, N., 339
Ericsson, K. A., 306
Erikson, E. H., 22, 23, 28, 31, 41, 43, 185, 186, 189, 201, 245, 269, 273, 317, 321, 348, 387, 389–391, 413, 457–459, 475, 480, 510, 511, 529, 591, 594, 596, 597, 602, 617, 642
Erikson, J., 22, 597
Eriksson, U. J., 87
Erixon-Lindroth, N., 497
Ernst, E., 85
Eron, L. D., 335
Eschuzur, J., 37
Escobar-Chaves, S. L., 272
Esther, R. R., 549
Estigarribia, B., 60
Estrada, S., 377
Etaugh, C., 525
Ethington, C. A., 163
Ettekal, I., 268, 335
Evaldsson, A-C., 209
Evangelista, L. S., 607
Evans, A. N., 487
Evans, D. A., 603
Evans, G. D., 492
Evans, G. W., 12, 267
Evans, J. R., 487
Evans, W. D., 11
Evans, W. J., 546
Evenson, K. R., 89, 639
Everett, C. J., 556
Evers, C., 54
Eviatar, Z., 112
Ewen, D., 235
Eymard, A. S., 559
Ezell, G., 213

Fabbri, R., 285
Fabes, R. A., 253
Fabiani, M., 572
Fabiano, G. A., 289
Fabricius, W. V., 264
Fagan, A. A., 407
Fagan, J. F., 159, 160, 172
Fagot, B. I., 253
Fahey, T. D., 428, 429
Faith, M. S., 285
Fakhoury, J., 541
Falbo, T., 262
Falck-Yttere, T., 132
Falk, M. C., 577
Fall, A. M., 380
Fancy, S. P. J., 112–113
Fantz, R. L., 130, 133, 140
Fargas, G., 197, 198
Farias, S. T., 546

Farkas, G., 11, 236
Farley, F., 377
Farley-Hackel, P., 623
Farney, T. M., 556
Faroogi, A., 97
Farr, R. H., 264
Farrell, M. P., 512
Farrell, S. K., 581
Farrell, S. W., 554
Farrow, C. V., 213
Fasig, L., 186
Fassino, S., 373
Fatusi, A. O., 426
Fauci, J., 628
Faulkner, G., 429
Faulkner, G. E., 368
Fauth, R. C., 236
Fava, J. L., 428
Fava, N. M., 363
Faveault, M. M., 465
Fay, S., 544–555, 578
Fayard, J. V., 520
Fecho, K., 92
Federmeier, K. D., 580
Fedoravicius, N., 409
Feeney, S., 234, 237, 269
Fees, B., 214
Feijo, L., 98
Feil, R., 71
Fein, S. B., 116
Feinberg, I., 113, 568
Feinberg, M., 194
Feinberg, M. E., 371
Feinglass, J., 18
Feingold, E., 88
Feinstein, E. E., 357, 371
Feiring, C., 191, 453
Feldman, D. H., 223
Feldman, L., 17, 538–540
Feldman, R., 193, 195
Feldman, S., 362
Feldman, S. S., 356, 363
Feldon, J. M., 2003, 635
Feng, L., 585
Fenning, R. M., 248
Ferber, T., 357
Ferguson, D. M., 119
Ferguson, M., 559
Fernandez, A. F., 553
Fernandez, M. E., 363
Fernandez-Martinez, F. J., 64
Ferrari, M., 573
Ferraro, K. F., 551
Ferreira, J. A., 271
Ferreira Lima, R. M., 542
Ferreiro, E., 586
Ferrie, J. E., 489
Ferriero, D., 111
Ferris, J., 260
Feve, J., 587
Field, A. E., 368
Field, D., 526
Field, T., 98
Field, T. M., 89
Field, T. M., 85, 89, 94, 98, 100, 133, 135, 150, 153
Fielding, R. A., 546–547
Figueiredo, B., 94, 95
Figueredo, V. M., 488
Finch, C. E., 497, 542, 567
Fincham, F. D., 432, 468
Fine, M., 334
Finger, B., 192
Fingeret, L., 298
Fingerman, K., 522
Fingerman, K. L., 522, 525–527, 610, 612
Finkel, E. J., 457
Finkelstein, E. A., 427
Finkelstein, L. M., 581
Fiori, K. L., 611
Firth, K. M. P., 514
Fisch, R. O., 101, 135
Fischer, K. W., 439
Fischer, L., 88

Fischhoff, B., 375, 631
Fisette, J. L., 213, 283
Fisher, B. S., 437
Fisher, C., 231
Fisher, C. B., 605
Fisher, D., 436
Fisher, H. L., 338
Fisher, P. A., 260
Fiske, A., 584, 585
Fitelson, E. M., 88
Fitzgerald, S. J., 554
Fitzmaurice, G. M., 118
Fitzpatrick, K. K., 371
Fivush, R., 155, 224, 225
Fjell, A. M., 543
Flack, W. F., 436
Flanagan, C., 381
Flavell, E., 227
Flavell, E. R., 227, 228
Flavell, J., 227, 293
Flavell, J. H., 227, 228, 298
Flegal, K. E., 570, 579
Flegal, K. M., 367
Fleming, A. S., 193
Fletcher, B. R., 497, 577
Fletcher, J. M., 232
Flicker, L., 556
Flicker, S., 366
Flint, M. S., 56
Flint-Wagner, H. G., 552
Flom, R., 154
Flook, L., 465
Flores, E., 363
Florsheim, P., 400
Flory, M. J., 158
Flouri, E., 525
Flowers, D. L., 283
Flynn, J., 302, 314
Flynn, J. R., 302
Focarelli, A., 487
Foehr, U. G., 271, 404
Fogel, A., 159
Foley, J. T., 214
Folsom, D. P., 583
Fonagy, P., 193
Fontana, L., 556
Fontenot, H. B., 67
Foong, N., 572
Foorman, B. R., 232
Forbes, S. C., 554
Forcella, R., 61
Ford, L., 246
Ford, R. M., 229
Forget-Dubois, N., 232
Forster, D. A., 86
Forsyth, A. L., 552
Forte, T., 444
Forzano, L. B., 29
Fosco, G. M., 407
Foshee, V. A., 372
Foster, E. M., 410
Foster, H., 360
Foster, J. D., 389
Foster, K. J., 330–331
Foster, S. E., 357, 371
Foster, W., 366
Fowler, C. D., 585
Fowler, C. G., 487, 548
Fox, B. J., 308, 309
Fox, M. K., 118, 213
Fox, N. A., 114, 152
Fozard, J. L., 550
Fraga, M. F., 71, 553
Fraiberg, S., 128
Frances, A. L., 295
Franchak, J. M., 131
Francis, D. J., 232
Francis, J., 391
Francisco, P., 119
Franco, D. L., 426
Franco, P., 116, 117
Frank, G. K. W., 373
Frank, J. L., 407
Frank, J. W., 12, 357
Frank, M. C., 132–133

McAuley, P. A., 556
McBean, A. M., 589
McBride-Chang, C., 232–233
McBurney, W., 537
McCabe, D. P., 498
McCabe, K., 266
McCaffery, K. J., 456
McCall, L. E., 295
McCarthy, M. R., 342
McCartney, K., 71, 191, 198, 199
McCartney, T. W., 200
McCauley, J. L., 436
McClain, C. S., 633
McClay, J. L., 408
McClearn, G. E., 183
McClellan, M. D. 2004, 595
McClelland, K., 58
McClelland, S. I., 362, 363
McCormack, L. A., 285
McCormack, T., 127
McCormick, C. B., 293, 298
McCourt, J., 623
McCourt, R., 623
McCourt, S. N., 411
McCoy, D. C., 248
McCrae, R. R., 512, 517, 530
McCullough, M. E., 502, 633
McCutcheon, V. V., 430
McDaniel, B., 327
McDaniel, M. A., 570–571
McDermott, B. M., 322
McDevitt, J., 429
McDonald, J., 612
McDonald, P. V., 127
McDonald, S., 65
McDonald, S. D., 65
McDonald, S. M., 558
McDonough, J. E., 606
McDonough, L., 156, 157
McDougall, S., 607
McDowell, M. A., 285
McElhaney, K. B., 395
McElwain, N. L., 180
McEvoy, C. L., 498, 569
McEvoy, M., 590
McFall, G. P., 566, 615
McGarry, J., 100
McGeary, J. E., 578
McGee, L. M., 232
McGee, T. R., 407
McGettigan, C., 112
McGillivray, G., 62
McGinley, M., 251
McGinty, A. S., 168
McGlinchey, R. E., 575
McGrath, S. K., 101
McGue, M., 52, 392
McGuffin, P., 68, 183
McGuire, B. A., 58
McHale, J., 258
McHale, S., 253, 263
McHale, S. M., 258, 395, 523
McIntosh, A. R., 578
McIntosh, C. G., 116
McIntosh, C. N., 342
McIntosh, E., 513
McIsaac, C., 399, 400
McKain, W. C. 1972, 609
McKelley, R. A., 196
McKelvie, R. S., 488
McKenna, K. Y. A., 457
McKenzie, B. E., 133
McKeon, C. A., 30
McKeon, C. A., 309
McKinney, E., 118
McKnight, A. J., 568
McKnight, J. R., 87
McKnight A. S., 568
McLachlan, H., 627
McLaughlin, K., 629
McLaughlin, K. A., 114
McLean, N., 373
McLellan, J. A., 394
McLeod, S., 285, 286
McLeskey, J. M., 290

McLoyd, V. C., 11, 343, 403
McLoyd, V. C., 257
McIver, K. L., 214
McMahon, E. M., 410
McMunn, A., 612
McNamara, F., 117
McNeil, D. A., 89
McNeill, K., 298
McNeill, K. L., 297–298
McNulty, J. K., 436, 457
McRae, K., 321
McRitchie, S. L., 368
McWilliams, L. A., 455
Meacham, J., 246
Meade, C. S., 364
Meador, K. G., 503
Meadows, S. O., 464
Meancker, F., 96
Meaney, M. J., 71
Measelle, J., 194, 195
Mechakra-Tahiri, S. D., 639, 640
Medina, L., 89
Mednick, S. A., 60
Meeks, S., 632
Meerlo, P., 99
Meeus, W. H. H., 391
Mehari, A., 61
Mehl, M. R., 473
Mehta, J. S., 487
Meiksins, P., 485
Meints, J., 520
Melhuish, E., 200
Melkevik, O., 194
Mellstrom, D., 88
Melton, B. F., 429
Meltzi, G., 308
Meltzoff, A. N., 150, 154–156, 171, 188, 329
Melzi, G., 195
Melzoff, A. N., 154, 156
Memari, A., 289
Menacker, F., 91–92
Menchola, M., 599
Mendelsohn, A. L., 255, 303
Mendes de Leon, C. F., 603
Mendez, M. A., 290
Mendle, J., 410
Menendez, S., 194
Menn, L., 131, 163, 230
Mennella, J. A., 136
Menon, M., 319
Menon, R., 79
Menon, V., 288
Menyuk, P., 164
Menzer, M., 268, 337
Mepham, S. O., 110
Mercy, J. A., 215
Meredith, N. V., 210
Merewood, A., 119
Merline, A. C., 429, 430
Merrill, D. A., 497
Merrill, D. M., 522, 526
Merrill, J. E., 430
Merriwether, A., 362
Mesman, J., 187
Messersmith, E. E., 371
Messiah, S. E., 85
Messier, C., 575
Metcalfe, J., 298
Metha, A., 341
Meyer, A. M., 580
Meyer, J., 607
Meyer, M. H., 614
Meyer, R. A., 369, 370
Meyer, S., 246, 248
Meyer, S. C., 251
Meyer, S. L., 94
Meyers, J., 338
Mezzacappa, E., 321
Michael, R. T., 432, 433, 493
Mickelson, K. D., 194
Midthassel, U. V., 338–339
Miga, E. M., 395
Miguel, R., 587
Mikami, A. Y., 405
Mikels, J. A., 599

Miki, T., 58, 62, 538
Mikulincer, M., 453–455
Milani, R. V., 555
Milberg, A., 637
Milberg, W. P., 575
Milburn, N. G., 410
Mill, J., 59
Miller, A., 237
Miller, A. M., 368, 371
Miller, B. C., 363
Miller, C., 13
Miller, C. F., 329
Miller, D. I., 575
Miller, G., 12, 267
Miller, G. T., 58
Miller, J., 326
Miller, J. B., 473–474
Miller, J. C., 549
Miller, J. G., 115
Miller, K. G., 559
Miller, L., 522
Miller, L. M., 607
Miller, M., 288–289
Miller, P. H., 23, 228, 375
Miller, R., 457, 636
Miller, R. A., 542
Miller, S., 411
Miller, T. L., 85
Miller-Johnson, S., 304
Milleron, B., 62
Miller-Perrin, C. L., 260
Mills, B., 377
Mills, C. M., 246, 319
Mills-Koonce, W. R., 181
Millstein, S. G., 375, 631
Milne, E., 89
Milner, C., 605
Milner, J., 605
Miltenberger, R. G., 25
Minaya-Rowe, L., 311
Mincic, M. M., 247
Minde, K., 97
Mindel, C. H., 11, 38, 266, 403
Mindell, J., 212
Mindell, J. A., 116
Miner, J. L., 197
Ming, L., 65
Minguez-Milio, J. A., 93
Miniussi, C., 544–545, 578
Minkler, M., 525
Minlussi, C., 544–555
Minnes, S., 85
Minor, R. K., 556
Miotto, E. C., 569
Mirfaxeli, F., 289
Mirman, J. H., 369
Mischel, W., 26
Mishra, G. D., 491
Mitchell, B. A., 521
Mitchell, D., 436
Mitchell, E. A., 117
Mitchell, O. S., 500
Mitchell, R. B., 117
Mitchell, V., 515
Mitchell, W., 198
Miura, M., 64
Miyake, K., 190, 398
Mize, K. D., 183
Moak, G. S., 589
Mock, S. E., 470
Moe, G., 117
Moen, P., 442–445, 485, 499–500, 582, 583
Moffitt, T. E., 71, 388, 453
Mogi, K., 193
Mohan, L., 298
Mok, A., 266
Molina, R. C., 365
Mollard, R. C., 283
Moller, J., 639
Molock, S. D., 409, 410
Monahan, C. J., 426–427
Monk, C., 88
Monserud, M. A., 524, 527
Montagna, P., 116
Montague, M., 287

Montani, J. P., 428
Montemitro, E., 116
Montero-Odasso, M., 575
Montessori, M., 234–235
Monti, J. M., 283
Montie, J., 237
Montine, T. J., 586
Montirosso, R., 95
Montoya Arizabaleta, A. V., 89
Moody, J, 371
Moon, J. S., 215, 431
Moon, R. Y., 116, 117, 125, 629
Moore, D., 56, 400
Moore, K. A., 11
Moore, M., 212
Moore, M. K., 150, 155
Moorefield, B. S., 334
Moos, B., 559
Mor, V., 558
Mora, F., 543
Morales-Campos, D. Y., 363
Moran, R., 290
Moran, S., 301
Moraros, J. S., 337, 338
Morasch, K. C., 114, 177, 180
Moravcik, E., 234, 237, 269
Moreau, C., 366, 460
Moreira, E. D., 494
Moreno, F., 444
Moreno, M. C., 194
Morgan, K., 97
Morgan, P. L., 11, 197, 198, 236
Morgante, J. C., 131
Morin, C. M., 545
Morin, F., 62
Morison, V., 131
Moroni, L., 60
Morra, L., 575
Morra, S., 293
Morrell, D., 65
Morris, A., 395
Morris, A. S., 327, 331
Morris, B. J., 135
Morris, D., 48
Morris, M. W., 266
Morris, P., 27
Morris, P. A., 27, 28
Morrison, D., 335
Morrison, G. S., 235, 303
Morrison, H., 368
Morrison, J. H., 31
Morrissey, D. A., 200
Morrissey, T. W., 197
Morrongiello, B. A., 136
Morrow, C. E., 85
Morrow, D., 576, 577
Morrow, d. G., 576–577
Morrow, L., 232, 269
Mortensen, E. L., 585
Mortensen, O., 194
Mortimer, J. A., 546, 555
Morton, R. A., 84
Moscovitch, M., 545
Moses, A. M. R., 566
Moses, L. J., 229
Mosher, W. D., 432, 462, 463
Moshman, D., 391
Mosing, M. A., 603
Moslehi, J., 542
Moss, P., 176, 197, 262, 369
Motowidlo, S. J., 443
Moulson, M., 187
Mouton, C. P., 639
Mouw, T., 487
Moxey, A., 590
Moyer, A., 462
Moyle, W., 607
Mroczek, D., 519–520
Mroczek, D. K., 517, 518, 520, 600
Mu, Y., 346
Mueller, M. R., 293
Mueller, P. S., 626
Muir, D. W., 127
Muir, H., 215
Mukherjee, A. D., 289

subject index

Schools. *See also* Colleges/universities; Early childhood education; Education
  accountability in, 341–342
  children with disabilities in, 290–291
  cultural diversity in, 344–346
  ethnic diversity in, 343–344
  high school, 379–381, 384
  in middle and late childhood, 340–346, 349
  service learning in, 381
  transition to middle or junior high, 378–379, 383
  for young adolescents, 379
Scientific method, 21, 22
Scientific thinking, 296–298
The Seasons of a Man's Life (Levinson), 511–512
Seattle Longitudinal Study, 495–497
Secondary circular reactions, 147
Second-language learning, in middle and late childhood, 309–310, 314
Secure attachment style, 454, 455
Securely attached babies, 190
Seekers, 471–472
Selective attention, 568
Selective optimization with compensation theory, 600–601, 617
Self
  in adolescence, 388–389
  in early childhood, 245–247, 273
  in late adulthood, 603–605, 617
  in middle and late childhood, 318–321, 347–348
  sense of, 185–186
Self-concept, 319
Self-conscious emotions, 178, 247
Self-control
  in children, 298
  in late adulthood, 604–605
Self-efficacy
  in late adulthood, 616
  in middle and late childhood, 320–321
Self-esteem
  in adolescence, 388–389, 412
  in late adulthood, 603–604
  in middle and late childhood, 319–320
Self-image. *See* Self-esteem
Self-regulation
  joint attention and, 154
  in middle and late childhood, 321
  use of language for, 220
Self-understanding
  in early childhood, 245–246
  in middle and late childhood, 318
Self-worth. *See* Self-esteem
Semantic memory, 569–570
Semantics, 161–162, 231. *See also* Language development
Senior Odyssey, 576–577
Sensation, 128
Sensitive periods, 26
Sensorimotor play, 269
Sensorimotor stage (Piaget)
  evaluation of, 148, 150, 171
  explanation of, 23–24, 146, 171
  object permanence in, 148, 149
  substages of, 146–147
Sensory development
  in infants, 128–136, 140
  in late adulthood, 547–549, 561
Sensory receptors, 128
Separation protest, 180
Seriation, 292
Service learning, 381, 384
Set point, 428
Sex education programs, 366
Sex-linked chromosomal abnormalities, 59–60
Sex-linked genes, 58–59
Sexual abuse, 259. *See also* Child maltreatment
Sexual activity
  in adolescence, 362–363, 383
  in early adulthood, 432
  in middle adulthood, 493–494
Sexual harassment, 436–437
Sexual identity, 362

Sexuality
  in adolescence, 362–366, 401
  in early adulthood, 431–437, 447
  in late adulthood, 550, 609
  in middle adulthood, 491–494
  romantic love and, 459
Sexually transmitted infections (STIs)
  in adolescence, 364
  explanation of, 434–435
  during pregnancy, 87
  strategies to avoid, 435–436
  types of, 434
Sexual maturation, 358–359. *See also* Puberty
Sexual orientation. *See also* Gays; Lesbians; Same-sex relationships
  research findings on, 432–433
  same-sex relationships and, 433–434
  sources of, 433
Shaken baby syndrome, 111
Shared environmental experiences, 70
Shared sleeping, 116
Short-term memory, 225, 295
Sibling relationships
  delinquency and, 407
  in early childhood, 261, 274
  in middle adulthood, 523–524
Sickle-cell anemia, 61
Similarity, attraction and, 456–457
Simple reflexes stage, 146–147
Single adults, 461
Single-parent families, ethnicity and, 266
SIRT1, 553
Size constancy, in infants, 133
Skinner's operant conditioning theory, 25, 153
Sleep
  in adolescence, 368–369
  in early childhood, 212
  in infancy, 115–117, 139
  in late adulthood, 545
  in middle adulthood, 489
  REM, 116
Slow-to-warm-up child type, 181
Small for date infants, 96, 97
Smell sense
  in infants, 136
  in late adulthood, 549
Smiling, in infants, 179
Smoking. *See* Tobacco
Social age, 19
Social clock, 515
Social cognition, in middle and late childhood, 336–337
Social cognitive theory
  explanation of, 26
  of gender, 253
Social constructivist approach, 221
Social contract or utility and individual rights stage (Kohlberg), 325
Social conventional reasoning, 327
Social developmental neuroscience, 361
Social influences, on gender development, 252–254
Social integration, 612, 618
Socialization, reciprocal, 194, 195
Social orientation, in infants, 187–188
Social play, 270
Social policy
  children in poverty and, 13
  explanation of, 11
Social referencing, in infants, 188
Social relationships. *See also* Friendship; Love; Peer relations
  emotional expression and, 178–179
Social role theory, 252, 253
Social smile, 179
Social support
  health and, 491
  in late adulthood, 611–612, 618
  during pregnancy, 89
  for widows and widowers, 639, 640
Social systems morality (Kohlberg), 324
Social workers, 45–46
Social work professors and administrators, 614

Sociocultural cognitive theory. *See* Vygotsky's sociocultural cognitive theory
Sociocultural contexts. *See also* Culture
  dating and, 400
Socioeconomic status (SES). *See also* Poverty
  delinquency and, 406
  ethnicity and, 403
  explanation of, 10–12
  families and, 267
  language development and, 164, 167
  memory and, 571
Socioemotional development. *See also* Emotional development; Emotions; Personality/personality development
  in adolescence, 388–411
  in early adulthood, 452–474
  in early childhood, 245–274
  gender differences in, 330–331
  in infants, 177–201
  in late adulthood, 596–616
  in middle adulthood, 510–530
  in middle and late childhood, 330–331
Socioemotional processes, 15
Socioemotional selectivity theory, 598–599, 617
Sociometric status, 335–336
Sounds, recognition of, 163
Source memory, 570
Special education teachers, 44
Speech. *See also* Language development
  inner, 220
  private, 220
Speech therapists, 46–47
Sperm, 57
Spina bifida, 61, 82
Spirituality. *See also* Religion
  explanation of, 501
  health and, 502
  in late adulthood, 590, 592
  life expectancy and, 539
  meaning of life and, 502, 506
  stress and, 503
Spoken vocabulary, 164
Stability-change issue
  from childhood to adulthood, 452–455
  explanation of, 20, 21
  in middle adults, 517–520
Stagnation, 510–511
Standardized tests, 31
Stanford-Binet tests, 299
Stepfamilies, 334–335
Stereotypes
  gender, 328–329, 331–332
  intelligence tests and, 304
  of older adults, 605, 607
Stranger anxiety, 179–180
Strange Situation, 190
Strategies, to improve memory, 294–295
Stress
  coping with, 322–323
  disease and, 490–491
  gender and, 514–515
  in midlife, 514–515, 529
  pregnancy and, 88, 90
  religion and, 503
Substance use/abuse. *See also* Alcoholism; Alcohol use/abuse; Tobacco
  in adolescence, 370–371, 383, 410
  in early adulthood, 429–432
  in late adulthood, 553, 562
Subtractive bilingualism, 310
Sucking, high-amplitude, 131
Sucking reflex, 123
Sudden infant death syndrome (SIDS), 116–117, 119, 630
Suicide
  in adolescence, 369–370, 409–410, 414
  gender and, 409
Suicide ideation
  in adolescence, 409, 410
  bullying and, 337–338
Supercentenarians, 538
Surveys, 30–31
Sustained attention, 153, 224, 225, 568
Symbolic function substage (Piaget), 216–217
Synapses, 113, 114

Syntax, 161, 162, 231
Syphilis, 87, 434

Taste
  in infants, 136
  in late adulthood, 549
Tay-Sachs disease, 61
Teaching strategies, based on Vygotsky's theory, 221
Technology use. *See also* Internet
  adolescents and, 404–405
  by older adults, 607
Teen Outreach Program (TOP), 366
Telegraphic speech, 165
Television viewing
  in early childhood, 271–272, 274
  exercise and, 429
Temperament
  biological influences on, 183
  classification of, 181–182
  in early adulthood, 452–453, 475
  explanation of, 181, 452
  gender, culture and, 183
  goodness of fit and, 184
  parenting and child's, 184
Temporal lobes, 112
Tend and befriend pattern, 515
Teratogens
  blood type incompatibility as, 86
  emotional states and stress as, 88
  environmental, 86
  explanation of, 82–83
  maternal diet and nutrition as, 87–88
  maternal diseases as, 86–87
  paternal factors as, 89
  prescription and nonprescription drugs as, 83
  psychoactive drugs as, 83–86
Tertiary circular reactions, novelty, and curiosity stage, 147
Testosterone, 359, 492, 493
Tests, standardized, 31
Theories, 21. *See also* Life-span development theories
Theory of mind
  autism and, 229
  developmental changes and, 226–228
  explanation of, 226, 247
  individual differences and, 228–229
Therapeutic/recreation therapists, 46
Thinking. *See also* Cognitive development; Cognitive function
  convergent, 296
  creative, 296, 297
  critical, 295–296
  divergent, 296
  moral, 326
  postformal, 439
  preoperational, 218
  scientific, 296–298
Three mountains task, 217
Time, perception of, 599
Tip-of-the-tongue phenomenon, 579
Tobacco
  adolescent use of, 370
  childhood exposure to, 215
  young adult use of, 431
Toddlers. *See also* Early childhood
  categorization in, 156–157
  language development in, 169 (*See also* Language development)
  motor skills in, 125–126
Tools of the Mind, 222
Touch
  in infants, 135–136
  in late adulthood, 549
Tracking method, 131–132
Transitivity, 292–293
Triarchic theory of intelligence, 300–301
Trimesters, of prenatal development, 81–82
Trophoblast, 78
Trust vs. mistrust stage (Erikson's theory), 22, 185
Turner syndrome, 60